Toward a Formal Science of Economics

Toward a Formal Science of Economics

The Axiomatic Method in Economics and Econometrics

Bernt P. Stigum

The MIT Press
Cambridge, Massachusetts
London, England

This book was set in Palatino by Asco Trade Typesetting Ltd. in Hong Kong and printed and bound in the United States of America.

Library of Congress Cataloging-in-Publication Data

Stigum, Bernt P.

Toward a formal science of economics: the axiomatic method in economics and econometrics/Bernt P. Stigum.

p. cm.

Bibliography: p.

Includes index.

ISBN 0-262-19284-5

1. Economics. 2. Economics, Mathematical. 3. Econometrics.

I. Title.

HB71.S84 1989

330—dc19 89-2404

CIP

To Olaug and Hilmar Stigum
—my parents

To Dartmouth College
—for all it gave me

To Betty and Dr. Ralph E. Miller
—for a home away from home

To Fia—my smashing wife—and Anne Olaug, Erik, and Tove—my three spunky children
—for years of adventure

Contents

Toward a Formal Science of Economics

1 Introduction

This is an essay in the philosophy of science in which I develop a formal unitary methodological basis for the theoretical and empirical sides of a science. The basis is built up from fundamental theorems in logic and model theory, and its vitality is proved in the analysis of interesting theoretical and empirical problems in economics.

My main purpose in writing the essay was to create a formal theoretical structure that would provide applied workers with guidance in methodical reasoning and with means to check the adequacy of statistical arguments. I also wanted to contribute to an orderly development of science by delineating efficient ways in which theorists, statisticians, and applied workers of any science could communicate. The results I present will demonstrate that I have succeeded in both endeavors, at least as far as the science of economics is concerned.

1.1 The Need for a Formal Unitary Methodological Basis for the Science of Economics

The existence of a formal unitary methodological basis for the theoretical and empirical sides of a science is not obvious. Moreover, the need for such a basis is a matter of scholarly dispute. This essay sets forth a formal unitary methodological basis for economic theory and econometrics, and the next few remarks will show why I believe there is a real need for such a basis.

Roughly speaking, economists can be divided into four almost separate groups. In one group we find the pure theorists, many of whom refer to themselves as mathematical economists. In another group the pure econometricians reside. Most of their work belongs in the realm of mathematical statistics. In a third group we find applied economists and applied econometricians, whose published work usually reports results from the analysis of economic data. Finally, in the fourth group reside "all the others"—for example, government policy makers, economic consultants, and bank employees. Their work is guided by methodological considerations that are of little interest here. Each of the other three groups has a methodological basis for their members' work that is inadequate for an orderly development of the science of economics.

The pure theorists' methodological basis is identical with the methodological basis of nonintuitionistic mathematics. Its main characteristics and its power and limitations are discussed in parts I and II of this book. This methodological basis may be adequate for the development of pure mathematics, but it is sorely inadequate for developing economic theory. To wit: Mathematics is created out of the empty set, and its assertions concern properties of symbols. Mathematicians interpret their symbols to see if their axioms are consistent. The symbols then become sets to some and real numbers to others. Mathematical economists also interpret their symbols—the undefined terms of their theories—to check whether their axioms are consistent. The symbols then become, say, money and capital. But "money" and "capital" are symbols just as much as x and y are symbols, and symbols per se are of no interest in economics. To be adequate, an interpretation of the symbols of an economic theory must describe at least one situation in which the empirical relevance of the theory can be tested. The methodological basis of mathematics provides no guidelines for formulating such an interpretation.

The methodological basis of the work of the applied economists and econometricians is described in Trygve Haavelmo's seminal treatise *The Probability Approach in Econometrics* (1944). There Haavelmo delineates the relationship between abstract economic theories and economic reality, discusses the nature of stochastic models and their applicability to economic data, and outlines a general scheme for testing economic theories. Haavelmo's unquestioned authority and the profoundness of his arguments notwithstanding, I believe that the methodological basis he constructed for applied economics and econometrics is inadequate because it does not provide economic researchers with a formal theoretical apparatus that can guide them in formulating their statistical models and provide them with an easy means of checking whether their arguments are sound. Evidence of the need for such an apparatus is the ample supply of meaningless estimates of statistical parameters in economic journals.

The pure econometricians' methodological basis is the methodological basis of nonintuitionistic mathematics. This basis may suffice for mathematical statistics, but it is inadequate for a meaningful development of econometrics. Econometrics is the theory of how to measure economic relations. Philosophical problems concerning the possibility of economic knowledge are as much a part of econometric theory as the asymptotic properties of parameter estimates and the power of statistical tests. Since the methodological basis of mathematics is not equipped to deal with epistemological problems, it is inadequate for the purposes of econometrics.

The formal unitary methodological basis of a science presented in parts I, II, and VI of this book will establish guidelines for both the economic theorist in search of empirical tests of his theory and the applied econometrician endeavoring to design economically meaningful statistical models. This basis will also provide the formal theoretical structure which the applied economist needs to determine the adequacy of his arguments. Finally, this basis will provide the framework within which the epistemological problems of econometrics can be tackled.

1.2 The Axiomatic Method and the Development of a Formal Science of Economics

I use the axiomatic method to construct the sought-for formal unitary methodological basis of a science. In addition, I envision that a scientist who accepts the basis will apply the means it provides *and* the axiomatic method to develop his theories and to formulate the required tests of these theories. For that reason this book has become a book about the axiomatic method, a book about the power and weaknesses of this method and about the uses to which it has been and can be put in economic theory and econometrics. The salient characteristics of the method are detailed in chapter 2, and its formal aspects are discussed in chapters 3–9 and 23–25; its informal use in economics and probability theory is illustrated in chapters 10–22 and 30–31 and its informal application in econometrics in chapters 26–29 and 32–34. In this section some of the highlights of the historical development of the method are briefly given, and the development of a formal science of economics is traced.

1.2.1 The Rise of Formal Economics

The axiomatic method is a systematic way of developing a concept such as natural number or consumer choice from a few basic propositions—axioms—using only generally accepted logical rules of inference. When and where this method originated is uncertain. However, Euclid's *Elements* of geometry (ca. 300 B.C.) and Archimedes' treatises in theoretical mechanics (ca. 240 B.C.) demonstrate that the method was well known to Greek mathematicians several hundred years before the Christian era. It was introduced to economics in A.D. 1836 by Nassau William Senior in his *Outline of the Science of Political Economy* and is today more or less consciously adopted by most economic theorists as the way of theorizing in economics.

Senior defined economics to be "the Science which treats of the Nature, the Production, and the Distribution of wealth" (1850, p. 1). To develop this science, he adopted as axioms four general propositions which he considered to be "the result of observation, or consciousness, and scarcely requiring proof" (1850, p. 3), and which he formulated as follows (see Senior 1850, p. 26):

1. Every "man desires to obtain additional Wealth with as little sacrifice as possible."

2. The "Population of the World ... is limited only by moral or physical evil, or by fear of a deficiency of those articles of wealth which the habits of the individuals of each class of its inhabitants lead them to require."

3. The "powers of Labour, and of the other instruments which produce wealth, may be indefinitely increased by using their Products as the means of further Production."

4. Agricultural "skill remaining the same, additional Labour employed on the land within a given district produces in general a less proportionate return...."

To derive meaningful theorems from these axioms Senior made use of the logical rules of inference that he had learned from Aristotelian logic.

From looking at Senior's four axioms, one cannot divine what kind of economics Senior intended to develop. To find out we must add definitional axioms that explicate Senior's idea of the terms "Wealth," "Labour," "Production," and "the other instruments of production" (see Senior 1850, pp. 6–22 and 50–81). We must also add axioms that delineate Senior's conception of the laws of production and of the behavior of man. When we do, we find that Senior's theory was developed to explicate the workings of an economy in which there are both consumers and producers, some of whom are laborers, others capitalists, and still others owners of natural agents of production, and in which services, farm products, and manufactured goods are produced and exchanged (for the most part) in perfectly competitive markets.

For the purposes of this essay it is not necessary to know the exact contours of Senior's economy. The important fact to observe is that Senior set out to formulate a theory which could describe the *actual* workings of the economy he had in mind. In this respect Senior's ideas concerning the nature of axioms were like the ideas of his fellow scientists who conceived of Euclid's geometry as an attempt to describe the *actual* physical space in which we live such as it appears to our senses.

The advent of the non-Euclidean geometries of N. I. Lobachevskij (1829) and B. Riemann (1854) shattered the pedestal on which resided the geometry of Euclid. They demonstrated that scientists' notions of straight lines, planes, and distances were vague and subject to a large number of tacit assumptions. They also showed that observations on physical space as it appears to the senses of a given individual would not enable this individual to decide whether Euclid's geometry or the new geometries provide *the* accurate description of his world. In doing that, the non-Euclidean geometries set the stage for acceptance of formal geometries on a par with the applied sciences of space and extension, even though such geometries are free of spacial intuition and their theorems lay down laws for imaginary matters only. Nineteenth-century examples are H. Grassmann's *Ausdehnungslehre* (1844) and M. Pasch's *Vorlesungen über Neuere Geometrie* (1882). (See Nagel 1939, pp. 142–222, for a discussion of the historical significance of Grassmann's and Pasch's contributions.)

Economists' understanding of the axiomatic method improved gradually after the appearance of Senior's treatise. Still it took them more than a century to grasp the significance of Lobachevskij's and Riemann's discoveries and to accept formal economics on a par with other branches of economics. Published discourses on methodology by leading economists attest to this fact. We shall mention three of them, Keynes, Weber, and Friedman, and contrast their ideas with the ideas underlying formal economic theories.

John Neville Keynes insisted in 1890 that an economic law, "notwithstanding the hypothetical element that it contains, still has reference to the actual course of events; it is an assertion respecting the actual relations of economic phenomena one to another" (1897, p. 221). About thirty years later Max Weber claimed that economic theory is an axiomatic discipline which exclusively utilizes ideal-type concepts such as Adam Smith' economic man, Marshall's representative firm, and Weber's own medieval-city economy. According to Weber, these ideal types are formed into analytic constructs "by the one-sided *accentuation* of one or more points of view and by the synthesis of a great many different, discrete, more or less present and occasionally absent *concrete individual* phenomena." In their conceptual purity, ideal types cannot be found anywhere in reality;

they are utopian (Weber 1949, pp. 43 and 90). Finally, as late as 1953 Milton Friedman declared that a theory, seen as a body of substantive hypotheses, should be judged by its predictive power alone; i.e., the only relevant test of the validity of the theory was a comparison of its predictions with experience (Friedman 1953, p. 8).

In contrast, a formal economic theory consists of a set of axioms and all the theorems that can be derived from the axioms with logical rules of inference. The axioms delineate the properties of certain undefined terms. These may or may not carry names that indicate the particular interpretation which the originator of the theory intended for them. The theory is meaningful only if the axioms are consistent, i.e., only if contradictory assertions cannot be derived from them. If the axioms are consistent, the theory can be made to talk about many different things simply by giving the undefined terms different interpretations. One of these interpretations will be the one for which the theory was developed. We shall refer to this interpretation as the *intended interpretation* of the axioms.

Keynes's, Weber's, and Friedman's ideas of the nature of axioms and the possibilities of the axiomatic method differ significantly from the ideas underlying the construction of a formal economic theory. This is obviously true of Keynes's ideas. It is true of Friedman's ideas too since to Friedman a substantive economic hypothesis is an hypothesis of the *actual* workings of some economic phenomena. As to Weber, it is fair to admit that the concept which an economic theorist has in mind when he develops his theory is probably an ideal-type concept. However, the moment the theory is formulated, it becomes a theory of undefined terms and takes on a life of its own—a life that is independent of the ideal type which originally guided the economist in his choice of axioms. Hence Weber's economic theory is not formal in the way we understand this term.

The preceding observations and the fact that the authority of Keynes, Weber, and Friedman was unquestioned in their time, justify my claim that a general acceptance of formal economic theory first came with the publication of Gerard Debreu's *Theory of Value* (1959).

1.2.2 The Rise of Formal Logic

The simplicity of the axiomatic method and the realization of its power that followed in the wake of the non-Euclidean geometries engendered the idea that every branch of mathematics could be developed in its totality from a finite set of axioms. George Boole (1847) and Ernst Schröder (1890) carried out this idea for the algebra of classes, Giuseppe Peano (1889) did it for natural numbers, and George Cantor (1895–97) tried to do it for set theory. At about the same time (1879, 1884, and 1893) Gottlob Frege axiomatized the propositional calculus, created a formal system of logic that incorporated both his propositional calculus and a first- and second-order quantification theory, and used the latter to formulate an axiomatic theory of sets. Finally, following in the footsteps of Frege and Cantor, Bertrand Russell (1903) and later Russell and Alfred North Whitehead (1910–1913) set out to demonstrate that there are axioms of formal logic that logicians must agree are true and from which all of mathematics can be derived.

Unfortunately the axiomatic method is not just simple and powerful. It is treacherous as well. Logical and semantic paradoxes that were discovered at the turn of the century attested to that. One of the logical paradoxes was due to Cesare Burali-Forti (1897) and can be paraphrazed as follows: Given any ordinal number, there is still a larger ordinal number; but the ordinal number determined by the set of all ordinal numbers is the largest ordinal number. One of the semantic paradoxes was due to K. Grelling (1908) and can be paraphrased as follows: An adjective is said to be *autological* or *heterological* according to whether the property denoted by the adjective holds or does not hold for the adjective itself. "Heterological" is an adjective. If "heterological" is heterological, it is not heterological. If "heterological" is not heterological, it is heterological.

The logical paradoxes demonstrated that the set theories of Cantor and Frege were inconsistent and guided mathematicians in their search for axioms of set theory that would outlaw troublesome objects such as the set of all ordinal numbers and the set of all sets. Similarly, the semantic paradoxes guided mathematical logicians in their search for a characterization of formal languages in which semantical concepts such as "truth" can be explicated. All of them contributed to a rapid development of mathematical logic in which new and exciting methods of proof were discovered and in which theorems were established that to the uninitiated must have sounded like pure magic. For ease of reference, three of them will be paraphrased here:

1. Gödel 1931: There is no finite set of axioms (formulated in a first-order language) from which all the true propositions about natural numbers can be derived.

2. Skolem 1922: There is a theory of real numbers (formulated in a first-order language) that has a model with a countable universe of discourse.

3. Skolem 1934: In a first-order language in which the theory of natural numbers can be formulated, there is no collection of well-formed formulas that can provide a complete characterization of natural numbers.

In the statement of Gödel's theorem, a first-order language is a symbolic language with individual variables, function and predicate symbols (one of which is equality), the logical connectives "not" and "imply," and the quantifier "for all." The language is described in chapter 3 and developed axiomatically in chapter 5. A proof of Gödel's theorem is outlined in chapter 8. The import of the theorem is that Russell and Whitehead's dream of creating in mathematical logic a basis for all of mathematics cannot be realized.

In Skolem's first theorem a model of a theory is an interpretation of the theory's undefined terms that renders its axioms (simultaneously) true statements. The theorem insists that if our comprehension of the continuum is as described in a first-order theory, then there is no loss in generality in assuming that the "continuum" is countable. A generalization of this theorem is stated and proved in chapter 6. As we shall see, the general version of Skolem's theorem has important implications for applied econometrics.

Skolem's second theorem can be paraphrased to say that any finitely axiomatized first-order theory of natural numbers has a model whose universe is uncountable. In proving it, Skolem established the existence of a universe of nonstandard natural numbers. This result and the generalizations that were to come at the hands of Abraham Robinson opened up a new branch of mathematical inquiry: nonstandard analysis. Skolem's theorem is established in chapter 7, and nonstandard analysis is presented from a modern point of view in part V of this book.

The three preceding theorems and others that I shall discuss in parts I and II greatly enhanced scientists' understanding of the axiomatic method. In addition, the theorems firmly established mathematical logic as a branch of mathematics on a par with geometry, algebra, and number theory.

1.2.3 The Development of a Formal Science of Economics

Webster's *New World Dictionary* insists that a science is a branch of knowledge concerned with establishing and systematizing facts, principles, and methods, as by experiments and hypotheses. For my purposes this definition is much too general because it allows fields of inquiry, such as the philosophy of history and Freudian psychoanalysis, to qualify as sciences.

I believe that a branch of knowledge, BK, is a *science* if and only if it satisfies the following conditions:

1. BK is concerned with establishing and systematizing facts and principles; its arguments are based on a relatively coherent body of logically consistent and precisely formulated theories.
2. BK's basic theories have empirical content; i.e., there exist data which can be used to determine the relevance of these theories in certain given situations.
3. There exist statistical methods that can be used to analyze data which are required for testing the empirical relevance of BK's basic theories.
4. In BK there is a tradition of collecting data and of analyzing them statistically for the purpose of deducing useful hypotheses.
5. There exists a unitary methodological basis for the theoretical and empirical sides of BK.

If a branch of knowledge is a science in accordance with the preceding definition, I shall say that it is a *formal science* if (1) its basic theories are formal in the sense given to this term above and (2) its unitary methodological basis in condition 5 is formulated as a formal axiomatic system.

There are many branches of knowledge that satisfy all the criteria listed above, e.g., classical mechanics and chemistry. I shall next demonstrate that economics became a science with the publication of Trygve Haavelmo's *The Probability Approach in Econometrics* (1944).

Economic theorizing in 1944 was based on (1) mathematically formulated theories of consumer and entrepreneurical choice, (2) less formal theories of variously structured markets in which consumers and firms exchanged goods and services for money, and (3) macroeconomic theories, most of which originated in J. M. Keynes's *The General Theory of Employment, Interest and Money* (1936). In these theories consumers maximized utility subject to their budget constraints, and firms maximized profits subject to their production constraints. Moreover, consumers were price takers in all markets. Firms were price takers in perfectly competitive markets, set prices in monopolistic markets, and colluded in different ways in oligopolistic markets. Finally, the existence of equilibria had been established for some markets—for example, for monopoly and duopoly—were taken on faith or postulated for other markets—for example, for monopolistically competitive markets—and were deduced by counting equations and variables in perfectly competitive markets. In addition, sufficient conditions for the stability of market equilibria had been established for monopoly, duopoly, and perfectly competitive markets.

The 1944 theories of consumer and entrepreneurial choice were essentially like the theories which Paul Samuelson developed in chapters III–VIII of his *Foundations of Economic Analysis* (1947). These theories had empirical content in the sense that they made predictions about individual behavior that could be tested with the data then available to economists, for example, with budget data on consumer expenditures and income and with time-series observations on prices and quantities of various commodities and services produced and sold.

The 1944 macroeconomic theories also had empirical content in the sense that they made predictions about the behavior of economic aggregates that could be tested with the data then available to economists, e.g., with Simon Kuznets's data on national income and capital formation in the United States, 1919–1933 (Kuznets 1934 and 1937) and Y. S. Leong's indices of the production of consumers' and producers' goods (Leong 1935). Wassily Leontief's work on input-output analysis (Leontief 1941) and Gottfried von Haberler's and Jan Tinbergen's work on the existence and structure of business cycles (Haberler 1937; Tinbergen 1939) attest to this.

In 1944 applied econometricians had a remarkable array of statistical methods at their disposal. They knew of R. A. Fisher's method of maximum likelihood, J. Neyman's theory of confidence intervals, and the Neyman-Pearson theory of testing statistical hypotheses. Moreover, they had learned of the problem of errors in variables and confluence analysis from Ragnar Frisch, and they had been taught interesting ways of analyzing economic time series by Herman Wold and H. B. Mann and A. Wald. Finally, Trygve Haavelmo's theory of simultaneous-equations estimation had made them aware of the consequences of ignoring the existence of simultaneous relations when estimating the parameters in single-equation econometric models.

Finally, in 1944 economists could look back on more than 150 years of data collection and more than 100 years of data analysis for the purpose of discovering useful economic hypotheses. An early example is E. Engel's study of the budgets of 153 Belgian families (Engel 1857), which resulted in Engel's famous law: "The poorer a family, the greater the proportion of its total expenditure that must be devoted to the provision of food." More recent examples are T. Schultz's study of demand (1939), R. G. D. Allen and A. Bowley's study of family expenditures (1935), C. W. Cobb and P. H. Douglas's (1928) and J. Marschak and W. H. Andrews's (1944) work on the production function, and Jan Tinbergen's (1939) study of business cycles in the United States, 1919–1932.

The preceding paragraphs demonstrate that economics in 1944 satisfied the first four conditions for a branch of knowledge to be a science. However, economics did not satisfy the fifth condition because there did not exist a theoretical framework within which economic theories could be formulated and their empirical relevance tested. In fact, there was then a division between mathematical statisticians and pure economic theorists which reflected the conviction of many that the nature of economic "laws" was such that the ideas of mathematical statistics could not be applied to test them. (see Frisch 1955, pp. 178–179, for a discussion of this anomaly.) Haavelmo wrote his treatise to obliterate the division between statisticians and economists. He succeeded magnificently, an in doing so, he also established economics as a science.

The vitality of the science of economics that Trygve Haavelmo and his fellow economists created has been amply demonstrated in the last forty years. Many memorable examples come to mind. Some of them concern the behavior of consumers—e.g., H. Wold and L. Juréen's *Demand Analysis* (1953) and S. J. Prais and H. S. Houthakker's *The Analysis of Family Budgets* (1955). Others deal with matters of entrepreneurial choice—e.g., G. H. Hildebrand and T. C. Liu's *Manufacturing Production Functions in the United States, 1957* (1965) and L. Johansen's *Production Functions* (1972). Still others are devoted to the study of economic growth and public policy—e.g., L. Johansen's *A Multi-sectoral Study of Economic Growth* (1960), H. Theil's *Economic Forecasts and Policy* (1961), and L. Klein and A. Goldberger's *An Econometric Model of the United States 1929–1952* (1955).

This science of economics was not "formal" in the sense we have given to formal science. However, its establishment constituted a first step toward creating a formal science of economics. The second step was taken with the publication of Gerard Debreu's *Theory of Value* (1959) and the resulting general acceptance of formal economics on a par with other branches of economics. Here I shall take the third and last step by formulating a formal unitary methodological basis for economics and econometrics.

A formal unitary methodological basis for science can be constructed in many ways. I formulate my basis in parts I, II, and VI and demonstrate its usefulness in part VII. This basis has two parts—a multi-sorted language for science, $L_{t,p}$, and a two-sorted modal-theoretic language, SEL, for talking about the meaningfulness of the assertions made in $L_{t,p}$. The vocabulary of $L_{t,p}$ consists of an observational part, a theoretical part, and a dictionary. We formulate scientific theories with the theoretical vocabulary, delineate characteristic features of a universe of observable objects with the observational vocabulary, and use the dictionary and the other two vocabularies to describe how the undefined terms of the theories and the observable objects are related to one another. The vocabulary of SEL is partly a vocabulary for discussing properties of real numbers and partly a vocabulary for describing salient characteristics of the sentences of $L_{t,p}$. The vocabulary of SEL is used to formulate a basis for statistical tests of the scientific hypotheses that are asserted in $L_{t,p}$.

The idea of constructing a language for science with a vocabulary that is partly observational, partly theoretical, and partly a dictionary is not new. For example, in 1929 F. P. Ramsey suggested that such a language should consist of a primary system, a secondary system, and a dictionary (Ramsey 1954, pp. 212–236). Ramsey's primary system is the analogue of my observational vocabulary; his secondary system is the analogue of my theoretical vocabulary; and his dictionary is basically the analogue of my dictionary. Ramsey's language differs from mine in that his language is single-sorted and mine is multisorted. From a mathematical point of view, this difference is not significant since—as demonstrated in chapter 25—anything that we can assert in our multisorted language can be asserted in a properly constructed single-sorted language. From a scientist's point of view, however, the difference is significant. It is easy to formulate empirical tests of hypotheses in a logical framework, such as $L_{t,p}$, in which the universes of theory and observation are kept far apart. It is difficult to formulate such tests with a single-sorted language in whose universe theoretical constructs and observational objects are mixed in confusing patterns.

To the best of my knowledge, the idea of using a two-sorted modal-theoretic language to formulate statistical tests of scientific hypotheses is new. However, in constructing and interpreting SEL I have made free use of ideas that I found in several seminal papers by S. A. Kripke on semantical analyses of modal logic (e.g., Kripke 1971, pp. 67–96) and by J. E. Fenstad on the structure of logical probabilities (e.g., Fenstad 1967, pp. 156–172). SEL differs from the language of Kripke's modal language. Moreover, the role which the modal operator $\square$ plays in SEL is much more involved than the role it plays in Kripke's logic. However, my interpretation of $\square$ is analogous to Kripke's interpretation of his modal operator. Similarly, the syntactic structure within which my logical probability measure functions differs from the context in which Fenstad's probability measure appears. Moreover, Fenstad's interpretation of his probability measure differs from the interpretation I give to mine. However, the axioms which Fenstad's probability measure must satisfy are analogues of the conditions I impose on my probability measure.

Both $L_{t,p}$ and SEL are constructed as formal axiomatic systems. Hence, to the extent that these languages constitute an adaquate formal unitary methodological basis for economics and econometrics, they also provide economists with the means, heretofore missing, to create a formal science of economics. In parts VI and VII of this book I give ample evidence of the adequacy of $L_{t,p}$ and SEL as a formal unitary methodological basis for economics and econometrics. Specifically, in chapters 26–28 I demonstrate how mathematical economists can use $L_{t,p}$ to describe situations in which the empirical relevance of their theories can be tested. I also exhibit ways in which $L_{t,p}$ and SEL can be used to guide applied economists and econometricians in their search for meaningful statistical models. Moreover, in chapters 23 and 24 I outline a way in which $L_{t,p}$ and an extended version of SEL can be used to study the epistemological problems of econometrics. Finally, in chapter 25 I establish syntactic and semantic theorems that demonstrate that $L_{t,p}$ has all the properties we should want to require of a language for science, that is, (1) $L_{t,p}$ is complete in the sense that it is impossible to derive more valid sentences by adding axioms and rules of inference, (2) any theory that is expressed in $L_{t,p}$ is consistent if and only if it has a model, and (3) if a theory that is expressed in $L_{t,p}$ has a model with an infinite universe, then it has a model with a denumerably infinite universe.

1.3 Formalism and the Unity of Science

I have talked much about formalism and economics. I have also insisted that I intend to develop a unitary methodological basis for the theoretical and empirical sides of any science—not just economics. Hence a few remarks concerning the unity of science and the advantages of formalism in scientific research are called for.

1.3.1 The Unity of Science

The unity of science as reflected in the methods of analysis employed by researchers in different branches of science is astounding. How come fundamental laws of statistical mechanics can be used to describe the dynamics of financial markets? How come game theory can be used both to develop a theory of oligopolistic markets and to resolve problems in evolutionary biology? How come the same statistical method can be used to estimate loading matrices in psychology, simultaneous-equation parameters in economics, and initial positions and velocities of the trajectories of celestial objects in astronomy? And how come the theory of electric circuits can be used to develop a theory of industrial dynamics that business firms in search of optimal organizational structures can apply?

Some philosophers would argue that this unity of science ultimately must be due to the unity of nature. Researchers in different sciences learn the same methods of mathematical and statistical analysis. These methods, however, do not come with tags that indicate where and when they can be applied. Each scientist must figure out for himself interesting ways of applying the methods in his field of inquiry. The unity of nature ensures that the same methods can be used in different branches of science.

Interesting applications of mathematical methods in the sciences are usually the end result of much imaginative thinking. Consider, for example, the simple idea of a constrained maximum of a function of several variables and the role it plays in biology and economics. In evolutionary biology fitness in the sense of expected descendant contribution is a function of certain physically determined design variables. An optimal form is a combination of values of the design variables that maximizes fitness subject to certain constraints that limit the values of the design variables. Finally, natural selection is taken to result in the predominance of optimal forms. In economics, fitness becomes utility for consumers and profits for firms, and design variable becomes a commodity or a service for consumers and an input or an output for firms. In addition, an optimal form is a vector of commodities and services that maximizes a consumer's utility subject to his budget constraint or a feasible input-output combination that maximizes a firm's profits subject to certain technical constraints. Finally, in perfectly competitive economies, Adam Smith's invisible hand ensures the predominance of optimal forms by finding prices for the economy's commodities and services at which their supply equals their demand.

The successful application of the idea of a constrained maximum in both biology and economics is a fact (Beatty 1980). Whether this success is a reflection of the unity of nature is another matter. Herman Weyl must think it is, judging from the following quotation: "The fact that in nature 'all is woven into one whole,' that space, matter, gravitation, the forces arising from the electromagnetic field, the animate and inanimate are all indissolubly connected, strongly supports the belief in the unity of nature and hence in the unity of the scientific method. There are no reasons to distrust it" (Weyl 1963, p. 214).

For the import of this essay, it is significant, to note that there is this unity of science; it is not essential to know why. The unitary methodological basis that I develop is meant for formal theories that pertain to some domain of science and *can* be formulated in a first-order language. I shall demonstrate its usefulness in economics and econometrics. The unity of science suggests that it can be applied to advantage in other sciences as well.

1.3.2 Advantages of Formalism in Science

A theory need not be elaborate. In fact, most theories of science are either based on a single hypothesis or derived from a small number of hypotheses. Examples are the kinematics of Albert Einstein's special theory of relativity and Robert Solow's theory of economic growth. The first is developed from the hypothesis that all who enjoy unaccelerated motion with respect to a point source of light will experience the same (finite) constant propagational velocity of light. The second is based on three assumptions concerning labor and capital: labor grows at an exponential rate, capital varies in proportion to net national product, and net national product is a linearly homogeneous function of capital and labor.

Theories in science also need not be formal. However, for theories that *can* be axiomatized, but are not, we can give good reasons why they ought to be. Some of these reasons are detailed below.

The formalism involved in axiomatizing a theory forces the theorist to make precise the ideas underlying his theory and to exhibit the implicit assumptions he employs in his informal search for interesting consequences of his hypotheses. Some of the implicit assumptions may be cause for concern and might, when exhibited, lead to outright rejection of the theory. Such was the fate of Sir Roy Harrod's theory of economic growth and his proof of the inherent instability of capitalistic systems. One of Harrod's implicit assumptions concerning the structure of the aggregate production function caused the virtual rejection of his theory and opened economists' eyes for the possibility of balanced economic growth.

A formal theory can be used to talk about many different subject matters. That increases research efficiency for obvious reasons. It also provides insight that can lead to surprising applications of the theory. For example, in physics the same differential equation can describe the behavior of both a forced harmonic oscillator (e.g., a mass on a spring) and the forced flow of current through an oscillatory electric circuit with resistance, inductance, and capacitance. Such insight allowed engineers to use analogue computers in their search for optimal designs of car springs and shock absorbers (Feynman, Leighton, and Sands 1964, pp. 25-6–25-8).

A formal theory can be derived from many different sets of axioms, and a scientific hypothesis can be rationalized by any number of different formal theories. Formalism in science increases research efficiency by making it easier to decide whether two theories about the same subject matter are alike, and if they are not, in what way they differ. For example, the two versions of quantum mechanics determined by the continuous mechanics of waves and the discrete mechanics of matrix representations were originally taken to be different. John von Neumann demonstrated that they were realizations of isomorphic Hilbert spaces and hence alike (Suppes 1968).

Two theories can differ in ways that cannot be detected by currently available data and statistical methods. Formalism in science increases research efficiency by making it easier to establish "empirical equivalences" of this kind. To wit: "For many of the experimental paradigms that have been intensively studied [in psychology] and for which extensive bodies of data exist, it is possible to show in a rigorous fashion that the models of precisely formulated versions of stimulus-response theory and the models of precisely formulated selection-of-strategy cognitive theories are isomorphic." (Suppes 1968).

Most of all, formalism in science is required for the purpose of confronting theories with data. Without axiomatizing both the theory and the empirical analysis, it is next to impossible for a scientist to simultaneously keep track of the implicit assumptions underlying his theory, the tacit assumptions he makes concerning the way his data are generated, and his ideas as to how data and theoretical variables are related to one another. The validity and import of the scientist's statistical inferences depend on all these assumptions. By not making them explicit, the scientist is likely to fool himself and to transmit meaningless information to his readers.

1.3.3 Formalism, Formalization, and the Scientific Method

Above I used "formalism" rather than "formalization" because I need the latter for another purpose. A *scientific theory* is a formal theory that pertains to some domain of science and can be formulated in a first-order language. A scientific theory is *formalized* if it actually is a first-order theory, i.e., if its axioms and theorems are well-formed formulas (wffs) in a first-order language. I do not insist that a theory, which pertains to some domain of science, be formalized. However, it ought to be axiomatized and preferably in such a way that it could be formalized if the need should arise.

Most scientific theories are not formalized. The same is true of most mathematical theories with which scientists become acquainted. In fact, mathematical theories of fundamental importance to all sciences, such as the theory of natural numbers and the theory of real numbers, are usually developed from axioms that cannot be expressed in a first-order language. Still I insist on the potential formalization of scientific theories—for the following reasons.

It is a fact that almost all known mathematical theories can be expressed by a first-order language, and in the course of the book I shall show how this is done for some of them. For example, in chapter 9 I demonstrate how the Kripke-Platek theory of sets is to be developed with a first-order language whose nonlogical vocabulary consists of just one binary predicate symbol and two unary function symbols. In chapter 20 I formulate the theory of real numbers and the theory of nonstandard real numbers within an equally simple first-order language. Such formalizations are obviously not necessary for the pursuit of mathematical ideas. However, they are essential to establishing the syntactic and semantic properties of theories, and they often lead to exciting new insights into the subject matter being studied. In chapters 21 and 22 I demonstrate the usefulness of our formalization of nonstandard analysis for foundational research in both mathematical economics and probability theory.

Since most mathematical theories can be formalized, my insistence on the potential formalization of scientific theories is not stringent. The significance of this potential formalization of scientific theories is twofold. For one thing, mathematical logic can be used both to check the validity of the arguments employed in developing a scientific theory and to establish the syntactic and semantic properties of the theory. For another, the methodological basis constructed in parts I, II, and VI of this book can be used to formulate theoretically sound empirical tests of a scientific theory. The latter is especially important because it makes it that much easier to effectuate the formalism I insist is required for the purpose of confronting theories with data.

In this context it is important to observe that my idea of a scientific theory differs from the so-called received view of scientific theories. According to the received view (see Suppe 1974, pp. 6–56), a scientific theory consists of two parts, a logical calculus whose vocabulary includes the primitive symbols of the theory and a set of rules—the bridge principles—that assign an empirical content to the logical calculus. In this book it is only the first part of the received view that constitutes a scientific theory. The bridge principles belong to the methodological basis but not to the theory.

The received view of scientific theories and the unitary methodological basis for the theoretical and empirical sides of a science that I create in this book are designed for different purposes. The received view of scientific theories is intended to provide an explication of certain logical and epistemological characteristics of theories, e.g., the way theoretical terms are assigned specific meanings with the help of an observational vocabulary. My methodological basis is designed to provide a means to formalize the scientific method. Scientists develop hypotheses, gather data, and use the data to test their hypotheses. Since the received view is void of ideas for carrying out tests of hypotheses, it is incapable of characterizing the scientific method.

"The scientific method" designates the way researchers in the sciences go about acquiring knowledge. In formalizing the scientific method, I allow for the possibility that scientists gather data in many different ways. They may observe the outcomes of experiments that nature conducts or the results of tests that teams of scientists have carried out. I also leave unspecified the methodology which scientists employ when they confront their theories with data. They may use statistical as well as nonstatistical methods; and if they use statistics, they may base their analyses on Bayesian as well as on classical principles of inference. The only restriction I insist on in my formalization of the scientific method is that scientists formulate their hypotheses in such a way that they can be rationalized by a formal axiomatic system. Thus, if a scientist chooses to give a semantic characterization of his theory, his way of acquiring knowledge will fall outside the scope of my unitary methodological basis unless there exists an equivalent axiomatic formalization of his theory (see in this respect Suppes 1967, pp. 60–62).

1.4 Noteworthy Results

I have written this essay to establish a formal unitary methodological basis for the theoretical and empirical sides of a science and to illustrate the uses of the axiomatic method in economics and econometrics. In doing that I have striven to present my ideas on a level of mathematical sophistication that is relatively uniform throughout the book and that should enable me to communicate with an audience that includes all those who have taken a college course in real analysis and a college course in probability and mathematical statistics. At times, therefore, I have sacrificed generality for uniformity and added introductory chapters for the sake of communication.

This is an essay in the philosophy of science and not a text book in mathematical economics and econometrics. It presents and discusses topics that are either essential to creating the sought-for formal unitary methodological basis for the theoretical and empirical sides of a science or efficient means to demonstrate its usefulness. The reader should also observe that, with the exception of a few introductory chapters, each chapter deals with a topic of fundamental importance to the foundations of the science of economics; each chapter illustrates some aspect of the axiomatic method; and different chapters discuss different topics and exhibit different ways of applying the axiomatic method.

In developing the various topics I have looked for interesting ways to demonstrate the potential of the axiomatic method and good ways to convey ideas of interest to theorists and applied workers alike. I have not insisted on establishing results which, from a theorist's viewpoint, are the best results obtainable. Even so, the reader will find novel insights in nearly all the nonintroductory chapters of the book. The most noteworthy of these insights are discussed below, and figure 1.1 outlines the interconnectedness of the parts of the book, suggesting various sequences of study.

1.4.1 Parts I and II: Mathematical Logic

The book begins (chapters 2–9) with an introductory course in mathematical logic, in which a symbolic language for mathematics is developed and the strengths and weaknesses of the axiomatic method are discussed. Most of the ideas presented here are discussed at length in A. Church's *Introduction to Mathematical Logic* (1956) and J. Shoenfield's *Mathematical Logic* (1967). I have added a few examples from nonstandard analysis, the ideas of which I learned from J. E. Fenstad and D. Norman, and have developed the elementary part of the Kripke-Platek theory of sets within my symbolic language.

These introductory chapters in logic may appear difficult to a reader with just the prerequisite knowledge of mathematics. Note, therefore, that while the content of chapters 2–9 is essential both for the construction of my formal unitary methodological basis and for the development of nonstandard analysis in chapters 20–22, only chapter 2 is required for an understanding of the material presented in parts III, IV, and VII–IX. Moreover, while the ideas discussed in chapters 4–9 and 23–25 are essential to a deeper understanding of the axiomatic method and the import of the unitary methodological basis for science, the content of chapter 2 and

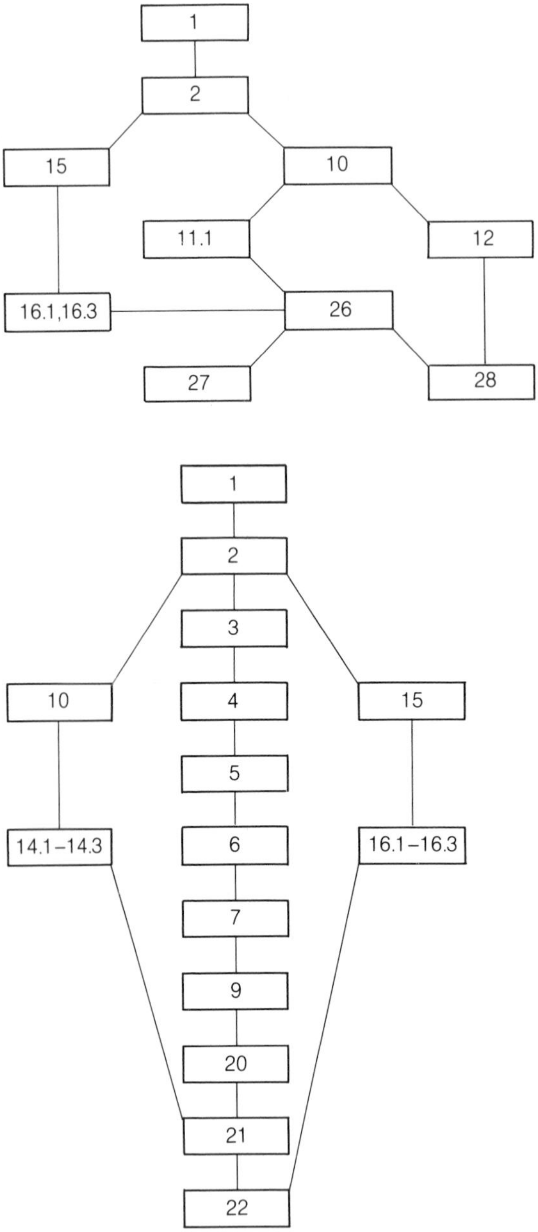

Figure 1.1
Various ways to read this book. The numbers stand for chapters (e.g. 15) and sections (e.g. 16.1).

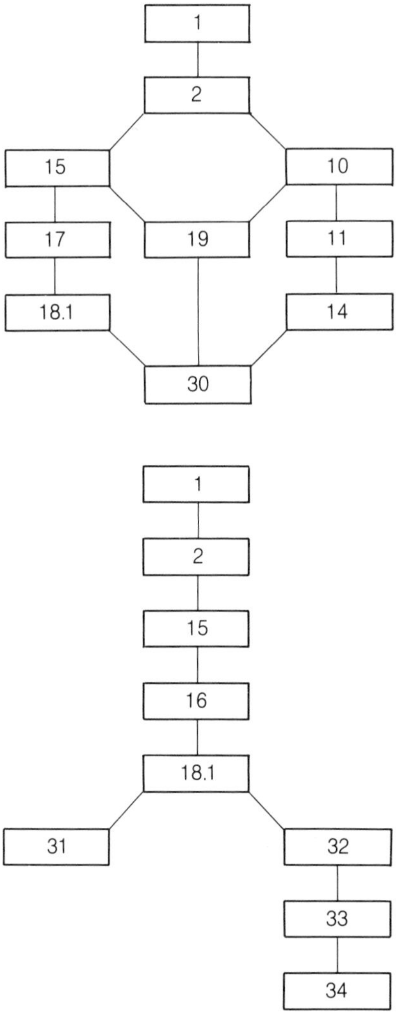

Figure 1.1 (continued)

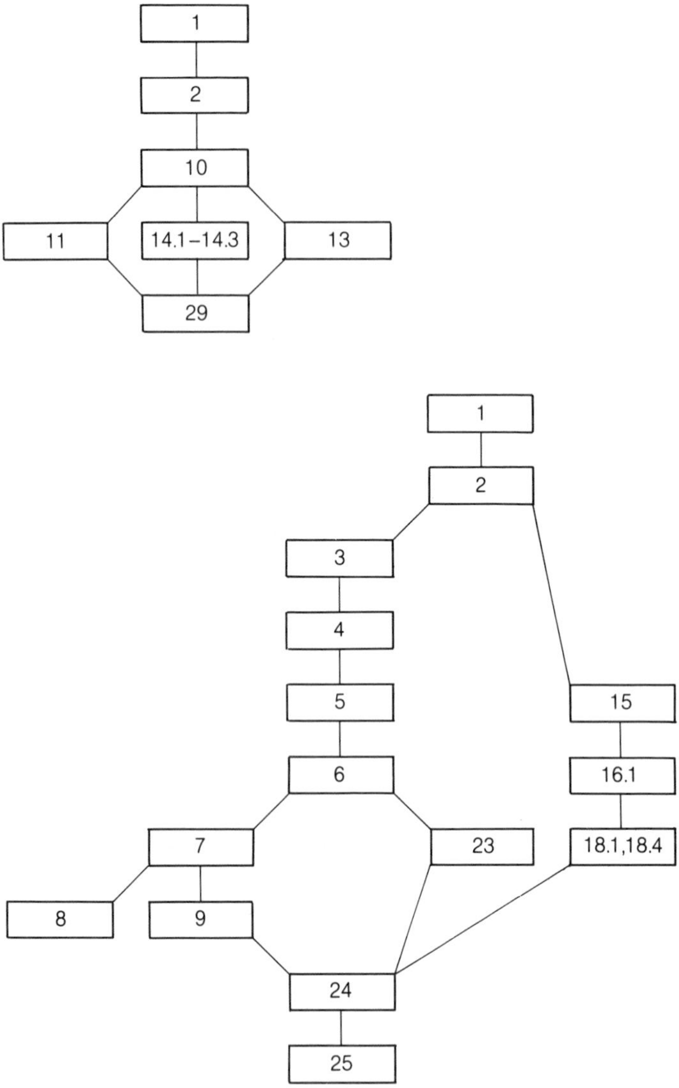

Figure 1.1 (continued)

of parts III, IV, and VII–IX suffices for acquiring a good understanding of the potential of the axiomatic method in economics and econometrics.

Chapter 9, in which I develop the Kripke-Platek theory of sets, KPU, may appear difficult even to a reader with a good formal background in mathematics. Such a reader may wonder why I have chosen to develop KPU in my language rather than developing the more standard Zermelo-Fraenkel theory, ZF. There are both mathematical and philosophical reasons for this. For example, the most obvious advantage of the axiomatic method is lost on ZF since ZF has so few recognizable models in which to interpret its theorems. Also in ZF large parts of mathematical practice are distorted by the demand that all mathematical objects be realized as sets. Finally, it is the case that KPU (and not ZF) provides the right setting for developing both nonstandard analysis and a formal theory of knowledge (see chapters 20 and 24). I learned of KPU from Jon Barwise's book *Admissible Sets and Structures* (1975) and can refer the reader to interesting applications of KPU to the semantics of natural language in Jon Barwise and John Perry's book *Situations and Attitudes* (1983).

1.4.2 Part III: Consumer Choice

In part III the standard certainty theory of consumer choice is presented. With the exception of the ideas of chapter 11 and the first half of chapter 14, the main ideas presented in this part are either novel or are taken from articles that I have published elsewhere. To wit: Both the formulations and proofs of the fundamental theorem of consumer choice and the Hicks-Leontief aggregation theorem in chapter 10 are novel. Similarly, the development of K. Arrow's theory of risk aversion in chapter 12 is new. Finally, the ideas of chapter 13 are taken from Stigum 1973 and the ideas of the last half of chapter 14 are obtained by specialization from Stigum 1974. Chapters 13 and 14 also contain an interesting revealed-preference characterization of additively separable utility functions, due to Bjørn Sandvik, and a simple proof by Bent Birkeland of a theorem of K. Arrow and L. Hurwicz concerning the stability of competitive equilibria.

My purpose in writing part III was to illustrate different aspects of the use of the axiomatic method in economics. Two aspects are especially noteworthy. One concerns the extraordinary sensitivity of theories to minor variations in their axioms. I demonstrate this sensitivity in chapers 10 and 12. In chapter 10 I postulate six axioms from which I derive the main theorems of the certainty theory of consumer choice. In chapter 12 I show that if we modify one of the axioms of chapter 10 a little, we can develop all of Arrow's theory of risk aversion within the certainty theory of consumer choice!

The other noteworthy aspect of part III concerns the status of theories of individual behavior. I contend that an economic theory of individual behavior is irrelevant if there does not exist an economy in which individuals who behave in accordance with the theory can function successfully, i.e., can succeed in carrying out their preferred actions. In chapter 14 I describe variously structured economies in which the consumers of chapters 10 and 11 interact, and I establish sufficient conditions so that these consumers can function successfully in their respective economies. For me, these results constitute an integral part of positive (as opposed to normative) economics!

1.4.3 Part IV: Chance, Ignorance, and Choice

Part IV of this book is devoted to problems that concern the foundations of econometrics and choice under uncertainty. Taken one at a time, most of the ideas presented here are well known to probabilists and mathematical statisticians. However, their significance for foundational research in economics and econometrics seems to have escaped the attention of economists. Here are three examples to substantiate this assertion:

Ever since the publication of the seminal papers of D. Ellsberg (1961) and W. Fellner (1961), economists have been aware that many individuals shade their probabilities in the face of uncertainty. Yet few seem to be aware that G. Shafer in his book A *Mathematical Theory of Evidence* (1976) has developed a complete theory of how such people assign probabilities to uncertain events. Shafer's theory is a theory of superadditive probability measures. I present this theory in chapter 15 and use it and ideas of K. A. Brekke, A. Chateauneuf, and I Gilboa in chapter 19 to formulate a theory of choice under uncertainty for individuals who shade their probabilities.

Kolmogorov's theory of probability (1933) plays a fundamental role in econometrics. In this theory there are three undefined terms: a state of the world, an event, and probability. An event is a subset of the set of all states of the world, and probability is a countably additive function from the family of events to the unit interval. The notion of uncertainty is completely absent from the theory. Moreover, on the surface of things, the possibility of interpreting the probability of an event A as the chance of A happening seems remote. But econometrics without chance and uncertainty makes little sense. Therefore in chapter 16 I use ideas of J. L. Doob, Paul Lévy, R. von Mises, and A. Church to develop an empirical characterization of chance that allows us to identify the probability of an event with the chance of the event occurring.

Many statisticians assign prior distributions to the unknown parameters of their statistical models. Some do it to incorporate in their data analyses the prior information which they possess concerning the values of the parameters in question. Others do it to express their ignorance about the likely values of these parameters. Whatever their reasons, statisticians who assign prior distributions to the parameters of their statistical models will *usually* analyze finite sets of data as if the data constitute a partial realization of an exchangeable process. Often they will also determine the asymptotic properties of their parameter estimates upon the hypothesis that their data are generated by a purely random process. From a methodological point of view, such statistical analyses are meaningless. Just how meaningless they are is shown in chapter 18 where ideas of D. G. Kendall, B. de Finetti, A. Rényi, and H. P. McKean are used to develop the theory of exchangeable processes, first on ordinary probability spaces and then on conditional probability spaces. The latter part is novel and fills a fundamental lacuna in the foundations of Bayesian econometrics.

1.4.4 Part V: Nonstandard Analysis

Part V begins with an introductory course in nonstandard analysis. Then we discuss exchange and probability in hyperspace. My main purpose in writing this part was to study the functioning of large economies and to introduce the reader to a method of analysis that I believe has important applications in mathematical statistics. Most of the ideas presented are discussed at length in A. Robinson's book *Non-standard Analysis* (1966), in S. Albeverio, J. E. Fenstad, R. Høegh-Krohn, and T. Lindstrøm's book, *Nonstandard Methods in Stochastic Analysis and Mathematical Physics* (1986), and in several seminal papers by D. Brown and A. Robinson (1974), P. Loeb (1975), and R. M. Anderson (1976). However, the relevance of these ideas for foundational research in economics and econometrics has not been explored fully. One of the results given in part V will attest to this relevance.

The economics of large economies have been studied from different points of view. One example is an economy consisting of a number of replicas of a finite exchange economy. G. Debreu and H. Scarf (1963) demonstrated that as the number of replicas (and hence the size of the economy) increases, the core of the economy converges to the set of competitive equilibria of the economy. Another example is R. Aumann's work on exchange economies with a measure space of economic agents; see, for example, Aumann's "Markets with a Continuum of Traders" (1964), in which he shows that in his economy the core equals the set of competitive equilibria. In chapters 21 and 22 we study exchange in hyperspace under different assumptions on the topology of the space. There we establish the fact that Aumann's result concerning the equality of the core and the set of competitive equilibria is a consequence of the topology which he imposes on his economy and has little to do with the number of agents in his economy.

This result does not detract from the unquestioned importance to mathematical economics of Robert Aumann's two seminal papers on exchange economies with a measure space of agents. Instead, the result provides evidence for the fact that when interpreting an economic theory, it is not sufficient to assign names to undefined terms and to check the mutual consistency of the axioms. The originator of an economic theory owes his readers a description of at least one situation in which the empirical relevance of the theory can be tested.

1.4.5 Part VI: Epistemology

Part VI completes the construction of a formal unitary methodological basis for the theoretical and empirical sides of a science that was begun in parts I and II. In the process of developing this methodological basis, we obtain results in formal philosophy that are of independent interest. Some of these results are discribed below.

Bertrand Russell (1976) begins his inquiry into the problems of philosophy by asking: Is there any knowledge in the world which is so certain that no reasonable man can doubt it? I believe that there is such knowledge. I also believe that if A denotes a declarative sentence, then a reasonable man *must agree* that he knows that A only if *it necessarily is the case* that A. If that is correct, then our analysis at the end of chapter 23 provides both a syntactic and a semantic characterization of the well-formed formulas (wffs) of a first-order language that express knowledge which no reasonable man can doubt.

In chapter 24 a two-sorted modal-theoretic language is formulated within which we develop a theory of rational belief and knowledge for some person I. Here rational belief is a numerical relation between pairs of propositions p and h that measures the degree of belief in p which I upon knowledge of h would entertain. Moreover, knowledge is a binary propositional function of pairs of propositions p and h, according to which

I knows that *p* upon knowledge of *h* if and only if (1) it is the case that *p* and (2) *I*'s rational belief in *p* upon knowledge of *h* equals 1. The theory is involved, but the rewards for developing it are gratifying. Three examples will attest to that.

First, conditional probability spaces and logical probabilities: Our characterization of *I*'s rational belief extends A. Rényi's theory of conditional probability spaces (Rényi 1970, pp. 33–99) to a theory of superadditive conditional probability measures on the wffs of a first-order language *L*. In this theory we delineate a well-defined collection of wffs of *L* that plays a role analogous to the role played by a bunch of events in Rényi's theory. Moreover, we demonstrate that the conditional probabilities on the wffs of *L* are generated by a uniquely determined superadditive probability measure on the closed wffs of *L*.

Next, epistemological truth and knowledge: According to the semantic conception of truth, a proposition "A" is true if and only if *A*; e.g., "snow is white" is true if and only if snow is white. According to the epistemological conception of truth, "A" is true if and only if it can be known that *A*. In our theory of knowledge "it can be known that A" is synonymous with "there is a proposition *h* such that *I* upon knowledge of *h* knows that *A*." We demonstrate that if *A* is a closed wff of a first-order language *L*, then "A" is true if and only if it can be known that *A*.

Finally, defective evidence and knowledge: Suppose that the proposition *p* is a disjunction of two propositions *q* and *r*, and that *q* is false and *r* is true. It is possible to know that *p* upon knowledge of *h* and at the same time to entertain a rational belief in *q* upon knowledge of *h* equal to 1. This possibility is disconcerting to most epistemologists. Therefore, at the end of chapter 24 we reformulate our concept of knowledge such that *I* can know that *p* upon knowledge of *h* only if the evidence for *p* provided by *h* is (in R. Chisholm's terminology) nondefective. After the change, our theory of knowledge becomes a symbolic rendition of Chisholm's theory of knowledge (Chisholm 1977) in which we can and do give syntactic and semantic characterizations of the wffs of a first-order language, which Chisholm calls self-presenting and nondefectively evident.

The theory of knowledge presented in chapter 24 leaves no room for partial knowledge. Either *I* knows that *p* upon knowledge of *h* or *I* does not know that *p* upon knowledge of *h*. If *I* is a scientist and *p* designates a postulate or a theorem of a scientific theory, *I* may know that *p* can be applied in some situations and not in others, but he usually cannot claim to know that *p*. It is, therefore, significant that the modal-theoretic language SEL, formulated in chapter 25, is a language for talking about scientists' search for knowledge concerning the applicability of their theories. Thus

SEL provides us with the means to theorize about both partial knowledge and the acquisition of new knowledge.

1.4.6 Part VII: Empirical Analysis of Economic Theories

Part VII was written to illustrate how useful the unitary methodological basis created in parts I, II, and VI is for economics and econometrics. In the process of writing part VII, I hit upon ideas that I believe are of particular interest to applied econometricians. I shall detail some of them next.

One of the themes that I try to develop in part VII is the idea that we cannot test the validity of a consistent formal economic theory. We can only test the empirical relevance of an interpretation of such a theory. In part VII I choose *one* formal economic theory—the certainty theory of consumer choice—and use observations on the choices made by members of *one* sample population—U.S. consumers in 1962—to test the empirical relevance of *three different* interpretations of the theory: the life-cycle hypothesis,[1] the permanent-income hypothesis, and Arrow's theory of risk aversion. I find that it is possible that the life-cycle hypothesis can be used to rationalize the consumption-savings choices of the sample population. I also show that the permanent-income hypothesis has little relevance for the same population. Finally, I demonstrate that if the U.S. consumers of 1962 made their balance-sheet choices in accordance with Arrow's theory, then their absolute and proportional risk-aversion functions must *both* be decreasing functions of net worth. In contrast, Arrow contented that an individual's absolute and proportional risk-aversion functions are, respectively, decreasing and increasing functions of his net worth.

The rejection of the relevance of Friedman's permanent-income hypothesis for the 1962 U.S. population is based on a statistical analysis that has several novel aspects. For example, in this analysis I demonstrate how instrumental variables can be introduced in a given factor-analysis model to ensure identification of the parameters of the model. I also use factor-analytic methods to estimate the parameters of a linear model in which the independent variables are nonobservable and the error terms need not be normally distributed. Finally, I derive the asymptotic distribution of my factor-analytic estimates and use bootstrap methods to obtain consistent estimates of their variances and covariances. The concept of an instrumental variable and the ideas of factor analysis are both well known and have been applied in various ways in econometrics. Relevant examples are found in Lin (1976) and Liviatan (1968). I believe, however, that the way I make use of instrumental variables and factor-analytic methods in testing the empirical relevance of Friedman's hypothesis is novel. The usefulness of bootstrapping techniques in the same context was pointed out to me by Petter Laake.

Part VII stresses the importance of writing down all (!) the axioms of an empirical analysis. The resulting formalism may seem unnecessary but is not. Chapters 12 and 28 attest to that. In chapter 12 I develop Arrow's theory of risk aversion and use ideas of D. Cass and J. Stiglitz and O. Hart to delineate the largest class of utility functions *D* that will ensure the relevance of Arrow's theory in a world—such as ours—in which individuals can invest in more than one risky asset. In chapter 28 we confront Arrow's theory with data from the 1962 population of U.S. consumers. We assume that the consumers in the sample behave in accordance with Arrow's theory and that their utility functions belong to *D*. Then we subject Arrow's hypotheses concerning the monotonicity of individuals' absolute and proportional risk-aversion functions to test. We also determine the relative degrees of risk aversion of various groups and show among other things that both absolute and proportional risk aversion increase with age. These results are interesting. It is therefore important to observe that not only is *D* the largest class of utility functions that will ensure the general applicability of Arrow's theory, *D* is also the largest class of utility functions for which our statistical (!) analysis can be justified. Without a full view of all the axioms of our empirical analysis, the significance of *D* for our statistical arguments would have been hard to fathom.

1.4.7 Part VIII: Determinism, Uncertainty, and the Utility Hypothesis

Much of economic theory is based on three questionable assumptions: (1) the world is deterministic; (2) decision makers act as if they know the values of all relevant parameters; and (3) consumers and firms, respectively, act as if they were maximizing utility and profit. In part VIII we use the axiomatic method to *speculate* about the sensitivity of some well-established doctrines of economics to a relaxation of these three assumptions. The results obtained are, from a methodological point of view, important both to economic theorists and to applied econometricians. I explain why below.

The confrontation of theory with data can happen in many ways. In chapters 26–28 we use *three* different *statistical* methods—least squares, factor analysis, and analysis of covariance—to test the empirical relevance of three different interpretations of one and the same theory—the certainty theory of consumer choice. In chapter 29 we consider two more interpretations of the same theory. For one of them we develop nonparametric, finite-sample tests. These tests, most of which are due to Sidney Afriat, are essentially *nonstatistical*. Even so, they reemphasize the fact that in chapters 26–28 it is the structure of the utility function and not the utility hypothesis per se that is at stake. More importantly, they demonstrate that the utility hypothesis cannot be tested with data from ordinary budget studies. Finally, for the fifth interpretation we combine economic-theoretic and statistical arguments to throw doubt on the possibility of using the usual time-series data on consumption expenditures of *groups* of consumers to test the utility hypothesis. These results provide new evidence for the need of writing down explicitly *all* the axioms of an empirical analysis.

Economists derive theorems, make predictions, and (!) suggest economic policies using arguments which explicitly or implicitly postulate the validity of the first two assumptions mentioned above. Such endeavors are unjustifiable unless it can be demonstrated that the most important doctrines of economics are insensitive to a relaxation of these two assumptions. Hence in chapters 30 and 31 we set out to determine whether a certainty theory of individual choice and macroeconomic growth suffices for all practical purposes. I begin in chapter 30 by introducing uncertainty into the environment of consumers and firms and by developing theories of consumer and entrepreneurial choice that are natural extensions of the standard certainty theories of the consumer and the firm. Then I demonstrate, among other things, that in an economy in which consumers and firms behave in accordance with my theories, neither the fundamental theorem of consumer choice nor the hallmark of welfare economics, which insists that competitive equilibria allocate resources Pareto-optimally, are generally valid. In chapter 31 I develop a theory of economic growth that allows us to test the robustness of, for example, Robert Solow's deterministic theory of economic growth (Solow 1956). Our theoretical results do not lead to a rejection of Solow's theory. Instead, they establish the existence of an observable parameter, the value of which can be used to determine whether a given economy, when large enough, will grow deterministically. Whatever the values of this parameter for developed and underdeveloped countries, the results presented in chapters 30 and 31 show beyond doubt that the foundations of welfare economics and public economics are shaky and may be irrelevant for most practical purposes.

Most of the ideas of part VIII I have either learned from others or borrowed from articles that I have published elsewhere. Specifically, the discussion of the utility hpothesis is based on ideas that I originally learned from H. Varian (1983) and H. Sonnenschein (1972). Moreover, the theories developed in chapter 30 are formalized versions of the theories of choice under uncertainty that I have presented earlier (1969, 1969a, and 1972). Finally, the ideas of chapter 31 are taken from Stigum (1972a) and from Kesten and Stigum (1974) and are as much the ideas of Harry Kesten as they are my own.

1.4.8 Part IX: Prediction, Distributed Lags, and Stochastic Difference Equations

In part IX we study four topics of fundamental importance to the analysis of economic time series: prediction; optimal distributed lags; modeling trends, cycles, and seasonal factors; and estimating parameters of a stochastic difference equation. This task involves us in delineating three classes of random processes—wide-sense stationary processes, ARIMA processes, and dynamic stochastic processes—and in establishing many interesting limit theorems for nonstationary processes. Our results ought to be of interest to both theoretical and applied econometricians. Two cases in point will explain why.

Trends, cycles, and seasonals in economic time series have been modeled in many ways. However, most of them can be rationalized by assuming that an economic time series is a partial realization of an ARIMA process or a dynamic stochastic process. In chapter 33 we establish the salient characteristics of such processes. Our results suggest that it is highly unlikely that an economic time series is generated by an ARIMA process but possible that it can be generated by a dynamic stochastic process. This is important, since so many prominent econometricians these days favor modeling trends, cycles, and seasonals by ARIMA processes.

Econometricians usually either wave their hands and pay lip service to, or simply ignore, the importance of asymptotic theory in the validation of their statistical methods. Some even believe that if they can establish that an estimate is best linear unbiased, their theoretical work has come to a happy ending. In chapter 34 we set out to determine whether the indifferent attitude of econometricians is justifiable when they estimate parameters of a stochastic difference equation. There we study the limiting behavior of such estimates and show that some of them converge exponentially fast, others with probability 1, and still others in probability to well-defined limiting values that need not equal the true values of the parameters in question. We also derive the limiting distribution of these estimates and demonstrate that it can, but need not, be normal and that it is often degenerate. These results exhibit the importance of asymptotic theory for least-squares estimation of the parameters of a stochastic difference equation. They also suggest interesting questions: How good is an inconsistent best linear unbiased estimate? And what is the real power of a finite-sample test of the sizes (or signs) of a set of parameters when the test is based on estimates whose limiting distribution is degenerate?

With the exception of the material discussed in chapter 32, the theories developed in part IX are theories that I have published before (Stigum 1974c, 1963, 1975, 1976, and 1976a). Since the proofs of my main theorems are involved and spelled out in these earlier publications, I omit them here unless they are essential for an understanding of the theorems in question.

1.5 Acknowledgments

It has taken more than fifteen years to write this long essay in the philosophy of science and I owe many friends and colleagues a hearty thanks for much help and moral support. Three of them, Henry P. McKean, Harry Kesten, and Jens Erik Fenstad taught me mathematics and have been an unending source of helpful suggestions, clarifying remarks, and useful references. Three others, Eyolf Steen-Olsen, Hans Jørgen Bakke, and Arne Strøm, provided the guidance and the computer programs I needed to carry out the applied econometric research for chapters 26–28. Still others made a significant impact on the content of the essay through their most constructive criticisms. I shall list them according to the parts they read: parts I and II—Jan Tore Lønning and Helle Frisak Sem; part III—Erik Grønn, Kjell Arne Brekke, Petter Frenger, Aanund Hylland, Atle Seierstad, and John Pratt; part IV—Kjell Arne Brekke, Geir Storvik, and Peter Fishburn; part V—Tom Lindstrøm; part VI—Jan Tore Lønning, Andrew Jones, Bjørn Hansen, and Roderick Chisholm; part VII—Jørgen Aasnes, Petter Laake, Harald Goldstein, and John Pratt; part VIII—Jørgen Aasnes, Kjell Arne Brekke, and Hal Varian; and part IX:—Keith McLaren, Clive Granger, Svend Hylleberg, Tore Schweder, and John Dagsvik. Finally, James T. Higginbotham introduced me to formal philosophy, Erling T. Thoresen provided data for the empirical analyses of chapters 26–28, and Marcia Stigum and Bruce Wolman edited early versions of the manuscript and helped me improve my presentation of many of the topics in the book.

At the suggestion of The MIT Press, nine distinguished scholars, whose names I do not know, agreed to read different parts of the essay. Their thoughtful comments and not always gentle prodding made me rewrite many of the chapters they read. I am grateful to these scholars for their constructive criticisms and to The MIT Press for having arranged this extraordinary refereeing process.

One circumstance of life made the writing of the essay more difficult than it might have been: I did not have an opportunity to give a series of lectures on most of the topics I cover in the essay. For that reason it was especially important to me that on various occasions I was invited to present my ideas to interested scholars in different parts of the world. I am most grateful to the following friends and colleagues both for inviting me to give talks in their seminars and for their thoughtful comments: Stanley Reiter, Walter Fisher, Richard Day, Mike Yohe, Dale Jorgenson, Michael Balch, Roy Radner, Christopher Sims, Jean Pierre Aubin, Edmond Malinvaud, Jean-Michel Grandmont, Ivar Ekeland, David Giles, Richard Manning, Ewen McGann, Eric Jones, Keith McLaren, Dean Terrell, Murrey Kemp, Jean Savin, Svend Hylleberg, Karl Vind, Birgit Grodal, and Agnar Sandmo.

My work on the book began during my sabbatical year at Northwestern University in 1973–74 and was completed at the University of Oslo in the fall of 1988. In between I had the privilege of spending three summers at the Mathematics Research Center (MRC) in Madison, Wisconsin, one summer at the University of Canterbury (UC) in Christchurch, New Zealand, four to five months at the Australian National University (ANU) in Canberra, Australia, and one year at the Massachusetts Institute of Technology. I am grateful to the Guggenheim Foundation and Northwestern University for financing my sabbatical year, to MRC, UC, and ANU for financing my stay at their respective institutions, and to the University of Oslo for financing my year at MIT.

Last but not least I want to thank Professor Wilhelm Keilhaus Minnefond and the Norwegian Research Council for Science and the Humanities for financial support. I also want to thank the most gracious young ladies who drew figures, made calculations, and typed the various versions of the manuscript: Marianne Ramstad, Inger Johanne Kroksjø, Rønnaug Teige, Tone Enger, Gro Winsnes, Randi Borgen, Inger Støen, Edel Mikkelsen, May-Bente Olsen, and Laila Jensen. Of them, Laila Jensen undoubtedly suffered the most and was responsible for typing the final manuscript.

2 The Axiomatic Method

2.1 Axioms and Undefined Terms

Consider a scientist developing a theory about some subject such as probability or consumer choice. He cannot prove rigorously each assertion of his theory. In fact, to avoid vicious-circle arguments, he must postulate some assertions and deduce from them the validity of others. This was recognized by Aristotle over 2000 years ago (see Aristotle 1964, pp. 165, 168, and 183; Wilder 1965, pp. 3–4):

> Every demonstrative science must proceed from primary, indemonstrable principles; otherwise the steps of demonstration would be endless. Of these indemonstrable principles some are a) common to all sciences, others are b) special to each science.

Originally, principles under (a) were called axioms. They were said to declare self-evident truths such as "the whole always exceeds each of its parts." Principles under (b) were called postulates. They pertained to facts considered so obvious that their validity could be assumed, e.g., "through a point P not on a given line L there is one and only one line parallel to L." Today all the basic assertions of a theory are called *axioms*.

A scientist is in the same situation vis-à-vis concepts as he is vis-à-vis assertions. He can define some concepts in terms of others, but he cannot define all his concepts that way. Instead he must start from certain undefined concepts, usually referred to as *undefined terms*, and use them to develop other concepts referred to as *defined terms*.

In choosing basic concepts (i.e., undefined terms), the scientist looks for concepts so simple that they can be understood without precise definition. Examples are "point" and "line" in geometry and "commodity" and "money" in economic theory. The number of concepts a researcher leaves undefined and the number of axioms he postulates are arbitrary. Their number depends on how the researcher wants to use his theory and how it may be used by others.

2.2 Rules of Inference and Definition

To go beyond axioms and basic concepts, a theorist needs certain *rules of inference* that tell him how to pass from axioms to theorems and from axioms *and* theorems to other theorems. He also needs some *rules of definition* that tell him how he may introduce new concepts based on existing ones.

Not all rules of inference are *valid* in that they lead from true premises to true conclusions. Only valid rules of inference interest our scientist. Whether a rule of inference is valid depends on the class of sentences to which it is applied. Examples 2.1 and 2.2 will illustrate this.

E 2.1 Each and every human being is mortal.
Per is a human being.
Therefore, Per is mortal.

In this example lines 1 and 2 state the premises, line 3 states the conclusion. Two rules of inference are used. The first is the *dictum de omni et nullo*: "What is true of all individuals is also true of any one individual"; i.e., from "each and every human being is mortal," we infer that "if Per is a human being, he is mortal." The other is the *Modus Ponens*: If assertion A is true and if A implies assertion B, we infer that B is true; i.e., from "Per is a human being" and "if Per is a human being, he is mortal," we infer "Per is mortal."

E 2.2 Let us call a set *regular* if it is not an element of itself. The set of all barbers in Paris is a regular set; the set of all abstract ideas is not. Sets that are not regular must be treated with care:

Each and every regular set belongs to F.
F is a regular set.
Therefore, F belongs to F.

In E 2.2 we use two premises and the same rules of inference as in E 2.1 to deduce a conclusion that contradicts one of the premises. Thus, unless two contradictory statements can both be true, E 2.2 illustrates a situation in which the given rules of inference cannot be applied.

Not all rules of definition are valid. For a definition to be valid it must meet several conditions: (1) it must be *dispensable*, that is, the scientist must be able to do without it; and (2) it must be *noncreative*, that is, the scientist cannot use the definition to establish formulas that do not contain the defined term, unless these formulas can be proved without using the definition.

Defined terms enter both in the statement of axioms and in the statement of theorems. For instance, in the set theory presented in chapter 9, there are only three basic concepts: an urelement, a set, and the predicate ε. "$\subset$" (set inclusion) is defined in terms of ε, and is used as thus defined to state the fourth axiom. In the probability theory presented in chapter 15, the basic concepts are a probable thing, an event, and a probability measure. The concepts of a random variable, expected value, conditional probability measure, and random processes are introduced as defined terms.

2.3 Universal Terms and Theorems

Equipped with undefined terms, axioms, rules of inference, and rules of definition, a scientist can begin to establish theorems. *Theorems* are assertions concerning the undefined and defined terms that can be proved from accepted premises with the help of the rules of inference. The accepted premises are in turn either axioms, already proved theorems, or so-called *universal theorems*; the latter are theorems that have been established in other areas of mathematical inquiry (e.g., the Implicit Function Theorem and Kakutani's Fixed Point Theorem that economists use in proving their theorems). When formulating his theorems the scientist often not only makes use of undefined and defined terms but also of a collection of so-called *universal terms*; these denote logical and mathematical objects such as set, field, function, there exists, etc. In a given situation the use of universal terms and theorems is not prescribed by logic; it depends on both the scientist's interests and the audience.

2.4 Theorizing and the Axiomatic Method

The undefined and defined terms, the axioms, and all the theorems that can be derived from them constitute a *theory*. The method of constructing such a theory from basic concepts and principles is called the *axiomatic method*. Our description of this method is summarized schematically in figure 2.1. In the figure the collecting and processing of information are represented by nodes I and II; in them rules for formulating sentences are prescribed. Node I operations use the rules of definition, node II operations the rules of inference. The arrows indicate information flows within the system.

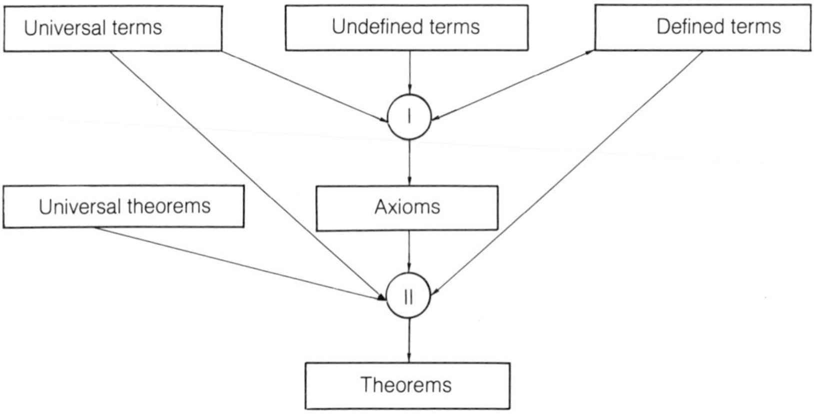

Figure 2.1
The axiomatic method.

2.5 Pitfalls in the Axiomatic Method

The axiomatic method is used to develop theories in such varied areas as mathematical logic, economics, and astronomy. Although appearing simple, the method has caused much controversy as self-evident postulates have turned out to be nonobvious, and carefully constructed theories have proved to be contradictory.

Many of the "self-evident truths" common to all sciences are not *generally* valid. The law of contradiction insists that nothing can both be and not be. Yet an Australian and a Norwegian will disagree on whether today is Sunday. Similarly, the law of the excluded middle insists that something must be or not be; but how can one be sure? Consider sentences such as "All angels have wings" and "There are natural numbers of which no one has ever thought." Finally, "the whole is always larger than any of its parts"; whether the whole is larger depends on the meaning of "larger," as witnessed by the one-to-one correspondence between positive and even integers.

The postulates that pertain to particular branches of science also often turn out to be neither simple nor obviously valid. For instance, non-Euclidean geometries shattered the idea that through a point P not on a given line L, one and only one line can be drawn that is parallel to L. In the geometry of Bolyai, Gauss, and Lobachevsky there exist infinitely many lines through P that are parallel to L; in Riemann's geometry there are no such lines.

Of the various theories whose axioms imply contradictory assertions, one of fundamental importance to modern mathematics is Cantor's set theory. As originally conceived, Cantor's theory contained contradictions such as E 2.2 and paradoxes such as "The power set of the set of all sets, U, has a greater cardinal than U itself." The contradiction was discovered by Russell, the paradox by Cantor. The contradiction and paradox are usually referred to as Russell's and Cantor's *antinomies*, respectively.

The preceding examples indicate not that the axiomatic method should never be used, but rather that it must be applied with care. Specifically, since most "obvious truths" are not generally valid, a scientist employing the axiomatic method must delineate the logic he is using to justify his rules of inference and rules of definition. He must also specify the mathematical theory which supplies the theorems in the universal-theorems box of figure 2.1, and he must check his axioms as a possible source of contradictory statements.

2.6 Theories and Models

The scientist must also bear in mind that, strictly speaking, any theory he constructs using the axiomatic method is a theory about undefined terms, not about anything specific in the world. He may give his undefined terms meaningful names, but in constructing his theory, these names must be treated as so many letter symbols. Consequently, his theory is a theory about symbols, nothing else.

The scientist can make his theory "talk about" objects of interest by giving the undefined terms an interpretation that renders all the axioms simultaneously true. Such an interpretation is called a *model* of the axioms and the theory derived from them. An axiom system that has one model usually has many. In naming his undefined terms, the scientist indicates the *intended model of his theory*. For instance, the intended model of the standard theory of consumer choice describes a consumer's choice of commodity bundles in various price-income situations. The theory can also be interpreted as describing a consumer's optimal investment in safe and risky assets in various price—net worth situations.

2.7 An Example

To conclude these introductory remarks on the axiomatic method I present an example that illustrates most of the ideas discussed above. The interested reader can find a variant of this example and a detailed discussion of the historical development of the axiomatic method in R. L. Wilder's *Introduction to the Foundations of Mathematics* (1965, pp. 3–22).

Look back at figure 2.1 and consider a scientist who wants to develop a theory about points and lines in a Euclidean plane. Let us say that he has stored "point" and "line" in the undefined-terms box and the following terms in the universal-terms box: every, collection, exist, same, distinct, equal, contains, one, two, on, only, if, at least, imply, not, assertion, in common.[1] He has also defined "to be parallel" to mean "to have no points in common" and has stored "parallel" in the defined-terms box. Finally, he has decided to adopt Modus Ponens as a rule of inference and to make use of only four universal theorems, one from set theory and three from mathematical logic:

UT 1 Two collections of points are equal if and only if they contain the same points.

UT 2 If A is an assertion, then A and not A cannot both be true.

UT 3 If A is an assertion, then either A or not A is true.

UT 4 If A and B are assertions, then A implies not B if and only if B implies not A.

These theorems he has stored in the universal-theorems box.

To develop his theory, our scientist now formulates the following axioms:

A 1 Every line is a collection of points.

A 2 There exist at least two points.

A 3 If p and q are distinct points, there exists one and only one line containing p and q.

A 4 If L is a line, there exists a point not on L.

A 5 If L is a line, and p is a point not on L, there exists one and only one line that contains p and is parallel to L.

The scientist knows that axioms can have many interpretations. So he observes that his axioms cannot be interpreted to be about books and libraries in a given town. He also observes that they cannot be about persons and clubs in a ghost town that contains just three people. However, his axioms can be made to talk about persons and clubs in a ghost town with four people. They can also be made to talk about points and lines in a Euclidean plane, as the scientist intended.

With the help of UT 1–UT 4, our scientist next uses Modus Ponens and A 1–A 5 to derive many interesting theorems. For example, from UT 1 and UT 2 and A 1–A 4, the scientist deduces T 1.

T 1 Every point is on at least two distinct lines.

Similarly, from UT 1–UT 4 and A 1–A 5, he deduces T 2.

T 2 Every line contains at least two points.

But if T 2 is true, it is easy to see that UT 2 and A 1–A 5 imply T 3.

T 3 There are at least four points.

Finally, from T 2, T 3, UT 1–UT 4, and A 1–A 5, he deduces T 4.

T 4 There are at least six lines.

The preceding theorems do not amount to much of a theory about points and lines in a Euclidean plane. However, they do illustrate how theorems can be proved from accepted premises. They also illustrate the use of universal theorems in developing mathematically formulated theories. Finally, they show that if a point is to be a person in a ghost town, the town must have at least four persons. Also if a line is to be a interpreted as a club in the same town, the club must have at least two members and there must be at least six clubs. In fact, each club must have the same number of members; and if n is the number of persons in the town and r is the number of members of each club, then $n = r^2$ and the number of clubs equals $n + r$.

I

Mathematical Logic I: First-Order Languages

3 Meaning and Truth

In part I we shall use the axiomatic method to develop a symbolic language that can be used to formulate all sorts of mathematical theories, e.g., set theory and probability theory. Our language will contain a logical and a nonlogical vocabulary. The logical vocabulary consists of symbols for a predicate of equality, a quantifier, sentence connectives, and a denumerable infinity of variables. The nonlogical vocabulary consists of symbols for constants, functions, and predicates. The sentences of our language are *formulas*. Not all such formulas are useful for our purposes. Those that are, we call *well-formed formulas*. They satisfy certain structural requirements (i.e., sentence-formation rules) that we impose on the sentences about which we theorize. Some of the well-formed formulas are singled out as axioms. Their structures delineate the meaning of the members of the logical vocabulary. From the axioms we derive theorems in accordance with specified rules of inference, one of which is the Modus Ponens described above. When the logical symbols are given their intended interpretation, these theorems provide us with rules of inference that can be used to prove theorems in other areas of mathematical inquiry.

3.1 A Technical Vocabulary

A symbolic language with its symbols, sentence formation rules, rules of inference, axioms, and theorems is usually referred to as an *object language*. In presenting it, we use some ordinary English words and certain other symbols. The symbols and the English words used belong to a poorly delimited language called the *metalanguage* of the object language. How extensive the metalanguage is depends on the use to which it is put. It must be used to present the object language, but it can also be used both to study the formal properties of the language and to interpret it.

Some of the English words that we use to describe and interpret our symbolic language require careful definition. In this chapter I define these words and discuss their meanings.

3.1.1 Names

We use the word *name* in the same way A. Church uses "proper name" (see Church 1956, p. 3). Examples are Oslo, the capital of Norway, nine, and four hundred thirty-nine. A name names something. We say that a name *denotes* that which it names, and we call the thing denoted its *denotation*. Different names may denote the same thing; for instance, "Oslo" and "the capital of Norway" denote the same city in Norway. In natural language a single name may also have different denotations. Thus Bergen denotes both a city in Norway and a town in New Hampshire.

Besides having a denotation, a name also has a *sense*. The sense of a name is "that which is grasped when one understands the name" (Church 1956, p. 6). It is possible to comprehend the sense of a name without knowing its denotation. For instance, it is logical to ask: Is Oslo the capital of Norway?

3.1.2 Declarative Sentences

Names of a particular kind are *declarative sentences*. Such sentences are aggregations of words that express an assertion, and they denote one or the other of two abstract objects called truth values; these are *truth* and *falsehood*. A true declarative sentence denotes truth, a false one falsehood. Thus "Oslo is the capital of Norway" is a name that denotes truth, while "Churchill was a Nazi" is a name that denotes falsehood.

The sense of a declarative sentence is called a *proposition*. A proposition is a function of the senses of the parts of the declarative sentence which expresses the proposition (Church 1956, p. 26); e.g., the sense of "a diamond is hard" is a function of the senses of diamond and hard. The same proposition may be expressed by different declarative sentences; e.g., "either the table is not immersed in water or it dissolves" expresses the same proposition as "the table is soluble." Also the same declarative sentence may express many different propositions; e.g., the sense of "I am right, and you are wrong" depends on the context in which it is uttered.

3.1.3 Constants and Variables

In mathematics and mathematical logic, a name is a *constant*. The *value of a constant* is its denotation. A *variable* is "a symbol whose meaning is like that of ... a constant except that the single denotation is replaced by the possibility of various values of the variable" (Church 1956, p. 9). Some variables can assume only one value; others have a range of possible values. The set of all names (i.e., constants) that can be substituted for a variable is called its *domain of definition*. The set of denotations of these names (i.e., the set of values of these constants) is called the *range* of the variable.

E 3.1 $\sqrt{2}$, Π, and e are constants that are the names of three different numbers. In contrast II, 2, $1 + 1$, and $\sqrt{4}$ are constants that are different names of the *same* natural number, 2.

E 3.2 Let x be a variable whose domain of definition is $\{1, 2, \ldots\}$. Then the range of values of x and $x + 2$, respectively, are the natural numbers denoted by 1, 2, ..., and 3, 4, ... Let p be a variable whose domain of definition is the set of declarative sentences of the form $1 < x < 50$. Then the range of values of p consists of the two truth values, truth and falsehood. The value of p is truth (or falsehood) when any one of the the names 2, 3, ..., 49 (or $1, 51, 52, \ldots$) is substituted for x.

3.1.4 Functions and Predicates

A *set* is a collection of objects. If A is a set, we write $x \in A$ for x is an object in A. If A and B are sets, we write $A \subset B$ if $x \in A$ only if $x \in B$. The set of objects that an axiom system talks about is called the *universe* of the axiom system. Its elements are usually referred to as *individuals*. The variables that vary over the universe are called *individual variables*.

If A and B are sets, a *function g from A to B* is an assignment of an object in B to *each* object in A. We denote it by $g(\cdot)$: $A \rightarrow B$ and we call A the *domain* of g. The set of objects in B that are assigned to some element of A is called the *range* of g. An *n-tuple in A* is an ordered set of n elements of A. We denote the n-tuple by $(a_1, \ldots, a_n)$ and we let A^n denote the set of all n-tuples in A. A function g from A^n to B is an *n-ary function from A to B*. The *graph* of g is the set of $(n + 1)$-tuples $(a_1, \ldots, a_n, b)$ with $(a_1, \ldots, a_n) \in A^n$ and $b \in B$ such that $b = g(a_1, \ldots, a_n)$. In our symbolic language, a function will always be a function from the universe to the universe. Such a function is called an *individual function*.

When A and B are sets and $A \subset B$, we say that A is a *subset* of B. An *n-ary predicate* P *in* A is a subset of A^n. If $(a_1, \ldots, a_n) \in P$, we say that $(a_1, \ldots, a_n)$ *satisfies* P and assert $P(a_1, \ldots, a_n)$; e.g., if P is the set of roses, a satisfies P if a is a rose. A predicate in the universe is an *individual predicate.*

E 3.3 Let R denote the set of real numbers and let $a < (=) b$ mean that the denotation of a is less than (or the same as) the denotation of b. Then $<$ and $=$ are binary predicates in R. We can truthfully assert $1 < \sqrt{2}$ and $\log e = 1$ but not $e^{-1} > 1$.

Finally, if A and B are sets, we let $A \cup B$ and $A \cap B$ denote, respectively, the *union* and the *intersection* of A and B. Thus, $x \in A \cup B$ if and only if $x \in A$ or $x \in B$; and $x \in A \cap B$ if and only if $x \in A$ and $x \in B$.

3.2 Logical Syntax

The study of the purely formal aspects of a symbolic language is called *logical syntax,* and the metalanguage used to carry out the logical syntax is called the *syntax language.* One problem in logical syntax is to ascertain that the formation rules of an object language are *effective*; i.e., that it is possible in a finite number of steps to decide whether a formula is well formed. Our formation rules begin by singling out a collection of formulas—the atomic formulas—that have a particularly simple structure. Examples of atomic formulas are a variable p that varies over declarative sentences and $P(x_1, \ldots, x_n)$, where P is an *n-ary* predicate and the x_i are individual variables. The rules declare that a formula A is well formed if and only if A is atomic, or if there are well-formed formulas B and C such that either A is $\sim B$ (not B) or A is $[B \supset C]$ (if B then C) or $(\forall x)B$ (for all xB). We can show that our formation rules are effective.

A much harder problem in logical syntax is to find an *effective characterization* of the theorems of an object language, i.e., a characterization that would enable us to determine in a finite number of steps whether a well-formed formula is a theorem. We shall insist that *a well-formed formula A in our language is a theorem if and only if A is a theorem follows from the following two laws*:

1. An axiom is a theorem.
2. If all the hypotheses of a rule of inference are theorems, then the conclusion is a theorem.

This characterization is not effective. However, it provides us with a simple method for deciding whether the theorems of our language possess a given property. For instance, a *proof* is a finite sequence of formulas, each of which is either an axiom or the conclusion of a rule of inference whose hypotheses precede that formula in the proof. A proof is said to be *a proof of the last formula in the sequence.* We can use the preceding characterization of a theorem to show that *a well-formed formula is a theorem if and only if it has a proof.*

In addition to the preceding problems, logical syntax is concerned with the establishment of various syntactical properties of the axioms of a symbolic language. For instance, the logical syntax of our object language will show that our axioms are *consistent* and *incomplete* (i.e., not complete). A given set of axioms is consistent if two contradictory assertions cannot be derived from them. A set of axioms is complete if there exists no formula A which is not a theorem and which can be adopted as an additional axiom without making the resulting set inconsistent.

3.3 Semantics

We interpret our symbolic language in steps. First, we single out a set of individuals as the universe of discourse and provide a name for each individual in the universe. Then we assign individuals, individual functions, and individual predicates in the universe to the various constants, functions, and predicates in the nonlogical vocabulary. Finally, we interpret the well-formed formulas by assigning truth values to them. The procedure we use for that purpose is inductive and described in detail in chapter 5. We begin by assigning truth values to the variable-free atomic formulas in accordance with the interpretation we have given to the nonlogical vocabulary. More complicated formulas are formed from them with the logical connectives, $\sim$ and $\supset$, the parentheses, [and], and the quantifier $\forall$. We interpret these formulas in the following manner, with t and f, respectively, denoting truth and falsehood: If A is a well-formed formula, $\sim A$ denotes f or t according as A denotes t or f. If B is another well-formed formula, $[A \supset B]$ denotes f if and only if A denotes t and B denotes f. Finally, if C is a unary predicate and x is an individual variable, then $(\forall x)C$ denotes t if and only if every individual in the universe satisfies C.

Strictly speaking, *to interpret* means to explain the meaning of. It is doubtful that the interpretation sketched above has assigned meanings to the members of the nonlogical vocabulary of our language. For instance, assigning denotation to a constant symbol does not determine the meaning of the constant. Similarly, assigning truth values to declarative sentences is not tantamount to giving meaning to them; e.g., "Scott is Scott" and "Scott is the author of *Waverly*" have the same denotation but different meanings. However, it is clear that *our interpretation has given meaning to the members of the logical vocabulary. Hence we have succeeded in interpreting the undefined terms of the axioms of our language.*

The study of the interpretation of a symbolic language *as* an interpretation is called *semantics.* Semantics is concerned with the semantical properties of symbolic languages. For instance, some well-formed formulas possess the characteristic that they assume the value truth because of their form alone. They are called *valid formulas.* The semantical study of our symbolic language shows that a well-formed formula is valid if and only if it is a theorem. This result establishes a remarkable equivalence between a syntactical concept, "theorem," and a semantical concept, "valid formula." It also provides justification for using the theorems of our symbolic language as a basis for formulating derived rules of inference in mathematics; e.g., we justify indirect proofs by the following theorem: Let A and B be assertions. Either it is false that $\sim A$ implies both B and $\sim B$ or A is true.

3.4 The Semantic Conception of Truth

In the intended interpretation of our language a variable-free well-formed formula is a declarative sentence which denotes one or the other of two abstract objects, truth and falsehood. *True* declarative sentences denote truth, the others falsehood. But what is the meaning of true?

The simplest declarative sentences predicate an attribute of some object; e.g., "Grass is green." Complicated declarative sentences are compounds of simpler sentences; e.g., "All the cats I know are ichthyophagous" is a compound of the sentences "x_i is a fish-eating cat," $i = 1, \ldots, n$, and "$x_1, \ldots, x_n$ are all the cats I know." Consequently, with a little stretch of the imagination we can think of a declarative sentence either as a sentence which predicates one or more relations between various objects or as a compound of such sentences. We say that *a declarative sentence is true if and only if the denotations of the names in the sentence satisfy the relations predicated of them by the sentence.*[1] Thus if p is a declarative sentence, we insist that the sentence "p" is true if and only if p.

E 3.4 The sentence "Othello believes that Desdemona loves Cassio" is true if and only if Othello believes that Desdemona loves Cassio. It is irrelevant whether there exists a complex unit—Desdemona's love for Cassio—corresponding to Othello's belief. See in this respect Bertrand Russell's correspondence theory of truth (1976, pp. 69–75).

I conceive of truth as an attribute of declarative sentences. As such my notion of truth accords with the spirit, if not the details, of Alfred Tarski's semantic conception of truth (Tarski 1964, pp. 52–65). It also accords with Aristotle's definition: Falsehood consists in saying of that which is that it is not, or of that which is not that it is. Truth consists in saying of that which is that it is, or of that which is not that it is not (Aristotle 1978, p. 142).

The idea of truth that emerges from my definition calls for two clarifying remarks. First, the notion of "truth" as defined here pertain to some given language and may change from one language to the next; a sentence which denotes truth in one language may be false, even nonsensical in another. In fact, my concept of truth may be explicated in one language but fall prey to seemingly iniquitous antinomies in another, as witnessed in E 3.5.

E 3.5 Let p declare: *the sentence written in italic on p. 49, ll. 14–15, of this chapter is false.* Then "p" is identical with the sentence written in italic on p. 49, *ll.* 14–15, of this chapter. Hence the following assertion: *the sentence 'p' is true if and only if p* insists that *"the sentence 'p' is true if and only if the sentence 'p' is not true."*

Thus "truth," as defined here, has a precise meaning only for a given language with a well-defined structure that rules out antinomies like the one in E 3.5. Characterization of such structures are given in Tarski 1964 (pp. 59–62).

Second, I define "true" in terms of the concept of "satisfying" a relation. In doing so, I assume that the idea of "satisfying a relation" is sufficiently clear to the reader that he is able to grasp the idea of truth. If so, I need only add that a complete explication of "satisfying" (i.e., of satisfying a relation) can only be obtained by pointing out the objects that are to satisfy all the various relations that occur in the language. This arduous task is solved differently by different authors.

Our concept of truth for a given language varies with the associated explication of "satisfying." Suppose that we want to determine the truth value of some declarative sentence p. This is easy for sentences such as (1) and (2).

(1) All widows have had husbands.
(2) Whatever is colored is extended.

Such sentences either are true by definition (e.g., (1)) or can be shown to be true by a *priori* reasoning alone (e.g., (2)). It is also easy to determine the truth value of sentences such as (3) and (4), since we can do that by applying tautologies which in our symbolic logic are either postulated as axioms (e.g., (3)), or deduced as theorems from our axioms (e.g., (4)).

(3) If there are four fish in this pond, Roald Amundsen was a great explorer.
(4) If Quisling was a patriot, all roses are red.

Furthermore, it is easy (at least in principle) to determine the truth value of sentences such as (5) and (6), since ascertaining their truth involves only checking whether a finite number of relations are satisfied.

(5) Max is a cat.
(6) All living Norwegians are less than a hundred years of age.

Determining the truth value of some other p seems formidable. Consider examples (7) and (8).

(7) This table is brown.
(8) He is a fascist.

The truth values of these sentences may depend on one's point of view, literally (e.g., (7)) or figuratively (e.g., (8)). It is also difficult to determine the truth value of p for sentences such as (9) and (10).

(9) There are three consecutive 7 in the decimal expansion of Π.
(10) If n is an integer greater than 2, there does not exist a triple of positive integers, (x, y, z), that satisfies the equation $x^n + y^n = z^n$.

At present the truth values of these sentences are unknown, and it is conceivable that no human being will ever determine them. Finally, finding the truth value of p is exceedingly difficult for sentences such as (11) and (12).

(11) If he had eaten the apple pie last Christmas Eve, he would have died.
(12) There are pebbles on this beach that no one will ever observe.

The truth value of (11) cannot be determined, and satisfying the predicated relation in (12) involves a contradiction. Moreover, determination of the falsehood of (12) is unlikely to occur.

So much for the problems of satisfying a relation. The upshot of our comments is that explication of "satisfying a relation" (and hence explication of our concept of truth) can be difficult in any language, may be arbitrary in some, and may be impossible in others. In the interpreted languages we shall use to describe choice under uncertainty, a complete explication of the term "satisfying a relation" is unavailable. Hence we must find ways to ascertain whether or not the relations that occur in our models are satisfied. Our intent in *this book is to construct a framework within which intelligent inferences as to the validity of such models (i.e., to the satisfaction of their relations) can be made.*

3.5 Truth and Meaning

The concept of truth sketched above is appropriate for mathematical arguments. However, it is inadequate for studying the structure of natural languages. It is also much too narrow for the purpose of constructing a language for science. To explain why, I must introduce two new concepts, extension and intension.

First, *extension*: The extension of a name is its denotation; the extension of a function is its graph; and the extension of a predicate is the collection of individuals that satisfy the predicate. When assigning truth values to the well-formed formulas of our language in section 3.3, we used only the extension of the members of the nonlogical vocabulary. Similarly, in section 3.4 we insisted that a declarative sentence be true if and only if the denotations of the names in the sentence satisfy the relations predicated of them by the sentence. Hence it makes sense to say that the concept of truth described in section 3.4 is extensional.

There are many situations in which an extensional concept of truth cannot be applied. Three examples attesting to this fact are given below.

1. It is true that "Peter owes Smith a horse." Yet there is no particular horse that Peter owes Smith.

2. It is true that in the universe of humans "Anne Olaug is a big baby." However, it is false that "Anne Olaug is big."

3. It is true that "Frank believes that Oslo is in Sweden" but it is false that "Frank believes that the capital of Norway is in Sweden."

The third example is of special interest to us because it exemplifies a semantical problem that we will face when we search for a formal language for science.

To ascertain the truth value of "Frank believes that Oslo is in Sweden" we must check whether *Frank* is in the relation belief to *Frank's understanding* of "Oslo is in Sweden." Frank's understanding of "Oslo is in Sweden" depends on his understanding of Oslo and Sweden. And since his understanding of Oslo differs from his understanding of "the capital of Norway," the latter cannot be substituted for Oslo in the given context, even though Oslo and "the capital of Norway" have the same denotation.

In example 3 it is the *denotation* of Frank and the *sense* of "Oslo is in Sweden" that determines the truth value of "Frank believes that Oslo is in Sweden." To have a semantic theory that accounts for such situations, we must formalize the idea of meaning. One way to do that is to identify the sense of an object (e.g., a name or a predicate) with its intension.

To explicate the idea of *intension* we let Ω denote the set of possible worlds. Moreover, for each $\omega \in \Omega$, we let U_ω denote the set of individuals in ω and we let U be the union of all the U_ω; i.e., we let U be such that $x \in U$ if and only if there is a ω so that $x \in U_\omega$. Then the intension of a constant is a function $\phi_a(\cdot)\colon \Omega \to U$ such that $\phi_a(\omega)$ is the extension of a in U_ω. In addition, the intension of an n-ary individual function g is a function $\phi_g(\cdot)\colon \Omega \to$ (family of subsets of U_ω^{n+1}) such that, for each $\omega \in \Omega$, $\phi_g(\omega)$ is the graph of g in U^{n+1}; and the intension of an n-ary predicate P is a function $\phi_P(\cdot)\colon \Omega \to$ (family of subsets of U^n) such that, for each $\omega \in \Omega$, $\phi_P(\omega)$ is the extension of P in U_ω^n. Finally, the intension of a declarative sentence A is a function $\phi_A(\cdot)\colon \Omega \to \{t, f\}$ such that, for each $\omega \in \Omega$, $\phi_A(\omega)$ is the extension (i.e., the truth value) of A in ω.

If we interpret Ω to be the set of all possible worlds compatible with Frank's beliefs, and if we identify the meaning of an object (e.g., the capital of Norway) with its intension, we can say: "Frank believes that A" denotes truth if and only if in all possible worlds that are compatible with Frank's beliefs it is the case that A.[2].

In the preceding paragraph we can substitute "he" or "we" or an unspecified individual for Frank. Hence the preceding discussion describes one way of using the idea of intension to analyze belief sentences. In analogous ways, the idea of intension can be used to develop the semantics of sentences such as "I know that ..." and "It is necessary that. . . ." We shall discuss these ideas in chapters 23 and 24. And in chapter 25 we shall use them to develop a symbolic language for science that is sufficiently rich for the purposes of econometric theory.

In concluding our discussion of truth and meaning, it is interesting to observe that we can apply the concepts of extension and intension to show how the axioms of a mathematical theory determine the meaning of the undefined terms of the theory. To wit: When we interpret a mathematical theory, we do it by delineating the extensions of the undefined terms of the theory. Such an interpretation is a model of the theory if the extensions of the undefined terms satisfy the relations predicated of them in the axioms. A mathematical theory which has one model has many. The extensions of the undefined terms vary with the models within the limits prescribed by the axioms. In that way the axioms determine the intensions and hence the meanings of the undefined terms. For instance, the undefined terms of the classical theory of natural numbers are a constant, 0, a unary function, S, two binary functions, $+$ and $\cdot$, and a binary predicate, $<$. A model of the theory delineates the extensions of these terms. The axioms of the theory insist that these extensions be such that we can interpret S as the "successor function," $+$ as "plus," $\cdot$ as "times," $<$ as "less than," and 0 as "zero." We shall discuss the semantics of mathematical theories at length in the second part of this book.

4 The Propositional Calculus

4.1 Symbols, Well-Formed Formulas, and Rules of Inference

In this chapter I begin the presentation of my symbolic language.

4.1.1 Symbols

We shall use three kinds of symbols. First, there are the members of the nonlogical vocabulary. These are given by the infinite list of *propositional variables*: $p, q, r, s, t, p_1, q_1, r_1, s_1, t_1, p_2, q_2, \ldots$.

Second, there are the members of the logical vocabulary. They are parentheses and sentence connectives that combine with members of the nonlogical vocabulary to form longer expressions which we call *formulas*. Initially we shall make use of four logical symbols: [,], $\supset$, $\sim$.

Third, there are symbols such as Γ, Δ, A, B, a, b, $s^b_B A|$, S, T that we use to denote syntactical variables. Logical and nonlogical symbols belong to the object language, while symbols denoting syntactical variables form part of the syntax language.

4.1.2 Well-Formed Formulas

To develop the first half of my symbolic language, we need three *language axioms* (LA):

LA 1 $[p \supset [q \supset p]]$

LA 2 $[[p \supset [q \supset r]] \supset [[p \supset q] \supset [p \supset r]]]$

LA 3 $[[\sim p \supset \sim q] \supset [q \supset p]]$

Whatever their meanings, the expressions in these axioms are called *for-*

mulas. They are *well formed* (wf) if and only if their being well formed follows from the following *formation rules*:

FR 1 A propositional variable standing alone is a wf formula (wff).

FR 2 If Γ is wf, then $\sim\Gamma$ is wf.

FR 3 If Γ and Δ are wf, then $[\Gamma \supset \Delta]$ is wf.

It is easy to verify that the formulas in axioms LA 1–LA 3 are wf. For more complicated formulas, a method exists by which one may determine in a finite number of steps whether such formulas are wf. The procedure is described in Church 1956 (pp. 70–71, 121–123).

4.1.3 Rules of Inference

The formation rules tell us how to produce new well-formed formulas (wffs) out of existing wffs. Some of the wffs are theorems. A *theorem* is either an axiom or derived from the axioms with the help of the rules of inference that we postulate. For the propositional calculus developed in this chapter, we assume the following two rules of inference:

RI 1 (Modus Ponens): Let A and B be wffs. *From* $[A \supset B]$ *and* A, *we infer* B.

RI 2 Let B be a wff, and let b be a propositional variable. Moreover, let $S^b_B A|$ *be the wff that results from substituting* B for each occurrence of b in A. *From* A, *we infer* $S^b_B A|$.

The meaning of RI 1 is clear, but the idea behind RI 2 might not be. In short, RI 2 insists that if we can assert A no matter what b expresses, we can also assert $S^b_B A|$ no matter what B asserts. Examples of the way in which RI 1 and RI 2 are applied are given in section 4.2. In section 4.3 I show how one can determine in a finite number of steps whether a wff of the propositional calculus is a theorem.

4.2 Sample Theorems

There are many theorems in my symbolic language. Examples are the axioms LA 1–LA 3 given above and T 4.1 and T 4.2 given below. The latter theorems have been chosen to illustrate different aspects of how theorems can be proved in the propositional calculus.

T 4.1 $[p \supset p]$

Proof $[[p \supset [q \supset r]] \supset [[p \supset q] \supset [p \supset r]]]$

$[[p \supset [q \supset p]] \supset [[p \supset q] \supset [p \supset p]]]$

$[p \supset [q \supset p]]$

$[[p \supset q] \supset [p \supset p]]$

$[[p \supset [q \supset p]] \supset [p \supset p]]$

$[p \supset p]$

The proof of this theorem is constructed in strict adherence to the definition of a proof given in chapter 3. We begin with LA 2. Then we substitute p for r and use RI 2. Thereafter we assert LA 1, apply LA 1 and Modus Ponens, substitute $[q \supset p]$ for q, and use RI 2. Finally we apply LA 1 and use Modus Ponens to conclude $[p \supset p]$. Notice that there are no commas, periods, or semicolons in the proof; our symbolic language lacks these symbols.

Proofs in mathematical logic of even simple theorems are quite involved. To facilitate and streamline such proofs, logicians frequently use *derived rules of inference.* These rules are established in the metalanguage as theorems about the object language. In proofs they are used on equal footing with the postulated rules of inference. It is understood, however, that the derived rules can be dispensed with. In the next theorem we establish a *derived rule of inference*:

DRI 1 From a theorem T infer $[q \supset T]$.

I label the theorem TM 4.1 rather than T 4.2 in order to make explicit that the theorem belongs to the metalanguage, not the object language.

TM 4.1 Let T be a theorem. Then $[q \supset T]$ is a theorem.

Proof T

$[p \supset [q \supset p]]$

$[T \supset [q \supset T]]$

$[q \supset T]$

In this proof we assert T and LA 1. We then substitute T for p and use RI 2. Finally we apply Modus Ponens to conclude $[q \supset T]$. Note that we omitted the sequence of formulas that constitute the proof of T. For cases in which TM 4.1, can be used, T often emerges at the end of such a sequence. Then TM 4.1 allows us to pass directly from T to $[q \supset T]$ without the two intervening steps. In the proof of T 4.2 below we illustrate the usefulness of TM 4.1.

A variant of a wff A is a wff obtained from A by alphabetic changes of the variables such that any two occurrences of the same variable in A remain occurrences of the same variable and such that any two occurrences of distinct variables in A remain occurrences of distinct variables.

A *variant proof* is a proof in which a variant of an axiom rather than the axiom itself is asserted in one or more steps. To establish the validity of a variant proof, it suffices to show that a variant of a theorem is a theorem. From this it follows that the final wff in a variant proof must be a theorem as well.

The validity of a variant proof is an immediate consequence of the following metatheorem:

TM 4.2 Let $b_1, \ldots, b_n$ denote n different variables and let $S^{b_1, \ldots, b_n}_{B_1, \ldots, B_n} A|$ denote the formula that results from the simultaneous substitution of the wffs, $B_1, \ldots, B_n$, for $b_1, \ldots, b_n$ in A. If T is a theorem, then $S^{b_1, \ldots, b_n}_{B_1, \ldots, B_n} T|$ is also a theorem.

A proof of TM 4.2 can be obtained in a finite number of steps by repeated applications of RI 2 (see Church 1956, pp. 82–83). The theorem therefore establishes the validity not just of variant proofs, but of a derived rule of inference:

DRI 2 From a theorem T infer $S^{b_1, \ldots, b_n}_{B_1, \ldots, B_n} T|$.

Below we use both DRI 1 and DRI 2 to construct a variant proof of a theorem belonging to the object language:

T 4.2 $[\sim p \supset [p \supset q]]$

Proof $[[\sim q \supset \sim p] \supset [p \supset q]]$

$[r \supset [[\sim q \supset \sim p] \supset [p \supset q]]]$

$[[r \supset [s \supset t]] \supset [[r \supset s] \supset [r \supset t]]]$

$[[r \supset [[\sim q \supset \sim p] \supset [p \supset q]]] \supset [[r \supset [\sim q \supset \sim p]] \supset$
$[r \supset [p \supset q]]]]$

$[[r \supset [\sim q \supset \sim p]] \supset [r \supset [p \supset q]]]$

$[[\sim p \supset [\sim q \supset \sim p]] \supset [\sim p \supset [p \supset q]]]$

$[p \supset [q \supset p]]$

$[\sim p \supset [\sim q \supset \sim p]]$

$[\sim p \supset [p \supset q]]$

In this proof we first assert a variant of LA 3 and apply a variant of DRI 1. We then assert a variant of LA 2 and substitute $[\sim q \supset \sim p]$ and $[p \supset q]$ for s and t in accordance with DRI 2. Thereafter we use Modus Ponens, substitute $\sim p$ for r, and use RI 2. Finally we assert LA 1, substitute $\sim p$ for p and $\sim q$ for q in accordance with DRI 2, and apply Modus Ponens to infer $[\sim p \supset [p \supset q]]$.

4.3 The Intended Interpretation

The intended interpretation of my symbolic language is as follows: The variables $p, q, r, s, \ldots$ have as their domain a set of declarative sentences which are written in some definite language, say English, and have as their range two truth values, truth and falsehood. Let t denote truth, f falsehood. A wff consisting of a variable a alone has the value t for the value t of a, the value f for the value f of a. For a given assignment of values to the variables of the wff A, the value of $\sim A$ is f if the value of A is t. The value of $\sim A$ is t if the value of A is f. Finally, for a given assignment of values to the variables of the wffs A and B, the value of $[A \supset B]$ is t if the value of A is f or if the value of B is t. The value of $[A \supset B]$ is f if the value of B is f and the value of A is t.

In the interpreted language, the symbol $\sim$ is used as "not" is used in English. Thus if A is a declarative sentence written in English, $\sim A$ can be read "not A."

The meaning of $\supset$, the *material implication sign,* is less clear. Often $[A \supset B]$ is read, "if A, then B." Whenever A denotes t, this makes sense, because in this case $[A \supset B]$ denotes t if and only if B is true. However, when A denotes f, $[A \supset B]$ is true whether B is true or false. This seems to stretch the meaning of "if ..., then." However, if one is committed to a two-valued logic and insists that theorems denote truth and contradictions falsehood, TM 4.1 and TM 4.3 and TM 4.4 below show that ours is the only possible interpretation of $\supset$.

TM 4.3 If T is a theorem, $[\sim T \supset q]$ is a theorem.

TM 4.4 If T is a theorem, $\sim[T \supset \sim T]$ is a theorem.

The validity of TM 4.3 and TM 4.4 can easily be established with the help of two useful theorems:

T 4.3 $[p \supset \sim\sim p]$

T 4.4 $[[p \supset [q \supset r]] \supset [q \supset [p \supset r]]]$

I leave the proofs of T 4.3 and T 4.4 and TM 4.4 to the reader. To prove TM 4.3, we assert T 4.3, substitute T for p, and use RI 2 and RI 1 to deduce that $\sim\sim T$. Then we assert T 4.2, substitute $\sim T$ for p, and use RI 2 to deduce that $[\sim\sim T \supset [\sim T \supset q]]$. Finally, we apply RI 1 to conclude that $[\sim T \supset q]$. Strange or not strange, our interpretation of $\supset$ has an interesting property: it allows one to assign a definite truth value to a wide class of sentences that under any other interpretation might have been considered incomplete or nonsensical. E 4.1 illustrates such a case.

E 4.1 According to our interpretation, the sentence "If the weather is sunny and bright tomorrow, Borg will beat Tanner in the tennis finals" assumes the value f if and only if the weather tomorrow is sunny and bright and Borg does not beat Tanner. If the weather is bad, the prediction assumes the value t no matter who wins the match.

To avoid misunderstanding, we usually take $[A \supset B]$ to read "*A* materially implies *B*" rather than "if *A*, then *B*."

4.3.1 Tautologies

At each point in its intended domain of definition, a variable p is a declarative sentence. From this and from the formation rules, it follows that once declarative sentences are substituted for variables in a well-formed formula, this formula becomes, in the intended interpretation of my symbolic language, a declarative sentence as well. In studying these formulas, we are interested in their abstract form, not their meaning. Our main intent is to ascertain what structure a declarative sentence must have in order that it denote truth no matter what it asserts.

A wff that denotes truth no matter what it asserts is called a *tautology*. We show in table 4.1 that the interpreted versions of LA 1 and LA 3 are tautologies. Similar arguments show that LA 2 is also a tautology. In table 4.1 the formulas are the column heads, and their values for different combinations of values of p and q are listed below them. As asserted above, $[p \supset [q \supset p]]$ denotes t regardless of the values assumed by p and q. The same is the true for $[[\sim p \supset \sim q] \supset [q \supset p]]$.

Table 4.1
Truth table for LA 1 and LA 3.

p	q	$\sim p$	$\sim q$	$[q \supset p]$	$[p \supset [q \supset p]]$	$[\sim p \supset \sim q]$	$[[\sim p \supset \sim q] \supset [q \supset p]]$
t	t	f	f	t	t	t	t
t	f	f	t	t	t	t	t
f	t	t	f	f	t	f	t
f	f	t	t	t	t	t	t

4.3.2 Theorems and Tautologies

It is easy to demonstrate that RI 1 and RI 2 preserve tautologies; i.e., if their premises are tautologies, so are their conclusions (Church 1956, pp. 97 and 127). From this and from the fact that the axioms are tautologies, it follows that, in the intended interpretation of the propositional calculus, all the theorems we can derive are tautologies. Thus, as the reader can verify, T 4.1, T 4.2, and all the other theorems stated in this chapter are tautologies.

The converse of the preceding observation (i.e., a wff is a tautology only if it is a theorem) is also true and is proved in section 4.7. Consequently, we have TM 4.5, the *Tautology Theorem.*

TM 4.5 A wff A is a theorem if and only if it is a tautology in the intended interpretation of the language.

This result is startling. I have previously defined the term "theorem" as it applies to my *uninterpreted* symbolic language. In this section we have interpreted the language and used the interpretation to give a complete characterization of the language's theorems. Moreover, *this characterization provides a foolproof method for checking in a finite number of steps whether a wff is a theorem: compute the wff's truth table.*

4.4 Interesting Tautological Structures

Sentences that denote truth because of their structure alone are interesting because they can be used to formulate derived rules of inference in mathematics. To see how, I shall next describe in English the characteristics of some of the most important tautologies in my symbolic language.

I begin with T 4.1. According to our interpretation of $\supset$, $[p \supset p]$ can be a tautology if and only if it is *always* the case that either p is false or p is true, i.e., if and only if no excluded middle exists. Thus in our interpreted language $[p \supset p]$ provides a succinct statement of the *law of the excluded middle.*

To obtain a statement of the *law of contradiction,* we first observe that p and $\sim\sim p$ have the same denotation. Thus both $[p \supset \sim\sim p]$ and $[\sim\sim p \supset p]$ must be theorems in our language. Bearing that observation in mind, we can state the law of contradiction (T 4.5).

T 4.5 $\sim\sim[p \supset \sim\sim p]$

According to our interpretation, this law is a tautology if and only if the assertion, p is true and not not p is false, is always false, i.e., if and only if p and not p cannot ever both be true.

Our translations of T 4.1 and T 4.5 may seem unconvincing even though they accord with the received "doctrine." The reason is that any two theorems in my symbolic language, say S and T, are equivalent in the sense that both $[S \supset T]$ and $[T \supset S]$ are theorems as witnessed by TM 4.1. It is hard to make the law of the excluded middle and the law of contradiction sound different when we (1) insist that the denotation of a name is unique, (2) allow only two truth values, and (3) insist that their symbolic prototypes, T 4.1 and T 4.5, mutually imply each other.

The interpreted version of LA 3 is called *the converse law of contraposition.* Its positive half asserts that, if not q materially implies not p, then p materially implies q. Thus to show that q is a consequence of p, it suffices to show that not q implies not p. From this we see that the interpreted version of LA 3 postulates the validity of one of the most applied methods of proof in mathematics.

Axiom LA 3 has a converse: T 4.6.

T 4.6 $[[p \supset q] \supset [\sim q \supset \sim p]]$

By combining the interpreted versions of LA 3 and T 4.6, we can deduce that p materially implies q if and only if not q materially implies not p. Or said another way: $[p \supset q]$ and $[\sim q \supset \sim p]$ have the same denotation. This is verified by table 4.2.

In addition to those just presented, we can derive several other laws which in their interpreted versions establish the validity of well-known methods of proof in mathematics. Two examples are *the transitive law of material implication* (T 4.7) and the *law of reductio ad absurdum* (T 4.8).

T 4.7 $[[p \supset q] \supset [[q \supset r] \supset [p \supset r]]]$

T 4.8 $[[p \supset q] \supset [[p \supset \sim q] \supset \sim p]]$

A third example is the *law of assertion* (T 4.9).

Table 4.2
Truth table for $[p \supset q]$ and $[\sim q \supset \sim p]$.

p	q	$\sim p$	$\sim q$	$[p \supset q]$	$[\sim q \supset \sim p]$
t	t	f	f	t	t
t	f	f	t	f	f
f	t	t	f	t	t
f	f	t	t	t	t

T 4.9 $[p \supset [[p \supset q] \supset q]]$

The names of T 4.7 and T 4.9 give good characterizations of the structures of the sentences expressed by these laws. In T 4.8 we insist that p cannot materially imply both q and not q unless p denotes f and hence $\sim p$ denotes truth.

4.5 Disjunction, Conjunction, and Material Equivalence

In my propositional calculus we can assert "Per is a philosopher" and "Per is a physicist." We can also combine these two sentences into assertions such as "either Per is a physicist or Per is a philosopher" or "Per is a physicist and Per is a philosopher." The next section indicates how.

4.5.1 Either-Or and Both-And Sentences

To formulate either-or sentences, let us agree that, *for any wff B,*

$A =_{\mathbf{df}} B$

means that "A is an abbreviation for B" and implies that A may be substituted for B whether B stands alone or forms part of a longer wff. Let

$[A \vee B] =_{\mathbf{df}} [\sim A \supset B]$

In our interpreted language $[A \vee B]$ is true if and only if either A or B or both denote t; it is false if and only if both A and B denote f. Consequently, in our interpreted language $[A \vee B]$ can be read as if it declared "either A or B or both."

To formulate both-and sentences, we let

$[A \wedge B] =_{\mathbf{df}} \sim [A \supset \sim B]$

In our interpreted language $[A \wedge B]$ denotes truth if and only if both A and B denote t. It is false if and only if either $\sim A$ or $\sim B$ or both are true. Consequently, the formula $[A \wedge B]$ can be read as if it declared "both A and B."

The following useful theorems describe some of the properties of $\vee$ and $\wedge$:

T 4.10 $[p \supset [q \vee p]]$

T 4.11 $[[p \vee p] \supset p]$

T 4.12 $[[p \wedge q] \supset q]$

T 4.13 $[[[p \vee q] \wedge [\sim p \vee r]] \supset [q \vee r]]$

The meaning of these theorems is self-explanatory. For later reference it is interesting to note that T 4.10, T 4.11, and T 4.13, respectively, form the basis of three rules of inference which J. R. Shoenfield calls the *expansion rule*, the *contraction rule*, and the *cut rule*, i.e., *infer* $[B \vee A]$ *from* A, *infer* A *from* $[A \vee A]$, and *infer* $[B \vee C]$ *from* $[A \vee B]$ and $[\sim A \vee C]$. (Shoenfield 1967, p. 21.)

4.5.2 Material Equivalence

In our interpreted language two sentences are said to be *materially equivalent* if they have the same denotation. We can express *material equivalence* in our language by letting

$$[A \equiv B] =_{\mathrm{df}} \sim[[A \supset B] \supset \sim[B \supset A]].$$

By consulting the truth table of the right-hand side of the definition of $\equiv$, we see immediately that $[A \equiv B]$ denotes truth if and only if A and B have the same denotation. It is false if and only if A and B have different denotations. Thus the expression $[A \equiv B]$ can be read as if it declared "A if and only if B." From our definition of $\wedge$, it follows that $[A \equiv B]$ is a different way of writing $[[A \supset B] \wedge [B \supset A]]$.

The sentence $[A \equiv B]$ declares a relationship between two assertions A and B. Thus we can think of $\equiv$ as a relation among declarative sentences. This relation is reflexive, symmetric, and transitive according to the following theorems:

T 4.14 $[p \equiv p]$

T 4.15 $[[p \equiv q] \supset [q \equiv p]]$

T 4.16 $[[[p \equiv q] \wedge [q \equiv r]] \supset [p \equiv r]]$

A relation with the properties displayed in T 4.14–T 4.16 is called an *equivalence relation*. Since this particular relation is constructed from material implication, $\equiv$ is usually referred to as the *relation of material equivalence*. T 4.17–T 4.22 are examples of materially equivalent assertions.

T 4.17 $[[p \vee q] \equiv [q \vee p]]$

T 4.18 $[[[p \vee q] \vee r] \equiv [p \vee [q \vee r]]]$

T 4.19 $[\sim[p \wedge q] \equiv [\sim p \vee \sim q]]$

T 4.20 $[\sim[p \vee q] \equiv [\sim p \wedge \sim q]]$

T 4.21 $[[p \wedge [q \vee r]] \equiv [[p \wedge q] \vee [p \wedge r]]]$

T 4.22 $[[p \vee [q \wedge r]] \equiv [[p \vee q] \wedge [p \vee r]]]$

Of these, the first two are usually referred to as the *complete commutative* and *associative laws of disjunction*, the next two as *de Morgan's laws for declarative sentences*, and the last two as the *distributive laws of conjunction and disjunction*. We also note that T 4.18 can be used to formulate J. R. Shoenfield's *associative rule* of inference: *infer* $[[A \vee B] \vee C]$ *from* $[A \vee [B \vee C]]$ (Shoenfield 1967, p. 21).

Besides possessing the three properties of an equivalence relation, $\equiv$ also has a fundamental substitutive property which is described in the next two metatheorems:

TM 4.6 If B results from A by substitution of C for D at zero or more places, and if $[C \equiv D]$ is a theorem, then $[A \equiv B]$ is also a theorem.

TM 4.7 If B results from A by substitution of C for D at zero or more places, and if $[C \equiv D]$ and A are theorems, then B is also a theorem.

These two theorems cannot be established simply by consulting the truth tables of the relevant wffs. However, since TM 4.6 is a special case of TM 5.15, which we prove in chapter 5, and since TM 4.7 is an easy consequence of TM 4.6, I omit their proofs.

4.6 Syntactical Properties of the Propositional Calculus

Logistic systems such as the one I have described in this chapter may or may not have certain properties that a user would require of a meaningful language. One is consistency: A language is *consistent* if it contains no sentence A with the property that both A and $\sim A$ are theorems. This property is important, since if both A and $\sim A$ are theorems, B is a theorem no matter what it asserts. This is demonstrated by applying T 4.2 and Modus Ponens:

$[\sim A \supset [A \supset B]]$

$\sim A$

$[A \supset B]$

A

B.

Our propositional calculus is consistent inasmuch as not all wffs are tautologies.

Another property the reader might want a language to have is completeness: A language is *complete* if there is no wff *A* that is not a theorem and at the same time can be added as an axiom without causing inconsistency in the language. This property expresses the idea that everything we might justly hope to assert in the language actually can be said. How desirable a property it is, is debatable. More about that later. Here we merely observe that the completeness of my propositional calculus is a simple corollary of TM 4.5 (see Church 1956, pp. 110 and 128).

A third property of a language that may be important is independence concerning the relations between its axioms, its rules of inference, and the theorems that can be derived from them. A set of axioms and a set of rules of inference are *independent* if it is impossible to delete one axiom or one rule of inference and still derive all the theorems that can be derived from the two original sets. This property is less vital than consistency and less interesting than completeness. A logician or mathematician might for convenience choose to work with a set of axioms and rules of inference that are not independent. Our LA 1–LA 3 and RI 1 and RI 2 are independent (see Church 1956, pp. 112–114 and 127).

4.7 Proof of the Tautology Theorem

In this section I shall outline a proof of the Tautology Theorem, i.e., TM 4.5. My proof makes use of two auxiliary theorems, T 4.23 and T 4.24. The first is an obvious strengthening of T 4.4.

T 4.23 $[[\mathrm{p} \supset [q \supset \mathrm{r}]] \equiv [q \supset [\mathrm{p} \supset \mathrm{r}]]]$

The second insists that p and ~p cannot both imply q unless q is true.

T 4.24 $[[\mathrm{p} \supset q] \supset [[\sim \mathrm{p} \supset q] \supset q]]$

I state both T 4.23 and T 4.24 without proof since the arguments needed to established these theorems are easy to come by.

We observed in section 4.3 that the axioms are tautologies and that the rules of inference preserve tautologies. From this and our inductive definition of a theorem, it follows that a theorem of the propositional calculus is a tautology.

To prove the converse—i.e., that a tautology is a theorem—we begin by establishing the following auxiliary result.

TM 4.8 Let A be a wff and let $p_1, \ldots, p_k$ be the propositional variables appearing in A. Moreover, let B be A or $\sim A$ according as A denotes t or f and, for each $i = 1, \ldots, k$, let B_i be p_i or $\sim p_i$ according as p_i denotes t or f. Then $[B_1 \supset [B_2 \supset [\ldots \supset [B_k \supset B]\ldots]]]$ is a theorem.

The proof of TM 4.8 goes by induction on the number of connectives occurring in A. If there is no connective in A, then $k = 1$, A is p_1, B_1 is B, and $[B_1 \supset B]$ becomes $[B \supset B]$, which is a theorem by T 4.1 and RI 2.

Suppose next that TM 4.8 is true for all wffs that contain less than n ocurrences of connectives and let A be a wff that contains exactly n occurrences of connectives. Then there exist wffs C and D containing less than n occurrences of connectives such that A is $\sim C$ or $[C \supset D]$. In either case, C and D are uniquely determined. (See Church 1956, pp. 122–123, for a proof of this fact.)

Suppose that A is $\sim C$. Then C contains $n - 1$ occurrences of connectives. Let C^* be C or $\sim C$ according as C denotes t or f. Then B is $\sim\sim C^*$ or C^* according as C denotes t or f. Moreover, by the induction hypothesis, we can assert that $[B_1 \supset [B_2 \supset [\ldots \supset [B_k \supset C^*]\ldots]]]$ is a theorem. From this, the material equivalence of C^* and $\sim\sim C^*$, and TM 4.7 follows the validity of TM 4.8 for the present case.

Suppose next that A is $[C \supset D]$ and let C^* and D^*, respectively, be C or $\sim C$ and D or $\sim D$ according as C denotes t or f and D denotes t or f. Moreover, let p_{t_i}, $i = 1, \ldots l$, and p_{s_j}, $j = 1, \ldots m$, be the propositional variables occurring, respectively, in C and D. Then, by the induction hypothesis, we can assert that both $[B_{t_1} \supset [B_{t_2} \supset [\ldots \supset [B_{t_l} \supset C^*]\ldots]]]$ and $[B_{s_1} \supset [B_{s_2} \supset [\ldots \supset [B_{s_m} \supset D^*]\ldots]]]$ are theorems. From these theorems and repeated use of TM 4.1, T 4.23, DRI 2, and TM 4.7, we deduce that $[B_1 \supset [B_2 \supset [\ldots \supset [B_k \supset C^*]\ldots]]]$ and $[B_1 \supset [B_2 \supset [\ldots \supset [B_k \supset D^*]\ldots]]]$ are theorems as well. There are several subcases. Suppose first that D^* is D. Then B is $[C \supset D]$ and $[D^* \supset B]$ is a theorem by LA 1 and TM 4.2. From this it follows by standard arguments that TM 4.8 is valid for the given case.

Suppose next that C^* is $\sim C$ and D^* is $\sim D$. Then B is $[C \supset D]$ and, by T 4.2 and TM 4.2, $[C^* \supset B]$ is a theorem. From this and the arguments used when D^* is D, it follows that TM 4.8 is valid in this case as well.

Finally, suppose that C^* is C and D^* is $\sim D$. Then B is $[C^* \wedge D^*]$ and $[C^* \supset [D^* \supset B]]$ is a theorem. From this and obvious arguments, it follows that TM 4.8 is valid now too and hence generally valid.

So much for TM 4.8. To prove the if part of the Tautology Theorem, we now let A and the B_i, $i = 1, \ldots, k$, be as described in TM 4.8 and assume that A is a tautology. Then $[B_1 \supset [B_2 \supset [\ldots \supset [B_k \supset A]\ldots]]]$ is a theorem.

Since A is a tautology, it must also be the case that $[\sim B_1 \supset [B_2 \supset [\ldots \supset [B_k \supset A]\ldots]]]$ is a theorem. Consequently, by T 4.24 we deduce that $[B_2 \supset [B_3 \supset [\ldots \supset [B_k \supset A]\ldots]]]$ is a theorem as well. Repeated use of the same arguments suffices to demonstrate that A is a theorem.

The proof of TM 4.8 was obtained by "induction on the number of connectives occurring in A." Such a proof may be unfamiliar to the reader. Hence I shall conclude the chapter with a remark on generalized inductive definitions and proofs by induction.

A *generalized inductive definition* of a collection C of objects consists of a set of laws, each of which says that, under suitable hypotheses, an object x belongs to C. Examples are my definitions of theorems in section 3.2 and wffs in section 4.1. When we give such a definition, it is always understood that $x \in C$ only if it follows from the laws that x belongs to C.

Suppose that a collection C of objects has been defined by a generalized inductive definition. To ascertain that all the members of C have a property P, it suffices to demonstrate that the objects having P satisfy the laws of the definition. Such a proof is called a proof *by induction on objects in* C. "The hypotheses in the laws that certain objects belong to C become, in such a proof, hypotheses that certain objects have property P; these hypotheses are called *induction hypotheses*" (Shoenfield 1967, p. 5).

5 The First-Order Predicate Calculus

The symbolic language I presented in chapter 4 is not rich enough to serve our purposes. For example, we can assert "All physicists are philosophers," but we cannot infer from this and the fact that Per is a physicist that Per is a philosopher as well. We cannot even infer from "All ravens are black" that there exists a black raven.

5.1 Symbols, Well-Formed Formulas, and Rules of Inference

In this chapter we shall fill the lacunae in my language. In fact, I shall present, and adopt as my own in this text, a language—the first-order predicate calculus—that is so rich it can be used to formalize all the mathematical theories of interest to us. This language need not contain any propositional variables. Yet it is an extension of the propositional calculus in the following sense: *Any theorem of the propositional calculus, e.g.,* $[p \supset p]$*, becomes a metatheorem of the predicate calculus when the propositional variables are replaced by syntactical variables varying through wffs, e.g.,* $[A \supset A]$*. Every value of the resulting metatheorem is a theorem of the predicate calculus.*

In presenting the predicate calculus, I shall list its logical and nonlogical symbols, describe its well-formed formulas, formulate its rules of inference, and postulate its axioms.

5.1.1 The Symbols

The nonlogical vocabulary of the predicate calculus consists of indexed sets of function symbols, $\{f^i\}_{i \in I_n}$, and indexed sets of predicate symbols, $\{P^j\}_{j \in J_n}$, $n = 0, 1, \ldots$. For each n and every $i \in I_n$, f^i is an n-ary function symbol. Similarly, for each n and every $j \in J_n$, P^j is an n-ary predicate symbol. A 0-ary function symbol is a constant, and a 0-ary predicate symbol is a propositional variable. The I_n and the J_n may be empty, finite, or denumerably infinite. In the mathematical theories which we discuss in this book, J_0 is empty.

E 5.1 A scientist's choice of index sets I_n and J_n depends on his subject matter. For instance, if he studies natural numbers, he may work with one constant, 0; one unary function, S; two binary functions, $+$ and $\cdot$; one binary predicate, $<$; and let J_0, J_1, J_n, and I_n, $n \geqslant 3$, be empty. If he studies elementary group theory, he may work with one binary function, $\cdot$, and let I_0, I_1, I_k, $k \geqslant 3$, and J_n, $n \geqslant 0$, be empty.

The logical vocabulary of the predicate calculus consists of a denumerable infinity of individual variables, x, y, z, u, v, x_1, y_1, ..., a binary predicate, $=$, a quantifier, $\forall$, left and right parentheses, ( ), the comma ,,, and the four symbols we used in the propositional calculus, i.e., [,], $\supset$, $\sim$.

5.1.2 The Well-Formed Formulas

To explicate the notion of a well-formed formula in the predicate calculus, I introduce a new concept, the *term*, which I define inductively by the following scheme:

DT 1 An individual variable is a term;

DT 2 If $t_1, \ldots, t_n$ are terms, and if f is an n-ary function symbol, then $f(t_1, \ldots, t_n)$ is a term, $n = 0, 1, \ldots$.

Terms are the elements of our language which denote individuals in the universe. Using them we can phrase the first formation rule as follows:

PFR 1 If $t_1, \ldots, t_n$ are terms, and if P is an n-ary logical or nonlogical predicate symbol, then $P(t_1, \ldots, t_n)$ is a wff, $n = 0, 1, \ldots$.

We note that PFR 1 generalizes FR 1 (chapter 4) of the propositional calculus. In the jargon of logicians $P(t_1, \ldots, t_n)$ is called an *atomic formula*.

Equipped with atomic formulas, we can give an inductive definition of the other well-formed formulas of the predicate calculus. This definition requires three formation rules. The first two are FR 2 and FR 3 of the propositional calculus; the third is new and concerns the use of $\forall$.

PFR 2 If A is wf, then $\sim A$ is wf.

PFR 3 If A and B are wf, then $[A \supset B]$ is wf.

PFR 4 If A is wf and a is an *individual variable*, then $(\forall a)A$ is wf.

Note that $\forall$ is applied only to individual variables and that $(\forall a)$ is to be read as "for all a." Note also that if A is a formula in a given predicate calculus, there exists a method by which one may determine in a finite number of steps whether A is wf (see Church 1956, pp. 170, 70–71, and 121–123).

5.1.3 The Axioms

In stating the axioms of the predicate calculus we make use of syntactical variables having wffs as values. The expressions that present the axioms are so-called *axiom schemata.* They belong to the syntax language but not to the object language. Only their values are axioms.

The first three axiom schemata generalize the three axioms of the propositional calculus:

PLA 1 $[A \supset [B \supset A]]$

PLA 2 $[[A \supset [B \supset C]] \supset [[A \supset B] \supset [A \supset C]]]$

PLA 3 $[[\sim A \supset \sim B] \supset [B \supset A]]$

Since every one of the values of these expressions is an axiom, LA 1–LA 3 are axioms in any predicate calculus containing 0-ary predicate symbols.

The next two axiom schemata concern the meaning of $\forall$. To state them we need two new concepts, a free variable and a bound variable, and a syntactical symbol, $A_a(b)$. An occurrence of an individual variable a in a wff A is *bound in A* if it occurs in a wf subformula of A of the form $(\forall a)B$; otherwise it is *free in A*. We say that a is a *free (or bound) variable of A* if some occurrence of a is free (or bound) in A. The symbol $A_a(b)$ denotes the wff that results from substituting the term h for all free occurrences of a in A.

Ideally $A_a(b)$ ought to say the same thing about b that A asserts of a. This does not always happen. For example, if a and b are individual variables that vary over natural numbers, and if A is expressed by

$$\sim(\forall b)\sim[[a = 2b] \vee [(a + 1) = 2b]]$$

then A insists that a is either even or odd, while $A_a(b)$ maintains that there is a value of b which equals 0 or 1.

We shall avoid anomalies, such as the one exhibited above, by introducing a convention: Let us say that b is *substitutable* for a in A if, for each variable x occurring in b, no part of A of the form $(\forall x)B$ contains an occurrence of a which is free in A. Then we agree that whenever we assert $A_a(b)$, it is implicitly assumed that b is substitutable for a in A.

Now the two axiom schemata:

PLA 4 Let A and B be wffs and let a be an individual variable that is not a free variable of A. Then

$[(\forall a)[A \supset B] \supset [A \supset (\forall a)B]]$.

PLA 5 Let A be a wff, let a be an individual variable, and let b be a term that is substitutable for a in A. Then $[(\forall a)A \supset A_a(b)]$.

The second of these is the predicate-calculus version of the *dictum de omni et nullo*.

Most mathematical theories treat equality, $=$, as a logical symbol. Therefore I have assumed that $=$ is one of the logical symbols of the predicate calculus. I write $[x = y]$ rather than $= (x, y)$ and postulate that $=$ satisfies the following axiom schemata:

PLA 6 If b is a term, $[b = b]$.

PLA 7 Let A be a wff, let a be an individual variable, and let b and c be terms that are substitutable for a in A. Then

$[[b = c] \supset [A_a(b) \supset A_a(c)]]$.

5.1.4 The Rules of Inference

There are two rules of inference in our predicate calculus. One is the Modus Ponens:

PRI 1 Let A and B be wffs. *From* $[A \supset B]$ *and* A, *we infer* B.

The other is the *Rule of Generalization*:

PRI 2 Let A be a wff. If *a is an individual variable, from A we infer* $(\forall a)A$.

In E 5.2 we illustrate the use of PRI 2:

E 5.2 There once was a town with many men and one barber. The barber shaved everyone who did not shave himself and only those. He had a problem that we shall use to illustrate PRI 2. Let the universe of discourse be all men in a given town, and let $P(\cdot)$ and $Q(\cdot)$ be unary predicates that, for each x in the universe, declare

x does not shave himself, and
x is shaved by the barber,

respectively. Moreover, let b denote the barber, let y denote any man in the universe different from b, and give $\equiv$ its intended interpretation. Then, according to the story, for all y

(i) $[P(y) \equiv Q(y)]$

denotes t; i.e., y does not shave himself if and only if he is shaved by the barber. As to b, note that, if b does not shave himself, $P(b)$ denotes t, $Q(b)$ denotes f, and

(ii) $[P(b) \equiv Q(b)]$

denotes f. If b shaves himself, $P(b)$, $\sim Q(b)$, and (ii) denote f. Hence we cannot assert $(\forall x)[P(x) \equiv Q(x)]$. However, if we let the barber shave himself, we can assert $[P \supset Q]$ and use PRI 2 to infer

$(\forall x)[P(x) \supset Q(x)]$.

The rules of inference of our predicate calculus do not include RI 2 of the propositional calculus. It is therefore important to note that in any predicate calculus with 0-ary predicate variables, RI 2 is a derived rule of inference. For a proof see Church 1956, pp. 149–150.

5.2 Sample Theorems

In this section we shall establish several metatheorems concerning $=$, $\forall$, and $\equiv$. We begin with equality.

5.2.1 Equality

In mathematics $=$ is an equivalence relation with a certain substitutive property. PLA 6 and TM 5.1, TM 5.2, and TM 5.4 below show that our $=$ has the same characteristics.

TM 5.1 Let a and b be terms. Then $[[a = b] \supset [b = a]]$.

TM 5.2 Let a, b, and c be terms. Then

$[[a = b] \supset [[b = c] \supset [a = c]]]$.

To prove TM 5.1 we record first the predicate-calculus version of T 4.23:

TM 5.3 $[[A \supset [B \supset C]] \equiv [B \supset [A \supset C]]]$

Then letting A assert $[x = a]$, we observe that when we substitute for x in PLA 7, then by PLA 7, TM 5.3, PLA 6, and PRI 1,

$[[a = b] \supset [[a = a] \supset [b = a]]]$

$[[a = a] \supset [[a = b] \supset [b = a]]]$

$[a = a]$

$[[a = b] \supset [b = a]]$.

To prove TM 5.2, let A assert $[x = c]$ and substitute for x in PLA 7 to infer

$$[[b = a] \supset [[b = c] \supset [a = c]]].$$

Then TM 4.1 with $[a = b]$ as q, PLA 2, TM 5.1, and two applications of PRI 1 suffice to establish $[[a = b] \supset [[b = c] \supset [a = c]]]$,

PLA 6, TM 5.1, and TM 5.2 show that $=$ is an equivalence relation. TM 5.4 demonstrates that $=$ also has the usual substitutive property.

TM 5.4 Let f be an n-ary function symbol and let t_i and s_i, $i = 1, \ldots, n$, be terms. Then

$$[[[t_1 = s_1] \wedge [[t_2 = s_2] \wedge [\ldots \wedge [t_n = s_n]\ldots]]] \supset [f(t_1, \ldots, t_n) = f(s_1, \ldots, s_n)]].$$

The proof of TM 5.4 is a generalization of the proofs of TM 5.1 and TM 5.2.

5.2.2 The Quantifiers

In interpreting our language, $(\forall a)$ is read as "for all a." Thus we can use $\forall$ to assert sentences such as "All ravens are black." To state sentences such as "There exists a raven," we must introduce a new symbol:

$$(\exists a)A =_{\text{df}} \sim (\forall a) \sim A.$$

In our interpreted language $(\exists a)$ will read as "there exists an a."

Next we shall state and prove several metatheorems concerning $\forall$ and $\exists$. In reading the proofs, note that only necessary details are spelled out, and that in every proof we make use of TM 5.5—the predicate-calculus version of T 4.7.

TM 5.5 $[[A \supset B] \supset [[B \supset C] \supset [A \supset C]]]$

Moreover, note that in the proof of TM 5.8 below we assert particular cases of the predicate-calculus versions of T 4.3 and T 4.6, i.e., TM 5.6 and TM 5.7.

TM 5.6 $[A \supset \sim\sim A]$

TM 5.7 $[[A \supset B] \supset [\sim B \supset \sim A]]$

In the first theorem, which concerns $\exists$, we ascertain that if we find a b satisfying A, we can be certain that $(\exists a)A$.

TM 5.8 Let a be an individual variable and let A be a wff. In addition, let b be a term that is substitutable for a in A. Then

$[A_a(b) \supset (\exists a)A]$.

Proof $[(\forall a){\sim}A \supset {\sim}A_a(b)]$

$[[(\forall a){\sim}A \supset {\sim}A_a(b)] \supset [{\sim}{\sim}A_a(b) \supset {\sim}(\forall a){\sim}A]]$

$[{\sim}{\sim}A_a(b) \supset {\sim}(\forall a){\sim}A]$

$[[A_a(b) \supset {\sim}{\sim}A_a(b)] \supset [[{\sim}{\sim}A_a(b) \supset {\sim}(\forall a){\sim}A] \supset$
$[A_a(b) \supset {\sim}(\forall a){\sim}A]]]$

$[A_a(b) \supset {\sim}{\sim}A_a(b)]$

$[A_a(b) \supset {\sim}(\forall a){\sim}A]$

In this proof we first assert PLA 5 for ${\sim}A$ and a version of TM 5.7. Then we apply PRI 1 to infer $[{\sim}{\sim}A_a(b) \supset {\sim}(\forall a){\sim}A]$. Finally we use TM 5.5 and TM 5.6 and apply PRI 1 twice to conclude that $[A_a(b) \supset (\exists a)A]$.

In PLA 4 and in TM 5.9 and TM 5.10 below, the distributive properties of $\forall$ are described.

TM 5.9 $[(\forall a)[A \supset B] \supset [(\forall a)A \supset B]]$

Proof $[(\forall a)[A \supset B] \supset [A_a(a) \supset B_a(a)]]$

$[[(\forall a)A \supset A_a(a)] \supset [[A_a(a) \supset B_a(a)] \supset [(\forall a)A \supset B_a(a)]]]$

$[(\forall a)A \supset A_a(a)]$

$[[A_a(a) \supset B_a(a)] \supset [(\forall a)A \supset B_a(a)]]$

$[[(\forall a)[A \supset B] \supset [A_a(a) \supset B_a(a)]] \supset [[[A_a(a) \supset B_a(a)] \supset$
$[(\forall a)A \supset B_a(a)]] \supset [(\forall a)[A \supset B] \supset [(\forall a)A \supset B_a(a)]]]]$

$[(\forall a)[A \supset B] \supset [(\forall a)A \supset B_a(a)]]$

In this proof we assert PLA 5 for $[A \supset B]$, a version of TM 5.5 and PLA 5. Then we apply PRI 1 to infer $[[A_a(a) \supset B_a(a)] \supset [(\forall a)A \supset B_a(a)]]$. Finally we assert a version of TM 5.5 and apply PRI 1 twice to deduce $[(\forall a)[A \supset B]] \supset [(\forall a)A \supset B]]$.

TM 5.10 $[(\forall a)[A \supset B] \supset [(\forall a)A \supset (\forall a)B]]$

Proof $[(\forall a)[A \supset B] \supset [(\forall a)A \supset B]]$

$(\forall a)[(\forall a)[A \supset B] \supset [(\forall a)A \supset B]]$

$[(\forall a)[(\forall a)[A \supset B] \supset [(\forall a)A \supset B]] \supset [(\forall a)[A \supset B] \supset$
$(\forall a)[(\forall a)A \supset B]]]$

$[(\forall a)[A \supset B] \supset (\forall a)[(\forall a)A \supset B]]$

$[(\forall a)[(\forall a)A \supset B] \supset [(\forall a)A \supset (\forall a)B]]$

$$[[(\forall a)[A \supset B] \supset (\forall a)[(\forall a)A \supset B]] \supset [[(\forall a)[(\forall a)A \supset B] \supset$$
$$[(\forall a)A \supset (\forall a)B]] \supset [(\forall a)[A \supset B] \supset [(\forall a)A \supset (\forall a)B]]]]$$
$$[(\forall a)[A \supset B] \supset [(\forall a)A \supset (\forall a)B]]$$

In this proof we assert TM 5.9, apply PRI 2, and use PLA 4 and PRI 1 to infer $[(\forall a)[A \supset B] \supset (\forall a)[(\forall a)A \supset B]]$. Then we assert a version of PLA 4 and a version of TM 5.5 and apply PRI 1 twice to establish $[(\forall a)[A \supset B] \supset [(\forall a)A \supset (\forall a)B]]$.

It is clear from our definition of $\exists$ that $\exists$ must have the same distributive properties as $\forall$. I leave it to the reader to establish this fact and conclude our discussion of $\forall$ and $\exists$ with TM 5.11.

TM 5.11 $[(\forall a)A \supset (\exists a)A]$

Proof $[(\forall a)A \supset A_a(b)]$

$[A_a(b) \supset (\exists a)A]$

$[[(\forall a)A \supset A_a(b)] \supset [[A_a(b) \supset (\exists a)A] \supset [(\forall a)A \supset (\exists a)A]]]$

$[(\forall a)A \supset (\exists a)A]$

In this proof we assert PLA 5, TM 5.8, and a version of TM 5.5. Then we apply PRI 1 twice to infer $[(\forall a)A \supset (\exists a)A]$.

While reading the preceding theorems, it is helpful to note the following: Suppose that we give $\sim$ and $\supset$ their intended interpretations and read $(\forall x)$ as "for all x" and $(\exists x)$ as "there exists an x." Suppose also that in each relevant case we choose the universe appropriately. Then we can use PLA 5 and PRI 1 to justify the inference from "All physicists are philosophers" and "Per is a physicist" to "Per is a philosopher." Similarly, from TM 5.11 and PRI 1 we can infer "There is a black raven" from "All ravens are black." We can also apply TM 5.9 and PRI 1 to infer from "All human beings are mortal" and "Everybody in the universe is a human" that "If y is a member of the universe, y will die." Finally we can use TM 5.10 and PRI 1 to infer from "All human beings are mortal" and "Everybody in the universe is human" that "Everybody in the universe will die."

We note in passing that, if all individuals are not ravens, the symbolic rendition of all ravens (R) are black (B) is $(\forall x)[R(x) \supset B(x)]$. From this assertion, TM 5.11, and PRI 1, we can infer that $(\exists x)[R(x) \supset B(x)]$ and that if this x is a raven, it is black. We cannot, however, deduce that there is a black raven; i.e., we cannot deduce that $(\exists x)[R(x) \wedge B(x)]$.

5.2.3 Material Equivalence

In chapter 4 I showed that the material equivalence relation of the propositional calculus is an equivalence relation with a certain substitutive property. Next I shall demonstrate that the $\equiv$ relation of my predicate calculus has the same characteristics. The results are stated in TM 5.12–TM 5.15. I leave the proofs of the first three to the reader and outline a proof of the fourth.

The axiom schemata PLA 1–PLA 3 and PRI 1 can be used to establish TM 5.12–TM 5.14, the predicate-calculus analogues of T 4.14–T 4.16.

TM 5.12 If A is a wff, $[A \equiv A]$.

TM 5.13 If A and B are wffs, $[[A \equiv B] \supset [B \equiv A]]$.

TM 5.14 If A, B, and C are wffs, then
$[[A \equiv B] \supset [[B \equiv C] \supset [A \equiv C]]]$.

Hence $\equiv$ is a material equivalence relation. This relation also has a substitutive property that we record in TM 5.15—a predicate-calculus analogue of TM 4.6.

TM 5.15 Let A be a wff and let $B_1, \ldots, B_n$ be wf subformulas of A. Also let $\hat{A}$ be a wff that is obtained from A by respectively substituting the wffs $\hat{B}_1, \ldots, \hat{B}_n$ for $B_1, \ldots, B_n$ at some of the occurrences in A of the latter formulas. Finally, suppose that, for every $i = 1, \ldots, n$, $[B_i \equiv \hat{B}_i]$ is a theorem. Then $[A \equiv \hat{A}]$ is also a theorem.

We shall prove this theorem by *induction on the length of wffs*. The idea of such a proof is simple. Think of the wffs as being distributed in layers. In the first layer, S_1, are all the atomic formulas. In the second layer, S_2, we observe all the wffs that are constructed from atomic formulas with the help of $\sim$, $\supset$, and $\forall$. In the third layer are all the wffs that are formed from the wffs in S_1 and S_2 with the help of $\sim$, $\supset$, and $\forall$. And so on. We establish the theorem first for atomic formulas. Then we assume that the theorem is valid for all wffs in all layers up to and including some given level and show that it is valid for the wffs in the next layer as well. The antecedent clause in this last step is referred to as *the induction hypothesis*.

In carrying out the last step in the proof described above, we make tacit use of the following facts, the proof of which I leave to the reader. (See Church 1956, pp. 180 and 122–123.)

1. Every wff A is either an atomic formula or there exist wffs B, C, and D and an individual variable a such that A is $\sim B$, $[B \supset C]$, or $(\forall a)D$. In each case, A is of that form in one and only one way.

2. A wf part of $\sim B$ either is $\sim B$ or is a wf part of B.

3. A wf part of $[B \supset C]$ either is $[B \supset C]$ or is a wf part of B or C but not of both.

4. A wf part of $(\forall a)D$ either is $(\forall a)D$ or is a wf part of D.

Now the proof: If $\hat{A}$ is A, then TM 5.12 implies that $[A \equiv \hat{A}]$ is a theorem. So in the remainder of the proof we assume that $\hat{A}$ differs from A. Suppose first that A is atomic. Then A is B_i for some i, $\hat{A}$ is $\hat{B}_i$, and $[A \equiv \hat{A}]$ is a theorem by hypothesis. Suppose next that A is $\sim C$ for some wff C. If B_i occurs in A, either A is B_i or B_i is contained in C. If A is B_i, $\hat{A}$ is $\hat{B}_i$, and $[A \equiv \hat{A}]$ is a theorem by hypothesis. If the occurrences of the B_i are contained in C and $\hat{C}$ is obtained from C by substituting $\hat{B}_i$ for B_i, $i = 1, \ldots, n$, then by the induction hypothesis $[C \equiv \hat{C}]$ is a theorem. From this, TM 5.13, and the fact that $\hat{A}$ is $\sim \hat{C}$, it follows by T 4.12, TM 5.7, and repeated use of PRI 1 that $[A \equiv \hat{A}]$ is a theorem as well. A similar argument suffices for the case when A is $[C \supset D]$ for two wffs C and D. Finally, if A is $(\forall a)C$ for some wff C, A is B_i for some i, and the proof goes through as above, or the B_i are contained in C. If the B_i are contained in C, $\hat{A}$ is $(\forall a)\hat{C}$, and $[C \equiv \hat{C}]$ is a theorem by the induction hypothesis. Consequently, by TM 5.13, T 4.12, PRI 2, TM 5.10 and repeated use of PRI 1, it follows that $[A \equiv \hat{A}]$ is a theorem as well.

Theorem TM 5.15 is used in many ways, e.g., to facilitate the application of PLA 5 in proofs. To wit: In the predicate calculus a *variant* of a wff A is a wff B that is obtained from A by a sequence of replacements in each of which a part $(\forall x)C$ is replaced by $(\forall y)C_x(y)$, where y is a variable that is not free in C. When a term b is not substitutable for a variable a in a wff A, we replace A by a variant of A in which none of the variables in b are bound and apply PLA 5 to the variant formula. The justification for this procedure is obtained from TM 5.15 and from the metatheorem TM 5.16, whose proof I leave to the reader.

TM 5.16 Let A be a wff and let a and y be individual variables. Moreover, suppose that A contains no free occurrence of y and that y is substitutable for a in A. Then

$$[(\forall a)A \equiv (\forall y)A_a(y)].$$

Another way in which TM 5.15 is used in proofs is to justify replacing wffs by wffs in which the quantifiers appear at the front of the formulas. For example, if A is $[B \supset (\exists x)C]$ and x is not free in B, TM 5.15 and TM 5.17 below justify replacing A by $(\exists x)[B \supset C]$. Similarly, if D is $[(\forall x)C \supset B]$ and x is not free in B, D can be replaced by $(\exists x)[C \supset B]$.

TM 5.17 Let B and C be wffs and let x be an individual variable. If x is not free in B,

$[[B \supset (\exists x)C] \equiv (\exists x)[B \supset C]]$.

I leave the demonstration of $[(\exists x)[B \supset C] \supset [B \supset (\exists x)C]]$ to the reader. To prove the converse relation we proceed as follows: First, by applying in succession TM 5.7, PRI 1, the tautology $[\sim\sim B \equiv B]$, and TM 4.7, we deduce from $[\sim B \supset [B \supset C]]$ that $[\sim[B \supset C] \supset B]$. From this it follows by application of PRI 2, TM 5.9, PRI 1, and TM 5.7 that $(S)[\sim B \supset (\exists x)[B \supset C]]$. By similar arguments, we deduce from $[C \supset [B \supset C]]$ that $(T)[(\exists x)C \supset (\exists x)[B \supset C]]$. Then we apply TM 4.1 to S and T and infer

(i) $[[B \supset (\exists x)C] \supset [\sim B \supset (\exists x)[B \supset C]]]$

and $[B \supset [(\exists x)C \supset (\exists x)[B \supset C]]]$. From the last assertion, PLA 2, and PRI 1, it follows that

(ii) $[[B \supset (\exists x)C] \supset [B \supset (\exists x)[B \supset C]]]$.

But if that is so, then (i), (ii), TM 5.3, TM 4.7, and the predicate-calculus version of T 4.24 suffice to demonstrate that $[[B \supset (\exists x)C] \supset (\exists x)[B \supset C]]$.

5.3 Semantic Properties

In this section I shall discuss some of the semantic properties of my first-order predicate calculus. In this discussion I use the term *first-order language* to denote a first-order predicate calculus with a specified set of nonlogical symbols. Two first-order languages differ only if they have different index sets I_n and J_n, i.e., if they do not have the same number of function and predicate symbols.

5.3.1 Structures

To interpret a given first-order language L, I first introduce the concept of a structure for L. A *structure* $\mathscr{D}$ for L is a quadruple $(|\mathscr{D}|, N_{\mathscr{D}}, F^{\mathscr{D}}, G^{\mathscr{D}})$, where $|\mathscr{D}|$ is a set of individuals; $N_{\mathscr{D}}$ is a set of names of the individuals in $|\mathscr{D}|$, with one name for each individual and different names for different individuals; $F^{\mathscr{D}}$ is a family of functions from $|\mathscr{D}|$ to $|\mathscr{D}|$; and G is a family of predicates in $|\mathscr{D}|$. To each *n-ary* f in $\{f^i\}_{i \in I_n}$ corresponds an n-ary $f^{\mathscr{D}}$ in $F^{\mathscr{D}}$, and to each n-ary P in $\{P^j\}_{j \in J_n}$ corresponds an n-ary $P^{\mathscr{D}}$ in $G^{\mathscr{D}}$, $n = 0, 1, \ldots$. The $f^{\mathscr{D}}$ exhaust $F^{\mathscr{D}}$ as f varies through the $\{f^i\}_{i \in I_n}$, and the $P^{\mathscr{D}}$ exhaust $G^{\mathscr{D}}$ as P varies through the $\{P^j\}_{j \in J_n}$.[1]

E 5.3 Let L be a first-order language with I_0, J_0, I_n, J_n, $n \geqslant 2$, empty, with five unary function symbols f^i, $i = 1, \ldots, 5$, and with six unary predicate symbols, P^j, $j = 1, \ldots, 6$. We construct a structure $\mathscr{D}$ for L in the following way:

Let $|\mathscr{D}| = \{x_1, x_2\}$, $N_{\mathscr{D}} = \{a_1, a_2\}$ and observe that there are only four unary functions from $|\mathscr{D}|$ to $|\mathscr{D}|$. They are described in table 5.1. There the value of k at x_1 is x_2, and the value of k at x_2 is x_1.

Similarly, there are only four unary predicates in $|\mathscr{D}|$. They are described in table 5.2. There a t in the x_1 row and P_2 column indicates that x_1 satisfies P_2; and an f in the x_2 row and P_2 column indicates that x_2 does not satisfy P_2.

We obtain a structure $\mathscr{D}$ for L by assigning x_1 to a_1; x_2 to a_2; f to f^1 and f^2; g, h, and k to f^3, f^4, and f^5, respectively; P_1 to P^1; P_2 to P^2; P_3 to P^3 and P^4; and P_4 to P^5 and P^6.

5.3.2 Structures and the Interpretation of a First-Order Language

Using the structure $\mathscr{D}$ for L, we obtain in interpretation of L in a manner described below. In this interpretation we first add the names in $N_{\mathscr{D}}$ to the 0-ary functions of L and denote the expanded first-order language by $L(\mathscr{D})$. Then we interpret

(i) each $a \in N_{\mathscr{D}}$ as the individual which it names, $\mathscr{D}(a)$; and
(ii) each variable-free term $a \in L(\mathscr{D})$ of the form $f(a_1, \ldots, a_n)$ as $f^{\mathscr{D}}(\mathscr{D}(a_1), \ldots, \mathscr{D}(a_n))$, $n = 0, 1, \ldots$.

It can be shown that, if a is a variable-free term in $L(\mathscr{D})$, then either a is a

Table 5.1
The unary individual functions in $F^{\mathscr{D}}$.

	F			
x	f	g	h	k
x_1	x_1	x_2	x_1	x_2
x_2	x_1	x_2	x_2	x_1

Table 5.2
The unary predicates in $G^{\mathscr{D}}$.

	P			
x	P_1	P_2	P_3	P_4
x_1	t	t	f	f
x_2	t	f	t	f

name or there exist an n, a uniquely determined n-ary function symbol f, and variable-free terms $a_1, \ldots, a_n$ such that a is $f(a_1, \ldots, a_n)$. (See Shoenfield 1967, p. 19.) From this it follows that (i) and (ii) determine the interpretation $\mathscr{D}(a)$ of all variable-free terms in L($\mathscr{D}$).

Next let b be a term in L with n free variables $x_1, \ldots, x_n$ in L; let $\theta_1, \ldots, \theta_n$ be names in $N_{\mathscr{D}}$; and let $b_{x_1,\ldots,x_n}(\theta_1, \ldots, \theta_n)$ be the term we obtain by substituting θ_i for x_i at each occurrence of x_i in b, $i = 1, \ldots, n$. Then $b_{x_1,\ldots,x_n}(\theta_1, \ldots, \theta_n)$ is a *$\mathscr{D}$-instance of b*. Conditions i and ii determine the interpretation of every $\mathscr{D}$ instance of b. In that way they determine the interpretation of b as well.

To interpret the wffs of L, we must first interpret the *closed formulas* in $L(\mathscr{D})$, i.e., the wffs in $L(\mathscr{D})$ in which no variable is free. This we do by induction on the length of wffs.

(iii) Let A be the closed wff $[a = b]$, where a and b are terms. Since A is closed, a and b must be variable-free. We interpret A by insisting that $\mathscr{D}(A) = t$ if $\mathscr{D}(a) = \mathscr{D}(b)$. Otherwise $\mathscr{D}(A) = $ f.

(iv) Let A be the closed atomic formula $P(a_1, \ldots, a_n)$, where P is not $=$. Since A is closed, the a_j are variable-free. We interpret A by insisting that $\mathscr{D}(A) = t$ if $P^{\mathscr{D}}(\mathscr{D}(a_1), \ldots, \mathscr{D}(a_n))$. Otherwise $\mathscr{D}(A) = $ f.

(v) If A and B are closed wff, then $\mathscr{D}(\sim A) = $ f if $\mathscr{D}(A) = t$ and $\mathscr{D}(\sim A) = $ t if $\mathscr{D}(A) = $ f. Also $\mathscr{D}([A \supset B]) = $ f if $\mathscr{D}(A) = t$ and $\mathscr{D}(B) = $ f. Otherwise $\mathscr{D}([A \supset B]) = $ t.

(vi) If C is a wff that contains only one free individual variable x, then $\mathscr{D}((\forall x)C) = $ t if and only if $\mathscr{D}(C_x(a)) = $ t for all $a \in N_{\mathscr{D}}$. Otherwise $\mathscr{D}((\forall x)C) = $ f.

It is clear that conditions iii–vi determine the interpretation of all closed wffs in $L(\mathscr{D})$ and hence in L. But if that is true, then those conditions determine the interpretation of the remaining formulas in L as well. To show how for a formula B with n free variables, let a *$\mathscr{D}$ instance of B* be a closed formula of the form $B_{x_1,\ldots,x_n}(a_1, \ldots, a_n)$, where $(a_1, \ldots, a_n)$ is an n-tuple of names in $N_{\mathscr{D}}$. Conditions iii–vi determine the interpretation of every $\mathscr{D}$ instance of B. In that way they determine the interpretation of B as well.

In TM 5.18 we see that the interpretation of $\mathscr{D}$ instances of terms and wffs described above is unambiguous.

TM 5.18 Let $\mathscr{D}$ be a structure for L; let a be a variable-free term of $L(\mathscr{D})$; and let $\theta \in N_{\mathscr{D}}$ be the name of $\mathscr{D}(a)$. If b is a term of $L(\mathscr{D})$ in which no variable except x occurs, then $\mathscr{D}(b_x(a)) = \mathscr{D}(b_x(\theta))$. Furthermore, if A is a wff in $L(\mathscr{D})$ in which no variable except x is free, then

$$\mathscr{D}(A_x(a)) = \mathscr{D}(A_x(\theta)).$$

We shall establish the validity of the theorem for terms by induction on the length of b. If b is a name, $b_x(a)$ and $b_x(\theta)$ are both b and there is nothing to prove. If b is a variable, $b_x(a)$ is a, $b_x(\theta)$ is θ, and $\mathscr{D}(a) = \mathscr{D}(\theta)$ by our choice of θ. Finally, if there is an n-ary function symbol f and terms $b_1, \ldots, b_n$ such that b is $f(b_1, \ldots, b_n)$, then by the induction hypothesis,

$$\begin{aligned}\mathscr{D}(b_x(a)) &= \mathscr{D}(f(b_{1x}(a), \ldots, b_{nx}(a))) \\ &= f^{\mathscr{D}}(\mathscr{D}(b_{1x}(a)), \ldots, \mathscr{D}(b_{nx}(a))) \\ &= f^{\mathscr{D}}(\mathscr{D}(b_{1x}(\theta)), \ldots, \mathscr{D}(b_{nx}(\theta))) \\ &= \mathscr{D}(f(b_{1x}(\theta), \ldots, b_{nx}(\theta))) \\ &= \mathscr{D}(b_x(\theta)).\end{aligned}$$

To establish the theorem for wffs we proceed by induction on the length of A. If A is atomic, then there are terms b and c such that A is $[b = c]$ or there are terms $b_1, \ldots, b_n$ and an n-ary predicate symbol P such that A is $P(b_1, \ldots, b_n)$. In either case, $\mathscr{D}(A_x(a))$ and $\mathscr{D}(A_x(\theta))$ declare equivalent sentences. Hence $\mathscr{D}(A_x(a)) = t$ if and only if $\mathscr{D}(A_x(\theta)) = t$. If A is not atomic, there are wffs B, C, and D such that A is $\sim B$ or $[B \supset C]$ or $(\forall y)D$. I leave it to the reader to use the induction hypothesis to establish the validity of the theorem when A is $\sim B$ or $[B \supset C]$. When A is $(\forall y)D$, we may assume that y and x are not the same variable, since otherwise $A_x(a)$ and $A_x(\theta)$ are both A. Let α be a variable that varies through the names in $N_{\mathscr{D}}$. Then $\mathscr{D}(A_x(a)) = t$ if and only if $\mathscr{D}(D_{x,y}(a, \alpha)) = t$ for all $\alpha \in N_{\mathscr{D}}$. Hence, by the induction hypothesis, $\mathscr{D}(A_x(a)) = t$ if and only if $\mathscr{D}(D_{x,y}(\theta, \alpha)) = t$ for all $\alpha \in N_{\mathscr{D}}$; i.e., $\mathscr{D}(A_x(a)) = t$ if and only if $\mathscr{D}(A_x(\theta)) = t$.

5.3.3 Tautologies and Valid Well-Formed Formulas

In presenting the propositional calculus, I insisted that a tautology be a wff that denotes truth no matter what it asserts. For the propositional calculus this amounts to demanding that a tautology be a wff that denotes truth because of the meaning of $\sim$ and $\supset$ alone. Then to ascertain whether a given wff is a tautology it suffices to check its truth table.

In our predicate calculus the meaning of $\sim$ and $\supset$ is determined by PLA 1–PLA 3 and PRI 1. Any two-valued interpretation of $\sim$ and $\supset$, in which the values of PLA 1–PLA 3 denote truth, their negations falsehood, and PRI 1 is a valid rule of inference, must be as described in condition v above. In this interpretation a *wff is a tautology if and only if it is a value of*

Table 5.3
Truth table for PLA 4.

A	P	$(\forall x)[A \supset P]$	$[A \supset (\forall x)P]$	$[(\forall x)[A \supset P] \supset [A \supset (\forall x)P]]$
t	P_1	t	t	t
f	P_1	t	t	t
t	P_2	f	f	t
f	P_2	t	t	t
t	P_3	f	f	t
f	P_3	t	t	t
t	P_4	f	f	t
f	P_4	t	t	t

one of our first three axiom schemata or it is a value of a theorem schemata that can be derived from PLA 1–PLA 3 with the help of PRI 1. Examples of such theorem schemata are TM 5.3, TM 5.5–5.7, and TM 5.12–TM 5.14.

Not all the theorems of our predicate calculus are tautologies. Hence to give a semantic characterization of the theorems of our language, I must introduce several new terms. We say that *a wff B is valid in* $\mathscr{D}$ if and only if $\mathscr{D}(B') = \text{t}$ for every $\mathscr{D}$ instance B' of B. It follows from this definition that a closed formula A is valid in $\mathscr{D}$ if and only if $\mathscr{D}(A) = \text{t}$.

E 5.4 Let L be as described in E 5.3, and let $\mathscr{D}$ be a structure for L such that $|\mathscr{D}| = \{x_1, x_2\}$. The truth table for PLA 4, table 5.3, shows that PLA 4 is valid in all such $\mathscr{D}$.

As E 5.4 showed, for the given pair $\{x_1, x_2\}$, PLA 4 was valid in every $\mathscr{D}$, with $|\mathscr{D}| = \{x_1, x_2\}$. Henceforth we shall say that *a wff A is valid in* $|\mathscr{D}|$ if it is valid in every structure for L with the same individuals as $|\mathscr{D}|$.

A *valid* wff is a wff that is valid in every structure. It is clear that a tautology is valid. Hence the values of PLA 1–PLA 3 are valid wffs. We next show that the values of PLA 4 and PLA 5 are also valid wffs.

A value of PLA 5 denotes f only if $(\forall a)A$ denotes t and $A_a(b)$ denotes f. According to our interpretation of $\forall$, however, $(\forall a)A$ denotes t only if $A_a(b)$ denotes t for all values of b. Hence the values of PLA 5 must be valid in every domain.

To show that the values of PLA 4 are valid, we begin by assuming the contrary. Thus there exist a domain E, a structure $\mathscr{D}$ for L with $|\mathscr{D}| = E$, wffs A and B, and an individual variable a that is not free in A such that $\mathscr{D}([(\forall a)[A \supset B] \supset [A \supset (\forall a)B]]) = \text{f}$. That can happen in $\mathscr{D}$ only if $(\forall a)$

$[A \supset B]$ denotes t and $[A \supset (\forall a)B]$ denotes f. $[A \supset (\forall a)B]$ denotes f in $\mathscr{D}$ only if A denotes t and $(\forall a)B$ denotes f. But if A and $(\forall a)[A \supset B]$ denote t in $\mathscr{D}$, then, for all b, $\mathscr{D}([A \supset B]_a(b)) = \mathscr{D}[A \supset B_a(b)] = \text{t}$ and $\mathscr{D}(B_a(b)) = \text{t}$. Consequently, $\mathscr{D}((\forall a)B) = \text{t}$ as well. This is a contradiction which demonstrates that E, $\mathscr{D}$, and the pair A, B with the required properties do not exist; i.e., the values of PLA 4 are valid, as was to be shown.

The validity of PLA 6 is obvious. The validity of the values of PLA 7 is an easily demonstrated consequence of TM 5.15. To see why, let $\mathscr{D}$ be a structure for L, let A be a wff in which a is a free variable, and let b and c be terms that are substitutable for a in A. Then TM 5.18 implies that, for every $\mathscr{D}$ instance of b, c, and A, either $\mathscr{D}(b)$ differs from $\mathscr{D}(c)$ or $\mathscr{D}(A_a(b)) = \text{t}$ only if $\mathscr{D}(A_a(c)) = \text{t}$. Hence the given value of PLA 7 is valid in $\mathscr{D}$. Since $\mathscr{D}$ is arbitrary, the same value of PLA 7 must be valid in all structures of L.

5.3.4 Valid Well-Formed Formulas and Theorems

It is easy to verify that the rules of inference, PRI 1 and PRI 2, preserve validity; i.e., if the premises are valid formulas, so too are the conclusions. From this and the validity of the values of PLA 1–PLA 7, it follows that the theorems of my language are valid wffs. The converse—i.e., a valid wff is a theorem—is true and will be proved in section 6.6. Consequently, we have TM 5.19.

TM 5.19 A wff A is a theorem if and only if it is valid.

This theorem is as remarkable as TM 4.5 of chapter 4. It uses one interpretation (of many possible) to characterize a class of wffs that was defined in terms of concepts of the uninterpreted predicate calculus. However, in contrast to TM 4.5, TM 5.19 does not provide an algorithm for checking whether a wff is a theorem. This is so because the number of individuals in the universe is unbounded.

5.4 Philosophical Misgivings

I believe that sections 5.1–5.3, together with our discussion of the interpretation of the propositional calculus, establish that a first-order language, such as the one presented above, can serve as a guide to sound scientific reasoning. There are, however, others who disagree. They have misgivings about the meaning and about the use of for-all and there-exist sentences in a formalized language. We look at those misgivings next.

5.4.1 For-All Sentences

Frank Ramsey (1954, p. 241) would have disputed our treating sentences such as $(\forall a)[A \supset B]$ as conjunctions. He considered that acceptable only when the universe D is finite. When D is infinite, he would have argued, such expressions may look like conjunctions but are not. They cannot be written out as conjunctions and asserted as such. And if they are not conjunctions, they are not declarative sentences. Instead they are rules for judging: if I meet an A, I shall regard it as a B. In particular, to Ramsey a sentence such as "all men are mortal" has no truth value; instead it is a prescription for behavior: if I meet a man, I shall regard him as mortal.

To assert a finite conjunction,

$$A_x(a_1) \quad \text{and} \quad A_x(a_2) \quad \text{and} \ldots \text{and } A_x(a_n),$$

we must be able to identify the a_i's; i.e., we must be able to name the n objects concerned. Since we cannot write down the names of infinitely many objects, we cannot declare an infinite conjunction of sentences in the way we asserted the finite conjunction above. We must use an auxiliary device such as the quantifier $\forall$. To justify such use I shall give examples that show that we *can* assert, understand, and assign a truth value to $(\forall a)A$ even in cases where we cannot name all the a's involved.

I begin with a trivial sentence. Its validity is *analytic* in the sense that "the predicate is part of the subject of which it is asserted" (Russell 1976, p. 46). Hence we can both understand it and assign a truth value to it without knowledge of any instances of it.

E 5.5 Let the universe consist of all human beings. According to Webster, no matter what value x assumes,
"Either x is not a widow or x has had a husband." By PRI 2 it follows that
"For all x, either x is not a widow or x has had a husband."

Next I give an example from elementary number theory. This sentence is also easy to understand. Moreover, we can infer its truth from just a few instances of it, and we can establish its validity by mathematical induction.

E 5.6 Let the universe consist of all the positive integers. Then "For all x, $1 + 2 + \cdots + x = x(x + 1)/2$."

My third example is one of Russell's stock examples (Russell 1976, p. 62). His sentence is easy to comprehend and undeniably true. Yet we cannot mention an instance of it.

E 5.7 Only a finite number of pairs of integers have been or will be thought of by human beings. Hence there are pairs of integers that nobody ever will have thought of:

All products of two integers, of which no human being ever will have thought, are over 100.

5.4.2 There-Exist Sentences

An existence sentence is a disjunction of assertions concerning the individuals in the universe; e.g., if the universe contains n individuals, the sentence "There is an a such that $A_x(a)$" asserts that

"Either $A_x(a_1)$ or $A_x(a_2)$ or $\cdots$ or $A_x(a_n)$."

According to our discussion in section 4.5, we can express finite but not infinite disjunctions in my language. Consequently, when the universe is infinite, we must use auxiliary devices, such as the quantifier $\exists$, to express there-exist sentences.

In this chapter we have used and interpreted $\exists$-formulas as if they were negations of $\forall$ statements. That is all right as long as the universe is finite, but in the eyes of the Dutch intuitionists it is an abuse of language when the universe is infinite. The infinite—according to them and to Aristotle (1980, p. 57)—is forever growing and exists only potentially, not actually. Thus an infinite totality, such as the set of positive integers, is to be viewed as being constructed step by step from the finite without hope of the construction ever being completed. The totality exists only as a possibility of an unbounded extension of the finite. This allows the assertion of $\forall$ sentences, since they use only the potentiality of the infinite. It renders the negation of such statements meaningless since the negation refers to the actuality of the infinite. An $\exists$ sentence—as I conceive it—is in the view of Dutch intuitionists not a declarative sentence. It is a *propositional abstract* resembling a document, which indicates the presence of a treasure without disclosing its location. The document is worthless until we discover where the treasure is hidden (Weyl 1949, pp. 50–51).[2]

One consequence of the intuitionists' refusal to allow the negation of sentences over an infinite universe is that in their logic the law of the excluded middle is not a generally valid principle. They insist that a declarative sentence denotes truth or falsehood according as it, or its negation, can be verified. If neither the sentence nor its negation is verifiable, the sentence is neither true nor false. Cases in point are sentences (9) and (12) of chapter 3. The first, which concerns the decimal expansion of Π, is at the moment neither true nor false, even though in time it may be proved true. The second, which concerns pebbles on a beach, is neither true nor false because verification is inconceivable.

The important point to note here about the intuitionists' attitude toward the law of the excluded middle is that their notion of truth belongs to the theory of knowledge while mine belongs to semantics. Thus, in spite of their objections, I insist on the general validity of $[A \supset A]$.

5.5 Concluding Remarks

Church has shown that my language is consistent in the sense that it contains no wff A with the property that both A and $\sim A$ are theorems (Church 1956, pp. 182 and 283). He has also shown that my language is not *complete*—i.e., complete in the sense that there is no wff A that is not a theorem which can be added as an axiom without causing the language to be inconsistent (Church 1956, pp. 185 and 284). For some this result may be disappointing; for me it seems fortuitous, since it is the incompleteness of the language that enables us to use it as a framework for mathematical and economic theories.

In this respect, it is interesting to observe that TM 5.19 is often referred to as *Gödel's Completeness Theorem*. To see why, note that TM 5.19 insists that the predicate calculus is complete in the sense that it is impossible to derive more valid wffs by adding axioms and rules of inference to PLA 1–PLA 7 and PRI 1 and PRI 2. Our axioms and rules of inference account for all the valid wffs there are.

In the next three chapters I shall state some difficult theorems without proof. The proofs can be found in Joseph R. Shoenfield's book *Mathematical Logic* (1967). Shoenfield bases his arguments on different axioms and different rules of inference, so I conclude this chapter by showing Shoenfield's predicate calculus to be equivalent to my own.

We observe first that the sentence-formation rules of the two calculi are equivalent. Hence a formula A is wf in my predicate calculus if and only if it is a wff in Shoenfield's predicate calculus.

Next I will show that a theorem in Shoenfield's calculus is also a theorem in my calculus. This fact follows from the following observations. Shoenfield's axioms are the values of $[A \supset A]$, $[A_x(a) \supset (\exists x)A]$, PLA 6, and PLA 7. His rules of inference are the following:

(i) Infer $[B \vee A]$ from A.
(ii) Infer A from $[A \vee A]$.
(iii) Infer $[[A \vee B] \vee C]$ from $[A \vee [B \vee C]]$.

(iv) Infer $[B \vee C]$ from $[[A \vee B] \wedge [\sim A \vee C]]$.
(v) If x is not free in B, infer $[(\exists x)A \supset B]]$ from $[A \supset B]$.

Theorems T 4.1 and TM 5.8 show that Shoenfield's axiom schemata are metatheorems in my predicate calculus. Furthermore, theorems T 4.10, T 4.11, T 4.13, and T 4.18 and the metatheorem TM 5.20 demonstrate that Shoenfield's rules of inference are derived rules of inference in my predicate calculus.

TM 5.20 If x is not free in B, $[[A \supset B] \supset [(\exists x)A \supset B]]$

Hence a theorem in Shoenfield's calculus is a theorem in my calculus, as was to be shown.

Finally I show that a theorem in my predicate calculus is also a theorem in Shoenfield's. Shoenfield proves that every tautology is a theorem (see Corollary, Shoenfield 1967, p. 27). Consequently, PLA 1–PLA 3 are theorem schemata in his predicate calculus. Shoenfield also shows that PLA 4 and PLA 5 are theorem schemata in his calculus (see Shoenfield's ∀-Introduction Rule and Substitution Rule, 1967, p. 31). Finally, Shoenfield's Detachment Rule and Generalization Rule demonstrate that my rules of inference are derived rules of inference in his calculus (Shoenfield 1967, pp. 28 and 31). From these observations it follows that a theorem in my predicate calculus is a theorem in Shoenfield's calculus.

II

Mathematical Logic II: Theories and Models

6 Consistent Theories and Models

In this part we shall study the syntactical and semantic properties of theories developed by the axiomatic method. If T is such a theory, we think of T as having been embedded in a first-order language; i.e., I have assigned symbols to the undefined terms of T and used them and the logical vocabulary of the predicate calculus to formulate wffs that express the ideas of the axioms and the theorems of T. Moreover, to PLA 1–PLA 7 of chapter 5, I have added as new axioms the set Γ of wffs that express the axioms of T. In the expanded axiom system, a theorem is either a theorem of the predicate calculus or a symbolic rendition of a theorem of T. Moreover, a wff that expresses a theorem of T is a theorem in the expanded axiom system. Finally, the syntactical and semantic properties of T are reflected in the syntactical and semantic properties of Γ.

In this chapter and in chapter 7 we study the relationship between the syntactical and semantic properties of a given subset Γ of the wffs of my symbolic language. I show in this chapter that Γ is consistent if and only if it has a *model*, i.e., if and only if there is a structure $\mathscr{D}$ in which all members of Γ are valid. In chapter 7 I show that, if Γ is consistent, Γ is complete if and only if every two models of Γ are *elementarily equivalent*, i.e., if and only if they assign truth to the same closed wffs.

In chapter 8 we discuss some of the shortcomings of the axiomatic method. For instance, I show that any finite set of axioms for the natural numbers is incomplete. Hence, no matter how we choose the set of axioms Γ, there is a true assertion concerning natural numbers that is not a logical consequence of Γ. I also show that, if Γ is a set of wffs that can be used as axioms for the theory of natural numbers, my symbolic language with Γ added to the original axioms cannot be used to establish the consistency of Γ.

Finally, in chapter 9 I show how the Kripke-Platek theory of sets can be embedded in a first-order language.

6.1 First-Order Theories

A first-order theory $T(\Gamma)$ consists of a first-order language L_Γ, a set of *nonlogical axioms* Γ, and all the theorems that by the rules of inference can be derived from Γ and the axioms of L_Γ. The axioms and theorems of L_Γ are, respectively, *the logical axioms* and the *logical theorems* of $T(\Gamma)$. The nonlogical axioms Γ are nontautological postulates pertaining to a particular theory under consideration. They are phrased in the vocabulary of L_Γ and single out a set V of function and predicate symbols that are to be the undefined terms of the theory. The theorems that can be derived with the help of both logical and nonlogical axioms are the *nonlogical theorems* of $T(\Gamma)$. They concern properties of the elements of V and certain objects that are defined in terms of members of V. In the development of $T(\Gamma)$, the members of the nonlogical vocabulary of L_Γ that do not belong to V play no useful role. Therefore, when we specify the language of a first-order theory, we usually insist that the nonlogical vocabulary contain only symbols for the undefined terms of the theory.

A simple example of a first-order theory is given in E 6.1. Observe that in specifying the nonlogical symbols, I adopt symbols that belong to number theory rather than f's and P's. Also, in stating the axioms and the theorems, I use the syntactical variable A to denote a wff. The syntactical variable is free to vary through all the wffs of L_P.

E 6.1 The classical axiom system for natural numbers, $T(P)$, concerns five undefined terms: a constant, 0; a unary function, S; two binary functions, $+$ and $\cdot$; and one binary predicate, $<$. Its nonlogical axioms are P 1–P 8 and the values in L_P of the axiom schemata of P 9:

P 1 $\sim[S(x) = 0]$

P 2 $[[S(x) = S(y)] \supset [x = y]]$

P 3 $[x = (x + 0)]$

P 4 $[(x + S(y)) = S(x + y)]$

P 5 $[0 = (x \cdot 0)]$

P 6 $[(x \cdot S(y)) = ((x \cdot y) + x)]$

P 7 $\sim[x < 0]$

P 8 $[[x < S(y)] \equiv [[x < y] \vee [x = y]]]$

P 9 $[[A_x(0) \wedge (\forall x)[A \supset A_x(S(x))]] \supset A]$

From these axioms we can derive many interesting theorems. Two of them are of particular interest to us:

PT 1 $[[[x < y] \vee [x = y]] \vee [y < x]]$

PT 2 $[(\exists x)A \supset (\exists z)[A_x(z) \wedge (\forall y)[[y < z] \supset \sim A_x(y)]]]$

The last of these asserts the validity of the *least-number principle.*

The paucity of nonlogical symbols in L_P is striking. However, the other symbols that we need to develop elementary number theory can be introduced by definitions. When properly formulated, such definitions increase the nonlogical vocabulary of L_P without affecting the set of theorems of $T(P)$. We shall discuss proper definitional schemes in chapter 7.

Strictly speaking, the classic axiom system for natural numbers is the system Peano proposed in his *Arithmetices Principia* in 1889. Peano's system differs from P 1–P 9 in two interesting ways. Firstly, in Peano's system addition, multiplication, and order are defined terms. In P 1–P 9, $+$, $\cdot$, and $<$ are undefined terms whose properties are as prescribed in P 3–P 8. Secondly, in Peano's system the principle of induction applies to *all* properties of natural numbers. In P 9, A varies over wffs in L_P and nothing else. Hence in P 1–P 9 the principle of induction applies only to those properties of natural numbers that can be described by wffs in L_P. The second difference is the reason why Peano's axioms in contradistinction to P 1–P 9 determine the natural numbers up to isomorphism. I shall have more to say about that in chapter 8.

6.2 Proofs and Proofs from Hypotheses

In chapter 3 a *proof* was defined to be a finite sequence of one or more wffs, each of which is either an axiom or is deduced from formulas preceding it in the sequence in accordance with one of the rules of inference of the language. Thus a proof in a first-order theory $T(\Gamma)$ is a proof in which the axioms used are either values of PLA 1–PLA 7 in L_Γ or are members of Γ, and the rules of inference are PRI 1 and PRI 2. A proof is a proof of the last wff in the sequence. If B is the last wff in a proof in $T(\Gamma)$, B is a consequence of Γ because of the meaning of the logical symbols, and B is said to be a *logical consequence* of Γ. We denote the set of logical consequences of Γ by $C_n(\Gamma)$.

The concept of a proof in $T(\Gamma)$ must be clearly distinguished from the concept of a *proof from hypotheses,* which is defined as follows: Let A_j, $j = 1, \ldots, n$, be wffs; and let $B_1, \ldots, B_m$ be another sequence of wffs which satisfy the conditions: for each i, $i = 1, \ldots, m$, either

1. B_i is one of the A_j;

2. B_i is an axiom or a variant of an axiom;

3. B_i is inferred by Modus Ponens from major premise B_j and minor premise B_k, $j < i$ and $k < i$; or

4. B_i is inferred, in accordance with the rule of generalization, from the premise B_j, $j < i$, where the variable that is generalized upon does not occur as a free variable in $A_1, \ldots, A_n$.

The sequence $B_1, \ldots, B_m$ is called a *proof of* B_m from the hypotheses $A_1, \ldots, A_n$. Such a proof is a proof in $T(A_1, \ldots, A_n)$. However, the converse need not be true; i.e., there may be proofs in $T(A_1, \ldots, A_n)$ that do not follow from the hypotheses $A_1, \ldots, A_n$. E 6.2, which follows, attests to that.

To illustrate a proof from hypotheses, we shall establish the validity of the so-called *simple constructive dilemma*: If A then C; if B then C; A or B. Therefore C. To state this dilemma we let

$$A_1, \ldots, A_n \vdash B$$

be a symbolic rendition of the assertion "There is a proof of B from the hypotheses $A_1, \ldots, A_n$." The dilemma can then be expressed as in TM 6.1.

TM 6.1 $[A \supset C], [B \supset C], [\sim A \supset B] \vdash C$

Proof $[\sim A \supset B]$

$[B \supset C]$

$[[\sim A \supset B] \supset [[B \supset C] \supset [\sim A \supset C]]]$

$[[B \supset C] \supset [\sim A \supset C]]$

$[\sim A \supset C]$

$[A \supset C]$

$[[A \supset C] \supset [[\sim A \supset C] \supset C]]$

$[[\sim A \supset C] \supset C]$

C

Another example of assertions that follow from hypotheses is given in TM 6.2.

TM 6.2 $[A \supset C], [B \supset D], [A \vee B] \vdash [C \vee D]$

TM 6.2 provides a symbolic statement of the so-called *complex constructive dilemma*.

6.3 The Deduction Theorem

In chapter 3 I insisted that a wff A be a theorem if and only if A is a theorem followed from the following two laws: (1) An axiom is a theorem and (2) if the hypotheses of a rule of inference are theorems, the conclusion is a theorem too. From this characterization of theorems it follows that to ascertain that all the theorems of a first-order theory have a property P, it suffices to check whether conditions i and ii below are satisfied.

(i) Every axiom has P.
(ii) If the hypotheses of a rule of inference have P, so does the conclusion.

A proof by this method is called *a proof by induction on theorems;* and the antecedent clause of condition ii is referred to as *the induction hypothesis.*

Suppose that we want to establish that the theorems of a first-order theory $T(\Gamma)$ have a certain property P. Suppose also that we are not sure that it suffices to check whether conditions i and ii hold. To see that it is sufficient, we proceed as follows: First we let S_0 contain the values of PLA 1–PLA 7 in L_Γ and the members of Γ. According to the first law of theorems (1), the wffs in S_0 are theorems of $T(\Gamma)$. Next we let S_1 contain all the wffs that are conclusions of PRI 1 or PRI 2 when the hypotheses belong to S_0. According to the second law of theorems (2), these wffs are theorems. Then we proceed to construct $S_2, S_3, \ldots, S_{n-1}$ and let S_n contain all the wffs that are conclusions of PRI 1 and PRI 2 when the hypotheses are in one of the previously formed S_j. These again are theorems by (2). Continuing in the same way until no new theorems can be obtained by (2), we eventually end up with all the theorems of $T(\Gamma)$. But if that is the case, we see immediately that, if conditions i and ii are satisfied, all the members of S_j will have P no matter what the value of j is. Hence all the theorems of $T(\Gamma)$ will have property P, as was to be shown.

We shall use the method of proof described above to establish the metatheorem TM 6.3. In stating it, I use $\vdash A$ to mean "A is a logical theorem."

TM 6.3 Let A and B be wffs in a first-order language, and suppose that A is closed. Then $A \vdash B$ if and only if $\vdash [A \supset B]$.

Usually TM 6.3 is referred to as the *Deduction Theorem.* Its proof goes as follows: It is obvious that if $\vdash [A \supset B]$, then $A \vdash B$. So it suffices to show that if $A \vdash B$, then $\vdash [A \supset B]$. We shall do that by induction on the theorems of $T(A)$. Suppose first that B is an axiom. If B is A, then $\vdash [A \supset A]$ by T 4.1. Otherwise $\vdash [B \supset [A \supset B]]$ by PLA 1 and $\vdash [A \supset B]$

by PRI 1. Suppose next that C is a wff and that $A \vdash C$ and $A \vdash [C \supset B]$. By the induction hypothesis, $\vdash [A \supset C]$ and $\vdash [A \supset [C \supset B]]$. But then, by PLA 2, $\vdash [[A \supset [C \supset B]] \supset [[A \supset C] \supset [A \supset B]]]$, and by two applications of PRI 1, $\vdash [A \supset B]$. Finally, suppose that C is a wff with one free variable x and suppose that B is $(\forall x)C$. Suppose also that $A \vdash C$. By the induction hypothesis, $\vdash [A \supset C]$ and by PRI 2, $\vdash (\forall x)[A \supset C]$. But then by PLA 4 and PRI 1, $\vdash [A \supset (\forall x)C]$; i.e., $\vdash [A \supset B]$, as was to be shown.

We can prove TM 6.4 (a generalization of TM 6.1) by induction on n.

TM 6.4 If $A_1, \ldots, A_n$ and B are wffs of a first-order language, and if the A_i are closed, then $A_1, \ldots, A_n \vdash B$ if and only if

$\vdash [A_1 \supset [A_2 \supset [\ldots[A_n \supset B]\ldots]]]$.

In passing we note that TM 6.1 and TM 6.4 imply the validity of TM 6.5.

TM 6.5 $[[A \supset C] \supset [[B \supset C] \supset [[\sim A \supset B] \supset C]]]$

The latter is a much less transparent assertion than TM 6.1. A direct proof of TM 6.5 would be lengthy, but theorems TM 6.1 and TM 6.4 provide a shortcut to establishing it.

When we use TM 6.4 to prove theories in the object language, it is important to bear in mind in what way a proof from the hypotheses Γ differs from a proof in $T(\Gamma)$. E 6.2 illustrates this point.

E 6.2 Let A be a wff with one free individual variable x. The following sequence of wffs illustrate a proof of $A_x(y)$ in $T(A)$:

A
$(\forall x)A$
$[(\forall x)A \supset A_x(y)]$
$A_x(y)$.

Yet $\vdash [A \supset A_x(y)]$ is false. That is as it should be. Otherwise TM 6.4 would imply an absurd result: that $[A_x(z) \supset A_x(y)]$ is a theorem of the first-order predicate calculus. Note, therefore, that

$A_x(y) \vdash [A_x(z) \supset A_x(y)]$

is true. So too is

$\vdash [A_x(y) \supset [A_x(z) \supset A_x(y)]]$,

as it should in accordance with TM 6.4.

E 6.2 illustrates that, in a proof from hypotheses, PRI 2 can be used only when the variables generalized upon are not free variables in the given set of hypotheses.

6.4 Consistent Theories and Their Models

We shall next use the Deduction Theorem to give a semantic characterization of $C_n(\Gamma)$ when Γ consists of a finite number of formulas, $\Gamma_1, \ldots, \Gamma_m$. To do so we let $M(\Gamma)$ denote the set of models of $T(\Gamma)$. A *model of* $T(\Gamma)$ is a structure $\mathscr{D}$ with the property that all the Γ_i are valid in $\mathscr{D}$. Hence

$$\mathscr{D} \in M(\Gamma) \text{ if and only if } \Gamma_i \text{ is valid in } \mathscr{D}, \qquad i = 1, \ldots, m.$$

It is easy to show that if $B \in C_n(\Gamma_1, \ldots, \Gamma_m)$ and if $\mathscr{D} \in M(\Gamma_1, \ldots, \Gamma_m)$, then B is valid in $\mathscr{D}$. The converse is also true: if $M(\Gamma_1, \ldots, \Gamma_m)$ is not empty and if B is valid in $\mathscr{D}$ for all $\mathscr{D} \in M(\Gamma_1, \ldots, \Gamma_m)$, then $B \in C_n(\Gamma_1, \ldots, \Gamma_m)$. Thus we have TM 6.6.

TM 6.6 If $M(\Gamma_1, \ldots, \Gamma_m)$ is nonempty, then $B \in C_n(\Gamma_1, \ldots, \Gamma_m)$ if and only if B is valid in $\mathscr{D}$ for all $\mathscr{D} \in M(\Gamma_1, \ldots, \Gamma_m)$.

To see why the sufficiency part of TM 6.6 is true, suppose that the Γ_i contain no free individual variables. Then

$$B \in C_n(\Gamma_1, \ldots, \Gamma_m) \text{ if and only if } \Gamma_1, \ldots, \Gamma_m \vdash B.$$

Consequently, by TM 6.4,

$$B \in C_n(\Gamma_1, \ldots, \Gamma_m) \text{ if and only if}$$

$$\vdash [\Gamma_1 \supset [\Gamma_2 \supset [\ldots[\Gamma_{m-1} \supset [\Gamma_m \supset B]]\ldots]]].$$

From this and from TM 5.19 it follows that $B \in C_n(\Gamma_1, \ldots, \Gamma_m)$ if and only if

$$[[\Gamma_1 \wedge [\Gamma_2 \wedge [\ldots[\Gamma_{m-1} \wedge \Gamma_m]\ldots]]] \supset B]$$

is a valid wff. This last wff in turn is valid if and only if B is valid in $\mathscr{D}$ for all $\mathscr{D} \in M(\Gamma_1, \ldots, \Gamma_m)$.

When the Γ_i contain free variables, we let $\hat{\Gamma}_i$ denote the *closure* of Γ_i; i.e.,

$$\hat{\Gamma}_i = (\forall x_1)\ldots(\forall x_k)\Gamma_i, \qquad i = 1, \ldots, m,$$

where $x_1, \ldots, x_k$ are the free variables of the Γ_i. To establish the sufficiency part of TM 6.6 when the Γ_i contain free variables, we appeal to TM 6.7 and use roughly the same arguments that we used in the special case above.

TM 6.7 $B \in C_n(\Gamma_1, \ldots, \Gamma_m)$ if and only if $\hat{\Gamma}_1, \ldots, \hat{\Gamma}_m \vdash B$.

The validity of TM 6.7 can be obtained by elaborating on the following observations: If $\hat{\Gamma}_1, \ldots, \hat{\Gamma}_m \vdash B$, then PRI 2 and TM 6.4 imply that both the $\hat{\Gamma}_i$ and $[\hat{\Gamma}_1 \supset [\ldots[\hat{\Gamma}_{m-1} \supset [\hat{\Gamma}_m \supset B]]\ldots]]$ belong to $C_n(\Gamma_1, \ldots, \Gamma_m)$. By repeated use of PRI 1, it follows from this that $B \in C_n(\Gamma_1, \ldots, \Gamma_m)$ as well. The converse is an immediate consequence of the fact that $B \in C_n(\Gamma_1, \ldots, \Gamma_m)$ only if $B \in C_n(\hat{\Gamma}_1, \ldots, \hat{\Gamma}_m)$, which can be intuited from PLA 5 and TM 5.10.

In TM 6.6 we insisted that $M(\Gamma_1, \ldots, \Gamma_m)$ be nonempty. That was not necessary. According to the next theorem, TM 6.8, if $M(\Gamma_1, \ldots, \Gamma_m)$ is empty, then $B \in C_n(\Gamma_1, \ldots, \Gamma_m)$ no matter what wff B denotes.

TM 6.8 $M(\Gamma_1, \ldots, \Gamma_m)$ is nonempty if and only if $T(\Gamma_1, \ldots, \Gamma_m)$ is consistent.

To establish this, suppose first that $M(\Gamma_1, \ldots, \Gamma_m)$ is nonempty and that $\mathscr{D} \in M(\Gamma_1, \ldots, \Gamma_m)$. If $T(\Gamma_1, \ldots, \Gamma_m)$ is inconsistent, there is a formula B without free variables such that $B \in C_n(\Gamma_1, \ldots, \Gamma_m)$ and $\sim B \in C_n(\Gamma_1, \ldots, \Gamma_m)$. But then $\mathscr{D}(B) = t$ and $\mathscr{D}(\sim B) = t$, which is absurd. Thus $T(\Gamma_1, \ldots, \Gamma_m)$ must be consistent. Next, suppose that $M(\Gamma_1, \ldots, \Gamma_m)$ is empty; then for all structures $\mathscr{D}$, there is an i such that $\mathscr{D}(\sim \hat{\Gamma}_i) = t$. From this and from TM 5.19 follows $\vdash [\sim \hat{\Gamma}_1 \vee [\sim \hat{\Gamma}_2 \vee [\ldots[\sim \hat{\Gamma}_{m-1} \vee \sim \hat{\Gamma}_m]\ldots]]]$. But then both the $\hat{\Gamma}_i$, $i = 1, \ldots, m$, and $\sim \hat{\Gamma}_m$ belong to $C_n(\Gamma_1, \ldots, \Gamma_m)$, which can happen only if $T(\Gamma_1, \ldots, \Gamma_m)$ is inconsistent. Thus $T(\Gamma_1, \ldots, \Gamma_m)$ is inconsistent if and only if $M(\Gamma_1, \ldots, \Gamma_m)$ is empty.

In proving TM 6.8, we observed the validity of one half of TM 6.9.

TM 6.9 $M(\Gamma_1, \ldots, \Gamma_m)$ is inconsistent if and only if $\vdash [\sim \hat{\Gamma}_1 \vee [\sim \hat{\Gamma}_2 \vee [\ldots[\sim \hat{\Gamma}_{m-1} \vee \sim \hat{\Gamma}_m]\ldots]]]$.

The validity of the other half can be established as follows: If $T(\Gamma_1, \ldots, \Gamma_m)$ is inconsistent, $\sim \hat{\Gamma}_m \in C_n(\Gamma_1, \ldots, \Gamma_m)$. Hence, by TM 6.7, $\hat{\Gamma}_1, \ldots, \hat{\Gamma}_m \vdash \sim \hat{\Gamma}_m$. From this, and from TM 6.4 we conclude that $\vdash [\sim \hat{\Gamma}_1 \vee [\sim \hat{\Gamma}_2 \vee [\ldots[\sim \hat{\Gamma}_{m-1} \vee \sim \hat{\Gamma}_m]\ldots]]]$.

6.5 The Compactness Theorem

In section 6.4 we established an equivalence between the concept of a consistent theory and a theory with a model when the theory is based on a finite sequence of wffs, $\Gamma_1, \ldots, \Gamma_m$. As TM 6.10 asserts, this equivalence holds for any first-order theory.

TM 6.10 Let Γ be a set of wffs. Then $T(\Gamma)$ is consistent if and only if $M(\Gamma)$ is nonempty.

TM 6.11 makes a similar assertion.

TM 6.11 If Γ is a set of wffs, and if $M(\Gamma)$ is nonempty, then $B \in C_n(\Gamma)$ if and only if B is valid in $\mathscr{D}$ for all $\mathscr{D} \in M(\Gamma)$.

The preceding results, which are proved in the appendix, are remarkable not only because they establish an equivalence between a syntactical and a semantical concept, but because they suggest shortcuts to verifying difficult facts, as witnessed in E 6.3.

E 6.3 It is impossible (as we shall see in TM 8.7) to establish the consistency of $T(P\,1\text{–}P\,9)$ as a theorem of $T(P)$. It is possible, but hard, to prove this consistency within a larger axiomatic system. Yet the existence of the standard model of $T(P)$ and TM 6.10 suffice to establish the consistency of $T(P\,1\text{–}P\,9)$.

In reading TM 6.11, note that, if $B \in C_n(\Gamma)$, there exists a finite sequence of formulas $\Gamma_i \in \Gamma$, $i = 1, \ldots, m$, such that $B \in C_n(\Gamma_1, \ldots, \Gamma_m)$. Thus if $T(\Gamma)$ is inconsistent, there must be a finite subset of formulas in Γ, say $\Gamma_1, \ldots, \Gamma_m$, such that $T(\Gamma_1, \ldots, \Gamma_m)$ is inconsistent as well. Since the converse is obviously true also, we can deduce from TM 6.10 and TM 6.11 the validity of TM 6.12.

TM 6.12 Let Γ be a set of wffs. Then $T(\Gamma)$ is consistent if and only if, for every finite sequence $\Gamma_i \in \Gamma$, $i = 1, \ldots, m$, $M(\Gamma_1, \ldots, \Gamma_m)$ is not empty.

TM 6.12 is called the *Compactness Theorem*. It has many interesting applications. I illustrate one of them in E 6.4.

E 6.4 Let L_P denote the first-order language of $T(P\,1\text{–}P\,9)$ and let η denote the standard model of $T(P)$. In addition, let $T(N)$ denote $T(P\,1\text{–}P\,8, \text{NA})$, where

NA $[[x < y] \vee [[x = y] \vee [y < x]]]$

Since NA is a theorem of $T(P)$ (see PT 1 of section 6.1), η is a model of $T(N)$ as well. Finally, let L_{PN} denote the language we obtain by adding a constant α to the vocabulary of L_P, and, for each $n = 0, 1, \ldots$, let AP_n assert:

$AP_n : [k_n < \alpha]$,

where k_n is defined inductively by

$k_0 =_{\text{df}} 0$

$k_n =_{\text{df}} S(k_{n-1}), \quad n = 1, 2, \ldots.$

We shall use the Compactness Theorem to show that the theory $T(NS)$, whose language is L_{PN} and whose nonlogical axioms comprise all the AP_n and all the closed wffs in L_P that are true in η, is consistent.

Let Γ_N denote the collection of closed wffs in L_P that are true in η and let A be any finite subset of $\Gamma_N \cup \{AP_1, AP_2, \ldots\}$. There is an n such that, if AP_m is in A, then $k_m < k_n$. Hence we obtain a model of $T(A)$ if we interprete α as n and let η interpret the remaining parts of L_{PN}. Since A is arbitrary, we conclude from TM 6.12 and TM 6.10 that $T(NS)$ is consistent and has a model.

In reading E 6.4, note that $T(NS)$ is a theory of nonstandard natural numbers. A model of $T(NS)$ has a universe that contains representatives of each and every natural number in addition to representatives of numbers that are larger than any natural number.

If a first-order theory $T(\Gamma)$ has one model, it is sure to have many. How these models differ is a topic we discuss in chapter 7. An astonishing theorem of T. Skolem, given here as TM 6.13, bears on this problem.

TM 6.13 Let Γ be a finite or denumerably infinite set of wffs and suppose that $T(\Gamma)$ is consistent. If Γ has a model with an infinite universe, there exists a $\mathscr{D} \in M(\Gamma)$ whose universe of discourse $|\mathscr{D}|$ is denumberably infinite.

Skolem's theorem is an extension of a theorem of Löwenheim. Therefore, TM 6.13 is usually referred to as the Löwenheim-Skolem theorem. I sketch a proof of the theorem in the appendix.

TM 6.13 has many paradoxical consequences. One of them is exemplified in the following observation: It is possible to formulate a first-order theory with countably many nonlogical symbols in which we can prove that the set of real numbers is uncountable. Yet, according to TM 6.13, any such theory has a model with a countably infinite number of individuals. This is paradoxical but not contradictory. To wit: The mapping used to enumerate the individuals in the universe does not belong to the model. Hence the enumeration does not invalidate the theorem that insists that there is no one-to-one mapping of the set of real numbers onto the set of natural numbers.

6.6 Appendix: Proofs

In section 6.4 we used TM 5.19 to establish TM 6.8—the finite version of TM 6.10. In this appendix we shall sketch a proof of TM 6.10 and show that the validity of TM 6.10 implies the validity of TM 5.19. We shall also sketch a proof of TM 6.13. The details left out of the proofs can be found on pp. 44–47 and pp. 78–79 of Shoenfield 1967.

6.6.1 A Proof of TM 6.10

The proof of TM 6.10 is obtained in steps. We begin with the sufficiency part. Let $\mathscr{D}$ be a model of $T(\Gamma)$ and observe that

(i) If A is a closed wff, $A \in C_n(\Gamma)$ only if $\mathscr{D}(A) = t$.

Since, for all closed wffs A, $\mathscr{D}([A \wedge -A]) = f$, it follows from (i) that A and $\sim A$ cannot both be theorems of $T(\Gamma)$. Consequently,

(ii) If $T(\Gamma)$ has a model, $T(\Gamma)$ is consistent.

To establish the necessity part of TM 6.10, I introduce some new concepts and prove several auxiliary results. Let L and $\hat{L}$ be first-order languages. Then $\hat{L}$ is an *extension* of L if the vocabulary of L is contained in the vocabulary of $\hat{L}$. Next, let $T(\Gamma)$ and $T(\hat{\Gamma})$ be first-order theories. Then $T(\hat{\Gamma})$ is an *extension* of $T(\Gamma)$ if $L_{\hat{\Gamma}}$ is an extension of L_Γ and every theorem of $T(\Gamma)$ is a theorem of $T(\hat{\Gamma})$. Moreover, $T(\hat{\Gamma})$ is a *conservative extension* of $T(\Gamma)$ if (1) $T(\hat{\Gamma})$ is an extension of $T(\Gamma)$ and (2) any wff A of L_Γ that is a theorem of $T(\hat{\Gamma})$ is also a theorem of $T(\Gamma)$. Finally, $T(\hat{\Gamma})$ is a *simple extension* of $T(\Gamma)$ if L_Γ and $L_{\hat{\Gamma}}$ are identical and $T(\hat{\Gamma})$ is an extension of $T(\Gamma)$.

One useful example of a conservative extension of a theory is described in TM 6.14.

TM 6.14 Let L and Γ be, respectively, a first-order language and a consistent set of wffs of L. Moreover, let $\hat{L}$ be the language we obtain by adding a denumerable number of new constants to the vocabulary of L. Finally, let T and $\hat{T}$ be $T(\Gamma)$ as developed, respectively, in L and $\hat{L}$. Then $\hat{T}$ is a conservative extension of T.

To see why TM 6.14 is valid, we need only demonstrate that if A is a wff of L with n free variables, $x_1, \ldots, x_n$, then for any sequence of distinct new constants, $e_1, \ldots, e_n$,

$$T \vdash A \text{ if and only if } \hat{T} \vdash A_{x_1,\ldots,x_n}(e_1,\ldots,e_n),$$

where $T \vdash A$ is short for "A is a theorem of T." It is obvious that $T \vdash A$ only if $\hat{T} \vdash A$. Consequently, by applying first PRI 2 and then PL 5 and PRI 1, we find that

$$T \vdash A \text{ only if } \hat{T} \vdash A_{x_1,\ldots,x_n}(e_1,\ldots,e_n).$$

Conversely, suppose that $\hat{T} \vdash A_{x_1,\ldots,x_n}(e_1,\ldots,e_n)$ and let $y_1, \ldots, y_n$ be distinct variables that do not occur in A or in the proof of $A_{x_1,\ldots,x_n}(e_1,\ldots,e_n)$. Then it is easy to verify that if we replace each occurrence of e_i in the proof of $A_{x_1,\ldots,x_n}(e_1,\ldots,e_n)$ by y_i, $i = 1, \ldots, n$, we obtain a proof of $T \vdash A_{x_1,\ldots,x_n}(y_1,\ldots,y_n)$. From this, PRI 2, PLA 5, and PRI 1 we deduce that

$$\hat{T} \vdash A_{x_1,\ldots,x_n}(e_1,\ldots,e_n) \text{ only if } T \vdash A.$$

Our first auxiliary result concerns the existence of complete simple extensions of consistent theories. A theory is *complete* if it is consistent and if every closed wff is either a theorem or the negation of a theorem.

TM 6.15 If $T(\Gamma)$ is consistent, then $T(\Gamma)$ has a complete simple extension.

Let $\mathscr{F}$ be a family of subsets of the wffs in L_Γ and suppose that $A \in \mathscr{F}$ if and only if $T(\Gamma, A)$ is consistent. To establish TM 6.15, we begin by showing that $\mathscr{F}$ is of *finite character*, i.e., that $A \in \mathscr{F}$ if and only if every finite subset of A belongs to $\mathscr{F}$. If $A \in \mathscr{F}$ and $B \subset A$, then $B \in \mathscr{F}$, since $T(\Gamma, A)$ is an extension of $T(\Gamma, B)$. If $A \notin \mathscr{F}$, then $T(\Gamma, A)$ is inconsistent. Hence there is a closed wff B such that $B \in C_n(\Gamma, A)$ and $\sim B \in C_n(\Gamma, A)$. If $\hat{A} \subset A$ and $\hat{\Gamma} \subset \Gamma$ together contain the axioms that are used in proving B and $\sim B$, then $T(\Gamma, \hat{A})$ is inconsistent. Hence $\hat{A} \notin \mathscr{F}$.

Since $\mathscr{F}$ is of finite character and obviously contains the empty set, we can use a theorem of Teichmüller and Tukey (see Kelley 1955, pp. 33–34) to claim the existence of a maximal set in $\mathscr{F}$, i.e., a set that is not a subset of any other member of $\mathscr{F}$. Let A be such a maximal set and observe that $T(\Gamma, A)$ is a consistent, simple extension of $T(\Gamma)$. Next, suppose that B is a closed wff that is neither a theorem nor the negation of a theorem of $T(\Gamma, A)$. Then $T(\Gamma, A, \sim B)$ is consistent and, hence $(A \cup \{\sim B\}) \in \mathscr{F}$. But this contradicts the maximality of A unless $\sim B \in A$. Since $\sim B$ is not a theorem, $\sim B \notin A$, and we have arrived at a contradiction which demonstrates that $T(\Gamma, A)$ is complete.

Our next auxiliary result establishes the existence of a useful conservative extension of $T(\Gamma)$. To state the result we introduce a sequence of so-called *special constants for* L_Γ. The *special constants of level* n are defined by induction on n. Suppose that the special constants of all levels less than n have been defined, and let $(\exists x)A$ be a closed wff formed with these constants and the symbols of L_Γ. If $n > 0$, suppose also that $(\exists x)A$ contains at least one special constant of level $n-1$. Then let $c_{(\exists x)A}$ be a special constant of level n and call it *the special constant for* $(\exists x)A$.

Next we add all the special constants to the nonlogical vocabulary of L_Γ and denote the resulting language by L_Γ^c. If $(\exists x)A$ is a closed wff of L_Γ^c, there is a unique special constant for $(\exists x)A$ in L_Γ^c. Let this constant be r. We shall refer to the formula $[(\exists x)A \supset A_x(r)]$ as *the special axiom for* r. Moreover, we shall denote by $T^c(\Gamma)$ the theory whose language is L_Γ^c and whose nonlogical axioms consist of the wffs in Γ and the special axioms for the special constants of L_Γ^c. Then

(iii) $T^c(\Gamma)$ is a conservative extension of $T(\Gamma)$.

To establish (iii) we first let T^c be the theory whose language is L_Γ^c and whose nonlogical axioms are the wffs in Γ. Then from TM 6.14 it follows that T^c is a conservative extension of $T(\Gamma)$.

Since T^c is a conservative extension of $T(\Gamma)$, we can verify (iii) by showing that every wff of L_Γ that is a theorem $T^c(\Gamma)$ is a theorem of T^c. Let A be a wff of L_Γ that is a theorem of $T^c(\Gamma)$, and suppose that $B_1, \ldots, B_k$ are the special axioms which are used in the proof of A. Then, by TM 6.7, $B_1, \ldots, B_k \vdash A$ is a theorem in T^c. Hence, by TM 6.4,

$T^c \vdash [B_1 \supset [B_2 \supset [\ldots \supset [B_k \supset A]\ldots]]]$.

To show that $T^c \vdash A$, we proceed by induction on k. If $k = 0$, there is nothing to prove. Therefore, suppose that $k \geqslant 1$ and that B_1 is $[(\exists x)C \supset C_x(r)]$, where r is the special constant for $(\exists x)C$. We may suppose that the level of r is at least as great as the levels of the special constants for which $B_2, \ldots, B_k$ are the special axioms. Then r does not occur in A and the B_i for $i = 2, \ldots, k$. But if that is so and if y is a variable that does not occur in the proof of A, we can replace r by y in this proof to obtain a proof in T^c of

$T^c \vdash [[(\exists x)C \supset C_x(y)] \supset [B_2 \supset [\ldots \supset [B_k \supset A]\ldots]]]$.

From this, TM 5.20, and PRI 1, it follows that

$T^c \vdash [(\exists y)[(\exists x)C \supset C_x(y)] \supset [B_2 \supset [\ldots \supset [B_k \supset A]\ldots]]]$.

Now, for any given wff C, $[(\exists x)C \supset (\exists x)C]$ is a value of theorem schemata of T^c. Hence, by TM 5.15 and the obvious analogue of TM 5.16, $T^c \vdash [(\exists x)C \supset (\exists y)C_x(y)]$. But, if that is so, TM 5.17 and TM 5.15 imply that $T^c \vdash (\exists y)[(\exists x)C \supset C_x(y)]$. Hence, by PRI 1,

$T^c \vdash [B_2 \supset [\ldots \supset [B_k \supset A]\ldots]]$,

and then, by the induction hypothesis, $T^c \vdash A$, as was to be shown.

So much for $T^c(\Gamma)$. Next we show that

(iv) If T is a complete simple extension of $T^c(\Gamma)$, there is a structure $\mathscr{D}$ for L^c_Γ such that, for any closed wff A of L^c_Γ, $\mathscr{D}(A) = t$ if and only if $T \vdash A$.

The required structure is obtained in the following way. For any pair a, b of variable-free terms in L^c_Γ, let $a \sim b$ mean $[a = b]$ can be proved in T—i.e., $T \vdash [a = b]$—and observe that $\sim$ is an equivalence relation. We let $|\mathscr{D}|$ and $N_\mathscr{D}$, respectively, denote the set of all equivalence classes of $\sim$ and the names of equivalence classes. Moreover, for each variable-free term a, we designate the equivalence class of a by a^0; and for every n and n-ary f and P in L^c_Γ, we let

$f^\mathscr{D}(a_1^0, \ldots, a_n^0) = (f(a_1, \ldots, a_n))^0$

and insist that

$P^\mathscr{D}(a_1^0, \ldots, a_n^0)$ if and only if $T \vdash P(a_1, \ldots, a_n)$.

Then $\mathscr{D} = (|\mathscr{D}|, N_\mathscr{D}, F^\mathscr{D}, G^\mathscr{D})$ is well defined. To wit: let a_i, b_i, $i = 1, \ldots, n$, be variable-free terms and let f and P be n-ary function and predicate symbols. If $a_i^0 = b_i^0$, $i = 1, \ldots, n$, it follows from TM 5.4, PLA 7, and $T \vdash [a_i = b_i]$, $i = 1, \ldots, n$, that

$$T \vdash [f(a_1, \ldots, a_n) = f(b_1, \ldots, b_n)]$$

$$T \vdash [P(a_1, \ldots, a_n) \equiv P(b_1, \ldots, b_n)].$$

Hence $(f(a_1, \ldots, a_n))^0 = (f(b_1, \ldots, b_n))^0$ and $T \vdash P(a_1, \ldots, a_n)$ if and only if $T \vdash P(b_1, \ldots, b_n)$.

To show that if A is a closed wff, $\mathscr{D}(A) = t$ if and only if $T \vdash A$, we proceed as follows. First we observe that if a is a variable-free term, $\mathscr{D}(a) = a^0$. Next we suppose that A is a variable-free atomic formula. If A is $[a = b]$, then $\mathscr{D}(A) = t$ if and only if $\mathscr{D}(a) = \mathscr{D}(b)$, i.e., if and only if $T \vdash A$. If A is $P(a_1, \ldots, a_n)$, then $\mathscr{D}(A) = t$ if and only if $P^{\mathscr{D}}(\mathscr{D}(a_1), \ldots, \mathscr{D}(a_n))$, i.e., if and only if $T \vdash A$. Hence, for variable-free atomic formulas, $\mathscr{D}(A) = t$ if and only if $T \vdash A$. Finally we demonstrate (by induction on the lengths of wffs) that, for all closed wff, $\mathscr{D}(A) = t$ if and only if $T \vdash A$.

Let A be a closed wff of L_Γ^c. Then there exist closed wffs of L_Γ^c, B, C, and D and an individual variable x such that A is $\sim B$, $[B \supset C]$ or $(\forall x)D$. Suppose first that A is $\sim B$. Then $\mathscr{D}(A) = t$ if and only if $\mathscr{D}(B) = f$. By the induction hypothesis, $\mathscr{D}(B) = f$ if and only if B is not a theorem of T. Finally, by the completeness of T, B is not a theorem of T if and only if $T \vdash \sim B$. Consequently, $\mathscr{D}(A) = t$ if and only if $T \vdash A$.

With only obvious modifications, the arguments used above can be applied to A when A is $[B \supset C]$. Those details I leave to the reader.

Suppose that A is $(\forall x)D$. Then $\mathscr{D}(A) = f$ if and only if there is an $i \in N_{\mathscr{D}}$ such that $\mathscr{D}(D_x(i)) = f$. Now, i is the name of an individual a^0. Hence, by TM 5.18, $\mathscr{D}(A) = f$ if and only if there is a variable-free term a such that $\mathscr{D}(D_x(a)) = f$. By the induction hypothesis $\mathscr{D}(D_x(a)) = f$ if and only if $D_x(a)$ is not a theorem of T, and by the completeness of T, $D_x(a)$ is not a theorem of T if and only if $T \vdash \sim D_x(a)$. Hence $\mathscr{D}(A) = f$ if and only if there is a variable free term, a, such that $T \vdash \sim D_x(a)$. Now $T \vdash \sim D_x(a)$ only if $T \vdash (\exists x) \sim D$. Also if e denotes the special constant of $(\exists x) \sim D$, then $T \vdash (\exists x) \sim D$ only if $T \vdash \sim D_x(e)$. From this, the tautology $[\sim \sim D \equiv D]$, and TM 5.15, we deduce that $T \vdash \sim D_x(a)$ for some variable free term, a, if and only if $T \vdash \sim A$. Consequently $\mathscr{D}(A) = f$ if and only if $T \vdash \sim A$ and, by the completeness of T, $\mathscr{D}(A) = t$ if and only if $T \vdash A$.

It follows from (iv) that the $\mathscr{D}$ we constructed in the proof of (iv) is a model of T. But then $\mathscr{D}$ is a model of $T^c(\Gamma)$ as well. By omitting some of the functions and predicates of $\mathscr{D}$, we obtain a structure for L_Γ that is a model of $T(\Gamma)$. This concludes the proof of

(v) If $T(\Gamma)$ is consistent, $T(\Gamma)$ has a model.

Assertions (ii) and (v) represent the two halves of TM 6.10. Thus the proof of TM 6.10 is complete.

6.6.2 A Proof of TM 6.11

By appealing to PRI 2 and PLA 5, we can show that it suffices to establish TM 6.11 for closed wffs. Let B be a closed wff and suppose that B is a theorem of $T(\Gamma)$. Then $T(\Gamma, \sim B)$ is inconsistent and, by TM 6.10, possesses no model. Hence, for all $\mathscr{D} \in M(\Gamma)$, $\mathscr{D}(\sim B) = f$ and $\mathscr{D}(B) = t$.

Suppose next that, for all $\mathscr{D} \in M(\Gamma)$, $\mathscr{D}(B) = t$. If B is not a theorem of $T(\Gamma)$, $T(\Gamma, \sim B)$ is consistent and possesses a model $\mathscr{A}$ in which $\mathscr{A}(B) = f$. Since $\mathscr{A}$ is a model of $T(\Gamma)$, this contradicts our original hypothesis. Hence B must be a theorem of $T(\Gamma)$.

6.6.3 A Proof of TM 5.19

The validity of TM 5.19 follows from the validity of TM 6.11 by letting Γ be the empty set.

6.6.4 A Proof of TM 6.13

The proof of TM 6.13 is based on two facts that we may formulate as follows:

(vi) L_Γ^c contains a denumerable infinity of special constants.
(vii) $T^c(\Gamma)$ has a model $\mathscr{D}$ such that each individual in $|\mathscr{D}|$ is $\mathscr{D}(r)$ for infinitely many special constants r.

I shall sketch a proof of (vii) and leave (vi) to the reader. Let $\mathscr{D}$ be the structure for T that we constructed in proving assertion (iv). Then every individual in $|\mathscr{D}|$ is $\mathscr{D}(a)$ for some variable-free term a in L_Γ^c. By PLA 6 and TM 5.8, $T^c(\Gamma) \vdash (\exists x)[x = a]$. Hence $T^c(\Gamma) \vdash [r = a]$, where r is the special constant for $(\exists x)[x = a]$. From this and (iv), it follows that $\mathscr{D}(r) = \mathscr{D}(a) = a^0$. By replacing x with other variables, we find infinitely many other special constants with the same property, as was to be shown.

To prove TM 6.13, we first add a denumerable infinity of constants, e_1, $e_2, \ldots$ to L_Γ and denote the resulting language by $\hat{L}$. Next, for each pair e_i,

e_j of distinct new constants, we add to the axioms of $T(\Gamma)$ an axiom $\sim[e_i = e_j]$ and denote the resulting theory by $\hat{T}$. Then an easy application of the Compactness Theorem suffices to demonstrate that $\hat{T}$ is a consistent theory. Finally, we form $\hat{L}^c$ from $\hat{L}$ and $\hat{T}^c$ from $\hat{T}$ in the way we formed L_Γ^c from L_Γ and T^c from $T(\Gamma)$, and we obtain a language that contains a denumerable infinity of special constants and a consistent theory. From this and from (vii) applied to $\hat{T}^c$, we deduce that $\hat{T}^c$ has a model $\mathscr{D}$ with a denumerable number of individuals. Since $\mathscr{D}(e_i) \neq \mathscr{D}(e_j)$ when $\sim[e_i \neq e_j]$, the universe of $\mathscr{D}$ must contain infinitely many individuals. By eliminating some functions and predicates from $\mathscr{D}$—i.e., by restricting $\mathscr{D}$ to L_Γ—we obtain a model of $T(\Gamma)$ with a denumerable infinity of individuals.

7 Complete Theories and Their Models

A first-order theory $T(\Gamma)$ is *complete* if and only if there is no closed wff A in L_Γ such that (1) A does not belong to $C_n(\Gamma)$ and (2) $T(\Gamma, A)$ is consistent. In this chapter I shall give several model-theoretic characterizations of complete theories. We begin by studying a certain hierarchy of theories that we construct by means of definitions. We then discuss isomorphic and elementarily equivalent structures and establish the correspondence between characteristics of such structures and complete theories.

7.1 Extension of Theories by Definitions

Two first-order theories T and T' can differ in many ways. We say that T' *is an extension of* T if and only if (1) the vocabulary of T is contained in the vocabulary of T' and (2) the theorems of T are theorems of T'. We say that T' *is a conservative extension of* T if and only if (1) T' is an extension of T and (2) any formula A which is wf in the language of T and is a theorem of T' is also a theorem of T. Finally, T *and* T' *are equivalent* if they are extensions of each other.

E 7.1 Let $T(P)$ and $T(N)$ be as described in E 6.1 and E 6.4. It follows from PT 1 of section 6.1 that $T(P)$ is an extension of $T(N)$. The theories are not equivalent since P 9 is not a theorem schemata of $T(N)$.

7.1.1 Predicates

One way in which conservative extensions of a theory are obtained is via definitions of new constants, functional constants, and predicate constants. We shall begin with predicates.

Let $T(\Gamma)$ be a first-order theory in which the formulas in Γ are the only nonlogical axioms; let $x_1, \ldots, x_m$ denote distinct individual variables, and let A be a wff in L_Γ in which no variable other than $x_1, \ldots, x_m$ is free. In addition, insist that P be an m-ary predicate constant that satisfies AD 1.

AD 1 $[P(y_1, \ldots, y_m) \equiv A_{x_1,\ldots,x_m}(y_1, \ldots, y_m)]$

Finally, let $T(\Gamma, \text{AD } 1)$ denote the theory obtained from $T(\Gamma)$ by adding the symbol P to the vocabulary of L_Γ and the assertion AD 1, called the *defining axiom of P*, to the other nonlogical axioms of $T(\Gamma)$. Then $T(\Gamma, \text{AD } 1)$ is a conservative extension of $T(\Gamma)$. In fact, we now have TM 7.1.

TM 7.1 Let $T(\Gamma)$, A, P, and AD 1 be as above. Moreover, let B be a wff in $L_{(\Gamma, \text{AD } 1)}$; let A' be a variant of A in which no variable of B is bound; and let B^* be a wff in L obtained from B, by replacing each part $P(a_1, \ldots, a_m)$ of B by $A'_{x_1,\ldots,x_m}(a_1, \ldots, a_m)$. Then $B^* \in C_n(\Gamma)$ if and only if $B \in C_n(\Gamma, \text{AD } 1)$.

In the predicate calculus, a variant of a wff A is a wff obtained from A by a sequence of replacements in each of which a part $(\forall x)B$ is replaced by $(\forall y)B_x(y)$, where y is a variable which is not free in B. Therefore, AD 1, TM 5.16, and TM 5.15 imply that if B and B^* are as described in TM 7.1, then $[B \equiv B^*] \in C_n(\Gamma, \text{AD } 1)$. Hence $B \in C_n(\Gamma, \text{AD } 1)$ if and only if $B^* \in C_n(\Gamma, \text{AD } 1)$. From this it follows that, to establish TM 7.1, it suffices to demonstrate that $B^* \in C_n(\Gamma)$ if $B \in C_n(\Gamma, \text{AD } 1)$. This we shall do by induction on theorems.

We begin with the axioms. If B is a value of PLA 1–PLA 3, so is B^*, and there is nothing to prove. If B is a value of PLA 4, say $[(\forall x)[C \supset D] \supset [C \supset (\forall x)D]]$, then B^* is $[(\forall x)[C^* \supset D^*] \supset [C^* \supset (\forall x)D^*]]$, which is another value of PLA 4, since x is not free in C^*. If B is a value of PLA 5, say $[(\forall x)C \supset C_x(y)]$, then B^* is $[(\forall x)C^* \supset C_x(y)^*]$, $C^*_x(y)$ is a variant of $C_x(y)^*$, and TM 5.16 and TM 5.15 imply that B^* is a theorem of $T(\Gamma)$. Ditto for B and B^* when B is a value of PLA 7. Finally, if B is a member of Γ, B^* is B; and if B is the defining axiom of P, B^* is $[A' \equiv A]$, which, by TM 5.16, belongs to $C_n(\Gamma)$.

Suppose next that B has been inferred from C and $[C \supset B]$. By the induction hypothesis, $C^* \in C_n(\Gamma)$ and $[C \supset B]^* \in C_n(\Gamma)$. Since $[C \supset B]^*$ is $[C^* \supset B^*]$, we conclude, by PRI 1, that $B^* \in C_n(\Gamma)$.

Finally, suppose that B is $(\forall x)C$ and that $C \in C_n(\Gamma, \text{AD } 1)$. By the induction hypothesis, $C^* \in C_n(\Gamma)$. Hence, by PRI 2, $(\forall x)C^* \in C_n(\Gamma)$. Since B^* is $(\forall x)C^*$, this concludes the proof of TM 7.1.

The definitional scheme expressed in AD 1 differs from the definitional scheme used in chapter 4. To see how they differ, consider E 7.2.

E 7.2 The symbol $\leqslant$ does not appear in L_P. We could introduce it by

$[x \leqslant y] =_{\text{df}} [[x < y] \vee [x = y]]$

Then $[x \leqslant y]$ would denote an abbreviation for $[[x < y] \vee [x = y]]$, and $\leqslant$ would function as a defined symbol and not as a predicate in $T(P)$. If we wanted to introduce $\leqslant$ as a predicate in $T(P)$, we would add $\leqslant$ to the vocabulary of L_P and postulate PD 1.

PD 1 $[[x \leqslant y] \equiv [[x < y] \vee [x = y]]]$

Then $\leqslant$ would function as a well-defined predicate in T(P 1–P 9, PD 1).

7.1.2 Functions

The introduction of functional constants into the language is more involved than the introduction of predicates. Let $T(\Gamma)$ be a first-order theory, and let $x_1, \ldots, x_m, y, y'$ denote distinct individual variables. In addition, let A be a wff in L_Γ in which no variable other than $x_1, \ldots, x_m, y$ is free; let f denote an m-ary functional constant; and insist that AD 2 hold.

AD 2 $[[u = f(z_1, \ldots, z_m)] \equiv A_{x_1,\ldots,x_m,y}(z_1, \ldots, z_m, u)]$

To introduce f in L_Γ via AD 2, the *defining axiom for f*, conditions EC and UC must be satisfied.

EC $(\exists u)A_{x_1,\ldots,x_m,y}(z_1, \ldots, z_m, u) \in C_n(\Gamma)$.

UC $[[A_{x_1,\ldots,x_m,y}(z_1, \ldots, z_m, u) \wedge A_{x_1,\ldots,x_m,y}(z_1, \ldots, z_m, u')] \supset [u = u']] \in C_n(\Gamma)$.

The first one is called the *existence condition for f*; the other is called the *uniqueness condition for f*.

When EC and UC are satisfied for f, we can use AD 2 to introduce f into L_Γ. The resulting theory is a conservative extension of $T(\Gamma)$. In fact, we now have TM 7.2.

TM 7.2 Let $T(\Gamma)$, A, and f be as above and suppose that EC and UC are satisfied. Then $T(\Gamma, \text{AD } 2)$ is a conservative extension of $T(\Gamma)$. Moreover, for every B in $L_{(\Gamma, \text{AD } 2)}$, there is a wff B^* in L_Γ such that

$[B \equiv B^*] \in C_n(\Gamma, \text{AD } 2)$.

The idea of the theorem is obvious, but it is hard to picture the structure of B^*. To describe the construction of B^*, we begin with atomic formulas and use induction on the number of occurrences of $f(\cdot)$ in such formulas. If there are no occurrences of f in B, B^* is B. Suppose then that B is $C_u(f(a_1, \ldots, a_m))$, where the a_i do not contain $f(\cdot)$ and where C is an atomic formula with one less occurrence of $f(\cdot)$ than B, and let $\hat{A}$ be a variant of A in which no variable of B is bound. Then we choose as B^* the following wff:

$(\exists u)[\hat{A}_{x_1,\ldots,x_m,y}(a_1, \ldots, a_m, u) \wedge C^*]$.

For example, if L_Γ is L_P, $f(z)$ is z^2, C is $[\ldots u \ldots]$, B is $[\ldots z^2 \ldots]$, and A is $[y = x \cdot x]$, we choose B^* to be $(\exists u)[[u = z \cdot z] \wedge [\ldots u \ldots]]$.

Once we have defined B^* for all atomic formulas, the B^* of any wff B can be obtained by replacing each atomic part C of B by its C^*. A proof that the B^* we have constructed is materially equivalent to B in $T(\Gamma, \text{AD } 2)$ is given in Shoenfield 1967 (pp. 59–60).

I shall not prove that $T(\Gamma, \text{AD } 2)$ is a conservative extension of $T(\Gamma)$, since the reader can find a proof of that on p. 60 of Shoenfield 1967. Instead I present the example E 7.3, in which I introduce two useful symbols in L_P.

E 7.3 Let $x_1, \ldots, x_m, y$ be distinct individual variables; let A be a wff in L_P in which no variable other than $x_1, \ldots, x_m, y$ is free; let

$$[u = \mu v A_{x_1,\ldots,x_m,y}(z_1, \ldots, z_m, v)]$$
$$=_{\text{df}} [A_{x_1,\ldots,x_m,y}(z_1, \ldots, z_m, u) \wedge (\forall v)[[v < u] \supset \sim A_{x_1,\ldots,x_m,y}(z_1, \ldots, z_m, v)]]$$

and observe that PT 2 implies that

$$[(\exists v)A_{x_1,\ldots,x_m,y}(z_1, \ldots, z_m, v) \supset (\exists u)[u = \mu v A_{x_1,\ldots,x_m,y}(z_1, \ldots, z_m, v)]]$$

belongs to $C_n(\text{P } 1\text{–P } 9)$. Finally, let

PD 2 $[[z = (x \dot{-} y)] \equiv [z = \mu v[[[x < y] \wedge [v = 0]] \vee [(y + v) = x]]]]$

Then

PT 3 $(\exists v)[[[x < y] \wedge [v = 0]] \vee [(y + v) = x]]$

is a theorem of $T(\text{P } 1\text{–P } 9)$. Consequently, by PT 2,

PT 4 $(\exists z)[z = \mu v[[[x < y] \wedge [v = 0]] \vee [(y + v) = x]]]$

It is also easy to verify that $C_n(\text{P } 1\text{–P } 9)$ contains PT 5.

PT 5 $[[[z = \mu v[[[x < y] \wedge [v = 0]] \vee [(y + v) = x]]]$
$\wedge [w = \mu v[[[x < y] \wedge [v = 0]] \vee [(y + v) = x]]]] \supset [z = w]]$

From PT 4 and PT 5 it follows that $\dot{-}$ is well defined and can be introduced as a functional constant in L_P. We next add PD 2 to P 1–P 9 and form $T(\text{P } 1\text{–P } 9, \text{PD } 2)$. To conclude the example, we note that

$$[[[x < y] \wedge [(x \dot{-} y) = 0]] \vee [(y + (x \dot{-} y)) = x]] \in C_n(\text{P } 1\text{–P } 9, \text{PD } 2).$$

Since constants are special cases of functional constants, the preceding discussion specializes to the introduction of constants. Hence no further comments in that respect are necessary.

7.1.3 Valid Definitional Schemes

With respect to the definitional schemes discussed above, notice that they satisfy the criteria laid down for valid definitions in section 2.2. First they are dispensable in the sense that whatever can be asserted with them in the extended theory can be asserted without them in the original theory. This fact is a consequence of the substitutive property of material equivalence. Second, these definitional schemes are noncreative in the sense that a wff of the original theory cannot be proved in the extended theory unless it can be proved in the original theory; i.e., a formula that is stated without the use of the new concepts cannot be demonstrated with these concepts unless it can also be demonstrated without them. Similar remarks apply to the definitional scheme of chapter 4.

Even though the definitional schemes discussed above and in chapter 4 satisfy the criteria that I insisted on in chapter 2, their general usefulness for the purpose of constructing a language for science is problematic. I give reasons why in E 7.4.

E 7.4 Let P and Q be unary predicates and let R be defined by

(i) $[R(x) \equiv [P(x) \supset Q(x)]]$.

Suppose that this definition asserts that x has the property R if and only if x under the test conditions described in P exhibits the response predicated in Q; e.g., x is magnetic if and only if, whenever x is close to a small iron object, the iron object moves towards x. As a definitional scheme for science, (i) has the following characteristic:

(ii) $[R(x) \equiv [P(x) \supset Q(x)]] \vdash [\sim P(x) \supset R(x)]$,

i.e., if x is not subjected to the test prescribed in P, x has the property R.

We might try to avoid the anomalous situation described in (ii) by changing (i) to

(iii) $[R(x) \equiv [P(x) \wedge [P(x) \supset Q(x)]]]$.

But for a scientist, who believes that the existence of physical objects is independent of anybody perceiving them, (iii) is no better than (i). To wit:

(iv) $[R(x) \equiv [P(x) \wedge [P(x) \supset Q(x)]]] \vdash [\sim P(x) \supset \sim R(x)]$.

i.e., if x is not subjected to the test prescribed by P, x does not have the property R.

To escape the unfortunate situations described in (ii) and (iv), Carnap (1936, pp. 441–444) suggested that R be defined by a so-called *reduction sentence*,

(v) $[P(x) \supset [R(x) \equiv Q(x)]]$.

Then, if x is not tested, x need not satisfy R. But (v) provides only a partial definition of R. Hence as a prototype of a general definitional scheme, (v) does not satisfy the conditions imposed on valid definitions in chapter 2.

Difficulties such as those exhibited in E 7.4 are caused by the characteristics of material implication. Hence they are not particular to the problem of introducing scientific concepts by definition but pop up in many areas of scientific endeavor, e.g., in the theory of evidence. For illuminating discussions of definitional schemes for science, I refer the reader to Hempel 1952 and to Przelecki 1969 (pp. 63–87).

7.2 Isomorphic Structures

In chapter 3 I insisted that a declarative sentence is true if the denotations of the names in the sentence satisfy the relations predicated of them by the sentence. I also suggested that a complete explication of truth *for a given language* would require prescribing for each and every relation of the language the objects that satisfy them. These ideas can be specialized to suit our present purposes as follows: Let L be a first-order language. A structure $\mathscr{D}$ for L is a quadruple consisting of a set of individuals $|\mathscr{D}|$ (the universe of discourse), a set of names of individuals, and functional and predicate constants that are related in a definite way to the functional and predicate symbols of our first-order language L. By adding the names of the elements in $|\mathscr{D}|$ to the constants of L, we obtain a language which in section 5.3.2 we denoted by $L(\mathscr{D})$. If B is a wff in L, then B is valid in $\mathscr{D}$ (i.e., is true) if the individuals in $|\mathscr{D}|$ satisfy the relations which B predicates of them in $\mathscr{D}$. We shall identify the concept of truth in $\mathscr{D}$ with the triple $(|\mathscr{D}|, L, \mathrm{Tr}(\mathscr{D}))$, where $\mathrm{Tr}(\mathscr{D})$ designates the set of closed wffs in $L(\mathscr{D})$ that denote truth in $\mathscr{D}$. As $\mathscr{D}$ varies, the concept of truth varies, both because the individuals in the universe of discourse change and because the idea of a true sentence in $L(\mathscr{D})$ changes.

Here is an example to aid our intuition.

E 7.5 Let $T(G)$ be a first-order theory whose language L_G contains two nonlogical symbols—a constant, c and a binary function symbol $\cdot$. The nonlogical axioms of $T(G)$ are the following:

G 1 $[((x \cdot y) \cdot z) = (x \cdot (y \cdot z))]$.

G 2 $[(c \cdot x) = x]$.

G 3 $(\forall x)(\exists y)[(y \cdot x) = c]$.

(Here $(x \cdot y)$ is a synonym for $\cdot(x, y)$.) There are two structures for L_G, $\mathscr{A}$ and $\mathscr{B}$, which are models of $T(G)$ and which satisfy the following conditions:

(i) $|\mathscr{A}| = R_{++}$ and $|\mathscr{B}| = R$.

(ii) $\mathscr{A}(c) = 1$ and $\mathscr{B}(c) = 0$.

(iii) If a and b are variable-free terms, then

(a) $\mathscr{A}(\cdot(a, b)) = (\mathscr{A}(a) \cdot \mathscr{A}(b))$ and

(b) $\mathscr{B}(\cdot(a, b)) = (\mathscr{B}(a) + \mathscr{B}(b))$.

Here R and R_{++} denote, respectively, the set of real numbers and the set of positive real numbers. Also 1 and 0 are the real numbers usually named by these symbols. Finally, the function symbols on the right-hand sides of (a) and (b) denote the standard multiplication and addition signs.

In this section we shall study how the concept of truth changes from one structure to another. To do so, I introduce several new concepts. Let A and B be sets and suppose that $\phi(\cdot): A \to B$. Then ϕ is *injective* if it is one–one and *bijective* if it is injective and on to.

E 7.6 Let R and R_{++} be as in E 7.5. The mapping $\phi(\cdot): R \to R_{++}$, defined by $\phi(x) = e^x$ for $x \in R$ is bijective. Similarly, if N and M denote, respectively, the set of natural numbers and the set of even natural numbers, the mapping $\phi(\cdot): N \to M$ defined by $\phi(x) = 2x$ is bijective.

Next let $\mathscr{D} = (|\mathscr{D}|, N_{\mathscr{D}}, F^{\mathscr{D}}, G^{\mathscr{D}})$ and $\mathscr{A} = (|\mathscr{A}|, N_{\mathscr{A}}, F^{\mathscr{A}}, G^{\mathscr{A}})$ be structures for L and suppose that $\phi(\cdot): |\mathscr{D}| \to |\mathscr{A}|$ is bijective. Then ϕ is an *isomorphism* of $\mathscr{D}$ and $\mathscr{A}$ if it satisfies the following conditions for all m-ary f and P and all $a_i \in |\mathscr{D}|$, $i = 1, \ldots, m$:

$$f^{\mathscr{A}}(\phi(a_1), \ldots, \phi(a_m)) = \phi(f^{\mathscr{D}}(a_1, \ldots, a_m)) \tag{7.1}$$

and

$$P^{\mathscr{A}}(\phi(a_1), \ldots, \phi(a_m)) \equiv P^{\mathscr{D}}(a_1, \ldots, a_m) \tag{7.2}$$

where m varies over 0, 1, ... Finally, two structures $\mathscr{D}$ and $\mathscr{A}$ are *isomorphic* if and only if there is a bijective mapping $\phi(\cdot): |\mathscr{D}| \to |\mathscr{A}|$ that satisfies equations 7.1 and 7.2.

There are several things to note about equations (7.1) and (7.2) above. First, the symbols $=$ and $\equiv$ must not be taken to be symbols of the object language. They are shorthand expressions for "equals" and "if and only if," respectively. Second, $f^{\mathscr{D}}$ and $f^{\mathscr{A}}$ correspond to the same function symbol in L. Similarly, $P^{\mathscr{D}}$ and $P^{\mathscr{A}}$ correspond to the same predicate symbol in L. Third, $|\mathscr{D}|$ may consist of objects that are entirely different from the objects in $|\mathscr{A}|$. $|\mathscr{D}|$ can also be either identical with or a subset of $|\mathscr{A}|$. When $|\mathscr{D}|$ contains a finite number of individuals, $|\mathscr{A}|$ must contain the same number of objects. In that case, if $|\mathscr{D}|$ and $|\mathscr{A}|$ contain the same elements, ϕ is a permutation of the individuals in $|\mathscr{D}|$.

The mapping $\phi(\cdot): R \to R_{++}$, defined by $\phi(x) = e^x$, $x \in R$, is an isomorphism of the two structures in E 7.5. Another example is given in E 7.7.

E 7.7 Let L, f, g, h, k, ad $P_1 - P_4$ be as in E 5.3. Furthermore, let $\mathscr{D}$ be the structure obtained by assigning $\{x_1, x_2\}$ to $|\mathscr{D}|$; f to f^1 and f^2; g, h, and k to f^3,

f^4, and f^5, respectively; P_1 to P^1; P_2 to P^2; P_3 to P^3 and P^4; and P_4 to P^5 and P^6. Finally, let $\mathscr{A}$ be the structure obtained by assignng $\{x_1, x_2\}$ to $|\mathscr{A}|$; f to f^3; g to f^1 and f^2; h and k to f^4 and f^5, respectively; P_1 to P^1; P_2 to P^3 and P^4; P_3 to P^2; and P_4 to P^5 and P^6. Then the function ϕ, defined by $\phi(x_1) = x_2$ and $\phi(x_2) = x_1$, is an isomorphism of $\mathscr{D}$ and $\mathscr{A}$.

If $\mathscr{D}$ is a structure for L and if A is a set and ϕ is a bijection from $|\mathscr{D}|$ to A, we can use equations 7.1 and 7.2 to define a structure $\mathscr{A}$ for L that is isomorphic to $\mathscr{D}$ and satisfies $|\mathscr{A}| = A$.

E 7.8 Let $T(N)$ and $T(NS)$ be as in E 6.4, let η denote the standard model of $T(N)$, and let η' be a model of $T(NS)$ such that $|\eta| \cap |\eta'| = \varnothing$. In addition, let N^* denote the set of all $a \in |\eta'|$ so that $a = \eta'(k_n)$ for some $n = 0, 1, \ldots$, and let

$$A = |\eta| \cup (|\eta'| - N^*).$$

Finally, let $\phi(\cdot)\colon |\eta'| \to A$ be such that $\phi(a) = a$ if $a \in (|\eta'| - N^*)$, and $\eta(k_n) = \phi(\eta'(k_n))$, $n = 0, 1, \ldots$. Then ϕ is a bijection. Hence the conditions

$$f^{\eta^*}(\phi(a_1), \ldots, \phi(a_k)) = \phi(f^{\eta'}(a_1, \ldots, a_k)),$$

$$P^{\eta^*}[\phi(a_1), \ldots, \phi(a_k)) \equiv P^{\eta'}(a_1, \ldots, a_k),$$

$f^{\eta'} \in F^{\eta'}$, $P^{\eta'} \in G^{\eta'}$, $(a_1, \ldots, a_k) \in |\eta'|^k$, $k = 0, 1, \ldots$, together with $|\eta^*| = A$ and $N_{\eta^*} = N_\eta \cup (N_{\eta'} - \{k_n, n = 0, 1, \ldots\})$ define a structure η^* for L that is isomorphic to η'.

Let $\mathscr{D}$ and $\mathscr{A}$ be structures for L and let $\phi(\cdot)\colon |\mathscr{D}| \to |\mathscr{A}|$ be an isomorphism of $\mathscr{D}$ and $\mathscr{A}$. Equations 7.1 and 7.2 do not mention $N_{\mathscr{D}}$ and $N_{\mathscr{A}}$. So for each $a \in N_{\mathscr{D}}$, we let $a^\phi \in N_{\mathscr{A}}$ denote the name of $\phi(\mathscr{D}(a))$. Moreover, if u is a term or a wff in $L(\mathscr{D})$, we let u^ϕ denote the term or wff in $L(\mathscr{A})$ in which each name a in u has been replaced by a^ϕ. With this notation we can assert TM 7.3.

TM 7.3 Let $\mathscr{D}$ and $\mathscr{A}$ be structures for L; let $\phi(\cdot)\colon |\mathscr{D}| \to |\mathscr{A}|$ be an isomorphism of $\mathscr{D}$ and $\mathscr{A}$; and let a and B be, respectively, a variable-free term and a closed wff of $L(\mathscr{D})$. Then

$$\mathscr{A}(a^\phi) = \phi(\mathscr{D}(a)) \quad \text{and} \quad \mathscr{A}(B^\phi) = \mathscr{D}(B).$$

Thus, if two structures $\mathscr{D}$ and $\mathscr{A}$ are isomorphic, the set of formulas in L that are valid in $\mathscr{D}$ is identical to the set of formulas in L that are valid in $\mathscr{A}$. However, the concept of truth in $\mathscr{D}$ differs from the concept of truth in $\mathscr{A}$ to the extent that the individuals and the function and predicate constants of $\mathscr{D}$ differ from those of $\mathscr{A}$.

To prove the theorem, let a be a variable-free term and proceed by induction on the length of a. If a is a name, there is nothing to prove. If a is $f(a_1, \ldots, a_n)$, then by the induction hypothesis,

$$\begin{aligned}\phi(\mathscr{D}(a)) &= \phi(f^{\mathscr{D}}(\mathscr{D}(a_1), \ldots, \mathscr{D}(a_n)))\\ &= f^{\mathscr{A}}(\phi(\mathscr{D}(a_1)), \ldots, \phi(\mathscr{D}(a_n)))\\ &= f^{\mathscr{A}}(\mathscr{A}(a_1^{\phi}), \ldots, \mathscr{A}(a_n^{\phi}))\\ &= \mathscr{A}(a^{\phi}).\end{aligned}$$

The second half of the theorem can be established in a similar way by induction on the length of wffs. We first show how for an atomic formula, $P(a_1, \ldots, a_n)$, where the a_i are variable-free terms and P is not $=$. In this case,

$$\begin{aligned}\mathscr{D}(A) = t &\equiv P^{\mathscr{D}}(\mathscr{D}(a_1), \ldots, \mathscr{D}(a_n))\\ &\equiv P^{\mathscr{A}}(\phi(\mathscr{D}(a_1)), \ldots, \phi(\mathscr{D}(a_n)))\\ &\equiv P^{\mathscr{A}}(\mathscr{A}(a_1^{\phi}), \ldots, \mathscr{A}(a_n^{\phi}))\\ &\equiv \mathscr{A}(A^{\phi}).\end{aligned}$$

When B is $[a = b]$ for some variable-free terms a and b, we observe that ϕ is injective and apply the same arguments as above.

Suppose next that there exist closed wffs A, C, and D and an individual variable x such that B is $\sim C$, $[C \supset D]$ or $(\forall x)A$. Since $(\sim C)^{\phi}$ is $\sim C^{\phi}$ and $[C \supset D]^{\phi}$ is $[C^{\phi} \supset D^{\phi}]$, the validity of the theorem for the first two cases is an immediate consequence of the induction hypothesis. To deal with the third case, we observe first that $\mathscr{D}(B) = f$ if and only if $\mathscr{D}(\sim B) = t$ and that B^{ϕ} is $(\forall x)A^{\phi}$. Then we note that since ϕ is surjective, for all $j \in N_{\mathscr{A}}$, there is an $i \in N_{\mathscr{D}}$ such that j is i^{ϕ}. Finally, we appeal to the induction hypothesis and deduce that

$$\begin{aligned}\mathscr{D}(\sim B) = t &\equiv \mathscr{D}((\exists x) \sim A) = t\\ &\equiv \mathscr{D}(\sim A_x(i)) = t \text{ for some } i \in N_{\mathscr{D}}\\ &\equiv \mathscr{A}(\sim A_x^{\phi}(i^{\phi})) = t \text{ for some } i \in N_{\mathscr{D}}\\ &\equiv \mathscr{A}(\sim A_x^{\phi}(j)) = t \text{ for some } j \in N_{\mathscr{A}}\\ &\equiv \mathscr{A}(\sim B^{\phi}) = t.\end{aligned}$$

From these arguments it follows that $\mathscr{A}(B^{\phi}) = \mathscr{D}(B)$.

If $\mathscr{D}$ is a structure for L, $\mathscr{D}$ is isomorphic to itself since the identity mapping on $|\mathscr{D}|$ is a bijection. In addition, if $\mathscr{D}$ and $\mathscr{A}$ are structures for L such that $\mathscr{D}$ is isomorphic to $\mathscr{A}$, then $\mathscr{A}$ is isomorphic to $\mathscr{D}$. Finally, if $\mathscr{D}$, $\mathscr{A}$, and $\mathscr{B}$ are structures for L such that $\mathscr{D}$ is isomorphic to $\mathscr{A}$, and $\mathscr{A}$ is isomorphic to $\mathscr{B}$, then $\mathscr{D}$ is isomorphic to $\mathscr{B}$. Thus the relation of being isomorphic is an equivalence relation that partitions the set of all structures for L into equivalence classes. Some of these equivalence classes are of particular interest to us.

Let Γ be a set of wffs, let $T(\Gamma)$ be the corresponding theory, let E_L denote an equivalence class of isomorphic structures, let $\mathscr{D}$ belong to $M(\Gamma)$, and suppose that $\mathscr{D} \in E_L$. If $\mathscr{A} \in E_L$, then $\mathscr{A} \in M(\Gamma)$ as well. Thus if $\mathscr{D}$ is a model of $T(\Gamma)$ for one $\mathscr{D} \in E_L$, it is a model of $T(\Gamma)$ for all $\mathscr{D} \in E_L$. How large E_L is depends on the number of elements in $|\mathscr{D}|$. If $\mathscr{D}$ is finite, every permutation of $|\mathscr{D}|$ determines a structure $\mathscr{A}$ that is isomorphic to $\mathscr{D}$ and belongs to E_L. If $|\mathscr{D}|$ contains infinitely many individuals, every bijective mapping of $|\mathscr{D}|$ onto subsets of $|\mathscr{D}|$ determines a structure $\mathscr{A}$ that is isomorphic to $\mathscr{D}$ and belongs to E_L.

The fact that a consistent theory $T(\Gamma)$ has many models suggests that it can be used to talk about many things. This is especially interesting to mathematicians because the theorems they establish for $T(\Gamma)$ need not be proved anew for each different model of $T(\Gamma)$. To scientists, on the other hand, it is cause for concern because they view the numerousness of the models of a scientific theory to be a measure of how vague such a theory is. Note, therefore, that for a scientific theory the vagueness caused by the existence of structures that are isomorphic to its intended model cannot be avoided. It is a fact of life scientists must live with.

If $T(\Gamma)$ has models with infinitely many individuals, it has models that are not isomorphic. If two models of $T(\Gamma)$ are not isomorphic, the concepts of truth that they determine may differ because their respective universes, functions, and predicates differ. They may also differ in that the two sets of wffs in L, which correspond to the true formulas in the two models, are different. The latter situation is a characteristic feature of incomplete theories as evidenced in TM 7.4.

TM 7.4 Suppose that Γ consists of a denumerable number of formulas and that $T(\Gamma)$ has only models with infinitely many individuals. Suppose also that all models with a denumerable universe are isomorphic. Then $T(\Gamma)$ is complete.

We showed previously that, if a theory such as $T(\Gamma)$ has a model with an infinite universe, then it has a model with a denumerably infinite universe. Thus the conditions of the theorem are not empty. They provide model-theoretic conditions sufficient for a theory to be complete. Similar conditions suffice when Γ consists of nondenumerably many wffs too.

The validity of TM 7.4 is easy to prove. Suppose that the conditions of TM 7.4 hold and that $T(\Gamma)$ is incomplete. Then there is a closed formula $B \in L$ such that B is not a theorem in $T(\Gamma)$ and such that $T(\Gamma, B)$ and

$T(\Gamma, \sim B)$ are both consistent and possess, respectively, models $\mathscr{D}$ and $\mathscr{D}^*$, which are also models of $T(\Gamma)$. Hence these models have infinite universes of discourse. From this and TM 6.13, we conclude that there exist structures $\mathscr{A}$ and $\mathscr{B}$ with denumerably infinite universes that are models of $T(\Gamma, B)$ and $T(\Gamma, \sim B)$, respectively. Since these models are also models of $T(\Gamma)$, they are isomorphic. But if that is so, then $\mathscr{A}(B) = \mathscr{B}(\sim B) = t$ is a contradiction, which demonstrates that $T(\Gamma)$ is complete.

7.3 Elementarily Equivalent Structures

When $\mathscr{D}$ and $\mathscr{B}$ are structures for L, with the property that the closed wffs in L which are true in $\mathscr{D}$ are also true in $\mathscr{B}$ and vice versa, they are said to be *elementarily equivalent*. Two isomorphic structures are elementarily equivalent. There exist, however, elementarily equivalent structures that are not isomorphic.

To discuss elementarily equivalent structures, I must introduce several new concepts: Let $\mathscr{D}$ and $\mathscr{A}$ be structures for L that satisfy the following conditions:

(i) $|\mathscr{D}| \subset |\mathscr{A}|$ and $N_{\mathscr{D}} \subset N_{\mathscr{A}}$.
(ii) $f^{\mathscr{D}}(a_1, \ldots, a_i) = f^{\mathscr{A}}(a_1, \ldots, a_i)$ for all i-ary $f^{\mathscr{D}} \in F^{\mathscr{D}}$, $i = 0, 1, \ldots$; and all $(a_1, \ldots, a_i) \in |\mathscr{D}|^i$.
(iii) $P^{\mathscr{D}}(b_1, \ldots, b_i) \equiv P^{\mathscr{A}}(b_1, \ldots, b_i)$ for all i-ary $P^{\mathscr{D}} \in G^{\mathscr{D}}$, $i = 1, 2, \ldots$; and all $(b_1, \ldots, b_i) \in |\mathscr{D}|^i$.

Then $\mathscr{A}$ is an *extension* of $\mathscr{D}$. Moreover, $\mathscr{A}$ is an *elementary extension* of $\mathscr{D}$ if $\mathscr{A}$ is an extension of $\mathscr{D}$ and $\mathscr{A}(A) = \mathscr{D}(A)$ for every closed wff A of $L(\mathscr{D})$. Finally, if $\mathscr{A}$ is an (elementary) extension of $\mathscr{D}$, we shall say that $\mathscr{D}$ is an (elementary) *substructure* of $\mathscr{A}$.

E 7.9 Let η be the standard model of $T(N)$ and let η^* be the model of $T(NS)$ that we constructed in E 7.8. Then η is a substructure of η^*. To see why, observe that, by construction, $|\eta| \subset |\eta^*|$ and $N_\eta \subset N_{\eta^*}$. Furthermore, for $n \in |\eta|$,

$$\begin{aligned} S^\eta(n) &= S^\eta(\eta(k_n)) = \eta(S(k_n)) = \eta(k_{n+1}) = \phi(\eta'(k_{n+1})) \\ &= \phi(\eta'(S(k_n))) = \phi(S^{\eta'}(\eta'(k_n))) = S^{\eta^*}(\phi(\eta'(k_n))) \\ &= S^{\eta^*}(\eta(k_n)) = S^{\eta^*}(n). \end{aligned}$$

Similarly, for $n, m \in |\eta|$ and $+(\cdot, \cdot)$, we find that

$$\begin{aligned} +^\eta(n, m) &= \eta(+(k_n, k_m)) = \eta(k_{n+m}) = \phi(\eta'(k_{n+m})) \\ &= \phi(\eta'(+(k_n, k_m)) = \phi(+^{\eta'}(\eta'(k_n), \eta'(k_m))) \\ &= +^{\eta^*}(\phi(\eta'(k_n)), \phi(\eta'(k_m))) = +^{\eta^*}(\eta(k_n), \eta(k_m)) \\ &= +^{\eta^*}(n, m). \end{aligned}$$

With obvious modifications, the same arguments show that, when $n, m \in |\eta|$,

$$\cdot^{\eta}(n, m) = \cdot^{\eta^*}(n, m),$$

and

$$<^{\eta}(n, m) \equiv <^{\eta^*}(n, m).$$

Since by construction, $\eta(k_0) = \eta^*(0)$, we conclude that η is a substructure of η^*, as was to be shown.

The conditions i–iii above are necessary for $\mathscr{D}$ to be a substructure of $\mathscr{A}$, but are not sufficient. To see why, assume that $|\mathscr{D}|$ and $|\mathscr{A}|$ satisfy (i) and define $f^{\mathscr{D}}$ and $P^{\mathscr{D}}$ on $|\mathscr{D}|^i$ by (ii) and (iii), respectively. Let $F^{\mathscr{D}}$ and $G^{\mathscr{D}}$ be the sets of functions and predicates obtained by letting f and P vary over the vocabulary of L. Then $(|\mathscr{D}|, N_{\mathscr{D}}, F^{\mathscr{D}}, G^{\mathscr{D}})$ is a substructure of $\mathscr{A}$ only if every i-ary $f^{\mathscr{D}}$ in $F^{\mathscr{D}}$ maps $|\mathscr{D}|^i$ into $|\mathscr{D}|$, $i = 1, 2, \ldots$. Necessary and sufficient conditions for $\mathscr{D}$ to be a substructure of $\mathscr{A}$ are given in TM 7.5.

TM 7.5 Let $\mathscr{D}$ and $\mathscr{A}$ be structures for L such that $|\mathscr{D}| \subset |\mathscr{A}|$ and $N_{\mathscr{D}} \subset N_{\mathscr{A}}$. Then $\mathscr{D}$ is a substructure of $\mathscr{A}$ if and only if, for all variable-free formulas B of $L(\mathscr{D})$, $\mathscr{D}(B) = \mathscr{A}(B)$.

A variable-free formula is a closed wff without quantifiers and free variables. Hence the only-if part of TM 7.5 is a consequence of TM 7.3.

To establish the if part of the theorem, it suffices to show that $\mathscr{A}$ satisfies conditions ii and iii of the definition of an extension of $\mathscr{D}$. To that end, let P and f be n-ary predicate and function symbols; let a_i, $i = 1, \ldots, n$ be individuals in $|\mathscr{D}|$; let $k_i \in N_{\mathscr{D}}$ be the name of a_i, $i = 1, \ldots, n$; and let $j \in N_{\mathscr{D}}$ be the name of $f^{\mathscr{D}}(a_1, \ldots, a_n)$. Moreover, assume that $\mathscr{D}(B) = \mathscr{A}(B)$ for all variable-free wffs of $L(\mathscr{D})$. Then

$$\mathscr{D}(P(k_1, \ldots, k_n)) = t \equiv P^{\mathscr{D}}(a_1, \ldots, a_n)$$

and

$$\mathscr{A}(P(k_1, \ldots, k_n)) = t \equiv P^{\mathscr{A}}(a_1, \ldots, a_n)$$

imply that $\mathscr{A}$ satisfies condition iii. Moreover, from

$$\mathscr{A}(f(k_1, \ldots, k_n) = j) = \mathscr{D}(f(k_1, \ldots, k_n) = j) = \mathrm{t}$$

we deduce that $f^{\mathscr{A}}(a_1, \ldots, a_n) = f^{\mathscr{D}}(a_1, \ldots, a_n)$ and hence that $\mathscr{A}$ satisfies condition ii as well.

We can also give useful necessary and sufficient conditions that one structure for L be an elementary extension of another structure for L—to wit, TM 7.6.

TM 7.6 Let $\mathscr{D}$ and $\mathscr{A}$ be structures for L and suppose that $\mathscr{D}$ is a substructure of $\mathscr{A}$. Then $\mathscr{A}$ is an elementary extension of $\mathscr{D}$ if and only if the following condition holds for all m and all wffs A of L:

(i) Let A be a wff of L with exactly $m + 1$ free variables, $x_0, \ldots, x_m$; let a_i, $i = 0, \ldots, m - 1$, be individuals in $|\mathscr{D}|$ with names k_i, $i = 0, \ldots, m - 1$. Then there exists an individual $b \in |\mathscr{A}|$ with name k_b such that

$$\mathscr{A}(A_{x_0,\ldots,x_m}(k_0,\ldots,k_{m-1},k_b)) = \mathrm{t}$$

only if there is an $a \in |\mathscr{D}|$ with name k_a such that

$$\mathscr{A}(A_{x_0,\ldots,x_m}(k_0,\ldots,k_{m-1},k_a)) = \mathrm{t}.$$

To establish the necessity part of TM 7.6 I suppose that $\mathscr{A}$ is an elementary extension of $\mathscr{D}$, and let A and a_i and k_i be as described in (i). Then $(\exists x)A_{x_0,\ldots,x_{m-1}}(k_0,\ldots,k_{m-1})$ is a closed wff in $L(\mathscr{D})$ which is valid in $\mathscr{A}$ if and only if it is valid in $\mathscr{D}$. Also if $a \in |\mathscr{D}|$ and k_a is the name of a, then $A_{x_0,\ldots,x_m}(k_0,\ldots,k_{m-1},k_a)$ is a wff in $L(\mathscr{D})$ that is valid in $\mathscr{D}$ if and only if it is valid in $\mathscr{A}$. From this and obvious arguments follows the validity of condition i.

Next I suppose that $\mathscr{D}$ is a substructure of $\mathscr{A}$ and that condition i holds. To establish the sufficiency part of TM 7.6 we must demonstrate that

(ii) for all closed wffs A of $L(\mathscr{D})$, $\mathscr{A}(A) = \mathscr{D}(A)$.

I procede by induction on the length of wffs. If A is an atomic formula, $\mathscr{A}(A) = \mathscr{D}(A)$ follows immediately from TM 7.5. The cases when A is $\sim C$ or $[C \supset D]$ for some closed wffs C and D of $L(\mathscr{D})$, I leave to the reader. So suppose that A is $(\forall x)B$ for some wff B of $L(\mathscr{D})$ with just one free variable x. Then there is an m and a wff C of L with exactly $m + 1$ free variables, $x_0, \ldots, x_{m-1}, x$, such that for some individuals $a_i \in |\mathscr{D}|$ with names k_i, $i = 0, \ldots, m - 1$, B is $C_{x_0,\ldots,x_{m-1}}(k_0,\ldots,k_{m-1})$. But then $\mathscr{A}(A) = \mathrm{f}$ if and only if

$$\mathscr{A}(C_{x_0,\ldots,x_{m-1},x}(k_0,\ldots,k_{m-1},k_b)) = \mathrm{f}$$

for some $b \in |\mathscr{A}|$ with name k_b. From this, $|\mathscr{D}| \subset |\mathscr{A}|$, and condition (i), it follows that $\mathscr{A}(A) = f$ if and only if

$$\mathscr{A}(C_{x_0,\ldots,x_{m-1},x}(k_0,\ldots,k_{m-1},k_a)) = \mathrm{f}$$

for some $a \in |\mathscr{D}|$ with name k_a. By the induction hypothesis,

$$\mathscr{A}(C_{x_0,\ldots,x_{m-1},x}(k_0,\ldots,k_{m-1},k_a)) = \mathscr{D}(C_{x_0,\ldots,x_{m-1},x}(k_0,\ldots,k_{m-1},k_a))$$

Consequently $\mathscr{A}(A) = \mathrm{f}$ if and only $\mathscr{D}(A) = \mathrm{f}$; i.e., $\mathscr{A}(A) = \mathscr{D}(A)$.

The idea of elementary equivalence of structures has many interesting aspects. For example, let $\mathscr{D}$ be a structure for a first-order language L and assume that $|\mathcal{D}|$ contains infinitely many individuals. Moreover, let $\Gamma(\mathcal{D})$ denote the collection of closed wffs of L that are true in $\mathcal{D}$, and observe that $\mathcal{D}$ is a model of $T(\Gamma(\mathcal{D}))$. By TM 6.13, $T(\Gamma(\mathcal{D}))$ has a model $\mathcal{S}$ with a denumerably infinite universe of discourse $|\mathcal{S}|$. Evidently, $\mathcal{S}$ and $\mathcal{D}$ are elementarily equivalent structures for L.

We can use TM 7.5 and TM 7.6 to obtain a very interesting strengthening of the preceding result that is due to Skolem (1920, pp. 4–9). The proof we give is an analogue of the proof of Skolem's theorem in Bell and Machover 1977 (pp. 168–170).

TM 7.7 Let $\mathcal{D}$ be a structure for a first-order language L and assume that $|\mathcal{D}|$ contains infinitely many individuals. Then there exists an elementary substructure of $\mathcal{D}$ whose universe of discourse is denumerably infinite.

This theorem is usually referred to as the *Downward Löwenheim-Skolem Theorem*. Its proof goes as follows: If $|\mathcal{D}|$ is denumerable, there is nothing to prove. Hence suppose $|\mathcal{D}|$ contains nondenumerably many individuals and let B_0 be a subset of $|\mathcal{D}|$ with a denumerable infinity of individuals that contains $\mathcal{D}(a)$ for all constants a of L. Moreover, let $\mathcal{P}(|\mathcal{D}|)$ denote the family of all subsets of $|\mathcal{D}|$; let $H(\cdot)\colon (\mathcal{P}(|\mathcal{D}|) - \{\phi\}) \to |\mathcal{D}|$ be a choice function for the subsets of $|\mathcal{D}|$; and for each $n \geqslant 0$ let $B_{n+1} = \{b \in |\mathcal{D}| : b = H(Y)$ for some $Y \in (\mathcal{P}(|\mathcal{D}|) - \{\phi\})$ that satisfies the condition: There is an m, a wff A of L with $m+1$ free variables, $x_0, \ldots, x_m$, some individuals, $a_i \in B_n$, $i = 0, \ldots, m-1$, with names $k_i \in N_{\mathcal{D}}$, $i = 0, \ldots, m-1$, such that

$$Y = \{a \in |\mathcal{D}| \text{ with name } k_a \in N_{\mathcal{D}} : \mathcal{D}(A_{x_0,\ldots,x_m}(k_0, \ldots, k_{m-1}, k_a)) = \mathrm{t}\}\}.$$

Finally, let $B = \bigcup_{n=0}^{\infty} B_n$; let N_B designate the set of names in $\mathcal{D}$ of the individuals in B; let $F^{\mathcal{D}/B}$ consist of the restrictions to B of the functions in $F^{\mathcal{D}}$; and let $G^{\mathcal{D}/B}$ consist of the restrictions to B of the predicates in $G^{\mathcal{D}}$. We shall demonstrate (somewhat sketchily) that

$$\mathcal{B} = (B, N_B, F^{\mathcal{D}/B}, G^{\mathcal{D}/B})$$

is a well-defined structure for L, with a denumerable infinity of individuals, and that $\mathcal{D}$ is an elementary extension of $\mathcal{B}$.

First we note that, for all $n \geqslant 0$, $B_n \subset B_{n+1}$. To see why, let A be the wff $[x_1 = x_2]$; let b be an individual in B_n with name k_b in $N_{\mathcal{D}}$; and observe that

$$\{b\} = \{a \in |\mathcal{D}| \text{ with name } k_a \in N_{\mathcal{D}} : \mathcal{D}(A_{x_1,x_2}(k_b, k_a)) = \mathrm{t}\}.$$

Hence $b \in B_{n+1}$.

Next we must show that each B_n contains only a denumerable infinity of individuals. To that end, let X and Y be sets with a denumerable infinity of elements; and let $(Y \times X)$ denote the set of pairs whose first component belongs to Y and whose second component belongs to X. Then it is a fact that $(Y \times X)$, X^m and $\bigcup_{m=0}^{\infty} (Y \times X^m)$ are all denumerable. But if that is so and if $|Z|$ and Z_L denote, respectively, the number of elements in Z and the collection of wffs in L, the denumerability of B_0 and Z_L, the relations

$$|B_n| \leqslant \left| \sum_{m=0}^{\infty} (Z_L \times B_{n-1}^m) \right|, \qquad n = 1,2, \ldots$$

and an obvious inductive argument suffice to demonstrate that, for all $n \geqslant 0$, the members of B_n are denumerable.

The preceding observations imply that B is well defined and contains only a denumerable infinity of individuals. It remains to show that $\mathscr{B}$ is a structure for L and $\mathscr{D}$ is an elementary extension of $\mathscr{B}$. To do that, it suffices to show that $\mathscr{D}$ and $\mathscr{B}$ (with $\mathscr{D}$ for $\mathscr{A}$ and $\mathscr{B}$ for $\mathscr{D}$) satisfy condition (i) of TM 7.6. Then condition i and the definition of B imply that $\mathscr{B}$ is a structure for L. Moreover, condition i, the definition of B, and TM 7.5 imply that $\mathscr{B}$ is a substructure of $\mathscr{D}$. From this, condition i, and TM 7.6 it follows that $\mathscr{D}$ is an elementary extension of $\mathscr{B}$.

To demonstrate that $\mathscr{D}$ and $\mathscr{B}$ satisfy condition i of TM 7.6, we proceed as follows. Let A be a wff of L with exactly $m + 1$ free variables, $x_0, \ldots, x_m$; let a_i, $i = 0, \ldots, m - 1$, be individuals in B with names k_i, $i = 0, \ldots, m - 1$; and let $b \in |\mathscr{D}|$ with name k_b be such that $\mathscr{D}(A_{x_0,\ldots,x_m}(k_0, \ldots, k_{m-1}, k_b)) = \mathrm{t}$. Then there is an n and an $a \in B_{n+1}$ with name k_a such that $(a_0, \ldots, a_{m-1}) \in B_n$ and $\mathscr{D}(A_{x_0,\ldots,x_m}(k_0, \ldots, k_{m-1}, k_a)) = \mathrm{t}$. Since $a \in B_{n+1}$, $a \in B$, and we have shown that $\mathscr{B}$ and $\mathscr{D}$ satisfy condition i of TM 7.6.

The preceeding theorem demonstrates that two elementarily equivalent structures need not be isomorphic. However, it is a fact that two elementarily equivalent structures have isomorphic extensions—see TM 7.8.

TM 7.8 Let $\mathscr{D}$ and $\mathscr{B}$ be structures for L. They are elementarily equivalent if and only if they have isomorphic elementary extensions.

The sufficiency part of this theorem is easy to establish and its proof is left to the reader. We shall prove the necessity half of the theorem in the appendix.

If $\mathscr{D}$ is a structure for L, $\mathscr{D}$ is elementarily equivalent to $\mathscr{D}$. Also if $\mathscr{D}$ and $\mathscr{A}$ are structures for L such that $\mathscr{D}$ is elementarily equivalent to $\mathscr{A}$, then $\mathscr{A}$

is elementarily equivalent to $\mathscr{D}$. Finally, if $\mathscr{D}$, $\mathscr{A}$, and $\mathscr{B}$ are structures for L such that $\mathscr{D}$ is elementarily equivalent to $\mathscr{A}$ and $\mathscr{A}$ is elementarily equivalent to $\mathscr{B}$, then $\mathscr{D}$ is elementarily equivalent to $\mathscr{B}$. Hence the relation of elementary equivalence among structures for L is an equivalence relation that partitions all structures for L into equivalence classes. This partition is, in general, coarser than the partition induced by the relation of being isomorphic. One consequence is described in TM 7.9.

TM 7.9 Let $T(\Gamma)$ be a consistent first-order theory with language L_Γ. Then $T(\Gamma)$ is complete if and only if any two models of $T(\Gamma)$ are elementarily equivalent.

This theorem is easy to prove. Observe first that in a complete theory a closed formula is either a theorem or the negation of a theorem. Also a theorem is valid in all models of the theory. Hence, if $T(\Gamma)$ is complete, if B is a closed wff in L_Γ, and if $\mathscr{D}$ and $\mathscr{A}$ are structures in $M(\Gamma)$, then $\mathscr{D}(B) = \mathscr{A}(B)$. Conversely, if $\mathscr{D}(B) = \mathscr{A}(B)$ for any closed wff B in L_Γ and any pair of structures for L_Γ in $M(\Gamma)$, then $T(\Gamma)$ must be complete. Otherwise we could find a closed wff A in L_Γ and two structures $\mathscr{D}$ and $\mathscr{A}$ such that the following hold: not $A \in C_n(\Gamma)$, $T(\Gamma, A)$ is consistent, $\mathscr{D} \in M(\Gamma)$, $\mathscr{A} \in M(\Gamma, A)$, $\mathscr{D}(A) = \text{f}$, and $\mathscr{A}(A) = \text{t}$.

The idea of elementarily equivalent structures has many interesting applications. I will conclude this chapter by giving an example of these applications. The example concerns the structures η, η', and η^* described in E 7.8. By construction, η and η' are elementarily equivalent relative to L_P; i.e., any closed wff B in L_P is true in η if and only if it is true in η'. According to E 7.8, η' and η^* are isomorphic and hence elementarily equivalent with respect to L_P. Consequently, η and η^* are elementarily equivalent as well. In E 7.10 I use this equivalence with respect to L_P of η and η^* to establish several astounding characteristics of $|\eta^*|$.

E 7.10 Let η and η^* be as described in E 7.8 and let $a = \eta^*(\alpha)$, where α is the constant in the axioms of $T(NS)$. Then $|\eta| \subset |\eta^*|$ by construction. Moreover, for all $n \in |\eta|$, $n < a$. To establish this inequality, note first that the closed wff in L_P,

(i) $(\forall x)(\forall y)[[x < y] \vee [[x = y] \vee [y < x]]]$

is true in η and hence in η^*; i.e., $<$ orders the individuals in both $|\eta|$ and $|\eta^*|$. Next note that, for all $n \in |\eta|$, the closed wff in L_P,

(ii) $(\forall x)[[x < k_n] \supset [[x = 0] \vee [[x = k_1] \vee [\ldots[x = k_{n-1}]\ldots]]]]$

is true in η and hence in η^*. Since not $a \in |\eta|$, it follows from (i) that either $a < n$ or $n < a$ and from (ii) that not $a < n$. Hence $n < a$ for all $n \in |\eta|$, as was to be shown.

The preceding observations imply that $|\eta|$ is an initial segment of $|\eta^*|$. To figure out what $(|\eta^*| - |\eta|)$ looks like, observe that the closed wff in L_P,

(iii) $(\forall x)[(\exists z)[S(x) = z] \wedge [\sim[x = 0] \supset (\exists y)[S(y) = x]]]$

is true in η and hence in η^*. Consequently, the set of b such that $b = a \pm n$ for some $n \in |\eta|$ is a subset of $|\eta^*|$. Denote this set by $N(a)$ and observe that, if k, $l \in |\eta|$ and not $k = l$, then $N(ka) \cap N(la) = \varnothing$. In particular, $|\eta| \cap N(ka) = \varnothing$ for all $k \geqslant 1$. Next note that the closed wff

(iv) $(\forall x)(\exists y)[[(y + y) = x] \vee [(y + y) = S(x)]]$

belongs to L_P and is true in η. Hence (iv) is also true in η^*. This can be used to establish the following facts: If b and c are elements of $|\eta^*|$, then either $N(b) = N(c)$ or $N(b) \cap N(c) = \varnothing$. Moreover, if $N(b) \cap N(c) = \varnothing$ and $b < c$, there is a $d \in |\eta^*|$ such that $b < d < c$ and $N(d)$ is disjoint from both $N(b)$ and $N(c)$. Simple proofs of these assertions are given in Boolos and Jeffrey 1974 (p. 196).

7.4 Concluding Remarks

In chapter 6 we used a semantic concept, model, to characterize two syntactic concepts, consistency and logical consequence. The results we obtained showed that our predicate calculus is complete in the following sense: PLA 1–PLA 7, together with PRI 1 and PRI 2, suffice for the determination of all the logical consequences $C_n(\Gamma)$ of any consistent collection of wffs, Γ.

In this chapter we used two semantic relations, isomorphism and elementary equivalence of structures, to characterize a syntactical concept, completeness of theories. A first-order theory $T(\Gamma)$ with a consistent collection of nonlogical axioms Γ is complete if there is no closed wff A so that neither A nor $\sim A$ belongs to $C_n(\Gamma)$. We related the idea of the completeness of $T(\Gamma)$ to properties of two equivalence relations among structures of L_Γ, one consisting of disjoint classes of isomorphic structures, the other consisting of disjoint classes of elementarily equivalent structures. For example, we observed that $T(\Gamma)$ is complete if and only if the models of $T(\Gamma)$ belong to one and the same class of elementarily equivalent structures. We also observed that if all the models of $T(\Gamma)$ have universes with infinitely many individuals, and if the models with denumerably infinite universes belong to one and the same class of isomorphic structures, then $T(\Gamma)$ is complete.

The semantic idea of isomorphic structures differs in one significant respect from the idea of elementarily equivalent structures. Two structures of L_Γ are isomorphic if they satisfy certain purely mathematical relations;

i.e., there is a bijection of their universes relating their respective functions and predicates in the way described in equations 7.1 and 7.2 of section 7.2. Two structures of L_Γ are elementarily equivalent, however, only if any closed wff of L_Γ that is true in one structure is also true in the other. How different the two ideas are is discussed in TM 7.8.

At last we must point out that our discussion of $T(NS)$ in E 7.8–E 7.10 suggests the validity of a very interesting result of Skolem: *There is no collection of wffs in L_P that can provide a complete characterization of the natural numbers*; i.e., if K is any collection of wffs in L_P such that $T(K)$ is a consistent extension of $T(N)$, then there are models of $T(K)$ with countable universes that are not isomorphic to η (see Skolem 1933, pp. 73–82). To see why, suppose that η is a model of $T(K)$ and let $\tilde{\eta}$ be a model of $T(NS)$ with a denumerably infinite universe. The restriction of $\tilde{\eta}$ to L_P is a model of $T(K)$ that is not isomorphic to η. I shall have more to say about this in the next chapter.

7.5 Appendix

In this appendix I shall demonstrate that if $\mathscr{D}$ and $\mathscr{B}$ are elementarily equivalent structures for L, then they have isomorphic elementary extensions. The proof, the ideas of which I have learned from J. E. Fenstad and D. Norman, is obtained in several steps, in two of which we apply TM 6.14 and TM 6.10 to a first-order language that might have nondenumerably many constant symbols. We have stated and proved the theorems for languages with at most a denumerable infinity of nonlogical symbols. Proofs that are valid for the cases of relevance here can be found in Shoenfield (1967, pp. 33–34 and 43–48).

First a few definitions. Let $\mathscr{D} = (|\mathscr{D}|, N_{\mathscr{D}}, F^{\mathscr{D}}, G^{\mathscr{D}})$ and $\mathscr{B} = (|\mathscr{B}|, N_{\mathscr{B}}, F^{\mathscr{B}}, G^{\mathscr{B}})$ be elementarily equivalent structures for L. Next let

$$T = \{A \in L(\mathscr{D})\text{: } A \text{ is closed and } \mathscr{D}(A) = t\}$$

$$T' = \{A \in L(\mathscr{B})\text{: } A \text{ is closed and } \mathscr{B}(A) = t\}$$

and

$$\hat{T} = \{A \in \hat{L}(\mathscr{D})\text{: } A \text{ is a logical consequence of } T \text{ in } \hat{L}(\mathscr{D})\}$$

where $\hat{L}(\mathscr{D})$ is obtaned from $L(\mathscr{D})$ by adding the names in $N_{\mathscr{B}}$ as constants to the constants of $L(\mathscr{D})$. We can, without loss in generality, assume that the members of $N_{\mathscr{B}}$ are distinct from the constants of $L(\mathscr{D})$. Finally, let $T'' = \hat{T} \cup T'$; i.e., let T'' be the first-order theory whose language is $\hat{L}(\mathscr{D})$ and whose nonlogical axioms are the wffs in $\hat{T} \cup T'$.

I claim that T'' is consistent and shall prove it by contradiction. If T'' is inconsistent, then there exist closed wffs $A'_i \in L(\mathscr{B})$, $i = 1, \ldots, k$, such that $\mathscr{B}(A'_i) = t$, $i = 1, \ldots, k$, and such that

(i) $\hat{T} \vdash [\sim A'_1 \vee [\sim A'_2 \vee [\ldots[\sim A'_{k-1} \vee \sim A'_k]\ldots]]]$.

Now if that is so, we can use first TM 6.14 and then PRI 2 to establish

(ii) $T \vdash [\sim A_1 \vee [\sim A_2 \vee [\ldots[\sim A_{k-1} \vee \sim A_k]\ldots]]]^c$,

where A_i denotes the wff obtained from A'_i by substituting variables for the members of $N_{\mathscr{B}}$ that occur in A'_i.[1] Since the A_i in (ii) belong to L, it follows from (ii) and the elementary equivalence of $\mathscr{D}$ and $\mathscr{B}$ with respect to L that

(iii) $\mathscr{B}([\sim A_1 \vee [\sim A_2 \vee [\ldots[\sim A_{k-1} \vee \sim A_k]\ldots]]]^c) = t$.

But (iii) cannot be the case unless there is an i such that $1 \leqslant i \leqslant k$ and such that $\mathscr{B}(A'_i) = \text{f}$. This contradicts the assumption that $\mathscr{B}(A'_i) = \text{t}$ for all $i = 1, \ldots, k$.

From the consistency of T'' and TM 6.10, it follows that T'' has a model, i.e., that there exists a structure for $\hat{L}(\mathscr{D})$,

$$\mathscr{B}'' = (|\mathscr{B}''|, N_{\mathscr{B}''}, F^{\mathscr{B}''}, G^{\mathscr{B}''})$$

that is a model of T''. We shall demonstrate that we can choose $\mathscr{B}''$ such that the restriction of $\mathscr{B}''$ to L, which we denote by $\mathscr{B}''/L$, is an elementary extension of $\mathscr{B}$. To do that we observe first that if $i, j \in N_{\mathscr{B}}$, and $i \neq j$, then $\sim[i = j] \in T'$ and $\mathscr{B}''(i) \neq \mathscr{B}''(j)$. Consequently, by replacing $\mathscr{B}''$ by an isomorphic structure, we may assume that

(iv) $|\mathscr{B}| \subset |\mathscr{B}''|$ and $N_{\mathscr{B}} \subset N_{\mathscr{B}''}$

and

(v) if $i \in N_{\mathscr{B}}$, then $\mathscr{B}''(i)$ is the individual which i names.

Next we note that if $A \in L(\mathscr{B})$ is closed, $\mathscr{B}(A) = \text{t}$ only if $\mathscr{B}''(A) = \text{t}$. The converse is obviously also true. Hence we conclude that

(vi) $\mathscr{B}(A) = (\mathscr{B}''/L)(A)$ for every closed wff A of $L(\mathscr{B})$.

From conditions iv–vi and TM 7.5, it follows that $\mathscr{B}''/L$ is an elementary extension of $\mathscr{B}$.

To conclude the proof of the only-if part of TM 7.8 we now observe that if $i, j \in N_{\mathscr{D}}$, and $i \neq j$, then $\sim[i = j] \in \hat{T}$ and $\mathscr{B}''(i) \neq \mathscr{B}''(j)$. Consequently, we can find a model of T'', $\mathscr{B}'''$, that is isomorphic to $\mathscr{B}''$ and satisfies the conditions

(vii) $|\mathscr{D}| \subset |\mathscr{B}'''|$ and $N_{\mathscr{D}} \subset N_{\mathscr{B}'''}$;

and

(viii) if $i \in N_{\mathscr{D}}$, then $\mathscr{B}'''(i)$ is the individual which i names.

But if that is so and if $\mathscr{B}'''/L$ denotes the restriction of $\mathscr{B}'''$ to L, we find by arguments similar to those used to establish condition (vi), that

(ix) $\mathscr{D}(A) = (\mathscr{B}'''/L)(A)$ for every closed wff A of $L(\mathscr{D})$.

From conditions vii, viii, and ix and from TM 7.5, it follows that $\mathscr{B}'''/L$ is an elementary extension of $\mathscr{D}$. Since $\mathscr{B}''/L$ and $\mathscr{B}'''/L$ are isomorphic, that concludes the proof of the only-if part of TM 7.8.

8 The Axiomatic Method and Natural Numbers

In the preceding chapters we considered two sets of axioms for natural numbers, $T(N) = (\text{P}\,1, \ldots, \text{P}\,8, \text{N}A)$ and $T(P) \equiv T(\text{P}\,1, \ldots, \text{P}\,9)$. We observed that $T(P)$ is an extension of $T(N)$ and that P 9 is not a theorem schemata of $T(N)$. Yet η is a model of both $T(N)$ and $T(P)$. From this we conclude that there are true assertions about natural numbers that are not theorems of $T(N)$ and hence that $T(N)$ is incomplete.

In this chapter we show that $T(P)$ and any other (so-called) axiomatized, consistent extensions of $T(N)$ are incomplete. We also demonstrate that the consistency of $T(P)$ cannot be established as a theorem of $T(P)$. These results are due to K. Gödel. They reveal a startling limitation on the power of the axiomatic method.

8.1 Recursive Functions and Predicates

To delineate the class of consistent, axiomatized extensions of $T(N)$, we begin with a discussion of *recursive functions and predicates*. They are, respectively, functions from $|\eta|^n$ to $|\eta|$ and relations in $|\eta|$, with the interesting property that they are *calculable*. Specifically, if $f(\cdot)\colon |\eta|^n \to |\eta|$ is recursive, there is a method by which the value of $f(\cdot)$ at any $a \in |\eta|^n$ can be determined in a finite number of steps. Similarly, if $P \subset |\eta|^n$ is recursive, there is a method by which we can determine in a finite number of steps whether $P(a)$ or $\sim P(a)$ for any $a \in |\eta|^n$.

8.1.1 Recursive Functions

We define *recursive functions* inductively by the rules R 1–R 3.

R 1 The binary functions $+$ and $\cdot$ are recursive. So are the functions $K_<(\cdot)$ and $I_i^n(\cdot)$, where

$$K_{<}(a_1, a_2) = \begin{cases} 0 & \text{if } a_1 < a_2 \\ 1 & \text{if } a_2 \leqslant a_1 \end{cases}$$

and

$$I_i^n(a_1, \ldots, a_n) = a_i, \qquad 1 \leqslant i \leqslant n, \quad n \in |\eta|.$$

R 2 If $G(\cdot)\colon |\eta|^k \to |\eta|$ and $H_i(\cdot)\colon |\eta|^n \to |\eta|$, $i = 1, \ldots, k$, are recursive, and if $F(\cdot)\colon |\eta|^n \to |\eta|$ is defined by

$$F(a) = G(H_1(a), \ldots, H_k(a)), \qquad a \in |\eta|^n,$$

then $F(\cdot)$ is recursive.

R 3 If $G(\cdot)\colon |\eta|^{n+1} \to |\eta|$ is recursive, if for all $a \in |\eta|^n$, there is an $x \in |\eta|$ such that $G(a, x) = 0$, if $\mu(\cdot)$ is as defined in E 7.3, and if $F(\cdot)\colon |\eta|^n \to |\eta|$ is defined by

$$F(a) = \mu x(G(a, x) = 0), \qquad a \in |\eta|^n,$$

Then $F(\cdot)$ is recursive.

There are all sorts of recursive functions. For instance, every constant function is recursive. Moreover, all functions that have an explicit definition using only variables, symbols for recursive functions, and μ operators are recursive.

E 8.1 Suppose that $F(\cdot)\colon |\eta|^3 \to |\eta|$ is defined by

$$F(a, b, c) = G(H(b, c), a), \qquad (a, b, c) \in |\eta|^3,$$

where G and H are recursive. Then F is recursive. To see why, let $F_1(a, b, c) = a$; $F_2(a, b, c) = b$; $F_3(a, b, c) = c$; and $F_4(a, b, c) = H(F_2(a, b, c), F_3(a, b, c))$. Then F_1, F_2, and F_3 are recursive by R 1 and F_4 is recursive by R 2. Since

$$F(a, b, c) = G(F_4(a, b, c), F_1(a, b, c)),$$

F is recursive by R 2.

8.1.2 Gödel's β function

For the purposes of this chapter the most important recursive function is Gödel's β function. We assert its existence and describe its properties in TM 8.1.

TM 8.1 Let $\dot{-}$ be as defined in E 7.3. There is a binary recursive function $\beta(\cdot)\colon |\eta|^2 \to |\eta|$ such that, for all $(a, i) \in |\eta|^2$, $\beta(a, i) \leqslant a \dot{-} 1$, and such that, for any $(n + 1)$-tuple of natural numbers, $a_0, \ldots, a_n$, there is an $a \in |\eta|$ such that $\beta(a, i) = a_i$, $i = 0, 1, \ldots, n$.

This theorem sounds like magic and its proof is rather involved. (See Shoenfield 1967, pp. 115–116, for details.) Even so we can give an explicit definition of a function $\beta(\cdot)\colon |\eta|^2 \to |\eta|$ that has the properties ascribed to $\beta(\cdot)$ in TM 8.1. In this definition we use a recursive function,

$$\text{op}(a, b) = (((a + b)^2 + a) + 1), \qquad (a, b) \in |\eta|^2,$$

and a predicate, div$(\cdot)$, that satisfies

$$\text{div}(a, b) \equiv (\exists y)[[y \leqslant a] \wedge [a = by]],$$

and for each pair $(a, i) \in |\eta|^2$ we let

$$\beta(a, i) = \mu x([[x \leqslant a \dot{-} 1] \wedge (\exists y)(\exists z)[[[y < a] \wedge [z < a]] \wedge [[a = \text{op}(y, z)] \wedge \text{div}(y, (1 + (\text{op}(x, i) + 1) \cdot z))]]]).$$

Note that $\beta(\cdot)$ is not monotonic. Note also that, for any given sequence, $a_0, \ldots, a_n$, the a that satisfies $\beta(a, i) = a_i$ for $i = 0, \ldots, n$, is a very large number (see E 8.2).

E 8.2 Suppose that $n = 1$ *and that both* a_0 and a_1 equal 1. Then $a = 1722$. If $n = 2$, and if $a_0 = 2$, $a_1 = 1$, and $a_2 = 2$, then $a = 8{,}723{,}162$.

It is important that the reader not get hung up on the definition of $\beta(\cdot)$. Here the only thing that matters is that there is a function $\beta(\cdot)$ with the properties prescribed in TM 8.1. In the next subsection we shall demonstrate that the $\beta(\cdot)$ we defined is recursive. A proof that it also has the other required properties is given in Shoenfield 1967 (pp. 115–116).

8.1.3 Recursive Predicates

It is not obvious that the $\beta(\cdot)$ we defined is recursive. To show that it is, we must first say what we mean by a recursive predicate: An n-ary predicate P is recursive if and only if *the representing function of P,*

$$K_P(a) = \begin{cases} 0 & \text{if } P(a) \\ 1 & \text{if } \sim P(a) \end{cases}$$

is recursive. From this definition and from R 1–R 3, it follows easily that if $Q \subset |\eta|^k$ and $H_i(\cdot)\colon |\eta|^n \to |\eta|$, $i = 1, \ldots, k$, are recursive, and if $P \subset |\eta|^n$ is defined by $P(a) \equiv Q(H_1(a), \ldots, H_k(a))$, $a \in |\eta|^n$, then P is recursive. In fact, any predicate that has an explicit definition in terms of variables, symbols for recursive functions and predicates, and μ operators is recursive.

E 8.3 If P and Q are recursive predicates, it is easy to show that $\sim P$, $[P \supset Q]$, $[P \vee Q]$, and $[P \wedge Q]$ are recursive; e.g., $K_{\sim P}(a) = K_<(0, K_P(a))$ and $K_{P \supset Q}(a) = K_{\sim P}(a) \cdot K_Q(a)$. Since $<$ is recursive and since $\leqslant$ and $=$ can be given an explicit definition in terms of $\sim$ and $<$, it follows from the preceding observation that $\leqslant$ and $=$ also are recursive predicates.

If P is an $(n+1)$-ary recursive predicate, $(\exists x)P(a,x)$ and $(\forall x)P(a,x)$ need not be recursive. They are recursive, however, if the quantifiers can be restricted to finite intervals. Specifically, we have R 4.

R 4 Let R be an $(n+1)$-ary recursive predicate and let P and Q be defined by $P(a,z) \equiv (\exists x)[[x < a] \wedge R(z,x)]$ and $Q(a,z) \equiv (\forall x)[[x < a] \supset R(z,x)]$, where $z \in |\eta|^n$. Then P and Q are $(n+1)$-ary recursive predicates.

I shall show that $P(\cdot)$ is recursive and leave Q to the reader. To see why $P(\cdot)$ is recursive, we define $U(\cdot)$ by

$$U(a,z,x) \equiv [[[x < a] \wedge R(z,x)] \vee [x = a]], \qquad (a,z,x) \in |\eta|^{n+2}.$$

Then $U(\cdot)$ is an $(n+2)$-ary recursive predicate with the property that, for all pairs (a,z), there is an x such that $K_U(a,z,x) = 0$. Hence, by R 3, the $(n+1)$-ary function $G(\cdot)$, defined by

$$G(a,z) = \mu x(K_U(a,z,x) = 0),$$

is recursive. Furthermore, $P(a,z) \equiv G(a,z) < a$, which shows that $P(\cdot)$ is recursive.

By changing $[y \leqslant a]$ to $[y < a + 1]$, we can use the preceding results to show that $\mathrm{div}(\cdot)$ is recursive. But, if this is so, it is easy to see that the argument of $\mu x(\cdot)$ in the definition of $\beta(\cdot)$ is recursive. Moreover, for all pairs $(a,i) \in |\eta|^2$, there is an x that satisfies the argument of $\mu x(\cdot)$. (See Shoenfield 1967, pp. 115–116, for a proof.) From these facts and from R 3 (applied to the representing function of the argument of $\beta(\cdot)$), it follows that $\beta(\cdot)$ is recursive.

8.1.4 Sequence Numbers

Gödel used $\beta(\cdot)$ to assign sequence numbers to n-tuples of natural numbers and sequence numbers to assign expression numbers to the terms and wffs of a given axiomatized extension of $T(N)$.

To explicate the meaning of a sequence number, we define for each $n \in |\eta|$ a function, $\langle\cdot\rangle\colon |\eta|^n \to |\eta|$, by

$$\langle b_1,\ldots,b_n\rangle = \mu x([[\beta(x,0) = n] \wedge [[\beta(x,1) = b_1]\ldots \wedge [\beta(x,n) = b_n]\ldots]]),$$
$$(b_1,\ldots,b_n) \in |\eta|^n.$$

Then a is a *sequence number* if there is an $n \in |\eta|$ and an n-tuple $(a_1,\ldots,a_n)$

in $|\eta|^n$ such that $a = \langle a_1, \ldots, a_n \rangle$. For each n, the function $\langle \cdot \rangle$ is recursive since it is defined in terms of μ and $\beta(\cdot)$. Additionally, if a is a sequence number, a determines the values of n and the a_i via a family of recursive functions, $lh(\cdot)$ and $(\cdot)_i$, which we define as follows:

$$lh(a) = \beta(a, 0)$$

and

$$(a)_i = \beta(a, i), \qquad 1 \leqslant i \leqslant lh(a), \quad a \in |\eta|.$$

E 8.4 Look back at E 8.2 and observe that $\langle 1 \rangle = 1722$ and $\langle 1, 2 \rangle = 8{,}723{,}162$. Also $lh(1722) = 1$ and $(1722)_1 = 1$. Finally, $lh(8{,}723{,}162) = 2$, $(8{,}723{,}162)_1 = 1$, and $(8{,}723{,}162)_2 = 2$.

Above I defined a sequence number. Later we use L_P to talk about such numbers. For that purpose I now define the recursive predicate:

$$\text{seq}(a) \equiv (\forall x)[[x < a] \supset [\sim[lh(x) = lh(a)] \vee (\exists i)[[[i \leqslant lh(a)] \wedge [1 \leqslant i]] \wedge \sim[(x)_i = (a)_i]]]]].$$

Seq(a) asserts that a is a sequence number.

8.2 Expression Numbers

In this section we consider a theory T with first-order language L. We assume that L contains only finitely many function and predicate symbols and that $L_P \subset L$. We also assume that T is a consistent extension of $T(N)$. Our intention is to show how we can assign numbers to the terms and wffs of L so that L_P and $T(N)$ can be used to talk about the syntactic properties of T.

We begin by assigning the numbers 1, 3, 5, 7, 11, 13, 17, and 19 to the symbols (,), , [,], $\sim$, $\supset$, and $\forall$, respectively. Then we arrange the variables of L in alphabetical order, $x_1, x_2, \ldots$ and assign the number $2i$ to x_i. Finally, we assign arbitrary (but different) prime numbers to the function and predicate symbols of L, e.g., 23, 29, 31, 37, 41, and 43 to 0, $+$, $\cdot$, S, $=$, and $<$, respectively.

With the help of the preceding numbers and $\beta(\cdot)$, we assign *expression numbers* to the terms and wffs of L. We begin with terms. Let a be a term and suppose first that a is a constant or a variable. Then the expression number of a, which we denote by $\ulcorner a \urcorner$, is given by $\ulcorner a \urcorner = \langle \text{sn}(a) \rangle$, where sn$(a)$ designates the number assigned to a above. Suppose next that

$a = f(z_1, \ldots, z_n)$ and let sn(f) be the number assigned to f. Then $\ulcorner a \urcorner = \langle \text{sn}(f), 1, \ulcorner z_1 \urcorner, 5, \ldots, 5, \ulcorner z_n \urcorner, 3\rangle$, where $\ulcorner z_i \urcorner$ is the expression number of z_i, $i = 1, \ldots, n$. In this way the expression numbers of all terms are obtained by induction on the length of terms.

E 8.5 Suppose that a is the term $(x_1 + x_2)$; i.e., suppose that a is $+(x_1, x_2)$. Then

$\ulcorner a \urcorner = \langle 29, 1, \langle 2\rangle, 5, \langle 4\rangle, 3\rangle$.

If a is $(x_3 \cdot x_4)$, we write it as $\cdot(x_3, x_4)$ and give it the expression number $\langle 31, 1, \langle 6\rangle, 5, \langle 8\rangle, 3\rangle$. Similarly, if a is $S(x_{50})$, we give it the expression number $\langle 37, 1, \langle 100\rangle, 3\rangle$.

The numbers which we assign to the wffs of L are determined by induction on the length of the formulas. We begin with atomic formulas. If A is $P(z_1, \ldots, z_n)$, where P is an n-ary predicate and the z_i are terms, we assign the expression number $\ulcorner A \urcorner = \langle \text{sn}(P), 1, \ulcorner z_1 \urcorner, 5, \ldots, 5, \ulcorner z_n \urcorner, 3\rangle$ to A, where sn(P) is the number assigned to P above.

E 8.6 Suppose that A is the atomic formula $[z = z]$. We write it as $=(z, z)$ and assign the number $\langle 41, 1, \ulcorner z \urcorner, 5, \ulcorner z \urcorner, 3\rangle$ to it. Similarly, if A is the atomic formula $[z_1 < z_2]$, we write it as $<(z_1, z_2)$ and give it the number $\langle 43, 1, \ulcorner z_1 \urcorner, 5, \ulcorner z_2 \urcorner, 3\rangle$.

If A is a wff with expression number $\ulcorner A \urcorner$, we give $\sim A$ the expression number $\langle 13, \ulcorner A \urcorner\rangle$. And if B is another wff with expression number $\ulcorner B \urcorner$, we assign $\langle 7, \ulcorner A \urcorner, 17, \ulcorner B \urcorner, 11\rangle$ to $[A \supset B]$ and $\langle 7, \ulcorner A \urcorner, 17, \langle 7, \ulcorner B \urcorner, 17, \ulcorner A \urcorner, 11\rangle, 11\rangle$ to $[A \supset [B \supset A]]$. Finally, if C is a wff with a free variable x, we assign $\langle 1, 19, \ulcorner x \urcorner, 3, \ulcorner C \urcorner\rangle$ to $(\forall x)C$.

In order to use L_P and the preceding numbers to talk about the syntactic properties of T, we must introduce several new functions and predicates. One of the predicates is vble$(\cdot)$:

$$\text{vble}(a) \equiv [[a = \langle (a)_1\rangle] \wedge (\exists y)[[y < a] \wedge [(a)_1 = 2y]]].$$

Vble(a) asserts that $a = \ulcorner x \urcorner$ for some variable x. One of the functions is num$(\cdot)$, which we define inductively by

$$\text{num}(0) = \langle 23\rangle \text{ and } \text{num}(S(a)) = \langle 37, 1, \text{num}(a), 3\rangle.$$

For a given a, num(a) designates the expression number of the term in which S is applied a times in succession to 0; i.e., $S(S(\ldots(S(0))\ldots))$. Since vble$(\cdot)$ is defined in terms of recursive functions and predicates, it is recursive. So is num$(\cdot)$, as can be seen from the proposition R 5.

R 5 Let $G(\cdot)\colon |\eta|^n \to |\eta|$ and $H(\cdot)\colon |\eta|^{n+2} \to |\eta|$ be recursive functions, and define $F(\cdot)\colon |\eta|^{n+1} \to |\eta|$ inductively by

$F(0, b) = G(b)$

and

$F(a + 1, b) = H(F(a, b), a, b).$

Then $F(\cdot)$ is recursive.

To prove this proposition, I shall use arguments that I have learned from G. Boolos and R. Jeffrey (1974, p. 166). Let $F(\cdot)$, $G(\cdot)$, and $H(\cdot)$ be as described in R 5. Then the properties of $\beta(\cdot)$ imply that, for any $k \in |\eta|$, there is a $c \in |\eta|$ such that

$$\beta(c, 0) = k + 1 \quad \text{and} \quad \beta(c, j + 1) = F(j, b), \qquad j \leqslant k.$$

Consequently, if we define $P \subset |\eta|^{n+2}$ by

$$P(b, k, c) \equiv [[\beta(c, 0) = k + 1] \wedge [[\beta(c, 1) = G(b)]$$
$$\wedge (\forall j)[[j < k] \supset [\beta(c, j + 2) = H(\beta(c, j + 1), j, b)]]]],$$

then P is well defined and, by E 8.3, R 2, and R 4, recursive. Moreover, for every pair $(b, k) \in |\eta|^{n+1}$, there is a $c \in |\eta|$ such that $P(b, k, c)$. From this and from R 3, it follows that if $d(\cdot)\colon |\eta|^{n+1} \to |\eta|$ is defined by

$$d(b, k) = \mu x(K_P(b, k, x) = 0),$$

then $d(\cdot)$ is well defined and recursive. In addition, for all $(k, b) \in |\eta| \times |\eta|^n$,

$$F(k, b) = \beta(d(b, k), I_{n+1}^{n+1}(b, k + 1)).$$

But if that is so, then R 1, R 2, and the recursiveness of $d(\cdot)$ and $\beta(\cdot)$ imply that $F(\cdot)$ is recursive as well.

Besides vble$(\cdot)$, we must introduce predicates such as $\text{term}_T(a)$, $\text{for}_T(a)$, $\text{nax}_T(a)$, and $\text{ax}_T(a)$. The first asserts that $a = \ulcorner b \urcorner$ for some term b. The other three assert, respectively, that $a = \ulcorner A \urcorner$ for some wf formula A, for some nonlogical axiom A of T, and for some axiom A of T. The first two are recursive. The last two need not be. When $\text{nax}_T(\cdot)$ is recursive, T is said to be *axiomatized*. Obviously T is axiomatized when it is developed from a finite number of axioms. Hence $T(N)$ is axiomatized. So is $T(P)$ since it is possible to give an explicit definition of the set of expression numbers of induction axioms which demonstrates that this set is recursive.

Also needed are predicates such as $MP(a, b, c)$ and $\text{RG}(a, b)$, which we define by

$$\text{MP}(a, b, c) \equiv b = \langle 7, a, 17, c, 11 \rangle$$

and

$\mathrm{RG}(a, b) \equiv b = \langle 1, 19, \ulcorner x \urcorner, 3, a \rangle.$

The first asserts that, if $a = \ulcorner A \urcorner$, $b = \ulcorner [A \supset C] \urcorner$, and $c = \ulcorner C \urcorner$ for some wffs A and C, then C can be inferred by Modus Ponens from A. The latter insists that b is the expression number of a formula that can be inferred by the Rule of Generalization from the formula whose expression number is a. Both these predicates are recursive.

If we assign the number $\langle \ulcorner u_1 \urcorner, \ldots, \ulcorner u_n \urcorner \rangle$ to a sequence of wffs, $u_1, \ldots u_n$, then the preceding predicates can be used to define

$$\begin{aligned} \mathrm{prf}_T(a) \equiv [&\mathrm{seq}(a) \wedge [\sim [lh(a) = 0] \wedge (\forall i)[[[i \leqslant lh(a)] \wedge [1 \leqslant i]] \\ &\supset [\mathrm{for}_T((a)_i) \wedge [\mathrm{ax}_T((a)_i) \vee (\exists j)[[j < i] \\ &\wedge [\mathrm{MP}((a)_j, \langle 7, (a)_j, 17, (a)_i, 11 \rangle, (a)_i) \\ &\vee \mathrm{RG}((a)_j, (a)_i)]]]]]]] \end{aligned}$$

and

$$\mathrm{pr}_T(a, b) \equiv [\mathrm{prf}_T(b) \wedge [a = (b)_{lh(b)}]].$$

The first of these insists that a is the expression number of a proof and the latter insists that if $a = \ulcorner A \urcorner$ for some wff A, then b is the expression number of a proof of A. Whenever T is axiomatized, these two predicates are recursive. However, the predicate $\mathrm{thm}_T(\cdot)$, defined by

$$\mathrm{thm}_T(a) \equiv (\exists x)\mathrm{pr}_T(a, x),$$

need not be recursive since $\exists$ is not restricted to a finite interval. $\mathrm{Thm}_T(a)$ asserts that a is the expression number of a theorem of T.

8.3 Representable Functions and Predicates

In the next section we shall use the predicates of the last section to show that any consistent axiomatized extension of $T(N)$ is incomplete. One difficulty in doing this is the fact that these predicates do not belong to L_P. We can circumvent the difficulty by finding ways to represent them in L_P. Therefore in this section we shall discuss the idea of functions and predicates which are representable in L_P. Throughout our discussion, $\vdash B$ asserts that B is a theorem of $T(N)$.

Let $k_0, k_1, k_2, \ldots$ denote the terms 0, $S(0)$, $S(S(0))$, $\ldots$ and let $x_1, \ldots, x_n$ and y be distinct variables. Also let A be a wff of L_P and let $F(\cdot)$ be an n-ary function. Then A with $x_1, \ldots, x_n, y$ *represents* $F(\cdot)$ if, for every $(a_1, \ldots, a_n) \in |\eta|^n$,

$\vdash [A_{x_1,\ldots,x_n}(k_{a_1},\ldots,k_{a_n}) \equiv [y = k_b]]$,

where $b = F(a_1,\ldots,a_n)$. If $G(\cdot)$ is n-ary and if there is a wff A and distinct variables $x_1, \ldots, x_n$ and y such that A with $x_1, \ldots, x_n, y$ represents $G(\cdot)$, then $G(\cdot)$, is *representable.*

Next let $P(\cdot)$ be an n-ary predicate, let $x_1, \ldots, x_n$ be distinct variables, and let A be a wff of L_P. Then A with $x_1, \ldots, x_n$ *represents* $P(\cdot)$ if for every $(a_1,\ldots,a_n) \in |\eta|^n$

$P(a_1,\ldots,a_n)$ implies $\vdash A_{x_1,\ldots,x_n}(k_{a_1},\ldots,k_{a_n})$

and

$\sim P(a_1,\ldots,a_n)$ implies $\vdash \sim A_{x_1,\ldots,x_n}(k_{a_1},\ldots,k_{a_n})$.

If $Q(\cdot)$ is an n-ary predicate and if there are a wff A and distinct variables $x_1, \ldots, x_n$ such that A with $x_1, \ldots, x_n$ represents $Q(\cdot)$, then $Q(\cdot)$ is *representable.*

E 8.7 In this example we show that $[x = y]$ with x and y represents $=$. From PLA 6 it follows that

$m = n$ implies $\vdash [k_m = k_n]$.

To show that $\vdash \sim[k_m = k_n]$ when $n \neq m$, we suppose first that $n < m$ and argue by induction on n. If $n = 0$, then P 1 implies that $\vdash \sim[k_m = k_n]$. If $n > 0$, then it follows from P 2 that $\vdash [[k_m = k_n] \supset [k_{m-1} = k_{n-1}]]$. Consequently by PLA 3, $\vdash [\sim[k_{m-1} = k_{n-1}] \supset \sim[k_m = k_n]]$. But if that is so, then the induction hypothesis, $\vdash \sim[k_{m-1} = k_{n-1}]$, and Modus Ponens imply that $\vdash \sim[k_m = k_n]$. Thus $n < m$ implies $\vdash \sim[k_m = k_n]$. By symmetry we obtain for all n and m that

$m \neq n$ implies $\vdash \sim[k_m = k_n]$.

Finally, let $F(\cdot)$ be an n-ary function; let a be a term of L_P, and let $x_1, \ldots, x_n$ be distinct variables. Then a with $x_1, \ldots, x_n$ *represents* $F(\cdot)$ if

$\vdash [a_{x_1,\ldots,x_n}(k_{a_1},\ldots,k_{a_n}) = k_b]$,

where $b = F(a_1,\ldots,a_n)$. In that case, if y is a new variable, $[y = a]$ with $x_1, \ldots, x_n, y$ represents $F(\cdot)$.

E 8.8 In this example we shall show that the term $(x + y)$ with x and y represents $+$. To do that we must show that

$\vdash [(k_m + k_n) = k_{m+n}]$.

We use induction on n. When $n = 0$, the assertion follows from P 3. Suppose the assertion is true for some n. Then TM 5.4 implies that

$\vdash [S(k_m + k_n) = k_{m+n+1}]$.

This, TM 5.2, and P 4 imply that

$\vdash [(k_m + k_{n+1}) = k_{m+n+1}]$,

which shows that the assertion is true for $n + 1$.

The importance of representable functions and predicates for our purposes is explicated in TM 8.2.

TM 8.2 Every recursive function and predicate is representable.

The proof of this theorem is obtained in four steps. I shall carry out the first two, leave the third to the reader, and suggest that the reader consult Shoenfield (1967, pp. 129–130) for the details needed to complete the fourth step.

In the first step of the proof of TM 8.2, we shall establish the auxiliary theorem TM 8.3.

TM 8.3 Let P be an n-ary predicate. Then P is representable if and only if $K_P(\cdot)$ is representable.

Suppose that A with $x_1, \ldots, x_n$ represents P and let B be

$[[A \wedge [y = k_0]] \vee [\sim A \wedge [y = k_1]]]$.

Then B with $x_1, \ldots, x_n, y$ represents $K_P(\cdot)$. To see why, suppose that

$K_P(a_1, \ldots, a_n) = 0$.

Then $P(a_1, \ldots, a_n)$ and $\vdash A_{x_1,\ldots,x_n}(k_{a_1}, \ldots, k_{a_n})$. From this, from TM 4.5, and from obvious arguments, it follows that

$\vdash [B_{x_1,\ldots,x_n}(k_{a_1}, \ldots, k_{a_n}) \equiv [y = k_0]]$.

The same reasoning applies when $K_P(a_1, \ldots, a_n) = 1$.

To establish the converse, we suppose that $K_P(\cdot)$ can be represented by A and $x_1, \ldots, x_n$ and y and procede to demonstrate that $A_y(k_0)$ with $x_1, \ldots, x_n$ represents $P(\cdot)$. If $P(a_1, \ldots, a_n)$, then $K_P(a_1, \ldots, a_n) = 0$. Hence $\vdash [A_{x_1,\ldots,x_n}(k_{a_1}, \ldots, k_{a_n}) \equiv [y = k_0]]$. By substituting k_0 for y and applying PLA 6 and TM 4.5, we find that

$\vdash A_{x_1,\ldots,x_n,y}(k_{a_1}, \ldots, k_{a_n}, k_0)$.

With obvious modifications, the same arguments apply when $\sim P(a_1, \ldots, a_n)$ and $K_P(a_1, \ldots, a_n) = 1$.

To fix these ideas, consider E 8.9.

E 8.9 In this example we shall demonstrate that $[x < y]$ with x and y represents $<$. To do that we must prove that

$\vdash [k_m < k_n]$, when $m < n$

and

$\vdash \sim [k_m < k_n]$, when $n \leqslant m$.

We proceed by induction on n. When $n = 0$, $m < n$ cannot happen and $\vdash \sim [k_m < k_0]$ follows from P 7. Suppose that the two assertions are true for some n. Then, by P 8,

$\vdash [[k_m < k_{n+1}] \equiv [[k_m < k_n] \vee [k_m = k_n]]]$.

Consequently, if $m < n + 1$ and hence $m < n$ or $m = n$, we can apply the induction hypothesis, PLA 6, and T 4.10 to conclude that

$\vdash [k_m < k_{n+1}]$ if $m < n + 1$.

With obvious modifications the same arguments can be used to show that

$\vdash \sim [k_m < k_{n+1}]$ when $(n + 1) \leqslant m$.

The preceding results demonstrate that $[x < y]$ with x and y represents $<$. From this and TM 8.3, it follows that $K_<(\cdot)$ is representable.

The validity of TM 8.3 implies that to prove TM 8.2 we need only demonstrate that the recursive functions are representable. To do that we proceed by induction on recursive functions. We begin with the functions that satisfy R 1.

In E 8.8 we showed that the binary function $+$ is representable. Similar arguments suffice to show that the binary function $\cdot$ is representable as well. In E 8.9 we demonstrated that $K_<(\cdot)$ is representable. Hence it remains to show that $I_i^n(\cdot)$ is representable. To do that just let A be $[[x_1 = x_1] \wedge [[x_2 = x_2] \wedge \cdots \wedge [[x_n = x_n] \wedge [y = x_i]]\ldots]]$. Then A with $x_1, \ldots, x_n$ and y represents $I_i^n(\cdot)$.

The preceding results complete the first two steps in the proof of TM 8.2. In the next two steps we must show that the functions described in R 2 and R 3 are representable. For brevity's sake I leave those steps to the reader. The first is not too difficult, but the second is a bit involved. The necessary details to complete both steps can be found in Shoenfield 1967 (pp. 129–130).

8.4 Incompleteness of Consistent, Axiomatized Extensions of $T(N)$

In this section we show that any consistent, axiomatized extension of $T(N)$ is incomplete. Throughout our discussion we let T denote a given extension of $T(N)$ and we let L denote its first-order language. We also assume that L has a finite set of nonlogical symbols.

To establish the incompleteness of T we make use of recursive function, $\mathrm{sub}(\cdot)\colon |\eta|^3 \to |\eta|$, with the property that $\mathrm{sub}(\ulcorner a \urcorner, \ulcorner x \urcorner, \ulcorner b \urcorner) = \ulcorner a_x(b) \urcorner$ and $\mathrm{sub}(\ulcorner A \urcorner, \ulcorner x \urcorner, \ulcorner b \urcorner) = \ulcorner A_x(b) \urcorner$ for any term a and wff A of L. If L has only unary and binary function and predicate symbols, $\mathrm{sub}(\cdot)$ can be defined as follows:

$$\mathrm{sub}(a, b, c) = \begin{cases} c \text{ if } [\mathrm{vble}(a) \wedge [a = b]] \\ \langle (a)_1, 1, \mathrm{sub}((a)_3, b, c), 3 \rangle \text{ if } a = \langle (a)_1, 1, (a)_3, 3 \rangle \\ \langle (a)_1, 1, \mathrm{sub}((a_3), b, c), 5, \mathrm{sub}((a_5), b, c), 3 \rangle \\ \quad \text{if } a = \langle (a)_1, 1, (a)_3, 5, (a)_5, 3 \rangle \\ \langle 13, \mathrm{sub}(d, b, c) \rangle \text{ if } a = \langle 13, d \rangle \\ \langle 7, \mathrm{sub}(d, b, c), 17, \mathrm{sub}(e, b, c), 11 \rangle \text{ if} \\ \quad a = \langle 7, d, 17, e, 11 \rangle, \text{ and} \\ \langle 1, 19, (a)_3, 3, \mathrm{sub}((a)_5, b, c) \rangle \text{ if } a = \langle 1, 19, (a)_3, 3, (a)_5 \rangle \\ \quad \text{and } {\sim}[b = (a)_3] \\ a \text{ otherwise.} \end{cases}$$

For more general languages, the definition of $\mathrm{sub}(\cdot)$ is more complicated. However, since the scheme we use to define $\mathrm{sub}(\cdot)$ for languages such as L_P is general, we can without fear assume the existence of $\mathrm{sub}(\cdot)$ for any relevant language L.

In addition to $\mathrm{sub}(\cdot)$, we make use of two interesting predicates, $P(\cdot)$ and $Q(\cdot)$, which we define as follows:

$$P(a, b) \equiv \mathrm{thm}_T(\mathrm{sub}(b, \ulcorner z \urcorner, \mathrm{num}(a))),$$

$$Q(a) \equiv {\sim}\mathrm{thm}_T(\mathrm{sub}(a, \ulcorner z \urcorner, \mathrm{num}(a))).$$

The first asserts that the formula whose expression number equals $\mathrm{sub}(b, \ulcorner z \urcorner, \mathrm{num}(a))$ is a theorem in T; e.g., if $b = \ulcorner A \urcorner$ and $c = \ulcorner A_z(k_a) \urcorner$, then $\mathrm{thm}_T(c)$ if and only if $A_z(k_a)$ is a theorem in T. The second predicate asserts that the wff whose expression number is $\mathrm{sub}(a, \ulcorner z \urcorner, \mathrm{num}(a))$ is not a theorem in T; e.g., if $a = \ulcorner A \urcorner$, then $Q(a)$ if and only if $A_z(k_a)$ is not a theorem in T.

TM 8.4 is a fact.

TM 8.4 If T is a consistent, axiomatized extension of $T(N)$, then $\mathrm{thm}_T(\cdot)$ is recursive if T is complete.

To see why, suppose that T is a consistent, axiomatized, and complete extension of $T(N)$, and let $F(\cdot)\colon |\eta|^2 \to |\eta|$ and $G(\cdot)\colon |\eta| \to |\eta|$, be defined by

$$F(0, a) = a,$$

$$F(n + 1, a) = \langle 1, 19, \langle 2n + 2\rangle, 3, F(n, a)\rangle,$$

and

$$G(a) = F(a, a).$$

Then R 5 implies that $F(\cdot)$ is recursive. Hence $G(\cdot)$ is recursive. Moreover, if $a = \ulcorner A \urcorner$ for some wff A, it is easy to see that

$$G(a) = \ulcorner (\forall x_a) \cdots (\forall x_1) A \urcorner.$$

Next observe that if $a = \ulcorner A \urcorner$ for some wff A and if x_1 is a free variable of A, then $i < \ulcorner x_i \urcorner < \ulcorner A \urcorner = a$. From this it follows that $(\forall x_a) \cdots (\forall x_1) A$ is closed and hence, by PRI 2, PLA 5, and the completeness of T, that

$$\sim \text{thm}_T(a) \equiv [\sim \text{for}_T(a) \vee \text{thm}_T(\langle 13, G(a)\rangle)]$$

$$\equiv (\exists x)[\sim \text{for}_T(a) \vee \text{pr}_T(\langle 13, G(a)\rangle, x)].$$

But if that is so, we can define a function $H(\cdot)\colon |\eta| \to |\eta|$ by

$$H(a) = \mu x([\text{pr}_T(a, x) \vee [\sim \text{for}_T(a) \vee \text{pr}_T(\langle 13, G(a)\rangle, x)]],$$

observe that $H(\cdot)$ is well defined and recursive, and show that

$$\text{thm}_T(a) \equiv \text{pr}_T(a, H(a)).$$

Evidently, $\text{pr}_T(a, H(a))$ only if $(\exists x)\text{pr}_T(a, x)$. Hence,

$$\text{pr}_T(a, H(a)) \text{ only if } \text{thm}_T(a).$$

Conversely, if $\sim \text{pr}_T(a, H(a))$, then $[\sim \text{for}_T(a) \vee \text{pr}_T(\langle 13, G(a)\rangle, H(a)))]$ and $\sim \text{thm}_T(a)$. Consequently, by PLA 3,

$$\text{thm}_T(a) \text{ only if } \text{pr}_T(a, H(a)),$$

and the required material equivalence is established. To conclude the proof it suffices now to note that since $H(\cdot)$ and $\text{pr}_T(\cdot)$ are recursive, $\text{thm}_T(\cdot)$ must be recursive as well.

Since $\text{sub}(\cdot)$ and $\text{num}(\cdot)$ are recursive, it follows from TM 8.4 that T can be ascertained to be incomplete by showing that $Q(\cdot)$ is not recursive. This we do in two steps. First let z be the first variable alphabetically, let $\vdash_T A$

assert that A is a theorem of T, and let $E(A)$ denote the set of natural numbers n which satisfy $\vdash_T A_z(k_n)$. Then observe that if T is inconsistent, $E(A)$ contains all natural numbers. Moreover, if T is consistent, every recursive set is an $E(A)$. To see why, let $\underline{A}$ be a recursive set and choose A so that A with z represents $\underline{A}$. If $n \in \underline{A}$, $\vdash A_z(k_n)$, and hence $\vdash_T A_z(k_n)$. Consequently, $n \in E(A)$. If $\sim[n \in \underline{A}]$, then $\vdash \sim A_z(k_n)$, and hence $\vdash_T \sim A_z(k_n)$. Since T is consistent, $\sim[n \in E(A)]$.

Next, for each b let $P_b(a) = P(a, b)$. Whenever $b = \ulcorner A \urcorner$ for some wff A, $P_b(\cdot)$ is $E(A)$. In addition, $Q(b) = \sim P_b(b)$. If $Q(\cdot)$ is recursive, there is a formula A such that A with z represents $Q(\cdot)$. Let $b = \ulcorner A \urcorner$ as above and note that if $n \in E(A)$, then $Q(n)$ and $P_b(n)$. Suppose that $\sim[b \in E(A)]$. Then $\sim P_b(b)$ and $Q(b)$. But $Q(b)$ implies that $b \in E(A)$, a contradiction. If $b \in E(A)$, then $P_b(b)$ and $Q(b)$. The latter implies $\sim P_b(b)$, another contradiction. From the two contradictions, we conclude that $Q(\cdot)$ cannot be recursive, and that T is incomplete—see TM 8.5.

TM 8.5 (Rosser and Gödel) Let T be a first-order theory with language L and assume that $L_P \subset L$ and that L contains only finitely many nonlogical symbols. If T is a consistent, axiomatized extension of $T(N)$, T is incomplete.[1]

One interesting corollary of this theorem is as follows: *If T is any consistent, axiomatized extension of $T(N)$ with language L_P and intended model η, then there are true assertions about natural numbers that are not theorems of T.* To see why, let $\mathrm{Th}(\eta)$ denote the first-order theory whose language is L_P and whose axioms are the wffs in L_P that are valid in η. Then $\mathrm{Th}(\eta)$ is complete. A theorem of T is also a theorem of $\mathrm{Th}(\eta)$. Since T is incomplete by TM 8.5, T, is not equivalent to $\mathrm{Th}(\eta)$. Consequently, there must be at least one axiom of $\mathrm{Th}(\eta)$ which is not a theorem of T; i.e., there is a wff in L_P that is valid in η but is not a theorem of T.

8.5 The Consistency of *T(P)*

We have shown that any consistent, axiomatized extension of $T(N)$, such as $T(P)$, is incomplete. In this section we show that the consistency of $T(P)$ cannot be demonstrated within $T(P)$. Specifically, we show that the assertion "$T(P)$ is consistent" can be formulated as a wff in the language of $T(P)$. This formula is satisfied by the standard model of $T(P)$, η. Yet we show that it is not a theorem of $T(P)$.

To formulate "$T(P)$ is consistent" as a wff in L_P we must first show that the recursive functions and predicates discussed in the preceding sections can be introduced in L_P. For that purpose we make use of the idea of a *recursive extension* of $T(P)$. Such an extension is an extension by definition of $T(P)$ in which the defining axioms for predicate symbols are open and the defining axioms for function symbols are of the form shown in PD, where A is an open wff in which no variables other than $x_1, \ldots, x_n$ and y are free.[2]

PD $[[z = f(x_1, \ldots, x_n)] \equiv [A_y(z) \wedge (\forall y)[[y < z] \supset \sim A]]]$.

Whenever $(\exists y)A$ is a theorem of $T(P)$, PT 1 and PT 2 of E 6.1 can be used to establish the existence and uniqueness conditions that are required for the introduction of $f(\cdot)$ via PD. Once that is done, we may assert

$$[f(x_1, \ldots, x_n) = \mu z(A_y(z))].$$

The recursive functions and predicates we discussed in the preceding sections can be introduced in recursive extensions of $T(P)$. For instance, $I_i^n(\cdot)$ can be introduced by the defining axiom

$$[[z = I_i^n(x_1, \ldots, x_n)] \equiv [[z = x_i] \wedge (\forall y)[[y < z] \supset \sim [y = x_i]]]],$$

in which case A is $[y = x_i]$. Similarly, if we let A be the wff $[[[x_1 < x_2] \wedge [y = 0]] \vee [\sim [x_1 < x_2] \wedge [y = 1]]]$, we can introduce $K_<(\cdot)$ by the axiom

$$[[z = K_<(x_1, x_2)] \equiv [A_y(z) \wedge (\forall y)[[y < z] \supset \sim A]]].$$

The existence and uniqueness conditions for $I_i^n(\cdot)$ and $K_<(\cdot)$ are easily established.

Since we already have $+$, $\cdot$, and $<$, the preceding observations show that the recursive functions of R 1 belong to recursive extensions of $T(P)$. And so do the recursive functions of R 2 and R 3, as can be seen from the following arguments: For R 2 let A be $[y = G(H_1(x_1, \ldots, x_n), \ldots, H_k(x_1, \ldots, x_n))]$ and assume that $G(\cdot)$ and the $H_i(\cdot)$ belong to some recursive extension of $T(P)$. Then $F(\cdot)$ can be introduced by

$$[[z = F(x_1, \ldots, x_n)] \equiv [A_y(z) \wedge (\forall y)[[y < z] \supset \sim A]]].$$

For R 3 we let A be $[G(x_1, \ldots, x_n, y) = 0]$ and assume that $G(\cdot)$ belongs to a recursive extension of $T(P)$ and that $(\exists y)A$ is a theorem in this extension. Then $F(\cdot)$ can be introduced as above.

E 8.10 In Section 8.1.2 we defined the predicate div$(\cdot)$ by

$$\text{div}(a, b) \equiv (\exists y)[[y \leqslant a] \wedge [a = by]].$$

We can introduce div$(\cdot)$ in a recursive extension of $T(P)$ in the following way: We first introduce $F(\cdot)$ by

$$[[z = F(a, b)] \equiv [[[a = bz] \vee [z = a]] \wedge (\forall y)[[y < z] \supset [\sim [a = by] \wedge \sim [y = a]]]]].$$

Here $A = [[a = by] \vee [y = a]]$. Since $\vdash A_y(a)$, $\vdash (\exists x)A$. Hence we can use PT 1 and PT 2 of E 6.1 to justify the introduction of $F(\cdot)$ in $T(P)$. The existence of $F(\cdot)$ allows us to introduce $\text{div}(\cdot)$ by the axiom

$$[\text{div}(a, b) \equiv [[F(a, b) < a] \vee [b = 1]]].$$

The method used in E 8.10 to introduce $\text{div}(\cdot)$ can, with some obvious modifications, be used to introduce $\beta(\cdot)$ as well. To show how, we first introduce the function $\text{op}(\cdot)$ by

$$[[z = \text{op}(a, b)] \equiv [z = \mu y[y = ((((a + b) \cdot (a + b)) + a) + 1)]]],$$

where 1 is an abbreviation for $S(0)$. Since $\cdot$ and $+$ are in L_P, we can introduce $\text{op}(\cdot)$ as defined. Next we introduce $\dot{-}$ by PD 2 of E 7.3. This is possible since $+$ and $<$ belong to L_P. Finally, we let B be an abbreviation of the expression

$$[[x \leqslant a \dot{-} 1] \wedge [[y < a] \wedge [[z < a] \wedge [[a = \text{op}(y, z)] \wedge \text{div}(y, (1 + (\text{op}(x, \text{i}) + 1) \cdot z))]]]],$$

and let $A(x, a)$ be defined by $[A(x, a) \equiv (\exists y)(\exists z)B]$ and observe that $A(\cdot)$ can be introduced in a recursive extension of $T(P)$ in the same way that $\text{div}(\cdot)$ was introduced. But if this is so, we can introduce $\beta(\cdot)$ with the axiom

$$[[v = \beta(a, \text{i})] \equiv [A_x(v) \wedge (\forall u)[[u < v] \supset \sim A]]].$$

The existence of an x that, for a given a, satisfies $A(\cdot, a)$ can be established as a theorem in the given recursive extension of $T(P)$. So can the uniqueness of v in the defining axiom of $\beta(\cdot)$.

For our purpose, the basic property of $\beta(\cdot)$ can be expressed as $(\exists x)(\forall y)[[y < z] \supset [\beta(x, y) = a]]$, where a is a term and where x, y, z are distinct and x and z do not occur in a. This gives the existence condition for introducing the functions $\langle a_1, \ldots, a_n \rangle$. The remaining recursive functions and predicates concerned with sequence numbers can then be introduced in the obvious way. In the sequel we take for granted that this has been done; i.e., we assume always that we are reasoning within a recursive extension of $T(P)$ in which we find the functions, $\langle \cdot \rangle$, $\text{sub}(\cdot)$, and $\text{num}(\cdot)$ and the predicates $\text{for}_P(\cdot)$ and $\text{pr}_P(\cdot)$.

The assertion that $T(P)$ is consistent can be formalized as

$$\sim (\forall x)[\text{for}_P(x) \supset (\exists y)\text{pr}_P(x, y)];$$

i.e., there is a formula that is unprovable. We let

$$\text{con}_P =_{\text{df}} \sim (\forall x)[\text{for}_P(x) \supset (\exists y)\text{pr}_P(x, y)]$$

and proceed to show that the translation of con_P into L_P is not a theorem in $T(P)$. To do that we must introduce the idea of an R formula. Such formulas are defined inductively by RC 1–RC 4.

RC 1 Every formula $[f(x_1, \ldots, x_n) = y]$ or $P(x_1, \ldots, x_n)$ or $\sim P(x_1, \ldots, x_n)$ is an R formula.

RC 2 If A and B are R formulas, so are $[A \vee B]$ and $[A \wedge B]$.

RC 3 If A is an R formula and x and y are distinct, then $(\forall x)[[x < y] \supset A]$ is an R formula.

RC 4 If A is an R formula, then $(\exists x)A$ is an R formula.

R formulas have several interesting syntactical properties. For instance, if P' is a recursive extension of $T(P)$, then every existential formula in $L_{P'}$—the language of P'—is materially equivalent in P' to an R formula.[3] Moreover, every R formula in $L_{P'}$ is materially equivalent in P' to an R formula in L_P. Finally, if A is an R formula of L_P in which $x_1, \ldots, x_n$ are the only free variables, then every instance of A of the form $A_{x_1,\ldots,x_n}(k_{a_1}, \ldots, k_{a_n})$, that is true in η is a theorem of $T(P)$. These assertions are proved in Shoenfield 1967 (pp. 209–211). Together they imply the validity of TM 8.6.

TM 8.6 Let P' be a recursive extension of $T(P)$, and let η' be the expansion of η to a model of P'. Then every closed existensial wff of $L_{P'}$ that is valid in η' is a theorem of P'.

In reading TM 8.6, note that, by TM 5.17, con_P is materially equivalent to

$$(\exists x)(\forall y) \sim [\mathrm{for}_P(x) \supset \mathrm{pr}_P(x, y)].$$

The latter formula is not existensial since the quantifiers are not all existensial.

Next let $\mathrm{thm}_P(a)$ abbreviate $(\exists y)\mathrm{pr}_P(a, y)$ and recall that $Q(\cdot)$ was defined by

$$Q(a) \equiv \sim \mathrm{thm}_P(\mathrm{sub}(a, \ulcorner x \urcorner, \mathrm{num}(a))).$$

In addition, let P' be a given recursive extension of $T(P)$, let B be the $L_{P'}$ formula

$$\sim (\exists y)\mathrm{pr}_P(\mathrm{sub}(x, k_{\ulcorner x \urcorner}, \mathrm{num}(x)), y),$$

where y is distinct from x, and let A be the translation of B into L_P. Finally, let η' be the expansion of η to a model of P' and let us agree that a wff of $L_{P'}$ is true if it is valid in η' and that a wff of L_P is true if it is valid in η. Then $B_x(k_n)$ and $A_x(k_n)$ are true if and only if $Q(n)$.

To show that the consistency of $T(P)$ cannot be proved in $T(P)$, we now let $a = \ulcorner A \urcorner$. Then

$B_x(k_a) \equiv \sim(\exists y)\mathrm{pr}_P(\mathrm{sub}(k_a, k_{\ulcorner x \urcorner}, \mathrm{num}(k_a), y)$.

From this (and the recall of $\mathrm{sub}(a, \ulcorner z \urcorner, \mathrm{num}(a)) = \ulcorner A_z(k_a) \urcorner$) it follows that $A_x(k_a)$ asserts of itself that it is not provable. According to the properties of R formulas that we recorded above, there is an R formula C in L_P that is materially equivalent in P' to $\sim B_x(k_a)$. Clearly C is materially equivalent to $\sim A_x(k_a)$ in P' and hence in $T(P)$ as well. If $A_x(k_a)$ is false, C is true, and hence C is a theorem of $T(P)$. But then $\sim A_x(k_a)$ is also a theorem of $T(P)$. On the other hand, if $A_x(k_a)$ is false, $Q(a)$ is false and $A_x(k_a)$ is a theorem of $T(P)$. Since $A_x(k_a)$ and $\sim A_x(k_a)$ cannot both be theorems of $T(P)$ if $T(P)$ is consistent, we conclude that the assertion $[\mathrm{con}_P \supset A_x(k_a)]$ must be true.

By formalizing the preceding steps (see Shoenfield 1967, pp. 212–213, for details), we can show that $[\mathrm{con}_P \supset A_x(k_a)]$ is a theorem of P'. From this and from the fact that $A_x(k_a)$ is not a theorem of P', it follows that con_P is not a theorem of P'. Hence we can assert TM 8.7.

TM 8.7 The wff of L_P that asserts that $T(P)$ is consistent is not a theorem of $T(P)$.

8.6 Concluding Remarks

In this chapter we first showed how metamathematical assertions about the theory of natural numbers can be represented by wffs *within* the theory. Then we established the fact that there exists no finite set of axioms from which we can derive as theorems all arithmethical truths; i.e., no matter how the axioms of the theory of natural numbers are chosen, we can always find true statements about natural numbers that are not logical consequences of the axioms. Finally, we showed that the wff that expresses the consistency of the first-order version of Peano's arithmetic (i.e., $T(P)$) is not a theorem of $T(P)$.

One discouraging implication of the result concerning axioms and arithmetical truths is that it is not possible to give an ultimate logical explication of valid mathematical proofs. The inventiveness of mathematicians in devising new rules of proof has no natural boundaries (Shoenfield 1967, p. 99). Another implication concerns the use of computers to establish arithmetical facts. To the extent that a calculating machine functions in accordance with a fixed set of rules, no such machine can match the human brain in mathematical intelligence (Shoenfield 1967, p. 102).

One seemingly discouraging implication of the result concerning consistency and the first-order version of Peano's arithmetic is the following:

The metamathematical statement expressing the consistency of P 1–P 9 cannot be established without assuming rules of inference that do not belong to *T*(*P*). Hence to prove the consistency of *T*(*P*), we must employ rules of inference and axioms whose consistency may be as doubtful as the consistency of *T*(*P*). In the next chapter we show that the consistency of *T*(*P*) is a logical consequence of the consistency of the axioms we postulate for elementary set theory. We also construct a model of our set-theoretic axioms to show that the latter are consistent.

In the present context it is also interesting to observe that the elementary set theory I shall present in chapter 9, KPU, is axiomatized. In developing KPU I begin with a language without function symbols and with just three predicate symbols and proceed to introduce a finite number of functions and predicates that enable me to delineate the properties of natural numbers within a conservative extension of KPU. From this, from the consistency of KPU, and from TM 8.5 it follows that KPU is incomplete.

9 Elementary Set Theory

In this chapter rudiments of elementary set theory are presented. The language of this theory contains all the logical symbols of the first-order predicate calculus. However, it has no functional symbols, no n-ary predicate symbols, for $n = 0, 3, 4, \ldots$, only two unary predicates, U and S, and one binary predicate, $\in$. The wffs of set theory are either of the form $U(x)$, $S(x)$, $[x = y]$ or $[x \in y]$, where x and y are individual variables, or are constructed from such formulas with the quantifiers and the logical connectives of the language in accordance with PFR 1–PFR 4 (given in section 5.1.2). One example of a constructed formula is $[x \subset y]$, where $\subset$ is the symbol for a binary predicate that we define with the help of S, $\forall$, and $\in$. In the intended interpretation of our language, U and S read, respectively, "is an urelement" and "is a set," while $\in$ and $\subset$ read, respectively, "belongs to" and "is a subset of." Finally, the rules of inference of set theory are PRI 1 and PRI 2 (section 5.13), and the axioms are PLA 1–PLA 7 (section 5.1.3) and a subset of Jon Barwise's axioms for admissible sets with urelements (see Barwise 1975, pp. 9–11).

There are several noteworthy features of this presentation of elementary set theory: First, many terms and predicates are introduced. Most of them are defined in accordance with the schemes described in chapters 4 and 7. Some are defined by induction. When used with care, our definitional schemes allow us to state theorems more succinctly. They do not, however, enlarge the set of logical consequences of the original axioms.

Second, even though we intend $[x \in y]$ to read "x belongs to y," we feel free to (and do) interpret the formula as saying "x is an ancestor of y" or "x is smaller than y" or other reasonable things. In any interpretation of the theory suggested in this chapter, however, it must be understood that the logical symbols have been given their intended interpretation. Otherwise we could not talk of true and false sentences.

Third, the concepts of an urelement and a set are undefined. For instance, in one context a set may be a human being, in another a real number, and in a third a collection of apples. Many mathematicians like to think of a set as a thing that lives and functions in a so-called *cumulative structure of types*. If we were to enter such a structure, we would—at level 0—meet certain individuals. They are the *urelements* of the structure. At level 1 we would encounter the same urelements and in addition various collections of such individuals. And, if we kept climbing the structure, we would find that each level contains the elements of its sublevels, all possible collections of these elements and nothing else. Moreover, there would seem to be no end to the levels. A particularly interesting cumulative structure of types is one that is constructed on top of the empty set.

9.1 The Axioms of KPU

The language of our set theory is the first-order language just described. We denote it by L. To simplify the wffs of L, many new symbols must be introduced. One of these is $\subset$. It is defined by SD 1.

SD 1 $[[x \subset y] \equiv [[S(x) \wedge S(y)] \wedge (\forall z)[[z \in x] \supset [z \in y]]]]$

In the intended interpretation of L, $[x \subset y]$ reads "x is a subset of y." ST 1 and ST 2 follow from SD 1.

ST 1 $[S(x) \supset [x \subset x]]$

ST 2 $[[[x \subset y] \wedge [y \subset z]] \supset [x \subset z]]$

When interpreted, ST 1 asserts that either x is not a set or x is a subset of itself; and ST 2 insists that if x is a subset of y and y is a subset of z, then x is a subset of z. Since x in ST 1 and y, z in ST 2 are arbitrary, it follows from PRI 2 that the same assertions, with $(\forall x)$ and $(\forall x)(\forall y)(\forall z)$ respectively prefixed, are also theorems. In this chapter I shall usually state axioms and theorems for arbitrary elements in the universe and leave the inference for all elements to the reader.

I shall sketch formal proofs of most of the set-theoretic theorems of this and the next section. To keep the length of these proofs within reasonable limits, I use certain English expressions in need of explanation: "To assert a theorem or a tautology" means to assert a value of a theorem schemata or a tautology. Furthermore, "to apply or use a theorem or a tautology" means to apply the derived rule of inference which results from the theorem or the tautology as the case may be. Finally, "by a theorem T" and "by a rule of inference R" mean, respectively, by asserting T and by applying R.

To prove ST 1, we assert the tautology

$$[[y \in x] \supset [y \in x]],$$

apply PRI 2, and declare

$$(\forall y)[[y \in x] \supset [y \in x]].$$

Then we apply TM 4.1, with q equal to $S(x)$, and obtain

$$[S(x) \supset (\forall y)[[y \in x] \supset [y \in x]]].$$

Next we assert another tautology,

$$[S(x) \supset [S(x) \wedge S(x)]],$$

and apply $[[[A \supset B] \wedge [A \supset C]] \supset [A \supset [B \wedge C]]]$ to deduce

$$[S(x) \supset [[S(x) \wedge S(x)] \wedge (\forall y)[[y \in x] \supset [y \in x]]]].$$

From this, SD 1, and TM 5.15, it follows that

$$[S(x) \supset [x \subset x]].$$

Theorem ST 2 can be proved in the same manner as ST 1. I leave those details to the reader.

For later reference, I shall denote our set theory by KPU. The first five axioms of KPU concern the meaning of U, S, $\in$, and $=$. In KA 5 below, φ denotes a wff in which y does not occur free.

KA 1 $(\forall y)[U(x) \supset \sim[y \in x]]$

KA 2 $(\exists x)S(x)$

KA 3 $[[S(x) \wedge U(y)] \supset \sim[x = y]]$

KA 4 $[[[x \subset y] \wedge [y \subset x]] \supset [x = y]]$

KA 5 $[(\exists x)\varphi \supset (\exists x)[\varphi \wedge (\forall y)[[y \in x] \supset \sim\varphi_x(y)]]]$

Here KA 1 says that an urelement contains no objects; KA 2 asserts that there is a set; and KA 3 insists that an urelement is not a set. Furthermore, KA 4—the *axiom of extensionality*—says that if x and y are sets and have the same elements, they are equal. Finally, KA 5—the *axiom of foundation*—insists that if there is an x which satisfies φ, then there is also an x which satisfies φ and contains no object which also satisfies φ. For example, if z is a nonempty set and φ asserts $[x \in z]$, then KA 5 insists that there is an x in z which has no element in common with z; i.e., $[(\exists x)[x \in z] \supset (\exists x)[[x \in z] \wedge (\forall y)[[y \in x] \supset \sim[y \in z]]]]$.

Axiom KA 4 sounds innocuous. To see that it is not, consider E 9.1.[1]

E 9.1 Consider a universe that consists of all human beings who were, are, or will be; and suppose that $(\forall x) \sim U(x)$. In addition, let $[x \in y]$ mean that x is an ancestor of y; i.e., x is either a father or a mother of y, or a grandfather or grandmother of y, etc. Finally, let a and b be a girl and a boy with the same parents. Then $[a = b]$.

Since it is not clear how a brother and a sister can be alike, recall that, in L, $=$ is a logical symbol that denotes a binary predicate with the properties described in PLA 6 and PLA 7. Axiom KA 4 concerns the relationship between $\in$ and $=$. This relationship is as it ought to be (see ST 3); i.e., if x and y are sets, they are equal if and only if they have the same elements.

ST 3 $[[S(x) \wedge S y)] \supset [[x = y] \equiv [[x \subset y] \wedge [y \subset x]]]]$

To prove ST 3, we assert PLA 7 with A equal to $[z \in x]$, apply PRI 2 and PLA 4, and declare

$$[[x = y] \supset (\forall z)[[z \in x] \supset [z \in y]]].$$

Next we use TM 4.1, with q equal to $[S(x) \wedge S(y)]$, and apply TM 5.3 to obtain

$$[[x = y] \supset [[S(x) \wedge S(y)] \supset (\forall z)[[z \in x] \supset [z \in y]]]].$$

Then the tautology $[[S(x) \wedge S(y)] \supset [S(x) \wedge S(y)]]$, an application of $[[[B \supset C] \wedge [A \supset [B \supset D]]] \supset [A \supset [B \supset [C \wedge D]]]]$, and SD 1 suffice to establish

$$[[x = y] \supset [[S(x) \wedge S(y)] \supset [x \subset y]]].$$

By similar arguments,

$$[[y = x] \supset [[S(y) \wedge S(x)] \supset [y \subset x]]],$$

and by $[[S(x) \wedge S(y)] \equiv [S(y) \wedge S(x)]$ and use of TM 5.15,

$$[[y = x] \supset [[S(x) \wedge S(y)] \supset [y \subset x]]].$$

Hence, if we apply TM 4.1, with q equal to $[x = y]$, and use PLA 2 to ascertain that

$$[[[x = y] \supset [y = x]] \supset [[x = y] \supset [[S(x) \wedge S(y)] \supset [y \subset x]]]],$$

we can, by TM 5.1 and PRI 1, deduce

$[[x = y] \supset [[S(x) \wedge S(y)] \supset [y \subset x]]]$.

But, if that is so, then

$[[x = y] \supset [[S(x) \wedge S(y)] \supset [[x \subset y] \wedge [y \subset x]]]]$,

and other application of TM 5.3 yields

$[[S(x) \wedge S(y)] \supset [[x = y] \supset [[x \subset y] \wedge [y \subset x]]]]$.

Since KA 4 and TM 4.1, with q equal to $[S(x) \wedge S(y)]$, imply that

$[[S(x) \wedge S(y)] \supset [[[x \subset y] \wedge [y \subset x]] \supset [x = y]]]$,

we can conclude that

$[[S(x) \wedge S(y)] \supset [[x = y] \equiv [[x \subset y] \wedge [y \subset x]]]]$,

as was to be shown.

To state the remaining axioms of KPU, I must first introduce the idea of a Δ_0 formula: *The collection of Δ_0 formulas of L is the smallest collection Y containing the atomic formulas of L which is closed under the following operations*: (1) if φ is in Y, so is $\sim\varphi$; (2) if φ and ψ are in Y, so is $[\varphi \supset \psi]$; and (3) if φ is in Y, so are $(\forall u)[[u \in v] \supset \varphi]$ and $(\exists u)[[u \in v] \wedge \varphi]$. One example of a Δ_0 formula is the wff used to define $\subset$. Hence the wff $[x \subset y]$ is equivalent in L to a Δ_0 formula. Another such equivalence is described in E 9.2.

E 9.2 It is easy to show that in L

$[\sim[y \in z] \equiv [[y \in z] \supset \sim[y = y]]]$.

Consequently, the wff $(\forall y) \sim [y \in z]$ is equivalent in L to the Δ_0 formula

$(\forall y)[[y \in z] \supset \sim[y = y]]$.

The writing of Δ_0 formulas is facilitated if we agree to the following abbreviations in which u and v are individual variables:

$(\forall u \in v)\varphi =_{\text{df}} (\forall u)[[u \in v] \supset \varphi]$,

$(\exists u \in v)\varphi =_{\text{df}} (\exists u)[[u \in v] \wedge \varphi]$.

Also, if we observe that $(\forall u \in v)$ and $(\exists u \in v)$ are so-called *bounded quantifiers*, we can characterize the set of Δ_0 formulas briefly as the smallest set of wffs that contains the atomic formulas of L and is closed under negation, material implication, and bounded quantification.

So much for Δ_0 formulas. Now the remaining axioms:

KA 6 $(\exists z)[S(z) \wedge [[x \in z] \wedge [y \in z]]]$

KA 7 $[S(z) \supset (\exists u)[S(u) \wedge (\forall y \in z)(\forall x \in y)[x \in u]]]$

Next let φ and ψ be Δ_0 formulas in which u does not occur free.

KA 8 $[S(z) \supset (\exists u)[S(u) \wedge (\forall x)[[x \in u] \equiv [[x \in z] \wedge \varphi]]]]$

KA 9 $[[S(z) \wedge (\forall x \in z)(\exists y)\psi] \supset (\exists u)[S(u) \wedge (\forall x \in z)(\exists y \in u)\psi]]$

Of these, the first is usually referred to as the *axiom of pairs.* The second is the *axiom of unions,* and the third and fourth are called, respectively, the *axiom of Δ_0 separation* and the *axiom of Δ_0 collection.* Although they appear difficult, they have simple interpretations and interesting consequences.

9.2 The Null Set and Russell's Antinomy

In the intended interpretation of L, KA 8 reads "there exists a set u that consists of all those elements x of z for which φ denotes truth." From PRI 2 it follows that KA 8 must also be true when we prefix it by $(\forall z)$.

Axioms KA 2 and KA 8 can be used to establish three interesting theorems:

ST 4 $(\exists x)[S(x) \wedge (\forall y)\sim[y \in x]]$

ST 5 $[S(z) \supset [[S(x) \wedge (\forall y)\sim[y \in x]] \supset [x \subset z]]]$

ST 6 $[S(z) \supset (\exists y)[S(y) \wedge \sim[y \in z]]]$

To show how ST 4 is established, we first assert an instance of KA 8:

$$[S(z) \supset (\exists u)[S(u) \wedge (\forall x)[[x \in u] \equiv [[x \in z] \wedge \sim[x = x]]]]].$$

Next we assert $[x = x]$; use $[A \equiv \sim\sim A]$, TM 4.1, with q equal to $[x \in z]$, and $[A \equiv \sim\sim A]$; and conclude that

$$\sim[[x \in z] \wedge \sim[x = x]].$$

Then TM 4.1, with q equal to $[[x \in u] \equiv [[x \in z] \wedge \sim[x = x]]]$, and use of $[[[A \equiv B] \supset \sim B] \supset [[A \equiv B] \supset \sim A]]$ allow us to declare

$$[[[x \in u] \equiv [[x \in z] \wedge \sim[x = x]]] \supset \sim[x \in u]].$$

By PRI 2 and with the use of TM 5.10, it follows that

$$[(\forall x)[[x \in u] \equiv [[x \in z] \wedge \sim[x = x]]] \supset (\forall x)\sim[x \in u]].$$

Hence,

$$[[S(u) \wedge (\forall x)[[x \in u] \equiv [[x \in z] \wedge \sim[x = x]]]] \supset [S(u) \wedge (\forall x)\sim[x \in u]]].$$

Next we apply PLA 3, PRI 2, TM 5.10, and PLA 3 again to deduce

$$[(\exists u)[S(u) \wedge (\forall x)[[x \in u] \equiv [[x \in z] \wedge \sim[x = x]]]] \supset (\exists u)[S(u) \wedge (\forall x)\sim[x \in u]]].$$

From this we obtain

$$[S(z) \supset (\exists u)[S(u) \wedge (\forall x)\sim[x \in u]]]$$

by first applying TM 4.1, with q equal to $S(z)$, and PLA 2 and then by asserting the noted instance of KA 8 and using PRI 1. But, if that is so, the theorem follows by an appeal to PLA 3, PRI 2, PLA 4, PLA 3 again, $[\sim\sim A \equiv A]$, TM 5.15, KA 2, and PRI 1.

In the case of ST 5, we first use T 4.2, PRI 2, and TM 5.10 to deduce that

$$[(\forall y)\sim[y \in x] \supset (\forall y)[[y \in x] \supset [y \in z]]]$$

and, hence, that

$$[[S(x) \wedge (\forall y)\sim[y \in x]] \supset [S(x) \wedge (\forall y)[[y \in x] \supset [y \in z]]]].$$

By applying TM 4.1, with q equal to $S(z)$, and TM 5.3 to this assertion we find that

$$[[S(x) \wedge (\forall y)\sim[y \in x]] \supset [S(z) \supset [S(x) \wedge (\forall y)[[y \in x] \supset [y \in z]]]]].$$

Since we also can assert $[S(z) \supset S(z)]$, apply TM 4.1 to it, and establish

$$[[S(x) \wedge (\forall y)\sim[y \in x]] \supset [S(z) \supset S(z)]],$$

we conclude that

$$[[S(x) \wedge (\forall y)\sim[y \in x]] \supset [S(z) \supset [S(z) \wedge [S(x) \wedge (\forall y)[[y \in x] \supset [y \in z]]]]]].$$

But if this is so, the tautologies $[[A \wedge [B \wedge C]] \equiv [[A \wedge B] \wedge C]]$ and $[[A \wedge B] \equiv [B \wedge A]]$, SD 1, TM 5.15, and another application of TM 5.3 suffice to establish ST 5.

To establish ST 6, we begin by asserting an instance of KA 8,

$$[S(z) \supset (\exists y)[S(y) \wedge (\forall x)[[x \in y] \equiv [[x \in z] \wedge \sim[x \in x]]]]],$$

and observe that

$$[(\forall x)[[x \in y] \equiv [[x \in z] \wedge \sim[x \in x]]] \supset \sim[y \in y]].$$

We then use the observation to give a simple proof of

$$(\forall x)[[x \in y] \equiv [[x \in z] \wedge \sim[x \in x]]] \vdash \sim[y \in z].$$

By the Deduction Theorem, it follows that

$$[(\forall x)[[x \in y] \equiv [[x \in z] \wedge \sim[x \in x]]] \supset \sim[y \in z]].$$

Hence,

$$[[S(y) \wedge (\forall x)[[x \in y] \equiv [[x \in z] \wedge \sim[x \in x]]]] \supset [S(y) \wedge \sim[y \in z]]].$$

But if that is so, we can use PLA 3, PRI 2, TM 5.10, and PLA 3 again to establish

$$[(\exists y)[S(y) \wedge (\forall x)[[x \in y] \equiv [[x \in z] \wedge \sim[x \in x]]]] \supset (\exists y)[S(y) \wedge \sim[y \in z]]].$$

From this assertion and the asserted instance of KA 8, the theorem follows by applying TM 4.1, with q equal to $S(z)$, and PLA 2.

In the intended interpretation of L, ST 4 asserts that a set exists that contains no elements. According to ST 5, such a set is a subset of all sets. The third theorem states that no matter how we choose the set x, there is a set y in the universe that does not belong to x. Consequently, the universe is not a set. Hence we cannot substitute the universe for x in KA 8 and assert the existence of the set of all sets that are not elements of themselves; no such set exists. This result precludes Russell's *antinomy* in this elementary set theory.

A set that has no elements is called a *null set* and is usually denoted by $\emptyset$. I will introduce $\emptyset$ in L as in SD 2.

SD 2 $[[z = \emptyset] \equiv [S(z) \wedge (\forall y)[[y \in z] \supset \sim[y = y]]]]$

Then ST 4, E 9.2, and TM 5.15 supply the existence condition for the introduction of $\emptyset$; and KA 2, KA 4, and KA 8 imply the validity of the required uniqueness condition, ST 7.

ST 7 $[[S(x) \wedge [(\forall y)\sim[y \in x] \wedge [S(z) \wedge (\forall y)\sim[y \in z]]]] \supset [x = z]]$

That is, two sets that have no elements are equal.

In order that $\emptyset$ be an efficient means of communication, we must be able to assert ST 8.

ST 8 $[S(\emptyset) \wedge (\forall y)\sim[y \in \emptyset]]$

We next show how SD 2 and ST 4 can be used to prove ST 8. Similar arguments suffice to establish ST 9.

ST 9 $[S(z) \supset [\varnothing \subset z]]$

To prove ST 8, we let $B(z)$ abbreviate $[S(z) \wedge (\forall y) \sim [y \in z]]$, and deduce from PLA 7 that

$$[[z = \varnothing] \supset [B \supset B_z(\varnothing)]].$$

Consequently, by an application of PLA 2,

$$[[[z = \varnothing] \supset B] \supset [[z = \varnothing] \supset B_z(\varnothing)]].$$

Now SD 2, the material equivalence of $(\forall y)[[y \in z] \supset \sim[y = y]]$ and $(\forall y) \sim [y \in z]$, and TM 5.15 allow us to assert $[[z = \varnothing] \supset B]$. Hence, by PRI 1,

$$[[z = \varnothing] \supset B_z(\varnothing)].$$

From this we can, by applying in succession PLA 3, PRI 2, PLA 4, and PLA 3 again, establish

$$[(\exists z)[z = \varnothing] \supset B_z(\varnothing)].$$

Finally, appealing to ST 4 and PRI 1 allows us to deduce $B_z(\varnothing)$, as was to be demonstrated.

We have sketched the proofs of ST 1, ST 3–ST 6, and ST 8 to illustrate how proofs of KPU theorems can be written as sequences of wffs in strict adherence to the definition of a proof given in chapter 3. These proofs are lengthy. Therefore, in the remainder of the chapter, I shall present only informal proofs of the theorems asserted. The details necessary to transform our proofs into sequences of wffs are left to the reader.

9.3 Unions, Intersections, and Differences

In the intended interpretation of L, KA 6 insists that there is a set that contains x and y. By KA 8, there is a set that contains only x and y. By KA 4, there can be only one such set. I denote this set by $\{x, y\}$ and introduce the term $\{x, y\}$ in L by SD 3.

SD 3 $[[z = \{x, y\}] \equiv [S(z) \wedge [[[x \in z] \wedge [y \in z]] \wedge (\forall u \in z)[[u = x] \vee [u = y]]]]]$

Then arguments similar to those used to prove ST 8 can be used to prove ST 10.

ST 10 $[S(\{x,y\}) \wedge (\forall u)[[u \in \{x,y\}] \equiv [[u = x] \vee [u = y]]]]$

When $[x = y]$, $\{x,y\}$ contains only one element. We usually denote the *singleton* $\{x,x\}$ by $\{x\}$. This notation is unambiguous as witnessed in the following simple theorems, the proofs of which I leave to the reader.

ST 11 $[[\{x\} = \{y\}] \equiv [x = y]]$

ST 12 $[[\{x\} = \{x,y\}] \equiv [x = y]]$

ST 13 $[[\{\{x\}\} = \{\{x\},\{x,y\}\}] \equiv [x = y]]$

9.3.1 Unions

Axiom KA 7 introduces the existence of unions of sets in a subtle way. In the intended interpretation of the axioms, it postulates that if x is not empty, there exists a set z which equals the union of the elements of x. The presumption that x exists and is nonempty is important. If $x_1, \ldots, x_n$ is a sequence of sets, the axiom *alone* does not allow us to infer that there is a set z that equals the union of these sets. Such an inference is possible only if we first establish the existence of a set w whose elements are the x_j's. Without this restriction on the existence of unions, we could prove that the universe is a set and thus establish a result that contradicts ST 6.

We can introduce notation for the union of a pair of sets, x and y, by SD 4.

SD 4 $[[S(x) \wedge S(y)] \supset [[z = (x \cup y)] \equiv [S(z) \wedge [(\forall u \in x)[u \in z]$

$\wedge [(\forall v \in y)[v \in z] \wedge (\forall w \in z)[[w \in x] \vee [w \in y]]]]]]]$

To establish the existence condition for $x \cup y$ we note first that the existence of $\{x,y\}$ and KA 7 imply that there is a set $\tilde{z}$ such that $[(\forall u \in x)[u \in \tilde{z}] \wedge (\forall v \in y)[v \in \tilde{z}]]$. Then we use $\tilde{z}$ and KA 8 to form a set z such that $[[u \in z] \equiv [[u \in \tilde{z}] \wedge (\exists w \in \{x,y\})[u \in w]]$. This z is the union of x and y we are searching for. Its uniqueness is a consequence of KA 4. From this it follows that the union of a pair of sets is well defined by SD 4. Moreover, arguments similar to those used to establish ST 8 suffice to prove the validity of ST 14.

ST 14 $[[S(x) \wedge S(y)] \supset [S((x \cup y)) \wedge (\forall u)[[u \in (x \cup y)] \equiv [[u \in x] \vee [u \in y]]]]]$

From ST 14 and the properties of $\vee$ (see T 4.8, T 4.9, and T 4.15), we infer ST 15 and ST 16.

ST 15 $[S(x) \supset [x = (x \cup x)]]$

ST 16 $[[S(x) \wedge S(y)] \supset [(x \cup y) = (y \cup x)]]$

In reading SD 4 and the theorems that followed, note that I provide only a partial definition of $\cup$. To introduce $\cup$ as a function symbol in L, I must also specify the value of $\cup$ on pairs x, y that are not sets; e.g.,

$$[\sim[S(x) \wedge S(y)] \supset [[z = (x \cup y)] \equiv [z = \varnothing]]].$$

Here, as well as in the remainder of the chapter, I shall leave it to the reader to add such details.

9.3.2 Intersections and Differences

From the existence of the sets x and y and from KA 8, we can deduce the existence of the intersection of x and y and the difference of x and y. Since the uniqueness of intersections and differences is a consequence of KA 4, I can introduce notation for such sets by SD 5 and SD 6.

SD 5 $[[S(x) \wedge S(y)] \supset [[z = (x \cap y)] \equiv [S(z) \wedge [(\forall u \in x)[[u \in y] \supset [u \in z]] \wedge (\forall w \in z)[[w \in x] \wedge [w \in y]]]]]]$

SD 6 $[[S(x) \wedge S(y)] \supset [[z = (x - y)] \equiv [S(z) \wedge [(\forall u \in x)[\sim[u \in y] \supset [u \in z]] \wedge (\forall w \in z)[[w \in x] \wedge \sim[w \in y]]]]]]$

Then arguments similar to those used to establish ST 8 suffice to prove ST 17 and ST 18.

ST 17 $[[S(x) \wedge S(y)] \supset [S((x \cap y)) \wedge (\forall u)[[u \in (x \cap y)] \equiv [[u \in x] \wedge [u \in y]]]]]$

ST 18 $[[S(x) \wedge S(y)] \supset [S((x - y)) \wedge (\forall u)[[u \in (x - y)] \equiv [[u \in x] \wedge \sim[u \in y]]]]]$

From ST 17 and the properties of $\wedge$, we deduce ST 19–ST 21.

ST 19 $[S(x) \supset [x = (x \cap x)]]$

ST 20 $[[S(x) \wedge S(y)] \supset [(x \cap y) = (y \cap x)]]$

ST 21 $[S(x) \supset [\varnothing = (x \cap \varnothing)]]$

9.4 Product Sets

As soon as notation for *singletons* $\{x\}$ and *unordered pairs* $\{x, y\}$ have been introduced, notation for ordered pairs can be introduced. I denote the *ordered pair* in which x is the first component and y the second by (x, y) and define it as in SD 7.

SD 7 $[[z = (x, y)] \equiv [S(z) \wedge [z = \{\{x\}, \{x, y\}\}]]]$

Then KA 6 and the existence of $\{x\}$ and $\{x, y\}$ imply the existence of a set that equals $\{\{x\}, \{x, y\}\}$. Since $\{x\}$ and $\{x, y\}$ are well defined, we deduce from KA 4 that there is only one such set. Consequently, we can introduce the term (x, y) in L via SD 7, and we can show ST 21.

ST 22 $[S(x, y) \wedge [(x, y) = \{\{x\}, \{x, y\}\}]]$

Ordered pairs, although they look strange, have two important properties. First, they are sets; i.e., they belong to the universe. Second, they possess all the properties usually associated with ordered pairs. One of these is given as ST 23.

ST 23 $[[(x, y) = (u, v)] \equiv [[x = u] \wedge [y = v]]]$

To establish ST 23, observe first that ST 3, $x = u$, and $y = v$ imply that $(x, y) = (u, v)$. Next suppose that $(x, y) = (u, v)$. Then by ST 3, $\{x\} = \{u\}$ or $\{x\} = \{u, v\}$. If $\{x\} = \{u\}$, $x = u$ by ST 11. If $\{x\} = \{u, v\}$, $x = u$, or $x = v$. If $x = v$, $x = u$ also by ST 12. Hence $(x, y) = (u, v)$ only if $x = u$. By ST 3, we must also have $\{x, y\} = \{u\}$ or $\{x, y\} = \{u, v\}$. If $\{x, y\} = \{u\}$, then $\{x, y\} = \{x\}$, and by ST 3, $\{u, v\} = \{x\}$. Hence, by ST 12, $y = x$ and $x = v$; that is, $y = v$. If $\{x, y\} = \{u, v\}$, $y = u$ or $y = v$. If $y = u$, then $y = x$, $\{u, v\} = \{x\}$, and $v = x$ by ST 12. So $y = v$ again, and we have shown that $(x, y) = (u, v)$ only if $y = v$.

A *product set* is a set of ordered pairs. To be more precise, we proceed as follows: Let x and y be sets. The cross product of x and y is a set of ordered pairs denoted by $x \times y$ and defined by SD 8.

SD 8 $[[S(x) \wedge S(y)] \supset [[z = (x \times y)] \equiv [S(z) \wedge [(\forall u \in x)(\forall v \in y)[(u, v) \in z]$
$\wedge (\forall w \in z)(\exists u \in x)(\exists v \in y)[w = (u, v)]]]]]$

It is not obvious that there is a set with the properties specified in SD 8. We shall sketch an outline of a proof that such a set exists.[2] In doing this, we illustrate the meaning of KA 9.

To show that $x \times y$ exists, we must first show that if x and y are sets, there is a set c such that

(i) $(\forall u \in x)(\forall v \in y)(\exists z \in c)[z = (u, v)]$.

Let $u \in x$ be given and let φ abbreviate $[z = (u, v)]$. Then φ is a Δ_0 formula and $(\forall v \in y)(\exists z)\varphi$. Hence, by KA 9,

(ii) $(\exists d)[S(d) \wedge (\forall v \in y)(\exists z \in d)[z = (u, v)]]$.

Next let ψ abbreviate $[S(d) \wedge (\forall v \in y)(\exists z \in d)[z = (u, v)]]$. Then ψ is a Δ_0 formula and $(\forall u \in x)(\exists d)\psi$. Hence, by KA 9,

(iii) $(\exists e)[S(e) \wedge (\forall u \in x)(\exists d \in e)\psi]$.

By KA 7, $(\exists c)[S(c) \wedge (\forall d \in e)(\forall z \in d)[z \in c]]$. By combining assertions (ii) and (iii), we see that this c satisfies (i), as was to be shown.

Let c be a set that satisfies (i). By KA 8 there is a set f that satisfies

(iv) $[S(f) \wedge (\forall z)[[z \in f] \equiv [[z \in c] \wedge (\exists u \in x)(\exists v \in y)[z = (u, v)]]]]$.

By combining assertions (i) and (iv), we see that, according to SD 8, $[f = (x \times y)]$.

The uniqueness of $(x \times y)$ follows from KA 4. Hence, for pairs of sets, the term $(x \times y)$ is well defined by SD 8. Moreover, standard arguments suffice to prove ST 24.

ST 24 $[[S(x) \wedge S(y)] \supset [S((x \times y)) \wedge (\forall u)[[u \in (x \times y)]$
$\equiv (\exists v \in x)(\exists w \in y)[u = (v, w)]]]]$

We can also show that if x is a set of ordered pairs, there is a pair y, z in the universe such that $[x \subset (y \times z)]$; i.e.,

ST 25 $[[S(x) \wedge (\forall u \in x)(\exists c \in u)(\exists v \in c)(\exists w \in c)[u = (v, w)]]$
$\supset (\exists y)(\exists z)[[S(y) \wedge S(z)] \wedge [x \subset (y \times z)]]]$

Finally, ST 24 and the properties of $\wedge$ imply ST 26 and ST 27.

ST 26 $[[[S(x) \wedge S(y)] \supset [[x = \emptyset] \vee [y = \emptyset]]] \supset [(x \times y) = \emptyset]]$

ST 27 $[[[x \subset u] \wedge [y \subset v]] \supset [(x \times y) \subset (u \times v)]]$

9.5 Relations and Functions

A *binary relation* is a set of ordered pairs. Conversely, a set of ordered pairs is a binary relation. In symbols this becomes

$[\mathrm{rel}(R) \equiv [S(R) \wedge (\forall u \in R)(\exists c \in u)(\exists x \in c)(\exists y \in c)[u = (x, y)]]]$.

If R is a binary relation, then by ST 25 there are sets A_R and B_R such that $R \subset (A_R \times B_R)$. We use A_R and B_R to define the domain of R, $\mathrm{dom}(R)$, and the range of R, $\mathrm{rang}(R)$:

$$[[z = \mathrm{dom}(R)] \equiv [S(z) \wedge [(\forall x \in z)(\exists y \in B_R)[(x, y) \in R] \wedge (\forall x \in A_R)(\forall y \in B_R)[[(x, y) \in R] \supset [x \in z]]]]],$$

$$[[z = \text{rang}(R)] \equiv [S(z) \wedge [(\forall y \in z)(\exists x \in A_R)[(x, y) \in R]$$
$$\wedge (\forall x \in A_R)(\forall y \in B_R)[[(x, y) \in R] \supset [y \in z]]]]].$$

The pair (A_R, B_R) is not uniquely determined. However, dom(R) and rang(R) are the same, no matter how we choose A_R and B_R.

E 9.3 Let x and y be sets and suppose that

$$[[R_\varepsilon \subset (x \times y)] \wedge (\forall u)(\forall v)[[(u, v) \in R_\varepsilon] \equiv [[[u \in x] \wedge [v \in y]] \wedge [u \in v]]]].$$

Then R_ε is a set of ordered pairs. Hence it is a relation. Also $(\forall u)(\forall v)[[(u, v) \in (x \times y)] \supset [[(u, v) \in R_\varepsilon] \equiv [u \in v]]]$. Next suppose that

$$[[R_= \subset (x \times y)] \wedge (\forall u)(\forall v)[[(u, v) \in R_=] \equiv [[[u \in x] \wedge [v \in y]] \wedge [u = v]]]].$$

Then $R_=$ is a set of ordered pairs. Hence it too is a relation. Also, $(\forall u)(\forall v)[[(u, v) \in (x \times y)] \supset [[(u, v) \in R_=] \equiv [u = v]]]$. In concluding, we note that the existence of x, y and $x \times y$, together with KA 8, ensure that R_ε and $R_=$ denote objects in the universe.

For any given set x, a relation R in $(x \times x)$ is said to be *reflexive* if and only if $(\forall u \in x)[(u, u) \in R]$. R is *symmetric* if and only if

$$(\forall u \in x)(\forall v \in x)[[(u, v) \in R] \supset [(v, u) \in R]].$$

R is *antisymmetric* if and only if

$$(\forall u \in x)(\forall v \in x)[[[(u, v) \in R] \wedge [(v, u) \in R]] \supset [u = v]].$$

Finally, R is *transitive* if and only if

$$(\forall u \in x)(\forall v \in x)(\forall w \in x)[[[(u, v) \in R] \wedge [(v, w) \in R]] \supset [(u, w) \in R]].$$

We shall often refer to these properties of relations. Here we merely observe that, if $[x = y]$ in E 9.3, R_ε need have none of the properties above, whereas $R_=$ has three of them: reflexivity, symmetry, and transitivity. A relation with the properties of $R_=$ is called an *equivalence relation*. A relation that is reflexive, antisymmetric, and transitive is called a *partial order*. One example of a partial order is the predicate $\leqslant$ in $(|\eta| \times |\eta|)$. A partial order R in $(x \times x)$ is a *total order* if and only if

$$(\forall u \in x)(\forall v \in x)[[(u, v) \in R)] \vee [(v, u) \in R]].$$

The predicate $\leqslant$ is a total order in $(|\eta| \times |\eta|)$.

A *unary function* F is a binary relation with the following property:

$$[[[(x, y) \in F] \wedge [(u, v) \in F]] \supset [[x = u] \supset [y = v]]].$$

If F is a unary function and $(x, y) \in F$, we usually write $y = F(x)$. We also write $F(\cdot)\colon A \to B$ to say that F is a function with $\mathrm{dom}(F) = A$ and $\mathrm{rang}(F) \subset B$. Finally, we shall insist that

$$[\mathrm{func}(F) \equiv [\mathrm{rel}(F) \wedge (\forall z \in F)(\forall w \in F)[[[[z = (x, y)] \wedge [w = (u, v)]] \wedge [x = u]] \supset [y = v]]]].$$

9.6 Extensions

In the preceding sections we considered unordered and ordered pairs of sets and unions and intersections of pairs of sets. The results we obtained can be generalized to n-tuples of sets. We consider triples of sets here; I leave the general case to the reader.

Unordered and ordered triples are defined so that

$$[\{x_1, x_2, x_3\} = (\{x_1, x_2\} \cup \{x_3\})] \quad \text{and} \quad [(x_1, x_2, x_3) = ((x_1, x_2), x_3)].$$

Similarly, unions and intersections of triples of sets are defined so that

$$\left[\left(\bigcup_{i=1}^{3} x_i\right) = \left(\left(\bigcup_{i=1}^{2} x_i\right) \cup x_3\right)\right] \quad \text{and} \quad \left[\left(\bigcap_{i=1}^{3} x_i\right) = \left(\left(\bigcap_{i=1}^{2} x_i\right) \cap x_3\right)\right].$$

Finally, the product of a triple of sets is defined so that

$$[(x_1 \times x_2 \times x_3) = ((x_1 \times x_2) \times x_3)].$$

For later reference we note that the operations $\cup$ and $\cap$ are associative; see ST 28 and ST 29.

ST 28 $[[[S(x) \wedge S(y)] \wedge S(z)] \supset [((x \cup y) \cup z) = (x \cup (y \cup z))]]$

ST 29 $[[[S(x) \wedge S(y)] \wedge S(z)] \supset [((x \cap y) \cap z) = (x \cap (y \cap z))]]$

In addition, $\cap$ distributes over $\cup$ and $\cup$ distributes over $\cap$ as in ST 30 and ST 31.

ST 30 $[[[S(x) \wedge S(y)] \wedge S(z)] \supset [(x \cap (y \cup z)) = ((x \cap y) \cup (x \cap z))]]$

ST 31 $[[[S(x) \wedge S(y)] \wedge S(z)] \supset [(x \cup (y \cap z)) = ((x \cup y) \cap (x \cup z))]]$

Finally, ordered triples satisfy ST 32.

ST 32 $[[(u, v, w) = (x, y, z)] \equiv [[u = x] \wedge [[v = y] \wedge [w = z]]]]$

Sets of ordered triples are *ternary relations*. Some of these in turn are binary functions. In the next section we shall find sets in the universe that can represent natural numbers, and we shall construct the binary functions that add and multiply them.

9.7 Natural Numbers

There are many ways of defining sets that can represent natural numbers in our universe. One of them is as follows. We begin by defining a unary functional symbol as in SD 9.

SD 9 $[S(x) \supset [[z = \mathscr{S}(x)] \equiv [S(z) \wedge [z = (x \cup \{x\})]]]]$

For all sets x there is a set z that equals $(x \cup \{x\})$. Since this set is uniquely determined, $\mathscr{S}$ is well defined on sets by SD 9. We also have ST 33.

ST 33 $[S(x) \supset [[y \in \mathscr{S}(x)] \equiv [[y \in x] \vee [y = x]]]]$

Next we define two useful unary predicates, trans$(\cdot)$ and ord$(\cdot)$, in SD 10 and SD 11.

SD 10 $[\text{trans}(x) \equiv [S(x) \wedge (\forall y \in x)(\forall z \in y)[z \in x]]]$

SD 11 $[\text{ord}(x) \equiv [\text{trans}(x) \wedge (\forall y \in x)\,\text{trans}(y)]]$

SD 10 asserts that x is *transitive*, and SD 11 insists that x is an *ordinal number*. Since $S(\emptyset)$, $\sim[y \in \emptyset]$, and

$[\sim[y \in \emptyset] \supset [[y \in \emptyset] \supset (\forall z \in y)[z \in \emptyset]]]$,

we have trans$(\emptyset)$, Similarly, trans$(\emptyset)$, $\sim[y \in \emptyset]$, and $[\sim[y \in \emptyset] \supset [[y \in \emptyset] \supset \text{trans}(y)]]$ imply ord$(\emptyset)$. Also, $[\text{trans}(x) \supset \text{trans}(\mathscr{S}(x))]$ and $[\text{ord}(x) \supset \text{ord}(\mathscr{S}(x))]$ are easy consequences of SD 10, SD 11, and ST 33. For later reference, we record two of these observations in ST 34 and ST 35.

ST 34 ord$(\emptyset)$

ST 35 $[\text{ord}(x) \supset \text{ord}(\mathscr{S}(x))]$

Finally, we define the unary predicate nat$(\cdot)$ in SD 12.

SD 12 $[\text{nat}(x) \equiv [\text{ord}(x) \wedge [[x = \emptyset] \vee [(\exists y \in x)[x = \mathscr{S}(y)]$

$\wedge\ (\forall y \in x)[[y = \emptyset] \vee (\exists z \in y)[y = \mathscr{S}(z)]]]]]]$

In the intended interpretation of KPU, nat(x) asserts that x is a natural number. Evidently, we have ST 36 and ST 37.

ST 36 nat$(\emptyset)$

ST 37 $[\text{nat}(x) \supset \text{nat}(\mathscr{S}(x))]$.

Furthermore, since $[\text{ord}(x) \wedge [y \in x]]$ materially implies ord(y), we have ST 38.

ST 38 $[[\text{nat}(x) \wedge [y \in x]] \supset \text{nat}(y)]$

The natural numbers in KPU have many interesting properties. The first three (ST 39–ST 41) are easily proved. They show that the natural numbers in KPU with the obvious interpretation satisfy P 1, P 2, and P 8 of T(P 1, ..., P 9) (i.e., of the $T(P)$ in section 6.1).

ST 39 $[\text{nat}(x) \supset \sim[\mathscr{S}(x) = \varnothing]]$

ST 40 $[[\text{nat}(x) \wedge \text{nat}(y)] \supset [[\mathscr{S}(x) = \mathscr{S}(y)] \supset [x = y]]]$

ST 41 $[[\text{nat}(x) \wedge \text{nat}(y)] \supset [[x \in \mathscr{S}(y)] \equiv [[x \in y] \vee [x = y]]]]$

The fourth property, described in ST 42, can be established with the help of KA 5. It asserts that the natural numbers in KPU satisfy the *principle of complete induction.*

ST 42 Let ψ be a wff in which x is free. Then
$[(\forall x)[\text{nat}(x) \supset [(\forall y \in x)\psi_x(y) \supset \psi]] \supset (\forall x)[\text{nat}(x) \supset \psi]]$.

In outlining a proof of ST 42, we illustrate the meaning of KA 5. We begin by observing that if we substitute $\sim[\text{nat}(x) \supset \psi]$ for φ in KA 5, the assertion in KA 5 becomes materially equivalent to

$$[(\forall x)[(\forall y \in x)[\text{nat}(y) \supset \psi_x(y)] \supset [\text{nat}(x) \supset \psi]] \supset (\forall x)[\text{nat}(x) \supset \psi]].$$

Hence, TM 5.3 and TM 5.15 allow us to assert

(i) $[(\forall x)[\text{nat}(x) \supset [(\forall y \in x)[\text{nat}(y) \supset \psi_x(y)] \supset \psi]] \supset (\forall x)[\text{nat}(x) \supset \psi]]$.

Next, we observe that $[[A \supset [B \supset C]] \supset [A \supset [[B \supset [C \supset D]] \equiv [B \supset D]]]]$ is a tautology and deduce, first, that

$$[[\text{nat}(x) \supset [[y \in x] \supset \text{nat}(y)]] \supset [\text{nat}(x) \supset [[[y \in x] \supset [\text{nat}(y) \supset \psi_x(y)]] \equiv [[y \in x] \supset \psi_x(y)]]]]$$

and then by ST 38, PRI 2, PLA 4, and TM 5.10, that

(ii) $[\text{nat}(x) \supset [(\forall y \in x)[\text{nat}(y) \supset \psi_x(y)] \equiv (\forall y \in x)\psi_x(y)]]$.

From assertion ii and the fact that $[[[A \supset [B \equiv C]] \supset [[A \supset B] \equiv [A \supset C]]]$ is a tautology, we deduce that

(iii) $[[\text{nat}(x) \supset (\forall y \in x)[\text{nat}(y) \supset \psi_x(y))]] \equiv [\text{nat}(x) \supset (\forall y \in x)\psi_x(y)]]$.

But, if that is so, (i), (iii), the tautology $[[[A \supset B] \equiv [A \supset C]] \supset [[A \supset [B \supset D]] \equiv [A \supset [C \supset D]]]$, and TM 5.15 suffice to establish the validity in KPU of the principle of complete induction.

Theorem ST 42 and easy arguments demonstrate that the natural numbers in KPU also satisfy the principle of induction expressed in P 9 (section 6.1); see ST 43.

ST 43 Let ψ be a wff in which x is free. Then $[[\psi_x(\emptyset) \wedge (\forall x)[\text{nat}(x) \supset [\psi \supset \psi_x(\mathscr{S}(x))]]] \supset (\forall x)[\text{nat}(x) \supset \psi]]$.

If ST 43 is false, $(\exists y) \sim [\text{nat}(x) \supset \psi]$. Hence, by ST 42, PLA 3, and PRI 1,

$$(\exists x)[\text{nat}(x) \wedge [(\forall y \in x)\psi_x(y) \wedge \sim\psi]].$$

From this we deduce that either $\sim\psi_x(\emptyset)$ or $(\exists x)[\text{nat}(x) \wedge [\psi \wedge \sim\psi_x(\mathscr{S}(x))]$, i.e., that the antecedent in ST 43 is false. Hence it must be true that if the antecedent in ST 43 is satisfied, then ψ holds for all natural numbers.

To establish the KPU equivalents of P 3–P 6, we must show that there are functions in KPU that add and multiply natural numbers. We begin with addition.

To characterize addition of natural numbers in KPU, we must demonstrate the existence of a function $F(\cdot)$ that, for all pairs of natural numbers x and u, satisfies the following conditions:

(i) $F(x, \emptyset) = x$.

(ii) $F(x, \mathscr{S}(u)) = \mathscr{S}(F(x, u))$.

The existence of such a function in KPU is not obvious, so a few remarks are called for.

Let x and y be given natural numbers and suppose that we have constructed $F(x, u)$ for $u \in y$ recursively, in accordance with the stated conditions. Then $F(x, \emptyset) = x$, $F(x, \mathscr{S}(\emptyset)) = \mathscr{S}(x)$, $F(x, \mathscr{S}(u)) = \mathscr{S}(F(x, u))$ for all $u \in y$ and

$$F(x, y) = \mathscr{S}(F(x, v))$$

for the $v \in y$ at which $\mathscr{S}(v) = y$. All these sets are well defined in KPU and satisfy $F(x, z) \in F(x, u)$ if $z \in u$, and $F(x, u) \in F(x, y)$ for all natural numbers z, $u \in y$.

From the preceding observations we deduce first that $(y \times F(x, y))$ and $(u \times F(x, u))$ exist for every $u \in y$. Then we denote by $F_x \restriction y$ and $F_x \restriction u$ the sets consisting, respectively, of all ordered pairs $(v, F(x, v))$ with $v \in y$ and $v \in u$, and use KA 8 to demonstrate that $F_x \restriction y$ and $F_x \restriction u$ are well-defined in KPU for y and every $u \in y$. Finally, we let $\bigcup z$ denote the union of all the elements of z and use KA 7 to ascertain that $\bigcup F_x \restriction y$ and $\bigcup F_x \restriction u$ and

$\bigcup(\bigcup F_x \restriction y)$ and $\bigcup(\bigcup F_x \restriction u)$ are well defined in KPU for y and every $u \in y$.

It is now easy to verify that

(iii) $F(x, u) = (x \cup (\bigcup(\bigcup F_x \restriction u)))$

for every $u \in y$ and that

(iv) $F(x, y) = (x \cup (\bigcup(\bigcup F_x \restriction y)))$.

From this it follows that any function $F(\cdot)$ which, for a given pair x and y, satisfies conditions i and ii for all $u \in y$ must also satisfy conditions iii and iv. Since the converse is obviously also true, we may assert that, for any given pair of natural numbers x and y, a function $F(\cdot)$ will satisfy conditions i and ii for all $u \in y$ if and only if it satisfies conditions iii and iv.

The existence of a function $F(\cdot)$ that satisfies conditions iii and iv for every pair of natural numbers x and y is no more obvious than the existence of an $F(\cdot)$ that satisfies conditions i and ii. Hence, the theorem STM 1 requires a proof.

STM 1 There exists a function $F(\cdot)$ in the universe of KPU that satisfies the condition

(i) $(\forall x)(\forall y)[[\text{nat}(x) \wedge \text{nat}(y)] \supset [F(x, y) = (x \cup (\bigcup(\bigcup F_x \restriction y)))]]$

Moreover, the restriction of $F(\cdot)$ to pairs of natural numbers is uniquely determined.

We shall prove this theorem in several steps. We begin with the uniqueness part.

Suppose that there are two functions $F(\cdot)$ and $G(\cdot)$ that satisfy condition i of the theorem. We shall use ST 43 to demonstrate that they must agree on pairs of natural numbers. To that end, let x and y be natural numbers. Then $F(x, \varnothing) = x = G(x, \varnothing)$. So suppose that $\sim[y = \varnothing]$ and that $F(x, u) = G(x, u)$ for all $u \in y$. Then

$$F(x, y) = (x \cup (\bigcup(\bigcup F_x \restriction y))) = (x \cup (\bigcup(\bigcup G_x \restriction y))) = G(x, y).$$

From this and from ST 43, we conclude that

$$(\forall y)[\text{nat}(y) \supset [F(x, y) = G(x, y)]].$$

Since x was chosen arbitrarily, we must also have

$$(\forall x)(\forall y)[[\text{nat}(x) \wedge \text{nat}(y)] \supset [F(x, y) = G(x, y)]],$$

as was to be shown.

To establish the existence of $F(\cdot)$, we first define a Δ_0 predicate in KPU:

$$[P(x,u,z,f) \equiv [\text{nat}(x) \wedge [\text{nat}(u) \wedge [\text{nat}(z) \wedge [[\text{func}(f) \wedge [\text{dom}(f) = u]]$$
$$\wedge [(\forall v \in u)[f(v) = (x \cup (\bigcup (\bigcup f \restriction v)))]$$
$$\wedge [z = (x \cup (\bigcup (\bigcup f \restriction u)))]]]]]]].$$

This predicate has several interesting properties. The first is an easy consequence of the uniqueness of $F(\cdot)$, which we established above:

(ii) $[[P(x,u,z,f) \wedge P(x,u,\tilde{z},g)] \supset [[z = \tilde{z}] \wedge [f = g]]]$.

The second is an obvious consequence of the definition of P:

(iii) $[[P(x,u,z,f) \wedge [v \in u]] \supset P(x,v,f(v),f \restriction v)]$.

From these two properties of P we deduce that

(iv) $[[P(x,u,z,f) \wedge [P(x,v,\tilde{z},g) \wedge [v \in u]]] \supset [[w \in v] \supset [f(w) = g(w)]]]$.

Next we shall demonstrate that, for every pair of natural numbers x and y, there exists a unique z and an f such that $P(x,y,z,f)$. Our proof is obtained by induction on y. Let x and y be given natural numbers and suppose that we have shown that

(v) $(\forall u \in y)(\exists z_u)(\exists f_u)P(x,u,z_u,f_u)$.

Moreover, let $v \in y$ be such that $\mathscr{S}(v) = y$, and let $\varphi(\cdot)$ be the Δ_0 predicate defined by

$$[\varphi(u,z) \equiv [[[u \in y] \wedge \text{nat}(z)] \wedge [[[u = v] \wedge [z = z_v]] \vee P(x,u,z,f_v \restriction u)]]].$$

Then from (ii)–(v), it follows, first, that $f_u = f_v \restriction u$ for all $u \in v$, and then that

$$(\forall u \in y)(\exists z)\varphi(u,z)$$

and

$$(\forall u \in y)[[\varphi(u,z) \wedge \varphi(u,w)] \supset [z = w]].$$

But if that is so, we can use, first KA 9 to establish the existence in KPU of a set $B(y)$ such that

$$(\forall u \in y)(\exists z \in B(y))\varphi(u,z)$$

and, then, KA 8 to establish the existence of an f in KPU such that

$$[[\text{func}(f) \wedge [\text{dom}(f) = y]] \wedge (\forall w)[[w \in f] \equiv [[w \in (y \times B(y))] \wedge \varphi(w)]]].$$

It follows from the definition of $\varphi(\cdot)$ and from conditions ii–v above that

$$z_u = f(u) \qquad \text{and} \qquad f \upharpoonright u = f_v \upharpoonright u$$

for all $u \in y$. Consequently, we may extend f to $\mathscr{S}(y)$ by

$$f(y) = (x \cup (\bigcup(\bigcup f \upharpoonright y)))$$

and deduce that

(vi) $P(x, y, f(y), f \upharpoonright y)$.

From conditions ii, v, and vi and from ST 42, it follows that, for every pair of natural numbers x and y, there exist a unique z and an f such that $P(x, y, z, f)$, as was to be shown.

The preceding observations imply that there is a function $F(\cdot)$ in KPU that is well defined on pairs of natural numbers by

(vii) $[[\text{nat}(x) \wedge \text{nat}(y)] \supset [[F(x, y) = z] \equiv (\exists f)P(x, y, z, f)]]$

and satisfy condition i of STM 1. To wit: if x, y, and z are natural numbers and f is a function with domain y that satisfies $P(x, y, z, f)$, then

$$F(x, y) = (x \cup (\bigcup(\bigcup f \upharpoonright y)))$$

and, by (ii) and (iii), $F(x, u) = f(u)$ for every $u \in y$. Hence,

$$F(x, y) = (x \cup (\bigcup(\bigcup F_x \upharpoonright y))).$$

So much for STM 1. Next we let $F(\cdot)$ denote a function in KPU that satisfies condition vii and hence condition i of STM 1. Moreover, we let

$$R_+(x, y, z) =_{\text{df}} [\text{nat}(x) \wedge [\text{nat}(y) \wedge [\text{nat}(z) \wedge [F(x, y) = z]]]].$$

Then the operation $+$ on natural numbers is well defined by

SD 13 $[[\text{nat}(x) \wedge \text{nat}(y)] \supset [[z = (x + y)] \equiv R_+(x, y, z)]]$

To see why, consider E 9.4.

E 9.4 Let $0 =_{\text{df}} \emptyset$, $1 =_{\text{df}} \mathscr{S}(\emptyset)$, and $(n + 1) =_{\text{df}} \mathscr{S}(n)$ for $n = 2, 3, \ldots$. Then $1 = \{0\}$, $2 = \{0, 1\}$, and $(n + 1) = \{0, 1, \ldots, n\}$. Furthermore
$F(n, 0) = (n \cup \emptyset) = n$:

$$\begin{aligned} F(n, 1) &= (n \cup (\{0\} \cup \{0, F(n, 0)\})) \\ &= (n \cup (\{0\} \cup \{F(n, 0)\})) \\ &= (n \cup \{n\}) = (n + 1) \end{aligned}$$

$$F(n, 2) = (n \cup ((\{0\} \cup \{0, F(n, 0)\}) \cup (\{1\} \cup \{1, F(n, 1)\})))$$
$$= (n \cup (\{n\} \cup \{n \cup \{n\}\}))$$
$$= ((n \cup \{n\}) \cup \{n \cup \{n\}\})$$
$$= ((n + 1) + 1) = (n + 2).$$

But if our definition of + is well defined by SD 13, the KPU analogues of P 3 and P 4 become ST 44 and ST 45.

ST 44 $[\mathrm{nat}(x) \supset [x = (x + 0)]]$

ST 45 $[[\mathrm{nat}(x) \wedge \mathrm{nat}(y)] \supset [(x + \mathscr{S}(y)) = \mathscr{S}(x + y)]]$

To establish the KPU equivalents of P 5 and P 6 we first record the theorem STM 2.

STM 2 There is a binary function G in the universe of KPU such that

$$\left[[\mathrm{nat}(x) \wedge \mathrm{nat}(y)] \supset \left[G(x, y) = \bigcup_{z \in y} (G(x, z) + x)\right]\right].$$

The restriction of G to natural numbers is uniquely determined.

Here $\bigcup_{z \in y}(G(x, z) + x)$ denotes the union of all the sets $(G(x, z) + x)$ for $z \in y$. When $y = \varnothing$, this union is empty; and when $v \in y$ and $\mathscr{S}(v) = y$, the union equals $(G(x, v) + x)$. The proof of the existence of $G(\cdot)$ is analogous to the proof of STM 1. Hence for brevity's sake, I leave the proof of STM 2 to the reader.

Next I introduce a ternary predicate $R_{.}$ by

$$R_{.}(x, y, z) =_{\mathrm{df}} [\mathrm{nat}(x) \wedge [\mathrm{nat}(y) \wedge [\mathrm{nat}(z) \wedge [G(x, y) = z]]]].$$

Then $R_{.}$ is well defined and the operation $\cdot$ on natural numbers can be defined by SD 14.

SD 14 $[[\mathrm{nat}(x) \wedge \mathrm{nat}(y)] \supset [[z = (x \cdot y)] \equiv R_{.}(x, y, z)]]$

To see why, consider E 9.5.

E 9.5 Let 0, 1, 2, and $(n + 1)$ be as defined in E 9.4. Then

$$G(n, 0) = 0$$

$$G(n, 1) = (G(n, 0) + n) = n$$

$$G(n, 2) = ((G(n, 0) + n) \cup (G(n, 1) + n))$$
$$= (n \cup (n + n)) = (n + n).$$

But if this is so, then the KPU equivalents of P 5 and P 6 can be stated, respectively, as ST 46 and ST 47.

ST 46 $[\mathrm{nat}(x) \supset [(x \cdot 0) = 0]]$

ST 47 $[[\mathrm{nat}(x) \wedge \mathrm{nat}(y)] \supset [(x \cdot \mathscr{S}(y)) = ((x \cdot y) + x)]]$

From ST 36–ST 47 and the obvious equivalent of P 7, ST 48, we see that there is an interpretation of P 1, ..., P 9 in KPU in which 0, S, and $<$ correspond, respectively, to $\varnothing$, $\mathscr{S}$, and the restriction of ε to the natural numbers in KPU, and in which $+$ and $\cdot$ correspond to the operations $+$ and $\cdot$ defined above.

ST 48 $[\mathrm{nat}(x) \supset \sim[x \in \varnothing]]$

Specifically, if $\mathscr{D}$ is any model of KPU, we can use the individuals in $|\mathscr{D}|$ that satisfy nat$(\cdot)$ to represent natural numbers and we can associate 0, S, $<$, $+$, and $\cdot$ with the interpretation of $\varnothing$, $\mathscr{S}$, ε, $+$, and $\cdot$ in $\mathscr{D}$.

9.8 Admissible Structures and Models of KPU

If KPU is consistent, any interpretation of P 1, ..., P 9 in KPU is a model of $T(P)$. To show that KPU is consistent, we establish the existence of a model of KPU.

To describe the intended models of KPU we must step outside KPU for a moment. Let α denote an ordinal; let λ denote a *limit ordinal,* i.e., an ordinal that is different from 0 and has the property that, if $\alpha \in \lambda$, $(\alpha + 1) \in \lambda$ as well; and let M be a set of urelements. In addition, define V_M recursively as follows:

$$V_M(0) = \varnothing,$$

$$V_M(\alpha + 1) = \text{power set of } (M \cup V_M(\alpha)),$$

$$V_M(\lambda) = \bigcup_{\alpha \in \lambda} V_M(\alpha) \text{ if } \lambda \text{ is a limit ordinal,}$$

$$V_M = \bigcup_{\alpha} V_M(\alpha),$$

where the last union is over all ordinals and where the power set of $(M \cup V_M(\alpha))$ is the collection of all subsets of $(M \cup V_M(\alpha))$. Finally, let A be a subset of V_M and let

$$\mathscr{A}_M = (|\mathscr{A}_M|, N_{\mathscr{A}_M}, F^{\mathscr{A}_M}, G^{\mathscr{A}_M})$$

be a structure for L in which $|\mathscr{A}_M| = (M \cup A)$, $(M \cap A) = \varnothing$, $U^{\mathscr{A}_M}(x)$ if and only if $x \in M$, $S^{\mathscr{A}_M}(x)$ if and only if $x \in A$, $\varepsilon^{\mathscr{A}_M}$ is the restriction of the membership relation on V_M to $(M \cup A)$, and $F^{\mathscr{A}_M}$ is empty. Then $\mathscr{A}_M$ is *admissible* if and only if (1)$(M \cup A)$ is transitive in V_M and (2) $\mathscr{A}_M$ is a model of KPU.

It is not obvious that an admissible structure exists. However, ST 49 shows there are many such structures.

ST 49 Let $\mathscr{A}_M$ be the structure for L described above; let ω denote the first limit ordinal; and define HF_M recursively by

$HF_M(0) = \varnothing$,

$HF_M(n + 1) =$ set of all finite subsets of $(M \cup HF_M(n))$,

and

$$HF_M = \bigcup_{n \in \omega} HF_M(n).$$

Then $\mathscr{A}_M$ with $|\mathscr{A}_M| = (M \cup HF_M)$ is admissible.

Since $(M \cup HF_M)$ is transitive in V_M and $(M \cap HF_M) = \varnothing$, it is easy to see that the $\mathscr{A}_M$ of ST 49 is a model of KA 1–KA 5. Thus to establish ST 49 we need only check the validity in $\mathscr{A}_M$ of KA 6–KA 9. If x and y belong to HF_M, they belong to $HF_M(n)$ for some n. But then $\{x, y\} \in HF_M(n + 1)$. Similarly, if z is an element of $HF_M(n)$, the union of the elements of z is a finite subset of $HF_M(n)$ and hence an element of $HF_M(n + 1)$. We conclude that KA 6 and KA 7 are valid in $\mathscr{A}_M$. If x and y are sets such that $x \subset y$ and $y \in HF_M(n)$, then $x \in HF_M(n)$ as well. Consequently, KA 8 is satisfied in $\mathscr{A}_M$. Similarly, if x is a set with k elements $x_1, \ldots, x_k$ and if, for each x_i, there is a y_i such that $\varphi(x_i, y_i)$ holds, then all the y_i occur in some $HF_M(n)$ and $\{y_1, \ldots, y_k\} \in HF_M(n + 1)$, which shows that KA 9 is valid in $\mathscr{A}_M$ as well.

In reading ST 49, note that for a given M the $\mathscr{A}_M$ described in the theorem is the smallest admissible structure for L there is. Observe also that in defining HF_M we need not assume the existence of ω. Certainly ω need not exist in KPU. Hence when we assert the existence in KPU of an interpretation of $T(P)$, we do not insist that every model of KPU contains a set which we can denote by ω.

In this respect, it is interesting to note that, if $S(x)$, the set of all finite subsets of x need not exist. Hence we cannot derive the existence of HF_x from the axioms of KPU. This fact shows that in constructing the admissible structure of ST 49 we *choose* a set of urelements M *and* employ means of construction that do not belong to KPU.

9.9 Concluding Remarks

In presenting the axioms of KPU, I divided them into two groups, KA 1–KA 5 and KA 6–KA 9. The first describes the properties of urelements and sets. The second makes sure that there are enough sets. For our present purposes it is interesting to note that KA 5 expresses the idea that sets occur in levels; KA 4 insists that when the same set occurs at different levels it is to be treated as the same set; and the restriction in KA 8 and KA 9 that φ and ψ be Δ_0 formulas ensures that when we form new sets at a given level α, we use sets created at levels preceding α and wffs whose meanings are determined solely on the basis of the sets created before α.

Our insistence on Δ_0 formulas in KA 8 and KA 9 puts restrictions on our usual definitional schemes. To see why, let φ be a wff with n free variables $x_1, \ldots, x_n$ and define the predicate $P(\cdot)$ by AD.

AD $[P(y_1, \ldots, y_n) \equiv \varphi_{x_1, \ldots, x_n}(y_1, \ldots, y_n)]$.

In (KPU + AD), P is a Δ_0 formula even if φ is not a Δ_0 formula in KPU; and if φ is not a Δ_0 formula, we cannot be sure that (KPU + AD) is a conservative extension of KPU.

We used Δ_0 formulas in defining $\subset$, $\varnothing$, $\{x, y\}$, $\cup$, $\cap$, $-$, (x, y), and product sets. Similarly, we used Δ_0 formulas in defining $\mathscr{S}$, trans, ord, and nat. In all these cases, when the partial definitions are properly completed, the introduction of new symbols results in theories that are conservative extensions of KPU. We defined + and $\cdot$ in terms of two functions F and G, whose definition was obtained by induction and not by Δ_0 formulas. Note, therefore, that the two theorems STM 1 and STM 2 ascertain that the introduction of + and $\cdot$ result in conservative extensions of KPU.

There is no conservative extension of KPU in which we can introduce the first limit ordinal ω and the set of all finite subsets of M. A few remarks concerning the existence of these sets are, therefore, in order. I begin with ω.

To establish the existence of ω in KPU, we must add a tenth axiom, KA 10.

KA 10 $(\exists x)[S(x) \wedge [[\varnothing \in x] \wedge (\forall y \in x)[\mathscr{S}(y) \in x]]]$.

Suppose that KA 10 holds. Then ω is the smallest of the sets whose existence is predicated in KA 10. More specifically, if W is any set that satisfies the conditions of KA 10,

$$[[z = \omega] \equiv [S(z) \wedge (\forall x)[[x \in z] \equiv [[x \in W] \wedge \text{nat}(x)]]]].$$

KA 10 can also be used to establish the existence of the set of finite subsets of any set in KPU. The definition of such a set is obtained as follows. Let x be a set and let

$$F(x, 0) = \{\varnothing\}$$

and

$$F(x, n+1) = \{b \cup \{y\}: b \in F(x, n),\ y \in x, \text{ and } \sim[y \in b]\},$$

where $n = 1, 2, \ldots$ and where $\{u: \varphi(u)\}$ is short for "the set of all u such that φ." Then $F(x, n)$ is the set of all n-element subsets of x, and

$$\mathscr{P}_F(x) = \bigcup_{n<\omega} F(x, n)$$

is the set of all finite subsets of x. It can be shown that $F(\cdot)$ can be introduced in KPU in such a way that the theory which results from adding the defining axiom of $F(\cdot)$ to KPU is a conservative extension of KPU. From this it follows that $\mathscr{P}_F(\cdot)$ can be introduced in a conservative extension of KPU + KA 10.

Finally a notational matter: In this chapter we have defined the terms $(x \cup y)$, $(x \cap y)$, $(x - y)$, $(y \times z)$, $(x + y)$, and $(x - y)$. Expressions such as $x \cup y$ and $y \times z$ are, therefore, meaningless in the context of our elementary set theory. In the chapters to come, however, we shall adhere to custom and omit parentheses whenever that is possible without destroying the readability of the pertinent formulas. We shall also adhere to custom and use terms such as $\{u \in y: \varphi_x(u)\}$ to denote the set of all u in y that satisfy φ. Finally, when A denotes a set, we shall (often without say) use the terms $\mathscr{P}(A)$ and $\mathscr{P}_F(A)$ to denote the family of all subsets of A and the family of all finite subsets of A, respectively.

A remark concerning the semantics of admissible structures is also in order. Let $\mathscr{A}_M$ be an admissible model of KPU with universe $(M \cup A)$ and write $\in$ both for the membership relation in V_M and for its restriction to $(M \cup A)$. In $\mathscr{A}_M$, $(M \cup A)$ is assumed to be transitive in V_M. Hence, for any set a, that is, for any member of V_M, if $a \in A$, then $a \subset A$. The significance of this assumption is that $\in$ and all the predicates and functions we introduced in KPU have, when applied in $(M \cup A)$, the same meaning in $\mathscr{A}_M$ as in any other admissible structure $\mathscr{B}_M$ whose universe, $(M \cup B)$, contains $(M \cup A)$. For example, if $S(a)$ and $a \in A$, then a has the same members in $(M \cup A)$ as it has in $(M \cup B)$. Also, a will satisfy nat$(\cdot)$ (or any other Δ_0 formula $\varphi(\cdot)$) in $\mathscr{A}_M$ if and only if it satisfies nat$(\cdot)$ (or $\varphi(\cdot)$) in $\mathscr{B}_M$. Similarly, if $F^{\mathscr{A}_M}(\cdot)$ and $F^{\mathscr{B}_M}(\cdot)$ denote the interpretation in $\mathscr{A}_M$ and $\mathscr{B}_M$, respectively, of the function whose existence we established in STM 1, $F^{\mathscr{A}_M}(\cdot)$ and $F^{\mathscr{B}_M}(\cdot)$ assume the same values on pairs of natural numbers in $(M \cup A)$. Hence, adding natural numbers in $(M \cup A)$ has the same meaning in $\mathscr{A}_M$ as it has in $\mathscr{B}_M$.

III Economic Theory I: Consumer Choice

10 Consumer Choice under Certainty

We have used the axiomatic method (1) to construct a symbolic language in which we can formalize mathematical theories and (2) to develop elementary set theory. Now we shall use the axiomatic method to characterize a consumer's choice of goods and services in various price-income situations. The presentation of consumer theory will differ in several respects from our discussion of set theory. For instance, we formulated the axioms of set theory as wffs of our symbolic language, and we envisioned that the proofs of our set-theoretic theorems could be written in accord with the definition of a proof given in section 3.2. In contrast, I assert the axioms of consumer theory using standard mathematical symbols, ordinary English words, and universal terms borrowed from other parts of mathematical inquiry. Similarly, I insist on writing informal proofs of consumer-choice theorems using the axioms of the theory, derived rules of inference of my symbolic language, and universal theorems that belong to real analysis. We shall not write the proofs as sequences of wffs in accord with our definition of a proof. Note, therefore, that our informal use of the axiomatic method in developing consumer theory adheres to the description of the method given in chapter 2.

The purpose of part III is to illustrate how the axiomatic method is used in economics. I shall begin by listing the universal terms and theorems that are needed. Then I shall present the axioms of consumer choice and describe the intended interpretation of their undefined terms. With this interpretation, the axioms and the theorems which follow from them describe various aspects of an individual's or a family's search for an optimal consumer-goods budget. The optimal budget varies both with the funds the consumer possesses and the prices that he faces. In the principal theorem of this chapter we analyze how such variations are related to one another.

In chapter 11 we adopt the axioms of consumer choice as stated in the present chapter and interpret the undefined terms so that the axioms and their logical consequences describe various aspects of a family's search for an optimal allocation of its resources over time. The purpose of chapter 11 is to show how a different interpretation of the undefined terms of an axiom system can suggest new questions to ask and new theorems to prove. To that end we consider theorems that characterize the time structure of consumer preferences and relate this structure to properties of the family's optimal consumption strategies. We also discuss the effect of the age of the head of the family on the family's current consumption. Finally we give sufficient conditions on consumer preferences so that valid predictions of future price indices and knowledge of current-period prices enable the family to determine its optimal level of current consumption.

In chapter 12 I again postulate the same axioms as in chapter 10 and add a constraint on the extension of the term "consumer." Then we interpret the undefined terms so that the axioms and the theorems that follow from them describe various aspects of a family's search for an optimal allocation of its net worth between risky and nonrisky assets. This interpretation suggests many new and interesting questions. For example: How can we measure risk aversion? And how can we determine the way an individual's risk aversion varies with his net worth? To answer these questions I first define two functions, the absolute and the proportional risk-aversion functions, and show that they can be used to measure an individual's risk aversion. Then we establish various relationships between the monotonic properties of these functions and the way an individual's porfolio varies with his net worth.

The axioms of consumer choice insist that a consumer is a triple, consisting of a constant, a set of commodities, and a utility function. The latter is a theoretical construct. Hence those who frown on the use of theoretical constructs will wonder whether there is an equivalent system that is free of such constructs. In chapter 13 I formulate an alternative axiom system that describes the undefined terms of chapter 10 in terms of characteristics of the consumer's market behavior. I show that the axioms of chapter 10 are logical consequences of the new axioms, but that the converse is not true. I also show that there are ways to restrict the extension of the term "consumer" so that the axioms of chapter 10 and the new axioms become equivalent.

In chapter 14 I conclude the discussion of consumer theory by showing that the consumers of chapters 10 and 11 can function effectively in variously structured exchange economies. Specifically, for each such economy we establish the existence of competitive equilibria. We also investigate the stability and the allocational properties of such equilibria.

10.1 Universal Terms and Theorems

Before I present the axioms, I must introduce certain notational conventions and define several concepts of real analysis for ease of reference.

Throughout this chapter we imagine that we are theorizing within a model $\mathscr{D}$ of KPU and the Axiom of Infinity. We assume that the universe of $\mathscr{D}$ contains a finite set of urelements U and a set of objects R which satisfy the axioms of a complete ordered field. We also assume that L contains symbols for all the functions on R to R and predicates in R which we need for our analysis, e.g., 0, 1, $+$, $\cdot$, ε, $<$. The interpretations in $\mathscr{D}$ of these function and predicate symbols are defined on $|\mathscr{D}|$. Thus, strictly speaking, it is the restriction of the functions and predicates in L to R that we discuss in the theory of consumer choice. Finally, we assume that the vocabulary of L is countable. This assumption is in accord with our description of the first-order predicate calculus, and it allows us to assume that $|\mathscr{D}|$ is countable, if need be.

We shall refer to R as the set of real numbers and let R_+ and R_{++}, respectively, denote the set of nonnegative and positive real numbers; i.e., $R_+ = \{x \in R : x \geqslant 0\}$ and $R_{++} = \{x \in R : x > 0\}$. In addition, we let R^n denote the set of all ordered n-tuples of real numbers, and we refer to such n-tuples as (n-dimensional) vectors. Moreover, if $x, y \in R^n$, we let $x \geqslant (>)$ y mean that $x_i \geqslant (>)\ y_i$, $i = 1, \ldots, n$. In particular, if $x \in R^n$, $x \geqslant (>)\ 0$ means that $x_i \geqslant (>)\ 0$, $i = 1, \ldots, n$. Consequently, the set of nonnegative and strictly positive vectors in R^n can be denoted, respectively, by R^n_+ and R^n_{++} and defined by $R^n_+ = \{x \in R^n : x \geqslant 0\}$ and $R^n_{++} = \{x \in R^n : x > 0\}$. Finally, if $x, y \in R^n$, we let $x \neq y$ and $x \nless y$, respectively, mean $\sim[x = y]$ and $\sim[x < y]$.

We constantly use certain operations on R^n: *addition of* two or more *vectors, scalar multiplication of* a vector by a constant, and the *inner product of two vectors.* These operations are defined as follows: If $a \in R$ and x, $y \in R^n$, $ax = (ax_1, \ldots, ax_n)$, $x + y = (x_1 + y_1, \ldots, x_n + y_n)$ and $xy = \sum_{i=1}^n x_i y_i$. If $a = -1$, we write $-x$ for $(-1)x$. We also write $x - y$ instead of $x + (-y)$. From these definitions it follows that, if $x, y \in R^n$ and $a \in R$, then $x + y \in R^n$ and $ax \in R^n$; i.e., *R^n is closed under vector addition and scalar multiplication.* It also follows that the inner product maps $R^n \times R^n$ onto R.

With the inner product we associate a function $\|\cdot\|: R^n \to R$ that is defined by $\|x\| = +\sqrt{xx}$, $x \in R^n$. The value of $\|\cdot\|$ at x is called the *norm* of x and is a measure of the size of x. The value of $\|\cdot\|$ at x-y measures the distance between x and y. When $n = 1$, we write $|\cdot|$ for $\|\cdot\|$.

UT 1 If $a \in R$ and $x, y \in R^n$, then
(i) $\|x\| \geqslant 0$, and $\|x\| = 0$ if and only if $x = 0$;
(ii) $\|ax\| = |a|\,\|x\|$;
(iii) $\|x + y\| \leqslant \|x\| + \|y\|$; and
(iv) $|xy| \leqslant \|x\|\,\|y\|$.

The inequalities in (iii) and (iv) are called the *triangle inequality* and *Schwarz inequality*, respectively. *If neither x nor y is the zero vector, equality holds in* (*iv*) *if and only if there is a constant* α *such that* $x = \alpha y$. *Equality holds in* (*iii*) *if and only if* $xy = \|x\|\,\|y\|$.

In this book we use $\|\cdot\|$ to define what we mean by convergence of vectors, closed sets, and continuous functions.

UD 1 Let $x^m, y \in R^n$, $m = 1, 2, \ldots$. Then x^m *converges* to y if and only if $\lim_{m\to\infty} \|x^m - y\| = 0$, i.e., if and only if, for every $\varepsilon > 0$, there is an m^0 so that, for all $m > m^0$, $\|x^m - y\| < \varepsilon$.

UD 2 Let $x^m \in R^n$, $m = 1, 2, \ldots$. The sequence x^m is *convergent* if and only if there is a vector $x \in R^n$ such that x^m converges to x. The vector x is the *limit* of x^m, and we write $\lim_{m\to\infty} x^m = x$.

UD 3 If X is a subset of R^n, X is *closed* if and only if every convergent sequence of vectors in X has a limit in X. It is *open* if and only if its complement is closed. Finally, it is *bounded* if and only if there is an integer N such that $\|x\| \leqslant N$ for all $x \in X$.

Note that conditions i and iii of UT 1 imply that *the limit of a convergent sequence is uniquely determined*. Note also that a *finite union* (intersection) *of closed* (open) *sets is closed* (open). Moreover, note that R^n as well as $\varnothing$ are both closed and open, R^n_+ is closed, and R^n_{++} is open. In addition, for $a, b \in R$ and $a < b$, the set $\{x \in R : a < x < b\}$, denoted (a, b), is open, and the set $\{x \in R : a \leqslant x \leqslant b\}$, denoted $[a, b]$, is closed.

UT 2 Suppose that $x^m \in R^n$ is a bounded sequence. Then x^m contains a convergent subsequence. Furthermore, x^m converges to $x \in R^n$ if and only if the limit points of all convergent subsequences of x^m equal x.

We shall encounter many functions on R^n to R. They can be characterized in various ways.

UD 4 Suppose that $X \subset R^n$ and that $f(\cdot)\colon X \to R$. Then $f(\cdot)$ is *increasing* (*decreasing*) if $x \leqslant y$ implies that $f(x) \leqslant (\geqslant) f(y)$. It is *strictly increasing* (*decreasing*) if $x \leqslant y$, $x \neq y$ imply $f(x) < (>) f(y)$. Finally, f is *monotonic* if it is increasing or decreasing.

UD 5 Suppose that $X \subset R^n$ and that $f(\cdot): X \to R$. Then $f(\cdot)$ is *continuous at* $y \in X$ if and only if, for every sequence $x^m \in X$ such that $\lim_{m\to\infty} x^m = y$, $\lim_{m\to\infty} f(x^m) = f(y)$. Moreover, we say that f is *continuous* if it is continuous at every $y \in X$.

UD 6 If $X \subset R^n$ and $g(\cdot): X \to R^m$, $g(\cdot)$ is continuous if and only if $g_i(\cdot)$ is continuous, $i = 1, \ldots, m$.

Since $| \|y\| - \|x^m\| | \leqslant \|y - x^m\|$, it is clear that *$\|\cdot\|$ is a continuous function on R^n*. It is also clear that *a convergent sequence is bounded*. From this and $|xy - x^m y^m| \leqslant \|y\| \|x - x^m\| + \|x^m\| \|y - y^m\|$, it follows that the inner-product function is continuous on $R^n \times R^n$. Also, *if $X \subset R^n$, $f(\cdot): X \to R$, $g(\cdot): X \to R$, $h(\cdot): X \to R^m$, and $F(\cdot)$:* $\{y \in R^m : y = h(x)$ for some $x \in X\} \to$ *R^k are continuous functions,* then $(f+g)(\cdot)(=f(\cdot)+g(\cdot))$, $(fg)(\cdot)$ $(=f(\cdot)g(\cdot))$, *and $F(h(\cdot))$ are continuous on X, while $(f/g)(\cdot)$ $(=f(\cdot)/g(\cdot))$ is continuous on* $\{x \in X: g(x) \neq 0\}$. Finally, *if A is a closed, bounded subset of X,* then $\{y \in R^m : y = h(x)$ for some $x \in A\}$ is *closed and bounded, and if B is an open subset of R^m, $\{x \in X : h(x) \in B\}$ is open.*

UT 3 Let X be a closed, bounded subset of R^n. If $f(\cdot): X \to R$ is continuous, there exist $y, z \in X$ such that $f(y) \leqslant f(x) \leqslant f(z)$ for all $x \in X$.

Certain classes of sets and functions are particularly important in economic theory. We define some of them below.

UD 7 Let X be a nonempty subset of R^n. Then X is *convex* if and only if $x, y \in X$ and $\lambda \in [0, 1]$ imply $\lambda x + (1 - \lambda)y \in X$.

UD 8 Let X be a nonempty convex subset of R^n and let $f(\cdot): X \to R$. Then $f(\cdot)$ is *(strictly) quasi-concave* if and only if $x, y \in X$, $x \neq y$, and $\lambda \in (0, 1)$ imply

$$f(\lambda x + (1 - \lambda)y) \geqslant (>) \min(f(x), f(y)).$$

$f(\cdot)$ is *(strictly) concave* if and only if $x, y \in X$, $x \neq y$, and $\lambda \in (0, 1)$ imply

$$\lambda f(x) + (1 - \lambda)f(y) \leqslant (<) f(\lambda x + (1 - \lambda)y).$$

The closure of a set X consists of the set X itself and all points that are limits of convergent sequences of points in X. *The interior of a set* is the complement of the closure of the set's complement. It is easy to show that *both the closure and the interior of a convex set are convex*. It is also easy to verify that if $X \subset R^n$ is convex and $f(\cdot): X \to R$ is quasi-concave, then the set $\{x \in X: f(x) \geqslant f(y)\}$ is convex for all $y \in X$. Finally, it is clear that a concave function is quasi-concave. The converse is untrue, as witnessed in $X = R^2_{++}$ and $f(\cdot): R^2_{++} \to R$ defined by $f(x) = (x_1 x_2)^2$. This function is strictly quasi-concave but not concave.

There is one property of convex sets and several properties of concave functions that we shall frequently use. We record them in UT 4–UT 6 for ease of reference.

UT 4 Suppose that X is a convex subset of R^n and that $y \in R^n$. There is a $z \in R^n - \{0\}$ such that X is contained in $\{x \in R^n : zy \leqslant zx\}$ if and only if y does not belong to the interior of X.

UT 5 Suppose that X is a nonempty convex subset of R^n and that $f(\cdot)\colon X \to R$ is concave. Then $f(\cdot)$ is continuous on the interior of X.

A function on an open subset X of R to R is *differentiable* if its first derivative is continuous on X. It is *twice differentiable* if its second derivative is continuous on X. Twice-differentiable concave functions can be characterized as in UT 6.

UT 6 Suppose that X is a nonempty, open, convex subset of R and let $f(\cdot)\colon X \to R$ be a twice-differentiable function. Then $f(\cdot)$ is concave if and only if $f''(x) \leqslant 0$ for all $x \in X$. It is strictly concave if $f''(x) < 0$ for all $x \in X$.

To conclude our discussion of universal terms and theorems, we look at three useful lemmas. The first, UT 7, concerns a property of certain sequences of sets.[1]

UT 7 For each pair $(p, A) \in R^n_{++} \times R_+$, let $F(p, A) = \{x \in R^n_+ : px \leqslant A\}$. Suppose $(p^m, A^m) \in R^n_{++} \times R_+$ is a sequence that converges to $(p^0, A^0) \in ((R^n_+ - \{0\}) \times R_{++}) \cup (R^n_{++} \times R_+)$. If $x^0 \in F(p^0, A^0)$, then there exists a sequence x^m such that $x^m \in F(p^m, A^m)$ and $\lim_{m \to \infty} x^m = x^0$.

The second, UT 8, establishes an equivalence relation among real-valued functions on R^n_+.

UT 8 Suppose that $f(\cdot)\colon R^n_+ \to R$ and $g(\cdot)\colon R^n_+ \to R$ are continuous, strictly increasing functions. Then there exists a continuous, strictly increasing function $G(\cdot)\colon \{\text{range of } g(\cdot)\} \to R$ such that, for all $x \in R^n_+$, $f(x) = G(g(x))$ if and only if, for all $y \in R^n_+$, $\{z \in R^n_+ : f(z) \geqslant f(y)\} = \{z \in R^n_+ : g(z) \geqslant g(y)\}$.

The third, UT 9, describes necessary and sufficient conditions that a vector in R^n_+ solves a quasi-concave programming problem.[2] In the statement of the lemma a function on an open subset X of R^n to R is taken to be differentiable if its partial derivatives are continuous on X.

UT 9 Let $A \subset R^n$ be open and suppose that $R^n_+ \subset A$. Moreover, let $U(\cdot)\colon A \to R$ and $G(\cdot)\colon A \to R$ be differentiable quasi-concave functions such that $\partial G(x)/\partial x_i \neq 0$ for all $x \in \{x \in R^n_+ : G(x) \geqslant 0\}$, $i = 1, \ldots, n$. Finally, suppose that there is an $\hat{x} \in R^n_+ - \{0\}$ such that $G(\hat{x}) > 0$. If $x^0 \in R^n_+$ and $\partial U(x^0)/\partial x_i \neq 0$ for some i for which $\hat{x}_i > 0$, then a necessary and sufficient condition that x^0 maximizes $U(\cdot)$, subject to the conditions $x \in R_+^n$ and $G(x) \geqslant 0$, is that there is a $\lambda^0 \in R_+$ such that

$$\frac{\partial U(x^0)}{\partial x_i} + \lambda^0 \cdot \frac{\partial G(x^0)}{\partial x_i} \leqslant 0, \qquad i = 1, \ldots, n$$

$$\sum_{i=1}^{n} x_i^0 \left(\frac{\partial U(x^0)}{\partial x_i} + \lambda^0 \cdot \frac{\partial G(x^0)}{\partial x_i} \right) = 0,$$

and

$$\lambda^0 G(x^0) = 0.$$

10.2 A Theory of Choice, T(H 1, . . . , H 6)

Next I present the axioms of the theory of consumer choice under certainty. The axioms chosen as a basis for the theory are less general than they could have been. However, they allow me to present the theory as simply as possible.

10.2.1 Axioms

The axioms of the theory of consumer choice under certainty concern the characteristics of various undefined terms named *commodity bundle, price, consumer,* and *consumption bundle.* These terms satisfy the postulates H 1–H 6.

H 1 A commodity bundle is a vector $x \in R_+^n$.

H 2 A price is a vector $p \in R_{++}^n$.

H 3 A consumer is a triple $(V(\cdot), X, \hat{A})$, where $X \subset R_+^n$; $\hat{A} \in R_+$; and $V(\cdot): X \to R_+$.

H 4 A consumption bundle is a vector $c \in R_+^n$ which, for some pair $(p, A) \in R_{++}^n \times R_+$, satisfies $c \in X$, $pc \leqslant A$, and $V(c) = \max_{x \in \Gamma(p,A)} V(x)$, where $\Gamma(p, A) = \{x \in X : px \leqslant A\}$.

H 5 $X = R_+^n$.

H 6 $V(\cdot)$ is continuous, strictly increasing, and strictly quasi-concave and has differentiable level sets in $(R_+^n - R_{++}^n) - \{0\}$.[3]

In reading these axioms, note that UT 4 and the properties of $V(\cdot)$ postulated in H 6 ensure that every commodity bundle is a consumption bundle in some (p, A) situation; i.e., T 10.1.

T 10.1 If $x \in R_+^n$, there is a pair $(p, A) \in R_{++}^n \times R_+$ for which x is a consumption bundle.

Example E 10.1 illustrates this fact.

E 10.1 Let $n = 2$ and let $V(x) = (x_1 + 2)(x_2 + 2)$, $x \in R_+^2$. If $x^0 \in R_+^2$, it is a consumption bundle for $p = (1, (x_1^0 + 2)/(x_2^0 + 2))$ and $A = x_1^0 + p_2 x_2^0$. To see why, let $\lambda^0 = x_2^0 + 2$ and apply UT 9 with $G(x) = (x_1^0 - x_1) + [(x_1^0 + 2)/(x_2^0 + 2)](x_2^0 - x_2)$.

The properties of $V(\cdot)$ also imply T 10.2.

T 10.2 For each pair $(p, A) \in R_{++}^n \times R_+$ there is one and only one consumption bundle.

To see why, observe first that $p > 0$ and the continuity of the inner product, respectively, imply that $\Gamma(p, A)$ is bounded and closed. From this, UT 3, and the continuity of $V(\cdot)$ follows the existence of a consumption bundle for (p, A). The uniqueness of this consumption bundle is a consequence of the convexity of $\Gamma(p, A)$ and the strict quasi-concavity of $V(\cdot)$.

T 10.3 follows from T 10.1 and T 10.2.

T 10.3 Let $f(\cdot)$: $R_{++}^n \times R_+ \to R_+^n$ be so that, for every pair $(p, A) \in R_{++}^n \times R_+$, $f(p, A)$ is the consumption bundle corresponding to (p, A). Then $f(\cdot)$ is well defined and maps $R_{++}^n \times R_+$ onto R_+^n.

It is usually difficult to describe the way a given consumer's consumption bundle varies with (p, A). However, as E 10.2 shows, it is easy for the consumer in E 10.1.

E 10.2 Let $n = 2$ and $V(x) = (x_1 + 2)(x_2 + 2)$, $x \geqslant 0$, as in E 10.1. In addition, let $f(p, A)$ be the consumption bundle corresponding to (p, A). Then

$$f(p, A) = \begin{cases} (0, A/p_2) & \text{if } p_1 \geqslant p_2 + A/2,\ p_2 > 0,\ A \geqslant 0 \\ ((A/2p_1) + (p_2/p_1) - 1, (A/2p_2) + (p_1/p_2) - 1) & \\ \quad \text{if } 0 < p < (p_2 + (A/2), p_1 + (A/2)) & \\ (A/p_1, 0) & \text{if } p_2 \geqslant p_1 + A/2,\ p_1 > 0,\ A \geqslant 0. \end{cases}$$

To see why, apply UT 9 with $G(x) = A - p_1 x_1 - p_2 x_2$ and $\lambda = 2/p_2$, $[A + 2(p_1 + p_2)]/2p_1 p_2$ and $2/p_1$ according as $f_1(p, A) = 0$, $f(p, A) > 0$, or $f_2(p, A) = 0$.

10.2.2 The Intended Interpretation of T(H 1, . . . , H 6)

One can find many different interpretations of T(H 1, . . . , H 6) in the economic literature. We shall discuss several of these interpretations in this and the next chapter and others in later chapters. Traditionally, the components of x in H 1 have been interpreted as denoting units of ordinary commodities such as apples, oranges, cheddar cheese, wheat flour, pencils, shoes, or hockey sticks. The units of measurement could be a pound for the first four, a pair for shoes, and the natural unit for pencils and hockey sticks. In modern treatments of consumer theory, the components of x can also denote such varied items as hours of leisure, gallons of gasoline, (driven) miles of a privately owned car, and hours of various recreational activities.

For each component of a commodity vector, there is a component of the price vector p in H 2 which denotes the number of units of account that is needed to purchase one unit of the commodity in question. The unit of account may be an American dollar, a Norwegian krone, a horse, or a cow, depending on which real-life situation is to be described.

A consumer is usually considered to be an individual living alone—or a family living together with a common household budget—who has available funds equal to $\hat{A}$. This supply of funds may be taken to be the consumer's income during a certain period, or alternatively, the amount that the consumer has decided to spend on commodities.

The function $V(\cdot)$ in H 3 is the consumer's utility function. Economists used to insist that the value of $V(\cdot)$ at a vector x measured the utility which the consumer derived from consuming x. Today $V(\cdot)$ is taken to be a utility indicator which shows how the consumer ranks different commodity vectors. We shall later see that the latter is the only sensible interpretation of $V(\cdot)$.

The set X consists of all currently available commodity bundles. I insisted that X be R^n_+ in order to simplify the presentation of the theory. In mathematically more advanced discussions of consumer choice, X is taken to be a closed, convex subset of R^n whose shape or form reflects various unspecified constraints on what commodity bundles the consumer can consume. Some of these constraints may be physiological. Others may be technical. Some may be prescribed by law and others may be imposed by religious customs. What they are will differ from one model of the axioms to another.

Finally, in the traditional interpretation of T(H 1, ..., H 6), it is assumed that the consumer in the market will purchase the commodity bundle that maximizes the value of $V(\cdot)$ subject to his budget constraint, $px \leqslant A$ and $x \geqslant 0$. Therefore, a consumption bundle in H 4 is a commodity bundle which the consumer would want to purchase in a certain (p, A) situation. Theorem T 10.2 showed that the consumption bundle is uniquely determined. Below, T 10.5 adds that the consumer's choice of c is independent of the unit in which we measure p and A and that the consumer always spends all his funds on c.

10.2.3 Sample Theorems

We can derive many theorems from H 1–H 6. In this section I present theorems that provide interesting characterizations of two new concepts, the consumer's set of consumption bundles and the demand function.

D 1 The consumer's *set of consumption bundles*, $C(\hat{A})$, consists of all commodity bundles that are consumption bundles relative to some pair $(p, A) \in R^n_{++} \times R_+$, with $A = \hat{A}$.

D 2 Let $f(\cdot)$: $R^n_{++} \times R_+ \rightarrow R^n_+$ be such that, for each $(p, A) \in R^n_{++} \times R_+$, $f(p, A)$ is the consumption bundle corresponding to (p, A). Then $f(\cdot)$ is the *demand function*. Moreover, $f(\cdot, \hat{A})$: $R^n_{++} \rightarrow R^n_+$ is the *consumer's demand function*.

According to T 10.3 there is only one function with the properties specified in D 2. Hence, the name "*the* demand function" is appropriate. T 10.3 also implies T 10.4.

T 10.4 $C(\hat{A}) = \{x \in R^n_+ : x = f(p, \hat{A}) \text{ for some } p \in R^n_{++}\}$.

The demand function has many interesting properties, the most important of which are described in T 10.5–T 10.8.

T 10.5 Let $f(\cdot)$: $R^n_{++} \times R_+ \rightarrow R^n_+$ be the demand function. Then $f(\cdot)$ is continuous and satisfies

(i) $pf(p, A) = A, \quad (p, A) \in R^n_{++} \times R_+$; and

(ii) $f(\lambda p, \lambda A) = f(p, A), \quad \lambda > 0, (p, A) \in R^n_{++} \times R_+$.

The monotonicity of $V(\cdot)$ and the fact that $\Gamma(\lambda p, \lambda A) = \Gamma(p, A)$ imply, respectively, the validity of conditions i and ii. Thus to establish T 10.5 we need only sketch a proof of the continuity of $f(\cdot)$ at a given pair $(p^0, A^0) \in R^n_{++} \times R_+$. To that end, let $(p^m, A^m) \in R^n_{++} \times R_+$ be a sequence of pairs that converges to (p^0, A^0). We must show that the sequence $x^m = f(p^m, A^m)$ converges to $x^0 = f(p^0, A^0)$. Since $p^0 > 0$, the x^m are uniformly bounded. By UT 2 there is a subsequence x^{m_k} and a vector x^* such that $\lim_{k \rightarrow \infty} x^{m_k} = x^*$. Obviously $x^* \in R^n_+$. Moreover, the continuity of the inner product implies that $p^0 x^* \leqslant A^0$. Consequently, $V(x^*) \leqslant V(x^0)$. On the other hand, UT 7 implies that there exists a sequence y^{m_k} such that $y^{m_k} \in \Gamma(p^{m_k}, A^{m_k})$ and $\lim_{k \rightarrow \infty} y^{m_k} = x^0$. But then $V(x^0) = \lim_{k \rightarrow \infty} V(y^{m_k}) \leqslant \lim_{k \rightarrow \infty} V(x^{m_k}) = V(x^*)$. Hence $V(x^*) = V(x^0)$. This fact, $x^* \in \Gamma(p^0, A^0)$, and the strict quasi-concavity of $V(\cdot)$ imply that $x^* = x^0$. Since x^{m_k} is an arbitrary subsequence of x^m, we can use UT 2 again to conclude that x^m converges to x^0, as was to be shown.

Theorem T 10.5 has an interesting corollary, the proof of which I leave to the reader.

T 10.6 Let $f(\cdot)$: $R^n_{++} \times R_+ \rightarrow R^n_+$ be the demand function and let

$P = \left\{ p \in R^n_{++} : \sum_{i=1}^{n} p_i = 1 \right\}$. If $\hat{A} > 0$,

$C(\hat{A}) = \{x \in R^n_+ : x = f(p, A) \text{ for some } (p, A) \in P \times R_{++}\}$.

The next two theorems study the behavior of $f(\cdot)$ at the boundaries of R^n_+ and P. They have no immediate economic interpretation but are useful as means to determine whether a function $g(\cdot)$: $R^n_{++} \times R_+ \rightarrow R^n_+$ is a demand function. We discuss that problem in chapter 13, and for the sake of brevity I omit the proofs of T 10.7 and T 10.8.

T 10.7 Let $f(\cdot)$: $R^n_{++} \times R_+ \rightarrow R^n_+$ be the demand function, and suppose that x, $z \in R^n_+$, $x \not> 0$, $x = f(p, A)$, and $px > pz$. Then there exist $u \in R^n_+$ and $(p^u, A^u) \in R^n_{++} \times R_+$ such that $u \leqslant x$, $u \neq x$, $u = f(p^u, A^u)$, and $p^u u > p^u z$.

T 10.8 Let $f(\cdot)$: $R^n_{++} \times R_+ \rightarrow R^n_+$ be the demand function; let $p^0 \in R^n_+$ and $p^m \in R^n_{++}$, $m = 1, 2, \ldots$; and assume that $p^0 \not> 0$ and that $\lim_{m \to \infty} \|p^m - p^0\| = 0$. Then $\lim_{m \to \infty} \|f(p^m, A)\| = \infty$ for all $A \in R_{++}$.

T 10.9 asserts that the demand function satisfies a certain consistency requirement.

T 10.9 Let $f(\cdot)$: $R^n_{++} \times R_+ \rightarrow R^n_+$ be the demand function and suppose that $c^k = f(p^k, A^k)$, $k = 0, \ldots, m$, and $A^k \geqslant p^k c^{k+1}$, $k = 0, \ldots, m - 1$. If the c^k are not all equal, $A^m < p^m c^0$.

To prove T 10.9, note that $c^i = f(p^i, A^i)$, $i = k$, $k + 1$, $c^k \neq c^{k+1}$, and $A^k \geqslant p^k c^{k+1}$ only if $V(c^k) > V(c^{k+1})$. Hence the conditions of the theorem are satisfied only if $V(c^0) > V(c^m)$. The conclusion, $A^m < p^m c^0$, follows immediately from this observation.

By referring back to the traditional interpretation of T(H 1, ..., H 6) we can give an interesting restatement of T 10.9. Suppose that we have observed the consumer's choices c^i, $i = k$, $k + 1$ in the two (p, A) situations (p^i, A^i), $i = k$, $k + 1$. Then $c^i = f(p^i, A^i)$, $i = k$, $k + 1$. Suppose also that $c^k \neq c^{k+1}$ and that $A^k \geqslant p^k c^{k+1}$. The latter conditions imply that the consumer has chosen c^k in a (p, A) situation where he could have just as well chosen c^{k+1}. His choice, therefore, *reveals* that he prefers c^k to c^{k+1}, and we say that *c^k is revealed preferred to c^{k+1}*. In the statement of T 10.9, we suppose that, if $c^0 \neq c^m$, either $m = 1$ and c^0 is revealed preferred to c^m or there is a sequence of vectors c^k, $k = 0, \ldots, m - 1$, such that, for all k, either c^k equals c^{k+1} or c^k is revealed preferred to c^{k+1}. Since the c^k are not all equal, it makes sense to say that *c^0 is indirectly revealed preferred to c^m* in the latter case. With this interpretation of the conditions of T 10.9, the theorem expresses the following: If c^0 is revealed preferred to c^m or if c^0 is indirectly revealed preferred to c^m, the consumer will acquire c^m only in a (p, A) situation in which he cannot afford c^0.

Finally, it is important to note that two consumers whose utility functions differ only by a monotonically increasing transformation have the same ordering of commodity vectors and hence the same demand function. In fact, we now have T 10.10.

T 10.10 Consider two consumers in T(H 1, ..., H 6) with utility functions $V_I(\cdot)$ and $V_{II}(\cdot)$ and demand functions $f_I(\cdot)$ and $f_{II}(\cdot)$. Then $f_I(p, A) = f_{II}(p, A)$ for all $(p, A) \in R^n_{++} \times R_+$ if there exists a continuous, increasing function

$G(\cdot)$: {range of $V_I(\cdot)$} $\to R$

such that $V_{II}(x) = G(V_I(x))$ for all $x \in R^n_+$.

Thus two consumers have the same consumption bundle in every (p, A) situation if they have the same ordering of commodity bundles. This is the reason why I insisted above that the only sensible interpretation of $V(\cdot)$ in H 1–H 6 is as a utility indicator that shows how the consumer ranks different commodity bundles. The proof of T 10.10 is based on UT 8. Details are left to the reader.

10.3 The Fundamental Theorem of Consumer Choice

In this section we study how the demand function varies with p and A. My main result is the *Fundamental Theorem of Consumer Choice*: Any commodity that is known always to increase in demand when income alone rises must definitely shrink in demand when its price alone rises (Samuelson 1953, p. 107). To establish this theorem we need several auxiliary results that we record in T 10.11–T 10.15.

In the first two theorems we establish the existence of a function on $R^n_{++} \times R^n_+$ that traces out the indifference surface of $V(\cdot)$ through x for each $x \in R^n_+$.

T 10.11 Let $f(\cdot): R^n_{++} \times R_+ \to R^n_+$ be the demand function. In addition, for each $x \in R^n_+$, let $G(x) = \{y \in R^n_+ : V(y) \geqslant V(x)\}$, and let $g(\cdot): R^n_{++} \times R^n_+ \to R^n_+$ be such that, for all $(p, x) \in R^n_{++} \times R^n_+$,

(i) $g(p, x) \in G(x)$, and

(ii) $pg(p, x) = \min_{y \in G(x)} py$.

Then $g(\cdot)$ is well defined and continuous. Moreover, for all $(p, x) \in R^n_{++} \times R^n_+$ and for all $A \in R_+$ and $\lambda \in R_{++}$,

(iii) $g(p, f(p, A)) = f(p, A)$;
(iv) $g(\lambda p, x) = g(p, x)$;
(v) $V(g(p, x)) = V(x)$; and
(vi) $pg(p, x) < py$ for $y \in G(x) - \{g(p, x)\}$ if $x \neq 0$.

It is easy to verify that, for each pair $(p, x) \in R^n_{++} \times R^n_+$, there is one and only one vector $y \in R^n_+$ that satisfies conditions i and ii. Hence $g(\cdot)$ is well defined. It is also easy to show that the properties of $V(\cdot)$ imply the validity of conditions iii–vi. So here we shall only sketch a proof of the continuity of $g(\cdot)$.

To show that $g(\cdot)$ is continuous, we must verify that if $(p^m, x^m) \in R^n_{++} \times R^n_+$ is a sequence which converges to $(p^0, x^0) \in R^n_{++} \times R^n_+$, and if $y^m = g(p^m, x^m)$ and $y^0 = g(p^0, x^0)$, then y^m converges to y^0. To that end we observe first that the y^m are bounded and, by UT 2, contain a convergent subsequence y^{m_k}. If $y^* = \lim_{m_k \to \infty} y^{m_k}$, then $y^* \in R^n_+$. Furthermore, since $V(y^{m_k}) \geqslant V(x^{m_k})$, $V(y^*) \geqslant V(x^0)$. Hence $y^* \in G(x^0)$.

Next we note that when $y^0 \neq x^0$, there is a sequence z^{m_k} such that $z^{m_k} \in G(x^{m_k})$ and $\lim_{m_k \to \infty} z^{m_k} = y^0$. To wit: Let $U(\lambda) = \lambda x^0 + (1 - \lambda) y^0$ and, for each $t \geqslant 2$, let l_t be such that $V(x^{m_k}) \leqslant V(U(1/t))$ for all $k > l_t$. Also let $z^{m_k} = U(1/t)$ for $l_t < k \leqslant l_{t+1}$, $t = 2, 3, \ldots$. Then $z^{m_k} \in G(x^{m_k})$ for all k and $\lim_{k \to \infty} z^{m_k} = y^0$.

To conclude the proof of the continuity of $g(\cdot)$, we let $w = x$ or z according as $y^0 = x^0$ or $y^0 \neq x^0$ and note that, by condition (vi), $p^{m_k} y^{m_k} \leqslant p^{m_k} w^{m_k}$, since $w^{m_k} \in G(x^{m_k})$ and $y^{m_k} = g(p^{m_k}, x^{m_k})$. Hence $p^0 y^* \leqslant p^0 y^0$. The last inequality, $y^* \in G(x^0)$, and condition (vi) imply that $y^* = y^0$. From this and from UT 2 follows the continuity of $g(\cdot)$.

T 10.12 Let $g(\cdot): R^n_{++} \times R^n_+ \to R^n_+$ be as specified in T 10.11 (i) and (ii), and let $P = \{p \in R^n_{++} : \sum_{i=1}^n p_i = 1\}$. If $x \in R^n_+$ and $x \neq 0$, then $\{y \in R^n_+ : y = g(p, x)$ for some $p \in P\} = \{y \in R^n_+ : V(y) = V(x)\}$.

By letting A vary with p in some determinate way, say $A(\cdot)$, we can also make $f(\cdot, A(\cdot))$ trace out the indifference surfaces of $V(\cdot)$. This fact, stated in T 10.14, is a simple corollary of T 10.12 and 10.13.[4]

T 10.13 Let $f(\cdot): R^n_{++} \times R_+ \to R^n_+$ be the demand function and let $g(\cdot): R^n_{++} \times R^n_+ \to R^n_+$ be as described in T 10.11 (i) and (ii). Moreover, let $A(\cdot): R^n_{++} \times R^n_{++} \times R_+ \to R_+$ be so that

$$f(p, A(p, p^0, A^0)) = g(p, f(p^0, A^0)), \quad (p, p^0, A^0) \in R^{2n}_{++} \times R_+.$$

Then $A(\cdot)$ is well defined and continuous. In addition,

(i) $A(p, p^0, A^0) \leqslant (\geqslant) A^0$ if $p \leqslant (\geqslant) p^0$

with equality holding only if $f(p^0, A^0) = g(p, f(p^0, A^0))$. Finally, for every $(p^0, A^0) \in R^{n+1}_{++}$,

(ii) $A(\cdot, p^0, A^0)$ is concave and homogeneous of degree 1.

To establish T 10.13, observe that T 10.5 and T 10.11 imply that $A(p, p^0, A^0) = pg(p, f(p^0, A^0))$ for all $(p, p^0, A^0) \in R^{2n}_{++} \times R_+$. From this and from the continuity of $g(\cdot)$ and the inner product, it follows that $A(\cdot)$ is well defined and continuous. Next note that, for any triple $(p, p^0, A^0) \in R^{2n}_{++} \times R_+$ such that $p^0 \leqslant p$ and $f(p^0, A^0) \neq g(p, f(p^0, A^0))$, T 10.5 and T 10.11 imply that

$$A^0 = p^0 f(p^0, A^0) < p^0 g(p, f(p^0, A^0)) \leqslant pg(p, f(p^0, A^0)) = A(p, p^0, A^0).$$

Similarly, when $p \leqslant p^0$ and $f(p^0, A^0) \neq g(p, f(p^0, A^0))$,

$$A(p, p^0, A^0) = pg(p, f(p^0, A^0)) < pf(p^0, A^0) \leqslant p^0 f(p^0, A^0) = A^0.$$

Finally, if $\tilde{p} = \lambda p + (1 - \lambda)p^*$, where $\lambda \in (0, 1)$, $p \in R^n_{++}$, and $p^* \in R^n_{++}$, if $(p^0, A^0) \in R^n_{++} \times R_+$, and if $a \in R_{++}$, then

$$\begin{aligned}&\lambda A(p, p^0, A^0) + (1 - \lambda)A(p^*, p^0, A^0)\\ &\quad = \lambda pg(p, f(p^0, A^0)) + (1 - \lambda)p^* g(p^*, f(p^0, A^0)) \leqslant \tilde{p}g(\tilde{p}, f(p^0, A^0))\\ &\quad = A(\tilde{p}, p^0, A^0)\end{aligned}$$

and

$$A(ap, p^0, A^0) = apg(ap, f(p^0, A^0)) = apg(p, f(p^0, A^0)) = aA(p, p^0, A^0).$$

For a given triple (p, p^0, A^0), $A(p, p^0, A^0)$ equals the level of income which the consumer, when faced with prices p, would need to achieve the same level of satisfaction—i.e., the same value of $V(\cdot)$—as at $f(p^0, A^0)$.

T 10.14 Let $f(\cdot)$ be the demand function, and let $A(\cdot)$ be as specified in T 10.13. Then, for all $(p^0, A^0) \in R^{n+1}_{++}$,

$$\begin{aligned}&\{y \in R^n_+ : y = f(p, A(p, p^0, A^0)) \text{ for some } p \in R^n_{++}\}\\ &\qquad = \{y \in R^n_+ : V(y) = V(f(p^0, A^0))\}.\end{aligned}$$

The function $A(\cdot, p^0, A^0)$ has an interesting interpretation which we should note. Let $x^0 = f(p^0, A^0)$ and $x^1 = f(p^1, A^1)$. The price-of-living-index number in going from x^0 to x^1 "is familiarly defined as the ratio of the cost of the cheapest bundle of goods at the prices of the second situation which will yield satisfaction equivalent to that of the initial situation, to the cost of the initial bundle at the initial prices" (Samuelson 1947, p. 156). In symbols the price-of-living-index number in going from x^0 to x^1 equals $A(p^1, p^0, A^0)/A^0$. According to T 10.13, the price-of-living index is an increasing function of p^1, as one should expect.

I next give an example of $g(\cdot)$ and $A(\cdot)$. Note that the utility function is the same one used in E 10.1 and E 10.2. Hence the demand function is as specified in E 10.2. Recalling E 10.2, we see that the g and A functions of E 10.3 satisfy T 10.11 (i)–(vi) and T 10.13 (i) and (iii), respectively.

E 10.3 Let $n = 2$ and let $V(x_1, x_2) = (x_1 + 2)(x_2 + 2)$, $x \in R_+^2$. Also, let $x^0 = (1, 1)$, $p^0 = (1, 1)$ and $A^0 = 2$. Then it is easy to verify that

$$g(p, x^0) = \begin{cases} (5/2, 0) \text{ if } 0 < p_1/p_2 \leqslant 4/9 \\ \left(3\sqrt{\dfrac{p_2}{p_1}} - 2,\ 3\sqrt{\dfrac{p_1}{p_2}} - 2\right) \text{ if } 4/9 < p_2/p_1 < 9/4 \\ (0, 5/2) \text{ if } 0 < p_2/p_1 \leqslant 4/9 \end{cases}$$

and that

$$A(p, (1, 1), 2) = \begin{cases} (5/2)p_1 \text{ if } 0 < p_1/p_2 \leqslant 4/9 \\ 6\sqrt{p_1 p_2} - 2p_1 - 2p_2 \text{ if } 4/9 < p_2/p_1 < 9/4 \\ (5/2)p_2 \text{ if } 0 < p_2/p_1 \leqslant 4/9. \end{cases}$$

It is clear from the definitions of $g(\cdot)$ in T 10.11 and $A(\cdot)$ in T 10.13 that they are unobservable theoretical constructs which have interesting interpretations but little empirical relevance. They provide, however, essential building blocks in our proof of the Fundamental Theorem, as can be seen from T 10.13 (i) and the next theorem.

T 10.15 Let $f(\cdot)$: $R_{++}^n \times R_+ \to R_+^n$ be the demand function and let $A(\cdot)$: $R_{++}^{2n+1} \to R_+$ be as specified in T 10.13. Moreover, let (p^0, A^0) be any vector in R_{++}^{n+1}, let $p \in R_{++}^n$ and $\Delta p = p - p^0$, and let $x^0 = f(p^0, A^0)$. If $g(p, x^0) \neq x^0$,

(i) $\Delta p(f(p, A(p, p^0, A^0)) - x^0) < 0$, and

(ii) $f(p, A^0) - f(p^0, A^0) = [f(p, A(p, p^0, A^0)) - x^0]$
$$+ [f(p, A^0) - f(p, A(p, p^0, A^0))].$$

To establish this theorem it suffices to observe that if $g(p, x^0) \neq x^0$,

$$\Delta p(f(p, A(p, p^0, A^0)) - x^0) = (pg(p, x^0) - px^0) + (p^0x^0 - p^0g(p, x^0)) < 0.$$

In condition ii we have just added and deducted $f(p, A(p, p^0, A^0))$.

In reading T 10.15 note that, when $\Delta p = (0, \ldots, 0, \Delta p_i, 0, \ldots, 0)$, $A(p, p^0, A^0) \leqslant (\geqslant)\ A^0$ according as $\Delta p_i \leqslant (\geqslant)\ 0$. Hence, if $f_i(p, \cdot)$ is an increasing function on R_+, $\Delta p_i(f_i(p, A^0) - f_i(p, A(p, p^0, A^0)) \leqslant 0$. From these remarks follows T 10.16, our version of the Fundamental Theorem.

T 10.16 Let $f(\cdot)$: $R_{++}^n \times R_+ \to R_+^n$ be the demand function, let $(p^0, A^0) \in R_{++}^{n+1}$, and let $\Delta p_i \neq 0$ be such that $p^1 = p^0 + (0, \ldots, \Delta p_i, \ldots, 0) = (p_1^0, \ldots, p_i^0 +$

$\Delta p_i, \ldots, p_n^0) \in R_{++}^n$. If $f_i(p, \cdot)$ is increasing on R_+ for all $p \in R_{++}^n$, and $g(p^1, f(p^0, A^0)) \neq f(p^0, A^0)$, then

$\Delta p_i(f_i(p^1, A^0) - f_i(p^0, A^0)) < 0.$

Theorem T 10.15 (ii) tells us how $f_i(\cdot, A)$ varies as p_i changes, with the other components of p remaining constant. It suggests that this variation can be looked upon as occurring in two steps. The first, $f_i(p, A(p, p^0, A^0)) - x_i^0$, is called the *substitution effect*. It measures the change in $f_i(\cdot, A^0)$ due to a change in p_i from p_i^0 to $p_i^0 + \Delta p_i$ when A is simultaneously changed so that the consumer is indifferent between his situation before and after the change in p_i and A. The second step, $f_i(p, A^0) - f_i(p, A(p, p^0, A^0))$, is called the *income effect*. It measures the change in $f_i(\cdot)$ when A is restored to its original level. It is clear from T 10.6 that if $f_i(p, \cdot)$ is an increasing function of A for all $p \in R_{++}^n$, then $f_i(p_1, \ldots, p_{i-1}, \cdot, p_{i+1}, \ldots, p_n, A)$ is a strictly decreasing function of p_i for all $(p_1, \ldots, p_{i-1}, p_{i+1}, \ldots, p_n, A) \in R_{++}^n$, as was asserted at the beginning of this section in the original statement of the Fundamental Theorem for simple commodities.

We do not know of instances in history when consmers have responded to a price hike by buying more of the commodity in question (Dwyer and Lindsay 1983, pp. 188–192). Nevertheless, it is important to note that if $f(\cdot)$ is a demand function, $f_i(p_1, \ldots, p_{i-1}, \cdot, p_{i+1}, \ldots, p_n, A)$ need not be a strictly decreasing function of p_i. To establish this fact, we next give an example of a utility function which generates a demand function that has the property that $f_1(\cdot, A)$ increases with p_1 when p_1 varies over a certain subset of R_{++} and p_2 remains constant. The example is due to Wold (1953, p. 102).

E 10.4 Let $V(x) = (x_1 - 1)/(x_2 - 2)^2$, $x_1 > 1$, $0 \leqslant x_2 < 1.6$. In

$\{p \in R_{++}^2 : A/2 < p_1 + p_2 < A \text{ and } A < 1.8p_2 + p_1\}$

the demand function is given by

$f(p, A) = ((2(p_1 + p_2) - A)/p_1, 2(A - (p_1 + p_2))/p_2),$

and the partial derivatives of $f(\cdot)$ are given by

$\partial f(p, A)/\partial p_1 = ((A - 2p_2)/p_1^2, -2/p_2),$

$\partial f(p, A)/\partial p_2 = (2/p_1, 2(p_1 - A)/p_2^2),$

$\partial f(p, A)/\partial A = (-1/p_1, 2/p_2).$

Note that

$\partial f_1(1/2, 1/3, 1)/\partial p_1 > 0$ and $\partial f_2(1/2, 1/3, 1)/\partial p_2 < 0.$

10.4 The Hicks-Leontief Aggregation Theorem

We suggested above that in the standard interpretation of T(H 1, ..., H 6) the components of x in H 1 are considered to denote units of commodities such as apples, oranges, and shoes. Strictly speaking, these nouns denote families of different commodities, e.g., McIntosh and Golden Delicious apples, Florida and Jaffa oranges, and Thom McAn and Bali shoes. Therefore we conclude our discussion of H 1–H 6 by stating an aggregation theorem of J. R. Hicks and W. W. Leontief.[5] This theorem shows that what T 10.5 and T 10.16 assert about simple commodities is also true of *composite commodities*, provided that the prices of the components of the composite commodities always vary in the way specified by T 10.17, i.e., proportionately within the respective groups.

T 10.17 Let $V(\cdot)\colon R_+^n \to R_+$ and $f(\cdot)\colon R_{++}^n \times R_+ \to R_+^n$ be, respectively, the utility function and the demand function in H 1–H 6 and let $p^0 = (p_1^0, \ldots, p_k^0) \in R_{++}^n$, where $p_i^0 \in R_{++}^{n_i}$, $i = 1, \ldots, k$, and $n = \sum_{i=1}^k n_i$. In addition, let

$$\Gamma_i(p_i^0, z_i) = \{y \in R_+^{n_i} : p_i^0 y \leqslant z_i\}, \quad i = 1, \ldots, k$$

and let $\hat{V}(\cdot)\colon R_+^k \to R_+$ be defined by

$$\hat{V}(z_1, \ldots, z_k) = \max_{x_i \in \Gamma_i(p_i^0, z_i), i=1,\ldots,k} V(x_1, \ldots, x_k). \tag{10.1}$$

Then $\hat{V}(\cdot)$ is a strictly increasing, continuous, strictly quasi-concave function. Moreover, if in H 1–H 6 we let $n = k$ and replace $V(\cdot)$ by $\hat{V}(\cdot)$, then the demand function in the new system, $\hat{f}(\cdot)\colon R_{++}^k \times R_+ \to R_+^k$, satisfies

$$\hat{f}_i(\lambda, A) = \sum_{j=1}^{n_i} p_{ij}^0 f_{ij}(\lambda_1 p_1^0, \ldots, \lambda_k p_k^0, A), \quad i = 1, \ldots, k \tag{10.2}$$

for all $(\lambda, A) \in R_{++}^k \times R_+$, where p_{ij}^0 and $f_{ij}(\cdot)$ are, respectively, the ijth component of p^0 and $f(\cdot)$.

In my proof of T 10.17 we first establish the properties of $\hat{V}(\cdot)$. It is obvious that $\hat{V}(\cdot)$ is strictly increasing. To see that $\hat{V}(\cdot)$ is strictly quasi-concave as well, let $\Gamma(p^0, \cdot)\colon R_+^k \to \mathscr{P}(R_+^n)$ be defined by

$$\Gamma(p^0, z) = \{x = (x_1, \ldots, x_k) : x_i \in R_+^{n_i}, i = 1, \ldots, k, \text{ and } p_i^0 x_i \leqslant z_i, i = 1, \ldots, k\}.$$

In addition, pick z^0 and $z^1 \in R_+^k$ such that $z^0 \neq z^1$, and let $x^0 \in \Gamma(p^0, z^0)$ and $x^1 \in \Gamma(p^0, z^1)$ be the corresponding solutions to equation (10.1). Then $x^0 \neq x^1$ and, for all $\lambda \in (0, 1)$, $\lambda x^0 + (1 - \lambda)x^1 \in \Gamma(p^0, \lambda z^0 + (1 - \lambda)z^1)$. From this and H 6 it follows that

$$\min(\hat{V}(z^0), \hat{V}(z^1))$$
$$= \min(V(x^0), V(x^1)) < V(\lambda x^0 + (1 - \lambda)x^1) \leqslant \hat{V}(\lambda z^0 + (1 - \lambda)z^1).$$

The continuity of $\hat{V}(\cdot)$ can be established in two steps. First let $z^m \in R_+^k$ be a sequence that converges to $z^0 \in R_+^k$. Then (1) the continuity of the inner product and the fact that $R_+^{n_i}$ is closed imply that if $y^m \in \Gamma(p^0, z^m)$ and y^m converges to y^0, then $y^0 \in \Gamma(p^0, z^0)$. Moreover, (2) if $y^* \in \Gamma(p^0, z^0)$, by UT 7, there exists, for each $m = 1, 2, \ldots,$ and $i = 1, \ldots, k$, $u_i^m \in R_+^{n_i}$ so that $p_i^0 u_i^m \leqslant z_i^m$ and so that $\lim_{m\to\infty} u_i^m = y_i^*$; i.e., there exists a sequence u^m such that, for each $m = 1, 2, \ldots$, u^m belongs to $\Gamma(p^0, z^m)$ and such that the u^m converge to y^*.

Next let z^m and z^0 be as above. Also let x^m and x^0, respectively, be the vectors in $\Gamma(p^0, z^m)$ and $\Gamma(p^0, z^0)$ at which $V(\cdot)$ assumes its maximum value in equation (10.1). The x^m are bounded and, by UT 2, contain a convergent subsequence, x^{m_l}. Let $x^* = \lim_{k\to\infty} x^{m_l}$. By (1) above, $x^* \in \Gamma(p^0, z^0)$. Hence $V(x^*) \leqslant V(x^0)$. On the other hand, by (2) above, there is a sequence u^{m_l} such that $u^{m_l} \in \Gamma(p^0, z^{m_l})$ and such that $x^0 = \lim_{l\to\infty} u^{m_l}$. Since $V(u^{m_l}) \leqslant V(x^{m_l})$ and $V(x^0) = \lim_{k\to\infty} V(u^{m_l})$, it follows that $V(x^0) \leqslant V(x^*)$. Consequently, $V(x^*) = V(x^0)$. By the strict quasi-concavity of $V(\cdot)$ and by the linearity of the constraints in $\Gamma(p^0, z^0)$, this equality holds only if $x^* = x^0$. Thus $\lim_{m\to\infty} \hat{V}(z^m) = \hat{V}(z^0)$.

It remains to show that $\hat{f}(\cdot)$ satisfies equation (10.2). To that end, let $(\lambda, A) \in R_{++}^k \times R_+$ be given and let

$$x_i^0 = \sum_{j=1}^{n_i} p_{ij}^0 f_{ij}(\lambda_1 p_1^0, \ldots, \lambda_k p_k^0, A), \quad i = 1, \ldots, k.$$

Then

$$\sum_{i=1}^{k} \lambda_i x_i^0 = A$$

implies that $\hat{V}(x_1^0, \ldots, x_k^0) \leqslant \hat{V}(\hat{f}_1(\lambda, A), \ldots, \hat{f}_k(\lambda, A))$. On the other hand, if $x^* \in R_+^n$ is the vector at which $V(\cdot)$ attains its maximum value in $\Gamma(p_1^0, \ldots, p_k^0, \hat{f}_1(\lambda, A), \ldots, \hat{f}_k(\lambda, A))$, then

$$\hat{V}(\hat{f}_1(\lambda, A), \ldots, \hat{f}_k(\lambda, A)) = V(x^*) \leqslant V(f(\lambda_1 p_1^0, \ldots, \lambda_k p_k^0, A)) \leqslant \hat{V}(x_1^0, \ldots, x_k^0).$$

Consequently, by the strict quasi-concavity of $V(\cdot)$, $x^* = f(\lambda_1 p_1^0, \ldots, \lambda_k p_k^0, A)$, and hence, by the montonicity of $V(\cdot)$, $\hat{f}_i(\lambda, A)$ satisfies equation (10.2), $i = 1, \ldots, k$, as was to be shown.

The prices of the components of composite commodities such as cheese, meat, and shoes do not usually vary in the way assumed by T 10.17. Even so, the theorem is useful. For example, consider an econometrician who studies consumer behavior. He has information on what each one of a sample of consumers spent on various composite commodities during a given period, and he knows the income of each consumer during that period. If the sample consumers are from the same town or city, it may be true that they all faced the same prices in the market and that these prices were constant over the period in question. It may also be true that their demand functions differ in some stochastically determinate way. If so, the econometrician can study how some representative consumer's demand function for the composite commodities, $\hat{f}(\lambda^0, \cdot)$, varies with A, where $\lambda_i^0 p_i^0$, $i = 1, \ldots, k$, denotes the observed values of prices during the period. Whenever $\hat{f}_i(\lambda^0, \cdot)$ is monotonic, such information also tells how, in a neighborhood of λ^0, $\hat{f}_i(\cdot, A)$ varies with the different components of λ, all other components being constant. Finally, T 10.17 shows that it makes sense to talk about demand for composite commodities in the given situation, and it describes how the inferred properties of $\hat{f}(\cdot)$ are related to the properties of $f(\cdot)$. Note in particular that if $\hat{f}_i(\lambda^0, \cdot)$ is an increasing function,

$$f_{ij}(\lambda_1^0 p_1^0, \ldots, \lambda_{i-1}^0 p_{i-1}^0, \lambda_i^0 p_{i1}^0, \ldots, \lambda_i^0 p_{i(j-1)}^0, \cdot, \lambda_i^0 p_{i(j+1)}^0, \ldots, \lambda_k^0 p_k^0, A)$$

need not be a strictly decreasing function of p_{ij}.

11 Time Preference and Consumption Strategies

In chapter 10 I presented axioms for a theory of choice and described their intended interpretation. Almost all the theorems we derived from the axioms were formulated with this interpretation in mind and were motivated by questions related to it. Now I shall propose a different interpretation and show how it leads to new questions and new theorems.

11.1 An Alternative Interpretation of T(H 1, ..., H 6)

Let $x \in R_+^n$ be a commodity bundle; assume that $n = m\xi$; and write $x = (x_1, \ldots, x_\xi)$, where $x_i \in R_+^m$, $i = 1, \ldots, \xi$. In the new interpretation of T(H 1, ..., H 6) the components of x_i, x_{ij}, $j = 1, \ldots, m$, denote so many units of ordinary commodities such as apples and oranges which the consumer can buy and consume in "period" i. (A period stands for a year that begins on January 1 and ends on December 31.) The first period is the *current period*; period ξ is the year during which the consumer dies. We assume that the kinds of commodities that are available in one period are available in all other periods as well, and we let x_{ij} and x_{kj} denote so many units of the same kind of commodity. The only difference between them is that x_{ij} is a period i commodity, while x_{kj} is a period k commodity.

Next, let $p \in R_{++}^n$ be a price and write $p = (p_1, \ldots, p_\xi)$, where $p_i \in R_{++}^m$, $i = 1, \ldots, \xi$. Let $\tilde{p}_i = (\tilde{p}_{i1}, \ldots, \tilde{p}_{im}) \in R_{++}^m$, $i = 1, \ldots, \xi$, where $\tilde{p}_{ij}$ denotes the number of units of the i-period unit of account that it takes to purchase one unit of x_{ij}, $j = 1, \ldots, m$. Let r_i denote the interest rate in period i; i.e., let $1/(1 + r_i)$ equal the number of units of the i-period unit of account that it takes to buy one unit of the $(i + 1)$-period unit of account. Then in the new interpretation of T(H 1, ..., H 6),

$$p_1 = \tilde{p}_1 \qquad \text{and} \qquad p_i = \left(\prod_{j=1}^{i-1} (1 + r_j)^{-1} \right) \tilde{p}_i, \qquad i = 2, \ldots, \xi.$$

Here $\prod_{j=1}^{i-1} (1 + r_j)^{-1}$ equals the number of units of the current-period unit of account that one receives in exchange for one unit of the i-period unit of account.

As before, a consumer is an individual living alone—or a family living together with a common budget—who has available funds of current-period units of account equal to $\hat{A}$. The function $V(\cdot)$ is the consumer's utility indicator. In addition,

$$\hat{A} = W_{-1} + y_1 + \sum_{i=2}^{\xi} \left(\prod_{j=1}^{i-1} (1 + r_j)^{-1} \right) y_i,$$

where W_{-1} denotes the value (in current-period units of account) of the consumer's initial net worth in period 1 and where y_i, $i = 1, \ldots, \xi$, denotes the income (in i-period units of account) that the consumer will receive in period i.

In the current period, the consumer chooses a consumption bundle c that will maximize the value of $V(\cdot)$ subject to his budget constraint. The vector c can be interpreted in two ways: (1) the consumer buys c at the *current-period prices* p, consumes c_1, and then expects to have c_i delivered to him for consumption in period i; or (2) the consumer buys c_1 at the current-period price p_1 and plans to acquire c_i, $i = 2, \ldots, \xi$, in period i at prices $\tilde{p}_i$. In the first case we must assume that the consumer knows the value of (p, A). In the second case we must assume that he knows the value of (p_1, W_{-1}, y_1, r_1) and that either he knows the values of $(\tilde{p}_i, r_i, y_i)$, $i = 2, \ldots, \xi$, with certainty or his expectations with respect to their values are point expectations. Since interpretation 1 has little empirical relevance in a world where there are relatively few futures markets, we adopt interpretation 2 here.

The preceding interpretation of T(H 1, . . . , H 6) suggests many new questions. Some concern the consumer's ordering of commodity bundles in different periods. How are they related to each other? Are they independent and stationary? Furthermore, can the notion of time preference be defined in T(H 1, . . . , H 6)?

Other questions pertain to the construction of price indices, $P_i(\cdot)\colon R^m_{++} \to R_{++}$, for each period $i = 1, \ldots, \xi$. Do price indices exist with the property that the consumer, upon knowledge of the actual value of $P_1(\cdot)$ and of the forecasted values of $P_i(\cdot)$, $i = 2, \ldots, \xi$, can decide how many units of the current-period unit of account to spend on current commodities? If such indices do exist, does $P_i(\cdot)$, $i = 1, \ldots, \xi$, provide a meaningful measure of the cost of living in period i?

11.2 The Time Structure of Consumer Preferences

The ordering of commodity bundles induced by the $V(\cdot)$ of H 3 and H 6 is a *preference order*. We shall refer to this order as the consumer's preference order or simply as the consumer's preferences.

Our questions concerning consumer preferences and price indices involve several new concepts which require precise definitions. A quick look at the definitions D 2 and D 4 below suffice for us to see that independence and stationarity are not necessary properties of a consumer's preference order. Hence to answer our questions we must first find conditions on $V(\cdot)$ that will ensure that the consumer's preferences are independent and stationary. That we do in this section with the help of a tenth universal theorem:

UT 10 Suppose that $\preceq$ is a reflexive and transitive binary relation in R_+^n. Also suppose that, if $x, y \in R_+^n$, then either $x \preceq y$ or $y \preceq x$. Finally suppose that, for all $x \in R_+^n$, the sets $\{y \in R_+^n : y \preceq x\}$ and $\{y \in R_+^n : x \preceq y\}$ are closed. Then there exists a continuous function $U(\cdot): R_+^n \to R$ such that, for all $x, y \in R_+^n$, $x \preceq y$ if and only if $U(x) \leqslant U(y)$.

This theorem is due to Gerard Debreu. (The proof can be found in Debreu 1959, pp. 56–59.) When $x, y \in R_+^n$ and $x \leqslant y$ imply $x \preceq y$ and not $y \preceq x$ (unless $x = y$), then

$$U(x) = \max\{z \in R_+ : z\cdot(1, \ldots, 1) \preceq x\}, \qquad x \in R_+^n,$$

is a continuous function that satisfies $x \preceq y$ if and only if $U(x) \leqslant U(y)$. (See Wold 1943, pp. 223–226.)

11.2.1 Independent Preference Structures

To characterize independent consumer preferences, we first introduce the idea of a separable preference ordering. To that end, let $\phi = \{\phi_1, \ldots, \phi_k\}$ denote a nonempty subset of $\{1, \ldots, \xi\}$, with $\phi_i < \phi_{i+1}$, $i = 1, \ldots, k-1$, and let ϕ^c denote its complement. Moreover, for every $x \in R_+^n$, let $x_\phi = (x_{\phi_1}, \ldots, x_{\phi_k})$, where $x_{\phi_i} \in R_+^m$ denotes the ϕ_ith component of $x = (x_1, \ldots, x_\xi)$, and define x_{ϕ^c} the same way. Finally, for every $x \in R_+^n$, write (x_ϕ, x_{ϕ^c}) for x even though the components of x_ϕ and x_{ϕ^c} may be intermixed in x; and, for all $x, y, z \in R_+^n$ with $z_\phi = x_\phi$ and $z_{\phi^c} = y_{\phi^c}$, write (x_ϕ, y_{ϕ^c}) for (z_ϕ, z_{ϕ^c}). Then separable consumer preference orders can be characterized as in D 1.

D 1 Let $\phi = \{i\}$ for some $i \in \{1, \ldots, \xi\}$. The ordering of R_+^n induced by $V(\cdot)$ is *separable* if and only if, for all i and all vectors $x, y, z, u \in R_+^n$, $V(x_\phi, z_{\phi^c}) \leqslant V(y_\phi, z_{\phi^c})$ only if $V(x_\phi, u_{\phi^c}) \leqslant V(y_\phi, u_{\phi^c})$.

If we let $\preceq$ denote the ordering of R_+^n that is induced by $V(\cdot)$, the ordering satisfies

$$x \preceq y \text{ iff } V(x) \leqslant V(y), \qquad x, y \in R_+^n. \tag{11.1}$$

Similarly, if ϕ is as in D 1, and if we let $\preceq_\phi$ denote the ordering of R_+^m that is induced by $V(\cdot, w_{\phi^c})$, where $w \in R_+^n$, the ordering satisfies

$$z \preceq_\phi u \text{ iff } V(z, w_{\phi^c}) \leqslant V(u, w_{\phi^c}), \qquad z, u \in R_+^m. \tag{11.2}$$

According to D 1, $\preceq$ is separable if and only if $\preceq_\phi$ is independent of w_{ϕ^c} for all $\phi \subset \{1, \dots, \xi\}$. Such orderings of R_+^n are characterized in T 11.1.

T 11.1 Let $\preceq$ be the ordering of R_+^n induced by $V(\cdot)$. Then $\preceq$ is separable if and only if there exist a continuous, strictly increasing, real-valued function $F(\cdot)$ and continuous, strictly increasing, strictly quasi-concave functions $U_i(\cdot)\colon R_+^m \to R$, $i = 1, \dots, \xi$, such that

$$V(x) = F(U_1(x_1), \dots, U_\xi(x_\xi)), \qquad x \in R_+^n. \tag{11.3}$$

It is obvious that, if $V(\cdot)$ satisfies equation 11.3, then $\preceq$ is separable. So to establish T 11.1 we need only show that, if $\preceq$ is separable, $V(\cdot)$ must have the structure that is described in equation 11.3. This we do as follows: Let $\preceq_\phi$ be as defined in equation 11.2 for $\phi = \{i\}$, $i = 1, \dots, \xi$, and a given $w \in R_+^n$. Moreover, let

$$U_i(y) = V(y, w_{\phi^c}), \qquad y \in R_+^m, \qquad \phi = \{i\}, \qquad i = 1, \dots, \xi. \tag{11.4}$$

Then $U_i(\cdot)$ is continuous, strictly increasing, and strictly quasi-concave. In addition, the ordering of R_+^m induced by $U_i(\cdot)$ is identical with $\preceq_\phi$ when $\phi = \{i\}$. Next, let $Y = \{z \in R^\xi : z = (U_1(x_1), \dots, U_\xi(x_\xi)) \text{ for some } x \in R_+^n\}$ and define $\preceq^*$ on Y as in equation 11.5.

If $z = (U_1(x_1), \dots, U(x_\xi))$ and $u = (U_1(y_1), \dots, U_\xi(y_\xi))$, then

$$z \preceq^* u \text{ iff } V(x) \leqslant V(y). \tag{11.5}$$

It is easy to verify that the separability of $\preceq$ implies that, for $x, y \in R_+^n$,

$$(U_1(x_1), \dots, U_\xi(x_\xi)) = (U_1(y_1), \dots, U_\xi(y_\xi)) \text{ iff } V(x) = V(y).$$

Hence $\preceq^*$ is well defined on Y. It is also a routine matter to ascertain that $z \leqslant u$ and $z \neq u$ imply not $u \preceq^* z$ and that $\preceq^*$ satisfies the conditions of UT 10. Consequently, there exists a continuous, strictly increasing function $G(\cdot)\colon Y \to R$ such that, for $z, u \in Y$, $z \preceq^* u$ if and only if $G(z) \leqslant G(u)$. From this, from UT 8, and from the fact that $\preceq$ and the ordering of R_+^n induced by $G(U_1(\cdot),\ldots,U_\xi(\cdot))$ are identical, it follows easily that there is a continuous, strictly increasing function $F(\cdot)$ that satisfies equation 11.3, with the $U_i(\cdot)$ as defined in equation 11.4.

E 11.1 Let $m = 2$, $\xi = 2$, and $n = 4$. Moreover, let $V(\cdot)\colon R_+^4 \to R$ be defined by

$$V(x) = F((x_1 + 2)^\alpha (x_2 + 2)^\beta, (x_3 + 2)^\gamma (x_4 + 2)^\phi), \qquad x \in R_+^4$$

where $0 < \alpha, \beta, \gamma, \phi$; $\alpha + \beta = \gamma + \phi = 1$; and $F(\cdot)\colon R_+^2 \to R$ is continuous, increasing, and strictly concave. Then $\preceq$ is separable.

When $\preceq$ in equation 11.1 is separable (independent) we say that $V(\cdot)$ is separable (independent). Separable utility functions are often said to be weakly independent, while independent (i.e., strongly independent) utility functions are described as additively separable. I will explain why in a moment, but first a definition.

D 2 Let ϕ denote a nonempty subset of $\{1,\ldots,\xi\}$ and suppose that $\xi \geqslant 3$. The ordering of R_+^n induced by $V(\cdot)$ is *independent* if and only if, for all ϕ and all vectors $x, y, z, u \in R_+^n$, $V(x_\phi, z_{\phi^c}) \leqslant V(y_\phi, z_{\phi^c})$ only if $V(x_\phi, u_{\phi^c}) \leqslant V(y_\phi, u_{\phi^c})$.

Such utility functions have an additive structure, as witnessed by T 11.2, another theorem of Debreu's (1959a, p. 21).

T 11.2 Suppose that $\xi \geqslant 3$ and let $\preceq$ be the ordering of R_+^n induced by $V(\cdot)$. Then $\preceq$ is independent if and only if there exist continuous, strictly increasing, strictly quasi-concave functions $U_i(\cdot)\colon R_+^m \to R$, $i = 1, \ldots, \xi$, and a continuous, strictly increasing function $G(\cdot)$: {range of $V(\cdot)$} $\to R$ such that

$$G(V(x)) = \sum_{i=1}^{\xi} U_i(x_i), \qquad x \in R_+^n. \tag{11.6}$$

The function $G(V(\cdot))$ is determined up to an increasing linear transformation.

In reading T 11.2 note that, by UT 8, if $H(\cdot)$: {range of $V(\cdot)$} $\to R$ is continuous and strictly increasing, the orderings of R_+^n induced by $V(\cdot)$ and $H(V(\cdot))$ are identical. Note also that if $V(\cdot)$ satisfies equation 11.3, $H(V(\cdot))$ satisfies (11.3) with $F(\cdot)$ replaced by $H(F(\cdot))$. Finally, observe that if $V(\cdot)$ satisfies equation 11.6, there need not exist continuous, strictly increasing, strictly quasi-concave functions $\tilde{U}_i(\cdot)\colon R_+^m \to R$, $i = 1, \ldots, \xi$, such that $H(V(x)) = \sum_{i=1}^{\xi} \tilde{U}_i(x_i)$, $x \in R_+^n$. The theorem asserts that, if $H(\cdot)$ and $G(\cdot)$ are two real valued, strictly increasing, continuous functions on the range of $V(\cdot)$ such that both $H(V(\cdot))$ and $G(V(\cdot))$ can be decomposed into the required sum of continuous, increasing, strictly quasi-concave functions, then there exist constants a and b, with $b > 0$, such that $G(t) = a + bH(t)$ for all $t \in$ {range of $V(\cdot)$}.

A proof of T 11.2 can be found in Debreu 1959a (pp. 20–25). Since the proof is rather involved, I will not repeat it here. Instead I present E 11.2, an example that brings out the main ideas of the theorem.

E 11.2 Let $m = 1$, $\xi = 3$, and $n = 3$. Also let $V(\cdot): R_+^3 \to R$ be defined by

$$V(x) = (x_1 + 2)^\alpha (x_2 + 2)^\beta (x_3 + 2)^\gamma, \qquad x \in R_+^3$$

where $0 < \alpha, \beta, \gamma$ and $\alpha + \beta + \gamma = 1$. Finally, let $F(t) = t^2$ and $G(t) = \log t$, $t > 0$. Then $V(\cdot)$ and $F(V(\cdot))$ induce the same ordering of R_+^3, but $F(V(\cdot))$ is not decomposable. Similarly, $V(\cdot)$ and $G(V(\cdot))$ induce the same ordering of R_+^3. However, $G(V(\cdot))$ is decomposable, as demonstrated by

$$G(V(x)) = \alpha \log(x_1 + 2) + \beta \log(x_2 + 2) + \gamma \log(x_3 + 2),$$

which holds for all $x \in R_+^3$. If $H(\cdot)$ is another continuous, strictly increasing function on R_{++} to R, then $H(V(\cdot))$ is decomposable if and only if there exist a, b, with $b > 0$, such that $H(t) = a + b \log t$, $t > 0$.

11.2.2 Stationary Preference Structures

If $\phi = \{i\}$ and if $\preceq$ is independent, the ordering $\preceq_\phi$ of R_+^m satisfies $z \preceq_\phi u$ if and only if $U_i(z) \leqslant U_i(u)$, $z, u \in R_+^m$. For two different values of i, we obtain two orderings of R_+^m which may be, but are not necessarily, the same.

D 3 Let $\preceq$ be the ordering of R_+^n induced by $V(\cdot)$ and suppose that it is independent. Furthermore, let $\phi = \{i\}$ and let $\preceq_\phi$ be the ordering of R_+^m induced by $V(\cdot, x_{\phi^c})$, where x is some vector in R_+^n. Then $\preceq$ is *persistent* if and only if $\preceq_\phi$ does not vary with i as i varies over $\{1, \ldots, \xi\}$.

Orderings of R_+^n that are independent and persistent can be characterized as in T 11.3.

T 11.3 Suppose that $\xi \geqslant 3$ and let $\preceq$ be the ordering of R_+^n induced by $V(\cdot)$. Then $\preceq$ is independent and persistent if and only if there exists a continuous, strictly increasing, strictly quasi-concave function $U(\cdot): R_+^m \to R$ and continuous, strictly increasing functions $G(\cdot)$: {range of $V(\cdot)$} $\to R$ and $F_i(\cdot)$: {range of $U(\cdot)$} $\to R$, $i = 2, \ldots, \xi$ such that

$$G(V(x)) = U(x_1) + \sum_{i=2}^{\xi} F_i(U(x_i)), \qquad x \in R_+^n. \tag{11.7}$$

The validity of this theorem is an immediate consequence of UT 8 and T 11.2: Choose $U(\cdot)$ to be the $U_1(\cdot)$ in T 11.2 and choose $F_i(\cdot)$ in accordance with UT 8 so that $U_i(\cdot) = F_i(U(\cdot))$, $i = 2, \ldots, 3$. That establishes the necessity of the conditions specified in T 11.3. The sufficiency of the same conditions is obvious.

E 11.3 Let $n = 6$, $m = 2$, $\xi = 3$, and let $V(\cdot)$ be defined by

$$V(x) = (x_{11} + a)^{\alpha_1}(x_{12} + a)^{\beta_1}(x_{21} + b)^{\alpha_2}(x_{22} + b)^{\beta_2}(x_{31} + c)^{\alpha_3}(x_{32} + c)^{\beta_3}$$

for all $x \in R_+^6$, where $0 < a, b, c$ and $0 < \alpha_i, \beta_i$, $i = 1, 2, 3$. The ordering of R_+^6 induced by $V(\cdot)$ is independent, since $\log V(x) = U_1(x_1) + U_2(x_2) + U_3(x_3)$, with

$$U_i(x_i) = \alpha_i \log(x_{i1} + e) + \beta_i \log(x_{i2} + e), \qquad i = 1, 2, 3$$

where $e = a, b$, or c according as $i = 1, 2$, or 3. It is also persistent if $a = b = c$ and $\beta_1/\alpha_1 = \beta_2/\alpha_2 = \beta_3/\alpha_3$. Finally, it is stationary in accordance with D 4 below if, in addition, $\alpha_2/\alpha_1 = \alpha_3/\alpha_2$.

In defining persistence, we compared the orderings $\preceq_{\{i\}}$ of R_+^m for different values of i. To ascertain that a persistent ordering is stationary, we must show that the orderings $\preceq_{\{i,i+1\}}$ of R_+^{2m} do not vary with i; see D 4.

D 4 Let $\preceq$ be the ordering of R_+^n induced by $V(\cdot)$ and suppose that it is independent and persistent. Also let $\phi = \{i, i + 1\}$, and let $\preceq_\phi$ denote the ordering of R_+^{2m} induced by $V(\cdot, x_{\phi^c})$ for some $x \in R_+^n$.

Then $\preceq$ is *stationary* if and only if $\preceq_{\{i,i+1\}}$ does not vary with i as i varies over $\{1, \ldots, \xi - 1\}$.

Thus an independent ordering $\preceq$ is stationary if and only if $\preceq_{\{i\}}$ and $\preceq_{\{i,i+1\}}$ do not vary with i as i varies over $\{1, \ldots, \xi\}$ and $\{1, \ldots, \xi - 1\}$, respectively. Orderings that are independent and stationary can be characterized as in T 11.4. An example of a function that induces such an ordering was given in E 11.3.

T 11.4 Suppose that $\xi \geqslant 3$ and let $\preceq$ be the ordering of R_+^n induced by $V(\cdot)$. Then $\preceq$ is independent, persistent, and stationary if and only if there exist a continuous, strictly increasing, strictly quasi-concave function $U(\cdot)\colon R_+^m \to R$, a continuous, strictly increasing function $G(\cdot)\colon \{\text{range of } V(\cdot)\} \to R$, and a positive constant α such that

$$G(V(x)) = \sum_{i=1}^{\xi} \alpha^{i-1} U(x_i), \qquad x \in R_+^n. \tag{11.8}$$

When $\preceq$ in (11.1) is persistent (stationary), we shall say that $V(\cdot)$ is persistent (stationary). Persistent (stationary) utility functions are often said to be weakly (strongly) stationary. It is easy to verify that $V(\cdot)$ is independent and stationary if $G(\cdot)$, $U(\cdot)$, and α exist. When $G(\cdot)$, $V(\cdot)$, $U(\cdot)$, and the $F_i(\cdot)$ in T 11.3 are differentiable, it is also easy to show that if $V(\cdot)$ is strongly stationary, there must exist constants α and β_i such that $F_i(t) = \beta_i + \alpha^{i-1}t$, $i = 2, \ldots, \xi$. From this follows the necessity of the existence of $G(\cdot)$, $U(\cdot)$, and α. When $G(\cdot)$, $V(\cdot)$, $U(\cdot)$, and the $F_i(\cdot)$ in T 11.3 are not differentiable, the proof of the necessity part of T 11.4 is rather involved. Therefore, I shall only sketch the outline of a proof here.

We begin by observing that if $\precsim$ is independent and persistent, we can choose $G(\cdot)$, $U(\cdot)$, and the $F_i(\cdot)$ in equation 11.7 so that $G(V(0)) = 0$, $U(0) = 0$, and $F_i(0) = 0$, $i = 2, \ldots, \xi$. Suppose that we have already done so, and note that the hypotheses of the theorem imply that there exists an increasing continuous function $H(\cdot)$: {range of $(F_2(U(\cdot)) + F_3(U(\cdot)))$ on R_+^{2m}} $\rightarrow R$ such that

$$U(x) + F_2(U(y)) = H(F_2(U(x)) + F_3(U(y))), \qquad x, y \in R_+^m. \tag{11.9}$$

But then $U(x) = H(F_2(U(x)))$, $F_2(U(y)) = H(F_3(U(y)))$ and $H(F_2(U(x)) + F_3(U(y))) = H(F_2(U(x))) + H(F_3(U(y)))$ for all $x, y \in R_+^m$. Consequently, for all $a, b \in R_+$ such that $(a + b) \in$ {range of $F_2(U(\cdot)) + F_3(U(\cdot))$ on R_+^{2m}}, $H(a + b) = H(a) + H(b)$ and $H(a) = 2H(a/2) = \cdots = 2^n H(a/2^n)$. This and $H(0) = 0$ imply that there is a positive constant c such that $H(a) = ca$. To conclude the proof, we use equation 11.9 to show that $F_2(U(x)) = c^{-1}U(x)$ and $F_3(U(x)) = c^{-2}U(x)$. Repeated use of the same arguments suffices to establish the validity of equation 11.8 with $\alpha = c^{-1}$.

11.3 The Rate of Time Preference and Consumption Strategies

Without empirical evidence we can only speculate about the characteristics of the utility function of an average consumer. The independence condition seems reasonable but the stationarity conditions appear restrictive. The physiology of a consumer changes with his age and so do his activities. If he lives in a mobile society, his work and his residence change also. To the extent that such changes are foreseen, they must be reflected in the shape of the utility function. Therefore it is hard to imagine a consumer whose V function satisfies the stationarity conditions.

Speculation alone will not enable us to determine whether a consumer's V function is likely to be stationary. In this section I present a theorem that will allow us to use data on consumer behavior to test whether a consumer's ordering of R_+^n is both independent and stationary.

11.3.1 The Induced Ordering of Consumption Strategies

To establish the required theorem, we need several auxiliary results. The first, T 11.5, concerns structural properties of the U function in T 11.4.

T 11.5 Suppose that $\xi \geqslant 3$ and that the ordering of R_+^n induced by $V(\cdot)$ is both independent and stationary. Moreover, let

$$G(V(x)) = \sum_{i=1}^{\xi} \alpha^{i-1} U(x_i), \qquad x \in R_+^n$$

be a representation of this ordering. Then $U(\cdot)$ is strictly concave.

It follows from a theorem of G. Debreu and T. C. Koopmans (see Debreu and Koopmans 1982, p. 80) that, with at most one exception, all the $U_i(\cdot)$ in equation 11.6 are concave. Consequently, both the $U(\cdot)$ and the $G(V(\cdot))$ in equation 11.8 are continuous concave functions. The concavity of $G(V(\cdot))$ implies that, for any pair $(x^0, x^1) \in R_+^n \times R_+^n$ such that $x^0 \neq x^1$, the function $f(\cdot)$: $[0, 1] \to R$, defined by $f(\lambda) = G(V(x^0 + \lambda(x^1 - x^0)))$, $\lambda \in [0, 1]$, is concave and hence absolutely continuous. This property of $G(V(\cdot))$, the strict quasi-concavity of $V(\cdot)$, and theorem 1 in Stigum 1972 (pp. 253–256) suffice to establish the strict concavity of $U(\cdot)$.

A *consumption strategy* is a vector $C \in R_+^{\xi}$. The next result, T 11.6, establishes the existence of the ordering of consumption strategies induced by $V(\cdot)$, and describes some of the ordering's structural properties.

T 11.6 Suppose that $\xi \geqslant 3$ and that the ordering of R_+^n induced by $V(\cdot)$ is both independent and stationary. Let $G(\cdot)$, α, and $U(\cdot)$ be as in T 11.4. Furthermore, let $\tilde{p} = (\tilde{p}_1, \ldots, \tilde{p}_{\xi})$, where $\tilde{p}_i \in R_{++}^m$, $i = 1, \ldots, \xi$; let $\Gamma_i(\tilde{p}_i, C_i) = \{x_i \in R_+^m : \tilde{p}_i x_i = C_i\}$, $i = 1, \ldots, \xi$; let

$$W(C_1, \ldots, C_{\xi}, \tilde{p}) = \max_{x_i \in \Gamma_i(\tilde{p}_i, C_i), i=1,\ldots,\xi} G(V(x)), \qquad C_i \geqslant 0, i = 1, \ldots, \xi$$

and let

$$\hat{V}(C, \tilde{p}_1) = \max_{x_1 \in \Gamma_1(\tilde{p}_1, C)} U(x_1), \qquad C \in R_+.$$

Then $W(\cdot)$ and $\hat{V}(\cdot)$ are well defined and continuous on $R_+^{\xi} \times R_{++}^n$ and $R_+ \times R_{++}^m$, respectively. Also, for each $\tilde{p} \in R_{++}^n$, $W(\cdot, \tilde{p})$ and $\hat{V}(\cdot, \tilde{p}_1)$ are strictly increasing and strictly concave functions on R_+^{ξ} and R_+, respectively. Finally, if $\tilde{p}_1 = \tilde{p}_i$, $i = 2, \ldots, \xi$,

$$W(C_1, \ldots, C_{\xi}, \tilde{p}) = \sum_{i=1}^{\xi} \alpha^{i-1} \hat{V}(C_i, \tilde{p}_1), \qquad (C_1, \ldots, C_{\xi}) \in R_+^{\xi}. \tag{11.10}$$

We shall sketch a proof of the properties of $\hat{V}(\cdot)$. With only obvious modifications, the same arguments suffice to establish the properties of $W(\cdot)$. The proof of equation 11.10 is left to the reader. Let $x_1(\tilde{p}_1, C)$ be the vector at which $U(\cdot)$ assumes its maximum value in $\Gamma_1(\tilde{p}_1, C)$. By T 10.3 and T 10.5 $x_1(\cdot)$ is well defined and continuous on $R_{++}^m \times R_+$. Since $\hat{V}(C, \tilde{p}_1) = U(x_1(\tilde{p}_1, C))$, it follows that $\hat{V}(\cdot)$ is continuous on $R_+ \times R_{++}^m$. The monotonicity of $\hat{V}(\cdot, \tilde{p}_1)$ is an immediate consequence of the monotonicity of $U(\cdot)$ and of the fact that $C^0 < C^1$ implies that $\Gamma_1(\tilde{p}_1, C^0) \subset \Gamma_1(\tilde{p}_1, C^1)$. Finally, if $C^0 \neq C^1$ and $C^{\lambda} = \lambda C^0 + (1 - \lambda) C^1$, $\lambda \in (0, 1)$, then

$y \in \Gamma(\tilde{p}_1, C^0)$ and $z \in \Gamma_1(\tilde{p}_1, C^1)$ imply that $(\lambda y + (1 - \lambda)z) \in \Gamma_1(\tilde{p}_1, C^\lambda)$. Hence the strict concavity of $\hat{V}(\cdot, \tilde{p}_1)$ follows from the following inequalities:

$$\begin{aligned}\lambda\hat{V}(C^0, \tilde{p}_1) + (1 - \lambda)\hat{V}(C^1, \tilde{p}_1) &= \lambda U(x_1(\tilde{p}_1, C^0)) + (1 - \lambda)U(x_1(\tilde{p}_1, C^1)) \\ &< U(\lambda x_1(\tilde{p}_1, C^0) + (1 - \lambda)x_1(\tilde{p}_1, C^1)) \\ &\leqslant U(x_1(\tilde{p}_1, C^\lambda)) = \hat{V}(C^\lambda, \tilde{p}_1).\end{aligned}$$

In reading the last theorem, recall our interpretation of p; that is,

$$p = (p_1, \ldots, p_\xi), \quad p_i = \left[\prod_{j=1}^{i-1} (1 + r_j)^{-1}\right]\tilde{p}_i, \quad i = 2, \ldots, \xi, \text{ and } p_1 = \tilde{p}_1,$$

where $\tilde{p}$ denotes the prices which the consumer expects to prevail in period $i = 2, \ldots, \xi$. The C_i denotes the consumer's planned expenditures on commodity bundles in period i. Furthermore, the assumption $\tilde{p}_1 = \tilde{p}_i$, $i = 2, \ldots, \xi$, means that the consumer has stationary price expectations. We call $W(\cdot)$ the *induced utility function* of consumption strategies.

11.3.2 Irving Fisher's Rate of Time Preference

According to Irving Fisher, the *rate of time preference* "is the percentage excess of the present marginal want for one more unit of present goods over the present marginal want for one more unit of future goods" (Fisher 1961, p. 62); i.e., for a differentiable $W(\cdot)$ the rate of time preference is either measured by the ratio

$$\frac{\partial W(C, \tilde{p})}{\partial C_1} - \frac{\partial W(C, \tilde{p})}{\partial C_2} \Bigg/ \frac{\partial W(C, \tilde{p})}{\partial C_2}$$

or represented by the sequence

$$\left[\prod_{j=1}^{i-1} \left(\frac{\partial W(C, \tilde{p})}{\partial C_j} - \frac{\partial W(C, \tilde{p})}{\partial C_{j+1}}\right) \Bigg/ \frac{\partial W(C, \tilde{p})}{\partial C_{j+1}}\right]^{1/i-1}, \qquad i = 2, \ldots, \xi.$$

So defined, the concept of a rate of time preference has a place in our second interpretation of T(H 1, ..., H 6) whether or not the consumer's ordering of R_+^n is stationary. However, if this ordering is independent and stationary, then at a vector C, where $C_i = C_1$, $i = 2, \ldots, \xi$, and $C_1 > 0$, Fisher's rate of time preference equals β, where $1/(1 + \beta) = \alpha$ and α is the α of T 11.5.

11.3.3 Stationary Price Expectations and Monotonic Optimal Consumption Strategies

Note that if $f(\cdot) = (f_1(\cdot), \ldots, f_\xi(\cdot))$ and $f(\cdot)\colon R^n_{++} \times R_+ \to R^n_+$ is the demand function, the vector $(C_1, \ldots, C_\xi)$ with $C_i = \tilde{p}_i f_i(p, A)$, $i = 1, \ldots, \xi$, denotes the point at which $W(\cdot, \tilde{p})$ assumes its maximum value in the set $\tilde{\Gamma}(r_1, \ldots, r_{\xi-1}, A)$, where

$$\tilde{\Gamma}(r_1, \ldots, r_{\xi-1}, A) = \left\{ C \in R^\xi_+ : C_1 + \sum_{i=2}^{\xi} \left[\prod_{j=1}^{i-1} (1 + r_j)^{-1} \right] C_i \leqslant A \right\}. \tag{11.11}$$

Thus, relative to the given $\tilde{p}$ and $(r_1, \ldots, r_{\xi-1})$, $(C_1, \ldots, C_\xi)$ represents the consumer's optimal consumption strategy. In T 11.7 we see how C_i varies with i when the consumer's price expectations are stationary.

T 11.7 Suppose that $\xi \geqslant 3$ and that the ordering of R^n_+ induced by $V(\cdot)$ is both independent and stationary. Let $W(\cdot)$, $V(\cdot)$, $G(\cdot)$, and α be as in T 11.6 and assume that $r_i = r$ and $\tilde{p}_i = \tilde{p}_1$, $i = 1, \ldots, \xi$. Then there exists a continuous function $C(\cdot)\colon R_+ \times R_+ \times R^n_{++} \to R^\xi_+$ with the following properties:

(i) $C(r, A, \tilde{p}) \in \tilde{\Gamma}(r, \ldots, r, A)$;

(ii) $W(C(r, A, \tilde{p}), \tilde{p}) = \max_{C \in \tilde{\Gamma}(r, \ldots, r, A)} W(C, \tilde{p})$; and

(iii) for all $i = 1, \ldots, \xi - 1$,

$$C_i(r, A, \tilde{p}) \geqslant (\leqslant)\, C_{i+1}(r, A, \tilde{p}) \tag{11.12}$$

according as $\alpha \leqslant (\geqslant)\, 1/(1 + r)$. In the subset of $R_+ \times R^{n+1}_{++}$ where $C_i(r, A, \tilde{p}) > 0$, $i = 1, \ldots, \xi$, strict inequalities hold almost everywhere for all i if $\alpha \neq (1/1 + r)$.[1]

Hence a consumer's planned expenditures on commodity bundles are likely to decrease (increase) over time if his preferences are independent and stationary with $\beta > (<)\, r$.

It is not difficult to establish the validity of T 11.7: With only obvious modifications, the arguments used to prove T 10.5 can be used to establish the existence and continuity of $C(\cdot)$. In addition, the proof of T 11.7 (iii) can be obtained by elaborating on the following observations: Suppose that $C, \Delta \in R_{++}$ and that $C - \Delta(1 + r) > 0$. Then the strict concavity of $\hat{V}(\cdot, \tilde{p}_1)$ implies that

$$(\Delta/1 + r)^{-1} \left[\hat{V}(C, \tilde{p}_1) - \hat{V}\left(C - \frac{\Delta}{1 + r}, \tilde{p}_1 \right) \right]$$
$$> \Delta^{-1}(\hat{V}(C + \Delta, \tilde{p}_1) - \hat{V}(C, \tilde{p}_1)) \tag{11.13}$$

and

$$[\Delta(1+r)]^{-1}[\hat{V}(C,\tilde{p}_1) - \hat{V}(C-\Delta(1+r),\tilde{p}_1)]$$
$$> \Delta^{-1}(\hat{V}(C+\Delta,\tilde{p}_1) - \hat{V}(C,\tilde{p}_1)). \qquad (11.14)$$

From $\alpha < 1/(1+r)$ and equation 11.13 we deduce that

$$\hat{V}(C,\tilde{p}_1) + \alpha\hat{V}(C,\tilde{p}_1) > \hat{V}\left(C - \frac{\Delta}{1+r}, \tilde{p}_1\right) + \alpha\hat{V}(C+\Delta,\tilde{p}_1), \qquad (11.15)$$

and from $\alpha > 1/(1+r)$ and equation 11.14 we deduce that

$$\hat{V}(C,\tilde{p}_1) + \alpha\hat{V}(C,\tilde{p}_1) > \hat{V}(C+\Delta,\tilde{p}_1) + \alpha\hat{V}(C-\Delta(1+r),\tilde{p}_1). \qquad (11.16)$$

With the exception of, at most, a denumerable set of values of C, the inequalities in equations 11.13 and 11.14 can be made arbitrarily small by letting Δ approach zero. Hence, for nonexceptional values of C and small Δ, we can reverse the inequality in 11.15 when $\alpha > 1/(1+r)$ and the inequality in 11.16 when $\alpha < 1/(1+r)$.

E 11.4 Suppose that $\xi = 2$, that the consumer has stationary price expectations, and that $\alpha \neq 1/(1+r)$. Suppose also that

$$W(C_1, C_2, \tilde{p}) = \log(C_1 + 2) + \alpha\log(C_2 + 2).$$

Then $C_1(\cdot)$ and $C_2(\cdot)$ satisfy the equalities below and the inequalities in equation 11.12:

$$C_1(r,A,\tilde{p}) = \begin{cases} A & \text{if } A \leqslant 2[1-\alpha(1+r)]/\alpha(1+r) \\ (1+\alpha)^{-1}\{A + 2[1/(1+r-\alpha)]\} & \text{if } \dfrac{2[1-\alpha(1+r)]}{\alpha(1+r)} \leqslant A \text{ and} \\ \quad 0 \leqslant A + 2[1/(1+r-\alpha)] & \\ 0 & \text{otherwise} \end{cases}$$

$$C_2(r,A,\tilde{p}) = \begin{cases} 0 & \text{if } A \leqslant \dfrac{2[1-\alpha(1+r)]}{\alpha(1+r)} \\ \dfrac{1+r}{1+\alpha}\left[\alpha A + 2\left(\alpha - \dfrac{1}{1+r}\right)\right] & \text{if } \dfrac{2[1-\alpha(1+r)]}{\alpha(1+r)} \leqslant A \text{ and} \\ \quad 0 \leqslant A + 2[1/(1+r-\alpha)] & \\ A & \text{otherwise.} \end{cases}$$

11.3.4 Optimal Consumption Strategies and Age

The planned expenditure pattern of a consumer is unobservable. Hence we cannot use T 11.7 to test the validity of the stationarity of preference hypothesis. However, we can construct such a test by examining how the first component of $C(\cdot)$ varies with the consumer's age. In T 11.8 we show that the current expenditure plans of a consumer with independent, stationary preferences and stationary price expectations are likely to increase with age.

T 11.8 Consider two consumers, I and II, with independent, stationary preferences. Suppose that both have the same stationary price and interest expectations and that their preferences for consumption strategies $W_{\text{I}}(\cdot)$ and $W_{\text{II}}(\cdot)$, satisfy

$$W_{\text{I}}(C_1, \ldots, C_\xi, \tilde{p}) = \sum_{i=1}^{\xi} \alpha^{i-1} \hat{V}(C_i, \tilde{p}_1), \qquad (C_1, \ldots, C_\xi) \in R_+^\xi$$

$$W_{\text{II}}(C_1, \ldots, C_\eta, \tilde{p}) = \sum_{i=1}^{\eta} \alpha^{i-1} \hat{V}(C_i, \tilde{p}_1), \qquad (C_1, \ldots, C_\eta) \in R_+^\eta,$$

where $3 \leqslant \xi < \eta$. Suppose also that $\hat{V}(\cdot, \tilde{p}_1)$ is strictly concave for every $\tilde{p}_1 \in R_{++}^m$. Then

$$C_{\text{I},1}(r, A, \tilde{p}_1) > C_{\text{II},1}(r, A, \tilde{p}_1)$$

at any triple $(r, A, \tilde{p}_1)$ in the region of $R_+ \times R_{++}^{m+1}$ where $C_{\text{II}}(r, A, \tilde{p}_1) > 0$.

In our interpretation of ξ as the last period in the consumer's life, ξ is a measure of the number of periods left to live. This number decreases with the consumer's age. T 11.8 can therefore be interpreted as saying that if a consumer in two consecutive periods faced the same (r, A), his expenditures on commodity bundles in the first period would be less than in the second.

It is important to note that the conclusion of T 11.8 is independent of the relative value of α and r. Note also that T 11.8 does not suggest that consumption increases with age. Hence it does not contradict the conclusion of T 11.7 (iii). Instead, T 11.8 implies that, if two groups of consumers with independent and stationary preference orderings of R_+^n differ only in that the members of one group are older than the members of the other, then the older group will have larger expenditures for current consumption than the younger group.

The validity of T 11.8 is a simple consequence of the following observation: In the region of $R_+ \times R_{++}^{m+1}$ where $C_{\text{II}}(r, A, \tilde{p}_1) > 0$, the components of $C_{\text{II}}(r, \cdot, \tilde{p}_1)$ are strictly increasing functions of A. This fact is due to the strict concavity of $\hat{V}(\cdot, \tilde{p}_1)$, as is easy to verify. For brevity I omit the proof.

E 11.5 Suppose that $W(C) = \sum_{i=1}^{\xi} \alpha^{i-1} \log C_i$, $C \in R_{++}$. Then it is easy to show that

$$C_1(r, A) = A \Big/ \sum_{i=1}^{\xi} \alpha^{i-1}$$

and

$$C_i(r, A) = \alpha(1 + r)C_{i-1}(r, A), \qquad i = 2, \ldots, \xi$$

in accordance with both T 11.7 (iii) and T 11.8. Note also that, for $\xi \geqslant 3$,

$$\begin{aligned} C_2(r, A) &= \alpha(1 + r)C_1(r, A) \\ &= \alpha(1 + r)A \Big/ \sum_{i=1}^{\xi} \alpha^{i-1} \\ &= \left(1 - \frac{1}{\sum_{i=1}^{\xi} \alpha^{i-1}}\right) A(1 + r) \Big/ \sum_{i=1}^{\xi-1} \alpha^{i-1}, \end{aligned}$$

where $(1 - (1/(\sum_{i=1}^{\xi} \alpha^{i-1})))A(1 + r)$ is the value of the consumer's net worth in period 2 if he consumed $A/\sum_{i=1}^{\xi} \alpha^{i-1}$ in the first period.

11.4 Consumption Strategies and Price Indices

We shall now answer the questions concerning price indices, current consumption, and the cost of living by establishing and commenting on a theorem whose idea originated with Robert Strotz (1957, pp. 269–285). Our proof of this theorem is based on the proposition T 11.9.

T 11.9 Let $f(\cdot)$: $R^n_{++} \times R_+ \to R^n_+$ be the demand function and suppose that $V(\cdot)$ is *homothetic*; i.e., suppose that, for all $x \in R^n_+$, all $\lambda \in R_{++}$ and all $z \in R^n_+$, $V(z) \geqslant V(x)$ if and only if $V(\lambda z) \geqslant V(\lambda x)$. Then there exists a continuous function $g(\cdot)$: $R^n_{++} \to R^n_+$ such that

$$f(p, A) = g(p) \cdot A, \qquad \text{with } (p, A) \in R^n_{++} \times R_+. \tag{11.17}$$

The proof of T 11.9 is easy: Let $g(p) = f(p, 1)$, $p \in R^n_{++}$, and pick an arbitrary pair $(p, A) \in R^n_{++} \times R_+$. Then $A^{-1}pf(p, A) = 1$ implies that $V(A^{-1}f(p, A)) \leqslant V(f(p, 1))$. Hence, $V(f(p, A)) \leqslant V(Af(p, 1))$. Similarly, $Apf(p, 1) = A$ implies that $V(Af(p, 1)) \leqslant V(f(p, A))$. From these two inequalities and the strict quasi-concavity of $V(\cdot)$, we deduce that $f(p, A) = Af(p, 1)$.

If $V(\cdot)$ is homothetic, it need not be true that, for all $x \in R^n_{++}$, $V(\lambda x) = \lambda V(x)$; i.e., $V(\cdot)$ need not be linearly homogeneous.[2] However, there exists a linearly homogeneous function $G(\cdot)$: $R^n_+ \to R$ and a strictly increasing, continuous function $H(\cdot)$: $\{\text{range of } G(\cdot)\} \to R$ such that $V(x) = H(G(x))$. We use this observation in proving the next theorem,[3] T 11.10.

T 11.10 Suppose that $n = \xi m$; let $f(\cdot)$: $R^n_{++} \times R_+ \to R^n_+$ be the demand function; let $f_i(\cdot)$: $R^n_{++} \times R_+ \to R^m_+$, $i = 1, \ldots, \xi$, be such that $f(\cdot) = (f_1(\cdot), \ldots, f_\xi(\cdot))$; and, for each $i = 1, \ldots, \xi$, let

$$C_i(p, A) = p_i f_i(p, A), \qquad (p, A) \in R^n_{++} \times R_+. \tag{11.18}$$

Suppose also that $V(\cdot)$ is separable; i.e., suppose that there exist strictly increasing, continuous, strictly quasi-concave functions $U_i(\cdot)\colon R_+^m \to R$ and a strictly increasing, continuous function $F(\cdot)$ such that

$$V(x) = F(U_1(x_1), \ldots, U_\xi(x_\xi)), \qquad x \in R_+^n. \tag{11.19}$$

Finally, assume that the $U_i(\cdot)$ are homothetic. Then there exist continuous functions, $P_i(\cdot)\colon R_{++}^m \to R_{++}$, $k_i(\cdot)\colon R_{++}^\xi \times R_+ \to R_+$ and $g_i(\cdot)\colon R_{++}^m \to R_+^m$, that are, respectively, homogeneous of degree 1, 1, and -1 and that satisfy the relations

$$C_i(p, A) = k_i(P_1(p_1), \ldots, P_\xi(p_\xi), A) \tag{11.20}$$

and

$$f_i(p, A) = g_i(p_i)C_i(p, A) \tag{11.21}$$

for all $(p, A) \in R_{++}^n \times R_+$ and $i = 1, \ldots, \xi$.

When the $U_i(\cdot)$ are linearly homogeneous, $F(\cdot)$ must be strictly quasi-concave. Note, therefore, that we can without loss in generality assume that $F(\cdot)$ and the U_i have been chosen such that the $U_i(\cdot)$ are linearly homogeneous and satisfy $U_i(0) = 0$, $i = 1, \ldots, \xi$. With this assumption made, we first sketch a proof that equation 11.19 implies equation 11.20: Let $\tilde{f}_i(\cdot)\colon R_{++}^m \times R_+ \to R_+^m$ be the function that, for each pair $(p_i, A) \in R_{++}^m \times R_+$, satisfies the following conditions:

(i) $\tilde{f}_i(p_i, A) \in \Gamma_i(p_i, A)$, where $\Gamma_i(p_i, A) = \{y \in R_+^m : p_i y \leqslant A\}$

(ii) $U_i(\tilde{f}_i(p_i, A)) = \max_{y \in \Gamma_i(p_i, A)} U_i(y)$.

Then $\tilde{f}_i(\cdot)$ is well defined and continuous on $R_{++}^m \times R_+$. Since $U_i(\cdot)$ is linearly homogeneous, there exists a continuous function $g_i(\cdot)\colon R_{++}^m \to R_+^m$ such that, for all $(p_i, A) \in R_{++}^m \times R_+$ and $\lambda \in R_{++}$,

$$\tilde{f}_i(p_i, A) = g_i(p_i)A, \quad p_i g_i(p_i) = 1, \quad \text{and} \quad g_i(\lambda p_i) = \lambda^{-1} g_i(p_i). \tag{11.22}$$

From now on we consider equations 11.22 to hold for $i = 1, \ldots, \xi$.

Next let

$$P_i(p_i) = 1/U_i(g_i(p_i)), \qquad p_i \in R_{++}^m \text{ and } i = 1, \ldots, \xi. \tag{11.23}$$

Since the $U_i(\cdot)$ and $g_i(\cdot)$ are continuous functions of their arguments, and since $U_i(g_i(p_i)) > 0$ for all $i = 1, \ldots, \xi$, and $p_i \in R_{++}^m$, the $P_i(\cdot)$ are well defined and continuous on R_{++}^m. In addition, since the $U_i(\cdot)$ are linearly homogeneous and since $g_i(\lambda p_i) = \lambda^{-1} g_i(p_i)$ for $\lambda \in R_{++}$ and for all i, the $P_i(\cdot)$ are linearly homogeneous. Thus the $P_i(\cdot)$ have the properties that the theorem requires.

To establish the existence of the $k_i(\cdot)$, proceed as follows: Observe first that, for a given p, the function of $(A_1, \ldots, A_\xi)$, $F(U_1(g_1(p_1)A_1), \ldots,$

$U_\xi(g_\xi(p_\xi)A_\xi))$, is strictly quasi-concave, increasing, and continuous on R_+^ξ. Hence there exists a continuous function $k(\cdot)$: $R_{++}^\xi \times R_+ \to R_+^\xi$ which satisfies the following conditions:

$$\text{(i)} \sum_{i=1}^{\xi} k_i(P_1(p_1), \ldots, P_\xi(p_\xi), A) = A, \qquad (p, A) \in R_{++}^n \times R_+;$$

$$\text{(ii)} \; F(U_1(g_1(p_1))k_1(P_1(p_1), \ldots, P_\xi(p_\xi), A), \ldots, U_\xi(g_\xi(p_\xi))k_\xi(P_1(p_1), \ldots,$$
$$P_\xi(p_\xi), A)) = \max_{x \in R_+^\xi, \sum_{i=1}^{\xi} x_i = A} F(U_1(g_1(p_1))x_1, \ldots, U_\xi(g_\xi(p_\xi))x_\xi).$$

Next observe that, for all $(p, A) \in R_{++}^n \times R_+$,

$$f_i(p, A) = g_i(p_i)k_i(P_1(p_1), \ldots, P_\xi(p_\xi), A), \qquad i = 1, \ldots, \xi. \tag{11.24}$$

To see why, fix p and A^0 and let $A_i^0 = k_i(P_1(p_1), \ldots, P_\xi(p_\xi), A^0)$ and $A_i^* = p_i f_i(p, A^0)$, $i = 1, \ldots, \xi$. Let $y_i = g_i(p_i)A_i^0$ and $x_i = f_i(p, A^0)$, $i = 1, \ldots, \xi$. Then $p_i y_i = A_i^0$ and $\sum_{i=1}^{\xi} A_i^0 = A^0$ imply that $V(y) \leqslant V(x)$. On the other hand, $p_i x_i = A_i^*$ and $\sum_{i=1}^{\xi} A_i^* = A^0$ imply that

$$\begin{aligned} V(x) &= F(U_1(x_1), \ldots, U_\xi(x_\xi)) \\ &\leqslant F(U_1(g_1(p_1)A_1^*), \ldots, U_\xi(g_\xi(p_1)A_\xi^*)) \\ &\leqslant F(U_1(g_1(p_1)A_1^0), \ldots, U_\xi(g_\xi(p_1)A_\xi^0)) = V(y). \end{aligned}$$

Hence $V(x) = V(y)$ and $x = y$, as equation 11.24 requires. But then

$$C_i(p, A) = k_i(P_1(p_1), \ldots, P_\xi(p_\xi), A), \quad (p, A) \in R_{++}^n \times R_+, \quad i = 1, \ldots, \xi,$$

since $p_i g_i(p_i) = 1$, $i = 1, \ldots, \xi$. Hence equation 11.20 is valid too.

The proof of T 11.9 can now be concluded as follows: Equations (11.20) and (11.24) imply the validity of equations 11.21. Moreover, the linear homogeneity of the $P_i(\cdot)$, equations 11.18 and 11.20, and T 10.5 imply that the $k_i(\cdot)$ are homogeneous of degree 1. Finally, the relations in equation 11.22 imply that the $g_i(\cdot)$ are homogeneous of degree -1. Hence the $g_i(\cdot)$, the $P_i(\cdot)$, and the $k_i(\cdot)$ have the properties which the theorem requires of them.

Theorem T 11.10 insists that if a consumer's preferences are separable and homothetic, there exists a sequence of price indices, one index for each period, such that the consumer can deal with his budgeting problem in two stages. To wit: According to equation 11.20, knowledge of the values of the respective price indices suffices for him to determine his optimal consumption strategy; and according to equation 11.21, for each $i = 1, \ldots, \xi$, the funds he has allocated to consumption in period i and knowledge of the i-period prices suffice for him to determine his consumption bundle in period i.

Thus T 11.10 provides sufficient conditions that there exist price indices such that the consumer upon knowledge of the values of these indices and current-period prices can determine his consumption bundle for the current period. To show that the given price indices can be used to measure the price of living in the respective periods, we must establish another theorem, T 11.11.

T 11.11 Let $V(\cdot)$, $F(\cdot)$, and the $U_i(\cdot)$ be as in T 11.10 and suppose that the $U_i(\cdot)$ are linearly homogeneous and satisfy $U_i(0) = 0$, $i = 1, \ldots, \xi$. In addition, let $g_i(\cdot)\colon R^m_{++} \to R^m_+$ and $P_i(\cdot)\colon R^m_{++} \to R_{++}$, $i = 1, \ldots, \xi$, be as described in equations 11.22 and 11.23. Then there exists a continuous function $h(\cdot)\colon R^\xi_{++} \times R_+ \to R^\xi_+$ that is homogeneous of degree 0 and satisfies

(i) $h(q_1, \ldots, q_\xi, A) \in \left\{z \in R^\xi_+ : \sum_{i=1}^{\xi} q_i z_i \leqslant A\right\}$;

(ii) $F(h(q_1, \ldots, q_\xi, A)) = \max_{z \in \{y \in R^\xi_+ : \sum_{i=1}^{\xi} q_i y_i \leqslant A\}} F(z)$; and

(iii) $h_i(P_1(p_1), \ldots, P_\xi(p_\xi), A) = U_i(g_i(p_i)C_i(p, A))$, $i = 1, \ldots, \xi$, where $C_i(\cdot)$ is as described in equation 11.18.

It follows from T 10.5 that there exists a continuous function $h(\cdot)$ that satisfies conditions i and ii. To establish condition iii we recall that $F(\cdot)$ must be strictly quasi-concave and observe that, since the $U_i(\cdot)$ are linearly homogeneous,

$$\sum_{i=1}^{\xi} P_i(p_i)U_i(g_i(p_i)C_i(p, A)) = \sum_{i=1}^{\xi} C_i(p, A) = A.$$

Consequently,

$$F(U_1(g_1(p_1)C_1(p, A)), \ldots, U_\xi(g_\xi(p_\xi)C_\xi(p, A))) \leqslant F(h(P_1(p_1), \ldots, P_\xi(p_\xi), A)). \tag{11.25}$$

By a similar argument, based on equation 11.20 and the properties of $k_i(\cdot)$ and $F(\cdot)$, it follows that

$$\begin{aligned} &F(U_1(g_1(p_1))P_1(p_1)h_1(P_1(p_1), \ldots, P_\xi(p_\xi), A), \ldots, \\ &\quad U_\xi(g_\xi(p_\xi))P_\xi(p_\xi)h_\xi(P_1(p_1), \ldots, P_\xi(p_\xi), A)) \\ &\qquad \leqslant F(U_1(g_1(p_1))C_1(p, A), \ldots, U_\xi(g_\xi(p_\xi))C_\xi(p, A)). \end{aligned} \tag{11.26}$$

From equations (11.25), (11.26), and (11.23) and the strict quasi-concavity of $F(\cdot)$, we conclude that condition (iii) of T 11.11 is true as stated.

It follows from T 11.11 and $P_i(p_i) = (1 + r)^{-(i-1)}P_i(\tilde{p}_i)$ that $P_i(\tilde{p}_i)$ is the unit price at $\tilde{p}_i$ of i-period utilities. This observation and the definition of a price-of-living index (see section 10.3) show that, in terms of the cost of i-period utilities at $\tilde{p}_i^0$, $P_i(\tilde{p}_i)/P_i(\tilde{p}_i^0)$ represents the price-of-living index at $\tilde{p}_i$. In fact, the value of this index equals the value of $P_i(p_i)/P_i(p_i^0)$ and

$$\frac{P_i(p_i)}{P_i(p_i^0)} = P_i(p_i)U_i(g_i(p_i^0)).$$

12 Risk Aversion and Choice of Safe and Risky Assets

In his Yrjø Jahnsson Lectures, Kenneth Arrow proposed a simple and beautiful model of how consumers choose their equilibrium balance sheets (Arrow 1965, pp. 28–44). The model is simple because it requires so few assumptions. It is beautiful because it yields such interesting insights into choice under uncertainty. We shall develop a modified version of Arrow's model to be used as a theoretical basis for an empirical analysis of consumer choice among risky and nonrisky assets.

To develop our version of Arrow's model, I begin by presenting Arrow's model as an axiomatic system. The axioms of this system include all the axioms of the standard theory of consumer choice. In addition, they specify that the consumer's utility indicator is an integral, i.e., an expected utility function. I show in the first half of the chapter that Arrow's and John Pratt's theorems concerning risk aversion and choice of risky and nonrisky assets (see Arrow 1965, pp. 43–44, and Pratt 1964, pp. 128, 135–136) are logical consequences of the axioms.

Our system of axioms can be interpreted as describing a consumer's choice of an equilibrium balance sheet in a world in which there is one safe asset, one risky asset, and no debt instruments. Since consumers in the real world have numerous assets from which to choose, we conclude this chapter by discussing a second axiom system which permits consumers to choose among several risky securities. The second system, when properly interpreted, provides the modified version of Arrow's model that we shall use as a basis for our statistical analysis in chapter 28.

Arrow's and Pratt's theorems establish a definite relationship between the structure of a consumer's demand functions for safe and risky assets and the structure of his risk preferences. At the end of the chapter we see that natural analogues of these theorems can be derived from the axioms of the modified version of Arrow's axiom system if and only if the consumer's utility function belongs to a class of functions that possess a certain separation property which D. Cass and J. E. Stiglitz (1970, p. 128) have invented. Our results represent extensions of theorems due to Cass and Stiglitz (1970, p. 142) and to O. D. Hart (1975, pp. 615–621).

In chapter 28 we shall analyze statistically data on the balance sheets of U.S. consumers at the end of 1962 and 1963. There we postulate that U.S. consumers are Arrow consumers in the sense that their choices of risky and nonrisky assets can be described by the modified version of Arrow's model, and we assume that our balance-sheet data represent observations on the respective consumer's equilibrium balance sheets. Based on these assumptions, we establish plausible hypotheses concerning the structure of U.S. consumers' risk preferences. We also compare the relative risk aversion of individuals in different consumer groups.

12.1 An Axiomatization of Arrow's Theory

Arrow's theory of how a consumer chooses an equilibrium balance sheet can be viewed as a model of a simple axiomatic system.

12.1.1 The Axioms

The axioms of this system and the associated theorems involve the undefined terms of T(H 1, ..., H 6), i.e., consumer, commodity bundle, price, and the consumer's consumption bundle. These terms satisfy the first four axioms of T(H 1, ..., H 6). For ease of reference we rename them A 1, ..., A 4:

A 1 A commodity bundle is a vector $x \in R_+^n$.

A 2 A price is a vector $p \in R_{++}^n$.

A 3 A consumer is a triple $(V(\cdot), X, \hat{A})$, where
$X \subset R_+^n$; $\hat{A} \in R_+$; and $V(\cdot): X \to R$.

A 4 A consumption bundle is a commodity bundle c which, for some pair $(p, A) \in R_{++}^n \times R_+$, satisfies the conditions:

$$c \in X,\ pc \leqslant A \text{ and } V(c) = \max_{x \in \Gamma(p, A)} V(x),$$

where $\Gamma(p, A) = \{x \in X : px \leqslant A\}$.

The undefined terms also satisfy three axioms added by Arrow. These open up the somewhat sterile theory of consumer choice to new and interesting theorems:

A 5 $n = 2$; $X = R_+^n$; and $p = (1, a) \in \{1\} \times R_{++}$.

A 6 There exists a nondegenerate probability distribution $F(\cdot)\colon R_+ \to [0, 1]$ with compact support and a thrice-differentiable function $U(\cdot)\colon R_+ \to R$ such that, for $x \in R_+^2$,

$$V(x_1, x_2) = \int_0^\infty U(x_1 + x_2 r)\, dF(r).$$

A 7 $U'(\cdot) > 0$ and $U''(\cdot) < 0$.

12.1.2 The Intended Interpretation

The above axiom system can be interpreted as describing different phenomena. Among the possible interpretations, there is a subset of intended interpretations. One of these can be described as follows: Name the first component of x μ and the second component m. Let m denote a risky asset such as shares, μ a nonrisky asset such as cash. Since the first component of p is "1," think of μ as the unit of account, and let a denote the number of units of account for which one unit of m exchanges. Finally, let "a consumer" denote a family unit which orders pairs (μ, m), according to the values assumed by a function $V(\cdot)$, and which has a certain number of units of account $\hat{A}$ to spend on μ and m. With each pair (μ, m), the family associates a random variable $\mu + mr$ with the probability distribution, $F((\cdot) - \mu)/m) : [\mu, \infty) \to [0, 1]$. The pairs (μ, m) are for sale in the current period, and for each value of r, $\mu + mr$ denotes the number of units of account which (μ, m) will command next period. The family chooses (μ, m) so as to maximize the value of $V(\cdot)$ subject to the constraints $\mu + am = \hat{A}$ and $(\mu, m) \geqslant 0$.

With this interpretation of the axioms A 1–A 7, the system describes a consumer's choice among risky and nonrisky assets. In a world where there is one safe asset and in which the consumer cannot borrow, this choice is the choice of an equilibrium balance sheet, with $\hat{A}$ representing the consumer's net worth. In fact, in such a world we can think of the consumer as having already made his current-period consumption-savings choice and as now allocating his end-of-period net worth ($\equiv$beginning-of-period net worth plus current-period savings) between μ and m. For each value of r and for a chosen pair (μ, m), $\mu + mr$ represents the value of the consumer's net worth at the beginning of the next period.

When we later speak about choice among risky and nonrisky assets and about consumer aversion to risk, we shall always be referring implicitly to the interpretation sketched above. Arrow's model differs from this interpretation in that he insists that $a \equiv 1$. This difference is important because, if we do not allow a to vary over R_+, we can not justify interpreting Arrow's measures of risk aversion as measures of risk aversion in our system. We also cannot establish the analogues of Arrow's and Pratt's theorems concerning the relationship between a consumer's absolute and proportional risk aversion and his choice of μ and m as functions of A.

For ease of reference in chapter 28 and to simplify our subsequent discussion, we shall henceforth write (μ, m) for x. This change in notation permits us to talk about μ as the safe asset and m as the risky asset without referring back to the interpretation of A 1–A 7 given above.

12.1.3 Sample Theorems

To give a preliminary idea of what the axioms imply about consumer behavior, I conclude this section by stating two theorems. Proofs of these and other theorems in the chapter are given in the appendix, section 12.7.

The first theorem T 12.1, shows that $V(\cdot)$ has the standard properties of a utility function (e.g., convex indifference curves between μ and m) and that the consumer's demand functions for μ and m are continuous and differentiable.

T 12.1 Both $U(\cdot)$ and $V(\cdot)$ are strictly increasing, thrice-differentiable, strictly concave functions on R_+ and R_+^2, respectively. Moreover, there exists a vector-valued function

$$(\mu, m)(\cdot) \colon R_{++} \times R_+ \to R_+^2$$

which is continuous everywhere, differentiable on $\{(a, A) \in R_{++} \times R_+ \colon (\mu, m)(a, A) > 0\}$, and for each and every pair $(a, A) \in R_{++} \times R_+$, satisfies $c = (\mu, m)(a, A)$, where c is the consumption bundle at (a, A).

The next theorem T 12.2, and corollary T 12.3, provide an example of some interesting implications of Arrow's system that cannot be derived from the axioms of the standard theory of consmer choice. Note that T 12.2 insists no matter how close a is to Er, if $a < Er$ and if $A > 0$, $m(a, A) > 0$.[1]

T 12.2 Let Ef denote $\int_0^\infty r\,dF(r)$. For all $(a, A) \in R_{++}^2$, $m(a, A) > 0$ if and only if $a < Er$.

T 12.3 For all $A \in R_+$, $\lim_{a \uparrow Er} m(a, A) = 0$.

When a consumer invests in a pair (μ, m) *with* $m > 0$, *he gambles, since* $\mu + mr$ *is a random variable. This gamble is favorable, fair, or unfair according as* $\mu + mEr$ *is* $>$, $=$, *or* $< \mu + am$. Theorem T 12.2 shows that the consumer will acquire a pair (μ, m) with $m > 0$ only if this pair represents a favorable gamble. *A consumer who refuses gambles that are either fair or unfair is said to be "risk-averse."* Hence in our interpretation of T(A 1, ..., A 7), T 12.2 insists that the consumer is risk-averse.

E 12.1 Let $U(A) = \log A$ for $A \in R_{++}$ and assume that r takes on the values 1.6 and 1.4 with probability 0.75 and 0.25, respectively. Then, for all pairs (μ, m) that satisfy $\mu + am = A$ and $(\mu, m) \geqslant 0$, we have $EU(\mu + mr) = 0.75 \log(A + m(1.6 - a)) + 0.25 \log(A + m(1.4 - a))$. It is easy to verify that the value of m that maximizes the right-hand side of this equation, subject to $0 \leqslant m \leqslant A/a$, is given by

$$m(a, A) = \begin{cases} 0 & \text{for } a \geqslant 1.55 \\ \left(\dfrac{a - 1.55}{a^2 - 3a + 2.24}\right)A & \text{for } 1.544828 \leqslant a < 1.55 \\ A/a & \text{for } 0 < a < 1.544828 \end{cases}$$

Since $Er = 1.55$, the description of $m(\cdot)$ is consistent with T 12.2.

12.2 Absolute and Proportional Risk Aversion

If it makes sense to say that one consumer is more risk-averse than another, then, all else being equal, the more risk-averse consumer will invest less in m than the other consumer. In fact, it ought to be true that, all else being equal, if one family always invests less in risky assets than another family, it is because the one is more risk-averse than the other. In this section I show that there exist at least two reasonable measures of risk aversion which permit us to compare the risk aversion of different consumers with the same value of A. I also show that there is a way to make precise what I mean by "all else being equal" so that our two presumptions can be shown to be true statements.

12.2.1 The Absolute Risk-Aversion Function

For simplicity we henceforth refer to a consumer who satisfies A 1–A 7 as an Arrow consumer. For such a consumer we can define a function $R(\cdot): R_+ \rightarrow R_+$ by

$$R(A) = -\frac{U''(A)}{U'(A)}, \qquad A \in R_+.$$

This function is called the consumer's *absolute risk-aversion function.* We propose to follow Arrow (1965, pp. 33–34) and Pratt (1964, pp. 125–126) in using this function as a measure of the consumer's risk aversion at different values of A.

E 12.2 Let $U_1(A)$, $U_2(A)$, and $U_3(A)$ be, respectively, $\log(1 + A)$, $-e^{-A}$, and $-e^{+A^{-1}}$; and let $R_i(\cdot)$, $i = 1, 2, 3$, be the corresponding absolute risk-aversion functions. Then $R_1(A) = (1 + A)^{-1}$, $R_2(A) = 1$, and $R_3(A) = A^{-2} + 2A^{-1}$.

12.2.2 Absolute Risk Aversion and Ordering of (μ, m) Pairs

To make sure that $R(\cdot)$ is a good measure of risk aversion in T(A 1, ..., A 7), we must ascertain that there is a one-to-one correspondence between absolute risk-aversion functions and orderings of (μ, m) pairs. Specifically, we must show that two Arrow consumers with the same ordering of (μ, m) pairs have identical absolute risk-aversion functions. We must also demonstrate that two Arrow consumers with the same absolute risk-aversion functions have the same ordering of (μ, m) pairs. Theorem T 12.4 shows that such a one-to-one relationship exists for consumers with the same probability distribution $F(\cdot)$.

T 12.4 Consider two Arrow consumers with the following two orderings of (μ, m) pairs:

$$V(\mu, m) = \int_0^\infty U(\mu + mr)\, dF(r), \qquad (\mu, m) \in R_+^2$$

and

$$W(\mu, m) = \int_0^\infty H(\mu + mr)\, d\tilde{F}(r), \qquad (\mu, m) \in R_+^2.$$

Suppose that $\tilde{F}(r) = F(r)$ for all $r \in$ support of $F(\cdot)$. Then there exists a strictly increasing, thrice-differentiable function $G(\cdot)$: range of $V(\cdot) \to R$ such that

$$W(\mu, m) = G(V(\mu, m)), \qquad (\mu, m) \in R_+^2$$

if and only if

$$\frac{H''(A)}{H'(A)} = \frac{U''(A)}{U'(A)}, \qquad A \in R_+.$$

If $G(\cdot)$ exists, $G(t) = d + bt$ for some pair (d, b), with $b > 0$.

Arrow took for granted that his consumer's utility function was measurable up to a positive linear transformation, and used this property to justify the use of $R(\cdot)$ as a measure of risk aversion (see Arrow 1965, p. 33). Theorem T 12.4 shows that in A 1–A 7, $V(\cdot)$ and $U(\cdot)$ are measurable up to a positive linear transformation.

12.2.3 Absolute Risk Aversion and Investment in Risky Assets

The one-to-one correspondence between absolute risk-aversion functions and orderings of (μ, m) pairs established in T 12.4 allows us to identify the consumer with a quadruple, $(R(\cdot), F(\cdot), R^2_+, \hat{A})$. It also enables us to compare two consumers with the same probability distribution $F(\cdot)$ in terms of the characteristics of their absolute risk-aversion functions. As witnessed in theorems T 12.5 and T 12.6 below, such comparisons justify using $R(\cdot)$ as a measure of a consumer's risk aversion at different values of A.

T 12.5 Consider two Arrow consumers with the same probability distribution $F(\cdot)$. Call them I and II, and name their absolute risk-aversion functions $R_{\text{I}}(\cdot)$ and $R_{\text{II}}(\cdot)$ and their demand functions for m, $m_{\text{I}}(\cdot)$ and $m_{\text{II}}(\cdot)$. Then the following conditions are equivalent, in either the weak or strong (indicated in brackets) form:

(i) $R_{\text{I}}(A) \geqslant [>] R_{\text{II}}(A)$ for all $A \in R_+$;

(ii) $m_{\text{I}}(a, A) \leqslant m_{\text{II}}(a, A)$ for all $(a, A) \in R_{++} \times R_+$
[and $<$ if $0 < m_{\text{I}}(a, A) < A/a$].

Theorem T 12.5 is my analogue to Pratt's theorem 7 (Pratt 1964, p. 136). In Pratt's theorem the random variable $\tilde{l}$, "return per unit invested," varies over all possible random variables with finite mean. In my theorem the random return per unit invested, $r - a$, varies only as a varies over R_+ because $F(\cdot)$, the distribution of r, is fixed and given. Since $F(\cdot)$ is arbitrary, the fact that $F(\cdot)$ is fixed and a is allowed to vary over all of R_+ matters only when we demonstrate that condition (ii) implies condition (i).

12.2.4 The Proportional Risk-Aversion Function

A second useful measure of risk aversion was proposed by Arrow (1965, pp. 33–34) and Pratt (1964, p. 134). It is defined by

$$R_p(A) = AR(A), \qquad A \in R_+$$

and it is called the consumer's *proportional risk-aversion function.*

E 12.3 Let $U_i(\cdot)$, $i = 1, 2, 3$, be as in E 12.2 and let $R_{pi}(\cdot)$ denote the corresponding proportional risk aversion functions. Then $R_{pl}(A) = A/(1 + A)$, $R_{p2}(A) = A$, and $R_{p3}(A) = A^{-1} + 2$.

The same one-to-one relationship exists between a consumer's proportional risk-aversion function $R_p(\cdot)$ and his orderings of (μ, m) pairs as exists between his absolute risk-aversion function $R(\cdot)$ and his ordering of (μ, m) pairs. Furthermore, T 12.6, which is a simple analogue to T 12.5, holds.

T 12.6 Consider two Arrow consumers with the same probability distribution $F(\cdot)$. Call them I and II. Name their proportional risk-aversion functions $R_{p\mathrm{I}}(\cdot)$ and $R_{p\mathrm{II}}(\cdot)$, and label their demand functions for μ, $\mu_{\mathrm{I}}(\cdot)$ and $\mu_{\mathrm{II}}(\cdot)$. Then the following conditions are equivalent, in either the strong (indicated in brackets) or the weak form.

(i) $R_{p\mathrm{I}}(A) \geqslant [>] R_{p\mathrm{II}}(A)$ for all $A \in R_{+}$;

(ii) $\mu_{\mathrm{I}}(a, A)/A \geqslant \mu_{\mathrm{II}}(a, A)/A$ for all $(a, A) \in R_{++} \times R_{+}$ [and $>$ if $0 < \mu_{\mathrm{II}}(a, A) < A$].

For completeness and to justify later examples, we note here that T 12.5 and 12.6 have interval analogues. Specifically, they are true if the domain of $R(\cdot)$ (or $R_p(\cdot)$) is taken to be an interval $[b, d]$ with $b \geqslant 0$ and $d > b$, and if the arguments of $m(\cdot)$ (or $\mu(\cdot)/A$) are allowed to vary in a region in $R_{++} \times R_{+}$ where $\{x\colon x = A + m(a, A)(r - a)$ for some $r \in$ support of $F(\cdot)\}$ is a subset of $[b, d]$. (See also in this respect Pratt's theorems 6 and 7, 1964, pp. 135–136.)

12.3 The Fundamental Theorems of Arrow

It is disappointing to have to insist that the two consumers in T 12.5 and the two in T 12.6 have the same probability distribution $F(\cdot)$, because in an interpretation of A 1–A 7 that might have empirical relevance, $F(\cdot)$ must be a subjective probability distribution that is likely to vary from one individual to the next. However, while we may be unable to use T 12.5 and T 12.6 as a basis for comparing different individuals' risk aversion, we can use them to determine how a consumer's optimal portfolio varies as A changes.

12.3.1 Risky Assets and Absolute Risk Aversion

To see how T 12.5 can be used to determine how a consumer's investment in risky assets varies with A, suppose that consumer I in T 12.5 has the ordering

$$V_{\mathrm{I}}(\mu, m) = \int_{0}^{\infty} U_{\mathrm{I}}(\mu + mr)\, dF(r), \qquad (\mu, m) \in R_{+}^{2}$$

of (μ, m) pairs, and suppose that the second consumer has the ordering

$$V_{\mathrm{II}}(\mu, m) = \int_{0}^{\infty} U_{\mathrm{II}}(\mu + mr)\, dF(r), \qquad (\mu, m) \in R_{+}^{2}$$

where $U_{\mathrm{II}}(A) = U_{\mathrm{I}}(\gamma + A)$, $A \in R_{+}$, for some $\gamma > 0$. Then we can think of consumer II as consumer I with γ more units of account, since $R_{\mathrm{II}}(A) =$

$R_{\mathrm{I}}(\gamma + A)$ and $m_{\mathrm{II}}(a, A) = m_{\mathrm{I}}(a, \gamma + A)$ for all pairs, $(a, A) \in R_{++} \times R_+$ with $m_{\mathrm{II}}(a, A) < A/a$. When we think of consumer II this way, T 12.5 becomes a statement about the relationship between the monotonicity of $R(\cdot)$ and that of $m(a, \cdot)$. Properly reformulated for our purposes, this statement is T 12.7.

T 12.7 For any Arrow consumer the following relations hold: In the set $\{(a, A) \in R^2_{++} : (\mu, m)(a, A) > 0\}$ $m(a, \cdot)$ is a strictly increasing (constant, (strictly decreasing)) function of A if and only if $R(\cdot)$ is a strictly decreasing (constant, (strictly increasing)) function of A on R_+.

The sufficiency part of this theorem was established by Arrow (1965, p. 43), the necessity by Pratt (1964, p. 136).

E 12.4 Consider the consumer in E 12.1. His $U(A) = \log A$ for $A \in R_{++}$, and r takes the values 1.6 and 1.4 with probability 0.75 and 0.25, respectively. Moreover, $R(A) = A^{-1}$ and $R'(A) < 0$ for all $A \in R_{++}$. Since, for $1.544828 < a < 1.55$, $a^2 - 3a + 2.24 < 0$, we see that, for all $(a, A) \in R_{++} \times R_+$ with $0 < m(a, A) < A/a$, $\partial m(a, A)/\partial A > 0$.

12.3.2 Safe Assets and Proportional Risk Aversion

Theorem T 12.6 can also be made to describe the way a consumer's portfolio changes with A. To show this, we redefine $U_{\mathrm{II}}(\cdot)$ as follows:

$$U_{\mathrm{II}}(A) = U_{\mathrm{I}}(kA), \qquad A \in R_+$$

for some $k > 0$. Then consumer II can be thought of as consumer I with a multiple of his original holdings of units of account, since $R_{p\mathrm{II}}(A) = R_{p\mathrm{I}}(kA)$ for all $A \in R_+$, and $\mu_{\mathrm{II}}(a, A)/A = \mu_{\mathrm{I}}(a, kA)/kA$ for all pairs $(a, A) \in R^2_{++}$ such that $0 < \mu_{\mathrm{II}}(a, A) < A$. When we think of consumer II in this manner, T 12.6 becomes a statement about how the monotonicity of $R_p(\cdot)$ is related to that of the function $\mu(a, \cdot)/(\cdot)$ and, a fortiori, to that of the function $\mu(a, \cdot)/am(a, \cdot)$. We record this relationship in T 12.8.

T 12.8 For any Arrow consumer, the following relations hold on the set $\{(a, A) \in R^2_{++} : (\mu, m)(a, A) > 0\}$:

(i) $\mu(a, \cdot)/am(a, \cdot)$ is a strictly increasing (constant, (strictly decreasing)) function of A if and only if $R_p(\cdot)$ is a strictly increasing (constant, (strictly decreasing)) function on R_+; and

(ii) $\mu(a, \cdot)/(\cdot)$ is a strictly increasing (constant, (strictly decreasing)) function of A if and only if $R_p(\cdot)$ is a strictly increasing (constant, (strictly decreasing)) function on R_+.

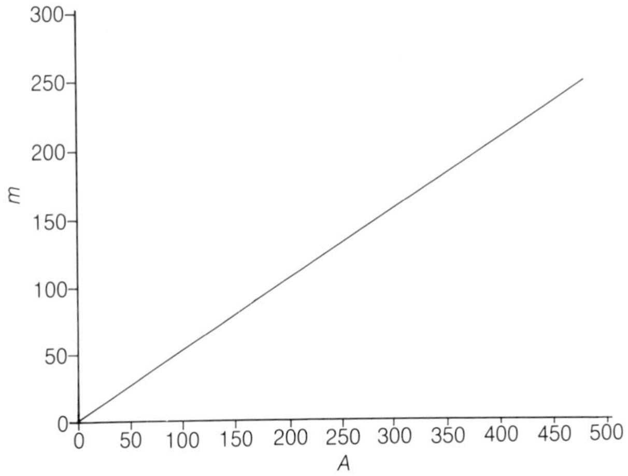

Figure 12.1

Example E 12.5 below illustrates how $m(a,\cdot)$ and $\mu(a,\cdot)/am(a,\cdot)$ might vary with A when both $R'(\cdot) < 0$ and $R_p'(\cdot) < 0$.

E 12.5 Let $U(A) = -e^{A^{-1}}$, $A \in R_{++}$, and suppose that r can take the values 1.1 and 0.9 with probability 0.55 and 0.45, respectively. Then $R_p(A) = 2 + A^{-1}$, $A \in R_{++}$, and $R_p'(\cdot) < 0$. Moreover, if we let $a = 1$, then the way the consumer's optimal portfolio varies with A can be characterized as in figures 12.1 and 12.2 below, where we have plotted $m(1,\cdot)$ and $\mu(1,\cdot)/m(1,\cdot)$ against A.[2]

We have stated T 12.7 and T 12.8 in terms of strictly increasing (constant, (strictly decreasing)) functions instead of positive (zero, (negative)) derivatives because it is awkward to state them in terms of derivatives. To see why, note that, if $R(\cdot)$ is strictly decreasing (constant, (strictly increasing)) on R_+, then $\partial m(a,\cdot)/\partial A > 0$ $(=0, (<0))$ on $\{(a,A) \in R_{++}^2 : (\mu, m)(a,A) > 0\}$. Theorem T 12.7 shows that the converse is true; it does not, however, show that $\partial m(a,\cdot)/\partial A > 0$ $(=0,(<0))$ for the relevant pairs (a,A) implies $R'(A) < 0$ $(=0,(>0))$ for all $A \in R_+$. The most we can demonstrate is that if $\partial m(a,\cdot)/\partial A > 0$ (<0) (or $\geqslant 0$, $(\leqslant 0)$) for all relevant pairs (a,A), then there does not exist an interval $[\alpha,\beta] \subset R_+$ such that $R'(A) \geqslant 0$ $(\leqslant 0)$ for all $A \in [\alpha,\beta]$. Analogous remarks apply to T 12.8.

Taking the preceding into consideration, we can state T 12.9 which is a corollary to T 12.8 (ii).

T 12.9 For any Arrow consumer the following relations hold: In the set, $\{(a,A) \in R_{++}^2 : (\mu,m)(a,A) > 0\}$, $(A/\mu(a,A))\,\partial\mu(a,A)/\partial A > 1$ $(=,(<1))$ if and only if $R_p(\cdot)$ is a strictly increasing (constant, (strictly decreasing)) function on R_+.

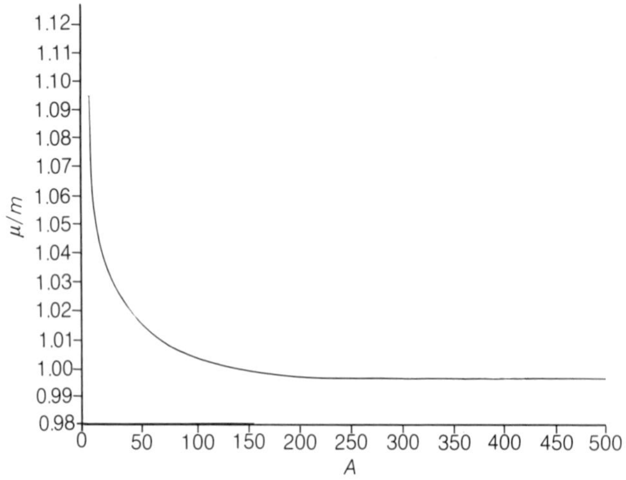

Figure 12.2

Arrow established the if part of this corollary; i.e., he showed that $(A/\mu(a, A))\, \partial\mu(a, A)/\partial A > 1$ for all relevant pairs (a, A) if $R_p(\cdot)$ is a strictly increasing function on R_+ (see Arrow 1965, pp. 43–44). To Arrow this result was significant for several reasons. First, according to him a consumer's U function must be bounded; and if it is, the consumer's $R_p(\cdot)$ cannot have a limit above 1 as A tends to 0 and cannot have a limit below 1 as A tends to infinity. Therefore, "it is broadly permissible to assume that relative risk aversion increases with" A (Arrow 1965, p. 37). Second, studies "of the movements of cash balance holdings, wealth and income (taken as a measure of wealth) by Selden, Friedman, Latané, and Meltzer, by different methods and under different assumptions agree in finding a wealth elasticity of demand for cash balances of at least 1." From these two observations, one conclusion emerges: "The notion that security, in the particular form of cash balance, has a wealth elasticity of at least one, seems to be the only ... explanation of the historical course of money holdings" (Arrow 1965, p. 44).

Arrow hypothesized that most consumers' R_p functions are strictly increasing functions of A and justified the hypothesis, as noted above, partly on theoretical grounds and partly on empirical evidence. He also hypothesized that the R functions of most consmers are strictly decreasing functions of A. This hypothesis, he thought, seemed to be "supported by everyday observation" (Arrow 1965, p. 35). In our empirical analysis of consumer choice of risky and nonrisky assets we shall test these hypotheses.

Theorems T 12.7–T 12.9 say little about $\partial\mu/\partial A$ (only that $\partial\mu(a, A)/\partial A \geqslant 0$ for all $(a, A) \in R^2_{++}$ with $(\mu, m)(a, A) > 0$ if $R'_p(A) \geqslant 0$ for all $A \in R_+$). They say nothing about $\partial\mu/\partial a$ and $\partial m/\partial a$; only by involving T 10.16 can we infer from T 12.7 that $\partial m(a, A)/\partial a < 0$ for all $(a, A) \in R^2_{++}$ such that $(\mu, m)(a, A) > 0$ if $R'(A) \leqslant 0$ for all $A \in R_+$. Even so, these theorems provide all we need know about Arrow consumers in order to carry out our empirical analysis.

12.4 New Axioms

In sections 12.1–12.3 we discussed a model of consumer choice in which the consumer allocated his net worth between a risky and a nonrisky asset. Since in reality consumers choose among many risky assets, we next discuss a model in which the consumer allocates his net worth between one safe and several risky assets. In doing so, we hope to establish analogues of T 12.1–T 12.9 that could be relevant to consumer choice in the actual world.

Instead of considering a model in which the number of risky assets is finite but otherwise undetermined, we simplify the exposition by taking the number to be 2. With only obvious changes in notation, our results are valid for a model in which any number of risky assets exist.

A quick look at A 1–A 7 shows that we only need to rephrase A 5 and A 6 to obtain a model of consumer choice among one safe and two risky assets. The new versions of these axioms are A 5* and A 6*.

A 5* $n = 3$, $X = R^3_+$, and $p = (1, a) \in \{1\} \times R^2_{++}$.

A 6* There exists a nondegenerate probability distribution $F(\cdot): R^2_+ \to [0, 1]$ with compact support, and a thrice-differentiable function $U(\cdot): R_+ \to R$ such that, for $x \in X$,

$$V(x_1, x_2, x_3) = \int_0^\infty \int_0^\infty U(x_1 + x_2 r_1 + x_3 r_2)\, dF(r_1, r_2).$$

Again we name the first component of x μ and refer to it as the *nonrisky asset*. We name the last two components of x $m = (m_1, m_2)$ and refer to them as the *risky assets*. In addition, we write am for $a_1 m_1 + a_2 m_2$ and mr for $m_1 r_1 + m_2 r_2$.

The analogue of T 12.1 in the new axiom system is T 12.10.

T 12.10 Suppose that A 1–A 4, A 5*, A 6*, and A 7 hold. Then $U(\cdot)$ and $V(\cdot)$ are strictly increasing, thrice-differentiable, strictly concave functions on R_+ and R^3_+, respectively. Moreover, there exists a vector-valued function $(\mu, m)(\cdot): R^2_{++} \times R_+ \to R^3_+$ which is continuous everywhere, differentiable in $\{(a, A) \in R^2_{++} \times R_+:$

$(\mu, m)(a, A) > 0\}$, and for each and every pair $(a, A) \in R^2_{++} \times R_+$, satisfies $c = (\mu, m)(a, A)$, where c is the unique consumption bundle at (a, A).

We shall henceforth refer to the components of $(\mu, m)(\cdot)$ as the consumer's *demand functions*. They satisfy T 12.11, which is an analogue of T 12.2.

T 12.11 Suppose that A 1–A 4, A 5*, A 6*, and A 7 hold, and let $(\mu, m)(\cdot)$ be the consumer's demand functions. Then, for all $(a, A) \in R^3_{++}$, $m(a, A) = 0$ if and only if $Er_1 \leqslant a_1$ and $Er_2 \leqslant a_2$. Moreover, if r_1 and r_2 are independently distributed relative to $F(\cdot)$, then, for all $(a, A) \in R^3_{++}$, $m_i(a, A) > 0$ if and only if $Er_i > a_i$, $i = 1, 2$.

It may seem surprising that we can have $Er_1 \leqslant a_1$, $Er_2 > a_2$, and $m(a, A) > 0$ if r_1 and r_2 are not independently distributed relative to $F(\cdot)$. Here is an example. In reading it, note that the m_1 component of the optimal portfolio is positive when $A \in (51.85185185, 200)$ even though $Er_1 = 0.0875 < 0.1 = a_1$.

E 12.6 Let $U(A) = -(200 - A)^2$ for $0 \leqslant A \leqslant 200$, and let the probability distribution of r be given by

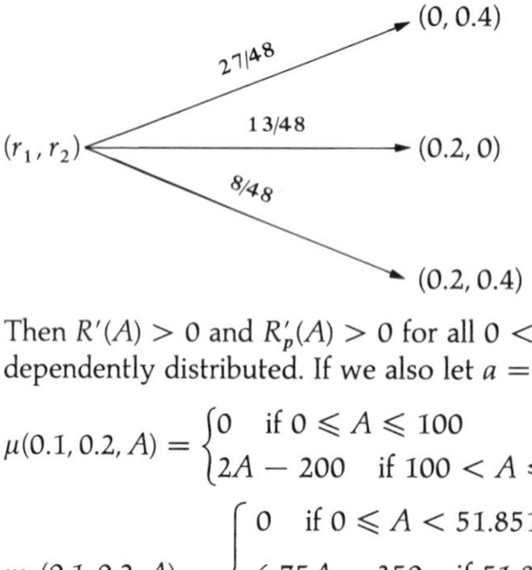

Then $R'(A) > 0$ and $R_p'(A) > 0$ for all $0 < A \leqslant 200$, and r_1 and r_2 are not independently distributed. If we also let $a = (0.1, 0.2)$, then we can easily show that

$$\mu(0.1, 0.2, A) = \begin{cases} 0 & \text{if } 0 \leqslant A \leqslant 100 \\ 2A - 200 & \text{if } 100 < A \leqslant 200 \end{cases}$$

$$m_1(0.1, 0.2, A) = \begin{cases} 0 & \text{if } 0 \leqslant A < 51.85185185 \\ 6.75A - 350 & \text{if } 51.85185185 \leqslant A \leqslant 100 \\ 3.25(200 - A) & \text{if } 100 < A \leqslant 200 \end{cases}$$

$$m_2(0.1, 0.2, A) = \begin{cases} 5A & \text{for } 0 \leqslant A < 51.85185185 \\ 175 + 1.625A & \text{if } 51.85185185 \leqslant A \leqslant 100 \\ 3.375(200 - A) & \text{if } 100 \leqslant A \leqslant 200 \end{cases}$$

In taking a closer look at T 12.2 and T 12.11, we see that T 12.11 is a poor analogue of T 12.2. Besides allowing anomalies such as the one exemplified in E 12.6, when r_1 and r_2 are not independently distributed, T 12.11 also allows the combination, $Er_1 > a_1$, $Er_2 > a$, and $m(a, A) \not> 0$, for an interval of values of A. An analogue of T 12.2 that is better than T 12.11 for the purposes of this chapter and chapter 28 is stated in T 12.12. In the statement of this theorem and in the remainder of the chapter,

$$\tilde{m}(a, A) = a_1 m_1(a, A) + a_2 m_2(a, A), \qquad (a, A) \in R^2_{++} \times R_+.$$

T 12.12 Suppose that A 1–A 4, A 5*, A 6*, and A 7 hold. Then $\tilde{m}(a, A) > 0$ for all $A \in R_+$ if and only if either $Er_1 > a_1$ or $Er_2 > a_2$ or both. Moreover,

$$\lim_{a \uparrow (Er_1, Er_2)} \tilde{m}(a, A) = 0.$$

12.5 An Aggregation Problem

In our empirical analysis in chapter 28 of choice among risky and nonrisky assets, we shall give data on the investment of individual consumers in various groups of risky securities (e.g., publicly traded stocks and bonds) and, a fortiori, on their total investment in risky securities. We have no information on the number of units of various assets acquired by the respective consumers. Therefore we are particularly interested in analogues of T 12.1–T 12.9 which ascertain that we can make the same assertions about $(\mu, \tilde{m})$ as T 12.1–T 12.9 make of (μ, m). To find such analogues is an *aggregation problem.*

The sum and product of continuous (or differentiable) functions are continuous (or differentiable). Hence T 12.10 solves the aggregation problem for T 12.1 by implication: what is true of $(\mu, m)(\cdot)$ in T 12.1 is true of $(\mu, \tilde{m})(\cdot)$. Similarly, T 12.12 solves the aggregation problem for T 12.2 and T 12.3 by showing that, what is asserted in T 12.2 and T 12.3 about investment in the one risky asset m is true of $\tilde{m}$, the units of account invested in all risky assets in the second axiom system. Note in particular that, so long as one of the components of a is less than the corresponding component of Er, the consumer will use some part of A to invest in m. Moreover, for each pair (a, A), he will always allocate his funds to m in a way such that, if $\tilde{m}(a, A) > 0$, then $\tilde{m}(a, A)$ represents a favorable gamble; that is, $\tilde{m}(a, A) < m_1(a, A)Er_1 + m_2(a, A)Er_2$. The last inequality is a consequence of

$$U(A) < EU(A + m(a, A)(r - a)) < U(A + m(a, A)(Er - a)).$$

We can use T 12.10–T 12.12 to establish the analogue of T 12.4 in the new axiom system. In doing this we take the first step toward establishing the usefulness of $R(\cdot)$ and $R_p(\cdot)$ as measures of risk aversion in this system:

T 12.13 Suppose that A 1–A 4, A 5*, A 6*, and A 7 hold, and consider two consumers with the following orderings of (μ, m) vectors:

$$V_{\mathrm{I}}(\mu, m) = \int_0^\infty \int_0^\infty U_{\mathrm{I}}(\mu + mr)\,dF(r), \qquad (\mu, m) \in R_+^3$$

and

$$V_{\mathrm{II}}(\mu, m) = \int_0^\infty \int_0^\infty U_{\mathrm{II}}(\mu + mr)\,d\tilde{F}(r), \qquad (\mu, m) \in R_+^3.$$

Suppose also that $F(r) = \tilde{F}(r)$ for all $r \in \{\text{support of } F(\cdot)\}$. Then there exists a strictly increasing, thrice-differentiable function $G(\cdot)$: $\{\text{range of } V_{\mathrm{I}}(\cdot)\} \to R$, such that

$$V_{\mathrm{II}}(\mu, m) = G(V_{\mathrm{I}}(\mu, m)), \qquad (\mu, m) \in R_+^3$$

if and only if

$$\frac{U_{\mathrm{II}}''(A)}{U_{\mathrm{II}}'(A)} = \frac{U_{\mathrm{I}}''(A)}{U_{\mathrm{I}}'(A)}, \qquad A \in R_+.$$

Moreover, if $G(\cdot)$ exists, then there also exist constants α and β with $\beta > 0$ such that, on the range of $V_{\mathrm{I}}(\cdot)$, $G(t) = \alpha + \beta t$.

As in the case of T 12.4, T 12.3 establishes a one-to-one correspondence between $R(\cdot)$ and orderings of (μ, m) vectors. This alone does not establish the usefulness of $R(\cdot)$ as a measure of risk aversion in the second system. We must also find an analogue to at least one of the theorems T 12.5–T 12.9.

We begin with T 12.7 and T 12.8. To figure out what analogues of these theorems might be like, consider E 12.6. In E 12.6, $R'(A) > 0$ and $R_p'(A) > 0$ for all $A \in [0, 200)$. Yet $\partial m_i(0.1, 0.2, A)/\partial A > 0$, $i = 1, 2$, when $A \in [51.85185185, 100]$. Only at values of A where $(\mu, m)(0.1, 0.2, A) > 0$, do we observe the expected inequalities: $\partial m_i(0.1, 0.2, A)/\partial A < 0$, $i = 1, 2$, and $\partial(\mu(0.1, 0.2, A)/\tilde{m}(0.1, 0.2, A))/\partial A > 0$. These observations suggest that relationships analogous to those described in T 12.7 and T 12.8 may hold in $\{(a, A) \in R_{++}^3 : (\mu, m)(a, A) > 0\}$ but not elsewhere. They do hold in this set for the utility function of E 12.6 regardless of what the distribution of r looks like. (see T 12.14–T 12.17 below.) Nevertheless, there are utility functions for which such relationships cannot be established, as witnessed in E 12.7.

E 12.7 Let $U(A) = \int_0^A \exp(-0.023801984x + 0.0000297525x^2)\,dx$ for $A \in [0, 399.9997311]$. Then $U'(\cdot) > 0$ and $U''(\cdot) < 0$. Moreover,

$$R(A) = 0.023801984 - 0.000059505A,$$

$$R_p(A) = 0.023801984A - 0.000059505A^2,$$

$$R_p'(A) = 0.023801984 - 0.000119010A.$$

Evidently $R'(A) < 0$ for $A \in [0, 399.9997311]$, while $R_p'(A) > 0$ for $A \in [0, 199.9998656)$ and <0 for $A \in (199.9998656, 399.9997311)$.

Next, let $a = (2, 0.1)$ and let the probability distribution of r be given by

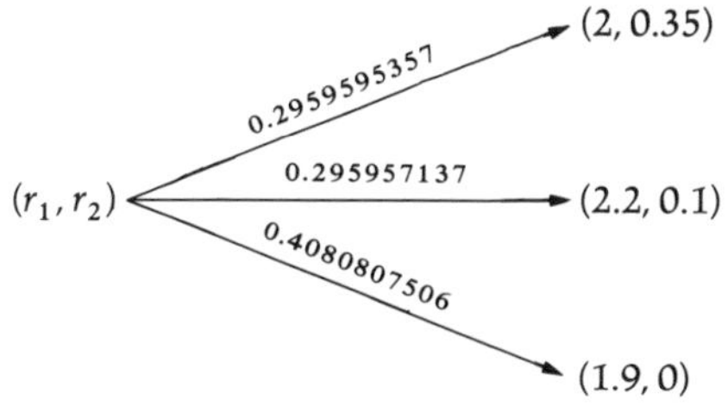

Then the behavior of $m(2, 0.1, A)$ for $A \in [250, 300]$ is as described in figure 12.3.[3]

The corresponding behavior of $\tilde{m}(2, 0.1, \cdot)$ and $\mu(2, 0.1, \cdot)/\tilde{m}(2, 0.1, \cdot)$ is illustrated in figures 12.4 and 12.5, respectively.

Figures 12.3 and 12.4 show that decreasing $R(\cdot)$ does not imply that $\partial m_i(a, A)/\partial A > 0$, $i = 1, 2$, or that $\partial \tilde{m}(a, A)/\partial A > 0$ whenever $(\mu, m)(a, A) > 0$. Similarly, figure 12.5 demonstrates that decreasing $R_p(\cdot)$ does not imply that $\partial(\mu(a, A)/\tilde{m}(a, A))\, \partial A < 0$ in the same region. Thus these figures con-

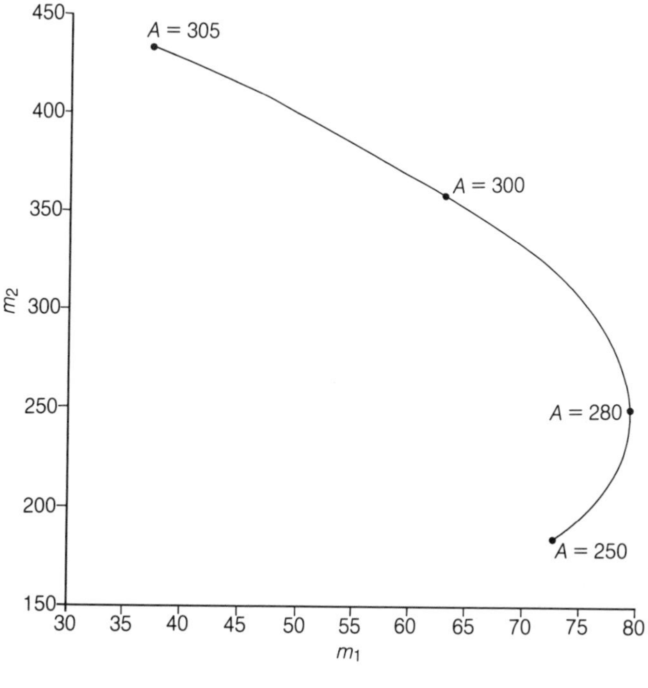

Figure 12.3

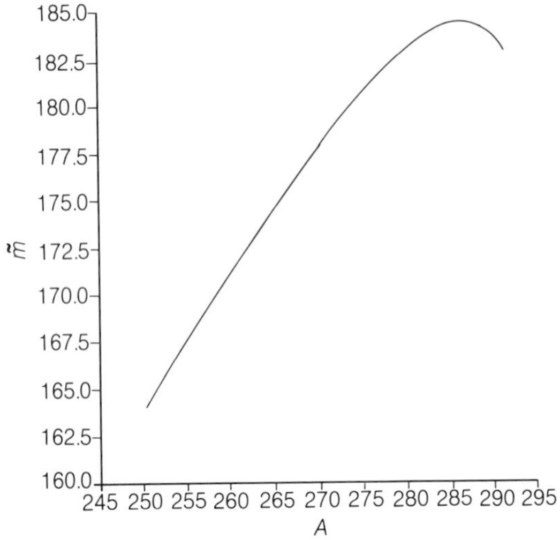

Figure 12.4

clusively demonstrate that what T 12.7 and T 12.8 assert of $(\mu, m)(\cdot)$ is not true in general of $(\mu, \tilde{m})(\cdot)$. In fact, they show that T 12.7 and T 12.8 have no *obvious* counterparts in the second axiom system.

Since we can take the two consumers in T 12.5 and T 12.6 to be the same consumer with two different levels of net worth (A and $A + \gamma$ in the case of T 12.5 and A and kA in the case of T 12.6), E 12.7 also shows that what T 12.5 and T 12.6 assert of $(\mu, m)(\cdot)$ and $(R(\cdot), R_p(\cdot))$ is not generally true of $(\mu, \tilde{m})(\cdot)$ and $(R(\cdot), R_p(\cdot))$. Thus in the case of T 12.5 and T 12.6, as well as in that of T 12.7 and T 12.8, we have an unresolved aggregation problem on our hands.

12.6 Resolution of the Aggregation Problem

We solve the aggregation problem for T 12.7 and T 12.8 in this section. By doing so we demonstrate that $R(\cdot)$ and $R_p(\cdot)$ are useful measures of risk aversion in the second axiom system.

12.6.1 Preliminary Remarks

Before we tackle the aggregation problem, we must look again at E 12.7. It is important to note that it is not the utility function alone that produces

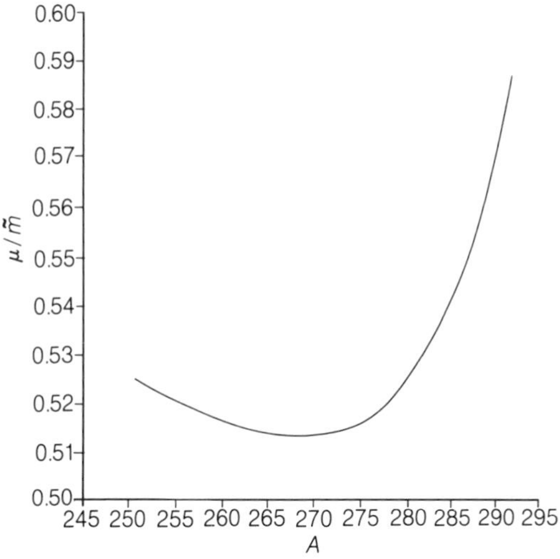

Figure 12.5

the unexpected result. If, for example, we changed the definition of a to $a = (1, 0.4)$, and changed the probability tree of r to

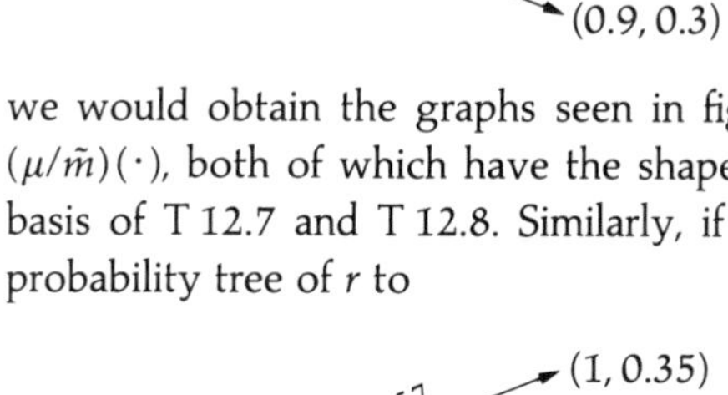

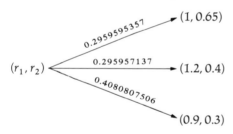

we would obtain the graphs seen in figures 12.6 and 12.7 for $\tilde{m}(\cdot)$ and $(\mu/\tilde{m})(\cdot)$, both of which have the shape we might have predicted on the basis of T 12.7 and T 12.8. Similarly, if we changed a to $(1, 0.1)$ and the probability tree of r to

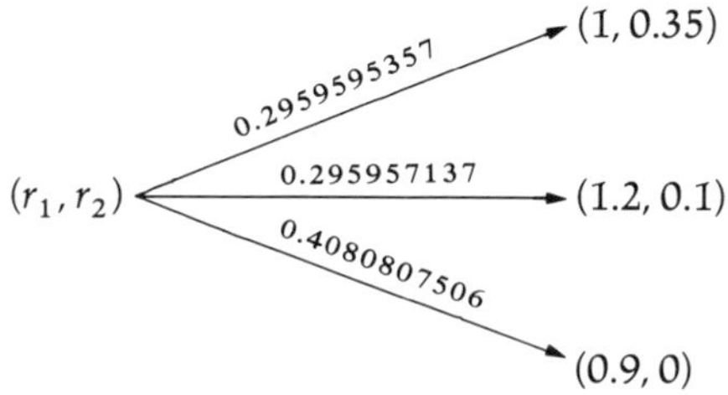

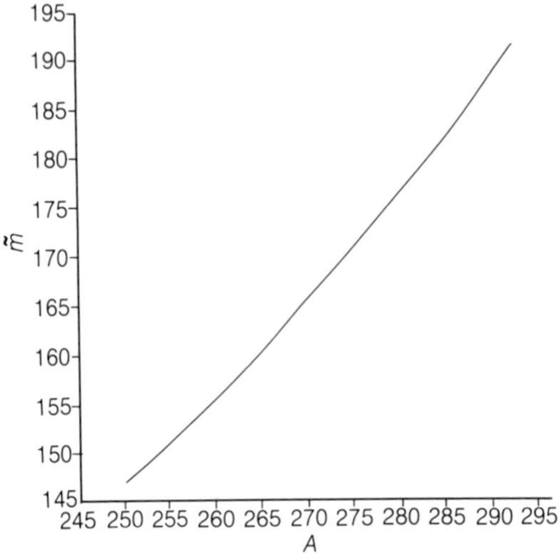

Figure 12.6

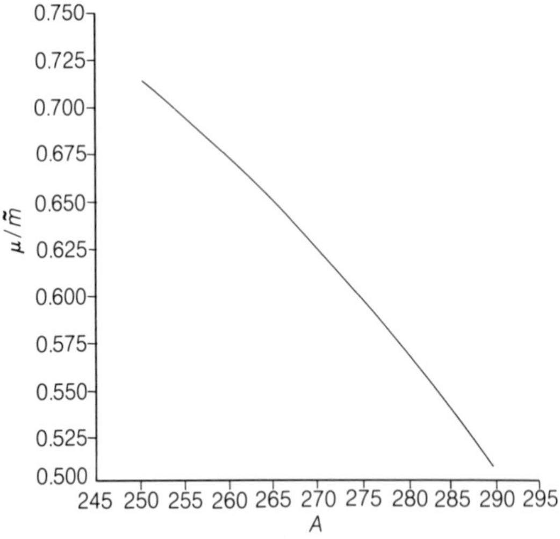

Figure 12.7

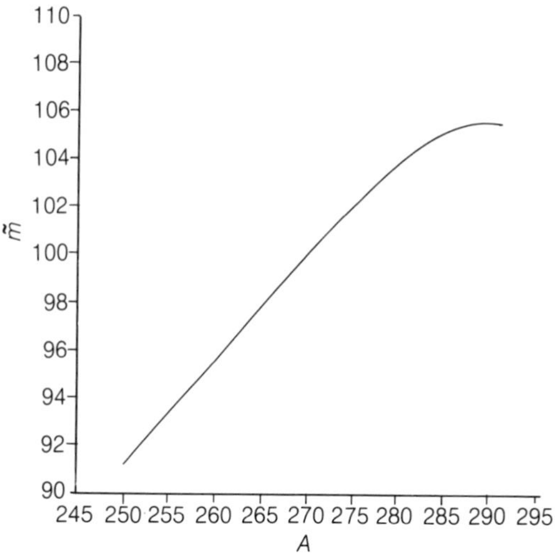

Figure 12.8

we would obtain the graphs seen in figures 12.8 and 12.9 for $\tilde{m}(\cdot)$ and $(\mu/\tilde{m})(\cdot)$. The first displays the kind of behavior anticipated by T 12.7, whereas the second is contrary to what might have been expected on the basis of T 12.8.

Thus we have in E 12.7 a utility function that, for some combinations of a and $F(\cdot)$, produces expected results for $(\mu, \tilde{m})$ and that, for other combinations of a and $F(\cdot)$, produces unexpected results. In looking for a solution to our aggregation problem, we attempt to delineate a class of U functions which have the property that, no matter how we choose $(a, F(\cdot))$, $(\mu, \tilde{m})(a, \cdot)$ and $(R(\cdot), R_p(\cdot))$ satisfy the relations which T 12.7 and T 12.8 insisted that $(\mu, m)(a, \cdot)$ and $(R(\cdot), R_p(\cdot))$ satisfy.

12.6.2 The Separation Property

In this section we characterize a class of utility functions with the following separation property: The consumer chooses among safe and risky assets as if he proceeded in two steps. In the first step he determines in what proportion to buy the two risky assets. In the second step he decides how to divide his net worth between safe and risky assets. To delineate the required class of utility functions, we must establish two new theorems, T 12.14 and T 12.15. In T 12.14 we assert that a certain class of utility functions have the separation property, and in T 12.15 we insist that this is

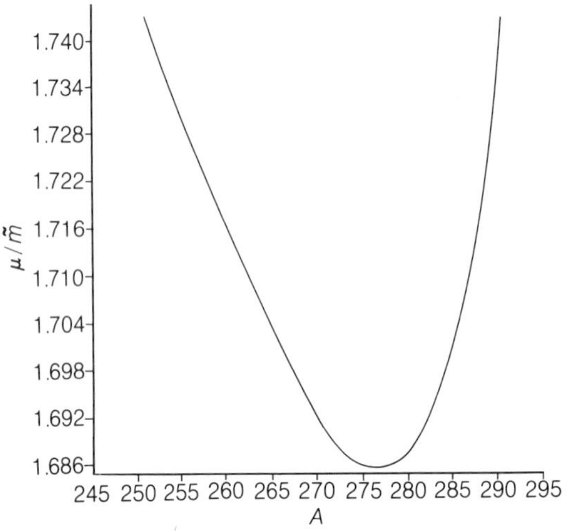

Figure 12.9

the largest such class. An analogue of T 12.15 for consumers who may borrow to invest in risky assets was established by Cass and Stiglitz (1970, p. 142).

T 12.14 Let $U(\cdot)\colon R_+ \to R$ be the utility function of a consumer in A 1–A 4, A 5*, A 6*, and A 7 and let $(\mu, m)(\cdot)\colon R^2_{++} \times R_+ \to R^3_+$ denote his demand functions. Suppose that $U(\cdot)$ satisfies either

(i) $U'(A) = D(\alpha + \beta A)^\gamma$, $A \in R_+$, where D, α, β, and γ are constants; or

(ii) $U'(A) = be^{dA}$, $A \in R_+$, where b and c are constants.

Then, for all $(a, A) \in R^3_{++}$ such that $(\mu, m)(a, A) > 0$, there exists a constant $k = k(a)$, which depends on a but not on A, such that $m_1(a, A) = k(a)m_2(a, A)$.

Note that, when $D = +2$, $\alpha = 200$, $\beta = -1$, and $\gamma = 1$, then $U(A) = -(200 - A)^2$, as in E 12.6. When $D = \frac{1}{2}$, $\alpha = 1$, $\beta = 1$, and $\gamma = -\frac{1}{2}$, then $U(A) = \sqrt{A + 1}$. And when $D = \beta = 1$, $\alpha = 0$, and $\gamma = -1$, then $U(A) = \log A$, as in E 12.1. Finally, we note that, when $U(\cdot)$ satisfies the equation in condition ii above, then $R(A) = -d$ for all $A \in R_+$.

In order that $U(\cdot)$ be a utility function, the constants in T 12.14 must satisfy definite conditions. For example, in T 12.14 (ii), $b > 0$ and $d < 0$. In T 12.14 (i), $\gamma \neq 0$ and $\gamma \neq 1$. If $-1 < \gamma < 1$, then $D > 0$, $\gamma < 0$, $\beta > 0$, and $\alpha > 0$. Similarly, if $\gamma = -1$, then either $D > 0$, $\beta > 0$, and $\alpha > 0$ or $D < 0$, $\beta < 0$, and $\alpha < 0$.

The set of values which the constants in T 12.14 (i) may assume can be enlarged considerably if we do not insist that the domain of $U(\cdot)$ be all of

R_+. For example, if we let the domain of $U(\cdot)$ be $[0, -\alpha/\beta]$, the following combinations are possible: $0 < \gamma < 1$, $D > 0$, $\beta < 0$, and $\alpha > 0$; and $\gamma = 1$ with either $D > 0$, $\beta < 0$, and $\alpha > 0$ or $D < 0$, $\beta > 0$, and $\alpha < 0$. Similarly, if we take the domain of $U(\cdot)$ to be $[-\alpha/\beta, \infty)$, we can allow the combination $-1 \leqslant \gamma < 0$, $D > 0$, $\beta > 0$, and $\alpha < 0$.

In our empirical analysis in chapter 28 we shall allow our consumers to have utility functions with domains $[h, \infty)$ or $[0, h]$. The behavior of such consumers does not distinguish itself from the behavior of those considered in this chapter inasmuch as their demand functions satisfy inconsequential modifications of T 12.1–T 12.3, T 12.5–T 12.9, or T 12.10–T 12.12, as the case may be. (See E 12.5 and E 12.8 below.) However, including them in our statistical analysis enlarges the scope of our empirical work significantly, as can be seen in the following: Suppose first that the domain of $U(\cdot)$ is R_+, and that $U(\cdot)$ satisfies T 12.14 (i). Then $R(A) = -\beta\gamma/(\alpha + \beta A)$, $R'(A) = \beta^2\gamma/(\alpha + \beta A)^2$, $R_p(A) = -\beta\gamma A/(\alpha + \beta A)$, and $R_p'(A) = -\beta\gamma\alpha/(\alpha + \beta A)^2$. Hence for $\gamma \in [-1, 0)$ $R'(\cdot) < 0$ and $R_p'(\cdot) > 0$ according to our calculation above. When the domain of $U(\cdot)$ is $[0, -\alpha/\beta]$ and $\gamma \in (0, 1]$, $R'(\cdot) > 0$ and $R_p'(\cdot) > 0$. Finally, if the domain of $U(\cdot)$ is $[-\alpha/\beta, \infty)$ and $\gamma \in [-1, 0)$, then $R'(\cdot) < 0$ and $R_p'(\cdot) < 0$. Only in this last case are both $R'(\cdot)$ and $R_p'(\cdot)$ negative. Note therefore that our empirical work in Chapter 28 is based on hypotheses that are true only if these two derivatives are both negative.

The preceding ideas are illustrated in E 12.8, which concerns a consumer in our first axiom system, i.e., in A 1–A 7. Note that the utility functions in E 12.8 are translates of the utility function in E 12.1, and the probability distribution in E 12.8 is the same as the probability distribution in E 12.1.

E 12.8 Let $\varepsilon > 0$ and consider a consumer in A 1–A 7 with utility function $U(A) = \log(\varepsilon + A)$ and probability distribution

$$F(r) = \begin{cases} 0 & \text{if } 0 \leqslant r < 1.4 \\ 0.25 & \text{if } 1.4 \leqslant r < 1.6 \\ 1 & \text{if } 1.6 \leqslant r \end{cases}$$

His demand function for m in the set $B = \{(a, A) \in R_{++}^2 : (\mu, m)(a, A) > 0\}$ is given by

$$m(a, A) = \frac{1.55 - a}{(1.6 - a)(a - 1.4)}(\varepsilon + A).$$

Note that $R'(A) < 0$ and $R_p'(A) > 0$ for all $A \in R_+$ and that $\partial m(a, A)/\partial A > 0$ and $\partial(m(a, A)/A)/\partial A < 0$, as they should be according to T 12.7 and T 12.8. Note also that the utility function is obtained from T 12.14 (i) by letting $\gamma = -1$, $\beta = 1$, $\alpha = \varepsilon$, and $D = 1$.

Next consider an individual with utility function $U(A) = \log(-\varepsilon + A)$ on $A > \varepsilon$. To allow him to be a consumer in A 1–A 7 we change the domain of definition of $U(\cdot)$ to $[\delta, \infty)$, where $\delta > \varepsilon$. We also change the specification of X from R_+^2 to $[\delta, \infty) \times R_+$. If this new consumer has the same probability distribution $F(\cdot)$ as the first, his demand function for m in the set $B = \{(a, A) \in R_{++} \times [\delta, \infty) : (\mu, m)(a, A) > (\delta, 0)\}$ is given by

$$m(a, A) = \frac{1.55 - a}{(1.6 - a)(a - 1.4)}(-\varepsilon + A).$$

This function is a simple translate of the first consumer's demand function. Yet $\partial m(a, A)/\partial A > 0$ *and* $\partial(m(a, A)/A)/\partial A > 0$, in accordance with T 12.7 and T 12.8, since $R'(A) < 0$ *and* $R_p'(A) < 0$ for all $A \in R_+$. The utility function of the second consumer is obtained from T 12.14 (i) by letting $\gamma = -1$, $\beta = 1$, $\alpha = -\varepsilon$, and $D = 1$.

The sensitivity of $R(\cdot)$ and the consumer's choice among safe and risky assets to translations of the argument of the utility function is remarkable. For that reason the following observation is in order: The utility function in T 12.14 (i) is a utility function with displaced origin and constant proportional risk-aversion function. If a consumer has a utility function that satisfies T 12.14 (i) for some values of D, α, β, and γ, then the constant proportional risk aversion is the reason why his preferred risky-asset mix does not vary with his net worth. The displaced origin accounts for the fact that the consumer's mix of safe and risky assets varies with his net worth. To see how, let $a \in R_{++}^2$ and $A^i \in R_{++}$, $i = 0, 1$, be such that $0 < (\mu, m)(a, A^i)$, $i = 0, 1$, then

$$m(a, A^1) = \frac{\alpha + \beta A^1}{\alpha + \beta A^0} m(a, A^0).$$

The right-hand side of this equality need not equal $(A^1/A^0)m(a, A^0)$.

Theorem T 12.14 has a converse that is formulated in T 12.15.

T 12.15 Let $U(\cdot)$: $R_+ \to R$ be thrice differentiable, with $U'(\cdot) > 0$ and $U''(\cdot) < 0$. Furthermore, let $\mathscr{F}$ denote the set of all nondegenerate probability distributions $F(\cdot)$: $R_+^2 \to [0, 1]$ with compact support. Finally, for each $F(\cdot) \in \mathscr{F}$, let $(\mu, m)(\cdot, F)$: $R_{++}^3 \to R_+^3$ denote the demand function of a consumer in A 1–A 4, A 5*, A 6*, and A 7 with utility function $U(\cdot)$ and probability distribution $F(\cdot)$. Suppose that, for each $F(\cdot) \in \mathscr{F}$ and for all $(a, A) \in \{(a, A) \in R_{++}^3 : (\mu, m)(a, A, F) > 0\}$, there exists a constant $k = k(a, F)$ which depends on (a, F) but not on A such that

$$m_1(a, A, F) = k(a, F)m_2(a, A, F)$$

Then $U'(\cdot)$ must satisfy either condition (i) or (ii) of T 12.14.

When reading T 12.14 and T 12.15 note that the utility functions in E 12.1 and E 12.5 have the separation property. This property specifies a relation between $U(\cdot)$ and characteristics of $(\mu, m)(\cdot, F)$ that $(\mu, m)(\cdot, F)$ must satisfy for *all* $F \in \mathscr{F}$ but only for those values of (a, A) where, for a given $F(\cdot)$, $(\mu, m)(a, A, F) > 0$. It is, therefore, not surprising that $(\mu, m)(0.1, 0.2, \cdot)$ in E 12.6 does not display the required characteristics as A varies over $[51.85185185, 100]$.

12.6.3 Arrow's Theorems and the Separation Property

It is true that if a consumer has a utility function with the separation property, his demand for μ and $\tilde{m}$ and his absolute and proportional risk-aversion function will satisfy T 12.7 and T 12.8—to wit T 12.16.

T 12.16 Let $(\mu, m)(\cdot): R^2_{++} \times R_+ \to R^3_+$ be the demand functions of a consumer in A 1–A 4, A 5*, A 6*, and A 7, and let $\tilde{B} = \{(a, A) \in R^3_{++} : (\mu, m)(a, A) > 0\}$. Suppose that, for all $(a, A) \in \tilde{B}$ there exists a constant $k = k(a)$, which depends on a but not on A, such that

$$m_1(a, A) = k(a) m_2(a, A).$$

Then in $\tilde{B}$ the following relations hold:

(i) $\tilde{m}(a, \cdot)$ is a strictly increasing (constant, (strictly decreasing)) function of A if and only if $R(\cdot)$ is a strictly decreasing (constant, (strictly increasing)) function on R_+;

(ii) $\mu(a, \cdot)/(\cdot)$ is a strictly increasing (constant, (strictly decreasing)) function of A if and only if $R_p(\cdot)$ is a strictly increasing (constant, (strictly decreasing)) function on R_+; and

(iii) $\mu(a, \cdot)/\tilde{m}(a, \cdot)$ is a strictly increasing (constant, (strictly decreasing)) function of A if and only if $R_p(\cdot)$ is a strictly increasing (constant, (strictly decreasing)) function on R_+.

Since $m_1(a, \cdot)$ in T 12.16 is a constant multiple of $m_2(a, \cdot)$ when $(\mu, m)(a, \cdot) > 0$, it is clear that, what is asserted of $\tilde{m}(a, \cdot)$ in T 12.16 (i) is true of $m_1(a, \cdot)$ and $m_2(a, \cdot)$ as well.

It is also true that if a consumer's utility function does not have the separation property, we can find a pair (a, F) such that his demand for μ and $\tilde{m}$ and his absolute and proportional risk-aversion functions do not satisfy T 12.7 and T 12.8—to wit T 12.17.

T 12.17 Let $U(\cdot): R_+ \to R$ be a thrice-differentiable function, with $U'(\cdot) > 0$ and $U''(\cdot) < 0$. In addition, let $\mathscr{F}$ denote the set of all nondegenerate probability distributions $F(\cdot): R^2_+ \to [0, 1]$ with compact support. Finally, consider the set of all consumers in A 1–A 4, A 5*, A 6*, and A 7 with utility function $U(\cdot)$ and some distribution $F(\cdot) \in \mathscr{F}$, and let their demand functions for (μ, m) be denoted by $(\mu, m)(\cdot): R^2_{++} \times R_+ \times \mathscr{F} \to R^3_+$, as in T 12.15. Suppose that there exist two triples, (a, A^0, F) and (a, A^1, F), such that $0 < A^0 < A^1$, $0 < (\mu, m)(a, A^i, F)$, $i = 0$, 1, and

$$\frac{m_1(a, A^0, F)}{m_2(a, A^0, F)} \neq \frac{m_1(a, A^1, F)}{m_2(a, A^1, F)}.$$

Then there exist distributions $F^*(\cdot)$, $F^{**}(\cdot) \in \mathscr{F}$ and vectors a^* and $a^{**} \in R^2_{++}$ such that $0 < (\mu, m)(a^*, A^i, F^*)$, $0 < (\mu, m)(a^{**}, A^i, F^{**})$, $i = 0, 1$,

$$m(a^*, A^0, F^*) \nleq m(a^*, A^1, F^*)$$

and

$$m(a^{**}, A^1, F^{**}) \nleq m(a^{**}, A^0, F^{**}).$$

Moreover, if

$$\tilde{m}(a, A^0, F) \leqslant \tilde{m}(a, A^1, F),$$

i.e., if $am(a, A^0, F) \leqslant am(a, A^1, F)$, then there exists a pair $(\hat{a}, \hat{F}) \in R^2_{++} \times \mathscr{F}$ such that $0 < (\mu, m)(\hat{a}, A^i, \hat{F})$, $i = 0, 1$, and

$$\tilde{m}(\hat{a}, A^1, \hat{F}) < \tilde{m}(\hat{a}, A^0, \hat{F}).$$

An analogue of the first half of T 12.17 for consumers who can borrow to invest in risky assets was established by 0. Hart (1975, p. 621). The second half of T 12.17, which concerns $\tilde{m}(\cdot)$, is novel.

From T 12.16 and T 12.17 we obtain T 12.18 which is a partial analogue to T 12.7.

T 12.18 Let $U(\cdot): R_+ \to R$ be a thrice-differentiable function, with $U'(\cdot) > 0$ and $U''(\cdot) < 0$. Also let $\mathscr{F}$ denote the set of all nondegenerate probability distributions $F(\cdot): R^2_+ \to [0, 1]$ with compact support. Finally, consider all consumers in A 1–A 4, A 5*, A 6*, and A 7 with utility function $U(\cdot)$ and some $F(\cdot) \in \mathscr{F}$; denote their demand functions by $(\mu, m)(\cdot): R^2_{++} \times R_+ \times \mathscr{F} \to R^3_+$ as in T 12.15; and let $\tilde{B}_{aF} = \{A \in R_{++} : (\mu, m)(a, A, F) > 0\}$, $(a, F) \in R^2_{++} \times \mathscr{F}$. Then (1) the condition, $R(\cdot)$ is a strictly decreasing (constant, (strictly increasing)) function on R_+, implies that $m_i(a, \cdot, F)$, $i = 1, 2$, and $\tilde{m}(a, \cdot, F)$ are strictly increasing (constant, (strictly decreasing)) functions on $\tilde{B}_{aF}$ for all $(a, F) \in R^2_{++} \times \mathscr{F}$, if and only if $U'(\cdot)$ satisfies T 12.14 (i) or (ii); and (2) the condition, $\tilde{m}(a, \cdot, F)$ is a strictly increasing (constant, (strictly decreasing)) function on $\tilde{B}_{aF}$ for all $(a, F) \in R^2_{++} \times \mathscr{F}$, implies that $R(\cdot)$ is a strictly decreasing (constant, (strictly increasing)) function on R_+ if and only if $U'(\cdot)$ satisfies T 12.14 (i) or (ii).

With obvious modifications, a similar analogue of T 12.8 is true. Hence T 12.18 concludes our search for a solution to our aggregation problem.

12.7 Appendix: Proofs

In this section we shall sketch proofs of most of the theorems discussed above. For that purpose we need an other universal theorem, UT 11.

UT 11 Suppose that $A \subset R^{n+m}$ is open and that $f(\cdot)\colon A \to R^n$ is differentiable. Suppose also that $x^0 \in R^n$, $y^0 \in R^m$, $(x^0, y^0) \in A$ and $f(x^0, y^0) = 0$. Finally, suppose that the $n \times n$ matrix $(\partial f_i(x^0, y^0)/\partial x_j)$ is invertible. Then there exists an open set $U \subset R^m$ and a unique differentiable function $g(\cdot)\colon U \to R^n$ such that $y^0 \in U$ and $x^0 = g(y^0)$, and such that, for all $y \in U$, $f(g(y), y) = 0$ and

$$\left(\frac{\partial g(y)}{\partial y}\right) = \left(\frac{\partial f_i(g(y), y)}{\partial x_j}\right)^{-1} - \left(\frac{\partial f(g(y), y)}{\partial y}\right),$$

where $(\partial g(y)/\partial y)$ is the $n \times m$ matrix $(\partial g_j(y)/\partial y_l)$, and $(\partial f(g(y), y)/\partial y)$ is the $n \times m$ matrix $(\partial f_i(g(y), y)/\partial y_l)$.

The theorem is called the *Implicit Function Theorem*. A proof of it can be found in (Rudin 1964, pp. 196–197).

In writing the proofs of T 12.1–T 12.18 we use "compact" as shorthand for closed and bounded. Moreover, we use $EU(A + m(r - a))$ as shorthand for

$$\int_0^\infty U(A + m(r - a))\, dF(r) \qquad \text{or} \qquad \int_0^\infty \int_0^\infty U(A + m(r - a))\, dF(r)$$

according as $r \in R_+$ or $r \in R_+^2$. Finally, we say that a function $f(\cdot)\colon X \to R^n$ is uniformly continuous on X if for every $\varepsilon > 0$ there is a $\delta > 0$ such that $x, y \in X$ and $\|x - y\| < \delta$ imply that $\|f(x) - f(y)\| < \varepsilon$.

12.7.1 Proof of T 12.1

Since $F(\cdot)$ is a probability distribution with compact support; since $U(\cdot)$ has continuous first, second, and third derivatives; and since a continuous function on a compact set is uniformly continuous and has compact range—as witnessed in UT 3, the obvious inequalities show that $V(\cdot)$ is thrice differentiable.

It is well known that the conditions specified for $U(\cdot)$ in A 7 imply that $U(\cdot)$ is strictly increasing and strictly concave. Since $F(\cdot)$ is nondegenerate, it follows that $V(\cdot)$ must be strictly incresasing. Moreover, the inequality,

$$\lambda V(\mu^0, m^0) + (1 - \lambda) V(\mu^1, m^1)$$

$$= \int_0^\infty (\lambda U(\mu^0 + m^0 r) + (1 - \lambda) U(\mu^1 + m^1 r))\, dF(r)$$

$$\leqslant \int_0^\infty U(\lambda\mu^0 + (1 - \lambda)\mu^1 + (\lambda m^0 + (1 - \lambda) m^1) r)\, dF(r)$$

$$= V(\lambda\mu^0 + (1 - \lambda)\mu^1, \lambda m^0 + (1 - \lambda) m^1),$$

which is valid for any two pairs (μ^0, m^0), $(\mu^1, m^1) \in R_+^2$ and for any $\lambda \in [0, 1]$, implies that $V(\cdot)$ is a concave function. If $(\mu^0, m^0) \neq (\mu^1, m^1)$ and if $\lambda \in (0, 1)$, the inequality is an equality only if, for all r in the set where $F(\cdot)$ increases,

$$\mu^0 + m^0 r = \mu^1 + m^1 r.$$

Since $F(\cdot)$ is nondegenerate, it is easy to check that such an equality cannot hold for all r in the set of increase of $F(\cdot)$, and that $V(\cdot)$ is strictly concave.

The continuity of $(\mu, m)(\cdot)$ on $R_{++} \times R_+$ is a consequence of the preceding results and T 10.5. The differentiability of $(\mu, m)(\cdot)$ on $B = \{(a, A) \in R_{++} \times R_+ : (\mu, m)(a, A) > 0\}$ is shown as follows: For any $(a, A) \in R_{++} \times R_+$, the pair $(\mu, m)(a, A)$ can be found by maximizing $EU(A + m(r - a))$ subject to $0 \leqslant m \leqslant A/a$ to find $m(a, A)$ and by then setting $\mu(a, A) = A - am(a, A)$. In B, $m(a, A)$ satisfies both the first-order necessary condition,

$$E(r - a)U'(A + m(a, A)(r - a)) = 0,$$

for a maximum and $E(r - a)^2 U''(A + m(a, A)(r - a)) < 0$. From these conditions and the Implicit Function Theorem, UT 11, it follows that $m(\cdot)$ is differentiable in B. Since $\mu(a, A) = A - am(a, A)$, $\mu(\cdot)$ must also be differentiable in B.

12.7.2 Proof of T 12.2

Let $(a, A) \in R_{++} \times R_+$ be such that $m(a, A) > 0$, and let $(\mu, m) = (\mu, m)(a, A)$. It follows from A 4, the definition of $(\mu, m)(\cdot)$, the monotonicity of $V(\cdot)$, the strict concavity of $U(\cdot)$, and the nondegeneracy of $F(\cdot)$ that

$$U(A) \leqslant EU(\mu + mr) = EU(A + m(r - a)) < U(A + m(Er - a)).$$

From this inequality, from $m > 0$, and from $U'(\cdot) > 0$, we deduce $a < Er$.

Conversely, suppose that $(a, A) \in R_{++}^2$, and that $a < Er$. Also suppose that $m(a, A) = 0$. Then the necessary condition for a maximum of $EU(A + m(r - a))$ at $m = 0$,

$$E(r - a)U'(A) \leqslant 0,$$

shows that $Er \leqslant a$, which is a contradiction. Thus $a < Er$ and $m(a, A) = 0$ cannot both hold.

12.7.3 Proof of T 12.4

It is clear that if $H''(A)/H'(A) = U''(A)/U'(A)$ for all $A \in R_+$, there exist constants d and b with $b > 0$ such that

$$H(A) = d + bU(A), \qquad A \in R_+.$$

In this case, therefore, $W(\mu, m) = d + bV(\mu, m)$ for all $(\mu, m) \in R_+^2$. Clearly, the function $G(t) = d + bt$, $t \in \{\text{range of } U(\cdot)\} \cup \{\text{range of } V(\cdot)\}$, is strictly increasing and thrice differentiable.

To establish the converse, let N be so large that $\{\text{support of } F(\cdot)\} \subset [0, N]$, and let

$$R_U(A) = \frac{-U''(A)}{U'(A)} \quad \text{and} \quad R_H(A) = \frac{-H''(A)}{H'(A)}, \qquad A \in R_+.$$

If $R_U(\cdot) \neq R_H(\cdot)$, then there is an interval $[\alpha, \beta]$ where one function is larger than the other. Suppose that

$$R_U(A) > R_H(A) \text{ for all } A \in [\alpha, \beta]. \tag{12.1}$$

Next, let $A^0 = (\alpha + \beta)/2$ and pick $m^0 > 0$ so small that $2m^0N < (\beta - \alpha)/2$. Also pick $a^0 < Er$ so large that $0 < m(a^0, A^0) < m^0$ and $\mu(a^0, A^0) > 0$. That such an a^0 exists follows from the definition of $(\mu, m)(\cdot)$, from the monotonicity of $V(\cdot)$, and from T 12.1–T 12.3. Finally, define the functions,

$$V_U(m) = \frac{EU(A^0 + m(r - a^0))}{U'(A^0)}, \qquad m \in R_+,$$

and

$$V_H(m) = \frac{EH(A^0 + m(r - a^0))}{H'(A^0)}, \qquad m \in R_+.$$

If, as we now assume, $V(\cdot)$ and $W(\cdot)$ represent identical orderings of (μ, m) pairs, $V_U(\cdot)$ and $V_H(\cdot)$ will both assume their maximum value at $m(a^0, A^0)$. Since, by choice of (a^0, A^0), $(\mu, m)(a^0, A^0) > 0$, we must have $V_U'(m(a^0, A^0)) - V_H'(m(a^0, A^0)) = 0 - 0 = 0$. On the other hand, if equation 12.1 holds, then (see equation 20 in Pratt 1964, p. 129)

$$\frac{U'(y)}{U'(z)} < \frac{H'(y)}{H'(z)} \quad \text{for all } z < y, \qquad z, y \in [\alpha, \beta].$$

This inequality implies that, for $m \in (0, m^0)$,

$V'_U(m) - V'_H(m)$

$$= E(r - a^0)\left(\frac{U'(A^0 + m(r - a^0))}{U'(A^0)} - \frac{H'(A^0 + m(r - a^0))}{H'(A^0)}\right) < 0,$$

which is a contradiction. Thus we cannot assume that $V(\cdot)$ and $W(\cdot)$ order (μ, m) pairs in the same way and assume at the same time that equation 12.1 holds.

12.7.4 Proof of T 12.5

Let N be as in the proof of T 12.4 and suppose that T 12.5 (i) holds. Then

$$\frac{U'_{\mathrm{I}}(y)}{U'_{\mathrm{I}}(z)} \leqslant [<] \frac{U'_{\mathrm{II}}(y)}{U'_{\mathrm{II}}(z)} \quad \text{for } z < y, \qquad z, y \in R_+ \tag{12.2}$$

where $U_i(\cdot)$ denotes the $U(\cdot)$ function of consumer i, $i = \mathrm{I}, \mathrm{II}$. Next, let

$$V_i(m, a, A) = \frac{EU_i(A + m(r - a))}{U'_i(A)}, \qquad (m, a, A) \in R_+ \times R_{++} \times R_+$$

for $i = \mathrm{I}, \mathrm{II}$, and observe that, for all pairs $(a, A) \in R_{++} \times R_+$, $V_i(\cdot, a, A)$ takes its maximum value where $EU_i(A + (\cdot)(r - a))$ does. It follows from equation 12.2 that, for all $(a, A) \in R^2_{++}$ and $m \in R_{++}$,

$$\frac{\partial(V_{\mathrm{I}}(m, a, A) - V_{\mathrm{II}}(m, a, A))}{\partial m}$$

$$= E(r - a)\left(\frac{U'_{\mathrm{I}}(A + m(r - a))}{U'_{\mathrm{I}}(A)} - \frac{U'_{\mathrm{II}}(A + m(r - a))}{U'_{\mathrm{II}}(A)}\right) \leqslant [<] 0,$$

that is, $\partial V_{\mathrm{I}}(m, a, A)/\partial m \leqslant [<] \partial V_{\mathrm{II}}(m, a, A)/\partial m$ for all $(m, a, A) \in R^3_{++}$. From these inequalities and $E(r - a)^2\, U''_i(A + m(r - a)) < 0$, $i = \mathrm{I}, \mathrm{II}$, we conclude that $m_{\mathrm{I}}(a, A) \leqslant m_{\mathrm{II}}(a, A)$ for all $(a, A) \in R_{++} \times R_+$. Moreover, if strict inequality holds in T 12.5 (i), then $m_{\mathrm{I}}(a, A) < m_{\mathrm{II}}(a, A)$ whenever $(a, A) \in R^2_{++}$ and $0 < m_{\mathrm{I}}(a, A) < A/a$.

Next suppose that, T 12.5 (ii) holds but (i) does not. Then there is an interval $[\alpha, \beta]$ such that

$$R_{\mathrm{I}}(A) < [\leqslant] R_{\mathrm{II}}(A) \quad \text{for all } A \in [\alpha, \beta].$$

Consequently,

$$\frac{U'_{\mathrm{II}}(y)}{U'_{\mathrm{II}}(z)} < [\leqslant] \frac{U'_{\mathrm{I}}(y)}{U'_{\mathrm{I}}(z)}, \qquad z < y,\ z, y \in [\alpha, \beta].$$

If we now choose A^0 and m^0 as in the proof at T 12.4, and if we choose $a^0 < Er$ so large that $m_{\mathrm{I}}(a^0, A^0) < m^0$ and $\mu_{\mathrm{I}}(a^0, A^0) > 0$, then $\partial V_{\mathrm{I}}(m_{\mathrm{I}}(a^0, A^0), a^0, A^0)/\partial m = 0$ and $\partial(V_{\mathrm{I}}(m, a^0, A^0) - V_{\mathrm{II}}(m, a^0, A^0))/\partial m >$ $[\geqslant] 0$ for $m \in (0, m^0)$, which implies that $\partial V_{\mathrm{II}}(m_{\mathrm{I}}(a^0, A^0), a^0, A^0)/\partial m <$ $[\leqslant] 0$, and that $m_{\mathrm{II}}(a^0, A^0) < [\leqslant] m_{\mathrm{I}}(a^0, A^0)$. The last inequalities contradict our original assumption and conclude the proof of T 12.5.[4]

12.7.5 Proof of T 12.6

The weak form of the theorem follows from T 12.5 and from the following relations: $R_{p\mathrm{I}}(A) \geqslant R_{p\mathrm{II}}(A)$ for all $A \in R_+$ if and only if $R_{\mathrm{I}}(A) \geqslant R_{\mathrm{II}}(A)$ for all $A \in R_+$; $m_{\mathrm{I}}(a, A) \leqslant m_{\mathrm{II}}(a, A)$ if and only if $\mu_{\mathrm{I}}(a, A) \geqslant \mu_{\mathrm{II}}(a, A)$; and $\mu_{\mathrm{I}}(a, A) \geqslant \mu_{\mathrm{II}}(a, A)$ if and only if $\mu_{\mathrm{I}}(a, A)/A \geqslant \mu_{\mathrm{II}}(a, A)/A$.

The strong form is proved in essentially the same way.

12.7.6 Proof of T 12.7

I shall prove the case of increasing $m(a, \cdot)$ and decreasing $R(\cdot)$. The proofs of the other cases, which are similar, are left to the reader.

Let N be as in the proof of T 12.4 and consider an Arrow consumer and name his U, R, and m functions $U_{\mathrm{I}}(\cdot)$, $R_{\mathrm{I}}(\cdot)$, and $m_{\mathrm{I}}(\cdot)$, respectively. Suppose that $m_{\mathrm{I}}(a, \cdot)$ is a strictly increasing function for all $(a, A) \in R^2_{++}$, with $0 < m_1(a, A) < A/a$, and that there exist A^*, $A^{**} \in R_+$, with $A^* < A^{**}$ such that $R_{\mathrm{I}}(A^*) \leqslant R_{\mathrm{I}}(A^{**})$. Then there exists an interval $[\alpha, \beta] \subset [A^*, A^{**}]$ such that $R_{\mathrm{I}}(\cdot)$ is nondecreasing on $[\alpha, \beta]$.

Next, let $\gamma > 0$ be a small number so that $\alpha < \beta - 4\gamma$; let $A^0 = (\alpha + \beta)/2$; let $0 < 2m^0 N < (\beta - \gamma - \alpha)/2$; and choose $a^0 < Er$ so large that $0 < m_{\mathrm{I}}(a^0, A^0 + \gamma) < A^0/a^0$ and such that $m_{\mathrm{I}}(a^0, A^0 + \gamma) < m^0$. Since by assumption $m_{\mathrm{I}}(a^0, A^0) < m_{\mathrm{I}}(a^0, A^0 + \gamma)$, and since $a^0 < Er$, $0 < m_{\mathrm{I}}(a^0, A^0) < A^0/a^0$ also.

Finally, consider a second Arrow consumer with U, R, and m functions $U_{\mathrm{II}}(\cdot)$, $R_{\mathrm{II}}(\cdot)$, and $m_{\mathrm{I}}(\cdot)$, where $U_{\mathrm{II}}(A) = U_{\mathrm{I}}(\gamma + A)$, $A \in R_+$. It easy to show that $R_{\mathrm{II}}(A) = R_{\mathrm{I}}(\gamma + A)$ and that, for all $(a, A) \in R^2_{++}$ with $0 < m_{\mathrm{II}}(a, A) < A/a$, $m_{\mathrm{II}}(a, A) = m_{\mathrm{I}}(a, \gamma + A)$. According to our original hypothesis, $R_{\mathrm{I}}(\cdot)$ is a nondecreasing function on $[\alpha, \beta]$. Hence $R_{\mathrm{II}}(A) \geqslant R_{\mathrm{I}}(A)$ for all $A \in [\alpha, \beta - \gamma]$. Consequently,

$$\frac{U'_{\mathrm{II}}(y)}{U'_{\mathrm{II}}(z)} \leqslant \frac{U'_{\mathrm{I}}(y)}{U'_{\mathrm{I}}(z)} \quad \text{for all } z < y, \qquad z, y \in [\alpha, \beta - \gamma].$$

We now define the functions $V_i(\cdot)$, $i = \mathrm{I}, \mathrm{II}$, as in the proof of T 12.5, and deduce that

$$\frac{\partial V_{\mathrm{I}}(m, a^0, A^0)}{\partial m} - \frac{\partial V_{\mathrm{II}}(m; a^0, A^0)}{\partial m} \geqslant 0, \qquad m \in (0, m^0).$$

This inequality, together with the facts $m_{\mathrm{II}}(a^0, A^0) < m^0$ and

$$\frac{\partial V_{\mathrm{II}}(m_{\mathrm{II}}(a^0, A^0), a^0, A^0)}{\partial m} = 0,$$

imply that $m_{\mathrm{I}}(a^0, A^0) \geqslant m_{\mathrm{II}}(a^0, A^0) = m_{\mathrm{I}}(a^0, A^0 + \gamma)$, which contradicts the original hypothesis. Thus the hypotheses $m_{\mathrm{I}}(a, \cdot)$ strictly increasing in the relevant region and $R_{\mathrm{I}}(\cdot)$ not decreasing on R_+ cannot hold simultaneously.

To prove the converse, we observe that in $\{(a, A) \in R^2_{++}: (\mu, m)(a, A) > 0\}$

$$\frac{\partial m(a, A)}{\partial A} = -\frac{E(r-a)U''(A+m(a, A)(r-a))}{E(r-a)^2U''(A+m(a, A)(r-a))}$$

$$= -\frac{E(R(A)-R(A+m(a, A)(r-a)))(r-a)U'(A+m(a, A)(r-a))}{E(r-a)^2U''(A+m(a, A)(r-a))}.$$

Since $F(\cdot)$ is nondegenerate, it is easy to show that the last fraction is positive if $R(\cdot)$ is a decreasing function in R_+. (See Arrow 1965, p. 43.)

12.7.7 Proof of T 12.8 and T 12.9

Note first that

$$\frac{\partial(\mu/A)}{\partial A} = A^{-2}\left\{A\frac{\partial \mu}{\partial A} - \mu\right\} = (\mu/A^2)\left\{\frac{A}{\mu}\frac{\partial \mu}{\partial A} - 1\right\}$$

and

$$\frac{\partial(\mu/am)}{\partial A}$$

$$= (am)^{-2}\left\{am\frac{\partial \mu}{\partial A} - a\mu\frac{\partial m}{\partial A}\right\} = (am)^{-2}\left\{(A-\mu)\frac{\partial \mu}{\partial A} - \mu\left(1 - \frac{\partial \mu}{\partial A}\right)\right\}$$

$$= (am)^{-2}\left\{A\frac{\partial \mu}{\partial A} - \mu\right\} = \left(\frac{A}{am}\right)^2\frac{\partial(\mu/A)}{\partial A}.$$

From these equalities, which hold for all $(a, A) \in R^2_{++}$ with $(\mu, m)(a, A) > 0$, it follows that, to prove T 12.8 and T 12.9, we need only prove T 12.8 (ii). We shall do so for strictly increasing $\mu(a, \cdot)/(\cdot)$ and $R_p(\cdot)$ only. The other two cases can be handled similarly.

Consider an Arrow consumer, and denote his U, R_p, μ, and m functions by $U_{\mathrm{I}}(\cdot)$, $R_{p\mathrm{I}}(\cdot)$, $\mu_{\mathrm{I}}(\cdot)$, and $m_{\mathrm{I}}(\cdot)$. Assume also that $\mu_{\mathrm{I}}(a, \cdot)/(\cdot)$ is an increasing function for all $(a, A) \in \{(a, A) \in R_{++}^2 : (\mu_{\mathrm{I}}, m_{\mathrm{I}})(a, A) > 0\}$, and that there exist A^* and $A^{**} \in R_+$ such that $A^* < A^{**}$ and such that $R_{p\mathrm{I}}(A^*) \geqslant R_{p\mathrm{I}}(A^{**})$. Consequently, there also exists an interval $[\alpha, \beta] \subset [A^*, A^{**}]$ on which $R_{p\mathrm{I}}(\cdot)$ is a nonincreasing function.

Next consider a second Arrow consumer with U, R_p, μ, and m functions $U_{\mathrm{II}}(\cdot)$, $R_{p\mathrm{II}}(\cdot)$, $\mu_{\mathrm{II}}(\cdot)$, and $m_{\mathrm{II}}(\cdot)$, respectively, where

$$U_{\mathrm{II}}(A) = U_{\mathrm{I}}(kA), \qquad A \in R_+,$$

for some constant $k > 1$ that satisfies $k\alpha < \beta$. It is easily shown that $R_{p\mathrm{II}}(A) = R_{p\mathrm{I}}(kA)$ and that, for all $(a, A) \in R_{++}$ with $0 < m_{\mathrm{II}}(a, A) < A/a$, $m_{\mathrm{II}}(a, A) = k^{-1} m_{\mathrm{I}}(a, kA)$, and $\mu_{\mathrm{II}}(a, A)/A = \mu_{\mathrm{I}}(a, kA)/kA$. Moreover, since $R_{p\mathrm{I}}(\cdot)$ is a nonincreasing function of A on $[\alpha, \beta]$, it follows that $R_{p\mathrm{II}}(A) \leqslant R_{p\mathrm{I}}(A)$, $A \in [\alpha, \beta k^{-1}]$, and hence

$$\frac{U_{\mathrm{I}}'(y)}{U_{\mathrm{I}}'(z)} \leqslant \frac{U_{\mathrm{II}}'(y)}{U_{\mathrm{II}}'(z)} \quad \text{for all } z < y, \qquad z, y \in [\alpha, \beta k^{-1}]. \tag{12.3}$$

Finally, let $A^0 = (\beta k^{-1} + \alpha)/2$; let $0 < 2m^0 N < (\beta k^{-1} - \alpha)/2$, where N is as in the proof of T 12.4; choose $a^0 < Er$ so large that $0 < m_{\mathrm{II}}(a^0, A^0) < m^0$; and define the functions $V_i(\cdot)$, $i = \mathrm{I}, \mathrm{II}$, as in the proof of T 12.5. It then follows from equation 12.3 that

$$\frac{\partial V_{\mathrm{I}}(m, a^0, A^0)}{\partial m} - \frac{V_{\mathrm{II}}(m, a^0, A^0)}{\partial m} \leqslant 0, \qquad m \in (0, m^0),$$

and hence that $m_{\mathrm{I}}(a^0, A^0) \leqslant m_{\mathrm{II}}(a^0, A^0) = k^{-1} m_{\mathrm{I}}(a^0, kA^0)$. From this we deduce that $a^0 m_{\mathrm{I}}(a^0, A^0)/A^0 \leqslant a^0 m_{\mathrm{I}}(a^0, kA^0)/kA^0$ and that $\mu_{\mathrm{I}}(a^0, A^0)/A^0 \geqslant \mu_{\mathrm{I}}(a^0, kA^0)/kA^0$. The latter inequality contradicts our original assumption, and thus we have shown that $\mu(a, \cdot)/(\cdot)$ cannot be a strictly increasing function on the relevant set unless $R_p(\cdot)$ is an increasing function on R_+.

To establish the converse, we observe (dropping subscripts and writing z for $A + m(a, A)(r - a)$, that for all $(a, A) \in R_{++}^2$ with $(\mu, m)(a, A) > 0$,

$$\begin{aligned}
\frac{\partial(\mu(a, A)/A)}{\partial A} &= A^{-2}\left\{A\frac{\partial \mu(a, A)}{\partial A} - \mu(a, A)\right\} = \frac{a}{A^2}\left\{m(a, A) - A\frac{\partial m(a, A)}{\partial A}\right\} \\
&= \frac{a}{A^2}\,\frac{Em(r - a)^2 U''(z) + EA(r - a)U''(z)}{E(r - a)^2 U''(z)} \\
&= \frac{a}{A^2}\,\frac{E(R_p(A) - R_p(z))(r - a)U'(z)}{E(r - a)^2 U''(z)}.
\end{aligned}$$

It is easy to show that, if $R_p(\cdot)$ is a strictly increasing function on R_+, the last fraction must be positive.

12.7.8 Proof of T 12.10

The proof of the monotonicity, concavity, and differentiability properties of $U(\cdot)$ and $V(\cdot)$ can be taken verbatim from the proof of T 12.1. The same is true of the continuity of $(\mu, m)(\cdot)$. The differentiability of $(\mu, m)(\cdot)$ on $\tilde{B} = \{(a, A) \in R^3_{++} : (\mu, m)(a, A) > 0\}$ is shown as follows: For any $(a, A) \in R^2_{++} \times R_+$, the vector $(\mu, m)(a, A)$ can be found by first maximizing $EU(A + m(r - a))$ subject to $0 \leqslant m$ and $am \leqslant A$ to find $m(a, A)$ and then setting $\mu(a, A) = A - am(a, A)$. In $\tilde{B}$, $m(a, A)$ satisfies the first-order necessary conditions,

$$E(r_i - a_i)U'(A + m(a, A)(r - a)) = 0, \qquad i = 1, 2, \tag{12.4}$$

and the inequality

$$\begin{aligned} &[E(r_1 - a_1)(r_2 - a_2)U''(A + m(a, A)(r - a))]^2 \\ &\quad < E(r_1 - a_1)^2U''(A + m(a, A)(r - a)) \\ &\qquad \cdot E(r_2 - a_2)^2U''(A + m(a, A)(r - a)). \end{aligned} \tag{12.5}$$

The latter follows from the Schwartz Inequality (which is a strict inequality in this case) once we observe that

$$(r_1 - a_1)(r_2 - a_2)U''(\cdot) = (-(r_1 - a_1)\sqrt{-U''(\cdot)})((r_2 - a_2)\sqrt{-U''(\cdot)}).$$

From equations 12.4 and 12.5, and from the Implicit Function Theorem, UT 11, we deduce that $m(\cdot)$ is differentiable in $\tilde{B}$. So is $\mu(\cdot)$, since $\mu(a, A) = A - am(a, A)$.

12.7.9 Proof of 12.11

For some $(a, A) \in R^2_{++} \times R_+$, let $m^0 = m(a, A)$ and suppose that $Er_i \leqslant a_i$, $i = 1, 2$, and that $m^0 \neq 0$. Then

$$U(A) \leqslant EU(A + m^0(r - a)) < U(A + m^0(Er - a)) \leqslant U(A),$$

which is an impossibility. Hence $Er_i \leqslant a_i$, $i = 1, 2$, implies $m^0 = 0$.

Suppose next that $m^0 = 0$. Then the necessary conditions for a maximum of $EU(A + m(r - a))$ in $\{m \geqslant 0, am \leqslant A\}$ at $m = 0$, $E(r_i - a_i)U'(A) \leqslant 0$, $i = 1, 2$, imply that $Er_i \leqslant a_i$, $i = 1, 2$.

The preceding arguments show that if one of the conditions $Er_i \leqslant a_i$, $i = 1, 2$, is not satisfied, then $m^0 \neq 0$. Suppose that $Er_1 > a_1$ and that r_1 and r_2 are independently distributed. We shall show that $m_1^0 > 0$. To do that we assume that $m_1^0 = 0$ and $m_2^0 > 0$. Then the necessary condition for a constrained maximum of $EU(A + m(r - a))$ at m^0,

$$0 \geqslant E(r_1 - a_1)U'(A + m_2^0(r_2 - a_2)) = E(r_1 - a_1) \cdot EU'(A + m_2^0(r_2 - a_2)),$$

implies that $Er_1 \leqslant a_1$, which is a contradiction. Hence $m_1^0 > 0$.

Next we shall show that if $m_1^0 > 0$ and if r_1 and r_2 are independently distributed, then $Er_1 > a_1$. The last paragraph showed that if $m_1^0 > 0$ and $m_2^0 = 0$, then $Er_1 > a_1$. So suppose $m^0 > 0$ and $Er_1 \leqslant a_1$. Then

$$\begin{aligned} EU(A + m^0(r - a)) &= E\{E\{U(A + m(r - a))|r_2\}\} \\ &< E\{U(A + m_1^0(E\{r_1|r_2\} - a_1) + m_2^0(r_2 - a_2))\} \\ &= EU(A + m_1^0(Er_1 - a_1) + m_2^0(r_2 - a_2)) \\ &\leqslant EU(A + m_2^0(r_2 - a_2)) \leqslant EU(A + m^0(r - a)), \end{aligned}$$

which is an impossibility. Hence $m_1^0 > 0$ implies $Er_1 > a_1$ if r_1 and r_2 are independently distributed.

The arguments used in the last two paragraphs apply to m_2^0 as well. Hence we have shown that, if r_1 and r_2 are independently distributed, $m_i^0 > 0$ if and only if $Er_i > a_i$, $i = 1, 2$.

12.7.10 Proof of T 12.13

Let

$$R_{\text{I}}(A) = \frac{-U_{\text{I}}''(A)}{U_{\text{I}}'(A)} \quad \text{and} \quad R_{\text{II}}(A) = \frac{-U_{\text{II}}''(A)}{U_{\text{II}}'(A)}, \qquad A \in R_+.$$

We shall show that if $G(\cdot)$ exists, then $R_{\text{I}}(A) = R_{\text{II}}(A)$ for all $A \in R_+$. The proof is obtained by contradiction.

Suppose that $G(\cdot)$ exists and that $R_{\text{I}}(\cdot) \neq R_{\text{II}}(\cdot)$. Then there is an interval $[\alpha, \beta]$ where one function is larger than the other, say

$$R_{\text{I}}(A) > R_{\text{II}}(A) \quad \text{for all } A \in [\alpha, \beta]. \tag{12.6}$$

Next, let N and M be so large that $\{\text{support of } F(\cdot)\} \subset [0, N] \times [0, M]$; let $A^0 = (\alpha + \beta)/2$; pick $m^0 > 0$ so small that $m_1^0 N + m_2^0 M < (\beta - \alpha)/4$; and choose $a^0 < Er$ so large that $0 \neq m(a^0, A^0) < m^0$ and $\mu(a^0, A^0) > 0$.

That such an a^0 exists follows from the definition of $(\mu, m)(\cdot)$, T 12.10–12.12 and the monotonicity of $V(\cdot)$. Finally, define the functions,

$$W_{\mathrm{I}}(m) = \frac{EU_{\mathrm{I}}(A^0 + m(r - a^0))}{U_{\mathrm{I}}'(A^0)}, \qquad m \in R_+^2$$

and

$$W_{\mathrm{II}}(m) = \frac{EU_{\mathrm{II}}(A^0 + m(r - a^0))}{U_{\mathrm{II}}'(A^0)}, \qquad m \in R_+^2.$$

If $G(\cdot)$ exists, both $W_{\mathrm{I}}(\cdot)$ and $W_{\mathrm{II}}(\cdot)$ take on their maximum value at $m(a^0, A^0)$. Therefore, since $\mu(a^0, A^0) > 0$,

$$\sum_{i=1}^{2} m_i(a^0, A^0) \frac{\partial W_j(m(a^0, A^0))}{\partial m_i} = 0, \qquad j = \mathrm{I}, \mathrm{II}. \tag{12.7}$$

On the other hand, if equation 12.6 holds, then

$$\frac{U_{\mathrm{I}}'(y)}{U_{\mathrm{I}}'(z)} < \frac{U_{\mathrm{II}}'(y)}{U_{\mathrm{II}}'(z)} \quad \text{for all } z < y, \qquad z, y \in [\alpha, \beta].$$

This inequality implies that

$$\sum_{i=1}^{2} m_i \frac{\partial(W_{\mathrm{I}}'(A^0 + m(r - a^0)) - W_{\mathrm{II}}'(A^0 + m(r - a^0)))}{\partial m_i} < 0$$

for all $m \in [0, m^0) - \{0\}$, which contradicts equation 12.7. Thus $G(\cdot)$ cannot exist unless $R_{\mathrm{I}}(A) = R_{\mathrm{II}}(A)$ for all $A \in R_+$.

The remainder of the proof of T 12.13 can be taken almost verbatim from the proof of T 12.4.

12.7.11 Proof of T 12.14

Consider a consumer in the second axiom system whose U function satisfies $U'(A) = be^{dA}$, $A \in R_+$. In the set $\tilde{B} = \{(a, A) \in R_{++}^3 : (\mu, m)(a, A) > 0\}$, the necessary conditions for a maximum of $EU(A + m(r - a))$ subject to $0 \leqslant m$ and $am \leqslant A$ are satisfied. Thus

$$E(r_i - a_i)be^{d(A+m(r-a))} = be^{dA}E(r_i - a_i)e^{dm(r-a)} = 0, \qquad i = 1, 2.$$

Since the solution to these equations is independent of A, the existence of the required constant $k(a)$ is obvious.

Next consider a consumer in the second axiom system whose U function satisfies $U'(A) = D(\alpha + \beta A)^\gamma$, $A \in R_+$; pick two pairs (a, A^0) and $(a, A^1) \in$

$\tilde{B}$ with $A^0 < A^1$, $\alpha + \beta A^0 \neq 0$, and $\alpha + \beta A^1 \neq 0$; and let $m^0 = m(a, A^0)$ and $m^1 = m(a, A^1)$. Also let $m^{0^*} = \beta m^0$ and $m^{1^*} = \beta m^1$, and define λ by

$$\lambda = \frac{\alpha + \beta A^1}{\alpha + \beta A^0}.$$

Finally, observe that the necessary conditions for a maximum of $EU(A + m(r - a))$ subject to $0 \leqslant m$ and $am \leqslant A$ are satisfied and have a unique solution for all $(a, A) \in \tilde{B}$. But, if that is true, then the relations

$$\begin{aligned} 0 &= E(r_i - a_i)D(\alpha + \beta(A^1 + m(a, A^1)(r - a)))^\gamma \\ &= DE(r_i - a_i)((\alpha + \beta A^1) + m^{1^*}(r - a))^\gamma \\ &= D\lambda^\gamma E(r_i - a_i)\left((\alpha + \beta A^0) + \left(\frac{m^{1^*}}{\lambda}\right)(r - a)\right)^\gamma \\ &= D\lambda^\gamma E(r_i - a_i)\left(\alpha + \beta\left(A^0 + \left(\frac{m^1}{\lambda}\right)(r - a)\right)\right)^\gamma, \qquad i = 1, 2 \end{aligned}$$

imply that $m^0 = m^1/\lambda$. Since $\alpha + \beta A = 0$ for at most one A, and since (a, A^0) and $(a, A^1) \in \tilde{B}$ were arbitrarily chosen, this result and the continuity of $m(a, \cdot)$ establish the existence of the required constant $k(a)$.

12.7.12 Proof of T 12.15

Let $F(\cdot)\colon R_+^2 \to [0, 1]$ be a nondegenerate probability distribution with compact support, and let $U(\cdot)\colon R_+ \to R$ be thrice differentiable, with $U'(\cdot) > 0$ and $U''(\cdot) < 0$. Also for any function $f(\cdot)$ that is integrable with respect to $F(\cdot)$, let $E_F f = \int_0^\infty \int_0^\infty f(r_1, r_2)\, dF(r_1, r_2)$. Finally note that if $U''(\cdot)/U'(\cdot)$ is a constant on R_+, $U'(\cdot)$ must have the form specified in T 12.14 (ii). Hence for the purposes of this proof we may assume that $U''(\cdot)/U'(\cdot)$ takes at least two values on R_+.

The proof of T 12.15 is obtained in several steps. First a few preliminary remarks: A consumer in A 1–A 4, A 5*, A 6*, and A 7 with utility function $U(\cdot)$ and probability distribution $F(\cdot)$ will, when faced with a pair $(a, A) \in R_{++}^2 \times R_+$, choose m so as to maximize $E_F U(A + m(r - a))$ subject to $0 \leqslant m$ and $am \leqslant A$. We denote this choice of m by $m(a, A, F)$. For each $F(\cdot)$, the theorem concerns only those values of $(a, A) \in R_{++}^3$ with the property that $0 < m(a, A, F)$ and $am(a, A, F) < A$. With respect to such pairs, $m(a, A, F)$ is the unique solution of

$$E_F(r_i - a_i)U'(A + m(r - a)) = 0, \qquad i = 1, 2. \tag{12.8}$$

Note that in equation 12.8 the random variable that enters is $r - a$ and not r. Let $\tilde{z}$ be the random variable $(r - a)$, and suppose that $\tilde{z}$ relative to $F(\cdot)$ has the distribution

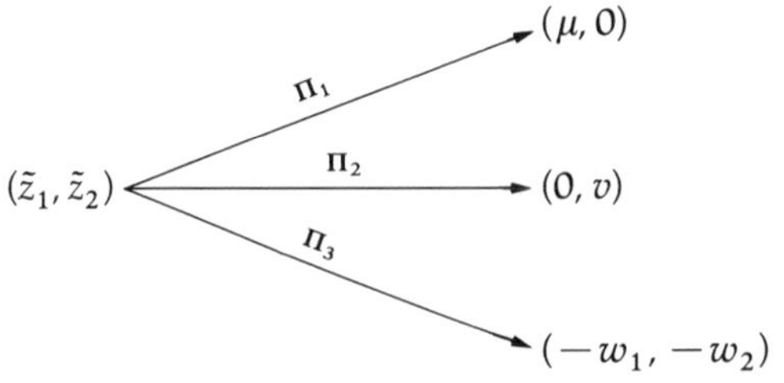

with $(\mu, v, w_1, w_2) > 0$, $\Pi_1 u - \Pi_3 w_1 > 0$ and $\Pi_2 v - \Pi_3 w_2 > 0$. For this $F(\cdot)$, equation 12.8 can be written as

$$U'(A + m_1 u) = \left(\frac{\Pi_3 w_1}{\Pi_1 u}\right) U'(A - mw) \tag{12.9}$$

and

$$U'(A + m_2 v) = \left(\frac{\Pi_3 w_2}{\Pi_2 v}\right) U'(A - mw). \tag{12.10}$$

If $U(\cdot)$ has the property specified in the statement of the theorem, we can find a constant k such that, for all A for which there is an interior solution to equations 12.9 and 12.10, there is a one-dimensional $m = m(A)$ which satisfies

$$U'(A + mu) = \left(\frac{\Pi_3 w_1}{\Pi_1 u}\right) U'(A - m(w_1 + kw_2)) \tag{12.11}$$

and

$$U'(A + kmv) = \left(\frac{\Pi_3 w_2}{\Pi_2 v}\right) U'(A - m(w_1 + kw_2)). \tag{12.12}$$

These equations play an important role in our proof of T 12.15.

Next let $y = A - m(A)(w_1 + kw_2)$, $x = A + m(A)u$, and $z = A + km(A)v$ and assume that $y < x < z$ and that $R(y) \neq R(z)$. Then we can use equations 12.11 and 12.12 and the Implicit Function Theorem to show that $dm(A)/dA$ satisfies the following two equations:

$$\frac{dm(A)}{dA} = \left\{\frac{R(y) - R(x)}{uR(x) + (w_1 + kw_2)R(y)}\right\} \tag{12.13}$$

and

$$\frac{dm(A)}{dA} = \left\{\frac{R(y) - R(z)}{kvR(z) + (w_1 + kw_2)R(y)}\right\}. \tag{12.14}$$

From equations 12.13 and 12.14 it follows that $A\,dm(A)/dA - m(A)$ satisfies

$$\frac{A\,dm(A)}{dA} - m(A) = \left\{\frac{R_p(y) - R_p(x)}{uR(x) + (w_1 + kw_2)R(y)}\right\} \tag{12.15}$$

and

$$\frac{A\,dm(A)}{dA} - m(A) = \left\{\frac{R_p(y) - R_p(z)}{kvR(z) + (w_1 + kw_2)R(y)}\right\}. \tag{12.16}$$

Since $R(y) \neq R(z)$, equations 12.13 and 12.14 imply that $R(x) \neq R(y)$. Hence, we can divide 12.13 into 12.15 and 12.14 into 12.16 to get

$$\left\{\frac{R_p(y) - R_p(x)}{R(y) - R(x)}\right\} = \left\{\frac{R_p(y) - R_p(z)}{R(y) - R(z)}\right\}$$

from which we deduce that

$$xR(x) = -\left\{\frac{(z - y)R(y)R(z)}{R(z) - R(y)}\right\} + \left\{\frac{zR(z) - yR(y)}{R(z) - R(y)}\right\} R(x). \tag{12.17}$$

So much for preliminary remarks. In the first step of the proof of T 12.15 we shall show that, for any triple $y, x, z \in R_+$ which satisfies $y < x < z$ and $R(y) \neq R(z)$, $R(x)$ must satisfy equation 12.17. This can be established as follows: Let $y, x, z \in R_{++}$ be numbers which satisfy $y < x < z$ and $R(y) \neq R(z)$. Then note that there are numbers $A, m, k, u, v, w_1, w_2, \Pi_1, \Pi_2, \Pi_3$ that are all positive and satisfy the equations $A + mu = x$; $A + kmv = z$; $A - m(w_1 + kw_2) = y$; $\Pi_1 + \Pi_2 + \Pi_3 = 1$, and equations 12.11 and 12.12. To show why, we first choose α and β so that

$$\frac{U'(x)}{U'(y)} = \alpha \qquad \text{and} \qquad \frac{U'(z)}{U'(y)} = \beta.$$

Then $0 < \beta < \alpha < 1$ according to A 7. Next we choose u, v, w_1, and w_2 so that

$$\frac{w_1}{u} = \alpha \qquad \text{and} \qquad \frac{w_2}{v} = \gamma,$$

where γ is a number that satisfies

$$0 < \gamma < \beta \qquad \text{and} \qquad \left(\frac{1}{1+\gamma}\right)y + \left(\frac{\gamma}{1+\gamma}\right)z < x.$$

We also let

$$\Pi_1 = \Pi_3 = \frac{\beta}{2\beta + \gamma} \qquad \text{and} \qquad \Pi_2 = \frac{\gamma}{2\beta + \gamma}$$

and

$$A = \frac{y + \alpha x + \gamma z}{1 + \alpha + \gamma}. \tag{12.18}$$

Finally we let

$$u = v = 2 \qquad w_1 = 2\alpha \qquad \text{and} \qquad w_2 = 2\gamma,$$

and we choose the values of m and k from

$$m = \frac{x - A}{2} \qquad \text{and} \qquad k = \frac{z - A}{x - A}. \tag{12.19}$$

It is easy to verify that the values of A, m, k, u, v, w_1, w_2, Π_1, Π_2, and Π_3 satisfy the required conditions; i.e. they are positive and satisfy $\Pi_1 + \Pi_2 + \Pi_3 = 1$, $A + mu = x$, $A + kmv = z$, $A - m(w_1 + kw_2) = y$, and equations 12.11 and 12.12.

To show that $R(x)$ must satisfy equation 12.17, we now choose $a \in R^2_{++}$ so small that

$$a_1 m + a_2 km < A \tag{12.20}$$

and we let the distribution of (r_1, r_2) be

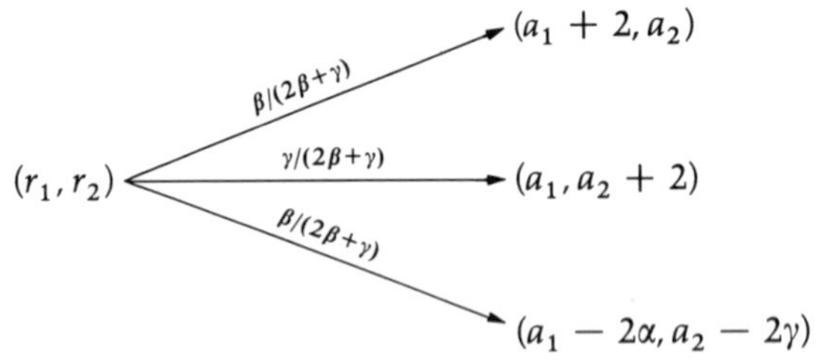

(12.21)

From the hypothesis of the theorem it follows that a consumer with $F(\cdot)$, as specified in equation 12.21, and with the given utility function will, when facing the triple (a_1, a_2, A) specified in equations 12.20 and 12.18 choose the vector $(A - a_1 m - a_2 km, m, km)$, where m and k are as specified in equation 12.19. With (a_1, a_2) and $F(\cdot)$ fixed, the consumer's choice of (m_1, m_2) will vary with A. However, in the set, $\tilde{B} = \{A \in R_+ : (m_1, m_2)(a, A, F) > 0$ and $a_1 m_1(a, A, F) + a_2 m_2(a, A, F) < A\}$, $m_2(a, A, F) = k(a, F) m_1(a, A, F)$. Since $U''(\cdot) < 0$ on R_+ and since (m, km) satisfies equation 12.8, $k = k(a, F)$. Consequently, with k, u, v, w_1, w_2, Π_1, Π_2, and Π_3 as specified above, there is a uniquely determined function $m(\cdot)$: $\tilde{B} \to R_{++}$ whose derivative at the value of A specified in equation 12.18 satisfies equations 12.13 and 12.14. From this result it follows that $R(x)$ must satisfy equation 12.17, as shown by equations 12.13–12.17.

Let $y, z \in R_{++}$ be so that $y < z$ and $R(y) \neq R(z)$: We have shown that for all $x \in (y, z)$, $R(x)$ satisfies equation 12.17. If we now let $b = R(z) - R(y)$, $e = (y - z)R(y)R(z)$, and $d = yR(y) - zR(z)$, this result can be formulated as follows:

$$R(x) = \frac{e}{d + bx}, \qquad x \in (y, z). \tag{12.22}$$

It easy to show that

$$R(y) = \lim_{x \to y} \frac{e}{d + bx} \qquad \text{and} \qquad R(z) = \lim_{x \to z} \frac{e}{d + bx}.$$

Hence, with $h = -e/b$ and $D = U'(y)/(d + by)^h$, we can deduce that

$$U'(x) = D(d + bx)^h, \qquad x \in [y, z]$$

i.e., that the derivative of $U(\cdot)$ in $[y, z]$ has the form described in T 12.14 (i).

With the provisions that $y < z$ and $R(y) \neq R(z)$, y and z were chosen arbitrarily from R_+. Consequently, we might have chosen $y = 0$ and deduced that $U'(\cdot)$ had the required form on $[0, z]$. We now claim that $U'(\cdot)$ has the required form on all of R_+. The proof of this is obtained by contradiction. Since z could be chosen arbitrarily large if it were not for the requirement that $R(z) \neq R(0)$, $U'(\cdot)$ can fail to have the required form in all of R_+ only if there is some number T such that for all $u \geqslant T$, $R(u) = R(0)$. Suppose that such a T exists. By the continuity of $R(\cdot)$ there must be a smallest such number. Let T denote this smallest number, and observe that it must differ from zero.

Next note that if $v \in (0, T)$, then $R(v) \neq R(0)$ because, if it were not, then we could take a $z \in (v, T)$ with $R(z) \neq R(0)$ and deduce that v must satisfy

$$R(0) = \frac{e}{d} = \frac{e}{d + bv}, \tag{12.23}$$

where $b = R(z) - R(0)$, $e = -zR(0)R(z)$, and $d = -zR(z)$. Since $b \neq 0$, equation 12.23 is satisfied only for $v = 0$, and that contradicts $v \in (0, T)$.

Suppose now that we have chosen a $z \in (0, T)$ and that $R(x)$ satisfies equation 12.22 for all $x \in [0, z]$. Moreover, let v be an element of (z, T) and observe that by repeating the arguments which led to equation 12.22 we can establish the existence of nonzero constants $\tilde{e}$, $\tilde{d}$, and $\tilde{b}$ such that

$$R(x) = \frac{\tilde{e}}{\tilde{d} + \tilde{b}x} \quad \text{for all } x \in [0, v]. \tag{12.24}$$

It is easily shown that

$$\frac{e}{d} = \frac{\tilde{e}}{\tilde{d}} \quad \text{and} \quad \frac{b}{d} = \frac{\tilde{b}}{\tilde{d}}. \tag{12.25}$$

From equations 12.24 and 12.25, from the fact that $e/(d + bx) = (e/d)/(1 + (b/d)x)$, from the continuity of $R(\cdot)$ on R_+, and from the fact that v was chosen arbitrarily in (z, T), we deduce that

$$R(x) = \frac{e}{d + bx} \quad \text{for all } x \in [0, T].$$

But then equation 12.23 must be satisfied for $v = T$, which is impossible, since $T > 0$.

The last contradiction shows that

$$R(x) = \frac{e}{d + bx} \quad \text{for all } x \in R_+$$

and hence that

$$U'(x) = D(d + bx)^h \quad \text{for all } x \in R_+,$$

as we set out to show.

12.7.13 Proof of T 12.16

Theorem T 12.16 (i) can be proved by modifying the arguments used to establish the validity of T 12.7. An analogous modification of the proof of T 12.8 and T 12.9 suffices to establish T 12.16 (ii) and (iii). I leave those proofs to the reader.

To establish T 12.16 (i) for $\tilde{m}(\cdot)$ strictly increasing and $R(\cdot)$ strictly decreasing, consider a consumer in A 1–A 4, A 5*, A 6*, and A 7 with U, R, m_1, m_2, and $\tilde{m}$ functions $U_I(\cdot)$, $R_I(\cdot)$, $m_{1I}(\cdot)$, $m_{2I}(\cdot)$, and $\tilde{m}_I(\cdot)$, respectively. For this consumer, assume that $\tilde{m}_I(a, \cdot)$ is a strictly increasing function of A for all $(a, A) \in R^3_{++}$ with $0 < (m_{1I}, m_{2I})(a, A)$ and with $\tilde{m}_I(a, A) < A$ and that there exist $A^*, A^{**} \in R_+$, with $A^* < A^{**}$ such that $R_{\mathrm{I}}(A^*) \leqslant R_{\mathrm{I}}(A^{**})$. Then there exists an interval $[\alpha, \beta] \subset [A^*, A^{**}]$ such that $R_{\mathrm{I}}(\cdot)$ is nondecreasing on $[\alpha, \beta]$.

Next let N and M be as in the proof of T 12.13; let $\gamma > 0$ be such that $\alpha + \gamma < \beta$; let $A^0 = (\beta - \gamma + \alpha)/2$ and $0 < 2\tilde{m}^0(k(a^0)N + M) < (\beta - \gamma - \alpha)/2$; and choose $a^0 < Er$ so large that $\tilde{m}_{\mathrm{I}}(a^0, A^0 + \gamma) < \min((k(a^0)a_1^0 + a_2^0)\tilde{m}^0, A^0)$. Since $A^0 > 0$ and $a^0 < Er$, T 12.12 implies that $\tilde{m}_{\mathrm{I}}(a^0, A^0) > 0$. From this and from the fact that $m_{1\mathrm{I}}(a^0, A^0) = k(a^0)m_{2\mathrm{I}}(a^0, A^0)$, we deduce that $m_{i\mathrm{I}}(a^0, A^0) > 0$, $i = 1, 2$, as well.

Finally, consider a second consumer in the new axiom system with U, R, m_1, m_2, and $\tilde{m}$ functions $U_{\mathrm{II}}(\cdot)$, $R_{\mathrm{II}}(\cdot)$, $m_{1\mathrm{II}}(\cdot)$, $m_{2\mathrm{II}}(\cdot)$, and $\tilde{m}_{\mathrm{II}}(\cdot)$, respectively, where $U_{\mathrm{II}}(A) = U_{\mathrm{I}}(\gamma + A)$, $A \in R_+$. It is easy to show that $R_{\mathrm{II}}(A) = R_{\mathrm{I}}(\gamma + A)$, $A \in R_+$, and that, for all $(a, A) \in R_{++}^3$ with $0 < (m_{1\mathrm{II}}, m_{2\mathrm{II}})(a, A)$ and with $\tilde{m}_{\mathrm{II}}(a, A) < A$, $m_{i\mathrm{II}}(a, A) = m_{i\mathrm{I}}(a, A + \gamma)$, $i = 1, 2$, and hence $\tilde{m}_{\mathrm{II}}(a, A) = \tilde{m}_{\mathrm{I}}(a, A + \gamma)$. Since $R_{\mathrm{I}}(\cdot)$ is a nondecreasing function on $[\alpha, \beta]$, $R_{\mathrm{I}}(A) \leqslant R_{\mathrm{II}}(A)$, $A \in [\alpha, \beta - \gamma]$. From this inequality we deduce

$$\frac{U'_{\mathrm{II}}(y)}{U'_{\mathrm{II}}(z)} \leqslant \frac{U'_{\mathrm{I}}(y)}{U'_{\mathrm{I}}(z)} \quad \text{for all } y > z, \qquad y, z \in [\alpha, \beta - \gamma]. \tag{12.26}$$

We now define the functions

$$V_{\mathrm{I}}(x, a^0, A^0) = \frac{EU_{\mathrm{I}}(A^0 + x(k(a^0)(r_1 - a_1^0) + (r_2 - a_2^0)))}{U'_{\mathrm{I}}(A^0)}, \qquad x \in R_+,$$

and

$$V_{\mathrm{II}}(x, a^0, A^0) = \frac{EU_{\mathrm{II}}(A^0 + x(k(a^0)(r_1 - a_1^0) + (r_2 - a_2^0)))}{U'_{\mathrm{II}}(A^0)}, \qquad x \in R_+,$$

and deduce from equation 12.26 that

$$\frac{\partial V_{\mathrm{I}}(x, a^0, A^0)}{\partial x} - \frac{\partial V_{\mathrm{II}}(x, a^0, A^0)}{\partial x} \geqslant 0 \quad \text{for all } x \in (0, \tilde{m}^0).$$

Since $\tilde{m}_{\mathrm{I}}(a^0, A^0 + \gamma) < \min((k(a^0)a_1^0 + a_2^0)\tilde{m}, A^0)$, $0 < m_{2\mathrm{II}}(a^0, A^0) = m_{2\mathrm{I}}(a^0, A^0 + \gamma) < \tilde{m}^0$ and $\partial V_{\mathrm{II}}(m_{2\mathrm{II}}(a^0, A^0), a^0, A^0) = 0$. From these two facts, T 12.10, and equation 12.8, it follows that $m_{2\mathrm{I}}(a^0, A^0) \geqslant m_{2\mathrm{II}}(a^0, A^0) = m_{2\mathrm{I}}(a^0, A^0 + \gamma)$, which contradicts our original hypothesis, since then $\tilde{m}_{\mathrm{I}}(a^0, A^0) \geqslant \tilde{m}_{\mathrm{I}}(a^0, A^0 + \gamma)$ as well. Thus, if $\tilde{m}(a, \cdot)$ is increasing in $\tilde{B}$, $R(\cdot)$ is decreasing in R_+.

The converse is obtained as in the proof of T 12.7: We first observe that, for all $(a, A) \in R_{++}^3$ with $0 < (m_{1\mathrm{I}}, m_{2\mathrm{I}})(a, A)$ and with $\tilde{m}_{\mathrm{I}}(a, A) < A$, by assumption

$$\frac{\partial m_{2\mathrm{I}}(a,A)}{\partial A}$$

$$= -\frac{E(k(a)(r_1-a_1)+(r_2-a_2))U_{\mathrm{I}}''(A+m_{2\mathrm{I}}(a,A)(k(a)(r_1-a_1)+(r_2-a_2)))}{E(k(a)(r_1-a_1)+(r_2-a_2))^2U_{\mathrm{I}}''(A+m_{2\mathrm{I}}(a,A)(k(a)(r_1-a_1)+(r_2-a_2)))}$$

$$= -\frac{E(R_{\mathrm{I}}(A)-R_{\mathrm{I}}(z))(k(a)(r_1-a_1)+(r_2-a_2))U_{\mathrm{I}}'(z)}{E(k(a)(r_1-a_1)+(r_2-a_2))^2U_{\mathrm{I}}''(z)},$$

where $z = A + m_{2\mathrm{I}}(a,A)(k(a)(r_1 - a_1) + (r_2 - a_2))$. Again it is easily shown that the last fraction is positive if $R_{\mathrm{I}}(\cdot)$ is a decreasing function on R_+. Since $\tilde{m}_{\mathrm{I}}(a,A) = m_{2\mathrm{I}}(a,A)(k(a)a_1 + a_2)$, we conclude that $\partial\tilde{m}_{\mathrm{I}}(a,A)/\partial A > 0$ in the relevant region if $R_{\mathrm{I}}(\cdot)$ is a decreasing function on R_+.

The remaining cases of T 12.16 (i) are obtained by similar arguments.

12.7.14 Proof of T 12.17

Let $m^0 = m(a, A^0, F)$ and $m^1 = m(a, A^1, F)$. We shall establish the existence of (a^*, F^*) and $(\hat{a}, \hat{F})$. The existence of (a^{**}, F^{**}) can be demonstrated with similar arguments. I leave those details to the reader.

By assumption, $m^0 \neq m^1$. If $m^0 \nleq m^1$, there is nothing to prove. Hence, suppose that $m^0 < m^1$. Moreover, let

$$\tau = m_2^0 m_1^1 - m_1^0 m_2^1.$$

The sign of τ will influence our choice of m^* below but is otherwise unimportant for our arguments. Hence we can, without loss in generality, assume that $\tau > 0$. Finally, let $m^* \in R_+^2$ be a vector that satisfies the conditions

$$0 < m^* \qquad m_1^* > m_1^1 \qquad \text{and} \qquad m_2^* < m_2^0,$$

and let

$$\alpha = \tau^{-1}\{m_1^* m_2^0 - m_1^0 m_2^1\}$$

$$\beta = \tau^{-1}\{m_1^0 m_1^1 - m_1^* m_1^0\}$$

$$\gamma = \tau^{-1}\{m_2^* m_2^0 - m_2^0 m_2^1\}$$

$$\delta = \tau^{-1}\{m_1^1 m_2^0 - m_2^* m_1^0\}$$

and

$$B = \begin{pmatrix} \alpha & \gamma \\ \beta & \delta \end{pmatrix}.$$

It is easy to verify that

$$\alpha > 0 \qquad \beta < 0 \qquad \gamma < 0 \qquad \delta > 0 \qquad \text{and} \qquad \alpha\delta - \beta\gamma > 0,$$

$$B^{-1} = (\alpha\delta - \beta\gamma)^{-1}\begin{pmatrix} \delta & -\gamma \\ -\beta & \alpha \end{pmatrix} > 0,$$

and

$$m^0 = m^0 B \qquad \text{and} \qquad m^* = m^1 B.$$

where m^0, m^1, and hence m^* are taken to be row vectors.

Next let $\tilde{z}$ be the column vector $(r - a)'$, let

$$\tilde{z}^* = B^{-1}\tilde{z},$$

and name the probability distributions of $\tilde{z}$ and $\tilde{z}^*$, respectively, F^0 and $\tilde{F}^0$. Moreover, let

$$C^0 = \{m \in R^2_+ : am \leqslant A^0\}$$

and

$$\tilde{C}^0 = \{m \in R^2_+ : m(B^{-1}a') \leqslant A^0\},$$

where a' denotes the transpose of a. Then $m^0 \in \tilde{C}^0 \cap C^0$, and the transformation $m \to mB^{-1}$ maps $\tilde{C}^0$ one to one into C^0 and m^0 into itself. Moreover, since the determinant of B^{-1} equals 1 and the ranges of $\tilde{z}$ and $\tilde{z}^*$ are contained in a compact subset of R^2, $E_{F^0}U(A^0 + m\tilde{z})$ and $E_{\tilde{F}^0}U(A^0 + m\tilde{z}^*)$ are well defined and satisfy

$$E_{\tilde{F}^0}U(A^0 + mz^*) = E_{F^0}U(A^0 + mB^{-1}\tilde{z}) \tag{12.27}$$

for all $m \in \tilde{C}^0$. From this and from the fact that

$$E_{F^0}U(A^0 + m\tilde{z}) \leqslant E_{F^0}U(A^0 + m^0\tilde{z})$$

for all $m \in C^0$, it follows that

$$E_{\tilde{F}^0}U(A^0 + m\tilde{z}^*) \leqslant E_{F^0}U(A^0 + m^0\tilde{z}) \tag{12.28}$$

for all $m \in \tilde{C}^0$. Since B^{-1} maps m^0 into itself, equations 12.27 and 12.28 imply that, for all $m \in \tilde{C}^0$,

$$E_{\tilde{F}^0}U(A^0 + m\tilde{z}^*) \leqslant E_{\tilde{F}^0}U(A^0 + m^0\tilde{z}^*).$$

From this, the strict concavity of $U(\cdot)$, and the nondegeneracy of the distribution of $\tilde{z}^*$, it follows that

$$m^0 = m(B^{-1}a', A^0, F_{\tilde{z}^* + B^{-1}a'}), \tag{12.29}$$

where $F_{\tilde{z}^* + B^{-1}a'}$ denotes the distribution of $\tilde{z}^* + B^{-1}a'$.

As for A^1, we let

$$C^1 = \{m \in R_+^2 : ma' \leqslant A^1\}$$

and

$$\tilde{C}^1 = \{m \in R_+^2 : m(B^{-1}a') \leqslant A^1\}$$

and observe that $m^* \in \tilde{C}^1$ and that $m^* B^{-1} = m^1$. Then arguments similar to those used above suffice to demonstrate that, for all $m \in \tilde{C}^1$,

$$E_{\tilde{F}^0} U(A^1 + m\tilde{z}^*) \leqslant E_{\tilde{F}^0} U(A^1 + m^*\tilde{z}^*)$$

and that

$$m^* = m(B^{-1}a', A^1, F_{\tilde{z}^* + B^{-1}a'}). \tag{12.30}$$

By construction, $0 < m^*$ and $m^0 \nleqslant m^*$. Therefore, equations 12.29, 12.30, and

$$(a^*, F^*) = (B^{-1}a', F_{\tilde{z}^* + B^{-1}a'})$$

establish the existence of a price a^* and a distribution F^* with the property that

$$m(a^*, A^0, F^*) \nleqslant m(a^*, A^1, F^*). \tag{12.31}$$

Since $a^* > 0$ and $m^*(B^{-1}a') = (m^* B^{-1})a' = m^1 a$, and since F^* is nondegenerate and has compact support, the pair (a^*, F^*) has all the properties which T 12.17 requires.[5]

We have established the existence of a pair (a^*, F^*) which satisfies equation 12.31 when $m^0 < m^1$. When $m^0 \leqslant m^1$ and $m^0 \nless m^1$, similar arguments suffice to establish the existence of a pair (a^*, F^*) which satisfies equation 12.31. For the sake of brevity, I leave those details to the reader.

To establish the existence of $(\hat{a}, \hat{F})$ we must consider two cases: $m^0 < m^1$ and $m^0 \nless m^1$. We begin with the latter.

Suppose that $m^0 \nless m^1$. Then a possible value of $\hat{a}$ can be obtained in the following way. Let α, β, γ, and δ be positive numbers such that

$$\max\left(\frac{m_1^0}{m_2^0}, \frac{m_1^1}{m_2^1}\right) < \frac{\alpha}{\beta}$$

and

$$\min\left(\frac{m_1^0}{m_2^0}, \frac{m_1^1}{m_2^1}\right) > \frac{\gamma}{\delta}.$$

Moreover, let

$$D = (\alpha\delta - \beta\gamma)^{-1}\begin{pmatrix} \alpha & \beta \\ \gamma & \delta \end{pmatrix}$$

and observe that

$$\alpha\delta - \beta\gamma > 0$$

and

$$m^i D^{-1} > 0, \qquad i = 0, 1. \tag{12.32}$$

Finally, pick $\hat{a} \in R^2_{++}$ such that

$$(m^i D^{-1})\hat{a}' < A^i, \qquad i = 0, 1 \tag{12.33}$$

and

$$((m^0 - m^1)D^{-1})\hat{a}' > 0. \tag{12.34}$$

The fact that $m^0 \neq m^1$, $\tilde{m}(a, A^0, F) \leqslant \tilde{m}(a, A^1, F)$ and $m^0 \nless m^1$ ensures that there is an $\hat{a} \in R^2_{++}$ which satisfies equations 12.33 and 12.34.

To find a possible choice of $\hat{F}$ we first let

$$\tilde{z}^{**} = D\tilde{z},$$

where $\tilde{z}$ is the column vector $(r - a)'$; and we let F^0 and F^{**}, respectively, be the distribution of $\tilde{z}$ and $\tilde{z}^{**}$. Then F^{**} has compact support and $E_{F^{**}} U(A + m\tilde{z}^{**})$ is well defined for all $A \in R_+$ and $m \in R^2_+$. Moreover, since the determinant of D equals 1,

$$E_{F^{**}} U(A + m\tilde{z}^{**}) = E_{F^0} U(A + mD\tilde{z}). \tag{12.35}$$

Next we shall demonstrate that if $M(\hat{a}, A)$ denotes the value of m at which $E_{F^{**}} U(A + m\tilde{z}^{**})$ attains its maximum value in $\{m \in R^2_+ : m\hat{a}' \leqslant A\}$, then

$$M(\hat{a}, A^i) = m^i D^{-1}, \qquad i = 0, 1. \tag{12.36}$$

To see why, note that equation 12.35, $\tilde{m}(a, A^i, F) < A^i$, $i = 0, 1$, and the strict concavity in m of $E_{F^0} U(A + m\tilde{z})$ imply that

$$\begin{aligned} E_{F^{**}} U(A^i + M(\hat{a}, A^i)\tilde{z}^{**}) &= E_{F^0} U(A^i + M(\hat{a}, A^i)D\tilde{z}) \\ &\leqslant E_{F^0} U(A^i + m^i\tilde{z}), \qquad i = 0, 1. \end{aligned} \tag{12.37}$$

On the other hand, equations 12.32 and 12.33 imply that

$$\begin{aligned} E_{F^{**}} U(A^i + M(\hat{a}, A^i)\tilde{z}^{**}) &\geqslant E_{F^{**}} U(A^i + (m^i D^{-1})\tilde{z}^{**}) \\ &= E_{F^0} U(A^i + m^i\tilde{z}), \qquad i = 0, 1. \end{aligned} \tag{12.38}$$

From equations 12.37 and 12.38 and from the uniqueness of $M(\hat{a}, A)$ follows the validity of equation 12.36.

Finally, we let $\hat{F}$ be the distribution of $\tilde{z}^{**} + \hat{a}$. Then equations 12.32–12.34 and 12.36 imply that

$$m^i D^{-1} = m(\hat{a}, A^i, \hat{F}), \qquad i = 0, 1,$$

$$0 < \tilde{m}(\hat{a}, A^i, \hat{F}) < A^i, \qquad i = 0, 1,$$

and

$$\tilde{m}(\hat{a}, A^1, \hat{F}) < \tilde{m}(\hat{a}, A^0, \hat{F}),$$

as was to be shown.

So much for the case $m^0 \nless m^1$. If $m^0 < m^1$, we first replace (a, F) by the (a^*, F^*) of equation 12.31 and observe that

$$m(a^*, A^0, F^*) = m^0 \nless m^* = m(a^*, A^1, F^*)$$

and

$$\tilde{m}(a, A^i, F) = \tilde{m}(a^*, A^i, F^*), \qquad i = 0, 1.$$

Then we produce $(\hat{a}, \hat{F})$ from (a^*, F^*) in the same way we produced $(\hat{a}, \hat{F})$ from (a, F) above.

13 Consumer Choice and Revealed Preference

A theory about certain undefined terms consists of all the axioms together with all the theorems that can be derived from the axioms. In chapter 2 I pointed out that the formulation of the theory may vary from one researcher to the next. What is an axiom in one formulation may be a theorem in another and conversely. The choice of axioms depends both on the skill and temparament of the theorist and on the use he intends to make of the theory. Our axioms, H 1–H 6 (section 10.2.1) are simple and easy to handle. From an empiricist's point of view, however, they have the disadvantage that H 3 contains an unobservable element $V(\cdot)$ that plays a pivotal role in the development of the theory. So the question arises:

Q 1 Is it possible to build the theory of consumer choice on axioms whose elements can be given a denotation that is defined entirely in terms of observable objects?

We shall attempt to answer Q 1 in this chapter.

The demand function is under ideal conditions observable as soon as we give x, p, and A denotations that are defined in terms of observable objects. Thus three reasonable steps in the search for an answer to Q 1 suggest themselves: First write down a minimal set of axioms S 1–S N in which an (observable) function $f(\cdot)$: $R^n_{++} \times R_+ \to R^n_+$ takes the place of $V(\cdot)$. Next show that $f(\cdot)$ is a demand function, i.e., show that there is a function $V(\cdot)$ with the properties we postulated in H 6 such that the value of $f(\cdot)$ at any $(p, A) \in R^n_{++} \times R_+$ is the vector in $\Gamma(p, A)$ at which $V(\cdot)$ takes its maximum value. Finally show that S 1–S N can be derived as theorems from H 1–H 6. If we choose S 1–S N appropriately, and manage to complete the three steps successfully, we will have a definite "yes" answer to Q 1.

Many theorists have sought to answer Q 1. Together they have found ways to carry out the first two steps of the three-step procedure described above. However, they have not discovered a way to complete the procedure. The main reason for this failure seems to be that H 6 is too weak. Therefore, in this chapter we shall attempt to answer Q 1 when H 6 is reformulated as the following postulate:

$\tilde{\text{H}}$ 6 $V(\cdot)$ is continuous, strictly increasing, and strictly quasi-concave and has differentiable level sets in R^n_+.

The level sets of $V(\cdot)$ are differentiable in R^n_+ only if they are differentiable in both $(R^n_+ - R^n_{++}) - \{0\}$ and R^n_{++}. A level set of $V(\cdot)$, A, is *differentiable* at $y \in R^n_{++}$ if and only if $A = \{z \in R^n_+ : V(z) \geqslant V(y)\}$ and if the conditions $A \subset \{z \in R^n : qz \geqslant qy\}$, $A \subset \{z \in R^n : pz \geqslant py\}$, and $p, q \in R^n_{++}$ imply that $p = \lambda q$ for some $\lambda \in R_{++}$.

In our attempt to answer Q 1 we follow in the footsteps of P. Samuelson (1947, pp. 107–116) and H. Houthakker (1950, pp. 159–174). The basic ideas of our argumentation are taken from Samuelson's and Houthakker's theories of revealed preference.

13.1 An Alternative Set of Axioms, S 1, . . . , S 11

A function $f(\cdot)$: $R^n_{++} \times R_+ \to R^n_+$ is a demand function only if it satisfies the conditions of T 10.3–T 10.9. I have shown elsewhere (Stigum 1973, pp. 411–423) that, if $f(\cdot)$ satisfies T 10.3, T 10.5, T 10.7–T 10.9, a strong version of T 10.1, and a certain Lipschitz condition, then $f(\cdot)$ is a demand function. These two results and the preceding comments suggest that we start our quest for an answer to Q 1 by postulating the following system of axioms as an alternative to H 1–H 5 and $\tilde{\text{H}}$ 6.

S 1 A commodity bundle is a vector $x \in R^n_+$.

S 2 A price is a vector $p \in R^n_{++}$.

S 3 A consumer is a triple $(f(\cdot), X, \hat{A})$, where $X \subset R^n_+$, $f(\cdot)$: $R^n_{++} \times R_+ \to X$, and $\hat{A} \in R_+$.

S 4 A consumption bundle is a vector $c \in R^n_+$ that, for some pair $(p, A) \in R^n_{++} \times R_+$, satisfies $c = f(p, A)$.

S 5 $X = R^n_+$,

S 6 $f(\cdot)$ is continuous, homogeneous of degree 0, and satisfies $pf(p, A) = A$ for all $(p, A) \in R^n_{++} \times R_+$.

S 7 Every commodity bundle x is a consumption bundle in some (p, A) situation. If $x > 0$, the pair (p, A) is uniquely determined up to a multiplicative constant.

S 8 If $p^0 \in R^n_+$, $p^m \in R^n_{++}$, $m = 1, 2, \ldots$, $p^0 \not> 0$, and

$\lim_{m\to\infty} \|p^m - p^0\| = 0$, then $\lim_{m\to\infty} \|f(p^m, A)\| = \infty$ for all $A \in R_{++}$.

S 9 If $c^k = f(p^k, A^k)$, $k = 0, \ldots, m$, $A^k \geqslant p^k c^{k+1}$, $k = 0, \ldots, m-1$, and the c^k are not all equal, then $A^m < p^m c^0$.

S 10 If $x, z \in R^n_+$, $x \not> 0$, $x = f(p, A)$, and $px > pz$, then there exist $u \in R^n_+$ and $(p^u, A^u) \in R^n_{++} \times R_+$ such that $u \leqslant x$, $u \neq x$, $u = f(p^u, A^u)$, and $p^u u > p^u z$.

S 11 Let $p^0, p^1 \in R^n_{++}$ and let $p(t) = p^0 + t(p^1 - p^0)$. There exists a positive constant K such that, for all $t \in [0, 1]$ and all $A, A^0 \in R_+$,

$\|f(p(t), A) - f(p(t), A^0)\| \leqslant K|A - A^0|$.

K may depend on p^0 and p^1 but not on t.

In this axiom system we have renamed H 1, H 2, and H 5 as S 1, S 2, and S 5, and replaced H 3 and $\tilde{\text{H}}$ 6 with two postulates, S 3 and S 6, that characterize a consumer in terms of potentially observable elements. Also we have used T 10.2 as an axiom, S 4, instead of H 4, and we have postulated the validity of a strong version of T 10.1 and T 10.3, S 7, and the validity of T 10.5 and T 10.7–T 10.9, respectively, in S 6, S 8, S 10, and S 9. Finally we have imposed a strong Lipschitz condition on $f(\cdot)$ in S 11. The consistency of the axioms is certain since the demand function in E 10.2 satisfies S 3, S 4, and S 6–S 11.

Axiom S 9, and hence T 10.9 as an axiom, is called Houthakker's *Strong Axiom of Revealed Preference*. When $m = 1$, it is called Samuelson's *Weak Axiom of Revealed Preference*. I gave the reason for the term "revealed preference" at the end of section 10.2. Here it remains to add that Samuelson, who originated this line of inquiry, proposed to build the theory of consumer choice on S 1–S 6 and the Weak Axiom (Samuelson 1947, p. 116). Houthakker observed that the Weak Axiom was not strong enough and suggested that it be replaced with the Strong Axiom (Houthakker 1950, pp. 159–274). He also contended that a Lipschitz condition on $f(\cdot)$ was a necessary ingredient of an axiom system from which H 1–H 5 and $\tilde{\text{H}}$ 6 could be derived as theorems. I have added S 8 and S 10 and formulated my version of the Lipschitz condition in S 11.

It is clear that Houthakker's axiom implies Samuelson's axiom. When $n = 2$, the converse is also true; i.e., in two-dimensional commodity spaces Houthakker's axiom can be derived from S 1–S 11 with the indefinite m in S 9 replaced by 1. A proof of this is given in Afriat 1965 (pp. 24–28). When $n \geqslant 3$, the converse is known to be false. To show that it is false when $n = 3$, we paraphrase in E 13.1 a counterexample by D. Gale (1960, pp. 348–354).

There is an essential difference between the Strong and the Weak Axiom of revealed preference that we can explicate if we adopt the following definition:

D 1 For $x, y \in R_+^n$, xQy if and only if there exists a sequence of consumption bundles $x^i = f(p^i, A^i)$, $i = 1, \ldots, k$, not all equal, such that $x^0 = x$, $x^k = y$, and $p^0x^0 \geqslant p^0x^1, \ldots, p^{k-1}x^{k-1} \geqslant p^{k-1}x^k$.

The relation Q need not be total. However, if S 1–S 11 are valid, then Q satisfies the conditions of T 13.1 below; and xQy can be read as "x is indirectly revealed preferred to y."

T 13.1 If S 1–S 11 hold and Q is as defined in D 1, then for all $x, y, z \in R_+^n$,

(i) $\sim xQx$;

(ii) xQy implies $\sim yQx$; and

(iii) xQy and yQz imply xQz.

Hence Q is irreflexive, antisymmetric, and transitive. If the indefinite m in S 9 is replaced by 1, Q will satisfy T 13.1 (iii), but, as evidenced in E 13.1, it need not satisfy T 13.1 (i) and (ii). The proof of T 13.1 is easy, so I leave it to the reader.

E 13.1 Suppose first that $n = 3$, and that the $f(\cdot)$ and $\hat{A}$ of S 3 satisfy $\hat{A} = 1$ and $f(p, 1) = Bp/pBp$, where B is a 3×3 nonsingular matrix. A necessary condition that $f(\cdot, 1)$ be the demand function of a consumer is that B be symmetric (see Gale 1960, p. 350). An example is $\tilde{f}(p, 1) = \tilde{B}p/p\tilde{B}p$, where

$$\tilde{B} = \begin{pmatrix} -3 & 2 & 2 \\ 2 & -3 & 2 \\ 2 & 2 & -3 \end{pmatrix}.$$

$\tilde{f}(\cdot, 1)$ is the demand function of a consumer with

$$V(x) = 4(x_1x_2 + x_2x_3 + x_3x_1) + x_1^2 + x_2^2 + x_3^2, \qquad x \in R_+^3.$$

Next let $\hat{f}(p, 1) = \hat{B}p/p\hat{B}p$, $p \in \{p \in R_{++}^3 : \hat{B}p \geqslant 0\}$, where

$$\hat{B} = \begin{pmatrix} -3 & 4 & 0 \\ 0 & -3 & 4 \\ 4 & 0 & -3 \end{pmatrix}.$$

Since $\hat{B}$ is not symmetric, $\hat{f}(\cdot)$ is not part of some consumer's demand function. However, $\hat{f}(\cdot, 1)$ satisfies the Weak Axiom of revealed preference; i.e., if $p, q \in \{p \in R_{++}^3 : \hat{B}p \geqslant 0\}$, then $p\hat{f}(q, 1) \leqslant 1$ and $q\hat{f}(p, 1) \leqslant 1$ imply that $\hat{f}(p, 1) = \hat{f}(q, 1)$. Also $\hat{f}(\cdot, 1)$ can be extended to a function $\bar{f}(\cdot, 1) : R_{++}^3 \to R_+^3$ that is continuous and satisfies the Weak Axiom in all of R_{++}^3 (see Gale 1960, pp. 351–353). The example below shows that $\hat{f}(\cdot, 1)$ does not satisfy the Strong Axiom of revealed preference.

Consider the pairs (p^i, x^i), $i = 1, \ldots, 4$:

$((1, 16/9, 12/9), (1, 0, 0))$, $((340/303, 440/303, 330/303), (0.6, 0, 0.3))$

$((1230/909, 1200/909, 900/909), (0.3, 0, 0.6))$

$((16/9, 12/9, 1), (0, 0, 1))$

For all $i = 1, \ldots, 4$, $x^i = \hat{f}(p^i, 1)$; for $i = 1, \ldots, 3$, $p^i\hat{f}(p^{i+1}, 1) \leqslant 1$; and $p^4\hat{f}(p^1, 1) > 1$. Hence x^1Qx^4 and x^1 is indirectly revealed preferred to x^4. By exploiting the structure of $\hat{B}$, we can extend the sequence of pairs and show first that $x^4Q(0, 1, 0)$ and then that $(0, 1, 0)Qx^1$. Hence x^4Qx^1, which contradicts T 13.1 (ii), and x^1Qx^1, which contradicts T 13.1 (i).

13.2 The Fundamental Theorem of Revealed Preference

Axioms S 1–S 11 constitute the first step in our search for an answer to Q 1. In this section we shall carry out the second step; i.e., we shall show that if S 1–S 11 hold, then there is a function $V(\cdot)$ with the properties postulated in $\tilde{\text{H}}$ 6 such that the value of $f(\cdot)$ at any $(p, A) \in R^n_{++} \times R_+$ is the vector in $\Gamma(p, A)$ at which $V(\cdot)$ takes its maximum value. To obtain this result we must first establish seven auxiliary theorems concerning properties of two families of sets that we define as follows:

D 2 Suppose $x^0 \in R^n_+$. Then $S^+(x^0) = \{y \in R^n_+ : yQx^0\}$ and $S^-(x^0) = \{y \in R^n_+ : x^0Qy\}$.

The basic idea of our argumentation in step 2 is to find a function $V(\cdot)$ whose family of level sets coincides with the family of closures of $S^+(\cdot)$. Our seven auxiliary theorems show that if S 1–S 11 hold, then, for any $x^0 \in R^n_+ - \{0\}$, the closure of $S^+(x^0)$, denoted $\overline{S^+(x^0)}$, has the necessary characteristics of the level sets of a utility function that satisfies $\tilde{\text{H}}$ 6.

13.2.1 A Rough Contour of $S^+(x^0)$

We begin by sketching the outline of $S^+(x^0)$ for some given but otherwise arbitrary vector $x^0 \in R^n_+$.

T 13.2 Suppose that $x^0 = f(p^0, A^0)$ for some $(p^0, A^0) \in R^n_{++} \times R_+$. Then the following assertions are valid:

(i) $\{x \in R^n_+ : x^0 \leqslant x, x \neq x^0\} \subset S^+(x^0)$;

(ii) $S^+(x^0)$ is convex;

(iii) $S^+(x^0) \subset \{x \in R^n_+ : A^0 \leqslant p^0x\}$; and

(iv) if $x^0 \in R^3_{++}$, if $a \in R^n_{++}$ and $S^+(x^0) \subset \{x \in R^n_+ : ax^0 \leqslant ax\}$, then $a = \lambda p^0$ for some $\lambda \in R_{++}$.

Here assertion (i) is an immediate consequence of S 4, S 6, and S 7, and assertion (iii) follows from D 1 and S 9. Also, assertion (ii) can be established by referring to D 1, S 7, and the fact that, if $x, y, z \in R^n_+$, if $z = \lambda x + (1 - \lambda)y$ for some $\lambda \in (0, 1)$, and if $z = f(p^z, A^z)$, then either $p^z x \leqslant A^z$ or $p^z y \leqslant A^z$ or both. If $x \in S^+(x^0)$ and $y \in S^+(x^0)$, either one of these inequalities yields zQx^0. Finally, assertion (iv) follows from the following arguments: Suppose that $a \neq \lambda p^0$ for all $\lambda \in R_{++}$ and let $z = f(a, ax^0)$. Then S 7 implies that $z \neq x^0$ and D 1 shows that $z \in S^+(x^0)$. Next let $p(t) = p^0 + t(a - p^0)$ and observe that the continuity of $f(\cdot)$ implies that there is a $t^0 \in (0, 1)$ such that $x(p(t^0), p(t^0)x^0) \neq x^0$. Finally, let $w = x(p(t^0), p(t^0)x^0)$ and observe that S 9 and the equality

$$(1 - t^0)p^0w + t^0aw = (1 - t^0)p^0x^0 + t^0ax^0$$

implies that $aw < ax^0 = az$. Since by construction $w \in S^+(x^0)$, the last inequality contradicts the relation $S^+(x^0) \subset \{x \in R^n_+ : ax^0 \leqslant ax\}$. We conclude that the assumption $a \neq \lambda p^0$ for all $\lambda \in R_{++}$ is untenable.

In reading T 13.2, note that T 13.1 (i) implies that $x^0 \notin S^+(x^0)$. Also, assertions T 13.2 (i) and (ii) imply that $x^0 \in \overline{S^+(x^0)}$ and that $\overline{S^+(x^0)}$ is convex. Other properties of $S^+(\cdot)$ are described in the next theorem. In the statement of T 13.3 below a lower boundary point of $S^+(x^0)$ is defined as follows:

D 3 If $x^1 \in \overline{S^+(x^0)}$, then x^1 is a lower boundary point of $S^+(x^0)$ if and only if $x \in \overline{S^+(x^0)}$ and $x \leqslant x^1$ imply that $x = x^1$.

We shall see in T 13.3 that, if $x^0 \neq 0$, then $S^+(x^0)$ possesses numerous lower boundary points. Specifically, for all $x \in R^n_{++}$, there is a unique positive constant λ—depending on x—such that λx is a lower boundary point of $S^+(x^0)$.

T 13.3 If $x^0 \neq 0$, and if $0 < x$, then there exists a finite positive number $\lambda(x)$ such that $\lambda(x)x \in \overline{S^+(x^0)}$ and such that

(i) $\lambda x \in S^+(x^0)$ if $\lambda > \lambda(x)$; and

(ii) $\lambda x \notin \overline{S^+(x^0)}$ if $\lambda < \lambda(x)$.

Also, either $\lambda(x)x = x^0$ or $\lambda(x)x_i < x_i^0$ for some i.

To see why T 13.3 must be true, we pick $x \in R^n_{++}$ and let $Z = \{z \in R^n_+ : z = \lambda x \text{ for some } \lambda \in R_+\}$. Then Z is closed and, by T 13.2 (i), $Z \cap \overline{S^+(x^0)}$ is not empty. Next we let $\lambda(x) = \min\{\lambda \in R_+ : \lambda x \in \overline{S^+(x^0)}\}$ and observe that $\lambda(x)$ is well defined and that T 13.2 (iii) implies that $\lambda(x) > 0$. Finally we let $z^0 = \lambda(x)x$ and claim that either $z^0 = x^0$ or $z^0 \notin \{y \in R_+^n : y \geqslant x^0\}$. A proof of this assertion is given below.

Suppose first that $x^0 = \lambda x$ for some $\lambda > 0$. Then T 13.2 (i) and (iii) imply that $z^0 = x^0$.

Suppose next that $z^0 \neq x^0$. Suppose that $z^0 \geqslant x^0$. We shall obtain a contradiction which shows that the last hypothesis is false. Let λ^n, $n = 1, 2, \ldots$ be a sequence of numbers such that $\lambda^n < \lambda(x)$ and $\lim_{n\to\infty} \lambda^n = \lambda(x)$. Moreover, for each $n = 1, 2, \ldots$, let $y^n \in R_+^n$ and $p^n \in R_{++}^n$ be such that $\lambda^n x = y^n$ and $y^n = f(p^n, p^n y^n)$. Finally, let $p^z \in R_{++}^n$ be such that $z^0 = f(p^z, p^z z^0)$. We can, without loss in generality, assume that the p^n's are chosen such that, for all n, $\|p^n\| = \|p^z\|$. Then the p^n contain a convergent subsequence, p^{n_k}, which, by S 8, S 7, and the fact that $z^0 \in R_{++}^n$, must converge to p^z. But if that is true, then $z^0 \geqslant x^0$ and $z^0 \neq x^0$ imply that $p^z z^0 > p^z x^0$, and hence that there exists an m so large that, for all $n_k \geqslant m$, $p^{n_k} y^{n_k} > p^{n_k} x^0$. Thus, for all $n_k \geqslant m$, $y^{n_k} \in S^+(x^0)$, which is impossible since $\lambda^{n_k} < \lambda(x)$.

To complete the proof of T 13.3 we must demonstrate that $\lambda x \in S^+(x^0)$ if $\lambda > \lambda(x)$. This fact, however, is an immediate consequence of T 13.2 (i) and T 13.5 (i) below and needs no additional proof here.

The set of lower boundary points of $S^+(x^0)$ contains x^0 and the set

$$\{z \in R_{++}^n : z = \lambda(x)x \text{ for some } x \in R_{++}^n\},$$

where $\lambda(\cdot)\colon R_{++}^n \to R_{++}$ is as described in T 13.3. The latter set together with x^0 and the boundary of R_+^n provide us with the rough contour of $S^+(x^0)$ for which we searched. To get a better idea of the contour of $S^+(x^0)$ we shall next establish several salient characteristics of the lower boundary points of $S^+(x^0)$.

13.2.2 Salient Characteristics of the Lower Boundary Points of $S^+(x^0)$

Lower boundary points of $S^+(x^0)$ have interesting characteristics. Theorems T 13.5 and T 13.6 will attest to that. But first a definition and a useful auxiliary theorem:

D 4 If $y^1 = f(p, A^1)$ and $y^2 = f(p, A^2)$, then $y^2 H y^1$ if and only if $A^1 < A^2$.

The relations Q and H are related in interesting ways—to wit T 13.4.

T 13.4 If $y, z \in R_+^n$ and yQz, there exist $u, v \in R_+^n$ such that yHu and uQz, and yQv and vHz.

To prove this theorem suppose that $y = f(p^y, A^y)$, $z = f(p^z, A^z)$ and $p^y y \geqslant p^y z$. Then the existence of u is obtained by the following argument: Let $p(t) = p^z + t(p^y - p^z)$ and observe that, for some $t_0 \in (0, 1)$ and $w = f(p(t_0), p(t_0)z)$, $w \neq z$. For this w, $p(t_0)w = p(t_0)z$ and S 9 imply that

$$p^y w = p(t_0)w + (1 - t_0)(p^y - p^z)w < p(t_0)z + (1 - t_0)(p^y - p^z)z$$
$$= p^y z.$$

Hence, if we let $u = f(p^y, p^y w)$, then yHu and uQz.

To show that v exists when $p^y y \geqslant p^y z$, proceed as follows: Let $x = \alpha y + (1 - \alpha)z$ for some $\alpha \in (0, 1)$ and let $p^x \in R^n_{++}$ and $A^x \in R_+$ be such that $x = f(p^x, A^x)$. Then $p^y y \geqslant p^y x$ and, by S 9 and the equality $p^x x = \alpha p^x y + (1 - \alpha)p^x z$, $p^x x > p^x z$. Consequently, there is an $A^v > A^z$ such that if $v = f(p^z, A^v)$, then $p^x x > p^x v$. For this v we find that yQx, xQv, and vHz, and hence that yQv and vHz.

The arguments used above can be generalized to establish the existence of u and v when y is only indirectly revealed preferred to z. Those details I leave to the reader.

T 13.5 Suppose that $x^0, x^1 \in R^n_+$ and that $x^0 \neq x^1$. Suppose also that x^1 is a lower boundary point of $S^+(x^0)$. Then

(i) $S^+(x^1) \subset S^+(x^0)$; and

(ii) $x^0 \notin (S^-(x^1) \cup S^+(x^1))$.

To prove T 13.5 (i) we pick an $x^2 \in S^+(x^1)$ and find an x^3 such that $x^2 Q x^3$ and $x^3 H x^1$. Since $x^1 \in \overline{S^+(x^0)}$, every neighborhood of x^1 contains a vector $u \in S^+(x^0)$. The relation $x^3 H x^1$ implies that there is a $u \in S^+(x^0)$ such that $x^3 Q u$. Hence $x^2 Q x^3$, $x^3 Q u$, $u Q x^0$, and $x^2 Q x^0$, as was to be shown.

To establish T 13.5 (ii) we must show that neither $x^1 Q x^0$ nor $x^0 Q x^1$ obtains. To do that, we first observe that if $z \in R^n_+$, D 3, S 4–S 7 and S 10 imply that zQx^0 and $x^1 H z$ cannot both be true. Hence $S^+(x^0) \subset \{x \in R^n_+ : p^1 x \geqslant A^1\}$. From this and T 13.4 it follows that it is not the case that $x^1 Q x^0$. Suppose next that $x^0 Q x^1$. Then by T 13.4 there exists $x^2 \in R^n_+$ such that $x^0 Q x^2$ and $x^2 H x^1$. This implies that there is a $u \in S^+(x^0)$ such that $x^2 Q u$. But then $x^0 Q x^2$, $x^2 Q u$, and $u Q x^0$, which contradicts T 13.1 (i); i.e., $x^0 Q x^1$ cannot obtain.

T 13.6 Suppose that $x^0, x^1 \in R^n_+$ and that $x^0 \neq x^1$. Suppose also that $x^1 \neq 0$ and x^1 is a lower boundary point of $S^+(x^0)$.

Then

$S^+(x^1) = S^+(x^0)$ and $\overline{S^+(x^1)} = \overline{S^+(x^0)}$.

A proof of this theorem is given in Stigum (1973, pp. 417–422). Since the proof is both lengthy and involved, I shall only mention here the main ideas of the proof when $x^0, x^1 \in R^n_{++}$.

Suppose that $x^0 = f(p^0, A^0)$, $x^1 = f(p^1, A^1)$, and x^0, $x^1 \in R^n_{++}$. Then $S^+(x^1) \subset S^+(x^0)$ by T 13.5 (i). Hence to establish T 13.6 we need only demonstrate that $S^+(x^0) \subset S^+(x^1)$.

The difficult part of the proof that $S^+(x^0) \subset S^+(x^1)$ consists in showing that $x^0 \in \overline{S^+(x^1)}$. To do that we begin by constructing several sequences of functions on [0, 1] to R^n_+ and R_+ with interesting properties. Let $p(t) = p^1 + t(p^0 - p^1)$, $t \in [0, 1]$, and $t^m_k = (k/2^m)$, $k = 0, 1, \ldots, 2^m$, $m = 0, 1, \ldots$. Also let

$$A^m(t^m_0) = p(t^m_0)x^1 = p^1 x^1$$

and

$$A^m(t^m_k) = p(t^m_k) f(p(t^m_{k-1}), A^m(t^m_{k-1})), \qquad k = 1, \ldots, 2^m.$$

Finally, let

$$A^m(t) = p(t) f(p(t^m_k), A^m(t^m_k)), \quad t^m_k \leqslant t \leqslant t^m_{k+1}, \qquad k = 0, 1, \ldots, 2^m - 1$$

and

$$x^m(t) = f(p(t), A^m(t)), \qquad t \in [0, 1]$$

For all m and t, $x^m(t)Qx^1$. Also, the $A^m(\cdot)$ are equicontinuous and contain a subsequence, $A^{m_j}(\cdot)$, that converge uniformly on [0, 1] to a continuous function $A(\cdot)$: $[0, 1] \to R_+$. Hence, if we let

$$x(t) = f(p(t), A(t)), \qquad t \in [0, 1]$$

then $x(t)$ is well defined and continuous on [0, 1] and satisfies

$$x(t) = \lim_{m_j \to \infty} f(p(t), A^{m_j}(t)) = \lim_{m_j \to \infty} x^{m_j}(t), \qquad t \in [0, 1].$$

To show that $x^0 \in \overline{S^+(x^1)}$, it suffices to show that $x(1) = x^0$. Evidently $x^0 H x(1)$ cannot obtain, since then $x^0 Q x^1$. So to ascertain that $x(1) = x^0$, we must show that $x(1) H x^0$ cannot happen either. For that purpose we first define a second pair of sequences of functions on [0, 1]: Let $t^m_k = k/2^m$ be as above. Also let $z^m(t^m_k)$, $k = 0, \ldots, 2^m$, be a sequence of vectors in R^n_+ such that $p^1 x^1 = p^1 z^m(t^m_1)$, $p(t^m_1) z^m(t^m_1) = p(t^m_1) z^m(t^m_2)$, $\ldots$, $p(t^m_{2^m-1}) z^m(t^m_{2^m-1}) = p(t^m_{2^m-1}) z^m(1)$, and such that $z^m(t^m_k) = f(p(t^m_k), A^{-m}(t^m_k))$, where

$$A^{-m}(t) = p(t)z^m(t_k^m), \quad t_{k-1}^m \leqslant t \leqslant t_k^m, \qquad k = 1, \ldots, 2^m.$$

Finally let

$$z^m(t) = f(p(t), A^{-m}(t)), \qquad t \in [0, 1].$$

For all m and t, $x^1 Q z^m(t)$. Also, the $A^{-m}(t)$ are equicontinuous and contain a subsequence, $A^{-m_j}(t)$, that converge uniformly on [0, 1] to a continuous function $A^-(\cdot)$: $[0, 1] \to R_+$. Hence the function,

$$z(t) = f(p(t), A^-(t)), \qquad t \in [0, 1]$$

is well defined and continuous on [0, 1] and satisfies

$$z(t) = \lim_{m_j \to \infty} f(p(t), A^{-m_j}(t)) = \lim_{m_j \to \infty} z^{m_j}(t), \qquad t \in [0, 1].$$

To show that $x(1)Hx^0$ cannot happen, it suffices to show that $x(t) = z(t)$, $t \in [0, 1]$. This we do by showing that $A(\cdot)$ and $A^-(\cdot)$ are solutions to the same differential equation,

$$\frac{dA(t)}{dt} = (p^0 - p^1)x(t), \qquad t \in [0, 1] \tag{13.1}$$

and by observing that, because of the Lipschitz condition we impose on $f(\cdot)$ in S 11, there can be only one solution to equation 13.1.

I shall demonstrate that $A(\cdot)$ satisfies equation 13.1 and leave it to the reader to prove that $A^-(\cdot)$ satisfies the same equation. Now it is a fact and easy to verify that

$$p(t)x(t) \leqslant p(t)x(s), \qquad t, s \in [0, 1] \tag{13.2}$$

and that $A(\cdot)$ is a concave function. From this and the continuity of $A(\cdot)$, it follows that the right-hand and left-hand derivatives of $A(\cdot)$ are continuous from the right and from the left, respectively, on [0, 1]. Consequently, it suffices to establish equation 13.1 for $t \in (0, 1)$. To that end, fix $t_0 \in (0, 1)$, let

$$F(t) = p(t_0)\frac{x(t) - x(t_0)}{t - t_0}$$

$$= \frac{A(t) - A(t_0)}{t - t_0} - (p^0 - p^1)x(t), \tag{13.3}$$

and let $A_+(t_0)$ and $A_-(t_0)$ denote the right-hand and left-hand derivatives of $A(\cdot)$ at t_0. Then equations 13.2 and 13.3 and the continuity of $x(t)$ imply that

$$F(t_0+) = \lim_{t>t_0,\, t\to t_0} F(t) \geqslant 0, \tag{13.4}$$

$$F(t_0-) = \lim_{t<t_0,\, t\to t_0} F(t) \leqslant 0, \tag{13.5}$$

and, for all $h > 0$,

$$F(t_0 - h) - F(t_0 + h) = \frac{p(t_0)}{h}\{(x(t_0) - x(t_0 - h)) - (x(t_0 + h) - x(t_0))\} \leqslant 0. \tag{13.6}$$

Similarly, from equation 13.3 and well-known properties of concave functions, it follows that

$$F(t_0-) - F(t_0+) = A_-(t_0) - A_+(t_0) \geqslant 0. \tag{13.7}$$

But if equations 13.3–13.7 are valid, then equation 13.1 must be valid as well.

To conclude the proof of T 13.6 for the case $x^0 > 0$ and $x^1 > 0$, we now pick an $x^2 \in S^+(x^0)$ and find an $x^3 \in R^n_+$ such that x^2Qx^3 and x^3Hx^0. There is an m_j so large that $x^3Hx^{m_j}(1)$ and $x^{m_j}(1)Hx^0$. Hence $x^2Qx^{m_j}(1)$ and $x^{m_j}(1)Qx^1$, which proves that $S^+(x^0) \subset S^+(x^1)$.

13.2.3 Characteristics of Vectors in $S^+(x^0) \cup (R^n_+ - \overline{S^+(x^0)})$

So much for lower boundary points of $S^+(x^0)$. Characteristics of the other points in $\overline{S^+(x^0)}$ are described in T 13.7.

T 13.7 Suppose that $x^0, x^1 \in R^n_+$ and that $x^0 \neq x^1$. Suppose also that $x^1 \in \overline{S^+(x^0)}$. Then

(i) $x^1 \in S^+(x^0)$ or x^1 is a lower boundary point of $S^+(x^0)$; and

(ii) $x^1 \in S^+(x^0)$ only if $\overline{S^+(x^1)} \subset S^+(x^0)$.

The validity of T 13.7 (i) is an immediate consequence of D 3, T 13.2 (i), and T 13.5 (i). The validity of T 13.7 (ii) results from the following arguments: Suppose that x^1Qx^0 and that $x^2 \in \overline{S^+(x^1)}$. If x^2Qx^1, then x^2Qx^0 as well. So suppose that x^2Qx^1 does not hold. Then, by the first half of T 13.4, there exists an $x^3 \in R^n_+$ such that x^1Hx^3 and x^3Qx^0. By arguments analogous to the arguments we used to show that $x(1) = x^0$ in the proof of T 13.6, this x^3 must satisfy both x^2Qx^3 and x^3Qx^0. Hence $x^2 \in S^+(x^0)$, as was to be shown.

We have shown that, if $x^1 \in \overline{S^+(x^0)}$ and if x^1 is not a lower boundary point of $S^+(x^0)$, then $x^1 \notin S^-(x^0)$. Also, if x^1 is a lower boundary point of

$S^+(x^0)$, then neither $x^1 Q x^0$ nor $x^0 Q x^1$ obtains. In T 13.8 we show that, if $x^1 \notin \overline{S^+(x^0)}$, then $x^0 Q x^1$.

T 13.8 Suppose that $x^0 \in R^n_+ - \{0\}$. Then the following assertions are valid:

(i) $S^-(x^0) \cap \overline{S^+(x^0)} = \varnothing$; and

(ii) $\overline{S^-(x^0)} \cup S^+(x^0) = S^-(x^0) \cup \overline{S^+(x^0)} = R^n_+$,

where $\overline{S^-(x^0)}$ denotes the closure of $S^-(x^0)$.

We begin by proving T 13.8 (i). Suppose that $x^2 \in S^-(x^0)$. Then S 9 implies that $x^2 \notin S^+(x^0)$, and T 13.5 (ii) implies that x^2 is not a lower boundary point of $S^+(x^0)$. Hence $x^2 \notin \overline{S^+(x^0)}$.

To establish T 13.8 (ii) we let $z = f(p, A^z)$ and consider the function $f(p, \cdot): R_+ \to R^n_+$. For A large enough, $pf(p, A) \gg px^0$. Therefore for A large enough, $f(p, A) \in S^+(x^0)$. Since $f(p, \cdot)$ is continuous, there is a smallest A, say A^y, such that $f(p, A^y) \in \overline{S^+(x^0)}$. Let $y = f(p, A^y)$. Then the arguments used to show that $x(1) = x^0$ in the proof of T 13.6 can be used to prove the following assertions:

(i) if $z = y$, $z \in \overline{S^-(x^0)} \cap \overline{S^+(x^0)}$;

(ii) if zHy, then $z \in S^+(x^0)$; and

(iii) if yHz, then $z \in S^-(x^0)$.

Since there is no need to elaborate, this establishes T 13.8 (ii).

13.2.4 The Fundamental Theorem

So much for auxiliary theorems. Next we define an ordering of commodity bundles and show that it is induced by a utility function.

D 5 For $x, y \in R^n_+$, $x \preceq y$ if and only if $\overline{S^+(y)} \subset \overline{S^+(x)}$.

It follows from T 13.2 (i) and from T 13.5–T 13.8 that $\preceq$ is a complete, reflexive, and transitive ordering of R^n_+. Also T 13.2 (i), T 13.6, and T 13.7 imply that

$$\{y \in R^n_+ : x \preceq y\} = \overline{S^+(x)};$$

and T 13.2 (i) and T 13.6–T 13.8 imply that

$$\{y \in R^n_+ : y \preceq x\} = \overline{S^-(x)}.$$

Since $\overline{S^-(x)}$ and $\overline{S^+(x)}$ are closed, we can apply UT 10 (section 11.2) and deduce that there exists a continuous function $V(\cdot): R^n_+ \to R$ such that, for all $x, y \in R_{+}^{n}$, $x \precsim y$ if and only if $V(x) \leqslant V(y)$. But if that is so, then T 13.2 (i), T 13.6, and T 13.7 imply that $V(\cdot)$ is strictly increasing, and T 13.2 (ii), T 13.6, T 13.7, and S 9 can easily be seen to imply that $V(\cdot)$ is strictly quasi-concave. Finally, T 13.2 (iv) and S 7 show that $V(\cdot)$ must have differentiable levels sets in R_{+}^{n}. The properties of $V(\cdot)$ and T 13.2 (i) and (iii) imply that $f(\cdot)$ is a demand function relative to $V(\cdot)$. These results we record in the *Fundamental Theorem of Revealed Preference*, T 13.9.

T 13.9 Suppose that S 1–S 11 hold, and let $\precsim$ be as defined in D 5. Then there exists a strictly increasing, continuous, strictly quasi-concave function $V(\cdot)\colon R_{+}^{n} \to R$ with differentiable level sets in R_{+}^{n} such that

$$x \precsim y \text{ iff } V(x) \leqslant V(y), \qquad x, y \in R_{+}^{n} \tag{13.8}$$

and

$$V(f(p, A)) = \max_{x \in \Gamma(p, A)} V(x), \qquad (p, A) \in R_{++}^{n} \times R_{+}. \tag{13.9}$$

$V(\cdot)$ is uniquely determinded up to a monotone, strictly increasing transformation.

Here several mental notes are called for. The $V(\cdot)$ of T 13.9 is uniquely determined up to a monotone, strictly increasing transformation *relative* to $\precsim$; i.e., if there is a continuous function $W(\cdot)\colon R_{+}^{n} \to R_{+}$ that satisfies

$$W(x) \leqslant W(y) \text{ iff } x \precsim y, \qquad x, y \in R_{+}^{n}$$

then there is a strictly increasing and continuous function $G(\cdot)$: {range of $W(\cdot)$} $\to R_{+}$ such that

$$V(x) = G(W(x)), \qquad x \in R_{+}^{n}.$$

The ordering of commodity bundles $\precsim$, which we defined in D 5, is well defined and uniquely determined by S 1–S 11 in the following sense: There exists no continuous function $H(\cdot)\colon R_{+}^{n} \to R_{+}$ that is not a monotone, strictly increasing transformation of $V(\cdot)$ and yet satisfies the relation

$$H(f(p, A)) = \max_{x \in \Gamma(p, A)} H(x), \qquad (p, A) \in R_{++}^{n} \times R_{+}.$$

Theorems 2 and 3 in Mas-Colell 1977 (pp. 1409–1429) attest to that. Consequently, the utility function of the S 1–S 11 consumer is unique up to a monotone, strictly increasing transformation.

13.3 The Equivalence of T(S 1, ..., S 11) and T(H 1, ..., H 5, $\tilde{\text{H}}$ 6)

With the establishment of T 13.9, we have completed two of the three steps required to answer "yes" to Q 1; i.e., we have formulated and alternative axiom system whose elements are potentially observable, and we have shown that H 1–H 5, $\tilde{H}$ 6 can be derived as theorems from these new axioms. Next we must show that S 1–S 11 are consequences of H 1–H 5 and $\tilde{H}$ 6.

It is clear from T 10.1 and the differentiability of the level sets of $V(\cdot)$, which we postulate in $\tilde{H}$ 6, from T 10.3 and T 10.5, and from T 10.7–T 10.9 that S 1–S 10 are logical consequences of H 1–H 5 and $\tilde{H}$ 6. However, S 11 is not; i.e., S 11 cannot be derived as a theorem from H 1–H 5 and $\tilde{H}$ 6. Consequently, H 1–H 5, $\tilde{H}$ 6, and S 1–S 11 are not equivalent. The latter set of axioms is stronger than the former.

The nonequivalence of the two axiom systems is disappointing. In this section we shall see what we can do about it. We shall check whether we can do without S 11 and—if not—whether we can find a reasonable substitute for the pair $\tilde{H}$ 6, S 11 that will enable us to establish the required equivalence.

13.3.1 A Counterexample

We begin by paraphrasing a theorem of Leonid Hurwicz and Marcel K. Richter's (theorem 1, 1971, p. 61) that describes some of the consequences of dropping S 11. Since the theorem is easy to understand and the proof is a bit involved, I state the theorem without proof. With some obvious modifications, Hurwicz and Richter's arguments can be used to prove my version of their theorem (see Richter 1966, p. 641, and Hurwicz and Richter 1971, pp. 61–63).

T 13.10 Suppose that S 1–S 10 are valid. Then there exists an increasing, upper semicontinuous, and strictly quasi-concave function $U(\cdot)\colon R_+^n \to R$ that has differentiable level sets in R_+^n and is such that, for each $(p, A) \in R_{++}^n \times R_+$,

$$U(f(p, A)) = \max_{x \in \Gamma(p, A)} U(x). \tag{13.10}$$

Actually there exist many increasing, upper semicontinuous, and strictly quasi-concave functions on R_+^n to R that satisfy equation (13.10), and these functions need not all be increasing transformations of each other!

It is not possible to change "upper semicontinuous" to "continuous" in T 13.10. In fact, there are strictly increasing, strictly quasi-concave functions $V(\cdot)\colon R_+^n \to R$ with differentiable level sets in R_+^n that are not continuous and that still determine demand functions which satisfy S 6–S 10. Hence H 1–H 5, $\tilde{H}$ 6 cannot be derived from S 1–S 10. So we cannot do without S 11 or some suitable substitute for S 11. The following example attests to this.[1]

E 13.2 Let $n = 2$ and let $V(\cdot)\colon R_+^n \to R$ be defined by

$$V(x_1, x_2) = \begin{cases} (x_1+3)(x_2+3) & \text{in } \{x \in R_+^2 : (x_1+3)(x_2+3) \leqslant 16\} \\ 14+(x_1+2)(x_2+2) & \text{in } \{x \in R_+^2 : (x_1+2)(x_2+2) \geqslant 9\} - \{(1,1)\} \\ 32-\left(x_1+\dfrac{1-x_1x_2}{x_1+x_2-2}\right)\left(x_2+\dfrac{1-x_1x_2}{x_1+x_2-2}\right) & \text{for all other } x \in R_+^2. \end{cases}$$

Then $V(\cdot)$ is strictly increasing and strictly quasi-concave, and has differentiable level sets in R_{++}^2. Also $V(\cdot)$ is continuous everywhere except at $x = (1, 1)$. The value of $V(\cdot)$ at $(1, 1)$ is 16. Yet $\lim_{n\to\infty} V(1 + (1/n), 1 + (1/n)) = 23$. The demand function $f(\cdot): R_{++}^2 \times R_+ \to R_+^2$ determined by $V(\cdot)$ satisfies S 6–S 10, as witnessed by the following equations for $(p, A) \in \{1\} \times R_{++} \times R_+$:

$$f(p,A) = \begin{cases} \left(\dfrac{A}{2} + \left(\dfrac{3}{2}\right)(p-1), \left(\dfrac{A}{2p}\right) + \left(\dfrac{3}{2}\right)\left(\dfrac{1}{p} - 1\right)\right) \quad \text{if} \\ \quad 0 < 1 - \dfrac{A}{3} < p < 1 + \dfrac{A}{3},\ A^2 + 6A(p+1) + 9p^2 - 46p + 9 \leqslant 0; \\ \left(\dfrac{A}{2} + p - 1, \left(\dfrac{A}{2p}\right) + \left(\dfrac{1}{p} - 1\right)\right) \quad \text{if } 0 < 1 - \dfrac{A}{2} < p < 1 + \dfrac{A}{2}, \\ \quad A^2 + 4A(p+1) + 4p^2 - 28p + 4 \geqslant 0; \\ \left(-\dfrac{A-2p}{p-1} - \sqrt{\left(\dfrac{A-2p}{p-1}\right)^2 + \dfrac{A^2 - (1+2A)p + p^2}{p-1}},\right. \\ \qquad \left.\dfrac{A-2}{p-1} + \dfrac{1}{p}\sqrt{\left(\dfrac{A-2p}{p-1}\right)^2 + \dfrac{A^2 - (1+2A)p + p^2}{p-1}}\right), \\ \quad \text{if } A^2 + 4A(p+1) + 4p^2 - 28p + 4 < 0,\ A^2 + 6A(p+1) \\ \quad + 9p^2 - 46p + 9 > 0 \text{ and either } p + \sqrt{p} < A \\ \quad \text{and } \dfrac{7}{3} \leqslant \dfrac{A}{p} \leqslant \dfrac{5}{2} \text{ or } 1 + \sqrt{p} < A \text{ and } \dfrac{7}{3} \leqslant A \leqslant \dfrac{5}{2}; \\ (A, 0) \quad \text{if } p \geqslant 1 + \dfrac{A}{3} \text{ and } 0 \leqslant A \leqslant \dfrac{7}{3}, \text{ or } p \geqslant 1 + \dfrac{A}{2} \\ \quad \text{and } A \geqslant \dfrac{5}{2}, \text{ or } p \geqslant (A-1)^2 \text{ and } \dfrac{7}{3} \leqslant A \leqslant \dfrac{5}{2}; \\ \left(0, \dfrac{A}{p}\right) \quad \text{if } 0 < p \leqslant 1 - \dfrac{A}{3} \text{ and } A \leqslant \dfrac{7}{3}p, \\ \quad \text{or } 0 < p \leqslant 1 - \dfrac{A}{2} \text{ and } A \geqslant \dfrac{5}{2}p, \text{ or } 0 < A \leqslant p + \sqrt{p} \\ \quad \text{and } \dfrac{7}{3} \leqslant \dfrac{A}{p} \leqslant \dfrac{5}{2}. \end{cases}$$

In reading this example, note that $f(\cdot)$ does not satisfy S 11. When $p^0 =$

$(1, 1)$, $p^1 = (1, 1600/961)$ and $A^0 = 2$, there is no constant K that satisfies the required inequality for all $t \in (0, 1)$ and all $A \in [1, 3]$.

13.3.2 Homothetic Utility Functions and the Fundamental Theorem

Since H 1–H 5 and $\tilde{\text{H}}$ 6 cannot be derived from S 1–S 10, we must search for reasonable substitutes for $\tilde{\text{H}}$ 6 and S 11. We begin by recording T 13.11, which is a theorem developed by H. Uzawa (1960, p. 133).

T 13.11 Let $f(\cdot): R^n_{++} \times R_+ \to R^n_+$ be the demand function in H 1–H 6, and suppose that $A^0 < A^1$ implies that

$$f(p, A^0) \leqslant f(p, A^1), (p, A^0, A^1) \in R^n_{++} \times R^2_+. \quad (13.11)$$

Then $f(\cdot)$ satisfies S 11.

Since $p(f(p, A^1) - f(p, A^0)) = A^1 - A^0$, the validity of T 13.11 is obvious. It is also clear that if we could characterize the class of utility functions whose demand functions satisfy equation 13.11, we could substitute equation 13.11 for S 11 and obtain two equivalent axiom systems by reformulating $\tilde{\text{H}}$ 6 appropriately.

At the moment we know only subclasses of utility functions whose demand functions satisfy equation 13.11. We shall discuss two of them: the class of homothetic utility functions and the class of additively separable utility functions whose components are strictly concave. First homothetic utility functions:

Suppose that we substitute $\hat{\text{H}}$ 6 for $\tilde{\text{H}}$ 6.

$\hat{\text{H}}$ 6 $V(\cdot)$ is continuous, strictly increasing, strictly quasi-concave and homothetic, and has differentiable level sets in R^n_+.

Suppose also that we add a condition on $f(\cdot)$ to S 6 in accordance with T 11.9 such that S 6 becomes S* 6.

S* 6 $f(\cdot)$ is continuous, homogeneous of degree 0, and satisfies $pf(p, A) = A$ for all $(p, A) \in R^n_{++} \times R_+$. Moreover, there exists a continuous function $g(\cdot): R^n_{++} \to R^n_+$ such that

$$f(p, A) = g(p) \cdot A, \qquad (p, A) \in R^n_{++} \times R_+.$$

Then we would obtain two equivalent systems: H 1–H 5, $\hat{\text{H}}$ 6 and S 1–S 5, S* 6, S 7–S 10. The reason we can dispense with S 11 in this case is clear from the statements of T 11.9 and T 13.12.

T 13.12 Let $V(\cdot): R^n_+ \to R$ and $f(\cdot): R^n_{++} \times R_+ \to R^n_+$ be the utility function and the demand function, respectively, in H 1–H 5, $\tilde{\text{H}}$ 6. Then $V(\cdot)$ is homothetic if and only if there exists a continuous function $g(\cdot)$: $R^n_{++} \to R^n_+$ such that

$$f(p, A) = g(p)A, \qquad (p, A) \in R^n_{++} \times R_+. \tag{13.12}$$

Some prominent economists contend that the suggested modification of H 1–H 6 is not drastic. We shall examine their views later in this book.

The proof of T 13.12 is easy. Suppose that $f(\cdot)$ satisfies equation 13.12 and observe that $V(\cdot)$ induces the same ordering of commodity vectors as the utility function we constructed in T 13.9. Next let $x^0 \in R^n_+$ and suppose that $y \in \{x \in R^n_+ : V(x) \geqslant V(x^0)\}$. Then $y \in \overline{S^+(x^0)}$ and there exist vectors $x^k \in R^n_+$, $k = 1, 2, \ldots$, such that $x^k Q x^0$ and $\lim_{k\to\infty} x^k = y$. From equation 13.12 it follows easily that, for any $\lambda \in R_{++}$, $\lambda x^k Q \lambda x^0$, $k = 1, 2, \ldots$. This fact and $\lim_{k\to\infty} \lambda x^k \to \lambda y$ imply that $\lambda y \in \overline{S^+(\lambda x^0)}$; that is, $\lambda y \in \{x \in R^n_+ : V(x) \geqslant V(\lambda x^0)\}$. With obvious modifications, the same arguments will ascertain that, if $\lambda \in R_{++}$ and $\lambda y \in \{x \in R^n_+ : V(x) \geqslant V(\lambda x^0)\}$, then $y \in \{x \in R^n_+ : V(x) \geqslant V(x^0)\}$. Hence equation 13.12 implies that $V(\cdot)$ must be homothetic. Since the converse was established in T 11.9, the proof of T 13.12 is complete.

13.3.3 Additively Separable Utility Functions and the Fundamental Theorem

Another way to obtain two equivalent axiom systems is to require $V(\cdot)$ to be additively separable with strictly concave components. The reason that might work can be intuited from T 13.13.

T 13.13 Suppose that there exists a strictly increasing, continuous function $G(\cdot)$: {range of $V(\cdot)$} $\to R$ and strictly increasing, continuous, strictly concave functions $U_i(\cdot)$: $R_+ \to R$, $i = 1, \ldots, n$, such that

$$G(V(x)) = \sum_{i=1}^{n} U_i(x_i), \qquad x \in R^n_+. \tag{13.13}$$

Then the demand function in T(H 1, ..., H 6) satisfies equation 13.11.

In fact, if $V(\cdot)$ satisfies the conditions of T 13.13, then the demand function in T(H 1, ..., H 6) satisfies equation 13.11 with strict inequality if $0 < f(p, A^0)$. For brevity I leave the proof of this fact and of T 13.13 to the reader.

Suppose now that we add to H 1–H 5 and H̃ 6 the axiom H̃ 7.

H̃ 7 There exists a strictly increasing, continuous function $G(\cdot)$: {range of $V(\cdot)$} $\to R_+$ and strictly increasing, continuous, strictly concave functions $U_i(\cdot)$: $R_+ \to R_+$, $i = 1, \ldots, n$, such that $G(V(\cdot))$ and the $U_i(\cdot)$ satisfy equation 13.13.

Then we can find a triple of substitutes for S 11–S̃ 11, S̃ 12, and S̃ 13—such that T(H 1, ..., H 5, H̃ 6, H̃ 7) is equivalent to T(S 1, ..., S 10, S̃ 11, S̃ 12,

$\tilde{S}$ 13). This equivalence, which we shall delineate in T 13.14 and T 13.15, is due to Bjørn Sandvik (lemmas 8 and 9, 1988, pp. 13–14).

To formulate the required substitutes for S 11, I must introduce new notation. Let I be a variable that varies over the subsets of $\{1, \ldots, n\}$; for example, $I = \{i\}$ or $I = \{k_1, k_2\}$, where i, k_1, $k_2 \in \{1, \ldots, n\}$ and $k_1 \neq k_2$. Moreover, for any $y \in R^n$, let y_I, $y_{-I} \in R^n$ be the vectors obtained from y by letting $y_i = 0$ for $i \in I^c$ and $i \in I$, respectively; for example, if $I = \{2\}$, then $y_I = (0, y_2, 0, \ldots, 0)$, $y_{-I} = (y_1, 0, y_3, \ldots, y_n)$ and $y = y_I + y_{-I}$. With this notation we can state the new axioms.

$\tilde{S}$ 11 Let $x, y \in R^n_{++}$ and $(p^x, A^x), (p^y, A^y) \in R^n_{++} \times R_+$ be such that $x = f(p^x, A^x)$ and $y = f(p^y, A^y)$. Moreover, let I be a subset of $\{1, \ldots, n\}$. Then

$$\frac{p^x_I}{p^x_I x_I} = \frac{p^y_I}{p^y_I y_I} \quad \text{only if } x_I = y_I.$$

$\tilde{S}$ 12 Let $x, y \in R^n_{++}$ and let I be a subset of $\{1, \ldots, n\}$. Moreover, let $z \in R^n_{++}$ be such that $z = x_I + y_{-I}$, and let $(p^x, A^x), (p^z, A^z) \in R^n_{++} \times R_+$ be such that $x = f(p^x, A^x)$ and $z = f(p^z, A^z)$. Then

$$\frac{p^x_I}{p^x_I x_I} = \frac{p^z_I}{p^z x_I}.$$

$\tilde{S}$ 13 If $x, y \in R^n_+$, $p \in R^n_{++}$, and $A^x, A^y \in R_+$ are such that $x = f(p, A^x)$, $y = f(p, A^y)$, and $A^x < A^y$, then $x \leqslant y$. Moreover, if $0 < x$, then $x < y$.

One half of the equivalence for which we search is expressed in T 13.14.

T 13.14 Let $f(\cdot)\colon R^n_{++} \times R_+ \to R^n_+$ be the demand function in T(H 1, ..., H 5, $\tilde{H}$ 6, $\tilde{H}$ 7). Then $f(\cdot)$ satisfies $\tilde{S}$ 11–$\tilde{S}$ 13.

We have already observed that $f(\cdot)$ satisfies $\tilde{S}$ 13. Hence it remains to show that $f(\cdot)$ satisfies $\tilde{S}$ 11 and $\tilde{S}$ 12. We begin with $\tilde{S}$ 11.

Let $U(\cdot)\colon R^n_+ \to R_+$ be $G(V(\cdot))$ and assume that $G(\cdot)$ and the $U_i(\cdot)$ in equation 13.13 have been chosen such that $U_i(0) = 0$, $i = 1, \ldots, n$. Then, for all $x \in R^n_+$ and all nonempty $I \subset \{1, \ldots, n\}$,

$$U(x) = U(x_I) + U(x_{-I}).$$

Next let x, $y \in R^n_{++}$ and (p^x, A^x), $(p^y, A^y) \in R^n_{++} \times R_+$ be such that $x = f(p^x, A^x)$ and $y = f(p^y, A^y)$; and assume that

$$\frac{p^x_I}{p^x_I x_I} = \frac{p^y_I}{p^y_I y_I}$$

for some $I \subset \{1, \ldots, n\}$. Then $p^y_I x_I = p^y_I y_I$. Hence $p^y(x_I + y_{-I}) = A^y$ and $U(x_I) \leqslant U(y_I)$. Similarly, $p^x_I x_I = p^x_I y_I$. Hence $p^x(y_I + x_{-I}) = A^x$ and

$U(y_I) \leqslant U(x_I)$. Consequently, $U(x_I) = U(y_I)$. This equality, $p^x x_I = p_I^x y_I$, and the strict concavity of the $U_i(\cdot)$ imply that $x_I = y_I$.

To show that $f(\cdot)$ satisfies $\tilde{S}$ 12 as well, we let x, y, and z be such that $x, y \in R_{++}^n$ and $z = x_I + y_{-I}$ for some $I \subset \{1, \ldots, n\}$. Moreover, we let (p^x, A^x), $(p^z, A^z) \in R_{++}^n \times R_+$ be such that $x = f(p^x, A^x)$ and $z = f(p^z, A^z)$. Then the differentiability of the level sets of $U(\cdot)$ and equation 13.13 imply that there is a constant $\lambda > 0$ such that

$$\frac{p_I^x}{p_I^x x_I} = \lambda \left(\frac{p_I^z}{p_I^z x_I} \right).$$

Obvious arguments, which I leave to the reader, suffice to verify that λ must equal 1.

The converse of T 13.14 is also valid—see T 13.15.

T 13.15 Suppose that S 1–S 10 and $\tilde{S}$ 11–$\tilde{S}$ 13 are valid. Suppose also that $n \geqslant 3$. Then there exist functions $V(\cdot)$: $R_+^n \to R_+$, $G(\cdot)$: {range of $V(\cdot)$} $\to R_+$ and $U_i(\cdot)$: $R_+ \to R_+$, $i = 1, \ldots, n$, such that $V(\cdot)$ satisfies $\tilde{H}$ 6 and equation 13.9 and such that $V(\cdot)$, $G(\cdot)$, and the $U_i(\cdot)$ satisfy $\tilde{H}$ 7.

To establish the theorem, we first observe that S 1–S 10 and $\tilde{S}$ 13, together with T 13.9 and T 13.11, suffice to establish the existence of a function $V(\cdot)$: $R_+^n \to R_+$ that satisfies $\tilde{H}$ 6 and equation 13.9.

Next let $|I|$ denote the number of elements in I. For each nonempty $I \subset \{1, \ldots, n\}$, $\tilde{S}$ 11 and $\tilde{S}$ 12 imply that the ordering of vectors in $R_+^{|I|}$ induced by $V(x_I + x_{-I})$ is independent of x_{-I}. From this, the monotonicity of $V(\cdot)$, and T 11.2, it follows that there exist continuous, strictly increasing functions $G(\cdot)$: {range of $V(\cdot)$} $\to R_+$ and $U_i(\cdot)$: $R_+ \to R_+$, $i = 1, \ldots, n$, such that $U_i(0) = 0$, $i = 1, \ldots, n$, and such that

$$G(V(x)) = \sum_{i=1}^{n} U_i(x_i) \quad \text{for all } x \in R_+^n.$$

But if that is true, then $\tilde{H}$ 6 and theorem 2 in Debreu and Koopmans 1982 (p. 9) imply that all but at most one $U_i(\cdot)$, say $U_j(\cdot)$, are strictly concave. Moreover, the differentiability properties of $U_j(\cdot)$ established in theorem 3 in Debreu and Koopmans 1983 (p. 10) and $\tilde{S}$ 13 can easily be seen to imply that $U_j(\cdot)$ is strictly concave as well. The last details I leave to the reader.

13.4 Concluding Remarks

We have been only partially successful in answering Q 1. It should not go unnoticed, however, that for most empirical purposes, the two systems,

H 1–H 5, $\tilde{H}$ 6 and S 1–S 11, are equivalent. Every theorem that can be derived from the first set of axioms can be deduced from the second set. Also, every theorem that can be derived from S 1–S 11 is a consequence of H 1–H 5, $\tilde{H}$ 6, provided the consumer's utility function belongs to the right class of functions—a class that varies from case to case. Therefore, since the axioms of T(H 1–H 6) are easier than the axioms of T(S 1–S 11) to manipulate, we shall keep T(H 1–H 6) as our theory of consumer choice under certainty.[2]

14 Consumer Choice and Resource Allocation

In the preceding chapters on consumer choice, we theorized about how a consumer's choice of commodity bundles varies with the prices he faces. These prices were not affected by his choice and we did not ask how their values were determined. In this chapter we shall discuss price formation in variously structured exchange economies whose constituent consumers behave in accordance with the principles of T(H 1, ..., H 6). We shall also discuss characteristics of resource allocation in such economies.

14.1 Competitive Equilibria in Exchange Economies

An *exchange economy* is an m-tuple,

$$E = ((V^1(\cdot), X^1, w^1), \ldots, (V^m(\cdot), X^m, w^m)),$$

that satisfies the following conditions: For each $i = 1, \ldots, m$,

EE 1 $w^i \in R^n_{++}$;

EE 2 $X^i = R^n_+$; and

EE 3 $V^i(\cdot)\colon X^i \to R_+$ is continuous, strictly increasing, and strictly quasi-concave.

In the intended interpretation of E, $(V^i(\cdot), X^i, w^i)$ is a consumer, i.e., an individual or a family, with a utility indicator $V^i(\cdot)$, a set of available commodity bundles X^i, and some initial holdings of commodities w^i.

14.1.1 A Scenario for Commodity Exchange

Economists like to think of the consumers in E as having formed a market and having agreed to exchange commodities at the rates prescribed by some price p. Each consumer i offers to trade his initial resources for his consumption bundle at (p, pw^i). The consumers will succeed in carrying out these exchanges if and only if their offers are mutually consistent, i.e., if and only if the consumers' consumption bundles at (p, pw^i), $i = 1, \ldots, m$, add up to the sum total of initial resources.

E 14.1 Consider an exchange economy with $n = m = 2$, and suppose that $V^1(x) = V^2(x) = (x_1 + 2)(x_2 + 2)$, $x \in R_+^2$. Suppose also that $w^1 = (1, 2)$ and $w^2 = (2, 1)$. At $p = (1, 1)$ the consumption bundles of consumer 1 and 2 are, respectively, $(3/2, 3/2)$ and $(3/2, 3/2)$. Hence consumer 1 offers to give consumer 2 one half of a unit of commodity 1 in exchange for one half of a unit of commodity 2; and consumer 2 is willing to accept the offer.

In Max Weber's fetching phraseology, the scenario sketched above *seems* both objectively possible and adequate from a nomological point of view. To make sure that this scenario *is* objectively possible, we establish below the existence of *equilibrium prices* in E, i.e., the existence of prices at which the offers of all E consumers would be mutually consistent. Whether the scenario is nomologically adequate depends on the ability of E consumers to find equilibrium prices and on the desirability of the allocation of resources that results from the corresponding commodity exchanges. We shall discuss those problems in sections 14.2 and 14.3.

14.1.2 Competitive Equilibria in E

To discuss price formation in exchange economies, I must introduce two new concepts: an allocation and a competitive equilibrium. An *allocation* is an m-tuple $(x^1, \ldots, x^m)$ that satisfies

EA 1 $x^i \in X^i$, $i = 1, \ldots, m$; and

EA 2 $\sum_{i=1}^{m} (x^i - w^i) = 0.$

Thus, if we let $w = \sum_{i=1}^{m} w^i$ and think of w as the exchange economy's initial resources, an allocation is a distribution of these resources in which the ith consumer receives the commodities in x^i, $i = 1, \ldots, m$.

A *competitive equilibrium* is an $(m + 1)$-tuple, $(p, x^1, \ldots, x^m)$ satisfying the following conditions:

CE 1 $p \in R_{++}^n$;

CE 2 $(x^1, \ldots, x^m)$ is an allocation;

CE 3 $px^i \leqslant pw^i$, $i = 1, \ldots, m$; and

CE 4 $V^i(x^i) = \max_{y \in \Gamma(p, pw^i)} V^i(y)$, $i = 1, \ldots, m$, where $\Gamma(p, pw^i) = \{y \in R^n_+ : py \leqslant pw^i\}$.

Thus, in the lingo of chapter 10, a competitive equilibrium is a price p and an allocation $(x^1, \ldots, x^m)$ in which the ith consumer receives the consumption bundle that he would have chosen in the price-income situation (p, pw^i), $i = 1, \ldots, m$. In terms of our scenario for commodity exchange, a competitive equilibrium is an equilibrium price and the allocation which would result from the exchanges E's consumers propose at p.

With the help of a twelfth universal theorem, *Brouwer's Fixed-Point Theorem*, we can show that there is a competitive equilibrium in E. First Brouwer's theorem, UT 12.

UT 12 Suppose that $S \subset R^n$ is a closed, bounded convex set. Moreover, suppose that $g(\cdot): S \to S$ is continuous. Then there is an $x \in S$ such that $x = g(x)$.

When $n = 1$ and $S = [0, 1]$, it is easy to see that any continuous function, $g(\cdot): [0, 1] \to [0, 1]$, must have a fixed point, i.e., a point $x \in [0, 1]$ at which $x = g(x)$. When $n > 1$, it is hard to fathom and difficult to prove the validity of UT 12. For a standard proof of Brouwer's theorem, I refer the interested reader to Berge (1959, p. 183).

Next, the existence of a competitive equilibrium—see T 14.1.

T 14.1 There exists a competitive equilibrium in the exchange economy E.

To establish T 14.1 we let $\grave{P} = \{p \in R^n_+ : \sum_{j=1}^n p_j = 1\}$ and we let $\grave{E} = ((V^1(\cdot), \grave{X}^1, w^1), \ldots, (V^m(\cdot), \grave{X}^m, w^m))$ be an auxiliary exchange economy in which $\grave{X}^i = \{x \in X^i : x \leqslant 2\sum_{i=1}^m w^i\}$, $i = 1, \ldots, m$. Furthermore, for each consumer i in $\grave{E}$, we let $\grave{f}^i(p, pw^i)$ denote i's consumption bundle at (p, pw^i), and we let $z^i(p) = \grave{f}^i(p, pw^i) - w^i$ and $z(p) = \sum_{i=1}^m z^i(p)$. Then $z^i(p)$ measures i's excess demand at (p, pw^i) and $z(p)$ records $\grave{E}$'s aggregate excess demand at $(p, w^1, \ldots, w^m)$. It is easy to verify that $\grave{f}^i(p, pw^i)$ is well defined for all $p \in \grave{P}$. Hence $z^i(\cdot): \grave{P} \to R^n$ and $z(\cdot): \grave{P} \to R^n$.

The function $z(\cdot)$ has some interesting properties. To wit: for all $p \in \grave{P}$,

(i) $z(\lambda p) = z(p)$ if $\lambda \in R_{++}$;

(ii) $pz(p) = 0$;

(iii) $z_j(p) > 0$ if $p_j = 0$ for some $j \in \{1, \ldots, n\}$; and

(iv) $z(\cdot)$ is continuous at p.

The first of these assertions follows from the fact that the consumers' budget constraints do not vary with λ. The next two are obvious consequences of the monotonicity of the $V^i(\cdot)$'s. Finally, the continuity of $z(\cdot)$ follows from the continuity of the $z^i(\cdot)$'s, and the continuity of $z^i(\cdot)$ can be established by applying arguments similar to those we used in chapter 10 to establish the continuity of $f(\cdot)$. For brevity I leave the details to the reader.

We shall use properties ii, iii, and iv of $z(\cdot)$ to establish the validity of T 14.1: Let $g(\cdot)$: $\grave{P} \to \grave{P}$ be defined by

$$g_j(p) = \frac{p_j + \max(0, z_j(p))}{1 + \sum_{k=1}^{n} \max(0, z_k(p))}, \qquad j = 1, \ldots, n. \tag{14.1}$$

Then $g(\cdot)$ is well defined and, by property (iv) above, continuous. Moreover, since $\grave{P}$ is a closed, bounded, convex subset of R^n, it follows from UT 12 that there exists a $p \in \grave{P}$ such that $p = g(p)$. Such a p must be positive because equation 14.1 and $p_j = 0$ imply that $z_j(p) \leqslant 0$ and because $z_j(p) \leqslant 0$ and $p_j = 0$ cannot happen according to property (iii) above.

When $p \in R^n_{++}$, the following equations, which we derive from equation 14.1,

$$p_j\left(\sum_{k=1}^{n} \max(0, z_k(p))\right) = \max(0, z_j(p)), \qquad j = 1, \ldots, n,$$

imply that if $z_j(p) \leqslant 0$ for one j, $z_k(p) \leqslant 0$ for all $k = 1, \ldots, n$. Since, on account of property (ii), the $z_k(p)$ cannot all be positive, $z_k(p) \leqslant 0$ for all k. But, if that is so, then a second application of (ii) suffices to ascertain that $z_k(p) = 0$, $k = 1, \ldots, n$.

The conditions $p \in R^n_{++}$ and $z(p) = 0$ imply both that $(\grave{f}^1(p, pw^1), \ldots, \grave{f}^m(p, pw^m))$ is an allocation and that, for each $i = 1, \ldots, m$, $\grave{f}^i(p, pw^i)$ is the ith consumer's consumption bundle *in E* at (p, pw^i).

14.2 Resource Allocation in Exchange Economies

In section 14.1.1 we described a scenario for commodity exchange in E, and T 14.1 established its objective possibility. To show that the scenario is also adequate from a nomological point of view, we must verify (1) that there is a method by which the consumers in E can locate a competitive equilibrium and (2) that the allocation of commodities in a competitive equilibrium cannot be improved upon. We shall discuss the second condition in this section and the first in section 14.3.

14.2.1 Pareto-Optimal Allocations and Fair Allocations

A Pareto-optimal allocation in E is an allocation that cannot be improved upon. We denote by Q the set of all Pareto-optimal allocations and define Q as follows: Let A be the set of allocations in E; i.e., let

$$A = \left\{ x \in R_+^{nm} : x = (x^1, \dots, x^m) \text{ with } x^i \in R_+^n,\ i = 1, \dots, m \text{ and } \sum_{i=1}^{m} (x^i - w^i) = 0 \right\}.$$

Then

$$Q = \{x \in A : \text{there is no } z \in A \text{ with } V^i(z^i) \geqslant V^i(x^i),\ i = 1, \dots, m, \text{ and } V^k(z^k) > V^k(x^k) \text{ for some } k \in \{1, \dots, m\}\}.$$

The definition of Q explicates in what sense a Pareto-optimal allocation in E cannot be improved upon.

There are many allocations in Q. We shall discuss some of them to make sure that the optimality of an $x \in Q$ is not misunderstood. If $x \in A$ and $V^i(x^i) < V^i(x^j)$ for some pair (i, j), then at x consumer i *envies* consumer j.[1] There are allocations in Q at which one consumer envies another; for example, $x = (x^1, \dots, x^m)$, with $x^j = 0$ for $j \neq i$ and $x^i = w$. In fact, envy is a characteristic feature of most allocations in Q—see T 14.2.

T 14.2 If $x \in Q$, there is a pair (i, k) such that consumer i envies nobody and nobody envies consumer k.

To see this, observe first that if everybody envies somebody, then there is a sequence $\{t_1, \dots, t_k\} \subset \{1, \dots, m\}$ such that $V^{t_i}(x^{t_i}) < V^{t_i}(x^{t_{i+1}})$, $i = 1, \dots, k-1$, and $V^{t_k}(x^{t_k}) < V^{t_k}(x^{t_1})$. Furthermore, there is a $z \in A$ so that $z^i = x^i$ if $i \in \{1, \dots, m\} - \{t_1, \dots, t_k\}$, $z^{t_i} = x^{t_{i+1}}$, $i = 1, \dots, k-1$, and $z^{t_k} = x^{t_1}$. But then $V^j(z^j) \geqslant V^j(x^j)$ for all j and $V^{t_i}(z^{t_i}) > V^{t_i}(x^{t_i})$ for $i = 1, \dots, k$, which contradicts the Pareto-optimality of x. The existence of a consumer whom nobody envies can be established in the same way.

When $x \in A$ and $V^i(x^i) \geqslant V^i(x^j)$ for all $j \neq i$, $i = 1, \dots, m$, x is *equitable*. If $x \in Q$ and x is equitable, *then x is fair.*

T 14.3 There exist fair allocations.

To see why, let $\dot{w}^i = w/m$, $i = 1, \dots, m$, and let $(p, x^1, \dots, x^m)$ be a competitive equilibrium relative to the distribution of w given by $(\dot{w}^1, \dots, \dot{w}^m)$.

For all pairs (i, j), $px^i = px^j$. Hence $V^i(x^i) \geqslant V^i(x^j)$ and $V^j(x^j) \geqslant V^j(x^i)$. From this and from the fact that competitive equilibria belong to Q, it follows that $(x^1, \ldots, x^m)$ is a fair allocation.

14.2.2 Pareto-Optimal Allocations and Competitive Equilibria

The fact that competitive equilibria belong to Q is one of the fundamental building blocks of welfare economics. It also provides an explication of why a competitive equilibrium allocation of w cannot be improved upon. We record this fact in T 14.4.

T 14.4 If $(p, x^1, \ldots, x^m)$ is a competitive equilibrium relative to some distribution of w, then $(x^1, \ldots, x^m) \in Q$.

The proof of T 14.4 is easy: Suppose that there is a $z \in A$ such that $V^j(z^j) \geqslant V^j(x^j)$ for all j and $V^k(z^k) > V^k(x^k)$ for some k. The first inequality implies that $pz^j \geqslant px^j$ and the latter implies that $pz^k > px^k$. Hence $pw = \sum_{i=1}^m px^i < \sum_{i=1}^m pz^i = pw$—a contradiction that demonstrates that there is no $z \in A$ with the required properties.

The optimality of competitive equilibria can be explicated in another interesting way. Let x be an arbitrary allocation and let S be a subset of $\{1, \ldots, m\}$. In the jargon of game theorists, the consumers whose indices are in S form a *coalition*. This coalition *blocks* the given allocation if there exist vectors $\dot{x}^i$, $i \in S$, such that $\dot{x}^i \in X^i$, $V^i(\dot{x}^i) \geqslant V^i(x^i)$ for all $i \in S$ with strict inequality for some i, and $\sum_{i \in S} \dot{x}^i = \sum_{i \in S} w^i$. The set of all allocations that cannot be blocked by any coalition is called the *core of E*. Evidently the core of E is a subset of Q. Moreover, the competitive equilibria in E belong to the core of E—to wit T 14.5.

T 14.5 If $(p, x^1, \ldots, x^m)$ is a competitive equilibrium in E, then $(x^1, \ldots, x^m)$ belongs to the core of E.

The properties of core allocations ensure that once the consumers have exchanged commodities in accordance with a competitive equilibrium price, trading will cease.

With only obvious modifications, the arguments used to establish T 14.4 can also be used to prove T 14.5. Therefore, I leave the proof of T 14.5 to the reader and conclude our discussion of Pareto-optimal allocations with another fundamental theorem of welfare economics, T 14.6.

T 14.6 If $\tilde{x} \in Q$, then there exists a $p \in R^n_{++}$ and a distribution of w relative to which $(p, \tilde{x})$ is a competitive equilibrium.

Thus any Pareto-optimal allocation can be sustained as a competitive equilibrium. To prove T 14.6, we let $\tilde{x}$ be as specified in the theorem and define $G \subset R^n$ by

$$G = \left\{ z \in R^n : \text{ there exist } x^i \in R^n_+, i = 1, \ldots, m, \text{ such that } z = \sum_{i=1}^{m} x^i, V^1(x^1) > V^1(\tilde{x}^1), \text{ and } V^i(x^i) \geqslant V^i(\tilde{x}^i), i = 2, \ldots, m \right\}.$$

It follows from the monotonicity and strict quasi-concavity of the $V^i(\cdot)$ that

(i) $z \in G$, $v \in R^n$ and $z \leqslant v$ imply $v \in G$; and

(ii) G is convex.

Moreover, it follows from the Pareto-optimality of $\tilde{x}$ that $w \notin G$. But then, by UT 4 (section 10.1), there is a $p^0 \in R^n - \{0\}$ such that $p^0 z \geqslant p^0 w$ for all $z \in G$. We observe that, by (i), $p^0 \in R^n_+$. In addition, for all $i = 1, \ldots, m$,

$$p^0 \tilde{x}^i = \min_{y \in \{x \in R^n_+ : V^i(x) \geqslant V(\tilde{x}^i)\}} p^0 y. \tag{14.2}$$

To ascertain the validity of equation 14.2, we suppose that there is a j and an x^j such that $p^0 x^j < p^0 \tilde{x}^j$ and such that $V^j(x^j) \geqslant V^j(\tilde{x}^j)$. Also we let $\varepsilon = p^0 \tilde{x}^j - p^0 x^j$ and we let $\delta \in R_{++}$ be so small that, if $z^j = (x^j_1 + \delta, x^j_2, \ldots, x^j_n)$, then $p^0 \tilde{x}^j - p^0 z^j \geqslant (2/3)\varepsilon$. Finally, we let $z^k = \tilde{x}^k$ for $k \neq j$ and 1 and, if $j \neq 1$, we let $z^1 = (\tilde{x}^1_1 + \delta, \tilde{x}^1_2, \ldots, \tilde{x}^1_n)$. Then the monotonicity of the $V^i(\cdot)$ implies that, if $z = \sum_{i=1}^m z^i$, then $z \in G$ and $p^0 z < p^0 w$—a contradiction that establishes equation 14.2.

Next we shall show that $p^0 > 0$. Suppose that $p^0_i = 0$ and that $p^0_k > 0$. Let $\tilde{x}^j$ be such that $\tilde{x}^j_k > 0$ and observe that we can find $\delta_1, \delta_2 \in R_{++}$ such that if $x = (x_1, \ldots, x_n)$ with $x_k = \tilde{x}^j_k - \delta_1$, $x_i = \tilde{x}^j_i + \delta_2$ and $x_l = \tilde{x}^j_l$ for all $l = 1, \ldots, n; l \neq i, k$, then $V^j(x) > V^j(\tilde{x}^j)$ and $p^0 x < p^0 \tilde{x}^j$—a contradiction, which shows that $p^0 > 0$.

To conclude the proof, we let $\tilde{w}^i = \tilde{x}^i$, $i = 1, \ldots, m$ and observe that $p^0 > 0$ and equation 14.2 imply that, for $i = 1, \ldots, m$, $\tilde{x}^i$ is consumer i's consumption bundle in the price-income situation $(p^0, p^0 \tilde{w}^i)$. This and the fact that $(\tilde{x}^1, \ldots, \tilde{x}^m)$ is an allocation imply that $(p^0, \tilde{x}^1, \ldots, \tilde{x}^m)$ is a competitive equilibrium relative to $(\tilde{w}^1, \ldots, \tilde{w}^m)$.

14.3 The Formation of Prices in an Exchange Economy

In section 14.1 we established the existence of competitive equilibria in E in order to establish the objective possibility of our exchange scenario for E. In section 14.2 we delineated various characteristics of resource allocation in E to determine the nomological adequacy of the same scenario. It remains to be seen whether there exists a scheme by which the consumers in E can find competitive equilibrium prices. We discuss that problem in this section.

14.3.1 On the Stability of Competitive Equilibria

Some hundred years ago, Leon Walras suggested that consumers in E could find competitive equilibrium prices by hiring an auctioneer who would call out a price p, record the resulting excess demand, and—without any trading having occurred—raise or lower his price quotations according as excess demand was positive or negative. Supposedly, after sufficiently many price quotes, the auctioneer would zero in on a price p^0 at which excess demand was zero. Only then would trading occur. The resulting allocation, together with p^0, would constitute a competitive equilibrium in E.

We shall describe the behavior of Walras's auctioneer symbolically by the following system of ordinary differential equations:

$$\frac{dp(t)}{dt} = z(p), \qquad t \geqslant 0 \tag{14.3}$$

where $z(\cdot)\colon (R^n_+ - \{0\}) \to R^n$ is as described in section 14.1.2; i.e., for each $p \in (R^n_+ - \{0\})$,

$$z(p) = \sum_{i=1}^{m} (\tilde{f}^i(p, pw^i) - w^i),$$

where $\tilde{f}^i(p, pw^i)$ denotes consumer i's consumption bundle at (p, pw^i) when his choice is restricted to be in $\tilde{X}^i = \{x \in X^i : x \leqslant 2 \sum_{i=1}^{m} w^i\}$. Walras thought that equation 14.3 would have a solution $p(\cdot)\colon R_+ \to R^n_{++}$ such that $p(t)$, as $t \to \infty$, would converge to a $p^0 \in R^n_{++}$ at which $z(p^0) = 0$. We next ask whether Walras's conjecture is reasonable. In reading our answer, it is important to keep in mind that, at any $p \in (R^n_+ - \{0\})$, $z(\cdot)$ satisfies conditions i–iv listed in section 14.1.2; i.e., $z(\cdot)$ is continuous, homogeneous of degree 0, and satisfies $pz(p) = 0$ and $z_j(p) > 0$ if $p_j = 0$, $j = 1, \ldots, n$. Moreover, $\|z(\cdot)\|$ is bounded.

Walras's idea is useless for *E*'s consumers if equation 14.3 does not have a solution defined on all of R_+. To help our intuition about the existence of such a solution, we next record and discuss two useful universal theorems, UT 13 and UT 14.

UT 13 Suppose that $F(\cdot)\colon R^n_{++} \to R^n$ is continuous. Moreover, suppose that there are constants M and $K \in R_{++}$ such that, for all $y, y^0 \in R^n_{++}$,

$$\|F(y)\| \leqslant M \tag{14.4}$$

and

$$\|F(y) - F(y^0)\| \leqslant K\|y - y^0\|. \tag{14.5}$$

Finally, for each $(\xi, x) \in R_+ \times R^n_{++}$, let $J(\xi, x)$ be the interval $(\xi - a(x), \xi + a(x))$, where $a(x) = (\min_{1 \leqslant i \leqslant n} x_i/M + 1)$. Then there exists a unique family $y(t; \xi, x)$ of solutions to the differential equation,

$$\frac{dy}{dt} = F(y), \tag{14.6}$$

defined for all $(\xi, x) \in R_+ \times R^n_{++}$ such that

$$y(\xi; \xi, x) = x$$

and

$$y(\cdot\,; \xi, x) : J(\xi, x) \to R^n_{++}.$$

Moreover, the functions on $\{(t; \xi, x) \in R \times R_+ \times R^n_{++} : t \in J(\xi, x)\}$ to R^n_{++} and R^n, $y(\cdot)$ and $dy(\cdot)/dt$, are continuous.

In the statement of the theorem, (ξ, x) determines the initial condition, $(\xi; \xi, x) = x$, which insists that the solution to equation 14.6 pass through x at "time" t equal to ξ. Moreover, the interval $J(\xi, x)$ is chosen such that we can be sure that, for all $t \in J(\xi, x)$, $y(t; \xi, x) \in R^n_{++}$. To show why, we consider the integral equation,

$$y(t) = x + \int_\xi^t F(y(s))\,ds, \qquad t \in [\xi, a). \tag{14.7}$$

If $y(\cdot)\colon [\xi, a) \to R^n_{++}$ is continuous and satisfies equation 14.7, then $y(\xi) = x$ and $dy(t)/dt = F(y(t))$, $t \in [\xi, a)$. Conversely, if $y(\cdot)\colon [\xi, a) \to R^n_{++}$ is a continuous solution to equation 14.6 that satisfies $y(\xi) = x$, then

$$y(t) - x = \int_\xi^t \frac{dy(s)}{ds}\,ds = \int_\xi^t F(y(s))\,ds,$$

which demonstrates that $y(\cdot)$ is a solution to equation 14.7 as well. Now equation 14.7 makes sense only for intervals $[\xi, a)$ in which the values of $y(\cdot)$ belong to R^n_{++}. Since, by equation 14.4, a solution to equation 14.7 must satisfy the inequalities

$$\| y(t) - x\| \leqslant \int_{\xi}^{t} \|F(y(s))\|\, ds \leqslant M(t - \xi),$$

we see that $[\xi, \xi + a(x))$ is such an interval. Analogous remarks are valid for $(\xi - a(x), \xi]$ as well.

A function $F(\cdot)\colon R^n_{++} \to R^n$ which satisfies equation 14.5 is said to be *Lipschitzian.* The condition that $F(\cdot)$ be Lipschitzian is important for the conclusions of UT 13. If $F(\cdot)$ does not satisfy equation 14.5, the solution to equation 14.7 need not be unique and it need not vary continuously with the initial conditions (ξ, x).

E 14.2 Suppose that $n = 1$ and let $J = R_+$ and $F(y) = (y - 1)^{2/3}$, $y \in R_{++}$. Then consider the equation

$$\frac{dy}{dt} = (y - 1)^{2/3}. \tag{14.8}$$

If $b > 1$ and $\xi = 0$,

$$y(t; 0, b) = 1 + \left(\frac{t + 3(b - 1)^{1/3}}{3}\right)^3, \qquad t \geqslant 0 \tag{14.9}$$

is the only solution to equation 14.8 through $(0, b)$. If $0 < b \leqslant 1$, $\xi = 0$, and $\bar{t} = -3(b - 1)^{1/3} \geqslant 0$, then, for each $a > \bar{t}$,

$$y(t; 0, b) = \begin{cases} 1 + ((t + 3(b - 1)^{1/3})/3)^3 \text{ when } 0 \leqslant t \leqslant \bar{t}, \\ 1 \text{ when } \bar{t} \leqslant t < a \\ 1 + ((t - a)/3)^3 \text{ for } a \leqslant t \end{cases}$$

is a solution to equation 14.8 through $(0, b)$.

If $F(\cdot)\colon R^n_{++} \to R^n$ is differentiable in an open neighborhood of $x^0 \in R^n_{++}$, there is a compact neighborhood of x^0 in which $F(\cdot)$ is Lipschitzian. Also if $F(\cdot)$ is differentiable in R^n_{++}, then $F(\cdot)$ is Lipschitzian on any compact subset of R^n_{++}. In a subset A of R^n_{++} in which $F(\cdot)$ is Lipschitzian, UT 13 is valid with R^n_{++} replaced by A; i.e., through any point in A there is one and only one solution in A to equation 14.6. Moreover, the solution varies continuously with the initial conditions. For example, in E 14.2, $(y - 1)^{2/3}$ is not Lipschitzian in a neighborhood of $y = 1$. However, it is Lipschitzian in any compact connected subset of R_{++} that does not contain $\{1\}$. Note, therefore, that the solution in equation 14.9 varies continuously with b on $\{r \in R_{++} : r > 1\}$.

According to T 10.5, $z(\cdot)\colon R^n_{++} \to R^n$ is continuous. However, $z(\cdot)$ need not be Lipschitzian on R^n_{++}, and it need not be differentiable in any open subset of R^n_{++}. When $z(\cdot)$ is neither Lipschitzian nor differentiable, we need UT 14 below to characterize the solutions to equation 14.3. The

Errata

Toward a Formal Science of Economics
by Bernt P. Stigum

- The following is to be added to step 1 on page 637:

Finally, a remark concerning $P^{\mathscr{L}}(\cdot|\cdot)$ and the possibility of assigning probabilities to the open wffs of $L_{t,p}(\xi)$ is called for. The probability measure $P^{\mathscr{L}}(\cdot|\varphi(K,\xi_e))$ induces in the obvious way an additive probability measure, $Q^{\mathscr{L}}(\cdot|K)$, on the closed wffs of $L_{t,p}(\xi)$. For the purpose of describing the kind of statistical experiment I have in mind for $T(\Gamma_t)$, I shall assume that there exists an additive probability measure $Q^{\mathscr{L}}(\cdot)$ on the wffs of $L_{t,p}(\xi)$ that agrees with $Q^{\mathscr{L}}(\cdot|K)$ on the latter's domain of definition, and that there is a probability measure $\mu(\cdot):\mathscr{P}(N_{\xi_t}\times N_{\xi_p})\rightarrow[0,1]$ such that, for all $A\in\Gamma_{t,p}$,

$$Q^{\mathscr{L}}(A)=\sum_{N_{\xi_t}\times N_{\xi_p}} Q^{\mathscr{L}}(A_{x_1,\ldots,x_{k+m}}(\eta)|K)\mu(\eta).$$

The existence of $Q^{\mathscr{L}}(\cdot)$ is not problematic. Since

$$[[x_1=\eta_1]\wedge[[x_2=\eta_2]\wedge[[\cdots[[x_{k+m-1}=\eta_{k+m-1}]\wedge[x_{k+m}=\eta_{k+m}]]\cdots]]]$$

is a wff in $L_{t,p}(\xi)$ for all $\eta\in N_{\xi_t}\times N_{\xi_p}$, the existence of $\mu(\cdot)$ is not problematic either as long as the members of $\Gamma_{t,p}$ have the simple structure insisted on in step 4 of section 25.6. See the discussion of logical probabilities in section 24.2.

- Also on page 637, the definition of $\tilde{Q}(B)$ should be

$$\tilde{Q}(B)=\sum_{\eta\in N(B)} P^{\mathscr{L}}(\{H\in\mathscr{X}:\xi_e RH \text{ and } H(A_{x_1,\ldots,x_{k+m}}(\eta))=t$$
$$\text{for all } A\in\Gamma_{t,p}\}|\varphi(K,\xi_e))\mu(\eta).$$

- On page 638, the definition of $Q(\cdot)$ should be

$$Q(A_S)=\tilde{P}(A_F)/\tilde{P}(\text{range of } F(\cdot)),\quad A\in\mathscr{F},\quad A_F=A\cap\text{range of } F(\cdot).$$

significance of the last half of the theorem will be borne out in T 14.7, where we insist that if a solution to equation 14.3 starts on a given sphere S, it stays on the sphere for all relevant t.

UT 14 Suppose that $F(\cdot)\colon R^n_{++} \to R^n$ is continuous. For each point $(\xi, x) \in R_+ \times R^n_{++}$, there is a maximal interval (α, β) with $\alpha < \xi < \beta$ on which there is a continuous solution to equation 14.6, $y(\cdot; \xi, x)\colon (\alpha, \beta) \to R^n_{++}$. If $\beta < \infty$, then given any compact set $A \subset R^n_{++}$, there is a $t \in (\alpha, \beta)$ at which $y(t; \xi, x) \notin A$.

Thus if $y(\cdot; \xi, x)\colon (\alpha, \beta) \to R^n_{++}$ and if $\beta < \infty$, then as $t \to \beta$ either $y(t; \xi, x)$ tends to the boundary of R^n_{++} or $\|y(t; \xi, x)\|$ tends to ∞ (or both). Proofs of UT 13 and UT 14 can be found in Graves (1956, pp. 152 and 159–160).

It is surprising that there need not exist a solution to equation 14.6 that is defined for all $t \in (\alpha, \infty)$. Here is an example of Hirsch and Smale's, which shows that this may be the case even when the function $F(\cdot)$ is differentiable (Hirsch and Smale 1974, p. 171).

E 14.3 Suppose that $n = 1$ and let $F(y) = 1 + y^2$, $y \in R_{++}$. Then consider the equation

$$\frac{dy}{dt} = 1 + y^2.$$

A solution to this equation is of the form

$$y(t; \xi, x) = \tan(t - c),$$

where c is a constant determined by the values of ξ and x. Such a solution cannot be extended over an interval larger than $(c - (\pi/2), c + (\pi/2))$ since $y(t; \xi, x)$ tends to $\pm\infty$ as t tends to $c \pm (\pi/2)$.

According to UT 14 and the properties of $z(\cdot)$ there is, for each $(\xi, \bar{p}) \in R_+ \times R^n_{++}$, a continuous solution to equation 14.3 that passes through $\bar{p}$ at $t = \xi$ and is defined on some maximal interval (α, β). In T 14.7–T 14.8 below we demonstrate that $\beta = \infty$.

It is awkward to write $p(\cdot; \xi, \bar{p})$ for a solution to equation 14.3. Hence in the sequel we shall say that "$p(\cdot)\colon (\alpha, \beta) \to R^n_{++}$ is a solution to equation 14.3 through $(\xi, \bar{p})$" if $\xi \in (\alpha, \beta)$ and $p(t) = p(t; \xi, \bar{p})$ for all $t \in (\alpha, \beta)$.

T 14.7 Suppose that $p(\cdot)\colon (\alpha, \beta) \to R^n_{++}$ is a solution to equation 14.3 through $(0, \bar{p}) \in R_+ \times R^n_{++}$. Then, for all $t \in (\alpha, \beta)$, $p(t) \cdot p(t) = \bar{p} \cdot \bar{p}$.

Hence a solution to equation 14.3 that begins on the sphere $\{p \in R^n_{++} : p \cdot p = \bar{p} \cdot \bar{p}\}$ stays on the sphere for all $t \in (\alpha, \beta)$. The proof is easy: Since $pz(p) = 0$ for all $p \in R^n_{++}$,

$$\sum_{i=1}^{n} p_i(t) \frac{dp_i(t)}{dt} = 0, \qquad t \in (\alpha, \beta).$$

Hence there is a constant k such that, for all $t \in (\alpha, \beta)$, $p(t) \cdot p(t) = k$. Evidently $k = \bar{p} \cdot \bar{p}$.

T 14.8 Suppose that $p(\cdot): (\alpha, \beta) \to R^n_{++}$ is a solution to equation 14.3 through $(0, \bar{p}) \in R_+ \times R^n_{++}$. If (α, β) is the maximal interval corresponding to $(0, \bar{p})$, $\beta = \infty$.

The proof goes as follows: Suppose that $\beta < \infty$, that $p^0 \in R^n_+$ is a limit point of $p(t)$ as t approaches β, and that $p^0_i = 0$ for some i. Moreover, let $M \in R_{++}$ be such that $\|z(p)\| \leqslant M$ for all $p \in R^n_+ - \{0\}$, and suppose that $\alpha < t < u < \beta$. Then (see equations 14.7)

$$\| p(u) - p(t)\| \leq \int_t^u \|z(p(s))\| \, ds \leqslant M(u - t).$$

From these inequalities it follows that if t_k, $k = 1, 2, \ldots,$ is a sequence of points in (α, β) that tend to β, then the corresponding p sequence, $p(t_k)$, $k = 1, 2, \ldots,$ is a Cauchy sequence.[2] Consequently, p^0 must be the only limit point of $p(t)$ as t tends to β. But if that is the case, $p^0_i = 0$ is an impossibility since then for t close enough to β, $z_i(p(t)) > 0$.

Suppose that $p(\cdot): R_+ \to R^n_{++}$ is a solution to equation 14.3 through $(0, \bar{p}) \in \{0\} \times R^n_{++}$. If $z(\bar{p}) = 0$, $p(t) = \bar{p}$ for all $t \in R_+$. If $z(\bar{p}) \neq 0$, there may or may not exist a $p^0 \in R^n_{++}$ such that $z(p^0) = 0$ and such that $\lim_{t \to \infty} p(t) = p^0$. We give evidence of this fact in E 14.4 and E 14.5.

E 14.4 Consider the consumers in E when $n = 2$, and let $r = p_2/p_1$, $g(r) = z_2(1, r)$, and $c^2 = \bar{p} \cdot \bar{p}$. Then $-rg(r) = z_1(1, r)$ and

$$\frac{dr}{dt} = c^{-1}(1 + r^2)^{3/2} g(r). \tag{14.10}$$

Since $g(\cdot)$ is continuous on R_{++}, positive for small r, and negative for large r, it is easy to verify that Walras's conjecture holds for this economy; i.e., for each $\bar{r} \in R_{++}$ there is an $r^0 \in R_{++}$ such that $g(r^0) = 0$ and such that if $r(\cdot): R_+ \to R_{++}$ is a solution to equation 14.10, through $(0, \bar{r}) \in R_+ \times R_{++}$, then $\lim_{t \to \infty} r(t) = r^0$. (This observation is due to Arrow and Hurwicz; theorem 6, 1958, p. 541.)

We may conclude from the preceding example that Walras's conjecture is valid for a two-commodity exchange economy. However, it is invalid for a three-commodity economy, as can be seen from an example by H. Scarf, E 14.5. In reading this example, note that the $V^i(\cdot)$ do not satisfy H 6. I have simplified the structure of the utility function only for simplicity's sake. A more elaborate example can be found in Scarf 1960 (pp. 163–172).

E 14.5 Consider a three-commodity, three-consumer economy in which the consumers' utility functions and initial resources are given by

$$V^1(x) = \min(x_1, x_2), \quad x \in R^3_+, \quad \text{and } \omega^1 = (1, 0, 0);$$
$$V^2(x) = \min(x_2, x_3), \quad x \in R^3_+, \quad \text{and } \omega^2 = (0, 1, 0); \text{ and}$$
$$V^3(x) = \min(x_1, x_3), \quad x \in R^3_+, \quad \text{and } \omega^3 = (0, 0, 1).$$

Assume that $\overline{p} \cdot \overline{p} = 3$ and that $\overline{p}_1 \cdot \overline{p}_2 \cdot \overline{p}_3 \neq 1$. Then

$$z(p) = \left(-\frac{p_2}{p_1 + p_2} + \frac{p_3}{p_1 + p_3}, \frac{p_1}{p_1 + p_2} - \frac{p_3}{p_2 + p_3}, \frac{p_2}{p_2 + p_3} - \frac{p_1}{p_1 + p_3} \right).$$

It is easy to verify that $p = (1, 1, 1)$ is the only equilibrium price on the sphere $\{p : p \cdot p = 3\}$, and that a solution to equation 14.3 through $(0, \overline{p}) \in R_+ \times R^3_{++}$ satisfies $p(t) \cdot p(t) = \overline{p} \cdot \overline{p}$ and $p_1(t) \cdot p_2(t) \cdot p_3(t) = \overline{p}_1 \cdot \overline{p}_2 \cdot \overline{p}_3$. Hence, for this economy Walras's conjecture is false.

From E 14.5, it follows that the consumers' utility functions must satisfy stronger conditions than H 6 for Walras's conjecture to be valid in E. Various conditions have been suggested (see, for instance, Karlin 1959, pp. 312–313). In T 14.9 I suggest an additional condition on $z(\cdot)$. This condition would be satisfied in E if we could find positive constants a_{ij} and a strictly concave function, $U(\cdot)\colon R_+ \to R_+$ such that

$$V^i(x_1, \ldots, x_n) = \sum_{j=1}^{n} a_{ij} U(x_j), \qquad i = 1, \ldots, m.$$

The theorem is due to K. Arrow and L. Hurwicz (1960, p. 640), the proof to Bent Birkeland.

T 14.9 Suppose that $p(\cdot)\colon R_+ \to R^n_{++}$ is a solution to equation 14.3 through $(0, \overline{p}) \in \{0\} \times R^n_{++}$. Suppose also that, for all $p^* \in R^n_{++}$ and $p \in \{p \in R^n_+ : p \cdot p = \overline{p} \cdot \overline{p}\}$, if $z(p^*) = 0$, $p^* z(p) > 0$ unless $z(p) = 0$. Then there is a $p^0 \in R^n_{++}$ such that $z(p^0) = 0$ and $\lim_{t \to \infty} p(t) = p^0$.

To prove T 14.9 we pick a $p^* \in R^n_{++}$ such that $p^* \cdot p^* = \overline{p} \cdot \overline{p}$ and $z(p^*) = 0$. Moreover, we let $V(p)\colon R^n_{++} \to R_+$ be defined by $V(p) = \| p - p^* \|^2$ and observe that $dV(p(t))/dt = -2p^* z(p(t))$, $t \in R_{++}$. Hence either $z(\overline{p}) = 0$ and $V(p(\cdot))$ is a constant or $V(p(\cdot))$ is a decreasing function of t in some maximal interval $[0, \alpha)$. If $z(\overline{p}) = 0$ or if $z(\overline{p}) \neq 0$ and $z(p(\alpha)) = 0$ for some finite α, there is nothing to prove. In the remainder of the proof we therefore assume that $\alpha = \infty$ and hence that $z(p(t)) \neq 0$ for all $t \in R_+$.

There is a sequence $t_k \in R_+$ such that $t_k + 1 \leqslant t_{k+1}$, $k = 1, 2, \ldots$, and such that $\lim_{k \to \infty} p^* z(p(t_k)) = \liminf_{t \to \infty} p^* z(p(t))$. Since the $p(t_k)$ are bounded, we can find a subsequence $p(t_{k_l})$ and a vector $p^0 \in \{p \in R^n_+ : p \cdot p = \overline{p} \cdot \overline{p}\}$ such that $p^0 = \lim_{k_l \to \infty} p(t_{k_l})$. The properties of $z(\cdot)$ and $p^* \in R^n_{++}$ then imply that $\liminf_{t\to\infty} p^*z(p(t)) = p^*z(p^0)$ as well. We shall show that $z(p^0) = 0$. From that and the properties of $z(\cdot)$, it follows that $p^0 > 0$.

Suppose that $z(p^0) \neq 0$ and let $\delta = p^*z(p^0)$. Moreover, let n_0 be so large that, for all $t \geqslant t_{n_0}$, $p^*z(p(t)) > \delta/2$. Then, for all $k_l > n_0$,

$$\begin{aligned} V(p(t_{k_{l+1}})) &= V(p(t_{k_l})) + \int_{t_{k_l}}^{t_{k_{l+1}}} \frac{dV(p(t))}{dt}\, dt \\ &\leqslant V(p(t_{k_l})) - \delta(t_{k_{l+1}} - t_{k_l})/2 \\ &\leqslant V(p(t_{n_0})) - \delta(t_{k_{l+1}} - t_{n_0})/2. \end{aligned}$$

But this is impossible, since $V(p) \geqslant 0$ for all $p \in R_+^n$ and $\lim_{k_l\to\infty} t_{k_{l+1}} = \infty$; consequently, the hypothesis $z(p^0) \neq 0$ is untenable.

The preceding arguments demonstrate that at least one of the limit points of $p(t)$ is an equilibrium point. Next we shall show that $p(t)$ has only one limit point as t tends to infinity.

Let p^0 be as above and suppose that p^1 is a limit point of $p(t)$ as t tends to ∞. Suppose also that $p^0 \neq p^1$ and let the sequences t_k^0 and t_l^1 be such that $t_k^0 + 1 \leqslant t_{k+1}^0$ and $t_l^1 + 1 \leqslant t_{l+1}^1$, $k, l = 1, 2, \ldots$, and such that

$$\lim_{k\to\infty} p(t_k^0) = p^0 \qquad \text{and} \qquad \lim_{l\to\infty} p(t_l^1) = p^1.$$

Since $z(p^0) = 0$ and $p^0 \neq \overline{p}$, $\partial(\| p(t) - p^0 \|^2)/\partial t < 0$ for all $t \in R_+^n$. Consequently, for every t_k^0 and $t_l^1 > t_k^0$,

$$\| p(t_k^0) - p^0 \|^2 \geqslant \| p(t_l^1) - p^0 \|^2.$$

But this is impossible, since

$$\lim_{k\to\infty} \| p(t_k^0) - p^0 \|^2 = 0 \qquad \text{and} \qquad \lim_{l\to\infty} \| p(t_l^1) - p^0 \|^2 = \| p^1 - p^0 \|^2.$$

Thus the assumption $p^1 \neq p^0$ is untenable.

In the preceding proof we used T 14.1 to claim the existence of a $p^* \in \{p \in R_{++}^n : p\cdot p = \overline{p}\cdot\overline{p}\}$ such that $z(p^*) = 0$. Then we showed (1) that a solution $p(\cdot)$ to equation 14.3 through $(0, \overline{p})$ has one and only one limit point p^0 as t tends to ∞ and (2) that $z(p^0) = 0$. The uniqueness of p^0 is remarkable. To see why, it suffices to observe that p^0 need not equal p^* and to note that if $p^0 \neq p^*$ and $p^\lambda = \lambda p^0 + (1 - \lambda)p^*$ for some $\lambda \in (0, 1)$, then the equality

$$p^\lambda z(p^\lambda) = \lambda p^0 z(p^\lambda) + (1 - \lambda)p^* z(p^\lambda)$$

and the conditions of T 14.9 imply that $z(p^\lambda) = 0$. From this and the continuity of $z(\cdot)$, it follows that if A^E denotes the set of competitive equilibrium prices in $\{p \in R^n_{++} : p \cdot p = \bar{p} \cdot \bar{p}\}$ and if

$$B = \left\{ p \in R^n_{++} : \sum_{i=1}^{n} p_i = 1 \text{ and } p = a\tilde{p} \text{ for some } a \in R_{++} \text{ and } \tilde{p} \in A^E \right\},$$

then B is closed and convex. This observation is due to Arrow and Hurwicz (1960, pp. 640).

An excess demand function $z(\cdot)$ which satisfies the conditions of T 14.9 is said to satisfy the Weak Axiom of revealed preference with respect to the prices in A^E. To understand why, suppose that $p^* \in A^E$ and that $p \in \{p \in R^n_{++} : p \cdot p = \bar{p} \cdot \bar{p}\} - A^E$. Then $pz(p) \geqslant pz(p^*)$ and—if the conditions of T 14.9 are satisfied—$p^*z(p^*) < p^*z(p)$ in accordance with the Weak Axiom. It is therefore interesting that $z(\cdot)$ will satisfy the Weak Axiom if all commodities are *gross substitutes,* i.e., if for all pairs $p^0, p^1 \in R^n_{++}$ such that $p^0 \neq \lambda p^1$ for all $\lambda \in R_{++}$, $p^0 \leqslant p^1$ and $p_i^0 = p_i^1$, $i \in N \subset \{1, \ldots, n\}$, imply that $z_i(p^0) < z_i(p^1)$ for all $i \in N$. For a proof of this fact, I refer the reader to Arrow, Block, and Hurwicz (1959, pp. 90–93).

In this context it is also interesting to note that if all commodities are gross substitutes, there is only one competitive equilibrium price in A^E. To show why, we suppose that $p^0, p^1 \in A^E$ and that $p^0 \neq p^1$. Then there is a $k \in \{1, \ldots, n\}$, a $\lambda \in R_{++}$ and a $\hat{p} \in R^n_{++}$ such that

$$\frac{p_k^0}{p_k^1} = \min_{i \in \{1, \ldots, n\}} \frac{p_i^0}{p_i^1}$$

and such that $\hat{p} = \lambda p^1$ and $\hat{p}_k = p_k^0$. But if this is so and if all commodities are gross substitutes, $\hat{p} \leqslant p^0$ and $z_k(\hat{p}) < z_k(p^0)$, which is impossible, since $z(p^0) = 0$ and $z(\hat{p}) = z(\lambda p^1) = z(p^1) = 0$.

The preceding theorem gives sufficient conditions so that even an incompetent auctioneer can carry out his job in E. As long as he quotes prices in accordance with equation 14.3, it does not matter where in R^n_{++} he starts out. Eventually his quotes will zero in on a competive equilibrium price. If the auctioneer is clever and always picks his initial price vector close to an equilibrium price, we can provide weaker sufficient conditions that enable him to successfully search for a competitive equilibrium price—see T 14.10.

T 14.10 Suppose that $p^0 \in R^n_{++}$ and that $z(p^0) = 0$. Suppose also that the $z^i(\cdot)$ are twice differentiable in an open neighborhood U of p^0. Finally, suppose that $\partial z_i(p^0)/\partial p_j > 0$ for all $i \neq j$, $j = 1, \ldots, n$, and for all $p \in U$. There is an open neighborhood $\tilde{U}$ of p^0 such that $\tilde{U} \subset U$ and such that if $(0, \bar{p}) \in \{0\} \times \tilde{U}$ and if $p(\cdot)$: $R_+ \to R^n_{++}$ is a solution to equation 14.3 through $(0, \bar{p})$, then $\lim_{t \to \infty} p(t) = p^0$.

If $\partial z_i(p)/\partial p_j > 0$ in E for all $i \neq j$ and all $p \in R^n_{++}$, the commodities in E are gross substitutes. The theorem insists that, if the commodities in E are gross substitutes in a neighborhood of p^0, the clever auctioneer in E will eventually find p^0. A proof of the theorem is given in Karlin 1959 (pp. 308–310). The first step in the proof consists in showing that there is an open neighborhood of p^0 in which $p^0 z(p) > 0$ for all p such that $p \neq \lambda p$ for all $\lambda \in R_{++}$. The second step is an analogue of our proof of T 14.9. Since the first step is rather involved, I omit the proof of T 14.10 and refer the reader to Karlin's proof for details.

14.3.2 Concluding Remarks

The arguments of sections 14.1–14.3 cannot be used to justify an economist's belief in free trade and the possibility of achieving a socially optimal resource allocation by once-and-for-all lump-sum tax-subsidy schemes. However, when a market-conditioned relationship of the type referred to in our scenario for exchange in E is discovered in reality, our discussion of consumer behavior in E makes the characteristic features of this relationship pragmatically clear. To that extent we have been successful in establishing the nomological adequacy of our scenario.

14.4 Temporary Equilibria in an Exchange Economy

We sketched our scenario of commodity exchange with the intended interpretation of T(H 1–H 6) in mind. Since the commodities in that interpretation are undated and taken to be available in the current period, it was easy to envision the consumers in E meeting in a market to exchange commodities at competitive equilibrium prices.

When we interpret T(H 1–H 6) the way it was done in chapter 11, the scenario is still objectively possible, since we can take w_1^i to be consumer i's possession of current commodities and w_t^i to be his claims on period-t commodities. Then the consumers in E meet in the market to exchange current commodities and claims on future commodities at competitive equilibrium prices.

From a nomological point of view, the last vision of consumer behavior in E is troublesome because it involves so many futures markets. Therefore, in this section I shall describe and establish the objective possibility of a scenario in which the consumers in E during each period meet to exchange current commodities and claims on units of the next-period unit of account at competitive equilibrium prices.[3] In sections 14.5 and 14.6 we discuss how adequate such a scenario is from a nomological point of view.

14.4.1 Consumption-Investment Strategies

With the promised scenario in mind I begin by characterizing an E consumer's current-period consumption-investment strategies. For that purpose we let $(V(\cdot), X, w)$ be one of the consumers in E and we suppose that $n = k \cdot N$. We also write $w = (w_1, \ldots, w_N)$ and $x = (x_1, \ldots, x_N)$, where $w_t \in R^k_{++}$ and $x_t \in R^k_+$, $t = 1, \ldots, N$. Finally, we let $R_{-1} = \{y \in R: -1 < y\}$ and introduce $W \in R^{N-1}$, $r_1 \in R_{-1}$, $p_1 \in R^k_{++}$, $r^e = (r^e_2, \ldots, r^e_{N-1})$ and $p^e = (p^e_2, \ldots, p^e_N)$, where $r^e_t \in R_{-1}$, $t = 2, \ldots, N-1$, and $p^e_t \in R^k_{++}$, $t = 2, \ldots, N$. In the intended interpretation of these symbols, x_t is a commodity bundle that is available in period t, and w_t is the initial commodity bundle that the consumer will receive in period t. Moreover, p_1 is the current price of x_1, p^e_t denotes the price of x_t that the consumer expects to face in period t, r_1 is the current-period interest rate, and r^e_t denotes the interest rate that the consumer expects to face in period t. Finally, W_t, $t = 1, \ldots, N-1$, denotes a security, each unit of which represents a claim on one unit of the $(t+1)$-period unit of account.

When we adopt the interpretation of w, x, W, r_1, p_1, r^e, and p^e given above, we can write the consumer's budget constraint as a sequence of N pairs of constraints:

$$p_1 x_1 + (1 + r_1)^{-1} W_1 \leqslant p_1 w_1$$

$$p^e_2 x_2 + (1 + r^e_2)^{-1} W_2 \leqslant p^e_2 w_2 + W_1$$

$$\vdots$$

$$p^e_{N-1} x_{N-1} + (1 + r^e_{N-1})^{-1} W_{N-1} \leqslant p^e_{N-1} w_{N-1} + W_{N-2} \qquad (14.11)$$

and

$$p^e_N x_N \leqslant p^e_N w_N + W_{N-1}$$

These constraints are interlocked so that the consumer will never borrow more than he is certain of being able to pay back; i.e., if, for $t = 2, \ldots, N-1$,

$$A_t(p^e, r^e, w^+) = \left\{ x \in R : x \geqslant -p^e_t w_t - \sum_{s=1}^{N-t} \left(\prod_{j=0}^{s-1} (1 + r^e_{t+j})^{-1} \right) p^e_{t+s} w_{t+s} \right\},$$

and if

$$A_N(p^e, r^e, w^+) = \{x \in R : x \geqslant -p_N^e w_N\},$$

where $w^+ = (w_2, \ldots, w_N)$, then $(x, W) \in R_+^{kN} \times R^{N-1}$ satisfies the inequalities in equation (14.11) only if $W_t \in A_{t+1}(p^e, r^e, w^+)$, $t = 1, \ldots, N-1$.

For a given vector (p_1, p^e, r_1, r^e, w), the consumer will search for a vector that maximizes his utility subject to the constraints in 14.11; i.e., he will attempt to solve the maximum problem,

$$\max_{(y,u) \in \Gamma(p_1, p^e, r_1, r^e, w)} V(y_1, \ldots, y_N), \tag{14.12}$$

where

$$\Gamma(p_1, p^e, r_1, r^e, w) = \{(x, W) \in R_+^{kN} \times R^{N-1} : (x, W) \text{ satisfies the inequalities in equation 14.11}\}.$$

If $((x_1, W_1), \ldots, (x_{N-1}, W_{N-1}), x_N)$ solves the maximum problem in equation 14.12, we can think of (x_1, W_1) as the vector of commodities and securities that the consumer will purchase in the current period at (p_1, r_1), and think of (x_t, W_t) and x_N as the vectors that the consumer plans to purchase in period t at (p_t^e, r_t^e) and in period N at p_N^e, respectively. Thus we can interpret the solution of the maximum problem in equation 14.12 as the consumer's *consumption-investment strategy at* (p_1, p^e, r_1, r^e, w).

The relationship between consumption-investment strategies and consumption bundles is interesting—to wit T 14.11.

T 14.11 Let $p = (p_1, \ldots, p_N)$, where $p_t \in R_{++}^k$, $t = 1, \ldots, N$, and suppose that

$$p_2 = (1 + r_1)^{-1} p_2^e$$

and (14.13)

$$p_t = (1 + r_1)^{-1} \left(\prod_{s=2}^{t-1} (1 + r_s^e)^{-1} \right) p_t^e, \qquad t = 3, \ldots, N.$$

In addition, let $c = (c_1, \ldots, c_N)$ and suppose that c is the consumption bundle at (p, pw). Then there is a vector $W \in R^{N-1}$ so that $((c_1, W_1), \ldots, (c_{N-1}, W_{N-1}), c_N)$ maximizes $V(\cdot)$ in $\Gamma(p_1, p^e, r_1, r^e, w)$. Conversely, if for some vector (p_1, p^e, r_1, r^e, w), $((x_1, W_1), \ldots, (x_{N-1}, W_{N-1}), x_N)$ solves the maximum problem in equation 14.12, then $(x_1, \ldots, x_N)$ is the consumer's consumption bundle at (p, pw) when p is as described in equation 14.13.

The proof of this theorem is easy, so I leave it to the reader.

14.4.2 The Current-Period Utility Function

So much for consumption-investment strategies. Next we shall construct a function that we can use to characterize our consumer's ordering of

(x_1, W_1) pairs. To do that I must introduce notation for some new sets and functions. First the sets:

$$\tilde{\Gamma}_N(W_{N-1}, p^e, r^e, w^+) = \{y \in R_+^k : p_N^e y \leqslant p_N^e w_N + W_{N-1}\}$$

and, for $t = 2, \ldots, N-1$,

$$\tilde{\Gamma}_t(W_{t-1}, p^e, r^e, w^+)$$
$$= \{(y, u) \in R_+^k \times A_{t+1}(p^e, r^e, w^+) : p_t^e y + (1 + r_t^e)^{-1} u \leq p_t^e w_t + W_{t-1}\},$$

where the $A_t(\cdot)$ are as described on pages 295–296 above. Next the functions:

$$F_1(x_1, \ldots, x_{N-1}, W_{N-1}; p^e, r^e, w^+) = \max_{y \in \tilde{\Gamma}_N(W_{N-1}, p^e, r^e, w^+)} V(x_1, \ldots, x_{N-1}, y)$$

and, for $s = 2, \ldots, N-2$,

$$F_s(x_1, \ldots, x_{N-s}, W_{N-s}; p^e, r^e, w^+)$$
$$= \max_{(y,u) \in \tilde{\Gamma}_{N-s+1}(W_{N-s}, p^e, r^e, w^+)} F_{s-1}(x_1, \ldots, x_{N-s}, y, u; p^e, r^e, w^+).$$

Then a theorem, T 14.12.

T 14.12 For each vector $(p^e, r^e, w^+) \in R_{++}^{k(N-1)} \times R_{-1}^{N-1} \times R_{++}^{k(N-1)}$, let $F(\cdot; p^e, r^e, w^+) : R_+^k \times A_2(p^e, r^e, w^+) \to R_+$ be defined by

$$F(x_1, W_1; p^e, r^e, w^+) = \max_{(y,u) \in \tilde{\Gamma}_2(W_1, p^e, r^e, w^+)} F_{N-2}(x_1, y, u; p^e, r^e, w^+).$$

Then $F(\cdot; p^e, r^e, w^+)$ is well defined, continuous, strictly increasing, and strictly quasi-concave.

We shall show that $F_1(\cdot; p^e, r^e, w^+)$ is well defined, continuous, strictly increasing, and strictly quasi-concave. Then a simple inductive argument suffices to establish the required properties of $F(\cdot; p^e, r^e, w^+)$. This part of the proof I leave to the reader. The continuity of $V(\cdot)$ and $p_N^e \in R_{++}^k$ imply that $F_1(\cdot; p^e, r^e, w^+)$ is well defined on $R_+^{k(N-1)} \times A_N(p^e, r^e, w^+)$. Also, the monotonicity and strict quasi-concavity of $V(\cdot)$, the linearity in y and W_{N-1} of the constraints in $\tilde{\Gamma}_N(W_{N-1}, p^e, r^e, w^+)$, and the fact that $W_{N-1}^0 < W_{N-1}^1$ entails $\tilde{\Gamma}_N(W_{N-1}^0, p^e, r^e, w^+) \subset$ (and $\neq$) $\tilde{\Gamma}_N(W_{N-1}^1, p^e, r^e, w^+)$ imply that $F_1(\cdot; p^e, r^e, w^+)$ is strictly increasing and strictly quasi-concave. Finally, with only obvious modifications, the arguments we used in the proof of T 10.5 to establish the continuity of the demand function can also be used to ascertain that the y which maximizes $V(x_1, \ldots, x_{N-1}, \cdot)$ in $\tilde{\Gamma}_N(W_{N-1}, p^e, r^e, w^+)$ varies continuously with p_N^e, $p_N^e w_N + W_{N-1}$ and x_1, $\ldots$, x_{N-1}. From this and the continuity of $V(\cdot)$ follows the continuity of $F_1(\cdot; p^e, r^e, w^+)$.

$F(\cdot;p^e,r^e,w^+)$ is the function we shall use to characterize our consumer's ordering of (x_1,W_1) pairs. To aid the reader's intuition and for later reference I give some examples of $F(\cdot;p^e,r^e,w^+)$ functions below.

E 14.6 Suppose that $n = 3$ and $m = 2$. Suppose also that there is one first-period commodity x and two second-period commodities y and z. Finally suppose that

$$V^1(x,y,z) = \sqrt{xy} + z, \qquad w^1 = (\bar{x}^1, \bar{y}, 0)$$

and

$$V^2(x,y,z) = \sqrt{x} - e^{-\sqrt{yz}}, \qquad w^2 = (\bar{x}^2, 0, \bar{z}).$$

If we drop the arguments p^e, r^e, and w^+ and assume that, for both consumers, $(p_y^e, p_z^e) = (1, 1)$, then

$$F^1(x,W_1) = \max_{\{(y,z)\in R_+^2 : y+z\leq \bar{y}+W_1\}} \sqrt{xy} + z$$
$$= \begin{cases} x/4 + \bar{y} + W_1 & \text{for } W_1 \geq -\bar{y},\ x < 4(\bar{y} + W_1) \\ \sqrt{x}\sqrt{(y + W_1)} & \text{for } W_1 \geq -\bar{y},\ x \geq 4(\bar{y} + W_1) \end{cases}$$

and

$$F^2(x,W_1) = \max_{\{(y,z)\in R_+^2 : y+z\leq \bar{z}+W_1\}} \sqrt{x} - e^{-\sqrt{yz}}$$
$$= \sqrt{x} - e^{-(\bar{z}+W_1)/2} \quad \text{for } x \in R_+ \text{ and } W_1 \geq -\bar{z}.$$

For each choice of (x_1,W_1), $F(x_1,W_1;p^e,r^e,w^+)$ records the maximum utility which the consumer can expect to obtain during the N periods of his planning horizon. To make this idea precise, I let

$$\Gamma_t(W_{t-1},p^e,r^e,w^+) = \{(y,u) \in R_+^{k(N-t+1)} \times R^{N-t} : p_t^e y_1 + (1 + r_t^e)^{-1}u_1$$
$$\leq p_t^e w_t + W_{t-1}, \ldots, p_{N-1}^e y_{N-t} +$$
$$(1 + r_{N-1}^e)^{-1}u_{N-t} \leq p_{N-1}^e w_{N-1} + u_{N-t-1},$$
$$\text{and } p_N^e y_{N-t+1} \leq p_N^e w_N + u_{N-t}\}$$

for $t = 2, \ldots, N-1$. Then $\Gamma_2(W_1,p^e,r^e,w^+)$ contains the vectors in $R_+^{k(N-1)} \times R^{N-2}$ which, for a given W_1, satisfy the last $N-1$ inequalities in equation 14.11; and my assertion concerning the values of $F(\cdot)$ can be stated as in T 14.13.

T 14.13 Let $F(\cdot)$ be the $F(\cdot)$ of T 14.12 and let the $\Gamma_t(\cdot)$ be as defined above. Then, for $(p^e,r^e,w^+) \in R_{++}^{k(N-1)} \times R_{-1}^{N-1} \times R_{++}^{k(N-1)}$ and $(x_1,W_1) \in R_+^k \times A_2(p^e,r^e,w^+)$,

$$F(x_1,W_1;p^e,r^e,w^+) = \max_{(y,u)\in\Gamma_2(W_1,p^e,r^e,w^+)} V(x_1,y). \tag{14.14}$$

To prove the theorem we show that

$$F_2(x_1,\ldots,x_{N-2},W_{N-2};p^e,r^e,w^+) = \max_{(y,u)\in\Gamma_{N-1}(W_{N-2},p^e,r^e,w^+)} V(x_1,\ldots,x_{N-2},y), \quad (14.15)$$

where $\Gamma_{N-1}(W_{N-2},p^e,r^e,w^+)$ contains the vectors in $R_+^{2k} \times R$ which, for a given W_{N-2}, satisfy the last two inequalities in equation 14.11. An easy inductive argument then suffices to establish equation 14.14. I leave that part of the proof to the reader. The proof of equation 14.15 goes as follows: Let $(y^0,z^0,W_{N-1}^0) \in R_+^{2k} \times R$ be such that

$$F_2(x_1,\ldots,x_{N-2},W_{N-2};p^e,r^e,w^+) = F_1(x_1,\ldots,x_{N-2},y^0,W_{N-1}^0;p^e,r^e,w^+)$$
$$= V(x_1,\ldots,x_{N-2},y^0,z^0). \quad (14.16)$$

Also, let $(y^*,z^*,W^*) \in R_+^{2k} \times R$ be the solution to the maximum problem in equation 14.15. Then $(y^0,z^0,W_{N-1}^0) \in \Gamma_{N-1}(W_{N-2};p^e,r^e,w^+)$, $z^* \in \tilde{\Gamma}_N(W^*,p^e,r^e,w^+)$ and $(y^*,W^*) \in \tilde{\Gamma}_{N-1}(W_{N-2},p^e,r^e,w^+)$, where $\tilde{\Gamma}_N(\cdot)$ and $\tilde{\Gamma}_{N-1}(\cdot)$ are as defined on p. 297 at the beginning of this section. But if that is so, then

$$V(x_1,\ldots,x_{N-2},y^0,z^0) \leqslant V(x_1,\ldots,x_{N-2},y^*,z^*)$$
$$\leqslant F_1(x_1,\ldots,x_{N-2},y^*,W^*;p^e,r^e,w^+)$$
$$\leqslant F_2(x_1,\ldots,x_{N-2},W_{N-2};p^e,r^e,w^+).$$

From this and from equation 14.16 follows the validity of equation 14.15.

The justification for using $F(\cdot;p^e,r^e,w^+)$ as our consumer's utility indicator of (x_1,W_1) pairs in $R_+^k \times A_2(p^e,r^e,w^+)$ is an easy corollary from the last two theorems. We record this justification in T 14.14, the proof of which is left to the reader.

T 14.14 Let $F(\cdot;p^e,r^e,w^+)$ be as in T 14.12 and T 14.13 and let

$$\hat{\Gamma}(p_1,p^e,r_1,r^e,w) = \{(y,u) \in R_+^k \times A_2(p^e,r^e,w^+) : p_1 y + (1+r_1)^{-1}u \leqslant p_1 w_1\}.$$

In addition, for a given vector (p_1,p^e,r_1,r^e,w), let $((x_1,W_1)^0,\ldots,(x_{N-1},W_{N-1})^0,x_N^0)$ be the consumer's consumption-investment strategy, i.e., the vector that maximizes $V(\cdot)$ in the $\Gamma(p_1,p^e,r_1,r^e,w)$ of equation 14.12. Then $(x_1,W_1)^0$ is the unique solution to

$$\max_{(x_1,W_1)\in\hat{\Gamma}(p_1,p^e,r_1,r^e,w)} F(x_1,W_1;p^e,r^e,w^+) \quad (14.17)$$

Conversely, if, for some vector (p_1,p^e,r_1,r^e,w), $(x_1,W_1)^*$ solves the maximum problem in equation 14.17, then there is a vector $((x_2,W_2),\ldots,(x_{N-1},W_{N-1}),x_N)$ such that $((x_1,W_1)^*,(x_2,W_2),\ldots,(x_{N-1},W_{N-1});x_N)$ maximizes $V(\cdot)$ in the

$\Gamma(p_1, p^e, r_1, r^e, w)$ of equation 14.12. Finally, if p is as defined in equation 14.13 relative to p_1, r_1, p^e, and r^e, then $(x_1, W_1)^*$ solves the maximum problem in equation 14.17 if and only if there is a vector $(c_2, \ldots, c_N) \in R_+^{k(N-1)}$ such that $(x_1^*, c_2, \ldots, c_N)$ is the consumer's consumption bundle at (p, pw).

14.4.3 Current-Period Temporary Equilibria

With T 14.14 in mind, we can envision the manner in which E consumers will behave in a market in which they may trade only in currently available commodities and securities. We begin by discussing behavior in the current period. Let $F^i(\cdot)$ and $(p^e, r^e, w^+)^i$ be the $F(\cdot)$ and the (p^e, r^e, w^+) of T 14.12 corresponding to the ith consumer. Furthermore, for each $i = 1, \ldots, m$, let

$$A^i = A_2((p^e, r^e, w^+)^i)$$

and let $\tilde{V}^i(\cdot)\colon R_+^k \times A^i \to R$ be defined by

$$\tilde{V}^i(x_1, W_1) = F^i(x_1, W_1; (p^e, r^e, w^+)^i).$$

Finally, let

$$\hat{E} = ((\tilde{V}^1(\cdot), R_+^k \times A^1, w_1^1), \ldots, (\tilde{V}^m(\cdot), R_+^k \times A^m, w_1^m)).$$

In the intended interpretation, $\hat{E}$ is an exchange economy that is populated by E consumers with utility functions $\tilde{V}^i(\cdot)$, sets of available commodities and securities $R_+^k \times A^i$, and initial resources w_1^i.

The consumers in $\hat{E}$ form a market to exchange commodities and securities. At any quoted price $(p_1, (1 + r_1)^{-1})$ they offer their initial commodity bundle in exchange for their consumption bundle of commodities and securities. They will be able to carry out their preferred trades if and only if the vector of consumption bundles in $\hat{E}$ represents an allocation in $\hat{E}$. Such an allocation is a vector, $((x_1, W_1)^1, \ldots, (x_1, W_1)^m)$, that satisfies the conditions:

ÊA 1 $(x_1, W_1)^i \in R_+^k \times A^i, \qquad i = 1, \ldots, m$; and

ÊA 2 $\sum_{i=1}^{m} (x_1, W_1)^i = (w_1, 0).$

A vector of consumption bundles at (p_1, r_1) will satisfy ÊA 1 and ÊA 2 if and only if (p_1, r_1) is a competitive equilibrium price. Such prices exist—to wit T 14.15.

T 14.15 There exists a competitive equilibrium in $\hat{E}$; i.e., there exists a vector $((p_1, r_1), (x_1, W_1)^1, \ldots, (x_1, W_1)^m)$ satisfying the following conditions:

(i) $(p_1, r_1) \in R^k_{++} \times R_{-1}$;

(ii) $((x_1, W_1)^1, \ldots, (x_1, W_1)^m)$ is an allocation;

(iii) $p_1 x_1^i + (1 + r_1)^{-1} W_1^i \leqslant p_1 w_1^i, \qquad i = 1, \ldots, m$; and

(iv) $\tilde{V}^i((x_1, W_1)^i) = \max_{(y,u) \in \Gamma^i(p_1, r_1, w_1^i)} \tilde{V}^i(y, u), \qquad i = 1, \ldots, m$

where $\Gamma^i(p_1, r_1, w_1^i) = \{(y, u) \in R^k_+ \times A^i : p_1 y + (1 + r_1)^{-1} u \leqslant p_1 w_1^i\}$.

With obvious modifications, the proof of T 14.1 can be used to establish the validity of T 14.15. I leave the details to the reader.

The existence of a competitive equilibrium in $\hat{E}$ justifies the scenario for $\hat{E}$ described above. Unfortunately, a competitive equilibrium in $\hat{E}$ is just a *temporary equilibrium for E*, since it only affects the distribution of E's first-period initial resources. Therefore, in order to justify using our vision of consumer behavior in $\hat{E}$ as a scenario for the first-period behavior of consumers in E, we must establish the existence of a sequence of temporary equilibria that allocates all the resources of E. This will be done in T 14.16.

14.4.4 Feasible Sequences of Temporary Equilibria

A temporary equilibrium in E during period t affects both the distribution of purchasing power and the consumers' ordering of commodity bundles in period $t + 1$. For example, if consumer i in period 1 consumed x_1^i and invested in W_1^i, in period 2 his utility indicator is $V^i(x_1^i, \cdot)$, his purchasing power equals $p_2 w_2^i + W_1^i$, and his $F(\cdot)$ function is $F_{N-2}(x_1^i, \cdot; p^e, r^e, w^+)$. Note that the conditions imposed on a temporary equilibrium in T 14.15 put restrictions on current exchanges of goods and securities but make no demands on price expectations. Moreover, the conditions do not insist that the consumers' consumption-investment strategies be mutually consistent. Inconsistent plans cannot all be carried out in later periods.

E 14.7 Consider the economy of E 14.6 and suppose that $\overline{x}^1 = \overline{x}^2 = \overline{y} = \overline{z} = 2$. Suppose also that consumer 1 starts out in periode 1 with a debt of $\tilde{x}^1$ units of x to consumer 2. If $\tilde{x}^1 = 2.52$, the vector

$$(p_x, r_1, (x_1, W_1)^1, (x_1, W_1)^2) = (1, 1.849, 0, -1.48, 4, 1.48)$$

is a temporary equilibrium in period 1. If $\tilde{x}^1 = 2.98$, there is no pair (p_x, r_1) at which consumer 2 would be willing to lend consumer 1 enough so that he could settle his first-period debt. This is true, moreover, regardless of consumer 1's future financial resources.

It follows from E 14.7 that, should the consumers in E during the current period arrive at a temporary equilibrium at which one consumer borrows funds from another, in the next period there need not exist a temporary equilibrium for E. The example also shows that whether the E economy in a given period will succeed in establishing an equilibrium without anyone being bankrupt, depends not just on the period's distribution of initial endowments of commodities and securities and the future earning power of the individual debtors, but also on the preferences of the individual creditors. Finally, the example illustrates that in E as in real life a consumer will not be forced into *bankruptcy* in a given period just because his net worth is negative.

A feasible sequence of temporary equilibria in E is a set

$$\{((p_t, r_t), (x_t, W_t)^1, \ldots, (x_t, W_t)^m),\ t = 1, \ldots, N-1, \text{ and } (p_N, x_N^1, \ldots, x_N^m)\}$$

such that, for each $t = 1, \ldots, N-1$, $((p_t, r_t), (x_t, W_t)^1, \ldots, (x_t, W_t)^m)$ is a temporary equilibrium in period t relative to the distribution of purchasing power $(p_t w_t^1 + W_{t-1}^1, \ldots, p_t w_t^m + W_{t-1}^m)$, and such that $(p_N, x_N^1, \ldots, x_N^m)$ is a competitive equilibrium relative to $(p_N w_N^1 + W_{N-1}^1, \ldots, p_N w_N^m + W_{N-1}^m)$. Such a sequence of temporary equilibria exists in E—see T 14.16.

T 14.16 There is a set of price expectations (p^e, r^e) which, if shared by all consumers, ensures the existence of a feasible sequence of temporary equilibria in E.

To establish this theorem we first let $(p, x^1, \ldots, x^m)$ be a competitive equilibrium in E and define (p^e, r^e) by $r_t^e = (\|p_{t+1}\|/\|p_t\|) - 1$, $t = 2, \ldots, N-1$, $p_2^e = (1 + r_1)p_2$ and $p_t^e = (1 + r_1)p_t \cdot \prod_{j=2}^{t-1}(1 + r_j^e)$, $t = 3, \ldots, N$, where $r_1 = (\|p_2\|/\|p_1\|) - 1$. Then (p^e, r^e) and (p, r_1) satisfy equation 14.13. Hence, for each $i = 1, \ldots, m$, we can find a vector $W^i \in R^{N-1}$ such that $((x_1, W_1)^i, \ldots, (x_{N-1}, W_{N-1})^i, x_N)$ maximizes $V^i(\cdot)$ subject to the inequalities in equation 14.11, with w_t replaced by w_t^i, $t = 1, \ldots, N$. The monotonicity of $V^i(\cdot)$ implies that, for the given vector, equality holds in equation 14.11. This fact and simple algebra suffice to show that, for each $t = 1, \ldots, N-1$, with $W_0^i = 0$, $i = 1, \ldots, m$,

(i) $(x_t, W_t)^i \in R_+^k \times A_{t+1}((p^e, r^e, w^+)^i)$, $\quad i = 1, \ldots, m$; and

(ii) $\sum_{i=1}^{m} (x_t, W_t)^i = (w_t, 0)$.

But, if that is so, then T 14.14 implies that $((p_1, r_1), (x_1, W_1)^1, \ldots, (x_1, W_1)^m)$ is a temporary equilibrium in period 1. Furthermore, the proofs of T 14.12 and T 14.13 and repeated use of the appropriate analogue of T 14.14 suffice to show that $((p_t^e, r_t^e), (x_t, W_t)^1, \ldots, (x_t, W_t)^m)$ and $(p_N^e, x_N^1, \ldots, x_N^m)$, respectively, are temporary equilibria in period t and N relative to the respective distributions of purchasing power $(p_t^e w_t^1 + W_{t-1}^1, \ldots, p_t^e w_t^m + W_{t-1}^m)$, $t = 2, \ldots, N-1$, and $(p_N^e w_N^1 + W_{N-1}^1, \ldots, p_N^e w_N^m + W_{N-1}^m)$. I leave the details to the reader.

In reading T 14.16 and the proof sketched above, observe that the consumers in E enter the first period without debts and that the price expectations are defined as belonging to $R_{++}^{k(N-1)} \times R_{-1}^{N-1}$. Observe also that the consumers' plans for future acquisitions of commodities and securities associated with each and every temporary equilibrium of the sequence are mutually consistent. Finally, observe that in each period the price expectations of consumers are validated and their plans are carried out. The last two properties are not intrinsic to feasible sequences of temporary equilibria. It is possible to have a feasible sequence of temporary equilibria with the property that consumer price expectations agree but the plans of consumers are always inconsistent. Along such a sequence, plans must be revised in each period , and consumer' price expectations are not validated.

E 14.8 Suppose that $n = 3$ and $m = 2$. Suppose also that there is one first-period commodity x and two second-period commodities y and z. Finally suppose that

$$w^1 = (2.14/3, 1.14, 1), \qquad w^2 = (3, 1, 0),$$

$$V^1(x, y, z) = -(1/3)e^{-3x} - e^{-(5+2\sqrt{yz})} \quad \text{on } R_+^3,$$

$$V^2(x, y, z) = -e^{-(5+x)} - (1/3)e^{-6\sqrt{yz}} \quad \text{on } R_+^3,$$

and $(p_y^e, p_z^e) = (1, 1)$ for both consumers. Then

$$F^1(x, W) = -(1/3)e^{-3x} - e^{-(7.14+W)} \quad \text{on } R_+ \times \{u: u \geqslant -2.14\},$$

and

$$F^2(x, W) = e^{-(5+x)} - (1/3)e^{-3(1+W)} \quad \text{on } R_+ \times \{u: u \geqslant -1\},$$

where W is a security, each unit of which will pay one unit of z the next period.

In this economy there are three possible temporary equilibria in the first period:

TE$_1$ $(p_x, (1+r)^{-1}, (x, W)^1 (x, W)^2) = (1, 0.169, (1.075, -2.14), (2.64, 2.14))$;

TE$_2$ $(p_x, (1+r)^{-1}, (x, W)^1, (x, W)^2) = (1, 1, (1.963, -1.25), (1.75, 1.25))$; and

TE$_3$ $(p_x, (1+r)^{-1}, (x, W)^1, (x, W)^2) = (1, 5.904, (2.854, -0.36), (0.86, 0.36))$.

If TE$_1$ obtained during the first period, the next period the consumers would not be able to find a temporary equilibrium in which consumer 1 could pay back his debt to consumer 2. Consequently, if TE$_1$ obtained, consumer 1 would be forced to declare bankruptcy during the second period. If TE$_2$ obtained in the first period, then in period 2.

TE$_2^*$ $(p_y, p_z, (y, z)^1, (y, z)^2) = ((1/2.14), 1, (0.3, 0.14), (1.84, 0.86))$

would be the one and only one temporary equilibrium relative to $(\hat{w}^1, \hat{w}^2) = ((1.14, -0.25), (1, 1.25))$. If TE$_3$ obtained during the first period, then in period 2

$\mathbf{TE}_3^*$ $(p_y, p_z, (y,z)^1, (y,z)^2) = ((1/2.14), 1, (1.25, 0.59), (0.89, 0.41))$

would be the one and only one temporary equilibrium relative to $(w^1, w^2) = ((1.14, 0.64), (1, 0.36))$.

From the preceding it follows that in E there are two feasible sequences of temporary equilibria,

$\{TE_2, TE_2^*\}$ and $\{TE_3, TE_3^*\}$.

In both of them price expectations are not validated and purchase plans for the second period must be revised.

14.5 Admissible Allocations and Temporary Equilibria

If we are to discuss the optimality of sequences of temporary equilibria, I must introduce the concept of an admissible allocation. For each $t = 1, \ldots, N-1$, let $B_t = \{(y,u) \in R_+^{km} \times A_{t+1}((p^e, r^e, w^+)^1) \times \cdots \times A_{t+1}((p^e, r^e, w^+)^m): \sum_{i=1}^m (y,u)^i = (w_t, 0)\}$ and let $x^i(t)$ denote consumer i's consumption of commodities in periods $s = 1, \ldots, t-1$. Then the set of admissible allocations in period t, Q_t, is defined as follows:

$$Q_t = \{(y,u) \in B_t : \exists \text{no}(z,v) \in B_t \text{ such that } F_t^i(x^i(t), z^i, v^i; (p^e, r^e, w^+)^i) \geqslant F_t^i(x^i(t), y^i, u^i; (p^e, r^e, w^+)^i) \text{ for all } i = 1, \ldots, m, \text{ with strict inequality for at least one } i\}$$

This set varies with $x^i(t)$ and $(p^e, r^e, w^+)^i$, $i = 1, \ldots, m$. However, since these vectors are data in period t, we write Q_t rather than $Q_t(x^1(t), (p^e, r^e, w^+)^1, \ldots, x^m(t), (p^e, r^e, w^+)^m)$ to simplify our notation.

It is obvious from the definition of Q_t that T 14.17 must be true.

T 14.17 In E, a temporary equilibrium in period t is admissible.

It is also obvious (see our discussion of T 14.4 and 14.6) that, once the consumers in E have arrived at a temporary equilibrium in period t, trading ceases. This is so even if, at the given temporary equilibrium, consumers' plans for future acquisitions of commodities and securities are inconsistent.

Theorem T 14.17 explicates the sense in which a temporary-equilibrium allocation cannot be improved upon. Next we shall see if the allocation of commodities over time, which a feasible sequence of temporary equilibria achieves, can be improved upon. It cannot if this allocation is Pareto-optimal. Hence we ask: Is an allocation of commodities which a feasible sequence of temporary equilibria prescribes necessarily Pareto-optimal? The answer is "no," as evidenced by E 14.9.

E 14.9 Consider the economy of E 14.8. The feasible sequences $\{TE_2, TE_2^*\}$ and $\{TE_3, TE_3^*\}$ do no allocate commodities Pareto-optimally. That this is a fact can be seen from the following simple calculations and a standard theorem of welfare economics:

$$(\partial V^1/\partial x/\partial V^1/\partial y)(1.96, 0.3, 0.14) = 0.91 \neq 3.25$$
$$= (\partial V^2/\partial x/\partial V^2/\partial y)(1.75, 1.84, 0.86)$$

and

$$(\partial V^1/\partial x/\partial V^1/\partial y)(2.85, 1.25, 0.59) = 0.23 \neq 0.16$$
$$= (\partial V^2/\partial x/\partial V^2/\partial y)(0.86, 0.89, 0.41)$$

Sufficient conditions so that a feasible sequence of temporary equilibria allocates E's resources Pareto-optimally exist. One such set of conditions is given in T 14.18.

T 14.18 Consider a feasible sequence of temporary equilibria in E, $\{((p_t, r_t), (x_t, W_{t-1})^1, \ldots, (x_t, W_{t-1})^m), t = 1, \ldots, N-1$, and $(p_N, x_N^1, \ldots, x_N^m)\}$. Suppose that the consumers share the price expectations (p^e, r^e) and that these are validated in each period. Suppose also that the plans of consumers in E for future acquisitions of commodities and securities at each and every temporary equilibrium of the sequence are mutually consistent. Then the allocation of commodities that the sequence prescribes is Pareto-optimal.

To prove the theorem, we let $p_t^e = p_t$, $t = 2, \ldots, N$, and $r_t^e = r_t$, $t = 2, \ldots, N-1$; and we let $((y_1, u_1), \ldots, (y_{N-1}, u_{N-1}), y_N)$ be the vector that, for the given sequence of pairs (p_t, r_t) and w^i, maximizes $V^i(\cdot)$ subject to the inequalities in equation 14.11. Since consumer i's price expectations are validated in each period, it follows first from T 14.14 that $(y_1, u_1) = (x_1, W_1)^i$, and then by repeated use of the appropriate analogue of T 14.14 and the proofs of T 14.12 and T 14.13, that $(y_t, u_t) = (x_t, W_t)^i$ for $t = 2, \ldots, N-1$ and that $y_N = x_N^i$. Hence $((x_1, W_1)^i, \ldots, (x_{N-1}, W_{N-1})^i, x_N^i)$ maximizes $V^i(\cdot)$ subject to the inequalities in equation 14.11 with $p_t^e = p_t$, $t = 2, \ldots, N$, $r_t^e = r_t$, $t = 2, \ldots, N-1$, p_1, r_1, and w^i as given.

Next we shall show that $(p, x^1, \ldots, x^m)$ is a competitive equilibrium in E when p is as defined in equation 14.13. By T 14.14, x^i is consumer i's consumption bundle at (p, pw^i), $i = 1, \ldots, m$. The preceding results and the fact that consumers' plans are mutually consistent imply that $\sum_{i=1}^m x^i = w$. Hence $(p, x^1, \ldots, x^m)$ satisfies the conditions of a competitive equilibrium in E.

But, if $(p, x^1, \ldots, x^m)$ is a competitive equilibrium, then $(x^1, \ldots, x^m) \in Q$, as was to be shown.

The conditions of T 14.18 are not necessary in order that a feasible sequence of temporary equilibria allocate resources Pareto-optimally. However, if a sequence allocates resources Pareto-optimally, there is a way to adjust consumers' price expectations so that the conditions of T 14.8 are satisfied—to wit, T 14.19.

T 14.19 If $x \in Q$ there is a pair (p_1, r_1), a distribution of $p_1 w_1$, $(y^1, \ldots, y^m)$, and a pair of expected prices (p^e, r^e) such that, if the consumers in E share these price expectations, then the feasible sequence of temporary equilibria that is determined by (p_1, r_1, p^e, r^e) and $(y, w^+)^i$, $i = 1, \ldots, m$, prescribes the same allocation over time of commodities as x.

This theorem is an easy consequence of T 14.6 and the arguments we used to establish T 14.16. Therefore I leave the proof to the reader.

14.6 On the Stability of Temporary Equilibria

Our discussion of the stability of competitive equilibria applies verbatim to the stability of temporary equilibria. The only matter left to discuss is the stability of sequences of temporary equilibria. For the sake of intuition take a look at E 14.10.

E 14.10 Consider the two first-period temporary equilibria of the feasible sequences of E 14.8, $\{TE_2, TE_2^*\}$ and $\{TE_3, TE_3^*\}$. Are TE_2 and TE_3 "more" stable than TE_1, a temporary equilibrium that leads to a bankruptcy situation in period 2? The answer is "no!" If $p(\cdot): R_+ \to R_{++}^2$ is a solution to equation 14.3 that goes through $(0, (1, \overline{r}))$, where $(1, \overline{r})$ is either in a small neighborhood of the price vector p^1 of TE_1 or p^3 of TE_3, $p(t)$ converges to p^1 or p^3, as the case may be. If $(1, \overline{r})$ belongs to a neighborhood of p^2, the price of TE_2, $p(t)$ will move away from p^2 as t increases.

The feasible sequences of temporary equilibria of E 14.8 did not allocate commodities according to the prescription of a Pareto-optimal allocation of E's resources. So a question arises: Might a Pareto-optimal sequence of temporary equilibria be as unstable as other feasible sequences of such equilibria? The answer is "yes," as witnessed by E 14.11.

E 14.11 Suppose that $n = 3$, $m = 2$, and that the consumers in E have the utility function of the consumers in E 14.8. Also assume that $w^1 = (2.14/3, 1.30, 0.84)$, $w^2 = (3, 0.27, 0.73)$ and $(p_y^e, p_z^e)^i = (1, 1)$, $i = 1, 2$. In this economy TE_1, TE_2, and TE_3 of E 14.8 are the first-period temporary equilibria. If TE_1 obtained,

TE_1^{**} $((p_y, p_z), (y, z)^1, (y, z)^2) = ((1, 1), (0, 0), (1.57, 1.57))$

would be the one, and only one, temporary equilibrium in period 2. If TE_2 obtained

TE_2^{**} $((p_y, p_z), (y, z)^1, (y, z)^2) = ((1, 1), (0.445, 0.445), (1.125, 1.125))$

would be the one, and only one, temporary equilibrium in period 2. If TE_3 obtained

$$\mathbf{TE_3^{**}} \quad ((p_y, p_z), (y_2, z_1)^1, (y, z)^2) = ((1, 1), (0.89, 0.89), (0.68, 0.68))$$

would be the one, and only one, temporary equilibrium in period 2.

The feasible sequences $\{TE_1, TE_1^{**}\}$, $\{TE_2, TE_2^{**}\}$, and $\{TE_3, TE_3^{**}\}$ allocate E's resources Pareto-optimally. Moreover, TE_1 and TE_3 are (locally) stable temporary equilibria, and TE_2 is a (locally) unstable temporary equilibrium.

In closing our discussion of the stability of temporary equilibria, it is interesting to observe the following: If the consumers in E were moving along a Pareto-optimal sequence of temporary equilibria and by some miscalculation of the auctioneer veered off it in period t, they would in most cases end up at a temporary equilibrium at which their plans for future acquisitions of goods and securities would be inconsistent. Since these plans obviously could not be carried out in subsequent periods, one might wonder if the consumers could be persuaded to move back on to the original Pareto-optimal sequence by informing them about the inconsistency of their plans. The answer is an emphatic "no!" Theorem T 14.17 explains why.

IV

Probability Theory: Chance, Ignorance, and Choice

15 The Measurement of Probable Things

In part IV we use the axiomatic method to develop certain aspects of probability theory that are of particular interest to economists and econometricians. I begin by introducing the notions of an experiment and a random variable. Then I present G. Shafer's theory of belief functions and show that such functions are efficient means to analyze the import of evidence and to represent beliefs in situations in which the idea of intrinsic probabilities of events is unintelligible. Finally, we discuss A. Kolmogorov's axiomatization of probability and describe ways in which probability distributions can be used to characterize the behavior of sequences of random variables.

Probability is an undefined term with many interpretations. In one situation the probability of an event A, $P(A)$, may represent an individual's subjective measure of the likelihood that A will occur. In another situation, $P(A)$ may denote the frequency with which A is expected to occur in repeated trials of a given experiment. Whether and when $P(A)$ can be interpreted as the chance of A occurring is, however, a matter of scholary dispute (see Allais 1983, pp. 35–65). Therefore, in chapter 16 we search for an empirical characterization of chance that can settle the matter for us. This search involves studying properties of sample paths of purely random processes and delineating several classes of gambling systems. At the end, we arrive at a resolution of the controversy that is due to A. Church.

Which is the best way to represent ignorance of intrinsic probabilities is another matter of scholarly dispute. In chapter 17 we use the axiomatic method to model ignorance. We begin by discussing S. Laplace's use of the Principle of Insufficient Reason to assign probabilities to events whose intrinsic probabilities are not known and cannot be known by reason alone. Then we axiomatize the concept of information and the concept of uncertainty and demonstrate that in the situations Laplace considered, his probabilities maximize our measure of uncertainty.

Mechanical application of Laplace's principles can have both uncomfortable and paradoxical consequences. The paradoxes arise in Bayesian statistical inference because of an inappropriate relationship between prior probabilities and the associated likelihood function. G. Box and G. Tiao believe that we can avoid such paradoxical situations if we measure ignorance of the intrinsic probabilities of the events of a given experiment, not absolutely in the manner of Laplace, but relative to the information which one or more performances of the experiment would provide. At the end of chapter 17 we discuss Box and Tiao's interesting idea and contrast their assignment of prior probabilities with the corresponding assignment of Laplace.

Bayesian econometricians, whether inspired by Laplace or Box and Tiao, analyze their data as if they were generated by exchangeable random processes. Such processes have many interesting characteristics, some of which we discuss in chapter 18. I begin by describing the salient properties of sequences of exchangeable random variables on ordinary probability spaces. Then I present A. Rényi's theory of conditional probability spaces and demonstrate how this theory can be used to formalize the use of improper priors in econometrics. Finally, I develop a theory of exchangeable processes on conditional probability spaces and state and prove an interesting theorem of H. P. McKean's concerning the "large-sample" properties of such processes. The latter theorem fills a fundamental lacuna in the theory of Bayesian statistical inference.

In chapter 19 I conclude our discussion of probability by presenting L. J. Savage's theory of choice under uncertainty. We begin with the axioms and relate them to the structural properties of utility functions described in chapter 11. Then I state Savage's expected-utility theorem and suggest ways to modify the theorem so that it can be applied to situations in which there are only finitely many states of the world. Finally we discuss (1) how Savage's theory can be used to elicit subjective probabilities, (2) whether existing tests of the expected-utility hypothesis constitute valid tests of Savage's theory, and (3) how the risk preferences of Savage's decision maker might differ from the risk preferences of a person whose subjective probabilities are superadditive. The results we obtain concerning risk preferences and superadditive probabilities fill a fundamental lacuna in Shafer's theory of belief functions.

15.1 Experiments and Random Variables

"The probable" or "probable things" has been given various definitions in the history of thought. Aristotle claimed that "the probable is that which for the most part happens" (Hacking 1975, p. 17). Thomas Aquinas insisted that a probable thing is an opinion which is approved by upright authorities (Hacking 1975, pp. 22–23). And Kant suggested that the probable was "that which, if it were held as truth, would be more than half certain" (von Mises 1951, p. 12). For us here, a *probable thing* is the outcome of an experiment.

An *experiment* is a pair $(\Omega, \mathscr{F})$, where Ω denotes a set of objects, the *outcomes* of the experiment, and where $\mathscr{F}$ denotes a collection of subsets of Ω called *events*.

15.1.1 Events

I shall always insist that the family $\mathscr{F}$ of events satisfies EX 1 and EX 2.

EX 1 $\Omega \in \mathscr{F}$; and

EX 2 If $A, B \in \mathscr{F}$, then $A \cup B \in \mathscr{F}$ and $A - B \in \mathscr{F}$.

Families of sets with these properties are called *fields*. They are closed under complementation and finite unions and intersections—see T 15.1.

T 15.1 If $A \in \mathscr{F}$, $A^c \in \mathscr{F}$, where $A^c = \Omega - A$. In addition, if $A_i \in \mathscr{F}$, $i = 1, \ldots, n$, $\bigcup_{i=1}^{n} A_i \in \mathscr{F}$.

Many experiments in real life can be given a mathematical representation as a pair $(\Omega, \mathscr{F})$. Such a representation is never uniquely determined.

E15.1 A blindfolded man is to pull one ball from an urn with fifty red balls and fifty white balls. In this case we may choose $(\Omega, \mathscr{F})$ so that Ω denotes the set of balls in the urn and $\mathscr{F}$ denotes the family of all subsets of Ω.

E 15.2 It is soccer season. Each week any Norwegian can bet on the outcomes of twelve soccer games being played at different locations in England. For each match there are three possible outcomes: the home team wins, H, the visiting team wins, V, or there is a tie, U. The games are numbered from 1 to 12. In this case we may choose $(\Omega, \mathscr{F})$ so that Ω denotes the set of all sequences of twelve letters taken from the triple (H, V, U); $\mathscr{F}$ denotes the family of all subsets of Ω.

In the two examples, $\mathscr{F}$ contains all subsets of Ω. This is not always so; and for some purposes we must insist that $\mathscr{F}$ satisfies a third condition, EX 3, to make sure that $\mathscr{F}$ contains enough sets.

EX 3 If $A_i \in \mathscr{F}$, $i = 1, 2, \ldots$, then $\bigcup_{i=1}^{\infty} A_i \in \mathscr{F}$.

If $\mathscr{F}$ satisfies EX 1–EX 3, it is closed under complementation and countable unions. It is also closed under countable intersections, as can be seen from the relation $(\bigcup_{i=1}^{\infty} A_i)^c = (\bigcap_{i=1}^{\infty} A_i^c)$.

I shall often insist that our experiments satisfy EX 3 in addition to EX 1 and EX 2. It is, therefore, important to note that EX 1–EX 3 are meaningful (i.e., noncontradictory) conditions. The family of all subsets of Ω satisfies them. Note also that the consequence of imposing EX 3 need not consist of trivial mathematical generalities. E 15.3 brings home this fact.

E15.3 Let Ω denote the set of real numbers and suppose that $\mathscr{F}$ contains all subsets of Ω that are either bounded left-closed, right-open intervals or are finite unions of such sets. If $\mathscr{F}$ satisfies EX 1–EX 3, it must also contain all open intervals, all closed intervals, and all denumerable subsets of Ω.

A family $\mathscr{F}$ that satisfies EX 1–EX 3 is called a *σ field.*

If $\mathscr{F}$ and $\mathscr{G}$ are families of subsets of Ω, their intersection $(\mathscr{F} \cap \mathscr{G})$ consists of all sets that are members of both $\mathscr{F}$ and $\mathscr{G}$. Similarly, if I is an index set, and if, for all $\alpha \in I$, $\mathscr{F}_\alpha$ is a family of subsets of Ω, then $\bigcap_{\alpha \in I} \mathscr{F}_\alpha$ consists of all sets that are members of each and every $\mathscr{F}_\alpha$. If $\mathscr{F}$, $\mathscr{G}$, and the $\mathscr{F}_\alpha$'s are σ fields, $(\mathscr{F} \cap \mathscr{G})$ and $\bigcap_{\alpha \in I} \mathscr{F}_\alpha$ are σ fields as well. From this and from the fact that the family of all subsets of Ω is a σ field, it follows that if $\mathscr{S}$ is a class of subsets of Ω, there is a smallest σ field that contains $\mathscr{S}$, namely, the intersection of all the σ fields that contain $\mathscr{S}$. When Ω is the set of real numbers and $\mathscr{F}$ is the smallest σ field that contains all subsets of Ω that are bounded left-closed, right-open intervals, an event is then called a *Borel set* and $\mathscr{F}$ is referred to as the *Borel field* in Ω. If Ω is a Borel set (e.g., $\Omega = [0, 1]$), the collection of subsets of Ω which are Borel sets is a σ field. We refer to this collection also as the *Borel field in* Ω.

15.1.2 Random Variables

If $\mathscr{F}$ and $\mathscr{G}$ are σ fields of subsets of Ω such that $\mathscr{F} \subset \mathscr{G}$, $\mathscr{F}$ is called a *sub-σ field of $\mathscr{F}$*. Sub-σ fields arise in many contexts. Some of these are important to us: Suppose that $(\Omega, \mathscr{F})$ is an experiment satisfying EX 1–EX 3, and let $f(\cdot)$ be a real-valued function on Ω; i.e., $f(\cdot): \Omega \to R$. Furthermore, let $\mathscr{F}(f)$ denote the smallest σ field that contains all sets of the form

$$\{\omega \in \Omega : f(\omega) < a\}, \qquad a \in R.$$

Then $\mathscr{F}(f)$ is called the *σ field generated by* $f(\cdot)$. This field may or may not be a sub-σ field of $\mathscr{F}$. If it is, $f(\cdot)$ is a *random variable.*

When $f(\cdot)$ and $g(\cdot)$ are random variables, we let $\mathscr{F}(f,g)$ denote the σ field generated by $f(\cdot)$ and $g(\cdot)$. It is the smallest σ field containing all sets of the form

$$\{\omega \in \Omega : f(\omega) < a, g(\omega) < b\}, \qquad a, b \in R.$$

Evidently, $\mathscr{F}(f,g) \subset \mathscr{F}$. Similarly, when for each $i = 1, 2, \ldots, f(i, \cdot)$ is a random variable, we let $\mathscr{F}(f(1), f(2), \ldots)$ denote the σ field generated by the $f(i, \cdot)$, $i = 1, 2, \ldots$. This field is the smallest σ field that contains all sets of the form

$$\{\omega: f(i_1, \omega) < a_{i_1}, \ldots, f(i_n, \omega) < a_{i_n}\},$$

where the a_{i_j} vary over all of R, and where $\{i_1, \ldots, i_n\}$ vary over all finite subsets of $\{1, 2, \ldots\}$ in such a way that $i_1 < i_2 < \cdots < i_n$. Again $\mathscr{F}(f(1), f(2), \ldots) \subset \mathscr{F}$.

There are many kinds of random variables on a fixed experiment $(\Omega, \mathscr{F})$. For instance, if $A \in \mathscr{F}$, the *indicator function of A*,

$$I_A(\omega) = \begin{cases} 1 & \text{if } \omega \in A \\ 0 & \text{otherwise} \end{cases}$$

is a random variable and $\mathscr{F}(I_A) = \{\phi, A, A^c, \Omega\}$. Similarly, if $a_1, \ldots, a_n$ are constants and $A_1, \ldots, A_n$ are disjoint events,

$$\sum_{i=1}^{n} a_i I_{A_i}(\omega), \qquad \omega \in \Omega$$

is a random variable. It is called a *simple function*, and the σ field it generates is the smallest σ field that contains all the A_i. Finally, if $g(\cdot): R \to R$ and if $\{x \in R : g(x) < a\}$ is a Borel set for all $a \in R$ and $f(\cdot)$ is a random variable, then $g(f(\cdot))$ is a random variable. In particular, if $g(\cdot)$ is a continuous, real-valued function on the range of $f(\cdot)$, then $g(f(\cdot))$ is a random variable.

15.1.3 Sequences of Events and Random Variables

Often we must study the limiting behavior of sequences of sets and sequences of random variables. We therefore conclude this section by defining and discussing some concepts that are relevant to that purpose. We begin with sets. Let $(\Omega, \mathscr{F})$ be an experiment that satisfies EX 1–EX 3, let $A_1, A_2, \ldots$ be a sequence of events, and let

$$\liminf A_n = \bigcup_{n=1}^{\infty} \bigcap_{k=n}^{\infty} A_k$$

and

$$\limsup A_n = \bigcap_{n=1}^{\infty} \bigcup_{k=n}^{\infty} A_k.$$

Then $\omega \in \bigcup_{n=1}^{\infty} \bigcap_{k=n}^{\infty} A_k$ if and only if there is an $n \geqslant 1$ such that $\omega \in \bigcap_{k=n}^{\infty} A_k$. Hence the lim inf of the given sequence consists of all outcomes that belong to all but a finite number of the A_k. From this and from $(\bigcup_{n=1}^{\infty} \bigcap_{k=n}^{\infty} A_k^c)^c = \bigcap_{n=1}^{\infty} \bigcup_{k=n}^{\infty} A_k$, it follows that the lim sup of the given sequence consists of all outcomes that belong to infinitely many of the A_k. For any m and all n, $\bigcap_{k=m}^{\infty} A_k \subset \bigcup_{k=n}^{\infty} A_k$. Consequently, $\liminf A_n \subset \limsup A_n$. We say that the sequence $A_1, A_2, \ldots$ converges to A if $\liminf A_n = \limsup A_n = A$. In that case we write $A = \lim A_n$.

Examples of convergent sequences are increasing sequences (with $A_i \subset A_{i+1}$ for all i) and decreasing sequences (with $A_{i+1} \subset A_i$ for all i). Their limits are, respectively, $\bigcup_{i=1}^{\infty} A_i$ and $\bigcap_{i=1}^{\infty} A_i$.

Suppose next that $f(1, \cdot), f(2, \cdot), \ldots$ is a sequence of random variables on $(\Omega, \mathscr{F})$, and let

$$\liminf f(n, \omega) = \sup_{n \geqslant 1} \inf_{k \geqslant n} f(k, \omega)$$

and

$$\limsup f(n, \omega) = \inf_{n \geqslant 1} \sup_{k \geqslant n} f(k, \omega).$$

Since

$$\sup_{k \geqslant n} f(k, \omega) = -\inf_{k \geqslant n} -f(k, \omega)$$

and

$$\left\{\omega \in \Omega : \inf_{k \geqslant n} f(k, \omega) < a\right\} = \bigcup_{k=n}^{\infty} \{\omega \in \Omega : f(k, \omega) < a\},$$

it is clear that $\liminf f(n, \cdot)$ and $\limsup f(n, \cdot)$ are both random variables. We say that $f(n, \omega)$ *converges* to $f(\omega)$ if $\liminf f(n, \omega) = \limsup f(n, \omega) = f(\omega)$. If so, we write $f(\omega) = \lim f(n, \omega)$. The subset of Ω on which $f(n, \cdot)$ converges can easily be shown to belong to $\mathscr{F}$.

E 15.4 Let $(\Omega, \mathscr{F})$ be an experiment that satisfies EX 1–EX 3; let $x(\cdot)$ be a bounded nonnegative random variable; and define $x(n, \cdot)$ by

$$x(n, \omega) = \begin{cases} (i-1)/2^n & \text{if } (i-1)/2^n \leqslant x(\omega) < i/2^n, \quad i = 1, \ldots, 2^n n \\ n & \text{if } x(\omega) \geqslant n \end{cases} \tag{15.1}$$

for all $n = 1, 2, \ldots$. Then $x(n, \cdot)$ is a nonnegative simple function, $x(n, \omega) \leqslant x(n+1, \omega)$, $n = 1, 2, \ldots$, and

$$0 \leqslant x(\omega) - x(n, \omega) < 2^{-n}$$

whenever $x(\omega) < n$. For each ω there is an n_0 such that $x(\omega) < n$ for all $n \geqslant n_0$. Consequently, for all $\omega \in \Omega$,

$$x(\omega) = \lim x(n, \omega).$$

From this example we deduce T 15.2.

T 15.2 A bounded, nonnegative random variable can be approximated arbitrarily close by a simple function.

15.2 Belief Functions

To measure probable things means to assign numbers to the events in the associated experiment $(\Omega, \mathscr{F})$. An assignment of numbers to the members of $\mathscr{F}$ is a function from $\mathscr{F}$ to the set of real numbers. In order to theorize about such functions, we must impose some restrictions on them. In this section we discuss the consequences of a particular set of restrictions proposed by Glenn Shafer (1976, p. 38).

15.2.1 Basic Probability Assignments and Belief Functions

Shafer's conditions concern an experiment $(\Omega, \mathscr{F})$ and two functions $m(\cdot)$ and $\text{bel}(\cdot)$ on $\mathscr{F}$ to [0, 1]. In stating them we let $\mathscr{P}(\Omega)$ and $\sum_{A \subset B} f(A)$ denote, respectively, the family of all subsets of Ω and the sum of the values which $f(\cdot)$ assumes on the various subsets of B (including B).

GS 1 $\Omega = \{\omega_1, \ldots, \omega_n\}$;

GS 2 $\mathscr{F} = \mathscr{P}(\Omega)$;

GS 3 $m(\cdot): \mathscr{F} \to [0, 1]$;

GS 4 $m(\phi) = 0$;

GS 5 $\sum_{A \subset \Omega} m(A) = 1$;

GS 6 $\text{bel}(\cdot): \mathscr{F} \to [0, 1]$; and

GS 7 if $A \in \mathscr{F}$, $\text{bel}(A) = \sum_{B \subset A} m(B)$.

Shafer assumes GS 1 and GS 2 to simplify his presentation. He refers to

$m(\cdot)$ as the *basic probability assignment* and calls bel$(\cdot)$ the *belief function over* Ω.

There are many sorts of belief functions. Two are described in E 15.5 and E 15.6. The first is the *vacuous belief function* and the second is a *simple support function.*

E 15.5 Suppose that $(\Omega, \mathscr{F})$ satisfies GS 1 and GS 2, and define $m(\cdot)$ by $m(\Omega) = 1$ and $m(A) = 0$ for all events A such that $\sim[A = \Omega]$. Then bel$(\Omega) = 1$ and bel$(A) = 0$ for all events A such that $\sim[A = \Omega]$.

E 15.6 Suppose that $(\Omega, \mathscr{F})$ satisfies GS 1 and GS 2; let A be a proper non-empty subset of Ω; and define $m(\cdot)$ by $m(A) = s$, $m(\Omega) = 1 - s$, and $m(B) = 0$ for all events B such that $\sim[[B = A] \vee [B = \Omega]]$. Finally, assume that $0 < s < 1$. Then

$$\text{bel}(B) = \begin{cases} 0 & \text{if} \sim [A \subset B] \\ s & \text{if } [[A \subset B] \wedge \sim[B = \Omega]] \\ 1 & \text{if } [B = \Omega] \end{cases}$$

From the postulates it follows that bel$(\varnothing) = 0$ and bel$(\Omega) = 1$. Also, if A and B are disjoint subsets of Ω, the possibility that $m(\cdot)$ may assign a positive number to a set that is a union of subsets of A and B implies that

$$\text{bel}(A) + \text{bel}(B) \leqslant \text{bel}(A \cup B).$$

These observations correctly suggest the validity of T 15.3, which we state below without proof. In the statement of T 15.3 $|I|$ is taken to denote the number of elements in I. A proof of the theorem is given in Shafer (1976, p. 51).

T15.3 bel$(\varnothing) = 0$ and bel$(\Omega) = 1$. Moreover, if $A_i \in \mathscr{F}$, $i = 1, \ldots, k$,

$$\sum_{\substack{I \subset \{1,\ldots,k\} \\ \sim[I = \varnothing]}} (-1)^{|I|+1} \text{bel}\left(\bigcap_{i \in I} A_i\right) \leqslant \text{bel}\left(\bigcup_{i=1}^{k} A_i\right).$$

An equally interesting theorem concerning $m(\cdot)$ and bel$(\cdot)$ follows:

T 15.4 If $A \in \mathscr{F}$, $m(A) = \sum_{B \subset A} (-1)^{|(A-B)|} \text{bel}(B)$.

Thus $m(\cdot)$ can be recovered from bel$(\cdot)$, and bel$(\cdot)$ can be obtained from $m(\cdot)$. To establish T 15.4, we observe first that if A is a finite set and $B \subset A$, then

$$\sum_{B \subset C \subset A} (-1)^{|C|} = \begin{cases} (-1)^{|A|} & \text{if } A = B \\ 0 & \text{otherwise.} \end{cases}$$

From this fact it follows that

$$\sum_{B\subset A} (-1)^{|(A-B)|} \operatorname{bel}(B) = (-1)^{|A|} \sum_{B\subset A} (-1)^{|B|} \operatorname{bel}(B)$$

$$= (-1)^{|A|} \sum_{B\subset A} (-1)^{|B|} \sum_{C\subset B} m(C)$$

$$= (-1)^{|A|} \sum_{C\subset A} m(C) \sum_{C\subset B\subset A} (-1)^{|B|}$$

$$= m(A)$$

as was to be shown.

15.2.2 Orthogonal Sums of Belief Functions

In Shafer's interpretation of GS 1–GS 7, $m(A)$ measures the belief that is committed exactly to A, and $\operatorname{bel}(A)$ measures the total belief committed to A. We shall explicate the meaning of $m(\cdot)$ and $\operatorname{bel}(\cdot)$ by describing a certain hierarchy of classes of belief functions, and begin by showing in T 15.5 below how two belief functions on the same Ω can be combined to form a third belief function. In the statement of the theorem, A is a *focal element of* $bel_i(\cdot)$ if $m_i(A) > 0$.

T15.5 Suppose that $\operatorname{bel}_1(\cdot)$ and $\operatorname{bel}_2(\cdot)$ are belief functions over Ω, with basic probability assignments $m_1(\cdot)$ and $m_2(\cdot)$ and focal elements $A_1, \ldots, A_k$ and $B_1, \ldots, B_l$, respectively. Moreover, suppose that

$$\sum_{\substack{i,j\\(A_i\cap B_j)=\varnothing}} m_1(A_i)m_2(B_j) < 1.$$

Finally, let $m(\varnothing) = 0$ and

$$m(A) = \sum_{\substack{i,j\\(A_i\cap B_j)=A}} m_1(A_i)m_2(B_j) \Bigg/ \left[1 - \sum_{\substack{i,j\\(A_i\cap B_j)=\varnothing}} m_1(A_i)m_2(B_j)\right] \tag{15.2}$$

for all nonempty $A \in \mathscr{F}$; and let

$$(\operatorname{bel}_1 \circ \operatorname{bel}_2)(A) = \sum_{B\subset A} m(B). \tag{15.3}$$

Then $m(\cdot)$ is a basic probability assignment, and $(\operatorname{bel}_1 \circ \operatorname{bel}_2)(\cdot)$ is a belief function on Ω.

Since $m_i(\cdot)\colon \mathscr{F} \to [0, 1]$, $i = 1, 2$, it is obvious that the $m(\cdot)$ of equation (15.12) satisfies $m(A) \geqslant 0$ for all $A \in \mathscr{F}$. Hence to prove T 15.5 it suffices to show that the $m(A)$ add to 1. Let k denote the denominator in equation (15.2). Then

$$\sum_{A\subset\Omega} m(A) = m(\varnothing) + \sum_{\substack{A\subset\Omega\\ A\neq\varnothing}} m(A) = k^{-1} \sum_{\substack{A\subset\Omega\\ A\neq\varnothing}} \sum_{\substack{i,j\\ (A_i\cap B_j)=A}} m_1(A_i)m_2(B_j)$$

$$= k^{-1} \sum_{\substack{i,j\\ (A_i\cap B_j)=\varnothing}} m_1(A_i)m_2(B_j) = 1$$

as was to be shown.

When it exists, $(\mathrm{bel}_1 \circ \mathrm{bel}_2)(\cdot)$ is called the *orthogonal sum* of $\mathrm{bel}_1(\cdot)$ and $\mathrm{bel}_2(\cdot)$. Note, therefore, that $(\mathrm{bel}_1 \circ \mathrm{bel}_2)(\cdot) = (\mathrm{bel}_2 \circ \mathrm{bel}_1)(\cdot)$.

It follows from theorem T 15.5 that if $\mathrm{bel}_1(\cdot)$ is the vacuous belief function, then $(\mathrm{bel}_1 \circ \mathrm{bel}_2)(\cdot)$ reduces to $\mathrm{bel}_2(\cdot)$. If $\mathrm{bel}_1(\cdot)$ and $\mathrm{bel}_2(\cdot)$ are both simple support functions with focal elements A, Ω and B, Ω, respectively, several possibilities emerge.

Suppose first that

$$\sim[[(A\cap B) = \varnothing] \vee [[A\subset B] \vee [B\subset A]]] \tag{15.4}$$

and

$$m_1(A) = s_1 \qquad \text{and} \qquad m_2(B) = s_2, \tag{15.5}$$

where $0 < s_1,\ s_2 < 1$. In this case the denominator in equation 15.2 reduces to 1. Furthermore,

$$m(C) = \begin{cases} s_1 s_2 & \text{if } [C = (A\cap B)] \\ s_1(1-s_2) & \text{if } [C = A] \\ s_2(1-s_1) & \text{if } [C = B] \\ (1-s_1)(1-s_2) & \text{if } [C = \Omega] \\ 0 & \text{otherwise} \end{cases} \tag{15.6}$$

and

$$(\mathrm{bel}_1 \circ \mathrm{bel}_2)(C)$$

$$= \begin{cases} 0 & \text{if } \sim[(A\cap B)\subset C] \\ s_1 s_2 & \text{if } [[(A\cap B)\subset C] \wedge \sim[[A\subset C] \vee [B\subset C]]] \\ s_1 & \text{if } [[A\subset C] \wedge \sim[B\subset C]] \\ s_2 & \text{if } [[B\subset C] \wedge \sim[A\subset C]] \\ 1-(1-s_1)(1-s_2) & \text{if } [[(A\cup B)\subset C] \wedge \sim[C=\Omega]] \\ 1 & \text{if } [C=\Omega] \end{cases} \tag{15.7}$$

The situation envisaged in equations 15.6 and 15.7 can be illustrated with a case taken from the annals of Sherlock Holmes—see E 15.7.

E 15.7 Sherlock Holmes is investigating a burglary in a sweetshop. He discovers two pieces of evidence. One suggests that the thief was left-handed, the other that he was an insider. Let $\Omega = \{\text{LI}, \text{RI}, \text{LO}, \text{RO}\}$, where L and R and I and 0 are short for left- and right-handed and insider and outsider, respectively. Moreover, let $\mathscr{F}$ denote the set of all subsets of Ω. Then Holmes's evidence can be represented by two simple support functions, one focused on $A = \{\text{LI}, \text{LO}\}$ to the degree, say 1/3, and the other focused on $B = \{\text{LI}, \text{RI}\}$ to the degree, say 1/4. Consequently, Holmes's basic probability assignment and belief function over Ω will (in face of the total evidence) be given by equations 15.6 and 15.7, respectively, with $s_1 = 1/3$ and $s_2 = 1/4$.

Next let us replace equation 15.4 by

$$[A \cap B = \varnothing] \tag{15.8}$$

and leave equation 15.5 as is, with $0 < s_1 < 1$ and $0 < s_2 < 1$. In this case the denominator in equation 15.2 equals $(1 - s_1 s_2)$. Moreover,

$$m(C) = \begin{cases} s_1(1 - s_2)/(1 - s_1 s_2) & \text{if } [C = A] \\ s_2(1 - s_1)/(1 - s_1 s_2) & \text{if } [C = B] \\ (1 - s_1)(1 - s_2)/(1 - s_1 s_2) & \text{if } [C = \Omega] \\ 0 & \text{otherwise} \end{cases} \tag{15.9}$$

and

$$(\text{bel}_1 \circ \text{bel}_2)(C)$$

$$= \begin{cases} 0 & \text{if } {\sim}[[A \subset C] \vee [B \subset C]] \\ s_1(1-s_2)/(1-s_1 s_2) & \text{if } [[A \subset C] \wedge {\sim}[B \subset C]] \\ s_2(1-s_1)/(1-s_1 s_2) & \text{if } [[B \subset C] \wedge {\sim}[A \subset C]] \\ (s_1(1-s_2)+s_2(1-s_1))/(1-s_1 s_2) & \text{if } [[(A \cup B) \subset C] \wedge {\sim}[C = \Omega]] \\ 1 & \text{if } [C = \Omega] \end{cases} \tag{15.10}$$

A possible interpretaton of equations 15.9 and 15.10 is given in E 15.8.

E 15.8 A jury is to decide whether a criminal defendant, named Charles, is guilty. The jurors have heard one witness claim that Charles was visiting the witness's apartment at the time of the crime. The testimonies of the other witnesses and the circumstantial evidence gathered by the police attest to the guilt of the defendant. Let $\Omega = \{G, I\}$, where G and I stand for guilty and not guilty, respectively, and let $\mathscr{F}$ denote the family of all subsets of Ω. The conflicting evidence faced by the jury can be represented by two simple support functions, one focused on $A = \{I\}$ to the degree s_1, and the other focused on $B = \{G\}$ to the degree s_2, where (presumably) $0 < s^1 < \cdots < s_2 < 1$. Different jurors may assign different values to s_1 and s_2. Whatever these values—based on the total evidence—are, each juror's basic probability assignment and belief function over Ω ought to be given by equations 15.9 and 15.10.

15.2.3 Support Functions

Shafer calls the union of the focal elements of a belief function, bel$(\cdot)$, the *core of bel*$(\cdot)$. It is easy to see from the statement of T 15.5 that if $\text{bel}_1(\cdot)$ and $\text{bel}_2(\cdot)$ are belief functions over Ω, then their orthogonal sum will exist if and only if their cores have a nonempty intersection. This observation can be generalized—to wit T 15.6.

T 15.6 Let $\text{bel}_1(\cdot), \ldots, \text{bel}_k(\cdot)$ be belief functions over Ω with cores $C_1, \ldots, C_k$, respectively. Then the orthogonal sum

$$(((\ldots((\text{bel}_1 \circ \text{bel}_2) \circ \text{bel}_3)\ldots) \circ \text{bel}_{k-1}) \circ \text{bel}_k)(\cdot)$$

exists if and only if $\sim[\bigcap_{i=1}^{k} C_i = \varnothing]$. Moreover, when the orthogonal sum of $\text{bel}_1(\cdot), \ldots, \text{bel}_k(\cdot)$ exists, the sum is invariant under permutations of the order in which the $\text{bel}_j(\cdot)$ appear in the sum.

A belief function that is either a simple support function or an orthogonal sum of simple support functions is called a *separable support function.* We have shown that the orthogonal sum of a simple support function $\text{bel}_1(\cdot)$ and the vacuous belief function equals $\text{bel}_1(\cdot)$. It is also easy to show that if $\text{bel}_2(\cdot)$ is a simple support function focused on the same event A as $\text{bel}_1(\cdot)$, then the orthogonal sum of $\text{bel}_1(\cdot)$ and $\text{bel}_2(\cdot)$ is a simple support function focused on A. From this it follows that the decomposition of a separable support function into an orthogonal sum of simple support functions is never unique. The most we can assert is described in T 15.7.

T 15.7 If bel$(\cdot)$ is a nonvacuous separable support function with core C, there exists a unique collection $\text{bel}_1(\cdot), \ldots, \text{bel}_k(\cdot)$ of nonvacuous simple support functions such that

(i) $k \geqslant 1$;

(ii) each $\text{bel}_i(\cdot)$ is focused on a subset of C;

(iii) if $i \neq j$, $\text{bel}_i(\cdot)$ and $\text{bel}_j(\cdot)$ are focused on different subsets of C; and

(iv) $\text{bel}(\cdot) = \text{bel}_1(\cdot)$ if $k = 1$ and is the orthogonal sum of the $\text{bel}_i(\cdot)$ if $k > 1$.

Not all belief functions are separable support functions. One counterexample will be given in E 15.9. Others can be easily be constructed on the basis of T 15.8.

T 15.8 Suppose that bel(·) is a separable support function and that A and B are two of its focal elements. If $\sim[(A \cap B) = \varnothing]$, then $(A \cap B)$ is a focal element of bel(·).

To prove this theorem we proceed as follows: Suppose that $\text{bel}_j(\cdot)$, $j = 1, \ldots, n$ are belief functions with basic probability assignments $m_j(\cdot)$, $j = 1, \ldots, n$. Suppose also that $\text{bel}_1(\cdot) \circ \text{bel}_2(\cdot) \circ \cdots \circ \text{bel}_n(\cdot)$ exists and denote its basic probability assignment by $m(\cdot)$. Equation 15.2 and induction over n suffice to show for all nonempty $A \in \mathscr{F}$,

$$m(A) = \frac{\displaystyle\sum_{\substack{A_j \in \mathscr{F}, j=1,\ldots,n \\ A_1 \cap A_2 \cap \cdots \cap A_n = A}} m_1(A_1)m_2(A_2)\cdots m_n(A_n)}{\displaystyle\sum_{\substack{B_j \in \mathscr{F}, j=1,\ldots,n \\ B_1 \cap B_2 \cap \cdots \cap B_n \neq \varnothing}} m_1(B_1)m_2(B_2)\cdots m_n(B_n)}. \tag{15.11}$$

When the $\text{bel}_j(\cdot)$ are simple support functions focused, respectively, on A_j, $j = 1, \ldots, n$, equation 15.11 reduces to equation 15.12, where $s_j = m_j(A_j)$, $(1 - s_j) = m_j(\Omega)$, $j = 1, \ldots, n$, $\bar{I} = \{1, \ldots, n\} - I$, $\prod_{j \in \varnothing} s_j = \prod_{j \in \varnothing}(1 - s_j) = 1$ and $\bigcap_{i \in \varnothing} A_i = \Omega$:

$$m(A) = \frac{\displaystyle\sum_{\substack{I \subset \{1,\ldots,n\} \\ \bigcap_{j \in I} A_j = A}} \left(\prod_{j \in I} s_j\right)\left(\prod_{j \in \bar{I}} (1 - s_j)\right)}{\displaystyle\sum_{\substack{I \subset \{1,\ldots,n\} \\ \bigcap_{j \in I} A_j \neq \varnothing}} \left(\prod_{j \in I} s_j\right)\left(\prod_{j \in \bar{I}} (1 - s_j)\right)}. \tag{15.12}$$

From equation 15.12 it follows that if A and B are focal elements of $m(\cdot)$, there exists $I \subset \{1, \ldots, n\}$ and $J \subset \{1, \ldots, n\}$ such that $s_j < 1$ if $j \in \bar{I} \cup \bar{J}$ and

$$A = \bigcap_{j \in I} A_j \qquad \text{and} \qquad B = \bigcap_{j \in J} A_j.$$

Then $A \cap B = \bigcap_{j \in (I \cup J)} A_j$ and $s_j < 1$ if $j \in \overline{(I \cup J)}$. We conclude from this and from equation 15.12 that $m(A \cap B) > 0$ if $\sim[(A \cap B) = \varnothing]$.

A support function is a belief function whose core is assigned a positive basic probability number. (See Shafer's definition (1976, p. 142) and his Theorem 7.1 (p. 143).) The class of support functions contains all separable support functions. It also contains the belief function displayed in E 15.9 below.

E 15.9 Let $\Omega = \{a, b, c\}$ and let $\mathscr{F}$ denote the set of all subsets of Ω. Moreover, let s_1, s_2 be positive numbers whose sum is less than 1. Finally, let $m(\cdot)$ be a basic probability assignment satisfying

$$m(C) = \begin{cases} s_1 & \text{if } [C = \{a, b\}] \\ s_2 & \text{if } [C = \{b, c\}] \\ (1 - s_1 - s_2) & \text{if } [C = \Omega] \\ 0 & \text{otherwise} \end{cases}$$

The associated belief function is not a separable support function.

15.2.4 Additive versus Nonadditive Belief Functions

Shafer believes that the class of support functions might be large enough to represent the impact of evidence on any experiment satisfying GS 1 and GS 2 (see Shafer 1976, p. 144). However, we are not only interested in the representation of evidence, but also want to measure such varied probable things as "a game of roulette," "the weather in Canberra tomorrow," and "Bjørn Borg's chances of accomplishing the Grand Slam in tennis next year." When contemplating the assignment of numbers to the events of such experiments in accordance with GS 1–GS 7, we become intensely aware that belief functions need not be additive and that most support functions are not. Thus if a person informs us that the odds are 7 to 3 that it will rain in Canberra tomorrow, GS 1–GS 7 do not allow us to infer that the same person believes the odds to be 3 to 7 that it will not rain. For all we know, he may insist instead that the odds are 2 to 7.

A belief function $\text{bel}(\cdot): \mathscr{F} \rightarrow [0, 1]$ is *additive* if and only if, for all disjoint events A and B,

$$\text{bel}(A) + \text{bel}(B) = \text{bel}(A \cup B).$$

$\text{bel}(\cdot)$ is *nonadditive* if it is not additive.

There are scholars (e.g., Fellner 1961, pp. 610–689, and Ellsberg 1961, pp. 643–669) who believe that nonadditive belief functions are a characteristic feature of individual choice under uncertainty. They base their arguments on evidence such as that presented in E 15.10.

E 15.10 Two urns A and B contain 100 balls that are either red or white. There are fifty red balls in A, but nobody knows how many there are in B. A blindfolded man is to pull a ball from one of the urns and you are to choose the urn for him. If he pulls a red ball, you will receive \$100, otherwise nothing. Of 140 colleagues, students, and friends in Evanston and Oslo who were faced with the given choice, eighty-two chose A, fourty-five could not make up their minds, and thirteen chose B.

Presumably, Fellner and Ellsberg would interpret the choice of the eighty-two in E 15.10 as indicating that their respective belief functions over B were nonadditive. Specifically, a choice of A suggests that bel(red ball in $B) < 0.5$ and (by symmetry—unless somebody prefers white to red) bel(white ball in $B) < 0.5$. Consequently, bel(red ball in B) + bel(white ball in B) < bel(ball in B). If we apply the same arguments to the choice of B by thirteen people, we find that their belief functions satisfy the same three relations, with $<$ replaced by $>$. Such belief functions do not satisfy GS 1–GS 7.

15.2.5 Additive Belief Functions

It is a matter of dispute among knowledgeable persons whether the results in E 15.10 can be interpreted as above. It is also a fact that many scholars refuse to accept Fellner's and Ellsberg's ideas concerning belief functions. Some of them claim that if a belief function is not additive, there usually are good reasons for modifying it (see, for instance, Raiffa 1961, pp. 690–694). We note, therefore, that GS 1–GS 7 allow additive belief functions. Such functions have a very characteristic structure—to wit, T 15.9.

T 15.9 A belief function $\text{bel}(\cdot)$ is additive if and only if there exists a function

$$p(\cdot): \Omega \to [0, 1]$$

such that, for all $A \in \mathscr{F}$,

$$\text{bel}(A) = \sum_{\omega \in A} p(\omega).$$

Since the validity of T 15.9 is obvious, I omit the proof.

Besides their structure, additive belief functions have one characteristic of particular interest to us: They need not be support functions—see T 15.10.

T 15.10 An additive belief function $\text{bel}(\cdot)$ is a support function if and only if there is a point $\omega \in \Omega$ such that $\text{bel}(\{\omega\}) = 1$.

Hence only degenerate additive belief functions are support functions. Since this fact is not easy to intuit, take a look a E 15.11 which shows why it is true.

E 15.11 Suppose that $\Omega = \{a, b\}$ and that $m(\varnothing) = 0$, $m(\{a\}) = m(\{b\}) = 1/2$, and $m(\Omega) = 0$. Then $m(\cdot)$ is a basic probability assignment and the associated belief function $\text{bel}(\cdot)$ is additive. Next let $\text{bel}_1(\cdot)$ and $\text{bel}_2(\cdot)$ be two simple support functions focused on $\{a\}$ and $\{b\}$, respectively, to the degree s_1 and s_2. There are no values of s_1 and s_2 in $(0, 1)$ that satisfy

$$0 = m(\Omega) = \frac{(1 - s_1)(1 - s_2)}{1 - s_1 s_2}.$$

Moreover, if $s_1 = 1$, there is no value of $s_2 \in (0, 1)$ which satisfies

$$0.5 = m(\{a\}) = \frac{1 \cdot (1 - s_2)}{1 - 1 \cdot s_2}.$$

Ditto for $s_2 = 1$ and $m(\{b\})$.

The belief functions that are not support functions are called *quasi support functions*. The class of quasi support functions includes the class of nondegenerate additive belief functions. More specifically, it contains all belief functions whose cores are assigned zero basic probability.

To conclude our discussion of belief functions, I give in E 15.12 an example of a nonadditive quasi support function. In reading E 15.12, note that the belief function cannot be decomposed into an orthogonal sum of simple support functions since its core is assigned zero basic probability.

E 15.12 Liverpool and Manchester United are playing the final in the English Soccer Cup. Before the game we are asked to reveal our beliefs in the possible outcomes, L, U, and M, where U is short for undecided. With $\Omega = \{L, U, M\}$ we figure out

$$m(A) = \begin{cases} 1/5 & \text{if } A = \{L\} \\ 1/5 & \text{if } A = \{U\} \\ 3/5 & \text{if } A = \{U, M\}, \\ 0 & \text{otherwise} \end{cases}$$

and confess that

$$\text{bel}(A) = \begin{cases} 0 & \text{if } \sim[[L \in A] \vee [U \in A]] \\ 1/5 & \text{if } [[[L \in A] \wedge \sim[U \in A]] \vee [[U \in A] \wedge [(\{L, M\} \wedge A) = \varnothing]]] \\ 2/5 & \text{if } [A = \{L, U\}] \\ 4/5 & \text{if } [A = \{U, M\}] \\ 1 & \text{if } [A = \Omega] \end{cases}$$

15.3 Probability Measures

Additive belief functions are probability measures on experiments satisfying GS 1 and GS 2. Such measures assign numbers to the members of $\mathscr{F}$ in accordance with axioms that differ considerably from GS 1–GS 7. We discuss their axioms next.

15.3.1 Finitely Additive Probability Measures

A *finitely additive probability measure* $P(\cdot)$ is an assignment of numbers to the events of an experiment $(\Omega, \mathscr{F})$ that satisfies two conditions, AK 1 and AK 2.

AK 1 $P(\cdot): \mathscr{F} \to [0, 1]$ and $P(\Omega) = 1$.

AK 2 If $A, B \in \mathscr{F}$ and if $A \cap B = \phi$, then

$P(A) + P(B) = P(A \cup B)$.

Since $\mathscr{F}$ is a field, AK 1 and AK 2 imply the validity of T 15.11 and T 15.12.

T 15.11 $P(\varnothing) = 0$.

T 15.12 If $A, B \in \mathscr{F}$ and $A \subset B$, then $P(A) \leqslant P(B)$.

Hence $P(\cdot)$ is monotone. It is also finitely additive—to wit T 15.13.

T 15.13 If $A_i \in \mathscr{F}$, $i = 1, \ldots, n$, and if $A_i \cap A_j = \varnothing$ for $i \neq j$, $i, j = 1, \ldots, n$, then

$$\sum_{i=1}^{n} P(A_i) = P\left(\bigcup_{i=1}^{n} A_i\right).$$

A probability measure—as described above—is an undefined object satisfying certain conditions. When we assign numbers to the events of an experiment, we interpret this object. Such an interpretation can be arbitrary. It can reflect our belief in the likelihood that the events in question will occur. Or it can be construed as a logical consequence of certain subsidiary hypotheses.

E 15.13 Consider the soccer games in E 15.2 and the experiment described there. We can assign numbers to the members of $\mathscr{F}$ according to the following considerations: There are 3^{12} possible sequences of letters taken from {H, V, U}. Hence $\Omega = \{\omega_1, \ldots, \omega_{3^{12}}\}$. We let

$$P(\{\omega_i\}) = 3^{-12}, \qquad i = 1, \ldots, 3^{+12}$$

and

$$P(A) = \sum_{\omega \in A} P(\{\omega\}). \qquad A \in \mathscr{F}.$$

Then $P(\cdot)$ satisfies AK 1 and AK 2.

15.3.2 The Bayes Theorem

We shall use the concept of a finitely additive probability measure to explicate the notion of independent events and to discuss the idea of conditional probabilities. For that purpose, let $(\Omega, \mathscr{F})$ be an experiment; let $P(\cdot)$ be a finitely additive probability measure on $(\Omega, \mathscr{F})$; and let A and B be events. Then A and B are *independent relative to* $P(\cdot)$ if and only if

$$P(A \cap B) = P(A) \cdot P(B).$$

E 15.14 A coin is to be tossed twice under uniform conditions. Let HT denote heads on first toss and tails on second toss; (with the obvious interpretation) let $\omega_1 = \text{HH}$, $\omega_2 = \text{HT}$, $\omega_3 = \text{TH}$, and $\omega_4 = \text{TT}$; let $\Omega = \{\omega_1, \ldots, \omega_4\}$; let $\mathscr{F} = \mathscr{P}(\Omega)$; and define $P(\{\omega_i\}) = 1/4$, $i = 1, \ldots, 4$. If A is the event heads on first toss, $P(A) = 1/2$. Similarly, if B is the event tails on second, $P(B) = 1/2$. But then $A \cap B$ is heads on first toss and tails on second toss, and $P(A \cap B) = 1/4$. So $P(A \cap B) = P(A) \cdot P(B)$, and A and B are independent.

Suppose next that $P(A) > 0$. Then the *conditional probability of B, given that A has occurred*, is defined by

$$P(B|A) = \frac{P(A \cap B)}{P(A)}.$$

When A and B are independent, the right-hand side reduces to $P(B)$. Hence in that case the probability of B occurring is independent of the occurrence of A, which is as it ought to be.

E 15.15 Let A and B be as in E 15.14. Then $P(B|A) = P(B)$; i.e., the conditional probability of tails on the second toss, given that heads has occurred on the first toss, equals the probability of tails on the second throw; i.e., 1/2. If C is the event heads on both tosses,

$$P(C|A) = \frac{P(A \cap C)}{P(A)} = \frac{(1/4)}{(1/2)} = 1/2$$

and $P(C) \neq 1/2$. So C and A are not independent.

It follows easily from our definition of conditional probability that $P(\cdot|A)$ is a finitely additive probability measure on $(\Omega, \mathscr{F})$—see T 15.14.

T 15.14 If $A \in \mathscr{F}$ and $P(A) > 0$, $P(\cdot|A)$ satisfies AK 1 and AK 2.

Moreover, since $A \subset \bigcup_{i=1}^n B_i$ implies $A = \bigcup_{i=1}^n (A \cap B_i)$, and since $P(B|A)P(A) = P(A|B)P(B)$ whenever $P(A) > 0$ and $P(B) > 0$, T 15.15—a version of the Bayes theorem must be true.

T 15.15 If $B_i \in \mathscr{F}$, $i = 1, \ldots, n$; if $B_i \cap B_j = \varnothing$ when $i \neq j$, $i, j = 1, \ldots, n$; if $A \in \mathscr{F}$ and $A \subset \bigcup_{i=1}^n B_i$; and if $P(B_i) > 0$, $i = 1, \ldots, n$, then

$$P(A) = \sum_{i=1}^n P(A|B_i)P(B_i), \qquad i = 1, \ldots, n$$

and (if $P(A) > 0$)

$$P(B_j|A) = P(A|B_j)P(B_j) \Big/ \sum_{i=1}^n P(A|B_i)P(B_i). \tag{15.13}$$

In most applications of the Bayes theorem $P(B_i)$ is referred to as the *prior measure* of B_i, i.e., the measure an individual would assign to B_i if he had no observations to guide him in assigning probabilities to events. In addition, $P(B_j|A)$ is referred to as the *posterior measure* of B_j, i.e., the measure that an individual with prior probabilities $P(B_i)$, $i = 1, \ldots, n$, would assign to B_j after having observed A. Finally, the conditional probabilities $P(A|B_i)$, $i = 1, \ldots, n$, measure the likelihood of A as a function of the B_i. Hence $P(A|\cdot)$ is often called a *likelihood function*. In most applications the conditional probability measures, $P(\cdot|B_i)$, $i = 1, \ldots, n$, are known probability measures.

E 15.16 Two indistinguishable urns B_1 and B_2 are standing in front of a blindfolded man. Each urn contains 100 balls that are identical except for color. Some are red; others are white. B_1 contains ten red balls and B_2 contains eighty red balls. The urns are shaken well and the blindfolded man picks a red ball from one of them. What is the probability that he sampled from B_1?

In this case our prior measures of the B_i are given by $P(B_1) = P(B_2) = 1/2$. Also

$$P(\text{red ball}|B_1) = 0.1$$

and

$$P(\text{red ball}|B_2) = 0.8.$$

Hence our posterior measure of B_1 is as follows:

$$P(B_1|\text{red ball}) = \frac{0.1 \cdot 0.5}{0.1 \cdot 0.5 + 0.8 \cdot 0.5} = \frac{1}{9}.$$

15.3.3 Posterior Probabilities and Conditional Belief Functions

It is interesting to contrast the way information is processed in T 15.15 with the way evidence is pooled in T 15.5. In T 15.15 the information we *have* and the information we *gain* are treated asymmetrically. We begin with the prior measures $P(B_i)$, $i = 1, \ldots, n$, observe A and compute the posterior probabilities $P(B_j|A)$, $j = 1, \ldots, n$. Moreover, we never question whether we actually have observed A. In T 15.5 when we form the orthogonal sum of $\text{bel}_1(\cdot)$ and $\text{bel}_2(\cdot)$, the evidence on which $\text{bel}_1(\cdot)$ is based and the evidence on which $\text{bel}_2(\cdot)$ is based are treated symmetrically. Moreover, neither $\text{bel}_1(\cdot)$ nor $\text{bel}_2(\cdot)$ insists that some particular subset of Ω must have happened.

The preceding contrast notwithstanding, there are situations in which the orthogonal sum of two belief functions can be interpreted as a posterior belief function. For example: Let $(\Omega, \mathscr{F})$ be an experiment that satisfies GS 1 and GS 2, and let $\text{bel}_1(\cdot): \mathscr{F} \to [0, 1]$ be a belief function with basic probability assignment $m_1(\cdot): \mathscr{F} \to [0, 1]$. In addition, let $E \in \mathscr{F}$ be an event that has a nonempty intersection with the core of $\text{bel}_1(\cdot)$, and let $\text{bel}_2(\cdot): \mathscr{F} \to [0, 1]$ be a belief function whose probability assignment, $m_2(\cdot): \mathscr{F} \to [0, 1]$, is given by

$$m_2(A) = \begin{cases} 1 & \text{if } A = E \\ 0 & \text{otherwise.} \end{cases}$$

Finally, assume that E is a proper subset of Ω and that $\text{bel}_1(E^c) < 1$. Then if $m(\cdot)$ denotes the basic probability assignment of $(\text{bel}_1 \circ \text{bel}_2)(\cdot)$, $m(\varnothing) = 0$ and for all nonempty $A \in \mathscr{F}$,

$$\begin{aligned} m(A) &= \sum_{B \in \mathscr{F}, B \cap E = A} m_1(B) \Bigg/ \left(1 - \sum_{B \in \mathscr{F}, B \cap E = \varnothing} m_1(B)\right) \\ &= \sum_{B \in \mathscr{F}, B \cap E = A} m_1(B)/(1 - \text{bel}_1(E^c)). \end{aligned}$$

Moreover,

$$\begin{aligned} (\text{bel}_1 \circ \text{bel}_2)(A) &= \sum_{D \subset A} m(D) \\ &= (1 - \text{bel}_1(E^c))^{-1} \sum_{\varnothing \neq D, D \subset A} \sum_{B \in \mathscr{F}, B \cap E = D} m_1(B) \\ &= (1 - \text{bel}_1(E^c))^{-1} \sum_{B \in \mathscr{F}, \varnothing \neq B \cap E, B \cap E \subset A} m_1(B) \\ &= (1 - \text{bel}_1(E^c))^{-1} \sum_{B \subset A \cup E^c, B \not\subset E^c} m_1(B) \\ &= (1 - \text{bel}_1(E^c))^{-1}(\text{bel}_1(A \cup E^c) - \text{bel}_1(E^c)). \end{aligned}$$

In this case $(\text{bel}_1 \circ \text{bel}_2)(\cdot)$ assigns numbers to events as if the only possible outcomes in Ω were the outcomes in E. That is, $(\text{bel}_1 \circ \text{bel}_2)(\cdot)$ assigns numbers to events as if it were a genuine conditional belief function, e.g., a posterior belief function.

Our observations concerning posterior probability measures and orthogonal sums of belief functions suggest that we define conditional belief as follows: Let $(\Omega, \mathscr{F})$ be an experiment that satisfies GS 1 and GS 2, and let $\text{bel}(\cdot): \mathscr{F} \to [0, 1]$ be a belief function. In addition, let A and E be events such that $\text{bel}(E^c) < 1$. Then the *conditional belief in A given E* is defined by

$$\text{bel}(A|E) = (1 - \text{bel}(E^c))^{-1}(\text{bel}(A \cup E^c) - \text{bel}(E^c)). \tag{15.14}$$

It is easy to verify that $\text{bel}(\cdot|E): \mathscr{F} \to [0, 1]$ is a well-defined belief function and that $\text{bel}(A|E)$ reduces to $\text{bel}(A \cap E)/\text{bel}(E)$ whenever $\text{bel}(\cdot)$ is additive. We shall return to conditional beliefs in chapter 24.[1]

15.3.4 σ-Additive Probability Measures

Probability measures—as we define them—need not be countably additive. Therefore, when $\mathscr{F}$ is a σ field, we usually also require that $P(\cdot)$ satisfy a third condition, AK 3.

AK 3 Suppose that $A_i \in \mathscr{F}$, $i = 1, 2, \ldots$, and that $A_i \cap A_j = \emptyset$ for $i \neq j$ and $i, j = 1, 2, \ldots$. Suppose also that $\mathscr{F}$ is a σ field, and that $P(\cdot)$ is a probability measure on $(\Omega, \mathscr{F})$. Then

$$P\left(\bigcup_{i=1}^{\infty} A_i\right) = \sum_{i=1}^{\infty} P(A_i).$$

Conditions EX 1–EX 3 and AK 1–AK 3 constitute A. Kolmogorov's axioms of probability (Kolmogorov 1933, pp. 2 and 13). A triple $(\Omega, \mathscr{F}, P(\cdot))$ which satisfies them is a *probability space.* An important example of a probability space is the space $(\Omega, \sigma(\mathscr{F}), \mu(\cdot))$ described in E 15.17 and E 15.18.

E 15.17 Let $\Omega = [0, 1)$; let S denote the family of all subsets of Ω of the form $[a, b)$, where $0 \leqslant a < b \leqslant 1$; and let $\mathscr{F}$ be the smallest field that contains all the sets in S. Moreover, let $P_S(\cdot)\colon S \to [0, 1]$ be defined by

$$P_S([a, b)) = b - a, \qquad 0 \leqslant a < b \leqslant 1 \tag{15.15}$$

Then there exists a unique countably additive probability measure $P(\cdot)\colon \mathscr{F} \to [0, 1]$ such that, for all $A \in S$, $P(A) = P_S(A)$.[2]

In the vernacular of probabilists, countably additive probability measures are σ-additive. They distinguish themselves from finitely additive probability measures in their continuity properties. Theorems T 15.16 and T 15.17 attest to this fact.

T 15.16 Consider an experiment $(\Omega, \mathscr{F})$ and a probability measure $P(\cdot)\colon \mathscr{F} \to [0, 1]$. Moreover, let $A_i, B_j \in \mathscr{F}$, $i, j = 1, 2, \ldots$, be sequences of events that satisfy the conditions:

(i) $A_i \subset A_{i+1}$, $\quad i = 1, 2, \ldots$, and $\bigcup_{i=1}^{\infty} A_i \in \mathscr{F}$,

(ii) $B_{j+1} \subset B_j$, $\quad j = 1, 2, \ldots$, and $\bigcap_{j=1}^{\infty} B_j \in \mathscr{F}$.

Then $P(\cdot)$ is σ-additive only if

$$P(\lim A_n) = \lim P(A_n) \tag{15.16}$$

and

$$P(\lim B_n) = \lim P(B_n). \tag{15.17}$$

I shall prove equation 15.16 and leave 15.17 to the reader. Let $A_0 = \emptyset$

and $C_i = A_i - A_{i-1}$, $i = 1, 2, \ldots$, and observe that $A_n = \bigcup_{i=1}^{n} C_i$, $n = 1, 2, \ldots$. From this and the σ-additivity of $P(\cdot)$, it follows that

$$P(\lim A_n) = P\left(\lim \bigcup_{i=1}^{n} C_i\right) = P\left(\bigcup_{i=1}^{\infty} C_i\right)$$

$$= \sum_{i=1}^{\infty} P(C_i) = \lim \sum_{i=1}^{n} P(C_i) = \lim P(A_n).$$

Theorem T 15.16 asserts that a σ-additive probability measure is continuous from above and below. The converse is also true—see T 15.17.

T 15.17 Consider an experiment $(\Omega, \mathscr{F})$ and a probability measure $P(\cdot): \mathscr{F} \to [0, 1]$. $P(\cdot)$ is σ-aditive if it is continuous from below at every $A \in \mathscr{F}$ or continuous from above at $\varnothing \in \mathscr{F}$.

To prove the theorem, let $A_i \in \mathscr{F}$, $i = 1, 2, \ldots$, be a sequence of events such that $\bigcup_{i=1}^{\infty} A_i \in \mathscr{F}$ and such that $A_i \cap A_j = \varnothing$ if $i \neq j$. Then $\bigcup_{i=1}^{n} A_i$ and $\bigcup_{i=n+1}^{\infty} A_i$ belong to $\mathscr{F}$ for all $n = 1, 2, \ldots$. Consequently, if $P(\cdot)$ is continuous from below at every $A \in \mathscr{F}$,

$$P\left(\bigcup_{i=1}^{\infty} A_i\right) = P\left(\lim \bigcup_{i=1}^{n} A_i\right) = \lim P\left(\bigcup_{i=1}^{n} A_i\right) = \lim \sum_{i=1}^{n} P(A_i) = \sum_{i=1}^{\infty} P(A_i).$$

And if $P(\cdot)$ is continuous from above at $\varnothing$,

$$P\left(\bigcup_{i=1}^{\infty} A_i\right) = P\left(\bigcup_{i=1}^{n} A_i\right) + P\left(\bigcup_{i=n+1}^{\infty} A_i\right) = \sum_{i=1}^{n} P(A_i) + P\left(\bigcup_{i=n+1}^{\infty} A_i\right)$$

and

$$\lim P\left(\bigcup_{i=n+1}^{\infty} A_i\right) = P(\varnothing) = 0.$$

For later reference it is important to note that if $\mathscr{F}$ is a σ field, equation 15.16 holds for any convergent sequence of events; i.e., if $A = \lim A_n$ and $P(\cdot)$ is σ-additive, then $P(A) = \lim P(A_n)$. To see why, note that, for all $m \geq n$,

$$P\left(\bigcap_{k=n}^{\infty} A_k\right) \leqslant P(A_m) \qquad \text{and} \qquad P(A_m) \leqslant P\left(\bigcup_{k=n}^{\infty} A_k\right). \tag{15.18}$$

Consequently,

$$P\left(\bigcap_{k=n}^{\infty} A_k\right) \leqslant \inf_{k \geqslant n} P(A_k) \qquad \text{and} \qquad \sup_{k \geqslant n} P(A_k) \leqslant P\left(\bigcup_{k=n}^{\infty} A_k\right). \tag{15.19}$$

Since by equations 15.16 and 15.17,

$$P(\liminf A_n) = \lim P\left(\bigcap_{k=n}^{\infty} A_k\right) \quad \text{and} \quad P(\limsup A_n) = \lim P\left(\bigcup_{k=n}^{\infty} A_k\right),$$

it follows from equations 15.18 and 15.19 that

$$P(\liminf A_n) \leqslant \liminf P(A_n) \leqslant \limsup P(A_n) \leqslant P(\limsup A_n). \qquad (15.20)$$

From equation 15.20 and from the fact that the A_n converge if and only if $\liminf A_n = \limsup A_n$, it follows that equation 15.16 is valid for all convergent sequences of events.

The structure of a field is much simpler than the structure of a σ field. Therefore, in proofs we often define probability measures on some field $\mathscr{F}$ and insist that they can be extended to $\sigma(\mathscr{F})$—the smallest σ field containing $\mathscr{F}$. Such extensions exist when the probability measures in question are σ-additive as witnessed in *Carathéodory's Extension Theorem*, UT 15.

UT 15 Let $(\Omega, \mathscr{F})$ be an experiment and let $P(\cdot)\colon \mathscr{F} \to [0, 1]$ be a σ-additive probability measure. There is one and only one σ-additive probability measure $\tilde{P}(\cdot)$ on $(\Omega, \sigma(\mathscr{F}))$ such that, for all $A \in \mathscr{F}$, $\tilde{P}(A) = P(A)$.

Since the arguments needed to establish this theorem are involved, I omit them and refer the reader to Loève (1960, pp. 87–90) for a detailed proof of UT 15.

E 15.18 Let $(\Omega, \mathscr{F})$ and $P(\cdot)$ be as in E 15.17. Since $P(\cdot)$ is σ-additive, we can use UT 15 to establish the existence of a unique σ-additive extension of $P(\cdot)$ to $\sigma(\mathscr{F})$. This extension is called the *Lebesgue measure*, and we shall always denote it by $\mu(\cdot)$.

The Lebesgue measure has many interesting properties. One of them is detailed below:

If $a \in [0, 1)$, then $\mu(\{a\}) = 0$.

To see why, observe that $\{a\} = \bigcap_{n=1}^{\infty} [a, a + n^{-1})$ and apply equations 15.15 and T 15.16.

15.3.5 Convergence in Probability and with Probability 1

We conclude this section with a brief discussion of two different concepts of the convergence of sequences of random variables.

Let $(\Omega, \mathscr{F}, P(\cdot))$ be a probability space, and let $x_1(\cdot)$, $x_2(\cdot)$, ... be a sequence of random variables. We say that *the $x_n(\cdot)$ converge in probability to a random variable $x(\cdot)$* and write

$$p \lim x_n = x$$

if and only if, for all $\varepsilon > 0$,

$$\lim P(\{\omega \in \Omega : |x_n(\omega) - x(\omega)| > \varepsilon\}) = 0.$$

We also say that *the* $x_n(\cdot)$ *converge with probability* 1 *to a random variable* $x(\cdot)$ and write

$$\lim x_n(\omega) = x(\omega) \quad \text{a.e.} \tag{15.21}$$

if and only if, for all $\varepsilon > 0$,

$$\lim P\left(\bigcup_{k=n}^{\infty} \{\omega \in \Omega : |x_k(\omega) - x(\omega)| > \varepsilon\right) = 0.$$

The "a.e." in (15.21) is short for "almost everywhere" and the latter is short for "everywhere except in a set of P measure zero."

To clarify the two concepts of convergence, we make the following observations: Let

$$A(\varepsilon) = \bigcap_{n=1}^{\infty} \bigcup_{k=n}^{\infty} \{\omega \in \Omega : |x_k(\omega) - x(\omega)| > \varepsilon\}.$$

Then the $x_n(\cdot)$ converge to $x(\cdot)$ with probability 1 if and only if $P(A(\varepsilon)) = 0$ for all $\varepsilon > 0$. $A(\varepsilon)$ consists of all ω with the property that infinitely many of the $x_n(\cdot)$ satisfy $|x_n(\omega) - x(\omega)| > \varepsilon$. Its complement satisfies

$$A(\varepsilon)^c = \bigcup_{n=1}^{\infty} \bigcap_{k=n}^{\infty} \{\omega \in \Omega : |x_k(\omega) - x(\omega)| \leqslant \varepsilon\}.$$

For all $\omega \in A(\varepsilon)^c$ there is an integer $n_0(\omega)$ such that for all $n \geqslant n_0(\omega)$ $|x_n(\omega) - x(\omega)| \leqslant \varepsilon$. Moreover, $P(A(\varepsilon)^c) = 1$. If $x(\omega) = \alpha$ for all ω, convergence of the $x_n(\cdot)$ with probability 1 implies that, for each $\varepsilon > 0$, there is a fixed (!) set, $A(\varepsilon)^c$, such that the values of the $x_n(\omega)$ for all $\omega \in A(\varepsilon)^c$ eventually lie within ε distance of α. If the $x_n(\cdot)$ just converged in probability to α, the most we could assert would be that, for all $\delta > 0$, there exists an integer $n(\delta, \varepsilon)$ such that, for all $n > n(\delta, \varepsilon)$,

$$P(\{\omega \in \Omega : |x_n(\omega) - \alpha| > e\}) < \delta. \tag{15.22}$$

The ω sets which satisfy equation 15.22 may differ from one n to the next. More about this in the next chapter.

15.4 Probability Distributions

We have discussed two different schemes for measuring probable things. In both schemes the task of assigning numbers to the events of an experiment

$(\Omega, \mathscr{F})$ is manageable when $\mathscr{F}$ is finite and formidable otherwise. In this section we discuss a way of assigning numbers to subfamilies of $\mathscr{F}$ that simplifies the task in most cases of interest to econometricians. The subfamilies we have in mind are the σ fields generated by random variables on $(\Omega, \mathscr{F})$, e.g., $\mathscr{F}(f(1), \ldots, f(n))$, the smallest σ field that contains all sets of the form $\{\omega \in \Omega : f(1, \omega) < a_1, \ldots, f(n, \omega) < a_n\}$, $a_i \in R$, $i = 1, \ldots, n$. For such subfamilies the assignment is determined by specifying the (joint) probability distributions of the random variables involved.

15.4.1 The Probability Distribution of a Random Variable

Let $x(\cdot): \Omega \to R$ be a random variable on a probability space $(\Omega, \mathscr{F}, P(\cdot))$. *The probability distribution of* $x(\cdot)$ is a function $F_x(\cdot): R \to [0, 1]$ that satisfies

$$F_x(a) = P(\{\omega \in \Omega : x(\omega) < a\}), \qquad a \in R. \tag{15.23}$$

It follows from equation 15.23 and T 15.12 that $a, b \in R$ and $a < b$ imply that $F_x(a) \leqslant F_x(b)$. Hence $F_x(\cdot)$ is monotonic and nondecreasing. Also, if $a_n \in R$ and $a_n \leqslant a_{n+1}$, $n = 1, 2, \ldots$, and if $a = \lim a_n$, then T 15.16 and the relation $\{\omega \in \Omega : x(\omega) < a\} = \bigcup_{n=1}^{\infty} \{\omega \in \Omega : x(\omega) < a_n\}$ imply that $F_x(a) = \lim F_x(a_n)$. Hence $F_x(\cdot)$ is continuous from the left. Finally, T 15.16,

$$\emptyset = \bigcap_{n=1}^{\infty} \{\omega \in \Omega : x(\omega) < -n\}, \qquad \text{and} \qquad \Omega = \bigcup_{n=1}^{\infty} \{\omega \in \Omega : x(\omega) < n\}$$

imply that

$$\lim_{a \to -\infty} F_x(a) = 0 \qquad \text{and} \qquad \lim_{a \to \infty} F_x(a) = 1. \tag{15.24}$$

For ease of reference we record these observations in T 15.18.

T 15.18 Let $(\Omega, \mathscr{F}, P(\cdot))$ be a probability space and let $x(\cdot)$ be a random variable. The probability distribution of $x(\cdot)$, $F_x(\cdot): R \to [0, 1]$, is monotone, nondecreasing, continuous from the left, and satisfies equation 15.24.

Two examples of probability distributions are given in E 15.19. The first is the probability distribution of an indicator function.

E 15.19 Let $(\Omega, \mathscr{F}, P(\cdot))$ be a probability space, and suppose that $A \in \mathscr{F}$. Then

$$F_{I_A}(a) = \begin{cases} 0 & \text{if } a \leqslant 0 \\ P(A^c) & \text{if } 0 < a \leqslant 1 \\ 1 & \text{if } 1 < a \end{cases}$$

Next, suppose that $0 < a_1 < a_2 < \cdots < a_n$ are constants and that $A_i \in \mathscr{F}$, $i = 1, \ldots, n$. If the A_i are disjoint and

$$x(\omega) = \sum_{i=1}^{n} a_i I_{A_i}(\omega) \tag{15.25}$$

then

$$F_x(a) = \begin{cases} 0 & \text{if } a \leqslant 0 \\ P\left(\bigcap_{i=1}^{n} A_i^c\right) & \text{if } 0 < a \leqslant a_1 \\ P\left(\bigcap_{j=1}^{n} A_j^c\right) + \sum_{j=1}^{i} P(A_j) & \text{if } a_i < a \leqslant a_{i+1},\ i = 1, \ldots, n-1 \\ 1 & \text{if } a_n < a \end{cases}$$

15.4.2 The Joint Probability Distribution of n Random Variables

If $x_1(\cdot), \ldots, x_n(\cdot)$ are random variables on the same probability space, $(\Omega, \mathscr{F}, P(\cdot))$, their *joint probability distribution* is defined by

$$F_{x_1,\ldots,x_n}(a) = P(\{\omega \in \Omega : x_1(\omega) < a_1, \ldots, x_n(\omega) < a_n\}), \qquad a \in R^n. \tag{15.26}$$

This function is nondecreasing and satisfies, for all $a, b \in R^n$ with $a < b$,

$$\Delta_{b-a} F_{x_1,\ldots,x_n}(a) \geqslant 0, \tag{15.27}$$

where[3]

$$\Delta_{b-a} = \Delta_{b_1-a_1} \cdot \Delta_{b_2-a_2} \cdots \Delta_{b_n-a_n}$$

$$\Delta_{b_i-a_i} F_{x_1,\ldots,x_n}(a) = F_{x_1,\ldots,x_n}(a_1, \ldots, a_{i-1}, b_i, a_{i+1}, \ldots, a_n) - F_{x_1,\ldots,x_n}(a)$$

and

$$\Delta_{b-a} F_{x_1,\ldots,x_n}(a) = \Delta_{b_1-a_1}(\Delta_{b_2-a_2}(\ldots(\Delta_{b_{n-1}-a_{n-1}}(\Delta_{b_n-a_n} F_{x_1,\ldots,x_n}(a)))\ldots)).$$

It is also continuous from below; i.e., for all $a, b \in R^n$ and $b \leqslant a$,

$$F_{x_1,\ldots,x_n}(a) = \lim_{b \to a} F_{x_1,\ldots,x_n}(b).$$

Moreover, for any $i = 1, \ldots, n$

$$0 = \lim_{a_i \to -\infty} F_{x_1,\ldots,x_n}(a_1, \ldots, a_n) \tag{15.28}$$

and

$$1 = \lim_{\substack{a_i \to \infty \\ i=1,\ldots,n}} F_{x_1,\ldots,x_n}(a_1, \ldots, a_n). \tag{15.29}$$

T 15.19 summarizes these observations.

T 15.19 Let $(\Omega, \mathscr{F}, P(\cdot))$ be a probability space, and let $x_i(\cdot)$, $i = 1, \ldots, n$ be random variables. Moreover, let $F_{x_1,\ldots,x_n}(\cdot)$ be the joint probability distribution of the $x_i(\cdot)$ as defined in equation 15.26. Then $F_{x_1,\ldots,x_n}(\cdot)$ is monotone, nondecreasing, continuous from below, and satisfies equations 15.27, 15.28, and 15.29.

An example of a two-dimensional distribution will be given in E 15.20. In reading the example, observe that $\lim_{b\to\infty} F_{I_A I_B}(a, b) = F_{I_A}(a)$, where $F_{I_A}(\cdot)$ is as described in E 15.19. This is as it ought to be, since if $F_{x_1,\ldots,x_n}(\cdot)$ is as defined in equation 15.26 and if

$$F_{x_1,\ldots,x_{i-1},x_{i+1},\ldots,x_n}(b) = P(\{\omega \in \Omega : x_1(\omega) < b_1, \ldots, x_{i-1}(\omega) < b_{i-1}, x_{i+1}(\omega) < b_i, \ldots, x_n(\omega) < b_{n-1}\}$$

for all $b \in R^{n-1}$, then, for all $a \in R^n$,

$$F_{x_1,\ldots,x_{i-1},x_{i+1},\ldots,x_n}(a_1, \ldots, a_{i-1}, a_{i+1}, \ldots, a_n) = \lim_{a_i \to \infty} F_{x_1,\ldots,x_n}(a_1, \ldots, a_n). \tag{15.30}$$

E 15.20 Let $(\Omega, \mathscr{F}, P(\cdot))$ be a probability space, and let A and B be events. Then

$$F_{I_A, I_B}(a, b) = \begin{cases} 0 & \text{if } a \leqslant 0 \text{ or } b \leqslant 0 \\ P(A^c \cap B^c) & \text{if } (a, b) \in (0, 1] \times (0, 1] \\ P(A^c) & \text{if } (a, b) \in (0, 1] \times (1, \infty) \\ P(B^c) & \text{if } (a, b) \in (1, \infty) \times (0, 1] \\ 1 & \text{if } (a, b) \in (1, \infty) \times (1, \infty) \end{cases}$$

15.4.3 Integrable Random Variables

Often the probability distributions of random variables can be characterized in terms of a few parameters. In this section we explicate the meaning of three such parameters: the mean and variance of a random variable and the covariance of two random variables. The first is used to describe such varied matters as the distribution of heads in n tosses of a coin and the distribution of incoming calls at a telephone exchange. All three parameters are used to characterize the asymptotic distribution of statistical estimates of various economic policy parameters, e.g., the marginal propensity to consume and the income elasticity of consumers' demand for cash balances.

We begin with the definition of the mean of a random variable: Let $(\Omega, \mathscr{F}, P(\cdot))$ be a fixed probability space; let $x(\cdot)$ be a random variable on this space; and, for all $(a, b) \in R^2$ such that $a < b$, let

$$F_x[a, b) = P(\{\omega \in \Omega : a \leqslant x(\omega) < b\}).$$

Then $F_x[a, b) = F_x(b) - F_x(a)$, where $F_x(\cdot): R \to [0, 1]$ is the probability distribution of $x(\cdot)$. Now let Ex denote the *mean of* $x(\cdot)$. The definition of Ex is obtained in several steps as follows: Suppose $x(\cdot)$ is the indicator function of an event A. Then

$$\begin{aligned} Ex &= P(A) \\ &= F_{I_A}[1, \infty). \end{aligned} \tag{15.31}$$

If $x(\cdot)$ is a simple function such as the one in equation 15.25, then

$$\begin{aligned} Ex &= \sum_{i=1}^{n} a_i EI_{A_i} \\ &= \sum_{i=1}^{n} a_i P(A_i) \\ &= \sum_{i=1}^{n-1} a_i F_x[a_i, a_{i+1}) + a_n F_x[a_n, \infty). \end{aligned} \tag{15.32}$$

The value of Ex in this case is easily seen to be independent of the chosen representation of $x(\cdot)$. Hence Ex is well defined for simple functions by equation 15.32. Next, suppose that $x(\cdot)$ is a bounded, nonnegative random variable and let $x(n, \cdot)$ be as defined in equation 15.1. Also, let $A_{i-1} = \{\omega \in \Omega : (i-1)/2^n \leqslant x(\omega) < i/2^n\}$, $i = 1, \ldots, n2^n$, and $A_{n2^n} = \{\omega \in \Omega : x(\omega) \geqslant n\}$. Then

$$\begin{aligned} Ex &= \lim Ex(n) \\ &= \lim \sum_{i=0}^{n2^n-1} (i/2^n)P(A_i) + nP(A_{n2^n}) \\ &= \lim \sum_{i=0}^{n2^n-1} (i/2^n)F_x[i/2^n, (i+1)/2^n) + nF_x[n, \infty). \end{aligned} \tag{15.33}$$

Since the $x(n, \cdot)$ constitute a nondecreasing sequence of functions, the limits in equation 15.33 exist. It can be shown that the common value of these limits is independent of the particular sequence of simple functions used to approximate $x(\cdot)$. Hence, for bounded nonnegative random variables, Ex is well defined by equation 15.33. Finally, suppose that $x(\cdot)$ is bounded and assumes negative as well as positive values. Also let

$$B = \{\omega: 0 \leqslant x(\omega)\},$$

and let

$$x^+(\omega) = x(\omega)I_B(\omega) \qquad \text{and} \qquad x^-(\omega) = -x(\omega)I_{B^c}(\omega).$$

Then define Ex by

$$Ex = Ex^+ - Ex^-. \tag{15.34}$$

Evidently Ex is well defined, since both Ex^+ and Ex^- are well defined and finite.

The steps we have used to define Ex are the steps measure theorists often use to define the integral of $x(\cdot)$ with respect to $P(\cdot)$. Hence—in standard notation—on the basis of equations 15.31–15.34, we can assert

$$Ex = \int_\Omega x(\omega)\,dP(\omega) \tag{15.35}$$

for any bounded random variable $x(\cdot)$.

With some obvious modifications, the definition of Ex for unbounded $x(\cdot)$ is obtained in the same way as for bounded $x(\cdot)$. When $x(\cdot)$ is unbounded, Ex is well defined if either Ex^+ or Ex^- or both are finite.

If Ex is well defined and finite, $x(\cdot)$ is an *integrable random variable*. When $x(\cdot)$ is integrable, we can use equations 15.31–15.34 and the standard definition of a Riemann-Stieltjes integral to show that

$$Ex = \int_{-\infty}^{\infty} t\,dF_x(t). \tag{15.36}$$

It follows easily from our definition of Ex that T 15.20 must be valid.

T 15.20 Let $x(\cdot)$ and $y(\cdot)$ be integrable random variables on a probability space $(\Omega, \mathscr{F}, P(\cdot))$ and let c be a constant. Then

(i) $x(\omega) = y(\omega)$ a.e. implies that $Ex = Ey$;

(ii) $x(\omega) \geqslant 0$ a.e. implies that $Ex \geqslant 0$;

(iii) $Ecx = cEx$; and

(iv) $E(x + y) = Ex + Ey$

For brevity's sake I leave the proof of the theorem to the reader.

To define the variance and covariance of random variables, we procede as follows: Let $x(\cdot)$ and $y(\cdot)$ be random variables on a probability space, $(\Omega, \mathscr{F}, P(\cdot))$, and suppose that both $x(\cdot)^2$ and $y(\cdot)^2$ are integrable. Then the *variance* of $x(\cdot)$, σ_x^2, is defined by

$$\begin{aligned}\sigma_x^2 &= E(x - Ex)^2 \\ &= \int_\Omega (x(\omega) - Ex)^2 \, dP(\omega) \\ &= \int_{-\infty}^{\infty} (t - Ex)^2 \, dF_x(t). \qquad (15.37)\end{aligned}$$

Also, the *covariance* of $x(\cdot)$ and $y(\cdot)$, σ_{xy}, is defined by

$$\begin{aligned}\sigma_{xy} &= E(x - Ex)(y - Ey) \\ &= \int_\Omega (x(\omega) - Ex)(y(\omega) - Ey) \, dP(\omega) \\ &= \iint_{-\infty}^{\infty} (t - Ex)(s - Ey) \, dF_{xy}(t, s), \qquad (15.38)\end{aligned}$$

where $F_{x,y}(\cdot)$ denotes the joint distribution function of $x(\cdot)$ and $y(\cdot)$ relative to $P(\cdot)$ and the double integral is the Riemann-Stieltjes integral of $(t - Ex)(s - Ey)$ with respect to $F_{x,y}(\cdot)$. Both σ_x^2 and σ_{xy} are well defined since the integrability of $(x(\omega) - Ex)^2$ and of $(x(\omega) - Ex)(y(\omega) - Ey)$ follows from the integrability of $x(\cdot)^2$ and $y(\cdot)^2$ and from the inequality of Schwarz:

$$(E(x - Ex)(y - Ey))^2 \leqslant E(x - Ex)^2 E(y - Ey)^2.$$

As soon as we observe that

$$F_x(a) = \lim_{b \to \infty} F_{xy}(a, b)$$

we can deduce from equations 15.35–15.38 that Ex, σ_x^2 (as well as Ey, σ_y^2), and σ_{xy} can be expressed in terms of the first and second moments of $F_{xy}(\cdot)$. Consequently, equations 15.35–15.38 show how the means, variances, and covariance of two random variables can be explicated in terms of characteristics of their joint probability distribution.

15.4.4 Probability Distributions in Econometrics

Econometricians usually specify the probability distributions of the random variables with which they work and then proceed without second thought about the appearance of the underlying probability space. We will next show how such a procedure can be justified.

The probability distributions most econometricians employ belong to well-defined classes of such distributions. Of these the most important class is described in E 15.21 and E 15.22.

E 15.21 Let $[\Omega, \mathscr{F}, P(\cdot))$ be a probability space and let $x(\cdot)$ be a random variable. Then $x(\cdot)$ is normally distributed if there exist constants $m \in R$ and $a \in R_{++}$ such that, for all $t \in R$,

$$F_x(t) = (2\pi a^2)^{-1/2} \int_{-\infty}^{t} \exp - \frac{(y-m)^2}{2a^2} d\mu(y). \tag{15.39}$$

In this case,

$$m = Ex \qquad \text{and} \qquad a^2 = \sigma_x^2. \tag{15.40}$$

E 15.22 Let $x_1(\cdot), \ldots, x_n(\cdot)$ be random variables on the same probability space $(\Omega, \mathscr{F}, P(\cdot))$, and suppose that there do not exist constants $a_1, \ldots, a_n$ such that

$$\sum_{i=1}^{n} a_i^2 > 0 \qquad \text{and} \qquad P\left(\left\{\omega \in \Omega : \sum_{i=1}^{n} a_i x_i(\omega) = 0\right\}\right) = 1. \tag{15.41}$$

Then the $x_i(\cdot)$ are jointly normally distributed if and only if there exists a positive, definite, symmetric, n-dimensional matrix, $A = (a_{ij})$, and a vector $m \in R^n$ such that, for all $b \in R^n$,

$$F_{x_1,\ldots,x_n}(b) = (2\pi)^{-n/2}|A|^{-1/2} \int_{-\infty}^{b_1} \cdots \int_{-\infty}^{b_n} \exp - [\tfrac{1}{2}(y-m)'A^{-1}(y-m)]\, d\mu(y_1)\cdots d\mu(y_n), \tag{15.42}$$

where $|A|$ denotes the determinant of A. In this case, for $1 \leqslant i, j \leqslant n$

$$m_i = Ex_i, \qquad a_{ii} = \sigma_{x_i}^2 \qquad \text{and} \qquad a_{ij} = \sigma_{x_i x_j} \quad \text{if } i \neq j. \tag{15.43}$$

With respect to examples E 15.21 and E 15.22 several remarks should be made. First, the conditions in equation 15.41 ensure that the joint distribution of the $x_i(\cdot)$ is not degenerate in the sense that it is concentrated on a subspace of R^n. Note, therefore, that there are degenerate normal distributions. We shall meet some of them in chapter 34. Second, if $x_1(\cdot), \ldots, x_n(\cdot)$ are jointly normally distributed, any subset of them is jointly normally distributed as well. In fact, if the joint distribution of the $x_i(\cdot)$ is as specified in equation 15.42, with $m = (m_1, \ldots, m_n)$ and $A = (a_{ij})$, then $x_i(\cdot)$ is normally distributed, with constants $m = m_i$ and $\sigma = a_{ii}^{1/2}$. Similarly, $x_i(\cdot)$ and $x_j(\cdot)$ are jointly normally distributed with $m = (m_i, m_j)$ and $A = \begin{pmatrix} a_{ii} & a_{ij} \\ a_{ji} & a_{jj} \end{pmatrix}$. Third, if $x(\cdot)$ and $y(\cdot)$ are normally distributed random variables, their joint distribution need not be normal. In E 15.23 I present a well-known example which establishes this fact.

E 15.23 Let $x(\cdot)$ and $y(\cdot)$ be random variables on the probability space $(\Omega, \mathscr{F}, P(\cdot))$ and suppose that the probability distribution of $x(\cdot)$ is normal with mean 0 and variance 1. Moreover, suppose that, for all $r \in R$,

$$P(y = r|x = r) = P(y = -r|x = r) = 0,5.$$

Then the probability distribution of $y(\cdot)$ is normal. However, the joint probability distribution of $x(\cdot)$ and $y(\cdot)$ is not.

Fourth and finally, if $x(\cdot)$ and $y(\cdot)$ are independently distributed random variables on the same probability space, their sum is normally distributed if and only if both $x(\cdot)$ and $y(\cdot)$ are normally distributed. A proof of this interesting fact is given in Cramér 1936 (pp. 405–409).

In E 15.21 and E 15.22 we postulated the existence of various random variables and prescribed the form their probability distributions must have in order that they be normally distributed. But how can we be sure that there exist random variables whose probability distributions are as specified in equations 15.39, 15.40, 15.42, and 15.43? That is, how do we know that the functions in equations 15.39 and 15.42 are probability distributions? We know because $F(x)$ in equation 15.39 satisfies the necessary conditions that we described in T 15.18, and $F_{x_1,\ldots,x_n}(\cdot)$ in equation 15.42 satisfies the necessary conditions that we specified in T 15.19, and because T 15.21 and T 15.22 below show that the necessary conditions are also sufficient conditions.

T 15.21 Suppose that $F(\cdot): R \to [0, 1]$ is monotone, nondecreasing, continuous from the left, and satisfies equation 15.43. Then there exist a probability space $(\Omega, \mathscr{F}, P(\cdot))$ and a random variable $x(\cdot)$ on it such that $F(\cdot)$ and $x(\cdot)$ satisfy equation 15.42, i.e., such that $F(\cdot)$ is the probability distribution of $x(\cdot)$.

According to the standard proof of this theorem, there is a σ-additive probability measure $P(\cdot)$ on R and its Borel field that satisfies, for all $(a, b) \in R^2$ such that $a < b$,

$$P([a, b)) = F(b) - F(a). \tag{15.44}$$

Relative to this $P(\cdot)$, the function, $x(\cdot): R \to R$, defined by

$$x(\omega) = \omega, \qquad \omega \in R$$

is a random variable whose probability distribution is $F(\cdot)$.

The n-dimensional analogue of T 15.21 is T 15.22.

T 15.22 Suppose that $F(\cdot)\colon R^n \to [0, 1]$ is monotone, nondecreasing, continuous from below, and satisfies equations 15.27, 15.28, and 15.29. Then there exist a probability space $(\Omega, \mathscr{F}, P(\cdot))$ and n random variables, $x_1(\cdot), \ldots, x_n(\cdot)$, on it such that $F(\cdot)$ and the $x_i(\cdot)$ satisfy equation 15.26, i.e., such that $F(\cdot)$ is the joint probability distribution of the $x_i(\cdot)$.

Its standard proof establishes the existence of a σ-additive probability measure $P(\cdot)$ on R^n and its Borel field that satisfies the n-dimensional analogue of equation 15.44: For all $a, b \in R^n$ with $a < b$,

$$P(\{x \in R^n : a \leqslant x < b\}) = \Delta_{b-a} F_{x_1, \ldots, x_n}(a) \tag{15.45}$$

where Δ_{b-a} is as described in equation 15.27. Relative to this $P(\cdot)$, the function $x(\cdot)\colon R^n \to R^n$ defined by

$$x(\omega) = \omega, \qquad \omega \in R^n$$

is a random vector whose probability distribution is $F(\cdot)$.

Theorems T 15.21 and T 15.22 show how the approach of econometricians to random variables can be justified. Note that these theorems assert the existence of a probability space and of certain variables on it which have a given joint probability distribution. These theorems do not insist that this space and those random variables are uniquely determined. They were not, for instance, in the example we gave of a probability space and a random variable for the $F(\cdot)$ in T 15.18. Another interesting example is the following: Let Ω be $(0, 1)$ and let $\mathscr{F}$ be the Borel field in Ω. Moreover, let $x(\cdot)\colon \Omega \to R$ be an inverse function of $F(\cdot)$. Then $x(\cdot)$ is a random variable whose probability distribution relative to the Lebesgue measure on Ω is $F(\cdot)$; i.e.,

$$\mu(\{\omega \in \Omega : x(\omega) < a\}) = \mu(\{\omega \in \Omega : \omega < F(a)\}), \qquad a \in R.$$

The interesting aspect of this example is that the probability space, $(\Omega, \mathscr{F}, \mu(\cdot))$, is kept fixed while we search for a random variable with the distribution $F(\cdot)$.

15.4.5 Convergence in Distributions

We conclude this section with a brief discussion of the notion of convergence in distribution.

Let $(\Omega, \mathscr{F}, P(\cdot))$ be a probability space and let $x_1(\cdot)$, $x_2(\cdot)$, ... be a sequence of random variables. We say that the $x_n(\cdot)$ *converge in distribution* to an F-distributed random variable if the probability distributions of the $x_n(\cdot)$, $F_{x_n}(\cdot)$, satisfy

$$F(x) = \lim F_{x_n}(x), \qquad x \in Cn(F),$$

where $Cn(F)$ denotes the set of continuity points of $F(\cdot)$. Moreover, we refer to $F(\cdot)$ as the *limiting* or the *asymptotic distribution* of the $x_n(\cdot)$.

E 15.24 Consider an experiment in which a coin is tossed n times under uniform conditions, and let $p \in (0, 1)$ denote the probability of heads. In addition, let S_n denote the number of tosses resulting in heads, and let $G_n(\cdot)$ and $F_n(\cdot)$, respectively, denote the probability distribution of S_n and $(S_n - np)/(np(1-p))^{1/2}$. Then

$$G_n(a) = \begin{cases} 0 & \text{if } a \leqslant 0 \\ \sum_{k=0}^{[a-1]} \binom{n}{k} p^k (1-p)^{n-k} & \text{if } 0 < a \leqslant n \\ 1 & \text{if } a > n \end{cases}$$

where $[a - 1]$ is the smallest natural number m such that $a - 1 \leqslant m$. Moreover,

$$\lim_{n\to\infty} F_n(a) = (2\pi)^{-1/2} \int_{-\infty}^{a} e^{-t^2/2}\, dt,$$

i.e., the random variables $(S_n - np)/(np(1-p))^{1/2}$ converge in distribution to a normally distributed random variable.

The three concepts of convergence, convergence with probability 1, convergence in probability, and convergence in distribution are not independent. Thus convergence with probability 1 implies convergence in probability, and the latter implies convergence in distribution. For the special case where the $x_n(\cdot)$ converge in probability to a constant α, convergence in probability and convergence in distribution are equivalent; i.e., with $F(a) = 0$ or 1, according as $a < \alpha$, $\alpha < a$, we have $p\lim x_n = \alpha$ if $\lim F_n(x) = F(x)$, $x \in Cn(F)$. More about this and related matters in the next section.

15.5 Random Processes and Kolmogorov's Consistency Theorem

Our discussion of convergence in sections 15.3.5 and 15.4.5 concerned the asymptotic behavior of an ever-expanding number of random variables; and the events we were asked to measure were determined by conditions imposed on the tail of the respective sequences. We conclude the chapter by discussing the problem of measuring events that are determined by conditions on a possibly infinite family of random variables.

15.5.1 Random Processes

A *random process* is a family of random variables, $\{x(t, \omega); t \in T\}$, on a probability space $(\Omega, \mathscr{F}, P(\cdot))$. Unless otherwise stated, it is assumed that the $x(t, \cdot)$ are real-valued and that T is a discrete index set such as $\{0, 1, \ldots\}$ or $\{\ldots, -1, 0, 1, \ldots\}$. Random processes can be classified in various ways. We shall distinguish between strictly and wide-sense stationary and nonstationary processes.

A random process is *strictly stationary* if and only if, for all n, all n-tuples $(t_1, \ldots, t_n)$ with $t_i \in T$, $i = 1, \ldots, n$, and all integers h with $t_i + h \in T$, $i = 1, \ldots, n$, the joint distributions of $x(t_1, \cdot), \ldots, x(t_n, \cdot)$ and $x(t_1 + h, \cdot), \ldots, x(t_n + h, \cdot)$ are identical. Examples of such a process are the sequences of identically and independently distributed random variables, which we discuss in chapter 16. They are called *purely random processes*. Other examples are the sequences of exchangeable random variables, which we discuss in chapter 18. They are called *exchangeable random processes*. Processes that are not strictly stationary are *strictly nonstationary*.

A *second-order process* is a random process whose random variables have finite first and second moments. Such a process is *wide-sense stationary* if and only if $Ex(t)$, $Ex(t)^2$ and $Ex(t)x(t+s)$, $t + s \in T$ are all independent of t. Strictly stationary second-order processes are wide-sense stationary. So is

$$x(t, \omega) = a(\omega)\cos\left(\frac{t\pi}{3}\right) + b(\omega)\sin\left(\frac{t\pi}{3}\right) + \eta(t, \omega), \qquad t \in T$$

where the $\eta(t, \cdot)$ are independently and identically distributed with mean 0 and variance 1 and where $a(\cdot)$ and $b(\cdot)$ have mean 0 and variance 1 and are distributed independently of one another and of the $\eta(t, \cdot)$. Second-order processes that are not wide-sense stationary are *nonstationary in the wide sense*. Examples are the dynamic stochastic processes discussed in chapter 33.

When we study a random process, our objective is often to delineate properties of the sample paths of the process. These are defined as follows: Let $\{x(t, \omega); t \in T\}$ be a random process on a probability space $(\Omega, \mathscr{F}, P(\cdot))$, let

$$\omega_t = x(t, \omega), \qquad t \in T$$

and let $\tilde{\omega}$ be the vector $(\omega_t; t \in T) \in R^T$. Then $\tilde{\omega}$ is the *sample path of values assumed by* $x(t, \omega)$ as t varies over T.

E 15.25 Consider an experiment in which a fair coin is tossed twenty times. Two of the roughly 1 million equally likely sample paths of outcomes are

0_1: H T H T H T H T H T H T H T H T H T H T
0_2: T H H H H T T T T H T T H T T T H T H H

In the preceding sections we would have noted that 0_1 contains ten H's, that 0_2 possesses nine, and that the probability of ten heads is greater than the probability of nine. For the purposes of this section, we note that 0_1 was obtained by writing down an alternating sequence of H's and T's, while 0_2 was determined by flipping a coin twenty times. One of the questions we discuss in chapter 16 is: What distinguishes sequences of outcomes that are generated by a random selection process from those determined by a deterministic selection process?

15.5.2 Kolmogorov's Consistency Theorem

To delineate characteristics of the sample paths of a random process and to answer questions such as the one in E 15.25, we must show how the probability distributions of the members of a process determine a unique probability measure on the space of sample paths of the process. For that purpose let $X = \{x(t, \omega); t \in T\}$ be a random process on a probability space $(\Omega, \mathscr{F}, P(\cdot))$ and, for each k-tuple of numbers in T, $t_1, \ldots, t_k$, let $F_{t_1,\ldots,t_k}(\cdot)$ denote the joint probability distribution of $x(t_1, \cdot), \ldots, x(t_k, \cdot)$ relative to $P(\cdot)$. Moreover, let $\Omega_t = R$ and $\tilde{\Omega} = \prod_{t \in T} \Omega_t$; let $\mathscr{F}_t$ be the Borel subsets of R; let C_T denote the class of cylinder sets

$$\prod_{j=1}^{k} A_{t_j} \times \prod_{\substack{t \neq t_j \\ j=1,\ldots,k}} \Omega_t, A_{t_j} \in \mathscr{F}_{t_j}; \quad t_j \in T; \quad j = 1, \ldots, k; \quad k \in \{1, 2, \ldots\}$$

let B_T denote the field of sets that consists of C_T and all sets that are finite disjoint unions of members of C_T; and let $\tilde{\mathscr{F}}$ denote the smallest σ field of subsets of $\tilde{\Omega}$ that contains B_T. Finally, let

$$\tilde{x}_t(\omega) = \omega_t, \qquad t \in T \text{ and } \omega \in \tilde{\Omega}.$$

Then $(\tilde{\Omega}, \tilde{\mathscr{F}})$ is the *sample space* of X, and the $\tilde{x}_t(\cdot)$ are random variables on $(\tilde{\Omega}, \tilde{\mathscr{F}})$, whose probability distributions are determined by a probability measure $\tilde{P}(\cdot)$ that we construct below.

To construct $\tilde{P}(\cdot)$ we first note that, with only obvious notational modifications, $F_{t_1,\ldots,t_k}(\cdot)$ satisfies the conditions specified in T 15.21 for $k = 1$ and in T 15.22 for $k > 1$. Furthermore, the family of all the joint probability distributions of the $x(t, \cdot)$ satisfies the following two consistency conditions, the latter one being a strengthening of equation 15.30:

(i) If $t_{\alpha_1}, \ldots, t_{\alpha_k}$ is a permutation of $t_1, \ldots, t_k$, then for all $(a_{t_1}, \ldots, a_{t_k}) \in R^k$,

$$F_{t_1,\ldots,t_k}(a_{t_1}, \ldots, a_{t_k}) = F_{t_{\alpha_1},\ldots,t_{\alpha_k}}(a_{t_{\alpha_1}}, \ldots, a_{t_{\alpha_k}}). \tag{15.46}$$

(ii) For any subset $\{s_1, \ldots, s_m\}$ of $\{t_1, \ldots, t_k\}$ and all $(a_{t_1}, \ldots, a_{t_k})$,

$$F_{s_1,\ldots,s_m}(a_{s_1}, \ldots, a_{s_m}) = \lim_{\substack{a_{t_i} \to \infty \\ t_i \neq s_j \\ j=1,\ldots,m \\ i=1,\ldots,k}} F_{t_1,\ldots,t_k}(a_{t_1}, \ldots, a_{t_k}). \tag{15.47}$$

Next, we use the joint probability distributions of the $x(t, \cdot)$ to assign numbers to the members of C_T in accordance with

$$P^*\left(\prod_{j=1}^{k} A_{t_j} \times \prod_{\substack{t \neq t_j \\ j=1,\dots,k}} \Omega_t\right) = \int_{A_{t_1}} \int_{A_{t_2}} \cdots \int_{A_{t_k}} dF_{t_1,\dots,t_k}(u_1, \dots, u_k),$$

$A_{t_j} \in \mathscr{F}_{t_j}$, $t_j \in T$ and $j = 1, \dots, k$; $k \in \{1, 2, \dots\}$. The properties of the $F_{t_1,\dots,t_k}(\cdot)$ ensure that $P^*(\cdot)$ is well defined on C_T and can be extended, first, to a σ-additive probability measure on $(\tilde{\Omega}, B_T)$ and, then, in one and only one way to a σ-additive probability measure $\tilde{P}(\cdot)$ on $(\tilde{\Omega}, \tilde{\mathscr{F}})$.

The $\tilde{P}(\cdot)$ constructed above is the probability measure we use to determine the joint probability distributions of the $\tilde{x}_t(\cdot)$. Specifically, for $k = 1, 2, \dots$, and each k-tuple, $t_1, \dots, t_k$, of numbers in T, we define the joint probability distribution of $\tilde{x}_{t_1}(\cdot), \dots, \tilde{x}_{t_k}(\cdot)$ by

$$\tilde{F}_{t_1,\dots,t_k}(a) = \tilde{P}(\{\omega \in \tilde{\Omega} : \tilde{x}_{t_1}(\omega) < a_1, \dots, \tilde{x}_{t_k}(\omega) < a_k\}), \qquad a \in R^k.$$

From this definition it follows that, for all k and each k-tuple $t_1, \dots, t_k$,

$$F_{t_1,\dots,t_k}(a) = \tilde{F}_{t_1,\dots,t_k}(a), \qquad a \in R^k. \tag{15.48}$$

Hence the $\tilde{x}_t(\cdot)$ have the same joint probability distributions as the corresponding $x(t, \cdot)$. Observe that, in constructing $\tilde{P}(\cdot)$, we used the joint probability distributions of the $x(t, \cdot)$ without referring to $P(\cdot)$. From this remark and from the discussion that preceded it, the validity of *Kolmogorov's consistency theorem*—T 15.23—follows.

T 15.23 Let $(\tilde{\Omega}, \tilde{\mathscr{F}})$ and the $\tilde{x}_t(\cdot)$, $t \in T$, be as specified above. In addition, let $\{F_{t_1,\dots,t_k}(\cdot), t_j \in T; j = 1, \dots, k; k \in \{1, 2, \dots\}\}$ be a family of probability distributions which, for $k = 1$ and $k > 1$, respectively, satisfy the conditions of T 15.21 and T 15.22 and the consistency requirements i and ii above. Then there exists a unique probability measure $\tilde{P}(\cdot)$ on $(\tilde{\Omega}, \tilde{\mathscr{F}})$, relative to which the joint probability distributions of the $\tilde{x}_t(\cdot)$ satisfy equation 15.48 for all k, each k-tuple $t_1, \dots, t_k$ in T and all $(a_1, \dots, a_k) \in R^k$.

15.5.3 The Measurement of Random Processes

To measure a random process means to assign numbers satisfying AK 1–AK 3 to the events of the experiment $(\tilde{\Omega}, \tilde{\mathscr{F}})$. Since the subsets of $\tilde{\Omega}$ in $\tilde{\mathscr{F}}$ are determined by conditions on infinitely many variables, the measurement of a stochastic (i.e., random) process sounds impossible, but it need not be. Kolmogorov's theorem shows that to do so we need only describe the finite-dimensional probability distributions of the process. Such a description can be obtained for many classes of processes which interest econometricians. Examples are the exchangeable processes of chapter 18, certain subclasses of the ARIMA processes and of the dynamic stochastic processes described in chapters 33 and 34, and purely random processes.

E 15.26 Let $\{x(t, \omega); t \in T\}$ be a purely random process on $(\Omega, \mathscr{F}, P(\cdot))$ and assume that every one of the $x(t, \cdot)$ relative to $P(\cdot)$ is normally distributed with mean μ and variance σ^2. The definition of a purely random process, given in section 16.1, shows that knowledge of μ and σ suffices to give a complete description of all the finite-dimensional probability distributions of the process.

15.6 Two Useful Universal Theorems

This chapter has provided a brief introduction to probability theory that touches on those basic ideas of the theory that are of particular interest to economists and econometricians. For the purposes of this book there are still two ideas we ought to mention: convergence in the mean and the Radon-Nikodym theorem.

To explicate the meaning of *convergence in the mean,* we let $x(\cdot)$ and $x_n(\cdot)$, $n = 1, 2, \ldots$, be integrable random variables on a probability space $(\Omega, \mathscr{F}, P(\cdot))$. The $x_n(\cdot)$ converge in the mean to $x(\cdot)$ if and only if

$$\lim_{n \to \infty} E|x_n - x| = 0.$$

When the $x_n(\cdot)$ converge in the mean to $x(\cdot)$, we shall write

$$\text{l.i.m.}\, x_n = x.$$

Examples of sequences of random variables that converge in the mean are easy to come by. For example, let $x(\cdot)$ be a bounded, nonnegative, random variable on a probability space $(\Omega, \mathscr{F}, P(\cdot))$, and let $x_n(\cdot)$ be the corresponding increasing sequence of simple functions that we defined in equation 15.1. Then the $x_n(\omega)$ converge a.e. to $x(\omega)$, and it is obvious that $\text{l.i.m.}\, x_n = x$ as well.

Other examples can be constructed with the help of the following consideration: Let $x(\cdot)$, $y(\cdot)$, and $x_n(\cdot)$, $n = 1, 2, \ldots$, be random variables on a probability space $(\Omega, \mathscr{F}, P(\cdot))$, and suppose that $p \lim x_n = x$. Suppose also that $y(\cdot)$ is integrable and that, for all $n = 1, 2, \ldots$, $|x_n(\omega)| \leqslant |y(\omega)|$ a.e. Then $x(\cdot)$ is integrable and $\text{l.i.m.}\, x_n = x$, an observation which is usually referred to as *Lebesgue's dominated convergence theorem* (see Loève 1960, p. 125, for a proof).

It is easy to see that if the $x_n(\cdot)$ converge in the mean to $x(\cdot)$, then

$$p\lim x_n = x \qquad \text{and} \qquad \lim_{n,m\to\infty} E|x_n - x_m| = 0.$$

The converse is also true—to wit, UT 16.

UT 16 If $x_n(\cdot)$, $n = 1, 2, \ldots$, is a sequence of integrable random variables on a probability space $(\Omega, \mathscr{F}, P(\cdot))$ and

$$\lim_{n,m\to\infty} E|x_n - x_m| = 0,$$

then there exists a random variable $x(\cdot)$ such that

$$\text{l.i.m.}\, x_n = x.$$

For a proof of this fact, see Loève 1960, p. 161.

There are several versions of the Radon-Nikodym theorem. The one most useful for our purposes can be phrased as follows:

UT 17 Let $(\Omega, \mathscr{F}, P(\cdot))$ be a probability space and let $\varphi(\cdot): \mathscr{F} \to R$ be σ-additive and bounded. Suppose that, for all $A \in \mathscr{F}$, $P(A) = 0$ only if $\varphi(A) = 0$. Then there exists an integrable random variable $h(\cdot)$ such that, for all $A \in \mathscr{F}$,

$$\varphi(A) = \int_A h(\omega)\, dP(\omega).$$

Moreover, if $g(\cdot)$ is another integrable random variable that, for all $A \in \mathscr{F}$, satisfies

$$\varphi(A) = \int_A g(\omega)\, dP(\omega),$$

then $h(\omega) = g(\omega)$ a.e..

In the statement of the theorem

$$\int_A h(\omega)\, dP(\omega) =_{df} \int_\Omega I_A(\omega) h(\omega)\, dP(\omega).$$

For a proof of UT 17 and other versions of the Radon-Nikodym theorem, the reader is referred to Loève 1960, pp. 130–134.

The Radon-Nikodym theorem has many useful applications. As an example, we shall here use UT 17 to obtain an interesting characterization of absolutely continuous probability distributions. To that end, let A be an interval, e.g., R, R_+ or $[a, b)$ for some finite reals a and b, with $a < b$, and let $f(\cdot): A \to R$. Then $f(\cdot)$ is *absolutely continuous* if and only if, for every $\varepsilon > 0$ there is a $\delta > 0$ such that, for each finite collection $[a_i, b_i)$, $i = 1, \ldots, k$, of nonoverlapping subintervals of A,

$$\sum_{i=1}^{k} |f(b_i) - f(a_i)| < \varepsilon \qquad \text{if} \qquad \sum_{i=1}^{k} (b_i - a_i) < \delta.$$

Examples of such functions are x and any $f(\cdot)$ for which there exists a positive constant K such that $|f(b) - f(a)| < K|b - a|$ for all pairs of reals in A such that $a < b$.

Absolutely continuous functions have many interesting properties. For example:

(i) If $A = [a, b)$ for some finite reals a and b and if $f(\cdot)\colon A \to R$ is absolutely continuous, then $f(\cdot)$ has a finite derivative a.e. (Lebesgue measure) in A (see Graves 1956, pp. 203 and 205).

(ii) If $A = R$, if $f(\cdot)\colon A \to [0, 1]$ is a probability distribution, and if $\mu_f(\cdot)$ is the probability measure of Lebesgue measurable subsets of A that satisfies $\mu_f([a, b)) = f(b) - f(a)$ for all pairs of reals with $a < b$, then $f(\cdot)$ is absolutely continuous if and only if $\mu_f(B) = 0$ whenever B has Lebesgue measure 0 (see Billingsley 1979, pp. 365–368).

From property ii and UT 17—with $\mathscr{F}$ being the σ field of Lebesgue measurable sets—we deduce:

(iii) If $A = R$ and $f(\cdot)\colon A \to [0, 1]$ is a probability distribution, then $f(\cdot)$ is absolutely continuous if and only if there exists an integrable random function $h(\cdot)\colon A \to R$ such that, for all $x \in R$,

$$f(x) = \int_{-\infty}^{x} h(t)\, d\mu(t)$$

where $\mu(\cdot)$ is the Lebesgue measure. In this case $f'(x) = h(x)$ a.e. (Lebesgue measure) and $h(\cdot)$ is called the *density*, or the *density function*, of $f(\cdot)$.

Throughout this chapter we have studiously avoided using the term "measurable function." This may be disconcerting to some. So I conclude the chapter by observing that in the context of this book a *measurable function* is simply a random variable. More specifically, if $(\Omega, \mathscr{F})$ is an experiment and $f(\cdot)$ is a real-valued function on Ω, then $f(\cdot)$ is *measurable with respect to* $\mathscr{F}$ if and only if $\mathscr{F}(f) \subset \mathscr{F}$. Moreover, $f(\cdot)$ is $\mathscr{F}$*-measurable* if and only if it is measurable with respect to $\mathscr{F}$. Finally, $f(\cdot)$ is a measurable function on $(\Omega, \mathscr{F})$ if and only if it is an $\mathscr{F}$-measurable function on Ω; and when $\mathscr{F}$ is the Borel field of [0, 1] or R (the field of Lebesgue measurable subsets of [0, 1] or R), an $\mathscr{F}$-measurable function is said to be *Borel measurable* (Lebesgue measurable).

16 Chance

Chance can mean an apparent absence of a cause or a fortuitous event. It can also mean the possibility of an occurrence or the intrinsic probability of an event, e.g., the probability of heads on a coin toss or a 6 on a dice roll. Finally, it can mean a dispositional property of an experiment that is to be repeated infinitely many times under uniform conditions. In this chapter we search for an explication of the concept of chance by studying characteristics of sample paths of a purely random process.

16.1 Purely Random Processes

To say what we mean by a purely random process, we must first explicate the meaning of independent events and variables.

16.1.1 Independent Events and Variables

Let $(\Omega, \mathcal{F}, P(\cdot))$ be a probability space, and recall that two events A and B are independent if and only if $P(A \cap B) = P(A) \cdot P(B)$. This condition generalizes to a finite number of events, $A_1, \ldots, A_n$. They are independent if and only if, for every subset $\{t_1, \ldots, t_k\}$ of $\{1, \ldots, n\}$,

$$P\left(\bigcap_{i=1}^{k} A_{t_i}\right) = \prod_{i=1}^{k} P(A_{t_i}). \tag{16.1}$$

Similarly, if T is an index set, the events A_t, $t \in T$, are independent if and only if, for all finite subsets $\{t_1, \ldots, t_k\}$ of T, equation 16.1 holds.

Consider next a family of classes of events, $\{C_t, t \in T\}$. These classes are said to be independent if and only if their members are independent. Evidently, if the C_t are independent, so are their subclasses. Moreover, their independence is preserved if to every C_t we adjoin $\emptyset$ and Ω, proper differences of its elements, countable disjoint unions of its elements, and limits of sequences of its elements. From these observations we can deduce the validity of T 16.1:

T 16.1 Let $(\Omega, \mathscr{F}, P(\cdot))$ be a probability space and let $\{C_t, t \in T\}$ be a family of classes of events. Assume that the C_t are closed under finite intersections and let $\mathscr{F}_t$ be the minimal σ field that contains C_t. If the C_t are independent, so are the members of the family, $\{\mathscr{F}_t, t \in T\}$.

Two random variables $x(\cdot)$ and $y(\cdot)$ on $(\Omega, \mathscr{F}, P(\cdot))$ are said to be independent if and only if $\mathscr{F}(x(\cdot))$ and $\mathscr{F}(y(\cdot))$ are independent. From this it follows that, if $x(\cdot)$ and $y(\cdot)$ are independent, then, for all $(a, b) \in R^2$,

$$P(\{\omega \in \Omega : x(\omega) < a, y(\omega) < b\})$$
$$= P(\{\omega \in \Omega : x(\omega) < a\}) \cdot P(\{\omega \in \Omega : y(\omega) < b\}).$$

Similarly, if $x_1(\cdot), \ldots, x_n(\cdot)$ are random variables, they are independent if and only if the σ fields $\mathscr{F}(x_1(\cdot)), \ldots, \mathscr{F}(x_n(\cdot))$ are independent. If the $x_i(\cdot)$, $i = 1, \ldots, n$, are independent, then for all subsets $\{t_1, \ldots, t_k\}$ of $\{1, \ldots, n\}$ and for all $(a_1, \ldots, a_k) \in R^k$,

$$P(\{\omega \in \Omega : x_{t_1}(\omega) < a_1, \ldots, x_{t_k}(\omega) < a_k\}) = \prod_{i=1}^{k} P(\{\omega \in \Omega : x_{t_i}(\omega) < a_i\}). \tag{16.2}$$

Finally, families of random variables $\{x_t(\cdot); t \in T\}$ are independent if and only if their finite subfamilies are mutually independent.

16.1.2 A Purely Random Process

A random process $\{x(t, \omega); t \in T\}$ on a probability space $(\Omega, \mathscr{F}, P(\cdot))$ is a *purely random process* if and only if the $x(t, \cdot)$ relative to $P(\cdot)$ are independently and identically distributed. This definition and equation 16.2 show why the finite-dimensional distributions of the random process in E 15.26 can be specified by assigning numbers to μ and σ.

It is difficult to understand the meaning of a random process. Consider, therefore, the following example:

E 16.1 Let $\Omega = [0, 1)$, let $\mathscr{F}$ denote the Borel subsets of Ω, and let $\mu(\cdot): \mathscr{F} \to [0, 1]$ be the Lebesgue measure. On the probability space $(\Omega, \mathscr{F}, \mu(\cdot))$ we define the random variables,

$$x(n,\omega) = \begin{cases} 0 & \text{if } \omega \in \bigcup_{\substack{i_j=0 \\ j=1,\dots,n-1}}^{9} \left[\sum_{j=1}^{n-1} i_j 10^{-j}, \sum_{j=1}^{n-1} i_j 10^{-j} + 10^{-n}\right) \\ \vdots \\ 9 & \text{if } \omega \in \bigcup_{\substack{i_j=0 \\ j=1,\dots,n-1}}^{9} \left[\sum_{j=1}^{n-1} i_j 10^{-j} + 9\cdot 10^{-n}, \sum_{j=1}^{n-1} i_j 10^{-j} + 10^{-(n-1)}\right) \end{cases}$$

for all $n = 1, 2, \ldots$. The $x_n(\cdot)$ are independent and have the common probability distribution

$$F_{x_1}(a) = \begin{cases} 0 & \text{if } a \leqslant 0 \\ 10^{-1} & \text{if } 0 < a \leqslant 1 \\ & \vdots \\ 9/10 & \text{if } 8 < a \leqslant 9 \\ 1 & \text{if } a > 9 \end{cases}$$

One way to envision the $x(n, \cdot)$ is to think of the value of $x(i, \omega)$ as denoting the number obtained in the ith draw (with replacement) from an urn that contains ten identical balls marked with the numerals 0, 1, ..., 9. Another way to envision the $x(n, \cdot)$ is to think of the sequence of values, $x(1, \omega), x(2, \omega), \ldots$, as representing the outcome of an experiment in which a number in $[0, 1)$ is chosen at random. To see why, observe that, for all $\omega \in \Omega$,

$$\omega = \sum_{n=1}^{\infty} x(n,\omega) 10^{-n}.$$

From our point of view it is important to note that the two experiments described in E 16.1 can be given a different mathematical representation. To wit: Let $T = \{1, 2, \ldots\}$ and, for all $t \in T$, let $\Omega_t = \{0, 1, \ldots, 9\}$ and $\mathscr{F}_t = \mathscr{P}(\Omega_t)$, and let $P_t(\cdot)$ be a probability measure on $(\Omega_t, \mathscr{F}_t)$ satisfying

$$P_t(\{i\}) = 10^{-1}, \qquad i = 0, 1, \ldots, 9. \tag{16.3}$$

Furthermore, let $\tilde{\Omega} = \prod_{t=1}^{\infty} \Omega_t$ and let $\tilde{\mathscr{F}}$ be the smallest σ field containing all the cylinder sets in $\prod_{t=1}^{\infty} \Omega_t$. The $P_t(\cdot)$ determine—in the manner described in section 15.5—a σ-additive probability measure $\tilde{P}(\cdot)$ on $(\tilde{\Omega}, \tilde{\mathscr{F}})$ satisfying the following conditions: (1) For all $t \in T$ and $A \in \mathscr{F}_t$,

$$\mu(\{\omega \in \Omega : x(t,\omega) \in A\}) = P_t(A)$$
$$= \tilde{P}\left(A \times \prod_{\substack{s \in T \\ s \neq t}} \Omega_s\right)$$

and (2) for all $k \in T$, $t_j \in T$, and $A_{t_j} \in \mathscr{F}_{t_j}$, $j = 1, \ldots, k$,

$$\mu(\{\omega \in \Omega : x(t_1, \omega) \in A_{t_1}, \ldots, x(t_k, \omega) \in A_{t_k}\}) = \prod_{j=1}^{k} P_{t_j}(A_{t_j})$$
$$= \tilde{P}\left(\prod_{j=1}^{k} A_{t_j} \times \prod_{\substack{s \in T \\ s \neq t_j \\ j=1,\ldots,k}} \Omega_s \right).$$

Hence, if we let

$$\tilde{x}(t, \tilde{\omega}) = \tilde{\omega}_t, \qquad t \in T \text{ and } \tilde{\omega} \in \tilde{\Omega}, \tag{16.4}$$

and observe that the $\tilde{x}(t, \cdot)$ are random variables on $(\tilde{\Omega}, \tilde{\mathscr{F}})$, we see that the joint probability distributions of the $x(t, \cdot)$ relative to $\mu(\cdot)$ are identical with the joint probability distributions of the $\tilde{x}(t, \cdot)$ relative to $\tilde{P}(\cdot)$. That is, $(\Omega, \mathscr{F}, \mu(\cdot))$ and the $x(n, \cdot)$ of E 16.1 and $(\tilde{\Omega}, \tilde{\mathscr{F}}, \tilde{P}(\cdot))$ and the $\tilde{x}(t, \cdot)$ of equation 16.4 provide two different descriptions of the same experiment.

16.2 Games of Chance

A glance at a sample path of a purely random process, e.g., the one recorded in figure 16.1, suggests that such paths are erratic. In fact, in figure 16.1 every event seems to have been fortuitous in two ways:

1. Each happened by chance; i.e., the event could not have been predicted on the basis of past events.
2. Its occurrence carried no information as to the likelihood of future events.

In this section we shall study characteristics of sample paths of a purely random process and discuss the way gamblers and ordinary people might experience these paths as they wage their luck in so-called games of chance.

16.2.1 The Absence of Successful Gambling Systems

We begin in T 16.2 by describing how luck and the absence of cause are reflected in the characteristics of sample paths of a purely random process. In the statement of this theorem $T = \{0, 1, \ldots\}$ and $(\tilde{\Omega}, \tilde{\mathscr{F}})$ is the space of sample paths of the process in question. Moreover, a *gambling sytem relative to* $P(\cdot)$ is a family $\{\varphi_i(\cdot); i \in T\}$ of random variables on $(\tilde{\Omega}, \tilde{\mathscr{F}})$ satisfying the following conditions:

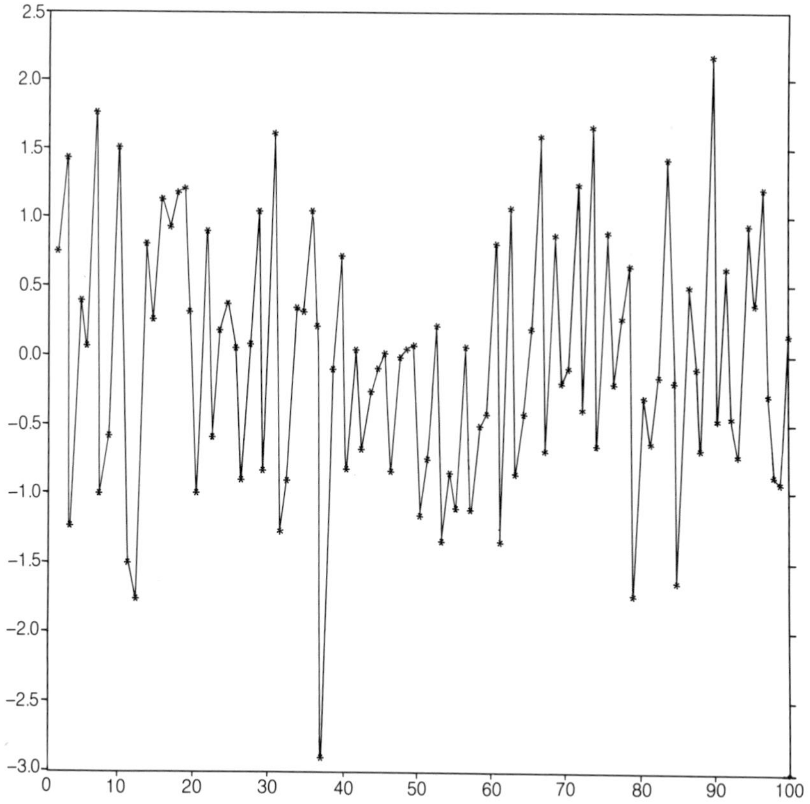

Figure 16.1
Sample path of a purely random process.

(i) $\varphi_i(\cdot): \tilde{\Omega} \to \{0, 1\}$;
(ii) $\varphi_0(\cdot)$ is a constant;
(iii) $\varphi_i(\tilde{\omega})$ varies with the first i components of $\tilde{\omega}$ only, and
(iv) $\limsup_i \varphi_i(\tilde{\omega}) = 1$ a.e. ($\tilde{P}$ measure), where $\tilde{P}(\cdot)$ is the (product) probability measure on $(\tilde{\Omega}, \tilde{\mathscr{F}})$ determined by $P(\cdot)$ and the process in question.

The theorem is due to J. L. Doob (1936, pp. 363–367).

T 16.2 Let $\{x(t, \omega); t \in T\}$ be a purely random process on $(\Omega, \mathscr{F}, P(\cdot))$, and let $\{\varphi_i(\cdot); i \in T\}$ be a gambling system relative to $P(\cdot)$. Moreover, let

$x(\omega) = (x(0, \omega), x(1, \omega), \ldots)$,

let $\theta(n, x)$ denote the nth value of i for which $\varphi_i(x) = 1$, and let

$\tilde{x}(\omega) = (x(\theta(0, x(\omega)), \omega), x(\theta(1, x(\omega)), \omega), \ldots)$.

Then, for all $B \in \tilde{\mathscr{F}}$,

$$P\{\omega \in \Omega : x(\omega) \in B\} = P\{\omega \in \Omega : \tilde{x}(\omega) \in B\}. \tag{16.5}$$

To prove the theorem it suffices to establish equation 16.5 for a cylinder set. So we suppose that

$$B = \prod_{j=1}^{k} A_{t_j} \times \prod_{\substack{s \in T \\ s \neq t_j \\ j=1,\ldots,k}} \Omega_s,$$

where $A_{t_j} \in \mathscr{F}$, $t_j \in T$, $j = 1, \ldots, k$; $k \in \{1, 2, \ldots\}$ and $t_1 < t_2 < \cdots < t_k$. Then we proceed by induction on k. If $k = 1$,

$$\begin{aligned}
&P(\{\omega \in \Omega : \tilde{x}(\omega) \in B\}) \\
&\quad = P(\{\omega \in \Omega : x(\theta(t_1, x(\omega)), \omega) \in A_{t_1}\}) \\
&\quad = \sum_{i=t_1}^{\infty} P(\{\omega \in \Omega : \theta(t_1, \omega) = i, x(i, \omega) \in A_{t_1}\}) \\
&\quad = \sum_{i=t_1}^{\infty} P(\{\omega \in \Omega : \theta(t_1, \omega) = i\}) \cdot P(\{\omega \in \Omega : x(i, \omega) \in A_{t_1}\}) \\
&\quad = P(\{\omega \in \Omega : x(t_1, \omega) \in A_{t_1}\}) \cdot \sum_{i=t_1}^{\infty} P(\{\omega \in \Omega : \theta(t_1, \omega) = i\}) \\
&\quad = P(\{\omega \in \Omega : x(t_1, \omega) \in A_{t_1}\}) \\
&\quad = P(\{\omega \in \Omega : x(\omega) \in B\}).
\end{aligned}$$

If equation (16.5) is valid for $k = 1, \ldots, n - 1$, and

$$B_{n-1} = \prod_{j=1}^{n-1} A_{t_j} \times \prod_{\substack{s \in T \\ s \neq t_j, j=1,\ldots,n-1}} \Omega_s,$$

then

$$P(\{\omega \in \Omega : \tilde{x}(\omega) \in B\})$$

$$= \sum_{i=t_n}^{\infty} P(\{\omega \in \Omega : \tilde{x}(\omega) \in B_{n-1}, \theta(t_n, \omega) = i, x(i, \omega) \in A_{t_n}\})$$

$$= P(\{\omega \in \Omega : x(t_n, \omega) \in A_{t_n}\}) \cdot \sum_{i=t_n}^{\infty} P(\{\omega \in \Omega : \tilde{x}(\omega) \in B_{n-1}, \theta(t_n, \omega) = i\})$$

$$= P(\{\omega \in \Omega : x(t_n, \omega) \in A_{t_n}\}) \cdot P(\{\omega \in \Omega : \tilde{x}(\omega) \in B_{n-1}\})$$

$$= P(\{\omega \in \Omega : x(t_n, \omega) \in A_{t_n}\}) \cdot P(\{\omega \in \Omega : x(\omega) \in B_{n-1}\})$$

$$= P(\{\omega \in \Omega : x(\omega) \in B\})$$

as was to be shown.

To the extent that we can represent games of chance by purely random processes, T 16.2 insists that there is no such thing as a successful gambling system. To see why, envision a game that is to be repeated infinitely many times under uniform conditions. Participants can partake in each and every game or just in some of them. A gambler who participates in the tth game receives the value assumed by $x(t, \cdot)$. Those who pass gain nothing and pay nothing. In deciding whether to participate in the various games, a gambler may use a gambling system. If he does, then at each t the gambler will record the outcomes of the first t trials of the game, $x(0, \omega), \ldots, x(t-1, \omega)$, and compute the value of $\varphi_t(x(0, \omega), \ldots, x(t-1, \omega), y)$ for some $y \in R^T$. If the value is 1, he will participate in the $(t+1)$st game; otherwise he will wait until the $(t+2)$nd game. Condition iv of a gambling system ensures that the gambler will participate in infinitely many games, and equation 16.5 shows that the conditions of the game (i.e., the gambler's chances for gains and losses) do not vary with his choice of a gambling system.

16.2.2 The Arc Sine Law

While observing successive outcomes of a game, gamblers and ordinary people often entertain the idea that the probability of success on the "next" trial increases with the length of consecutive failures. This idea is usually referred to as the *gambler's fallacy*. How fallacious it is is borne out by T 16.2. Another common belief is that in a prolonged, fair, symmetric game the accumulated gains of a gambler ought to be nonnegative roughly half the time. We next see how fallacious this belief is. First an example.

E 16.2 Consider a coin-tossing experiment with a balanced coin, i.e., a coin for which the probability of heads is 0.5. Let $x_i(\cdot)$, $i = 1, 2, \ldots$ be a representation on $(\Omega, \mathscr{F}, P(\cdot))$ of an infinite sequence of repetitions of this experiment, and assume that these variables assume the value $+1$ and -1 according as the respective tosses end in heads or tails. Moreover, let $S_0(\omega) = 0$, let $S_n(\cdot) = \sum_{i=1}^{n} x_i(\cdot)$, $n = 1, 2, \ldots$, and agree that the sequence $s_n(\omega)$, $n = 0, 1, \ldots$, spends the time from $k-1$ to k on the positive side if $S_k(\omega) \geqslant 0$ and $S_{k-1}(\omega) \geqslant 0$. Finally, assume that the first twenty outcomes of the game are as recorded in 0_2 in E 15.25. Then observe that $S_{20}(0_2)$ spends fourteen periods of time on the negative side. Notice also that, from the eighth toss on, $S_n(0_2)$ spends all the time on the negative side. The probability that $S_n(\cdot)$ spends at least fourteen periods on one and the same side is 0.8160.

In the example, the value of $S_n(\cdot)$ can be interpreted as the accumulated gains after n trials of a gambler who in each performance of the game wins (or loses) a dollar with probability $\frac{1}{2}$ $(\frac{1}{2})$. The example suggests that a gambler who participates in a sequence of fair symmetric games must be prepared to face long periods in which his losses outweighs his gains. How long these periods might be is borne out by T 16.3. The theorem is due to P. Erdøs and M. Kac. The proof is given in Erdøs and Kac 1947 (pp. 1011–1020).

T 16.3 Let $T = \{1, 2, \ldots\}$ and let $\{\eta(t, \omega); t \in T\}$ be a purely random process on a probability space $(\Omega, \mathscr{F}, P(\cdot))$. In addition, assume that the probability distribution of $\eta(1, \omega)$ is symmetric with mean 0 and finite variance. Finally, let $\{x(t, \omega); t \in T\}$ be a random process that satisfies the difference equations

$$x(t, \omega) = x(t-1, \omega) + \eta(t, \omega), \qquad t \in T \tag{16.6}$$

and

$$x(0, \omega) = 0, \tag{16.7}$$

and let $\psi(\cdot): R \to \{0, 1\}$ be such that, for all $y \in R$, $\psi(y) = 1$ if and only if $y \in R_{++}$. Then, for all $\alpha \in (0, 1)$,

$$\lim P\left(\left\{\omega \in \Omega : n^{-1} \sum_{t=1}^{n} \psi(x(t, \omega)) < \alpha\right\}\right) = 2\pi^{-1} \arcsin \alpha^{1/2}. \tag{16.8}$$

When the $\eta(t, \cdot)$ assume the values $+1$ and -1, each with probability $\frac{1}{2}$, T 16.3 implies that in one out of ten cases the path of the $x(t, \cdot)$ will spend 99.4 percent of the time on the same side of the origin; and in one of five cases the path of the $x(t, \cdot)$ will stay for roughly 97.6 percent of the time on the same side of the origin (see Feller 1957, pp. 80–81).

16.2.3 The Classical Ruin Problem

A gambler's ability to survive the periods in which his accumulated gains are negative depends on his net worth. We conclude this section by describing this for the game analogy of the experiment in E 16.2.

Suppose that the net worth of a gambler is \$z and let T, $\{\eta(t,\omega); t \in T\}$ and $\{x(t,\omega); t \in T\}$ be as in T 16.3, with the 0 in equation 16.7 replaced by \$z. Furthermore, assume that the $\eta(t,\cdot)$ assume the values $+\$1$ and $-\$1$, each with probability $\frac{1}{2}$. Then, for each $\omega \in \Omega$, $x(t,\omega)$ and $(x(t,\omega) - \$z)$, respectively, record the gambler's net worth and his accumulated gains at the end of the tth game. In a game in which the gambler can borrow funds to sustain arbitrarily large losses, the probability that $x(t,\omega) = \$a$ (with $a > z$) for the first time at $t = 2n - (a - z)$ equals, when $n \geqslant a - z$,

$$((a - z)/(2n - (a - z)))\binom{2n - (a - z)}{n}2^{-2n+(a-z)}.$$

Moreover, the probability that $x(t,\cdot)$ eventually will reach \$a is 1, but the expected value of the length of time the gambler might have to wait for it to happen is infinitely large.

Suppose next that our gambler has decided to play until his net worth equals \$a or \$0—whichever happens first. Assume that $1 \leqslant z \leqslant a - 1$ and let p_z and q_z, respectively, denote the probability that the gambler stops when his net worth equals \$a and when his net worth equals \$0. Then q_z satisfies the following difference equation:

$$q_z = \tfrac{1}{2}q_{z+1} + \tfrac{1}{2}q_{z-1} \tag{16.9}$$

and

$$q_0 = 1 \qquad \text{and} \qquad q_a = 0$$

with solution

$$q_z = 1 - \frac{z}{a}.$$

In addition, p_z satisfies equation 16.9 with the initial conditions

$$p_0 = 0 \qquad \text{and} \qquad p_a = 1.$$

The solution is given by

$$p_z = \frac{z}{a}.$$

Hence $p_z + q_z = 1$. Moreover, if the gambler's initial worth is, say, \$1000, the probability that $x(t, \cdot)$ will reach \$1250 before it hits 0 is 0.8.

The expected length of time D_z that it takes the gambler's net worth either to reach \$$a$ or to drop to \$0 can be calculated in a similar way. Specifically, D_z is finite and satisfies the following difference equation:

$$D_z = \tfrac{1}{2}D_{z+1} + \tfrac{1}{2}D_{z-1} + 1$$

$$D_0 = 0 \qquad \text{and} \qquad D_a = 0$$

with solution

$$D_z = z(a - z).$$

Hence, with $z = 1000$ and $a = 1250$, the expected number of games that it will take before either the gambler has won \$250 or his adversary has ruined him equals 250,000.[1]

16.3 The Law of Large Numbers

Sequences of independent events and independent random variables have many interesting statistical properties. We record some of them in theorems T 16.4–T 16.8.

16.3.1 Tail Events and Functions

Let $x_i(\cdot)$, $i = 1, 2, \ldots$, be an infinite sequence of random variables on a probability space $(\Omega, \mathscr{F}, P(\cdot))$ and observe that the sequence of σ fields, $\mathscr{F}(x_n(\cdot), x_{n+1}(\cdot), \ldots)$, $\mathscr{F}(x_{n+1}(\cdot), x_{n+2}(\cdot), \ldots)$, $\ldots$ is nonincreasing. Their intersection C is called the *tail σ field* or the *sub-σ field of events induced by the tail of the sequence $x_n(\cdot)$*. The members of C are called *tail events*, and the random variables on (Ω, C) are called *tail functions*.

E 16.3 Let $x_i(\cdot)$, $i = 1, 2, \ldots$, be an infinite sequence of random variables on a probability space $(\Omega, \mathscr{F}, P(\cdot))$. Then $\liminf x_n$ and $\limsup x_n$ are tail functions. The subset of Ω where the sequence $n^{-1}\sum_{i=1}^{n} x_i(\cdot)$, $n = 1, 2, \ldots$, converges is a tail event.

Both tail events and tail functions of purely random processes are degenerate—to wit T 16.4 and T 16.5.

T 16.4 The tail events of a sequence of independent random variables have probability 0 or 1. The tail functions are degenerate (i.e., they are constants with probability 1).

The proof is as follows: Let $x_i(\cdot)$, $i = 1, 2, \ldots$, be a sequence of independent random variables on a probability space $(\Omega, \mathscr{F}, P(\cdot))$ and let C denote the tail σ field of the sequence. Then $C \subset \mathscr{F}(x_n(\cdot), x_{n+1}(\cdot), \ldots)$ no matter what the value of n is. Hence C is independent of $\mathscr{F}(x_1(\cdot), \ldots, x_n(\cdot))$ for each and every n. It follows that C is independent of $\mathscr{F}(x_1(\cdot), x_2(\cdot), \ldots)$. But then C is independent of itself. So if $A \in C$, $P(A \cap A) = P(A) \cdot P(A)$, which can happen only if $P(A) = 0$ or 1. This establishes the first half of T 16.4. The second half is an immediate consequence of the first half.

T 16.5 If A_n, $n = 1, 2, \ldots$, are independent events, then $P(\limsup A_n) = 0$ or 1 according as $\sum_{n=1}^{\infty} P(A_n) < \infty$ or $= \infty$.

To see why, it suffices to observe that, for all n and m,

$$1 - \exp\left(-\sum_{i=n}^{m} P(A_i)\right) \leqslant 1 - \prod_{i=n}^{m} (1 - P(A_i)) \leqslant \sum_{i=n}^{m} P(A_i),$$

and that

$$P(\limsup A_i) = \lim_{n\to\infty} \lim_{m\to\infty} P\left(\bigcup_{i=n}^{m} A_i\right) = \lim_{n\to\infty} \lim_{m\to\infty} \left(1 - P\left(\bigcap_{i=n}^{m} A_i^C\right)\right).$$

Of the last two theorems, T 16.4 is Kolmogorov's 0–1 Law and T 16.5 presents Borel's 0–1 Criterion. Insight into the meaning of T 16.4 can be gained from Kolmogorov's *Strong Law of Large Numbers*, which we discuss next.

16.3.2 Kolmogorov's Strong Law of Large Numbers

There are many laws of large numbers. The one most interesting to us is due to Kolmogorov and is stated in T 16.6. A proof of the theorem can be found in Loève 1960 (pp. 239–240).

T 16.6 Let $x_1(\cdot), x_2(\cdot), \ldots$, be an infinite sequence of independent random variables on $(\Omega, \mathscr{F}, P(\cdot))$ with common probability distribution $F(\cdot)$. Then there is a finite constant c such that

$$\lim n^{-1} \sum_{i=1}^{n} x_i(\omega) = c \quad \text{a.e.} \tag{16.10}$$

if and only if $E|x_1| < \infty$; and then $c = Ex_1$.

One interesting corollary of T 16.6 can be deduced from the following observations: Let the $x_i(\cdot)$ be as in T 16.6 and let $g(\cdot)\colon R \to R$ be such that for all $a \in R$, $\{x \in R : g(x) < a\}$ is a Borel set. Then $\mathscr{F}(g(x_i(\cdot))) \subset \mathscr{F}(x_i(\cdot))$, $i = 1, 2, \ldots$. Since the σ fields, $\mathscr{F}(x_i(\cdot))$, $i = 1, 2, \ldots$, are independent, their sub-σ fields, $\mathscr{F}(g(x_i(\cdot)))$, $i = 1, 2, \ldots,$ are independent too. From this it follows that the random variables, $g(x_i(\cdot))$, $i = 1, 2, \ldots,$ are independent. Moreover, since the $x_i(\cdot)$ have a common distribution, so do the $g(x_i(\cdot))$. With this in mind we state the corollary:

T 16.7 Let the $x_i(\cdot)$ be as in T 16.6 and let

$$A(a) = (-\infty, a), \qquad a \in R.$$

Then the random variables, $I_{A(a)}(x_i(\cdot))$, $i = 1, 2, \ldots,$ are independent and have a common probability distribution. Moreover,

$$\lim n^{-1} \sum_{i=1}^{n} I_{A(a)}(x_i(\omega)) = F_{x_1}(a) \quad \text{a.e.} \tag{16.11}$$

E 16.4 serves to illustrate the import of T 16.6 and T 16.7.

E 16.4 Let $T = \{1, 2, \ldots\}$ and let $(\Omega, \mathscr{F}, \mu(\cdot))$ and $x(t, \cdot)$, $t \in T$, be as described in E 16.1. Then

$$\lim_{n\to\infty} n^{-1} \sum_{t=1}^{n} x(t, \omega) = 4.5 \quad \text{a.e.} \tag{16.12}$$

and

$$\lim_{n\to\infty} n^{-1} \sum_{t=1}^{n} I_{A(a)}(x(t, \omega)) = F_{x_1}(a) \quad \text{a.e., } a \in R. \tag{16.13}$$

Our discussion of E 16.1 shows that T 16.6 and T 16.7 can be considered as asserting that numerous observations on the values assumed by one random variable can be used to determine the intrinsic probability of observing any one of the events we associate with the random variable. Such an interpretation of T 16.6 and T 16.7 is interesting; e.g., it suggests that, by repeating an experiment in which we pick a ball from an urn with an uncertain composition of red and white balls, we would, after sufficiently many repetitions, eventually be able to determine the true proportion of red balls in the urn. Similarly, by tossing a coin sufficiently many times, we could determine the true probability of heads.

These observations sound good, but can be misunderstood. Let us, therefore, take another look at E 16.1 and interpret it as describing an experiment in which a number is drawn repeatedly (with replacement) from an urn containing ten identical balls marked with the numerals 0, 1, ..., 9. The probability of picking a prescribed infinite sequence of numbers is zero; i.e., the likelihood that we will observe the sequence $\omega_0 = 3333\ldots.$ is as large as the likelihood that we will observe $\omega_1 = 454545\ldots.$ or $\omega_2 = 012345678901234\ldots.$ Yet ω_0 will yield 3 as a limit in equation 16.12 and $F_{x_1}(a) = 0$ if $a \leqslant 3$ and $F_{x_1}(a) = 1$ if $3 < a \leqslant 9$ as a limit in equation

16.13, whereas ω_2 will yield the right limits in both equation 16.12 and 16.13. Note in this respect that ω_1 yields the right limit in equation 16.12 and the wrong limit in equation 16.13. Therefore the exceptional points in T 16.6 need not coincide with the exceptional points in T 16.7.

A second remark: In E 16.4 we picked the values of the $x(t, \cdot)$ in accordance with the $P_t(\cdot)$ in equation 16.3. Evidently, we could also have picked the values of the $x(t, \cdot)$ according to any other set of probabilities, $\{p_0, \ldots, p_9\}$, with $0 < p_i$, $i = 0, \ldots, 9$. Doing so would in no way alter the set of possible number sequences that we might observe. However, it would change the set of exceptional points in both equation 16.12 and 16.13.

16.3.3 The Central Limit Theorem

A third remark: The limits in equations 16.10 and 16.11 are completely independent of observations made on a finite number of the $x_n(\cdot)$, since for any fixed positive natural number N_0

$$\lim n^{-1} \sum_{i=1}^{n} x_i(\omega) = \lim n^{-1} \sum_{i=1}^{N_0} x_i(\omega) + \lim n^{-1} \sum_{i=N_0+1}^{n} x_i(\omega)$$

$$= 0 + \lim n^{-1} \sum_{i=N_0+1}^{n} x_i(\omega).$$

Even so, when the $x_i(\cdot)$ are independently and identically distributed with finite mean and variance, the limit in equation 16.10 can, within prescribed bounds, be determined for sufficiently large n. The reason why is explained in T 16.8, which extends the result we described in E 15.22.

T 16.8 Suppose that $x_i(\cdot)$, $i = 1, 2, \ldots$, are independently and identically distributed random variables on a probability space $(\Omega, \mathscr{F}, P(\cdot))$. Suppose also that they have finite mean μ and variance σ^2. Then the random variables $\sqrt{n}((n^{-1} \sum_{i=1}^{n} x_i(\cdot) - \mu)/\sigma)$, $n = 1, 2, \ldots$, converge in distribution to a normally distributed random variable with mean 0 and variance 1.

E 16.5 will aid our intuition concerning the significance of T 16.8:

E 16.5 We are asked to measure the probability that a given coin comes up heads. Since we have no idea of the physical constitution of the coin, we decide to determine the probability experimentally. We toss the coin once and record the result, 1 if heads and 0 if tails. Thereafter we repeat the experiment 9999 times. By then the first three decimals of the estimated frequency of heads seem to have settled on 0.376. So we decide to let $P(\text{heads}) = 0.376$.

In order to apply T 16.8, we observe that in this experiment $\mu = p$ and $\sigma^2 = p(1 - p)$, where p denotes the probability of our coin coming up heads.

Table 16.1
An excerpt of results.

	Number of tosses									
	1000	2000	3000	4000	5000	6000	7000	8000	9000	10,000
Frequency of heads	0.382	0.3745	0.379	0.3815	0.3774	0.3795	0.377	0.376	0.3763	0.3762

This fact, a little algebra, and a table of values of the normal distribution suffice to ascertain that the probability that $(10.000)^{-1}\sum_{i=1}^{10,000} x_i(\cdot)$ will differ from p by less than ± 0.01 is close to 0.95.

So much for the Law of Large Numbers. In the next section we shall use its corollary, T 16.7, and the ideas of Doob's theorem, T 16.2, to give an empirical characterization of chance.

16.4 An Empirical Characterization of Chance

There are probabilists, called *frequentists,* such as L. von Mises and Kolmogorov, who believe that the most reasonable way to interpret probability measures is the one suggested by T 16.7; i.e., the probability of an event A in a given experiment equals the frequency with which A would occur in repeated performances of the experiment. Von Mises even insisted that the concept of probability should only apply to problems in which either the same experiment repeats itself again and again or a great number of uniform elements are involved at the same time (von Mises 1951, pp. 8–9). Examples are:

1. A game of chance such as heads or tails.
2. A carefully defined actuarial problem such as: What is the chance that a 40-year-old man insured before his thirty-ninth birthday and living in Norway will die before he is 41 years old?
3. A carefully described mechanical or physical phenomenon such as the random motion of colloidal particles.

16.4.1 The Collectives of von Mises

To arrive at a meaningful probability measure for experiments such as those listed above, von Mises introduced the idea of a collective. A *collective* is a sequence of real numbers satisfying several conditions which we detail below. In stating these conditions we use certain symbols, R, T, φ, $\mathscr{A}$, $K(\cdot)$,

$\mathscr{B}$, and $Q(\cdot)$, whose meanings are as follows: R denotes the set of real numbers; $T = \{0, 1, \ldots\}$; $\varphi = \{\varphi_i(\cdot); i \in T\}$ denotes a gambling system (relative to some unspecified probability measure $P(\cdot)$); $\mathscr{A}$ denotes a family of gambling systems; $K(\cdot)$ denotes

$$K(n; \varphi, x) = \sum_{i=0}^{n} \varphi_i(x), \qquad \varphi \in \mathscr{A} \text{ and } x \in R^T \tag{16.14}$$

$\mathscr{B}$ denotes the Borel field of subsets of R, and $Q(\cdot)$ denotes

$$Q(A, x) = \lim n^{-1} \sum_{i=0}^{n} I_A(x_i), \qquad A \in \mathscr{B} \text{ and } x \in R^T. \tag{16.15}$$

Then $x \in R^T$ is a *collective in the sense of von Mises* if and only if

(i) $Q(\cdot, x)$ is well defined and finitely additive on $\mathscr{B}$,
(ii) for all $A \in \mathscr{B}$ and all $\varphi \in \mathscr{A}$

$$Q(A, x) = \lim K(n; \varphi, x)^{-1} \sum_{i=0}^{n} I_A(x_i)\varphi_i(x),$$

(iii) $\varphi \in \mathscr{A}$ if and only if $\lim_{n\to\infty} K(n, \varphi, x) = \infty$.

When x is a collective and $A \in \mathscr{B}$, von Mises insisted that $Q(A, x)$ measures the *chance* of observing an outcome in A in the experiment associated with x.

In order that von Mises' characterization of chance be meaningful, each and every purely random process with finite mean must possess a sample path that satisfies the conditions of a collective. For example, if $\{x(t, \omega); t \in T\}$ is a purely random process on a probability space $(\Omega, \mathscr{F}, P(\cdot))$, with $E|x_1| < \infty$ and sample space $(\tilde{\Omega}, \tilde{\mathscr{F}})$, there must be a $\tilde{\omega} \in \tilde{\Omega}$ such that, for all $A \in \mathscr{B}$ and $\hat{A} = \{\omega \in \Omega : x(1, \omega) \in A\}$,

$$P(\hat{A}) = Q(A, \tilde{\omega}). \tag{16.16}$$

Unfortunately, von Mises' collectives fail to satisfy this condition, as evidenced in E 16.6.

E 16.6 Let $T = \{0, 1, \ldots\}$ and $\Omega = [0, 1]$. In addition, let $\mathscr{B}$ denote the Borel subsets of Ω and let $\mu(\cdot)$ be the Lebesgue measure on $(\Omega, \mathscr{B})$. There exists no $\tilde{\omega} \in \Omega^T$ such that, for all $A \in \mathscr{B}$,

$$\lim n^{-1} \sum_{i=0}^{n} I_A(\omega_i) = \mu(A).$$

To see why, suppose that $\tilde{\omega} \in \Omega^T$ is such a sequence and let $A = \bigcup_{i=0}^{\infty} \{\omega_i\}$. Then $A \in \mathscr{B}$ and $\mu(A) = 0$. Yet $\lim n^{-1} \sum_{i=0}^{n} I_A(\omega_i) = 1$.

The crucial property of $(\Omega, \mathscr{B}, \mu(\cdot))$ in E 16.6 is that, for all $\omega \in \Omega$, $\{\omega\} \in \mathscr{B}$ and $\mu(\{\omega\}) = 0$. Since any other probability space $(\Omega, \mathscr{F}, P(\cdot))$, with $\{\omega\} \in \mathscr{F}$ and $P(\{\omega\}) = 0$ for all $\omega \in \Omega$, provides exceptions to equation 16.16 similar to the exception exhibited in E 16.6, the example suggests that von Mises' characterization of chance is meaningful for probability spaces with $\{\omega\} \in \mathscr{F}$ for all $\omega \in \Omega$ only if $P(\{\omega\}) > 0$ for at least one ω. Unfortunately, von Mises' ideas do not fare well then either—to wit E 16.7.

E 16.7 Let T and Ω be as in E 16.6 and let $\mathscr{B}$ denote the Borel subsets of Ω. Furthermore, let $P(\cdot)$ be a σ-additive probability measure on $(\Omega, \mathscr{B})$ such that, for some $\omega^0 \in \Omega$, $0 < P(\{\omega^0\}) < 1$. Finally, suppose that $\tilde{\omega}$ is a collective, with $P(A) = Q(A, \tilde{\omega})$ for all $A \in \mathscr{B}$. Then $\tilde{\omega}$ contains infinitely many components that equal ω^0. Hence we can find a gambling system φ such that, for all $i \in T$ with $\tilde{\omega}_i = \omega^0$, $\varphi_i(\tilde{\omega}) = 1$, and such that $\varphi_i(\tilde{\omega}) = 0$ for all other i. Then

$$P(\{\omega^0\}) < 1 = \lim K(n; \varphi, \tilde{\omega})^{-1} \sum_{i=0}^{n} I_{\{\omega^0\}}(\tilde{\omega}_i)\varphi_i(\tilde{\omega}),$$

which shows that $\tilde{\omega}$ cannot exist.

16.4.2 Church's Concept of Chance

The preceding examples suggest that von Mises' concept of a collective must be modified in several ways. Specifically, we must ensure that the experiments to which the concept of a collective applies are uncomplicated. We must also impose constraints on the set of eligible gambling systems. We shall next consider modifications of von Mises' collectives that are due to A. Church (1940, pp. 130–135).

To introduce Church's collectives we begin by letting $T = \{0, 1, \dots\}$, $\Omega = \{\alpha_1, \dots, \alpha_m\}$, $\mathscr{F} = \mathscr{P}(\Omega)$, and $\Omega^* = \bigcup_{i=1}^{\infty} \Omega^i$. Here, as well as in the remainder of the chapter, we shall think of Ω as the range space of a purely random process and identify $\tilde{\Omega}$ with Ω^T and $\tilde{\mathscr{F}}$ with the smallest σ field that contains all the cylinder sets in Ω^T. Next we let y and $\mathscr{A}_r$, respectively, denote a vector in Ω^T and a family of gambling systems. The latter is defined as follows: Let $\varphi = \{\varphi_i(\cdot); i \in T\}$ be a gambling system (relative to some unspecified probability measure on $(\Omega, \mathscr{F})$). Moreover, let $\psi(\cdot)$: $\Omega^* \to \{0, 1\}$ be given by

$$\psi(x) = \varphi_i(x, y), \qquad x \in \Omega^i,\ i = 1, 2, \dots.$$

Then $\varphi \in \mathscr{A}_r$ if and only if $\psi(\cdot)$ is recursive. Finally, we let $K(\cdot)$ and $Q(\cdot)$ be as described in equations 16.14 and 16.15 with $\mathscr{A}$, R, and $\mathscr{B}$ replaced by $\mathscr{A}_r$, Ω, and $\mathscr{F}$, respectively, and we insist that a sample path $\tilde{\omega} \in \Omega^T$ is a *collective in the sense of Church* if and only if

(i) $Q(\cdot, \tilde{\omega})$ is well defined and additive on $(\Omega, \mathscr{F})$;
(ii) for some $j \in \{1, \ldots, m\}$, $0 < Q(\{\alpha_j\}, \tilde{\omega}) < 1$; and
(iii) for all $A \in \mathscr{F}$ and all $\varphi \in \mathscr{A}_r$ with $\lim K(n; \varphi, \tilde{\omega}) = \infty$,

$$\lim K(n; \varphi, \tilde{\omega})^{-1} \sum_{i=0}^{n} I_A(\tilde{\omega}_i)\varphi_i(\tilde{\omega}) = Q(A, \tilde{\omega}).$$

The collectives of Church have many interesting properties. Those that are important to us are recorded in T 16.9.

T 16.9 Let $(\Omega, \mathscr{F}, P(\cdot))$ be a probability space with $\Omega = \{\alpha_1, \ldots, \alpha_m\}$, $\mathscr{F} = \mathscr{P}(\Omega)$, and $0 < P(\{\alpha_j\}) < 1$ for some j. Moreover, let $\tilde{P}(\cdot)$ be the product extension of $P(\cdot)$ to $(\tilde{\Omega}, \tilde{\mathscr{F}})$; i.e., let $\tilde{P}(\cdot)$ be a σ-additive probability measure on $(\tilde{\Omega}, \tilde{\mathscr{F}})$ that, for all $\{t_1, \ldots, t_k\} \subset T$ and $A_{t_j} \in \mathscr{F}$, $j = 1, \ldots, k$, satisfies

$$\tilde{P}\left(\left(\prod_{j=1}^{k} A_{t_j}\right) \times \Omega^T\right) = \prod_{j=1}^{k} P(A_{t_j}).$$

Finally, let $\mathscr{A}_r$ be as defined above and let $C(\mathscr{A}_r, P(\cdot))$ be the set of all $\tilde{\omega} \in \tilde{\Omega}$ such that (1) for all $A \in \mathscr{F}$,

$$P(A) = Q(A, \tilde{\omega})$$

and (2) for all $A \in \mathscr{F}$ and all $\varphi \in \mathscr{A}_r$ with $\lim K(n, \varphi, \tilde{\omega}) = \infty$,

$$P(A) = \lim K(n; \varphi, \tilde{\omega})^{-1} \sum_{i=0}^{n} I_A(\tilde{\omega}_i)\varphi_i(\tilde{\omega}).$$

Then $C(\mathscr{A}_r, P(\cdot)) \neq \varnothing$ and $\tilde{P}(C(\mathscr{A}_r, P(\cdot))) = 1$. Moreover, if $\tilde{\omega} \in C(\mathscr{A}_r, P(\cdot))$, $\tilde{\omega}$ is nonrecursive; i.e., the set $\{i \in T : \tilde{\omega}_i = \alpha_j\}$ is nonrecursive, $j = 1, \ldots, m$.

Thus if $(\Omega, \mathscr{F}, P(\cdot))$ is *any* probability space with finite Ω and nondegenerate $P(\cdot)$ and if $\tilde{x}(t, \tilde{\omega}) = \tilde{\omega}_t$, $t \in T$ and $\tilde{\omega} \in \tilde{\Omega}$, then $\{\tilde{x}(t, \tilde{\omega}); t \in T\}$ is a purely random process on $(\tilde{\Omega}, \tilde{\mathscr{F}}, \tilde{P}(\cdot))$, with the property that almost all its sample paths are collectives in the sense of Church. Moreover, these collectives are nonrecursive and hence nonprogrammable in the sense that no finite computer program exists that can reproduce a collective.

The proof of T 16.9 is obtained in two steps. In the first we compute the probability of $C(\mathscr{A}_r, P(\cdot))$. Let

$$\hat{\Omega} = \{\tilde{\omega} \in \tilde{\Omega} : P(A) = Q(A, \tilde{\omega}) \text{ for all } A \in \mathscr{F}\}.$$

Since $\mathscr{F}$ contains only a finite number of sets, it follows from T 16.7 and the additivity of $P(\cdot)$ that $\tilde{P}(\hat{\Omega}) = 1$.

Next, for each $\varphi \in \mathscr{A}_r$, let

$$B_{\varphi,\sim P} = \{\tilde{\omega} \in \hat{\Omega} : \lim K(n; \varphi, \tilde{\omega}) = \infty, \text{ and}$$

$$P(A) \neq \lim K(n; \varphi, \tilde{\omega})^{-1} \sum_{i=1}^{n} I_A(\tilde{\omega}_i)\varphi_i(\tilde{\omega})$$

$$\text{for some } A \in \mathscr{F}\}.$$

We shall show that $\tilde{P}(B_{\varphi,\sim P}) = 0$. This follows from T 16.2 when φ is a gambling system relative to $P(\cdot)$. When φ is not a gambling system relative to $P(\cdot)$, $\tilde{P}(\{\tilde{\omega} \in \tilde{\Omega} : \lim K(n; \varphi, \tilde{\omega}) = \infty\}) < 1$. For such a gambling system, the equality in equation 16.5 becomes an inequality; i.e., for all $B \in \tilde{\mathscr{F}}$, $P(\{\omega\colon \tilde{x}(\omega) \in B\}) \leqslant P(\{\omega \in \Omega : x(\omega) \in B\})$. This and T 16.7 imply that $\tilde{P}(B_{\varphi,\sim P}) = 0$. Thus, for all $\varphi \in \mathscr{A}_r$, $\tilde{P}(B_{\varphi,\sim P}) = 0$.

Finally, observe that $\hat{\Omega} - \bigcup_{\varphi \in \mathscr{A}_r} B_{\varphi,\sim P} \subset C(\mathscr{A}_r, P(\cdot))$ and that there are only countably many φ in $\mathscr{A}_r$. From this and the preceding comments, it follows that $\tilde{P}(C(\mathscr{A}_r, P(\cdot))) = 1$.

In the second step we show that the sample paths in $C(\mathscr{A}_r, P(\cdot))$ are nonrecursive. Suppose that $\tilde{\omega} \in C(\mathscr{A}_r, P(\cdot))$ and let y be an arbitrary vector in Ω^T. Moreover, for each pair (i, j) and $x \in \Omega^i$, $j = 1, \ldots, m$, $i = 1, 2, \ldots,$ let $\varphi_i^j(\cdot)\colon \Omega^T \to \{0, 1\}$ be defined by $\varphi_0^j(y) = 0$ and

$$\varphi_i^j(x, y) = \begin{cases} 1 & \text{if } \tilde{\omega}_i = \alpha_j \\ 0 & \text{otherwise.} \end{cases}$$

Then $\varphi^j = \{\varphi_i^j(\cdot); i \in T\}, j = 1, \ldots, m$, is a gambling system and, for some j, $\lim K(n; \varphi^j, \tilde{\omega}) = \infty$. Moreover, if $\tilde{\omega}$ is recursive, the functions

$$\varphi^j(x) = \varphi_i^j(x, y), \qquad x \in \Omega^i, \quad i = 0, 1, \ldots, \quad j = 1, \ldots, m$$

are recursive too. Since the recursiveness of the $\varphi^j(\cdot)$ and the unboundedness of one of the $K(n; \varphi^j, \tilde{\omega})$ contradict the assumptions of the theorem, $\tilde{\omega}$ cannot be recursive.

The two conclusions of the theorem have a bearing on our search for an empirical characterization of chance. To wit: The fact that Church's collectives are nonprogrammable captures the idea that the events that we may define on a collective are fortuitous in the sense that they happen by chance and they carry no information as to the likelihood of future events. Furthermore, the fact that $\tilde{P}(C(\mathscr{A}_r, P(\cdot))) = 1$ captures the notion of chance that we met in our discussion of games of chance: Gambling systems are of no strategic value in sequences of games performed under uniform conditions. This is so even though we restrict the gambler's choice of gambling systems to recursive $\varphi(\cdot)$'s. Any gambling system of which a gambler might conceive is likely to be recursive.

With the preceding observations in mind, we can propose two concepts of chance. The first is akin to C. S. Peirce's notion of probability as the "would-be" of a chance mechanism (Peirce 1955, pp. 164–173): Let the triple $(\Omega, \mathscr{F}, P(\cdot))$ be a mathematical idealization of an actual experiment and suppose that *the chance of an event in* $\mathscr{F}$ *happening is a dispositional property of the chance mechanism that we associate with the experiment.* Then, for all $A \in \mathscr{F}$, T 16.7 justifies our interpreting $P(A)$ as the chance of A occurring; i.e., in symbols,

$$\text{chance}(A) = P(A). \tag{16.17}$$

Our second concept of chance is analogous to von Mises' notion of probability (1951, pp. 18–20). To wit: Let $(\Omega, \mathscr{F})$ be an experiment with a finite number of outcomes and suppose that *the chance of an event in* $\mathscr{F}$ *happening is an intrinsic property of an ever-unfolding sequence of outcomes of repeated performances of this same experiment.* Then if $\hat{\omega} \in \hat{\Omega}$ is a collective in the sense of Church and $A \in \mathscr{F}$, T 16.9 and $\hat{\omega} \in C(\hat{\mathscr{A}}_r, Q(\cdot, \hat{\omega}))$ justify our interpreting $Q(A, \hat{\omega})$ as the chance of A occurring as $\hat{\omega}$ unfolds itself; i.e., in symbols,

$$\text{chance}(A, \hat{\omega}) = Q(A, \hat{\omega}). \tag{16.18}$$

This is so even though $Q(\cdot, \hat{\omega})$ need not equal the dispositional property of the chance mechanism associated with $(\Omega, \mathscr{F})$.

16.5 Chance and the Characteristics of Purely Random Processes

I believe that T 16.9 and equation 16.18 give an empirical characterization of chance; the resulting concept captures the idea of chance embodied in a purely random process. It is, therefore, important to note that this opinion might not be shared by others. One reason for disagreeing with me would be that Church's collectives need not satisfy the Law of the Iterated Logarithm, T 16.10.

T 16.10 Suppose that $\{x(t, \omega); t \in T\}$ is a purely random process on a probability space $(\Omega, \mathscr{F}, P(\cdot))$. Also suppose that $x(1, \cdot)$ has finite mean μ and variance σ^2. Then

$$P\left\{ \omega \in \Omega : \limsup \left| \frac{\sum_{i=1}^{n} (x(i, \omega) - \mu)}{\sigma(2n \log \log n)^{1/2}} \right| = 1 \right\} = 1.$$

In fact, J. Ville (1939) has shown that, for any triple $(\Omega, \mathscr{F}, P(\cdot))$ with $\Omega = \{0, 1\}$ and $\mathscr{F} = \mathscr{P}(\Omega)$, there are sample paths $\tilde{\omega} \in C(\mathscr{A}_r, P(\cdot))$ such that, with $p = P(\{1\})$,

$$\limsup \left| \sum_{i=1}^{n} (\tilde{\omega}_i - p)/(p(1-p)2n \log\log n)^{1/2} \right| = 0.$$

Be that as it may, Ville's result does not demonstrate that my seond concept of chance is inadequate. It establishes only that Church's concept of a collective provides an unsatisfactory characterization of the typical sample path of a purely random process.

Since the irrelevance of Ville's result for our empirical characterization of chance is important to us, we shall dwell on it for a moment. Consider an axiomatic system with undefined terms—*merkmalraum, experiment, probability, place selection*—and axioms MA 1—MA 4.

MA 1 A merkmalraum is a finite collection of objects, $M = \{\alpha_1, \ldots, \alpha_m\}$.

MA 2 Let $T = \{0, 1, \ldots\}$, $M_t = M$, $t \in T$, and $\mathscr{M}_t = \mathscr{P}(M)$, $t \in T$. Then an experiment is a pair $(\tilde{\Omega}, \tilde{\mathscr{F}})$, where $\tilde{\Omega} = \prod_{t \in T} M_t$ and $\tilde{\mathscr{F}} = \prod_{t \in T} \mathscr{M}_t$, the smallest σ field that contains the cylinder sets in $\tilde{\Omega}$.

MA 3 A probability is a σ-additive function $\tilde{P}(\cdot)\colon \tilde{\mathscr{F}} \to [0, 1]$ which satisfies two conditions: (1) $\tilde{P}(\tilde{\Omega}) = 1$ and (2) there exists a finitely additive function $P(\cdot)\colon \mathscr{P}(M) \to [0, 1]$ such that $P(M) = 1$, $0 < P(\{\alpha_j\}) < 1$ for some $j \in \{1, \ldots, m\}$, and for all cylinder sets,

$$A = \prod_{i=1,\ldots,n} A_{t_i} \times \prod_{\substack{t \in T \\ t \neq t_i \\ i=1,\ldots,n}} M_t, \qquad \tilde{P}(A) = \prod_{i=1,\ldots,n} P(A_{t_i}).$$

MA 4 A place selection is a recursive function

$$\varphi(\cdot)\colon \bigcup_{i=1}^{\infty} M^i \to \{0, 1\}.$$

Theorem T 16.9 demonstrates that T(MA 1, ..., MA 4) is equivalent to the theory we can derive from an axiom system with undefined terms—*merkmalraum, experiment, place selection, collective, chance*—and axioms CA 1—CA 3 which we list below.

CA 1 MA 1, MA 2, and MA 4.

CA 2 Let $\mathscr{A}_r$ denote the set of all place selections on $\bigcup_{i=1}^{\infty} M^i$. Moreover, for each $\varphi \in \mathscr{A}_r$ and $i = 0, 1, \ldots$, let $\varphi_i(\cdot)\colon \tilde{\Omega} \to \{0, 1\}$ be given by

$$\varphi_0(\tilde{\omega}) = 0, \qquad \tilde{\omega} \in \tilde{\Omega}$$

and

$\varphi_i(x, \tilde{\omega}) = \varphi(x), \qquad x \in M^i,\ \tilde{\omega} \in \tilde{\Omega}$, and $i = 1, 2, \ldots$

Finally, let $K(\cdot)$: $\{1, 2, \ldots\} \times \mathscr{A}_r \times \tilde{\Omega} \to \{1, 2, \ldots\}$ and $Q(\cdot)$: $\mathscr{P}(M) \times \tilde{\Omega} \to [0, 1]$, respectively, be defined by

$$K(n, \varphi, \tilde{\omega}) = \sum_{i=1}^{n} \varphi_i(\tilde{\omega})$$

and

$$Q(A, \tilde{\omega}) = \lim n^{-1} \sum_{t=1}^{n} I_A(\tilde{\omega}_t),$$

where $\tilde{\omega}_t$ is the tth component $\tilde{\omega}$ and $I_A(\cdot)$: $M \to \{0, 1\}$ is the indicator function of $A \subset M$. Then $\tilde{\omega} \in \tilde{\Omega}$ is a collective if and only if it satisfies conditions i–iii (section 16.4.2) of Church's collectives, with $\mathscr{A}_r$, $K(\cdot)$, $Q(\cdot)$, and the $\varphi_i(\cdot)$ as described above and with $\mathscr{P}(M)$ in place of $\mathscr{F}$.

CA 3 Let D denote the collection of all collectives in $\tilde{\Omega}$. Then chance is a function $C(\cdot)$: $\mathscr{P}(M) \times D \to [0, 1]$ such that, for each $\tilde{\omega} \in D$ and $A \in \mathscr{P}(M)$,

$$C(A, \tilde{\omega}) = Q(A, \tilde{\omega}).$$

Specifically, if MA 1—MA 4 are valid and $\tilde{P}(\cdot)$: $\tilde{\mathscr{F}} \to [0, 1]$ is a probability, then it follows from T 16.9 that there exists a subset of $\tilde{\Omega}$, E, such that $\tilde{P}(E) = 1$ and such that $E \subset D$ and

$$P(A) = C(A, \tilde{\omega}), \qquad \tilde{\omega} \in E \text{ and } A \in \mathscr{P}(M)$$

where $P(\cdot)$: $\mathscr{P}(M) \to [0, 1]$ is the finitely additive set function associated with $\tilde{P}$ in MA 3, and where D and $C(\cdot)$ are as described in CA 2 and CA 3. Conversely, if CA 1—CA 3 holds and if $\tilde{\omega} \in D$, then there exists a probability $\tilde{P}(\cdot)$ on $\tilde{\mathscr{F}}$ whose associated set function $P(\cdot)$ on $\mathscr{P}(M)$ satisfies

$$P(A) = C(A, \tilde{\omega}), \qquad A \in \mathscr{P}(M).$$

Moreover, there is a nonempty set $E \in \tilde{\mathscr{F}}$, such that $\tilde{P}(E) = 1$, $E \subset D$, $\tilde{\omega} \in E$, and $C(A, \cdot)$ does not vary with $\omega \in E$.

The preceding equivalence between T(MA 1–MA 4) and T(CA 1–CA 3) is analogous to the equivalence for which we searched in chapter 13. This equivalence explicates the sense in which we have been successful in giving an empirical characterization of chance. Our success is not affected by the existence of an $\hat{\omega} \in E$ that does not satisfy the Law of the Iterated Logarithm.

For a detailed account of the problem of how best to characterize the typical sample paths of a purely random process, the reader should consult C. P. Schnorr's *Zufälligkeit und Wahrscheinlichkeit* (1971, pp. 60–119) and Michiel van Lambalgen's article "Von Mises' Definition of Random Sequences Reconsidered" (1987, pp. 725–755).

17 Ignorance

Ignorance is the condition of being ignorant, and to be *ignorant* means to lack knowledge and/or experience. An individual can be ignorant of certain facts or of a particular subject matter. He can also be generally uninformed and be regarded as an *ignorant person*. In this chapter we shall discuss ignorance of intrinsic probabilities.

17.1 Epistemic versus Aleatory Probabilities

If $(\Omega, \mathscr{F})$ denotes an experiment that satisfies axioms GS 1 and GS 2 of section 15.2, a probability measure can be characterized as an additive belief function whose basic probability assignment satisfies

$$m(A) = \begin{cases} P(A) & \text{if } A = \{\omega_i\} \text{ for some } i \in \{1, \ldots, n\} \\ 0 & \text{otherwise.} \end{cases} \tag{17.1}$$

Conversely, an additive belief function, $\text{bel}(\cdot)$, is a probability measure. Its associated basic probability assignment satisfies equation 17.1 with $P(A)$ replaced by $\text{bel}(A)$.

In my intended interpretation, additive belief functions measure personal beliefs in various propositions such as "Australia's prime minister drowned in 1965." Applied probabilists classify such probabilities as *epistemic*, and refer to them as subjective or personal. This is to distinguish them from *aleatory* probabilities, which probabilists think of as objective and as measuring the intrinsic probabilities of occurrence of properly defined events, e.g., the intrinsic probability of a biased coin coming up heads.

In this section and the next, we shall discuss the relationship between epistemic and aleatory probabilities in situations where it makes sense to talk of intrinsic probabilities. My intention is to contrast the assignment of probabilities by leading probabilists (1) with the assignment of probabilities by ordinary people and (2) with the intrinsic probabilities.

17.1.1 Risk and Epistemic Probability

A *risky situation* is an experiment whose intrinsic probabilities either *are* known or *can be* known by analysis. For such situations Laplace suggested the following definition of epistemic probability: The probability of an event is the ratio of the number of cases that are favorable to it, to the number of possible cases, when there is nothing to make us believe that one case should occur rather than any other, so that the cases are, for us, equally possible (Laplace 1951, pp. 6–7 and 11). In some cases this definition leads to an assignment of numbers to events that most people would consider to be intrinsic probabilities. For instance, if the 100 balls in the urn of E 15.1 were identical except for color—fifty red and fifty white—and if the urn were shaken well, Laplace would have assigned 0.5 to the event that the blindfolded man pulls a red ball. Since the urn is shaken well only if the intrinsic probability of any one ball is 0.01, the intrinsic and epistemic probabilities of a red ball coincide in this experiment. They coincide also with the assignment of the ordinary man judging from the responses of the 140 subjects of E 15.10 to the question: On what event would you rather bet in E 15.1, that the blindfolded man pulls a red ball from the urn or that he pulls a white ball? Those questioned were all indifferent between the bets.

Coincidences of the sort described above do not always occur, as illustrated by the following example given by W. Feller (1957, pp. 39 and 59).

E 17.1 Consider a mechanical system of r indistinguishable particles; suppose that the phase space has been subdivided into a large number n of cells so that each particle is assigned to one cell. Our problem is to assign a number to the event that cells $1, \ldots, n$ contain $r_1, \ldots, r_n$ particles with $r = r_1 + \cdots + r_n$.

If we were to assign the required number in accordance with Laplace's definition, we would reason as follows: There are n^r different ways in which r particles can be arranged in n cells. We have no reason to believe that one way is more likely than another. So we take all ways to be equally likely. Since there are $r!/r_1!r_2!\ldots r_n!$ indistinguishable ways in which we can arrange r particles such that r_i particles are in cell i, $i = 1, \ldots, n$, the required probability is

$$(r!/r_1!\ldots r_n!)n^{-r}.$$

Feller claims that numerous experiments have shown beyond doubt that our epistemic probabilities are not the intrinsic probabilities of any known mechanical system of particles. For instance, photons, nuclei, and atoms containing an even number of elementary particles behave as if they only considered distinguishable arrangements. Since there are just $\binom{n+r-1}{r}$ distinguishable arrangements of r particles in n cells, and since all seem to be equally likely, the intrinsic probability ent in question is (for photons, nuclei, and atoms containing an even of elementary particles)

$$\binom{n + r - 1}{r}^{-1}.$$

Epistemic and aleatory probabilities differ in many situations. In Feller's mechanical system it appears that they should not differ, but in fact they do. We next consider cases in which it seems that epistemic and aleatory probabilities must differ—and usually they do.

17.1.2 Uncertainty and the Principle of Insufficient Reason

The *Principle of Insufficient Reason* asserts that two events A and B are equally probable if there is no reason why A should happen more than B and vice versa. This principle provides the justification of Laplace's assignment of probabilities in risky situations. It is also often used to assign epistemic probabilities in so called *uncertain situations*, i.e., in experiments whose intrinsic probabilities neither *are* known nor *can be* known by reason alone.

An example of an uncertain situation is the experiment associated with the urn in E 15.10 that contains an unknown proportion of red to white balls. If the choices of the 140 subjects in that example can be interpreted the way Ellsberg and Fellner claim they can, only 45 subjects assigned numbers to the various events in accordance with AK 1 and AK 2. The choices of these 45 subjects suggest that they appealed to the Principle of Insufficient Reason and assigned probability 0.5 to the event that the blindfolded man pulls a red ball from the urn.

Laplace would have agreed with the probability assignment of the 45 subjects for reasons similar to those given by Edgeworth in E 17.2.

E 17.2 "It is known that a box or urn contains a hundred balls of different colors, white and black, ninety-nine of one color and one of another; but which colour is in the majority is absolutely unknown. The probability of drawing a white ball is 1/2. I believe that the numerical value is justified by the fact that in a great number of experiences with urns one colour would as often be in the majority as another" (Edgeworth 1884, p. 231).

In order to understand Edgeworth's reasoning, we shall use conditional probabilities to idealize his arguments: Consider two urns C and D with 100 balls each. C has 99 white and one black ball; D has one white and 99 black balls. Both are well shaken. Edgeworth argues that the likelihood that his urn is C is as great as the likelihood that it is D. Consequently, by the Principle of Insufficient Reason,

$$P(C) = P(D) = 0.5.$$

He then figures that

$$P(\text{white ball}) = P(\text{white ball in } C|C)P(C) + P(\text{white ball in } D|D)P(D)$$

$$= 0.99 \cdot 0.5 + 0.01 \cdot 0.5 = 0.5.$$

This conclusion sounds convincing, but the fact remains that the intrinsic probability of Edgeworth's pulling a white ball from his urn is either 0.99 or 0.01, no matter how well he argues for 0.5.

17.1.3 Modeling Ignorance à la Laplace and Edgeworth

In Laplace's definition of epistemic probability, as well as in Edgeworth's assignment of probabilities to C and D, there is a definite conception of how to model ignorance. Laplace would keep dissecting his experiment into possible cases up to the point where he was unable to reason why one possibility was more likely than any other. He would then reveal his ignorance by assigning the same number to each possibility, ensuring they added to 1. Similarly, Edgeworth, unable to decide which of C and D was most likely to be his box, would disclose his ignorance by assigning 0.5 to both. This way of modeling ignorance can be adopted even when the number of possibilities is infinite, as witnessed in E 17.3.

E 17.3 We are to flip a coin once. It can come up heads H with probability p and tails T with probability $1 - p$. All we know about p is that $p \in [0, 1]$. So we assign Lebesgue measure to the Borel sets of possible values of p. Then

$$P(\{\text{H}\}) = \int_0^1 p\, d\mu(p) = 0.5 = \int_0^1 (1 - p)\, d\mu(p) = P(\{T\}). \tag{17.2}$$

Suppose next that we flip the coin n times in such a way that the probability of heads, p, is constant from one flip to the next. For each given p, the probability of r heads in n throws equals

$$\binom{n}{r} p^r (1 - p)^{n-r}. \tag{17.3}$$

Consequently,

$$P(r \text{ heads in } n \text{ flips}) = \binom{n}{r} \int_0^1 p^r (1 - p)^{n-r}\, d\mu(p) = (n + 1)^{-1}, \tag{17.4}$$

which is independent of r. This result reflects our ignorance of the value of p.

On the surface, Laplace's and Edgeworth's way of modeling ignorance sounds reasonable. However, many have criticized it for paradoxical consequences; e.g., ignorance of p in E 17.3 need not reflect similar ignorance of p^{-1}. Others have ridiculed it for some of the uses to which it has been put; e.g., after seeing the tide rise periodically ten succesive times at an interval of about twelve and a half hours, we might decide that the probability that it will rise for the eleventh time is 11/12. Finally, Shafer has criticized it because he believes that one cannot model ignorance by an additive belief function (Shafer 1976, pp. 22–25). Shafer might have assigned the number 0.001 to the event that a white ball is pulled from Edgeworth's box and 0.001 to the event that a black ball is pulled.

17.1.4 Measuring Uncertainty with Entropy

The problem of how to model ignorance is as important today as it was when Laplace formulated his epistemological definition of probability. Notwithstanding the severe criticism to which they have been subject, Laplace's and Edgeworth's ideas are not dead. In fact, judging from Arnold Zellner's authoritative account of Bayesian inference in econometrics (Zellner 1971), Laplace's and Edgeworth's assignment of probabilities to the events of E 17.2 and E 17.3 are accepted by many modern econometricians. The only difference is that an econometrician would not use the Principle of Insufficient Reason to justify his priors.[1] He would use Laplace's and Edgeworth's priors because they maximize C. E. Shannon's entropy function in the uncertain situations envisaged in E 17.2 and E 17.3.

It is not easy to understand what Shannon's entropy function has to do with epistemic probabilities. Hence, a few comments are in order. We begin by discussing a system of axioms that purports to characterize two undefined terms[2]: *information* and *uncertainty*.

P 1 Information is an extended continuous function

$I(\cdot)\colon [0, 1] \rightarrow R_+ \cup \{\infty\}$.

P 2 There is a $p \in (0, 1)$ such that $0 < I(p) < \infty$.

P 3 If $0 \leqslant p, q \leqslant 1$, and $p \leqslant q$, then $I(q) \leqslant I(p)$.

P 4 If $0 \leqslant p, q \leqslant 1$, then $I(pq) = I(p) + I(q)$.

P 5 Let $A_n = \{x \in R^n_+ : \sum_{i=1}^n x_i = 1\}$; and let $A = \bigcup_{n=1}^\infty A_n$. Then uncertainty is a function $H(\cdot)\colon A \rightarrow R_+$ such that, for all $p \in A_n$, $n = 1, 2, \ldots,$

$$H(p) = \sum_{i=1}^{n} p_i I(p_i). \tag{17.5}$$

It is easy to see from P 2 and P 4 that $I(1) = 0$ and $I(0) = \infty$. It is also easy to establish the validity of T 17.1.

T 17.1 There is a positive constant c so that

$$I(p) = -c \log p, \qquad p \in [0, 1]. \tag{17.6}$$

To prove the theorem, define $f(\cdot)\colon R_+ \to R_+$ by $f(u) = I(e^{-u})$, $u \in R_+$; and let $cu_p = f(u_p)$ where $u_p = -\log p$ and p satisfies $0 < I(p) < \infty$. Then, for all $u, v, \in R_+$, $f(u + v) = f(u) + f(v)$. Moreover, if r is a positive rational number $f(ru_p) = rf(u_p)$. Finally, if $u \in R_{++}$, there is a sequence of rational numbers r_n such that $r_n u_p$ converges to u and such that $f(r_n u_p)$ converges to $f(u) = (u/u_p)f(u_p)$. Hence $I(q) = -(I(p)/-\log p)\log q$ for all $q \in [0, 1]$, as was to be shown.

From equations 17.5 and 17.6 it follows that, for all $n = 1, 2, \ldots$

$$H(p) = -c \sum_{i=1}^{n} p_i \log p_i.$$

Hence, in the lingo of information theorists, $H(\cdot)$ *is the entropy function of Shannon.*

We shall adopt the standard convention that $0 \cdot \log 0$ equals 0. When we do, it is easy to verify that, for each $n = 2, 3, \ldots$, $H(\cdot)$ is a continuous concave function on A_n. We can also demonstrate that Edgeworth's prior in E 17.2, i.e., $(\frac{1}{2}, \frac{1}{2})$, maximizes $H(\cdot)$ subject to the constraints $p_1 + p_2 = 1$ and $0 \leqslant p_1, p_2$—to wit T 17.2.

T 17.2 For all n and all $p \in A_n$,

$$H(p) \leqslant H\left(\frac{1}{n}, \ldots, \frac{1}{n}\right) \leqslant H\left(\frac{1}{n+1}, \ldots, \frac{1}{n+1}\right).$$

The proof is easy, so I leave it to the reader.

The idea behind axioms P 1–P 5 is that a message saying that an event A has occurred carries information whose importance varies with the anticipated likelihood of the occurrence of A. Thus if A was considered unlikely, the message about the happening of A is almost unbelieveable; on the other hand if A was taken for granted, the message carries little information. Similarly, if A and B are events and $A \subset B$, information about the occurrence of A reveals that B has occurred as well. In that sense the message concerning A is more informative than an analogous message concerning B.

The value of $H(\cdot)$ at $p \in A_n$ is the expected value of the information carried by the components of p. According to T 17.2, the more diffuse p is, the higher is the value of $H(p)$. In that sense $H(p)$ is a measure of the uncertainty involved in assessing the likelihood of the occurrence of the various events in the experiment associated with p.

We have defined $H(\cdot)$ on discrete probability distributions. The natural extension of $H(\cdot)$ to differentiable probability distributions is given by $\int p(t)I(p(t))\,dt$. Note therefore that the Lebesgue measure on $[0, 1]$ maximizes $\int_0^1 p(t)I(p(t))\,dt$ subject to $p(t) \geqslant 0$ and $\int_0^1 p(t)\,dt = 1$; i.e., the prior in E 17.3 maximizes Shannon's entropy function over differentiable probability distributions on $[0, 1]$. It is also interesting to note that the normal distribution with mean m and variance σ^2 maximizes $\int_{-\infty}^{\infty} p(t)I(p(t))\,dt$ subject to $\int_{-\infty}^{\infty} p(t)\,dt = 1$, $\int_{-\infty}^{\infty} tp(t)\,dt = m$, and $\int_{-\infty}^{\infty} (t - m)^2 p(t)\,dt = \sigma^2$.

17.2 The Bayes Theorem and Epistemic Probabilities

In E 17.3 we began our experiment completely ignorant of the value of p. We also revealed our ignorance by using Lebesgue measure as a prior probability measure on the set of possible values of p. Then we computed the probability of heads on the first toss of the coin and the probability of r heads in n tosses. How do these probabilities differ from the probabilities we would have assigned if we previously had had the chance to observe the outcomes of repeated performances of the experiment? In this and the next section we present answers to this question from Laplace, ordinary people, and econometricians who take exception to Laplace's and Edgeworth's modeling of ignorance. First Laplace.

17.2.1 Learning by Observing

Consider the experiment in E 17.3 and suppose that we have used Lebesgue measure as a prior measure on the set of possible values of p. After having performed the experiment n times under uniform conditions and observed r heads in n tosses, we are less ignorant than before. This fact is reflected both in the probability measure we assign to the set of possible values of p and in the number we assign to the event heads on the next trial. To wit: Let A denote the event that the number of heads in n tosses of the coin is r, and change the sum in equation 15.13 to an integral. Then, for the present case, equation 15.13 becomes

$$P(dp|A) = \binom{n}{r} p^r(1-p)^{n-r}\mu(dp) \Big/ \int_0^1 \binom{n}{r} p^r(1-p)^{n-r}\,d\mu(p)$$

$$= (n+1)\binom{n}{r} p^r(1-p)^{n-r}\mu(dp). \qquad (17.7)$$

This measure is the posterior probability measure on Ω, given that A has been observed. Using $P(dp|A)$ to compute the probability of heads on the next throw, we find that

$$P(\text{heads on the } (n+1)\text{st toss}|A) = \int_0^1 p\, dp(P|A)$$
$$= \frac{r+1}{n+2}, \qquad (17.8)$$

which may differ both from $\frac{1}{2}$ and the true value of p. Finally,

$$P(r \text{ heads in the next } n \text{ tosses}|A) = \binom{n}{r} \int_0^1 p^r(1-p)^{n-r}\, dp(P|A)$$
$$= (n+1)\binom{n}{r}^2 \Big/ (2n+1)\binom{2n}{2r}, \qquad (17.9)$$

which differs considerably from the simple formula in equation 17.4.

17.2.2 An Example

The measures we exhibit in equations 17.8 and 17.9 are the measures Laplace and Edgeworth would have assigned in the envisaged situation. However, they need not correspond to the measures ordinary humans would have assigned in the same circumstances. To see how they might differ, we shall consider a simple example.

E 17.4 An urn is filled with black and white balls, 2/3 of one color and 1/3 the other. We do not know which color is in the majority. Nils draws a sample of five balls with replacement and obtains four white balls and one black ball. Ole draws a sample of twenty balls with replacement and obtains twelve white balls and eight black balls. The urn was well shaken between draws. Which person, Nils or Ole, ought to be more confident that the urn contains more white than black balls?

If both Nils and Ole argue in accord with Laplace's principles and use indifferent priors to reflect their ignorance about the composition of the urn, they should assign posterior probability 0.889 and 0.941, respectively, to the combination

(2/3 white, 1/3 black).

Hence Ole ought to be more certain than Nils that the urn contains more white than black balls.

To determine how an ordinary human might respond to the question posed in E 17.4, we asked 286 economics and statistics students.

Among them only 78 insisted that Ole ought to be more confident than Nils.

The rationale behind the choice of the majority of our students is controversial. Some scholars (e.g., D. Kahnemann and A. Tversky) insist that the choice of the majority supports their hypothesis that most individuals in assessing likelihoods and making predictions do not use sophisticated theorems from probability theory. Instead they rely on a limited number of heuristics which help them reduce complex computational tasks to manageable proportions.

One heuristic that can be used to explain the choice of Nils is called the *representativeness heuristic*: When the outcome A of an experiment is highly representative of the process B from which it originates, then the conditional probability of A given B is judged to be high. Hence, since 4 to 1 is more representative of 2 to 1 than is 12 to 8, Nils seems to be a reasonable guess (Kahnemann and Tversky 1972, pp. 430–454).

There is another way of rationalizing the choice of Nils. Binomial probabilities are hard to compute by hand. Subjective estimates of probabilities like those in equation 17.3 tend to be conservative, and the degree of conservatism increases with p and n (see, for instance, Peterson, DuCharme, and Edwards 1968, pp. 239–240). The possibility exists, therefore, that some of those who chose Nils used the right prior measure and Bayes's theorem, but also overly conservative binomial probabilities to make their choice. In fact, various psychometric tests seem to substantiate the reasonableness of such a hypothesis (see, for instance, Peterson, DuCharme, and Edwards 1968, pp. 241–242).

While the overwhelming majority of our subjects obviously did not reason precisely the way prescribed by Laplace and Edgeworth, there is a chance that many of the seventy-eight who voted for Ole did not either. Some of them were statistics students and might have argued as follows: Nils and Ole are testing the null hypothesis,

H_0: more black balls

against the alternative hypothesis,

H_1: more white balls.

Both reject H_0 at the 0.05 level of significance. However, since the power of Ole's test, 0.9, is much higher than the power of Nils' test, 0.5, Ole can reject H_0 with more confidence than Nils.

Other subjects were strong believers in Shafer's theory of evidence. They might have recalled Shafer (1976, pp. 77–78 and 85–86) and argued as follows: Let H_0, H_1 be as above and let $\Omega = \{H_0, H_1\}$. With each observed black ball Nils and Ole associate a simple support function whose basic probability assignment is given by

$$m_B(A) = \begin{cases} \frac{1}{2} & \text{if } A = \{H_0\} \\ 0 & \text{if } A = \{H_1\} \\ \frac{1}{2} & \text{if } A = \Omega \end{cases}$$

With each white ball they associate a simple support function whose basic probability assignment is given by

$$m_W(A) = \begin{cases} 0 & \text{if } A = \{H_0\} \\ \frac{1}{2} & \text{if } A = \{H_1\} \\ \frac{1}{2} & \text{if } A = \Omega \end{cases}$$

Finally, Nils and Ole pool evidence in accordance with the rule prescribed in T 15.5. Consequently, after the experiments, Nils' belief function on $(\Omega, \mathscr{F})$ is derived from a basic probability assignment given by

$$m^{\text{Nils}}(A) = \begin{cases} 15/17 & \text{if } A = \{H_1\} \\ 1/17 & \text{if } A = \{H_0\} \\ 1/17 & \text{if } A = \Omega \end{cases}$$

while Ole's belief function on $(\Omega, \mathscr{F})$ is based on the basic probability assignment

$$m^{\text{Ole}}(A) = \begin{cases} 4095/4351 & \text{if } A = \{H_1\} \\ 255/4351 & \text{if } A = \{H_0\} \\ 1/4351 & \text{if } A = \Omega \end{cases}$$

From this it follows that Ole must be more confident than Nils that there are more white than black balls in the urn.

17.2.3 A Paradox

In the preceding example the learned and the not-so-learned gave different answers to a simple question. Moreover, the learned gave the same answer possibly for very different reasons. There are also situations in which the learned will disagree. One such situation is of special interest to us and is described in E 17.5.

E 17.5 A burglary has occurred and we have a suspect. To determine the suspect's guilt we order that the refractive indices of a broken window at the scene of the crime and of the fragments of glass found on the suspect's clothing be measured. While waiting for the measurements we make the following mental notes.

(i) We know that the refractive indices must belong to a well-defined interval $A = (a, b)$, but we have no idea of the likelihood of observing an index in any one of the subsets of A.

(ii) It is likely that the refractive index of the broken window can be measured accurately. However, the measurements of the refractive indices of the glass fragments are subject to error. We presume that the mean of these measurements is approximately normally distributed, with mean θ and variance σ^2/n, where n is the number of glass fragments and σ is very small.

(iii) The chances are 50–50 that the glass fragments came from the broken window.

Now the measurements determine that the refractive index of the broken window equals θ_0 and that the mean of the other indices equals y. The difference $|y - \theta_0|$ is small, but still more than twice the size of $\sigma/\sqrt{n}$. That leaves us with a problem: Is it reasonable to insist that $\theta = \theta_0$? We don't know. A standard sampling-theory test of significance would reject the null hypothesis $\theta = \theta_0$. Yet a Bayesian econometrician might advise us not to reject the null hypothesis.

In E 17.5 we paraphrased a problem in forensic science that Dennis Lindley (1977, pp. 207–213) posed.[3] In taking a second look at the example it is easy to see why a standard sampling-theory test of the null hypothesis, $H_0\colon \theta = \theta_0$, against the alternative hypothesis, $H_1\colon \theta \in (a, b) - \{\theta_0\}$, would reject H_0. It is harder to see why a Bayesian econometrician might favor H_0. So the latter requires a clarifying remark.

The Bayesian econometrician observes that our prior distribution of θ assigns probability $\frac{1}{2}$ to $\{\theta_0\}$ and distributes $\frac{1}{2}$ uniformly over (a, b). He also notes that the probability density of the mean of the measurements of θ, Y, is given by

$$\left(\frac{2\pi\sigma^2}{n}\right)^{-1/2} \exp \frac{-n(Y - \theta)^2}{2\sigma^2}.$$

Finally, he records that σ is very small and that the observed value of Y, y differs from θ_0 by more than two times the size of $(\sigma/\sqrt{n})$. From this he concludes that the posterior odds in favor of H_0 over H_1 are given by

$$\frac{P(\theta = \theta_0 | Y = y)}{P(\theta \neq \theta_0 | Y = y)} = \frac{(\frac{1}{2})(2\pi\sigma^2/n)^{-1/2} \exp -n(y - \theta_0)^2/2\sigma^2}{(\frac{1}{2})(b - a)^{-1}(2\pi\sigma^2/n)^{-1/2} \int_a^b \exp -n(y - \theta)^2/2\sigma^2 \, d\mu(\theta)}$$

and that when $\min((y - a), (b - y)) > 4(\sigma/\sqrt{n})$, the posterior odds are approximately equal to

$$(b-a)\cdot\left(\frac{2\pi\sigma^2}{n}\right)^{-1/2}\exp\frac{-n(y-\theta_0)^2}{2\sigma^2}.$$

Consequently, for appropriate values of a, b, σ, and n, the posterior odds in favor of H_0 will be large enough for the Bayesian econometrician to advise us not to reject H_0.

The conflict between the sampling theory and Bayesian analysis of the problem in E 17.5 is discomforting to many and is called a paradox by Lindley (1957, pp. 187–192). Note, therefore, that Lindley's paradox is of great generality. The conflict it exhibits can arise in any test situation in which the prior distribution under an alternative hypothesis is very diffuse relative to the power of discrimination of the observations.

The fact that sufficiently diffuse priors can overwhelm strong statistical evidence is not just paradoxical. It is cause for concern to anyone who uses diffuse priors to model ignorance. Therefore, in the next section we shall discuss a new and very interesting idea for modeling ignorance in risky situations.

17.3 Noninformative Priors

Some econometricians, e.g., George Box and George Tiao (1972, pp. 20–60), take strong exception to Laplace's and Edgeworth's manner of modeling ignorance. They insist that knowing little *a priori* about the intrinsic probabilities of an experiment means to know little *relative* to the information that one or more performances of the experiment may provide. We show below how these econometricians would model ignorance in cases of interest to them and how their priors and the probabilities they assign change after a prescribed number of observations.

17.3.1 Locally Uniform Priors

Let $x(\cdot)$ be a random variable on an experiment $(\Omega, \mathscr{F})$, and suppose that the probability distribution of $x(\cdot)$ belongs to the family $\{F_\theta(\cdot); \theta \in A\}$, where A is a subset of R. Suppose also that we have performed the experiment n times under uniform conditions and that we have observed the values $x_1, \ldots, x_n$ of $x(\cdot)$. Finally, let $p(\cdot|\theta)$ denote the density of $F_\theta(\cdot)$; let $x = (x_1, \ldots, x_n)$; let

$$l(\theta|x) = \prod_{i=1}^{n} p(x_i|\theta), \qquad \theta \in A$$

let $p(\cdot)\colon A \to R_+$ denote the density of our prior distribution of θ, and let

$$P(\theta|x) = l(\theta|x)p(\theta) \bigg/ \int_A l(\theta|x)p(\theta)\,d\theta, \qquad \theta \in A. \tag{17.10}$$

Then, for the given x, $l(\cdot|x)$ is the likelihood function of θ and $P(\cdot|x)$ is the posterior density of θ relative to our prior density $p(\theta)$.

A prior distribution is said to be *locally uniform* if its density does not change much over the region in which the likelihood is appreciable and does not assume large values outside that range. An example is the Lebesgue measure in E 17.3. If a prior is locally uniform at some x, the corresponding posterior density is approximately equal to the standardized likelihood function. Thus, if our prior in equation 17.10 is locally uniform at x,

$$P(\theta|x) \approx l(\theta|x) \bigg/ \int_A l(\theta|x)\,d\theta, \qquad \theta \in A. \tag{17.11}$$

Then almost all the information about θ that we possess after n performances of the experiment is the information conveyed by the likelihood function. In that sense our locally uniform prior at x is *noninformative* relative to our data.

A locally uniform prior for θ at x need not be locally uniform at some other x. Furthermore, a locally uniform prior for θ at x need not be locally uniform for $\phi = \phi(\theta)$ at x, where $\phi(\cdot)$: $A \to R$ is monotonic. Hence equations 17.10 and 17.17 do not provide us with a theory for choosing noninformative priors. To construct such a theory we make use of an idea of Box and Tiao's (1972, pp. 26–27).

17.3.2 Exact Data-Translated Likelihoods

Box and Tiao's interesting idea can be paraphrased as follows: Look for a monotonic function $\phi(\cdot)$: $A \to R$ with the property that the likelihood function for $\phi(\cdot)$ is up to its location completely determined a priori. If such a function exists, then to say that we know little a priori relative to the information that can be gleaned from the data can be taken to mean we are almost equally willing to accept one value of ϕ as another. If we are, we should choose as our noninformative prior one that is locally uniform in ϕ. The corresponding noninformative prior in θ is obtained from

$$p(\theta)\,d\theta \propto |d\phi/d\theta|\,d\theta, \tag{17.12}$$

where $\propto$ asserts "is proportional to."

In symbols Box and Tiao's idea can be formulated as follows: Search for functions $g(\cdot): R \to R$, $f(\cdot): R^n \to R$, and $\phi(\cdot): A \to R$ such that, for all $(\theta, x) \in A \times R^n$,

$$l(\theta|x) \propto g(\phi(\theta) - f(x)). \tag{17.13}$$

If $g(\cdot)$, $f(\cdot)$, and $\phi(\cdot)$ exist, $l(\cdot|\cdot)$ is said to be *data-translated in* ϕ. Two examples of such functions and the corresponding noninformative priors in θ are given below.

E 17.6 The random variable $x(\cdot)$ is normally distributed with mean θ and known variance σ^2. Then

$$l(\theta|x) \propto \frac{\exp -n(\theta - \bar{x})^2}{2\sigma^2},$$

where $\bar{x} = n^{-1} \sum_{i=1}^{n} x_i$; and $g(\cdot)$, $f(\cdot)$, and $\phi(\cdot)$ can be choosen so that $g(y) = \exp -ny^2/2\sigma^2$, $f(x) = \bar{x}$ and $\phi(\theta) = \theta$. In addition, $p(\theta)\,d\theta \propto d\theta$.

E 17.7 The random variable $x(\cdot)$ is normally distributed with mean 0 and variance θ^2. Then

$$l(\theta|x) \propto \exp\left\{-n(\log\theta - \log s) - \frac{n}{2}\exp[-2(\log\theta - \log s)]\right\},$$

where $s^2 = n^{-1} \sum_{i=1}^{n} x_i^2$; and $g(\cdot)$, $f(\cdot)$, and $\phi(\cdot)$ can be chosen so that $g(y) = \exp\{-ny - (n/2)\exp[-2y]\}$, $f(x) = \log s$ and $\phi(\theta) = \log\theta$. In addition, $p(\theta)\,d\theta \propto \theta^{-1}\,d\theta$.

Often the functions in equation 17.13 do not exist. We must then look for good approximations. Below we see how to search for approximations for an important class of likelihood functions; the ideas underlying the search are due to Box and Tiao (1972, pp. 36–40).

17.3.3 Approximate Data-Translated Likelihoods

We assume throughout this section that, for each family of probability distributions $\{F_\theta(\cdot); \theta \in A\}$, there exist functions $h(\cdot): R \to R_+$, $u(\cdot): R \to R$, $w(\cdot): A \to R_{++}$, and $c(\cdot): A \to R$ such that, for all $(x, \theta) \in R \times A$,

$$p(x|\theta) = h(x)w(\theta)e^{c(\theta)u(x)}$$

where $p(\cdot|\theta): R \to R_+$ denotes the density of $F_\theta(\cdot)$. Examples are the binomial distribution with mean θ and the normal distribution with mean 0 and variance θ^2.

For the families of probability distributions described above we can find a functon $\phi(\cdot): A \to R$ such that the likelihood function in ϕ is approximately data-translated. To find ϕ we let $L(\theta|x) = \log l(\theta|x)$ and we let $\hat{\theta}$ denote the maximum likelihood estimate of θ; i.e., we let $\hat{\theta}$ be the solution to the equation: $\partial L(\theta|x)/\partial\theta = 0$. For any $n > 1$, $\partial^2 L(\hat{\theta}|x)/\partial\theta^2$ is a function of $\hat{\theta}$ only. Also, for large n, $\partial^2 L(\hat{\theta}|x)/\partial\theta^2 < 0$ and

$$L(\theta|x) \approx L(\hat{\theta}|x) - \left(\frac{n}{2}\right)(\theta - \hat{\theta})^2\left(-\frac{1}{n}(\partial^2 L(\hat{\theta}|x)/\partial\theta^2)\right)$$

in a neighborhood of $\hat{\theta}$. Next we let $\phi = k(\theta)$, $\theta \in A$, where $k(\cdot)$ is differentiable and strictly monotone; and we let $K(\phi|x) = L(k^{-1}(\phi)|x)$. Then, with $\hat{\phi} = k(\hat{\theta})$, we find that

$$L(\theta|x) = K(\phi|x) \approx K(\hat{\phi}|x) - \left(\frac{n}{2}\right)(\phi - \hat{\phi})^2\left(-\frac{1}{n}(\partial^2 K(\hat{\phi}|x)/\partial\phi^2)\right)$$

$$= L(\hat{\theta}|x) - \left(\frac{n}{2}\right)(\phi - \hat{\phi})^2\left(-\frac{1}{n}(\partial^2 L(\hat{\theta}|x)/\partial\theta^2)\right)|(\partial\theta/\partial\phi)|_{\hat{\phi}}^2 \qquad (17.14)$$

in a neighborhood of $\hat{\theta}$. From equation 17.14 we deduce that, if we choose $k(\cdot)$: $\{\text{range of } \hat{\theta}\} \to R$ so that $|k'(\hat{\theta})| = (-(1/n)(\partial^2 L(\hat{\theta}|x)/\partial\theta^2))^{1/2}$, we can approximate the functions in equation 17.13 by $g(y) = \exp -ny^2/2$, $f(x) \propto k(\hat{\theta}(x))$ and $\phi(\theta) \propto k(\theta)$. The corresponding noninformative prior in θ is obtained from equation 17.12 and satisfies, for all $\theta \in \{\text{range of } \hat{\theta}\}$,

$$p(\theta)\, d\theta \propto \left(-\frac{1}{n}\left(\frac{\partial^2 L(\theta|x)}{\partial\theta^2}\right)\right)^{1/2} d\theta.$$

An example of such a prior is given in E 17.8.

E 17.8 The random variable $x(\cdot)$ assumes the values 0 and 1 with probability $(1 - \theta)$ and θ, respectively. In the n performances of the experiment, 1 is observed r times. Hence

$$l(\theta|x) = \theta^r(1 - \theta)^{n-r}$$

and $\hat{\theta} = r/n$. Also

$$-\frac{1}{n}\frac{\partial^2 L(\hat{\theta}|x)}{\partial\theta^2} = (\hat{\theta}(1 - \hat{\theta}))^{-1}.$$

Consequently, we choose $\phi(\theta) = \sin^{-1}\sqrt{\theta}$ and let

$$p(\theta)\, d\theta \propto (\theta(1 - \theta))^{-1/2}\, d\theta \qquad (17.15)$$

be our noninformative prior in θ.

It is important to note that the prior in equation 17.15 is very different from the prior we used to reflect our ignorance in E 17.3. Note also that with the prior in equation 17.15 the probabilities in equations 17.2 and 17.4 become

$$P(\{H\}) = \pi^{-1} \int_0^1 p^{1/2}(1-p)^{-1/2}\, d\mu(p)$$
$$= \frac{1}{2} = P(\{T\})$$

and

$$P(r \text{ heads in } n \text{ tosses}) = \pi^{-1}\binom{n}{r}\int_0^1 p^{r-(1/2)}(1-p)^{(n-r)-(1/2)}\, d\mu(p)$$
$$= \pi^{-1}\binom{n}{r}\cdot\frac{\Gamma(r+\frac{1}{2})\Gamma(n-r+\frac{1}{2})}{\Gamma(n+1)}$$

where $\Gamma(\cdot)$ is the gamma function. Furthermore, the posterior in equation 17.7 and the probabilities in equations 17.8 and 17.9 change:

$$P(dp|A)$$
$$= \binom{n}{r} p^{r-(1/2)}(1-p)^{n-r-(1/2)}\mu(dp) \Big/ \int_0^1 \binom{n}{r} p^{r-(1/2)}(1-p)^{n-r-(1/2)}\, d\mu(p)$$
$$= \frac{\Gamma(n+1)}{\Gamma(r+\frac{1}{2})\Gamma(n-r+\frac{1}{2})} p^{r-(1/2)}(1-p)^{n-r-(1/2)}\mu(dp),$$

$$P(\text{heads on the } (n+1)\text{st toss}|A) = \int_0^1 p\, dP(p|A)$$
$$= \frac{\Gamma(n+1)\Gamma(r+1+\frac{1}{2})}{\Gamma(n+2)\Gamma(r+\frac{1}{2})}$$
$$= \frac{r+\frac{1}{2}}{n+1}, \tag{17.16}$$

$$P(r \text{ heads in the next } n \text{ tosses}|A)$$
$$= \binom{n}{r}\int_0^1 p^r(1-p)^{n-r}\, dP(p|A)$$
$$= \frac{\Gamma(n+1)\binom{n}{r}}{\Gamma(r+\frac{1}{2})\Gamma(n-r+\frac{1}{2})}\cdot\frac{\Gamma(2r+\frac{1}{2})\Gamma(2(n-r)+\frac{1}{2})}{\Gamma(2n+1)}. \tag{17.17}$$

Hence the posterior distribution is a β distribution with $(x, y) = (r + \frac{1}{2}, n - r + \frac{1}{2})$ and the prior distribution is a β distribution with $(x, y) = (\frac{1}{2}, \frac{1}{2})$. The probabilities in equations 17.8 and 17.9 change accordingly, as witnessed in equations 17.16 and 17.17.

Whatever their reasons for choice of priors, the probabilities of events which Laplace and Box and Tiao would assign differ in interesting ways from the corresponding intrinsic probabilities. The way they differ is of great importance to econometrics. We shall, therefore, devote the next chapter to studying these differences in detail.

17.4 Measuring the Performance of Probability Assessors

In their economic theories, economists usually do not care how well subjective probabilities approximate intrinsic probabilities. Moreover, chances are that most individuals neither have the occasion nor the ability to measure how good their probability assignments are.

There are, however, individuals, e.g., weather forecasters and stock-market analysts, who care about how good their probability assignments are and who strive to improve them. Concluding this chapter on ignorance, we look at an example of the performance of weathermen and discuss how they can measure and improve their performance.

E 17.19 During the months of November and December 1949 and January 1950 each of eight professionals in the Salt Lake City weather bureau was asked to indicate the probability 0.6, 0.8, or 1 he assigned to his twelve-hour forecasts of rain or not-rain. Together these professionals made 294 0.6-predictions and were right 59 percent of the time; they made 292 0.8-predictions and were right 74 percent of the time; finally they made 509 1-predictions, and were right 97 percent of the time.

We consider the performance of the weathermen in Salt Lake City good. Howard Raiffa, however, thinks they could do better. In commenting on the results, Raiffa says: "This is not too bad, but still if they were to continue this practice of dividing predictions into three categories, it would be well if they recalibrated the middle category into a 0.75 confidence level" (Raiffa 1969, p. 5).

Whatever the validity of Raiffa's remark, it suggests several interesting questions: Do there exist sound ways of measuring the performance of probability assessors? If such measures exist, can they be used to improve the skill of an assessor? Knowledgeable weathermen answer yes to both these questions (see, for instance, F. Sanders 1967) and justify their assertions by referring to their success in using the so-called Brier score, proposed by G. W. Brier (1950), to measure and improve their forecasts.

We next describe the Brier score. Suppose that a weatherman over a certain period has made N probability forecasts of the occurrence of various weather conditions such as rain, temperature, wind direction and speed, visibility, etc. Suppose that the forecasts concerned M different events, E_i, $i = 1, \ldots, M$, and that the probability forecasts could assume L values only, f_k, $k = 1, \ldots, L$. Let 0_{ki} be 1 or 0, according as the event E_i occurred or not at the time the forecaster assigned probability f_k that it would. Then the forecaster's Brier score can be expressed as

$$F =_{df} N^{-1} \sum_{k=1}^{L} \sum_{i=1}^{M} (f_k - 0_{ki})^2 \cdot I_{ki},$$

where $I_{ki} = 1$ if f_k pertained to E_i and 0 otherwise. If we now let

$$M_k = \sum_{i=1}^{M} I_{ki}, \; \overline{0}_k = M_k^{-1} \sum_{i=1}^{M} 0_{ki} I_{ki}$$

and

$$F_k =_{df} M_k^{-1} \sum_{i=1}^{M} (f_k - 0_{ki})^2 \cdot I_{ki}$$

$$= (f_k - \overline{0}_k)^2 + \overline{0}_k(1 - \overline{0}_k), \qquad k = 1, \ldots, L$$

we can write the Brier score as

$$F = N^{-1} \sum_{k=1}^{L} M_k[(f_k - \overline{0}_k)^2 + \overline{0}_k(1 - \overline{0}_k)]. \tag{17.18}$$

In the brackets $[\cdot]$ in equation 17.18, the first term is a measure of the validity of the forecast. To make F as small as possible, f_k ought to be as close to $\overline{0}_k$ as possible. The second term (in the same brackets) is a measure of the sharpness of the forecast. Its value is 0 only when $\overline{0}_k$ is 1 or 0, that is, "when all instances have been sorted into two categories in one of which the event always occurs and in the other of which the event never occurs" (Sanders 1963, p. 192).

The performance of the weathermen in E 17.9 can be evaluated in terms of the Brier score as follows: Let $f_1 = 1$, $f_2 = 0.8$, and $f_3 = 0.6$. Then

$$F_1 = (1 - 0.97)^2 + 0.97(1 - 0.97) = 0.03,$$

$$F_2 = (0.8 - 0.74)^2 + 0.74(1 - 0.74) = 0.196,$$

$$F_3 = (0.6 - 0.59)^2 + 0.59(1 - 0.59) = 0.242,$$

$$F = (1095)^{-1}\{509 \cdot 03 + 292 \cdot 0.196 + 294 \cdot 0.242\} = 0.131187.$$

These F numbers indicate that the Salt Lake City weathermen could have improved (i.e., lowered) their Brier score if they had changed 0.8 to 0.75 as suggested by Raiffa. Such a change would have increased the "validity" of their forecasts. To increase the "sharpness" of their forecasts, they should also have added a 0.9 category.

The Brier score has been used successfully both to train and to evaluate the performance of weather forecasters. Other scoring rules have been proposed and used successfully to measure the performance of students on objective tests, to rank the skill of stock-market analysts, and to evaluate the performance of a panel of experts. For a general discussion of the properties of different scoring rules, I refer the reader to Staël von Holstein 1970, pp. 15–74.

18 Exchangeable Random Processes

By assigning prior distributions to the parameters of a purely random process, Laplace and Box and Tiao treat the variables of the process as if they were just exchangeable. Such a procedure has problematic consequences for the statistical analysis of purely random processes. Below I demonstrate how problematic these consequences are by delineating the salient characteristics of exchangeable random processes on both ordinary and conditional probability spaces. We begin with a short discussion of conditional expectations and probabilities.

18.1 Conditional Expectations and Probabilities

Let $(\Omega, \mathscr{F}, P(\cdot))$ be a probability space and let $B \in \mathscr{F}$ be such that $P(B) > 0$. Then B determines a conditional probability measure $P(\cdot|B)\colon \mathscr{F} \to [0, 1]$ such that, for all $A \in \mathscr{F}$,

$$P(A|B) = \frac{P(A \cap B)}{P(B)}$$

and such that, if A_i, $i = 1, 2, \ldots$, is an infinite sequence of disjoint events, then

$$P\left(\bigcup_{i=1}^{\infty} A_i|B\right) = \sum_{i=1}^{\infty} P(A_i|B).$$

From this and $P(\varnothing|B) = 0$ and $P(\Omega|B) = 1$, it follows that $(\Omega, \mathscr{F}, P(\cdot|B))$ is a probability space.

Next let $x(\cdot)$ be an integrable random variable on $(\Omega, \mathscr{F}, P(\cdot))$. The conditional expectation of $x(\cdot)$ given B is denoted by $E_B x$ and defined by

$$E_B x = \int_\Omega x(\omega)\, dP(\omega|B). \tag{18.1}$$

Since $P(A|B) = 0$ for all $A \in \{D \in \mathscr{F} : D = (F \cap B^C)$, for some $F \in \mathscr{F}\}$ the right-hand side of equation 18.1 reduces to $\int_B x(\omega)\, dP(\omega|B)$ and, since $P(A|B) = P(A)/P(B)$ for all $A \in \{D \in \mathscr{F} : D = (F \cap B)$, for some $F \in \mathscr{F}\}$,

$$E_B x = P(B)^{-1} \int_B x(\omega)\, dP(\omega). \tag{18.2}$$

Evidently, when $x(\cdot)$ is the indicator function of an event A, the conditional expectation of $x(\cdot)$ equals the conditional probability of A; i.e.,

$$E_B I_A = P(B)^{-1} \int_B I_A(\omega)\, dP(\omega) = \frac{P(A \cap B)}{P(B)}.$$

The conditional expectation in equation 18.2 is a function of B. For our purposes it is better to think of the conditional expectation of a random variable as a function on Ω. Hence we shall assign the number $E_B x$ to every point of B and represent the conditional expectation of x given B by $(E_B x) I_B(\cdot)$.

We can use the idea of a conditional expectation as a function to define the conditional expectation of a random variable with respect to a σ field. To that end, suppose that B_i, $i = 1, 2, \ldots$, is a sequence of disjoint events such that $\Omega = \bigcup_{i=1}^{\infty} B_i$, and let $\mathscr{B}$ denote the smallest σ field which contains all the B_i. Then the conditional expectation of x given $\mathscr{B}$ is denoted by $E^{\mathscr{B}} x$ and defined by

$$E^{\mathscr{B}} x = \sum_{i=1}^{\infty} (E_{B_i} x) I_{B_i}(\cdot). \tag{18.3}$$

If $P(B_i) = 0$ for some i, $E_{B_i} x$ is not well defined. Hence $E^{\mathscr{B}} x$ is undetermined on the union of all the B_i with P measure zero. We give $E^{\mathscr{B}} x$ an arbitrary value on this union and insist that $E^{\mathscr{B}} x$ is determined up to a set of P measure zero.

If $\mathscr{A}$ is a sub-σ field of $\mathscr{F}$, there need not exist a countable sequence of disjoint sets A_i, $i = 1, 2, \ldots$, such that $\Omega = \bigcup_{i=1}^{\infty} A_i$ and such that $\mathscr{A}$ is the smallest σ field which contains all the A_i. For such an $\mathscr{A}$, the conditional expectation of x given $\mathscr{A}$ is defined by

$$\int_B (E^{\mathscr{A}} x)\, dP_{\mathscr{A}}(\omega) = \int_B x\, dP(\omega), \qquad B \in \mathscr{A} \tag{18.4}$$

where $P_{\mathscr{A}}(\cdot)\colon \mathscr{A} \to [0, 1]$ is the restriction of $P(\cdot)$ to $\mathscr{A}$; i.e.,

$$P_{\mathscr{A}}(A) = P(A) \quad \text{for all } A \in \mathscr{A}, \tag{18.5}$$

and $E^{\mathscr{A}} x$ is an $\mathscr{A}$-measurable function.

The preceding definition is meaningful and extends equation 18.3. To show why, we observe first that it follows from the integrability of x and the Radon-Nikodym theorem (see UT 17, chapter 15) that there is an $\mathscr{A}$-measurable function $E^{\mathscr{A}}x$ which satisfies equation 18.4 and that any two $\mathscr{A}$-measurable functions which satisfy equation 18.4 can differ at most on a set of $P_{\mathscr{A}}$ measure 0. Hence $E^{\mathscr{A}}x$ is determined up to a set of $P_{\mathscr{A}}$ measure 0 by equation 18.4.

Next we note that equation 18.4 reduces to equation 18.3 when there exists a partition of Ω, A_i, $i = 1, 2, \ldots$, such that $\mathscr{A}$ is the smallest σ field which contains all the A_i. To wit: If $B \in \mathscr{A}$ is a nonnull event, there exists a sequence of A_i, A_{i_j}, $j = 1, \ldots, n_B$, such that $B = \bigcup_{j=1}^{n_B} A_{i_j}$. Consequently, by equations 18.3 and 18.2,

$$\int_B (E^{\mathscr{A}}x)\,dP_{\mathscr{A}}(\omega) = \sum_{j=1}^{n_B} \int_{A_{i_j}} (E^{\mathscr{A}}x)\,dP_{\mathscr{A}}(\omega) = \sum_{j=1}^{n_B} (E_{A_{i_j}}x)P(A_{i_j})$$

$$= \sum_{j=1}^{n_B} \int_{A_{i_j}} x\,dP(\omega) = \int_B x\,dP(\omega)$$

as required by equation 18.4.

Some of the properties of $E^{\mathscr{A}}(\cdot)$ are easily established. For example, T 18.1(i)–(iv).

T 18.1 Let $(\Omega, \mathscr{F}, P(\cdot))$ be a probability space and let $\mathscr{A}$ be a sub-σ field of $\mathscr{F}$. Moreover, let x and y be integrable random variables, and let $E^{\mathscr{A}}(\cdot)$ and $P_{\mathscr{A}}$ be as defined in equations 18.4 and 18.5. Then

(i) $E(E^{\mathscr{A}}x) = Ex$; and with $P_{\mathscr{A}}$ measure 1

(ii) $E^{\mathscr{A}}(x + y) = E^{\mathscr{A}}x + E^{\mathscr{A}}y$.

(iii) If x is $\mathscr{A}$ measurable, then with $P_{\mathscr{A}}$ measure 1, $E^{\mathscr{A}}x = x$ and $E^{\mathscr{A}}x \cdot y = x \cdot E^{\mathscr{A}}y$.

(iv) If $\mathscr{B}$ is a sub-σ field of $\mathscr{A}$, then $E^{\mathscr{B}}(E^{\mathscr{A}}x) = E^{\mathscr{B}}x = E^{\mathscr{A}}(E^{\mathscr{B}}x)$ a.e.

I shall prove condition iv and leave the rest to the reader. Let B be a member of $\mathscr{B}$. Then the first half of condition iv follows from

$$\int_B (E^{\mathscr{B}}x)\,dP_{\mathscr{B}}(\omega) = \int_B x\,dP(\omega) = \int_B (E^{\mathscr{A}}x)\,dP_{\mathscr{A}}(\omega) = \int_B (E^{\mathscr{B}}(E^{\mathscr{A}}x))\,dP_{\mathscr{B}}(\omega)$$

and the second half follows from

$$\int_B (E^{\mathscr{A}}(E^{\mathscr{B}}x))\,dP_{\mathscr{A}}(\omega) = \int_B (E^{\mathscr{B}}x)\,dP(\omega) = \int_B (E^{\mathscr{B}}x)\,dP_{\mathscr{B}}(\omega).$$

Other properties of $E^{\mathscr{A}}(\cdot)$ are harder to demonstrate. Of them two are of particular interest to us. We shall describe one in T 18.2 and the other in T 18.5. But first a few preliminary remarks.

Let $(\Omega, \mathscr{F}, P(\cdot))$ be a probability space and let $\mathscr{A}$ be a sub-σ field of $\mathscr{F}$. The restriction of $E^{\mathscr{A}}(\cdot)$ to indicators of events determines a function $P^{\mathscr{A}}(\cdot)$ on $\mathscr{F}$ whose values are $\mathscr{A}$-measurable functions on Ω that are determined up to a set of $P_{\mathscr{A}}$ measure 0 by the relation

$$P^{\mathscr{A}}(A) = E^{\mathscr{A}} I_A.$$

Evidently, with $P_{\mathscr{A}}$ probability 1, $P^{\mathscr{A}}(\Omega) = 1$ and $P^{\mathscr{A}}(A) \geqslant 0$ for any $A \in \mathscr{F}$. Moreover, if $A_1 A_2, \ldots$ is a sequence of disjoint events of $\mathscr{F}$, then

$$P^{\mathscr{A}}\left(\bigcup_{i=1}^{\infty} A_i\right) = \sum_{i=1}^{\infty} P^{\mathscr{A}}(A_i) \quad \text{a.e. } (P_{\mathscr{A}} \text{ measure}).$$

As defined, $P^{\mathscr{A}}(\cdot)$ has properties that are analogous to the properties of a probability measure on $\mathscr{F}$. Note, therefore, there need not exist a $P_{\mathscr{A}}$ null set N such that, for all $\omega \in N^c$, $P^{\mathscr{A}}(\cdot)$ is a probability measure on $\mathscr{F}$. In other words, there need not exist a function $P(\cdot)$: $\mathscr{F} \times \Omega \rightarrow [0, 1]$ such that

(i) For all $A \in \mathscr{F}$, $P(A, \cdot)$ is $\mathscr{A}$-measurable, and for all $\omega \in \Omega$, $P(\cdot, \omega)$ is a probability measure on $\mathscr{F}$, and
(ii) for all $A \in \mathscr{F}$, $P(A, \omega) = P^{\mathscr{A}}(A)$ with $P_{\mathscr{A}}$ measure 1.

The preceding observation is disconcerting but not fatal to the purpose of this chapter, since $P(\cdot)$ exists in all cases of interest to us—to wit, T 18.2.

T 18.2 Let $X = \{x(t, \omega); t \in T\}$ be a sequence of integrable random variables on a probability space $(\Omega, \mathscr{F}, P(\cdot))$. Moreover, let $\mathscr{A}$ be the sub-σ field of $\mathscr{F}$ determined by X; i.e., let $\mathscr{A} = \mathscr{F}(x(t); t \in T)$. Finally, let $\mathscr{B}$ be a sub-σ field of $\mathscr{A}$ and assume that the range of X is a Borel subset of R^T. Then there exists a function, $P(\cdot)$: $\mathscr{A} \times \Omega \rightarrow [0, 1]$, that satisfies conditions i and ii above, with $\mathscr{A}$ in place of $\mathscr{F}$ and $\mathscr{B}$ in place of $\mathscr{A}$.

This theorem is due to J. L. Doob. Since proving it is involved, I refer the reader to Loève (1960, pp. 361–362) for a detailed proof.

18.2 Exchangeable Random Variables

So much for conditional expectations and probabilities. Next we shall study exchangeable processes on an ordinary probability space. I begin by delineating the properties of finite sequences of exchangeable random variables.

18.2.1 Finite Sequences of Binary Exchangeable Random Variables

Let $T = \{1, 2, \ldots\}$ and let $x_t(\cdot)$, $t \in T$ be random variables on a probability space $(\Omega, \mathscr{F}, P(\cdot))$. They are *exchangeable* if and only if, for all $k \in T$, and k-tuples $t_1, \ldots, t_k$ with k different components, the joint probability distribution of $x_{t_1}(\cdot), \ldots, x_{t_k}(\cdot)$ is identical with the joint probability distribution of $x_1(\cdot), \ldots, x_k(\cdot)$. Similarly, if $A_1, A_2, \ldots$ is a sequence of events, the A_i are *exchangeable* if and only if the indicator functions, $I_{A_1}(\cdot), I_{A_2}(\cdot), \ldots$ are exchangeable.

With T replaced by $\{1, 2, \ldots, n\}$ for some n, the preceding definition also applies to a finite sequence of random variables. However, even though the definition is the same, the properties of a finite sequence of exchangeable random variables may differ from those of an infinite sequence. Theorems T 18.3 and T 18.4 will substantiate this fact.

T 18.3 Let $x_1(\cdot), \ldots, x_n(\cdot)$ be a finite sequence of exchangeable random variables on a probability space $(\Omega, \mathscr{F}, P(\cdot))$, and assume that these variables take only the values 0 and 1. Then there exist nonnegative numbers w_j, $j = 0, 1, \ldots, n$, with $\sum_{j=0}^{n} w_j = 1$, and an integer-valued random variable $N(\cdot)$ such that

$$P(\{\omega: N(\omega) = j\}) = w_j, \qquad j = 0, 1, \ldots, n \tag{18.6}$$

and such that, for $k = 1, \ldots, N$, $t_i \in \{1, \ldots, n\}$, and all j for which $w_j > 0$,

$$P(\{\omega \in \Omega : x_{t_i}(\omega) = 1, i = 1, \ldots, k\} | N = j) = \frac{j\cdot(j-1)\cdots(j-k+1)}{n(n-1)\cdots(n-k+1)}. \tag{18.7}$$

One way to understand the meaning of T 18.3 is to envision an experiment in which a blindfolded man draws n balls in succession from an urn with $(n+1)\cdot n$ balls. One half of the balls in the urn are marked 1, the other half 0, and $x_i(\cdot)$ records the number observed on the ith draw. Theorem T 18.3 insists that if the $x_i(\cdot)$ are exchangeable, the sampling of balls is conducted as if the urn were divided in $(n+1)$ compartments U_j, $j = 0, 1, \ldots, n$, each containing n balls and U_j containing j 1-balls, and as if the blindfolded man first chooses a U_j in accordance with equation 18.6 and then samples from the chosen U_j at random and without replacement.

Both the theorem and the ideas of the proof I shall give are due to D. G. Kendall (1967, pp. 321–322). Let $\alpha_0 = 1$ and, for each $k = 1, \ldots, n$, let

$$\alpha_k = P(\{\omega \in \Omega : x_i(\omega) = 1, i = 1, \ldots, k\}). \tag{18.8}$$

Moreover, let $\delta\alpha_k = \alpha_k - \alpha_{k+1}$ and $\delta^r\alpha_k = \delta(\delta^{r-1}\alpha_k)$. Then

$\delta\alpha_k = P(\{\omega \in \Omega : x_i(\omega) = 1, i = 1, \ldots, k, \text{ and } x_{k+1}(\omega) = 0\})$

for $k = 0, 1, \ldots, n - 1$,

$\delta^2\alpha_k = P(\{\omega \in \Omega : x_i(\omega) = 1, i = 1, \ldots, k, \text{ and } x_{k+1}(\omega) = 0, x_{k+2}(\omega) = 0\})$

for $k = 0, 1, \ldots, n - 2$, and

$\delta^r\alpha_k = P(\{\omega \in \Omega : x_i(\omega) = 1, i = 1, \ldots, k; x_{k+j}(\omega) = 0, j = 1, \ldots, r\})$

for $r = 3, \ldots, n - k$, and $k = 0, 1, \ldots, n - 3$. It is obvious that

$$\delta^r\alpha_{n-r} \geqslant 0, \qquad r = 0, 1, \ldots, n. \tag{18.9}$$

Moreover, when the m_i are different,

$\delta^r\alpha_k = P(\{\omega \in \Omega : x_{m_i}(\omega) = 1, i = 1, \ldots, k; x_{m_{k+j}}(\omega) = 0, j = 1, \ldots, r\})$

for $r = 0, 1, \ldots, n$ and $k = 0, 1, \ldots, n - r$. Consequently, since $\alpha_0 = 1$,

$$\sum_{r=0}^{n} \binom{n}{r} \delta^r\alpha_{n-r} = 1. \tag{18.10}$$

Next note that $\alpha_k = \delta\alpha_k + \alpha_{k+1}$, $\delta\alpha_k = \delta^2\alpha_k + \delta\alpha_{k+1}$, and $\alpha_k = \delta^2\alpha_k + 2\delta\alpha_{k+1} + \alpha_{k+2}$. In fact,

$$\alpha_k = \sum_{r=0}^{n-k} \binom{n-k}{r} \delta^r\alpha_{n-r}, \qquad k = 0, 1, \ldots, n.$$

Hence, if we let

$$w_j = \binom{n}{j} \delta^{n-j}\alpha_j, \qquad j = 0, 1, \ldots, n$$

then, by equations 18.9 and 18.10, the w_j determine a probability measure on $(\{0, 1, \ldots, n\}, \mathscr{P}(\{0, 1, \ldots, n\}))$ and

$$\alpha_k = \sum_{r=k}^{n} \left[\frac{r(r-1)\ldots(r-k+1)}{n(n-1)\ldots(n-k+1)}\right] w_r, \qquad k = 0, 1, \ldots, n.$$

Finally, let $N(\cdot): \Omega \to \{0, 1, \ldots, n\}$ be such that $N(\omega)$ records the number of indices i with $x_i(\omega) = 1$. Then

$$P(\{\omega \in \Omega : N(\omega) = j\}) = \binom{n}{j} \delta^{n-j}\alpha_j = w_j \tag{18.11}$$

for all $j = 0, 1, \ldots, n$, and

$$P(\{\omega \in \Omega : x_{m_i}(\omega) = 1, i = 1, \ldots, k\} | N = j) = \binom{n-k}{j-k}\left(\frac{\delta^{n-j}\alpha_j}{w_j}\right)$$
$$= \binom{n-k}{j-k} \Big/ \binom{n}{j}.$$

But if this is so, then for $k = 0, 1, \ldots, n$, and $j = k + 1, \ldots, n$,

$$P(\{\omega \in \Omega : x_{m_i}(\omega) = 1, i = 1, \ldots, k\} | N = j) = \frac{j(j-1)\ldots(j-k+1)}{n(n-1)\ldots(n-k+1)}$$

as was to be shown.

E 18.1 Let $x_1(\cdot)$, $x_2(\cdot)$, and $x_3(\cdot)$ be random variables on the probability space $(\Omega, \mathscr{F}, P(\cdot))$ and suppose that they can only take the values 0 and 1. Moreover, let $A_i = \{\omega \in \Omega : x_i(\omega) = 1\}$, $i = 1, 2, 3$, and assume that

$P(A_i) = 0.5, \qquad i = 1, 2, 3$

$P(A_1 \cap A_2) = P(A_1 \cap A_3) = P(A_2 \cap A_3) = 0.2,$

and

$P(A_1 \cap A_2 \cap A_3) = 0.05.$

Then the $x_i(\cdot)$ are exchangeable random variables and the A_i are exchangeable events. In addition (in the notation of T 18.3),

$$P(\{\omega : N(\omega) = j\}) = \begin{cases} 0.05 & \text{if } j = 0 \\ 0.45 & \text{if } j = 1 \\ 0.45 & \text{if } j = 2 \\ 0.05 & \text{if } j = 3 \end{cases}$$

and

$$P(A_i|N) = \begin{cases} 1/3 & \text{if } N = 1 \\ 2/3 & \text{if } N = 2 \\ 1 & \text{if } N = 3 \end{cases}$$

$$P(A_{t_1} \cap A_{t_2}|N) = \begin{cases} 1/3 & \text{if } N = 2 \\ 1 & \text{if } N = 3 \end{cases}$$

$P(A_1 \cap A_2 \cap A_3 | N = 3) = 1.$

18.2.2 Sequences of Infinitely Many Binary Exchangeable Variables

The analogue of T 18.3 for an infinite sequence of random variables, T 18.4, is due to B. deFinetti and is both surprising and extremely interesting.

T 18.4 Let $x_i(\cdot)$, $i = 1, 2, \ldots$, be an infinite sequence of random variables on a probability space $(\Omega, \mathscr{F}, P(\cdot))$, and assume that the $x_i(\cdot)$ only take the values 0 and 1. Then the $x_i(\cdot)$ are exchangeable if and only if there exists a random variable $y(\cdot)$ with probability distribution $F_y(\cdot)$ such that

$$\lim n^{-1} \sum_{i=1}^{n} x_i(\omega) = y(\omega) \quad \text{a.e.} \tag{18.12}$$

and such that $F_y(\cdot)$ has all its points of increase in [0, 1] and satisfies

$$P(\{\omega \in \Omega : x_{t_i}(\omega) = 1, i = 1, \ldots, k, x_{t_{k+j}}(\omega) = 0, j = k+1, \ldots, n-k\})$$
$$= \int_0^1 p^k(1-p)^{n-k}\, dF_y(p), \tag{18.13}$$

and

$$P\left(\left\{\omega \in \Omega : \sum_{i=1}^{n} x_{t_i}(\omega) = k\right\}\right) = \binom{n}{k} \int_0^1 p^k(1-p)^{n-k}\, dF_y(p), \tag{18.14}$$

where the t_i are different positive integers.

It is obvious that if the $x_i(\cdot)$ satisfy equations 18.12–18.14, then they are exchangeable. Hence we shall only establish the necessity of equations 18.12–18.14 here. We begin by invoking the following universal theorem of F. Hausdorff (see Feller 1966, pp. 223–224):

UT 18 Let $\alpha_0, \alpha_1, \ldots$ be a sequence of numbers and let $\delta\alpha_k = \alpha_k - \alpha_{k+1}$ and $\delta^r\alpha_k = \delta(\delta^{r-1}\alpha_k)$. Then conditions i and ii below are equivalent:

(i) For all $r, k = 0, 1, \ldots, \delta^r\alpha_k \geqslant 0$ and $\alpha_0 = 1$.

(ii) There is a probability distribution $F(\cdot)$ with support in [0, 1] such that, for all $k = 0, 1, \ldots$

$$\alpha_k = \int_0^1 x^k\, dF(x). \tag{18.15}$$

Next, let $\alpha_0 = 1$ and, for all $k = 1, 2, \ldots$, define α_k as in equation 18.8. Then, by varying n in equation 18.9, observe that the α_k satisfy condition i of UT 18. Consequently, there is a probability distribution $F(\cdot)$ with support in [0, 1] such that α_k satisfies equation 18.15 for all $k = 0, 1, \ldots$. But if this is so, it is easy to verify

$$\delta^r\alpha_k = \int_0^1 x^k(1-x)^r\, dF(x)$$

for all $r, k = 0, 1, \ldots$. Hence $F(\cdot)$ satisfies equation 18.13 for all $n = 0, 1, \ldots$ such that $n \geqslant k$. Since the $x_i(\cdot)$ are exchangeable, $F(\cdot)$ obviously satisfies equation 18.14 as well.

It remains to establish equation 18.12 and to show that $F(\cdot)$ is the probability distribution of $y(\cdot)$. The validity of equation 18.12 is a corollary of T 18.5 below. To show that $F(\cdot)$ is the distribution of $y(\cdot)$, let n be fixed and let $N(\cdot): \Omega \to \{0, 1, \ldots, n\}$ and the w_i be as defined in the proof of T 18.3. Then, by equation 18.11,

$$P\left(\left\{\omega \in \Omega : n^{-1} \sum_{i=1}^{n} x_i(\omega) = \frac{k}{n}\right\}\right) = P(\{\omega \in \Omega : N(\omega) = k\})$$

$$= \binom{n}{k} \delta^{n-k} \alpha_k, \qquad k = 0, 1, \ldots, n.$$

Hence, for each $n = 0, 1, \ldots$, the probability distribution of $n^{-1} \sum_{i=1}^{n} x_i(\cdot)$ is given by

$$F_n(t) = \begin{cases} 0 & \text{if } t \leqslant 0 \\ \sum_{k \leqslant nt} \binom{n}{k} \delta^{n-k} \alpha_k & \text{if } t \in (0, 1] \\ 1 & \text{if } t > 1 \end{cases} \tag{18.16}$$

It is a fact (see Feller 1966, pp. 220–223, for a proof) that at each continuity point t of $F(\cdot)$

$$\lim F_n(t) = F(t). \tag{18.17}$$

From this and equation 18.12 it follows that $F(\cdot)$ is the distribution of $y(\cdot)$.

Looking back at T 18.3 and T 18.4, we make two mental notes. First: There is an essential difference between assuming that a finite number of random variables are exchangeable and assuming that they constitute a finite subset of an infinite sequence of exchangeable random variables. For example, the three variables in E 18.1 are exchangeable. They cannot form a subset of a sequence of more than six exchangeable random variables (Galambos 1978, pp. 127–128). Next: The $F_n(\cdot)$ of equation 18.16 is the probability distribution of $N(\cdot)/n$, where $N(\cdot)$ is as described in T 18.3. From this and from equations 18.17 and 18.7, it follows that when n is large and k is small relative to n, the joint probability distribution of any k of the variables in T 18.3 is similar in form to the joint probability distribution of any k of the variables in T 18.4.

More insight into the characteristics of infinite sequences of binary exchangeable random variables can be gained from the following considerations: Recall that we defined C to be the intersection, $\bigcap_{n \geqslant 1} \mathscr{F}(x_n, x_{n+1}, \ldots)$, i.e., the σ field of tail events. When the $x_n(\cdot)$ are independent, the tail events have probability 0 or 1, and the random variables on (Ω, C) are degenerate. When the $x_n(\cdot)$ are exchangeable, $(\Omega, C, P_C(\cdot))$ is much richer in structural detail. Note, therefore, that the random variable y in T 18.4 is a random variable on (Ω, C) and that y need not be degenerate relative to $P(\cdot)$.

We shall next show that y is a.e. equal to the conditional expectation of $x_1(\cdot)$ with respect to C and that, conditional upon the value of y, the $x_i(\cdot)$ are identically and independently distributed random variables. For that purpose we need an interesting theorem of M. Loève, T 18.5.

T 18.5 Let $x_1(\cdot), x_2(\cdot), \ldots,$ be a sequence of integrable exchangeable random variables on a probability space $(\Omega, \mathscr{F}, P(\cdot))$. Moreover, for each $n = 1, 2, \ldots,$ let

$$y_n(\cdot) = n^{-1} \sum_{i=1}^{n} x_i(\cdot) \qquad \text{and} \qquad \mathscr{B}_n = \mathscr{F}(y_n, y_{n+1}, \ldots).$$

Finally, let $\tilde{C} = \bigcap_{n=1}^{\infty} \mathscr{B}_n$. Then

$$\lim E^{\mathscr{B}_n} x_1 = E^{\tilde{C}} x_1 \quad \text{a.e.} \tag{18.18}$$

and

$$\lim y_n = E^{\tilde{C}} x_1 \quad \text{a.e.} \tag{18.19}$$

We note in passing that, since $y_n = E^{\mathscr{B}_n} y_n$ a.e. and since

$$E^{\mathscr{B}_n} y_n = n^{-1} \sum_{i=1}^{n} E^{\mathscr{B}_n} x_i = n^{-1} \sum_{i=1}^{n} E^{\mathscr{B}_n} x_1 = E^{\mathscr{B}_n} x_1, \quad \text{a.e.}$$

equation 18.19 is an immediate consequence of equation 18.18. Hence, it is only 18.18 which is in need of proof. We also note that, for all $n = 1, 2, \ldots,$

$$\mathscr{B}_n = \mathscr{F}(y_n, x_{n+1}, x_{n+2}, \ldots).$$

Consequently, $\mathscr{F}(x_{n+1}, x_{n+2}, \ldots) \subset \mathscr{B}_n$ and $C \subset \tilde{C}$. Finally we note that if $\lim y_n$ exists, then for any fixed m,

$$\lim y_n = \lim_{n \to \infty} n^{-1} \sum_{i=m}^{n} x_i(\cdot).$$

From this it follows that if $y = \lim y_n$, then y is measurable with respect to C.

The validity of equation 18.18 and hence the existence of $\lim y_n$ is an immediate consequence of the integrability of x_1, the fact that for all n, $\mathscr{B}_n \supset \mathscr{B}_{n+1}$ and a universal theorem of Doob's concerning convergence of martingales (see Doob 1953, theorem 4.3, p. 331). For brevity's sake I shall not elaborate.

Now on to the y of T 18.4, $E^C x_1$, and the structure of $P(\cdot|y)$. First, y and $E^C x_1$: Theorem T 18.5 demonstrates that the random variable $y(\cdot)$ in equation 18.12 exists and that it is a.e. equal to $E^{\tilde{C}} x_1$. From this, T 18.1(iv), and the fact that $C \subset \tilde{C}$ and y is C-measurable, it follows that

$$E^C x_1 = E^C(E^{\tilde{C}} x_1) = E^C y = y \quad \text{a.e. } (P_C \text{ measure})$$

as asserted above.

Next we shall show that, conditional upon y, the x_i in T 18.4 are independently and identically distributed.

T 18.6 Let $x_1(\cdot), x_2(\cdot), \ldots,$ be a sequence of exchangeable random variables on a probability space $(\Omega, \mathscr{F}, P(\cdot))$ and assume that the $x_i(\cdot)$ only take the values 0 and 1. Moreover, let $\tilde{C}$ be as defined in T 18.5 and let $y = E^{\tilde{C}} x_1$. Then, for $k = 1, 2, \ldots,$ and any n different positive integers, t_i, $i = 1, \ldots, n$,

$$P(\{\omega \in \Omega : x_{t_i}(\omega) = 1, i = 1, \ldots, k \text{ and } x_{t_{k+j}}(\omega) = 0, j = 1, \ldots, n-k\}|y)$$
$$= y^k(1-y)^{n-k} \qquad \text{a.e. } (P_{\mathscr{F}(y)} \text{ measure})$$

and

$$P\left(\left\{x \in \Omega : \sum_{i=1}^{n} x_{t_i}(\omega) = k\right\}\middle| y\right) = \binom{n}{k} y^k(1-y)^{n-k} \qquad \text{a.e. } (P_{\mathscr{F}(y)} \text{ measure}).$$

The proof of T 18.6, which we sketch below, is due to D. Kendall who attributes the theorem to A. Rényi and P. Révész (Kendall 1967, pp. 319–325). We begin by observing that if $1 \leqslant t_1 < t_2 \leqslant n$, and if, for each $n = 1, 2, \ldots, N(n) = \sum_{i=1}^{n} x_i$, then with probability 1

$$\begin{aligned} E^{\mathscr{B}_n}(x_{t_1} \cdot x_{t_2}) &= E^{\mathscr{B}_n}(x_1 \cdot x_n) = E^{\mathscr{B}_n}(x_n E^{\mathscr{B}_{n-1}} x_1) \\ &= E^{\mathscr{B}_n}(x_n \cdot (n-1)^{-1} N(n-1)) \\ &= E^{\mathscr{B}_n}(x_n \cdot (n-1)^{-1}(N(n)-1)) \\ &= (n-1)^{-1}(N(n)-1) \cdot n^{-1} N(n) \end{aligned}$$

since $N(n-1) = N(n) - 1$ unless $x_n = 0$. By induction we find that if $1 \leqslant t_1 < t_2 < \cdots < t_k \leqslant n$,

$$E^{\mathscr{B}_n}(x_{t_1} \cdot x_{t_2} \cdot \cdots \cdot x_{t_k}) = \prod_{j=0}^{k-1} (n-j)^{-1}(N(n)-j) \qquad \text{a.e.}$$

From this, T 18.5, and Doob's martingale theorem, it follows that for $k = 1$, 2, ... and any k different positive integers t_i, $i = 1, \ldots, k$,

$$E^{\tilde{C}}(x_{t_1} \cdot x_{t_2} \cdot \cdots \cdot x_{t_k}) = y^k \quad \text{a.e.} \tag{18.20}$$

Next we let $\mathscr{F}(y)$ and $E(x|y)$, respectively, denote the σ field generated by y and the conditional expectation of x with respect to $\mathscr{F}(y)$. Then by T 18.1(iv),

$$E(x_1|y) = E(E^{\tilde{C}}x_1|y) = E(y|y) = y \qquad \text{a.e.}$$

Hence,

$$E(x_1|y) = y \quad \text{a.e. } (P_{\mathscr{F}(y)} \text{ measure}).$$

By a similar argument and by equation 18.20, we find that, for any $k = 1, 2, \ldots$ and any k different positive integers $t_1, \ldots, t_k$,

$$E(x_{t_1} \cdot x_{t_2} \cdots x_{t_k}|y) = y^k \qquad \text{a.e. } (P_{\mathscr{F}(y)} \text{ measure}).$$

Consequently, since $E(x_{t_1}|y) = E(I_{\{\omega \in \Omega : x_{t_1}(\omega)=1\}}|y)$ and $E(x_{t_1} \cdot x_{t_2} \cdots x_{t_k}|y) = E(I_{\{\omega \in \Omega : x_{t_i}(\omega)=1, i=1,\ldots,k\}}|y)$, it follows that with $P_{\mathscr{F}(y)}$ probability 1

$$P(\{\omega \in \Omega : x_{t_1}(\omega) = 1\}|y) = y$$

and

$$P(\{\omega \in \Omega : x_{t_1}(\omega) = 1, \ldots, x_{t_k}(\omega) = 1\}|y) = y^k.$$

But if that is so, it must also be the case that

$$P(\{\omega \in \Omega : x_{t_i}(\omega) = 1,\, i = 1, \ldots, k \text{ and } x_{t_{k+j}}(\omega) = 0,\, j = 1, \ldots, n-k\}|y)$$
$$= y^k(1-y)^{n-k} \qquad \text{a.e. } (P_{\mathscr{F}(y)} \text{ measure}).$$

From this and the exchangeability of the $x_t(\cdot)$ follows the validity of the theorem.

18.2.3 Integrable Exchangeable Random Processes

The preceding results can be generalized in many interesting ways. Before I describe the one of most interest to us, a few preliminary remarks concerning n-symmetric random variables are called for. To that end, let $X = \{x_t(\omega);\, t = 1, 2, \ldots\}$ be an exchangeable random process on a probability space $(\Omega, \mathscr{F}, P(\cdot))$. A random variable on $(\Omega, \mathscr{F})$ is *n-symmetric* if and only if it is a function of X whose values are invariant under permutations of its first n variables. An example of such a function is $n^{-1}\sum_{t=1}^{n} f(x_t)$, where $f(\cdot)$ is a Borel-measurable function on the range of the $x_t(\cdot)$.

N-symmetric random variables have interesting properties. To wit: Let $g(X)$ be a bounded n-symmetric random variable and suppose that

$E|f(x_1)| < \infty$. Then the exchangeability of the $x_t(\cdot)$ implies that, for all $j = 1, \ldots, n$,

$$E(f(x_j)g(X)) = E(f(x_1)g(x_j, x_2, \ldots, x_{j-1}, x_1, x_{j+1}, \ldots)) = E(f(x_1)g(X))$$

and hence that

$$E\left(n^{-1} \sum_{t=1}^{n} f(x_t)g(X)\right) = E(f(x_1)g(X)). \tag{18.21}$$

Next, let $\mathscr{S}_n$ denote the smallest σ field relative to which all the n-symmetric random variables are measurable and observe that $\mathscr{S}_n \supset \mathscr{S}_{n+1}$. Since $n^{-1}\sum_{t=1}^{n} f(x_t)$ is an n-symmetric random variable, it follows easily from equations 18.4 and 18.21, with $g(\cdot)$ replaced by $I_A(\cdot)$ for some $A \in \mathscr{S}_n$, that

$$n^{-1} \sum_{t=1}^{n} f(x_t) = E^{\mathscr{S}_n} f(x_1) \quad \text{a.e. } (P^{\mathscr{S}_n} \text{ measure}). \tag{18.22}$$

Consequently, if we let $\mathscr{S} = \bigcap_{n=1}^{\infty} \mathscr{S}_n$ and apply Doob's martingale theorem, we find that with probability 1

$$\lim n^{-1} \sum_{t=1}^{n} f(x_t) = E^{\mathscr{S}} f(x_1). \tag{18.23}$$

In particular, for any $x \in R$ and $A_x = \{r \in R : r < x\}$, with probability 1,

$$\lim n^{-1} \sum_{t=1}^{n} I_{A_x}(x_t) = P^{\mathscr{S}}(\{\omega \in \Omega : x_1(\omega) < x\}). \tag{18.24}$$

The preceding observations can be generalized as follows: Let $f(\cdot)$ be a bounded Borel measurable function on R^k. Then arguments similar to those that led to equation 18.22 suffice to demonstrate that

$$(n(n-1)\ldots(n-k+1))^{-1} \sum f(x_{j_1}, \ldots, x_{j_k}) = E^{\mathscr{S}_n} f(x_1, \ldots, x_k) \qquad \text{a.e.,}$$

where the sum extends over distinct $j_1, \ldots, j_k \leqslant n$. From this and Doob's martingale theorem, we deduce that with probability 1,

$$\begin{aligned} E^{\mathscr{S}} f(x_1, \ldots, x_k) &= \lim\, (n(n-1)\ldots(n-k+1))^{-1} \sum f(x_{j_1}, \ldots, x_{j_k}) \\ &= \lim n^{-k} \sum_{j_1=1}^{n} \cdots \sum_{j_k=1}^{n} f(x_{j_1}, \ldots, x_{j_k}) \end{aligned}$$

the second equality being a consequence of the fact that the contribution from terms with coincidences among the j_i is of the order of n^{k-1}. But if that is true, then the last equation with $I_{A_{s_1}}(x_1) \ldots I_{A_{s_k}}(x_k)$ in place of

$f(x_1,\ldots,x_k)$, and equation 18.24 suffice to show that

$$P^{\mathscr{S}}(\{\omega \in \Omega : x_1(\omega) < s_1,\ldots,x_k(\omega) < s_k\}) = \prod_{t=1}^{k} P^{\mathscr{S}}(\{\omega \in \Omega : x_t(\omega) < s_t\}). \tag{18.25}$$

The relation depicted in equations 18.24 and 18.25 and their proofs demonstrate that if $X = \{x_t(\omega); t = 1,2,\ldots\}$ is an integrable exchangeable process, then there exists a σ field conditional upon which the components of X are independent and identically distributed. This observation is due to de Finetti (1964, pp. 130–140). The arguments used to establish it I have learned from J. F. C. Kingman (1978, pp. 185–187).

For our purpose it is awkward that the probabilities in equation 18.25 be conditioned on a σ field. Fortunately for us, the $\mathscr{S}$ in equation 18.25 can be replaced by a σ field generated by a random variable M—to wit T 18.7.

T 18.7 Let $x_1(\cdot), x_2(\cdot), \ldots$ be an infinite sequence of integrable exchangeable random variables on the probability space $(\Omega, \mathscr{F}, P(\cdot))$ and let C be the σ field of tail events of the sequence. Moreover, assume that the range of the $x_t(\cdot)$ is a Borel subset of R^∞. Then there exist random variables $\xi(\cdot)$ and $M(\cdot)$ on (Ω, C) such that with probability 1,

$$\lim n^{-1} \sum_{t=1}^{n} x_t(\omega) = \xi(\omega) \qquad \text{and} \qquad \xi(\omega) = E^C x_1 \tag{18.26}$$

and such that, for all $k = 1, 2, \ldots$, and any k different positive integers $t_1, \ldots, t_k$,

$$P(\{\omega \in \Omega : x_{t_i}(\omega) < a_i, i = 1,\ldots,k\}|M) = \prod_{i=1}^{n} P(\{\omega \in \Omega : x_{t_i}(\omega) < a_i\}|M) \quad \text{a.e..} \tag{18.27}$$

In reading this theorem, note that the validity of equation 18.26 is an immediate consequence of equation 18.23, $C \subset \mathscr{S}$, T 18.1 (iii) and (iv), and the fact that ξ is measurable with respect to C. The existence of a random variable M on (Ω, C) conditional on which the x_t are independent and identically distributed was first established by Richard Olshen. Olshen also demonstrated that M is essentially unique; i.e., if Y is a random variable conditional upon which the x_t are independent and identically distributed, a version of M is measurable with respect to $\mathscr{F}(Y)$. For proof of these and related results, I refer the reader to Olshen (1974, pp. 317–321).

18.3 Exchangeable Processes and Econometric Practice

To serious econometricians, theorems T 18.3–T 18.7 pose an uncomfortable philosophical question that may be paraphrased as follows: We usually assume that the probability distributions of the random variables being studied belong to well-defined classes whose extent is determined by the range of values assumed by certain parameters; e.g., $x(\cdot)$ is normally distributed with mean μ and variance σ^2, where $\mu \in R$ and $\sigma^2 \in R_{++}$. We also usually assume that—conditional upon the values of these parameters—the random variables in question are independently distributed. Some of us, the classical econometricians, treat them as independently distributed regardless of whether we know the values of the parameters. Others, the Bayesian econometricians, assign a prior distribution to the parameters and treat the variables as exchangeable random variables. We can justify the first procedure only if the random variables in question constitute a subset of an infinite sequence of exchangeable random variables with an associated degenerate σ field of tail events. We can justify the second procedure only if our prior distribution corresponds to the probability distribution of the M variable in T 18.7. Since the justification of either procedure involves properties of tail events, we shall never be able to decide which is correct. We can only ascertain in our analysis the differences to which they lead. Several such differences are illustrated below.

18.3.1 Consistent Parameter Estimates

Classical and Bayesian econometricians define consistency differently. To show how different they are, we let $Q = \{Q_\theta : \theta \in \Theta\}$ be a family of probability measures on a space $\mathscr{X}$, and we let Q_θ^∞ denote the infinite product probability measure on $\mathscr{X}^\infty$ which renders the coordinate random variables, $X_1, X_2, \ldots$, independent, with common probability distribution determined by Q_θ. Moreover, we let P_φ denote the joint distribution of the parameter θ and the data; i.e., for $A \subset \Theta$ and $B \subset \mathscr{X}^\infty$,

$$P_\varphi(A \times B) = \int_A Q_\theta^\infty(B)\, d\varphi(\theta),$$

where $\varphi(\cdot)$ denotes the prior measure on subsets of Θ. Finally, we denote by $\varphi_n(\cdot|x_1,\ldots,x_n)$ the posterior distribution of θ, given the observed values of $X_1, \ldots, X_n$, which we denote by $x_1, \ldots, x_n$.

A classical estimate of θ, $\hat{\theta}_c$, may be many things; e.g., it may be a function of the observations, $x_1, \ldots, x_n$, that maximizes the value of $\prod_{i=1}^n Q_\theta(\{x_i\})$; or it may be a function of the observations that minimizes the expected value of a quadratic loss function. Whatever it is, we shall denote the classical estimate by $\hat{\theta}_c(x_1,\ldots,x_n)$. In the setting of classical econometrics, this estimate is *consistent* if and only if, for any given $\theta \in \Theta$ and all $\varepsilon > 0$,

$$\lim_{n\to\infty} Q_\theta^\infty(\{x \in \mathscr{X}^\infty : \|\hat{\theta}_c(x_1,\ldots,x_n) - \theta\| > \varepsilon\}) = 0, \tag{18.28}$$

where $\|a - b\|$ designates a suitable measure of distance between a and b.

A Bayes estimate of θ can also be many different things. However, most of the time the Bayes estimate of θ is a function of the observations, $\hat{\theta}_B(x_1,\ldots,x_n)$, that satisfies the equation

$$\hat{\theta}_B(x_1,\ldots,x_n) = \int_\Theta \theta \, d\varphi_n(\theta|x_1,\ldots,x_n).$$

To a classical econometrician the Bayes estimate is consistent if and only if it satisfies equation 18.28, with $\hat{\theta}_c(\cdot)$ replaced by $\hat{\theta}_B(\cdot)$. But in the setting of Bayesian econometrics, the classical notion of consistency makes little sense. So a Bayesian will usually define consistency differently.

A Bayesian econometrician envisions that nature picks a point $\theta^0 \in \Theta$ in accordance with a chance mechanism which is governed by an alias of his own prior probability measure $\varphi(\cdot)$. To him the pair $(\theta^0, \varphi_n(\cdot))$ is consistent if and only if, for all bounded continuous functions $f(\cdot)\colon \Theta \to R$ and almost all $x \in \mathscr{X}^\infty$ ($Q_{\theta^0}^\infty$ measure),

$$\lim_{n\to\infty} \int_\Theta f(\theta)\, d\varphi_n(\theta|x_1,\ldots,x_n) = \int_\Theta f(\theta)\, d\delta_{\theta^0}(\theta), \tag{18.29}$$

where $\delta_{\theta^0}(\cdot)$ denotes a Dirac measure that assigns numbers to subsets of Θ in accordance with

$$\delta_{\theta^0}(A) = \begin{cases} 1 & \text{if } \theta^0 \in A \\ 0 & \text{otherwise.} \end{cases}$$

Thus, to a Bayesian, $(\theta^0, \varphi_n(\cdot))$ is consistent if and only if, for almost all sequences of observations in $\mathscr{X}^\infty$ ($Q_{\theta^0}^\infty$ measure), the posterior probability measure $\varphi_n(\cdot)$ eventually shrinks to a point measure at θ^0.

In most parametric statistical inference of interest to econometricians, the consistency of $(\theta, \varphi_n(\cdot))$ implies the consistency in the classical sense of $\hat{\theta}_B(x_1,\ldots,x_n)$ as well; i.e., if $(\theta, \varphi_n(\cdot))$ is consistent, then for the given(!) θ and all $\varepsilon > 0$, equation 18.28 holds, with $\hat{\theta}_c(\cdot)$ replaced by $\hat{\theta}_B(\cdot)$. It is, therefore, interesting to observe that for most parametric statistical inference in econometrics $(\theta, \varphi_n(\cdot))$ is consistent for almost all values of θ (φ measure). This observation is due to Doob (1949, pp. 23–27) and is stated precisely in T 18.8.

T 18.8 Let $\mathscr{X}$, Θ, Q_θ, φ_n, and $\hat{\theta}_B(x_1,\ldots,x_n)$ be as described above. Suppose that $\mathscr{X}$ and Θ are, respectively, Borel subsets of R and R^k for some $k \geqslant 1$, and let $\mathscr{B}$

denote the Borel subsets of Θ. Moreover, suppose that there is a function $q(\cdot)\colon \Theta \times \mathscr{X} \to R$ such that, for all $y \in \mathscr{X}$ and $A = \mathscr{X} \cap (-\infty, y)$,

$$Q_\theta(A) = \int_A q(\theta, x)\, dx$$

and such that, for each $y \in \mathscr{X}$, the function

$$Q(\theta, y) = Q_\theta(\mathscr{X} \cap (-\infty, y))$$

is measurable with respect to $\mathscr{B}$. Finally, let $\varphi(\cdot)\colon \mathscr{B} \to [0, 1]$ denote the prior measure on $\mathscr{B}$ and suppose that

(i) if $\theta_1, \theta_2 \in \Theta$ and $\theta_1 \neq \theta_2$, then $Q_{\theta_1} \neq Q_{\theta_2}$; and

(ii) there is a function $g(\cdot)\colon \Theta \to R$ such that

$$\varphi(A) = \int_A g(\theta)\, d\theta, \qquad A \in \mathscr{B}.$$

Then, for almost all θ (φ measure) $(\theta, \varphi_n(\cdot))$ is consistent. Moreover, if $\int_\Theta \theta g(\theta)\, d\theta < \infty$ and $(\theta, \varphi_n(\cdot))$ is consistent, then

$$\lim \hat{\theta}_B(x_1, \ldots, x_n) = \theta \quad \text{a.e. } (Q_\theta^\infty \text{ measure})$$

as well.

Since the statement of Doob's theorem is easy to understand and since the proof would not add to our understanding of the import of the theorem, I shall omit the proof for brevity's sake.

Doob's theorem allows us to compare the classical and Bayesian notions of consistency. According to the classical notion, $\hat{\theta}_c(\cdot)$ is consistent if it satisfies equation 18.28 for *all* $\theta \in \Theta$. However, since the classical econometrician does not know the true value of θ, the "for all θ" accompanying equation 18.28 does not carry much weight by itself. It is the assumption that there is really just one relevant value of θ that makes equation 18.28 meaningful as a definition of consistency. As to the Bayesian notion of consistency, equation 18.29, note that Doob's theorem provides no information about the null-θ-set which contains all θ for which $(\theta, \mu_n(\cdot))$ is inconsistent. This and the fact that the convergence in equations 18.28 and 18.29 happens only with Q_θ^∞-measure 1 imply that $(x_1, \ldots, x_n)$ and knowledge of equation 18.29 carry no more information about the value of θ chosen by nature than do $(x_1, \ldots, x_n)$ and equation 18.28 about the "true" value of θ in the classical context.

To conclude: What difference does it make if we adopt the classical as opposed to the Bayesian view on consistency? Our discussion suggests that in parametric inference the differences matter for the empirical analysis of a given set of data, $x_1, \ldots, x_n$, only when $\hat{\theta}_c(x_1, \ldots, x_n)$ and $\hat{\theta}_B(x_1, \ldots, x_n)$

have different limiting values. E 18.2 gives an example where they have the same limiting value.

E 18.2 Suppose that $\mathscr{X} = \{0, 1\}$, $\Theta = (0, 1)$, $\varphi(\cdot)$ is Lebesgue measure and

$$Q_\theta(A) = \begin{cases} \theta & \text{if } A = \{1\} \\ 1 - \theta & \text{if } A = \{0\} \end{cases}$$

Then let

$$\hat{\theta}_c(x_1, \ldots, x_n) = n^{-1} \sum_{i=1}^{n} x_i$$

and observe that by equation (17.11)

$$\hat{\theta}_B(x_1, \ldots, x_n) = (n + 2)^{-1} \left(1 + \sum_{i=1}^{n} x_i\right).$$

In this case $\hat{\theta}_c(\cdot)$ and $\hat{\theta}_B(\cdot)$ have the same limiting values along sequences of observations in $\mathscr{X}^\infty$.

18.3.2 Finite-Sample Interval Estimates

A Bayesian econometrician equipped with $(x_1, \ldots, x_n)$ and equation 18.29 might not be more knowledgeable about the value of θ chosen by nature than a classical econometrician equipped with $(x_1, \ldots, x_n)$ and equation 18.28 is about the "true" value of θ. However, even when the limiting values of $\hat{\theta}_c(x_1, \ldots, x_n)$ and $\hat{\theta}_B(\hat{x}_1, \ldots, x_n)$ are the same, the inferences concerning the most likely values of θ which a Bayesian makes will differ in interesting ways from the analogous inferences made by classical econometricians. We shall see how by looking at a special case.

Suppose that $\{x(t, \omega); t \in T\}$ is a purely random process on $(\Omega, \mathscr{F}, P(\cdot))$ and assume that the $x(t, \cdot)$ relative to $P(\cdot)$ are normally distributed with mean μ and variance σ^2. We do not know the values of μ and σ. Therefore we must estimate them. This can be done in several ways, depending on whether we insist on treating the process as a purely random process or we agree to follow Bayesian econometricians in treating the process as an exchangeable random process. In the first case we would proceed as follows: We let $x(0), \ldots, x(n)$ be observed values of $x(0, \cdot), \ldots, x(n, \cdot)$ and define the pair $(\bar{x}, s^2)$ by

$$(\bar{x}, s^2) = \left(n^{-1} \sum_{i=0}^{n-1} x(i), (n - 1)^{-1} \sum_{i=0}^{n-1} (x(i) - \bar{x})^2\right)$$

and use this pair as an estimate of (μ, σ^2). According to the Law of Large Numbers, the estimate converges to the true value of the pair with probability 1 when n goes to infinity. How good the estimate is depends on n. Specifically, $\bar{x}$ is normally distributed with mean μ and variance σ^2/n, $(n-1)s^2/\sigma^2$ is χ^2-distributed with $(n-1)$ degrees of freedom, and $\sqrt{n}(\bar{x}-\mu)/s$ is Student-t distributed with $(n-1)$ degrees of freedom. The last two distributions provide us with probabilistic bounds on σ^2 and μ, respectively; e.g.,

$$\tilde{P}\left(\left\{\omega \in \tilde{\Omega} : \sigma^2 < \frac{s^2(\omega)}{a}\right\}\middle| \mu, \sigma\right) = \int_{a(n-1)}^{\infty} \left(2^{v/2}\Gamma\left(\frac{v}{2}\right)\right)^{-1} x^{(v/2)-1}e^{-x/2}\,dx \tag{18.30}$$

and

$$\begin{aligned}&\tilde{P}(\{\omega \in \tilde{\Omega} : \bar{x}(\omega) - cs(\omega)/\sqrt{n} < \mu < \bar{x}(\omega) - bs(\omega)/\sqrt{n}\}|\mu, \sigma)\\ &\quad = \int_b^c \frac{\Gamma((v+1)/2)}{\sqrt{v\pi}\,\Gamma(v/2)}\left(1 + \frac{x^2}{v}\right)^{-(v+1)/2} dx,\end{aligned} \tag{18.31}$$

where $0 < a$, $b < c$, $v = n - 1$, and $\Gamma(\cdot)$ denotes the standard gamma function. In reading these equations, note that a, b, and c are chosen parameters. Note also that $s^2(\cdot)$ in equation 18.30, and $\bar{x}(\cdot)$ and $s^2(\cdot)$ in equation 18.31 are random variables while μ and σ^2 are unknown constants. The values of μ and σ^2 determine the values assumed by $\tilde{P}(\cdot)$ in equations 18.30 and 18.31. For that reason we have written $\tilde{P}(\cdot|\mu, \sigma)$. Because the right-hand sides of equations 18.30 and 18.31 do not depend on μ and σ, these equations provide probabilistic bounds on σ^2 and μ, respectively.

To obtain analogous bounds on μ and σ^2 a Bayesian econometrician might assign to (μ, σ) the prior probability distribution, $dF(\mu, \sigma) = k\sigma^{-1}\,d\mu\,d\sigma$, where k is a constant that is chosen so that with this prior distribution and the observations $x(0), \ldots, x(n)$, the econometrician's posterior distribution of (μ, σ) is given by

$$\begin{aligned}&F(a, b|x(0), \ldots, x(n))\\ &\quad = k_1 \int_{-\infty}^{a}\int_0^b \sigma^{-(n+1)} \exp\left(-\frac{vs^2 + n(\bar{x}-\mu)^2}{2\sigma^2}\right) d\mu\,d\sigma,\end{aligned} \tag{18.32}$$

where (a, b) ranges over $R \times R_{++}$, k_1 is a constant, $v = n - 1$, and $(\bar{x}, s^2)$ is as defined in equation 18.30. The corresponding marginal distributions of μ and σ are, respectively,

$$F_\mu(a|x(0), \ldots, x(n)) = k_2 \int_{-\infty}^{a} \left\{v + \frac{(\bar{x}-\mu)^2}{s^2/(v+1)}\right\}^{-(v+1)/2} d\mu, \tag{18.33}$$

and

$$F_\sigma(b|x(0),\ldots,x(n)) = k_3 \int_0^b \sigma^{-(v+1)} \exp - \left(\frac{vs^2}{2\sigma^2}\right) d\sigma, \tag{18.34}$$

where k_2 and k_3 are appropriately chosen constants. Probabilistic bounds on μ and σ can be obtained by finding the smallest intervals $[a, b]$ and $[c, d]$ that satisfy the equations

$$0.95 = \int_a^b dF_\mu(\mu|x(0),\ldots,x(n)) \quad \text{and} \quad 0.95 = \int_c^d dF_\sigma(\sigma|x(0),\ldots,x(n)).$$

These bounds need not differ much from the bounds obtained in equations 18.30 and 18.31 for appropriately chosen values of a, b, and c. Even so, there is a significant difference that ought not go unnoticed: In equations 18.30 and 18.31 the $x(i)$ are random variables and μ and σ are constants. In equations 18.33 and 18.34, the $x(i)$ are constants and μ and σ are random variables!

18.3.3 Concluding Remarks

Looking back at our discussion of consistency and interval estimates in econometrics, two remarks come to mind. First, consider a strictly stationary process $X = \{x_t(\omega); t \in T\}$ with mean μ, variance σ^2, and finite fourth moments, and let $(\bar{x}, s^2)$ be as described in section 18.3.2. When X is a purely random process, the asymptotic distribution of $(\bar{x}, s^2)$ can be used to justify interval estimates of μ and σ based on equations 18.30 and 18.31. In contrast, when the $x_t(\cdot)$ are just exchangeable, the asymptotic distribution of $(\bar{x}, s^2)$ cannot be used to justify the Bayesian interval estimates of μ and σ which we obtained from equations 18.33 and 18.34.

Second, we have been concerned with parametric inference in econometrics. Searching for the distribution of M in equation 18.27 is as likely to be a problem in nonparametric inference as a problem in parametric inference. A few observations concerning the consistency of Bayes estimates in nonparametric inference are, therefore, called for.

Suppose first that Θ is finite and that Q contains all probability measures on $\mathscr{X}$. Then for all $\theta \in \Theta$ and any prior measure $\mu(\cdot)$, $(\theta, \mu_n(\cdot))$ is consistent if and only if θ belongs to the support of $\mu(\cdot)$ (see Freedman 1963, theorem 1, p. 1389). For example, in E 18.2 $(\theta, \mu_n(\cdot))$ is consistent for all $\theta \in (0, 1)$.

Suppose next that Θ is denumerably infinite and that Q contains all probability measures on Θ. Then David Freedman has shown that, for essentially all priors, the Bayes estimates are consistent essentially nowhere (Freedman 1965, p. 454).

When Θ contains nondenumerably many points, the situation for consistent Bayes estimates is, if anything, bleaker still than the picture we painted in the preceding paragraph. Freedman's results and the results related by Diaconis and Freedman (1986, pp. 1–26) suggest that priors in nonparametric inference must be assigned with care. Suggestions as to how to choose priors are given in Diaconis and Freedman 1986.

18.4 Conditional Probability Spaces

In looking back at equation 18.32 and the discussion that followed, it is important to note (1) that the prior probability distribution of (μ, σ) is the product of the noninformative priors that we derived in E 17.6 and E 17.7 and (2) that both priors are improper in the sense that they integrate to ∞; that is, $\int_{-\infty}^{\infty} d\mu = \infty = \int_0^{\infty} \sigma^{-1}\, d\sigma$. This observation is disconcerting and requires comment.

18.4.1 Conditional Probability Spaces

We could justify the use of improper priors in statistics by waving our hands and insisting that they provide good approximations to their proper noninformative counterparts and that they simplify the analysis. Instead we shall use the axiomatic method to show that improper priors have a role to play in probability theory. We begin by defining the concepts of a bunch of events and a conditional probability space.

First a *bunch of events*: let $(\Omega, \mathscr{F})$ be an experiment and assume that $\mathscr{F}$ is a σ field. Also let $\mathscr{B}$ denote a subset of $\mathscr{F}$. Then $\mathscr{B}$ is a bunch of events if it satisfies the following conditions:

(i) If $B_1, B_2 \in \mathscr{B}$, then $B_1 \cup B_2 \in \mathscr{B}$.
(ii) There exists a sequence $B_n \in \mathscr{B}$, $n = 1, 2, \ldots$ such that $\bigcup_{n=1}^{\infty} B_n = \Omega$.
(iii) $\emptyset \notin \mathscr{B}$.

Examples of a bunch of events are easy to find—see E 18.3 and E 18.4.

E 18.3 Let $\Omega = \{1, 2, \ldots\}$; let $\mathscr{F} = \mathscr{P}(\Omega)$; and let $\mathscr{B}$ denote the family of all nonempty finite subsets of Ω. Then $(\Omega, \mathscr{F})$ is an experiment, $\mathscr{F}$ is a σ field, and $\mathscr{B}$ is a bunch of events.

E 18.4 Let $\Omega = R$; let $\mathscr{F}$ denote the family of Borel subsets of Ω; and let $\mathscr{B}$ denote the family of Borel subsets of Ω with positive Lebesgue measure. Then $(\Omega, \mathscr{F})$ is an experiment, $\mathscr{F}$ is a σ field, and $\mathscr{B}$ is a bunch of events.

Next a *conditional probability space*: In the sense given to the term by Alfred Rényi, a conditional probability space is a quadruple, $(\Omega, \mathscr{F}, \mathscr{B}, P(\cdot|\cdot))$, where $(\Omega, \mathscr{F})$ is an experiment, $\mathscr{F}$ is a σ field, $\mathscr{B}$ is a bunch of events, $P(\cdot|\cdot)$: $\mathscr{F} \times \mathscr{B} \to [0, 1]$ and, for each $B \in \mathscr{B}$, $P(\cdot|B)$ is a σ-additive probability measure satisfying the conditions

(i) $P(B|B) = 1$, and
(ii) if $C \subset B$ and $C \in \mathscr{B}$ and $A \in \mathscr{F}$,

$$P(C|B) > 0$$

and

$$P(A|C) = P(A \cap C|B)/P(C|B).$$

Two examples of conditional probability spaces are given below:

E 18.5 Let $(\Omega, \mathscr{F}, \mathscr{B})$ be as in E 18.3. Also, for each $A \in \mathscr{F}$, let $|A|$ denote the number of elements in A. Finally, let $P(\cdot|\cdot)$: $\mathscr{F} \times \mathscr{B} \to [0, 1]$ be defined by

$$P(A|B) = |A \cap B|/|B|.$$

Then $(\Omega, \mathscr{F}, \mathscr{B}, P(\cdot|\cdot))$ is a conditional probability space.

E 18.6 Let $(\Omega, \mathscr{F})$ be as in E 18.3 and let $\mathscr{B}$ be the family of all nonempty subsets of Ω. In addition, let p_i, $i = 1, 2, \ldots$, be such that $p_i > 0$ and $\sum_{i=1}^{\infty} p_i < \infty$. Finally, define $\lambda(\cdot)$: $\mathscr{F} \to R_+$ by

$$\lambda(A) = \sum_{i \in A} p_i, \qquad A \in \mathscr{F}$$

and, for each pair $(A, B) \in \mathscr{F} \times \mathscr{B}$, let

$$P(A|B) = \frac{\lambda(A \cap B)}{\lambda(B)}.$$

Then $(\Omega, \mathscr{F}, \mathscr{B}, P(\cdot|\cdot))$ is a conditional probability space.

From our point of view, the main difference between the preceding conditional probability spaces is that in E 18.5 $\Omega \notin \mathscr{B}$ and $|\Omega| = \infty$, while in E 18.6 $\Omega \in \mathscr{B}$ and $\lambda(\Omega) < \infty$. Thus in E 18.5, $P(\cdot|\Omega)$ is not defined, while in E 18.6 $(\Omega, \mathscr{F}, P(\cdot|\Omega))$ is a probability space.

18.4.2 Rényi's Fundamental Theorem

Rényi's Fundamental Theorem concerning the structure of conditional probabilities is stated in T 18.9. In the statement of the theorem, a *σ-finite measure* $v(\cdot)$ on $\mathscr{F}$ is taken to be a σ-additive function $v(\cdot)$: $\mathscr{F} \to R_+$ for which there exists a sequence of events A_i, $i = 1, 2, \ldots$, with $v(A_i) < \infty$ and $\bigcup_{i=1}^{\infty} A_i = \Omega$.

T 18.9 If $(\Omega, \mathscr{F}, \mathscr{B}, P(\cdot|\cdot))$ is a conditional probability space, there exists a σ-finite measure $v(\cdot)\colon \mathscr{F} \to R_+$ such that, for each $B \in \mathscr{B}$, $0 < v(B) < \infty$ and, for each $A \in \mathscr{F}$ and $B \in \mathscr{B}$,

$$P(A|B) = \frac{v(A \cap B)}{v(B)}. \tag{18.35}$$

The measure $v(\cdot)$ is uniquely detemined up to a multiplicative constant.

Since the sense of T 18.9 is easily understood, I shall give only a brief outline of Rényi's proof and refer the reader to Rényi (1970, pp. 40–43) for details.

First we pick an arbitrary $B_0 \in \mathscr{B}$ and define $\mu(\cdot)$ on $\mathscr{B}$ by

$$\mu(B) = \frac{P(B|B \cup B_0)}{P(B_0|B \cup B_0)}. \tag{18.36}$$

Second, on each $A \in \mathscr{F}$ for which there is a $B \in \mathscr{B}$ with $A \subset B$ we let

$$\mu(A) = P(A|B)\mu(B) \tag{18.37}$$

and show that the value of $\mu(\cdot)$ at A is independent of B; i.e., if $A \subset B_1 \cap B_2$, $P(A|B_1)\mu(B_1) = P(A|B_2)\mu(B_2)$.

Next, we let $\mathscr{F}^*$ be the family of events that are subsets of some $B \in \mathscr{B}$ and observe that unions and differences of sets in $\mathscr{F}^*$ belong to $\mathscr{F}^*$. From equations 18.36 and 18.37 it follows that $\mu(\cdot)$ is a nonnegative function on $\mathscr{F}^*$ to $[0, 1]$. Furthermore, if $A_1, A_2 \in \mathscr{F}^*$ and $A_1 \cap A_2 = \varnothing$,

$$\begin{aligned}\mu(A_1 \cup A_2) &= P(A_1 \cup A_2|B)\mu(B)\\ &= P(A_1|B)\mu(B) + P(A_2|B)\mu(B)\end{aligned}$$

for any $B \in \mathscr{B}$ such that $A_1 \cup A_2 \subset B$. Hence $\mu(\cdot)$ is finitely additive on $\mathscr{F}^*$. In fact, $\mu(\cdot)$ is σ-additive on $\mathscr{F}^*$. For, if $\{A_n\}$ is a sequence of sets in $\mathscr{F}^*$ such that $A_i \cap A_j = \varnothing$ for all $i, j = 1, 2, \ldots$ and $i \neq j$, and such that $\bigcup_{n=1}^{\infty} A_n \in \mathscr{F}^*$,

$$\begin{aligned}\mu\left(\bigcup_{n=1}^{\infty} A_n\right) &= P\left(\bigcup_{n=1}^{\infty} A_n|B\right)\mu(B)\\ &= \left(\sum_{n=1}^{\infty} P(A_n|B)\right)\mu(B)\\ &= \sum_{n=1}^{\infty} P(A_n|B)\mu(B) = \sum_{n=1}^{\infty} \mu(A_n)\end{aligned}$$

for any $B \in \mathscr{B}$ such that $\bigcup_{n=1}^{\infty} A_n \subset B$.

The preceding results imply that $\mu(\cdot)$ can be extended in one and only one way to a σ-additive measure $v(\cdot)$ on the smallest σ field that contains $\mathscr{F}^*$. This σ field is $\mathscr{F}$. Hence $\mu(\cdot)$ can be extended to a unique σ-additive measure $v(\cdot)$ on all of $\mathscr{F}$. To conclude the proof of T 18.9 we must show that $v(\cdot)$ has all the properties which the theorem requires. That is not too difficult. It follows from 18.36 that $0 < v(B) < \infty$ for all $B \in \mathscr{B}$ and from 18.36 and condition ii in the definition of a bunch of events that $v(\cdot)$ is σ-finite. Since, for each $A \in \mathscr{F}$ and all $B \in \mathscr{B}$, $A \cap B \subset B$, and by equation 18.37

$$P(A|B) = P(A \cap B|B) = \frac{v(A \cap B)}{v(B)},$$

$v(\cdot)$ must satisfy equation 18.35 as well. Finally, $v(\cdot)$ is determined up to a multiplicative positive constant. For brevity I leave the proof of that fact to the reader.

When the bunch of events in T 18.9 contains all events with finite positive $v(\cdot)$ measure, $(\Omega, \mathscr{F}, \mathscr{B}, P(\cdot|\cdot))$ is a *full* conditional probability space. Rényi calls it the full conditional probability space generated by $v(\cdot)$ and denotes it by $[\Omega, \mathscr{F}, v(\cdot)]$. Examples are the conditional probability spaces of E 18.5 and E 18.6. They are full and generated by $|\cdot|$ and $\lambda(\cdot)$, respectively. A third example of special interest to us is given in E 18.7.

E 18.7 Let $\Omega = R^{n+1}$; let $\mathscr{F}^i$ denote the Borel subsets of R^i, $i = 1, \ldots, n+1$; and define $\lambda(\cdot)\colon \mathscr{F}^{n+1} \to R_+$ by

$$\lambda\left(\left[\mu, \mu + d\mu\right) \times \prod_{i=1}^{n} [x_i, x_i + dx_i)\right)$$
$$= (2\pi)^{-n/2} \exp -\left(\sum_{i=1}^{n} (x_i - \mu)^2/2\right) dx_1, \ldots, dx_n\, d\mu.$$

In addition, let $\mathscr{B}$ contain all the Borel sets in $\mathscr{F}^{n+1}$ with finite positive $\lambda(\cdot)$ measure. Finally, let

$$P(A|B) = \frac{\lambda(A \cap B)}{\lambda(B)}, \qquad (A, B) \in \mathscr{F}^{n+1} \times \mathscr{B}. \tag{18.38}$$

Then $(\Omega, \mathscr{F}^{n+1}, \mathscr{B}, P(\cdot|\cdot))$ is the full conditional probability space generated by $\lambda(\cdot)$.

When A and B in equation (18.38) equal $[\mu^0, \mu^0 + d\mu) \times \prod_{i=1}^{n} [x_i, x_i + dx_i)$ and $[\mu^0, \mu^0 + d\mu) \times R^n$, respectively, we get

$$P(A|B) = (2\pi)^{-n/2} \exp -\left(\sum_{i=1}^{n} (x_i - \mu^0)^2/2\right) dx_1 \ldots dx_n.$$

Thus, conditional upon μ^0 being the value of μ, the x_i are independently distributed normal variables with mean μ^0.

When A and B in equation (18.38) equal $[\mu, \mu + d\mu) \times \prod_{i=1}^{n} [x_i^0, x_i^0 + dx_i)$ and $R \times \prod_{i=1}^{n} [x_i^0, x_i^0 + dx_i)$, respectively, we obtain

$$P(A|B) = (2\pi/n)^{-1/2} \exp -n(\mu - \bar{x})^2/2\, d\mu,$$

the posterior distribution of μ, given that the observed value of x_i is x_i^0, $i = 1, \ldots, n$. Here $\bar{x} = n^{-1} \sum_{i=1}^{n} x_i^0$.

Finally, for any k-tuple $\{t_1, \ldots, t_k\}$ and $D \in \mathscr{B}$,

$$P\left([\mu, \mu + d\mu) \times \prod_{i=1}^{k} [x_{t_i}, x_{t_i} + dx_{t_i}) \times R^{n-k} | D\right)$$

$$= P\left([\mu, \mu + d\mu) \times \prod_{i=1}^{k} [x_i, x_i + dx_i) \times R^{n-k} | D\right)$$

$$= \lambda(D)^{-1} (2\pi)^{-k/2} \exp -\left(\sum_{i=1}^{k} (x_i - \mu)^2/2\right) dx_1 \ldots dx_k\, d\mu.$$

Hence when we integrate out μ in D, we see that the x_i are exchangeable random variables.

18.5 Exchangeable Processes on a Full Conditional Probability Space

A superexchangeable process is an exchangeable process on a full conditional probability space. We shall next discuss some of the properties of such processes. For that purpose we introduce the idea of a translation of events.

Let $[\Omega, \mathscr{F}, v(\cdot)]$ be a full conditional probability space and let $\mathscr{B}$ be the associated bunch of events. A *translation* is a single-valued transformation S on the σ field $\mathscr{F}$ into itself that preserves complementations and countable intersections; i.e., if A and A_j, $j = 1, 2, \ldots$, are events, then

$$SA^c = (SA)^c \qquad \text{and} \qquad S\left(\bigcap_{j=1}^{\infty} A_j\right) = \bigcap_{j=1}^{\infty} SA_j.$$

Such a transformation is measure-preserving if and only if for all $A \in \mathscr{F}$

$$v(SA) = v(A).$$

A translation S may be considered as an operator acting on indicators of events. To wit: if $A \in \mathscr{F}$, and if $I_A(\cdot)$ denotes the corresponding indicator function, then the function $SI_A(\cdot)\colon \Omega \to R$ is well defined by the equation

$$SI_A(\omega) = I_{SA}(\omega), \qquad \omega \in \Omega.$$

Moreover, the S acting on indicator functions can be extended in one and only one way to a continuous linear transformation S on the family $\mathscr{M}$ of random variables on $(\Omega, \mathscr{F})$ such that, for each $y(\cdot) \in \mathscr{M}$, the measurable function $Sy(\cdot)$ satisfies the relation,

$$\{\omega \in \Omega : Sy(\omega) < a\} = S\{\omega \in \Omega : y(\omega) < a\}$$

for all $a \in R$ (see Loève 1960, pp. 430–432, for a proof).

A *superexchangeable process* on the full conditional probability space $[\Omega, \mathscr{F}, v(\cdot)]$ is a family of random variables $\{x_t(\omega); t = 1, 2, \ldots\}$ that satisfies the following conditions:

(i) There exists a measure-preserving translation S: $\mathscr{F} \to \mathscr{F}$ such that

a. $SB = B$, $B \in \mathscr{B}$; and

b. $x_t(\omega) = S^{t-1}x_1(\omega)$ a.e. (v measure), $t = 1, 2, \ldots$.

(ii) For each mapping π of the positive integers onto themselves that leaves all but a finite number of integers invariant, there exists a measure preserving translation S_π: $\mathscr{F} \to \mathscr{F}$ such that

a. $S_\pi B = B$, $B \in \mathscr{B}$; and

b. $S_\pi x_t(\omega) = x_{\pi(t)}(\omega)$ a.e. (v measure), $t = 1, 2, \ldots$.

For superexchangeable processes we can establish an interesting analogue of T 18.7 that is due to Henry P. McKean:

T 18.10 Let $\{x_t(\omega); t = 1, 2, \ldots\}$ be a superexchangeable process on a full conditional probability space $[\Omega, \mathscr{F}, v(\cdot)]$; and let $\mathscr{B}$ and $P(\cdot|\cdot)$ be the associated bunch of events and conditional probability measure respectively. Moreover, let

$$C = \bigcap_{n=1}^{\infty} \mathscr{F}(x_n, x_{n+1}, \ldots)$$

and assume that, for all $B \in \mathscr{B}$,

$$E(|x_1||B) < \infty \tag{18.39}$$

and that the range of the $x_t(\cdot)$ is a Borel subset of R^∞. Finally, let $\mathscr{C}$ be the smallest σ field containing C and $\mathscr{B}$, and for each $B \in \mathscr{B}$ and random variable x on $(\Omega, \mathscr{B})$, let

$$v(A|x) = v^{\mathscr{C}(x)}(A), \qquad A \in \mathscr{F}$$

$$v_B(A) = \frac{v(A \cap B)}{v(B)}, \qquad A \in \mathscr{F}$$

$$v_B(A|x) = v_B^{\mathscr{C}(x)}(A), \qquad A \in \mathscr{F}$$

where $v^{\mathscr{C}(x)}(A)$ and $v_B^{\mathscr{C}(x)}(A)$ denote, respectively, the v measure and the v_B measure of A conditioned on the sub-σ field of $\mathscr{C}$ generated by x.

Then there are random variables $\xi(\cdot): \Omega \to R$ and $M(\cdot): \Omega \to R$ on $(\Omega, \mathscr{C})$ such that

(i) $E^{\mathscr{C}} x_1 = \xi$ a.e. ($v_{\mathscr{C}}$ measure);

(ii) $\lim n^{-1} \sum_{i=1}^{n} x_i(\omega) = \xi(\omega)$ a.e. ($v_{\mathscr{C}}$ measure); and

(iii) for all $k = 1, 2, \ldots,$ all k-tuples $t_i \in \{1, 2, \ldots\}$, $i = 1, \ldots, k$, all $B \in \mathscr{B}$, and all Borel sets $A_i \subset R$, $i = 1, \ldots, k$,

$$v_B(\{\omega \in \Omega : x_{t_i}(\omega) \in A_i, i = 1, \ldots, k\} | M)$$
$$= \prod_{i=1}^{k} v_B(\{\omega \in \Omega : x_{t_i}(\omega) \in A_i\} | M)$$
$$= \prod_{i=1}^{k} v_B(\{\omega \in \Omega : x_i(\omega) \in A_i\} | M) \quad \text{a.e.}$$

Moreover, if the restriction of $v(\cdot)$ to $\mathscr{C}(M)$ is σ-finite and if there is a sequence $B_i \in \mathscr{B}$, $i = 1, 2, \ldots,$ such that $\Omega = \bigcup_{i=1}^{\infty} B_i$ and $B_i \cap B_j = \varnothing$ when $i \neq j$, i, $j = 1, 2, \ldots,$ then $v(\cdot | M)$ can be chosen such that

(iv) for all $k = 1, 2, \ldots,$ all k-tuples $t_j \in \{1, 2, \ldots\}$, $j = 1, \ldots, k$, and all Borel sets $A_j \subset R$, $j = 1, \ldots, k$,

$$v(\{\omega \in \Omega : x_{t_j}(\omega) \in A_j, j = 1, \ldots, k\} | M)$$
$$= \prod_{j=1}^{k} v(\{\omega \in \Omega : x_{t_j}(\omega) \in A_j, j = 1, \ldots, k\} | M)$$
$$= \prod_{j=1}^{k} v(\{\omega \in \Omega : x_j(\omega) \in A_j, j = 1, \ldots, k\} | M) \quad \text{a.e.}$$

The proof of this theorem is obtained in several steps: First we let B be an event in $\mathscr{B}$ and observe that equation 18.39 and the defining conditions of a superexchangeable process imply that the $x_t(\cdot)$ relative to $P(\cdot | B)$ constitute an integrable exchangeable process. Hence, by T 18.7, there exists a family of functions, $\xi(\cdot | B)$: $B \to R$, $B \in \mathscr{B}$, that satisfies the following conditions:

(i) $\xi(\cdot | B)$ is a random variable on (B, C_B), where C_B is the smallest σ field of subsets of B that contains B and $D \cap B$ whenever $D \in C$;
(ii) $E^{C_B} x_1 = \xi(\cdot | B)$ a.e. (v_{C_B} measure); and
(iii) $\lim n^{-1} \sum_{t=1}^{n} x_t(\omega) = \xi(\omega | B)$ a.e. (v_{C_B} measure).
(iv) If $B_1, B_2 \in \mathscr{B}$ and $B_1 \subset B_2$, then

$$\xi(\cdot | B_2) = \xi(\cdot | B_1) \quad \text{a.e. } (v_{C_{B_1}} \text{ measure}).$$

Next we recall from the definition of a bunch of events that there exists a sequence $B_i \in \mathscr{B}$, $i = 1, 2, \ldots,$ such that $\Omega = \bigcup_{i=1}^{\infty} B_i$. For such a sequence we let $B^n = \bigcup_{i=1}^n B_i$, $n = 1, 2, \ldots$, and define by recursion a sequence of functions, $\xi^n(\cdot)\colon \Omega \to R$, $n = 1, 2, \ldots$, as follows:

$$\xi^1(\omega) = \begin{cases} \xi(\omega|B^1) & \text{if } \omega \in B^1 \\ 0 & \text{otherwise} \end{cases}$$

$$\xi^{n+1}(\omega) = \begin{cases} \xi^n(\omega) & \text{if } \omega \in B^n \\ \xi(\omega|B^{n+1}) & \text{if } \omega \in (B^{n+1} - B^n) \\ 0 & \text{otherwise} \end{cases}$$

Moreover, we let $\xi(\cdot)\colon \Omega \to R$ be defined by

$$\xi(\omega) = \xi^n(\omega), \quad \omega \in B^n, \qquad n = 1, 2, \ldots$$

Then the $\xi^n(\cdot)$ and hence $\xi(\cdot)$ are well defined. In addition, $\xi(\cdot)$ is a random variable on $(\Omega, \mathscr{C})$. To see why, we shall first demonstrate that the $\xi^n(\cdot)$ are random variables on $(\Omega, \mathscr{C})$. We proceed by induction on n. Evidently, for all $a \in R$,

$$\{\omega \in \Omega : \xi^1(\omega) < a\} = \begin{cases} (\{\omega \in \Omega : \xi(\omega|B^1) < a\} \cup (\Omega - B^1)) & \textit{if } a > 0 \\ \{\omega \in \Omega : \xi(\omega|B^1) < a\} & \text{if } a \leqslant 0 \end{cases}$$

Hence, $\xi^1(\cdot)$ is a random variable on $(\Omega, \mathscr{C})$. Suppose next that we have demonstrated that $\xi^i(\cdot)$ is a random variable on $(\Omega, \mathscr{C})$ for $i = 1, 2, \ldots, n$. Then for all $a \in R$,

$$\{\omega \in \Omega : \xi^{n+1}(\omega) < a\}$$

$$= \begin{cases} (((\{\omega \in \Omega : \xi^n(\omega) < a\} \cap B^n) \cup (\{\omega \in \Omega : \xi(\omega|B^{n+1}) < a\} \\ \quad \cap (B^{n+1} - B^n))) \cup (\Omega - B^{n+1})) \qquad \text{if } a > 0\text{: and} \\ ((\{\omega \in \Omega : \xi^n(\omega) < a\} \cap B^n) \cup (\{\omega \in \Omega : \xi(\omega|B^{n+1}) < a\} \\ \quad \cap (B^{n+1} - B^n))) \qquad \text{if } a \leqslant 0 \end{cases}$$

Hence $\xi^{n+1}(\cdot)$ is a random variable on $(\Omega, \mathscr{C})$. But if all the $\xi^n(\cdot)$ are random variables on $(\Omega, \mathscr{C})$, so is $\xi(\cdot)$ because, for all $a \in R$,

$$\{\omega \in \Omega : \xi(\omega) < a\} = \bigcup_{n=1}^{\infty} (\{\omega \in \Omega : \xi(\omega) < a\} \cap B^n)$$

$$= \bigcup_{n=1}^{\infty} (\{\omega \in \Omega : \xi^n(\omega) < a\} \cap B^n).$$

From the definition of $\xi(\cdot)$ and from conditions iii and iv in our description of $\xi(\cdot|\cdot)$ on p. 417, we deduce that, for all $B \in \mathscr{B}$,

(i) $\lim n^{-1} \sum_{t=1}^{n} x_t(\omega) = \xi(\omega)$ a.e. (v_{C_B} measure).

Moreover, from the definition of $\xi(\cdot)$, from condition ii on p. 417, and from the measurability of $\xi(\cdot)$ with respect to $\mathscr{C}$, we deduce that the following condition is also true: For all $B \in \mathscr{B}$,

(ii) For all $A \in C_B$,

$$\int_A (E^{\mathscr{C}} x_1)\, dv_{\mathscr{C}} = \int_A x_1\, dv = v(B) \int_A x_1\, dv_B = v(B) \int_A (E^{C_B} x_1)\, dv_{C_B}$$

$$= v(B) \int_A \xi(\omega|B)\, dv_{C_B} = \int_A \xi(\omega|B)\, dv_{\mathscr{C}}$$

$$= \int_A \xi(\omega)\, dv_{\mathscr{C}}$$

since the restriction of $v_{\mathscr{C}}$ to C_B equals $v(B) \cdot v_{C_B}$ and $[\Omega, \mathscr{F}, v(\cdot)]$ is full. The preceding conditions establish the validity of T 18.10 (i) and (ii).

To establish condition iii of the theorem we observe that the exchangeability of the $x_t(\cdot)$ with respect to $P(\cdot|B)$, $B \in \mathscr{B}$, and T 18.7 imply that here exists a family of functions $M(\cdot|B)\colon B \to R$, $B \in \mathscr{B}$, that satisfy the following conditions:

(i) $M(\cdot|B)$ is a random variable on (B, C_B).
(ii) Conditional upon $M(\cdot|B)$, the $x_t(\cdot)$ on B are independently and identically distributed with common distribution:

$$F_B(x|M(\cdot|B)) = v_B(\{\omega \in \Omega : x_1(\omega) < x\}|M(\cdot|B)), \qquad x \in R.$$

(iii) If $B_1, B_2 \in \mathscr{B}$ and $B_1 \subset B_2$, then

$$M(\omega|B_1) = M(\omega|B_2) \quad \text{a.e. } (v_{C_{B_1}} \text{ measure}).^1$$

But if that is so, then in the way we used $\xi(\cdot|B)$ to define $\xi(\cdot)$ we can use the $M(\cdot|B)$ to construct a function $M(\cdot)\colon \Omega \to R$ that is measurable with respect to $\mathscr{C}$ and is such that, for any $B \in \mathscr{B}$,

$M(\omega) = M(\omega|B)$ a.e. (v_{C_B} measure).

From this and the properties of the $M(\cdot|B)$, it follows that, for any $B \in \mathscr{B}$, for any k integers t_i, $i = 1, \ldots, k$, and Borel sets A_i, $i = 1, \ldots, k$, and for a value of $M(\cdot)$, $\overline{M}$ such that $\{\omega \in B : M(\omega) = \overline{M}\} \in \mathscr{B}$,

$$P\left(\bigcap_{i=1}^{k} \{\omega \in \Omega : x_{t_i}(\omega) \in A_i\} | \{\omega \in B : M(\omega) = \overline{M}\}\right)$$

$$= \prod_{i=1}^{k} P(\{\omega \in \Omega : x_{t_i}(\omega) \in A_i\} | \{\omega \in B : M(\omega) = \overline{M}\})$$

$$= \prod_{i=1}^{k} P(\{\omega \in \Omega : x_i(\omega) \in A_i\} | \{\omega \in B : M(\omega) = \overline{M}\})$$

$$= v(\{\omega \in B : M(\omega) = \overline{M}\})^{-1}$$

$$\times \prod_{i=1}^{k} v(\{\omega \in B : x_i(\omega) \in A_i \text{ and } M(\omega) = \overline{M}\}).$$

The assertion of condition iii of T 18.10 generalizes this observation in the obvious way. Its validity is a simple consequence of theorem T 18.7.

To establish condition iv of the theorem, we observe that the σ finiteness of the restriction of $v(\cdot)$ to $\mathscr{C}(M)$ and the Radon-Nikodym theorem imply that, for all $A \in \mathscr{F}$, $v(A|M)$ is well defined a.e. ($v_{\mathscr{C}(M)}$ measure) and represents the v measure of A conditioned on $\mathscr{C}(M)$.[2] Moreover, the existence of $v(\cdot|M)$ and Loève's proof of the existence of regular conditional probabilities (i.e. of T 18.2) can be used to show that we can choose $v(\cdot|M)$ such that it satisfies the following condition:

(i) Let $X_1 = \{x_t, \omega); t = 1, 2, \ldots\}$ and $X_2 = \{I_{B_i}(\omega); i = 1, 2, \ldots\}$.

Moreover, let $\mathscr{F}(X_1, X_2)$ be the sub-σ field of $\mathscr{F}$ determined by the components of X_1 and X_2. Then, for all $A \in \mathscr{F}(X_1, X_2)$, $v(A|M)$ is a random variable on $(\Omega, \mathscr{C}(M))$. In addition, a.e. $v_{\mathscr{C}(M)}$ measure $v(\cdot|M)$ is a σ-additive probability measure on $\mathscr{F}(X_1, X_2)$.

In fact, since for all $A \in \mathscr{F}(X_1)$

$$v(A|M) = \sum_{i=1}^{\infty} v(A \cap B_i|M),$$

we can choose $v(\cdot|M)$ such that it also satisfies the following condition:

(ii) For all $A \in \mathscr{F}(X_1)$,

$$v(A|M) = \sum_{i=1}^{\infty} v_{B_i}(A|M)v(B_i|M) \quad \text{a.e. } (v_{\mathscr{C}(M)} \text{ measure}).$$

But if that is so, then condition iii of T 18.10 and obvious arguments suffice to establish the validity of condition iv of the theorem.

18.6 Probability versus Conditional Probability

Rényi seems to believe that all epistemic probability is conditional probability. This is obviously so in some situations; e.g., when a meteorologist says that there is a 0.8 chance of rain tomorrow, he probably means that roughly 80 percent of the past weather situations which he has observed and found similar to the one he observes today were followed by rain the next day. Rényi insists, however, that it is also true in other situations, such as those envisaged in E 15.1 and E 17.2. When we ask for the probability of picking a white ball from an urn, we tacitly assume that the urn is shaken well.

It is not important for our purposes to take a stand for or against Rényi's idea of the prevalence of conditional probabilities. What is important to us is that Rényi, by taking conditional probability as an undefined term and probability as a defined term in his theory, has enlarged the scope of probability theory. To wit: In Kolmogorov's theory, probability is an undefined term and conditional probability is a defined term. Also from a probability space $(\Omega, \mathscr{F}, P(\cdot))$ we can construct the full conditional probability space generated by $P(\cdot)$, $[\Omega, \mathscr{F}, P(\cdot)]$. However, the conditional probability spaces that are generated in this way are all generated by finite measures. Rényi's theory allows conditional probability spaces that are generated by unbounded measures. As suggested by our discussion in 18.3.2, such conditional probability spaces are important to Bayesian econometricians.

19 Choice under Uncertainty

A *decision maker* is usually thought of as a person who is confronted with an array of uncertain options from which he must choose the one that is most desirable. An *uncertain option* is a probability distribution specifying a set of possible returns and the likelihood of each return occurring. Sometimes this distribution is objectively determined, e.g., a lottery ticket. Other times it must be determined subjectively, e.g., a business investment. Probability distributions can be ranked in many ways. Nevertheless, most theories of choice contend, either as an axiom or as a consequence of other axioms, that the decision maker ranks probability distributions according to the expected utility which they offer. In this chapter we shall discuss Leonard Savage's expected-utility theory (Savage 1954, pp. 1–104). By doing so, we can elicit implications of the expected-utility hypothesis that were not apparent in our discussion of Arrow's theory of risk aversion. We shall also discuss the difficult problem of choice in situations in which subjective probabilities are nonadditive.

19.1 The Decision Maker and His Experiment

There are four undefined terms in Savage's axiom system: a decision maker, a state of the world, a consequence, and an act.

19.1.1 The Decision Maker

We can think of the decision maker as any person who must choose between options with uncertain outcomes. Thus he may be a person deciding whether to play another game of roulette, or agonizing about where to spend his skiing vacation, or deciding on his food budget for the week. He may also be the president of a firm pondering whether to make a major investment, or he may be a government official deciding whether to introduce price controls. Whoever he or she is in real life, in Savage's axiom system a decision maker is a special kind of triple:

SA 1 A decision maker is a triple $((\Omega, \mathcal{F}), X^{\Omega}, \preceq)$, where $(\Omega, \mathcal{F})$ is an experiment with $\mathcal{F} = \mathcal{P}(\Omega)$, X^{Ω} is the set of functions from Ω to X, and $\preceq$ is a total, reflexive, and transitive binary relation in X^{Ω}.

19.1.2 The State of the World

The *world* is the object about which the decision maker is concerned. A *state of the world* is a description of the world describing all relevant details. Sometimes the description of the world is easy to write down. At other times it is practically impossible. For instance, in roulette a state of the world may be one of the thirty possible outcomes. For someone about to go on a skiing vacation the relevant consideration may be the skiing conditions in different resorts. If so, describing the world for such a person would involve specifying the amount of snow on the slopes of these resorts at the beginning of his vacation and the weather during his vacation. On the other hand, what is in the mind of an official deciding whether to impose price controls is anyone's guess; for that person, it would be practically impossible to describe the world adequately. Be that as it may, in Savage's axiom system a state of the world is a probable thing:

SA 2 A state of the world is a possible outcome of $(\Omega, \mathcal{F})$.

19.1.3 Acts and Consequences

Whatever the description of the world, the decision maker must make a decision. By this we mean that he must choose an act.

SA 3 A consequence is an object in X. An act is an element of X^{Ω}, i.e., a function $x(\cdot): \Omega \to X$.

We denote points in X by $x, y, z, \ldots$. An act is denoted by $x(\cdot), y(\cdot), z(\cdot), \ldots$. In addition, we interpret the value of $x(\cdot)$ at ω to be the consequence of choosing the act $x(\cdot)$ when the state of the world is ω.

The problem of how to specify the set of consequences in a given situation can be as easy or as difficult as the problem of how to specify all the states of the world. E 19.1 will serve to fix our ideas.

E 19.1 A ball is pulled at random from an urn with ninety balls. We bet on the color of the ball and receive \$100 if our guess is right and \$0 otherwise. Of the balls in the urn thirty are red, and the remaining sixty are either black or yellow. We do not know how many are black and how many are yellow.

Table 19.1

Act	$\omega \in C_{\text{red}}$	$\omega \in C_{\text{black}}$	$\omega \in C_{\text{yellow}}$
$x_1(\cdot)$	\$100	\$0	\$0
$x_2(\cdot)$	\$0	\$100	\$0
$x_3(\cdot)$	\$100	\$0	\$100
$x_4(\cdot)$	\$0	\$100	\$100

For this choice situation Ω consists of three points (i.e., states of the world). Each state of the world specifies the color of the ball pulled from the urn. The set of all consequences X consists of two points, \$0 and \$100. Finally, with C_i, $i =$ red, black, yellow, denoting the subset of the urn containing the balls with color i, four of the available acts are as described in table 19.1.

19.2 The Decision Maker's Risk Preferences

To choose between acts in a meaningful way, the decision maker must be able to rank them in the order of his preference. We refer to the decision maker's ordering of acts as his *risk preferences*.

19.2.1 Risk Preferences

An ordering of acts is a binary relation in X^{Ω}. Hence we may interpret the relation $\preceq$ in SA 1 as the risk preferences of Savage's decision maker. According to SA 1, these preferences are total, reflexive, and transitive. In that respect several observations are relevant.

First, different people frequently order even the simplest set of acts differently. The next example illustrates this. In writing the example we use $x(\cdot) \sim y(\cdot)$ as shorthand for $x(\cdot) \preceq y(\cdot)$ and $y(\cdot) \preceq x(\cdot)$ and $z(\cdot) \prec u(\cdot)$ as shorthand for $z(\cdot) \preceq u(\cdot)$ and not $u(\cdot) \preceq z(\cdot)$.

E 19.2 We asked twenty-four economics students in Oslo to rank the four acts in E 19.1. Eight students insisted that

$$x_1(\cdot) \sim x_2(\cdot) \prec x_4(\cdot) \sim x_3(\cdot). \tag{19.1}$$

Thirteen said that

$$x_2(\cdot) \prec x_1(\cdot) \prec x_3(\cdot) \prec x_4(\cdot). \tag{19.2}$$

Of the remaining three, one told us that

$$x_2(\cdot) \sim x_1(\cdot) \prec x_3(\cdot) \prec x_4(\cdot) \tag{19.3}$$

and two presented us with an incomplete ordering:

$$x_2(\cdot) \prec x_1(\cdot) \prec x_3(\cdot) \qquad \text{and} \qquad x_2(\cdot) \prec x_4(\cdot) \prec x_3(\cdot). \tag{19.4}$$

Second, there are scholars (see Wolfowitz 1962, pp. 470–479) who claim that SA 1 is too strong. Although they consider it essential that the decision maker can order some acts and that his ordering among such acts is reflexive and transitive, they insist it is unnecessary to assume that the ordering is total. For instance, the ordering in equation 19.4 is incomplete. Even so, it is clear that $x_3(\cdot)$ is the best act. Analogous situations arise both in economics and statistics. To wit: A government policy maker, who can order Pareto-optimal allocations, can determine an optimal allocation of goods. Similarly, a statistician, who can order his admissible strategies, can find a best strategy.

19.2.2 The Sure-Thing Principle

The most controversial of Savage's axioms is called the *sure-thing principle.* It asserts that if $x(\cdot)$ and $y(\cdot)$ are two acts that agree (i.e., assume the same consequences) on a subset A of Ω, then the ranking of $x(\cdot)$ and $y(\cdot)$ is independent of the actual values assumed by $x(\cdot)$ and $y(\cdot)$ in A. Specifically,

SA 4 Suppose that $A \in \mathscr{F}$ and let $x(\cdot)$, $y(\cdot)$, $x^*(\cdot)$, and $y^*(\cdot)$ be acts such that

(i) for all $\omega \in A$, $x(\omega) = y(\omega)$ and $x^*(\omega) = y^*(\omega)$;
(ii) for all $\omega \in A^C$, $x(\omega) = x^*(\omega)$ and $y(\omega) = y^*(\omega)$; and
(iii) $x(\cdot) \precsim y(\cdot)$.

Then $x^*(\cdot) \precsim y^*(\cdot)$.

This axiom is exceedingly strong. To see how strong, we give several examples.

E 19.3 An ordering of the four acts in E 19.1 satisfying SA 4 must heed the following conditions:

$$x_1(\cdot) \prec x_2(\cdot) \text{ iff } x_3(\cdot) \prec x_4(\cdot). \tag{19.5}$$

Note, therefore, that the orderings in equations 19.1 and 19.4 satisfy equation 19.5. The orderings in equations 19.2 and 19.3 do not.

There is the possibility that we could convince the fourteen students whose orderings of $x_1(\cdot), \ldots, x_4(\cdot)$ violate SA 4 that they have committed an error of logic analogous to saying that $2 + 2 = 3$. Here is an argument suggested by Howard Raiffa (1960, p. 694). We show the students an unbiased coin and ask them to rank two bets:

A: $x_4(\cdot)$ if heads and $x_1(\cdot)$ if tails; and
B: $x_3(\cdot)$ if heads and $x_2(\cdot)$ if tails.

According to the orderings in equations 19.2 and 19.3, the students will say that they prefer A to B. Then we demonstrate for them that both A and B are elaborate versions of the same bet: \$100 if heads and \$0 if tails. So by closer scrutiny the students must admit that they are indifferent between A and B and that they erred in equations 19.2 and 19.3.

Raiffa's argument seems convincing to us, but it need not sway the opinion of others. According to Ellsberg, who originated the example, Savage insisted on equation 19.2 and could not be made to change his mind (Ellsberg 1961, p. 656).

Here is a second example that illustrates the power of SA 4:

E 19.4 Suppose that $X = R_+^n$ and that $\Omega = \{\omega_1, \dots, \omega_S\}$, where $S \geqslant 3$. Then an act is a vector

$$\tilde{x} = (x(\omega_1), \dots, x(\omega_S)) \in (R_+^n)^S.$$

Suppose that the decision maker's risk preferences can be represented by a strictly increasing, continuous function $U(\cdot) : (R_+^n)^S \to R$. If these risk preferences satisfy SA 4, they are (in the lingo of chapter 11) independent. Hence we can find continuous, strictly increasing functions $U_i(\cdot) : R_+^n \to R$, $i = 1, \dots, S$, and a strictly increasing, continuous function $F(\cdot)$: (range of $U(\cdot)$) $\to R$ such that, for all $\tilde{x} \in (R_+^n)^S$,

$$F(U(\tilde{x})) = \sum_{i=1}^{S} U_i(x(\omega_i)).$$

19.2.3 Constant Acts

A constant act is an act that assumes one and only one value in X. The decision maker's ordering of such acts induces an *ordering of consequences*. We denote this ordering by $\precsim^*$.

To establish the properties of $\precsim^*$ I must introduce two new concepts. For this purpose let $x(\cdot)$ and $y(\cdot)$ be acts and let B be an event. Then $x(\cdot) \precsim y(\cdot)$ *given* B if and only if $x(\cdot) \precsim y(\cdot)$ once they have been modified on B^C so as to agree with each other there. Moreover, B is a *null event* if and only if, for all acts $x(\cdot)$ and $y(\cdot)$, $x(\cdot) \precsim y(\cdot)$ given B. We note that if SA 4 is satisfied, then the relation $x(\cdot) \precsim y(\cdot)$ given B is independent of the choice of values of $x(\cdot)$ and $y(\cdot)$ in B^C.

According to Savage's theory of choice, the decision maker's ordering of consequences is independent of the state of the world—see SA 5.

SA 5 Let $x(\cdot)$ and $y(\cdot)$ be constant acts that assume the values x and y, respectively, in X, and let B be an event. If B is not a null event, $x(\cdot) \precsim y(\cdot)$ given B if and only if $x \precsim^* y$.

This postulate is both strong and controversial. Its power is illustrated in E 19.5:

E 19.5 Let Ω, X, $F(\cdot)$, $U(\cdot)$, and $U_i(\cdot)$, $i = 1, \ldots, S$, be as in E 19.4. Furthermore, let the decision maker's conditional ordering of X^S, given $\omega = \omega_i$, be defined by

$$V(\tilde{x}|\omega = \omega_i) = U_i(x(\omega_i)) + \sum_{\substack{j=1 \\ j \neq i}}^{S} U_j(\overline{x}),$$

where $\tilde{x} = (x(\omega_1), \ldots, x(\omega_i), \ldots, x(\omega_S))$ and $\overline{x}$ is an arbitrary vector in X. Finally, let

$$W(x) = \sum_{j=1}^{S} U_j(x), \qquad x \in X.$$

Then, for all $\tilde{x}$, $\tilde{y}$ in X^S,

$$V(\tilde{x}|\omega = \omega_i) \leqslant V(\tilde{y}|\omega = \omega_i) \text{ iff } U_i(x(\omega_i)) \leqslant U_i(y(\omega_i)). \tag{19.6}$$

Moreover, if SA 5 is satisfied and $x(\cdot)$ and $y(\cdot)$ are constant acts that assume the values x and y, respectively, then

$$V(\tilde{x}|\omega = \omega_i) \leqslant V(\tilde{y}|\omega = \omega_i) \text{ iff } W(x) \leqslant W(y). \tag{19.7}$$

From equations 19.6 and 19.7 and UT 8, it follows that if SA 5 is satisfied, then there exist continuous, strictly increasing functions $G_i(\cdot)$, $i = 1, \ldots, S$, such that

$$U_i(x) = G_i(W(x)), \qquad x \in X, i = 1, \ldots, S. \tag{19.8}$$

That is, if SA 5 is satisfied, then (in the lingo of chapter 11) the decision maker's ordering of X^S is independent and persistent.

We can gain still more insight into the meaning of SA 5 and its implications by being less general. Suppose, for instance, that the states of the world in E 19.5 describe for each and every hour of the day the weather during a certain month. Finally, suppose that one of the components of x represents hours playing at outdoor tennis and that another component represents hours playing at indoor tennis. If ω_i prescribes mostly rainy days and ω_j prescribes mostly sunny days, it is hard to see how $U_i(\cdot)$ and $U_j(\cdot)$ in E 19.5 could satisfy equation 19.8. However, SA 5 insists that they do.

Many students of choice under uncertainty wonder if there really are such things as constant acts. Savage discussed them at length without resolving the problem of their existence. From my point of view the discussion of the existence of constant acts is somewhat beside the point. I view Savage's axioms as an uninterpreted system whose undefined terms can be interpreted in many ways. The empirical relevance of any such interpretation must not be philosophically decided *a priori*, but by confronting the theory with the relevant data.

19.3 Risk Preferences and Subjective Probability

In this section we see how a decision maker's ordering of acts induces an ordering of events. We also establish sufficient conditions so that this ordering of events can be rationalized by a subjective probability measure.

19.3.1 Bets and Prizes

To offer a decision maker a prize $p \in X$ if event A occurs amounts to offering him an act $x_A(\cdot)$ which assumes the value p in A and the value q in A^c for some $q \in X$, with $q \prec^* p$. We call $x_A(\cdot)$ a *bet* and let $\mathscr{B}(p, q)$ denote the set of all bets obtained by varying A over $\mathscr{F}$.

The decision maker's ordering of acts induces an ordering of $\mathscr{B}(p, q)$. In Savage's axiom system, the induced ordering of $\mathscr{B}(p, q)$ is independent of (p, q)—to wit SA 6.

SA 6 Let p, q, r, and s be consequences such that $q \prec^* p$ and $r \prec^* s$. In addition, suppose that $x_A(\cdot)$ and $x_B(\cdot)$ belong to $\mathscr{B}(p, q)$ and that $y_A(\cdot)$ and $y_B(\cdot)$ belong to $\mathscr{B}(s, r)$. Then $x_A(\cdot) \preceq x_B(\cdot)$ if and only if $y_A(\cdot) \preceq y_B(\cdot)$.

This axiom looks innocuous, but is not; e.g., an independent and persistent ordering of the X^S of E 19.5 need not satisfy SA 6. We shall see that SA 6 has interesting implications. But first a seventh axiom and an example. The axiom makes sure that SA 6 is not empty:

SA 7 There exist consequences p and q such that $q \prec^* p$.

The example suggests that an ordering of the X^S in E 19.5 that is independent, persistent, and stationary satisfies SA 6.

E 19.6 Let Ω, X, $U(\cdot)$, $F(\cdot)$, $W(\cdot)$, and $G_i(\cdot)$, $i = 1, \ldots, S$, be as in E 19.4 and E 19.5, and suppose that there are constants $\alpha_i > 0$, $i = 1, \ldots, S$, such that $\sum_{i=1}^{S} \alpha_i = 1$ and $G_i(t) = \alpha_i t$, $t \in R$. Then

$$F(U(\tilde{x})) = \sum_{i=1}^{S} \alpha_i W(x(\omega_i)), \qquad \tilde{x} \in X^S. \tag{19.9}$$

Moreover, if $A = \{\omega_{i_1}, \ldots, \omega_{i_k}\}$, $B = \{\omega_{j_1}, \ldots, \omega_{j_r}\}$ and $\tilde{x}_A$ and $\tilde{x}_B$ belong to $\mathscr{B}(p, q)$, with $W(q) < W(p)$, then

$$F(U(\tilde{x}_B)) - F(U(\tilde{x}_A)) = \left[\left(\sum_{l=1}^{r} \alpha_{j_l}\right) - \left(\sum_{l=1}^{k} \alpha_{i_l}\right)\right](W(p) - W(q)).$$

Hence

$$F(U(\tilde{x}_B)) \geqslant F(U(\tilde{x}_A)) \text{ iff } \sum_{l=1}^{r} \alpha_{j_l} \geqslant \sum_{l=1}^{k} \alpha_{i_l}.$$

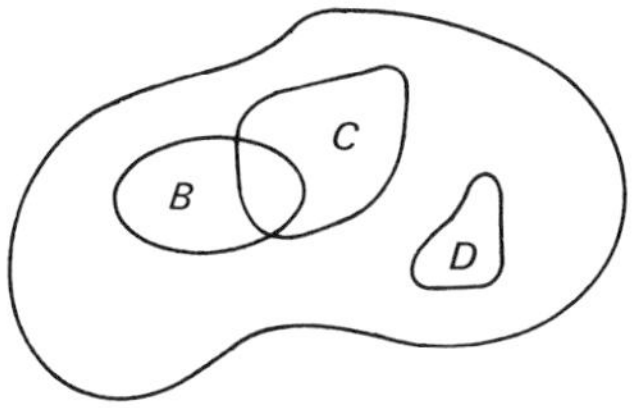

Figure 19.1

19.3.2 Qualitative Probability

When $x_A(\cdot)$ and $x_B(\cdot)$ belong to $\mathscr{B}(p, q)$ and $x_A(\cdot) \precsim y_B(\cdot)$, we say that A *is not more probable than* B and write $A \leqslant B$.

T 19.1 Suppose that $\precsim$ satisfies SA 1–SA 7 and let $\leqslant$ be as above. Then $\leqslant$ is a total, reflexive, and transitive binary relation in $\mathscr{F}$ that satisfies

(i) $\varnothing \leqslant B$ for all $B \in \mathscr{F}$ and $\varnothing < \Omega$;

(ii) $B \leqslant C$ if and only if $B \cup D \leqslant C \cup D$ for all $D \in \mathscr{F}$ with $B \cap D = C \cap D = \varnothing$.

It is obvious that $\leqslant$ is total, reflexive, and transitive in $\mathscr{F}$. It is also easy to show that $\leqslant$ satisfies condition i. To see that $\leqslant$ satisfies condition ii as well, consider figure 19.1.

Suppose $B \leqslant C$; that is, suppose that $x_B(\cdot) \precsim x_C(\cdot)$. Since $x_B(\cdot)$ and $x_C(\cdot)$ agree with each other in $(B \cup C)^c$ and take the value q there, we can—without changing the decision maker's preference for them—modify both acts so that they take on the value p on D. But then $x_B(\cdot)$ becomes $x_{B \cup D}(\cdot)$, $x_C(\cdot)$ becomes $x_{C \cup D}(\cdot)$, and our preceding remark implies that $x_{B \cup D}(\cdot) \precsim x_{C \cup D}(\cdot)$; i.e.,

$$B \cup D \leqslant C \cup D. \tag{19.10}$$

By reversing our steps we can show that equation 19.10 implies $B \leqslant C$. Since B, C, and D are arbitrary events such that $B \cap D = \varnothing = C \cap D$, we have established the validity of condition ii.

A binary relation in $\mathscr{F}$ that satisfies the conditions of T 19.1 is called a *qualitative probability*. We shall next see if a qualitative probability can be rationalized by a probability measure; i.e., we shall check to see if there is a finitely additive probability measure $Q(\cdot)\colon \mathscr{F} \to [0, 1]$ such that, for all A, B in $\mathscr{F}$,

$$A \leqslant B \text{ iff } Q(A) \leqslant Q(B). \tag{19.11}$$

19.3.3 Subjective Probability

A probability measure on $\mathscr{F}$ that satisfies equation 19.11 need not be uniquely determined. When it is, we refer to $Q(\cdot)$ as the *decision maker's subjective probability measure.*

In equation 19.9 we exhibit a preference order for which there is a probability measure that satisfies equation 19.11. To wit: Let

$$Q(A) = \sum_{i \in A} \alpha_i, \qquad A \in \mathscr{F}.$$

Then $Q(\cdot)$ is a probability measure on $\mathscr{F}$ that satisfies equation 19.11. However, there may be infinitely many probability measures that satisfy equation 19.11 in this case. More on that in section 19.4.3.

Another example where there exists a probability measure $Q(\cdot)$ that satisfies equation 19.11 is given in E 19.7. Again $Q(\cdot)$ is not unique.

E 19.7 Let Ω, X, and S be as in E 19.6 and assume that $S = 2$ and $n = 1$. Suppose also that

$$U(\tilde{x}) = (V(x(\omega_1) - 1) + (V(x(\omega_2))^2 - 1), \qquad \tilde{x} \in X^2,$$

where $V(\cdot)$ is continuous, increasing, and strictly concave, with $V(0) = 1$. Then the ordering in X^Ω induced by $U(\cdot)$ satisfies SA 4–SA 7, but there is no admissible transform of $U(\cdot)$ which satisfies equation 19.9. The measure $Q(\cdot)\colon \mathscr{F} \to [0, 1]$, defined by

$$Q(\{\omega_1\}) = \tfrac{1}{4} \qquad \text{and} \qquad Q(\{\omega_2\}) = \tfrac{3}{4},$$

satisfies equation 19.11.

Even if the risk preferences of Savage's decision maker satisfy SA 4–SA 7, there need not exist a probability measure $Q(\cdot)$ that satisfies equation 19.11. Here is a counterexample suggested by Kraft, Pratt, and Seidenberg (1959, pp. 414–415).

E 19.8 Let $\Omega = \{\omega_1, \ldots, \omega_5\}$, let $X = \{p, q\}$, and assume that $<^*$ is such that $q \prec^* p$. Moreover, let

$$x_i \equiv x_{\omega_i}(\cdot), \qquad i = 1, \ldots, 5$$

$$x_{ij} \equiv x_{\omega_i \cup \omega_j}(\cdot), \qquad 1 \leqslant i, j \leqslant 5$$

$$x_{ijk} \equiv x_{\omega_i \cup \omega_j \cup \omega_k}(\cdot), \qquad 1 \leqslant i, j, k \leqslant 5$$

$$x_{ijkm} \equiv x_{\omega_i \cup \omega_j \cup \omega_k \cup \omega_m}(\cdot), \qquad 1 \leqslant i, j, k, m \leqslant 5$$

$$x_{12345} \equiv x_\Omega(\cdot)$$

and assume that

$$\varnothing \prec x_2 \prec x_3 \prec x_4 \prec x_{23} \prec x_{24} \prec x_1 \prec x_{12} \prec x_{34} \prec x_5 \prec x_{234} \prec x_{13} \prec x_{14}$$
$$\prec x_{25} \prec x_{321} \prec x_{35} \prec x_{124} \prec x_{45} \prec x_{134} \prec x_{235} \prec x_{245} \prec x_{15} \prec x_{1234}$$
$$\prec x_{125} \prec x_{345} \prec x_{2345} \prec x_{135} \prec x_{145} \prec x_{1235} \prec x_{1245} \prec x_{1345} \prec x_{12345}. \quad (19.12)$$

The list of acts in equation 19.12 describes all possible acts. Thus $\preceq$ satisfies SA 1 and it is a routine matter to check that it satisfies SA 4–SA 7 as well. Hence, if we define $\leqslant$ as in T 19.1, $\leqslant$ is a qualitative probability. Yet there is no probability measure on $(\Omega, \mathscr{F})$ that satisfies equation 19.11. If such a measure did exist, the relations $x_{24} \prec x_1$, $x_{12} \prec x_{34}$, and $x_{14} \prec x_{25}$ would imply that $Q(\{\omega_1, \omega_2, \omega_4\}) < Q(\{\omega_3, \omega_5\})$, which contradicts $x_{35} \prec x_{124}$.

To ensure the existence of a subjective probability measure on $(\Omega, \mathscr{F})$ we need one more axiom. The one suggested by Savage is SA 8.

SA 8 If $x(\cdot) \prec y(\cdot)$ and z is any consequence, then there exists a partition of Ω such that if $x(\cdot)$ or $y(\cdot)$ is modified on any one element of the partition so as to take the value z at every ω there, other values being unchanged, then the modified $x(\cdot)$ remains $\prec y(\cdot)$, or $x(\cdot)$ remains $\prec$ the modified $y(\cdot)$, as the case may require.

In the next theorem we record the fact that SA 1–SA 8 imply that Savage's decision maker has a subjective probability measure on $(\Omega, \mathscr{F})$.

T 19.2 If $\preceq$ satisfies SA 1–SA 8, then there exists a unique probability measure $Q(\cdot)$ on $(\Omega, \mathscr{F})$ such that, for any two events A and B,
$A \leqslant B$ iff $Q(A) \leqslant Q(B)$.

The proof of this theorem, which is lengthy and technical, is given in Savage 1954 (pp. 34–40).

19.4 Expected Utility

We have given sufficient conditions so that Savage's decision maker ranks events as if he had a subjective probability measure. Our next question is: Do axioms SA 1–SA 8 imply that the decision maker ranks uncertain options according to their expected utility?

19.4.1 Savage's Fundamental Theorem

The answer to our question is "yes," as long as we restrict the decision maker's choices to acts with a finite number of consequences. To obtain a similar result for all acts, we need SA 9:

SA 9 Let $x(\cdot)$ and $y(\cdot)$ be acts; let $y_s(\cdot): \Omega \rightarrow \{y(s)\}$ be a constant act; and let B be an event. If $x(\cdot) \preceq (\prec)\ y_s(\cdot)$, given B for every $s \in B$, then $x(\cdot) \preceq (\prec)\ y(\cdot)$ given B.

With this axiom in our hands we can state Savage's fundamental theorem of bounded expected utility, T 19.3.

T 19.3 Suppose that SA 1–SA 9 are valid and let $Q(\cdot)$ denote the decision maker's subjective probability measure on $(\Omega, \mathscr{F})$. Then there exists a bounded function $U(\cdot)\colon X \to R$ such that, for all acts $x(\cdot)$ and $y(\cdot)$,

$$x(\cdot) \precsim y(\cdot) \text{ iff } \int_\Omega U(x(\omega))\, dQ(\omega) \leqslant \int_\Omega U(y(\omega))\, dQ(\omega). \tag{19.13}$$

A detailed proof of the theorem is given in Savage 1954 (pp. 206–210).[1]

One interesting consequence of equation 19.13 is this: If $x(\cdot)$ and $y(\cdot)$ are acts such that the probability distributions on X induced by $x(\cdot)$ and $Q(\cdot)$ and by $y(\cdot)$ and $Q(\cdot)$ are identical, then $x(\cdot) \sim y(\cdot)$. Similarly, $x(\cdot) \prec y(\cdot)$ if and only if the decision maker prefers the probability distribution on X induced by $y(\cdot)$ and $Q(\cdot)$ to the probability distribution on X induced by $x(\cdot)$ and $Q(\cdot)$. E 19.9 illustrates this.

E 19.9 Suppose that $x(\cdot)$ and $y(\cdot)$ are acts that assume the same finite number of consequences, z_i, $i = 1, \ldots, m$. Suppose also that, for $i = 1, \ldots, m$,

$$Q(\{\omega \in \Omega\colon x(\omega) = z_i\}) = Q(\{\omega \in \Omega\colon y(\omega) = z_i\}).$$

Then $x(\cdot) \sim y(\cdot)$ since

$$\int_\Omega U(x(\omega))\, dQ(\omega) = \sum_{i=1}^{m} U(z_i) Q(\{\omega \in x(\omega) = z_i\}) = \int_\Omega U(y(\omega))\, dQ(\omega).$$

19.4.2 Measurable Utility

The measure $Q(\cdot)$ in T 19.2 is uniquely determined, but $U(\cdot)$ is not. Theorem T 19.4 shows the latitude we have in choosing $U(\cdot)$:

T 19.4 Suppose that SA 1–SA 9 are valid; and let $U(\cdot)$ and $Q(\cdot)$ be as in T 19.3. Then $U(\cdot)$ is determined up to a positive linear transformation.

We sketch a proof of this theorem. Observe first that if a and b are constants such that $b > 0$, and if $F(\cdot)\colon X \to R$ satisfies

$$F(x) = a + bU(x), \qquad x \in X \tag{19.14}$$

then, for all acts $x(\cdot)$ and $y(\cdot)$,

$$x(\cdot) \precsim y(\cdot) \text{ iff } \int_\Omega F(x(\omega))\, dQ(\omega) \leqslant \int_\Omega F(y(\omega))\, dQ(\omega). \tag{19.15}$$

Therefore, it suffices to show that if $F(\cdot)$ satisfies equation 19.15 it satisfies equation 19.14 for some constants a and b, with $b > 0$.

If X contains just two points y and z, with $y \prec^* z$, and $F(\cdot)$ is *any* function on X to R, then

$$F(x) = \frac{U(z)F(y) - U(y)F(z)}{U(z) - U(y)} + \frac{F(z) - F(y)}{U(z) - U(y)} U(x), \qquad x \in X. \tag{19.16}$$

Suppose next that X contains more than two consequences, and let x, y, and z be three arbitrary consequences. We will show that

$$\det \begin{pmatrix} 1 & 1 & 1 \\ U(x) & U(y) & U(z) \\ F(x) & F(y) & F(z) \end{pmatrix} = 0, \tag{19.17}$$

where $\det(\cdot)$ denotes the determinant of $(\cdot)$. If any two of the consequences are equivalent, equation 19.17 must hold. Thus, without loss in generality, we can assume that $x \prec^* y \prec^* z$. Then there exists an event A such that $U(y) = Q(A)U(x) + (1 - Q(A))U(z)$ and $F(y) = Q(A)F(x) + (1 - Q(A))F(z)$. (See Savage 1954, pp. 74–75.) From this follows the validity of equation 19.17.

To conclude the proof we pick two consequences y and z such that $y \prec^* z$, and we let x be an arbitrary consequence. We then expand the determinant in equation 19.17 and find that $F(\cdot)$ satisfies equation 19.16. Since x is arbitrary, equation 19.16 is satisfied and hence equation 19.14 must hold for all $x \in X$.

Theorem T 19.4 provides us with a method we can use to construct an individual's utility function under various interpretations of the undefined terms of SA 1–SA 9. One example is given in E 19.10. In reading it, note that we confront the decision maker with a series of gambles in which the probabilities are objectively specified. I can justify our procedure by insisting that, for the gambles under consideration, subjective probabilities equal objective probabilities and by recalling that it is the distributions induced by $Q(\cdot)$ and the various relevant acts that matter to the decision maker, not the acts themselves.

E 19.10 Suppose that $X = [-200, 1000]$, where each $x \in X$ denotes so many dollars. Suppose also that S is a decision maker whose risk preferences satisfy SA 1–SA 9; and let $U(\cdot)\colon X \to R$ be his utility function. Without loss in generality, we may assume that

$U(-200) = 0 \qquad \text{and} \qquad U(1000) = 1.$

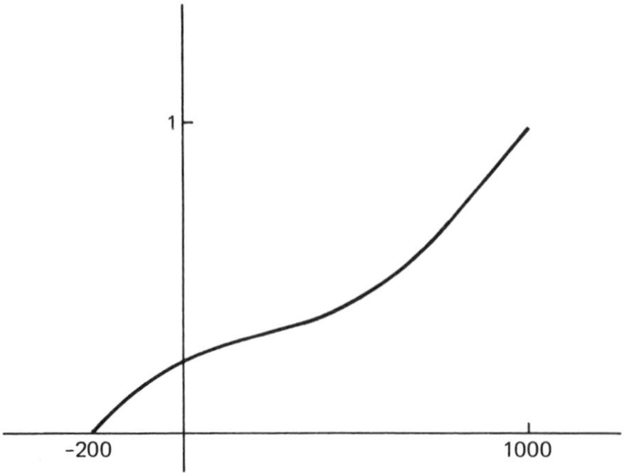

Figure 19.2

In addition, we assume that $U(\cdot)$ is continuous. From these assumptions it follows that, for each $p \in (0, 1)$, there is an $x \in X$ such that

$$U(x) = p.$$

Hence, by varying p and by asking S to specify the x that would make him indifferent between x for sure and the option \$1000 with probability p and $-$\$200 with probability $(1 - p)$, we can use the defining equations for $U(\cdot)$ to construct S's utility function on X.

A typical utility function of an economics student from Oslo is displayed in figure 19.2.

19.4.3 Expected Utility with a Finite Number of States of the World

Both SA 8 and SA 9 implicitly assume that there are infinitely many states of the world. To establish an analogue of T 19.4 when Ω has only a finite number of points, we must replace SA 8 and SA 9 by other axioms. There are many possibilities. I shall present one that is of interest to economists.

Before stating the theorem I must introduce new notation. Let Ω, X, and $\tilde{x}$ be as in E 19.4; i.e., let $\Omega = \{\omega_1, \ldots, \omega_S\}$, let $X = R_+^n$, and let $\tilde{x} = (x(\omega_1), \ldots, x(\omega_S)) \in (R_+^n)^S$. Then, for each $x \in X$, let

$$^j x = (x_1, \ldots, x_{j-1}, x_{j+1}, \ldots, x_n) \tag{19.18}$$

and denote x by $(x_j, {}^j x)$ even if $j \neq 1$, Moreover, let

$$\tilde{x}^{k,i} = (x(\omega_1), \ldots, x(\omega_{k-1}), x(\omega_{k+1}), \ldots, x(\omega_{i-1}), x(\omega_{i+1}), \ldots, x(\omega_S)) \tag{19.19}$$

and denote $\tilde{x}$ by $(x(\omega_k), x(\omega_i), \tilde{x}^{k,i})$ even if $(k, i) \neq (1, 2)$. Finally, let

$$\Gamma(x_j^0 | {}^j x, \tilde{x}^{k,i}) = \{(x_j, y_j) \geqslant 0; (x_j, {}^j x, y_j, {}^j x, \tilde{x}^{k,i}) \succeq (x_j^0, {}^j x, x_j^0, {}^j x, \tilde{x}^{k,i})\}, \tag{19.20}$$

where $(x_j, {}^j x)$ denotes the value of $x(\cdot)$ at $\omega = \omega_k$, and where $(y_j, {}^j x)$ denotes the value of $x(\cdot)$ at $\omega = \omega_i$. Then we can establish the following proposition:[2]

T 19.5 Consider a decision maker, $((\Omega, \mathscr{F}), X^\Omega, \preceq)$, for whom $\Omega = \{\omega_1, \ldots, \omega_S\}$, $S \geqslant 3$, $X = R_+^n$, and $n \geqslant 1$. Suppose that $\preceq$ satisfies SA 4, SA 5, and SA 6 and the following conditions:

SSA 1 If $\tilde{x}, \tilde{y} \in X^S$ are acts and $\tilde{x} \leqslant \tilde{y}$, $\tilde{x} \neq \tilde{y}$, then $\tilde{x} \preceq \tilde{y}$ and not $\tilde{y} \preceq \tilde{x}$.

SSA 2 If $\tilde{x}, \tilde{y} \in X^S$ are acts and $\lambda \in (0, 1)$, then the conditions $\tilde{x} \preceq \tilde{y}$, $\tilde{y} \preceq \tilde{x}$, and $\tilde{x} \neq \tilde{y}$ imply that $\tilde{x} \preceq (\lambda\tilde{x} + (1 - \lambda)\tilde{y})$ and not $(\lambda\tilde{x} + (1 - \lambda)\tilde{y}) \preceq \tilde{x}$.

SSA 3 For each $\tilde{x} \in X^S$ the sets $\{\tilde{y} \in X^S : \tilde{x} \preceq \tilde{y}\}$ and $\{\tilde{y} \in X^S : \tilde{y} \preceq \tilde{x}\}$ are relatively closed in $(R_+^n)^S$.

SSA 4 Let ${}^j x$, $\tilde{x}^{k,i}$ and $\Gamma(\cdot | {}^j x, \tilde{x}^{k,i})$ be as defined in equations 19.18–19.20. Then for each $k = 1, \ldots, S$ and $i \neq k$, there exists a positive constant α_{ik} such that, for some j and all $(x_j^0, {}^j x, x_j^0, {}^j x, \tilde{x}^{k,i}) \in X^S$,

$$\Gamma(x_j^0 | {}^j x, \tilde{x}^{k,i}) \subset \{(x_j, y_j) \in R_+^2 : (1 + \alpha_{ik})x_j^0 \leqslant y_j + \alpha_{ik} x_j\}. \tag{19.21}$$

Then there exist a continuous, strictly increasing, strictly concave function $U(\cdot): R_+^n \to R_+$ and positive constants α_i, $i = 1, \ldots, S$, such that $\sum_{i=1}^S \alpha_i = 1$ and such that, for all $\tilde{x}, \tilde{y} \in X^S$,

$$\tilde{x} \preceq \tilde{y} \text{ iff } \sum_{i=1}^S \alpha_i U(x(\omega_i)) \leqslant \sum_{i=1}^S \alpha_i U(y(\omega_i)). \tag{19.22}$$

The α_i are uniquely determined and $U(\cdot)$ is determined up to a positive linear transformation.

I shall only sketch an outline of a proof of this theorem since the ideas of the proof are simple and since the difficult details are available elsewhere.

To begin, we observe that SSA 1–SSA 3 and UT 10 of section 11.2 imply that there exists a continuous, strictly increasing, and strictly quasi-concave function $V(\cdot): X^S \to R$ such that, for all $\tilde{x}, \tilde{y} \in X^S$,

$$\tilde{x} \preceq \tilde{y} \text{ iff } V(\tilde{x}) \leqslant V(\tilde{y}).$$

Next we observe that, by SA 4 and T 11.4, there exist continuous, strictly increasing, strictly quasi-concave functions $U_i(\cdot): X \to R$, $i = 1, \ldots, S$, and a continuous, strictly increasing function $G(\cdot)$: {range of $V(\cdot)$} $\to R$ such that, for all $\tilde{x} \in X^S$,

$$G(V(\tilde{x})) = \sum_{i=1}^{S} U_i(x(\omega_i)).$$

Moreover, the function $G(V(\cdot))$ is determined up to a positive linear transformation and, by theorem 10 of Debreu and Koopmans 1982, with at most one exception, the $U_i(\cdot)$ are concave. Finally, if one of the $U_i(\cdot)$ is not concave, the others are strictly concave.

We now assume that $G(\cdot)$ and the $U_i(\cdot)$ have been picked such that $U_i(0) = 0$, $i = 1, \ldots, S$. Then we observe that UT 8, SA 5, and SA 6 imply that there is an integer i, $1 \leqslant i \leqslant S$, and a family of strictly increasing, absolutely continuous functions $F_{ik}(\cdot)$, $k \neq i$, $k = 1, \ldots, S$, such that

$$G(V(\tilde{x})) = U_i(x(\omega_i)) + \sum_{k \neq i} F_{ik}(U_i(x(\omega_k))), \qquad \tilde{x} \in X^S. \tag{19.23}$$

For any given i, the existence of continuous, strictly increasing functions $F_{ik}(\cdot)$ that satisfy equation 19.23 is a consequence of UT 8 and SA 5. The fact that, for some i, the $F_{ik}(\cdot)$ are absolutely continuous is a consequence of SA 6. To see why, let $\varphi_k = \{\omega_k\}$, $k = 1, \ldots, S$; pick $y, z \in X$ such that $z < y$; and let $\tilde{x}_{\varphi_k} \in X^S$, $k = 1, \ldots, S$, denote gambles in $\mathscr{B}(y, z)$. Then, for $i \neq k$,

$$G(V(\tilde{x}_{\varphi_i})) - G(V(\tilde{x}_{\varphi_k})) = (U_i(y) - U_i(z)) - (U_k(y) - U_k(z)). \tag{19.24}$$

For some i, $\tilde{x}_{\varphi_k} \preceq \tilde{x}_{\varphi_i}$, for all $k = 1, \ldots, S$. We let the i in equation 19.23 be one such i and deduce from equation 19.24 that, for all $k \neq i$, $k = 1, \ldots, S$, and for all $t, s \in \{\text{range of } U_i(\cdot)\}$,

$$|F_{ik}(t) - F_{ik}(s)| \leqslant |t - s|.$$

From this inequality follows the required absolute continuity of the $F_{ik}(\cdot)$.

The absolute continuity of the $F_{ik}(\cdot)$, well-known properties of concave functions, theorem 3 of Debreu and Koopmans 1982, and SSA 4 imply that, for all $t \in \{\text{range of } U_i(\cdot)\}$,

$$F_{ik}(t) = \alpha_{ik} t. \tag{19.25}$$

To show why, we fix i and $k \neq i$ and pick a j which, for the chosen pair (k, i), satisfies the condition described in SSA 4. Then we let $\hat{x} \in R_+^n$ be an arbitrary vector and define $f(\cdot)$: $\{\text{range of } U_i(\cdot, {}^j\hat{x})\} \to R$ by

$$f(x_j) = U_i(x_j, {}^j\hat{x}), \qquad x_j \in R_+$$

and $H(\cdot)$: $R_+^2 \to R$ by

$$H(x, y) = \; = F_{ik}(f(x)) + f(y), \qquad (x, y) \in R_+^2.$$

From the properties of $G(V(\cdot))$ it follows that $H(\cdot)$ is continuous, strictly increasing, and strictly quasi-concave. Moreover, both $f(\cdot)$ and $F_{ik}(\cdot)$ are continuous and strictly increasing, and at least one of them is concave. Finally, well-known properties of concave functions and theorem 3 of Debreu and Koopmans 1982 imply that outside a countable subset of R_+ both $f(\cdot)$ and $F_{ik}(f(\cdot))$ have strictly positive derivatives. These properties of $f(\cdot)$ and $F_{ik}(f(\cdot))$, the absolute continuity of $F_{ik}(\cdot)$, SSA 4, and standard arguments suffice to establish the validity of equation 19.25.

To conclude the proof of T 19.5, we first define a function $U(\cdot)$: $R_+^n \to R$ and S constants α_j, $j = 1, \ldots, S$, by

$$U(x) = \left(1 + \sum_{k \neq i} \alpha_{ik}\right) U_i(x), \qquad x \in R_+^n$$

$$\alpha_i = \left(1 + \sum_{k \neq i} \alpha_{ik}\right)^{-1}$$

and

$$\alpha_j = \frac{\alpha_{ij}}{1 + \sum_{k \neq i} \alpha_{ik}}, \qquad j \neq i, j = 1, \ldots, S.$$

Then equations 19.23 and 19.25 demonstrate that

$$G(V(\tilde{x})) = \sum_{j=1}^{S} \alpha_j U(x(\omega_j)), \qquad \tilde{x} \in X^S.$$

Since $G(V(\cdot))$ is determined up to a positive linear transformation and since the α_{ik} in equation 19.25 equals the α_{ik} of equation 19.21, it is obvious that $U(\cdot)$ is determined up to a positive linear transformation and that the α_j are uniquely determined. Finally, the required monotonicity and continuity of $U(\cdot)$ is an immediate consequence of the fact that $U_i(\cdot)$ is strictly increasing and continuous; and the strict concavity of $U(\cdot)$ follows from theorem 10 of Debreu and Koopmans 1982, theorem 1 of Stigum 1972b, and the arguments we used to establish the strict concavity of $U(\cdot)$ in T 11.5.

In reading T 19.5 and its proof, note that SSA 3 can be interpreted to be the finite-states of the world analogue of SA 8. Also SSA 4 can be interpreted as follows: Let $x(\cdot)$ be an act that assumes the value x^0 at ω_i and ω_k. Then there is a component j of x^0 such that (at the margin) the rate at which the decision maker would be willing to exchange a contingent claim on units of x_j—if ω_i were to occur—for a contingent claim on units of x_j—if ω_k were to occur—equals a constant α_{ik} that is independent of x^0 and the values of the other components of $\tilde{x}$. Finally, note that E 19.7 illustrates that it is not true that SA 4, SA 5, SA 6, and SSA 1–SSA 3 alone imply the validity of equation (19.22).

We have demonstrated that if $\Omega = \{\omega_1, \dots, \omega_s\}$, $X = R_+^n$, and the decision maker's preferences, $\precsim$ satisfy SA 4–SA 6 and SSA 1–SSA 4, then there exist constants $\alpha_i \in R_{++}$, $i = 1, \dots, S$, and continuous, strictly increasing functions $U(\cdot)$: $R_+^n \to R_+$, $V(\cdot)$: $(R_+^n)^s \to R_+$ and $G(\cdot)$: {range of $V(\cdot)\} \to R_+$ such that $U(\cdot)$ is strictly concave and

$$\tilde{x} \precsim \tilde{y} \text{ iff } G(V(\tilde{x}) \leqslant G(V(\tilde{y})),$$

$$G(V(\tilde{x})) = \sum_{i=1}^{S} \alpha_i U(x_i(\omega)),$$

and

$$\sum_{i=1}^{S} \alpha_i = 1.$$

It remains to be seen whether $G(V(\tilde{x}))$ can be interpreted as the decision maker's expected utility of $x(\cdot)$.

Let $\leqslant$ denote the ordering of events determined by $\precsim$, and define $Q(\cdot)$: $\mathscr{F} \to [0, 1]$ by

$$Q(A) = \sum_{i \in A} \alpha_i, \qquad A \in \mathscr{F}.$$

Then, for all $A, B \in \mathscr{F}$,

$$A \leqslant B \text{ iff } Q(A) \leqslant Q(B).$$

To demonstrate that $G(V(\cdot))$ is an expected utility function, we must show that $Q(\cdot)$ is the only probability measure on $(\Omega, \mathscr{F})$ that agrees with $\leqslant$.

Now, it is a fact that $Q(\cdot)$ need not be the only probability measure on $(\Omega, \mathscr{F})$ that agrees with $\leqslant$. For example, if $S = 2$, $Q(\cdot)$ is the one and only probability measure that agrees with $\leqslant$ if and only if $(\alpha_1, \alpha_2) = (\frac{1}{2}, \frac{1}{2})$. Similarly, if $S = 3$, $Q(\cdot)$ is the one and only probability measure that agrees with $\leqslant$ if and only if

$$(\alpha_1, \alpha_2, \alpha_2) \in \left\{(\tfrac{1}{3}, \tfrac{1}{3}, \tfrac{1}{3}), (\tfrac{1}{4}, \tfrac{1}{4}, \tfrac{1}{2}), (\tfrac{1}{2}, \tfrac{1}{4}, \tfrac{1}{4}), (\tfrac{1}{4}, \tfrac{1}{2}, \tfrac{1}{4})\right\}.$$

To show why this is so, I shall state and prove an interesting theorem, T 19.6, that is due to Peter Fishburn and A. M. Odlyzko (see Fishburn and Odlyzko 1989, lemma 1, p. 4):

T 19.6 Let $(\Omega, \mathscr{F})$, $\precsim$, and the α_i, $i = 1, \dots, S$, be as in T 19.5. Let $\leqslant$ be the ordering of events determined by $\precsim$, and define $Q(\cdot)$: $\mathscr{F} \to [0, 1]$ by

$$Q(A) = \sum_{i \in A} \alpha_i, \qquad A \in \mathscr{F}.$$

Then $Q(\cdot)$ is the only probability measure on $(\Omega, \mathscr{F})$ that agrees with $\leqslant$ if and only if the following condition is satisfied:

(i) There exist $S - 1$ pairs $(A_j, B_j) \in \mathscr{F} \times \mathscr{F}$ such that $A_j \cap B_j = \emptyset$ and such that the equations for $x \in R^S$,

$$\sum_{i \in A_j} x_i = \sum_{i \in B_j} x_i, \qquad j = 1, \ldots, S - 1$$

are linearly independent and satisfied by $(\alpha_1, \ldots, \alpha_s)$.

The proof goes as follows: Suppose that condition i is satisfied and observe that then

$$Q(A_j) = Q(B_j), \qquad j = 1, \ldots, S - 1$$

and

$$A_j \leqslant B_j \text{ and } B_j \leqslant A_j, \qquad j = 1, \ldots, S - 1.$$

From this it follows that if $P(\cdot)\colon \mathscr{F} \to [0, 1]$ is another probability measure that agrees with $\leqslant$, $P(\cdot)$ must satisfy

$$\sum_{i \in A_j} P(\{i\}) = \sum_{i \in B_j} P(\{i\}), \qquad j = 1, \ldots, S - 1.$$

Since these equations are linearly independent and $P(\cdot)$ is a probability measure, $P(\cdot) = Q(\cdot)$.

Suppose next that $Q(\cdot)$ is the only probability measure on $(\Omega, \mathscr{F})$ that agrees with $\leqslant$. If there do not exist $S - 1$ pairs $(A_j, B_j) \in \mathscr{F} \times \mathscr{F}$ that satisfy condition i, small perturbations of $Q(\cdot)$ will provide us with probability measures that agree with $\leqslant$ and are different from $Q(\cdot)$. Hence condition i must hold.

In reading the theorem and its proof, keep in mind the following possibilities for $S = 3$, where lip is short for *linearly independent*:

1. $\sum_{i \in \emptyset} x_i = x_1$ and $\sum_{i \in \emptyset} x_i = x_2$ are lip and satisfied by $(0, 0, 1)$;
2. $\sum_{i \in \emptyset} x_i = x_1$ and $x_2 = x_3$ are lip and satisfied by $(0, \frac{1}{2}, \frac{1}{2})$; and
3. $x_1 = x_2$ and $\sum_{i \in \{1,2\}} x_i = x_3$ are lip and satisfied by $(\frac{1}{4}, \frac{1}{4}, \frac{1}{2})$.

Since $\alpha_i \in R_{++}$, $i = 1, \ldots, S$, possibilities 1 and 2 are ruled out of court in T 19.6.

19.5 Assessing Probabilities and Measuring Utilities

To conclude our discussion of Savage's expected-utility theory we shall briefly discuss whether Savage's theory provides a framework within which we can assess subjective probabilities and measure utility functions. I shall also comment on some of the tests to which the expected-utility hypothesis has been put.

19.5.1 Assessing Subjective Probabilities

According to Ramsey, a person's degree of belief in a proposition is a causal property of his belief, which we can express vaguely as the extent to which he is prepared to act on it (Ramsey 1954, p. 169). If this is so, and if the person's risk preferences satisfy SA 1–SA 8, we can infer his subjective probabilities of events from his choices between bets—to wit E 19.11.

E 19.11 Gramley is knowledgeable in Norwegian politics; we want to determine the probability he assigns to the event E that the right-wing party will be in power after the coming elections. We choose a number C and present him with a series of bets of the form: $\$S$ if E and $-\$C$ if E^c. For some values of S, Gramley would be willing to gamble; for others he would not. However, there is also an S^0 at which he would be indifferent between gambling and not gambling. This must be an S^0 at which

$$U(w) = Q(E)U(w + S^0) + (1 - Q(E))U(w - C), \tag{19.26}$$

where $U(\cdot)$, w, and $Q(E)$ are, respectively, Gramley's utility function, his net worth, and his subjective probability of E. Hence, if C is not too large,

$$\hat{Q}(E) = \frac{C}{S^0 + C}$$

is a good estimate of $Q(E)$.

The method we describe in E 19.11 has one drawback: to justify using $\hat{Q}(E)$ as an estimate of $Q(E)$, we may have to make C so small that the estimate is rendered meaningless by Gramley's reluctance to bother about trifles. How small C must be varies from subject to subject. But some idea of the order of magnitude involved can be gathered from various psychometric studies, e.g., Mosteller and Nogee 1951 (pp. 371–404) and Edwards 1955 (pp. 201–214). These studies agreed that most of their subjects' utility of money expressed in 1956 dollars was approximately linear in the interval (−\$5.50, \$5.50).

Those who worry about Gramley's reluctance to bother about trifles can use other methods to determine $Q(E)$. One of them is based on an idea of E. Borel (1963, p. 57): Ask Gramley to choose between the two gambles, \$100 if E, nothing if E^c, and \$100 if he receives a 5 or a 6 in a toss of a die; nothing otherwise. If he prefers to bet on E, it must be because $Q(E) > 1/3$.

Borel's method is appealing but does not always produce the desired result. This is illustrated in E 19.12.

E 19.12 Peter believes that the probability of its raining tomorrow is 1/3. Yet when we ask him to choose between betting \$100 on rain tomorrow and betting \$100 on receiving a 5 or a 6 in a toss of a die, he chooses the latter without hesitation. His reasoning is as follows: If it rains tomorrow, he will spend the day at home catching up on paperwork. If it does not rain, he will spend \$100 taking his children to an amusement park. Ergo, if he bets on the weather, his expected utility is

$$(1/3)U(w + 100) + (2/3)U(w - 100).$$

If he bets on the die, his expected utility is

$$(1/9)U(w + 100) + (4/9)U(w) + (4/9)U(w - 100).$$

Since his utility function is strictly concave and increasing, the latter is larger than the former.

In assessing Gramley's and Peter's subjective probabilities, we assume that their risk preferences satisfy SA 1–SA 8. Note, therefore, that in the context of E 19.11 and E 19.12, SA 8 is a very strong assumption which we cannot easily do without.

To see why we need SA 8 in the situation envisioned in E 19.11, we suppose, for the sake of argument, that Gramley cannot think of more than a few factors that will be decisive for the outcome of the next election in Norway. If that is true, the choices which Gramley faces in E 19.11 must be represented by acts on a finite set of states of the world where SA 8 is inapplicable. Therefore, suppose that Gramley's risk preferences satisfy SA 1–SA 6 and instead of SA 8 the conditions added to SA 1–SA 6 in T 19.5. But then the $Q(E)$ in equation 19.26 equals $\sum_{i \in E} \alpha_i$, where the α_i are as described in equation 19.22, and $\hat{Q}(E)$ is an estimate of Gramley's subjective probability of E only if condition i of T 19.6 is satisfied.

19.5.2 Measuring Utility Functions

The utility function of Savage's decision maker is determined up to a positive linear transformation. Such a utility function is said to be measurable; and in E 19.10 I described a method by which a person's utility function can be measured. This method, which has been used in variously structured experimental situations by psychometricians, decision theorists, and economists, is suspect for many reasons. I detail some of them below.

In E 19.10 we fixed the values of $U(\cdot): [-200, 1000] \to R$ to be 0 at -200 and 1 at 1000. Then we determined other values of $U(\cdot)$ by finding, for various $p \in (0, 1)$, the certainty equivalent x of a bet yielding \$1000 with probability p and $-\$200$ with probability $(1 - p)$ and by observing that $U(x) = p$. Here the *certainty equivalent* of a bet is the x at which the decision maker would be indifferent between having x for sure and engaging in the given bet.

One reason to suspect the method of E 19.10 is that the p used to propose a bet need not be the p our subject perceives when he searches for his certainty equivalent of the bet. For example, our subject may overvalue small probabilities and undervalue high probabilities. If he does, the function we construct becomes an experimental artifact. To wit:

E 19.13 Consider a decision maker with a linear utility function $U(\cdot)\colon [0, 1000] \to [0, 1]$ given by

$$U(x) = \frac{1}{2}\left(1 + \frac{x - 500}{500}\right), \qquad x \in [0, 1000]$$

and suppose that we want to measure this function by the method described in E 19.10. Suppose also that the decision maker, when he hears p, perceives it to be $\pi(p)$, where

$$\pi(p) = \tfrac{1}{2} + 4(p - (\tfrac{1}{2}))^3, \qquad p \in (0, 1).$$

Then the "utility function" we measure is

$$W(x) = \frac{1}{2}\left(1 + \frac{(x - 500)^{1/3}}{500^{1/3}}\right), \qquad x \in [0, 1000].$$

Another reason to suspect the method of E 19.10 is that seemingly equivalent methods of determining the values of $U(\cdot)$ produce strikingly different functions. Consider, for example, the function $\hat{V}(\cdot)\colon [-200, 1000] \to [0, 1]$ constructed in the following way: let $p = \frac{1}{2}$; let $B(x, y)$ denote the uncertain option, x with probability $\frac{1}{2}$ and y with probability $\frac{1}{2}$; and let $C(x, y)$ denote the certainty equivalent of $B(x, y)$. Then we assign 0 and 1, respectively, to $\hat{V}(-200)$ and $\hat{V}(1000)$. Furthermore, whenever $\hat{V}(\cdot)$ has been defined at x and y, let $\hat{V}(C(x, y)) = \frac{1}{2}\hat{V}(x) + \frac{1}{2}\hat{V}(y)$. For example, if $x_1 = C(-200, 1000)$, $\hat{V}(x_1) = \frac{1}{2}$; and if $x_2 = C(-200, x_1)$ and $x_3 = C(x_1, 1000)$, $\hat{V}(x_2) = 1/4$ and $\hat{V}(x_3) = 3/4$. Similarly, if $x_4 = C(-200, x_2)$, $\hat{V}(x_4) = 1/8$; if $x_5 = C(x_2, x_1)$, $\hat{V}(x_5) = 3/8$; and so forth ad infinitum. Finally, if $x = \lim x_{i_n}$, let $\hat{V}(x) = \lim \hat{V}(x_{i_n})$. Most axiomatizations of the expected utility hypothesis for choice under risky conditions, i.e., for choices among uncertain options with objectively assigned probabilities of outcomes, agree that

1. $\hat{V}(\cdot)$ is well defined,
2. $\hat{V}(\cdot)$ is independent of our choice of p,
3. $\hat{V}(\cdot)$ is a utility function; i.e., $\hat{V}(x) = U(x)$ for $x \in [-200, 1000]$.

Nevertheless, attempts at establishing the empirical validity of 2 and 3 have failed. For instance, M. McCord and R. de Neufville (1983, p. 192)

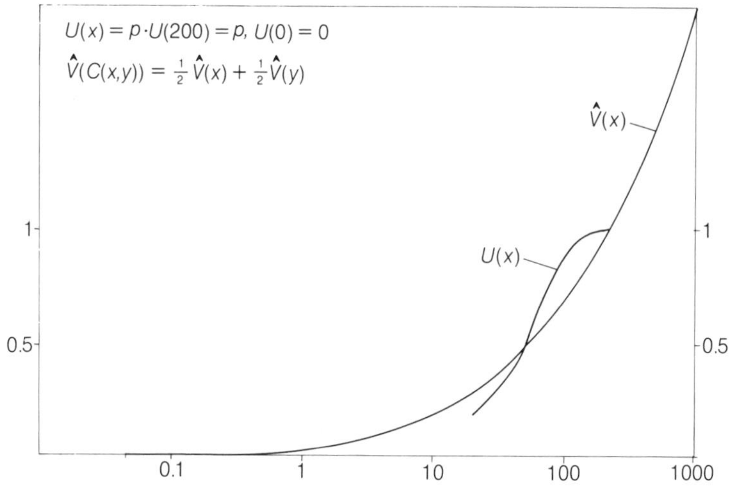

Figure 19.3
An Allais test of the expected-utility hypothesis. The U curve is a free drawing through the points $(x, p) \in \{(25, \frac{1}{4}), (50, \frac{1}{2}), (65, \frac{2}{3}), (100, 0.9), (160, 0.98), (200, 1)\}$. The $\hat{V}$ curve is a free drawing through the points $(x, \hat{V}) \in \{(3.2, \frac{1}{8}), (10, \frac{1}{4}), (28, \frac{3}{8}), (50, \frac{1}{2}), (100, \frac{3}{4}), (200, 1), (2000, 2)\}$, where $3.2 = C(0, 10)$, $10 = C(0, 50)$, $28 = C(0, 100)$, $50 = C(0, 200)$, $100 = C(50, 200)$, and $200 = C(0, 2000)$. The data are extrapolated from de Finetti's answers to Allais' questions in Allais 1979.

found that $\hat{V}(\cdot)$ increased as p varied from 0.0625 to 0.5; and M. Allais' data (Allais 1979, pp. 640–663) suggest that $\hat{V}(x) < U(x)$ for large x and that $U(x) < \hat{V}(x)$ for small values of x. An example of Allais' findings is given in figure 19.3. The different appearances of the $U(\cdot)$ and the $\hat{V}(\cdot)$ are remarkable.

19.5.3 A Test of Savage's Theory

Opponents of the expected-utility hypothesis will use Allais' and McCord and de Neufville's results to discredit the descriptive power of the hypothesis in risky situations. Whether their results can be used to discredit Savage's theory is a question we must attend to next. Suppose that we can formulate the questions in E 19.10 so that the choices which the decision maker must make appear to him as choices among acts on an experiment $(\Omega, \mathcal{F})$ and suppose that the decision maker's risk preferences satisfy SA 1–SA 9. Then the fact that $\hat{V}(\cdot)$ is well defined and equal to $U(\cdot)$ and the fact that $\hat{V}(\cdot)$ is independent of our choice of $\frac{1}{2}$ as the value of p can be deduced from theorems T 19.7 and T 19.8.

T 19.7 Suppose that the decision maker's risk preferences satisfy SA 1–SA 8 and let $Q(\cdot): \mathscr{F} \rightarrow [0, 1]$ be his subjective probability measure. For every $n > 1$ there exists a partition of Ω, $\{A_i, i = 1, \ldots, n\}$, such that $Q(A_i) = 1/n$ for all i.

This theorem paraphrases Savage's theorem 4 (Savage 1954, p. 38). Since the proof is technical and lengthy, I omit it here and refer the reader to Savage 1954, pp. 33–38, for details.

T 19.8 Suppose that the decision maker's risk preferences satisfy SA 1–SA 8 and let $Q(\cdot): \mathscr{F} \rightarrow [0, 1]$ be his subjective probability measure. Also let $p, q \in X$ and $A \in \mathscr{F}$ be so that $q \prec^* p$ and $Q(A)$ is positive and rational; let $x_A(\cdot) \in \mathscr{B}(p, q)$ and let $x \in X$ be a certainty equivalent of $x_A(\cdot)$. Finally, suppose that $y_A(\cdot) \in \mathscr{B}(p, x)$ and let y be a certainty equivalent of $y_A(\cdot)$. Then there is a $B \in \mathscr{F}$ and an $x_B(\cdot) \in \mathscr{B}(p, q)$ such that y is a certainty equivalent of $x_B(\cdot)$

The proof of this theorem is easy since it suffices to choose $B \in \mathscr{F}$ so that $Q(B) = 2Q(A) - Q(A)^2$. I leave the remaining details to the reader.

From the preceding comments it follows that, if we can formulate the construction of $U(\cdot)$ and $\hat{V}(\cdot)$ within the framework of SA 1–SA 9, we can use the identity of $U(\cdot)$ and $\hat{V}(\cdot)$ to test the empirical validity of Savage's theory. However, since it is unlikely that the subjects of Allais and McCord and de Neufville perceived their choices as choices among acts on a nondenumerable experiment, Allais' and McCord and de Neufville's results cannot be used to discredit the descriptive power of SA 1–SA 9 for choice under uncertainty.

It is unreasonable to assume that we can formulate the construction of $U(\cdot)$ and $\hat{V}(\cdot)$ within the framework of SA 1–SA 9. However, we may try to do it within the framework of SA 1–SA 6 and the conditions we added in T 19.5. If we do, we first use Borel's method to obtain the values of the α_i in equation 19.22. Then with the α_i on hand, we propose bets on events and determine any number of values of as many $\hat{V}(\cdot)$'s as there are events with different $Q(\cdot)$ values, where $Q(\cdot)$ is the probability measure on $(\Omega, \mathscr{F})$ determined by the estimated values of the α_i. Finally, we construct $U(\cdot)$ by the method described in E 19.10. The relationship between $U(\cdot)$ and the $\hat{V}(\cdot)$'s and between the different $\hat{V}(\cdot)$'s will appear uncertain unless condition i of T 19.6 holds. If the estimated α_i equal the true α_i, if condition i of T 19.6 is satisfied, and if the decision maker when he hears p always perceives it to be p, we can show that the $U(\cdot)$ and the $\hat{V}(\cdot)$'s we construct must be identical on the intersection of their domains of definition. That provides us with possible tests of the finite-states-of-the-world version of Savage's theory.

19.6 Belief Functions and Choice under Uncertainty

In section 15.2 we discussed various classes of belief functions and described a way by which two or more belief functions can be combined to form other belief functions. Such functions are superadditive probability measures and constitute the basis of Glenn Shafer's interesting theory of evidence.

Shafer's theory tells us how to assign probabilities to events but not how to act upon such probability assignments. We shall next fill this lacuna in Shafer's theory. Our discussion builds on a theorem of Kjell Arne Brekke and on ideas underlying the expected utility theories of Alain Chateauneuf (1986) and Itzhak Gilboa (1987).

Consider a decision maker DM who faces an experiment $(\Omega, \mathscr{F})$ and a set of acts X^{Ω}, where $\Omega = \{\omega_1, \ldots, \omega_n\}$, $\mathscr{F} = \mathscr{P}(\Omega)$, and X is a set of consequences. Assume that DM assigns probabilities to the events in accordance with a basic probability assignment, $m(\cdot)\colon \mathscr{F} \to [0, 1]$, and a belief function, $\mathrm{bel}(\cdot)\colon \mathscr{F} \to [0, 1]$, and that he ranks consequences in accordance with the values assumed by a utility function, $U(\cdot)\colon X \to R_+$. Moreover, for each $x \in X^{\Omega}$, let $w_x(\cdot)\colon \mathscr{F} \to R$ be defined by

$$w_x(A) = \min_{\omega \in A} U(x(\omega)), \qquad A \in \mathscr{F} \tag{19.27}$$

and assume that DM ranks acts in accordance with the values assumed by the function

$$V(x) = \sum_{A \subset \Omega} w_x(A)m(A), \qquad x \in X^{\Omega}. \tag{19.28}$$

[3]

Finally, to avoid trivialities, assume that there exist consequences x_*, x, and x^* such that

$$U(x_*) < U(x) < U(x^*)$$

and

$$U(x_*) \leqslant U(y) \quad \text{for all } y \in X.$$

DM's risk preferences possess many interesting characteristics: They do not satisfy Savage's axioms, cannot be rationalized by an expected utility index, and exhibit a remarkable aversion to uncertainty. Below we shall derive a modified version of Savage's axiom system which our DM's ordering of acts satisfies, establish an integral representation of his risk preferences, and characterize his aversion to uncertainty. We begin with the modified version of Savage's axiom system.

19.6.1 Belief Functions and the Axioms of Savage

To establish the required modification of Savage's axioms we need the following obviously valid theorem:

T 19.9 Let $\preceq$ denote the ordering of acts induced by the $V(\cdot)$ of equation 19.28 and let $\preceq^*$ denote the ordering of consequences induced by $U(\cdot)$. Then $\preceq$ and $\preceq^*$ are well defined and satisfy, respectively, Savage's axioms SA 1 and SA 7.

Next we give an example which demonstrates that our DM's risk preferences do not satisfy the sure-thing principle, SA 4.

E 19.14 Consider our DM; suppose that $\Omega = \{\omega_1, \omega_2, \omega_3\}$; and let $m(\cdot): \mathscr{F} \to [0, 1]$ be given by

$$m(\varnothing) = 0; \quad m(\{\omega_1\}) = 1/6, \quad i = 1, 2, 3; \quad m(\{\omega_1, \omega_2\}) = 1/4;$$

$$m(\{\omega_1, \omega_3\}) = m(\{\omega_2, \omega_3\}) = m(\Omega) = 1/12.$$

Moreover, let $x(\cdot): \Omega \to X$ and $y(\cdot): \Omega \to X$ be acts such that $x(\omega_2) = y(\omega_2)$ and assume that

$$U(x(\omega_1)) < U(x(\omega_2)) < U(x(\omega_3))$$

and

$$U(y(\omega_1)) > U(y(\omega_2)) > U(y(\omega_3)).$$

When $U(x(\omega_1)) = 6$, $U(x(\omega_2)) = 12$, $U(x(\omega_3)) = 15$, $U(y(\omega_1)) = 20$, and $U(y(\omega_3)) = 2$, then

$$V(x) = 8\tfrac{1}{2} > 8\tfrac{1}{3} = V(y).$$

Next let x_m and y_m be x and y modified so that they assume the value z at ω_2 and assume that $U(z) = 18$. Then

$$V(x_m) = 10\tfrac{1}{4} < 11\tfrac{2}{3} = V(y_m).$$

There is a modification of SA 4 which $\preceq$ satisfies. To state it succinctly, we need the following notation concerning an act $x \in X^\Omega$, a consequence $a \in X$, and an event $A \in \mathscr{F}$:

$$x|_A^a(\omega) = \begin{cases} a & \text{if } \omega \in A \\ x(\omega) & \text{if } \omega \in A^c. \end{cases}$$

T 19.10 Let $x(\cdot)$ and $y(\cdot)$ be acts and let a and b be consequences. Moreover, let A be an event in $\mathscr{F}$ and suppose that the following conditions are satisfied:

(i) $x(\omega) \preceq^* a$ and $x(\omega) \preceq^* b$ if $\omega \in A^C$;

(ii) $y(\omega) \preceq^* a$ and $y(\omega) \preceq^* b$ if $\omega \in A^C$; and

(iii) $x|_A^a(\cdot) \preceq y|_A^a(\cdot)$.

Then $x|_A^b(\cdot) \preceq y|_A^b(\cdot)$ as well. The same relation is true if $\preceq^*$ is replaced by ${}^*\succeq$.

I shall prove the theorem for the case when conditions i and ii are as stated and leave the case when $\preceq^*$ is replaced by ${}^*\succeq$ to the reader. Under the hypotheses of the theorem,

$$V(x|_A^a) = U(a)\,\mathrm{bel}(A) + \sum_{\substack{D\subset\Omega \\ D\not\subset A}} w_x(D)m(D)$$

and

$$V(y|_A^a) = U(a)\mathrm{bel}(A) + \sum_{\substack{D\subset\Omega \\ D\not\subset A}} w_y(D)m(D).$$

Hence $V(x|_A^a) \leqslant V(y|_A^a)$ if and only if

$$\sum_{\substack{D\subset\Omega \\ D\not\subset A}} w_x(D)m(D) \leqslant \sum_{\substack{D\subset\Omega \\ D\not\subset A}} w_y(D)m(D),$$

an inequality which is independent of a and b.

Before stating the next theorem we must redefine Savage's notion of conditional preference:

D 1 Let B be an event and let $x(\cdot)$ and $y(\cdot)$ be acts. Then $x(\cdot) \preceq y(\cdot)$ given B if and only if $x(\cdot) \preceq y(\cdot)$ once they have been modified on B^c so as to assume the value x_* there. Moreover, B is a null event if and only if, for all acts $x(\cdot)$ and $y(\cdot)$, $x(\cdot) \preceq y(\cdot)$ given B.

The motivation behind this definition can be seen from E 19.4 below and the next theorem, which I state without proof.

T 19.11 Let $x(\cdot)$ and $y(\cdot)$ be constant acts that assume the values x and y, respectively, in X; and let B be an event. If B is not a null event, $x(\cdot) \preceq y(\cdot)$ given B if and only if $x \preceq^* y$.

Hence the decision maker's ordering of consequences is independent of the event he might have observed.

Theorem T 19.11 differs from SA 5 only to the extent that I have changed the definition of conditional preference. How important this change is can be intuited from the following example.

E 19.15 Consider our DM and let $x(\cdot)$ and $y(\cdot)$ be acts such that

$$U(x(\omega)) = \begin{cases} a & \text{if } \omega \in B \\ d & \text{if } \omega \in B^C \end{cases}$$

$$U(y(\omega)) = \begin{cases} b & \text{if } \omega \in B \\ d & \text{if } \omega \in B^C. \end{cases}$$

Then

$$V(x) = a \cdot \sum_{A \subset B} m(A) + d \sum_{A \subset B^C} m(A) + (\min\{a, d\}) \cdot \sum_{\substack{A \cap B^C \neq \varnothing \\ A \not\subset B^C}} m(A),$$

$$V(y) = b \cdot \sum_{A \subset B} m(A) + d \cdot \sum_{A \subset B^C} m(A) + (\min\{b, d\}) \cdot \sum_{\substack{A \cap B^C \neq \varnothing \\ A \not\subset B^C}} m(A).$$

Suppose next that $x(\cdot)$ and $y(\cdot)$ do not vary on B and assume the values x and y, respectively, there. Moreover, assume that $a < b$, that $m(A) \neq 0$ for some A such that $A \cap B^C \neq \varnothing$ and that $\mathrm{bel}(B) = 0$. Then $x \prec^* y$ and $V(x) = V(y)$ or $V(x) < V(y)$ according as $d < a$ or $d > a$.

The preceding theorems demonstrate that our DM's risk preferences satisfy the conditions of SA 1–SA 3, SA 7, and modified versions of SA 4 and SA 5. Next we shall show that DM's ordering of acts satisfy SA 6.

T 19.12 Let $\preceq$ and $\preceq^*$ be as described in T 19.9 and let a, b, c, and d be consequences such that

$a \prec^* b$ and $c \prec^* d$.

Moreover, let $x(\cdot)$ and $y(\cdot)$ be constant acts that assume the values a and c, respectively. Finally, let A and B be events. Then

$x|_B^b \preceq x|_A^b$ iff $y|_B^d \preceq y|_A^d$.

The proof is as follows: Observe first that

$$V(x|_A^b) - V(x|_B^b) = U(b)(\mathrm{bel}(A) - \mathrm{bel}(B)) + U(a)\left[\sum_{\substack{D \subset \Omega \\ D \not\subset A}} m(D) - \sum_{\substack{D \subset \Omega \\ D \not\subset B}} m(D)\right]$$

$$= U(b)[\mathrm{bel}(A) - \mathrm{bel}(B)]$$

$$+ U(a)\left[\sum_{\substack{D \subset (A \cup B) \\ D \not\subset A}} m(D) - \sum_{\substack{D \subset (A \cup B) \\ D \not\subset B}} m(D)\right]$$

$$= (U(b) - U(a))(\mathrm{bel}(A) - \mathrm{bel}(B)). \tag{19.29}$$

By analogy, $V(y|_A^d) - V(y|_B^d) = (U(d) - U(c))(\mathrm{bel}(A) - \mathrm{bel}(B))$. The validity of the theorem follows from this and from equation 19.29.

From the preceding theorem we deduce that our DM's risk preferences satisfy SA 6. Hence we have shown that they satisfy SA 1–SA 3, SA 6 and SA 7, and the modified versions of SA 4 and SA 5 that we described in T 19.10 and T 19.11, respectively. Since Ω is finite, we cannot here present modified versions of SA 8 and SA 9 which DM's risk preferences satisfy.

19.6.2 Belief Functions, Qualitative Probability, and Expected Utility

Savage needed SA 8 to rationalize his DM's ordering of events by a subjective probability measure, and he needed SA 8 and SA 9 to rationalize his DM's ordering of acts by an expected-utility index. In this section I shall (1) show that our DM's belief function can be used to rationalize his ordering of events and (2) obtain an integral representation of his ordering of acts.

T 19.13 Let $a \in X$ be such that $x_* \prec^* a$ and suppose that $x(\cdot): \Omega \to x_*$. Moreover, let $\leqslant$ be a binary relation in $\mathscr{F}$ defined by

$$A \leqslant B \text{ iff } V(x|_A^a) \leqslant V(x|_B^a).$$

Then $\leqslant$ is well defined, total, reflexive, and transitive. Moreover,

$$A \leqslant B \text{ iff } \mathrm{bel}(A) \leqslant \mathrm{bel}(B) \tag{19.30}$$

and A is null if and only if $\mathrm{bel}(A) = 0$.

The fact that $\leqslant$ is total, reflexive, and transitive is obvious, and the validity of equation 19.30 is an easy consequence of equation 19.29 with $b \neq a$ and $a = x_*$.

In reading T 19.12 it is interesting to observe that the ordering of acts induced by $V(x|_{(\cdot)}^a)$ is not a qualitative probability. To wit: It is false that if A, B, and C are events such that $((A \cup B) \cap C) = \varnothing$, then

$$(A \cup C) \leqslant (B \cup C) \text{ iff } A \leqslant B.$$

Counterexamples are easy to construct since it is false that

$$\mathrm{bel}(A \cup C) \leqslant \mathrm{bel}(B \cup C) \text{ iff } \mathrm{bel}(A) \leqslant \mathrm{bel}(B).$$

Next we shall establish an integral representation of our DM's risk preferences that is due to Kjell Arne Brekke.

T 19.14 Let $(\Omega, \mathscr{F})$, $m(\cdot)$, $\mathrm{bel}(\cdot)$, X, and $U(\cdot)$ be as described above. Moreover, let $w_x(\cdot): \mathscr{F} \to R$ and $V(\cdot): X^\Omega \to R$, respectively, be as defined in equations 19.27 and 19.28. Then $w_x(\cdot)$ and $V(x)$ are well defined for all $x \in X^\Omega$. Moreover,

$$V(x) = \int_0^\infty \mathrm{bel}(\{\omega \in \Omega: U(x(\omega)) \geqslant t\})\, dt, \qquad x \in X^\Omega. \tag{19.31}$$

To see why equation 19.31 is valid, pick an $x \in X^\Omega$; let $U_i = U(x(\omega_i))$, $i = 1, \ldots, n$; let $U_0 = 0$; and assume for simplicity that $U_0 < U_1 < \cdots < U_n$. Then observe that

$$\int_0^\infty \text{bel}(\{\omega \in \Omega : U(x(\omega)) \geqslant t\})\,dt$$

$$= \sum_{i=1}^{n} \int_{U_{i-1}}^{U_i} \text{bel}(\{\omega \in \Omega : U(x(\omega)) \geqslant t\})\,dt$$

$$+ \int_{U_n}^{\infty} \text{bel}(\{\omega \in \Omega : U(x(\omega)) \geqslant t\})\,dt$$

$$= \sum_{i=1}^{n} (U_i - U_{i-1})\,\text{bel}(\{\omega \in \Omega : U(x(\omega)) \geqslant U_i\})$$

$$= \sum_{i=1}^{n} U_i(\text{bel}(\{\omega \in \Omega : U(x(\omega)) \geqslant U_i\})$$

$$- \text{bel}(\{\omega \in \Omega : U(x(\omega)) \geqslant U_{i+1}\}))$$

$$= \sum_{A \subset \Omega} w_x(A)m(A),$$

as was to be shown.[4]

It is easy to see from the proof of equation 19.31 that if bel(·) is additive, then our DM ranks acts according to their expected utility. From this we conclude that equations 19.27 and 19.28 represent the natural analogue of the expected-utility hypothesis in cases where subjective probabilities are superadditive.

19.6.3 Belief Functions and Uncertainty Aversion

Next I shall present a theorem in which I characterize our DM's aversion to uncertainty. The import of the theorem stems from the following considerations: A decision maker facing a risky situation (i.e., an experiment whose intrinsic probabilities either are known or can be known by analysis) is said to be risk-averse if (1) he ranks acts according to their expected utility and (2) his utility function is concave. Our DM faces an uncertain situation (i.e., an experiment whose intrinsic probabilities neither are known nor can be known by reason alone). He might, but need not, rank acts according to their expected utility and his utility function need not be concave. Hence it is not certain that our DM is risk-averse. However, his ordering of acts does reflect an aversion to uncertainty which is characteristic of people who shade their probability assignments in the face of uncertainty. To wit, note equation 19.31 and the following theorem, the idea of which I owe to Alain Chateauneuf (theorems 1 and 2, 1986, p. 17).

T 19.15 Let $(\Omega, \mathscr{F})$, $m(\cdot)$, $\text{bel}(\cdot)$, X, $U(\cdot)$, and $V(\cdot)$ be as in T 19.14. Moreover, let

$$P = \left\{p(\cdot)\colon \Omega \to [0, 1]\colon \sum_{i=1}^{n} p(\omega_i) = 1\right\}$$

and, for each $p \in P$, let $P_p(\cdot)\colon \mathscr{F} \to [0, 1]$ be such that

$$P_p(A) = \sum_{\omega_i \in A} p(\omega_i), \qquad A \in \mathscr{F}.$$

Finally, let

$$C = \{p \in P\colon \text{for all } A \in \mathscr{F},\ P_p(A) \geqslant \text{bel}(A)\}.$$

Then, for all $x \in X^{\Omega}$,

$$V(x) = \min_{p \in C} \sum_{i=1}^{n} U(x(\omega_i))p(\omega_i). \tag{19.32}$$

To prove the theorem we first show that, for all $x \in X^{\Omega}$ and $p \in C$,

$$V(x) \leqslant \sum_{i=1}^{n} U(x(\omega_i))p(\omega_i). \tag{19.33}$$

Let $x \in X^{\Omega}$ and $p \in C$ be given, and define j_i, $i = 0, 1, \ldots, n$, such that if $U_{j_i} = U(x(\omega_{j_i}))$, then $U_{j_0} = 0$ and $0 \leqslant U_{j_i} \leqslant U_{j_{i+1}}$, $i = 1, \ldots, n-1$. From these inequalities, the proof of equation 19.31, and the definition of C, it follows that

$$V(x) = \sum_{i=1}^{n} (U_{j_i} - U_{j_{i-1}})\,\text{bel}(\{\omega \in \Omega\colon U(x(\omega)) \geqslant U_{j_i}\})$$

$$\leqslant \sum_{i=1}^{n} (U_{j_i} - U_{j_{i-1}})\left[\sum_{k=i}^{n} p(\omega_{j_k})\right] = \sum_{k=1}^{n} U_{j_k}p(\omega_{j_k}).$$

Next we shall show that, for each $x \in X^{\Omega}$, there is a $p \in C$ such that equality holds in equation 19.33. To do that we fix $x \in X^{\Omega}$ and define the j_i and the U_{j_i} as above. Moreover, we let

$$p(\omega_{j_i}) = \text{bel}(\{\omega \in \Omega\colon U(x(\omega)) \geqslant U_{j_i}\}) - \text{bel}(\{\omega \in \Omega\colon U(x(\omega)) \geqslant U_{j_{i+1}}\}), \tag{19.34}$$

where $j = 1, \ldots, n$ and $U_{j_{n+1}}$ is some number greater than U_{j_n}. Then $p(\cdot)$: $\Omega \to [0, 1]$ and it is easy to verify that $\sum_{i=1}^{n} p(\omega_j) = 1$. To show that $p \in C$ we use induction. Observe first that equation 19.34 and the superadditivity of $\text{bel}(\cdot)$ imply that

$$p(\omega_{j_n}) = \text{bel}(\{\omega_{j_n}\}), \qquad p(\omega_{j_{n-1}}) \geqslant \text{bel}(\{\omega_{j_{n-1}}\})$$

and

$P_p(\{\omega_{j_n}, \omega_{j_{n-1}}\}) = \text{bel}(\{\omega_{j_n}, \omega_{j_{n-1}}\}).$

Hence $P_p(A) \geqslant \text{bel}(A)$ for all $A \in \mathscr{P}(\{\omega_{j_n}\})$ and for all $A \in \mathscr{P}(\{\omega_{j_n}, \omega_{j_{n-1}}\})$.

Suppose next that $P_p(A) \geqslant \text{bel}(A)$ for all $A \in \mathscr{P}(\{\omega_{j_n}, \ldots, \omega_{j_{n-i}}\})$. We shall show that it is also true for all $A \in \mathscr{P}(\{\omega_{j_n}, \ldots, \omega_{j_{n-i-1}}\})$. To do that, it suffices to consider sets of the form $(\{\omega_{j_{n-i-1}}\} \cup B)$, where $B \in \mathscr{P}(\{\omega_{j_n}, \ldots, \omega_{j_{n-i}}\})$. Let A be such a set. Then the inequality

$$\text{bel}(A) + \text{bel}(\{\omega_{j_n}, \ldots, \omega_{j_{n-i}}\}) - \text{bel}(B) \leqslant \text{bel}(\{\omega_{j_n}, \ldots, \omega_{j_{n-i-1}}\}),$$

equation 19.34, and the induction hypothesis imply that

$$\text{bel}(A) \leqslant p(\omega_{j_{n-i-1}}) + P_p(B) = P_p(A).$$

Since $p \in C$, equation 19.34 and

$$V(x) = \sum_{i=1}^{n} U_{j_i}(\text{bel}(\{\omega \in \Omega : U(x(\omega)) \geqslant U_{j_i}\}) - \text{bel}(\{\omega \in \Omega : U(x(\omega)) \geqslant U_{j_{i+1}}\})) \tag{19.35}$$

imply that equality must hold in equation 19.33 for the $p(\cdot)$ we defined in equation 19.34. This and the arbitrary choice of $x \in X^{\Omega}$ establish the validity of T 19.15.

19.6.4 Examples

In this section I shall give two examples which illustrate how the risk preferences described in equations 19.27 and 19.28 can be used to rationalize experimental behavior that does not accord with the expected-utility hypothesis. We begin with the Ellsberg Paradox.

E 19.16 Consider the experimental situation described in E 19.1 and suppose that a decision maker assigns the following basic probabilities to the subsets of Ω:

$$m(A) = \begin{cases} 1/3 & \text{if } A = C_{\text{red}} \\ \varepsilon/6 & \text{if } A = C_{\text{black}} \text{ or } A = C_{\text{yellow}} \\ (2-\varepsilon)/3 & \text{if } A = (C_{\text{black}} \cup C_{\text{yellow}}) \\ 0 & \text{otherwise} \end{cases}$$

where ε is a very small positive number and C_i is short for $\{\omega \in \Omega : \omega \in C_i\}$.

Moreover, suppose that the same decision maker's utility of consequences is given by

$$U(0) = 0 \qquad \text{and} \qquad U(\$100) = 100$$

and that he ranks acts in accordance with equations 19.27 and 19.28. Finally, let $\tilde{x}_1$, $\tilde{x}_2$, $\tilde{x}_3$, and $\tilde{x}_4$ be the acts described in E 19.1. Then

$V(\tilde{x}_2) < V(\tilde{x}_1) < V(\tilde{x}_3) < V(\tilde{x}_4)$,

which accords with the ranking of the thirteen "exceptional" cases in equation 19.2.

Next we shall consider a variation on the theme of the so-called Allais Paradox (see Allais 1979, pp. 437–638).

E 19.17 Consider an urn with 100 balls that differ only in color and assume that there are eighty-nine red balls, ten black balls, and one white ball. The urn is shaken well and a blindfolded man is to pull one ball from it. We ask a decision maker, Peter, to rank the components of the following two pairs of acts in which he will receive

α_1: \$1000 regardless of which ball is drawn;

α_2: nothing, \$1000, or \$5000 according as the ball drawn is white, red, or black,

β_1: nothing if the ball is red and \$1000 otherwise;

β_2: nothing if the ball is either red or white and \$5000 if the ball is black.

To rank these acts, Peter lets $\Omega = \{\omega_1, \ldots, \omega_{100}\}$ and insits that ω_i is the name of a red, black, or white ball according as $0 < i \leqslant 89$, $90 \leqslant i \leqslant 99$, and $i = 100$, respectively. Moreover, he lets

$X = \{0, \$1000, \$5000\}$

and notes that his utility function on X is given by

$U(0) = 0, \quad U(\$1000) = 0.85, \quad \text{and} \quad U(\$5000) = 1.$

Finally, Peter decides for himself that the expression "the urn is shaken well" is vague and assigns the following basic probabilities to the subsets of Ω:

$$m(A) = \begin{cases} 0.7 & \text{if } A = \{\omega_1, \ldots, \omega_{89}\} \\ 0.2 & \text{if } A = \{\omega_{90}, \ldots, \omega_{99}\} \\ 0.02 & \text{if } A = \{\omega_{100}\} \\ 0.05 & \text{if } A \text{ is } \{\omega_1, \ldots, \omega_{99}\} \\ 0.03 & \text{if } A \text{ is } \{\omega_1, \ldots, \omega_{89}, \omega_{100}\} \\ 0.01 & \text{if } A \text{ is } \{\omega_{90}, \ldots, \omega_{100}\} \\ 0 & \text{otherwise} \end{cases}$$

Now Peter ranks acts in accordance with equations 19.27 and 19.28. Therefore he needs little time to figure that

$V(\tilde{x}_{\alpha_2}) < V(\tilde{x}_{\alpha_1}) \qquad \text{and} \qquad V(\tilde{x}_{\beta_1}) < V(\tilde{x}_{\beta_2}).$

This ranking of α_1 and α_2 and β_1 and β_2 cannot be rationalized by the expected-utility hypothesis.

It cannot be rationalized by risk preferences which satisfy axioms SA 4–SA6 and SSA 1–SSA 4 either!

One aspect of the two preceding examples must not go unnoticed: The uncertainty involved in ranking acts in E 19.16 is different from the uncertainty involved in ranking pairs of acts in E 19.17. Both examples describe an experiment in which a ball is to be pulled from an urn. The ball is red, black, or yellow in one experiment and red, black, or white in the other. In E 19.17 there are 100 balls in the urn and equally many states of the world. In E 19.16 there are 90 balls and just three states of the world. The difference reflects the fact that in E 19.17 the balls are numbered as well as colored, while in E 19.16 the balls are just colored and the composition of colors is uncertain.

19.6.5 Concluding Remarks

In this section we have discussed the risk preferences of an individual, DM, who assigns numbers to events in accordance with GS 1–GS 7 in chapter 15. These numbers need not be the values of a probability measure. When they are not, they are the values of a superadditive belief function; and we may think of DM as a decision maker who shades his probabilities in the face of uncertainty. We have shown that DM's ordering of events agrees with his belief function. We have also demonstrated that DM's ordering of acts displays a remarkable aversion to uncertainty. These results help us fill a lacuna in Shafer's theory of belief functions: how to choose among uncertain options with a superadditive probability measure.

In filling the lacuna in Shafer's theory we have ended up with a theory of choice that, for people who shade their probabilities in the face of uncertainty, represents a viable alternative to the expected utility hypothesis. Maurice Allais both initiated and spearheaded the last four decades' search for good alternatives to the expected utility hypothesis. Therefore, a few comments concerning the formal similarities between our theory and Allais' theory of choice among random prospects (1988, pp. 231–289) are in order.

In Allais' theory a random prospect P is an n-tuple of pairs (x_i, p_i), $i = 1, \ldots, n$, where $0 \leqslant x_1 \leqslant x_2 < \cdots \leqslant x_n, p_i \geqslant 0$, $i = 1, \ldots, n$ and $\sum_{i=1}^{n} p_i = 1$. The utility of such a prospect, $W(P)$, is given by

$$W(P) = u(x_1) + \theta(p_2 + \cdots + p_n)(u(x_2) - u(x_1)) + \cdots$$
$$+ \theta(p_n)(u(x_n) - u(x_{n-1})),$$

where $u(\cdot)$: $[1, \infty) \to [0, \infty)$ and $\theta(\cdot)$: $[0, 1] \to [0, 1]$ are strictly increasing continuous functions, $\theta(0) = 0$, and $\theta(1) = 1$. This expression is formally similar to the relation

$$V(x) = \sum_{i=1}^{n} (U_{j_i} - U_{j_{i-1}}) \text{bel}(\{\omega \in \Omega : U(x(\omega)) \geqslant U_{j_i}\}),$$

which we, with the U_{j_i} as described in the proof of T 19.15, established in the course of proving T 19.14.

Allais refers to $\theta(\cdot)$ as the "specific probability function" and insists that it "represents the subject's greater or lesser preference for risk or security." He also observes that if we let $p_{n+1} = 0$ and

$$p_i^* = \theta(p_i + \cdots + p_n) - \theta(p_{i+1} + \cdots + p_n), \qquad i = 1, \ldots, n$$

then $p_i^* \geqslant 0$, $i = 1, \ldots, n$, $\sum_{i=1}^{n} p_i^* = 1$, and

$$W(P) = \sum_{i=1}^{n} p_i^* u(x_i).$$

This expression is formally similar to

$$V(x) = \sum_{i=1}^{n} U_{j_i}(\text{bel}(\{\omega \in \Omega : U(x(\omega)) \geqslant U_{j_i}\}) \\ - \text{bel}(\{\omega \in \Omega : U(x(\omega)) \geqslant U_{j_{i+1}}\})),$$

which we established in the proof of T 19.15. There is, however, a significant difference. In Allais' theory the p_i^* are ordinary weights with no particular meaning (see Allais 1988, p. 237). The corresponding weights in our theory solves an interesting minimization problem (see equations 19.32 and 19.35) and thus reveals our DM's remarkable aversion to uncertainty.

V Nonstandard Analysis

20 Nonstandard Analysis

In this part we shall study nonstandard analysis and some of its applications to economics and probability theory. We begin by delineating the main characteristics of the nonstandard universe. Then we discuss exchange in hyperspace, Loeb probability spaces, and a hyperfinite characterization of the Brownian motion.

Roughly speaking, the nonstandard universe is a transitive subset of an admissible set that satisfies the axioms of KPU, the axiom of infinity, and an axiom which insists that the totality of urelements constitutes a set. The set of urelements is an ordered field of hyperreal numbers containing a complete ordered field of real numbers as a proper subset. It also contains a subset satisfying the axioms of $T(NS)$—the theory of nonstandard natural numbers that was described in E 6.4 and discussed at length in E 7.8–E 7.10.

In pursuit of structural properties of the nonstandard universe we use a strategy that is similar to the one we used in E 7.10 to describe salient properties of $|\eta^*|$. Specifically, we replace the notion of elementarily equivalent structures with a principle of transfer and pass in and out of the universe in search of nonstandard analogues to the theorems in real analysis. The relation of transfer and the idea of elementarily equivalent structures is interesting. Hence we shall discuss it in some detail in this chapter.

There are three features of the set of hyperreal numbers that are important for the applications of nonstandard analysis that we consider: The set contains infinitesimals, infinitely large numbers, and infinite hyperfinite subsets that possess all the properties of finite sets; e.g., infinite hyperfinite sums of numbers are well defined. We shall use these and other properties of the hyperreal numbers to study exchange in an economy with infinitely many agents and to obtain a hyperfinite construction of the Brownian motion.

The purpose of writing the chapters on nonstandard analysis is twofold. I shall introduce the reader to three fundamental ideas of semantics—the transfer principle, the saturation principle, and the standard version of a Loeb probability space. With their help we develop exciting far-from-standard ways of using the axiomatic method and demonstrate the usefulness of semantics in our search for knowledge in economics and econometrics. In addition, we shall provide foolproof evidence in support of the thesis that, *to be adequate, an interpretation of an economic theory must describe one situation in which the empirical relevance of the theory can be tested.* The evidence consists in our demonstrating that the hallmark of most measure-theoretic conceptions of large economies, the idea that core allocations are competitive equilibria, is a topological artifact and not a fundamental property of large economies!

Because of this emphasis on the methodological aspects of nonstandard analysis we shall at times prove theorems that are short of the best available. We shall also, for lack of space, leave unmentioned some topics of importance to mathematical economics. Even so, the following three chapters ought to provide a good, short introduction to nonstandard analysis that will enable an *economist* to delve into any of the problem areas which Robert M. Anderson discusses in his survey article on notions of core convergence (Anderson 1986) and a *physicist* to tackle the problems in mathematical physics that are discussed in *Nonstandard Methods in Stochastic Analysis and Mathematical Physics* (Albeverio et al. 1986).

20.1 The Set of Urelements *U*

In our description of KPU in chapter 9, the set of urelements M came without a structure. For our purposes in part V, the structural characteristics of the set of urelements are of primary importance. Thus I begin this chapter by describing these characteristics.

Let L be a first-order language with two constants, 0 and 1, two binary functions, $+$ and $\cdot$, two unary predicates, U and S, and two binary predicates, $<$ and $\in$. We assume that U, S, and $\in$ satisfy the axioms of KPU, KA 1–KA 9, and the axiom of infinity, KA 10. We also assume that the collection of urelements constitutes a set; i.e.,

NSA 1 $(\exists x)[S(x) \wedge (\forall y)[[y \in x] \equiv U(y)]]$.

By the Axiom of Extension, KA 4, there is only one set that satisfies NSA 1. We denote it by U and take $[x \in U]$ and $U(x)$ to be materially equivalent expressions. In the intended interpretation of L, the set U with $+$, $\cdot$, and $<$ is to be an ordered-field extension of a complete ordered field.

To ensure that it will be, we insist that U satisfy the conditions detailed next.

20.1.1 The Axioms for U

We need twelve axioms to ensure that U with $+$ and $\cdot$ is a field. Here they are:

NSA 2 $[U(0) \wedge U(1)]$

NSA 3 $(\forall x \in U)(\forall y \in U)[[(x + y) \in U] \wedge [(x \cdot y) \in U]]$

NSA 4 $(\forall x \in U)(\forall y \in U)[(x + y) = (y + x)]$

NSA 5 $(\forall x \in U)(\forall y \in U)(\forall z \in U)[(x + (y + z)) = ((x + y) + z)]$

NSA 6 $(\forall x \in U)[(x + 0) = x]$

NSA 7 $(\forall x \in U)(\exists y \in U)[(x + y) = 0]$

NSA 8 $(\forall x \in U)(\forall y \in U)[(x \cdot y) = (y \cdot x)]$

NSA 9 $(\forall x \in U)(\forall y \in U)(\forall z \in U)[(x \cdot (y \cdot z)) = ((x \cdot y) \cdot z)]$

NSA 10 $(\forall x \in U)[(x \cdot 1) = x]$

NSA 11 $(\forall x \in U)[\sim[x = 0] \supset (\exists y \in U)[(x \cdot y) = 1]]$

NSA 12 $\sim[0 = 1]$

NSA 13 $(\forall x \in U)(\forall y \in U)(\forall z \in U)[(x \cdot (y + z)) = ((x \cdot y) + (x \cdot z))]$

To be an ordered field, U must also satisfy the following axioms:

NSA 14 $(\forall x \in U) \sim [x < x]$

NSA 15 $(\forall x \in U)(\forall y \in U)(\forall z \in U)[[[x < y] \wedge [y < z]] \supset [x < z]]$

NSA 16 $(\forall x \in U)(\forall y \in U)[[x < y] \vee [[x = y] \vee [y < x]]]$

NSA 17 $(\forall x \in U)(\forall y \in U)(\forall z \in U)[[x < y] \supset [(x + z) < (y + z)]]$

NSA 18 $(\forall x \in U)(\forall y \in U)(\forall z \in U)[[[x < y] \wedge [0 < z]] \supset [(x \cdot z) < (y \cdot z)]]$

When $+$, $\cdot$, and $<$ are given their intended standard interpretation, the meanings of these axioms become clear. I leave it to the reader to read the axioms aloud.

Finally, U with $+$, $\cdot$, and $<$ is to be an extension of a complete ordered field. To ensure that it is, we insist on the next axiom:

NSA 19 $(\exists z)[[[[[[S(z) \wedge (\forall x \in z)[x \in U]] \wedge \sim[z = U]] \wedge [[0 \in z] \wedge [1 \in z]]] \wedge (\forall x \in z)(\forall y \in z)[[(x + y) \in z] \wedge [(x \cdot y) \in z]]] \wedge (\forall x \in z)[\sim[x = 0] \supset [(\exists y \in z)[(x + y) = 0] \wedge (\exists y \in z)[(x \cdot y) = 1]]]] \wedge [[S(A) \wedge [(\forall x \in A)[x \in z] \wedge (\exists a \in z)(\forall x \in A)[x < a]]] \supset (\exists b \in z)[(\forall x \in A)[[x < b] \vee [x = b]] \wedge [[[a \in z] \wedge (\forall x \in A)[x < a]] \supset [[b < a] \vee [b = a]]]]]]]$

In brief, we insist that there is a proper subset of U that satisfies the conditions of a complete ordered field. Since any two complete ordered fields are isomorphic, there is only one subset of U that constitutes, with $+$, $\cdot$, and $<$, a complete ordered field. For reference I name this subset V.

20.1.2 Structural Characteristics of U

We shall refer to U as the set of *hyperreal numbers* and describe its main characteristics informally. In this discussion we assume that the functional symbols for minus, absolute value, and inverse (that is, $-$, $|\cdot|$, and $(\cdot)^{-1}$) have been introduced in L in such a way that, if $[x \in V]$, then $[-x \in V]$, $[|x| \in V]$, and $[\sim[x = 0] \supset [(x)^{-1} \in V]]$; and if $[x \in U]$, then $[-x \in U]$, $[|x| \in U]$, and $[\sim[x = 0] \supset [(x)^{-1} \in U]]$. We also assume that a predicate symbol V_{++} has been introduced so that $[S(V_{++}) \wedge [(\forall x \in V_{++})[x \in V] \wedge (\forall x \in V)[[x \in V_{++}] \equiv [0 < x]]]]$. Finally, we write $(x - y)$ for $(x + (-y))$, $|x - y|$ for $|(x - y)|$, and x^{-1} for $(x)^{-1}$.

To characterize the set of hyperreal numbers, we use the following concepts:

1. x is *infinitesimal* if $[[x \in U] \wedge (\forall r \in V_{++})[|x| < r]$;
2. x is *finite* if $[[x \in U] \wedge (\exists r \in V_{++})[|x| < r]]$;
3. x is *infinite* if $[[x \in U] \wedge (\forall r \in V_{++})[r < |x|]$; and
4. x, y are *infinitely close* if $[[[x \in U] \wedge [y \in U]] \wedge (\forall r \in V_{++})[|x - y| < r]]$.

When x, y are infinitely close, we write $[x \approx y]$; that is, we have NSD 1:

NSD 1 $[[x \approx y] \equiv [[[x \in U] \wedge [y \in U]] \wedge (\forall r \in V_{++})[|x - y| < r]]]$

Evidently, if $x \in U$, $[x \approx x]$. Also, $[x \approx y]$ if and only if $[y \approx x]$. Finally, if $[x \approx y]$ and $[y \approx z]$, the properties of $|\cdot|$ imply that $[x \approx z]$ as well. Hence $\approx$ is an equivalence relation in U. The set of all y such that $x \approx y$ is called the *monad* of x and is introduced in L by NSD 2.

NSD 2 $[[z = \text{monad}(x)] \equiv [S(z) \wedge (\forall y \in U)[[y \in z] \equiv [y \approx x]]]]$

By KA 8 there is a set z that satisfies the right-hand side of NSD 2. Since $\approx$ is an equivalence relation, there can be only one such set. Hence we can introduce monad$(\cdot)$ in L via NSD 2; we then show the following:

T 20.1 $(\forall y \in U)[[y \in \text{monad}(x)] \equiv [y \approx x]]$

Since $\approx$ is an equivalence relation, T 20.2 follows easily:

T 20.2 $(\forall x \in U)(\forall y \in U)[[\text{monad}(x) = \text{monad}(y)] \vee [(\text{monad}(x) \cap \text{monad}(y)) = \varnothing]]$

Moreover, it is not difficult to show T 20.3:

T 20.3 $[[[x \in U] \wedge (\exists r \in V_{++})[|x| < r]] \supset [(\exists s \in V)[s \in \text{monad}(x)] \wedge [[[r \in V] \wedge [r \in \text{monad}(x)]] \supset [r = s]]]]$

i.e., if x is finite, there is one and only one element in V that belongs to monad(x). This element is called the *standard part* of x and is denoted by st(x); we then have NSD 3:

NSD 3 $[[y = \text{st}(x)] \equiv [[y \in V] \wedge [y \in \text{monad}(x)]]]$

To see that there is such a number, fix x and let A denote the set of $r \in V$ such that $r < x$. Then A is nonempty and has an upper bound. By NSA 19, it has a least upper bound $c \in V$. For all $s > 0$, $s \in V$, it is easy to see that $x - c < s$ and $-(x - c) < s$. Hence $|x - c| < s$ and c is infinitely close to x; that is, $c \in \text{monad}(x)$. There can be only one real number in monad(x).

Above we talked about infinitesimals and infinite hyperreals. Such number exist:

T 20.4 $[[(\exists x \in U)(\forall r \in V_{++})[|x| < r] \wedge (\exists y \in U)(\forall r \in V_{++})[|y| > r]]$

To see why, recall that U is a proper extension of V and pick any x in $(U - V)$. If x is infinite, x^{-1} is infinitesimal. If x is finite, let $c \in V$ belong to monad(x). Then $(x - c)$ is infinitesimal and $(x - c)^{-1}$ is an infinite element of U.

It is suggestive to think of the set of finite hyperreal numbers as the union of disjoint monads, one monad for each $x \in V$; that is, $[[[y \in U] \wedge (\exists r \in V_{++})[|y| < r]] \supset [y \in \bigcup_{x \in V} \text{monad}(x)]]$. Similarly, we can think of U as the union of disjoint galaxies. Here the *galaxy* of an x in U, galaxy(x), is the set of hyperreal y such that $|x - y|$ is finite. Evidently, $V \subset \text{galaxy}(0)$. Furthermore, if x and y are hyperreal and $\sim[x = y]$, their galaxies are either identical or disjoint. Hence U can be covered by a suitable union of disjoint galaxies.

20.2 A Model of the Axioms for U

We know that there exist complete ordered fields. Let R with the standard version of $+$, $\cdot$, and $<$ be one of them. In this section we use R to show that there are interpretations of U, V, $+$, $\cdot$, and $<$ in which V with $+$, $\cdot$, and $<$ is a complete ordered field and U with the same $+$, $\cdot$, and $<$ is an ordered-field extension of V. Our discussion will be informal. Moreover, we shall argue outside KPU. Our arguments can be made precise by formulating them in a set theory based on KA 2, KA 4–KA 7, KA 8 with unrestricted φ, KA 10, an axiom that asserts the existence of the power set of any set, and Zorn's Lemma. The latter asserts that if X is a partially ordered set and if every totally ordered subset of X has an upper bound, then X contains a maximal element. We need Zorn's Lemma to establish the existence of free ultrafilters over the set of natural numbers, and we need free ultrafilters to construct an ordered-field extension of R.

20.2.1 Free Ultrafilters over N

If we let N denote the set of natural numbers, we can define free ultrafilters over N as follows:

UD 9 Let $\mathcal{U}$ be a family of subsets of N with the following properties:
(i) $A \in \mathcal{U}$, $B \subset N$, and $A \subset B$ imply $B \in \mathcal{U}$;
(ii) $A, B \in \mathcal{U}$ imply $(A \cap B) \in \mathcal{U}$;
(iii) $N \in \mathcal{U}$ and $\sim[\varnothing \in \mathcal{U}]$;
(iv) $A \subset N$ implies that either $A \in \mathcal{U}$ or $(N - A) \in \mathcal{U}$;
(v) if $A \subset N$ and A is finite, then $\sim[A \in \mathcal{U}]$.
Then $\mathcal{U}$ is a free ultrafilter over N.

In this definition conditions i–iii assert that $\mathcal{U}$ is a *filter*; condition iv adds that $\mathcal{U}$ is an *ultrafilter*; and condition v insists that $\mathcal{U}$ is *free*. An example of a filter that is not an ultrafilter is the family of all subsets of N containing all but a finite number of elements of N. For $\mathcal{U}$ to be an ultrafilter, either the set of all odd numbers or the set of all even numbers and zero, but not both, must belong to $\mathcal{U}$. An example of an ultrafilter is the family of subsets of N that has $\{x_0\}$ as a subset, where $x_0 \in N$ is an arbitrarily chosen number. This ultrafilter is not free, however.

We have the following for a fact:

UT 19 There exists a free ultrafilter over N.

To see why, let $\mathscr{A}$ be the set of all filters over N that contain the complements of all finite subsets of N. If $A_i \in \mathscr{A}$, $i = 1, 2, \ldots$, and $A_i \subset A_{i+1}$, $i = 1, 2, \ldots$, then $\bigcup_{i=1}^{\infty} A_i \in \mathscr{A}$. More generally, $\mathscr{A}$ is partially ordered by $\subset$; and any totally ordered subset has an upper bound with respect to $\subset$, the union of the members of the set. By Zorn's Lemma, $\mathscr{A}$

contains a maximal element $\mathscr{U}$. We shall see that $\mathscr{U}$ is an ultrafilter. Since $\mathscr{U}$ is a filter containing all complements of finite sets and not containing $\emptyset$, we observe that $\mathscr{U}$ contains no finite sets. Hence if $\mathscr{U}$ is an ultrafilter, it is a free ultrafilter.

Let $X \subset N$. We shall show that either X or $(N - X)$ belongs to $\mathscr{U}$. To do that we must consider two cases:

Case 1 For all $Y \in \mathscr{U}$, $(X \cap Y)$ is infinite, i.e., contains infinitely many numbers. Then

$\tilde{V} = \{Z \subset N: X \cap Y \subset Z \text{ for some } Y \in \mathscr{U}\}$

is a free filter that has X as an element and contains $\mathscr{U}$. Since $\mathscr{U}$ is maximal, $\tilde{V} = \mathscr{U}$ and $X \in \mathscr{U}$.

Case 2 For some $Y \in \mathscr{U}$, $(X \cap Y)$ is finite. Then $(N - X) \cap Y$ is infinite. Suppose that $(N - X) \cap Z$ is finite for some $Z \in \mathscr{U}$. Then $(N - X) \cap Z \cap Y$ and $X \cap Y \cap Z$ are both finite. Hence $Y \cap Z$ is finite, which is a contradiction showing that $(N - X) \cap Y$ is infinite for all $Y \in \mathscr{U}$. By the argument used above, we conclude that $(N - X) \in \mathscr{U}$.

20.2.2 An Ordered Field of Hyperreal Numbers *R

There exists at least one free ultrafilter over N. In fact, infinitely many exist. We shall use one of these free ultrafilters to establish the validity of a fundamental universal theorem of A. Robinson:

UT 20 There exists an ordered-field extension of R.

In the proof of the theorem we let $\mathscr{U}$ be a given free ultrafilter over N. We also let $R^N = \{\{a_n\}: a_n \in R \text{ for } n = 0, 1, \ldots\}$ and we let ${}^*R = R^N/\mathscr{U}$ be the set of $\mathscr{U}$-equivalence classes in R^N.

The definition of *R is obtained in the following way: Let $\{a_n\}$ and $\{b_n\}$ belong to R^N. We say that

$\{a_n\} \sim_{\mathscr{U}} \{b_n\}$ iff $\{n \in N: a_n = b_n\} \in \mathscr{U}$.

Since $N \in \mathscr{U}$, $\{a_n\} \sim_{\mathscr{U}} \{a_n\}$. In addition, $\{a_n\} \sim_{\mathscr{U}} \{b_n\}$ if and only if $\{b_n\} \sim_{\mathscr{U}} \{a_n\}$. Finally, properties i and ii of $\mathscr{U}$ (see UD 9 in the previous section) can be seen to imply that if $\{a_n\} \sim_{\mathscr{U}} \{b_n\}$ and $\{b_n\} \sim_{\mathscr{U}} \{c_n\}$, then $\{a_n\} \sim_{\mathscr{U}} \{c_n\}$ as well. Hence $\sim_{\mathscr{U}}$ is an equivalence relation on R^N. Next, for each $a \in R^N$, we let $a_{\mathscr{U}} = \{b \in R^N: a \sim_{\mathscr{U}} b\}$. Then *R is well defined by ${}^*R = \{a_{\mathscr{U}}: a \in R^N\}$ since if $\{a_n\} \in a_{\mathscr{U}}$ and $\{b_n\} \in b_{\mathscr{U}}$,

(i) $a_{\mathscr{U}} = b_{\mathscr{U}}$ if and only if $\{n \in N: a_n = b_n\} \in \mathscr{U}$.

Next let $\tilde{L}$ be L without the predicates U, S, and $\in$. Also let $\mathscr{D}$ be a structure for $\tilde{L}$ in which

(ii) $|\mathscr{D}| = {}^*R$, $\mathscr{D}(0) = \{0\}_{\mathscr{U}}$, and $\mathscr{D}(1) = \{1\}_{\mathscr{U}}$;
(iii) $a_{\mathscr{U}} < b_{\mathscr{U}}$ if and only if $\{n \in N: a_n < b_n\} \in \mathscr{U}$;
(iv) $(a_{\mathscr{U}} + b_{\mathscr{U}}) = c_{\mathscr{U}}$ if and only if $\{n \in N: (a_n + b_n) = c_n\} \in \mathscr{U}$; and
(v) $(a_{\mathscr{U}} \cdot b_{\mathscr{U}}) = c_{\mathscr{U}}$ if and only if $\{n \in N: (a_n \cdot b_n) = c_n\} \in \mathscr{U}$.

Then it is a routine matter to verify that $\mathscr{D}$ is a model of NSA 4–NSA 18, with $(\forall u \in U)$ and $(\exists u \in U)$, respectively, replaced by $(\forall u)$ and $(\exists u)$, where u varies over x, y, and z.

The preceding observation shows that $^*R$, with 0, 1, $<$, $+$, and $\cdot$ as depicted in conditions ii–v above, is an ordered field. To show that $^*R$ is an ordered-field extension of a complete ordered field, we proceed as follows: Let $^*: R \to {}^*R$ be a one-to-one mapping of R into $^*R$ in which $^*r = r_{\mathscr{U}}$ for each $r \in R$ and $r_{\mathscr{U}}$ is short for $\{r\}_{\mathscr{U}}$. Then $^*0 = 0_{\mathscr{U}}$ and $^*1 = 1_{\mathscr{U}}$. Also, since $N \in \mathscr{U}$, $^*r = {}^*s$ if and only if $r = s$; $^*r < {}^*s$ if and only if $r < s$; $({}^*r + {}^*s) = {}^*t$ if and only if $(r + s) = t$; and $({}^*r \cdot {}^*s) = {}^*t$ if and only if $(r \cdot s) = t$. Finally, if we let $^{\sigma}R$ denote the * image of R in $^*R$, $^*: R \to {}^{\sigma}R$ is a bijection. Consequently, the structures $\mathscr{A} = (R, N_{\mathscr{A}}, F^R, G^R)$ and $\mathscr{B} = ({}^{\sigma}R, N_{\mathscr{B}}, F^{\mathscr{B}}, G^{\mathscr{B}})$, where F^R and G^R contain the standard versions of $+$, $\cdot$, and $<$, are isomorphic; that is, $^{\sigma}R$ with the definition of 0, 1, $<$, $+$, and $\cdot$ given in conditions ii–v above is isomorphic to the complete ordered field R with the standard versions of 0, 1, $<$, $+$, and $\cdot$. From this it follows that $^{\sigma}R$ with the given definitions of 0, 1, $<$, $+$, and $\cdot$ is a complete ordered field. Since $^{\sigma}R \subset {}^*R$ and $\sim[{}^{\sigma}R = {}^*R)$, we have shown that $^*R$ is an ordered-field extension of a complete ordered field.

E 20.1 If $\varepsilon = \{n^{-1}\}_{\mathscr{U}}$ and $\delta = \{n^{-2}\}_{\mathscr{U}}$ then both are infinitesimal and $(\varepsilon + \delta) = \{n^{-1} + n^{-2}\}_{\mathscr{U}}$, $(\varepsilon \cdot \delta) = \{n^{-3}\}_{\mathscr{U}}$, $(\delta \cdot \varepsilon^{-1}) = \{n^{-1}\}_{\mathscr{U}}$, and $(\varepsilon \cdot \delta^{-1}) = \{n\}_{\mathscr{U}}$. Notice that $\varepsilon > \delta$ and that $\{r\}_{\mathscr{U}} < \{n\}_{\mathscr{U}}$ for all $r > 0$, $r \in R$. Hence $\{n\}_{\mathscr{U}}$ is an infinite number in $^*R$. So is $\varphi = \{n^2\}_{\mathscr{U}}$. Finally, $\varphi \cdot \varepsilon = \{n\}_{\mathscr{U}}$ and $\varphi \cdot \delta = \{1\}_{\mathscr{U}}$.

The preceding arguments conclude our proof of the existence of interpretations of U, V, $+$, $\cdot$, and $<$ in which V with $+$, $\cdot$, and $<$ is a complete ordered field and U with the same $+$, $\cdot$, and $<$ is a ordered-field extension of V. In the sequel we usually use $^*R$, R, $+$, $\cdot$, and $<$ to denote such an interpretation of U, V, $+$, $\cdot$, and $<$. However, we feel free to interpret U as $^*R$; V as the * image in $^*R$ of some complete ordered field; and $+$, $\cdot$, and $<$ as in conditions iii–v whenever that seems useful.

20.3 Elementarily Equivalent Structures and Transfer

Before we proceed to construct the nonstandard universe, it would be useful to take a second look at $\tilde{L}$ and the structures, $\mathscr{A} = (R, N_{\mathscr{A}}, F^R, G^R)$, $\mathscr{B} = ({}^\sigma R, N_{\mathscr{B}}, F^{\mathscr{B}}, G^{\mathscr{B}})$, and $\mathscr{D} = ({}^*R, N_{\mathscr{D}}, F^{\mathscr{D}}, G^{\mathscr{D}})$.

20.3.1 Two Elementarily Equivalent Structures

We have observed that $\mathscr{A}$ is isomorphic to $\mathscr{B}$. Hence a closed wff A in $\tilde{L}$ is valid in $\mathscr{A}$ if and only if A is valid in $\mathscr{B}$. In the next theorem we insist that A is valid in $\mathscr{A}$ if and only if A is vaid in $\mathscr{D}$. In fact, we postulate the following theorem:

T 20.5 $\mathscr{D}$ is an elementary extension of $\mathscr{B}$ and $\mathscr{A}$ and $\mathscr{D}$ are elementarily equivalent.

We saw above the $\mathscr{B}$ is a substructure of $\mathscr{D}$. To demonstrate that $\mathscr{D}$ is an elementary extension of $\mathscr{B}$, we shall apply TM 7.6 and make use of a theorem of J. Łos's, T 20.9, which I state and prove below.

Suppose that A is a wff of $\tilde{L}$ with exactly $(m + 1)$ free variables, $x_1, \ldots, x_m$, x, and let $a_1, \ldots, a_m$ be individuals in $|\mathscr{B}|$ with names $k_{a_1}, \ldots, k_{a_m}$. Suppose also that b is an individual in $|\mathscr{D}|$ with name k_b and that

$$\mathscr{D}(A_{x_1,\ldots,x_m,x}(k_{a_1}, \ldots, k_{a_m}, k_b)) = t.$$

By Łos's theorem this can happen only if $\{n \in N: \mathscr{A}(A_{x_1,\ldots,x_m,x}(k_{a_1}, \ldots, k_{a_m}, k_{b_n})) = t\} \in \mathscr{U}$, where b_n is an individual in $|\mathscr{A}|$ with name k_{b_n}, $n = 1, 2, \ldots$, and $b \sim_{\mathscr{U}} \{b_n\}$. But if that is the case, there is an $n_0 \in N$ and $a \in |\mathscr{B}|$ with name k_a such that $a \sim_{\mathscr{U}} \{b_{n_0}\}$ and such that, first, $\{n \in N: \mathscr{A}(A_{x_1,\ldots,x_m,x}(k_{a_1}, \ldots, k_{a_m}, k_{b_{n_0}}) = t\} \in \mathscr{U}$, and then, by Łos's theorem, T 20.9,

$$\mathscr{D}(A_{x_1,\ldots,x_m,x}(k_{a_1}, \ldots, k_{a_m}, k_a)) = t.$$

From this and TM 7.6 it follows that $\mathscr{D}$ is an elementary extension of $\mathscr{B}$.

Since $\mathscr{A}$ and $\mathscr{B}$ are isomorphic, the preceding result obviously implies that $\mathscr{A}$ and $\mathscr{D}$ are elementarily equivalent.

20.3.2 Transfer

So much for the $\mathscr{A}$, $\mathscr{B}$, and $\mathscr{D}$ of section 20.2.2. Next let $\hat{L}$ be $\tilde{L}$ with a finite or denumerably infinite number of additional functional and predicate constants. Let $\mathscr{A}$ and $\mathscr{D}$ be structures for $\hat{L}$ so that $|\mathscr{A}| = R$, and $|\mathscr{A}|$ with the $\mathscr{A}$ versions of 0, 1, +, ·, and <, is a complete ordered field; $|\mathscr{D}| = {}^*R$, and $|\mathscr{D}|$ with the $\mathscr{D}$ versions of 0, 1, +, ·, and <, is an ordered-field extension of R; and $N_{\mathscr{A}} \subset N_{\mathscr{D}}$, with identical constants naming the same objects. In addition, let $^*(\cdot)$ be the identity mapping from $|\mathscr{A}|$ to $|\mathscr{D}|$, and observe that for each constant term z of $\hat{L}(\mathscr{A})$, $^*(\cdot)$ maps $\mathscr{A}(z)$ into itself. Finally, if f is one of the functional symbols and P is one of the predicate symbols of $\hat{L}$, let f and P denote their interpretations in $\mathscr{A}$ and $^*f$ and $^*P$ denote their interpretations in $\mathscr{D}$. Then $^*(\cdot)$ is an *embedding* of $\mathscr{A}$ in $\mathscr{D}$ if and only if, for any n and n-ary f and P and for all variable-free terms $z_1, \ldots, z_n$ in $\hat{L}(\mathscr{A})$,

(i) $f(\mathscr{A}(z_1), \ldots, \mathscr{A}(z_n)) = {}^*f({}^*\mathscr{A}(z_1), \ldots, {}^*\mathscr{A}(z_n))$, and
(ii) $P(\mathscr{A}(z_1), \ldots, \mathscr{A}(z_n))$ if and only if ${}^*P({}^*\mathscr{A}(z_1), \ldots, {}^*\mathscr{A}(z_n))$,

that is, if and only if the functions and predicates of $\mathscr{D}$ are extensions of the corresponding functions and predicates in $\mathscr{A}$. When they are, we will refer to $^*(\cdot)$ as the *natural embedding of* $\mathscr{A}$ *in* $\mathscr{D}$.

Next suppose that $^*(\cdot)$ is the natural embedding of $\mathscr{A}$ in $\mathscr{D}$, and let φ be a closed wff of $\hat{L}(\mathscr{A})$ concerning 0, 1, +, ·, =, <, the function symbols $f_1, \ldots, f_n$, the predicate symbols $P_1, \ldots, P_k$, and the constant symbols $\theta_1, \ldots, \theta_m$. In $\mathscr{A}$, φ denotes the same sentence with quantifiers ranging over R and with the θ_i replaced by the real numbers, $r_1, \ldots, r_m$. The * *transform* of φ, denoted $^*\varphi$, is the image of φ under $^*(\cdot)$, that is, the $\mathscr{D}$ version of φ with the same real numbers, with the f's and P's replaced by $^*f_1, \ldots, {}^*f_n$ and $^*P_1, \ldots, {}^*P_k$, respectively, and with quantifiers ranging over $^*R$. Since the quantifiers of φ and $^*\varphi$ range over different sets, it is not certain that φ and $^*\varphi$ have the same truth value. Note, therefore, that *φ and $^*\varphi$ have the same truth value if $\mathscr{D}$ is an elementary extension of $\mathscr{A}$. They also have the same truth value if $^*(\cdot)$ satisfies the following principle*:

Transfer Principle Let $\mathscr{A}$ and $\mathscr{D}$ be structures for $\hat{L}$ such that $|\mathscr{A}| \subset |\mathscr{D}|$, and let $^*(\cdot)$ be the natural embedding of $\mathscr{A}$ in $\mathscr{D}$. Furthermore, let φ be a closed wff of $\hat{L}(\mathscr{A})$ and let $^*\varphi$ be its * transform. Then φ is valid in $\mathscr{A}$ if and only if $^*\varphi$ is valid in $\mathscr{D}$.

When $^*(\cdot)$ satisfies the transfer principle and φ is a closed wff of $\hat{L}(\mathscr{A})$ that is valid in $\mathscr{A}$, we say that *$^*\varphi$ is true by transfer.*

E 20.2 Let $\hat{L}$, $\mathscr{A}$, and $\mathscr{D}$ be as above and let $^*(\cdot)$ be the natural embedding of $\mathscr{A}$ in $\mathscr{D}$. Assume that $^*(\cdot)$ satisfies the transfer principle. Then the following interesting theorem is true:

T 20.6 Suppose that f is a function symbol of $\hat{L}$ and that in $\mathscr{A}$ $f(\cdot)\colon R \to R$. Then f is continuous at $x \in R$ if and only if $^*f(x) \simeq {}^*f(y)$ for all y in $^*R$ with $y \simeq x$.

Proof: Suppose first that $f(\cdot)$ is continuous at x. Then, for given $\varepsilon > 0$, we can find $\delta > 0$ such that

$$(\forall y)[[|x-y| < \delta] \supset [|f(x) - f(y)| < \varepsilon]]$$

is true, in $\mathscr{A}$. By transfer,

$$(\forall y)[[|x-y| < \delta] \supset [|{}^*f(x) - {}^*f(y)| < \varepsilon]]$$

is true in $\mathscr{D}$. But then

$$(\forall y)[[x \approx y] \supset [|{}^*f(x) - {}^*f(y)| < \varepsilon]]$$

is true in $\mathscr{D}$ as well. Since ε is arbitrary, in $\mathscr{D}$

$$(\forall y)[[x \approx y] \supset [{}^*f(x) \approx {}^*f(y)]]. \tag{20.1}$$

Suppose next that equation 20.1 is true in $\mathscr{D}$ and let $\varepsilon > 0$ be a real number. Then

$$(\exists\delta)(\forall y)[[|x-y| < \delta] \supset [|{}^*f(x) - {}^*f(y)| < \varepsilon]]$$

is true in $\mathscr{D}$. By transfer in reverse,

$$(\exists\delta)(\forall y)[[|x-y| < \delta] \supset [|f(x) - f(y)| < \varepsilon]]$$

is true in $\mathscr{A}$. Since ε was chosen arbitrarily, $f(\cdot)$ is continuous at x, as was to be shown.

20.3.3 Transfer versus Elementary Extension of Structures

Our result concerning elementarily equivalent structures of $\tilde{L}$ can be summarized and extended in the following way:

T 20.7 Let $\tilde{L}$ be L without the predicates U, S, and $\in$. In addition, let $\tilde{T}$ be a first-order theory whose language is $\tilde{L}$ and whose nonlogical axioms are NSA 4–NSA 18, with $(\forall u \in U)$ and $(\exists u \in U)$ replaced by $(\forall u)$ and $(\exists u)$, where u varies over x, y, and z. Finally, let $\hat{L}$ be an extension of $\tilde{L}$ whose additional nonlogical vocabulary has been introduced in accordance with the schemes of chapter 7 and let $\hat{T}$ be the corresponding extension of $\tilde{T}$. Then there exist models of $\hat{T}$, $\mathscr{A}$, and $\mathscr{D}$, such that (i) $|\mathscr{A}|$ with the $\mathscr{A}$ versions of 0, 1, $+$, $\cdot$, and $<$ is a complete ordered field; (ii) $|\mathscr{D}|$ with the $\mathscr{D}$ versions of 0, 1, $+$, $\cdot$, and $<$ is an ordered-field extension of $|\mathscr{A}|$; and (iii) $\mathscr{D}$ is an elementary extension of $\mathscr{A}$.

The relationship between the idea of an elementary extension of structures and transfer is described in T 20.8 below. In reading the theorem, note that the conditions which determine the properties of the functional and predicate symbols of $\hat{L}$ that do not belong to $\tilde{L}$ are not even mentioned in the theorem statement. Yet in T 20.7 I insisted that they have been introduced by the schemes of chapter 7. The difference provides one reason why nonstandard analysts use transfer rather than the notion of elementarily equivalent structures when they present their theories.

T 20.8 Let $\tilde{L}$ and $\tilde{T}$ be as in T 20.7, and let $\hat{L}$ be an extension of $\tilde{L}$ with a finite or denumerably infinite number of additional functional and predicate constants. Moreover, let $\mathscr{A}$ and $\mathscr{D}$ be structures of $\hat{L}$ which are models of $\tilde{T}$ and satisfy the following conditions:

(i) $|\mathscr{A}|$ with the $\mathscr{A}$ versions of 0, 1, $+$, $\cdot$, and $<$ is a complete ordered field, and

(ii) $|\mathscr{D}|$ with the $\mathscr{D}$ versions of 0, 1, $+$, $\cdot$ and $<$ is an ordered-field extension of $|\mathscr{A}|$.

Finally, let $^*(\cdot)$ be the natural embedding of $\mathscr{A}$ in $\mathscr{D}$. Then $^*(\cdot)$ satisfies the transfer principle if and only if $\mathscr{D}$ is an elementary extension of $\mathscr{A}$.

20.4 Superstructures and Superstructure Embeddings

In this section we discuss superstructures over V and U, $W(V)$ and $W(U)$, and determine whether there exist superstructure embeddings of $W(V)$ in $W(U)$. Again we argue informally and outside KPU. If called upon to do so, we could make our arguments precise by formulating them in a set theory based on KA 2, KA 4–KA 7, KA 8 with unrestricted φ, KA 10, the power-set axiom, and Zorn's Lemma.

20.4.1 Superstructures $W(\cdot)$ over Sets of Urelements

Let M be a set of urelements; let $V_M(\alpha)$ be as described in chapter 9; and let ω denote the first-limit ordinal. In addition, define $W_k(M)$ inductively by

$$W_0(M) = M \cup V_M(0),$$

$$W_n(M) = \left(\bigcup_{k=0}^{n-1} W_k(M) \right) \cup V_M(n), \qquad n = 1, 2, \ldots$$

$$W(M) = \bigcup_{n<\omega} W_n(M).$$

Then $W(M)$ is the *superstructure over* M. It is obvious that

$$W_0(M) = M, \quad W_n(M) \subset W_{n+1}(M), \quad \text{and} \quad W_n(M) \subset W(M).$$

It is also easy to verify that $W_{n+1}(M) = W_n(M) \cup \mathscr{P}(W_n(M))$, $n = 0, 1, \ldots$, and hence that

$$M \in W_1(M), \quad W_n(M) \in W_{n+1}(M), \quad \text{and} \quad W_n(M) \in W(M).$$

Finally, it is true that $W(M) = M \cup V_M(\omega)$. We use these facts to construct an embedding of $W(V)$ in $W(U)$ which has many interesting characteristics.

20.4.2 The Superstructure over R

Before we construct the promised embedding of $W(V)$ in $W(U)$, we must take a closer look at $W(R)$, where R with the standard versions of $+, \cdot, =$, and $<$ is a complete ordered field. For that purpose, let $\check{L}$ denote an expansion of L containing a finite or denumerably infinite number of additional function and predicate symbols. In addition, let $\mathscr{A}$ be the intended structure for $\check{L}$ and assume that $W(R) \subset |\mathscr{A}|$. For the purposes of this discussion, we shall not distinguish between a symbol of $\check{L}$ and its interpretation in $\mathscr{A}$.

To begin our investigation of $W(R)$ we note that 0 and 1 belong to $W_0(R)$. Moreover, if r, s, and t are in R, then $\{r\}$ and $\{r, s\}$ belong to $W_1(R)$, (r, s) is an element of $W_2(R)$, and (r, s, t) resides in $W_3(R)$. Hence, if we define $\tilde{<}$ by

$$(r, s) \in \tilde{<} \text{ iff } [[[r \in R] \wedge [s \in R]] \wedge [r < s]]$$

and $\tilde{+}$ by

$$(r, s, t) \in \tilde{+} \text{ iff } [[[[r \in R] \wedge [s \in R]] \wedge [t \in R]] \wedge [t = (r + s)]],$$

we see that there is a version in $W_2(R)$ of the restriction of $<$ to R and a version in $W_3(R)$ of the restriction of $+$ to R. Similarly, there is a version in $W_3(R)$ of the restriction of $\cdot$ to R.

Next note that if $A \subset R$, $A \in W_1(R)$. Furthermore, if $\mathscr{F}$ is a family of subsets of A—for example, $\mathscr{P}_F(A)$ or $\mathscr{P}(A)$—then $\mathscr{F} \in W_2(R)$. Hence, if $\mu \in F^{\mathscr{A}}$ and if the restriction of μ to $\mathscr{F}$ is a probability measure on $(A, \mathscr{F})$, we can define a function $\tilde{\mu}$ by

$$(x, y) \in \tilde{\mu} \text{ if } [[[x \in \mathscr{F}] \wedge [y \in R]] \wedge [\mu(x) = y]]$$

and show that there is in $W_4(R)$ a version of the restriction of μ to $\mathscr{F}$.

Finally, note that a version of the n-fold product of R with itself, R^n, is an element of $W_{n+1}(R)$. Moreover, versions of the operations of scalar multiplication and vector addition in R^n, respectively, reside in $W_{n+3}(R)$ and $W_{3n}(R)$. Finally, in $W_{2n+3}(R)$ we can find a version of the inner product of vectors in R^n, and in $W_{2n+4}(R)$ we can find a version of the inner-product topology in R^n. Thus for most topics in real analysis there is an n and a $W_n(R)$ within which the respective topics can be presented and where versions of the associated functions and predicates in $F^{\mathscr{A}}$ and $G^{\mathscr{A}}$ can be analyzed.

There is no good reason why we should prefer the functions and predicates in $F^{\mathscr{A}}$ and $G^{\mathscr{A}}$ to their aliases in $W(R)$. Instead there is a reason why the aliases are preferable: The functions and predicates in $F^{\mathscr{A}}$ and $G^{\mathscr{A}}$ are defined on all of $|\mathscr{A}|$. Usually it is only the restriction of these functions and predicates to their "natural" domains—e.g., $<$ to R, μ to $(A, \mathscr{F})$, and the inner product of vectors in R^n to R^n—that is of interest to mathematicians. In the remainder of this chapter we shall adopt L rather than $\check{L}$ as our language and use the $W(R)$ versions of the functions and predicates needed for illustrative purposes.

20.4.3 Superstructure Embeddings

Let U and V be as described in section 20.1.1. A *superstructure embedding of* $W(V)$ *in* $W(U)$ is a mapping *: $W(V) \to W(U)$ satisfying these conditions:

(1) $^*r = r$ for all r in V.
(2) For all x, y in $W(V)$, $x \in y$ if and only if $^*x \in {}^*y$.

We will show that there is an interpretation, $^*R$, R, $+$, $\cdot$, $=$, $<$, and $\in$, of U, V, $+$, $\cdot$, $=$, $<$, and $\in$ and a mapping *: $W(R) \to W(^*R)$ so that R with $+$, $\cdot$, and $<$ is a complete ordered field, $^*R$ with $+$, $\cdot$, and $<$ is an ordered-field extension of R, and $^*(\cdot)$ is a superstructure embedding.

Let R with the standard versions of $+$, $\cdot$, and $<$ be a complete ordered field, let $\mathscr{U}$ be a free ultrafilter over n, and let $^*R = R^N/\mathscr{U}$. In addition, let $W_k(R)^N$ denote the set of functions $A(\cdot)$: $N \to W_k(R)$; let $W_k(R)^N/\mathscr{U}$ denote the set of $\mathscr{U}$-equivalence classes in $W_k(R)^N$; and define $W_{\mathscr{U}}$ by

$$W_{\mathscr{U}} = \bigcup_{k=0}^{\infty} W_k(R)^N/\mathscr{U}.$$

It is obvious that $^*R = W_0(R)^N/\mathscr{U}$ and that $W_n(R)^N/\mathscr{U} \subset W_{n+1}(R)^N/\mathscr{U}$. Hence $W_{\mathscr{U}} = \lim_{n\to\infty} W_n(R)^N/\mathscr{U}$. Furthermore, $^*R$, with $+$, $\cdot$, and $<$ as defined in conditions ii–v in section 20.2.2, is an ordered-field extension of a complete ordered field which is isomorphic to R with the standard versions of $+$, $\cdot$, and $<$.

In order to construct the superstructure embedding we next define the predicate of belonging in $W_{\mathscr{U}}$ and two mappings $i(\cdot)$: $W(R) \to W_{\mathscr{U}}$ and $j(\cdot)$: $W_{\mathscr{U}} \to W(^*R)$. Let $a = \{a_n\}$ and $b = \{b_n\}$ belong to $W_k(R)^N$ for some $k \geqslant 1$; and let $a_{\mathscr{U}}$ and $b_{\mathscr{U}}$, respectively, denote the $\mathscr{U}$-equivalence class in $W_k(R)^N$ determined by a and b. Then we define the required predicate in $W_{\mathscr{U}}$ by

(vi) $a_{\mathscr{U}} \in b_{\mathscr{U}}$ if and only if $\{n \in N\colon a_n \in b_n\} \in \mathscr{U}$,

where we write ε rather than $\varepsilon_{\mathscr{U}}$ for simplicity. It is easy and left to the reader to show that $\in$ so defined depends on the equivalence classes $a_{\mathscr{U}}$ and $b_{\mathscr{U}}$ and not on a and b. That is, if $a \sim_{\mathscr{U}} a'$ and $b \sim_{\mathscr{U}} b'$, then $\{n \in N: a_n \in b_n\} \in \mathscr{U}$ if and only if $\{n \in N: a'_n \in b'_n\} \in \mathscr{U}$. Hence $\in$ is well defined in $W_{\mathscr{U}}$ by condition vi. The mapping $i(\cdot)$ is to be a one-to-one embedding of $W(R)$ in $W_{\mathscr{U}}$. We define it by

(vii) $i(x) = x_{\mathscr{U}}, \qquad x \in W(R)$;

i.e., $i(x)$ is the equivalence class of $\{x\}_{\mathscr{U}}$ in $W_{\mathscr{U}}$; and I leave it to the reader to show that $i(\cdot)$ so defined is one-to-one. Finally, we define $j(\cdot)$ by recursion so that it satisfies the following conditions:

(viii) $j(r) = r$ for all $r \in {}^*R$.

(ix) For all $a_{\mathscr{U}} \in W_{\mathscr{U}} - {}^*R$, $j(a_{\mathscr{U}}) = \{ j(b_{\mathscr{U}}): b_{\mathscr{U}} \in a_{\mathscr{U}}\}$.

Specifically, we define $j(\cdot)$ to be the identity on $^*R$; and once we have defined $j(\cdot)$ on $W_k(R)^N/\mathscr{U}$, we define it on $(W_{k+1}(R)^N/\mathscr{U} - W_k(R)^N/\mathscr{U})$ as suggested in condition (ix) above. This procedure clearly determines $j(\cdot)$ as a one-to-one mapping of $W_{\mathscr{U}}$ into $W({}^*R)$.

Since $i(\cdot)$ is into and since the domain of $j(\cdot)$ is $W_{\mathscr{U}}$, the one-to-oneness of both $j(\cdot)$ and $i(\cdot)$ ensure that their composition $j(i(\cdot))$ is well defined and maps $W(R)$ into a proper subset of $W({}^*R)$. In particular, $j(i(r)) = r_{\mathscr{U}}$ for all $r \in R$, and, for all x, y in $W(R)$, $x \in y$ if and only if $j(i(x)) \in j(i(y))$. Hence if we let $^*(A) = j(i(A))$ for all $A \in W(R)$ and identify R with its * image in $^*R$, we see that $^*(\cdot)$ is a superstructure embedding of $W(R)$ in $W({}^*R)$ that we can picture as follows:

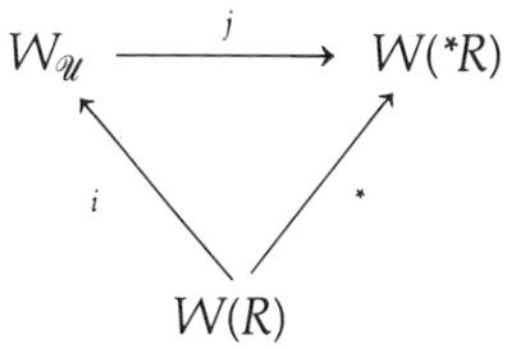

E 20.3 The mapping $j(i(\cdot))$ maps a real interval $[a, b]$ into a hyperreal interval $^*[a, b]$. Specifically,

$c_{\mathscr{U}} \in i([a, b])$ iff $\{n \in N: a \leqslant c_n \leqslant b\} \in \mathscr{U}$

and

$s \in j(i([a, b]))$ iff $s = j(c_{\mathscr{U}})$ for some $c_{\mathscr{U}} \in i([a, b])$.

But $c_{\mathscr{U}} \in {}^*R$. Hence $c_{\mathscr{U}} = j(c_{\mathscr{U}})$. We conclude

$^*[a, b] = j(i([a, b])) = \{s \in {}^*R: a_{\mathscr{U}} \leqslant s \leqslant b_{\mathscr{U}}\}$.

When a and b belong $({}^*R - R)$, there is no interval $[c, d] \subset R$ such that $^*[a, b] = j(i([c, d]))$.

We shall identify V with the * image of R; U with $^*R$; $+$, $\cdot$, and $<$ with the functions and the predicate defined by conditions iii–v in section 20.2.2; $=$ on $^*R$ with the predicate defined by condition i in section 20.2.2; $=$ on $W(^*R) - {}^*R$ with the predicate determined by $\in$ and the axiom of extension; and $\in$ with the restriction to $W(^*R) - {}^*R$ of the extension of $\in$ in an admissible-set model of KPU, NSA 1, and KA 10, whose universe of discourse contains $W(^*R)$. In that way we obtain interpretations of U, V, $+$, $\cdot$, $<$, $=$, and $\in$ for which the $^*(\cdot)$ in the figure above is a superstructure embedding of $W(V)$ in $W(U)$.

20.5 Transfer and Superstructure Embeddings

Superstructure embeddings need not have all the properties we require of them. In this section we reformulate the transfer principle so that it applies to superstructure embeddings, and we establish the existence of superstructures and embeddings that satisfy the principle.

20.5.1 Leibniz's Principle

To state the new transfer principle I must introduce two structures for L and say what I mean by the * transform of a wff. We denote the structures of L by $\mathscr{A}_R = (W(R), N_{\mathscr{A}_R}, F^R, G^R)$ and $\mathscr{A}_{^*R} = (W(^*R), N_{\mathscr{A}_{^*R}}, R^{^*R}, G^{^*R})$, and we assume that the $\in$'s in G^R and $G^{^*R}$ represent the standard membership relation in $W(R)$ and $W(^*R)$. We also assume that $R \subset {}^*R$; that R with the restriction to R of $+$, $\cdot$, $<$, and $=$ is a complete ordered field; that $^*R$ with the restriction to $^*R$ of $+$, $\cdot$, $<$, and $=$ is an ordered-field extension of R; and that there is a superstructure embedding $^*(\cdot)$ of $W(R)$ in $W(^*R)$. The * *transform* of a closed wff φ in $L(\mathscr{A}_R)$ is the $^*(\cdot)$ image of φ in $L(\mathscr{A}_{^*R})$. Specifically, the * transform of φ, $^*\varphi$, is the closed wff in $L(\mathscr{A}_{*R})$ that results from exchanging the functions and predicates in φ with their images under $^*(\cdot)$.

I give examples of * transforms of wffs in E 20.4 below. In reading the example, note that E, $W_k(R)$, and $\mathscr{P}(E)$ are not nonlogical symbols of L. They are constants of $L(\mathscr{A}_R)$ that denote sets in $W(R)$. Hence ψ is a Δ_0 formula in $L(\mathscr{A}_R)$ but not in L. Note also the $^*\varphi$ asserts that $^*\mathscr{P}(E) = \mathscr{P}(^*E)$. This equality holds only if E is finite.

E 20.4 Let E and $\mathscr{P}(E)$, respectively, denote a set in $W(R)$ and the family of all subsets of E. In addition, let $k > 1$ be so large that $\mathscr{P}(E) \in W_k(R)$ and consider the following closed wffs in $L(\mathscr{A}_R)$:

φ: $(\forall y)[[y \in \mathscr{P}(E)] \equiv (\forall x \in y)[x \in E]]$

ψ: $(\forall y \in W_k(R))[[y \in \mathscr{P}(E)] \equiv (\forall x \in y)[x \in E]]$.

Their * transforms are, respectively,

$^*\varphi$: $(\forall y)[[y \in {}^*(\mathscr{P}(E))] \equiv (\forall x \in y)[x \in {}^*E]]$,

$^*\psi$: $(\forall y \in {}^*W_k(R))[[y \in {}^*(\mathscr{P}(E))] \equiv (\forall x \in y)[x \in {}^*E]]$.

The transfer principle for superstructure embeddings is called Leibniz's Principle. We denote it by LP and formulate it as follows:

LP If φ is a closed bounded wff in $L(\mathscr{A}_R)$, φ is valid in $\mathscr{A}_R$ if and only if $^*\varphi$ is valid in $\mathscr{A}_{^*R}$.

Here a *bounded wff* is a wff in which all the quantifiers are bounded. Thus the ψ in E 20.4 is bounded, while φ is not. Note, therefore, that both φ and ψ are valid in $\mathscr{A}_R$, $^*\varphi$ is valid in $\mathscr{A}_{^*R}$ only if E is finite, and $^*\psi$ is valid in $\mathscr{A}_{^*R}$ for all E if $^*(\cdot)$ satisfies LP.

20.5.2 Łos's Theorem and the Validity of Leibniz's Principle

The existence of superstructure embeddings that satisfy LP can be deduced from a theorem of Jerzy Łos, T 20.9. In the statement and proof of T 20.9, $\varphi(a_1, \ldots, a_k)$ and $\varphi(x, a_1, \ldots, a_k)$ are to be read as $\varphi_{x_1,\ldots,x_k}(a_1, \ldots, a_k)$.

T 20.9 Let R, $^*R$, and $^*(\cdot)$ be as described in the preceding section. Moreover, let φ be a bounded wff of $L(\mathscr{A}_R)$ with k free variables and let $^*\varphi$ be its $j(i(\cdot))$ transform. If $a_{i_\mathscr{U}} \in W_\mathscr{U}$, $i = 1, \ldots, k$, $^*\varphi(j(a_{1_\mathscr{U}}), \ldots, j(a_{k_\mathscr{U}}))$ is true if and only if $\{n \in N\colon \varphi(a_{1n}, \ldots, a_{kn})\} \in \mathscr{U}$ for any versions $\{a_{in}\}$ of $a_{i\mathscr{U}}$, $i = 1, \ldots, k$.

Standard proofs of this theorem can be found in the literature (see Keisler 1976, p. 54–55). Therefore I only sketch the outline of a proof here. Throughout the proof we assume that $+$, $\cdot$, and $<$ are restricted to $^*R$ and defined on $^*R$ in the way described in conditions iii–v in section 20.2.2. We also assume that the relation of belonging in $W_\mathscr{U}$ is as defined in condition vi at the beginning of section 20.4.3. The proof of T 20.9 is obtained by induction on the length of wffs in $L(\mathscr{A}_R)$. We begin with atomic formulas. If $a_\mathscr{U}$ and $b_\mathscr{U}$ belong to $^*R$, $[j(a_\mathscr{U}) < j(b_\mathscr{U})]$ if and only if $\{n \in N\colon a_n < b_n\} \in \mathscr{U}$, where $\{a_n\}$ and $\{b_n\}$ are versions of $a_\mathscr{U}$ and $b_\mathscr{U}$. Similarly, $[j(a_\mathscr{U}) = j(b_\mathscr{U})]$ if and only if $\{n \in N\colon a_n = b_n\} \in \mathscr{U}$. If $a_\mathscr{U}$ and $b_\mathscr{U}$ are sets in $W_\mathscr{U}$, then by construction and the axiom of extension $[a_\mathscr{U} = b_\mathscr{U}]$ if and only if $[j(a_\mathscr{U}) = j(b_\mathscr{U})]$. Furthermore, if $\{a_n\}$ and $\{b_n\}$ are versions of $a_\mathscr{U}$ and $b_\mathscr{U}$, $[a_\mathscr{U} = b_\mathscr{U}]$ if and only if $\{n \in N\colon a_n = b_n\} \in \mathscr{U}$. Similar arguments suffice to show that $[j(a_{\mathscr{U}}) \in j(b_{\mathscr{U}})]$ if and only if $\{n \in N: a_n \in b_n\} \in \mathscr{U}$. Hence Łos's theorem is valid for atomic sentences.

Suppose next that the two bounded wffs of $L(\mathscr{A}_R)$, φ and ψ, satisfy the theorem. It is then a routine matter, which I leave to the reader, to ascertain that $\sim\varphi$ and $[\varphi \supset \psi]$ satisfy the theorem as well. The interesting part of the demonstration is that the proof for $\sim\varphi$ uses in an essential way that $\mathscr{U}$ is an ultrafilter and not just a filter.

Finally, suppose that φ is a bounded wff with $(k + 1)$ free variables and suppose that $a_{i\mathscr{U}} \in W_{\mathscr{U}}$, $i = 1, \ldots, k$, and that $A_{\mathscr{U}} \in W_{\mathscr{U}}$. I shall next demonstrate that if $A_{\mathscr{U}} \sim_{\mathscr{U}} \{A_n\}$ and $a_{i\mathscr{U}} \sim_{\mathscr{U}} \{a_{in}\}$, $i = 1, \ldots, k$, then

$$(\exists x \in j(A_{\mathscr{U}}))^*\varphi(x, j(a_{1\mathscr{U}}), \ldots, j(a_{k\mathscr{U}}))$$

if and only if

$$\{n \in N : (\exists x \in A_n)\varphi(x, a_{1n}, \ldots, a_{kn})\} \in \mathscr{U}.$$

Suppose first that $b \in j(A_{\mathscr{U}})$ is such that $^*\varphi(b, j(a_{1\mathscr{U}}), \ldots, j(a_{k\mathscr{U}}))$ and let $b_{\mathscr{U}} \in A_{\mathscr{U}}$ and $b_n \in A_n$, $n = 1, 2, \ldots$, be such that $b_{\mathscr{U}} \sim_{\mathscr{U}} \{b_n\}$ and $b = j(b_{\mathscr{U}})$. By the induction hypothesis $\{n \in N : [[b_n \in A_n] \wedge \varphi(b_n, a_{1n}, \ldots, a_{kn})]\} \in \mathscr{U}$. Since also

$$\{n \in N : [[b_n \in A_n] \wedge \varphi(b_n, a_{1n}, \ldots, a_{kn})]\}$$
$$\subset \{n \in N : (\exists x \in A_n)\varphi(x, a_{1n}, \ldots, a_{kn})\},$$

we conclude that $\{n \in N : (\exists x \in A_n)\varphi(x, a_{1n}, \ldots, a_{kn})\} \in \mathscr{U}$. To establish the converse for each $n \in N$ for which $(\exists x \in A_n)\varphi(x, a_{1n}, \ldots, a_{kn})$, we pick an $a_n \in A_n$ such that $\varphi(a_n, a_{1n}, \ldots, a_{kn})$; and for all other n we pick an arbitrary $a_n \in A_n$. Then, by construction and hypothesis, $\{n \in N : [[a_n \in A_n] \wedge \varphi(a_n, a_{1n}, \ldots, a_{kn})]\} \in \mathscr{U}$. Hence, by the induction hypothesis, $[[j(a_{\mathscr{U}}) \in j(A_{\mathscr{U}})] \wedge {}^*\varphi(j(a_{\mathscr{U}}), j(a_{1\mathscr{U}}), \ldots, j(a_{k\mathscr{U}})]$, where $a_{\mathscr{U}} = \{a_n\}$. This implies that $(\exists x \in j(A_{\mathscr{U}}))^*\varphi(x, j(a_{1\mathscr{U}}), \ldots, j(a_{k\mathscr{U}}))$, as was to be shown.

By using the material equivalence of $(\forall x)\varphi$ and $\sim(\exists x) \sim \varphi$ and obvious arguments, we can demonstrate that $(\forall x \in j(A_{\mathscr{U}}))^*\varphi(x, j(a_{1\mathscr{U}}), \ldots, j(a_{k\mathscr{U}}))$ if and only if $\{n \in N : (\forall x \in A_n)\varphi(x, a_{1n}, \ldots, a_{kn})\} \in \mathscr{U}$ and conclude the proof of T 20.9. Those details I leave to the reader.

From Łos's theorem it follows that there is a superstructure embedding that satisfies Leibniz's Principle. For ease of reference I record that fact here:

T 20.10 The superstructure embedding, $j(i(\cdot))$ that we constructed in section 20.4 satisfies the Leibniz Principle.

20.6 Internal Subsets of $W(^*R)$

In this section our discussion pertains to the two structures for L, $\mathscr{A}_R$ and $\mathscr{A}_{^*R}$, that we described in section 20.5. We also assume that the superstructure embedding of $W(R)$ in $W(^*R)$, $^*(\cdot)$, satisfies LP.

20.6.1 A Classification of the Elements of $W(^*R)$

For many purposes it is useful to classify the elements of $W(^*R)$ according to the following scheme: If $b \in W(^*R)$, then b is

1. *real* if $b \in W(R)$,
2. *standard* if $b = {}^*a$ for some $a \in W(R)$,
3. *internal* if $b \in {}^*a$ for some $a \in W(R)$,
4. *external* if b is not internal.

For example, if $a_i \in R$, $i = 1, \ldots, n$, then each a_i and the set $\{a_1, \ldots, a_n\}$ are standard and real. Also N and R are real and external, while $^*N$ and $^*R$ are standard but not real. Similarly, if a, b in R, then $^*[a, b]$ is standard but not real, while for c, d in $^*R - R$, the subset of $^*R$, $[c, d]$, is internal but not real. Finally, if b is standard, it is internal as well, but the converse is untrue, as evidenced by $[c, d]$.

20.6.2 Elementary Properties of Internal Sets

Internal subsets of $W(^*R)$ have many interesting characteristics, some of which are described below. First, two useful auxiliary results.

Suppose that $b \in W(^*R)$ and that $b \in {}^*a$ for some $a \in W(R)$. Then $b \in j(a_{\mathscr{U}})$, where $a_{\mathscr{U}}$ denotes the $\mathscr{U}$-equivalence class of a, and $a_{\mathscr{U}} \in W_k^N/\mathscr{U}$ for some $k \geqslant 1$. From this and the one-to-oneness of $j(\cdot)$, it follows that if $b \in W(^*R)$, then b is internal if and only if there is a $b_{\mathscr{U}} \in W_{\mathscr{U}}$ and a $k \geqslant 1$ such that $b = j(b_{\mathscr{U}})$ and $b_{\mathscr{U}} \in W_k^N/\mathscr{U}$. In particular, we have T 20.11.

T 20.11 If $A \subset {}^*R$ and A is internal, then $A \in {}^*W_1(R)$.

To establish T 20.11, we fix A and pick a $B \in W(R)$ such that $A \in {}^*B$. The following sentence is the * transform of a true sentence in $\mathscr{A}_R$:

$$(\forall x \in {}^*B)[(\forall y \in x)[y \in {}^*R] \supset [x \in {}^*W_1(R)]].$$

This sentence is, therefore, true in $\mathscr{A}_{^*R}$. Since A was arbitrary, we conclude that T 20.11 is true as stated.

Suppose next that A, B are sets in $W(^*R)$ and that $f(\cdot): A \to B$. Then $f(\cdot) \in W(^*R)$ and $f(\cdot)$ is internal if and only if its graph, $G(f)$, is internal. From this and arguments similar to those used above, it follows that a function $f(\cdot) \in W(^*R)$ is internal if and only if there exists a $k \geqslant 1$ and a sequence of functions $f_n(\cdot)$ whose graphs (1) belong to W_k and (2) determine an element of $W_{\mathscr{U}}$, $G_{\mathscr{U}}$ that satisfies $G(f) = j(G_{\mathscr{U}})$.

Our preceding observations describe the way in which internal sets and functions in $W(^*R)$ can be constructed from sequences of sets and functions that belong to $W(R)$. Another way of generating internal sets and functions is delineated in T 20.12—the so-called *Internal Definition Principle.*

T 20.12 Let φ be a bounded wff of $L(\mathscr{A}_{^*R})$ with one free variable, and suppose that the constants of φ are all internal. For all internal sets C, $\{v \in C : \varphi_x(v)\}$ is internal.

To prove T 20.12, let $b_1, \ldots, b_n$ be the constants in φ and write φ as $\varphi(b_1, \ldots, b_n)$. For some k, C and the b_i's will all belong to $^*W_k(R)$. Moreover, by the construction of $W(R)$,

$$(\forall y_1 \in W_k(R)) \ldots (\forall y_n \in W_k(R))(\forall z \in W_k(R))(\exists u \in W_{k+1}(R))$$

$$(\forall v \in W_k(R))[[v \in u] \equiv [[v \in z] \wedge \varphi_x(v, y_1, \ldots, y_n)]]$$

is valid in $\mathscr{A}_R$. By LP, the * transform is true in $\mathscr{A}_{*R}$. The validity of T 20.12 follows from this.

The preceding auxiliary results can be used to construct simple proofs of the assertions made in T 20.13 and T 20.14.

T 20.13 Suppose that A is an internal set in $W(R^*)$:

(i) If $A \subset {}^*N$ and A is not empty, it has a least element.

(ii) If $N \subset A$, there is an $a \in {}^*N - N$ such that $\{n \in {}^*N : n \leqslant a\} \subset A$.

(iii) If $({}^*N - N) \subset A$, there is a $k \in N$ such that $\{n \in {}^*N : n \geqslant k\} \subset A$.

To wit: To prove property i, it suffices to observe that the assertion

$$(\forall x \in {}^*W_1(R))[[\sim[x = \varnothing] \wedge (\forall y \in x)[y \in {}^*N]]$$

$$\supset (\exists n \in {}^*N)[[n \in x] \wedge (\forall y \in x)[n \leqslant y]]]$$

is the * transform of a wff that is valid in $\mathscr{A}_R$. To prove properties ii and iii it suffices to note that N and $^*N - N$ are external and that, by T 20.12, the sets

$$\{n \in {}^*N : (\forall k \leqslant n)[k \in A]\} \text{ and } \{n \in {}^*N : (\forall k \geqslant n)[k \in A]\}$$

are internal and, respectively, contain N and $^*N - N$.

T 20.14 Suppose that $\{a_n; n \in {}^*N\}$ is an internal sequence in $W({}^*R)$ such that $a_n \approx 0$ for all $n \in N$. Then there is a $\gamma \in N^* - N$ and a $\delta \in {}^*R$ such that $0 < \delta \leqslant \gamma^{-1}$ and $|a_n| \leqslant \delta$ for all $n \leqslant \gamma$, $n \in {}^*N$.

To prove this theorem it suffices to observe that, by T 20.12, $\{n \in {}^*N : |a_n| \leqslant n^{-1}\}$ is internal and contains N. Then T 20.14 becomes a consequence of T 20.13 (ii). Slightly more involved arguments are needed to establish the next theorem.

T 20.15 If $A \in \mathscr{P}(R)$, then A is internal if and only if it is finite.

I shall prove the necessity half and leave the sufficiency half to the reader. Evidently, if $A \subset R$, it must be the case that $A \subset {}^*A$. If $A \subset R$ and A is internal, the converse is also true. To see why, we pick a $b \in A$ and let $A_i \in W_1(R)$, $i = 1, 2, \ldots$, and $A_{\mathscr{U}} = \{A_i\}_{\mathscr{U}}$ be such that $j(A_{\mathscr{U}}) = A$. Then $j(\{b\}_{\mathscr{U}}) = b$ and $\{b\}_{\mathscr{U}} \in A_{\mathscr{U}}$. Consequently, $\{A\}_{\mathscr{U}} \subset A_{\mathscr{U}}$ and ${}^*A \subset A$. But $A \subset R$ and $A = {}^*A$ can happen only if A is finite. If there did exist an infinite sequence of different elements of A, $a_1, a_2, \ldots$, then $j(\{a_i\}_{\mathscr{U}})$ would belong to ${}^*A$ but not to A. We conclude that if $A \subset R$, A is internal only if A is finite.

20.6.3 Hyperfinite Sets in $W({}^*R)$

Internal sets of particular interest to us are the hyperfinite sets in $W({}^*R)$. They are defined as follows:

UD 10 An element B of $W({}^*R)$ is hyperfinite if and only if (i) B is internal and (ii) there is an internal bijection from an initial segment of ${}^*N$ onto B.

This definition is the * transform of a standard definition of finite sets. To see that it is, let

$$P(x, y) =_{\text{df}} [[[x \in N] \wedge [y \in N]] \wedge [x \leqslant y]];$$

$$\begin{aligned} A(z, x, y) =_{\text{df}} &[[[S(z) \wedge S(x)] \wedge [y \in N]] \\ &\wedge (\forall u \in z)(\exists v \in x)(\exists w \in N)[P(w, y) \wedge [u = (v, w)]]]; \end{aligned}$$

$$\begin{aligned} B(z, x, y) =_{\text{df}} &[[A(z, x, y) \wedge [(\forall v \in x)(\exists w \in N)[P(w, y) \wedge [(v, w) \in z]] \\ &\wedge (\forall w \in N)[P(w, y) \supset (\exists v \in x)[(v, w) \in z]]]] \\ &\wedge (\forall u \in z)(\forall v \in z)[[[u = (u_1, w_1)] \wedge [v = (u_2, w_2)]] \\ &\supset [[u_1 = u_2] \equiv [w_1 = w_2]]]]]. \end{aligned}$$

Then the standard definition of a finite set can be formulated as

$$(\forall x \in W_k(R))[[x \in \mathscr{P}_F(x)] \equiv (\exists z \in \mathscr{P}(x \times N))(\exists y \in N)B(z, x, y)].$$

The * transform of this assertion is the symbolic rendition of UD 10. To wit:

$$(\forall x \in {}^*W_k(R))[[x \in {}^*\mathscr{P}_F(x)] \equiv (\exists z \in {}^*\mathscr{P}(x \times N))(\exists y \in {}^*N){}^*B(z, x, y)].$$

Here an x that belongs to ${}^*W_k(R)$ for some k is internal. Also the bijection z is internal because it is an element of ${}^*\mathscr{P}(x \times N)$.

In this context it is interesting to record the validity of T 20.16.

T 20.16 Let E and $\mathscr{P}_F(E)$ denote, respectively, a set in $W(R)$ and the family of all finite subsets of E. Suppose that A is a hyperfinite subset of ${}^*E$. Then

$A \in {}^*\mathscr{P}_F(E)$.

The proof goes as follows: Let $k > 1$ be so large that $\mathscr{P}_F(E) \in W_k(R)$ and $A \in {}^*W_k(R)$. Then it is true in $\mathscr{A}_R$ that

$$(\forall x \in W_k(R))[[x \in \mathscr{P}_F(E)] \equiv (\exists z \in \mathscr{P}(E \times N))(\exists y \in N)B(z, x, y)].$$

Hence, by LP, it is true in $\mathscr{A}_{{}^*R}$ that

$$(\forall x \in {}^*W_k(R))[[x \in {}^*\mathscr{P}_F(E)] \equiv (\exists z \in {}^*\mathscr{P}(E \times N))(\exists y \in {}^*N){}^*B(z, x, y)].$$

Since A is a hyperfinite subset of ${}^*E$ that belongs to ${}^*W_k(R)$, it follows from the preceding observation that $A \in {}^*\mathscr{P}_F(E)$ is true in $\mathscr{A}_{{}^*R}$.

The A in T 20.16 may contain infinitely many members. Hence ${}^*\mathscr{P}_F(E)$ need not equal $\mathscr{P}_F({}^*E)$. In fact, ${}^*\mathscr{P}_F(E) = \mathscr{P}_F({}^*E)$ only if E is finite. To intuit the reason why, consider the following example.

E 20.5 Let R, ${}^*R$, and ${}^*(\cdot)$ be as described in section 20.4.3 and let $E = [0, 1]$. Then $A \in {}^*\mathscr{P}_F(E)$ if and only if there is a $B_{\mathscr{U}} \in i(\mathscr{P}_F(E))$ so that $A = j(B_{\mathscr{U}})$. If $\{B_n\}$ is a member of the equivalence class of $B_{\mathscr{U}}$ and if, for all $n \in N$, $B_n = \{0, 1/n, 2/n, \ldots, 1\}$, then $B_{\mathscr{U}} \in i(\mathscr{P}_F(E))$ and $j(B_{\mathscr{U}})$ contains infinitely many members.

20.7 Admissible Structures and the Nonstandard Universe

Let $T = $ T(KPU, KA 10, NSA 1–NSA 19) and let $\mathscr{A}_R$ and $\mathscr{A}_{{}^*R}$ be the structures for L described in section 20.5. Neither $\mathscr{A}_R$ nor $\mathscr{A}_{{}^*R}$ is a model of T. Thus to complete our description of the nonstandard universe we must show that $\mathscr{A}_{{}^*R}$ has an extension that is a model of T. We begin with a few remarks concerning admissible structures.

20.7.1 Admissible Structures

In section 20.1 we described the language of T, L, as a single-sorted language with two constants, 0 and 1, two binary functions, $+$ and $\cdot$, two unary predicates, U and S, and two binary predicates, $<$ and $\in$. We insisted that 0 and 1 be urelements and described the extension of $+$, $\cdot$, and $<$ in the set of urelements. We also postulated that U, S, and $\in$ satisfy the axioms of KPU, KA 10, NSA 1, and NSA 19.

Since the extension of $+$, $\cdot$, and $<$ in the universe of sets is irrelevant as far as T is concerned, we may think of a model of T as a quintuple, $(\mathcal{M}, A, \mathcal{U}, \mathcal{S}, \in)$, where

(i) $\mathcal{M}$ is a structure for a first-order language with two constants, 0 and 1, two binary functions, $+$ and $\cdot$, and one binary predicate, $<$,

(ii) $\mathcal{M}$ is a model of NSA 4–NSA 18 without the bounded quantifiers,

(iii) $\mathcal{U}$, $\mathcal{S}$, and $\in$ are interpretations of U, S, and $\in$ that satisfy the conditions

a. $(\forall x)[\mathcal{U}(x) \equiv [x \in |\mathcal{M}|]]$;
b. $(\forall x)[\mathcal{S}(x) \equiv [x \in A]]$; and
c. axioms KA 1–KA 10, NSA 1, and NSA 19, and

(iv) $A \subset V_{|\mathcal{M}|}$ and $(|\mathcal{M}| \cup A)$ is a transitive in $V_{|\mathcal{M}|}$.

We showed in section 20.2 that there is a structure $\mathcal{M}$ that satisfies conditions i and ii and is such that $|\mathcal{M}|$ with $+$, $\cdot$, and $<$ is an ordered-field extension of a complete ordered field. Hence to establish the existence of a model of T, it remains to show that there exists a quadruple $(A, \mathcal{U}, \mathcal{S}, \in)$ satisfying conditions iii and iv. For that purpose we need the concept of a cardinal number.

20.7.2 Cardinal Numbers

Our discussion of cardinal numbers will be brief and informal, and we shall argue outside KPU. Our arguments can be made precise by formulating them in a set theory based on KA 2, KA 4–KA 7, KA 8 with unrestricted φ, KA 10, an axiom that asserts the existence of the power set of any set, and the Axiom of Choice. The latter insists that if z is a set of nonempty, pairwise disjoint sets, there is a set u which has exactly one member in common with each member of z.

Two sets, x and y, are *similar* if and only if there exist functions f and g which are one-to-one and map, respectively, x into y and y into x. Evidently, x is similar to x. Moreover, if x and y are similar and y and z are similar, then x and z are also similar.

The *cardinal number* of a set x, denoted card(x), is the least ordinal to which x is similar. If x and y are similar, card(x) = card(y). Moreover, if card(x) = card(y), then x and y are similar. Hence card(x) = card(y) if and only if x and y are similar.

Our concept of a cardinal number represents a generalization of the concept of a natural number. To wit: if x is similar to the natural number n, card(x) = n. In addition, if x is similar to the set of all natural numbers, ω, card(x) = ω. ω is the smallest infinite cardinal number. The second smallest is the least-uncountable ordinal.

The infinite cardinal numbers are named by the letters $\mathcal{N}_\alpha$, where α varies over ordinals. They are obtained recursively by the following definitional scheme:

$$\mathcal{N}_0 = \omega,$$

$$\mathcal{N}_{\alpha+1} = \mathcal{N}(\mathcal{N}_\alpha),$$

where $\mathcal{N}(x)$ denotes the set of all ordinals that are similar to subsets of x; and

$$\mathcal{N}_\lambda = \bigcup_{\alpha<\lambda} \mathcal{N}_\alpha \text{ if } \lambda \text{ is a limit ordinal.}$$

20.7.3 An Admissible Model of T

Next we shall use the idea of cardinal numbers to construct a model of T. Our construction is outlined in T 20.17. In reading the theorem, note that the construction is analogous to the construction of HF_M presented in ST 49 in section 9.8. Recall that a model of KPU was said to be admissible if its universe was transitive in V_M. We say that a model of T is *admissible* if and only if $|\mathcal{M}| \cup A$ is transitive in $V_{|\mathcal{M}|}$.

T 20.17 Let $\mathcal{M}$ be as described in the first two conditions of a model of T and suppose that $|\mathcal{M}|$ with $+, \cdot$, and $<$ is an ordered-field extension of a complete ordered field. In addition, let $k = \mathcal{N}_{\alpha+1}$ for some ordinal α and assume that $k > \text{card}(|\mathcal{M}|)$. Finally, let $H(k)_{|\mathcal{M}|}$ be defined by the following recursive scheme:

$$G(0) = \varnothing;$$

$$G(\beta + 1) = \{x \subset |\mathcal{M}| \cup G(\beta) : \text{card}(x) < k\};$$

$$G(\lambda) = \bigcup_{\beta \subset \lambda} G(\beta) \text{ if } \lambda \text{ is a limit ordinal;}$$

$$H(k)_{|\mathcal{M}|} = \bigcup_{\beta<k} G(\beta).$$

Then, with $A = H(k)_{|\mathcal{M}|}$, with $\mathcal{U}$ and $\mathcal{S}$ as described in the third condition of a model of T (section 20.7.1), and with ε as the standard membership relation in $H(k)_{|\mathcal{M}|}$, the quintuple $(\mathcal{M}, H(k)_{|\mathcal{M}|}, \mathcal{U}, \mathcal{S}, \varepsilon)$ is an admissible model of T.

I refer the reader to Barwise 1975 (pp. 52–54) for a proof of T 20.17 and examples of other admissible models of T.

20.7.4 Admissible Models of T and Superstructures

Let $\mathcal{A}_R$ and $\mathcal{A}_{*R}$ be the structures for L that we described in section 20.5 and suppose that the $\mathcal{M}$ of T 20.17 is such that $*R = |\mathcal{M}|$. Then $W(*R)$ need not be a subset of $|\mathcal{M}| \cup H(k)_{|\mathcal{M}|}$. If it is not, then $(\mathcal{M}, H(k)_{|\mathcal{M}|}, \mathcal{U}, \mathcal{S}, \varepsilon)$ is not an extension of $\mathcal{A}_{*R}$. However, by choosing α so large that $k >$ card$(W(*R))$, the model of T that we described in T 20.17 becomes an extension of $\mathcal{A}_{*R}$, with $+$, $\cdot$, and $<$ restricted to $*R$.

In thinking about the model of T described in T 20.17 and the extension of $\mathcal{A}_{*R}$ proposed above, several observations are relevant. To justify the construction of $H(k)_{|\mathcal{M}|}$, we must assume the validity of the Axiom of Choice. Hence we cannot use T to establish the existence of a model of T. Moreover, to find a k that is large enough for the construction of an extension of $\mathcal{A}_{*R}$, we may need Tarski's axiom concerning the existence of inaccessible cardinals. For a discussion of inaccessible cardinals, see Drake 1974 (pp. 65–68). The need for additional axioms to establish the existence of models of T is analogous to our needing KA 10 to construct a model of KPU in section 9.8 (see ST 49 and the discussion that followed).

21 Exchange in Hyperspace

In chapter 14 we studied the objective possibility and nomological adequacy of a scenario in which a finite number of consumers meet in the market to exchange goods at competitive equilibrium prices. The scenario has one disquieting feature: All consumers act as price takers even though any one of them acting alone could, if he chose to, influence the price at which trading occurs. In this chapter we shall use nonstandard analysis to study exchange in an economy with infinitely many consumers. Our purpose is (1) to model behavior in economies in which a single consumer by his own actions cannot influence the price at which trading occurs; and (2) to show that in sufficiently large economies a core allocation is a competitive-equilibrium allocation.

21.1 The Saturation Principle

To study exchange in hyperspace we must first impose a new condition on superstructure embeddings and discuss useful topological characteristics of hyperspace. Throughout our discussion L is the first-order language described in section 20.1. Also $\mathscr{A}_R = (W(R), N_{\mathscr{A}_R}, F^R, G^R)$ and $\mathscr{A}_{^*R} = (W(^*R), N_{\mathscr{A}_{^*R}}, F^{^*R}, G^{^*R})$ are the structures for L delineated in section 20.5.1. Finally, $^*(\cdot)$: $W(R) \rightarrow W(^*R)$ is a superstructure embedding that satisfies LP.

21.1.1 The Saturation Principle

The new condition that we impose on superstructure embeddings is called the *Saturation Principle*. We formulate it as follows:

SP Suppose that $A_i \in W(^*R)$, $i \in N$, is nonempty and internal. Suppose also that $A_0 \supset A_1 \supset \cdots$. Then $\sim[\bigcap_{i \in N} A_i = \varnothing]$; i.e., there is an internal object that belongs to all the A_i.

As evidenced in the following theorem, this is a meaningful principle.

T 21.1 There are superstructure embeddings that satisfy both LP and SP.

In fact, the superstructure embedding $j(i(\cdot))$ constructed in section 20.4.3 satisfies SP as well as LP. This is shown as follows: Let A_i, $i \in N$, be a decreasing sequence of nonempty internal sets, and assume that, for some $k > 1$ and all $i \in N$, $A_i \in {}^*W_k(R)$. Then there are sets $B_{ij} \in W_k(R)$, $j \in N$, $i \in N$, such that, if $\tilde{B}_i = \{B_{ij}\}_{\mathscr{U}}$, $A_i = j(\tilde{B}_i)$, $i \in N$. Without loss in generality we can assume that $\tilde{B}_0 = \{W_k(R)\}_{\mathscr{U}}$. If we do so, and if we let

$$I_n = \{j \in N : [[[j \geqslant n] \wedge [B_{0j} \supset B_{1j} \supset \cdots \supset B_{nj}]] \wedge \sim[B_{nj} = \varnothing]]\},$$

$n \in N$, then $I_0 = N$, $I_n \in \mathscr{U}$, $I_{n+1} \subset I_n$, and $\bigcap_{n \in N} I_n = \varnothing$. Also the function $m(\cdot)$: $N \to N$, defined by

$$m(j) = \max\{m \in N : j \in I_m\}, \qquad j \in N$$

is well defined and satisfies $(\forall j \in N)(\forall n \in N)[[j \in I_n] \supset [n \leqslant m(j)]]$. It follows that if we pick $C_j \in B_{m(j)j}$, $j \in N$, and let $C_{\mathscr{U}} = \{C_j\}_{\mathscr{U}}$, then $I_n \subset \{j \in N : C_j \in B_{nj}\}$ and $C_{\mathscr{U}} \in \tilde{B}_i$ for all $i \in N$. But if this is so, and if $C = j(C_{\mathscr{U}})$, then C is an internal set that belongs to all the A_i.[1]

21.1.2 Useful Consequences

The Saturation Principle has many interesting consequences. One concerns the cardinality of internal sets.

T 21.2 Let $E \in W({}^*R)$ be internal and suppose that E is countable from the outside; i.e., suppose that $E = \{e_0, e_1, \ldots\}$. If ${}^*(\cdot)$ satisfies LP and SP, E is finite.

To see why, let $E_n = E - \{e_0, \ldots, e_n\}$, $n \in N$, and observe that E_n is internal and that $E_0 \supset E_1 \supset \cdots$. By SP, $\sim[\bigcap_{n \in N} E_n = \varnothing]$. But that is impossible, so T 21.2 is true as stated.

E 21.1 Suppose that $E \in W({}^*R)$ is a hyperfinite set. Then there exists an *internal* bijection of E onto an initial segment of ${}^*N$, say $\{n \in {}^*N : n \leqslant m\}$. m is called the *internal cardinality* of E and denoted by $|E|$. If ${}^*(\cdot)$ satisfies LP and SP, E is countable from the outside only if $m \in N$. If $m \in {}^*N - N$, no *external* map of N onto E exists.

For us, the most important consequence of SP is recorded in T 21.3.

T 21.3 Let $A_n \in W({}^*R)$, $n \in N$, be a sequence of internal sets, and suppose that there is a $k \in N$ such that, for all $n \in N$, $A_n \in {}^*W_k(R)$. If ${}^*(\cdot)$ satisfies LP and SP, this sequence can be extended to an internal sequence on all of ${}^*N$.

The proof is easy: Let $l > k$ be so large that $(N \times W_k(R)) \in W_l(R)$. Also for each $n \in N$, let B_n denote the set

$$\{f \in {}^*W_l(R) : f(\cdot): {}^*N \to {}^*W_k(R) \qquad \text{and} \qquad (\forall i \leqslant n)[f(i) = A_i]\}.$$

Then B_n is nonempty; and, by T 20.12, B_n is internal. Also, $B_0 \supset B_1 \supset \cdots$. Hence, by SP, the intersection $\bigcap_{n \in N} B_n$ is not empty. Any member of this intersection may serve as the extension of $\{A_n, n \in N\}$.

We conclude this section with a startling consequence of SP which we shall need in order to discuss probability in hyperspace in chapter 22.

T 21.4 Let Ω, B, and A_i, $i \in N$, be internal sets in $W({}^*R)$. Suppose that Ω is internal and that B and the A_i are internal subsets of Ω. In addition, suppose that $B \subset \bigcup_{i \in N} A_i$. Then there is an $m \in N$ such that $B \subset \bigcup_{i=1}^m A_i$.

To prove the theorem observe that

$$\varnothing = B - \bigcup_{i \in N} A_i = \bigcap_{i \in N} (B - A_i).$$

It follows from SP that there is an $m \in N$ such that

$$\bigcap_{i=0}^{m} (B - A_i) = B - \bigcup_{i=1}^{m} A_i = \varnothing.$$

21.2 Two Nonstandard Topologies

Let X be a set and let $\mathscr{T}$ be a family of subsets of X. Then $(X, \mathscr{T})$ is a *topological space* and $\mathscr{T}$ is *a topology* for X if $\mathscr{T}$ satisfies these conditions:

(i) $\varnothing \in \mathscr{T}$ and $X \in \mathscr{T}$.
(ii) If $G_i \in \mathscr{T}$, $i = 1, \ldots, n$, then $\bigcap_{i=1}^n G_i \in \mathscr{T}$.
(iii) If I is an index set and $G_i \in \mathscr{T}$, $i \in I$, then $\bigcup_{i \in I} G_i \in \mathscr{T}$.

The members of $\mathscr{T}$ are the *open* subsets of X in this topology. Also a set A is *closed* in this topology if and only if its complement A^c is open. We note that any finite union of closed sets is closed; and any intersection of closed sets is closed. Finally the *closure of a set* A, denoted clo(A), is the intersection of all closed subsets of X that contain A; and the *interior of* A, denoted int(A), is the union of all the open subsets of A. For all $A \in \mathscr{P}(X)$, int(A) is open, clo(A) is closed, and int$(A) \subset A \subset$ clo(A). Also $A =$ int(A) if A is open, and $A =$ clo(A) if A is closed.

E 21.2 If X is a nonempty set, there are all sorts of topologies for X. Suppose that $\mathscr{T}_1$ and $\mathscr{T}_2$ are different topologies for X such that $\mathscr{T}_1 \subset \mathscr{T}_2$; then $\mathscr{T}_1$ is *weaker* than $\mathscr{T}_2$ and $\mathscr{T}_2$ is *stronger* than $\mathscr{T}_1$. The weakest topology for X is

$\mathscr{T} = \{\varnothing, X\}$; the strongest is $\mathscr{T} = \mathscr{P}(X)$. The latter is called the *discrete* topology for X.

Next let X be a nonempty set and let $\mathscr{B}$ be a family of subsets of X with the following properties:

(i) If $x \in X$, there is a $B \in \mathscr{B}$ with $x \in \mathscr{B}$.
(ii) If $B_1, B_2 \in \mathscr{B}$ and $x \in B_1 \cap B_2$, there is a $B_3 \in \mathscr{B}$ with $x \in B_3$ and $B_3 \subset B_1 \cap B_2$.

Moreover, for each subset A of X, let A be open if and only if, for each $x \in A$, there is a $B \in \mathscr{B}$ such that $x \in B$ and $B \subset A$. Finally, let $\mathscr{T}$ consist of all the open subsets of X. Then $\mathscr{T}$ is a topology for X. Specifically, $\mathscr{T}$ is *the topology* for X *generated* by $\mathscr{B}$. Also $\mathscr{B}$ is a *base* for $(X, \mathscr{T})$.

E 21.3 Let R and Q be, respectively, the set of real numbers and the set of rational numbers in R. In addition, for each $x \in R^n$ and $q \in Q \cap R_{++}$, let

$S(x, q) = \{y \in R^n : \|y - x\| < q\}$,

where $\|\cdot\|$ is the norm of UT 1 in chapter 10. Finally, define $\mathscr{S}$ by

$B \in \mathscr{S}$ if there is an $x \in Q^n$ and a $q \in Q \cap R_{++}$ such that $B = S(x, q)$.

Then $\mathscr{S}$ satisfies a and b above; and the topology for R^n generated by $\mathscr{S}$ is the *standard topology for* R^n described in section 10.1. We denote this topology by $\mathscr{T}_{R^n}$.

For the remainder of the chapter we assume that $^*(\cdot)$ satisfies LP and SP. We also assume that R^n is endowed with its standard topolgoy. With these assumptions in hand we consider two topologies for $^*R^n$, the * topology and the S topology.

21.2.1 The * Topology

Let $\mathscr{S}$ be as described in E 21.3. Then, by LP, $^*\mathscr{S}$ satisfies a and b above. Next, for each $A \subset {}^*R^n$, let A be open if and only if A is internal and, for each $x \in A$, there is a $B \in {}^*\mathscr{S}$ such that $x \in B$ and $B \subset A$. Finally, let $\mathscr{T}_{^*R^n}$ be the family of open subsets of $^*R^n$. Then $\mathscr{T}_{^*R^n}$ satisfies the following conditions:

(i) $\varnothing \in \mathscr{T}_{^*R^n}$ and $^*R^n \in \mathscr{T}_{^*R^n}$.
(ii) If $m \in {}^*N$ and if G_i is internal and $G_i \in \mathscr{T}_{^*R^n}$, $i = 0, \ldots, m$, then $\bigcap_{i=0}^m G_i \in \mathscr{T}_{^*R^n}$.
(iii) If I is an internal index set and $G_i \in \mathscr{T}_{^*R^n}$ for all $i \in I$, then $\bigcup_{i \in I} G_i \in \mathscr{T}_{^*R^n}$ if $\bigcup_{i \in I} G_i$ is internal.

A family of internal sets satisfying conditions i–iii is an *internal topology* for $^*R^n$. We will refer to $\mathcal{T}_{^*R^n}$ as the * *topology* of $^*R^n$.

Since the union of a set of open internal sets need not be internal, $\mathcal{T}_{^*R^n}$ is not a topology in the ordinary sense. It is, therefore, interesting to observe that $\mathcal{T}_{^*R^n}$ constitutes a base for a topology in $^*R^n$. A. Robinson called the topology generated by $\mathcal{T}_{^*R^n}$ the Q topology for $^*R^n$ and showed that an internal set B is open in the Q topology if and only if B belongs to $\mathcal{T}_{^*R^n}$ (see Robinson 1966, theorem 4.2.9, p. 99).

The relationship between the * topology of $^*R^n$ and the standard topology of R^n is described in the following theorem:

T 21.5 $\mathcal{T}_{^*R^n} = {}^*(\mathcal{T}_{R^n})$.

The proof is as follows: Let A be an internal subset of $^*R^n$. Then $A \in {}^*W_k(R)$ for some $k > 1$; and the following assertion is the * transform of an assertion that is true in $\mathscr{A}_R$:

$$(\forall z \in {}^*W_k(R))[[z \in {}^*(\mathcal{T}_{R^n})] \equiv (\forall x \in z)(\exists B \in {}^*\mathscr{S})[[x \in B] \wedge [B \subset z]]].$$

From this and LP follows the validity of T 21.5.

For each $x \in {}^*R^n$ let $^*S(x, l^{-1}) = \{y \in {}^*R^n : \|y - x\| < l^{-1}\}$. Then the monad of x is defined as

$$m(x) = \bigcap_{l \in N} {}^*S(x, l^{-1}).$$

By SP, $m(x) \neq \varnothing$. If $y \in m(x)$, we write $y \approx x$ and read aloud, "y is infitesimally close to x." For all $x \in {}^*R^n$, $x \approx x$. Also, $y \approx x$ if and only if $x \approx y$. Finally, if $x \approx y$ and $y \approx z$, then $x \approx z$. Hence $\approx$ is an equivalence relation. From this we can infer T 21.6.

T 21.6 If $x, y \in {}^*R^n$, either $m(x) = m(y)$ or $m(x) \cap m(y) = \varnothing$.

The monad of an $x \in {}^*R^n$ need not be an internal subset of $^*R^n$. However, for each $x \in {}^*R^n$, there is an internal open set $B \subset m(x)$—see T 21.7.

T 21.7 If $x \in {}^*R^n$, there is a $B \in \mathcal{T}_{^*R^n}$ such that $x \in B$ and $B \subset m(x)$.

The proof is as follows: Let $\mathscr{S}_x = \{A \in \mathcal{T}_{^*R^n} : x \in A\}$ and, for each $l \in N$, let $B_l = \{A \in \mathscr{S}_x : A \subset {}^*S(x, l^{-1})$. Then by T 20.12 $\mathscr{S}_x$ and the B_l are internal and nonempty. Moreover, $B_{l+1} \subset B_l$, $l \in N$. By SP there is an internal set $B \in \bigcap_{l \in N} B_l$. Since $B \in B_l$, $B \in \mathscr{S}_x$. From this and $\mathscr{S}_x \subset \mathcal{T}_{^*R^n}$ follows the validity of the theorem.

E 21.4 Let $n = 1$ and consider the set $^*(0, 1)$. By transfer this set is open in the * topology. Note, therefore, that $m(0) \cap {}^*(0, 1) \neq \varnothing$. Also, if $x \in R \cap {}^*(0, 1)$, $m(x) \subset {}^*(0, 1)$ and there is a $B \in {}^*(\mathcal{T}_{R^n})$ such that $x \in B$ and $B \subset m(x)$.

It follows from T 21.5 and LP that a subset A of R^n is open (closed) if and only if $^*A$ is open (closed) in the * topology. For later purposes we give another characterization of the open (closed) subsets of R^n in T 21.8:

T 21.8 For an $A \subset R^n$, the following assertions are true:

(i) $A \in \mathcal{T}_{R^n}$ if and only if, for all $x \in A$, $m(x) \subset {}^*A$; and

(ii) $A^C \in \mathcal{T}_{R^n}$ if and only if, for all $x \in R^n$ and all $y \in {}^*A$, $y \in m(x)$ implies $x \in A$.

The proof of assertion i is easy: If $A \in \mathcal{T}_{R^n}$ and $x \in A$, there is a $q \in R_{++} \cap Q$ such that $S(x, q) \subset A$. By LP, $m(x) \subset {}^*S(x, q) \subset {}^*A$. Conversely, if $m(x) \subset {}^*A$, by T 21.7, there is a $B \in {}^*(\mathcal{T}_{R^n})$ such that $x \in B$ and $B \subset m(x) \subset {}^*A$. By LP, there is a $\tilde{B} \in \mathcal{T}_{R^n}$ such that $x \in \tilde{B}$ and $\tilde{B} \subset A$.

The validity of assertion ii is an immediate consequence of the validity of assertion i and needs no further proof.

A vector $x \in {}^*R^n$ is *near-standard* if and only if $x \in m(y)$ for some $y \in R^n$. If $x \in {}^*R^n$ is near-standard, $y = {}^\circ x$ if and only if $y \in R^n$ and $x \in m(y)$. Also, $x \in Ns({}^*R^n)$ if and only if $x \in {}^*R^n$ and x is near-standard. Finally, if $A \subset {}^*R^n$, A is *near-standard* if and only if $A \subset Ns({}^*R^n)$, and ${}^\circ A = \{y \in R^n : y = {}^\circ x$ for some $x \in A \cap Ns({}^*R^n)\}$.

E 21.5 Let $A \subset {}^*R$ be ${}^*(0, \frac{1}{2}) \cup {}^*(\frac{1}{2}, 1)$. Then A is internal and ${}^\circ A = [0, 1]$.

For internal subsets of $^*R^n$ we can establish the following interesting theorem:

T 21.9 If $A \subset {}^*R^n$ is internal, ${}^\circ A$ is closed in $\mathcal{T}_{R^n}$.

The proof goes as follows: Suppose that ${}^\circ A$ is not closed. Then there is an $x \in R^n - {}^\circ A$ such that $S(x, l^{-1}) \cap {}^\circ A \neq \emptyset$ for all $l \in N$. If $y \in S(x, l^{-1}) \cap {}^\circ A$, there is a $z \in A$ such that $y = {}^\circ z$. Hence $m(y) \cap A \neq \emptyset$. From this and the fact that $m(y) \subset {}^*S(x, l^{-1})$, it follows that ${}^*S(x, l^{-1}) \cap A \neq \emptyset$ for all $l \in N$. But then, by SP and the internality of A, it follows that $m(x) \cap A \neq \emptyset$ and that $x \in {}^\circ A$, contrary to our initial assumption.

It is obvious that $A \subset R^n$ is *compact* (i.e., closed and bounded) in $\mathcal{T}_{R^n}$ only if $^*A$ is closed in the * topology and bounded by an $m \in N$. In fact, we come to the following:

T 21.10 A set $A \subset R^n$ is compact in $\mathcal{T}_{R^n}$ if and only if, for all $x \in {}^*A$, there is a $y \in A$ such that $x \in m(y)$.

The proof is easy. I leave it to the reader.

We shall say that an internal set B is **-compact* if and only if B is closed in the * topology and there is an $m \in {}^*N$ such that $B \subset \{x \in {}^*R^n : \|x\| \leqslant m\}$.

For internal sets the following theorem is the * transform of an assertion that is valid in $\mathscr{T}_{R^n}$.

T 21.11 Suppose that $A \subset {}^*R^n$ is internal and *-compact and let $\mathscr{G}$ be an internal family of *-open sets that cover A. There is an $m \in {}^*N$ and a sequence of sets G_i, $i = 0, 1, \ldots, m$, such that $G_i \in \mathscr{G}$ and $A \subset \bigcup_{i=0}^{m} G_i$.

If A is a subset of R^n, A is convex if and only if, for all $x, y \in A$ and all $\lambda \in (0, 1)$, $\lambda x + (1 - \lambda)y \in A$. Similarly, if B is an internal subset of ${}^*R^n$, B is *-convex if and only if, for all $x, y \in B$ and all $\lambda \in {}^*(0, 1)$, $\lambda x + (1 - \lambda)y \in B$. In R^n the convex hull of a set A consists of all $x \in R^n$ for which there exist an $m \in N$, $x_i \in A$, and $\lambda_i \in [0, 1]$, $i = 1, \ldots, m$, such that

$$\sum_{i=1}^{m} \lambda_i = 1 \qquad \text{and} \qquad x = \sum_{i=1}^{m} \lambda_i x_i.$$

Similarly, the *-convex hull of an internal subset B of ${}^*R^n$ consists of all $x \in {}^*R^n$ for which there exist $m \in {}^*N$, $x_i \in B$, and $\lambda_i \in {}^*[0, 1]$ such that

$$\sum_{i=1}^{m} \lambda_i = 1 \qquad \text{and} \qquad x = \sum_{i=1}^{m} \lambda_i x_i.$$

For *-convex internal subsets of ${}^*R^n$ we can establish an important separation theorem, T 21.12.

T 21.12 Let B be a *-convex internal subset of ${}^*R^n$ and suppose that $x \in {}^*R^n - B$. Then there is a $p \in {}^*R^n - \{0\}$ such that $B \subset \{y \in {}^*R^n : px \leqslant py\}$.

The proof is easy: Let B be an internal subset of ${}^*R^n$ and let $C(A)$ assert that A is convex; i.e.,

$$C(A) =_{\text{df}} (\forall x \in A)(\forall y \in A)(\forall \lambda \in (0, 1))[(\lambda x + (1 - \lambda)y) \in A].$$

Suppose also that $B \in {}^*W_k(R)$ for some $k > 1$. Then

$$(\forall z \in W_k(R))[[[[z \subset R^n] \wedge C(z)] \wedge [x \in R^n - z]]$$

$$\supset (\exists p \in R^n - \{0\})(\forall y \in z)[px \leqslant py]]$$

is true in $\mathscr{A}_R$. Its * transform, which is a symbolic rendition of T 21.12 is, by LP, true in $\mathscr{A}_{{}^*R}$.

An internal function $f(\cdot)$: $A \to B$ is **-continuous* if it is continuous in the * topology. Thus, if $A \subset {}^*R^n$ and $B \subset {}^*R$, $f(\cdot)$ is *-continuous at $x \in A$ if and only if, for all $\varepsilon \in {}^*R_{++}$, there is a $\delta \in {}^*R_{++}$ such that, for all $y \in A$ with $\|y - x\| < \delta$, $|f(y) - f(x)| < \varepsilon$. Also $f(\cdot)$ is *-continuous if it is *-continuous at every $x \in A$. For *-continuous functions we can establish the following extension of Brouwer's Fixed-Point Theorem, UT 12.

T 21.13 Let A be an internal *-compact convex subset of $^*R^n$ and suppose that $f(\cdot)\colon A \to A$ is internal and *-continuous. Then there is an $x \in A$ such that $x = f(x)$.

The proof is as follows: Let $k_1 > 1$ and $k_2 > k_1$ be such that $A \in {}^*W_{k_1}(R)$ and $f \in {}^*W_{k_2}(R)$. In addition, let $C(A)$ be as above and let

$$\psi(f, A) =_{\text{df}} [[f(\cdot)\colon A \to A] \wedge (\forall V \in \mathscr{T}_{R^n})(\forall x \in A)[[f(x) \in V] \supset (\exists U \in \mathscr{T}_{R^n})[[x \in U] \wedge [U \cap A) \subset f^{-1}(V \cap A)]]]].$$

Then the assertion

$$(\forall z \in W_{k_1}(R))[[C(z) \wedge [[z^c \in \mathscr{T}_{R^n}] \wedge (\exists m \in N)[z \subset S(0, m)]]] \supset (\forall f \in W_{k_2}(R))[\psi(f, z) \supset (\exists x \in z)[x = f(x)]]]$$

is valid in $\mathscr{A}_R$. By LP, its * transform, which is a symbolic rendition of T 21.13, is valid in $\mathscr{A}_{^*R}$.

21.2.2 The S Topology

For an $A \subset {}^*R^n$ we shall say that A is *S-open* if and only if, for all $x \in A$, there is a $q \in Q \cap R_{++}$ such that $^*S(x, q) \subset A$. The S-open sets form a topology for $^*R^n$ that we call the S topology and denote by $\mathscr{T}_S$.

We note in passing that our S topology is the same as A. Robinson's S topology (Robinson 1966, pp. 106–107). To wit: Robinson insisted that a set $A \subset {}^*R^n$ is an S ball if and only if there exists a $q \in R_{++}$ and an $a \in A$ such that $A = \{x \in {}^*R^n : \text{st}(\|x - a\|) < q\}$. He also demonstrated that the family of S balls constitute a base for a topology which he named the S topology. Since

$$\{x \in {}^*R^n : \|x - a\| < (q/2)\} \subset \{x \in {}^*R^n : \text{st}(\|x - a\|) < q\} \subset \{x \in {}^*R^n : \|x - a\| < q\}$$

when $q \in R_{++}$, an $A \subset {}^*R^n$ is open in Robinson's S topology if and only if it is open in our S topology.

The * transform of an open set need not be S-open; e.g., $^*(0, 1)$ is not S-open. However, an S-open internal subset of $^*R^n$ is open in the * topology. The following four theorems describe how the S topology differs from the * topology.

T 21.14 For $A \in \mathscr{P}(^*R^n)$ let $S\text{-int}(A)$ be the union of all the S-open subsets of A. If $x \in {}^*R^n$ and $x \notin S\text{-int}(A)$, then $m(x) \cap S\text{-int}(A) = \varnothing$.

To prove this theorem suppose that $y \in m(x) \cap S\text{-int}(A)$. Then there is an $l_0 \in N$ so large that, for all $l \geqslant l_0$, $^*S(y, l^{-1}) \subset S\text{-int}(A)$. Hence, for any $l > l_0$, $x \notin S(y, l^{-1})$; i.e., $\|y - x\| \geqslant l^{-1}$, which contradicts $y \in m(x)$.

It follows from the proof of T 21.14 that, if $A \in \mathscr{T}_S$, then, for all $x \in A$, $m(x) \subset A$. When A is internal, the latter condition is sufficient for $A \in \mathscr{T}_S$ as well, and we have the following theorem:

T 21.15 If $A \in \mathscr{P}(^*R^n)$ is internal, $x \in S\text{-int}(A)$ if and only if $m(x) \subset A$.

The proof is as follows: If $x \in S\text{-int}(A)$, there is an $l \in N$ such that $m(x) \subset {}^*S(x, l^{-1}) \subset A$. If $m(x) \subset A$, then by T 20.12 the set $\{l \in {}^*N : {}^*S(x, l^{-1}) \subset A\}$ is internal and contains all infinitely large numbers in $^*N$. By T 20.13 (iii) there is an $l \in N$ such that $^*S(x, l^{-1}) \subset A$.

A set $A \subset {}^*R^n$ is S-closed if and only if its complement is S-open. From this and T 21.15 we deduce the validity of T 20.16:

T 21.16 If $A = \mathscr{P}(^*R^n)$ is internal and $x \in {}^*R^n$, then $x \in S\text{-clo}(A)$ if and only if $m(x) \cap A \neq \emptyset$.

For later reference, I give examples of the S closure of several internal sets below: Note that one of the sets is *-open. The other is *-closed.

E 21.6 Suppose that $a \in {}^*R$ and $p \in {}^*R^n_{++} - m(0)$ are near-standard. Then in $^*R$

$S\text{-clo}(^*(0, 1)) = m(0) \cup {}^*(0, 1) \cup m(1);$

and if $A = \{x \in {}^*R^n : a \leqslant px\}$,

$S\text{-clo}(A) = \{x \in {}^*R^n : a \lesssim px\}$

in $^*R^n$, where $a \lesssim b$ means that either $a < b$ or $b \approx a$.

The *boundary* of a set A is defined to equal the intersection of clo(A) and clo(A^c). From this definition and from T 21.15 and T 21.16 follows the validity of T 21.17 below:

T 21.17 If $A \in \mathscr{P}(^*R^n)$ is internal, and $x \in {}^*R^n$, then x is in the S boundary of A if and only if both $m(x) \cap A \neq \emptyset$ and $m(x) \cap A^c \neq \emptyset$.

Evidently the content of the boundary of a set depends on the relevant topology. Here is an example to illustrate this fact.

E 21.7 In the * topology of $^*R$, the boundary of $^*(0, 1)$ is $\{0, 1\}$; in the S topology, the boundary is $m(0) \cup m(1)$. Also, if A is as in E 21.6, in $\mathscr{T}_{^*R^n}$ the boundary of A is $\{x \in {}^*R^n : px = a\}$; in $\mathscr{T}_S$ the boundary of A is $\{x \in {}^*R^n : px \approx a\}$.

In A, $B \in \mathscr{P}(^*R^n)$, a function $f(\cdot): A \to B$ is S-continuous if and only if it is continuous in the S topology. Thus, if $A \subset {}^*R^n$ and $B \subset {}^*R$, $f(\cdot)$ is

S-continuous at $x \in A$ if and only if, for all $\varepsilon \in R_{++}$, there is a $\delta \in R_{++}$ such that, for all $y \in A$, $\|y - x\| < \delta$ implies $|f(y) - f(x)| < \varepsilon$. Also $f(\cdot)$ is S-continuous if and only if it is S-continuous at every $x \in A$. An S-continuous function need not be *-continuous, and a *-continuous function need not be S-continuous, as illustrated below:

E 21.8 Suppose that $H \in {}^*N - N$ and consider the two internal functions

$f(x) = \sin Hx, \qquad x \in {}^*(0, 1);$

and

$$g(x) = \begin{cases} H^{-1} & \text{if } x \in {}^*Q \cap {}^*[0, 1] \\ 0 & \text{if } x \in {}^*[0, 1] - {}^*Q. \end{cases}$$

Then $f(\cdot)$ is *-continuous on $^*(0, 1)$ and S-continuous nowhere, whereas $g(\cdot)$ is S-continuous on $^*[0, 1]$ and *-continuous nowhere.

For internal functions we can establish several interesting theorems concerning their S-continuity.

T 21.18 Suppose that $A \subset {}^*R^n$ is internal and that $f(\cdot): A \to {}^*R$ is internal. Moreover, for any $B \in \mathscr{P}({}^*R^n)$, let $f(B) = \{r \in {}^*R : r = f(x) \text{ for some } x \in B\}$. Then $f(\cdot)$ is S-continuous at $x \in A$ if and only if $f(m(x) \cap A) \subset \tilde{m}(f(x))$, where $\tilde{m}(f(x))$ denotes the monad in $^*R$ of $f(x)$.

I shall prove the necessity of the condition and leave the sufficiency to the reader. Let $^*\tilde{S}(r, l^{-1}) = \{y \in {}^*R : |y - r| < l^{-1}\}$ and observe that, for any given $k \in N$, $\{l \in {}^*N : f({}^*S(x, l^{-1}) \cap A) \subset {}^*\tilde{S}(f(x), k^{-1})\}$ is internal. If $f(\cdot)$ is S-continuous at x, the set contains $^*N - N$. By T 20.13 (iii) it contains an $l \in N$. Since $m(x) \subset {}^*S(x, l^{-1})$, it follows that $f(m(x) \cap A) \subset {}^*\tilde{S}(f(x), k^{-1})$. By the arbitrariness of k we conclude that $f(m(x) \cap A) \subset \tilde{m}(f(x))$ as well.

T 21.19 Suppose that $A \in \mathscr{P}({}^*R^n)$ is internal and that $f(\cdot): A \to {}^*R$ is internal and S-continuous. Then $f(\cdot)$ is uniformly S-continuous on A.

This proof is easy: By T 20.12, for any given k, the set

$$\{l \in {}^*N : (\forall x \in A)[f({}^*S(x, l^{-1}) \cap A) \subset {}^*\tilde{S}(f(x), k^{-1})]\}$$

is internal and contains $^*N - N$. Hence, by T 20.13 (iii) it also contains an $l \in N$. From this and the arbitrariness of k follows T 21.19.

If $A \subset {}^*R^n$, the S-convex hull of A consists of all $x \in {}^*R^n$ for which there is an $m \in N$ and pairs $(x_i, \lambda_i) \in A \times {}^*[0, 1]$, $i = 1, \ldots, m$, such that

$$\sum_{i=1}^{m} \lambda_i = 1 \qquad \text{and} \qquad x = \sum_{i=1}^{m} \lambda_i x_i.$$

A set $A \subset {}^*R^n$ that contains its S-convex hull is said to be S-convex. S-convex sets have several interesting properties that we detail next.

T 21.20 If $A \in \mathscr{P}({}^*R^n)$ is S-convex, S-int(A) is S-convex.

The proof is as follows: If S-int(A) is empty, there is nothing to prove. Suppose that $x, y \in S\text{-int}(A)$ and that $\lambda \in {}^*(0, 1)$. There are two cases to consider: $\lambda \not\simeq 1$ and $\lambda \not\simeq 0$. I will take the first case and leave the second to the reader. If $\lambda \not\simeq 1$, then, for sufficiently large k, $y + k^{-1}((1 + \lambda)/(1-\lambda)){}^*S(0, 1) \subset A$ and $\lambda x + (1-\lambda)y + k^{-1}{}^*S(0, 1) \subset \lambda(A + k^{-1}{}^*S(0, 1)) + (1-\lambda)y + k^{-1}{}^*S(0, 1) = (1-\lambda)(y + k^{-1}((1+\lambda)/(1-\lambda)){}^*S(0, 1)) + \lambda A \subset (1 - \lambda)A + \lambda A = A$. Hence $\lambda x + (1 - \lambda)y \in S\text{-int}(A)$, as was to be shown.

T 21.21 If $A \subset {}^*R^n$ is S-convex, ${}^\circ A$ is convex in R^n.

When A is empty or consists of just one point, there is nothing to prove. So to prove the theorem we assume that $x, y \in {}^\circ A$ and $\lambda \in (0, 1)$. Then there are vectors ε_1 and ε_2 in $m(0)$ such that $x + \varepsilon_1$ and $y + \varepsilon_2$ belong to A. Consequently, $\lambda x + (1 - \lambda)y + (\lambda\varepsilon_1 + (1 - \lambda)\varepsilon_2) \in A$ as well. Since $\lambda \in R$, $\lambda\varepsilon_1 + (1 - \lambda)\varepsilon_2 \in m(0)$, which shows that $\lambda x + (1 - \lambda)y \in {}^\circ A$.

The preceding results can be used to construct a simple proof of a separation theorem which will prove important for our purposes.

T 21.22 If $A \subset {}^*R^n$ is near-standard and S-convex; and if $x \in R^n$ and $x \notin S\text{-int}(A)$, then there is a $p \in R^n - \{0\}$ such that $px \lesssim py$ for all $y \in S\text{-int}(A)$.

If S-int(A) is empty, there is nothing to prove. Hence, suppose that $S\text{-int}(A) \neq \varnothing$. Then, by T 21.20, S-int(A) is S-convex and, by T 21.21, ${}^\circ(S\text{-int}(A))$ is convex. Furthermore, by T 21.14, $x \notin {}^\circ(S\text{-int}(A))$. Hence, by UT 4, there is a $p \in R^n - \{0\}$ such that $px \leqslant py$ for all $y \in {}^\circ(S\text{-int}(A))$. Since p is real, $p\delta \simeq 0$ for all $\delta \in m(0)$. Consequently, $px \lesssim py$ for all $y \in S$-int(A), as was to be shown.[2]

21.3 Exchange in Hyperspace by Transfer

In this section we shall use the method of transfer to study resource allocation in a hyperfinite exchange economy.

21.3.1 A Hyperfinite Exchange Economy

A hyperfinite exchange economy E is a triple $(U(\cdot), T \times {}^*R^n_+, A(\cdot))$, where $T = \{1, \ldots, \gamma\}$ for some $\gamma \in {}^*N - N$, $U(\cdot)\colon T \times {}^*R^n_+ \to {}^*R_+$, and

$A(\cdot)$: $T \to {}^*R^n_{++}$. We assume that both $^*R$ and $^*R^n$ are endowed with the * topology and that

(i) $A(\cdot)$ is internal;
(ii) there is a pair $(\delta, r) \in R^2_{++}$ such that, for all $t \in T$, $\delta \leqslant A(t) \leqslant r$;
(iii) $U(\cdot)$ is internal; and
(iv) for each $t \in T$, $U(t, \cdot)$ is strictly increasing, strictly quasi-concave and continuous in the * topology. Specifically:
   a. If $x, y \in {}^*R^n_+$, $x \geqslant y$, and $x \neq y$, then $U(t, x) > U(t, y)$.
   b. If $x \in {}^*R^n_+$, then $\{z \in {}^*R^n_+ : U(t, z) \geqslant U(t, x)\}$ is *-convex.
   c. If $x, y \in {}^*R^n_+$, $x \neq y$ and $\lambda \in {}^*(0, 1)$, then

$$U(t, \lambda x + (1 - \lambda)y) > \min(U(t, x), U(t, y)).$$

   d. $U(t, \cdot)$ is *-continuous.

In our intended interpretation of E, T is an index set, each point of which names a particular consumer in E. Different points in T name different consumers; and each consumer in E is named by some point in T. The set $^*R^n_+$ represents the consumers' commodity space and the value of $A(\cdot)$ at t describes the initial commodity bundle of the tth consumer. Finally, for each t, $U(t, \cdot)$ is the utility indicator of consumer t.

To study resource allocation in E we must first formulate the properties of $U(\cdot)$ symbolically: The monotonicity of $U(t, \cdot)$ is expressed by the * transform of

$$\psi_1(t, U) =_{\text{df}} (\forall x \in R^n_+)(\forall y \in R^n_+)[[[x \leqslant y] \wedge \sim[x = y]] \supset [U(t, x) < U(t, y)]].$$

Similarly the quasi-concavity of $U(t, \cdot)$ is expressed by the * transform of

$$\psi_2(t, U) =_{\text{df}} (\forall x \in R^n_+)(\forall y \in R^n_+)(\forall \lambda \in (0, 1))[\sim[x = y] \supset [[U(t, \lambda x + (1 - \lambda)y) > U(t, x)] \vee [U(t, \lambda x + (1 - \lambda)y) > U(t, y)]]].$$

Finally, the * continuity of $U(t, \cdot)$ is expressed by the * transform of

$$\psi_3(t, U) =_{\text{df}} (\forall z \in \mathscr{T}_R)(\forall x \in R^n_+)[[f(x) \in z] \supset (\exists y \in \mathscr{T}_{R^n}[[x \in y] \wedge [(y \cap R^n_+) \subset U(t, \cdot)^{-1}(z \cap R_+)]]].$$

Next we must say what we mean by a * allocation and a * competitive equilibrium. In our hyperfinite exchange economy, E, a * allocation is an internal function $X(\cdot)$: $T \to {}^*R^n_+$ such that $\sum_{t \in T} X(t) = \sum_{t \in T} A(t)$. Also, a

* competitive equilibrium is a pair $(p, X(\cdot))$, where $p \in {}^*R^n_{++}$ and $X(\cdot)$ is a * allocation that, for all $t \in T$, satisfies these conditions:

(i) $pX(t) = pA(t)$.
(ii) $U(t, X(t)) = \max_{y \in \{x \in {}^*R^n_+ : px \leqslant pA(t)\}} U(t, y)$.

We can show the following:

T 21.23 There exists a * competitive equilibrium in E.

To do that we let

$\psi_4(y, p, A) =_{\text{df}} [py \leqslant pA]$,

where $y \in R^n_+$, $p \in R^n_{++}$, and $A \in R^n_+$. Then we pick k_1 and k_2 so that $A(\cdot) \in {}^*W_{k_1}(R)$ and $U(\cdot) \in {}^*W_{k_2}(R)$ and assert

$$(\forall A \in W_{k_1}(R))(\forall U \in W_{k_2}(R))(\forall T \in \mathscr{P}_F(N))[[[[A(\cdot): T \to R^n_{++}]$$
$$\wedge [U(\cdot): T \times R^n_+ \to R_+]] \wedge (\forall t \in T)[\psi_1(t, U) \wedge [\psi_2(t, U)$$
$$\wedge \psi_3(t, U)]]] \supset (\exists p \in R^n_{++})(\exists X \in W_{k_1}(R))[[[X(\cdot): T \to R^n_+]$$
$$\wedge [\sum_{t \in T} X(t) = \sum_{t \in T} A(t)]] \wedge (\forall t \in T)[\psi_4(X(t), p, A(t))$$
$$\wedge (\forall y \in R^n_+)[\psi_4(y, p, A(t)) \supset [U(t, y) \leqslant U(t, X(t))]]]]]].$$

By T 14.1 this assertion is valid in $\mathscr{A}_R$. By LP its * transform, which is a symbolic rendition of T 21.23, is valid in $\mathscr{A}_{{}^*R}$.

A *-Pareto-optimal allocation is a * allocation $X(\cdot)$ for which there exists no other * allocation $Y(\cdot)$ such that, for all $t \in T$, $U(t, X(t)) \leqslant U(t, Y(t))$ with strict inequality for some t. If we let k_1 be as in the proof of T 21.23 and define

$$A = \left\{X \in {}^*W_{k_1}(R) : \left[[X(\cdot): T \to {}^*R^n_+] \wedge \left[\sum_{t \in T} X(t) = \sum_{t \in T} A(t)\right]\right]\right\},$$

the set of *Pareto-optimal allocations, Q, is given by

$$Q = \{X \in A : \sim(\exists Y \in A)[(\forall t \in T)[U(t, X(t)) \leqslant U(t, Y(t))]$$
$$\wedge (\exists t \in T)[U(t, X(t)) < U(t, Y(t))]]\}.$$

By T 20.12, both A and Q are internal.

With only obvious modifications, the proof of T 14.4 can be used to establish the following theorem:

T 21.24 If $(p, X(\cdot))$ is a * competitive equilibrium in E, then $X(\cdot) \in Q$.

The converse of T 21.24 is also true, so we have T 21.25:

T 21.25 If $X(\cdot) \in Q$, there is a $p \in {}^*R^n_{++}$ and a distribution of $p(\sum_{t \in T} A(t))$ relative to which $(p, X(\cdot))$ is a * competitive equilibrium.

To prove T 21.25 we use T 14.6 and transfer. For that purpose we let

$$\psi_5(X, A, T) =_{\mathrm{df}} \left[[X(\cdot)\colon T \to R^n_+] \wedge \left[\sum_{t \in T} X(t) = \sum_{t \in T} A(t) \right] \right]$$

and

$$\psi_6(X, Y, U, T) =_{\mathrm{df}} [(\forall t \in T)[U(t, X(t)) \leqslant U(t, Y(t))]$$
$$\wedge\ (\exists t \in T)[U(t, X(t)) < U(t, Y(t))]].$$

Then we apply T 14.6 to infer the validity in $\mathscr{A}_R$ of the following assertion:

$$(\forall A \in W_{k_1}(R))(\forall U \in W_{k_2}(R))(\forall T \in \mathscr{P}_F(N))[[[[A(\cdot)\colon T \to R^n_{++}]$$
$$\wedge\ [U(\cdot)\colon T \times R^n_+ \to R_+]] \wedge (\forall t \in T)[\psi_1(t, U) \wedge [\psi_2(t, U) \wedge \psi_3(t, U)]]]$$
$$\supset (\forall X \in W_{k_1}(R))[[\psi_5(X, A, T) \wedge \sim(\exists Y \in W_{k_1}(R))[\psi_5(Y, A, T)$$
$$\wedge\ \psi_6(X, Y, U, T)]] \supset (\exists p \in R^n_{++})(\forall t \in T)(\forall z \in R^n_+)[\psi_4(z, p, X(t))$$
$$\supset [U(t, z) \leqslant U(t, X(t))]]]]].$$

By LP the * transform of this assertion, which is a symbolic rendition of T 21.25, is valid in $\mathscr{A}_{^*R}$.

From my point of view, the most interesting theorems of nonstandard economic analysis concern the relationship between the set of competitive equilibria and the core of E. The definition of the core of E depends on the topological basis of our analysis. In this section a * allocation $X(\cdot)$ is in the * core of E if and only if there is no internal subset S of T and a * allocation $Y(\cdot)$ such that

(i) $\sum_{t \in S} Y(t) = \sum_{t \in S} A(t)$ and

(ii) for all $t \in S$, $U(t, X(t)) \leqslant U(t, Y(t))$ with strict inequality for some $t \in S$.

If there is an internal set $S \subset T$ and a * allocation $Y(\cdot)$ that satisfy conditions i and ii, we shall say that S *blocks* $X(\cdot)$. Furthermore, we shall call an internal subset of T a *coalition*.

With some obvious modifications we can use the proof of T 14.4 to show T 21.26:

T 21.26 If $(p, X(\cdot))$ is a * competitive equilibrium in E, then $X(\cdot)$ belongs to the * core of E.

However, there is no way to establish the converse—that a core allocation necessarily is a competitive equilibrium allocation. This is interesting because it suggests that it is not the number of consumers alone that ensures the equivalence of core and competitive equilibrium allocations in E.

21.3.2 A Nonstandard Version of a Theorem of Debreu and Scarf

In a path-breaking study of large economies, Debreu and Scarf obtained an interesting result that we can paraphrase as follows: Let E be the standard exchange economy of section 14.1, and let E_n be the economy consisting of n replicas of E. For large n, the core of E_n is approximately equal to the set of competitive equilibria in E_n (Debreu and Scarf 1963). We shall next establish a nonstandard analogue of Debreu and Scarf's result. The arguments we use are nonstandard translations of Debreu and Scarf's arguments.

Suppose that $\gamma = \eta k$ for some $k \in {}^*N$ and $\eta < \gamma$ and suppose that E contains k different types of consumers and η consumers of each type. To keep consumers of different types apart, we index consumers by pairs (i, j), where $i = 1, \ldots, k$, and $j = 1, \ldots, \eta$. Also, we denote the utility function and initial quantities of type i consumers by $U_i(\cdot)$ and $A_i(\cdot)$, respectively. Then, for $i = 1, \ldots, k$, $U_i(\cdot)\colon \{1, \ldots, \eta\} \times {}^*R_+^n \to {}^*R_+$ and $A_i(\cdot)\colon \{1, \ldots, \eta\} \to {}^*R_{++}^n$ are internal functions that do not vary with the index in $\{1, \ldots, \eta\}$. Also, for a fixed pair (i, j), $U_i(j, \cdot)$ is strictly increasing, strictly quasi-concave, and *-continuous.

T 21.27 Suppose that E is as described above, with k different types of consumers and η consumers of each type. Also suppose that $X_i(\cdot)\colon \{1, \ldots, \eta\} \to {}^*R_+^n$, $i = 1, \ldots, k$, is a * allocation in the * core of E. Then $X_i(j) = X_i(1)$ for all $j \in \{1, \ldots, \eta\}$, $i = 1, \ldots, k$; that is, consumers of the same type receive identical commodity bundles.

The proof is as follows: For each i there is an l such that $U_i(1, X_i(l)) \leqslant U_i(1, X_i(j))$ for all $j \in \{1, \ldots, \eta\}$. Let $x_i = X_i(l)$ for such an l, $i = 1, \ldots, k$, and suppose that there is a consumer j of type r whose commodity bundle $X_r(j) \neq x_r$. Then the strict quasi-concavity of the $U_i(1, \cdot)$ implies that $U_i(1, \eta^{-1} \sum_{j=1}^{\eta}, X_i(j)) \geqslant U_i(1, x_i)$ for all $i = 1, \ldots, k$, with strict inequality for $i = r$. Next let S be a coalition consisting of k consumers, one consumer from each type and each consumer having been allocated the x_i of his type in $X(\cdot)$. Since

$$\sum_{i=1}^{k}\left[\eta^{-1}\sum_{j=1}^{\eta} X_i(j) - A_i(1)\right] = 0,$$

S blocks $X(\cdot)$—a contradiction that establishes the theorem.

In the next theorem we consider a sequence of economics, E_ξ, $\xi \in {}^*N$, with k different types of consumers and ξ consumers of each type. We denote a * allocation in E_ξ by $X^\xi(\cdot)$ and let $X^\xi = (X_1^\xi(1),, \ldots, X_k^\xi(1))$. In addition, we let

$$C_\xi = \{x \in {}^*R_+^{kn} : x = X^\xi \text{ for some } X^\xi(\cdot) \text{ in the * core of } E_\xi\}$$

and we assume that the E_ξ have the same types of consumers as E. Then E_η and E denote the same economy and $C_\xi \subset C_\psi$ when $\psi \leqslant \xi$. Since $(p, X^\eta(\cdot))$ is a * competitive equilibrium in E_η only if (p, X^η) is a * competitive equilibrium in E_1, it follows from T 21.28 below that as ξ grows, C_ξ shrinks to the set of * competitive equilibrium allocations in E_1.

T 21.28 Suppose that E satisfies the conditions of T 21.27 and let the sequence of pairs, (E_ξ, C_ξ), $\xi \in {}^*N$, be as described above. If $X(\cdot)$ is a * core allocation in E and

$$(X_1(1), \ldots, X_k(1)) \in C_\xi$$

for all $\xi \geqslant \eta$, then there is a $p \in {}^*R_{++}^n$ such that $(p, X(\cdot))$ is a * competitive equilibrium in E.

We begin the proof by letting $G = \sum_{i=1}^k G_i$, where

$$G_i = \{z \in {}^*R^n : U_i(1, X_i(1)) < U_i(1, A_i(1) + z)\},$$

$i = 1, \ldots, k$. We also let $\hat{G}$ denote the *-convex hull of G and observe that $z \in \hat{G}$ if and only if there exist pairs (z_i, λ_i), $i = 1, \ldots, k$, such that $z_i \in G_i$, $\lambda_i \in {}^*[0, 1]$, $\sum_{i=1}^k \lambda_i = 1$, and $z = \sum_{i=1}^k \lambda_i z_i$. Then G is internal and $0 \notin \hat{G}$.

To show that $0 \notin \hat{G}$, we assume that $0 \in \hat{G}$ and deduce a contradiction. Suppose that $0 \in \hat{G}$ and let the pairs (z_i, λ_i), $i = 1, \ldots, k$, be such that $\lambda_i \in {}^*[0, 1]$, $z_i \in G_i$, $\sum_{i=1}^k \lambda_i = 1$, and $0 = \sum_{i=1}^k \lambda_i z_i$. Furthermore, let I be the set of i for which $\lambda_i > 0$ and, for each $i \in I$, let a_i^m be the smallest integer greater than or equal to $m\lambda_i$. Finally, let $z_i^m = ((m\lambda_i)/a_i^m)z_i$, $i \in I$, and pick m so large that, for all $i \in I$,

$$U_i(1, X_i(1)) < U_i(1, A_i(1) + z_i^m).$$

From these inequalities and from

$$\sum_{i \in I} a_i^m z_i^m = m \sum_{i \in I} \lambda_i z_i = 0,$$

it follows that a coalition S consisting of a_i^m consumers of each type $i \in I$

can block $X^{\xi}(\cdot)$ for sufficiently large ξ if $X^{\xi}(\cdot)$ is the * core allocation in E_{ξ} with $X^{\xi} = (X_1(1), \ldots, X_k(1))$. This contradicts the hypotheses of the theorem and demonstrates that $0 \notin \hat{G}$.

If $0 \notin \hat{G}$, we can use T 21.12 to deduce the existence of a $p \in {}^*R^n - \{0\}$ such that $pz \geqslant 0$ for all $z \in \hat{G}$. We show below that this p and $X(\cdot)$ satisfy the conditions of a * competitive equilibrium.

We first show that $p \in {}^*R^n_+$ and that $pX_i(1) = pA_i(1)$, $i = 1, \ldots, k$. To do that we use the monotonicity and the continuity of the $U_i(1, \cdot)$ together with $\sum_{i=1}^{k} (X_i(1) - A_i(1)) = 0$ and the following observation: If $x \in {}^*R^n_+$, $U_i(1, X_i(1)) < U_i(1, x)$ implies that $x - A_i(1) \in G_i$. Hence $px \geqslant pA_i(1)$. I leave the details to the reader.

Next we show that $U_i(1, X_i(1)) < U_i(1, x)$ implies that $pA_i(1) < px$: Since $A_i(1) \in {}^*R^n_{++}$, there is a $y \in {}^*R^n_{++}$ such that $py < pA_i(1)$. Let $z = \lambda y + (1 - \lambda)x$ and suppose that $px = pA_i(1)$ and $U_i(1, X_i(1)) < U_i(1, x)$. For λ sufficiently close to 0, $pz < pA_i(1)$ and $U_i(1, X_i(1)) < U_i(1, z)$, which is a contradiction.

The preceding results and the monotonicity of the $U_i(\cdot)$ imply that $p \in {}^*R^n_{++}$ and that $(p, X(\cdot))$ satisfies the conditions of a * competitive equilibrium.

In comparing T 21.28 with Debreu and Scarf's theorem, it is important to note that Debreu and Scarf insisted that, for a sufficiently large *standard* n, the core of E_n is approximately equal to the set of competitive equilibria in E_n. Theorem T 21.28 demonstrates that, for a sufficiently large *hyperfinite* η, the *core of E_η is approximately equal to the set of *competitive equilibria in E_η. Since we cannot replace the hyperfinite η in T 21.28 by a finite n and restrict the domain of ξ to natural numbers, T 21.28 provides another example of how important topological considerations are for the study of large economies.[3]

21.4 Exchange in Hyperspace without Transfer

With the *topology as a topological base, I have used transfer to show that the characteristics of resource allocation in nonstandard economies with infinitely many consumers and standard economies with finitely many consumers are similar; e.g., in both economies competitive equilibria exist and Pareto-optimal allocations can be sustained by perfectly competitive economies. In this section we adopt the S topology as a topological base for studying exchange in hyperspace. The primary aim is to show that in the S topology we can, by ignoring coalitions of relatively few consumers, establish the identity of the core and the set of competitive equilibrium allocations without restricting the number of types of consumers in the economy.

21.4.1 On Exchange in the S Topology

In the S topology a nonstandard exchange economy E_S is a triple $(U(\cdot), T \times {}^*R^n_+, A(\cdot))$, where $T = \{1, \ldots, \gamma\}$ for some $\gamma \in N^* - N$, $U(\cdot)$: $T \times {}^*R^n_+ \to ({}^*R_+ \cap Ns({}^*R))$ and $A(\cdot)$: $T \to {}^*R^n_{++}$. We assume that

(i) $A(\cdot)$ is internal;
(ii) there is a pair $(\delta, r) \in R^2_{++}$ such that, for all $t \in T$, $\delta \leqslant A(t) \leqslant r$;
(iii) $U(\cdot)$ is internal; and
(iv) for each $t \in T$, $U(t, \cdot)$ is strictly increasing, strictly quasi-concave, and continuous in the S topology. Specifically,
   a. If $x, y \in {}^*R^n$, $y \leqslant x$, and $x \neq y$, then $U(t,x) > U(t,y)$; if in addition, $m(x) \cap m(y) = \varnothing$, then $U(t,x) \not\approx U(t,y)$.
   b. If $x \in {}^*R^n_+$, then $\{z \in {}^*R^n_+ : U(t,z) \geqslant U(t,x)\}$ is S-convex.
   c. If $x, y \in {}^*R^n_+$, $x \neq y$, and $\lambda \in {}^*(0,1)$, then

$$U(t, \lambda x + (1-\lambda)y) > \min(U(t,x), U(t,y));$$

   if, in addition, $\lambda x + (1-\lambda)y \not\approx x$ and $\lambda x + (1-\lambda)y \not\approx y$, then

$$U(t, \lambda x + (1-\lambda)y) \not\approx \min(U(t,x), U(t,y)).$$

   d. $U(t, \cdot)$ is S-continuous.

In addition, we endow both ${}^*R^n$ and ${}^*R$ with the S topology.

Except for topological differences, E_S is identical with the E discussed in section 21.2.1. These differences seem innocuous, but are not. They have profound effects on our ideas both of competitive equilibria and of core allocations. We explain why next.

First a few remarks on relative topologies: Suppose that $(X, \mathscr{T})$ is a topological space and that $A \subset X$. Then let $\mathscr{T}(A)$ consist of all sets of the form $A \cap B$, where $B \in \mathscr{T}$, and observe that $\mathscr{T}(A)$ is a topology for A. This topology is called the *relative topology for A induced by* $\mathscr{T}$. A subset of A that is open (or closed) in the $\mathscr{T}(A)$ topology is said to be *relatively open* (or relatively closed) in A in the $\mathscr{T}$ topology.

E 21.9 For a given pair $(p, A) \in {}^*R^n_{++} \times {}^*R_+$, the set $B = \{x \in {}^*R^n_+ : px \leqslant pA\}$ is closed in the * topology but not in the S topology of ${}^*R^n$. Also B is closed in $\mathscr{T}_{{}^*R^n}({}^*R^n_+)$; i.e., B is relatively closed in ${}^*R^n_+$ in the * topology. Finally, the set $\{x \in {}^*R^n_+ : px \lesssim A\}$ is relatively closed in ${}^*R^n_+$ in the S topology when $p \in {}^*R^n_{++} - m(0)$.

It is reasonable to insist that the budget set of a consumer be relatively closed in $^*R^n_+$. Hence, for each $t \in T$ and for each $p \in {}^*R^n_{++}$, we let

$$\Gamma(t, p) = \{x \in {}^*R^n_+ : px \lesssim pA(t)\}$$

be the tth consumer's budget set. This set is closed in $\mathscr{T}_S({}^*R^n_+)$ and standardly bounded whenever p is real or there is a $\delta \in R_{++}$ such that $\delta \leqslant p$.

As a budget set, $\Gamma(t, p)$ has several disturbing features. First, it allows the tth consumer to spend more funds than he owns. Second, $U(t, \cdot)$ assumes maximal values but has no unique maximum in $\Gamma(t, p)$. To see why, note that in the present context *x is maximal in $\Gamma(t, p)$* means that $x \in \Gamma(t, p)$ and there is no $y \in \Gamma(t, p)$ such that, for all $w \in m(y)$, $U(t, w) > U(t, x)$ and $U(t, w) \not\approx U(t, x)$. A maximal vector in $\Gamma(t, p)$ is a consumption bundle at $(p, pA(t))$ for consumer t. If x is maximal in $\Gamma(t, p)$, then by T 21.18, any $y \in [m(x) \cap \Gamma(t, p)]$ is maximal in $\Gamma(t, p)$.

E 21.10 Let $n = 1$, $p = 1$, and $A(t) = 1$. Then $\Gamma(t, 1) = \{x \in R^*_+ : x \lesssim 1\} = {}^*[0, 1) \cup m(1)$. Next, suppose that $U(t, x) = \sqrt{x}$. Then $U(t, \Gamma(t, 1)) = {}^*[0, 1] \cup m(1)$. Any value in $m(1)$ is a maximal value of $U(t, \cdot)$ in $\Gamma(t, 1)$. There is no unique maximum value of $U(t, x)$ as x varies over $\Gamma(t, 1)$.

An S allocation in E_S is an internal function $X(\cdot)\colon T \to {}^*R^n_+$ that is uniformly bounded by some $r \in R_{++}$ and satisfies

$$\gamma^{-1} \sum_{t \in T} X(t) \approx \gamma^{-1} \sum_{t \in T} A(t).$$

Also, an S competitive equilibrium in E_S is a pair $(p, X(\cdot))$ that satisfies the following conditions:

(i) $p \in {}^*R^n_{++} - m(0)$.
(ii) $X(\cdot)$ is an S allocation.
(iii) There is an internal set $K \subset T$ such that $|K|/\gamma \approx 1$, and such that, for all $t \in K$, $X(t)$ is maximal in $\Gamma(t, p)$.

In reading these definitions, note that the mean values of the $X(t)$ and the $A(t)$ may differ by an infinitesimal amount. In addition, $T - K$ is an internal set that is either empty, finite, or nondenumerably infinite.

A coalition is an internal set $H \subset T$. H is *nonnegligible* if and only if $|H|/\gamma \not\approx 0$. A nonnegligible coalition H *blocks* an S allocation $X(\cdot)$ if and only if there is an S allocation $Y(\cdot)$ such that

(i) $\gamma^{-1} \sum_{t \in H} Y(t) \approx \gamma^{-1} \sum_{t \in H} A(t)$ and

(ii) for all $t \in H$, $U(t, Y(t)) > U(t, X(t))$ and $U(t, Y(t)) \not\approx U(t, X(t))$.

The S core of E_S consists of all S allocations that cannot be blocked by a nonnegligible coalition.

To establish the identity of the S core and the set of S competitive equilibrium allocations in E_S we need an auxiliary lemma which I shall state and then prove. Both the lemma and the proof are due to D. Brown and A. Robinson, who originated the study of nonstandard exchange economies (Brown and Robinson 1975, pp. 47–49).

21.4.2 An Auxiliary Lemma

T 21.29 Let E_S be as described above; and let $X(\cdot)$ be an S core allocation. Moreover, for each $t \in T$ and $m \in {}^*N$, let

$$G_m(t) = \{z \in Ns({}^*R^n) : (\forall w \in {}^*S(z, m^{-1}))[U(t, X(t)) < U(t, A(t) + w)]\};$$

and let $G(t) = \bigcup_{m \in N} G_m(t)$. Finally, for each $A \in \mathscr{P}(T)$, let

$$\mathscr{G}(A) = \bigcup_{t \in A} G(t);$$

and let $\hat{\mathscr{G}}(A)$ denote the S-convex hull of $\mathscr{G}(A)$. Then there is an internal $A \in \mathscr{P}(T)$ such that $(|A|/\gamma) \approx 1$ and such that $0 \notin S\text{-int}(\hat{\mathscr{G}}(A))$.

The proof of the theorem is obtained in several steps. In the first we delineate the set A. For that purpose let

$$G_m^{-1}(x) = \{t \in T : x \in G_m(t)\}, \qquad x \in Ns({}^*R^n),\ m \in {}^*N;$$

and let $M = \{q \in Q^n : |G_m^{-1}(q)|/\gamma \approx 0 \text{ for all } m \in N\}$. Since $U(\cdot)$ is internal, it follows from T 20.12 that, for all $q \in M$ and all $m \in {}^*N$, $G_m^{-1}(q)$ is internal. From this fact and from T 20.12 and T 20.13 (ii), we deduce that, for each $q \in M$, the set $\{m \in {}^*N : |G_m^{-1}(q)|/\gamma < m^{-1}\}$ is internal and contains an infinite number η. Hence, if we express M by $M = \{q_i\}_{i \in N}$ and let $B_n = \bigcup_{i=1}^n G_{\eta_i}^{-1}(q_i)$, $n \in N$, then B_n is internal and $|B_n|/\gamma \approx 0$. By T 21.3, the B_n can be extended to an internal sequence on ${}^*N$, $\{B_n; n \in {}^*N\}$, such that if $\xi \in {}^*N - N$, $B_n \subset B_\xi$ for all $n \in N$. Also, by T 20.12 and T 20.13 (ii), the set $\{n \in {}^*N : |B_n|/\gamma < n^{-1}\}$ is internal and contains an infinite number ξ. We let $A = T - B_\xi$ and observe that A is internal and $|A|/\gamma \approx 1$.

Next suppose that $0 \in S\text{-int}(\hat{\mathscr{G}}(A))$. Then there is an $m \in N$, a $z \in {}^*R^n_{++}$, a $k \in N$, and pairs $(\lambda_i, z_i) \in {}^*(0,1) \times \bigcup_{t \in A} G(t)$, $i = 1, \ldots, k$, such that $z \geqslant m^{-1}$, $-z \in S\text{-int}(\hat{\mathscr{G}}(A))$, $-z = \sum_{i=1}^k \lambda_i z_i$ and $\sum_{i=1}^k \lambda_i = 1$. Furthermore, there are consumers in A, $t_1, \ldots, t_k$ such that $z_i \in G(t_i)$, $i = 1, \ldots, k$. But $z_i \in G(t_i)$ implies that there is an $m_i \in N$ such that $z_i \in G_{m_i}(t_i)$. Hence we can find $r_i \in Q^n \cap G_{m_i}(t_i)$, $\alpha_i \in Q \cap R_{++}$, $i = 1, \ldots, k$, and $l \in N$ such that r_i is close to z_i, α_i is close to λ_i, $\sum_{i=1}^k \alpha_i = 1$, and $-l^{-1} \geqslant \sum_{i=1}^k \alpha_i r_i$.

Let $-r = \sum_{i=1}^{k} \alpha_i r_i$ and choose some consumer $t_0 \in A$. For a sufficiently large $a \in Q \cap R_{++}$, $ar \in G(t_0)$. Let $r_0 = ar$, $\beta_0 = (a+1)^{-1}$, and $\beta_i = a\alpha_i/(a+1)$, $i = 1, \ldots, k$. Then $\beta_i \in Q \cap (0, 1)$, $i = 0, \ldots, k$, $\sum_{i=0}^{k} \beta_i = 1$, $r_i \in \mathcal{G}(A)$, $i = 0, \ldots, k$, and $0 = \sum_{i=0}^{k} \beta_i r_i$. In addition, for all $i = 0, \ldots, k$, there is an $m_i \in N$ such that $t_i \in G_{m_i}^{-1}(r_i)$. Since $t_i \in A$, $r_i \notin M$ and $\sim[|G_{m_i}^{-1}(r_i)|/\gamma \approx 0]$, $i = 0, \ldots, k$.

The preceding results can be used to construct a coalition H that can block $X(\cdot)$. To obtain this coalition we let

$$\delta = (k+1)^{-1} \min_{0 \leqslant i \leqslant k} \{|G_{m_i}^{-1}(r_i)|/\gamma\beta_i\}$$

and choose disjoint internal subsets of A, $B_0, \ldots, B_k$, such that $|B_i|/\gamma \approx \delta\beta_i$ and $B_i \subset G_{m_i}^{-1}(r_i)$, $i = 0, \ldots, k$. Then we let $H = \bigcup_{i=0}^{k} B_i$ and distribute the economy's resources in the following way:

$$Y(t) = \begin{cases} r_i + A(t) \text{ for } t \in B_i,\ i = 0, 1, \ldots, k \\ A(t) \text{ for } t \notin H. \end{cases}$$

Then for $t \in H$, $U(t, Y(t)) >$ (and $\not\approx$) $U(t, X(t))$ and

$$\begin{aligned} \gamma^{-1} \sum_{t \in H} Y(t) &= \gamma^{-1} \sum_{i=0}^{k} \sum_{t \in B_i} (r_i + A(t)) \\ &= \gamma^{-1} \sum_{i=0}^{k} |B_i| r_i + \gamma^{-1} \sum_{t \in H} A(t) \\ &\approx \delta \sum_{i=0}^{k} \beta_i r_i + \gamma^{-1} \sum_{t \in H} A(t) \\ &= \gamma^{-1} \sum_{t \in H} A(t), \end{aligned}$$

which shows that $Y(\cdot)$ is an S allocation which enables H to block $X(\cdot)$. Since $X(\cdot)$ is in the S core of E, the preceding result is a contradiction that establishes $0 \notin S\,\mathrm{int}(\hat{\mathcal{G}}(A))$.

21.4.3 The Fundamental Equivalence

With the preceding auxiliary theorem in our minds, we can establish the following equivalence between general equilibrium and core allocations:

T 21.30 Let E_S be as described above. If $(p, X(\cdot))$ is an S competitive equilibrium, $X(\cdot)$ is an S core allocation. If $X(\cdot)$ is in the S core of E_S, there is a $p \in {}^*R_{++}^n - m(0)$ such that $(p, X(\cdot))$ is an S competitive equilibrium.

For brevity I sketch a proof of the second half of the theorem and leave the first half to the reader. The omitted details are spelled out in Brown and Robinson 1975 (pp. 49–50).

Suppose that $X(\cdot)$ is in the S core of E_S and let A, $G(\cdot)$, $\mathscr{G}(A)$, and $\hat{\mathscr{G}}(A)$ be as in T 21.29. Then $0 \notin S\text{-int}(\hat{\mathscr{G}}(A))$ and, by T 21.22, there is a $p \in R^n - \{0\}$ such that $0 \lesssim py$ for all $y \in S\text{-int}(\hat{\mathscr{G}}(A))$. For all $t \in A$, $G(t) = S\text{-int}(G(t)) \subset S\text{-int}(\hat{\mathscr{G}}(A))$. Hence, for all $t \in A$ and $y \in G(t)$, $0 \lesssim py$. This and the monotonicity of $U(t, \cdot)$ imply that $p \geqslant 0$. Moreover, if $z \in R_+^n$, $U(t, X(t)) < U(t, z)$ and $U(t, X(t)) \not\approx U(t, z)$, then $(z - A(t)) \in G(t)$ and $0 \lesssim p(z - A(t))$, from which we deduce that $pA(t) \lesssim pz$.

Next we show that if we neglect a negligible subset of A, for all $t \in A$, $pX(t) \approx pA(t)$. Suppose that $pX(t) < pA(t)$ and $pX(t) \not\approx pA(t)$. Then there is a $z \in (R_+^n - \{0\})$ such that $p(X(t) + z) < pA(t)$, $p(X(t) + z) \not\approx pA(t)$, $U(t, X(t)) < U(t, X(t) + z)$ and $U(t, X(t)) \not\approx U(t, X(t) + z)$—a contradiction. Thus, $pA(t) \lesssim pX(t)$. If $pA(t) \not\approx pX(t)$ for all t in a nonnegligible set $S \subset A$, there is a $\delta \in R_{++}$ such that $\gamma^{-1} \sum_{t \in A} pA(t) + \delta \lesssim \gamma^{-1} \sum_{t \in A} pX(t)$, which contradicts the fact that $X(\cdot)$ is in the S core of E_S.

Finally we show that, for all $t \in A$ modulo a negligible subset, $X(t)$ is maximal in $\Gamma(t, p)$. To do that we must first show that $p \in R_{++}^n$. Suppose that $p_1 = 0$. Then $p \neq 0$ implies that there is a coordinate, say p_2, that is positive. Next recall that, for all $t \in T$, there is a pair $(\delta, r) \in R_{++}^2$ such that $\delta \leqslant A(t) \leqslant r$. Hence there is a $\delta_1 \in R_{++}$ and a nonnegligible coalition $S \subset A$ such that, for all $t \in S$, $\delta_1 \leqslant X(t)$. But, if that is so, then, for any $t \in S$, we can find a $\delta_2 \in R_{++}$ such that $\delta_2 < \delta_1$ and with $z = (1, -\delta_2, 0, \ldots, 0)$, $U(t, X(t)) < U(t, X(t) + z)$ and $U(t, X(t)) \not\approx U(t, X(t) + z)$. Therefore, by a previous result $p(X(t) + z) \gtrsim pA(t)$. Hence, $0 \lesssim pz$ and $\delta_2 p_2 \lesssim p_1$—a contradiction, which shows that $p \in R_{++}^n$.

If for some $t \in A$ (modulo the negligible subset we have alluded to above), $X(t)$ is not maximal in $\Gamma(t, p)$, there is a $z \in \Gamma(t, p)$ such that $U(t, X(t)) < U(t, z)$ and $U(t, X(t)) \not\approx U(t, z)$. Since $\delta \leqslant A(t)$, there is a pair $(\delta_3, v) \in R_{++}^{n+1}$ such that $v + \delta_3 < A(t)$. For some $\lambda \in {}^*(0, 1)$, $p(\lambda v + (1-\lambda)z) < pA(t)$, $p(\lambda v + (1-\lambda)z) \not\approx pA(t)$, $U(t, X(t)) < U(t, \lambda v + (1-\lambda)z)$ and $U(t, X(t)) \not\approx U(t, \lambda v + (1 - \lambda)z)$—a final contradiction.

In looking back at T 21.29, T 21.30, and their proofs, we need to keep several remarks in mind. Except for topological differences, the assumptions we make concerning E_S are appropriate analogues of the hypotheses about E that we postulated in section 21.3. The latter in turn are hyperfinite versions of the conditions we imposed on our finite exchange economy in chapter 14. I have insisted on this uniformity in order that the topological aspects of the equivalence between core allocations and competitive equilibria come out as clearly as possible.

This insistence on uniformity has drawbacks. Seen with the eyes of a mathematical economist, the conditions I impose on E_S are distressingly strong and prevent the reader from acquiring a feel for the real power of nonstandard analysis. It is, therefore, interesting to observe that in proving T 21.29 and T 21.30 we did not use assumptions (iv)b and c (section 21.3.1). Hence these theorems are valid for an economy populated by consumers whose utility functions need not be quasi-concave. According to Brown and Robinson, T 21.30 is true even for economies whose consumers' preferences cannot be represented by continuous utility functions. For these and other matters of interest concerning the Brown-Robinson equivalence theorem, I refer the reader to Brown and Kahn 1980 (pp. 167–172).

21.5 Concluding Remarks

In this chapter we set out to study exchange in economies with infinitely many consumers. Our purpose was (1) to model behavior in economies in which a single consumer by his own actions cannot influence the price at which trading occurs and (2) to show that in sufficiently large economies a core allocation is a competitive-equilibrium allocation. Now we must take stock of our results.

In section 21.3 we studied an economy in which the consumers' commodity space was endowed with the * topology and the utility functions were *-continuous. We saw that such an economy possesses all the characteristics of a finite economy; e.g., competitive equilibria exist and belong to the core, and Pareto-optimal allocations can be sustained as competitive equilibria. We also saw that if the economy contains a given number of types of consumers and infinitely many consumers of each type its core allocations are not too different from its competitive-equilibrium allocations.

Whether the economy of section 21.3 satisfies the condition that a single consumer by his own actions has only negligible influence on the prices at which trading occurs depends on the meaning of "negligible." If we measure price changes in terms of nonstandard ε neighborhoods, the actions of a single consumer have as much effect on prices in a hyperfinite economy as they have in a standard finite economy. If we measure price changes in terms of standard ε neighborhoods, even coalitions with uncountably many consumers might have a negligible influence on the prices at which trading occurs.

In section 21.4 we studied a hyperfinite economy in which price changes are measured in terms of standard ε neighborhoods. Specifically, we studied an economy in which the consumers' commodity space is endowed with the S topology and the utility functions are S-continuous. We saw for such an economy that if we ignore negligible coalitions, all core allocations are competitive-equilibrium allocations.

The economy of section 21.4 possesses the expected characteristics of an economy with infinitely many consumers. Note, therefore, that the theory I developed is incomplete to the extent that I have not shown that the core is nonempty. In the next chapter we establish the nonemptiness of the core by ascertaining the existence of a competitive equilibrium in the given economy.

22 Probability and Exchange in Hyperspace

In this chapter we study probability and exchange in hyperspace. We begin with a discussion of Loeb probability spaces and integration in hyperspace. The results we obtain have varied applications. We use them first to establish the existence of a competitive equilibrium in the economy of section 21.4 and then to delineate a hyperfinite construction of the Brownian motion.

22.1 Loeb Probability Spaces

To discuss the measurement of probable things in hyperspace I must introduce several new terms. Let Ω be a nonempty internal set and let $\mathscr{A}$ be a field of internal subsets of Ω. Then $\mathscr{A}$ is closed under finite unions and complementation. If $\mathscr{A}$ is internal, $\mathscr{A}$ is closed under hyperfinite unions and intersections as well. To fix these ideas concerning internal fields, here is an example:

E 22.1 Let $\Omega = {}^*[0, 1]$ and let $\mathscr{A}$ be a field of internal subsets of Ω containing all interval subsets of Ω which are left-closed and right-open in the *topology. If $\mathscr{A}$ is internal, it contains all internal subsets of Ω which are hyperfinite unions of intervals in Ω that are left-closed and right-open in the *topology. Thus, if $a, b \in \Omega$, $a < b$, and $\gamma \in {}^*N - N$, then $\mathscr{A}$ contains both

$$\bigcap_{1 \leqslant n \leqslant \gamma} \left({}^*\left[a - \frac{1}{n}, a + \frac{1}{n} \right) \cap \Omega \right) \quad \text{and} \quad \bigcup_{1 \leqslant n \leqslant \gamma} \left({}^*\left[a + \frac{1}{n}, b - \frac{1}{n} \right) \cap \Omega \right).$$

However, $\mathscr{A}$ does not contain

$$m(a) = \bigcap_{n \in N} {}^*\left(a - \frac{1}{n}, a + \frac{1}{n} \right) \quad \text{and} \quad \Omega - m(1) = \bigcup_{n \in N} {}^*\left[1 - \frac{1}{n}, 1 - \frac{1}{n+1} \right).$$

In fact, except for $\varnothing$ and Ω, $\mathscr{A}$ does not contain any subset of Ω that is relatively closed or relatively open in the S topology.

The reason why the internal field of subsets of Ω in E 22.1 does not contain any S-open or S-closed subsets of Ω other than $\emptyset$ and Ω is given in the following theorem of Robinson's:

T 22.1 $\emptyset$ and $^*R^n$ are the only S-open internal subsets of $^*R^n$.

For brevity I omit the proof and refer the reader to Robinson 1966 (p. 121) for details.

A triple $(\Omega, \mathscr{A}, v(\cdot))$ is called an *internal probability space* if Ω is a nonempty internal set, $\mathscr{A}$ is an internal field of subsets of Ω, and $v(\cdot)\colon \mathscr{A} \to {}^*[0, 1]$ is an internal, finitely additive function such that $v(\emptyset) = 0$ and $v(\Omega) = 1$. For internal probability spaces we can establish the following theorem:

T 22.2 If $(\Omega, \mathscr{A}, v(\cdot))$ is an internal probability space, then $v(\cdot)$ is σ-additive on $\mathscr{A}$.

To see why, suppose that $A_i \in \mathscr{A}$, $i \in N$, and that $A_i \cap A_j = \emptyset$ for all $i, j \in N$ such that $i \neq j$. If $A = \bigcup_{i \in N} A_i$ and $A \in \mathscr{A}$, then, by T 21.5, there is an $m \in N$ such that $A = \bigcup_{i=1}^{m} A_i$. Hence $v(A) = \sum_{i=1}^{m} v(A_i)$ and, *by default*, $v(\cdot)$ is σ-additive on $\mathscr{A}$.

E 22.2 Let $\mathscr{A}$ and Ω be as in E 22.1 and assume that $\mathscr{A}$ is internal. Also define $v(\cdot)\colon \mathscr{A} \to {}^*[0, 1]$ by

$$v({}^*[a, b)) = b - a \text{ for } a, b \in \Omega, \qquad a < b$$

and insist that $v(\cdot)$ be finitely additive and internal. Then $v(\cdot)$ is hyperfinitely additive as well; e.g.,

$$v\Bigl(\bigcup_{1 \leq n \leq \gamma} {}^*[1 - n^{-1}, 1 - (n + 1)^{-1})\Bigr) = \sum_{1 \leq n \leq \gamma} (n^{-1} - (n + 1)^{-1})$$
$$= 1 - (\gamma + 1)^{-1}.$$

However, $v(\bigcup_{n \in N} {}^*[1 - n^{-1}, 1 - (n + 1)^{-1}))$ is not defined since the argument of $v(\cdot)$, ${}^*[0, 1) - m(1)$, does not belong to $\mathscr{A}$.

Next let $(\Omega, \mathscr{A}, v(\cdot))$ be an internal probability space; let $\sigma(\mathscr{A})$ be the smallest σ field of subsets of Ω that contains $\mathscr{A}$ and observe that $\sigma(\mathscr{A})$ contains both internal and external sets. Moreover, let ${}^\circ v(\cdot)\colon \mathscr{A} \to [0, 1]$ be defined by

$$ {}^\circ v(A) = {}^\circ(v(A)), \qquad A \in \mathscr{A}. \tag{22.1}$$

Then ${}^\circ v(\cdot)$ is finitely additive and hence σ-additive on $\mathscr{A}$. From this and UT 15 we deduce the validity of the following theorem:

T 22.3 Let $(\Omega, \mathscr{A}, v(\cdot))$ be an internal probability space and let ${}^\circ v(\cdot)$ be as defined in equation 22.1. Moreover, let $\sigma(\mathscr{A})$ be the smallest σ field containing $\mathscr{A}$. Then there is a unique σ-additive probability measure $\tilde{P}_v(\cdot)$: $\sigma(\mathscr{A}) \to [0, 1]$ such that $\tilde{P}_v(A) = {}^\circ v(A)$ for all $A \in \mathscr{A}$.

It is important to keep in mind that $\tilde{P}_v(\cdot)$ assigns standard numbers to nonstandard events. For example, consider E 22.3.

E 22.3 Let $(\Omega, \mathscr{A}, v(\cdot))$ be the internal probability space of E 22.2, and suppose that $a \in (0, 1)$. Then ${}^*[1/3, 1/2) \in \mathscr{A}$, $m(a) \in \sigma(\mathscr{A})$ and $\bigcup_{n \in N} {}^*[1 - (1/n), 1 - (1/(n + 1)) \in \sigma(\mathscr{A})$. Furthermore, $\tilde{P}_v({}^*[1/3, 1/2)) = 1/6$, $\tilde{P}_v(\bigcup_{n \in N} {}^*[1 - (1/n), 1 - (1/(n + 1)) = 1$ and $\tilde{P}_v(m(a)) = 0$.

It is also interesting to note that sets in $\sigma(\mathscr{A})$ can be approximated in $\tilde{P}_v$ measure by sets in $\mathscr{A}$:

T 22.4 Let $(\Omega, \mathscr{A}, v(\cdot))$ be an internal probability space; let $\sigma(\mathscr{A})$ be the smallest σ field containing $\mathscr{A}$, and let $\tilde{P}_v(\cdot)$ be the extension of ${}^\circ v(\cdot)$ to $\sigma(\mathscr{A})$. For each $A \in \sigma(\mathscr{A})$ and each $n \in N$, there exist $B, C \in \mathscr{A}$ such that $B \subset A \subset C$ and $\tilde{P}_v(C) - (1/n) < \tilde{P}_v(A) < \tilde{P}_v(B) + (1/n)$. Also there is a $D \in \mathscr{A}$ such that

$$\tilde{P}_v((A - D) \cup (D - A)) = 0.$$

I establish the existence of C and leave the rest of the proof to the reader. Suppose that $A \in \sigma(\mathscr{A})$ and observe that the construction of $\tilde{P}_v(\cdot)$ is such that, for each $\delta \in R_{++}$, there exists a sequence of sets in $\mathscr{A}$, A_m, $m \in N$, such that $A_m \subset A_{m+1}$, $A \subset \bigcup_{m \in N} A_m$ and $\tilde{P}_v(\bigcup_{m \in N} A_m) < \tilde{P}_v(A) + \delta$. In addition, $\mathscr{A} \in {}^*W_k(R)$ for some $k \in N$. Hence, by an obvious extension of T 21.3, the sequence of A_m can be extended to a sequence $\{A_m; m \in {}^*N\}$ such that (1) for all $m \in {}^*N$, $A_m \in \mathscr{A}$ and $A_m \subset A_{m+1}$, and (2) for all $m \in {}^*N - N$, $A \subset A_m$. Consequently, if we let $r = \tilde{P}_v(A)$ and observe that, by T 20.12, the set $\{m \in {}^*N : v(A_m) < r + \delta\}$ is internal and contains N, we can use T 20.13 (ii) to find a w in ${}^*N - N$ such that $v(A_w) < r + \delta$. Since r and δ are standard reals, it follows that $\tilde{P}_v(A_w) < \tilde{P}_v(A) + \delta$, as was to be shown.

For the purposes of this chapter, it will be convenient to work with a slightly larger family of sets than $\sigma(\mathscr{A})$. This larger σ field, which we denote by $\mathscr{F}_{\mathscr{A}}$, is the smallest σ field that contains $\sigma(\mathscr{A})$ and all subsets of sets in $\sigma(\mathscr{A})$ with $\tilde{P}_v$-measure 0. We denote by $P_v(\cdot)$ the σ-additive extension of $\tilde{P}_v(\cdot)$ to $\mathscr{F}_{\mathscr{A}}$.

If $(\Omega, \mathscr{F}, P(\cdot))$ is a probability space, $P(\cdot)$ is said to be *complete* if $E \subset \mathscr{F}$, $F \subset E$, and $P(E) = 0$ imply that $F \in \mathscr{F}$. It follows from the construction of $P_v(\cdot)$: $\mathscr{F}_{\mathscr{A}} \to [0, 1]$ that $P_v(\cdot)$ is a complete probability measure on $(\Omega, \mathscr{F}_{\mathscr{A}})$. Another example of a complete probability measure is the Lebesgue measure $\mu(\cdot)$ on $([0, 1], \mathscr{L})$, where $\mathscr{L}$ denotes the smallest σ field containing the Borel subsets of $[0, 1]$, $\mathscr{B}$, and all subsets of sets in $\mathscr{B}$ of μ measure 0.

For ease of reference we note that $(\Omega, \mathscr{F}_{\mathscr{A}}, P_v(\cdot))$ is called the *Loeb probability space* associated with $(\Omega, \mathscr{A}, v(\cdot))$.[1] The family of sets that we denote by $\mathscr{L}$ is called the family of *Lebesgue measurable* subsets of $[0, 1]$. Finally, we denote by $\mu(\cdot)$ the extension to $([0, 1], \mathscr{L})$ of the Lebesgue measure $\mu(\cdot)$ on $([0, 1], \mathscr{B})$.

22.2 Standard Versions of Loeb Probability Spaces

A Loeb probability space, $(\Omega, \mathscr{F}_{\mathscr{A}}, P_v(\cdot))$, is an ordinary probability space with a twist: $(\Omega, \mathscr{F}_{\mathscr{A}})$ is a nonstandard experiment with an internal set of outcomes. When $\Omega \subset {}^*R^n$ for some $n \in N$ a *standard version of a Loeb probability space,* $(\Omega, \mathscr{F}_{\mathscr{A}}, P_v(\cdot))$, is a standard probability space, $(X, \mathscr{F}, \mu_v(\cdot))$, that satisfies the following conditions:

(i) $X = {}^\circ\Omega$.
(ii) For all $B \in \mathscr{F}$, $\{\omega \in \Omega : {}^\circ\omega \in B\} \in \mathscr{F}_{\mathscr{A}}$.
(iii) For all $B \in \mathscr{F}$,

$$\mu_v(B) = P_v(\{\omega \in \Omega : {}^\circ\omega \in B\}).$$

In this definition X is taken to be nonempty. In addition, $\mathscr{F}$ is a σ field and $\mu_v(\cdot)$: $\mathscr{F} \rightarrow [0, 1]$ is a σ-additive probability measure.

22.2.1 Examples

To aid intuition concerning Loeb probability spaces and their standard versions, I present several examples and state a useful theorem. First a follow-up to E 22.2:

E 22.4 Let $(\Omega, \mathscr{A}, v(\cdot))$ be the internal probability space of E 22.2 and let $(\Omega, \mathscr{F}_{\mathscr{A}}, P_v(\cdot))$ be its associated Loeb probability space. Then $[0, 1] = {}^\circ\Omega$, and, for all $A \in \mathscr{L}$, $\{\omega \in \Omega : {}^\circ\omega \in A\} \in \mathscr{F}_{\mathscr{A}}$ and $\mu(A) = P_v(\{\omega \in \Omega : {}^\circ\omega \in A\})$. Hence $([0, 1], \mathscr{L}, \mu(\cdot))$ is a standard version of $(\Omega, \mathscr{F}_{\mathscr{A}}, P_v(\cdot))$.

In reading our definition of standard versions of Loeb probability spaces and E 22.4, it is important to recall that $y \in {}^\circ\Omega$ if and only if y is standard and there is near-standard $x \in \Omega$ such that $y \in m(x)$. When $\Omega \subset {}^*R$, we take $m(x)$ to be the monad of x in ${}^*R$ and insist that $X \subset R$. When $\Omega \subset {}^*R^n$, we take $m(x)$ to be the monad of x in ${}^*R^n$ and insist that $X \subset R^n$. However, we do not require X to be a subset of Ω; e.g., if $\Omega = {}^*(0, 1)$, $X = [0, 1]$.

The importance of the set of near-standard points in Ω for delineating standard versions of a Loeb probability space is illustrated below:

E 22.5 Let γ be a nonstandard integer in $^*N - N$ and let $\Omega = \{1, \ldots, \gamma\}$. Also let $\mathscr{A}$ be the family of all internal subsets of Ω, and, for each $A \in \mathscr{A}$, let $v(A) = |A|/\gamma$. Then $(\Omega, \mathscr{A}, v(\cdot))$ is an internal probability space. Next let $(\Omega, \mathscr{F}_{\mathscr{A}}, P_v(\cdot))$ be the associated Loeb probability space and let $X = {}^\circ\Omega$, $\mathscr{F} = {}^\circ\mathscr{F}_{\mathscr{A}}$, and

$$\mu_v(B) = P_v(\{\omega \in \Omega : {}^\circ\omega \in B\}), \qquad B \in \mathscr{F}.$$

Then X, $\mathscr{F}$, and $\mu_v(\cdot)\colon \mathscr{F} \to [0, 1]$ are well defined, but $\mu_v(\cdot)$ is not a probability measure. In fact, $\mu_v(B) = 0$ for all $B \in \mathscr{F}$ even though there are infinitely many $C \in \mathscr{F}_{\mathscr{A}}$ with $P_v(C) > 0$.

One reason why the Loeb probability space of E 22.5 fails to have a standard version is that the P_v measure of the set of near-standard points of Ω differs from 1. This fact is borne out in the next theorem.

T 22.5 Suppose that X is a closed, nonempty interval in R and that $(\Omega, \mathscr{A}, v(\cdot))$ is an internal probability space with $\Omega = {}^*X$. Let $(\Omega, \mathscr{F}_{\mathscr{A}}, P_v(\cdot))$ be the associated Loeb probability space and suppose that $P_v(Ns(\Omega)) = 1$ and that $\{\omega \in \Omega : {}^\circ\omega \in B\} \in \mathscr{F}_{\mathscr{A}}$ for all relatively closed $B \subset X$. Finally, let $\mathscr{B}_X$ be the family of all Borel subsets of X and define $\mu_v(\cdot)\colon \mathscr{B}_X \to [0, 1]$ by

$$\mu_v(B) = P_v(\{\omega \in \Omega : {}^\circ\omega \in B\}), \qquad B \in \mathscr{B}_X.$$

Then $(X, \mathscr{B}_X, \mu_v(\cdot))$ is a standard version of $(\Omega, \mathscr{F}_{\mathscr{A}}, P_v(\cdot))$.

The proof is easy once we observe that the relatively closed subsets of X generate $\mathscr{B}_X$. I leave the details to the reader.[2]

22.2.2 A Hyperfinite Alias of Lebesgue's Probability Space

A standard probability space may be the standard version of many Loeb probability spaces. For example, we observed above that Lebesgue's probability space, $([0, 1], \mathscr{L}, \mu(\cdot))$, is a standard version of the Loeb probability space of E 22.2. Below we show that Lebesgue's probability space may also be a standard version of a Loeb probability space with a hyperfinite set of outcomes. In doing that, we demonstrate that *the Lebesgue measure on* [0, 1] *is the natural extension of Laplace's counting measure.*

Let γ, η in $^*N - N$ be so that $\gamma = \eta!$ and let $\Omega = \{0, 1/\gamma, \ldots, 1\}$. Then Ω is an internal subset of $^*[0, 1]$, $|\Omega| = \gamma + 1$ and all the standard rationals in $[0, 1]$ belong to Ω. Also if $r \in [0, 1]$ is irrational, there is a unique $t \in \Omega$ such that $t < r < t + \gamma^{-1}$. Finally, if A is an internal subset of Ω, then, by T 21.9, ${}^\circ A$ is a relatively closed subset of $[0, 1]$ and ${}^\circ\Omega = [0, 1]$. In fact, we have T 22.6:

T 22.6 Let $\Omega = \{0, 1/\gamma, \ldots, 1\}$, where $\gamma = \eta!$ for some $\eta \in {}^*N - N$; let $\mathscr{A}$ denote the family of all internal subsets of Ω; and let $v(\cdot)\colon \mathscr{A} \to {}^*[0, 1]$ be defined by $v(A) = |A|/(\gamma + 1)$, $A \in \mathscr{A}$. Then $(\Omega, \mathscr{A}, v(\cdot))$ is an internal probability space. Let $(\Omega, \mathscr{F}_{\mathscr{A}}, P_v(\cdot))$ be the associated Loeb probability space. Both $([0, 1], \mathscr{B}, \mu(\cdot))$ and $([0, 1], \mathscr{L}, \mu(\cdot))$ are standard versions of this Loeb space. Also $B \in \mathscr{L}$ if and only if $\{\omega \in \Omega : {}^\circ\omega \in B\} \in \mathscr{F}_{\mathscr{A}}$.

It is obvious that $(\Omega, \mathscr{A}, v(\cdot))$ is a well-defined internal probability space. So to establish the theorem we need only show that $([0, 1], \mathscr{B}, \mu(\cdot))$ is a standard version of $(\Omega, \mathscr{F}_{\mathscr{A}}, P_v(\cdot))$ and that $B \in \mathscr{L}$ if and only if $\{\omega \in \Omega : {}^\circ\omega \in B\} \in \mathscr{F}_{\mathscr{A}}$. Then the completeness of $\mu(\cdot)$ and $P_v(\cdot)$ implies that $([0, 1], \mathscr{L}, \mu(\cdot))$ is a standard version of $(\Omega, \mathscr{F}_{\mathscr{A}}, P_v(\cdot))$.

To ascertain that $([0, 1], \mathscr{B}, \mu(\cdot))$ is a standard version of $(\Omega, \mathscr{F}_{\mathscr{A}}, P_v(\cdot))$, we must first show that $A \in \mathscr{B}$ implies that $\{\omega \in \Omega : {}^\circ\omega \in B\} \in \mathscr{F}_{\mathscr{A}}$. For that purpose, let q and r be rationals in $(0, 1)$ such that $q < r$ and observe that

$$\{\omega \in \Omega : {}^\circ\omega \in [q, r)\} = \bigcup_{m \in N} \bigcap_{n \in N} \left\{\omega \in \Omega : \omega \in {}^*\!\left[q - \frac{1}{n}, r - \frac{1}{m}\right)\right\}.$$

It follows from T 20.12 that, for each pair $(m, n) \in N^2$, $\{\omega \in \Omega : \omega \in {}^*[q - 1/n, r - 1/m)\}$ is internal. Consequently, $\{\omega \in \Omega : {}^\circ\omega \in [q, r)\} \in \mathscr{F}_{\mathscr{A}}$. Since $\mathscr{F}_{\mathscr{A}}$ is a σ field, it follows that if A is a countable union or intersection of left-closed, right-open intervals with rational end points in $(0, 1)$, then $\{\omega \in \Omega : {}^\circ\omega \in A\} \in \mathscr{F}_{\mathscr{A}}$. But if that is so, it is a routine matter to verify that if A is either a left-closed, right-open interval of $[0, 1]$, a finite union of such intervals, or a difference of such sets, then $\{\omega \in \Omega : {}^\circ\omega \in A\} \in \mathscr{F}_{\mathscr{A}}$. From this and from the fact that $\mathscr{B}$ is the smallest σ field that contains all finite unions and differences of left-closed, right-open subintervals of $[0, 1]$, it follows for all $A \in \mathscr{B}$ that $\{\omega \in \Omega : {}^\circ\omega \in A\} \in \mathscr{F}_{\mathscr{A}}$.

Next we must show that the Lebesgue measure $\mu(\cdot)$ satisfies $\mu(B) = P_v(\{\omega \in \Omega : {}^\circ\omega \in B\})$ for all $B \in \mathscr{B}$. By appealing to the σ additivity of $\mu(\cdot)$ and $P_v(\cdot)$, it is easy to ascertain that this equality holds, first for all left-closed, right-open intervals with rational end points in $(0, 1)$, then for all left-closed, right-open intervals with end points in $[0, 1]$ and their finite unions and differences, and finally for all $B \in \mathscr{B}$.

The preceding arguments show that $([0, 1], \mathscr{B}, \mu(\cdot))$ is a standard version of $(\Omega, \mathscr{F}_{\mathscr{A}}, P_v(\cdot))$. To conclude the proof of the theorem, we must show that a subset A of $[0, 1]$ is Lebesgue-measurable if and only if $\{\omega \in \Omega : {}^\circ\omega \in A\} \in \mathscr{F}_{\mathscr{A}}$. Suppose that $A \subset [0, 1]$. If A is Lebesgue-measurable, for each $\varepsilon \in R_{++}$, we can find a closed set B and an open set C in $\mathscr{B}$ such that $B \subset A \subset C$ and $\mu(C) - \varepsilon < \mu(A) < \mu(B) + \varepsilon$. Let $\tilde{B} = \{\omega \in \Omega : {}^\circ\omega \in B\}$,

$\tilde{A} = \{\omega \in \Omega : {}^\circ\omega \in A\}$ and $\tilde{C} = \{\omega \in \Omega : {}^\circ\omega \in C\}$ and observe that $\tilde{B} \subset \tilde{A} \subset \tilde{C}$, $\tilde{B} \in \mathscr{F}_{\mathscr{A}}$, $\tilde{C} \in \mathscr{F}_{\mathscr{A}}$, and $P_v(\tilde{C}) - \varepsilon < \mu(A) < P_v(\tilde{B}) + \varepsilon$. Since ε is arbitrary and $P_v(\cdot)$ is complete, it follows by easy arguments that $\tilde{A} \in \mathscr{F}_{\mathscr{A}}$ and $\mu(A) = P_v(\tilde{A})$. Conversely, if $\tilde{A} \in \mathscr{F}_{\mathscr{A}}$ and $\varepsilon \in R_{++}$, by T 22.4, there are internal sets B, $C \in \mathscr{A}$ such that $B \subset \tilde{A} \subset C$ and $P_v(C) - \varepsilon < P_v(\tilde{A}) < P_v(B) + \varepsilon$. Since B and C are internal, T 21.9 implies that ${}^\circ B$ and ${}^\circ C$ are relatively closed subsets of [0, 1] and belong to $\mathscr{B}$. Moreover, ${}^\circ B \subset A \subset {}^\circ C$ and $\mu({}^\circ C) - \varepsilon < P_v(\tilde{A}) < \mu({}^\circ B) + \varepsilon$. From this and the completeness of $\mu(\cdot)$, it follows by standard arguments that $A \in \mathscr{L}$ and $\mu(A) = P_v(\tilde{A})$.[3]

Many things can go wrong in nonstandard analysis. To make sure that the preceding theorem will not be misunderstood, I present an example found in Keisler 1984 (p. 14):

E 22.6 Let $(\Omega, \mathscr{A}, v(\cdot))$ and $(\Omega, \mathscr{F}_{\mathscr{A}}, P_v(\cdot))$ be as described in T 22.6 and let $K \in {}^*N - N$ be such that $K/\gamma \approx 0$. Also suppose that $C \in \mathscr{L}$ is nonempty and let $\tilde{C} = \{\omega \in \Omega : {}^\circ\omega \in C\}$ and

$$\hat{C} = \{\omega \in \Omega : \omega = nK/\gamma \text{ for some } n \in {}^*N \text{ and } {}^\circ\omega \in C\}. \tag{22.2}$$

Then $\tilde{C} \in \mathscr{F}_{\mathscr{A}}$ and $\hat{C} \in \mathscr{F}_{\mathscr{A}}$. Moreover, $P_v(\tilde{C}) = \mu(C)$ and $P_v(\hat{C}) = 0$. Finally, $C = {}^\circ\hat{C}$!

22.3 Random Variables and Integration in Hyperspace

In this section we study random variables and integration in hyperspace. Our intent is to gain insight and to acquire tools that we shall need for our study of exchange in hyperspace and Brownian motion. Throughout our discussion we assume that $\Omega \subset {}^*R^n$ for some $n \in N$.

22.3.1 Random Variables in Hyperspace

Let Ω be a nonempty set and let $\mathscr{F}$ be a field of subsets of Ω. In addition, let $f(\cdot): \Omega \to {}^*R$ be such that $\{\omega \in \Omega : f(\omega) < a\} \in \mathscr{F}$ for all $a \in {}^*R$. Then $f(\cdot)$ is said to be *$\mathscr{F}$-measurable*. Whenever $\mathscr{F}$ is a σ field, an $\mathscr{F}$-measurable function is a random variable. A *random variable in hyperspace* is a random variable on a nonstandard experiment.

We are not interested in random variables for their own sake. Instead we want to establish correspondences between measurable functions on pairs of related nonstandard probability spaces. Our first result concerns measurable functions on an internal probability space $(\Omega, \mathscr{A}, v(\cdot))$ and its associated Loeb probability space, $(\Omega, \mathscr{F}_{\mathscr{A}}, P_v(\cdot))$. In reading the statement of the theorem, note that an internal function $F(\cdot): \Omega \to {}^*R$ is $\mathscr{A}$-measurable when $\mathscr{A}$ contains all internal subsets of Ω. Note also that if $f(\cdot): \Omega \to R$,

$F(\cdot)\colon \Omega \to {}^*R$ is a *lifting* of $f(\cdot)$ if and only if $F(\cdot)$ is internal, $\mathscr{A}$-measurable, and satisfies $f(\omega) = {}^\circ F(\omega)$ a.e.—P_v measure.

T 22.7 Let $(\Omega, \mathscr{A}, v(\cdot))$ be an internal probability space where $\mathscr{A}$ contains all internal subsets of Ω. Moreover, let $(\Omega, \mathscr{F}_{\mathscr{A}}, P_v(\cdot))$ be the associated Loeb probability space and let $f(\cdot)\colon \Omega \to R$. Then $f(\cdot)$ is a random variable on $(\Omega, \mathscr{F}_{\mathscr{A}}, P_v(\cdot))$ if and only if $f(\cdot)$ has a lifting $F(\cdot)\colon \Omega \to {}^*R$.

To prove the theorem, we suppose that $f(\cdot)\colon \Omega \to R$ has a lifting $F(\cdot)\colon \Omega \to {}^*R$. Then, for each $a \in R$, $\{\omega \in \Omega : {}^\circ F(\omega) < a\} = \bigcup_{n \in N} \{\omega \in \Omega : F(\omega) < a - 1/n\}$. Since $F(\cdot)$ is $\mathscr{A}$-measurable, $\{\omega \in \Omega : F(\omega) < a - 1/n\} \in \mathscr{A}$. Hence $\{\omega \in \Omega : {}^\circ F(\omega) < a\} \in \sigma(\mathscr{A})$. From this and the construction of $\mathscr{F}_{\mathscr{A}}$ it follows that $\{\omega \in \Omega : f(\omega) < a\} \in \mathscr{F}_{\mathscr{A}}$ for all $a \in R$.

To establish the converse, we use an argument of R. M. Anderson's (Anderson 1977, p. 47–48). Suppose that $f(\cdot)\colon \Omega \to R$ is a random variable on $(\Omega, \mathscr{F}_{\mathscr{A}}, P_v(\cdot))$ and let N_i, $i \in N$, be a base of open sets for the standard topology of R. Also let $A_i = \{\omega \in \Omega : f(\omega) \in N_i\}$, $i \in N$. The A_i belong to $\mathscr{F}_{\mathscr{A}}$. Hence, by T 22.4, for each $i \in N$, we can find a $\tilde{D}_i \in \mathscr{A}$ such that $P_v((A_i - \tilde{D}_i) \cup (\tilde{D}_i - A_i)) = 0$. We may choose a new sequence D_i, $i \in N$, such that $D_i \in \mathscr{A}$, $P_v((A_i - D_i) \cup (D_i - A_i)) = 0$ and, whenever $A_{j_1} \cap A_{j_2} \cap \cdots \cap A_{j_k} = \varnothing$, $D_{j_1} \cap D_{j_2} \cap \cdots \cap D_{j_k} = \varnothing$; e.g., by defining inductively, for all $i \in N$,

$$D_i = \tilde{D}_i - \bigcup \{D_{j_1} \cap \cdots \cap D_{j_k} : j_l < i \text{ and } A_i \cap A_{j_1} \cap \cdots \cap A_{j_k} = \varnothing\}.$$

For each $m \in N$, let $G_m = \{\text{internal } F(\cdot)\colon \Omega \to {}^*R : F(D_i) \subset {}^*N_i,\ i \leqslant m\}$. Then the G_m are internal and nonempty and $G_1 \supset G_2 \supset \cdots$. Hence, by SP (section 21.1.1), there is an internal $F(\cdot) \in \bigcap_{m \in N} G_m$. For a $\omega \in \Omega - \bigcup_{m \in N} ((A_m - D_m) \cup (D_m - A_m))$, $F(\omega) \in \bigcap \{{}^*N_i : f(\omega) \in N_i\}$ and (hence) $f(\omega) = {}^\circ F(\omega)$. From this and $P_v(\Omega - \bigcup_{m \in N} ((A_m - D_m) \cup (D_m - A_m))) = 1$ it follows that $f(\omega) = {}^\circ F(\omega)$ a.e. (P_v measure). Hence $F(\cdot)$ is a lifting of $f(\cdot)$.

Next we shall establish a theorem that relates $\mathscr{A}$-measurable functions on an internal probability space $(\Omega, \mathscr{A}, v(\cdot))$ to random variables on one of the standard versions of $(\Omega, \mathscr{F}_{\mathscr{A}}, P_v(\cdot))$.

T 22.8 Let $(\Omega, \mathscr{A}, v(\cdot))$ be an internal probability space where $\mathscr{A}$ contains all internal subsets of Ω and let $(\Omega, \mathscr{F}_{\mathscr{A}}, P_v(\cdot))$ be the associated Loeb probability space. In addition, let $(X, {}^\circ\mathscr{F}_{\mathscr{A}}, \mu_v(\cdot))$ be a standard version of $(\Omega, \mathscr{F}_{\mathscr{A}}, P_v(\cdot))$ and suppose that $f(\cdot)\colon X \to R$. Finally, suppose that the points in Ω are near-standard; i.e., suppose that ${}^\circ\omega$ is well defined for all $\omega \in \Omega$. Then $f(\cdot)$ is a random variable on $(X, {}^\circ\mathscr{F}_{\mathscr{A}}, \mu_v(\cdot))$ if and only if there is an internal function $F(\cdot)\colon \Omega \to {}^*R$ such that $f({}^\circ\omega) = {}^\circ F(\omega)$ a.e. (P_v measure).

To prove the theorem, we let $f_1(\cdot)\colon \Omega \to R$ be defined by $f_1(\omega) = f({}^\circ\omega)$, $\omega \in \Omega$. Then $f_1(\cdot)$ is well defined and, by T 22.7, $f_1(\cdot)$ is a random variable on $(\Omega, \mathscr{F}_{\mathscr{A}}, P_v(\cdot))$ if and only if there is an internal function $F(\cdot): \Omega \to {}^*R$ on $(\Omega, \mathscr{A})$ such that $f_1(\omega) = {}^\circ F(\omega)$ for almost all $\omega \in \Omega$—P_v measure. Consequently, we can establish T 22.8 by showing that $f(\cdot)$ is a random variable on $(X, {}^\circ\mathscr{F}_{\mathscr{A}}, \mu_v(\cdot))$ if and only if $f_1(\cdot)$ is a random variable on $(\Omega, \mathscr{F}_{\mathscr{A}}, P_v(\cdot))$. But that is obviously true, since by condition ii of the definition of standard versions of Loeb probability spaces, $\{x \in X : f(x) < a\}$, $a \in R$, belongs to ${}^\circ\mathscr{F}_{\mathscr{A}}$ if and only if $\{\omega \in \Omega : f({}^\circ\omega) < a\} \in \mathscr{F}_{\mathscr{A}}$ and since $\{\omega \in \Omega : f_1(\omega) < a\} = \{\omega \in \Omega : f({}^\circ\omega) < a\}$.

For ease of reference we say that $F(\cdot)$ is a lifting of $f(\cdot)$ if $f(\cdot)$ and $F(\cdot)$ satisfy the conditions of T 22.8. The fact that we have two concepts of lifting should not cause confusion later.

In reading T 22.8 it is important to note that if $F(\cdot)$ is an internal function on $(\Omega, \mathscr{A}, v(\cdot))$, there need not exist a random variable $f(\cdot)$ on $(X, {}^\circ\mathscr{F}_{\mathscr{A}}, \mu_v(\cdot))$ such that $F(\cdot)$ is a lifting of $f(\cdot)$.

E 22.7 Let $(\Omega, \mathscr{A}, v(\cdot))$, $(\Omega, \mathscr{F}_{\mathscr{A}}, P_v(\cdot))$, and $([0, 1], \mathscr{L}, \mu(\cdot))$ be as in T 22.6 and let $C \in \mathscr{L}$ be such that $\mu(C) > 0$. Furthermore, let $\tilde{C} = \{\omega \in \Omega : {}^\circ\omega \in C\}$ and let $\hat{C}$ be as in equation 22.2. Finally, let $I_A(\cdot)$ denote the indicator function of A, and let $F_{\tilde{C}}(\cdot)$ and $F_{\hat{C}}(\cdot)$, respectively, be liftings of $I_{\tilde{C}}(\cdot)$ and $I_{\hat{C}}(\cdot)$. Then $F_{\tilde{C}}(\cdot)$ is a lifting of $I_C(\cdot)$, but $F_{\hat{C}}(\cdot)$ is not.

22.3.2 Integration in Hyperspace

In this section we establish certain basic results concerning nonstandard integration that we shall need for our study of exchange in hyperspace.

Let $(\Omega, \mathscr{A}, v(\cdot))$ be an internal probability space, let $F(\cdot): \Omega \to {}^*R$ be an internal function; and suppose that $F(\cdot)$ is $\mathscr{A}$-measurable. Then $F(\cdot)$ is *finite* if and only if there is an $n \in N$ such that, for all $\omega \in \Omega$, $-n \leqslant F(\omega) \leqslant n$. For finite functions the following relationship holds:

T 22.9 Let $(\Omega, \mathscr{A}, v(\cdot))$ be an internal probability space and let $(\Omega, \mathscr{F}_{\mathscr{A}}, P_v(\cdot))$ be its associated Loeb space. Suppose that $F(\cdot): \Omega \to {}^*R_+$ is internal and $\mathscr{A}$-measurable. If $F(\cdot)$ is finite

$$ {}^\circ\left(\int_A F(\omega)\, dv(\omega)\right) = \int_A {}^\circ F(\omega)\, dP_v(\omega) \tag{22.3}$$

for all $A \in \mathscr{A}$.

I prove equation 22.3 for $A = \Omega$ and leave the concluding details for the reader. The theorem and the arguments used are due to Peter Loeb (Loeb 1975, pp. 117–118). Let $B = \{r \in R : P_v(\{\omega \in \Omega : {}^\circ F(\omega) = r\}) > 0\}$ and observe that B is either finite or countably infinite. Next fix $\delta \in R_{++}$ and let y_i, $i = 0, \ldots, m$, be such that $y_i \in R - B$, $0 = y_0 < y_1 < \cdots < y_m$, $\sup_{\omega \in \Omega} {}^\circ F(\omega) < y_m$ and $y_i - y_{i-1} < \delta/3$ for $1 \leqslant i \leqslant m$.

Also let $\underline{S}_v = \sum_{i=1}^{m} y_{i-1} v(F^{-1}(^*[y_{i-1}, y_i)))$, $\overline{S}_v = \sum_{i=1}^{m} y_i v(F^{-1}(^*[y_{i-1}, y_i)))$, $\underline{S}_P = \sum_{i=1}^{m} y_{i-1} P_v(^\circ F^{-1}([y_{i-1}, y_i)))$, and $\overline{S}_P = \sum_{i=1}^{m} y_i P_v(^\circ F^{-1}([y_{i-1}, y_i)))$. Then $\underline{S}_v \leqslant \int_\Omega F(\omega)\, dv(\omega) \leqslant \overline{S}_v$ and $\underline{S}_P \leqslant \int_\Omega {}^\circ F(\omega)\, dP_v(\omega) \leqslant \overline{S}_P$. Moreover, $\overline{S}_v - \underline{S}_v < \delta/3$ and $\overline{S}_P - \underline{S}_P < \delta/3$. Finally, observe that, for all $i \in \{1, \ldots, m\}$, $^\circ F^{-1}((y_{i-1}, y_i)) \subset F^{-1}(^*(y_{i-1}, y_i)) \subset F^{-1}(^*[y_{i-1}, y_i]) \subset {}^\circ F^{-1}([y_{i-1}, y_i])$. Hence

$$\begin{aligned} P_v(^\circ F^{-1}([y_{i-1}, y_i])) &= P_v(^\circ F^{-1}((y_{i-1}, y_i))) \\ &\leqslant P_v(F^{-1}(^*(y_{i-1}, y_i))) \approx v(F^{-1}(^*(y_{i-1}, y_i))) \\ &\leqslant v(F^{-1}(^*[y_{i-1}, y_i])) \approx P_v(F^{-1}(^*[y_{i-1}, y_i])) \\ &\leqslant P_v(^\circ F^{-1}([y_{i-1}, y_i])), \end{aligned}$$

from which it follows that $\underline{S}_v \approx \underline{S}_P$ and $\overline{S}_v \approx \overline{S}_P$. Consequently, $|\int_\Omega F(w)\, dv(\omega) - \int_\Omega {}^\circ F(\omega)\, dP_v(w)| < \delta$ and equation 22.3 with $A = \Omega$ follows from the fact that our choice of δ was arbitrary.

To extend the preceding result to internal functions that are not necessarily finite, we need a definition and an auxiliary theorem. First the definition: Let $(\Omega, \mathscr{A}, v(\cdot))$ be an internal probability space and let $F(\cdot)\colon \Omega \to {}^*R$ be an internal $\mathscr{A}$-measurable function on $(\Omega, \mathscr{A})$. Then $F(\cdot)$ is *S-integrable* if and only if it satisfies these conditions:

(i) $^\circ(\int_\Omega |F(\omega)|\, dv(\omega)) < \infty$.
(ii) For all $A \in \mathscr{A}$ with $v(A) \approx 0$, $\int_A |F(\omega)|\, dv(\omega) \approx 0$.

Necessary and sufficient conditions for a function $F(\cdot)$ to be S-integrable are given in the next theorem. The theorem is due to R. M. Anderson. For a proof see Anderson 1976 (pp. 18–19).

T 22.10 Let $(\Omega, \mathscr{A}, v(\cdot))$ be an internal probability space and let $F(\cdot)\colon \Omega \to {}^*R$ be an internal $\mathscr{A}$-measurable function. Then $F(\cdot)$ is S-integrable if and only if there is a sequence of finite, internal, $\mathscr{A}$-measurable functions, $F_n(\cdot)\colon \Omega \to {}^*R$, $n \in N$, such that

$$\lim {}^\circ\left(\int_\Omega |F(\omega) - F_n(\omega)|\, dv(\omega)\right) = 0.$$

With the help of the last two theorems we can establish the following relation between integration on an internal probability space and integration on the associated Loeb space.

T 22.11 Let $(\Omega, \mathscr{A}, v(\cdot))$ be an internal probability space and let $(\Omega, \mathscr{F}_{\mathscr{A}}, P_v(\cdot))$ be the associated Loeb probability space. In addition, let $f(\cdot)\colon \Omega \to R$ be a random variable on $(\Omega, \mathscr{F}_{\mathscr{A}}, P_v(\cdot))$. Then $f(\cdot)$ is integrable if and only if it has an S-integrable lifting $F(\cdot)\colon \Omega \to {}^*R$. When $f(\cdot)$ is integrable and $F(\cdot)$ is its S-integrable lifting, then

$$\int_A f(\omega)\,dP_v(\omega) = {}^\circ\left(\int_A F(\omega)\,dv(\omega)\right)$$

for all $A \in \mathscr{A}$.

Suppose that $f(\cdot)$ has an S-integrable lifting $F(\cdot)$, and let $F_n(\cdot)$, $n \in N$, be a sequence of internal finite $\mathscr{A}$-measurable functions such that $\lim {}^\circ(\int_\Omega |F(\omega) - F_n(\omega)|\,dv(\omega)) = 0$. Moreover, for all $n \in N$, let $f_n(\cdot)\colon \Omega \to R$ be defined by $f_n(\omega) = {}^\circ F_n(\omega)$. Then, by T 22.9 and T 22.7, $f_n(\cdot)$ is a random variable on $(\Omega, \mathscr{F}_\mathscr{A}, P_v(\cdot))$ and, for all $A \in \mathscr{A}$, $\int_A f_n(\omega)\,dP_v(\omega) = {}^\circ(\int_A F_n(\omega)\,dv(\omega))$. We shall see (1) that there is an integrable random variable $g(\cdot)\colon \Omega \to R$ on $(\Omega, \mathscr{F}_\mathscr{A}, P_v(\cdot))$ such that $\lim \int_\Omega |g(\omega) - f_n(\omega)|\,dP_v(\omega) = 0$ and (2) that $f(\omega) = g(\omega)$ a.e. (P_v measure). The validity of the first assertion, that is, point 1 follows from a universal theorem of measure theory (see UT 16, section 15.6) and the inequalities,

$$\begin{aligned}\int_\Omega |f_n(\omega) - f_m(\omega)|\,dP_v(\omega) &= {}^\circ\left(\int_\Omega |F_n(\omega) - F_m(\omega)|\,dv(\omega)\right)\\ &\leqslant {}^\circ\left(\int_\Omega |F_n(\omega) - F(\omega)|\,dv(\omega)\right)\\ &\quad + {}^\circ\left(\int_\Omega |F_m(\omega) - F(\omega)|\,dv(\omega)\right).\end{aligned}$$

The validity of point 2 follows from the fact that $p\lim f_n(\omega) = g(\omega)$ in P_v measure, $p\lim F_n(\omega) = F(\omega)$ in v measure and, for any $\delta \in R_{++}$,

$$\begin{aligned}P_v(\{\omega \in \Omega : |f(\omega) - f_n(\omega)| > \delta\}) &= P_v(\{\omega \in \Omega : |{}^\circ F(\omega) - {}^\circ F_n(\omega)| > \delta\})\\ &= P_v(\{\omega \in \Omega : {}^\circ|F(\omega) - F_n(\omega)| > \delta\})\\ &\leqslant P_v(\{\omega \in \Omega : |F(\omega) - F_n(\omega)| > \delta\})\\ &\approx v(\{\omega \in \Omega : |F(\omega) - F_n(\omega)| > \delta\}).\end{aligned}$$

From points 1 and 2, we deduce both that $f(\cdot)$ is integrable and that

$$\begin{aligned}\int_A f(\omega)\,dP_v(\omega) &= \lim \int_A f_n(\omega)\,dP_v(\omega)\\ &= \lim {}^\circ\left(\int_A F_n(\omega)\,dv(\omega)\right) = {}^\circ\left(\int_A F(\omega)\,dv(\omega)\right) \qquad (22.4)\end{aligned}$$

for $A = \Omega$. The same arguments applied to $f(\omega)I_A(\omega)$ show that equation 22.4 is valid for any $A \in \mathscr{A}$.

To prove the converse, we suppose that $f(\cdot)$ is integrable and let $f_n(\omega) = n$ or $-n$ according as $f(\omega) > n$, $f(\omega) < -n$ and $f_n(\omega) = f(\omega)$ if $|f(\omega)| \leqslant n$, $n \in N$. Then the $f_n(\cdot)$ are integrable random variables on $(\Omega, \mathscr{F}_{\mathscr{A}}, P_v(\cdot))$ such that $\lim \int_\Omega |f(\omega) - f_n(\omega)| dP_v(\omega) = 0$. Next, for each $n \in N$, let $F_n(\cdot)$: $\Omega \to {}^*R$ be an integrable lifting of $f_n(\cdot)$ and observe that ${}^\circ(\int_\Omega |F_n(\omega) - F_m(\omega)|\, dv(\omega)) = \int_\Omega |f_n(\omega) - f_m(\omega)|\, dP_v(\omega)$ and that $\int_\Omega |f_n(\omega) - f_m(\omega)|\, dP_v(\omega)$ tends to zero as n, m tend to infinity. By T 21.3, the internal sequence, $F_n(\cdot)$, $n \in N$, can be extended to an internal sequence, $F_n(\cdot)$, $n \in {}^*N$. For some $\eta \in {}^*N - N$, $F_\eta(\cdot)$ is an $\mathscr{A}$-measurable function on $(\Omega, \mathscr{A}, v(\cdot))$ and $\lim {}^\circ(\int_\Omega |F_n(\omega) - F_\eta(\omega)|\, dv(\omega)) = 0$. Thus $F_\eta(\cdot)$ is S-integrable and, by the first half of our proof, ${}^\circ F_\eta(\cdot)$ is an integrable random variable on $(\Omega, \mathscr{F}_{\mathscr{A}}, P_v(\cdot))$. From this and the inequalities

$$\begin{aligned}\int_\Omega |f(\omega) - {}^\circ F_\eta(\omega)|\, dP_v(\omega) &\leqslant \int_\Omega |{}^\circ F_\eta(\omega) - {}^\circ F_n(\omega)|\, dP_v(\omega) \\ &\quad + \int_\Omega |f(\omega) - {}^\circ F_n(\omega)|\, dP_v(\omega) \\ &= {}^\circ\left(\int_\Omega |F_\eta(\omega) - F_n(\omega)|\, dv(\omega)\right) \\ &\quad + \int_\Omega |f(\omega) - {}^\circ F_n(\omega)|\, dP_v(\omega),\end{aligned}$$

it follows that ${}^\circ F_\eta(\omega) = f(\omega)$ a.e. (P_v measure) and that $F_\eta(\cdot)$ is an S-integrable lifting of $f(\cdot)$. This concludes the proof of the converse.

Next we establish for integration an analogue of T 22.7:

T 22.12 Let $(\Omega, \mathscr{A}, v(\cdot))$ be an internal probability space and let $(\Omega, \mathscr{F}_{\mathscr{A}}, P_v(\cdot))$ be the associated Loeb probability space. In addition, let $(X, {}^\circ\mathscr{F}_{\mathscr{A}}, \mu_v(\cdot))$ be a standard version of $(\Omega, \mathscr{F}_{\mathscr{A}}, P_v(\cdot))$ and let $f(\cdot)$: $X \to R$ be a random variable on $(X, {}^\circ\mathscr{F}_{\mathscr{A}})$. Finally, suppose that the points in Ω are near-standard. Then $f(\cdot)$ is integrable if and only if $f(\cdot)$ has an S-integrable lifting $F(\cdot)$: $\Omega \to {}^*R$. If $f(\cdot)$ is integrable and $F(\cdot)$ is its S-integrable lifting, then

$$\int_A f(x)\, d\mu_v(x) = {}^\circ\left(\int_{\tilde{A}} F(\omega)\, dv(\omega)\right)$$

for all pairs $(A, \tilde{A})$ such that $A \in {}^\circ\mathscr{F}_{\mathscr{A}}$, $\tilde{A} \in \mathscr{A}$, and $\tilde{A} = \{\omega \in \Omega : {}^\circ\omega \in A\}$.

If we define $f_1(\cdot)$: $\Omega \to R$ by $f_1(\omega) = f({}^\circ\omega)$, $\omega \in \Omega$, it follows from T 22.8 and T 22.11 that the only things we need to prove are (1) that $f(\cdot)$ is integrable if and only if $f_1(\cdot)$ is integrable in P_v measure and (2) that if $f(\cdot)$ is integrable, $\int_A f(x)\, d\mu_v(x) = \int_{\tilde{A}} f_1(\omega)\, dP_v(\omega)$ for all pairs $(A, \tilde{A})$ such that $A \in {}^\circ\mathscr{F}_{\mathscr{A}}$, $\tilde{A} \in \mathscr{F}_{\mathscr{A}}$ and $\tilde{A} = \{\omega \in \Omega : {}^\circ\omega \in A\}$. It follows easily from T 22.8

that with $A = X$ and $\tilde{A} = \Omega$, both items 1 and 2 above are true when $f(\cdot)$ is a simple function. But, if that is so, then standard approximations suffice to verify that items 1 and 2 with $A = X$ and $\tilde{A} = \Omega$ are true for all random variables on $(X, {}^\circ\mathscr{F}_{\mathscr{A}}, \mu_v(\cdot))$. The same arguments applied to $f(\cdot)I_A(\cdot)$ show that item 2 is valid for all pairs $(A, \tilde{A})$ with the required properties.

22.4 Exchange in Hyperspace Revisited

In this section we use theorems T 22.6, T 22.8, and T 22.12 to fill an important lacuna in our theory of exchange in hyperspace. Specifically, we see that the core of the economy of section 21.4 is nonempty when the internal cardinality of the set of consumers, $|T|$, equals $\eta!$ for some $\eta \in {}^*N - N$, and $A(\cdot)$ and $U(\cdot)$ are liftings of real-valued functions on $[0, 1]$ and $([0, 1] \times R_+^n)$, respectively.

The economy in section 21.4 was a triple, $(U(\cdot), T \times {}^*R_+^n, A(\cdot))$, where $T = \{1, \ldots, \gamma\}$ for some $\gamma \in {}^*N - N$, $U(\cdot): T \times {}^*R_+^n \to ({}^*R_+ \cap Ns({}^*R))$, and $A(\cdot): T \to {}^*R_{++}^n$. We endowed ${}^*R$ and ${}^*R^n$ with the S topology and assumed that

(i) $A(\cdot)$ is internal;
(ii) there is a pair $(\delta, r) \in R_{++}^2$ such that, for all $t \in T$, $\delta \leqslant A(t) \leqslant r$;
(iii) $U(\cdot)$ is internal; and
(iv) for each $t \in T$, $U(t, \cdot)$ is continuous, strictly quasi-concave, and strictly increasing in the S topology, as specified in conditions iva–ivd in section 21.4.1.

In this section we rename the consumers in the economy so that

$$T = \{1/\gamma, \ldots, 1\}; \tag{22.5}$$

we let $(T, \mathscr{A}, v(\cdot))$ be an internal probability space where $\mathscr{A}$ consists of all the internal subsets of T and where $v(A) = |A|/\gamma$, $A \in \mathscr{A}$; and we let $(T, \mathscr{F}_{\mathscr{A}}, P_v(\cdot))$ be the associated Loeb probability space. We also add an assumption:

(v) $\gamma = \eta!$ for some $\eta \in N^* - N$ and there are functions $V(\cdot): ([0, 1] \times R_+^n) \to R_+$ and $w(\cdot): [0, 1] \to R_{++}^n$ such that $w({}^\circ t) = {}^\circ A(t)$ a.e. (P_v measure), and such that, for some P_v null set $\mathscr{N}$,

$$V({}^\circ t, {}^\circ x) = {}^\circ U(t, x), \qquad (t, x) \in (T - \mathscr{N}) \times Ns({}^*R^n). \tag{22.6}$$

The preceding economy has a standard alias, $(V(\cdot), [0, 1] \times R_+^n, w(\cdot))$, that we describe next. First $V(\cdot)$: By T 22.6, ${}^\circ T = [0, 1]$, ${}^\circ(T - \mathscr{N}) \in \mathscr{L}$, and $\mu({}^\circ(T - \mathscr{N})) = 1$. From this, equation 22.6, and the S continuity of

$U(t, \cdot)$, it follows that $V(t, \cdot)$ is continuous for almost all $t \in [0, 1]$.[4] It is also easy to verify that conditions iv and v above imply that, for almost all $t \in [0, 1]$, $V(t, \cdot)$ is strictly quasi-concave and strictly increasing; that is, x, $y \in R_+^n$, $x \geqslant y$, and $x \neq y$ imply that $V(t,x) > V(t,y)$; and $x, y \in R_+^n$, $x \neq y$, and $\lambda \in (0, 1)$ imply that $V(t, \lambda x + (1 - \lambda)y) > \min(V(t,x), V(t,y))$.

Next $w(\cdot)$: Since ${}^\circ T = [0, 1]$ and $A(\cdot)$ is internal, it follows from condition (v) above and T 22.6 and T 22.8 that $w(\cdot)$ is $\mathscr{L}$-measurable.

For ease of reference we record these facts in the next theorem.

T 22.13 Let $V(\cdot)$: $[0, 1] \times R_+^n \to R_+$ and $w(\cdot)$: $[0, 1] \to R_{++}^n$ be as described in condition v. Then for almost all $t \in [0, 1]$ μ measure, $V(t, \cdot)$ is strictly quasi-concave, strictly increasing, and continuous. Moreover, $w(\cdot)$ is $\mathscr{L}$-measurable.

It follows from conditions v and ii that

$$\delta \leqslant w(t) \leqslant r \quad \text{a.e. } (\mu \text{ measure}). \tag{22.7}$$

From this and T 22.12 we conclude that

$$\int_{[0,1]} w(t)\, d\mu(t) = {}^\circ\left(\int_T A(t)\, dv(t)\right). \tag{22.8}$$

Let E denote the nonstandard economy of section 21.4 and let $\hat{E}$ denote its standard alias. An allocation in $\hat{E}$ is an $\mathscr{L}$-measurable function $x(\cdot)$: $\Omega \to R_+^n$ such that $\int_\Omega x(t)\, d\mu(t) = \int_\Omega w(t)\, d\mu(t)$. Furthermore, a competitive equilibrium in $\hat{E}$ is a triple, $(p, x(\cdot), K)$, where $p \in R_{++}^n$, $K \in \mathscr{L}$, $\mu(K) = 1$, and $x(\cdot)$ is an allocation such that, for all $t \in K$,

$$px(t) \leqslant pw(t), \qquad \text{and} \qquad V(t, x(t)) = \max_{\{y \in R_+^n :\, py \leqslant pw(t)\}} V(t, y).$$

We shall see that there is a competitive equilibrium in $\hat{E}$. For that purpose we must establish the following auxiliary theorem:

T 22.14 Let $\Omega = [0, 1]$; let $V(\cdot)$: $\Omega \times R_+^n \to R_+$ be as described in equation 22.6; and let $x(\cdot)$ and $y(\cdot)$ be integrable functions on $(\Omega, \mathscr{L}, \mu(\cdot))$. Then $\{t \in \Omega : V(t, x(t)) > V(t, y(t))\}$ belongs to $\mathscr{L}$.

To prove the theorem we note that, by T 22.12, there exist S-integrable random variables on $(T, \mathscr{A}, v(\cdot))$, denoted $F_x(\cdot)$ and $F_y(\cdot)$, such that a.e.—P_v measure, ${}^\circ F_x(t) = x({}^\circ t)$ and ${}^\circ F_y(t) = y({}^\circ t)$ and such that $\int_\Omega x(t)\, d\mu(t) = {}^\circ(\int_T F_x(t)\, dv(t))$ and $\int_\Omega y(t)\, d\mu(t) = {}^\circ(\int_T F_y(t)\, dv(t))$. Let $A = \{t \in \Omega : V(t, x(t)) > V(t, y(t))\}$, $\tilde{A} = \{t \in T : {}^\circ t \in A\}$, and $\hat{A} = \{t \in T : {}^\circ U(t, F_x(t)) > {}^\circ U(t, F_y(t))\}$. Then it is easy to verify that $P_v((\tilde{A} - \hat{A}) \cup (\hat{A} - \tilde{A})) = 0$. Also, by T 22.6, $A \in \mathscr{L}$ if and only if $\tilde{A} \in \mathscr{F}_{\mathscr{A}}$. From these two observations and the completeness of $P_v(\cdot)$ it follows that, to show that $A \in \mathscr{L}$ it suffices to show that $\hat{A} \in \mathscr{F}_{\mathscr{A}}$. The latter relation follows from the properties of $F_x(\cdot)$, $F_y(\cdot)$, and $U(\cdot)$, which imply that, for all $n \in N$, $\{t \in T : U(t, F_x(t)) > U(t, F_y(t)) + n^{-1}\} \in \mathscr{A}$, and from

$$\hat{A} = \bigcup_{n \in N} \{t \in T : U(t, F_x(t)) > U(t, F_y(t)) + n^{-1}\}.$$

Theorems T 22.13 and T 22.14 show that $\hat{E}$ satisfies the conditions of Aumann's economy in Aumann 1966 (pp. 2–17). From this and Aumann's Main Theorem (Aumann 1966, p. 4) we deduce the validity of theorem T 22.15:

T 22.15 Let $\hat{E} = (V(\cdot), \Omega \times R^n_+, w(\cdot))$ be as described in equations 22.4–22.8. Then there exists a competitive equilibrium $(p, x(\cdot), K)$ in $\hat{E}$.

Next, let $(p, x(\cdot), K)$ be a competitive equilibrium in $\hat{E}$ and let $F_x(\cdot): T \to {}^*R^n_+$ be an S-integrable lifting of $x(\cdot)$. We shall show that $(p, F_x(\cdot))$ is an S competitive equilibrium in E. To do that we show first that $F_x(\cdot)$ is an S allocation. It follows from $px({}^\circ t) \leqslant pw({}^\circ t)$, $x({}^\circ t) = {}^\circ F_x(t)$, and $w({}^\circ t) = {}^\circ A(t)$ that

$$pF_x(t) \lesssim pA(t); \tag{22.9}$$

and from $\int_\Omega x(t)\, d\mu(t) = \int_\Omega w(t)\, d\mu(t)$, T 22.11, and equation 22.8 that

$$\int_T F_x(t)\, dv(t) \approx \int_T A(t)\, dv(t). \tag{22.10}$$

Also from equations 22.7, 22.9, and $p \in R^n_{++}$, it follows that on the set of $t \in T$, where $px({}^\circ t) \leqslant pw({}^\circ t)$ and $x({}^\circ t) = {}^\circ F_x(t)$, $F_x(\cdot)$ is uniformly bounded. Since this set has P_v measure 1 and since $F_x(\cdot)$ is determined up to a set of P_v measure 0, we can without loss in generality assume that there is an $a \in R_{++}$ such that

$$F_x(t) \leqslant a, \qquad t \in T. \tag{22.11}$$

Finally, from equation 22.11 and the fact that $F_x(\cdot)$ is a lifting of $x(\cdot)$ that satisfies equation 22.10, it follows that $F_x(\cdot)$ is an S allocation in E.

Next we show that on a T set of P_v measure 1, $F_x(t)$ is maximal with respect to $U(t, \cdot)$ in the set $\{y \in {}^*R^n_+ : py \lesssim pA(t)\}$. Let $A \in \mathscr{L}$ denote the set of $t \in [0, 1]$ at which $px(t) \leqslant pw(t)$ and $V(t, x(t)) \geqslant V(t, y)$ for all $y \in R^n_+$ such that $py \leqslant pw(t)$, and let $\tilde{A} = \{t \in \mathscr{N} : {}^\circ t \in A, x({}^\circ t) = {}^\circ F_x(t), w({}^\circ t) = {}^\circ A(t)\}$. Then $\tilde{A} \in \mathscr{F}_{\mathscr{A}}$ and $P_v(\tilde{A}) = 1$. For all $t \in \tilde{A}$, $py \leqslant pw({}^\circ t)$ implies that ${}^\circ U(t, y) \leqslant {}^\circ U(t, F_x(t))$ and hence that $U(t, y) \lesssim U(t, F_x(t))$. Consequently, since $y \in {}^*R^n_+$ and $py \lesssim pA(t)$ implies $p^0 y \leqslant p^\circ A(t)$, we can use T 21.18 to deduce

$$\text{for all } t \in \tilde{A},\ y \in {}^*R^n_+ \text{ and } py \lesssim pA(t) \text{ implies } U(t, y) \lesssim U(t, F_x(t)). \tag{22.12}$$

From equations 22.12 and 22.9 it follows that in $\tilde{A}$ $F_x(t)$ is maximal with respect to $U(t, \cdot)$ in the set $\{y \in {}^*R^n_+ : py \lesssim pA(t)\}$.

Finally, using standard arguments, we can find an internal set $\hat{A} \in \mathscr{A}$ such that $\hat{A} \subset \tilde{A}$ and $v(\hat{A}) \approx 1$. From this, and from equations 22.11 and 22.10, we deduce that $\int_{\hat{A}} F_x(t)\,dv(t) \approx \int_{\hat{A}} A(t)\,dv(t)$ and conclude the proof of the following theorem:

T 22.16 Let $E = (U(\cdot), T \times {}^*R^n_+, A(\cdot))$ be as described in assumptions i–v above. Then there is an S competitive equilibrium $(p, F_x(\cdot))$ in E.

From T 22.16 and T 21.30 it follows that the S core of E is nonempty. Also the S core of E and the set of S competitive-equilibrium allocations in E are identical.

Since E differs a bit from E_S, several remarks concerning E and the import of T 22.16 are in order. First the condition imposed on $U(\cdot)$ in condition v: The existence of a function $V(\cdot)$ that satisfies equation 22.6 ensures that the preferences of the individuals in E_S are not too different. To see why, just observe that for a $U(\cdot)$ which is S-continuous on all of $(T \times {}^*R^n_+)$ we can *define* $V(\cdot)$ by equation 22.6 and demonstrate that the resulting $V(\cdot)$ is well defined and continuous on $([0, 1] \times R^n_+)$.

Next condition v and the existence of competitive equilibria: Neither condition v nor conditions ivb–ivd (section 21.4.1) are necessary for demonstrating the existence of an S competitive equilibrium in a hyperfinite exchange economy. Using nonstandard arguments, Donald Brown has established the existence of an S competitive equilibrium in an economy populated by consumers whose endowments and utility functions need not satisfy condition v and whose utility functions are *-continuous but need not be S-continuous and quasi-concave. For details concerning Brown's economy I refer the reader to Brown 1976 (p. 540).

Here it is worth noting that in establishing T 22.16 we did not really use assumptions ivb–ivd. To wit: Aumann does not assume that his consumers' preferences are quasi-concave. Hence both T 22.15 and our proof of T 22.16 are valid without our insisting on the quasi-concavity of $U(t, \cdot)$. Also if $U(\cdot)$ satisfies conditions iii, iva, and v, it is easy to verify that, for all $t \in (T - \mathscr{N})$, $V(t, \cdot)$ is continuous and increasing and $U(t, \cdot)$ is S-continuous. Hence our proof of T 22.16 is valid without our insisting on the S continuity of $U(t, \cdot)$ in condition ivd.[4]

We might also note that if $U(\cdot)$: $(T \times {}^*R^n_+) \to ({}^*R_+ \cap Ns({}^*R))$ is internal and satisfies condition v, then $U(\cdot)$ is said to be a *uniform lifting* of $V(\cdot)$. It is, therefore, interesting that if $W(\cdot)$: $([0, 1] \times R^n_+) \to R_+$ and $W(\cdot, x)$ is Lebesgue-measurable for each and every $x \in R^n_+$, then for almost all $t \in$

[0, 1] (μ measure) $W(t, \cdot)$ is continuous on R_+^n if and only if $W(\cdot)$ has a uniform lifting. For a proof of this fact I refer the reader to Albeverio et al. 1986 (pp. 136–137).[5]

My reasons for imposing strong conditions on E are methodological. I insisted on conditions i–iv for the sake of uniformity with the conditions imposed on E and E_S in chapters 14 and 21. I imposed condition v so that we could relate our economy to Robert Aumann's economy and use T 21.28, T 21.30, and T 22.16 to demonstrate that Aumann's fundamental result concerning the equivalence of core allocations and competitive equilibria is a topological artifact and not a characteristic of large economies.

The topological aspect of the equivalence of core allocations and competitive equilibria that we have established is a general feature of most measure-theoretic characterizations of exchange economies.[6] Our result, therefore, does not detract from the unquestioned importance to mathematical economics of Aumann's two seminal papers on exchange economies with a measure space of agents. Instead, our result provides evidence for the fact that when interpreting an economic theory, it is not sufficient to assign names to undefined terms and to check the mutual consistency of the axioms. The originator of an economic theory owes his readers a description of at least one situation in which the empirical relevance of the theory can be tested.

22.5 A Hyperfinite Construction of the Brownian Motion

So much for exchange in hyperspace. Next we use the idea of a Loeb probability space to construct an interesting version of one of the most well-known random processes, Brownian motion. The construction delineated is due to R. A. Anderson and most of the arguments used are taken from Anderson 1976 (pp. 26–33).

A *Brownian motion* is a function, $\beta(\cdot): [0, 1] \times \Omega \to R$, on a standard probability space $(\Omega, \mathscr{F}, P(\cdot))$ that satisfies the following conditions:

(i) For each $t \in [0, 1]$, $\beta(t, \cdot)$ is a random variable on $(\Omega, \mathscr{F}, P(\cdot))$.

(ii) For each pair, $s, t \in [0, 1]$, such that $s < t$, the random variable, $\beta(t, \cdot) - \beta(s, \cdot)$, is normally distributed with mean zero and variance $t - s$.

(iii) For any n-tuple, $(s_1, t_1), \ldots, (s_n, t_n)$, in [0, 1] such that $s_1 < t_1 \leqslant s_2 < t_2 \leqslant \cdots < s_n < t_n$, the random variables, $\beta(t_1, \cdot) - \beta(s_1, \cdot), \cdots, \beta(t_n, \cdot) - \beta(s_n, \cdot)$, are independently distributed.

To construct such a process, I must introduce two new notions of stochastic independence and establish a hyperfinite central-limit theorem.

22.5.1 Independent Random Variables in Hyperspace

Let $I \subset {}^*N$ be an index set that contains N as a proper subset and let x_i, $i \in I$, be a family of $\mathscr{A}$-measurable functions on an internal probability space $(\Omega, \mathscr{A}, v(\cdot))$. This family is **-independent* if and only if every internal subcollection $\{x_{t_1}, \ldots, x_{t_m}\}$, $m \in {}^*N$, and every internal m-tuple, $(a_1, \ldots, a_m) \in {}^*R^m$, satisfies

$$v(\{\omega \in \Omega : x_{t_1}(\omega) < a_1, \ldots, x_{t_m}(\omega) < a_m\}) = \prod_{i=1}^{m} v(\{\omega \in \Omega : x_{t_i}(\omega) < a_i\}).$$

The family is *S-independent* if and only if every finite subcollection, $\{x_{t_1}, \ldots, x_{t_k}\}$, $k \in N$, and every k-tuple $(a_1, \ldots, a_k) \in R^k$ satisfy

$$v(\{\omega \in \Omega : x_{t_1}(\omega) < a_1, \ldots, x_{t_k}(\omega) < a_k\}) = \prod_{i=1}^{k} v(\{\omega \in \Omega : x_{t_i}(\omega) < a_i\}).$$

For S-independent, $\mathscr{A}$-measurable functions we can establish the following theorem:

T 22.17 Let $(\Omega, \mathscr{A}, v(\cdot))$ be an internal probability space and let $(\Omega, \mathscr{F}_{\mathscr{A}}, P_v(\cdot))$ be its associated Loeb probability space. Also, let $I \subset {}^*N$ be an index set and let x_i, $i \in I$, be a family of S-independent, $\mathscr{A}$-measurable functions on $(\Omega, \mathscr{A}, v(\cdot))$. Then ${}^\circ x_i$, $i \in I$, is a family of independent random variables on $(\Omega, \mathscr{F}_{\mathscr{A}}, P_v(\cdot))$.

To see why, pick $k \in N$ and $(a_1, \ldots, a_k) \in R^k$, and observe that

$$\begin{aligned}
&P_v(\{\omega \in \Omega : {}^\circ x_{t_1}(\omega) < a_1, \ldots, {}^\circ x_{t_k}(\omega) < a_k\}) \\
&\quad = P_v\left(\bigcup_{n \in N} \{\omega \in \Omega : x_{t_1}(\omega) < a_1 - 1/n, \ldots, x_{t_k}(\omega) < a_k - 1/n\}\right) \\
&\quad = \lim P_v(\{\omega \in \Omega : x_{t_1}(\omega) < a_1 - 1/n, \ldots, x_{t_k}(\omega) < a_k - 1/n\}) \\
&\quad = \lim {}^\circ v(\{\omega \in \Omega : x_{t_1}(\omega) < a_1 - 1/n, \ldots, x_{t_k}(\omega) < a_k - 1/n\}) \\
&\quad = \lim {}^\circ\left(\prod_{i=1}^{k} v(\{\omega \in \Omega : x_{t_i}(\omega) < a_i - 1/n\})\right) \\
&\quad = \prod_{i=1}^{k} \lim {}^\circ v(\{\omega \in \Omega : x_{t_i}(\omega) < a_i - 1/n\}) \\
&\quad = \prod_{i=1}^{k} P_v(\{\omega \in \Omega : {}^\circ x_{t_i}(\omega) < a_i\}),
\end{aligned}$$

as was to be shown.

A *-independent family of $\mathscr{A}$-measurable functions is S-independent. We shall use this fact, T 22.17, the standard central-limit theorem for purely random processes, and transfer to establish the following central-limit theorem for *-independent random variables.

T 22.18 Let $(\Omega, \mathscr{A}, v(\cdot))$ be an internal probability space. In addition, let x_n, $n \in {}^*N$, be an internal sequence of *-independent, $\mathscr{A}$-measurable functions on $(\Omega, \mathscr{A})$ with common standard probability distribution $F(\cdot)$: ${}^*R \to [0, 1]$. Suppose that $Ex_n = 0$, $Ex_n^2 = 1$ and x_n^2 is S-integrable. Then, for any $\eta \in {}^*N - N$ and $\alpha \in {}^*R$,

$$v\left(\left\{\omega \in \Omega : \eta^{-1/2} \sum_{i=1}^{\eta} x_i(\omega) < \alpha\right\}\right) \approx {}^*\psi(\alpha), \tag{22.13}$$

where $\psi(\cdot)$ denotes the normal distribution with mean 0 and variance 1.

The proof is as follows: By an argument similar to the one we used in the proof of T 22.17, we can show that if $(\Omega, \mathscr{F}_{\mathscr{A}}, P_v(\cdot))$ is the Loeb space associated with $(\Omega, \mathscr{A}, v(\cdot))$ and if

$$G(a) = P_v(\{\omega \in \Omega : {}^\circ x_i(\omega) < a\}), \qquad a \in R$$

then $G(\cdot)$: $R \to [0, 1]$ is the common distribution of the ${}^\circ x_m$, $m \in {}^*N$ and

$$G(a) = \lim {}^\circ v(\{\omega \in \Omega : x_i(\omega) < a - 1/n\}) = \lim {}^\circ F(a - 1/n) = {}^\circ F(a).$$

Hence $G(\cdot) = {}^\circ F(\cdot)$ and $F(\cdot) = {}^*G(\cdot)$.

It is easy to see that $E^\circ x_i = 0$ and $E^\circ x_i^2 = 1$. From this, T 22.17, and the fact that a *-independent family of random variables is S-independent, it follows that $\{{}^\circ x_n(\omega) : n \in N\}$ is a standard purely random process with mean 0 and variance 1. But if that is so, T 16.8 implies that, for any given $\delta \in R_{++}$ and $a \in R$, there is an $n_o \in N$ such that

$$(\forall m \in N)[[m \geqslant n_o] \supset [|G^m(\sqrt{m}\, a) - \psi(a)| < \delta]],$$

where $G^m(\cdot)$: $R \to [0, 1]$ denotes the mth convolution of $G(\cdot)$. By transfer,

$$(\forall m \in {}^*N)[[m \geqslant n_o] \supset [|F^m(\sqrt{m}a) - {}^*\psi(a)| < \delta]].$$

Since δ was chosen arbitrarily, we conclude that, for all $\eta \in {}^*N - N$, $F^\eta(\sqrt{\eta}\, a) \approx {}^*\psi(a)$. Now the *-independence of the x_i implies that $F^\eta(\cdot)$ is the probability distribution of $\sum_{i=1}^{\eta} x_i$. Consequently, equation 22.13 is valid for $\alpha = a$. Since a was arbitrary, equation 22.13 is true for all $\alpha \in R$. Moreover, since $\psi(\cdot)$ is continuous and both sides of equation 22.13 are increasing, and since ${}^*\psi(\alpha) \approx 1$ and ${}^*\psi(-\alpha) \approx 0$ whenever ${}^\circ\alpha = \infty$, equation 22.13 holds for all $\alpha \in {}^*R$.

22.5.2 Brownian Motion

We shall use the ideas of T 22.17 and T 22.18 to construct a model of the axioms of Brownian motion. For that purpose we pick an $\eta \in {}^*N - N$ and let $\Omega = \{-1, 1\}^\eta$ be the set of internal η-tuples of -1s and $+1$s. In addition, we let $\mathscr{A}$ be the field of all the internal subsets of Ω and we define the internal probability measure $v(\cdot)$: $\mathscr{A} \to {}^*[0, 1]$ by

$$v(A) = |A|/2^\eta, \qquad A \in \mathscr{A}.$$

Then $(\Omega, \mathscr{A}, v(\cdot))$ is an internal probability space with an associated Loeb probability space $(\Omega, \mathscr{F}_{\mathscr{A}}, P_v(\cdot))$.

Next we let $T = \{1/\eta, 2/\eta, \ldots, 1\}$ and assume that there is a $\gamma \in {}^*N - N$ such that

$$\eta = \gamma!$$

Also we let $\Delta t = \eta^{-1}$ and define $B(\cdot)$: $T \times \Omega \to {}^*R$ by

$$B(0, \omega) = 0, \qquad \omega \in \Omega \tag{22.14}$$

and

$$B(t, \omega) = \eta^{-1/2} \sum_{k=1}^{(t-\Delta t)} \omega_k, \qquad (t, \omega) \in T \times \Omega \tag{22.15}$$

where ω_k denotes the kth component of $\omega \in \Omega$. Then $B(\cdot)$ is well defined, and for each $t \in T$, $B(t, \cdot)$ satisfies the following conditions:

(i) $B(t, \cdot)$ is a random variable on $(\Omega, \mathscr{A})$.
(ii) $t > 0$ and $\omega_k = \omega'_k$, $k = 1, \ldots, \eta(t - \Delta t)$, imply $B(t, \omega) = B(t, \omega')$.
(iii) If $t < 1$, the conditional expectation of $B(t + \Delta t, \cdot)$ given the observed values of $B(0, \cdot), \ldots, B(t, \cdot)$, $E(B(t + \Delta t, \cdot)|B(0, \omega), \ldots, B(t, \omega)) = B(t, \omega)$ for almost all $\omega \in \Omega$—v measure.
(iv) If $t < 1$, $E((B(t + \Delta t, \cdot) - B(t, \cdot))^2|B(0, \omega), \ldots, B(t, \omega)) = \Delta t$, and $\max_{\omega, t}|B(t + \Delta t, \omega) - B(t, \omega)| \leqslant \Delta t^{1/2}$.

Since $B(t + \Delta t, \omega) - B(t, \omega) = \eta^{-1/2}\omega_{\eta t}$, these conditions are easily verified. I leave the proof to the reader.

A function $x(\cdot)$: $T \times \Omega \to R^*$ that satisfies the appropriate analogues of conditions i–iii above is a *hypermartingale* on $(\Omega, \mathscr{A}, v(\cdot))$.[7] Such a function is S-continuous if and only if there is an $A \in \mathscr{A}$ such that $v(A) = 1$ and such that, for all triples $(\omega, t, s) \in A \times T^2$, $x(t, \omega)$ is near-standard and $s \approx t$ implies $x(s, \omega) \approx x(t, \omega)$. From these definitions, conditions i–iv above, equation 22.14, and the universal theorem of Keisler (next) it follows that $B(\cdot)$ is an S-continuous hypermartingale.

UT 21 Let $(\Omega, \mathscr{A}, v(\cdot))$ be an internal probability space and let $T = \{0, 1/\eta, \ldots, 1\}$, where $\eta = \gamma!$ for some $\gamma \in {}^*N - N$. Also let $x(\cdot)$: $T \times \Omega \to {}^*R$ be a hypermartingale such that

(i) $x(0, \omega)$ is finite a.e.—v measure;

(ii) $\max_{\omega,t} |x(t + \Delta t, \omega) - x(t, \omega)| \approx 0$; and

(iii) there is a $K \in R_{++}$ such that, for all $0 \leqslant t < 1$,

$E((x(t + \Delta t, \cdot) - x(t, \cdot))^2 | x(0, \omega), \ldots, x(t, \omega)) \leqslant K \Delta t.$

Then $x(\cdot)$ is S-continuous.

This theorem is stated and proved in Keisler 1984 (pp. 35–37). Since the proof is technical, I omit the proof and refer the reader to Keisler's monograph for details.

The $B(\cdot)$ defined in equations 22.14 and 22.15 is a hypermartingale. It is also a random walk that from t to $t + \Delta t$ moves a distance $\eta^{-1/2}$ to the left or right according as $\omega_{\eta t}$ is $+1$ or -1. We can use $B(\cdot)$ to construct a Brownian motion in the following way:

T 22.19 Let $(\Omega, \mathscr{A}, v(\cdot))$ be an internal probability space and let $(\Omega, \mathscr{F}_{\mathscr{A}}, P_v(\cdot))$ be its associated Loeb probability space. In addition, let $B(\cdot)$: $T \times \Omega \to {}^*R$ be as defined in equations 22.14 and 22.15 and define $\beta(\cdot)$: $[0, 1] \times \Omega \to R$ by

$$\beta({}^\circ t, \omega) = {}^\circ B(t, \omega), \qquad (t, \omega) \in T \times \Omega. \tag{22.16}$$

Then $\beta(\cdot)$ is a well-defined Brownian motion on $(\Omega, \mathscr{F}_{\mathscr{A}}, P_v(\cdot))$.

To prove the theorem, we observe first that the S continuity of $B(\cdot)$ implies that $\beta(\cdot)$ is well defined and the $\mathscr{A}$ measurability of $B(t, \cdot)$ implies that $\beta({}^\circ t, \cdot)$ is $\mathscr{F}_{\mathscr{A}}$-measurable. From this and the fact that ${}^\circ T = [0, 1]$ it follows that $\beta(\cdot)$ satisfies the first condition of a Brownian motion.

Next we show that, for each $t, s \in T$ with ${}^\circ s < {}^\circ t$, the random variable $\beta({}^\circ t, \cdot) - \beta({}^\circ s, \cdot)$ is normally distributed with mean 0 and variance $({}^\circ t - {}^\circ s)$. To do that we observe that, by T 22.18, for all $a \in R$

$$
\begin{aligned}
&P_v(\{\omega \in \Omega : \beta({}^\circ t, \omega) - \beta({}^\circ s, \omega) < a\}) \\
&\quad = P_v(\{\omega \in \Omega : {}^\circ B(t, \omega) - {}^\circ B(s, \omega) < a\}) \\
&\quad = P_v\left(\left\{\omega \in \Omega : {}^\circ\left(\eta^{-1/2} \sum_{k=\eta s}^{\eta(t-\Delta t)} \omega_k\right) < a\right\}\right) \\
&\quad = \lim {}^\circ v\left(\left\{\omega \in \Omega : \left((\eta t - \eta s)^{-1/2} \sum_{k=\eta s}^{\eta(t-\Delta t)} \omega_k\right) < (a - 1/n)/(t - s)^{1/2}\right\}\right) \\
&\quad = \lim {}^{\circ *}\psi\left(\frac{(a - 1/n)}{(t - s)^{1/2}}\right) \\
&\quad = \lim \psi\left(\frac{(a - 1/n)}{({}^\circ t - {}^\circ s)^{1/2}}\right) = \psi\left(\frac{a}{({}^\circ t - {}^\circ s)^{1/2}}\right).
\end{aligned}
$$

Therefore, for all $t, s \in [0, 1]$ such that $s < t$ and for all $a \in R$,

$$P_v(\{\omega \in \Omega : \beta(t, \omega) - \beta)s, \omega) < a\sqrt{t - s}\}) = \psi(a),$$

as was to be shown.

To conclude the proof of the theorem, we suppose that $°s_1 < °t_1 \leqslant °s_2 < °t_2 \leqslant \cdots \leqslant °s_n < °t_n \in [0, 1]$ and observe that the random variables $B(t_1, \cdot) - B(s_1, \cdot), \ldots, B(t_n, \cdot) - B(s_n, \cdot)$ are *-independent and hence S-independent. From this and T 22.17 it follows that the random variables $\beta(°t_1, \cdot) - \beta(°s_1, \cdot), \ldots, \beta(°t_n, \cdot) - \beta(°s_n, \cdot)$ are independently distributed on $(\Omega, \mathscr{F}_{\mathscr{A}}, P_v(\cdot))$.

The preceding arguments establish the validity of our hyperfinite construction of a Brownian motion. By referring to the S continuity of $B(\cdot)$, we can also show that the Brownian motion that we have constructed is finite and continuous with P_v probability 1. For later reference we record this fact in the following theorem.

T 22.20 Let $\beta(\cdot)$: $[0, 1] \times \Omega \times R$ be as defined in equation 22.16. Then $\beta(\cdot, \omega)$ is finite and continuous with P_v probability 1.

22.5.3 The Wiener Measure

We can use theorems T 22.19 and T 22.20 to establish the existence of the Wiener measure on the experiment of Borel-measurable continuous functions on [0, 1], which we denote by $(C([0, 1]), \mathscr{C})$. Before we do that, however, a few remarks concerning $C([0, 1])$ and measures on $(C([0, 1]), \mathscr{C})$ are called for.

Let $C([0, 1])$ denote the set of all continuous functions on [0, 1] and let $\|\cdot\|: C([0, 1]) \to R_+$ be defined by

$$\|x\| = \sup_{0 \leqslant t \leqslant 1} |x(t)|, \qquad x \in C([0, 1]).$$

Then $\|\cdot\|$ is a norm on $C([0, 1])$; i.e., for all $x, y \in C([0, 1])$ and $\alpha \in R$, $\|\cdot\|$ satisfies the following conditions:

(i) $\|x\| \geqslant 0$ and $\|x\| = 0$ if and only $x(t) = 0$ for all $t \in [0, 1]$.
(ii) $\|\alpha x\| = |\alpha| \, \|x\|$.
(iii) $\|x + y\| \leqslant \|x\| + \|y\|$.

Next define $S(\cdot)$: $C([0, 1]) \times (Q \cap R_{++}) \to \mathscr{P}(C([0, 1]))$ by

$$S(x, q) = \{y \in C([0, 1]): \|y - x\| < q\}$$

and $\mathscr{B} \subset \mathscr{P}(C([0, 1]))$ by $B \in \mathscr{B}$ if and only if there is an $x \in C([0, 1])$ and a

$q \in Q \cap R_{++}$ such that $B = S(x, q)$. Then $\mathscr{B}$ satisfies the two conditions that are characteristic for a base of a topology—see section 21.2. The topology generated by $\mathscr{B}$, which we denote by $\mathscr{T}$, is the standard topology for $C([0, 1])$.

The topological space $(C([0, 1]), \mathscr{T})$ has several interesting properties:

(i) $(C([0, 1]), \mathscr{T})$ is perfectly separable; i.e., there exists a countable subfamily of $\mathscr{B}$ that forms a base for $(C([0, 1]), \mathscr{T})$.

An example of such a base is the family of spheres $S(x, q)$ that we obtain by varying x and q, respectively, over the set of polynomials in t with rational coefficients and $(Q \cap R_{++})$.

(ii) $(C([0, 1]), \mathscr{T})$ is complete; i.e., if $x_n \in C([0, 1])$, $n = 1, 2, \ldots,$ and $\lim_{n,m\to\infty} \|x_n - x_m\| = 0$, then there exists one and only one $x \in C([0, 1])$ such that $\lim \|x_n - x\| = 0$.

Thus $(C([0, 1]), \mathscr{T})$ is a perfectly separable, complete topological space.

The experiment of Borel-measurable continuous functions on $[0, 1]$ is a pair $(C([0, 1]), \mathscr{C})$, where $\mathscr{C}$ is the smallest σ-field that contains all the sets in $\mathscr{T}$. We shall use the properties of $(C([0, 1]), \mathscr{T})$ to prove an interesting theorem concerning probability measures on $(C([0, 1]), \mathscr{C})$. In the statement of the theorem, $\pi^t(\cdot)\colon C([0, 1]) \to R$ and $\pi^{t_1, \ldots, t_k}(\cdot)\colon C([0, 1]) \to R^k$ are defined, respectively, by

$$\pi^t(x) = x(t), \qquad t \in [0, 1] \text{ and } x \in C([0, 1])$$

and

$$\pi^{t_1, \ldots, t_k}(x) = (x(t_1), \ldots, x(t_k)), \quad t_i \in [0, 1], i = 1, \ldots, k, \text{ and } x \in C([0, 1]).$$

T 22.21 Let $(C([0, 1]), \mathscr{C})$, $\pi^t(\cdot)$, and $\pi^{t_1, \ldots, t_k}(\cdot)$ be as described above. Moreover, let $\mu(\cdot)\colon \mathscr{C} \to [0, 1]$ and $v(\cdot)\colon \mathscr{C} \to [0, 1]$ be σ-additive probability measures. Then $\mathscr{C}$ is the smallest σ field of subsets of $C([0, 1])$ with respect to which the $\pi^t(\cdot)$, $t \in [0, 1]$, are measurable. Moreover, a necessary and sufficient condition that μ and v coincide on $\mathscr{C}$ is that, for all $k = 1, 2, \ldots$ and $t_1, \ldots, t_k \in [0, 1]$, the measures $\mu^{t_1, \ldots, t_k}$ and $v^{t_1, \ldots, t_k}$ induced, respectively, by μ and $\pi^{t_1, \ldots, t_k}(\cdot)$ and v and $\pi^{t_1, \ldots, t_k}(\cdot)$ coincide on the Borel subsets of R^k.

To prove the first half of the theorem we let $\mathscr{A}$ be the smallest σ field of subsets of $C([0, 1])$ with respect to which all the $\pi^t(\cdot)$ are measurable. Since, for all $t \in [0, 1]$ and all $x, y \in C([0, 1])$,

$$|\pi^t(x) - \pi^t(y)| \leqslant \|x - y\|,$$

the $\pi^t(\cdot)$ are continuous functions on $C([0, 1])$ and $\mathscr{A} \subset \mathscr{C}$. It is also true that $\mathscr{C} \subset \mathscr{A}$. To see why, recall that $(C([0, 1]), \mathscr{T})$ is separable. From this it follows that every open set in $C([0, 1])$ is a union of countably many closed spheres. Therefore, to establish $\mathscr{C} \subset \mathscr{A}$ it suffices to demonstrate that $\mathscr{A}$ contains all closed spheres. Now, if $a \in R_{++}$, $x_0 \in C([0, 1])$, and $r_2, r_2, \ldots$ is an enumeration of the rationals in $[0, 1]$, and if $\overline{S(x_0, a)}$ denotes the set $\{x \in C([0, 1]) : \|x - x_0\| \leqslant a\}$, then

$$\overline{S(x_0, a)} = \bigcap_{n=1}^{\infty} \{x \in C([0, 1]) : |x(r_n) - x_0(r_n)| \leqslant a\}.$$

Since the right-hand side belongs to $\mathscr{A}$, $\overline{S(x_0, a)} \in \mathscr{A}$, as was to be shown.

We need only prove sufficiency for the second half of the theorem. To do that we let k vary over 1, 2, ..., and $(t_1, \ldots, t_k)$ over k-tuples in $[0, 1]$, and we let $\mathscr{A}_{t_1, \ldots, t_k} = \{(\pi^{t_1, \ldots, t_k})^{-1}A : A \text{ a Borel subset of } R^k\}$ and

$$\mathscr{F} = \bigcup_{k, t_1, \ldots, t_k} \mathscr{A}_{t_1, \ldots, t_k}.$$

It follows from the hypotheses of the theorem that $\mu(E) = v(E)$ for all $E \in \mathscr{F}$. Since $\mathscr{F}$ is a field that generates $\mathscr{A}$ and $\mathscr{A} = \mathscr{C}$, it must be the case that μ and v agree on $\mathscr{C}$ as well.

So much for preliminaries. Next we shall establish the existence of the Wiener measure on $(C([0, 1]), \mathscr{C})$. The *Wiener measure* is a probability measure, $W(\cdot)$: $\mathscr{C} \to [0, 1]$, that satisfies the following conditions:

(i) $W(\{x \in C([0, 1]): x(0) = 0\}) = 1$.

(ii) For all $t, s \in [0, 1]$ such that $s < t$ and all $a \in R$,

$$W(\{x \in C([0, 1]): (\pi^t(x) - \pi^s(s)) < a\}) = \psi(a/\sqrt{t - s}).$$

(iii) For all $k = 1, 2, \ldots$ and $t_0, t_1, \ldots, t_k \in [0, 1]$ such that $0 \leqslant t_0 < t_1 < \cdots < t_k \leqslant 1$, the random variables $(\pi^{t_i}(\cdot) - \pi^{t_{i-1}}(\cdot))$, $i = 1, \ldots, k$, are independently distributed relative to $W(\cdot)$.

It follows from T 22.21 that if $W(\cdot)$ exists, it is uniquely determined by conditions i–iii.

To establish the existence of $W(\cdot)$, we proceed as follows: For a given $k \geqslant 1$ and sequence $t_1, \ldots, t_k \in [0, 1]$ and for any $E \in \mathscr{A}_{t_1, \ldots, t_k}$,

$$\{\omega \in \Omega : \beta(\cdot, \omega) \in E\} \in \mathscr{F}_{\mathscr{A}}.$$

This follows from the fact that there is a Borel set $A \subset R^k$ such that

$$\{\omega \in \Omega : \beta(\cdot, \omega) \in E\} = \{\omega \in \Omega : \beta(\cdot, \omega) \in C([0, 1])\}$$
$$\cap \{\omega \in \Omega : (\beta(t_1, \omega), \ldots, \beta(t_k, \omega)) \in A\}$$

and from the obvious fact that the right-hand side of this equation belongs to $\mathscr{F}_{\mathscr{A}}$.

From the preceding observations and from the arbitrariness of k and the t_i, $i = 1, \ldots, k$, it follows that

$$\{\omega \in \Omega : \beta(\cdot, \omega) \in E\} \in \mathscr{F}_{\mathscr{A}}$$

for all $E \in \mathscr{F}$ and hence for all $E \in \mathscr{C}$. Consequently, the measure $W(\cdot)$: $\mathscr{C} \to [0, 1]$, defined by

$$W(E) = P_v(\{\omega \in \Omega : \beta(\cdot, \omega) \in E\}),$$

is a well-defined probability measure on $(C([0, 1]), \mathscr{C})$. The properties of $\beta(\cdot, \cdot)$ ensure that $W(\cdot)$ also satisfies the three conditions of the Wiener measure. The validity of the following theorem is therefore established.

T 22.22 There exists a unique probability measure $W(\cdot)$ on $(C([0, 1]), \mathscr{C})$ that satisfies the three conditions that are characteristic of Wiener measure.

We shall return to the Wiener measure and discuss some of its interesting extensions in chapter 33. There we use it to characterize the asymptotic properties of ARIMA processes.

VI Epistemology

23 Truth, Knowledge, and Necessity

In the preceding parts of this book, we discussed the most important characteristics of the axiomatic method, and used it (1) to create a formalized language for mathematical arguments and (2) to develop elementary set theory, the basic structure of the theory of natural numbers, and various aspects of consumer choice, probability theory, and nonstandard analysis. Next I shall show how the axiomatic method can be used in epistemology.

Epistemology is the study of the origin, nature, methods, and limits of knowledge. Therefore, in this chapter I begin by discussing the possibility of knowledge and the epistemological concept of truth. My aim is to describe problems with which epistemologists have struggled for centuries and to demonstrate that they have conceptual analogies in economics. I also want to show that our language is inadequate for the pursuit of knowledge. To use it in epistemology, as we use it in mathematics, we must add several rules of inference and postulates concerning the nature of the universe. I describe these rules of inference and formulate the new postulates. Then I propose a scheme for classifying different kinds of knowledge and conclude the chapter with a discussion of necessity and modal logic.

In chapter 24 I begin with a discussion of epistemological universes. They are theoretical constructs whose principal function is to serve as descriptive references for scientists who set out to test their theories. I suggest that all have a core structure that we can derive from our new postulates. Then I use the axiomatic method to characterize a concept of belief that we need to formulate inductive rules of inference in epistemology. My theory represents an extension of Shafer's theory of evidence and contains results that provide analogues of J. M. Keynes's sufficient conditions for rules of inference to be good. I conclude the chapter by delineating an epistemological language which we use to explicate the meaning of knowledge.

Chapter 25 is devoted to constructing a language for science that we can use as a basis for theorizing in econometrics. My aim is to create a framework within which we can formulate tests of scientific theories and determine the properties of such tests. That the framework is sufficient is amply demonstrated in chapters 26–28.

23.1 The Semantical Concept of Truth Revisited

According to the semantical concept of truth, an assertion "A" is true if and only if A; e.g., "snow is white" is true if and only if snow is white. The meaning of "true" in this sentence seems intuitively clear. To ensure that it is unambiguous, we must show that truth has a definition that agrees with our intuitive notion. Such a definition must be such that the meaning of true is independent of A. It may, however, depend on the set of sentences over which A varies. In chapter 5 we defined truth for a given structure $\mathscr{D}$ of our language. The resulting concept varies with $\mathscr{D}$ but is independent of any one sentence of $L(\mathscr{D})$.

Our semantic concept of truth jibes with intuition. Also (see chapters 6 and 7), it gives interesting semantic characterizations of many syntactical properties of our language. For instance, a wff is a theorem if and only if it is valid. Here a valid wff is a formula that denotes truth no matter what it asserts. Examples are the Law of Contradiction, $\sim\sim[A \supset \sim\sim A]$, the Law of the Excluded Middle, $[A \supset A]$, and the following variant of PLA 5:

$$[(\forall x)[P(x) \supset Q(x)] \supset [P(y) \supset Q(y)]]. \tag{23.1}$$

Also if $\Gamma_1, \ldots, \Gamma_n, A$ are closed wffs, then A is a logical consequence of $\Gamma_1, \ldots, \Gamma_n$ if and only if A is true in each and every structure $\mathscr{D}$ that forms the basis of a model of $T(\Gamma_1, \ldots, \Gamma_n)$. In fact, if we recall that a formula B is valid in a structure $\mathscr{D}$ if and only if every $\mathscr{D}$ instance of B is true, we can assert: B is a logical consequence of a collection of formulas, Γ, if and only if it is valid in every structure $\mathscr{D}$ in which all the formulas in Γ are valid. One example is the syllogistic equivalent of equation 23.1:

$$(\forall x)[P(x) \supset Q(x)],\ P(y) \vdash Q(y). \tag{23.2}$$

Here $Q(y)$ is a logical consequence of $(\forall x)[P(x) \supset Q(x)]$ and $P(y)$. It denotes truth in every structure $\mathscr{D}$ in which $(\forall x)[P(x) \supset Q(x)]$ and $P(y)$ denote truth (e.g., if all men are mortal and Per is a man, Per is mortal).

23.2 Truth and Knowledge

The semantic concept of truth can be used to define its epistemological counterpart. We shall say that *we know that* A if and only if (1) A is true in the semantic sense, (2) we believe that A, and (3) the best evidence available to us supports our belief (Chisholm 1982, p. 43). Also we shall insist that we cannot know that A without believing that we know that A. Finally, we shall say that A *is (epistemologically) true* if it can be known and false if it cannot be known. Thus (if Charles Peirce's overly optimistic view of the scientific method is valid) true ideas are those we would accept if we were able to pursue our inquiries to their ideal limit (Ayer 1968, p. 25). False ideas are ideas that we cannot assimilate, validate, corroborate, or verify.

E 23.1 It is easy to define epistemological truth. However, a long search may be required to determine whether a given proposition can be known. Consider equations 23.1 and 23.2 above and a structure $\mathscr{D}$ in which $|\mathscr{D}|$ denotes the set of human beings, y denotes a man named Peter who is alive and singing in New York, and $P(x)$ and $Q(x)$ assert, respectively, that "x is a man" and "x is mortal." Also, consider an epistemologist who accepts the validity of equations 23.1 and 23.2 and agrees that Peter satisfies $P(\cdot)$. To determine the truth value of $Q(y)$, he has only two options: to wait and see if Peter will die or to search for the truth value of $(\forall x)[P(x) \supset Q(x)]$. Chances are good that our epistemologist will never establish the truth value of $Q(y)$.

Our concept of knowledge has several interesting properties that we may describe as follows: Let L be a first-order language; and let CL be the set of all closed wffs in L. Also let $\text{Kn}(A)$ be a symbolic rendition of the assertion "we know that A." Finally, let DL be the smallest set of formulas that contains CL and that contains $\sim A$, $[A \supset B]$, and $\text{Kn}(A)$ whenever it contains A and B. Then our concept of knowledge is such that, for all $A \in DL$,

(i) $[\text{Kn}(A) \supset A]$ and
(ii) $[\text{Kn}(A) \supset \text{Kn}(\text{Kn}(A))]$;

i.e., either we do not know that A or A is true and we know that we know that A.

The assertions i and ii do not determine the subset of formulas in L that satisfy $\text{Kn}(\cdot)$. To delineate this set we must introduce a belief function on DL. Different belief functions determine different concepts of knowledge. In chapter 24 we shall describe a belief function that determines a concept of knowledge which in addition to assertions i and ii satisfies

(iii) $[\mathrm{Kn}([A \supset B]) \supset [\mathrm{Kn}(A) \supset \mathrm{Kn}(B)]]$, and
(iv) $\vdash A$ implies that $\mathrm{Kn}(A)$;

i.e., if we know that $[A \supset B]$ and that A, then we know that B as well. Also if $A \in CL$ is a theorem, then we know that A.

A concept of knowledge that satisfies conditions i–iv is akin to the idea of knowledge that Hintikka presents (see in particular Hintikka 1962, pp. 31, 43, 50). In reading these conditions, note that they do not imply that, for all $A \in CL$, $[\mathrm{Kn}(A) \vee \mathrm{Kn}(\sim\mathrm{Kn}(A))]$; i.e., it is not always the case that we either know that A or know that we don't know that A. However, we can establish the validity of the following theorem:

T 23.1 If $\mathrm{Kn}(\cdot)$ satisfies conditions i–iv, then, for all $A \in DL$, $[\sim\mathrm{Kn}(A) \vee \mathrm{Kn}(A)]$.

Our concept of knowledge is controversial. Some epistemologists object to T 23.1 and our acceptance of the Law of the Excluded Middle. Others complain because we allow the possibility that we might know that A for the wrong reasons, as evidenced in E 23.2 and Gettier 1963 (pp. 121–123).

E 23.2 Peter is a close relative. He has owned many cars. All of them were Fords. Now Peter and a friend of his, Gary, are coming to take us to the airport. We *believe* correctly that one of them owns a Ford. Since all the evidence we have supports our belief, we *know* that one of them owns a Ford. However, we know for the wrong reasons. Peter sold his Ford to Gary the day before yesterday.

Finally, some criticize our concept of knowledge because of their concern about the nonsubstitutivity of identity in referentially opaque contexts such as "believes that ..." and "knows that ..." (Quine 1979, pp. 17–22). To wit, it is possible to believe that Oslo is in Sweden without believing that the capital of Norway is in Sweden. It is also possible to know that Venus is the evening star without knowing that Venus is the morning star. These objections to our concept of knowledge cannot be taken lightly. We shall deal with them in due course in this and the next chapter.

23.3 The Possibility of Knowledge

Most epistemologists share doubts as to the usefulness of our language or an equivalent in their quest for knowledge, but they are at odds about the best way to modify it for their purposes. Our way to do that is to start with the intended interpretation of our first-order predicate calculus and to look for an augmented version of it that we can use in epistemology.

To find the desired modification of our language we shall next study some of the simplest atomic formulas that occur in epistemology. They are all propositional functions of one variable and concern physical objects and other minds. One may assert that x is a table. Another may assert that x is crazy. We want to see what is involved in determining their truth values, i.e., what rules of inference and postulates will allow us to assert such ideas and to insist that we know that they are valid.

23.3.1 The Universe Is Not Empty, PE 1

In order that any search for knowledge be feasible, the following must be the case:

PE 1 The universe is not empty.

This sounds like an innocuous postulate, but is not. In fact, PE 1 demarcates the limit of all knowledge. To see why, ask why there is something rather than nothing and probe for an answer. "Any factor introduced to explain why there is something will itself be part of the something to be explained, so it (or anything utilizing it) could not explain all of the something—it could not explain why there is *anything* at all" (Nozick 1981, p. 115). The quest for an answer, therefore, seems doomed to lead to endless regress. If it does, we have no choice but to adopt PE 1.

In his book Robert Nozick discusses many explanations of why there is something rather than nothing (Nozick 1981). They are all equally inconclusive. Even so, one of them is of relevance for us because it concerns the general validity of the Law of the Excluded Middle. In this explanation, Nozick observes first that pairs of contradictory predicates such as (colored, uncolored) and (loud, not loud) are applied only to parts of the universe. For instance, whatever is colored or uncolored (i.e., transparent) must have extension. Bethoven's Fifth Symphony is not extended. It is also neither colored nor uncolored. Next Nozick wonders whether every pair of contradictory predicates possesses preconditions that determine the subset of the universe to which the pair pertains. In particular, he wonders if there is something beyond existence and nonexistence in our universe (Nozick 1981, pp. 150–164).

It is plausible that what is beyond existence and nonexistence cannot be reconciled with ordinary ways of thinking. However, it is not difficult to give examples: For instance, before creation of the universe nonbeing existed not nor-being (Radhakrishnan and Moore 1957, p. 23). Also, the source of every existent thing must fall outside the categories of existence and nonexistence. Hence God must be beyond being (Plato 1974, p. 309). Similarly, the set of all sets is not a set and neither exists nor not exists. Finally, if the self reflexively synthesizes itself as a self, the self is beyond existence and nonexistence as well (Nozick 1981, p. 110).

If what is beyond existence and nonexistence cannot be reconciled with ordinary ways of thinking and made the subject of logical analysis (Pletcher 1973, pp. 201–211), it is unlikely that we can learn to know about it other than by experience. We ordinary people do not have such experiences. However, we can speculate about what they might contain. For instance, if nothing exists in the byond, the distinction between subject and object must disappear. Out there we would expect to lose our sense of self and *be* what we *see*. But how can we *be* where nothing *is*? The E 23.3 recap of an experience gives no answer.

E 23.3 In describing a mescaline experience that he had in his study, Aldous Huxley writes: "I spent several minutes—or was it several centuries?—not merely gazing at those bamboo legs, but actually *being* them—or rather being myself in them; or to be still more accurate (for 'I' was not involved in the case, nor in a certain sense were 'they') being my Not-self in the Not-self which was the chair" (Huxley 1954, pp. 15–16).

There is another possibility. If in the beyond nonbeing exists not, nor being, whatever is out there might have *both* being and nonbeing. In that case we need not lose our sense of self in an experience. Instead we might *remain* who we are and *become* who or what we are not. If this is so, any experience out there must have all sorts of contradictory properties. Most reports of mystical experiences attest to this possibility. So does the following beautiful passage from the *Isa Upanishad* (Stace 1961, p. 255):

That One, though never stirring
   is swifter than thought ...
Though standing still, it overtakes
   those who are running ...
It stirs and it stirs not.
It is far and likewise near.
It is inside all this, and it is outside all this.

Our speculations have not carried us far in our quest for knowledge about the beyond and between being and nonbeing. Also, the evidence presented to us by mystics is of little help in delineating the preconditions of the pair (existence, nonexistence). So we cannot explain why there is something rather than nothing. We are forced to accept PE 1 as it is and argue as if the Law of the Excluded Middle applied to the whole universe.

Since we already have learned to live without the set of all sets, and since we are prepared to assert that Bethoven's Fifth Symphony is *not* colored, for the purposes of this book the consequences seem minimal.

Postulate PE 1 does not indicate what we might find in the universe. What is there depends on the branch of epistemology to which our quest for knowledge belongs. In geology we find rocks. Botany abounds with flowers, and economics is full of consumers and firms.

23.3.2 Induction

If we look at, feel, tap, or smell a physical object such as the table we sit next to, we sense certain sense data that we perceive belong to a thing which we refer to as a "table." There is no doubt that we are aware of these sense data. Also, since sense data that belong to the same object vary from one individual to another, we cannot be aware of the table as such. We cannot even be sure it exists, and if it exists, we cannot know its real nature; it may be an idea in the mind of Berkeley's God, a community of souls in Leibnitz's monadic world, or simply a vast collection of electric charges in violent movement in the wonderful space of science (Russell 1976, p. 6).

Whatever the real nature of the table is, our sense data provide inductive evidence that it exists. Here *induction denotes a process of reasoning in which we argue from particulars of our experiences to similar particulars of as yet unrealized experiences.* Traditionally, this process has been formulated as a rule of inference in the way illustrated in E 23.4:

E 23.4 Jean, Philippe, and Pierre are all the Frenchmen I know.
They drink wine.
Chances are that all Frenchmen drink wine.

The words "chances are" in the traditional rule of inference ensure that the validity of the rule is a matter of logic rather than facts. They also render the rule too vague for our purposes. To us an inductive argument is a process of reasoning in which we, with the help of Shafer's or Bayes's rules of inference, pass *from* an initial belief in a proposition A, *over* factual evidence, A_i, $i = 1, \ldots, n$, *to* a better substantiated probabilistic evaluation of A. We give an example of the use of Shafer's rule below:

E 23.5 Let F and W be unary relations; let A denote $(\forall x)[F(x) \supset W(x)]$; and let $\Omega = \{A, \sim A\}$. Also, let $S_0(\cdot)$ and $S_i(\cdot)$, $i = 1, \ldots, n$, be simple support functions focused on A to the degree $0 < s_i < 1$, $i = 0, 1, \ldots, n$. Finally, suppose that $S_0(\cdot)$ measures our initial belief in A and that $S_i(\cdot)$ is the support function determined by the evidence $[F(x_i) \wedge W(x_i)]$. Following Shafer's rule of inference, we pass from $S_0(\cdot)$ over $[F(x_i) \wedge W(x_i)]$, $i = 1, \ldots, n$, to the simple support function, $S_0 \circ S_1 \circ \cdots \circ S_n(\cdot)$ The latter supports A to the degree $\prod_{i=0}^{n}(1 - s_i)$.

A scientist's initial belief in a proposition A depends on his knowledge. When properly formulated, that part of his knowledge which is relevant for assessing the validity of A consists of a set of wffs K. Therefore, in E 23.5, $S_0(\cdot)$ depends on K; so too do the $S_i(\cdot)$, $i = 1, \ldots, n$. For simplicity we have taken the import of $[F(x_i) \wedge W(x_i)]$ to be independent of $[F(x_j) \wedge W(x_j)]$ for all $j \neq i$. So $S_i(\cdot)$ depends on K but not on $[F(x_j) \wedge W(x_j)]$.

23.3.3 The Uniformity of Nature, PE 2

We have used sense data and induction to infer that the table next to us exists but only as an idea in our mind. To establish its existence as a physical object independent of our perceiving it, we need more sense data, the same inductive rule of inference, a basic postulate concerning the nature of the universe, and a schema to determine the identity over time of an object.

The postulate we have in mind has no standard formulation, but it does have a name, the *Principle of the Uniformity of Nature.* According to John Stuart Mill, the principle asserts that "there are such things in nature as parallel cases, that what happens once will, under a sufficient degree of similarity of circumstances, happen again, and not only again, but as often as the same circumstances recur" (Mill 1973, p. 306). For our purposes the most useful formulation of the principle is due to Keynes (1921, p. 226):

PE 2 Mere differences in time and space of our sense data are inductively irrelevant.

It is difficult to fathom what Mill had in mind when he talked of parallel cases. It is equally hard to delineate general criteria for ascertaining whether we face situations, which from an inductive point of view, differ only in time and space. For instance, it is easy to judge that the maple tree I see in my yard today is the same as the one I saw yesterday. That is so even though it has grown a smidge and lost a big branch in the storm that raged last night. However, it is hard to determine all those factors that would render time and space inductively irrelevant in inferences concerning the composition of consumer expenditures on goods and services. Be that as it may, in one form or another PE 2 will appear either explicitly or implicitly in the econometric models we analyze in this book.

23.3.4 Identity and the Closest-Continuer Schema

PE 2 justifies our making like inferences from similar sets of sense data, no matter when and where they are obtained. However, similar sense data, induction, and PE 2 do not suffice to establish the existence of a physical object independent of our perceiving it. We also need a schema for deciding whether the object whose existence we inferred at time t_1 is the same as the object whose existence we inferred at time t_2.

In mathematics, equality is a binary equivalence relation with an important substitutive property. Whether two individuals a and b are identical depends on who these individuals are and the context in which we refer to them. For instance, if a and b are numerals, they are equal if and only if they denote the same number. If a and b are functions on a measure space, they are equal if and only if their values differ at most on a set of measure zero. Also, the same functions may be equal in one measure space and different in another.

The identity relation in epistemology is also an equivalence relation with a substitutive property. It differs from its mathematical counterpart in that it has both an extensional and an intensional dimension, while the mathematical predicate is extensional. When we formulate our schema for identity below, we do not intend to provide a nut-shell characterization of the epistemological concept of identity. We only want to propose a schema for deciding problems of identity that arise in the process of establishing the existence of physical objects independent of our perceiving them. The schema is, for obvious reasons, called the *Closest-Continuer Schema*. Nozick formulates it roughly as in CCS, where the times t_1 and t_2 satisfy $t_1 < t_2$, and individual is short for object whose existence we inferred (Nozick 1981, p. 31):

CCS The individual b at t_2 is the same as the individual a at t_1 only if (1) b's properties at t_2 are causally dependent on a's properties at t_1, and (2) there is not another individual c at t_2 who stands in a closer or as-close relationship to a at t_1 than b at t_2 does.

Our schema and its global extension (Nozick 1981, pp. 50–51) are like a mathematical heuristic that is used to determine whether in a given context two functions of time are equivalent. We can use the schema to ascertain that the tree that lost its branch last night is the same as the tree we saw yesterday. We can also use it to decide on the identity of aging humans, even though the schema will not tell us in what this identity consists. Finally, we can use it to sort out the delightful Greek philosophical puzzle that we recap in E 23.6.[1]

E 23.6 Once upon a time there was a wooden ship whose planks were removed one by one at discrete points of time. Each time one plank was removed, another was put in its place. By CCS the different changes of planks did not affect the identity of the ship. That was true even when the last old plank of the ship was replaced.

Suppose now that the removed planks were not destroyed but stored in a warehouse. When the last plank entered the warehouse, the old shipbuilder proceeded to rebuild the original ship. When done, he launched the ship and watched it disappear over the horizon side by side with the rejuvenated version of the old ship. Which one is the original, he mused? Neither, insisted our oracle CCS.

23.3.5 Analogy

Sense data, induction, the two postulates concerning the universe, and CCS enable us to *infer* the truth or falsehood of assertions such as "the thing next to us appears to be brown" and "I perceive a large body at the other end of the thing next to me." However, to ascertain that the thing next to us is a table we must use both induction and analogy, where *analogy is a process of reasoning in which objects or events that are similar in one respect are judged to resemble each other in certain other respects as well.* Similarly, to make judgments as to the truth of declarative sentences, such as x is crazy, we must have reason to believe in the existence of other minds as well as of bodies. For that we need both induction and analogy. To wit, we cannot know from experience alone how other bodies tick. We can observe them moving about and hear them singing. We can cook meals for them and talk with them. However, we can infer from this that these bodies have minds only if we use both induction and analogy.

E 23.7 If we see the contorted face of a skier who has fallen and broken his legs, we cannot experience *his* pain, but we can get an idea of how he feels by envisioning how we would have felt in an *analogous* situation.

Keynes, in his theory of induction, distinguishes between *positive* and *negative* analogies. A propositional function, satisfied by all individuals in a group, is a positive analogy for the group. A negative analogy is a propositional function, satisfied by some but not all individuals in the group. In E 23.4, for example, x is a Frenchman and x drinks wine are positive analogies. If Jean and Philippe have brown eyes and Pierre has green eyes, x has brown eyes is a negative analogy. Keynes thought of induction as an argument in which we single out two sets of positive analogies, $P_1, \ldots, P_k$ and $Q_1, \ldots, Q_m$, for an observed group of individuals and then hypothesize that, chances are that the next individual we observe either will not satisfy one or more of the P's or will satisfy all the Q's. The given group may display many other positive analogies too. However, for the inductive argument in question they are either deemed irrelevant (e.g., x has ten fingers) or they are judged to be negative analogies for the group to which the observed individuals belong (e.g., x is not an alcoholic).

23.3.6 The Principle of Limited Variety, PLV

We can *ascertain* the validity of assertions that concern sense data alone; e.g., when I sit at my desk, the coffee table *looks* brown to me. In contrast, we can only *infer* the validity of assertions that concern physical objects and other minds; e.g., that woman is *angry*. How good our inferences are depends on the universe in which we live. If the universe is too complex, our inferences are likely to have little value. Therefore Keynes suggested that we adopt the *Principle of Limited Variety* as a third postulate concerning the nature of the universe. He formulated it roughly as follows (see Keynes 1921, pp. 252 and 256):

PLV The qualities of an object are bound together in a limited number of *groups*, a subclass of each group being an infallible symptom of the coexistence of certain other members of the group. Moreover, the objects in the field, over which our generalizations extend, have a finite number of independent qualities.

In short, the postulate insists that the characteristics, however numerous, of the objects in which we are interested, adhere in groups of invariable connection, which are finite in number (Keynes 1921, p. 256).

Keynes used PE 2 and PLV in his theory of induction to ensure that *any* inductive hypothesis would have a positive initial probability of being valid. In the context of this chapter, PLV together with PE 2 can be used to establish the possibility of ostensive definitions of universals such as table, dog, whiteness, and justice. The two posulates can also be used to explain scientists' successful search for useful classifications of both animate and inanimate matter. Hence they form a basis on which we can use induction and analogy to assign truth values to sentences such as "the object next to which I sit is a wooden table" and "the body I perceive in front is a woman wearing a white dress."

Lord Russell rejected the two postulates, PE 2 and PLV, on the grounds that they are prescientific (see (Russell 1948, p. 444). However, most reasoning done outside laboratories and the ivory towers of academia *is* prescientific. In adapting to life, people more or less consciously trust the validity of variants of these principles. This is implicit both in their belief in the existence of physical objects and other minds and in the confidence they place in their ability to recognize objects. Thus in preparing for a ski trip, we look for our skis where we think we left them. If we experience emotional problems, we may confide our woes to a friend and hope for comfort and advice. If we notice an object on the road that is the size of a soccer ball but looks like a stone, we do not kick it. The fact that most people manage to cope with life may be taken as testimony to the considerable extent to which PE 2 and PLV provide people with a reasonable basis for inference by induction and analogy in everyday situations.

23.4 Different Kinds of Knowledge

Equipped with the new postulates and rules of inference, we can transform our basic first-order predicate calculus into a language that expresses all sorts of ideas. Some we know to be sound, either because we have invented them or because we have derived them from valid premises. Others we are less certain about, either because they are based on flimsy evidence or because they are subject to the laws of chance. In this section I propose a scheme for classifying the stock of ideas that comprise our knowledge. In reading it, note that the transitive verb "know" does not always take objects that belong to the subject matter of epistemology. Examples are "I know my wife," "I know how to ski," and "I know right from wrong." In epistemology we study knowledge of propositions—e.g., "I know that Fia is my wife," "I know that I am a good skier," and "I know that I can distinguish right from wrong." Our discussion of knowledge is based on this observation.

23.4.1 Knowledge of Logical Propositions

We are looking for an augmented version of our language to use in epistemology. Therefore, we feel free to use our language with its intended interpretation as a basis for epistemological arguments. Our attitude has several interesting consequences. First, in accordance with it, we insist that we know that A, if A is a theorem of the first-order predicate calculus. Thus we know (1) that whatever is, is (i.e., $[x = x]$); (2) that nothing can both be and not be (i.e., $\sim\sim[A \supset \sim\sim A]$; and (3) that a thing either is or it is not (i.e., $[A \supset A]$). Such knowledge is a priori in the sense that it is independent of any factual knowledge we may possess, but it is dependent on the axioms we postulate, on the rules of inference we adopt, and on the interpretation we give to our language. Consider the next example:

E 23.8 A. Heyting has proposed the following axioms for the intuitionistic propositional calculus:

HLA 1 $[A \supset [A \wedge A]]$

HLA 2 $[[A \wedge B] \supset [B \wedge A]]$

HLA 3 $[[A \supset B] \supset [[A \wedge C] \supset [B \wedge C]]]$

HLA 4 $[[[A \supset B] \wedge [B \supset C]] \supset [A \supset C]]$

HLA 5 $[A \supset [B \supset A]]$

HLA 6 $[[A \wedge [A \supset B]] \supset B]$

HLA 7 $[A \supset [A \vee B]]$

HLA 8 $[[A \vee B] \supset [B \vee A]]$

HLA 9 $[[[A \supset C] \wedge [B \supset C]] \supset [[A \vee B] \supset C]]$

HLA 10 $[\sim A \supset [A \supset B]]$

HLA 11 $[[[A \supset B] \wedge [A \supset \sim B]] \supset \sim A]$

The rule of inference is Modus Ponens.

Heyting's axiom system concerns four undefined terms $\sim$, $\supset$, $\vee$, and $\wedge$. They are interpreted, respectively, as the negation, implication, disjunction, and conjuction signs, but they do not have all the properties we ascribed to these signs in chapter 4. Three of the differences are important to us and are detailed below:

1. From HLA 1–HLA 11 we can derive

HT 1 $[[A \vee B] \supset [\sim A \supset B]]$

HT 2 $[[A \wedge B] \supset \sim [A \supset \sim B]]$

but not their inverses. Hence $\vee$ and $\wedge$ cannot be defined in terms of $\sim$ and $\supset$.

2. From HLA 1–HLA 11 we can derive

HT 3 $[A \supset A]$

HT 4 $[[\sim A \vee A] \supset [A \supset A]]$

but not the inverse of HT 4. Hence in Heyting's propositional calculus $[A \supset A]$ cannot be interpreted as a symbolic rendition of the Law of the Excluded Middle. The latter, which is expressed by $[\sim A \vee A]$, is not provable in HLA 1, . . . , HLA 11.

3. From HLA 1–HLA 11 we can derive

HT 5 $[A \supset \sim\sim A]$

HT 6 $\sim\sim[A \supset \sim\sim A]$

HT 7 $[\sim\sim[A \supset \sim\sim A] \supset \sim[A \wedge \sim A]]$

but not the inverse of HT 5 and HT 7. Hence, in Heyting's propositional calculus $\sim\sim[A \supset \sim\sim A]$ cannot be interpreted as a symbolic rendition of the Law of

Contradiction. The latter, which is expressed by $\sim[A \wedge \sim A]$, is, however, provable in HLA 1–HLA 11, as evidenced by HT 6 and HT 7.

Heyting's intuitionistic logic was developed to deal with mathematical propositions (see Heyting 1956, p. 97). Hence the values of A, B, and C in HLA 1–HLA 11 are to be mathematical formulas. According to Heyting, a mathematical formula A denotes truth if and only if it has a constructive proof. Its negation, $\sim A$, denotes truth if and only if A can be used to establish a contradiction, as evidence by HLA 10 and HLA 11 when the B in HLA 10 is replaced by $[A \wedge \sim A]$.

Second, in accordance with our attitude, we also insist that, for every structure $\mathcal{D}$, we know that A if (1) A is a logical consequence of a consistent set of closed formulas, $\Gamma_1, \ldots, \Gamma_n$, and if (2) we know that $[\Gamma_1 \wedge [\Gamma_2 \wedge [\cdots[\Gamma_{n-1} \wedge \Gamma_n]\cdots]]]$. For instance, if $n = 9$, if $\Gamma_1, \ldots, \Gamma_9$ denote the axioms of elementary set theory, and if $\mathcal{D}$ denotes the type structure of hereditarily finite sets, we know that $[\Gamma_1 \wedge [\Gamma_2 \wedge \cdots[\Gamma_8 \wedge \Gamma_9]\cdots]]$. Hence we also know that A if A is a theorem of the elementary set theory. Such knowledge depends on the postulates, rules of inference, and interpretation of our first-order predicate calculus. It is a priori if our knowledge of $[\Gamma_1 \wedge \cdots \wedge \Gamma_n]$ is *a priori*. I will elaborate on this next.

In chapter 5 we discussed the Dutch intuitionists' refusal to think of there-exist formulas as negations of for-all formulas in situations in which the universe is infinite. According to them, a for-all sentence uses only the potentiality of the infinite, which is all right; a negation of a for-all statement uses the actuality of the infinite, which is nonsense. Consequently, it is an abuse of language to define $\exists$ in terms of $\forall$ as we did in section 5.2. The proper way (i.e., the intuitionistic way) to treat $\exists$ and $\forall$ is described in E 23.9.

E 23.9 In Heyting's propositional calculus, the connectives $\sim$, $\wedge$, $\vee$, and $\supset$ are primitive symbols. In his predicate calculus the quantifiers $\forall$ and $\exists$ are also primitive. They satisfy the following axioms:

HLA 12 $[(\forall x)A \supset A_x(y)]$

HLA 13 $[A_x(y) \supset (\exists x)A]$

The corresponding rule of inference is this: Suppose that A and B are wffs in which x is not free in A and not bound in any part of B. Then from $[A \supset B]$, we infer $[A \supset (\forall x)B]$ and, from $[B \supset A]$, we infer $[(\exists x)B \supset A]$. The interpretation of Heyting's quantifiers is the same as the interpretation of our $\forall$ and $\exists$. However, his quantifiers do not have all the properties we ascribe to ours. Thus

HT 8 $[(\forall x)A \supset \sim(\exists x) \sim A]$

HT 9 $[(\exists x)A \supset \sim(\forall x) \sim A]$

HT 10 $[\sim\sim(\forall x)A \supset (\forall x)\sim\sim A]$

But the inverse implications of these theorems are false.

Disagreements as to the content of the propositional calculus and the first-order predicate calculus necessarily lead to disagreements as to the content of mathematical theories and to the validity of mathematical assertions.

E 23.10 Heyting's first-order predicate calculus and the following axioms concerning the constant, 0, the functions, $S(\cdot)$, $+$, and $\cdot$, and the predicates, $=$, and $<$, can be used to develop the intuitionistic version of the theory of natural numbers, HT(P).

HP 1 "$=$" is an equivalence relation; i.e., $[x = x]$, $[[x = y] \supset [y = x]]$ and $[[[x = y] \wedge [y = z]] \supset [x = z]]$.

HP 2 $[[x = y] \supset [S(x) = S(y)]]$

HP 3 P1–P7 and P 9 (section 6.1)

HP 4 $[[x < S(y)] \equiv \sim[\sim[x < y] \wedge \sim[x = y]]]$

HP 5 $[[x < y] \supset [\sim[y < x] \wedge \sim[x = y]]]$

HP 6 $[[[x = y] \wedge [y < z]] \supset [x < z]]$

HP 7 $[[[x < y] \wedge [y = z]] \supset [x < z]]$

HP 8 $[[[x < y] \wedge [y < z]] \supset [x < z]]$

HP 9 $[[\sim[x < y] \wedge \sim[y < x]] \supset [x = y]]$

HP 10 $[[\sim[x < y] \wedge \sim[x = y]] \supset [y < x]]$

Here *Pi* refers to the *i*th axiom of T(P) in chapter 6 and $[A \equiv B] =_{\text{df}} [[A \supset B] \wedge [B \supset A]]$.

An idea of Heyting's a priori knowledge of natural numbers can be obtained from the following theorems:

HP 11 $[\sim\sim[x = y] \supset [x = y]]$

HP 12 $[\sim\sim[x < y] \supset [x < y]]$

HTM 1 Let A be a closed formula that does not contain $\vee$ or $\exists$. If A is a theorem in T(P), it is also a theorem in HT(P).

The first two are easy consequences of the axioms. Together with HT 8, HT 11 and HT 12 they demonstrate that the law of double negation is intuitionistically valid for the atomic formulas of HT(P). Gerhard Gentzen used this fact and HTM 2 below to establish HTM 1 (see Gentzen 1969, pp. 59–65).

HTM 2 If A, B, and C are wffs and if x is not bound in A, then the validity of $[\sim\sim A \supset A]$ and $[\sim\sim B \supset B]$ implies the validity of $[\sim\sim[A \wedge B] \supset [A \wedge B]]$, $[\sim\sim[C \supset A] \supset [C \supset A]]$, $[\sim\sim\sim C \supset \sim C]$, and $[\sim\sim(\forall x)A \supset (\forall x)A]$.

Since in the predicate calculus of T(P), $[A \vee B]$ and $(\exists x)A$ are, respectively, materially, equivalent to $\sim[\sim A \wedge \sim B]$ and an abbreviation for $\sim(\forall x) \sim A$, it is easy to intuit from HTM 1 and HTM 2 that if a closed wff A is a theorem in T(P), there is a wff A^* such that $[A \equiv A^*]$ is a theorem in T(P) and A^* is a theorem in HT(P). The arguments needed to establish this fact are outlined in Gentzen 1969 (pp. 60–63).

The preceding examples show that there is nothing absolute or apodictic about *a priori* knowledge. What one man believes he knows from *a priori* considerations alone, may be disputed by another. We have indicated how such disagreements arise in mathematical logic and number theory. From that and an appeal to analogy, we infer that similar controversies arise in all fields of mathematics. An example is Kant's contention that the world in which we live must be Euclidean because our perception of space accords with Euclid's principles of geometry. Such an idea is untenable, as evidenced by the existence of competing geometries.

23.4.2 Knowledge of Extralogical Propositions

According to Lord Russell, we have *knowledge by acquaintance* of present sense data, of remembered past sense data, and of the act of sensing sense data. We have *knowledge by description* of physical objects and other minds; e.g., the desk at which I sit is the object which I sense has the following sense data. . . . [2]

In economic matters: We have knowledge by acquaintance of the salary we received last year, but we have knowledge by description only of what our income was, i.e., of the maximum amount of money we could have spent last year and been as wealthy at the end of the year as we were at the beginning (Hicks 1946, p. 172). Similarly, we have knowledge by acquaintance of the price of our house but only knowledge by description of its current market value.

Besides knowledge of sense data, physical objects, and other minds, we have knowledge by description of the unary relations that are determined by universals such as table, metal, and music. We have knowledge by acquaintance of the unary relations that are characterized by qualities such as whiteness, justice, and magic. Similarly we have knowledge by acquaintance of binary relations such as left of, father of, and taller than, and of ternary relations such as between and parents of.

In economics: We have knowledge by description of universals such as salary, commodity, and market and knowledge by acquaintance of qualities such as scarcity, monopoly, and moral hazard. We also have knowledge by acquaintance of binary relations such as riskier than, more efficient than, and preferred to.

Knowledge of universals is problematic. To see why, observe that a universal has both an extension and an intension. In a given world the extension of a universal is the set of objects that satisfy the relation that it determines, e.g., the set of all just acts in the case of justice. The intension of the universal is the graph of a set-valued function on the set of all possible worlds whose values are the respective extensions of the universal. To know a universal means to know its intension. Obtaining such knowledge by description or by acquaintance is possible only if there exists a finite set of observable characteristics that provide necessary and sufficient conditions for an object (or an overt behavior or an event) to be an instance of the universal in question. According to PLV, such sets exist for table, cat, and most of the other "objects in the field, over which our generalizations extend." According to Russell, such sets also exist for sensible qualities such as white and hard and for relations such as to the left of and resemblance. And in comments above, I add that they must exist for universals such as anger, justice, and market as well.

In this respect it is interesting to observe that Kant insisted that our knowledge of the relations of the physical objects that we perceive is not obtained by description or by acquaintance. Instead such knowledge is a priori because the characteristics that delineate the relations of physical objects are due to our own nature. Our intellect does not *draw* its laws from nature. It *imposes* its laws on nature. Note, therefore, in our theory the set of characteristics that determine the intension of a universal are characteristics that human beings in the course of history have invented for the purpose of keeping order in the infinitude of particulars that they face. Knowledge of such a universal is a priori only if it is determined by a relation of universals that form integral parts of a scientific theory.

From the point of view of our theory, sense data, descriptions of physical objects and other minds, and universals are not proper objects of knowledge. Instead they are sources of knowledge about propositions concerning them. Thus knowledge of the universal "hard" and an appropriate sense datum allow us to assert: We know that we sense that the thing next to us is hard. Similarly, knowledge of universals and possession of appropriate sense data allow us to assert that we know that, whatever it is that is next to us, it is a thing that we sense possesses the following sensory characteristics .... Such knowledge and descriptive knowledge of the relavant universal, e.g., table, in turn allow us to assert that we know that the thing next to us appears to us to be a table. To claim that we know that the thing next to us *is* a table, we must also be able to ascertain that our sense data are veridical, i.e., that we are not dreaming or floating in the tank of a psychiatrist.

There are many situations in which we are not dreaming or being deceived in some other way and yet cannot be certain of what we are experiencing.

E 23.11 At dusk we sense a thing on our neighbor's roof that seems to have a long tail, four legs, and pointed ears. We believe that it is a cat. So we know that we believe that we are seeing a cat. However, our sense data provide insufficient evidence for us to know that we are seeing a cat.

A different but analogous situation was faced by the prosecutors of Alger Hiss. Their evidence sufficed to convict him of spying. It provided only partial support for their asserting that Hiss was a spy.

Similar examples abound in all fields of knowledge. The voyage of the *Kon-Tiki* across the Pacific and the other evidence which Thor Heyerdahl and his collaborators collected provide only partial support for Heyerdahl's thesis that "Polynesia was settled originally by people from the west coast of South America." Historical facts ensure that Jesus existed, but they provide only partial support for asserting that he was the son of God. Christians believe this, but Jews do not. In econometrics an interval estimate of the value of a parameter usually provides only partial support for asserting that the true value belongs to the given interval. In all these cases we cannot assert that we know that ..., but we can make a probabilistic evaluation of our knowledge in the way exemplified in E 23.13.

E 23.12 A Bayesian econometrican tosses a quarter a hundred times and obtains fifty-four heads. His prior probability that the intrinsic probability of heads, p, belonged to a given Borel subset, A, of $[0, 1]$ equaled the Lebesgue measure of A. His posterior probability that $p \in (0.49, 0.6)$ is 0.95.

23.4.3 Knowledge of Variable Hypotheticals

Variable hypotheticals can be divided in two groups, depending on whether their validity can or cannot be established with certainty.[3] We begin with the certain hypotheticals.

23.4.2.1 Knowledge by Definition, Analysis, Intuition, and Enumeration

Some variable hypotheticals can be known with certainty because they are *analytic* in the sense that their negations are self-contradictory. Examples are "all widows have had husbands" and the following naive form of Walras's law:

E 23.13 In any economy the value of all purchases equals the value of all sales.

Others are *known by analysis*. Examples are "for all integers n, $1 + 2 + \cdots + n = n(n + 1)/2$" and the theoretical version of Walras's law which we met in section 14.3.1:

E 23.14 In an economy without foreign trade the value of all *planned* purchases will (at a given set of prices) always equal the value of all *planned* sales.

Still other hypotheticals are *known by intuition*. Examples are "whatever is colored is extended" and the following version of the law of the (eventually) diminishing marginal product of labor:

E 23.15 Agricultural skill remaining the same, additional labor employed on the land within a given district produces in general a less-than-proportionate return.

If the latter were false, then in any country only the very best land would be cultivated. Also, the produce of the farm with the best land could be made to feed the whole country (Senior 1850, p. 26). Finally, some variable hypotheticals are established *by enumeration*. A typical example is given below. In reading it, note that the premises that warrant the conclusion are of two kinds: (1) all the *listed* members of a group satisfy a given condition, and (2) there are no other members of this group.

E 23.16 There are four members of the board of directors of the AFZ Corporation. Their names are Smith, Jones, Fitch, and Hammond; all are U.S. citizens. Consequently, all the members of the board of directors of the AFZ are U.S. citizens.

23.4.3.2 Accidental, Nomological, and Derivative Laws

The ∀ sentences that cannot be known with certainty can be grouped in various ways. We shall distinguish them according as the laws they assert are *accidental, nomological* or *derivative*.

Accidental Laws Prototypes of accidental laws are assertions such as "all ravens are black" and "all ruminants have cloven hooves." They have two important characteristics: (1) They can be inferred from factual evidence, and (2) at the moment there exists no good theoretical reason why they *must* be true. For instance, the current state of scientific inquiry does not warrant our insisting that any raven which inhabited polar regions and was exposed to x-ray radiation would be black (Nagel 1961, p. 70).

There are many examples of accidental laws in economics. Some of them are inferred by induction from factual evidence. One example is Malthus's

Principle of Population. Botero conceived it in 1589 at the end of several centuries during which Europe had experienced high population growth and rapidly rising prices (Schumpeter 1954, p. 254). Two centuries later the principle reappeared in the writings of Malthus in the following form (Malthus 1973, p. 6):

E 23.17 The population of a country has a constant tendency to increase beyond the means of subsistence.

Other accidental economic laws are inferred by analogy from introspection. One example is Senior's first fundamental postulate of political economy:[4]

E 23.18 Any man is either in selfless pursuit of some spiritual goal or desires to obtain additional wealth with as little sacrifice as possible.

Nomological Laws Prototypes of nomological laws are assertions such as "copper expands when heated" and "any living organism has or has had a parent." They resemble accidental laws in that they can be inferred from factual evidence. They differ from accidental laws in that there are good theoretical reasons why they must be true. Thus we may assert "an object either is not copper or would expand when heated" and "if x had been a living organism, it would have had a parent" (Nagel 1961, p. 51).

There are examples of nomological laws in economics. One is Gresham's Law, first enunciated by Sir Thomas Gresham in 1558. It may be formulated as follows:

E 23.19 A country with two metallic currencies, one of which is in ample supply and inferior to the other, either is populated by people in selfless pursuit of spiritual goals or will eventually experience a complete disappearance of the superior currency.

In different words, the law asserts that as soon as the specie value of one currency exceeds its currency value, its coins will be melted or exported (Schumpeter 1954, p. 343).

Derivative Laws Derivative laws are postulates or theorems of a mathematically formulated theory. One interesting example is "a body, under the action of no external forces, maintains a constant velocity." This assertion is a postulate of Newton's theory of mechanics. In the intended interpretation of the theory, it is (at best) true by default because Newton's theory of gravitation implies that there are no bodies that are not under the action of some external forces. The interpreted law receives its empirical relevance from the role it plays in Newton's theory (Nagel 1961, p. 61).

Another example is Snell's Law: "A ray of light, incident at a surface separating two media, is bent. The ratio of the sine of the angle of incidence to the sine of the angle of refraction is a constant for two given media." As stated, the law is a theorem in the theory of optics that can be derived from more fundamental principles such as the Principle of the Rectilinear Propagation of Light and Fermat's Principle of Least Time. In the intended interpretation of the theory, a ray of light may be a sunbeam and a medium can be air, water, or some other transparent substance.

In reading Snell's Law, note that a ray of light is an ideal in the same way a line and a point are ideals in geometry. Any experimentally determined sunbeam can only roughly approximate Snell's ray. Also, not air, nor water, nor any other transparent substance is homogeneous from the point of view of optics. It is, indeed, a difficult problem in experimental optics to characterize the shape and the physical and chemical composition of a substance that has a given refractive index (i.e., a given incidence-refraction sine ratio). On the basis of such observations, Stephen Toulmin suggested that it is inappropriate to ask whether Snell's Law is true. The only relevant question concerns the circumstances under which and the degree of exactness with which it can be applied (Toulmin 1960, p. 73).

Interesting examples of derivative laws in economics are the Fundamental Theorem of Consumer Choice, which we discussed at length in chapter 10, and the following assertion:

E 23.20 A consumer's absolute risk aversion is a *decreasing* function of his net worth if and only if his holdings of risky assets are an *increasing* function of his net worth.

This economic law is a (roughly formulated) theorem in Arrow's theory of risk aversion (Arrow 1965, p. 43), which we discussed in chapter 12.

In Arrow's theory, the consumer is an *ideal* person, the economic man in single-minded pursuit of an economic goal. He searches for the balance sheet that will maximize his expected utility subject to his budget constraint. This balance sheet consists of two assets (a safe and a risky one), no debt, and net worth. In most applications, the consumer is taken to be an individual living alone or a family with a common household budget. A consumer who lives in an industrialized country has both the opportunity to incur debt and to invest in an array of risky assets.

A person is risk-averse if he is averse to the chance of loss. Arrow proposed two measures of risk aversion, one of which he calls absolute risk aversion. E 23.20 above attests to the usefulness of this concept in characterizing individual choice under uncertainty. In reading E 23.20, note that Arrow's measure is a theoretical construct. We have no idea of how to measure a consumer's absolute risk aversion at different levels of his net worth. In fact, we even have difficulty measuring his net worth, since to do so we must determine the market values of used cars, durables, and houses.

We conclude, as we did in the case of Snell's Law, that it seems inappropriate to query whether a derivative law such as E 23.20 is true in an epistemological sense. Instead, we must seek to ascertain the circumstances and the exactness with which it can be applied.

The natural way to apply the law in E 23.20 is as follows. We are faced with two assertions:

(i) Either x is not a consumer or his absolute risk aversion decreases with his net worth.

This assertion prescribes a relationship between a theoretical construct, the consumer's absolute risk aversion, and the values assumed by an observable variable, his net worth.

(ii) Either x is not a consumer or his investment in risky assets increases with his net worth.

This second assertion describes a relationship between two observable variables, the consumer's investment in risky assets and his net worth. E 23.20 insists that we can infer the validity of (i) from the validity of (ii). Therefore, *seeking circumstances under which this law can be applied amounts to searching for observable interpretations of a consumer, his net worth, safe assets, and risky assets that satisfy Arrow's axioms and then testing the validity of* (i) by testing the validity of (ii). This we do in chapter 28.

23.5 Necessity and Modal Logic

In discussing different kinds of knowledge we encountered the notion of necessity in two places. I suggested that we can know a universal only if we can describe its instances in terms of a finite number of characteristics that are independent of the state of the world. Such a description will prescribe *necessary* properties of the instances of the universal; e.g., a human being is a rational animal. I also suggested that we can know nomological laws because they prescribe relations that hold necessarily; e.g., in any world if x were a piece of copper and x were heated, x would expand.

23.5.1 A Modal-Logical System, ML

The branch of mathematical logic in which logicians attempt to explicate the idea of necessity is called *modal logic*. Next we shall formulate a modal-logical language, ML, which we shall use to characterize the wffs in L_Γ—a given first-order language—that are necessarily true. In ML the terms are wffs. Moreover, there is a functional symbol $\Box$ which is meant to be the symbolic rendition of "necessarily"; i.e., if u is a term, then in the intended interpretation of ML $\Box u$ asserts "necessarily u." Roughly speaking, $\Box u$ will denote truth if u denotes truth in all possible worlds; it will denote falsehood otherwise.

A possible world can be so many things. It can be an undefined term, e.g., a point of reference in R. Montague's pragmatics (Montague 1974, pp. 98, 108). It can also be a state description, e.g., a maximal consistent set of atomic sentences in R. Carnap's theory of meaning and necessity (Carnap 1956, p. 9). And it can simply be a way that things could have been, as in D. Lewis's theory of counterfactuals (Lewis 1973, p. 84). To us a *possible world* is a structure of the given first-order language L_Γ; and two possible worlds are different if and only if they are not isomorphic.

To construct our modal-logical system, ML, we proceed as follows: The logical vocabulary of ML consists of the standard symbols—$\sim$, $\supset$, [ ], ( )—and an infinite list of propositional variables—$p, q, r, p_1, q_1, r_1, \ldots$. The nonlogical vocabulary of ML consists of two unary predicate symbols, *TCL* and *CL*, two unary function symbols, $\Box$ and *N*, and a binary function symbol, *I*.

The symbols of the vocabulary of ML combine to form propositional terms and wffs. The propositional terms are defined inductively as follows:

(ti) Propositionals and constants are propositional terms.
(tii) If u is a propositional term, then Nu and $\Box u$ are propositional terms.
(tiii) If u and v are propositional terms, then $I(u, v)$ is a propositional term.

In the intended interpretation of ML, Nu is short for "not u" and $I(u, v)$ is short for "u materially implies v."

The wffs are defined inductively by the following formation rules:

(fi) If u is a propositional term, then u, $TCL(u)$ and $CL(u)$ are wffs.
(fii) If A is wf, then $\sim A$ is a wff.
(fiii) If A and B are wffs, then $[A \supset B]$ is a wff.

The axioms of ML are as stated below. In the statement of M 1, $\equiv$ is the material equivalence sign that we introduced in section 4.5.2.

M 0 PLA 1—PLA 3 (section 5.1.3).

M 1 Let u and v be propositional terms. Then

(i) $[Nu \equiv \sim u]$

(ii) $[I(u, v) \equiv [u \supset v]]$

M 2 If u is a propositional term, then

$[TCL(u) \supset CL(u)]$

M 3 If u and v are propositional terms, then

(i) $[\Box u \supset u]$

(ii) $[\Box I(u, v) \supset [\Box u \supset \Box v]]$

(iii) $[\Box u \supset \Box\Box u]$

M 4 If u and v are propositional terms, then

(i) $[CL(u) \supset CL(Nu)]$

(ii) $[CL(u) \supset [CL(v) \supset CL(I(u, v))]]$

M 5 If u is a term, then

(i) $[TCL(u) \supset \Box u]$

(ii) $[CL(u) \supset [\Box u \supset TCL(u)]]$

The rules of inference of ML follow:

MRI 1 From A and $[A \supset B]$ we infer B.

MRI 2 If u is a term and a tautological consequence of M 0 and M 1, then from u we infer $\Box u$.

23.5.2 Sample Theorems in ML

In reading the axioms and the rules of inference of ML, note that M 0 and MRI 1 allow us to apply in ML any theorem schemata of the propositional calculus; e.g., in proving the following theorem, it suffices to assert the theorem schemata determined by T 4.1.

MLT 1 If u is a propositional term, then

$[\Box u \supset \Box u]$.

Similarly, in proving MLT 2, we begin by asserting $[\sim u \supset [u \supset v]]$.

MLT 2 If u and v are terms, then

$[\Box Nu \supset [\Box u \supset \Box v]]$.

Then we use M 1, TM 4.7, and MRI 2 to deduce first $I(Nu, I(u, v))$ and then

$\Box I(Nu, I(u, v))$. Next we assert $[\Box I(Nu, I(u, v)) \supset [\Box Nu \supset \Box I(u, v)]]$ and use M 3 (ii) and MRI 1 to infer $[\Box Nu \supset \Box I(u, v)]$. Finally, we assert M 3 (ii), apply TM 4.1 with q equal to $\Box Nu$, use PLA 2, and apply MRI 1 to deduce $[\Box Nu \supset [\Box u \supset \Box v]]$.

In the intended interpretation of ML the extensions of CL and TCL are, respectively, the closed wffs of L_Γ and the logical and nonlogical theorems in L_Γ. It is, therefore, interesting to observe the following:

MLT 3 If u and v are propositional terms, then

(i) $[CL(u) \supset [TCL(u) \equiv \Box u]]$

(ii) $[TCL(u) \supset \Box I(v, u)]$.

Hence, if our interpretation can be justified, then the logical and nonlogical theorems of L_Γ are true necessarily.

The validity of MLT 3 (i) is an immediate consequence of M 5 (i) and (ii) and needs no proof. To establish MLT 3 (ii) we proceed as follows: We begin by asserting $[u \supset [v \supset u]]$. Then we use M 1, TM 4.7, and MRI 2 to deduce $\Box I(u, I(v, u))$. Next we assert $[\Box I(u, I(v, u)) \supset [\Box u \supset \Box I(v, u)]]$ and use M 3 (ii) and MRI 1 to infer $[\Box u \supset \Box I(v, u)]$. Finally, we apply TM 4.1 (with q equal to $TCL(u)$) and use PLA 2, M 5 (i), and MRI 1 to infer MLT 3 (ii).

To demonstrate that our intended interpretation of TCL is not far-fetched we shall conclude this section by establishing analogues of TM 4.1 and TM 4.3.

MLT 4 Let u and v be propositional terms. Then
$[CL(v) \supset [TCL(u) \supset TCL(I(v, u))]]$.

To prove this theorem we first appeal to MLT 3 (ii), apply TM 4.1 (with q equal to $CL(I(v, u))$), and use TM 5.3 to deduce that

$$[TCLu) \supset [CL(I(v, u)) \supset \Box I(v, u)]].$$

Then, since by MLT 3 (i) and M 0,

$$[[CL(I(v, u)) \supset \Box I(v, u)] \supset [CL(I(v, u)) \supset TCL(I(v, u))]],$$

we can assert $[TCL(u) \supset [CL(I(v, u)) \supset TCL(I(v, u))]]$ and hence

$$[[TCL(u) \supset CL(I(v, u))] \supset [TCL(u) \supset TCL(I(v, u))]].$$

From this, $[CL(v) \supset [TCL(u) \supset CL(I(v, u))]]$, and standard arguments follows the validity of MLT 4.

Theorem MLT 4 is an analogue of TM 4.1. In the next theorem I state an analogue of TM 4.3. For brevity I omit the proof, which is similar to the one I gave of MLT 4.

MLT 5 Let u and v be propositional terms. Then

(i) $[TCL(u) \supset \sim TCL(Nu)]$

(ii) $[CL(v) \supset [TCL(u) \supset TCL(I(Nu, v))]]$.

23.5.3 The Intended Interpretation of ML

We have created ML for the purpose of characterizing the closed wffs of a first-order language L_Γ and the theorems of a theory $T(\Gamma)$ that is formulated in L_Γ. With that in mind we let a structure for ML be a twelve-tuple,

$$\mathscr{L}_{\mathscr{M}} = (|\mathscr{M}|, N_{\mathscr{M}}, N^{\mathscr{M}}, I^{\mathscr{M}}, \Box^{\mathscr{M}}, TCL^{\mathscr{M}}, CL^{\mathscr{M}}, \mathscr{X}, R, \xi, \phi, R_{\Box}),$$

where

1. $|\mathscr{M}|$ is the smallest set of wffs that contains the closed wffs of L_Γ and that contains $N^{\mathscr{M}}A$, $I^{\mathscr{M}}(A, B)$, and $\Box^{\mathscr{M}}A$ whenever it contains A and B. Here $N^{\mathscr{M}}$, $I^{\mathscr{M}}$, and $\Box^{\mathscr{M}}$ are the interpretations of N, I, and $\Box$ in $\mathscr{L}_{\mathscr{M}}$.

2. $N_{\mathscr{M}}$ contains all the names of the wffs in $|\mathscr{M}|$, one name for each wff and different names for different wffs.

3. $TCL^{\mathscr{M}}$ and $CL^{\mathscr{M}}$ are the interpretations of TCL and CL in $\mathscr{L}_{\mathscr{M}}$. We insist that $CL^{\mathscr{M}}$ consists of all the closed wffs of L_Γ and that $TCL^{\mathscr{M}}$ contains all the closed wffs in L_Γ that are tautologies. Moreover, $TCL^{\mathscr{M}} \subset CL^{\mathscr{M}}$ and $CL^{\mathscr{M}} \subset |\mathscr{M}|$. Finally, if A and B are in $CL^{\mathscr{M}}$, then $N^{\mathscr{M}}A$ and $I^{\mathscr{M}}(A, B)$ are to be the closed wffs of L_Γ, $\sim A$, and $[A \supset B]$, respectively.

4. $\mathscr{X}$ is a set of structures for L_Γ that may or may not be models of $T(\Gamma)$.

5. R is a reflexive, transitive relation in $\mathscr{X}$ and $\xi \in \mathscr{X}$.

6. $\phi(\cdot)$: $CL^{\mathscr{M}} \times \mathscr{X} \to \mathscr{P}(\mathscr{X})$ and satisfies

$$\phi(A, H) = \{H' \in \mathscr{X} : HRH' \text{ and } H'(A) = t\},$$

where $H'(A)$ denotes the truth value of A in H'.

7. $R_{\Box} \subset \mathscr{X} \times \mathscr{P}(\mathscr{X})$ and $(H, E) \in R_{\Box}$ if and only if $H \in \mathscr{X}$ and $E = \{H' \in \mathscr{X} : HRH'\}$.

Before we can use $\mathscr{L}_{\mathscr{M}}$ to interpret ML we must, for each $H \in \mathscr{X}$, extend its domain of definition to $|\mathscr{M}|$, and we must extend the domain of definition of $\phi(\cdot)$ to $|\mathscr{M}| \times \mathscr{X}$. This we do by induction as follows: Let Γ_i,

$i = 0, 1, \ldots,$ be an increasing sequence of sets of wffs that satisfy the conditions:

(i) $\Gamma_0 = CL^{\mathcal{M}}$,
(ii) if $A \in \Gamma_i$ for some $i \geqslant 1$, then there are wffs C and D in Γ_{i-1} such that A is C, $N^{\mathcal{M}}C$, $I^{\mathcal{M}}(C, D)$, or $\square^{\mathcal{M}}C$.

Then our characterization of $|\mathcal{M}|$ implies that $|\mathcal{M}| = \bigcup_{i=0}^{\infty} \Gamma_i$.

Next observe that, for each $H \in \mathcal{X}$, $H(\cdot)$ is defined on Γ_0. Moreover, $\phi(\cdot)$ is defined on $\Gamma_0 \times \mathcal{X}$. Suppose that we have extended the domain of definition of all the $H \in \mathcal{X}$ and $\phi(\cdot)$ to Γ_{n-1} and $\Gamma_{n-1} \times \mathcal{X}$, respectively. If $A \in \Gamma_n$, then by condition ii above there are wffs C and D in Γ_{n-1} such that A is C, $N^{\mathcal{M}}C$, $I^{\mathcal{M}}(C, D)$, or $\square^{\mathcal{M}}C$. To define $H \in \mathcal{X}$ on A we let $H(A) = H(C)$ if A is C. If A is $N^{\mathcal{M}}C$, we let $H(A) = \mathrm{t}(\mathrm{f})$ according as $H(C) = f(t)$. If A is $I^{\mathcal{M}}(C, D)$, we let $H(A) = \mathrm{t}$ if $H(C) = \mathrm{f}$ or $H(D) = \mathrm{t}$, and let $H(A) = \mathrm{f}$ if $H(C) = \mathrm{t}$ and $H(D) = \mathrm{f}$. If A is $\square^{\mathcal{M}}C$, we let $H(A) = \mathrm{t}$ if $(H, \phi(C, H)) \in R_{\square}$ and $H(A) = \mathrm{f}$ otherwise. Finally, we let

$$\phi(A, H) = \{H' \in \mathcal{X} : HRH' \text{ and } H'(A) = \mathrm{t}\}$$

as required in condition 6 above.

A structure $\mathcal{L}_{\mathcal{M}}$ with the function $H(\cdot)$ extended to $|\mathcal{M}|$ and with $\phi(\cdot)$ extended to $|\mathcal{M}| \times \mathcal{X}$ determines an interpretation of ML in the following way: We add the names in $N_{\mathcal{M}}$ as constants to the nonlogical vocabulary of ML and name the expanded language ML($\mathcal{M}$). Then we interpret the variable-free terms of ML($\mathcal{M}$) by induction on the length of terms:

(i) If $a \in N_{\mathcal{M}} \mathcal{M}(a)$ we let the individual be names, which a; and
(ii) if a is a variable-free term in ML($\mathcal{M}$) of the form Nb, $I(b, c)$ or $\square b$, we let $\mathcal{M}(a)$ be, respectively, $N^{\mathcal{M}}\mathcal{M}(b)$, $I^{\mathcal{M}}(\mathcal{M}(b), \mathcal{M}(c))$, or $\square^{\mathcal{M}}\mathcal{M}(b)$.

It can be shown that if a is a variable-free term in ML($\mathcal{M}$), then either a is a name or there exist variable-free terms b and c such that a is Nb, $I(b, c)$, or $\square b$. From this it follows that conditions i and ii determine the interpretation $\mathcal{M}(a)$ of all variable-free terms in ML($\mathcal{M}$).

Next let a be a term in ML with n free propositional variables, $p_1, \ldots, p_n$, and let $\theta_1, \ldots, \theta_n$, be names in $N_{\mathcal{M}}$. In addition, let $a_{p_1, \ldots, p_n}(\theta_1, \ldots, \theta_n)$ be the term we obtain by substituting θ_i for p_i at each occurrence of p_i in a, $i = 1, \ldots, n$. Then $a_{p_1, \ldots, p_n}(\theta_1, \ldots, \theta_n)$ is an $\mathcal{M}$ instance of a. Conditions i and ii determine the interpretation of every $\mathcal{M}$ instance of a. In that way they determine the interpretation of a as well.

To interpret the wffs in ML, we must first interpret the closed wffs in ML($\mathcal{M}$). I proceed by induction on the length of wffs.

(iii) Let A be closed wff and suppose that A is a term a. Then a is variable-free and we interpret A by insisting that $\mathscr{L}_{\mathscr{M}}(A) = \mathrm{t}$ if and only if $\xi(\mathscr{M}(a)) = \mathrm{t}$. Otherwise $\mathscr{L}_{\mathscr{M}}(A) = \mathrm{f}$.

(iv) Let A be the closed atomic formula $TCL(a)$. Since A is closed, a must be variable-free. We interpret A by insisting that $\mathscr{L}_{\mathscr{M}}(A) = \mathrm{t(f)}$ according as $\mathscr{M}(a) \in TCL^{\mathscr{M}}$ (or not).

(v) Let A be the closed atomic formula $CL(a)$. Since A is closed, a must be variable-free. We interpret A by insisting that $\mathscr{L}_{\mathscr{M}}(A) = \mathrm{t(f)}$ according as $\mathscr{M}(a) \in CL^{\mathscr{M}}$ (or not).

(iv) If A and B are closed wffs, then $\mathscr{L}_{\mathscr{M}}(\sim A) = \mathrm{f(t)}$ according as $\mathscr{L}_{\mathscr{M}}(A) = \mathrm{t(f)}$. Moreover, $\mathscr{L}_{\mathscr{M}}([A \supset B]) = \mathrm{t}$ if $\mathscr{L}_{\mathscr{M}}(A) = \mathrm{f}$ or $\mathscr{L}_{\mathscr{M}}(B) = \mathrm{t}$. Otherwise $\mathscr{L}_{\mathscr{M}}([A \supset B]) = \mathrm{f}$.

It is clear that conditions iii–v determine the interpretation of all the closed wffs of ML($\mathscr{M}$) and hence of ML. In the obvious way they interpret the other wffs in ML as well by interpreting their $\mathscr{M}$ instances.

23.5.4 Salient Properties of the Intented Interpretation of ML

In reading the preceding interpretation of ML, we should make several useful observations. First, the interpretation is unambiguous in the following sense.

TML 1 Let $\mathscr{L}_{\mathscr{M}}$ be a structure for ML; let a be a variable-free term of ML($\mathscr{M}$); and let $\theta \in N_{\mathscr{M}}$ be the name of $\mathscr{M}(a)$. If b is a term of ML($\mathscr{M}$) in which no variable except p occurs, then $\mathscr{M}(b_p(a)) = \mathscr{M}(b_p(\theta))$. Moreover, if A is a wff in ML($\mathscr{M}$) in which no variable except p is free, then $\mathscr{L}_{\mathscr{M}}(A_p(a)) = \mathscr{L}_{\mathscr{M}}(A_p(\theta))$.

The validity of this theorem is easily established, so I leave the proof to the reader.

Next note that in the intended structure $\mathscr{L}_{\mathscr{M}}$ for ML the content of $\mathscr{X}$ and the extension of R will depend on Γ and on the applications we have in mind for ML. For example, when we aim to explicate the idea of logical necessity, we let $\mathscr{X}$ be the set of all possible worlds and insist that $R = \mathscr{X} \times \mathscr{X}$. When Γ contains formulas that express natural laws and we aim to explicate the notion of physical necessity, we let $\mathscr{X}$ consist of all possible worlds in which at least one natural law is valid. Also we insist that, if $(\mathscr{D}_1, \mathscr{D}_2) \in \mathscr{X} \times \mathscr{X}$, then $(\mathscr{D}_1, \mathscr{D}_2) \in R$ if and only if the natural laws that are valid in $\mathscr{D}_1$ are valid in $\mathscr{D}_2$ as well. Finally, when we aim to explicate the idea of logical consequence, we choose $\mathscr{X}$ to be the set of all models of $T(\Gamma)$ and let $R = \mathscr{X} \times \mathscr{X}$.

The following theorems demonstrate that we can use ML both to explicate the idea of logical necessity and the idea of logical consequence. In the theorem we let $\vdash A$ mean that the wff A is a theorem in ML.

TML 2 If $\mathscr{L}_{\mathscr{M}}$ is a model of the axioms of ML and A is a wff, then $\vdash A$ only if $\mathscr{L}_{\mathscr{M}}(A) = \mathrm{t}$.

This theorem insists that the rules of inference of ML are truth-preserving. It is well known that MRI 1 is truth-preserving. Hence we need only check whether MRI 2 also possesses this property. But that is an immediate consequence of the fact that if a is a variable-free propositional term and a tautological consequence of M 0 and M 1, then $H(\mathscr{M}(a)) = \mathrm{t}$ for all $H \in \mathscr{X}$.

TML 3 If Γ is consistent, then there exist models of ML, $\mathscr{L}_{\mathscr{M}_1}$ and $\mathscr{L}_{\mathscr{M}_2}$, such that $TCL^{\mathscr{M}_1}$ consists of all the closed logical theorems of L_Γ and such that $TCL^{\mathscr{M}_2}$ consists of all the closed logical and nonlogical theorems of $T(\Gamma)$.

In the case of $\mathscr{L}_{\mathscr{M}_1}$ we choose $TCL^{\mathscr{M}_1}$ such that $\mathscr{M}_1(u) \in TCL^{\mathscr{M}_1}$ if and only if $\mathscr{M}_1(u)$ is a closed logical theorem of L_Γ and we insist that $\mathscr{X}$ contains all structures of L_Γ and that $R = \mathscr{X} \times \mathscr{X}$. In the case of $\mathscr{L}_{\mathscr{M}_2}$ we choose $TCL^{\mathscr{M}_2}$ such that $\mathscr{M}_2(u) \in TCL^{\mathscr{M}_2}$ if and only if $\mathscr{M}_2(u) \in C_n(\Gamma)$ and we insist that $\mathscr{X}$ consists of all the models of $T(\Gamma)$ and that $R = \mathscr{X} \times \mathscr{X}$. The possibility of characterizing $\mathscr{L}_{\mathscr{M}_1}$ and $\mathscr{L}_{\mathscr{M}_2}$ in this way is a consequence of MLT 3 (i).

Examples of $T(\Gamma)$ that we had in mind when we developed ML were the $T(P)$ of E 6.1 and the T(KA 1–KA 9) of chapter 9.

23.5.5 Universals, Nomological Laws, and Modal Logic

It is awkward that all the formulas in $|\mathscr{M}|$—the universe of ML—are closed. Next we shall discuss one of the consequences of having insisted on this feature of ML.

Consider the following two sentences:

1. $\Box(\forall x)[m(x) \equiv [r(x) \wedge a(x)]]$.
2. $(\forall x)\Box[m(x) \equiv [r(x) \wedge a(x)]]$.

We can assert sentence 1 but not 2. With the obvious interpretation of m, r, and a, sentence 1 insists that necessarily, for all x, x is human if and only if x is a rational animal. There is different way of saying the same thing: It is the essential characteristic of human beings that they are rational animals. When phrased in that way, our interpretation of sentence 1 shows that ML captures the notion of necessity that we met in our discussion of knowledge of universals.

Sentence 2 insists that, for all x, necessarily x is human if and only if it is a rational animal. In different words, sentence 2 asserts that, for all x, in any world that might occur x would be considered to be a human being if and only if it were a rational animal. That leaves open the possibility that x might be human in one world, a werewolf in another, and not exist at all in a third. But whether werewolf or nonexistent, x would have been human if it had been a rational animal; i.e., being a rational animal is the essential part of being human.

With the obvious interpretation of c, h, and e, we have two other sentences:

3. $\Box(\forall x)[[c(x) \wedge h(x)] \supset e(x)]$
4. $(\forall x)\Box[[c(x) \wedge h(x)] \supset e(x)]$

These sentences can be read in a way similar to the way we read the first two. For example, sentence 3 insists that it is necessary that, for all x, either x is not copper and heated or x will expand. And sentence 4 asserts that, for all x, necessarily either x is not copper and heated or x will expand. In fact, sentence 4 insists that, even in a world where x does not exist or where x is not copper and heated, it would have expanded if it had been copper and heated. Thus both sentences assert the nomological law we discussed in section 23.4.3.2. Besides, if true, sentence 4 can be interpreted to imply the validity of a counterfactual version of the same law.

Some philosophers believe that it is a characteristic feature of a nomological law that it supports a counterfactual version of itself. It is, therefore, important to understand why sentence 4 and not 3 can be read to assert the counterfactural version of the law about heated copper that necessarily expands. To ascertain the truth value of sentence 3 we must, for each possible world, evaluate a for-all statement where x varies over the universe that pertains to that particular world. It is irrelevant for this evaluation whether we know what might have happened if we had added an individual to the respective universe. This is so even though there may be x's (i.e., individuals) that exist in more than one world and assume different characters in different worlds. To ascertain the truth value of sentence 4 we must evaluate a for-all statement where x varies over a universe that is the union of the universes of the various possible worlds. To do that, we must, for each x and for each and every possible world, ascertain the truth value of an assertion about x and copper that expands when heated. Our ability to do that in a meaningful way for an x and a possible world in which x does not exist is questionable. But be that as it may. When we insist that sentence 4 supports the counterfactual—if x had been copper and heated, it would have expanded—we are implicitly assigning the truth value t to $[[c(x) \wedge h(x)] \supset e(x)]$ in any world in which x does not exist.

In this context the following observation is relevant: Let E be a predicate such that Ex asserts that x exists, and rewrite sentence 4 as follows:

4*. $(\forall x)\Box[Ex \supset [[c(x) \wedge h(x)] \supset e(x)]]$

In a world in which x does not exist, $[Ex \supset [[c(x) \wedge h(x)] \supset e(x)]]$ denotes truth. In a world in which x exists, the same expression will denote truth if and only if $[[c(x) \wedge h(x)] \supset e(x)]$ denotes truth. Consequently, we must assign the same truth value to sentence 4* as we did to 4. Note, therefore, that we cannot read sentence 4* so that it supports our counterfactual about heated copper that necessarily expands!

23.5.6 Concluding Remarks

We could introduce E in L_Γ and create a modal-logical system in which we assert both open and closed wffs. If we did, we could discuss in more detail the difficulties involved in quantifying into modal contexts that we encountered in our interpretation of sentences 2 and 4. We could also discuss the nonsubstitutivity of equality in referentially opaque modal contexts. For example, how can the number of planets be nine and $\Box[9 > 7]$ without $\Box$[the number of planets > 7] being true? However, doing all this would take too much time and divert attention from the main issues of epistemology that we want to study. So we will be content with ML as it is.

In looking back at ML there are several points to notice. First of all, ML provides a language and an axiomatic framework for explicating the meaning of necessity in L_Γ. It shows, therefore, how the axiomatic method can be used to study semantical properties of first-order languages and theories. In the next chapter we shall add functional symbols to ML and use the extended language to explicate the idea of knowledge that we have discussed in this chapter.

24 The Private Epistemological Universe, Belief, and Knowledge

In this chapter we develop a mathematical characterization of the concept of knowledge described in section 23.2. We begin with a discussion of the structure of the private epistemological universe. Then I present two axiomatic formalizations of belief that we need to formulate rules of inference in epistemic logic. Finally I delineate an epistemological language in which I explicate the meaning of knowledge.

24.1 The Private Epistemological Universe

In chapter 23 we discussed properties of the epistemological universe in which we live and indicated how we would use them in our pursuit of knowledge. The universe has other properties as well and I present an axiomatic description of them below. But first a second look at PE 2 and PLV.

24.1 A Reformulation of PLV, PE 3

In order that we obtain a good understanding of the import of PE 2 and PLV, we must express PLV more systematically than we did before. One way to do so is as follows: Let Γ_i, $i = 1, \ldots, k$, and C denote characteristics. The Γ_i are said to *generate* C when anything that has all the Γ_i has C and when anything that has only some of the Γ_i might lack C. In such a case the Γ_i are *generating factors* and C is a *generated characteristic.* Also $\{\Gamma_1, \ldots, \Gamma_k\}$ is *a generating set of* C. If only one set can generate C, the Γ_i constitute *the* generating set of C. Finally, an *inductive generalization* is a variable hypothetical that connects two mutually exclusive sets of generated characteristics; e.g., anything that has the characteristics C_1, C_2, and C_3 will have the characteristics C_4 and C_5. For the purpose of such generalizations, PLV can be formulated as follows:

PE 3 Consider the characteristics of individuals in the universe. There is a finite number of generating factors, $\Gamma_1, \ldots, \Gamma_n$, and a finite number of generated characteristics, $C_1, \ldots, C_N$, with $N > n$. Each of the C_j, $j = 1, \ldots, N$, is generated by one and only one generating set, $\{\Gamma_{t_1}, \ldots, \Gamma_{t_r}\}$, where $t_k \in \{1, \ldots, n\}$, $k = 1, \ldots, r$.[1]

When PLV is phrased in this way, PE 2 can be taken to assert that the characteristics, factors, and generating sets in the universe may be described independently of time and location. Hence together PE 2 and PE 3 insist that each and every object in which we are interested in epistemology can be described in terms of a finite number of characteristics. These characteristics adhere in groups of invariable connections that are generated by a finite number of factors. The number of characteristics in the universe is finite and greater than the number of generating factors.

The terms "factor" and "characteristics" in PE 3 are undefined terms. Their interpretations vary from one branch of epistemology to another; they also vary within a given branch both with the inclinations of scientists and with the content and level of sophistication of discourse; and they vary over time with the development of scientific knowledge. I shall illustrate these facts with examples from chemistry and physics.

In chemistry a factor might be one of the 105 elements in Mendelev's periodic table and a characteristic might be a chemical compound that can be formed by such elements. A factor might also be the atom of one of the elements in Mendelev's table and a characteristic might be a molecule formed by a combination of such atoms. Finally, a factor might be one of three subatomic particles—i.e., a proton, a neutron, or an electron—and a characteristic might be an atom of the periodic table or a molecule of such atoms.

E 24.1 Water is a colorless liquid that flows in rivers, forms lakes and oceans, and is either polluted, salty, or drinkable. Aristotle believed that water was one of five basic substances that could combine with other substances to form compounds but could not be broken down to simpler substances. His idea was dispelled when H. Cavendish in 1775 succeeded in showing that hydrogen and oxygen—two of Mendelev's elements—combined to form water.

Water can also be viewed as a collection of molecules, each one of which is put together by two hydrogen atoms and one oxygen atom. Atoms are composed of electrically charaged particles called neutrons (0), protons (+), and electrons (−). The hydrogen atom contains one proton and one electron; the oxygen atom contains one neutron, eight protons, and eight electrons.

A physicist might agree that matter is made of atoms and that atoms are composed of protons, neutrons, and electrons. However, he might equally well insist that the basic building blocks of matter are leptons and quarks and identify "factor" with lepton or quark and "characteristic" with subatomic particle. In fact, if he views the universe as consisting of both matter and antimatter, he will include among his factors antileptons and antiquarks and admit as characteristics the antiparticles they generate.

E 24.2 There are six leptons; one is the electron; another is the electron neutrino. There are also six quarks. They are called up, down, charm, strange, top, and bottom. Two up quarks and one down quark form a proton. Two down quarks and one up quark form a neutron.

To each lepton corresponds an antilepton. Thus an electron has an antielectron called the positron. Similarly, to each quark corresponds an antiquark, e.g., the antiup quark and the antidown quark. Two antiup quarks and one antidown quark form an antiproton. Two antidown quarks and one antiup quark form an antineutron.

Antimatter can be created in the laboratory by smashing particles together. Note, therefore, that if a particle collides with its antiparticle, the two will anihilate each other.

Once the terms "factor" and "characteristics" are interpreted, the condition $N > n$ guarantees that *some* inductive generalization must be true. Hence the condition also ensures that the prior probability of the truth of any one generalization will be positive. How large and how meaningful such probabilities are remains, however, unknown.

E 24.3 We have written on pieces of paper the names and ages at death of all Norwegian poets who died before January 1, 1976, crumbled each piece into a ball, and put the balls in an urn. After shaking the urn well, we draw five names —x, y, z, u, and v. The ages at death of these poets are, respectively, 48, 76, 84, 48, and 45. These five ages have the following characteristics in common:

(i) The difference of the two digits divided by 3 leaves a remainder of 1.

(ii) The first digit raised to the power indicated by the second leaves a remainder of 1 when divided by 3.

(iii) The sum of the prime factors of each age is divisible by 3 if we include 1 among the prime factors.

There is no reason to assign a high probability to the event that the next name we draw will have associated with it an age that possesses these three characteristics.[2]

If in E 24.3 we had further investigated the lives of the observed poets, we might have found that x, y, z, u, and v were all blue-eyed redheads. We might also have found that they all wrote poetry about Norwegian scenery and that they all were hard drinkers. There is almost no end to the qualities these five poets might have had in common. But unless we start out with a good hypothesis about Norwegian poets, the chance is small that our search for common traits among the five observed poets will identify traits that we could, with a high degree of confidence, believe were the traits of most Norwegian poets.

The preceding example and the comments that followed suggest that PE 1–PE 3 and observations alone will not get us far in our pursuit of knowledge. We need hypotheses and theories as well. Even with them we may encounter difficulties. However, examples of successful interplays of observations and theory, such as the development of Mendelev's periodic table, are cause for optimism in scientific research. The periodic table began in the 1860s as an interesting inductive generalization on the observation that all known elements could be ordered in a tabular form according to atomic weight and "similarity" of chemical properties. Today the table is a theoretically profound construct whose underlying theory grew out of *E.* Rutherford's conception of the atom as a tiny, positively charged nucleus with a surrounding "cloud" of negatively charged electrons and *N.* Bohr's partitioning of the cloud into shells and subshells, each with a definite electron capacity.

24.1.2 Epistemological Universes

There are all sorts of theories whose subject matter belongs to epistemology. Most of them are partial and only some are axiomatized. An axiomatized theory that can be formulated in a first-order language is a *scientific theory*. For example, the theory of consumer choice is a scientific theory. It is partial because it concerns only a fragment of the subject matter of economics.

If T is a scientific theory and L_T is the first-order language in which it is formulated, then the *epistemological universe of* T is a structure $\mathscr{D}$ for L_T which represents the intended model of T. Conversely, if $\mathscr{D}$ is a structure for a first-order language L, then $\mathscr{D}$ is an epistemological universe only if it is the intended model of an axiomatized scientific theory T that is formulated in L.

In reading the last definition, we should make several mental notes. First, the epistemological universe of a scientific theory T is a theoretical construct. Second, singling out *the* intended model of T is not easy. If $\mathscr{D}$ and $\mathscr{D}'$ are models of a scientific theory T, T by itself cannot distinguish between them since the axioms and the theorems of T are true in both $L(\mathscr{D})$ and $L(\mathscr{D}')$. When $\mathscr{D}$ and $\mathscr{D}'$ are isomorphic, even L_T cannot distinguish between them since $L(\mathscr{D})$ and $L(\mathscr{D}')$ have the same true sentences. However, the scientist who developed T might think of $\mathscr{D}$ rather than $\mathscr{D}'$ as his epistemological universe simply because $|\mathscr{D}|$, the universe of discourse of $\mathscr{D}$ contains the objects he wants to theorize about and $|\mathscr{D}'|$ does not.

There are situations in which a scientist would not care about the constitution of his theory's universe of discourse: If $\mathscr{D}$ and $\mathscr{D}'$ are isomorphic models of T, $|\mathscr{D}|$ and $|\mathscr{D}'|$ differ only in ways that are irrelevant as far as T is concerned. So chances are that a mathematician who insists that η be the standard model of $T(P)$ neither cares about nor knows what the natural numbers in $|\eta|$ look like. Similarly, if $\mathscr{D}$ is the intended model of a comprehensive theory T and if $\mathscr{D}'$ is the intended model of a partial theory T' whose axioms are logical consequences of the axioms of T, we might be able to use $\mathscr{D}$ to construct a model $\mathscr{D}''$ of T' whose universe of discourse differs significantly from $|\mathscr{D}'|$. Why should $\mathscr{D}'$ and not $\mathscr{D}''$ receive the honor of being an epistemological universe? Certainly, a mathematician would be hard put to explain why he should prefer $|\eta|$ to the natural numbers we constructed within KPU. Finally, if the intended interpretation of some of the terms of a theory T denote either unobservable objects or ideal elements, it is likely that the scientist who developed T would not be concerned about the representation of these objects in a model of T.

Outside pure mathematics the principal function of epistemological universes is to serve as descriptive references for scientists who are testing the empirical relevance of their theories. For that purpose, it is important that the universe be as simple as the tests allow. When a scientist tests his theory, he tests only whether the undefined terms of his theory possess the characteristics that his axioms prescribe. If the scientist's data are discrete and his axioms possess a model with a denumerable universe of discourse, the scientist ought to choose his epistemological universe so that it contains denumerably many individuals.

For the purpose of testing a scientific theory, the epistemological universe also ought to be chosen so that it satisfies PE 1–PE 3. In most fields of science PE 1–PE 3 are used, explicitly or implicitly, to justify scientists' search for simple ways to identify objects of interest and describe the relations of these objects to one another. Consequently, most epistemological universes will heed the imperatives postulated in PE 2 and PE 3. How they do it depends on the roles assigned to the two axioms by the respective theories. In some theories PE 2 and PE 3 combine with other postulates to determine interesting theorems. For instance, physicists deduce the principles of the conservation of energy and the conservation of linear momentum from PE 2 and the principles of quantum mechanics. The epistemological universes of such theories will satisfy PE 2 and PE 3 by design. In other theories, such as the theory of consumer choice, the axioms are formulated without reference to time and place. The description of the epistemological universes of such theories will satisfy PE 2 by omitting time and place from the list of factors that render the axioms true, all else being constant. The same description will satisfy PE 3 as well if the axioms of the theory use a finite number of characteristics to delineate the properties of the individuals in the universe.

For ease of reference and to fix our ideas concerning PE 1–PE 3 and epistemological universes, I give an example from classical mechanics.

E 24.4 Let T denote a set of points of *time*, let S denote a set of points in *space*, and assume that $T = R$ and $S = R^3$, where R denotes the set of real numbers. An *individual* is a function $x(\cdot)$: $T \to S$ that satisfies a second-order differential equation of the form

$$\ddot{x}(t) = f(x, \dot{x}, t), \qquad t \in T \tag{24.1}$$

where $x \in S$, $\dot{x}(t) = dx(t)/dt$, $\ddot{x}(t) = d^2x(t)/dt^2$ and $f(\cdot)$: $S \times R^3 \times T \to R^3$. Also, for some $n \in N$, the *universe* is a collection of n interacting individuals; i.e., the universe is a function $X(\cdot)$: $T \to S^n$ that satisfies a second-order differential equation of the form

$$\ddot{X}(t) = F(X, \dot{X}, t), \qquad t \in T \tag{24.2}$$

where $X = (x_1, \ldots, x_n)$, $\dot{X} = (\dot{x}_1, \ldots, \dot{x}_n)$, $\ddot{X}(t) = (\ddot{x}_1(t), \ldots, \ddot{x}_n(t))$, $F(\cdot) = (F_1(\cdot), \ldots, F_n(\cdot))$, and $F_i(\cdot)$: $S^n \times R^{3n} \times T \to R^3$, $i = 1, \ldots, n$.

We assume that the universe U satisfies several conditions. First U satisfies PE 1 and PE 2:

(i) The equations in 24.2 have solutions.

(ii) If $\varphi(\cdot)$: $T \to S^n$ is a solution to equation 24.2 and if, for some $s \in T$ and $r \in R^3$, $\Psi(\cdot)$: $T \to S^n$ and $\xi(\cdot)$: $T \to S^n$ satisfy $\Psi(t) = \varphi(t + s)$ and $\xi_i(t) = \varphi_i(t) + r$, $i = 1, \ldots, n$, $t \in T$, then $\Psi(\cdot)$ and $\xi(\cdot)$ are solutions to equation 24.2.

Next, U satisfies PE 3:

(iii) $F(\cdot)$ belongs to a finite-parameter family of functions. Also $F(\cdot)$ is sufficiently smooth so that the solution to equation 24.2 is uniquely determined by the values $X(0)$ and $\dot{X}(0)$.

Third, U satisfies Galileo's Principle of Relativity:

(iv) If $\varphi(\cdot)$: $T \to S^n$ is a solution to equation 24.2 and if, for some $v \in R^3_{++}$, $\eta(\cdot)$: $T \to S^n$ satisfies $\eta_i(t) = \varphi_i(t) + vt$, $i = 1, \ldots, n$, $t \in T$, then $\eta(\cdot)$ is a solution to equation 24.2.

Finally, U satisfies a condition that ensures that motion in space is invariant under changes in the coordinate system of R^3 that leave the origin and the units of measurement intact:

(v) Let G be a 3×3 orthogonal matrix and let $GF(\cdot)$, GX, and $G\dot{X}$, respectively, be short for $(GF_1(\cdot), \ldots, GF_n(\cdot))$, $(GX_1, \ldots, GX_n)$, and $(G\dot{X}_1, \ldots, G\dot{X}_n)$. Then $GF(X, \dot{X}, t) = F(GX, G\dot{X}, t)$.

In reading conditions i–v note that condition ii implies that $F(\cdot)$ is independent of t. Also conditions ii and iv imply that $F(\cdot)$ depends only on the relative coordinates, $x_j - x_k$, and the relative velocities, $\dot{x}_j - \dot{x}_k$, $j, k = 1, \ldots, n$.

Conditions i–v are not self-contradictory. To wit: The laws of motion of Newtonian mechanics satisfy them. There $F(\cdot)$ is parametrized by a constant G and the masses of the individuals in the universe, $m_1, \ldots, m_n$. Specifically,

$$m_i F_i(X, \dot{X}, t) = -\sum_{j \neq i} \frac{G m_i m_j (x_i - x_j)}{\|x_i - x_j\|^3}, \qquad i = 1, \ldots, n. \tag{24.3}$$

With this $F(\cdot)$ in equation 24.2 the equations have a unique solution through any point $X \in S^n$, with $x_i \neq x_j$, $i \neq j$, $i = 1, \ldots, n$.

24.1.3 A Private Universe for the Theory of Knowledge and PE 4

The preceding discussion left us with an extraordinary variety of epistemological universes. To explicate our concept of knowledge, we need a universe that is not specific to any particular theory and that can be used to talk about matters of interest to historians, sociologists, and weathermen, as well as about matters that pertain to the sciences.

The universe that we have in mind for the theory of knowledge differs in many ways from the epistemological universes we discussed in section 24.1.2. One of these ways is of particular interest to us: in an epistemological universe of the sciences the individuals in the universe of discourse and the functions and predicates that determine their properties are unobservable theoretical entities that are related by description to intersubjectively observable phenomena. In contrast, the individuals and the constants, functions, and predicates that constitute the universe of the theory of knowledge are related by description to objects, acts, and relations in the private world of the person about whose knowledge we are theorizing. Thus we may think of the epistemological universe of a science as objective and refer to the universe of the theory of knowledge as the *private epistemological universe*.

How private the universe of the theory of knowledge is is a matter of scholarly dispute. If the universe is too private, the theory of knowledge becomes meaningless. Therefore, when we develop our formal theory of knowledge in section 24.3, we shall implicitly make the five assumptions listed below. These assumptions limit the privacy of the universe just enough so that we can make sense of the interpretation we propose for the theory.

1. *Common cultural background*: Our theory of knowledge pertains to an individual who belongs to a group $\mathcal{G}$ of people with more or less the same cultural background; e.g., he or she is a literate grown-up citizen of a country in Western Europe or North America.

2. *Common language*: Let A and B be individuals in $\mathcal{G}$ and denote their languages (for the theory of knowledge) by L_Γ^A and L_Γ^B. There is a language

for $\mathscr{G}$, L_Γ, that is an extension of both L_Γ^A and L_Γ^B. Moreover, the logical vocabularies of L_Γ^A and L_Γ^B are identical and the nonlogical vocabularies of L_Γ^A and L_Γ^B have a nonempty intersection. Finally, the rules of formulating wffs, the logical axioms, and the rules of inference that we described in chapter 5 are accepted by both A and B.

3. *Common predicates and constants*: Let A and B be individuals in $\mathscr{G}$ and denote their nonlogical axioms by Γ^A and Γ^B, respectively. Moreover, let P be an n-ary predicate that belongs to the nonlogical vocabularies of both L_Γ^A and L_Γ^B. Then there exist constants, $\theta_1, \ldots, \theta_n$, such that $P(\theta_1, \ldots, \theta_n)$ belongs to both $Cn(\Gamma^A)$ and $Cn(\Gamma^B)$; that is, $P(\theta_1, \ldots, \theta_n)$ is for both A and B either an axiom or a logical consequence of a finite number of axioms.

4. *Common theorems*: Let A and B be individuals in $\mathscr{G}$ and denote their logical and nonlogical theorems by $T(\Gamma^A)$ and $T(\Gamma^B)$, respectively. Moreover, let α denote a formula that is wf in both L_Γ^A and L_Γ^B. Then $\alpha \in T(\Gamma^A)$ if and only if $\alpha \in T(\Gamma^B)$; i.e., if α is a theorem to A, then α is either a postulate or a theorem to B and conversely.

5. *Common facts*: Let A be an individual in $\mathscr{G}$ and denote A's private universe by $\mathscr{E}^A$. Moreover, let α be a wff in L_Γ^A. Finally, let Γ and $T(\Gamma)$, respectively, denote the nonlogical axioms and logical and nonlogical theorems of $\mathscr{G}$ as a whole. Then $T(\Gamma^A) \subset T(\Gamma)$, $\mathscr{E}^A(\alpha) = \mathrm{t}$ if $\alpha \in T(\Gamma)$, and $\mathscr{E}^A(\alpha) = \mathrm{f}$ if $\sim\alpha \in T(\Gamma)$.

Of these assumptions assumptions 1 and 2 ought to be self-explanatory, while assumptions 3–5 are in need of clarifying remarks. We begin with assumption 3.

Let A and B be individuals in $\mathscr{G}$. They need not agree on much. However, if they use the same n-ary predicate P, then there is in the common part of their nonlogical vocabularies an n-tuple of constants, $\theta_1, \ldots, \theta_n$, that they agree must satisfy P. Two examples suffice to illustrate the import of this agreement.

E 24.5 Let A and B be individuals in $\mathscr{G}$ and let P be an unary predicate in the nonlogical vocabularies of L_Γ^A and L_Γ^B. Moreover, let $\mathscr{E}^A$ and $\mathscr{E}^B$, respectively, denote the private epistemological universe of A and B. Finally, assume that both $P^{\mathscr{E}^A}(x)$ and $P^{\mathscr{E}^B}(x)$ assert that x is red. Then there exists a constant θ in L_Γ^A and L_Γ^B such that A insists that $\mathscr{E}^A(\theta)$ is red and such that B insists that $\mathscr{E}^B(\theta)$ is red.

In reading this example note that $|\mathscr{E}^A|$ may differ from $|\mathscr{E}^B|$. Hence A and B need not have the same perception of "red," and they need not agree on the extension of "red."

E 24.6 Let A and B be individuals in $\mathscr{G}$ and let P be an unary predicate in L_Γ^A and L_Γ^B. Moreover, let θ be the constant of assumption 3, and let $\mathscr{E}^A$ and $\mathscr{E}^B$, respectively, denote the private epistemological universes of A and B. Finally, assume that both $P^{\varepsilon^A}(x)$ and $P^{\varepsilon^B}(x)$ assert that x is a rock. Then A will insist that $\mathscr{E}^A(\theta)$ is a rock, and B will "agree" that $\mathscr{E}^B(\theta)$ is a rock.

A's justification for his claim that $P^{\varepsilon^A}(\varepsilon^A(\theta))$ may differ significantly from the arguments that B uses to demonstrate that $P^{\varepsilon^B}(\varepsilon^B(\theta))$. For example, to A a rock may be anything that is hard, solid, and composed of minerals. To B $\mathscr{E}^B(\theta)$ may be a piece of granite and granite may be an igneous rock with very high silica content that is composed of orthoclase, quartz, plagioclase, biotite, muscovite, and hornblende. Then (with the obvious interpretation), A would base his analysis of $P(\theta)$ on the two axioms

Aa: $(\forall x)[P(x) \equiv [H(x) \wedge [S(x) \wedge M(x)]]]$

Ab: $[H(\theta) \wedge [S(\theta) \wedge M(\theta)]]$,

and B would deduce the validity of $P(\theta)$ from the three axioms

Ba: $(\forall x)[G(x) \equiv [[IG(x) \wedge HS(x)] \wedge C^{OQPBMH}(x)]]$

Bb: $(\forall x)[IG(x) \supset P(x)]$

Bc: $G(\theta)$.

If the predicate M belongs to L_Γ^B as well as to L_Γ^A, it is reasonable to require that Γ^B contain

$(\forall x)[C^{OQPBMH}(x) \supset M(x)$.

Then $M(\theta)$ would belong to $Cn(\Gamma^B)$, as required by assumption 3.

Assumption 4 and 5 insist that, for any given individual A in $\mathscr{G}$, $\mathscr{E}^A$'s assignment of truth values to the wffs in L_Γ^A be in accordance with the factual knowledge of the group as a whole. These truth values are the truth values A would end up assigning to the wffs of L_Γ^A if he had the inclination and were to take the time to check all the sources of information available to the members of $\mathscr{G}$. Since A is not likely to pursue truth to this extent, we must interpret assumptions 4 and 5 such that they require $\mathscr{E}^A$'s assignment of truth values to be in accordance with A's potential knowledge. Then these assumptions limit the privacy of A's universe by delimitting the range of what can be known by A.

The factual knowledge of any group evolves over time. Therefore, the constraints which assumptions 1–5 impose on the privacy of an individual's universe will vary over time as well. This allows the possibility that a person's claim to knowledge may be justified in one period and proven wrong in a later period. Such is life. Still it is a matter of much concern to philosophers of science.

Assumptions 1–5 notwithstanding, the possibility of constructing an epistemological universe for the theory of knowledge seems farfetched.

However, a set of urelements with a rich structure, the axioms of KPU, and KA 10 can be used to develop most scientific theories. Hence a sufficiently rich admissible model of KPU*, i.e., of KPU and KA 10, with a highly structured set of urelements, ought to suffice as an epistemological universe for the theory of knowledge.

Since the usefulness of KPU for the theory of knowledge need not be obvious, a few remarks are called for. First the urelements: In chapter 9 the urelements came without a structure and in chapter 20 the urelements were structured in accordance with the axioms of nonstandard real analysis. For the purpose of the theory of knowledge, we shall think of the structure of the urelements as having been delineated in two steps. In the first step we formulate a multisorted language L—like the one we shall describe in section 25.4—to talk about the characteristics of a (given) finite number of different kinds of individuals. These individuals may be the factors and characteristics of PE 3, points in time, locations in space, commodity bundles, real numbers, and many others. Their properties are determined by functions and predicates that satisfy various nonlogical axioms and axiom schemata, Γ. In the second step we formulate—in the way described in section 25.8—a single-sorted first-order language $\hat{L}$ that is formally equivalent to L in the sense that whatever we can assert in L can be asserted in $\hat{L}$ and vice versa. The individuals about whom $\hat{L}$ talks are the urelements of our theory of knowledge. They are structured in accordance with a set of axioms and axiom schemata, $\hat{\Gamma}$, that are the translations in $\hat{L}$ of the axioms and axiom schemata in Γ.

Next KA 10: The structure of the model of KPU* determines the epistemological problems that we can and cannot talk about. We insist that the epistemological universe be a model of KA 10 as well as KPU, first of all because we want to use the methods of real analysis to develop our scientific theories. However, if we think of a whole, e.g., an atom or a molecule, as an object that is not just the sum of all its parts, then we also need KA 10 to form wholes and to ascertain the properties of such wholes in the universe.

There are problems that we cannot talk about within any model of KPU + KA 10. For example, the theory of sets that we formulate with KPU does not recognize the set of all sets as a set. Hence the collection of all sets does not belong in the epistemological universe. It is also likely that, for analogous reasons, most ideas of God will place God outside the universe. What is more uncertain is whether the "self" of a human being has a reasonable representative in the epistemological universe. According to R. Nozick (Nozick 1981, pp. 71–114), the essential characteristic of a person's self is its ability to reflexively self-refer: e.g., the denotation of I in "I know that I am sitting at a table" is the self of the person uttering the sentence and this self refers to itself reflexively. This characteristic of the self suggests that the self must be an element of itself. Nozick even envisions that the self is created in an act in which the self synthezises itself. Now if the self is an element of itself, it is ruled out of the epistemological universe by the axioms of KPU and we cannot discuss problems that involve knowledge of a person's self.

To conclude: For the theory of knowledge we insist that the epistemological universe satisfy PE 1–PE 3 and one other postulate:

PE 4 The universe is a subset of the universe of an admissible model of KPU and KA 10 with a structured set of urelements.

24.2 Logical Probabilities and Their Possible-World Interpretation

A scientist's belief in a proposition A depends on his knowledge. When properly formulated, that part of his knowledge which is relevant for the assessment of the validity of A consists of a set of wffs K. Some of these wffs the scientist knows are true. About others he is less certain. The truth of these wffs depends on the universe in which the scientist is theorizing. Whatever the true universe may be, we will denote the scientist's *belief in* A *on* K by $P(A|K)$.

It is important to keep in mind that the scientist believes in propositions and not in declarative sentences. Therefore we shall interpret $P(A|K)$ as the probability which the scientists, conditional upon the set of possible worlds in which the declarative sentences in K denote truth, assigns to the set of possible worlds in which the declarative sentence A denotes truth; i.e., in the notation of chapter 3, we shall interpret $P(A|K)$ as

$$P(\{\omega \in \Omega : \varphi_\omega(A) = t\} | \{\omega \in \Omega : \varphi_\omega(\Gamma) = t \text{ for all } \Gamma \text{ in } K\}).$$

The purpose of this section is to establish the possibility of interpreting $P(\cdot|\cdot)$ this way. We begin with additive logical probabilities.

24.2.1 Additive Logical Probabilities

Let L_Γ be the language of a consistent first-order theory $T(\Gamma)$; let $\vdash C$ be short for "C is a theorem of $T(\Gamma)$"; and let $P(\cdot)$ be a function, $P(\cdot)\colon L_\Gamma \to [0, 1]$, which satisfies the following conditions:

(i) $P(\sim A) = 1 - P(A)$.

(ii) $P(A) + P(B) - P([A \wedge B]) = P([A \vee B])$.

(iii) If $\vdash A$, then $P(A) = 1$.

(iv) If $\vdash [A \equiv B]$, then $P(A) = P(B)$.

We shall obtain the "possible-world" interpretation of $P(A)$ first for closed wffs of L_Γ and then for open wffs. The results we present are due to J. Łos (Łos 1962, pp. 225–229) and J. E. Fenstad (Fenstad 1968, pp. 156–172).

To obtain the possible-world interpretation of $P(A)$ for closed wffs of L_Γ we proceed as follows: Let Ω denote the set of models of $T(\Gamma)$ and, for each closed wff A, let $\Omega(A)$ denote the subset of Ω in which A is valid. Moreover, let

$$\mathscr{F} = \{S \in \mathscr{P}(\Omega) : S = \Omega(A) \text{ for some closed wff } A\}$$

and define $\lambda(\cdot)\colon \mathscr{F} \to [0, 1]$ by

$$\lambda(\Omega(A)) = P(A), \qquad A \text{ a closed wff in } L_\Gamma.$$

Then Ω represents the set of all possible worlds and $\mathscr{F}$ is a field of subsets of Ω. Moreover, since (by TM 6.11) $\Omega(A) = \Omega(B)$ only if $\vdash [A \equiv B]$, $\lambda(\cdot)$ is well defined and satisfies the conditions of a finitely additive probability measure on $(\Omega, \mathscr{F})$.

It is an interesting fact that $\lambda(\cdot)$ is σ-additive on $(\Omega, \mathscr{F})$. To show why, we let $(\Omega, \mathscr{T})$ denote the topological space generated by Ω and the members of $\mathscr{F}$. Next we observe that if A is a closed wff, then

$$\Omega(A)^c = \Omega(\sim A).$$

Consequently, if $\Omega = \bigcup_{i \in I} \Omega(A_i)$, then $\bigcap_{i \in I} \Omega(\sim A_i) = \varnothing$. From this and the Compactness Theorem, TM 6.12, it follows, first, that there exist an n and a sequence $i_j \in I$, $j = 1, \ldots, n$, such that

$$\bigcap_{j=1}^{n} \Omega(\sim A_{i_j}) = \varnothing;$$

and then, that $\Omega = \bigcup_{j=1}^{n} \Omega(A_{i_j})$. Thus Ω is compact in $(\Omega, \mathscr{T})$. But if Ω is compact and the members of $\mathscr{F}$ are both open and closed in the given topology, then for any closed wffs A and A_i, $i = 1, 2, \ldots$, such that

$$\Omega(A) = \bigcup_{i=1}^{\infty} \Omega(A_i),$$

we can find a finite subsequence of the A_i, A_{i_j}, $j = 1, \ldots, n$, such that

$$\Omega(A) = \bigcup_{j=1}^{n} \Omega(A_{i_j}).$$

The σ additivity of $\lambda(\cdot)$ follows from this and the relations

$$\lambda(\Omega(A)) = \lambda\left(\bigcup_{j=1}^{n} \Omega(A_{i_j})\right) \leqslant \lim_{N\to\infty} \lambda\left(\bigcup_{i=1}^{N} \Omega(A_i)\right) = \lambda(\Omega(A)).$$

The σ additivity of $\lambda(\cdot)$ on $(\Omega, \mathscr{F})$ and UT 15 imply that $\lambda(\cdot)$ can be extended in one and only one way to a σ-additive probability measure $\lambda(\cdot)\colon \sigma(\mathscr{F}) \to [0, 1]$. This result provides us with the required interpretation of $P(\cdot)$ on the set of closed wffs in L_Γ.

To obtain the required interpretation of $P(A)$ when A is not closed, we shall first establish a simple integral representation of $P(\cdot)$. To that end let A be any wff in L and define $\lambda_A(\cdot)\colon \mathscr{F} \to [0, 1]$ by

$$\lambda_A(\Omega(B)) = P([A \wedge B]),\ B \text{ a closed wff in } L_\Gamma.$$

Then $\lambda_A(\cdot)$ is well defined on $(\Omega, \mathscr{F})$ and can be extended in one and only one way to a σ-additive probability measure $\lambda_A(\cdot)$ on $(\Omega, \sigma(\mathscr{F}))$. Moreover, for all $S \in \sigma(\mathscr{F})$,

$$\lambda_A(S) \leqslant \lambda(S).$$

From this and the Radon-Nikodym theorem it follows that there exists a random function $f_A(\cdot)\colon \Omega \to R$ on $(\Omega, \sigma(\mathscr{F}))$ such that, for all $S \in \sigma(\mathscr{F})$,

$$\lambda_A(S) = \int_S f_A(\omega)\, d\lambda(\omega).$$

But if that is the case, then

$$P(A) = \lambda_A(\Omega) = \int_\Omega f_A(\omega)\, d\lambda(\omega),$$

since, for any theorem T in $T(\Gamma)$, $\vdash [A \equiv [A \wedge T]]$ and $\Omega(T) = \Omega$.

In the interpretation of $P(A)$ for which we are searching, $P(A)$ will be represented by an integral in which $f_A(\cdot)$ is replaced by a family of finitely additive probability measures on a suitably chosen family of experiments. To obtain such a representation of $P(A)$ we observe first that the random functions $f_A(\cdot)$ can be chosen such that they satisfy these conditions:

(i) $0 \leqslant f_A(\cdot) \leqslant 1$.

(ii) $f_{A \vee B}(\cdot) + f_{A \wedge B}(\cdot) = f_A(\cdot) + f_B(\cdot)$.

(iii) For any $C \in Cn(\Gamma)$, $f_C(\cdot) = 1$ and $f_{\sim C}(\cdot) = 0$.

Since it is a routine matter to establish this fact, I leave its verification to the reader.

Next we delineate the sought-for family of experiments. In doing that, we can without loss in generality assume that the individual variables of L_Γ are denoted by the sequence $v_1, v_2, \ldots$. So suppose that this is so and let A be a wff with n free variables, $v_{i_1}, \ldots, v_{i_n}$. Moreover, let X_ω denote the universe of discourse of $\omega \in \Omega$ and let

$$A[\omega] = \{x \in X_\omega^\infty : \omega(A_{v_{i_1},\ldots,v_{i_n}}(x_{i_1}, \ldots, x_{i_n})) = t\}.$$

Then $A[\omega]$ consists of all the sequences $x \in X_\omega^\infty$ that satisfy A in the sense that when x_{i_j} is substituted for v_{i_j} in A, $j = 1, \ldots, n$, the resulting wff denotes truth in ω. By varying the A in $A[\omega]$ over the wffs of L_Γ, we obtain a family of subsets of X_ω^∞ that form a field, which we denote by $\mathscr{B}_\omega$. The sought-for family of experiments is given by

$$\{(X_\omega^\infty, \mathscr{B}_\omega); \omega \in \Omega\}.$$

Finally, for each $\omega \in \Omega$, we define $\mu_\omega(\cdot)\colon \mathscr{B}_\omega \to [0, 1]$ by

$$\mu_\omega(A[\omega]) = f_A(\omega), \qquad A \text{ a wff in } L_\Gamma.$$

It can be shown that the $f_A(\cdot)$ can be chosen such that they satisfy conditions i and ii above and are such that $A[\omega] = B[\omega]$ entails $f_A(\omega) = f_B(\omega)$ (see Fenstad 1968, pp. 164–165, for a detailed proof). Suppose that the $f_A(\cdot)$ have been chosen in that way. Then $\mu_\omega(\cdot)\colon \mathscr{B}_\omega \to [0, 1]$ is well defined. Moreover, the properties of $f_A(\cdot)$ imply that $\mu_\omega(\cdot)$ is a finitely additive probability measure on $(X_\omega^\infty, \mathscr{B}_\omega)$ and that $\mu_{(\cdot)}(\cdot)$ satisfies the integral equation

$$P(A) = \int_\Omega \mu_\omega(A[\omega])\, d\lambda(\omega), \qquad A \text{ a wff in } L_\Gamma.$$

For each $\omega \in \Omega$ and wff A with n free variables, $\mu_\omega(A[\omega])$ measures the probability of finding n-tuples of individuals in X_ω that satisfy A in ω. According to the integral above, $P(A)$ equals a weighted average of the probability of finding n-tuples in the universes of different possible worlds that satisfy A in those worlds. Interestingly enough, $P(A)$ can also be interpreted as the probability of finding individuals that satisfy A by a process in which, first, a possible world is chosen in accordance with $\lambda(\cdot)$ and, then, the individuals in X_ω that satisfy A in ω are sampled in accordance with $\mu_\omega(\cdot)$.

The last integral representation of $P(A)$ provides us with the required interpretation of all open wffs in L_Γ. In that respect, a remark is in order:

Let A and B be wffs in L_Γ with n free variables, say $v_1, \ldots, v_n$ and $v_{i_1}, \ldots, v_{i_n}$, respectively, and suppose that B is obtained from A by a change of variables; i.e., suppose that B is $A_{v_1,\ldots,v_n}(v_{i_1}, \ldots, v_{i_n})$. Then the axioms for $P(\cdot)$ do not imply that $P(A) = P(B)$. Hence it need not be the case that $\mu_\omega(A[\omega]) = \mu_\omega(B[\omega])$ for any $\omega \in \Omega$. This is disconcerting. It is, therefore, interesting to note that the theory of exchangeable processes ensures that we can add axioms to the axioms of $P(\cdot)$ and obtain a consistent axiom system in which $P(A) = P(B)$ whenever B can be obtained from A simply by a change of variable. Interesting special cases of such systems are discussed at length in several of Fenstad's aticles on logical probability (see, for instance, Fenstad 1968, pp. 166–170).

When K denotes a collection of wffs in L_Γ such that $P(K) > 0$, we define $P(\cdot|K)$ by

$$P(A|K) = P([A \wedge K])/P(K), \qquad A \text{ in } L_\Gamma.$$

Then $P(\cdot|K)$ is a well-defined, additive logical probability on the wffs of L_Γ whose possible-world interpretation on closed wffs in L_Γ is as required in the introduction to this section.

24.2.2 Superadditive Logical Probabilities

The logical probabilities we shall use in section 24.3 to formalize the idea of belief in epistemology need not be additive. Hence in this subsection we shall consider the problem of establishing possible-world interpretations of superadditive conditional probability measures on first-order languages. To that end, let L_Γ be the language of a first-order theory $T(\Gamma)$; and let $Q(\cdot)\colon L_\Gamma \to [0, 1]$ be a function that satisfies the following conditions:

(i) $Q(\sim A) \leqslant 1 - Q(A)$.

(ii) $Q(A) + Q(B) - Q([A \wedge B]) \leqslant Q([A \vee B])$.

(iii) If $\vdash A$, then $Q(A) = 1$.

(iv) If $\vdash [A \supset B]$, then $Q([A \wedge B]) = Q(A)$.

(v) If $\vdash [A \equiv B]$, then $Q(A) = Q(B)$.

We shall obtain the possible-world interpretation of $Q(A)$ and $Q(A|K)$ for closed wffs A and K and describe a possible integral representation of $Q(A)$ when A is an open wff of L_Γ.

We begin with the representation of $Q(\cdot)$ on the closed wffs of L_Γ: Let Ω denote the set of models of $T(\Gamma)$ and, for each closed wff A of L_Γ, let

$\Omega(A)$ denote the subset of Ω in which A is valid. Moreover, let

$$\mathscr{F} = \{S \in \mathscr{P}(\Omega) : S = \Omega(A) \text{ for some closed wff } A\}$$

and define $\lambda(\cdot)\colon \mathscr{F} \to [0, 1]$ by

$$\lambda(\Omega(A)) = Q(A), \qquad A \text{ a closed wff of } L_\Gamma.$$

Then Ω represents the set of all possible worlds and $\mathscr{F}$ is a field of subsets of Ω. Moreover, since (again by TM 6.11) $\Omega(A) = \Omega(B)$ only if $\vdash [A \equiv B]$, $\lambda(\cdot)$ is well defined. Finally, the properties of $Q(\cdot)$ imply that $\lambda(\cdot)$ satisfies the following conditions for any $S, T \in \mathscr{F}$:

(i) $\lambda(S^c) \leqslant 1 - \lambda(S)$.

(ii) $\lambda(S) + \lambda(T) - \lambda(S \cap T) \leqslant \lambda(S \cup T)$.

(iii) $\lambda(\Omega) = 1$.

Hence $\lambda(\cdot)$ is a superadditive probability measure on $(\Omega, \mathscr{F})$ that provides us with a possible-world interpretation of $Q(\cdot)$ on the closed wffs of L_Γ.

Next the interpretation of $Q(\cdot|K)$: Let K denote a finite conjunction of closed wffs of L_Γ that satisfies the condition

$$0 \leqslant Q(\sim K) < 1.$$

Then, to allow for the possibility of strict inequality in condition ii for $Q(\cdot)$, we define $Q(\cdot|K)\colon L_\Gamma \to [0, 1]$ by

$$Q(A|K) = \frac{Q([A \wedge \sim K]) - Q(\sim K)}{1 - Q(\sim K)}, \qquad A \text{ a wff in } L_\Gamma.$$

When we do, we can easily demonstrate that $Q(\cdot|K)$ is a well-defined superadditive probability measure on L_Γ that satisfies the five conditions we imposed on $Q(\cdot)$ above. Also, the obvious possible-world interpretation of $Q(A|K)$ for closed wffs A of L_Γ becomes $\lambda(\Omega(A)|\,\Omega(K))$, where

$$\lambda(S|\Omega(K)) = \frac{\lambda(S \cup \Omega(\sim K)) - \lambda(\Omega(\sim K))}{1 - \lambda(\Omega(\sim K))} \qquad S \in \mathscr{F}$$

and $\lambda(\cdot|\Omega(K))$ is a superadditive probability measure on $(\Omega, \mathscr{F})$ that satisfies conditions i–iii above. This interpretation is in accord with our representation of conditional belief in equation 15.14.

Our ideas concerning the representation of $Q(A)$ and $Q(A|K)$ when A is not closed are still tentative. However, we believe that the following conjecture is valid: Let $(\Omega, \mathscr{F})$ and $\lambda(\cdot)$ be as described in this subsection; let $(X_\omega^\infty, \mathscr{B}_\omega)$ and $A[\omega]$ be as defined in section 24.2.1; and let

$$P = \{\phi(\cdot): \mathscr{F} \to [0, 1]: \phi(\cdot) \text{ is a probability measure and } \phi(S) \geqslant \lambda(S)$$
$$\text{for all } S \in \mathscr{F}\}.$$

Then there exists a family of functions $f_A(\cdot): \Omega \to [0, 1]$, A a wff in L_Γ, such that a.e. (λ measure)

(i) $0 \leqslant f_A(\omega) \leqslant 1$,

(ii) $f_A(\omega) + f_B(\omega) - f_{A \wedge B}(\omega) \leqslant f_{A \vee B}(\omega)$

and such that

(iii) $Q(A) = \int_0^1 \lambda(\{\omega \in \Omega : f_A(\omega) \geqslant t\}\, dt$,

(iv) $Q(A) = \inf_{\phi \in P} \int_\Omega f_A(\omega)\phi\,(d\omega)$.

Moreover, there exists a well-defined family of superadditive probability measures, $\mu_\omega(\cdot): \mathscr{B}_\omega \to [0, 1]$, $\omega \in \Omega$, such that

(v) $\mu_\omega(A[\omega]) = f_A(\omega)$,

(vi) $Q(A) = \inf_{\phi \in P} \int_\Omega \mu_\omega(A[\omega])\phi\,(d\omega)$, A a wff in L_Γ.

If our conjecture is valid—and the results of G. Choquet (Choquet 1953, pp. 264–290) and P. Huber and V. Strassen (Huber and Strassen 1973, pp. 251–254) suggest that it is—then $Q(A)$ can be interpreted as an infimum of admissible weighted averages of the probability of choosing individuals that satisfy A in the different possible worlds. This analysis of $Q(A)$ is analogous to the characterization of a decision maker's aversion to uncertainty which we developed in section 19.6.

24.2.3 Concluding Remarks

When the $Q(\cdot)$ of section 24.2.2 is additive, then $\lambda(\cdot)$ is additive as well, and the representation of $Q(\cdot|K)$ reduces to

$$\lambda(S|\Omega(K)) = \lambda(S \cap \Omega(K))/\lambda(\Omega(K)).$$

With that remark we conclude our discussion of the possible-world interpretation of $P(\cdot)$, $P(\cdot|K)$, $Q(\cdot)$, and $Q(\cdot|K)$. In the remainder of this chapter we shall only consider probabilities on closed wffs; and in the next chapter we shall work with additive probabilities. Therefore, the missing proof in section 24.2.2 notwithstanding, our discussion of the representation of logical probabilities does suffice for the immediate purposes of this book.

24.3 An Axiomatization of Knowledge

In this section we shall develop a two-sorted language, *EL*, to explicate the idea of knowledge that we discussed in chapter 23. The language is two-sorted because it conttains two kinds of variables—individual variables, whose values are taken to be real numbers, and propositional variables, whose values are intended to be closed wffs of some given first-order language L_{Γ}, e.g., L_{KPU^*}.

24.3.1 The Symbols

The logical vocabulary of EL consists of the standard symbols $\sim$, $\supset$, [ ], ( ), $\forall$, $=$, and one new symbol, $|$. In addition, there is an infinite list of individual variables, $x, y, z, x_1, y_1, z_1, \ldots$, and an infinite list of propositional variables, $p, q, r, p_1, q_1, r_1, \ldots$.

The nonlogical vocabulary consists of three sets of symbols. In the first set we find two individual constant symbols, 0, 1; one unary function symbol, $(\cdot)^{-1}$; three binary function symbols, $+, \cdot, -$; and a binary predicate symbol, $\leqslant$. In the second set we find two unary function symbols, N and $\Box$; three binary function symbols, I, Kn, and Bl; and four unary predicates CL, Γ, Ξ, TCL. In the third set we find one binary function symbol, P.

The nonlogical vocabulary generates two kinds of terms, individual terms whose values are individuals and propositional terms whose values are declarative sentences. Of these, the propositional terms are defined inductively as follows:

(ti) Propositional variables and constants are propositional terms.
(tii) If u and v are propositional terms, then Nu and $I(u, v)$ are propositional terms.
(tiii) If u and v are propositional terms, then $\Box u$, $\mathrm{Kn}(u, v)$, and $\mathrm{Bl}(u, v)$ are propositional terms.

The individual terms are defined inductively by the following:

(tiv) Individual variables and constants are individual terms.
(tv) If u and v are propositional terms, then $P(u|v)$ is an individual term.
(tvi) If u and v are individual terms, then $(u)^{-1}$. $(u + v)$, $(u \cdot v)$ and $(u - v)$ are individual terms.

Similarly, the nonlogical vocabulary determine two sets of atomic formulas. One set concerns individual terms and is described by the following:

(fi) If u and v are individual terms, then $[u = v]$ and $[u \leqslant v]$ are wffs.

The other set concerns propositional terms and is described as follows:

(fii) If u is a propositional term, then u, $CL(u)$, $\Gamma(u)$, $\Xi(u)$ and $TCL(u)$ are wffs.

From these two sets of wffs we obtain the remaining wffs inductively in accordance with the following rules:

(fiii) If A is wf, then $\sim A$ is a wff.
(fiv) If A and B are wffs, then $[A \supset B]$ is a wff.
(fv) If A is a wff and if a is an individual variable, then $(\forall a)A$ is a wff.

In reading these rules, note that if u is an individual term and v and w are propositional terms, then $[u = v]$, $[u \leqslant v]$, $[v = w]$, and $[v \leqslant w]$ are not wf. Similarly, u, $[u \supset u]$, and $[u \supset v]$ are not wf.

24.3.2 The Logical Axioms

With some obvious modifications the logical axioms of EL are the same as the axioms of our predicate calculus. Specifically, the axiom schemata PLA 1–PLA 3 are axiom schemata in EL as well:

ELA 1 PLA 1–PLA 3 (section 5.1.3).

The axiom schemata PLA 4 and PLA 5 are rephrased in ELA 2 and ELA 3. In reading these axioms, note that in this chapter a term b is taken to be substitutable for a variable a in a wff A only if a and b are terms of the same kind.

ELA 2 Let A and B be wffs and let a be an individual variable that is not a free variable of A. Then

$$[(\forall a)[A \supset B] \supset [A \supset (\forall a)B]].$$

ELA 3 Let A be a wff, let a be an individual variable, and let b be a term that is substitutable for a in A. Then

$$[(\forall a)A \supset A_a(b)].$$

In addition, the axiom schemata PLA 6 and PLA 7 are replaced by the following:

ELA 4 If a is an individual term, then $[a = a]$.

ELA 5 Let A be a wff; let a be and individual variable; and let b and c be individual terms that are substitutable for a in A. Then

$[[b = c] \supset [A_a(b) \supset A_a(c)]]$.

With these axioms and Modus Ponens we can demonstrate that $=$ *is an equivalence relation on individual terms and has the standard substitutive property*. We can also show that $\equiv$ *is an equivalence relation on wffs and has the standard substitutive property*. Proofs of these assertions are left to the reader.

24.3.3 The Nonlogical Axioms

The nonlogical axioms of EL are a varied lot. First there are the axioms for $0, 1, +, \cdot, -, (\cdot)^{-1}$, and $\leqslant$, which we summarize as follows:

ELA 6 If $\mathscr{L}$ is a model of EL and $|\mathscr{L}_1|$ denotes the universe of individuals, then $(|\mathscr{L}_1|, 0, 1, +, \cdot, -, (\cdot)^{-1}, \leqslant)$ is an ordered field.

Next the axioms concerning $\square$, CL, Γ, TCL, and Ξ. In stating them we use M k as shorthand for the M kth axiom schemata of ML, $k = 1, 3, 4, 5$.

ELA 7 If u is a propositional term, then

$[[TCL(u) \supset \Xi(u)] \wedge [[\Xi(u) \supset CL(u)] \wedge [CL(u) \supset \Gamma(u)]]]$.

ELA 8 M 1 and M 3–M 5 (section 23.5.1).

ELA 9 If u and v are propositional terms, then

(i) $[\Gamma(u) \supset [\Gamma(Nu) \wedge \Gamma(\square u)]]$;

(ii) $[[\Gamma(u) \wedge \Gamma(v)] \supset \Gamma(I(u, v))]$;

(iii) $[[\Gamma(u) \wedge \Xi(v)] \supset [\Gamma(Kn(u, v)) \wedge \Gamma(Bl(u, v))]]$.

ELA 10 If u and v are propositional terms, then

(i) $[\Xi(u) \supset \sim\Xi(Nu)]$;

(ii) $[[\Xi(u) \wedge \Xi(v)] \supset \Xi(I(Nu, v))]$;

(iii) $[\Xi(u) \supset N\square Nu]$;

(iv) $[CL(u) \supset [N\square Nu \supset \Xi(u)]]$.

In the intended interpretation of EL, the extensions of CL and TCL are, respectively, the closed wffs of L_Γ and the logical and nonlogical theorems in L_Γ. Moreover, in A. Rényi's phraseology, the extension of Ξ is to be the collection of wffs in L_Γ that constitute *admissible conditions for* $P(\cdot|\cdot)$. Finally, for each v such that $\Xi(v)$, the extension of Γ is to be the domain of $P(\cdot|v)$.

The axioms for $P(\cdot|\cdot)$ are involved. In order to ease the reading of these axioms we divide them in three groups. Moreover, we make use of three new binary function symbols, C, D, and E, that we define as follows: Let u and v be propositional terms. Then

$$C(u, v) =_{\text{df}} NI(u, Nv);$$

$$D(u, v) =_{\text{df}} I(Nu, v);$$

$$E(u, v) =_{\text{df}} C[I(u, v), I(v, u)].$$

In the intended interpretation of EL, $C(u, v)$ expresses the conjunction of u and v (that is, "$u \wedge v$"), $D(u, v)$ expresses the disjunction of u and v (that is, "$u \vee v$"), and $E(u, v)$ insists that u and v are materially equivalent (that is, "$u \equiv v$").

ELA 11 If u, v, and w are propositional terms, then

(i) $[[\Gamma(u) \wedge \Xi(v)] \supset [[0 \leqslant P(u|v)] \wedge [P(u|v) \leqslant 1]]];$

(ii) $[[\Gamma(u) \wedge \Xi(v)] \supset [(P(u|v) + P(Nu|v)) \leqslant 1]];$

(iii) $[[[\Gamma(u) \wedge \Gamma(w)] \wedge \Xi(v)] \supset [((P(u|v) + P(w|v)) - P(C(u, w)|v)) \leqslant P(D(u, w)|v)]].$

ELA 12 If u, v, and w are propositional terms, then

(i) $[[\Gamma(u) \wedge \Xi(v)] \supset [\Box I(v, u) \supset [P(u|v) = 1]]];$

(ii) $[[[\Gamma(u) \wedge \Gamma(w)] \wedge \Xi(v)] \supset [\Box I(v, I(u, w)) \supset [P(C(u, w)|v) = P(u|v)]]];$

(iii) $[[[\Gamma(u) \wedge \Gamma(w)] \wedge \Xi(v)] \supset [\Box I(v, E(u, w)) \supset [P(u|v) = P(w|v)]]].$

ELA 13 If u, v, and w are propositional terms, then

(i) $[[\Xi(u) \wedge \Xi(v)] \supset [\Box I(u, v) \supset [P(Nu|v) < 1]]];$

(ii) $[[\Gamma(w) \wedge [\Xi(u) \wedge \Xi(v)]] \supset [\Box I(u, v) \supset [P(w|u) = (1 - P(Nu|v))^{-1}(P(D(w, Nu)|v) - P(Nu|v))]].$

In the intended interpretation of EL, ELA 11 and ELA 12 insist that, for each admissible condition $v \in \Xi$, $P(\cdot|v)$ is a superadditive probability measure on Γ which—with $\vdash A$, $\vdash [A \supset B]$, and $\vdash [A \equiv B]$, respectively, replaced by $\Box I(v, u)$, $\Box I(v, I(u, w))$, and $\Box I(v, E(u, w))$—satisfies the conditions we imposed on $Q(\cdot)$ in section 24.2.2. Similarly, ELA 12 (i)—with u replaced by v—and ELA 13 impose conditions on $P(\cdot|\cdot)$ which for superadditive logical probabilities are appropriate analogues of the conditions we imposed on conditional probability measures in section 18.4.1. Here Ξ has taken the place of Rényi's bunch of events, v has replaced the event B, and $C \subset B$ has become $\Box I(u, v)$.

Finally, we postulate the axioms for $\mathrm{Bl}(\cdot,\cdot)$ and $\mathrm{Kn}(\cdot,\cdot)$:

ELA 14 If u and v are propositional terms, then

(i) $[[\Gamma(u) \wedge \Xi(v)] \supset [\mathrm{Bl}(u, v) \equiv [P(u|v) = 1]]]$;

(ii) $[[\Gamma(u) \wedge \Xi(v)] \supset [\mathrm{Bl}(u, v) \supset \mathrm{Bl}(\mathrm{Bl}(u, v), v)]]$.

ELA 15 If u and v are propositional terms, then

(i) $[[\Gamma(u) \wedge \Xi(v)] \supset [\mathrm{Kn}(u, v) \equiv [u \wedge \mathrm{Bl}(u, v)]]]$;

(ii) $[[\Gamma(u) \wedge \Xi(v)] \supset [\mathrm{Kn}(u, v) \supset \mathrm{Bl}(\mathrm{Kn}(u, v), v)]]$.

In the intended interpretation of EL, ELA 14 insists that if v is an admissible condition, then we would believe u on v if and only if we could be absolutely sure on v that u. Moreover, if we believe u on v, we must also believe on v that we believe u on v. Finally, ELA 15 insists that if v is an admissible condition, then we would know that u on v if and only if (1) it is the case that u and (2) we believe that u on v. Moreover, if we know that u on v, we must also believe on v that we know that u on v.

24.3.4 The Rules of Inference

The rules of inference of EL are the Modus Ponens, the rule of generalization for individuals, and a rule of inference for $\Box$. Specifically, we have the following:

ERI 1 Let A and B be wffs. From A and $[A \supset B]$ we infer B.

ERI 2 Let A be a wff. From A, if a is an individual variable, we infer $(\forall a)A$.

ERI 3 If u is a propositional term and a tautological consequence of ELA 1 and, M 1 then from u we infer $\Box u$.

24.5 The Intended Interpretation of EL

To interpret our epistemological language we must first say what we mean by a structure for EL. A structure for EL is a 10-tuple,

$$\mathscr{L}_{\mathrm{L}_\Gamma} = (\mathscr{L}_f, \mathscr{L}_l, \mathscr{X}, R, \mathscr{E}, \varphi, R_\Box, R_{\mathrm{Bl}}, R_{\mathrm{Kn}}, P^{\mathscr{L}}),$$

whose components are as follows:

1. L_Γ is a given first-order language, e.g., $L_{\mathbf{KPU}^*}$.

2. $\mathscr{L}_f = (|\mathscr{L}_f|, N_{\mathscr{L}_f}, F^{\mathscr{L}_f}, G^{\mathscr{L}_f})$ is a structure for a first-order language whose nonlogical vocabulary consists of the individual constant, function, and predicate symbols of EL.

3. $\mathscr{L}_l = (|\mathscr{L}_l|, N_{\mathscr{L}_l}, F^{\mathscr{L}_l}, G^{\mathscr{L}_l})$ is a structure for a language whose nonlogical vocabulary consists of the propositional function and predicate symbols of EL. Specifically, $F^{\mathscr{L}_l}$ contains the interpretations in $\mathscr{L}$ of N, I, Kn, Bl, and $\square$ which we denote by $N^{\mathscr{L}}$, $I^{\mathscr{L}}(\cdot)$, $\mathrm{Kn}^{\mathscr{L}}(\cdot)$, $\mathrm{Bl}^{\mathscr{L}}(\cdot)$, and $\square^{\mathscr{L}}$, respectively. Moreover, $G^{\mathscr{L}_l}$ contains the interpretations in $\mathscr{L}$ of TCL, Ξ, CL, and Γ which we denote, respectively, by $TCL^{\mathscr{L}}(\cdot)$, $\Xi^{\mathscr{L}}(\cdot)$, $CL^{\mathscr{L}}(\cdot)$, and $\Gamma^{\mathscr{L}}(\cdot)$. Finally, $N^{\mathscr{L}}$ and $I^{\mathscr{L}}$, respectively, designate the negation sign of L_Γ and the material implication sign of L_Γ; $|\mathscr{L}_l|$ is the smallest set of wffs that contains the closed wffs of L_Γ and that contains $N^{\mathscr{L}}A$, $I^{\mathscr{L}}(A, B)$, $\square^{\mathscr{L}}A$, $\mathrm{Kn}^{\mathscr{L}}(A, B)$, and $\mathrm{B}l^{\mathscr{L}}(A, B)$ if it contains A and B; and $N_{\mathscr{L}_l}$ consists of all the names of the elements of $|\mathscr{L}_l|$—one name for each wff and different names for different wffs.

For the sake of being concrete, we shall insist that the extensions of $CL^{\mathscr{L}}(\cdot)$ and $TCL^{\mathscr{L}}(\cdot)$, respectively, coincide with the collection of all the closed wffs of L_Γ and contain the collection of closed logical theorems of L_Γ. Moreover, we shall insist that the extension of $\Gamma^{\mathscr{L}}(\cdot)$ is a proper subset of $|\mathscr{L}_l|$.

4. $\mathscr{X}$ is a set of structures for L_Γ, R is a reflexive, transitive relation on $\mathscr{X}$, and $\mathscr{E}$ is a member of $\mathscr{X}$ that is taken to represent the epistemological universe. We assume that $\{H \in \mathscr{X} : \mathscr{E}RH\}$ is not empty.

5. Let $CL^{\mathscr{L}}$ denote the extension of $CL^{\mathscr{L}}(\cdot)$. Moreover, for each $H \in \mathscr{X}$, let $H(\cdot)$: $CL^{\mathscr{L}} \to \{t, f\}$ be such that $H(A)$ denotes the truth value of A in H. Then $\varphi(\cdot)$: $CL^{\mathscr{L}} \times \mathscr{X} \to \mathscr{P}(\mathscr{X})$ is defined by

$$\varphi(A, H) = \{H' \in \mathscr{X} : HRH' \text{ and } H'(A) = t\}.$$

6. $R_\square \subset \mathscr{X} \times \mathscr{P}(\mathscr{X})$ and $(H, E) \in R_\square$ if and only if $H \in \mathscr{X}$ and $E = \{H' \in \mathscr{X} : HRH'\}$.

7. $R_{\mathbf{Bl}} \subset \mathscr{X} \times \mathscr{P}(\mathscr{X}) \times \mathscr{P}(\mathscr{X})$, $R_{\mathbf{Kn}} \subset \mathscr{X} \times \mathscr{P}(\mathscr{X}) \times \mathscr{P}(\mathscr{X})$ and $(H, A, B) \in R_{\mathbf{Kn}}$ only if $H \in A$ and $(H, A, B) \in R_{\mathbf{Bl}}$.

8. $P^{\mathscr{L}}(\cdot|\cdot)$: $\mathscr{P}(\mathscr{X}) \times \mathscr{P}(\mathscr{X}) \to [0, 1]$.

Before we can use $\mathscr{L}$ to interpret EL we must, for each $H \in \mathscr{X}$, extend the domain of definition of $H(\cdot)$ to $|\mathscr{L}_l|$, and we must extend the domain of definition of $\varphi(\cdot)$ to $|\mathscr{L}_l| \times \mathscr{X}$. This we do by induction as follows: Let Γ_i, $i = 0, 1, \ldots$, be an increasing sequence of sets of wffs that satisfy the following conditions: (i) $\Gamma_0 = CL^{\mathscr{L}}$. (ii) If $A \in \Gamma_i$ for some $i \geqslant 1$, then there are wffs C and D in Γ_{i-1} such that A is C, $N^{\mathscr{L}}C$, $I^{\mathscr{L}}(C,D)$, $\Box^{\mathscr{L}}C$, $\mathrm{Kn}^{\mathscr{L}}(C,D)$, or $\mathrm{Bl}^{\mathscr{L}}(C,D)$. Then our characterization of $|\mathscr{L}_l|$ implies that $|\mathscr{L}_l| = \bigcup_{i=0} \Gamma_i$.

Next observe that, for each $H \in \mathscr{X}$, $H(\cdot)$ is defined on Γ_0 and $\varphi(\cdot)$ is defined on $\Gamma_0 \times \mathscr{X}$. Suppose that we have extended the definition of the $H(\cdot)$ and $\varphi(\cdot)$, respectively, to Γ_{n-1} and $\Gamma_{n-1} \times \mathscr{X}$. If $A \in \Gamma_n$, there are wffs C, $D \in \Gamma_{n-1}$ such that A is C, $N^{\mathscr{L}}C$, $\Box^{\mathscr{L}}C$, $I^{\mathscr{L}}(C,D)$, $\mathrm{Kn}^{\mathscr{L}}(C,D)$, or $\mathrm{Bl}^{\mathscr{L}}(C,\mathrm{D})$. If A is C, we let $H(A) = H(C)$. If A is $N^{\mathscr{L}}C$, we let $H(A) = \mathrm{t}$ or f, according as $H(C) = \mathrm{f}$ or t. If A is $I^{\mathscr{L}}(C,D)$, we let $H(A) = \mathrm{t}$ if $H(C) = \mathrm{f}$ or $H(D) = \mathrm{t}$, and we let $H(A) = \mathrm{f}$ otherwise. If A is $\Box^{\mathscr{L}}C$, we let $H(A) = \mathrm{t}$ or f, according as $(H, \varphi(C,H)) \in R_{\Box}$ or not. If A is $\mathrm{Kn}^{\mathscr{L}}(C,D)$ (or $\mathrm{Bl}^{\mathscr{L}}(C,D)$), we let $H(A) = \mathrm{t}$ or f, according as $(H, \varphi(C,H), \varphi(D,H)) \in R_{\mathrm{Kn}}$ (or $(H, \varphi(C,H), \varphi(D,H)) \in R_{\mathrm{Bl}}$) or not. Finally, we let $\varphi(A,H) = \{H' \in \mathscr{X} : HRH' \text{ and } H'(A) = t\}$.

In reading our description of $\mathscr{L}_{L_\Gamma}$, we make several mental notes. If C is a wff in L_Γ and $H \in \mathscr{X}$, the reflectivity of R implies that $(H, \varphi(C,H)) \in R_{\Box}$ only if $H(C) = t$. Moreover, if C, D are wffs in L_Γ and $H \in \mathscr{X}$, then $(H, \varphi(C,H), \varphi(D,H)) \in R_{\mathrm{Kn}}$ only if $H(C) = \mathrm{t}$ and $(H, \varphi(C,H), \varphi(D,H)) \in R_{\mathrm{Bl}}$. However, since we do not insist that $H \in \varphi(D,H)$, "Gettier cases" are not ruled out of order by our interpretation of EL. Finally, note that if $\mathscr{L}_{L_\Gamma}$ is a model of EL and if C and D are wffs in L_Γ such that $CL^{\mathscr{L}}(C)$ and $\Xi^{\mathscr{L}}(D)$, then $(\mathscr{E}, \varphi(C,\mathscr{E}), \varphi(D,\mathscr{E})) \in R_{\mathrm{Kn}}$ if and only if $\mathscr{E}(C) = \mathrm{t}$ and $(\mathscr{E}, \varphi(C,\mathscr{E}), \varphi(D,\mathscr{E})) \in R_{\mathrm{Bl}}$.

A structure $\mathscr{L}$ with the functions $H(\cdot)$ extended to $|\mathscr{L}_l|$ and with $\varphi(\cdot)$ extended to $|\mathscr{L}| \times \mathscr{X}$ determines an interpretation of EL in the following way: We add the names in $N_{\mathscr{L}_f}$ and $N_{\mathscr{L}_l}$, respectively, as individual and propositional constants to the vocabulary of EL and name the expanded language EL($\mathscr{L}$). Then we interpret the variable-free terms of EL($\mathscr{L}$) by induction on the length of terms. First the propositional terms:

(i) If $a \in N_{\mathscr{L}_l}$, then $\mathscr{L}_l(a)$ is the wff in $|\mathscr{L}_l|$ which a names.
(ii) If a and b are variable-free propositional terms, we let $\mathscr{L}_l(Na)$, $\mathscr{L}_l(I(a,b))$, $\mathscr{L}_l(\Box a)$, $\mathscr{L}_l(\mathrm{Kn}(a,b))$, and $\mathscr{L}_l(\mathrm{Bl}(a,b))$ be, respectively, $N^{\mathscr{L}}(\mathscr{L}_l(a))$, $I^{\mathscr{L}}(\mathscr{L}_l(a), \mathscr{L}_l(b))$, $\Box^{\mathscr{L}}(\mathscr{L}_l(a))$, $\mathrm{Kn}^{\mathscr{L}}(\mathscr{L}_l(a), \mathscr{L}_l(b))$, and $\mathrm{Bl}^{\mathscr{L}}(\mathscr{L}_l(a), \mathscr{L}_l(b))$.

It can be shown that if a is a variable-free propositional term of EL($\mathscr{L}$), then either a is a name or there exist variable-free propositional terms b and c such that a is Nb, $I(b,c)$, $\Box b$, $\mathrm{Kn}(b,c)$, or $\mathrm{Bl}(b,c)$. From this it follows that conditions i and ii determine the interpretation $\mathscr{L}_l(a)$ of all variable-free propositional terms of EL($\mathscr{L}$).

Next we interpret the variable-free individual terms of EL($\mathscr{L}$):

(iii) If $\alpha \in N_{\mathscr{L}_f}$, then $\mathscr{L}_f(\alpha)$ is the individual which α names.

(iv) If u and v are variable-free propositional terms and α is $P(u|v)$, then we interpret α such that

$$\mathscr{L}_f(\alpha) = \mathscr{L}_f(P(u|v)) = \begin{cases} P^{\mathscr{L}}(\varphi(\mathscr{L}_l(u), \mathscr{E})|\varphi(\mathscr{L}_l(v), \mathscr{E})) \text{ if this} \\ \quad \text{term is well-defined, and} \\ 0 \text{ otherwise.} \end{cases}$$

(v) If α and β are variable-free individual terms, than we interpret $(\alpha)^{-1}$, $(\alpha + \beta)$, $(\alpha \cdot \beta)$, and $(\alpha - \beta)$ in the usual way, e.g., by letting $\mathscr{L}_f(\alpha + \beta) = \mathscr{L}_f(\alpha) + \mathscr{L}_f(\beta)$.

It can be shown that if α is a variable-free individual term of EL($\mathscr{L}$), then either α is a name or there exist variable-free individual terms, β and γ, and variable-free propositional terms, u and v, such that α is either $P(u|v)$, $(\beta)^{-1}$, $(\beta + \gamma)$, $(\beta \cdot \gamma)$, or $(\beta - \gamma)$. From this it follows that conditions i–v above determine the interpretation $\mathscr{L}_f(\alpha)$ of all variable-free individual terms.

Next we interpret the closed atomic formulas of EL($\mathscr{L}$). If u and v are variable-free individual terms, we interpret the wffs $[u = v]$ and $(u \leqslant v)$ in the usual way. If u is a variable-free propositional term, we let $\mathscr{L}(u) = \mathscr{E}(\mathscr{L}_l(u))$, and we let $\mathscr{L}(TCL(u)) = \mathrm{t}$ or f according as $\mathscr{L}_l(u)$ satisfies $TCL^{\mathscr{L}}(\cdot)$ or not. Similarly, $\mathscr{L}(\Xi(u)) = \mathrm{t}$ or f according as $\mathscr{L}_l(u)$ satisfies $\Xi^{\mathscr{L}}(\cdot)$ or not. Finally, $\mathscr{L}(CL(u))$ and $\mathscr{L}(\Gamma(u))$, respectively, equal t or f according as $\mathscr{L}_l(u)$ satisfies $CL^{\mathscr{L}}(\cdot)$ and $\Gamma^{\mathscr{L}}(\cdot)$.

Once the variable-free terms and closed atomic formulas of EL($\mathscr{L}$) have been interpreted, the remaining terms and formulas of EL($\mathscr{L}$) and EL can be interpreted in the standard way. I need not repeat those details here.

24.3.6 Salient Properties of the Interpretation of EL

The interpretation of EL that we have described is unambiguous in the following sense:

MTEL 1 Let $\mathscr{L}_{L_T}$ be a structure for EL; let α and a, respectively, be a variable-free individual term and a variable-free propositional term in EL($\mathscr{L}$); and let $\theta_\alpha \in N_{\mathscr{L}_f}$ and $\theta_a \in N_{\mathscr{L}_l}$ be, respectively, the name of $\mathscr{L}_f(\alpha)$ and $\mathscr{L}_l(a)$. Next let b be a term in which no variable except u occurs. If b and u are both individual terms, then $\mathscr{L}_f(b_u(\alpha)) = \mathscr{L}_f(b_u(\theta_\alpha))$; if b is an individual term and u is a propositional term, then $\mathscr{L}_f(b_u(a)) = \mathscr{L}_f(b_u(\theta_a))$; and if both b and u are propositional terms, then $\mathscr{L}_l(b_u(a)) = \mathscr{L}_l(b_u(\theta_a))$. Finally, let A be a wff in EL($\mathscr{L}$) in which no variable except u is free. If u is an individual variable, then $\mathscr{L}(A_u(\alpha)) = \mathscr{L}(A_u(\theta_\alpha))$; and if u is a propositional term, then $\mathscr{L}(A_u(a)) = \mathscr{L}(A_u(\theta_a))$.

The proof of this theorem is standard and left to the reader. I shall also leave to the reader the proof of the next theorem. The necessary arguments can be obtained in the obvious way by generalizing upon the proof of TML 3 in chapter 23.

MTEL 2 If $\mathscr{L}_{L_\Gamma}$ is a model of the axioms of EL and A is a wff, then A is a theorem of EL only if $\mathscr{L}(A) = t$.

That is, the rules of inference of EL are truth-preserving.

The theorems of ML concerning $\Box$, TCL, and CL, are theorems of EL. In particular, we have the following:

MTEL 3 Let u be a propositional term. Then

$[CL(u) \supset [\Box u \equiv TCL(u)]]$.

From this theorem and MTEL 2 it follows that if $\mathscr{L}_{L_\Gamma}$ is a model of EL then all the closed tautologies of L_Γ belong to $TCL^{\mathscr{L}}$. Moreover, if $\mathscr{L}_{L_\Gamma}$ is a model of EL and if in addition $\mathscr{X}$ contains all structures of L_Γ and $R = \mathscr{X} \times \mathscr{X}$, then the closures of all the logical theorems of L_Γ and no others belong to $TCL^{\mathscr{L}}$. Finally, if $\mathscr{L}_{L_\Gamma}$ is a model of EL and if $\mathscr{X}$ consists of all models of $T(\Gamma)$, $R = \mathscr{X} \times \mathscr{X}$, and Γ is a consistent set of wffs, then the closures of all wffs in $Cn(\Gamma)$ and no others belong to $TCL^{\mathscr{L}}$.

Here is an example to help our intuition in these matters.

E 24.7 Let a and b be variable-free terms of L_Γ and let A be a wff of L_Γ with one free variable x. If a and b are substitutable for x in A, then

$[[a = b] \supset [A_x(a) \equiv A_x(b)]]$

is a theorem of L_Γ. Consequently, if u is a propositional term of EL such that, for some model $\mathscr{L}_{L_\Gamma}$ of EL,

$\mathscr{L}_l(u)$ is $[[a = b] \supset [A_x(a) \equiv A_x(b)]]$,

then $H(\mathscr{L}_l(u)) = \text{t}$ for all $H \in \mathscr{X}$ and (as well) $H[\Box^{\mathscr{L}} \mathscr{L}_l(u)) = \text{t}$ for all $H \in \mathscr{X}$. From this, the fact that $\mathscr{L}_l(u)$ is closed, and MTEL 3, we deduce that $\mathscr{L}_l(u) \in TCL^{\mathscr{L}}$.

Note also that if $[a = b]$ and hence $[A_x(a) \equiv A_x(b)]$ are theorems of L_Γ, then both $[a = b]$ and $[A_x(a) \equiv A_x(b)]$ belong to $TCL^{\mathscr{L}}$ if $\mathscr{X}$ is a subset of the collection of models of $T(\Gamma)$.

24.3.7 Theorems of EL

I have constructed a language for talking about the closed wffs of L_Γ. Therefore, even though the axioms and the rules of inference of EL determine all sorts of theorems concerning real numbers, I shall not state any of them here. The theorems that concern the closed wffs in L_Γ and that I state are easy to prove. So I shall provide only hints as to how they can be established. In stating the theorems, I use $\vdash A$ as a symbolic rendition of the assertion "A is a theorem in EL."

24.3.7.1 Useful Properties of $P(\cdot|\cdot)$

In the axioms of EL the collection of terms in Ξ plays the same role which a bunch of events played in Rényi's theory of conditional probability spaces. For ease of reference, I record here one of the properties of Ξ that we need for our discussion of $P(\cdot|\cdot)$.

ELT 1 Let u be a propositional term. Then

$[CL(u) \supset [\Xi(u) \equiv N\Box Nu]]$.

That is, either the propositional term u does not satisfy $CL(\cdot)$ or it satisfies $\Xi(\cdot)$ if and only if it is not the case that "necessarily not u." The significance of this theorem will be spelled out later.

The first properties of $P(\cdot|\cdot)$ recorded below are simple consequences of ELA 1, ELA 7, M 5 (i), ELA 11, ELA 12, and MLT 4. We express them as follows:

ELT 2 Let u, v, and w be propositional terms. Then

(i) $[TCL(I(v,u)) \supset [[\Gamma(u) \wedge \Xi(v)] \supset [P(u|v) = 1]]]$;

(ii) $[TCL(I(v,I(u,w))) \supset [[\Gamma(u) \wedge [\Gamma(w) \wedge \Xi(v)]] \supset [P(C(u,w)|v) = P(u|v)]]]$;

(iii) $[TCL(I(v,E(u,w))) \supset [[\Gamma(u) \wedge [\Gamma(w) \wedge \Xi(v)]] \supset [P(u|v) = P(w|v)]]]$.

Similarly, we have ELT 3:

ELT 3 Let u, v, and w be propositional terms. Then

(i) $[[TCL(u) \wedge \Xi(v)] \supset [[P(u|v) = 1] \wedge [P(Nu|v) = 0]]]$;

(ii) $[TCL(E(u,w)) \supset [[\Gamma(u) \wedge [\Gamma(w) \wedge \Xi(v)]] \supset [P(u|v) = P(w|v)]]]$;

(iii) $[TCL(I(u,w)) \supset [[\Gamma(u) \wedge [\Gamma(w) \wedge \Xi(v)]] \supset [P(C(u,w)|v) = P(u|v)]]]$;

(iv) $[TCL(I(u,w)) \supset [[\Gamma(u) \wedge [\Gamma(w) \wedge \Xi(v)]] \supset [P(D(u,w)|v) = P(w|v)]]]$.

Both ELT 2 and ELT 3 look forbidding, but are not. Just ignore the Γ's and the Ξ's and read them first aloud with "if" and "u is a tautological consequence of v" substituted for "$\supset$" and "$TCL(I(v,u))$." Then ELT 2 (i) becomes the following:

"If u is a tautological consequence of v, the probability of u on v equals 1."

and ELT 3 (iii) reads similarly:

> "If it is a tautology that u is materially equivalent to w, then the probability of u on v equals the probability of w on v."

I shall write down some of the steps in a formal proof of ELT 3 (i) and leave the proof of ELT 2 and ELT 3 (ii)–(iv) to the reader. To prove ELT 3 (i) we first appeal to MLT 3 (ii) and assert

$$[[TCL(u) \wedge \Xi(v)] \supset \Box I(v, u)].$$

Then it follows from ELA 7 that

$$[[TCL(u) \wedge \Xi(v)] \supset [\Gamma(u) \wedge \Xi(v)]]$$

and from ELA 12 (i) and TM 4.1 (with q equal to $[TCL(u) \wedge \Xi(v)]$) that

$$[[TCL(u) \wedge \Xi(v)] \supset [[\Gamma(u) \wedge \Xi(v)] \supset [\Box I(v, u) \supset [P(u|v) = 1]]]].$$

From the preceding three assertions and ELA 11 (i)–(ii), we deduce by repeated use of ELA 1 and Modus Ponens that ELT 3 (i) is valid as stated.

For completeness' sake we also observe that $P(\cdot|\cdot)$ has the following properties:

ELT 4 Let u, v, and w be propositional terms. Then

(i) $[TCL(I(v, NC(u, w))) \supset [[\Gamma(u) \wedge [\Gamma(w) \wedge \Xi(v)]]$
$\supset [(P(u|v) + P(w|v)) \leqslant P(D(u, w))|v)]]]$;

(ii) $[TCL(I(v, I(u, w))) \supset [[\Gamma(u) \wedge [\Gamma(w) \wedge \Xi(v)]]$
$\supset [P(C(w, Nu)|v) \leqslant (P(w|v) - P(u|v))]]]$;

(iii) $[[\Gamma(u) \wedge [\Gamma(w) \wedge \Xi(v)]] \supset [[P(C(u, w)|v) \leqslant P(u|v)]$
$\wedge [P(u|v) \leqslant P(D(u, w)|v)]]]$.

We shall write down some of the steps in a formal proof of ELT 4 (iii) and leave the proofs of ELT 4 (i) and (ii) to the reader. Suppose that ELT 4 (i) and (ii) are valid and observe that if u, v, and w are propositional terms, then in EL it is the case that

$$[v \supset [u \equiv [[u \wedge w] \vee [u \wedge \sim w]]]] \text{ and } [v \supset \sim[[u \wedge w] \wedge [u \wedge \sim w]]]$$

are tautological consequences of ELA 1. From this, M 1, ERI 1, and ERI 3 it follows that the following assertions are theorems of EL:

$$\Box I(v, E(u, D(C(u, w), C(u, Nw))) \text{ and } \Box I(v, NC(C(u, w), C(u, Nw))).$$

But if this is so, then ELA 9 (i) and (ii), ELA 11 (i) and (ii), ELA 12 (i), ELA 11 (iii), TM 4.1, ELA 1 and ELA 12 (iii) imply first that

$$[[\Gamma(u) \wedge [\Gamma(w) \wedge \Xi(v)]] \supset [P(C(C(u, w), C(u, Nw))|v) = 0]]$$

and then that

$$[[\Gamma(u) \wedge [\Gamma(w) \wedge \Xi(v)]] \supset [(P(C(u, w)|v) + P(C(u, Nw)|v)) \leqslant P(u|v)]].$$

From this and ELA 11 (i) follows the validity of the first inequality in ELT 4 (iii). By symmetry,

$$[[\Gamma(u) \wedge [\Gamma(w) \wedge \Xi(v)]] \supset [P(C(w, u)|v) \leqslant P(w|v)]].$$

Hence, by ELA 11 (iii), ELA 12 (iii), and the fact that $[v \supset [[u \vee w] \equiv [w \vee u]]$,

$$[[\Gamma(u) \wedge [\Gamma(w) \wedge \Xi(v)]] \supset [P(u|v) \leqslant P(D(u, w)|v)]],$$

as was to be shown.

24.3.7.2 Good Inductive Rules of Inference and the Properties of $P(\cdot|\cdot)$

The inductive rules of inference in EL are determined by the properties of $P(\cdot|\cdot)$. We shall deem these rules of inference *good* if they contain rules that are natural analogues of the Modus Ponens and if they also can be used to justify inductive inference in scientific research.

To determine whether the inductive rules of inference in EL are good, we must first establish the possibility of a sequential development of $P(\cdot|\cdot)$. That we do in the next two theorems.

ELT 5 Let u and w be propositional terms. Then

$$[[[\Xi(u) \wedge \Xi(w)] \wedge \Xi(C(u, w))] \supset [P(Nu|w) < 1]].$$

To prove this theorem, let the v in ELA 13 (ii) be $D(u, w)$ and observe that $I(w, D(u, w))$ is a tautological consequence of ELA 1 and M 1. From this, ERI 3, and TM 4.1, we first infer $\square I(w, D(u, w))$ and

$$[[\Gamma(Nu) \wedge [\Xi(w) \wedge \Xi(D(u, w))]] \supset \square I(w, D(u, w))]$$

and then, by M 3 (i), ELA 13 (i) and (ii), and an application of ELA 1 and ERI 1,

$$[[\Gamma(Nu) \wedge [\Xi(w) \wedge \Xi(D(u, w))]] \supset [P(Nu|w) = (1 - P(Nw|v))^{-1}(P(D(Nu, Nw)|v) - P(Nw|v))]].$$

But if this is so, then the fact that $TCL(E(D(Nu, Nw), NC(u, w)))$, ELT 3 (ii), and obvious arguments imply that

$$[[[\Xi(u) \wedge \Xi(w)] \wedge \Xi(C(u, w))] \supset [[P(NC(u, w)|v) < 1] \wedge [P(Nu|w) = (1 - P(Nw|v))^{-1}(P(NC(u, w)|v) - P(Nw|v))]]],$$

from which follows the validity of ELT 5.

ELT 6 Let u, a, and w be propositional terms. Then

$$[[\Gamma(w) \wedge [[\Xi(u) \wedge \Xi(a)] \wedge \Xi(C(u,a))] \supset [P(w|C(u,a)) = (1 - P(Nu|a))^{-1}(P(D(w,Nu)|a) - P(Nu|a))]]].$$

The proof of ELT 6 is simple. Let v be $D(u,a)$ and observe that $I(C(u,a), D(u,a))$, and $I(a, D(u,a))$ are tautological consequences of ELA 1. From this we infer $\Box I(C(u,a), D(u,a))$ and $\Box I(a, D(u,a))$. But if this is the case, then ELA 13 (i) and (ii), ELA 1, ERI 1, and MLT 4 can be used to demonstrate that the antecedent in ELT 6 materially implies that

$$[P(w|C(u,a)) = (1 - P(D(Nu,Na)|v))^{-1}(P(D(w,D(Nu,Na)))|v) - P(D(Nu,Na)|v))],$$

$$[P(Nu|a) = (1 - P(Na|v))^{-1}(P(D(Nu,Na))|v) - P(Na|v))],$$

$$[(1 - P(Nu|a))^{-1} = (1 - P(D(Nu,Na)|v))^{-1}(1 - P(Na|v))],$$

$$[P(D(w,Nu))|a) = (1 - P(Na|v))^{-1}(P(D(w,D(Nu,Na))|v) - P(Na|v))].$$

From these equalities it follows that the antecedent in ELT 6 materially implies that

$$[P(w|C(u,a)) = (1 - P(Nu|a))^{-1}(P(D(w,Nu)|a) - P(Nu|a))],$$

as was to be shown.

In the statement and proof of ELT 6 we wrote $P(w|C(u,a))$ rather than $P(w|u,a)$, which is the customary way of expressing the conditional probability of w given u and a. To simplify our notation, we shall from now on adhere to custom and write $P(w|u,a)$ rather than $P(w|C(u,a))$.

Theorem ELT 6 establishes the possibility of a sequential development of $P(\cdot|\cdot)$. This result, together with ELT 2 (i) and the easily established fact that

$$[TCL(I(v,I(w,u))) \supset [[\Gamma(u) \wedge [\Xi(w) \wedge [\Xi(v) \wedge \Xi(C(w,v))]]] \supset [P(u|w,v) = 1]]],$$

implies that the inductive rules of inference in EL contain rules that are natural analogues of the Modus Ponens.

We can also show that the inductive rules of inference in EL contain rules that can be used to justify inductive inference in scientific research. For that purpose we need the following interesting theorem.

ELT 7 Let u, a, and w be propositional terms. Then

$$[TCL(I(a, I(w, u))) \supset [[\Gamma(w) \wedge [[\Xi(u) \wedge \Xi(a)] \wedge \Xi(C(u, a)]]$$
$$\supset [P(w|a) \leqslant P(w|u, a)]]].$$

When $P(Nu|a) > 0$, the inequality in ELT 7 becomes a strict inequality.

The import of ELT 7 can be intuited from the next example:

E 24.8 Let $A(x)$ assert that either x lacks at least one of the characteristics C_1, C_2, and C_3 or x has the characteristics C_4 and C_5; and let w be $(\forall x)A$. Also, suppose that we have observed y and found that y has the characteristics $C_1, \ldots, C_5$. Finally, let u be $A_x(y)$ and think of a as expressing our knowldge before we observed y. Then, if $P(Nu|a) > 0$, ELT 7 insists that our observing u must increase the probability we assign to w.

As long as we insist on a *formal* justification of inductive inference in science, ELT 7 is as far as we can go with EL. However, if we are willing to argue informally, we can generalize upon ELT 7 and E 24.8 to establish interesting sufficient conditions for the validity of inductive inference in scientific research. This we do in the next example.

E 24.9 Suppose that L_Γ contains infinitely many constants, $\theta_1, \theta_2, \ldots$, and let A be a wff in L_Γ with just one free variable x.

In addition, let $\tilde{A}$ be $(\forall x)A$ and suppose that $\Xi(\sim \tilde{A})$. Finally, let $\prod_{i=1}^n A_x(\theta_i)$ be short for $[A_x(\theta_1) \wedge [\ldots[A_x(\theta_{n-1}) \wedge A_x(\theta_n)]\ldots]]$, and suppose that $\Xi(A_x(\theta_i))$, $i = 1, \ldots, n$, and that $\Xi(\prod_{i=1}^n A_x(\theta_i))$. Then, for any v such that $TCL(v)$,

$$\lim_{n\to\infty} P\left(\sim \prod_{i=1}^{n} A_x(\theta_i)|\tilde{A}, v\right) = 1$$

implies that

$$\lim_{n\to\infty} P(\tilde{A}|A_x(\theta_n), \ldots, A_x(\theta_1), v) = 1.$$

Easy informal arguments based on ELA 13, ELT 7, and ELT 8 (given below) suffice to establish this assertion. Hence I leave its proof to the reader and only note that the relevance of v will be explicated in ELT 8.

In reading E 24.9, the reader should observe that $\lim_{n\to\infty} P(\prod_{i=1}^n A_x(\theta_i)| \sim \tilde{A}, v) = 0$ constitutes J. M. Keynes's sufficient condition for the validity of his inductive rules of inference (see Keynes 1921, pp. 236–237). Our condition reduces to Keynes's condition when $P(\cdot|v)$ is additive.

Now, if the scientific method is such that a false hypothesis eventually will be found out, then ELT 7 and E 24.9 provide the sought-for justification of inductive inference in scientific research. With that remark, our discussion of good inductive rules of inference has come to a happy ending.

24.3.7.3 The Existence of $P(\cdot|\cdot)$

Our interpretation of logical probabilities in section 24.2 demonstrated the meaningfulness of the idea of additive and superadditive probability measures on first-order languages. In this subsection we shall see that the idea of a family of conditional probability measures that satisfies ELA 11–ELA 13 is equally meaningful. This we do by establishing an interesting analogue of A. Rényi's fundamental theorem on conditional probability spaces, T 18.9.

ELT 8 Let v, v_0, and w be propositional terms. Then

(i) $[[\Gamma(w) \wedge [TCL(v) \wedge TCL(v_0)]] \supset [P(w|v) = P(w|v_0)]]$;

(ii) $[[TCL(v_0) \wedge [\Gamma(w) \wedge \Xi(v)]] \supset [[P(Nv|v_0) < 1] \wedge [P(w|v)$
$= (1 - P(Nv|v_0))^{-1}(P(D(w, Nv)|v_0) - P(Nv|v_0))]$.

ELT 8 is an analogue of T 18.9 since it demonstrates the existence of a uniquely defined superadditive probability measure $Q(\cdot)$ "on Γ," $P(\cdot|v_0)$, such that, for all propositional terms w and v,

$$[[\Gamma(w) \wedge \Xi(v)] \supset [[Q(Nv) < 1] \wedge [P(w|v)$$
$$= (1 - Q(Nv))^{-1}(Q(D(w, Nv)) - Q(Nv))]]].$$

The proof of ELT 8 is easy. It follows from ELA 7 and ELT 3 (i) that

$$[[TCL(v) \wedge TCL(v_0)] \supset [P(Nv|v_0) = 0]].$$

Moreover, the easily established fact that

$$[[\Gamma(w) \wedge TCL(v)] \supset TCL(E(w, D(w, Nv)))]$$

and ELT 3 (ii) imply that

$$[[\Gamma(w) \wedge [TCL(v) \wedge TCL(v_0)]] \supset [P(w|v_0) = P(D(w, Nv)|v_0)]].$$

From these two observations, MLT 3 (ii), ELA 13 (ii), and the transitivity of $=$ follows the validity of ELT 8 (i).

The validity of ELT 8 (ii) is an immediate consequence of MLT 3 (ii) and ELA 13 (i) and (ii) and needs no further comment.

When interpreting ELA 8, it is interesting to make the following observations: Suppose that $\mathscr{L}_{L_\Gamma}$ determines a model of EL. Then, for all $\mathscr{L}_l(v) \in TCL^{\mathscr{L}}$,

$$\varphi(\mathscr{L}_l(v), \mathscr{E}) = \{H \in X; \mathscr{E}RH\}.$$

Consequently, for all $\mathscr{L}_l(v_0)$, $\mathscr{L}_l(v) \in TCL^{\mathscr{L}}$ and $\mathscr{L}_l(w) \in \Gamma^{\mathscr{L}}$,

$$\mathscr{L}_f(P(w|v)) = P^{\mathscr{L}}(\varphi(\mathscr{L}_l(w), \mathscr{E})|\varphi(\mathscr{L}_l(v), \mathscr{E})) = P^{\mathscr{L}}(\varphi(\mathscr{L}_l(w), \mathscr{E})|\varphi(\mathscr{L}_l(v_0), \mathscr{E}))$$
$$= \mathscr{L}_f(P(w|v_0))$$

in accordance with ELT 8 (i). Moreover, if we define $Q^{\mathscr{L}}(\cdot)\colon \Gamma^{\mathscr{L}} \to [0, 1]$ by

$$Q^{\mathscr{L}}(\mathscr{L}_l(w)) = P^{\mathscr{L}}(\varphi(\mathscr{L}_l(w), \mathscr{E})|\varphi(\mathscr{L}_l(v_0), \mathscr{E}))$$

for some $\mathscr{L}_l(v_0) \in TCL^{\mathscr{L}}$, then for all $\mathscr{L}_l(w) \in \Gamma^{\mathscr{L}}$ and $\mathscr{L}(v) \in \Xi^{\mathscr{L}}$, $Q^{\mathscr{L}}(\mathscr{L}_l(Nv)) < 1$ and

$$\mathscr{L}_f(P(w|v)) = (1 - Q^{\mathscr{L}}(\mathscr{L}_l(Nv)))^{-1}(Q^{\mathscr{L}}(\mathscr{L}_l(D(w, Nv))) - Q^{\mathscr{L}}(\mathscr{L}_l(Nv)))$$

in accordance with ELT 8 (ii). When $Q^{\mathscr{L}}(\cdot)$ is additive, the last equation reduces to

$$\mathscr{L}_f(P(w|v)) = Q^{\mathscr{L}}(\mathscr{L}_l(C(w, v)))/Q^{\mathscr{L}}(\mathscr{L}_l(v)).$$

24.3.7 Theorems concerning Kn(·) *and* Bl(·)

So much for $P(\cdot|K)$. Next we shall establish some of the salient properties of Kn(·). We begin by observing that if u and v are propositional terms such that $TCL(u)$ and $\Xi(v)$, then Kn(u, v). Hence if u is a tautological consequence of ELA 1 and M 1, then Kn(u, v). To wit, ELT 9.

ELT 9 Let u and v be propositional terms. Then

$[[TCL(u) \wedge \Xi(v)] \supset \text{Kn}(u, v)]$.

From ELA 9 (ii), MLT 4, ELA 7, and ELT 2 (i), it follows that

$[[TCL(u) \wedge \Xi(v)] \supset [P(u|v) = 1]]$.

Moreover, from ELA 9 (i) and ELA 8 we deduce that

$[[TCL(u) \wedge \Xi(v)] \supset u]$.

But if this is so, we can use ELA 14 (i), ELA 15 (i), and TM 5.15 to establish the theorem.

It ought to be the case that if u is a propositional term, then we either know that u or we do not know that u. Moreover, we shall know that u only if we do not know that not u. Finally, if we know that u, we shall know that we know that u. In the next three theorems we demonstrate the validity of these suppositions.

The predicate-calculus analogue of T 4.1 implies ELT 10.

ELT 10 Let u and v be propositional terms. Then

$[[\Gamma(u) \wedge \Xi(v)] \supset [\sim\text{Kn}(u, v) \vee \text{Kn}(u, v)]]$.

In addition, since $[[\Gamma(u) \wedge \Xi(v)] \supset [\text{Kn}(Nu, v) \supset \sim u]]$ and hence $[[\Gamma(u) \wedge \Xi(v)] \supset [u \supset \sim \text{Kn}(Nu, v)]]$, we can appeal to

$$[[[u \wedge \text{Bl}(u, v)] \supset u] \supset [[u \supset \sim \text{Kn}(Nu, v)] \supset [[u \wedge \text{Bl}(u, v)] \supset \sim \text{Kn}(Nu, v)]]],$$

TM 4.1, ELA 1, and TM 5.15 to establish the validity of ELT 11.

ELT 11 Let u and v be propositional terms. Then

$$[[\Gamma(u) \wedge \Xi(v)] \supset [\text{Kn}(u, v) \supset \sim \text{Kn}(Nu, v)]].$$

Finally, since

$$[[\Gamma(u) \wedge \Xi(v)] \supset [\text{Kn}(\text{Kn}(u, v), v) \supset \text{Kn}(u, v)]],$$

ELT 12 follows from ELT 10 and ELA 15 (i) and (ii).

ELT 12 Let u and v be propositional terms. Then

$$[[\Gamma(u) \wedge \Xi(v)] \supset [\text{Kn}(u, v) \equiv \text{Kn}(\text{Kn}(u, v), v)]].$$

Both $\text{Bl}(\cdot)$ and $\text{Kn}(\cdot)$ have interesting distributive properties that we record next. The first property is one that $\text{Bl}(\cdot)$ and $\text{Kn}(\cdot)$ share with $\Box$.

ELT 13 Let u, v, and w be propositional terms. Then

$$[[[\Gamma(u) \wedge \Gamma(v)] \wedge \Xi(w)] \supset [[\text{Bl}(I(u, v), w) \supset [\text{Bl}(u, w) \supset \text{Bl}(v, w)]] \wedge [\text{Kn}(I(u, v), w) \supset [\text{Kn}(u, w) \supset \text{Kn}(v, w)]]]].$$

To prove this theorem we write H for $[[\Gamma(u) \wedge \Gamma(v)] \wedge \Xi(w)]$ and observe that

$$[H \supset [[\text{Bl}(u, w) \wedge \text{Bl}(I(u, v), w)] \supset [[P(u|w) = 1] \wedge [P(I(u, v)|w) = 1]]]].$$

From this, the fact that $\vdash [[u \wedge [u \supset v]] \supset v]$, M 1, and

$$[H \supset [((P(u|w) + P(I(u, v)|w)) - P(C(u, I(u, v))|w) \leqslant 1]]$$

we deduce, first, that

$$[H \supset [[\text{Bl}(u, w) \wedge \text{Bl}(I(u, v), w)] \supset [P(C(u, I(u, v))|w) = 1]]]$$

and, then, that

$$[H \supset [[\text{Bl}(u, w) \wedge \text{Bl}(I(u, v), w)] \supset [P(v|w) = 1]]].$$

Similar arguments suffice to show that

$$[H \supset [[\text{Kn}(u, w) \wedge \text{Kn}(I(u, v), w)] \supset [v \wedge [P(v|w) = 1]]]].$$

But if this is so, we can use TM 5.3, TM 5.15, ELA 14 (i), and ELA 15 (i) to conclude the proof of the theorem. I leave the writing down of those details to the reader.

Next we observe that Bl(·) and Kn(·) distribute over conjunctions as in ELT 14.

ELT 14 Let u, v, and w be propositional terms. Then

$$[[\Gamma(u) \wedge [\Gamma(v) \wedge \Xi(w)]] \supset [[\mathrm{Bl}(C(u,v),w) \equiv [\mathrm{Bl}(u,w) \wedge \mathrm{Bl}(v,w)]]$$
$$\wedge [\mathrm{Kn}(C(u,v),w) \equiv [\mathrm{Kn}(u,w) \wedge \mathrm{Kn}(v,w)]]]].$$

That is, if u and v are propositional terms such that $\Gamma(u)$ and $\Gamma(v)$, then we know (believe) that both u and v is the case if and only if we both know (believe) that u and know (believe) that v. The proof is easy. Since $\vdash [[u \wedge v] \supset u]$ and $\vdash [[u \wedge v] \supset v]$, we can appeal to ELA 14 (i), ELT 4 (iii), and ELA 15 (i) to establish, first,

$$[[\Gamma(u) \wedge [\Gamma(v) \wedge \Xi(w)]] \supset [\mathrm{Bl}(C(u,v),w) \supset [\mathrm{Bl}(u,w) \wedge \mathrm{Bl}(v,w)]]]$$

and, then,

$$[[\Gamma(u) \wedge [\Gamma(v) \wedge \Xi(w)]] \supset [\mathrm{Kn}(C(u,v),w) \supset [\mathrm{Kn}(u,w) \wedge \mathrm{Kn}(v,w)]]].$$

Next we use ELA 11 (i) and (iii), ELA 14 (i), and ELA 15 (i) to infer, first,

$$[[\Gamma(u) \wedge [\Gamma(v) \wedge \Xi(w)]] \supset [[\mathrm{Bl}(u,w) \wedge \mathrm{Bl}(v,w)] \supset \mathrm{Bl}(C(u,v),w)]]$$

and, then,

$$[[\Gamma(u) \wedge [\Gamma(v) \wedge \Xi(w)]] \supset [[\mathrm{Kn}(u,w) \wedge \mathrm{Kn}(v,w)] \supset \mathrm{Kn}(C(u,v),w)]].$$

That concludes the proof of ELT 14.

Finally we observe that Bl(·) and Kn(·) do not distribute over disjunctions in the way they distribute over conjunctions. Instead, we have ELT 15:

ELT 15 If u, v, and w are propositional terms, then

$$[[\Gamma(u) \wedge [\Gamma(v) \wedge \Xi(w)]] \supset [[\mathrm{Bl}(D(u,v),w) \supset [\sim \mathrm{Bl}(Nu,w) \vee \mathrm{Bl}(v,w)]]$$
$$\wedge [\mathrm{Kn}(D(u,v),w) \supset [\sim \mathrm{Kn}(Nu,w) \vee \mathrm{Kn}(v,w)]]]].$$

That is, either we do not know (believe) that u or v is the case or we do not know (believe) that not u or know (believe) that v. This theorem is a simple corollary of ELT 13, and I leave the proof to the reader.

Theorems ELT 1–ELT 15 concerned the properties of $P(\cdot)$, Bl(·), and Kn(·). The next two theorems concern the relationship between Bl(·) and Kn(·). Of these, the first is a consequence of

$[[\Gamma(u) \wedge \Xi(v)] \supset [\mathrm{Kn}(\mathrm{Bl}(u, v), v) \supset \mathrm{Bl}(u, v)]]$,

the predicate-calculus analogue of T 4.1, and ELA 14 (ii).

ELT 16 Let u and v be propositional terms. Then

$[[\Gamma(u) \wedge \Xi(v)] \supset [\mathrm{Bl}(u, v) \equiv \mathrm{Kn}(Bl(u, v), v)]]$.

The second theorem, ELT 17, formalizes a remark of Jaakko Hintikka (see Hintikka 1962, p. 83).

ELT 17 Let u and v be propositional terms. Then

$[[\Gamma(u) \wedge \Xi(v)] \supset \sim\mathrm{Kn}(C(u, N\mathrm{Bl}(u, v)), v)]$.

That is, we cannot know both that u and that we do not believe that u is the case. This is obviously true since, by ELT 14,

$[[\Gamma(u) \wedge \Xi(v)] \supset [\mathrm{Kn}(C(u, N\mathrm{Bl}(u, v)), v) \equiv [\mathrm{Kn}(u, v) \wedge \mathrm{Kn}(N\mathrm{Bl}(u, v), v)]]]$

since, by ELA 15 (i),

$[[\Gamma(u) \wedge \Xi(v)] \supset [[\mathrm{Kn}(u, v) \wedge \mathrm{Kn}(N\mathrm{Bl}(u, v), v)] \supset [\mathrm{Bl}(u, v) \wedge N\mathrm{Bl}(u, v)]]]$

and since $\vdash \sim[\mathrm{Bl}(u, v) \wedge N\mathrm{Bl}(u, v)]$ and MRI 2, MLT 3, and M 3 (i) imply that

$[[\Gamma(u) \wedge \Xi(v)] \supset [[\mathrm{Kn}(u, v) \wedge \mathrm{Kn}(N\mathrm{Bl}(u, v), v)] \supset \sim[\mathrm{Bl}(u, v) \wedge N\mathrm{Bl}(u, v)]]]$.

Then from $\vdash [[u \supset v] \supset [[u \supset \sim v] \supset \sim u]]$ and repeated use of ERI 1 follows the validity of the theorem.

24.3.7.5 Substitution in Referentially Opaque Contexts

According to the *principle of the indiscernibility of identicals*, given a true statement of identity, one of its two terms may be substituted for the other in any true statement and the result will be true. This principle has many exceptions. Here are three of them.

The following statement is a fact:

Oslo = the captial of Norway.

However "the capital of Norway" cannot be substituted for "Oslo" in this statement:

"Oslo" contains four letters.

Similarly, we know the following for a fact:

Hesper = Lucifer.

However, "Lucifer" cannot be substituted for "Hesper" in Sappho's song:

"Oh Hesper! Thou art, I think, an evening star, of all stars the fairest."

Finally, the following can be stated as a fact:

Frank believes that Oslo lies in Sweden.

However, it is false that Frank believes that the capital of Norway lies in Sweden. The failure of the substitutivity of equality in these cases happens because the occurrence of Oslo in the first is not referential and the occurrences of Hesper and Oslo in the second and third examples are not purely referential.

W. V. O. Quine characterizes contexts such as "is unaware that ...," "believes that ...," and knows that ..." as referentially opaque. We shall next study the substitutivity of material equivalence in the referentially opaque context of $\mathrm{Bl}(\cdot)$ and $\mathrm{Kn}(\cdot)$.

ELT 18 Let u, v, and w be propositional terms. Then

$$[[\Gamma(u) \wedge [\Gamma(v) \wedge \Xi(w)]] \supset [TCL(E(u,v)) \supset [[\mathrm{Bl}(u,w) \equiv \mathrm{Bl}(v,w)] \wedge [\mathrm{Kn}(u,w) \equiv \mathrm{Kn}(v,w)]]]].$$

The proof goes as follows: Let u, v, and w be propositional terms such that $\Gamma(u)$, $\Gamma(v)$, and $\Xi(w)$. Then ELA 7 and MLT 4 imply that

$$[TCL(E(u,v)) \supset TCL(I(w, E(u,v)))].$$

From this, ELT 2 (iii), and ELA 14 (i), we deduce, first, that

$$[[\Gamma(u) \wedge [\Gamma(v) \wedge \Xi(w)]] \supset [TCL(E(u,v)) \supset [\mathrm{Bl}(u,w) \equiv \mathrm{Bl}(v,w)]]]$$

and then, by appeal to M 1 and $[TCL(E(u,v)) \supset E(u,v)]$, that

$$[[\Gamma(u) \supset [\Gamma(v) \wedge \Xi(w)]] \supset [TCL(E(u,v)) \supset [\mathrm{Kn}(u,w) \equiv \mathrm{Kn}(v,w)]]].$$

Thus in the referentially opaque contexts of $\mathrm{Bl}(\cdot)$ and $\mathrm{Kn}(\cdot)$, the substitutive property of material equivalence is valid for propositional terms u and v that satisfy $\Gamma(\cdot)$ and (!) $TCL(E(\cdot,\cdot))$.

The importance of $TCL(E(\cdot,\cdot))$ in ELT 18 must not be overlooked. One interesting illustration of why is the following: In spite of ELA 15 (i) we *cannot* demonstrate that $[\Gamma(u) \wedge \Xi(v)]$ materially implies that

$$[\mathrm{Bl}(C(u, \mathrm{Bl}(u,v)), v) \equiv \mathrm{Bl}(\mathrm{Kn}(u,v), v)].$$

This may sound strange, but it is in accord with our semantic analysis as well. To wit: Let $\mathscr{L}$ be the structure of EL described in section 23.3.5 and suppose that the interpretation of EL determined by $\mathscr{L}$ is a model of

ELA 1–ELA 15. Then $\mathscr{L}_l$ maps $[u \wedge \mathrm{Bl}(u, v)]$ and $\mathrm{Kn}(u, v)$ into two wffs in $|\mathscr{L}_l|$, $[\mathscr{L}_l(u) \wedge \mathrm{Bl}^{\mathscr{L}}(\mathscr{L}_l(u), \mathscr{L}_l(v))]$, and $\mathrm{Kn}^{\mathscr{L}}(\mathscr{L}_l(u), \mathscr{L}_l(v))$. These wffs need not be identical, but they must have the same truth value in $\mathscr{E}$. If they are not identical, their truth values may differ in any other member of $\mathscr{X}$; and that is the semantic reason why we cannot use ELA 15 (i) to justify substituting $\mathrm{Kn}(u, v)$ for $C(u, \mathrm{Bl}(u, v))$ in $\mathrm{Bl}(\cdot, v)$.

To see how the substitutivity of equality fares in the referentially opaque context of $\mathrm{Kn}(\cdot)$, we first note that (by ELT 18) if u and v are propositional terms such that $\Gamma(u)$ and $\Xi(v)$, then

$$\vdash [u \equiv v] \text{ implies } \vdash [\mathrm{Kn}(u, w) \equiv \mathrm{Kn}(v, w)].$$

From this and PLA 6 and PLA 7 of chapter 5 it follows that if $v \in \Xi$, if C is a wff in L_Γ with one free variable x, and if a and b are variable-free terms in L_Γ, then

$$\vdash [a = b] \text{ implies } \vdash [\mathrm{Kn}(C_x(a), v) \equiv \mathrm{Kn}(C_x(b), v)].$$

Consequently, if $[a = b]$ is a theorem of $T(\Gamma)$ we can be certain that $\mathrm{Kn}(C_x(a), v)$ if $\mathrm{Kn}(C_x(b), v)$ and conversely only if the structures in $\mathscr{X}$ are models of $T(\Gamma)$. However, if $[a = b]$ is not a theorem of $T(\Gamma)$ and/or if the structures in $\mathscr{X}$ are not models of $T(\Gamma)$, it is possible that $\mathscr{L}(\mathrm{Kn}(C_x(a), v)) =$ f even though $\mathscr{L}_l(\mathrm{Kn}(C_x(b), v)) =$ t. This is illustrated in E 24.10.

E 24.10 Assume that e, m, v are constants of L_Γ that in $\mathscr{L}_l$ denote, respectively, the evening star, the morning star, and Venus. Suppose that $\mathscr{L}_{L_\Gamma}$ is a model of EL and that $\mathscr{L}([v = e]) =$ t and $\mathscr{L}(\mathrm{Bl}([v = e], K)) =$ t, where $\Xi(K)$. Then $\mathscr{L}(\mathrm{Kn}([v = e], K)) =$ t. If in addition, $\mathscr{L}([e = m]) =$ t, it follows from the transitivity of $=$ that $\mathscr{L}([v = m]) =$ t but not that $\mathscr{L}(\mathrm{Bl}([v = m], K)) =$ t. Hence $\mathscr{L}(\mathrm{Kn}([v = m], K))$ need not equal t. However, if both $\mathscr{L}([e = m]) =$ t and $\mathscr{L}(\mathrm{Bl}([e = m], K)) =$ t, then we can show that $\mathscr{L}(\mathrm{Kn}([v = m], K)) =$ t as well.

24.3.7.6 *The Epistemological Concept of Truth*

In section 23.2 we insisted that a proposition A is epistemologically true if it can be known and epistemologically false if it cannot be known. In the context of EL a propositional term u can be known if and only if there is a propositional term v in Ξ such that $\mathrm{Kn}(u, v)$. I shall use this observation to give the following syntactic characterization of the epistemologically true propositional terms of EL.

ELT 19 Let u and v be propositional terms. Then

(i) $[CL(u) \supset [u \supset \Xi(u)]]$;

(ii) $[[CL(u) \wedge \Xi(v)] \supset [\mathrm{Kn}(u, v) \supset \Xi(u)]]$;

(iii) $[CL(u) \supset [u \equiv \mathrm{Kn}(u, u)]]$.

The proof is easy. First we prove (i): It follows from TM 5.5 that

$$[[\Box Nu \supset Nu] \supset [[Nu \supset \sim u] \supset [\Box Nu \supset \sim u]]].$$

From this, M 3 (i), M 1 (i), and repeated use of ERI 1, we deduce that

$$[\Box Nu \supset \sim u].$$

Next we observe that, by TM 5.7, $[[\Box Nu \supset \sim u] \supset [\sim\sim u \supset \sim\Box Nu]]$. Consequently, by ERI 1, $[\sim\sim u \supset \sim\Box Nu]$. Since also, by TM 5.5,

$$[[u \supset \sim\sim u] \supset [[\sim\sim u \supset \sim\Box Nu] \supset [u \supset \sim\Box Nu]]]$$

and, by TM 5.6, $[u \supset \sim\sim u]$, we can apply ERI 1 twice and deduce that $[u \supset \sim\Box Nu]$. From this, M 1(i), an obvious application of TM 5.7, and repeated use of ERI 1 we conclude that $[u \supset N\Box Nu]$. But if that is the case, then by TM 5.5,

$$[[u \supset N\Box Nu] \supset [[N\Box Nu \supset \Xi(u)] \supset [u \supset \Xi(u)]]]$$

and by an application of ERI 1, it follows that

$$[[N\Box Nu \supset \Xi(u)] \supset [u \supset \Xi(u)]].$$

To the last wff we apply TM 4.1 (with q equal to $CL(u)$) and conclude the proof of ELT 19 (i) by appealing to ELA 1 and ELT 1 and by using ERI 1 twice to deduce

$$[CL(u) \supset [u \supset \Xi(u)]].$$

The validity of ELT 19 (ii) is an immediate consequence of ELT 19 (i), ELA 15 (i), and ELA 1 and needs no further proof.

The proof of ELT 19 (iii) goes as follows: First we observe that, by ELA 12 (i), ELA 14 (i), and TM 5.15,

$$[\Xi(u) \supset [\Box[u \supset u] \supset \mathrm{Bl}(u, u)]].$$

From this, TM 5.3, T 4.1, ERI 3, and ERI 1 we deduce that

$$[\Xi(u) \supset \mathrm{Bl}(u, u)].$$

Next we observe that, by TM 5.5,

$$[[u \supset \Xi(u)] \supset [[\Xi(u) \supset \mathrm{Bl}(u, u)] \supset [u \supset \mathrm{Bl}(u, u)]]].$$

From this and the preceding observation, TM 5.3, and ERI 1 we obtain

$$[[u \supset \Xi(u)] \supset [u \supset \mathrm{Bl}(u, u)]].$$

But if that is so, then

$[CL(u) \supset [[u \supset \Xi(u)] \supset [u \supset \text{Bl}(u, u)]]]$.

and we can use ELA 1, ELT 19 (i), and ERI 1 to establish

$[CL(u) \supset [u \supset \text{Bl}(u, u)]]$.

The last assertion and the fact that $[CL(u) \supset [u \supset u]]$ suffice to establish the validity of ELT 19 (iii).

24.4 Other Concepts of Knowledge

The main purpose of constructing EL was to give a mathematical characterization of the concept of knowledge that we discussed in chapter 23. A brief review of section 24.3 suffices to see that we have succeeded. To wit, axioms ELA 14 and ELA 15, ERI 3, and theorems ELT 10 and ELT 13 show that the Kn(·) of EL has the four properties of the concept of knowledge that we insisted on in section 23.2. Also from MTEL 3 and ELT 9 it follows that, for any u in CL and v in Ξ, we can assert Kn(u, v) if u is either a nomological hypothetical or an assertion whose truth we can establish by a priori reasoning alone. Finally, if u is an accidental hypothetical that belongs to CL, ELT 7 gives sufficient conditions that our belief in u on v increases with the number of observations.

Our concept of knowledge has controversial features. I shall comment on some of them. Throughout our comments, L_Γ denotes the language for the theory of knowledge of a person A who belongs to some given group $\mathcal{G}$ (see section 24.1.3); $\mathcal{L}_{L_\Gamma}$ is a structure for EL that provides us with an interpretation of EL which satisfies all the axioms of EL; $\mathcal{X}$ is a set of models of the nonlogical axioms of $\mathcal{L}_\Gamma$; and $\mathcal{E}$ denotes the private epistemological universe of A.

24.4.1 Peirce's Concept of Knowledge

We believe that C. S. Peirce's ideas of knowledge and belief can be represented by a model of ELA 1–ELA 15 (i). Peirce certainly would have agreed to ELA 1–ELA 13 with equality instead of inequality in ELA 11–ELA 13. We believe that he also would have agreed to ELA 14 and ELA 15 (i) for reasons that are detailed below.

To Peirce belief is a "demi-cadence which closes a musical phrase in the symphony of our intellectual life" and has just three properties: (1) it is something of which we are aware; (2) it appeases the irritation of doubt in our mind; and (3) it involves the establishment of a habit in our nature (see Peirce 1955, p. 28). That is, if a person A believes that something, say u, is the case, then A believes that u is the case without a trace of doubt, A is willing to act on his belief if the occasion arises, and A is aware of the fact that he believes that u is the case. From this we conclude that Peirce's idea of belief is in accord with ELA 14.

To Peirce truth is what can be known, and what can be known is something which is fated to be ultimately agreed on by all who investigate (see Peirce 1955, p. 38). If that is correct, a person A cannot know that something, say u, is the case unless u *is* the case *and* A believes that u is the case. Conversely, if something, u, actually *is* the case and A believes that u is the case, then eventually all those who investigate will agree that A is right about u. Consequently, A knows that u is the case. From this, we conclude that Peirce's idea of knowledge is in accord with ELA 15 (i).

While Peirce might even have accepted all our axioms for the theory of knowledge as they are, he would have had serious reservations with respect to our description of the private epistemological universe in section 24.1.3. There we insisted that $\mathscr{E}$'s assignment of truth values to the wffs of L_Γ be in accordance with A's potential knowledge, as reflected in the factual knowledge of the totality of individuals in $\mathscr{G}$. Peirce agrees that reality can be meaningfully conceived only in relation to the possible interpretation of it by a community of intelligible beings. However, in contradistinction to us, he insists that the reference group must be without limits and extend to the whole communion of minds to which we belong (see, for example, Peirce 1955, p. 247).

24.4.2 Hintikka's Concept of Knowledge

Jaakko Hintikka has expounded his ideas about knowledge and belief in a treatise, *Knowledge and Belief* (Hintikka 1962), and in numerous other places (e.g., Hintikka 1969, pp. 87–111; Hintikka 1974, pp. 212–233). I believe that Hintikka's concept of belief is analogous to mine but that his notion of knowledge differs in an interesting way from my idea of knowledge. My reasons are detailed below. I begin with belief.

Let p be a proposition and let $B_A p$ assert that A believes that p. Then according to Hintikka (1962, p. 94) we have the following:

$B_A p$ is true in a possible world ξ if and only if p is true in all of A's doxastic alternatives to ξ.

Here a *doxastic alternative* to ξ for A is a possible world which is compatible with what A believes in ξ.

In my theory the set of alternatives to ξ is the set $\{H \in \mathscr{X} : \xi R H\}$. Moreover, for any pair of propositions u and v such that $\Gamma(u)$ and $\Xi(v)$,

$\mathscr{L}(\mathrm{Bl}(u, v)) = \mathrm{t}$ if and only if $P^{\mathscr{L}}(\varphi(\mathscr{L}_l(u), \xi) | \varphi(\mathscr{L}_l(v), \xi)) = 1$.

When $\mathscr{L}_l(u)$ is p and $\mathscr{L}_l(v)$ satisfies $TCL^{\mathscr{L}}$, the last expression becomes a symbolic rendition of the first. From this, and from the fact that Hintikka (1962, pp. 109–110) insists that

$B_A p \supset B_A B_A p$,

we infer that Hintikka's concept of belief accords with ELA 14.

Next, knowledge: Let $K_A p$ assert that A knows that p. Then Hintikka (see (C.KK*) and (C.K) in Hintikka 1962, p. 43) asserts the following:

$K_A p$ is true in a possible world ξ if and only if p is true in all of A's epistemic alternatives to ξ.

Here an *epistemic alternative* to ξ for A is a possible world which is compatible with what A knows in ξ. Hintikka (1962, p. 51) assumes that a doxastic alternative to ξ is an epistemic alternative to ξ. I shall add the assumption that an epistemic alternative to ξ is either ξ or a doxastic alternative to ξ.

In my theory I do not distinguish between doxastic and epistemic alternatives to ξ. They are just alternatives to ξ. Moreover, for any pair of propositions u and v such that $\Gamma(u)$ and $\Xi(v)$,

$\mathscr{L}(\mathrm{Kn}(u, v)) = \mathrm{t}$ if and only if $\xi(\mathscr{L}_l(u)) = \mathrm{t}$ and $\mathscr{L}(\mathrm{Bl}(u, v)) = \mathrm{t}$.

Since Hintikka (1962, p. 43) insists that

$K_A p \supset p$,

the second assertion becomes a symbolic rendition of the first once we equate p with $\mathscr{L}_l(u)$ and assume that $\mathscr{L}_l(v)$ satisfies $TCL^{\mathscr{L}}$. From this and from Hintikka's acceptance (see (C.KB) in Hintikka 1962, p. 50) of

$K_A p \supset B_A K_A p$,

it follows that Hintikka's characterization of knowledge accords with ELA 15

This demonstration of the equality of my concept of knowledge and Hintikka's depends crucially on the assumption that an epistemic alternative to ξ is either ξ or a doxastic alternative to ξ. When that assumption fails, we can show that

$K_A p \supset p \wedge B_A p$

and that

$K_A K_A p \equiv K_A p \wedge B_A K_A p$

are valid in Hintikka's theory, but we cannot establish the relation

$p \wedge B_A p \supset K_A p.$

24.4.3 Chisholm's Concept of Knowledge

According to Roderick Chisholm (see Chisholm 1977, p. 110) if p is a proposition and $K_A p$ is short for A knows that p, then we have the following;

$K_A p$ if and only if (1) it is the case that p; (2) A believes that p without a trace of doubt; and (3) p is nondefectively evident for A.

To explicate this notion of knowledge, we shall translate the assertion "p is nondefectively evident" into a statement about the wffs of L_Γ. We begin by translating "p is self-presenting for A."

Roughly speaking, in Chisholm's theory of knowledge (see Chisholm 1977, pp. 135–136) a proposition p is self-presenting for A if and only if (1) it is the case that p; and (2) the fact that p is true necessarily leads A to believe without a trace of doubt that p is the case. When u is a propositional term such that $\mathscr{L}_l(u) \in CL^{\mathscr{L}}$, then $\mathscr{E}(\mathscr{L}_l(u)) = \mathrm{t}$ implies that $\mathscr{E}(\mathscr{L}_l(N\Box Nu)) = \mathrm{t}$. From this and ELT 1 it follows that

$\mathscr{L}_l(u) \in CL^{\mathscr{L}}$ and $\mathscr{E}(\mathscr{L}_l(u)) = \mathrm{t}$ implies that $\mathscr{L}_l(u) \in \Xi^{\mathscr{L}}$.

Since $\mathrm{Bl}(v, v)$ for all propositional terms v such that $\Xi(v)$, we conclude that Chisholm's idea of self-presenting propositions can be translated as follows:

For any propositonal term u, $\mathscr{L}_l(u)$ *is self-presenting* if and only if (1) $\mathscr{L}_l(u) \in \Xi^{\mathscr{L}}$ and (2) $\mathscr{E}(\mathscr{L}_l(u)) = \mathrm{t}$.

Next we must translate "p is a basis of q for A." Roughly speaking, in Chisholm's theory of knowledge (see Chisholm 1977, p. 138), p is a basis of q for A if and only if (1) p is self-presenting for A and (2) if p is self-presenting for A, then A necessarily believes without a trace of doubt that it is the case that q. We translate this idea as follows:

Let u and v be propositional terms. Then $\mathscr{L}_l(v)$ *is a basis of* $\mathscr{L}_l(u)$ if and only if (1) $\mathscr{L}_l(v)$ is self-presenting and (2) $\mathscr{E}([[\mathscr{L}_l(v) \wedge \Xi^{\mathscr{L}}(\mathscr{L}_l(v))] \supset \Box \mathrm{Bl}^{\mathscr{L}}(\mathscr{L}_l(u), \mathscr{L}_l(v))]) = \mathrm{t}$.

In Chisholm's theory, a proposition p is *nondefectively evident* for A if and only if either it is certain for A that p is the case or (1) A believes without a trace of doubt that p and (2) p is entailed by a conjunction of propositions, each one of which has a basis for A which is not a basis of any false proposition for A (see Chisholm 1977, p. 138). The first half of this definition is easy to translate: A proposition $\mathscr{L}_l(u)$ is certain for A if and only if $\mathscr{L}(\mathrm{Bl}(u, v)) = \mathrm{t}$ for any v such that $\mathscr{L}_l(v)$ satisfies $TCL^{\mathscr{L}}$. The second half is complicated. However, I believe that we can capture its spirit by an assertion of the form

$$\mathscr{E}([\mathrm{Bl}^{\mathscr{L}}(\mathscr{L}_l(u), \mathscr{L}_l(v)) \wedge [[\Gamma^{\mathscr{L}}(\mathscr{L}_l(w)) \wedge [\mathscr{L}_l(v) \wedge \Xi^{\mathscr{L}}(\mathscr{L}_l(v))]]$$

$$\supset [\Box \mathrm{Bl}^{\mathscr{L}}(\mathscr{L}_l(w), \mathscr{L}_l(v)) \supset \mathscr{L}_l(w)]]]) = \mathrm{t},$$

where $\mathscr{L}_l(u)$ has taken the place of p.

If our translation of "p is a nondefectively evident proposition for A" is right, then we can characterize Chisholm's idea of knowledge, $\mathrm{CKn}(\cdot)$, as follows: Let $\tilde{\Xi}(v)$ assert that v is self-presenting; i.e., let

$$[\tilde{\Xi}(v) \equiv [v \wedge \Xi(v)]].$$

Then

$$[[\Gamma(u) \wedge \tilde{\Xi}(v)] \supset [\mathrm{CKn}(u, v) \equiv [[u \wedge \mathrm{Bl}(u, v)] \wedge [\Gamma(w)$$

$$\supset [\Box \mathrm{Bl}(w, v) \supset w]]]]].$$

In words, this assertion insists that if u and v are propositional terms such that $\Gamma(u)$ and $\tilde{\Xi}(v)$, then A knows that u on the basis of v if and only if (1) it is the case that u; (2) A believes that u on the basis v; and (3) v is a base of a propositional term w only if it is the case that w.

Chisholm formulated his notion of knowledge to deal with the wounds that E. L. Gettier had inflicted on the traditional theory of knowledge. Example E 23.2 describes a problematic situation which Gettier envisaged. By letting u be $D(p, w)$, p be "Gary owns a Ford," and w be "Peter owns a Ford," we see that, according to $\mathrm{CKn}(\cdot)$, we cannot claim in E 23.2 that we know that "Gary or Peter owns a Ford."

Chisholm's idea of knowledge is complicated. It is, therefore, interesting to make the following observations: Suppose that we substitute $\mathrm{CKn}(\cdot)$ for $\mathrm{Kn}(\cdot)$ in our description of EL and postulate ELA 1–ELA 14 and our characterization of $\mathrm{CKn}(\cdot)$ above. Then we can demonstrate that, for any propositional terms u, v, and p such that $\Gamma(u)$, $\tilde{\Xi}(v)$, and $\Gamma(p)$, the following assertions are valid:

$$[\mathrm{CKn}(u, v) \supset u],$$

$$[\mathrm{CKn}(I(u, p), v) \supset [\mathrm{CKn}(u, v) \supset \mathrm{CKn}(p, v)]],$$

$$[TCL(E(u,p)) \supset [\mathrm{CKn}(u,v) \equiv \mathrm{CKn}(p,v)]].$$

However, we cannot demonstrate that $[TCL(u) \supset \mathrm{CKn}(u,v)]$! Hence, without assuming that v is a nondefectively evident proposition, we cannot assert that $\mathrm{CKn}(u,v)$ if u is a tautological consequence of ELA 1 and M 1. To us that is a drawback of the notion of knowledge determined by $\mathrm{CKn}(\cdot)$.

24.4.4 Sundry Comments and a Look Ahead

In concluding our discussion of EL we shall briefly comment on four characteristics of EL and $\mathscr{L}$ that ought not to be overlooked. They concern the completeness of $\mathrm{Bl}(\cdot)$ and $\mathrm{Kn}(\cdot)$, $\mathscr{E}$'s assignment of truth values, missing quantifiers, and partial knowledge in EL.

First, the completeness of $\mathrm{Bl}(\cdot)$ and $\mathrm{Kn}(\cdot)$: Many epistemologists will object to the content of ELT 9 and to some of the consequences of ELT 13. Although they might admit that it is not wrong to suppose that an individual believes in a logical truth, they will consider it odd that it be provably the case (Jones 1983, p. 52). Similarly, they will think it odd that in EL it is provably the case that everyone knows the logical consequences of what he knows since such knowledge is beyond the information storage capacity of most humans (Jones 1983, p. 68). Well, it may be odd. Still I insist that it ought to be provable that an individual must believe in logical truths and know the logical consequences of all that he knows. Otherwise he would, sooner or later, find himself in an indefensible position (in court, on the job, or at home) from which he would gladly retreat.

Next, $\mathscr{E}$'s assignment of truth values: We have seen that both Hintikka and Chisholm object to ELA 15 (i). Andrew Jones agrees with them for reasons that are of particular interest to us. Using Hintikka's notation for knowledge and belief, Jones defines knowledge by

$$K_A p =_{\mathrm{df}} [[B_A p \wedge V_A p] \wedge O_A V_A p],$$

where $V_A p$ asserts that "p is true according to the information available to A" and $O_A V_A p$ insists that "it is optimal relative to A's interest in being informed, that $V_A p$." Jones also postulates that

$$O_A V_A p \supset p,$$

but he refuses to accept the converse. Hence

$$K_A p \supset [p \wedge [B_A p \wedge V_A p]],$$

but the converse need not hold. For all that *we* know, A might not want to know that p! This is interesting because of the light it throws on our discussion of private epistemological universes in section 24.1.3. If $\mathscr{L}$ determines a model of ELA 1–ELA 15 and $\mathscr{E}$ represents the private epistemological universe of A, then we insist that $\mathscr{E}$ assign truth values to the wffs in $|\mathscr{L}_l|$ in accordance with A's potential knowledge without regard to A's wishes.

Then the missing quantifiers in EL: Note that in EL the $\forall$ quantifier is applied to individuals in EL and not to individuals in L_Γ. Hence the problem of passing from $\mathrm{Kn}((\exists x)C, v)$ to $(\exists y)\mathrm{Kn}(C_x(y), v)$ and conversely does not arise in the context of EL; e.g., we can assert "Erik knows that there are spies," but we cannot infer from this that "there is a spy whom Erik knows." Not tackling this problem leaves us with an important lacuna in our theory. I chose not to fill it because filling it would divert attention from the main issues of epistemology that we want to study.

Finally, the absence of partial knowledge in EL: Note that there is no such thing as partial knowledge in EL. According to ELT 10, either we know that A or we do not know that A. Usually we do not know that A when A is a derivative law. So we must construct a different language for talking about scientists' search for knowledge concerning the applicability of derivative laws. That we will do in the next chapter.

25 An Epistemological Language for Science

In chapters 23 and 24 I discussed the possibility of knowledge, and I proposed a schema for classifying different kinds of knowledge. I also formulated a language for explicating our idea of knowledge. In this chapter I shall develop an epistemological language for science with which we can formulate and analyze tests of scientific hypotheses. These hypotheses may be accidental or nomological laws, in which case they can be falsified or known eventually. They may also be derivative laws. If they are, we can determine the circumstances under which, and the degree of exactness with which, they can be applied, but we cannot falsify or know such laws.

I shall begin by discussing two criteria, simplicity and autonomy, which scientific hypotheses ought to satisfy. Then I treat inference by analogy and describe ways in which analogy can be used to generate useful hypotheses. I also treat inductive inference and discuss the treacherous business of confronting scientific hypotheses with data. Finally, I formulate a multisorted language, discuss some of its semantic properties, and use a modified version of it to construct the sought-for epistemological language for science. In concluding the chapter, I delineate a probabilistic framework within which we can formulate statistical tests of scientific hypotheses.

25.1 Simple, Autonomous Relations

When we postulate theoretical relationships in L_{KPU^*}, we would like to formulate simple relationships that are valid for as large a collection as possible of the relevant models of KPU*. In Trygve Haavelmo's terminology (Haavelmo 1944, pp. 21–39), we would like our postulated relationships to be (1) *simple* and (2) *autonomous* with respect to as large a set of relevant KPU* models as possible.

Here is an example to fix our ideas:

E 25.1 Let B be a vector whose components denote the various assets and liabilities available to consumers in the universe. We are looking for a finite set of factors, $F_1, \ldots, F_n$, and a vector-valued function, $g(\cdot)$, such that a U.S. consumer's choice of balance sheet in 1962 can be represented by

$$B = g(F_1, \ldots, F_n) + u,$$

where $g(\cdot)$ is common to all consumers and the values of $F_1, \ldots, F_n$, and u vary from one individual to the next. There are many candidates to choose from. We would like to find one $(n + 2)$-tuple, $(g, F_1, \ldots, F_n, u)$ such that (in the U.S. population of 1962) each component of u has mean zero, finite variance, and zero covariance with the F_i.

Some of the factors we have in mind in E 25.1 are age, education, risk aversion, initial wealth, and current-period asset prices, interest rates, and disposable income. Other factors are listed in table 25.1, which summarizes the reasons for acquiring various assets and liabilities given by a group of U.S. consumers in 1962.

The requirement that theoretical relationships be simple suggests that in E 25.1 we choose as few factors as possible. The requirement that theoretical relationships be autonomous with respect to as large a set of relevant KPU* models as possible suggests that we include in our list of selected factors those most likely to have a significant effect on consumers' choice of equilibrium balance sheets. Note, therefore, that there might not have been one consumer in the U.S. population who in 1962 was influenced by *all* the factors in table 25.1. Note also that the factors were not equally important in determining the sample consumers' balance-sheet choices.

The presentation of a scientific hypothesis in L_{KPU^*} ought to include a description of the class of KPU* models relative to which the hypothesis is believed to be autonomous. When applied to economic matters, this maxim requires that economic hypotheses be presented with a specification of a class of economic structures relative to which the hypotheses are autonomous. Delineating such classes is difficult and economists have worked hard to prove theorems which were required for that purpose. Cases in point are T 10.17, T 11.9, and T 12.14–T 12.18. The first theorem considers economic structures in which the extension of "consumer" is not restricted but commodity prices must vary in certain prescribed ways to ensure that consumers' demand for composite commodities can be treated as if the composites were ordinary commodities. The second theorem and the third group of theorems consider various economic structures in which prices

Table 25.1
Assets associated with investment objectives (percentage distribution of consumer units).

	Investment objectives					
Assets	Maximum current cash return	Safe, steady return	Growth of capital through appreciation	Safety of capital	Liquidity or marketability	Minimizing income taxes
Cash and savings accounts	6	11	1	12	20	9
Securities (stock + others)	52	54	54	45	55	38
Investment in real estate	27	18	24	27	12	39
Other assets	7	11	5	8	9	5
No asset mentioned	6	5	15	7	5	9
$\sum$	100	100	100	100	100	100
Number of units	191	579	699	521	231	151

Source: Projector and Weiss 1966.

vary freely but the extension of "consumer" is restricted so that consumer demand for certain specified aggregates of commodities can be treated as if the aggregates were ordinary commodities.

In the epistemological language presented below the interpretation of the modal operator $\Box$ specifies the set of structures relative to which a given hypothesis is assumed to be autonomous. More specifically, the interpretation, $(\mathscr{X}, \xi, R, \varphi)$, singles out a structure ξ in which the hypothesis is valid and insists that it be valid in all structures in $\mathscr{X}$ that are in the relation R to ξ.

25.2 Analogy and the Generation of Scientific Hypotheses

There are many ways to generate useful scientific hypotheses. In this section we shall discuss one of them, inference by analogy.

25.2.1 Analogy and Inductive Inference

While discussing the possibility of knowledge in chapter 23 we defined inference by analogy as a process of reasoning in which objects or events that are similar in one respect are judged to resemble each other in certain other respects as well. We also suggested that induction may be thought of as an argument in which we single out two sets of positive analogies, $P_1, \ldots, P_k$ and $Q_1, \ldots, Q_m$, for an observed group of individuals and hypothesize that the next individual we meet either will not satisfy some of the P's or will satisfy all the Q's. For our present purposes it is important to note that such an inductive argument concerns properties of individuals in one and the same universe; e.g., all the individuals x that we have observed have either not been ravens, $\sim R(x)$, or have been black, $B(x)$; hence chances are that $(\forall x)[R(x) \supset B(x)]$. The characteristic feature of inference by analogy that we intend to stress in this section is that it is an argument by which we derive properties of individuals in one universe from the properties of individuals in some other universe.

25.2.2 Models

Arguments by analogy appear in different disguises in economic theory. We used such arguments in chapters 11 and 12 when we treated optimal expenditure strategies and equilibrium balance sheets as consumption bundles. In chapters 21 and 22 we used transfer to establish nonstandard analogues of well-known properties of standard economies. Linguistic limits to such analogies were discussed in sections 7.3 and 7.4.

The preceding examples illustrate different aspects of the role that models and arguments by analogy play in the construction of new economic theories. This role is as important in other sciences as it is in economics. For example, in physics Huygens used the familiar view of sound as a wave phenomenon to develop his wave theory of light. Similarly, Black's experimental discoveries concerning heat and Fourier's theory of heat conduction were motivated by their conception of heat as a fluid. In each case "the model served both as a guide for setting up the fundamental assumptions of a theory, as well as a source of suggestions for extending the range of their application" (Nagel 1961, pp. 108–109).

The epistemological language I present below provides a vehicle for systematic use of models and arguments by analogy in scientific research. In this language inferences by analogy from the properties of one kind of individuals to those of another are drawn in accordance with axioms that delineate the characteristics of members of an observational vocabulary and describe the relationship between the symbols of the observational and the theoretical vocabulary. These axioms determine both what kind of inferences the language allows and specify the conditions under which such inferences can be drawn. For example, some axioms may relate demand for single commodities to demand for aggregates of commodities. Others may explicate the relationship between single-vintage production functions and aggregate production functions.

25.2.3 Representative Individuals and Aggregates

We also use inference by analogy in many ways in econometrics. The idea of one of these ways dates back to A. Quetelet—the creator of the *abominable l'homme moyen*. Quetelet claimed that what related to the human species, considered en masse, was of the order of physical facts. "The greater the number of individuals," he said, "the more the individual will is effaced and leaves predominating the series of general facts which depend on the general causes, in accordance with which society exists and maintains itself. These are the causes we seek to ascertain, and when we shall know them, we shall determine effects for society as we determine effects by causes in the physical sciences." (Stigler 1965, p. 202)

Quetelet's dictum contains a postulate and a prescription. The postulate asserts that in the human race there are positive analogies worth knowing. The prescription tells us how to look for these analogies.

Table 25.2
Gradations of income and relative surplus.

Gradations ($)	Number of families	Their earnings ($)	Their expenses ($)	Average yearly surplus or debt ($)
300–500	10	4,308	4,466	−15.8
500–700	140	86,684	86,023	4.72
700–900	181	143,281	138,747	25.05
900–1100	54	52,708	49,720	55.33
1100–1300	8	9,729	8,788	117.63
> 1300	4	6,090	5,241	212.25
Total	397	302,800	292,987	24.72

Source: Wright 1875, p. 380

E 25.2 In 1875 the Massachusetts Bureau of Labor Statistics under the supervision of C. Wright conducted a survey of incomes and expenditures of families of the state's workers. Table 25.2 gives a summary statement of the workers' incomes and savings. The relationship between savings and incomes, which we observe in the table, and Quetelet's dictum gave Wright the idea of the following law: *The higher the income of a family, the greater is the amount it will save, actually and proportionately.*

Today few believe in Quetelet's statistical methods, as exemplified in Wright's use of the data in table 25.2. However, econometricians believe in his dictum and use it in the way we shall use it in the applied econometric part of the book, i.e., in chapters 26–28. There we postulate the existence of a *representative consumer* and describe how other consumers differ from him. Then we use data that pertain to many different individuals and test whether the positive analogies for consumers that are exhibited in the behavior of the representative consumer exist. Our representative consumer is the econometric counterpart of the economic man. He is also the personification of Quetelet's *l'homme moyen* in our econometric axiom system.

In this context it is interesting to note that the analogue of the representative consumer in our epistemological language is the ξ structure in the interpretation of SEL. The relation R and the set of structures $\mathcal{X}$ determine the extent to which inference by analogy from one structure to another is permitted.

25.2.4 Observations, Theoretical Hypotheses, and Analogy

Sometimes observations, theoretical hypotheses, and inference by analogy can combine to produce spectacular results. One example is Keynes's General Theory (Keynes 1936). Keynes used economic theory concerning the behavior of individual consumers and firms, observations, and inference by analogy to derive his macroeconomic relations, one of which was the aggregate version of Wright's Law. Another example, which we shall describe next, is Newton's derivation of his general law of gravity.

In Newton's case the observational inputs were supplied by Tycho Brahe's observations on planetary motion and the following three empirical laws that Johannes Kepler derived from them.

1. Each planet moves around the sun in an ellipse, with the sun at one focus.
2. The radius vector from the sun to the planet sweeps out equal areas in equal intervals of time.
3. The orbital periods of any two planets are proportional to the 3/2 power of the lengths of the semimajor axes of their respective orbits.

The theoretical inputs were provided by Newton's three laws of motion:

1. Principle of Inertia: An object that is left alone remains still if just standing still, and continues to move with constant velocity in a straight line if originally moving.
2. A force is needed to change the velocity and the direction of motion of an object. The time rate of change of the mass times the velocity of the object is proportional to the force.
3. The action (i.e., force exerted) of one object on another object equals the reaction (i.e., force exerted) of the second object on the first.

Newton used his two first laws to show that the motion of the planets would satisfy Kepler's Law of Areas if and only if the forces that acted on the planets were directed exactly toward the sun. Then he showed that Kepler's first and third laws held if and only if the forces that acted on the planets varied inversely as the square of the distance of the respective planets from the sun. Finally, Newton used his third law and an argument by analogy to show that "all objects attract each other with a force directly proportional to the product of their masses and inversely proportional to the square of their separation" (Cohen 1981, pp. 123–131). Newton's argument by analogy was the following: "And since the action of centripetal force upon the attracted body, at equal distances, is proportional to the matter in this body, it is reasonable, too, that it is also proportional to the matter in the attracting body. For the action is mutual, and causes the bodies by a mutual endeavor [by the second law] to approach each other, and accordingly it ought to be similar to itself in both bodies" (Cohen 1981, p. 128). The assertion which resulted from this argument and Newton's third law is called Newton's General Law of Gravity and is formulated in symbols in equation 24.3.

In presenting his theory, Newton distinguished between *absolute space*, which is immutable and immovable, and *relative space*, which is a movable representation of absolute space (see Newton 1968, pp. 9–18). His bodies moved about in absolute space while Tycho Brahe's planets circled the sun in relative space. It is, therefore, interesting to us that the positive analogies Newton's laws prescribe for celestial motion in absolute space do play a role in the analysis of celestial motion in relative space that is analogous to the role which our representative consumer plays in the characterization of individual behavior in a sample population.

25.3 Induction and Meaningful Sampling Schemes

Inductive rules of inference pass from assertions concerning characteristics of our observations to assertions concerning characteristics of observations to come. In section 24.3.7.2 we saw that the inductive rules of inference, which we delineated in the ELA 11–ELA 13 of EL in section 24.3.3, determine rules of inference for EL that are appropriate analogues of the Modus Ponens of our first-order predicate calculus. We also found sufficient conditions on the scientific method that these rules can be used to justify inductive inference in scientific research. The last result might have given the reader the impression that with "sufficiently many" observations we can determine the truth value of any variable hypothetical. But what do we mean by "sufficiently many"?

E 25.3 Let $\prod(x)$ denote the number of primes less than x, and let $l(x) = \int_0^x (\log t)^{-1}\, dt$. Gauss and other prominent mathematicians conjectured that

$$\prod(x) < l(x).$$

This conjecture was not only plausible, but was supported by the evidence. The primes up to 10^7 and their numbers at intervals up to 10^9 were known and the inequality held for all x for which data were available. Yet Littlewood proved in 1912 that the conjecture is false: that there are infinitely many values for which the inequality must be reversed. Later Skewes demonstrated that there is a number x less than $10^{10^{10^{34}}}$ which does not satisfy the inequality.

Even though Skewes' number may be reduced by refining his arguments, it is unlikely that we shall ever know an instance of Littlewood's theorem. The example, therefore, shows that we cannot, in a given case, count on the number of observations alone to determine the correct generalization.[1]

The moral of E 25.3 is not that ELT 7 and E 24.9 are irrelevant and that our inductive rules of inference are not good. Rather it is that, in processing evidence, we must consider both the data-generating process and the size of our sample of observations. In other words, in epistemology in general and econometrics in particular, it is not sufficient to introduce axioms concerning the characteristics of the universe and postulate properties of our inductive rules of inference. We must also hypothesize about the way our data are generated; e.g., the data may constitute a random sample or be generated by a stratified random sampling scheme.

C. Broad suggested in Broad 1928 (pp. 15–18) that the necessary hypothesis concerning the data-generating processes in nature could be introduced once and for all in the form of a *fundamental causal premise*. I do not choose to do so because the data-generating mechanisms we face in econometrics are much more varied than those Broad envisioned. Instead I shall introduce the postulates we need as they become relevant for the applied-econometric studies I present later. In each case the assumptions will be such that we can appeal to probabilistic limit theorems and show that our rules of inference are good in the situation considered.

To aid our intuition and to guide us in selecting the assumptions concerning the relevant data-generating processes that I introduce in subsequent chapters, I shall next introduce the idea of a meaningful sampling scheme. To that end, let $(\Omega, \mathscr{F}, P(\cdot))$ be a probability space; let $x_i(\cdot): \Omega \to R$, $i = 1, \ldots, n$, be random variables on $(\Omega, \mathscr{F})$; and let X_i denote the range of $x_i(\cdot)$, $i = 1, \ldots, n$. Moreover, let $Z = \prod_{i=1}^n X_i$; let $\mathscr{B}(Z)$ denote the smallest σ field that contains all sets of the form $\prod_{i=1}^n A_i$, with $A_i \subset X_i$ and $\{\omega \in \Omega : x_i(\omega) \in A_i\} \in \mathscr{F}$, $i = 1, \ldots, n$; and let $Q(\cdot)$ be a probability measure on $(Z, \mathscr{B}(Z))$. Then $(Z, \mathscr{B}(Z), Q(\cdot))$ is the sample space of an experiment in which we, in accordance with $Q(\cdot)$, obtain a sequence of n observations on the values assumed by the $x_i(\cdot)$. We shall say that $(Z, \mathscr{B}(Z), Q(\cdot))$ is a *meaningful sampling scheme* if and only if,

$$Q(A) = P(\{\omega \in \Omega : (x_1(\omega), \ldots, x_n(\omega) \in A\}), \qquad A \in \mathscr{B}(Z).$$

If the $x_i(\cdot)$ are independently distributed relative to $P(\cdot)$ and if $(Z, \mathscr{B}(Z), Q(\cdot))$ is a meaningful sampling scheme, then relative to Q an outcome of the experiment $(Z, \mathscr{B}(Z))$ is a random sample.

It is not always easy to design an experiment in which we sample in accordance with a given probability measure. We illustrate this in E 25.4.

E 25.4 Fifty sharks were observed in Oslo fjord during the summer of 1976. Twenty were blue sharks. Can we infer that about 40 percent of all sharks in Oslo fjord are blue sharks? If the observations constitute a random sample, 0.4 is a reasonable estimate of the true proportion of blue sharks in Oslo fjord, and the answer is "yes." If not, 0.4 is an estimate of the mean of the sampling distribution. The mean can differ from the true proportion of blue sharks inasmuch as areas with either relatively few or relatively many blue sharks may have been oversampled. For nonrandom samples the suggested inference cannot be justified.

For the shark sample in E 25.4 to constitute a random sample, the sharks would have had to be sampled in the way we sample with replacement from an urn with blue and white balls and with as many balls as there were sharks and as many blue balls as there were blue sharks in Oslo fjord in the summer of 1976. It is unlikely that the sharks were observed in accordance with such a scheme. Analogous remarks apply to most nonexperimental observations obtained from nature; e.g., any black ravens we observe are sampled from a limited area over a time horizon that excludes all future periods and all periods in the distant past.

Even in situations in which we have numerous observations and we have sampled in accordance with a meaningful sampling scheme, the probabilities that we may assign to the validity of the associated variable hypothetical might be low. Take E 25.5, for instance.

E 25.5 Consider an urn with a large number, M, of balls that are identical except for color. Assume that each ball is painted with one color and that the choice of color was made at random from v different colors. We do not know the color composition of the urn, and we sample balls at random without replacement. The balls drawn are all red. If we assume that $P(\cdot|K)$ is additive over the relevant propositions and drop K in the formulas for convenience, our rules of inference imply that

$$P\{\text{1st ball red}\}$$

$$= \sum_{s=0}^{M} P\{\text{1st ball red}|s \textit{ red balls}\} \cdot P\{s \text{ red balls}\}$$

$$= \sum_{s=0}^{M} \left(\frac{s}{M}\right)\binom{M}{s}\left(\frac{1}{v}\right)^{s}\left(1-\frac{1}{v}\right)^{M-s} = v^{-1};$$

$$P\{\text{1st } k \text{ balls red}\} = \sum_{s=k}^{M} \frac{s!(M-k)!}{M!(s-k)!}\binom{M}{s}\left(\frac{1}{v}\right)^{s}\left(1-\frac{1}{v}\right)^{M-s} = v^{-k}.$$

Consequently,

$$P(\text{all balls red}|\text{1st } n \text{ balls red}) = v^{-(M-n)}.$$

The latter probability converges to 1 as n goes to M. However, for reasonable values of n, $v^{-(M-n)}$ will be near to 0 if M is large.[2]

The preceding examples illustrate some problematic aspects of inductive inference. There are many others. We shall later discuss those that are particular to tests of scientific hypotheses. But first an introduction to many-sorted logic.

25.4 Many-Sorted Languages

A many-sorted language is a first-order language with more than one set of individuals. In this section we shall discuss some of the properties of such languages.

25.4.1 The Symbols

Let L be a many-sorted language with k disjoint sets of individuals. The logical symbols of L are

$\sim \supset [\quad](\ ,\ )\forall =$

and k nonoverlapping infinite lists of individual variables,

$x_1 y_1 z_1 \cdots ; x_2 y_2 z_2 \cdots ; \cdots ; x_k y_k z_k \cdots .$

The nonlogical vocabulary of L consists of a selection from the following lists of constants, function symbols, and predicate symbols:

1. k disjoint sequences of constants,

$\alpha_1 \beta_1 \gamma_1 \cdots ; \alpha_1 \beta_2 \gamma_2 \cdots ; \cdots ; \alpha_k \beta_k \gamma_k \cdots .$

2. Indexed sets of predicate symbols, $\{P^j\}_{j \in J_n}$, $n = 1, 2, \ldots$. For each n and every $j \in J_n$, P^j is an n-ary predicate symbol.

3. Indexed sets of function symbols, $\{f^{i_0, i_1, \ldots, i_n}\}_{i \in I_n}$, and indexed sets of predicate symbols, $\{R^{j_1, \ldots, j_n}\}_{j \in \hat{J}_n}$. For each $n = 1, 2, \ldots$ and every $i \in I_n$, $f^{i_0, i_1, \ldots, i_n}$ is an n-ary function symbol whose values are to be individuals of the i_0th kind and whose n arguments are to be individuals of kind i_m, $m = 1, \ldots, n$. Similarly, for each $n = 1, 2, \ldots$ and every $j \in \hat{J}_n$, $R^{j_1, \ldots, j_n}$ is an n-ary predicate symbol whose n arguments are to be individuals of the j_mth kind, $m = 1, \ldots, n$.

E 25.6 In presenting nonstandard analysis we used a single-sorted language. We could have used a two-sorted language instead. Then our logical vocabulary would have contained two sets of variables, $x_1 y_1 z_1 \ldots$ and $x_2 y_2 z_2 \ldots$, the first for urelements and the second for sets. Also our nonlogical vocabulary would have consisted of two constants, α_1, β_1 (i.e., 0 and 1), two binary function symbols,

$f^{1,1,1}$ and $g^{1,1,1}$ (i.e., + and ·), and two binary predicate symbols, P and $R^{1,1}$ (i.e., ε and $<$).

25.4.2 The Terms and the Well-Formed Formulas

A many-sorted language with k different kinds of individuals contains terms of k kinds. The terms of L are defined inductively as follows:

DMT 1 For each j, $j = 1, \ldots, k$, constants and variables of the jth kind are terms of the jth kind.

DMT 2 For each $i \in I_n$, $n = 1, 2, \ldots$, if t_{i_m} is a term of the i_mth kind, $m = 1, \ldots, n$, and if $f^{i_0, i_1, \ldots, i_n}$ is an n-ary function symbol, then $f^{i_0, i_1, \ldots, i_n}(t_{i_1}, \ldots, t_{i_n})$ is a term of the i_0th kind.

With this definition of terms on our hands we can define the wffs of L inductively as follows:

MPFR 1 If t_1 and t_2 are terms, $[t_1 = t_2]$ is a wff.

MPFR 2 If $t_1, \ldots, t_n$ are terms and if P is an n-ary predicate symbol, then $P(t_1, \ldots, t_n)$ is a wff, $n = 1, 2, \ldots$.

MPFR 3 If t_{j_l} is a term of the j_lth kind, $l = 1, \ldots, n$, and if $R^{j_1, \ldots, j_n}$ is an n-ary predicate symbol, then $R^{j_1, \ldots, j_n}(t_{j_1}, \ldots, t_{j_n})$ is a wff.

MPFR 4 If A is wf, then $\sim A$ is a wff.

MPFR 5 If A and B are wf, then $[A \supset B]$ is a wff.

MPFR 6 For each $j = 1, \ldots, k$, if a is an individual variable of the jth kind and if A is a wff, then $(\forall a)A$ is a wff.

These formation rules and the preceding definition of terms provide an unambiguous characterization of the terms and wffs of L. In reading the formation rules, note that the arguments of P in MPFR 2 need not be of the same kind. Note also that in DMT 2 the arguments of $f^{i_0, i_1, \ldots, i_n}$ may be of the same kind.

25.4.3 The Axioms and the Rules of Inference

With some obvious modification, the axioms and the rules of inference of L are the same as the axioms and the rules of inference of our predicate calculus. Specifically, the axiom schemata PLA 1–PLA 4 and PLA 6 are axiom schemata in L as well:

MPLA 1 PLA 1–PLA 4 and PLA 6 (section 5.1.3).

The axiom schema PLA 5 is rephrased in MPLA 2. In reading MPLA 2, note that in this chapter a term b *is taken to be substitutable for a variable* a in a wff A if and only if a and b are of the same kind and, for each variable x occurring in b, no part of A of the form $(\forall x)B$ contains an occurrence of a which is free in A.

MPLA 2 Let A be a wff, let a be a variable of the jth kind, $j \in \{1, \ldots, k\}$, and let b be a term that is substitutable for a in A. Then

$$[(\forall x)A \supset A_a(b)].$$

In addition, the axiom schemata of PLA 7 is replaced by the following three axiom schemata:

MPLA 4 If t and s are terms of different kinds, $\sim[t = s]$.

MPLA 4 Let $t_1, \ldots, t_n$ and $s_1, \ldots, s_n$ be terms and let P be an n-ary predicate symbol. Then

$$[[[t_1 = s_1] \wedge [[t_2 = s_2] \wedge [\cdots \wedge [t_n = s_n]]\cdots]]]$$
$$\supset [P(t_1, \ldots, t_n) \supset P(s_1, \ldots, s_n)]].$$

MPLA 5 Let A be a wff; let a_j be an individual variable of the l_jth kind, $j = 1, \ldots, n$; and let b_j, c_j be terms that are substitutable for a_j in A, $j = 1, \ldots, n$. Then

$$[[[b_1 = c_1] \wedge [[b_2 = c_2] \wedge [\cdots \wedge [b_n = c_n]]\cdots]]]$$
$$\supset [A_{a_1, \ldots, a_n}(b_1, \ldots, b_n) \supset A_{a_1, \ldots, a_n}(c_1, \ldots, c_n)].$$

Finally, the rules of inference of L are identical with the rules of inference of our predicate calculus; that is, we have MPRI 1:

MPRI 1 PRI 1 and PRI 2 (section 5.1.4).

25.4.4 Sample Theorems

With the help of MPRI 1 we can deduce from MPLA 1 and MPLA 5 that $=$ is an equivalence relation. Consider TM 25.1.

TM 25.1 If a, b, and c are terms,

(i) $[a = a]$;

(ii) $[[a = b] \supset [b = a]]$;

(iii) $[[[a = b] \wedge [b = c]] \supset [a = c]]$.

Also we can deduce from MPLA 1 and MPLA 5 that $=$ has the standard substitutive property. That is, we have TM 25.2.

TM 25.2 If t_j, s_j are terms of the i_jth kind, $j = 1, \ldots, n$, and if $f^{i_0, i_1, \ldots, i_n}$ is an n-ary function symbol,

$$[[[t_1 = s_1] \wedge [[t_2 = s_2] \wedge [\cdots \wedge [t_n = s_n]\cdots]]]$$

$$\supset [f^{i_0, i_1, \ldots, i_n}(t_1, \ldots, t_n) = f^{i_0, i_1, \ldots, i_n}(s_1, \ldots, s_n)]].$$

Similarly, from MPLA 1 and MPLA 2 we deduce the many-sorted analogues of TM 5.8 and TM 5.10. That is, we have TM 25.3 and TM 25.4.

TM 25.3 Let A be a wff and let a be an individual variable of the jth kind, $j \in \{1, \ldots, k\}$. Also let b be a term that is substitutable for a in A. Then

$$[A_a(b) \supset (\exists a)A].$$

TM 25.4 Let A and B be wffs and let a be an individual variable of the jth kind, $j \in \{1, \ldots, k\}$. Then

$$[(\forall a)[A \supset B] \supset [(\forall a)A \supset (\forall a)B]].$$

Finally we can use MPLA 1 and MPRI 1 to show that $\equiv$ is an equivalence relation in L, and we can use MPLA 1, MPLA 2, MPRI 1, and a proof by induction on the length of a wff to show that $\equiv$ has the standard substitutive property. Consider TM 25.5.

TM 25.5 Let A, B, and C be wffs. Then

(i) $[A \equiv A]$;

(ii) $[[A \equiv B] \supset [B \equiv A]]$;

(iii) $[[[A \equiv B] \wedge [B \equiv C]] \supset [A \equiv C]]$.

TM 25.6 Let A and $\hat{A}$ be wffs. Also let $B_1, \ldots, B_n$ be wf subformulas of A and let $\hat{B}_1, \ldots, \hat{B}_n$ be wffs. Finally, suppose that $\hat{A}$ has been obtained from A by substituting $\hat{B}_i$ for B_i at some of the occurrences of B_i, $i = 1, \ldots, n$. If, for all $i = 1, \ldots, n$, $[B_i \equiv \hat{B}_i]$ is a theorem, then $[A \equiv \hat{A}]$ is a theorem as well.

The proofs of TM 25.1–TM 25.6 are identical with the proofs of their predicate-calculus analogues. So for brevity I omit the proofs here.

25.4.5 Structures and the Interpretation of Many-Sorted Languages

A structure for our many-sorted language L is a $(2k + 3)$-tuple,

$$\mathscr{D} = (U_1, \ldots, U_k, N_{U_1}, \ldots, N_{U_k}, C^{\mathscr{D}}, F^{\mathscr{D}}, G^{\mathscr{D}}),$$

where U_i, $i = 1, \ldots, k$, denotes the universe of the ith kind of individuals, N_{U_i}, $i = 1, \ldots, k$, contains the names of the individuals in U_i—one name for each individual and different names for different individuals—and $C^{\mathscr{D}}$, $F^{\mathscr{D}}$, and $G^{\mathscr{D}}$ are collections of constants, functions, and predicates that provide the interpretation in $\mathscr{D}$ of the nonlogical vocabulary of L. We assume that these collections satisfy the following conditions:

(i) If c is a constant of the ith kind, its interpretation in $C^{\mathscr{D}}$, $\mathscr{D}(c)$, belongs to U_i.

(ii) If $f^{i_0,i_1,\ldots,i_n}$ is an n-ary function symbol, its interpretation in $\mathscr{D}$, $(f^{i_0,i_1,\ldots,i_n})^{\mathscr{D}}$, is a function whose mth argument varies through U_{i_m}, $m = 1, \ldots, n$, and whose values belong to U_{i_0}.

(iii) If $R^{j_1,\ldots,j_n}$ is an n-ary predicate symbol, its interpretation in $\mathscr{D}$, $(R^{j_1,\ldots,j_n})^{\mathscr{D}}$, is a subset of $U_{j_1} \times \cdots \times U_{j_n}$.

(iv) Moreover, we assume that $U_i \cap U_j = \varnothing$ and $N_{U_i} \cap N_{U_j} = \varnothing$ for all i, $j = 1, \ldots, k$ and $i \neq j$.

(v) Finally, we allow the possibility that both $C^{\mathscr{D}}$ and $F^{\mathscr{D}}$ are empty. However, $G^{\mathscr{D}}$ must contain at least one predicate.

For ease of reference we shall say that a structure for L that satisfies conditions i–v is a model of L.

The way $\mathscr{D}$ is used to interpret L is analogous to the way we used structures to interpret first-order languages in chapter 5. We begin with the variable-free terms of $L(\mathscr{D})$, where $L(\mathscr{D})$ denotes the language we obtain from L by adding the names in N_{U_i} to the constants of the ith kind in L, $i \in \{1, \ldots, k\}$. Let b be a variable-free term in $L(\mathscr{D})$ of the i_0th kind. If b is a name, $\mathscr{D}(b)$ is taken to be the individual that b names. If b is not a name, there are variable-free terms a_{i_j}, $j = 1, \ldots, n$, and a function symbol $f^{i_0,i_1,\ldots,i_n}$ such that b is $f^{i_0,i_1,\ldots,i_n}(a_{i_1}, \ldots, a_{i_n})$. Then $\mathscr{D}(b)$ is taken to be $(f^{i_0,i_1,\ldots,i_n})^{\mathscr{D}}(\mathscr{D}(a_{i_1}), \ldots, \mathscr{D}(a_{i_n}))$.

Next, let b be a term in L of the i_0th kind, with n free variables $x_{i_1}, \ldots, x_{i_n}$, and let $\theta_{i_1}, \ldots, \theta_{i_n}$, respectively, be names in $N_{U_{i_j}}$, $j = 1, \ldots, n$. Also, let $b_{x_{i_1},\ldots,x_{i_n}}(\theta_{i_n}, \ldots, \theta_{i_n})$ be the term we obtain by substituting θ_{i_j} for x_{i_j} at each occurrence of x_{i_j} in b, $j = 1, \ldots, n$. Then $b_{x_{i_1},\ldots,x_{i_n}}(\theta_{i_1}, \ldots, \theta_{i_n})$ is a $\mathscr{D}$ instance of b. Our interpretation of variable-free terms in $L(\mathscr{D})$ determines the interpretation of every $\mathscr{D}$ instance of b. In that way the interpretation of variable-free terms determines the meaning of b as well.

To interpret the wffs of L we first interpret the closed wffs in $L(\mathscr{D})$ by induction on the length of wffs. Let A be a closed atomic formula. If A is $[a = b]$, where a and b are terms, then a and b must be variable-free. We insist that $\mathscr{D}(A) = \mathrm{t}$ if a and b are terms of the same kind and $\mathscr{D}(a) = \mathscr{D}(b)$. Otherwise $\mathscr{D}(A) = \mathrm{f}$. If A is $P^j(a_1, \ldots, a_n)$ for some $j \in J_n$ and variable-free terms $a_1, \ldots, a_n$, we insist that $\mathscr{D}(A) = \mathrm{t}$ if $(P^j)^{\mathscr{D}}$ $(\mathscr{D}(a_1), \ldots, \mathscr{D}(a_n))$, where

$(P^j)^{\mathscr{D}}$ designates the member of $G^{\mathscr{D}}$ that interprets P^j in $\mathscr{D}$. Otherwise $\mathscr{D}(A) = \text{f}$. If A is $R^{j_1,\ldots,j_n}(a_{j_1},\ldots,a_{j_n})$ for some $j \in \hat{J}_n$ and variable-free terms a_{j_m} of the j_mth kind, $m = 1, \ldots, n$, we insist that $\mathscr{D}(A) = \text{t}$ if $(R^{j_1,\ldots,j_n})^{\mathscr{D}}(\mathscr{D}(a_{j_1}),\ldots,\mathscr{D}(a_{j_n}))$. Otherwise $\mathscr{D}(A) = \text{f}$.

So much for atomic formulas. If A is a closed nonatomic wff, there are closed wffs B, C, and D such that A is $\sim B$ or $[B \supset C]$ of $(\forall x_i)D$ for some $i \in \{1,\ldots,k\}$. In each case, the value of $\mathscr{D}(A)$ is determined in the obvious way. Thus, if A is $\sim B$, $\mathscr{D}(A) = \text{t}$ if $\mathscr{D}(B) = \text{f}$; otherwise $\mathscr{D}(A) = \text{f}$. Moreover, if A is $[B \supset C]$, $\mathscr{D}(A) = \text{t}$ if $\mathscr{D}(B) = \text{f}$ or $\mathscr{D}(C) = \text{t}$; otherwise $\mathscr{D}(A) = \text{f}$. Finally, if A is $(\forall x_i)D$, $\mathscr{D}(A) = \text{t}$ if $\mathscr{D}(D_{x_i}(a)) = \text{t}$ for all variable-free terms a that are substitutable for x_i in D. Otherwise $\mathscr{D}(A) = \text{f}$.

The preceding description shows how the closed wffs of $L(\mathscr{D})$ are interpreted. Suppose next that B is a wff in L with n free variables, $x_{i_1}, \ldots, x_{i_n}$, and let $\theta_{i_n}, \ldots, \theta_{i_n}$, respectively, be names in $N_{U_{i_j}}$, $j = 1, \ldots, n$. Also let $B_{x_{i_1},\ldots,x_{i_n}}(\theta_{i_1},\ldots,\theta_{i_n})$ be the wff that we obtain from B by substituting θ_{i_j} for x_{i_j} at all free occurrences of x_{i_j} in B, $j = 1, \ldots, n$. Then $B_{x_{i_1},\ldots,x_{i_n}}(\theta_{i_1}, \ldots, \theta_{i_n})$ is a $\mathscr{D}$ instance of B. Our interpretation of closed wffs in $L(\mathscr{D})$ determines the interpretation of every $\mathscr{D}$ instance of B. In that way the interpretation I described above determines the meaning of B as well.

In the next theorem I show that the interpretations of $\mathscr{D}$ instances of terms and wffs described above is unambiguous. The proof of the theorem is, with only obvious modifications, identical to the proof of TM 5.15 and is, therefore, omitted here.

TM 25.7 Let $\mathscr{D}$ be a structure for L; let a be a variable-free term of the ith kind; and let $\theta \in N_{U_i}$ be the name of $\mathscr{D}(a)$. If b is a term of $L(\mathscr{D})$ in which no variable except x_i occurs, then $\mathscr{D}(b_{x_i}(a)) = \mathscr{D}(b_{x_i}(\theta))$. Also, if A is a wff in $L(\mathscr{D})$ in which no variable except x_i is free, then $\mathscr{D}(A_{x_i}(a)) = \mathscr{D}(A_{x_i}\theta))$.

The wffs that can be deduced from PLA 1–PLA 3 with the help of PRI 1 are tautologies. Such wffs denote truth in any structure because of the meaning of $\sim$ and $\supset$ alone. Examples are the values of TM 25.1 and TM 25.5.

We shall say that a wff B is valid in a structure $\mathscr{D}$ for L if and only if $\mathscr{D}(B') = \text{t}$ for every $\mathscr{D}$ instance B' of B. Then a closed wff A is valid in $\mathscr{D}$ if and only if $\mathscr{D}(A) = \text{t}$.

Finally, a wff A is valid if and only if it is valid in every model of L. Thus a tautology is a valid wff. Other examples are the values of MPLA 2–MPLA 5 and all the theorems that can be derived from MPLA 1–MPLA 5 with the help of MPRI 1. In the next section we shall see that there are no other valid wffs.

25.5 Semantic Properties of Many-Sorted Languages

In this section we record a completeness theorem for many-sorted languages and discuss many-sorted theories and their models. The results we obtain are multisorted analogues of TM 5.19, TM 6.3, and TM 6.10–TM 6.13.

We begin with the completeness theorem:

TM 25.8 If B is a wff of L, B is a theorem if and only if B is valid.

We prove this theorem in the appendix (section 25.8) by first creating a predicate-calculus alias of L, denoted $\hat{L}$, in which every wff B of L has a well-defined translation, $\hat{B}$. Then we show that B is a theorem of L if and only if $\hat{B}$ is a theorem of $\hat{L}$. From this and the completeness theorem for first-order theories, TM 6.11, follows the validity of TM 25.8.

Next the deduction theorem for L:

TM 25.9 Let A and B be wffs of L and suppose that A is closed. Then

$A \vdash B$ if and only if $\vdash [A \supset B]$.

The arguments needed to prove TM 25.9 are, with only obvious modifications, identical to those we used to prove TM 6.3. Hence, for brevity's sake, I omit the proof.

Theorems TM 25.8 and TM 25.9 can be used to establish analogues of TM 6.6 and TM 6.8, which concerned the existence of models of consistent finite collections of wffs Γ. More generally, we can show TM 25.10:

TM 25.10 Let A and Γ be, respectively, a wff and a collection of wffs in L. Then Γ is consistent if and only if Γ has a model. Also $A \in C_n(\Gamma)$ if and only if A is valid in every model of Γ.

This theorem is the multisorted analogue of TM 6.10 and TM 6.11. With only obvious modifications, the arguments we use to prove TM 25.8 can be used to establish TM 25.10 as well. Therefore I shall leave the proof of TM 25.10 to the reader.

The analogue of the compactness theorem of the predicate calculus is valid for many-sorted languages too—see TM 25.11.

TM 25.11 Let Γ be a collection of wffs of L and suppose that every finite subcollection of wffs in Γ possesses a model. Then Γ possesses a model too.

By appeal to TM 6.12 we can establish this theorem in the way we proved TM 25.8, i.e. by relating the wffs in Γ to their translations in $\hat{L}$. The collection $\hat{\Gamma}$ of translations of wffs in Γ is consistent if and only if Γ is consistent. Moreover, by TM 6.12, $\hat{\Gamma}$ is consistent if and only if every finite subcollection of $\hat{\Gamma}$ is consistent. Ditto for Γ.

Finally we note that the multisorted analogue of TM 6.13 is valid.

TM 25.12 Let Γ be a finite or denumerably infinite set of wffs of L and suppose that $T(\Gamma)$ is consistent. Then there is a model of Γ whose universe of discourse is either finite or denumerably infinite.

The validity of this theorem can also be proved by relating Γ to the collection of translations in $\hat{L}$ of the wffs in Γ.

25.6 A Language for Science

To construct a language that we can use to formulate tests of scientific theories we proceed in steps.

Step 1: Let L_t be a many-sorted language with k sets of individuals. The logical symbols of L_t are

$\sim \ \supset [\quad] (\ , \ ) \forall =$

and k nonoverlapping lists of individual variables,

$x_1 y_1 z_1 \cdots ; \cdots ; x_k y_k z_k \cdots .$

The nonlogical vocabulary of L_t consists of a selection from the following lists of constants, function symbols, and predicate symbols:

1. k disjoint sequences of constants $\alpha_1 \beta_1 \gamma_1 \cdots ; \cdots ; \alpha_k \beta_k \gamma_k \cdots$.
2. Indexed sets of predicate symbols, $\{P^j\}_{j \in J_n^t}$, $n = 1, 2, \ldots$. For each n and every $j \in J_n^t$, P^j is an n-ary predicate symbol.
3. Indexed sets of function symbols, $\{f^{i_0, i_1, \ldots, i_n}\}_{i \in I_n^t}$, $n = 1, 2, \ldots$. For each n and every $i \in I_n^t$, $f^{i_0, i_1, \ldots, i_n}$ is an n-ary function symbol.
4. Indexed sets of predicate symbols, $\{R^{j_1, \ldots, j_n}\}_{j \in \hat{J}_n^t}$, $n = 1, 2, \ldots$. For each n and every $j \in \hat{J}_n^t$, $R^{j_1, \ldots, j_n}$ is an n-ary predicate symbol.

Moreover, the terms and the sentence-formation rules and hence the wffs of L_t are as described in section 25.4.2. Finally, the logical axioms and the rules of inference of L_t are as described in section 25.4.3.

In the intended interpretation of the language we have set out to construct, L_t will be the language of a given theory, e.g., Newtonian Dynamics or the Theory of Consumer Choice. We denote the axioms of the theory by Γ_t and the theory by $T(\Gamma_t)$. For later reference we also let $C_n(\Gamma_t)$ denote the set of logical consequences of Γ_t in L_t.

Step 2: Let L_p be a many-sorted language with m sets of individuals. The logical symbols of L_p are

$\sim \supset [\ \ ](\ ,\ )\forall =$

and m nonoverlapping lists of individual variables,

$x_{k+1}\, y_{k+1}\, z_{k+1} \cdots; \cdots; x_{k+m}\, y_{k+m}\, z_{k+m} \cdots.$

The nonlogical vocabulary of L_P consists of a selection from the following lists of constants, function symbols, and predicate symbols:

1. m disjoint sequences of constants

$\alpha_{k+1}\, \beta_{k+1}\, \gamma_{k+1} \cdots; \cdots; \alpha_{k+m}\, \beta_{k+m}\, \gamma_{k+m} \cdots.$

2. Indexed sets of predicate symbols, $\{Q^j\}_{j \in J_n^P}, n = 1, 2, \ldots$. For each n and every $j \in J_n^P$, Q^j is an n-ary predicate.
3. Indexed sets of function symbols, $\{g^{i_0, i_1, \ldots, i_n}\}_{i \in I_n^P}$, $n = 1, 2, \ldots$. For each n and every $i \in I_n^P$, $g^{i_0, i_1, \ldots, i_n}$ is an n-ary function symbol.
4. Indexed sets of predicate symbols, $\{S^{j_1, \ldots, j_n}\}_{j \in \hat{J}_n^P}$, $n = 1, 2, \ldots$. For each n and every $j \in \hat{J}_n^P$, $S^{j_1, \ldots, j_n}$ is an n-ary predicate symbol.

In addition, the terms and sentence-formation rules and hence the wffs of L_p are as described in section 25.4.2. Finally, the logical axioms and the rules of inference are as described in section 25.4.3.

In the intended interpretation of the language we search for, L_p will be designed to talk about real-world objects that are observable at least to those who know how and where to look. These objects possess certain characteristics and relate to each other in definite ways. We assume that both the characteristics and the relationships can be delineated by a set of wffs in L_P which we denote by Γ_P and refer to as the nonlogical axioms of L_P. The corresponding theory is denoted by $T(\Gamma_P)$ and the logical consequences in L_p of Γ_P are denoted by $C_n(\Gamma_P)$.

Step 3: Let $L_{t,p}$ be a many-sorted language with $k + m$ sets of individuals. The first k sets are the k sets of individuals of L_t and the next m sets are the m sets of individuals of L_p. The logical symbols of $L_{t,p}$ are $\sim \supset [\ \ ](\ ,\ )$ $\forall =$ and $(k + m)$ nonoverlapping lists of individual variables. We assume that the first k lists of variables are the k lists of individual variables of L_t and that the next m lists of variables are the m lists of individual variables of L_p.

The nonlogical vocabulary of $L_{t,p}$ consists of three collections of constants, function symbols, and predicate symbols. The first contains all the nonlogical vocabulary of L_t and pertains to the k first sets of individuals. The second collection consists of the nonlogical vocabulary of L_p and pertains to the next m sets of individuals. The third collection consists of $(k+m)$ finite sets of constants, which we denote by θ_{ij}, $j = 1, \ldots, n_i$, $i = 1, \ldots, k+m$, and a selection from the following indexed sets of predicate symbols:

$$\{V^{j_1,\ldots,j_n}\}_{j \in \hat{J}_n^{t,p}}, \qquad n = 2, 3, \ldots$$

where, for each n and every $j \in \hat{J}_n^{t,p}$, $V^{j_1,\ldots,j_n}$ is an n-ary predicate symbol with at least one $j_i \leqslant k$ and one $j_i > k$.

With the terms so defined, the wffs of $L_{t,p}$ can be described as follows:

SMPFR 1 If t_1 and t_2 are terms, $[t_1 = t_2]$ is a wff.

SMPFR 2 If $t_{j_1}, \ldots, t_{j_n}$ are terms, $j_i \leqslant k$, $i = 1, \ldots, n$, and if P is an n-ary predicate symbol, then $P(t_{j_1}, \ldots, t_{j_n})$ is a wff.
$i_l \in \{1, \ldots, k\}$, $l = 0, \ldots, n$, and if $f^{i_0,i_1,\ldots,i_n}$ is an n-ary function symbol, then $f^{i_0,i_1,\ldots,i_n}(t_{i_1}, \ldots, t_{i_n})$ is a term of the i_0th kind.

SDMT 3 For each $i \in I_n^p$, $n = 1, 2, \ldots$, if t_{i_l} is a term of the i_lth kind with $i_l \in \{k+1, \ldots, m\}$, $l = 0, \ldots, n$, and if $g^{i_0,i_1,\ldots,i_n}$ is an n-ary function symbol, then $g^{i_0,i_1,\ldots,i_n}(t_{i_1}, \ldots, t_{i_n})$ is a term of the i_0th kind.

With the terms so defined, the wffs of $L_{t,p}$ can be described as follows:

SMPFR 1 If t_1 and t_2 are terms, $[t_1 = t_2]$ is a wff.

SMPFR 2 If $t_{j_1}, \ldots, t_{j_n}$ are terms, $t_i \leqslant k$, $j_i = 1, \ldots, n$, and if P is an n-ary predicate symbol, then $P(t_{j_1}, \ldots, t_{j_n})$ is a wff.

SMPFR 3 If $t_1, \ldots, t_n$ are terms with $k < t_i \leqslant k + m$, $i = 1, \ldots, n$, and if Q is an n-ary predicate symbol, $Q(t_1, \ldots, t_n)$ is a wff.

SMPFR 4 If t_{j_i} is a term of the j_ith kind, with $j_i \leqslant k$, $i = 1, \ldots, n$, and if $R^{j_1,\ldots,j_n}$ is an n-ary predicate symbol, then $R^{j_1,\ldots,j_n}(t_{j_1}, \ldots, t_{j_n})$ is a wff, $n = 1, 2, \ldots$.

SMPFR 5 If t_{j_i} is a term of the j_ith kind, with $k < j_i \leqslant k + m$, $i = 1, \ldots, n$, and if $S^{j_1,\ldots,j_n}$ is an n-ary predicate symbol, $S^{j_1,\ldots,j_n}(t_{j_1}, \ldots, t_{j_n})$ is a wff, $n = 1, 2, \ldots$.

SMPFR 6 If t_{j_i} is a term of the j_ith kind, $i = 1, \ldots, n$, and if $V^{j_1,\ldots,j_n}$ is an n-ary predicate symbol, then $V^{j_1,\ldots,j_n}(t_{j_1}, \ldots, t_{j_n})$ is a wff, $n = 2, 3, \ldots$.

SMPFR 7 If A is wf, then $\sim A$ is a wff.

SMPFR 8 If A and B are wffs, then $[A \supset B]$ is a wff.

SMPFR 9 For each $j = 1, \ldots, k+m$, if a is an individual variable of the jth kind and if A is a wff, then $(\forall a)A$ is a wff.

These formation rules and the preceding definition of terms provide an unambiguous characterization of the terms and wffs of $L_{t,p}$. Note that the terms and wffs of L_t and L_p are terms and wffs of $L_{t,p}$.

The logical axioms of $L_{t,p}$ are MPLA 1–MPLA 5, as stated in section 25.4.3. Moreover, the rules of inference of $L_{t,p}$ are as described in MPRI 1 of section 25.4.3.

A structure for $L_{t,p}$ is a triple, $\mathscr{D} = ((\mathscr{D}_i, \mathscr{D}_p), F^{\mathscr{D}}, G^{\mathscr{D}})$, where

$$\mathscr{D}_t = (|\mathscr{D}_1|, \ldots, |\mathscr{D}_k|, N_{\mathscr{D}_1}, \ldots, N_{\mathscr{D}_k}, F^{\mathscr{D}_t}, G^{\mathscr{D}_t})$$

is a structure for L_t;

$$\mathscr{D}_p = (|\mathscr{D}_{k+1}|, \ldots, |\mathscr{D}_{k+m}|, N_{\mathscr{D}_{k+1}}, \ldots, N_{\mathscr{D}_{k+m}}, F^{\mathscr{D}_p}, G^{\mathscr{D}_p})$$

is a structure for L_p; $F^{\mathscr{D}}$ is a collection of constants that interpret the constant symbols θ_{ij}; and $G^{\mathscr{D}}$ is a collection of predicates that interpret the V-predicate symbols of $L_{t,p}$. In the obvious way $\mathscr{D}$ is used to interpret the terms and wffs of $L_{t,p}$. A wff B in $L_{t,p}$ is valid in $\mathscr{D}$ if and only if every $\mathscr{D}$ instance of B is true. In particular, a closed wff B in $L_{t,p}(\mathscr{D})$ is valid in $\mathscr{D}$ if and only if $\mathscr{D}(B) = \mathrm{t}$.

Step 4: In $L_{t,p}$ we can present the theory to be tested and describe salient properties of the data that are to be used in the test. For that purpose we need four sets of axioms: (1) The axioms of the theory; they are expressed entirely in terms of the vocabulary of L_t and denoted by Γ_t (see step 1). (2) The axioms which describe the characteristics and relationships of the observations; they are expressed entirely in terms of the vocabulary of L_p and denoted by Γ_p (see step 2). (3) A set of axioms $\Gamma_{t,p}$, that delineate the relationship between the observational and the theoretical vocabulary. And (4) a set of axioms $D_{t,p}$ that describe the salient properties of the θ_{ij}.

Several remarks concerning the wffs in $\Gamma_{t,p}$ and $D_{t,p}$ are in order. First, for the purpose of testing $T(\Gamma_t)$, it is important that the wffs in $\Gamma_{t,p}$ be open. Hence in this chapter we shall assume that if A is a wff in $\Gamma_{t,p}$, then A is open. Second, we call the fourth set of axioms by the name $D_{t,p}$ to indicate that the θ constants of $L_{t,p}$ are used solely to design the statistical experiment we use to test $T(\Gamma_t)$. Third, to simplify our description of the statistical experiment we shall assume that

(i) $\Gamma_{t,p}$ contains only a finite number of wffs; and
(ii) if $A \in \Gamma_{t,p}$ and x_i and y_j are free variables of A, then $i \neq j$.

We denote by $T(\Gamma_t, \Gamma_p, \Gamma_{t,p})$ the theory which results from the first sets of axioms and let $Cn(\Gamma_t, \Gamma_p, \Gamma_{t,p})$ denote the set of logical consequences in

$L_{t,p}$ of the wffs in Γ_t, Γ_p, and $\Gamma_{t,p}$. Evidently, $Cn(\Gamma_t) \subset Cn(\Gamma_t, \Gamma_p, \Gamma_{t,p})$ and $Cn(\Gamma_p) \subset Cn(\Gamma_t, \Gamma_p, \Gamma_{t,p})$. From the point of view of the test, it is important that there exist wffs A and B such that A in L_t, B in L_p, $A \notin Cn(\Gamma_t)$, $B \notin Cn(\Gamma_p)$, $A \in Cn(\Gamma_t, \Gamma_p, \Gamma_{t,p})$, and $B \in Cn(\Gamma_t, \Gamma_p, \Gamma_{t,p})$.

We shall give informal examples of $L_{t,p}$ and $T(\Gamma_t, \Gamma_p, \Gamma_{t,p})$ in the next three chapters. These examples are all taken from econometrics. They are informal because the theories we develop in chapters 26–28 are not formalized in a many-sorted first-order language.

25.7 A Modal-Logical Apparatus for Testing Scientific Hypotheses

The multisorted language $L_{t,p}$ with its nonlogical axioms is the epistemological language for science for which we searched. In this section we see how $L_{t,p}$ can be used to test scientific hypotheses. We proceed in steps and begin by constructing a modal-logical language, SEL, which is designed to discuss properties of the closed wffs of $L_{t,p}(\xi)$, where ξ is a structure for $L_{t,p}$ that denotes the universe which the scientist faces.

Step 1: In this step we give a brief description of SEL: With the exception that the function symbols Kn and Bl are missing, the vocabulary of SEL is the same as the vocabulary of EL. Moreover, the terms and wffs of SEL are terms and wffs of EL; and the terms and wffs of EL that do not contain the symbols Kn and Bl are terms and wffs of SEL. Finally, SEL and EL have the same logical axioms and almost the same nonlogical axioms.

The nonlogical axioms of SEL are as follows:

SELA 1 ELA 6–ELA 8, ELA 9 (i) and (ii) and ELA 10.

SELA 2 If u, v, and w are propositional terms, then

(i) $[[\Gamma(u) \wedge \Xi(v)] \supset [[0 \leqslant p(u|v)] \wedge [P(u|v) \leqslant 1]]$;

(ii) $[[\Gamma(u) \wedge \Xi(v)] \supset [(P(u|v) + P(Nu|v)) = 1]]$;

(iii) $[[[\Gamma(u) \wedge \Gamma(w)] \wedge \Xi(v)] \supset [\Box \sim C(u,w)$

$\supset [(P(u|v) + P(w|v)) = P(D(u,w)|v)]]]$.

SELA 3 ELA 12.

SELA 4 If u, v, and w are propositional terms, then

(i) $[[\Xi(u) \wedge \Xi(v)] \supset [\Box I(u,v) \supset [0 < P(u|v)]]]$;

(ii) $[[\Gamma(w) \wedge [\Xi(u) \wedge \Xi(v)]] \supset [\Box I(u,v)$

$\supset [P(w|u) = P(u|v)^{-1}P(C(w,u)|v)]]]$.

These axioms differ from the nonlogical axioms of EL in that ELA 9 (iii) and ELA 14 and ELA 15 are missing and in that $P(\cdot|v)$ is taken to be additive for every v in Ξ.

The rules of inference of SEL are the same as the rules of inference of EL. Consequently, it is easy to ascertain that MLT 1–MLT 5 and ELT 1–ELT 3 are theorems of SEL and that ELT 4 with $\leqslant$ replaced by $=$ in (i) and (iii) is a theorem of SEL. It is also easy to obtain the appropriate analogues of ELT 5 and ELT 6. That is, we have SELT 1.

SELT 1 Let u, a, and w be propositional terms. Then

(i) $[[[\Xi(u) \wedge \Xi(w)] \wedge \Xi(C(u, w))] \supset [0 < P(u|w)]]$;

(ii) $[[\Gamma(w) \wedge [[\Xi(u) \wedge \Xi(a)] \wedge \Xi(C(u, a))]]$

$\supset [P(w|C(u, a)) = (P(C(u, w)|a)/P(u|a))]]$.

Moreover, it is obvious that the real-number theorems of EL are theorems of SEL.

Finally a structure for SEL is an eight-tuple

$$\mathscr{L}(L_{t,p}) = (\mathscr{L}_f, \mathscr{L}_l, \mathscr{X}, R, \xi, \varphi, R_{\square}, P^{\mathscr{L}}),$$

whose components are as follows:

1. $L_{t,p}$ is the language we described in section 25.6, and ξ is a structure for $L_{t,p}$ that is intended to represent the world as it is.

2. $\mathscr{L}_f = (|\mathscr{L}_f|, N_{\mathscr{L}_f}, F^{\mathscr{L}_f}, G^{\mathscr{L}_f})$ is a structure for a first-order language whose nonlogical vocabulary consists of the individual constant, function, and predicate symbols of SEL.

3. $\mathscr{L}_l = (|\mathscr{L}_l|, N_{\mathscr{L}_l}, F^{\mathscr{L}_l}, G^{\mathscr{L}_l})$ is a structure for a language whose nonlogical vocabulary consists of the propositional constant, function, and predicate symbols of SEL. Specifically, $F^{\mathscr{L}_l}$ contains the interpretations in $\mathscr{L}_l$ of $\square$, N, I and the propositional constants. For simplicity we shall denote the interpretation of $\square$ by $\square$ rather than $\square^{\mathscr{L}_l}$. Moreover, $G^{\mathscr{L}_l}$ contains the interpretations in $\mathscr{L}_l$ of TCL, Ξ, CL, and Γ which we denote, respectively, by $TCL^{\mathscr{L}_l}(\cdot)$, $\Xi^{\mathscr{L}_l}(\cdot)$, $CL^{\mathscr{L}_l}(\cdot)$ and $\Gamma^{\mathscr{L}_l}(\cdot)$. Finally, $|\mathscr{L}_l|$ is a set of wffs that contains the closed wffs of $L_{t,p}(\xi)$ and contains $\sim A$, $[A \supset B]$ and $\square A$ whenever it contains A; and $N_{\mathscr{L}_l}$ consists of all the names of the elements of $|\mathscr{L}_l|$—one name for each wff and different names for different wffs. We insist that

(i) the domain of $TCL^{\mathscr{L}_l}$ contains the closures of the logical theorems of $L_{t,p}$ and the closures of the logical consequences of Γ_t and Γ_p in $L_{t,p}(\xi)$;

(ii) the domain of $CL^{\mathscr{L}_l}(\cdot)$ consists of all the closed wffs of $L_{t,p}(\xi)$; and

(iii) the domain of $\Gamma^{\mathscr{L}_l}(\cdot)$ is the smallest set of wffs that contains all the closed wffs of $L_{t,p}(\xi)$ and contains $\sim A$, $[A \supset B]$ and $\Box A$ whenever it contains A and B. For simplicity we also insist that the domain of $\Gamma^{\mathscr{L}_l}(\cdot)$ is all of $|\mathscr{L}_l|$.

4. $\mathscr{X}$ is a set of structures for $L_{t,p}(\xi)$; R is a reflexive, transitive relation on $\mathscr{X}$; and the expansion of ξ to a structure for $L_{t,p}(\xi)$, which we denote by ξ_e, is a member of $\mathscr{X}$. We assume that $\mathscr{X}$ and ξ satisfy the following conditions:

(i) The structures in $\mathscr{X}$ are nonisomorphic models of $T(\Gamma_t, \Gamma_p, D_{t,p})$.

(ii) ξ and the structures in $\mathscr{X}$ that are in the relation R to ξ_e have universes that contain only a denumerable infinity of individuals of each kind.

(iii) The structures in $\mathscr{X}$ that are in the relation R to ξ_e have the same universe as ξ and name the individuals in the universe by the same names as ξ.

5. Let $CL^{\mathscr{L}_l}$ denote the domain of definition of $CL^{\mathscr{L}}(\cdot)$. Moreover, for each $H \in \mathscr{X}$, let $H(\cdot)\colon CL^{\mathscr{L}_l} \to \{\mathrm{t}, \mathrm{f}\}$ be such that $H(A)$ denotes the truth value of A in H. Then $\varphi(\cdot)\colon CL^{\mathscr{L}_l} \times \mathscr{X} \to \mathscr{P}(\mathscr{X})$ is defined by

$$\varphi(A, H) = \{H' \in \mathscr{X} : HRH' \text{ and } H'(A) = t\}.$$

6. $R_\Box \subset \mathscr{X} \times \mathscr{P}(\mathscr{X})$ and $(H, E) \in R_\Box$ if and only if $H \in \mathscr{X}$ and $E = \{H' \in \mathscr{X} : HRH'\}$.

7. $P^{\mathscr{L}}(\cdot|\cdot) : \mathscr{P}(\mathscr{X}) \times \mathscr{P}(\mathscr{X}) \to [0, 1]$.

8. There is a distinguished member K of $\Xi^{\mathscr{L}}$ that describes our knowledge before the test and is such that $P^{\mathscr{L}}(\varphi(K, \xi_e)|\{H \in \mathscr{X} : \xi_e RH\}) > 0$ and $P^{\mathscr{L}}(\cdot|\varphi(K, \xi_e))$ is σ-additive.

Before we can use $\mathscr{L}$ to interpret SEL we must, for each $H \in \mathscr{X}$, extend the domain of definition of $H(\cdot)$ to $|\mathscr{L}_l|$, and we must extend the domain of definition of $\varphi(\cdot)$ to $|\mathscr{L}_l| \times \mathscr{X}$. This we do by induction as follows: Let Γ_i, $i = 0, 2, \ldots$, be an increasing sequence of sets of wffs that satisfy the conditions, (i) $\Gamma_0 = CL^{\mathscr{L}_l}$ and (ii) if $A \in \Gamma_i$ for some $i \geqslant 1$, then there are wffs C and D in Γ_{i-1} such that A is C, $\sim C$, $[C \supset D]$, or $\Box C$. Then our characterization of $|\mathscr{L}_l|$ implies that $|\mathscr{L}_l| = \bigcup_{i=0}^{\infty} \Gamma_i$.

Next observe that, for each $H \in \mathscr{X}$, $H(\cdot)$ is defined on Γ_0 and $\varphi(\cdot)$ is defined on $\Gamma_0 \times \mathscr{X}$. Suppose that we have extended the definition of the $H(\cdot)$ and $\varphi(\cdot)$, respectively, to Γ_{n-1} and $\Gamma_{n-1} \times \mathscr{X}$. If $A \in \Gamma_n$, there are wffs C and D in Γ_{n-1} such that A is C, $\sim C$, $[C \supset D]$ or $\Box C$. If A is C, we let $H(A) = H(C)$. If A is $\sim C$, we let $H(A) = \mathrm{t}$ or f according as $H(C) = \mathrm{f}$ or t. If A is $[C \supset D]$, we let $H(A) = \mathrm{t}$ if $H(C) = \mathrm{f}$ or $H(D) = \mathrm{t}$ and we let $H(A) = \mathrm{f}$ otherwise. If A is $\Box C$, we let $H(A) = \mathrm{t}$ if $(H, \varphi(C, H)) \in R_\Box$.

Otherwise we let $H(A) = \text{f}$. Finally, we let $\varphi(A, H) = \{H' \in \mathscr{X} : HRH'$ and $H'(A) = t\}$.

A structure $\mathscr{L}$ with the functions $H(\cdot)$ extended to $|\mathscr{L}_l|$ and with $\varphi(\cdot)$ extended to $|\mathscr{L}_l| \times \mathscr{X}$ determines an interpretation of SEL in the same way as a structure for EL determines an interpretation of EL. In this interpretation we let SEL($\mathscr{L}$) denote the language we obtain from SEL by adding to SEL's nonlogical vocabulary the names in $N_{\mathscr{L}_f}$ and $N_{\mathscr{L}_l}$ as individual and propositional constants, respectively. Moreover, when u is a variable-free propositional term, we let $\mathscr{L}_l(u)$ designate the wff in $L_{t,p}(\xi)$ which u denotes in $\mathscr{L}$, and we let $\mathscr{L}(u)$ record the truth value of u in $\mathscr{L}$ and insist that $\mathscr{L}(u) = \xi_e(\mathscr{L}_l(u))$. Finally, when u and v are variable-free propositional terms in SEL($\mathscr{L}$) and α is $P(u|v)$, we let $\mathscr{L}_f(\alpha)$ designate the individual in $|\mathscr{L}_f|$ which α denotes in $\mathscr{L}$ and we insist that

$$\mathscr{L}_f(\alpha) = \mathscr{L}_f(P(u|v))$$
$$= \begin{cases} P^{\mathscr{L}}(\varphi(\mathscr{L}_l(u), \xi_e)|\varphi(\mathscr{L}_l(v), \xi_e)) & \text{if this term is well defined} \\ 0 & \text{otherwise.} \end{cases}$$

With this much said about the interpretation of SEL, I leave the remaining details to the reader.

The reader might find the assumptions made about ξ and $\mathscr{X}$ in our interpretation of SEL stringent. Hence it is important that he or she understand that there are good reasons why they are not: First, if $T(\Gamma_t, \Gamma_p, D_{t,p})$ has models whose universes contain infinitely many individuals of each kind, then $T(\Gamma_t, \Gamma_p, D_{t,p})$ has a model whose universe contains only a denumerable infinity of individuals of each kind. In fact, each model of $T(\Gamma_t, \Gamma_p, D_{t,p})$ whose universe contains infinitely many individuals of each kind has an elementary substructure whose universe contains only a denumerable infinity of individuals of each kind. Second, if the structures in $\mathscr{X}$ that are in the relation R to ξ_e have universes with a denumerable infinity of individuals of each kind, we can, for the purposes of our tests, without loss in generality assume that they have the same universe as ξ. Third, the tests we might propose use only the properties of individuals that are prescribed in the wffs of Γ_t, Γ_p, and $D_{t,p}$. Hence, if $T(\Gamma_t, \Gamma_p, D_{t,p})$ has a model with a denumerable infinity of individuals of each kind, we can, for the purposes of our tests, without loss in generality assume that the universe of ξ has a denumerable infinity of individuals of each kind.

It goes without saying that the preceding remarks take for granted that there are nonisomorphic models of $T(\Gamma_t, \Gamma_p, D_{t,p})$ whose universes have a denumerable infinity of individuals of each kind. If this were not the case

$T(\Gamma_t, \Gamma_p, D_{t,p})$ would be complete and $L_{t,p}$ could not be used to construct a test of $T(\Gamma_t)$.

Step 2: In this step we shall delineate a probabilistic framework within which we can formulate statistical tests of the validity of $T(\Gamma_t)$. We begin by letting

$$\Omega_H = \{\omega \in |\xi_1| \times \cdots \times |\xi_{k+m}|: \text{if } \eta \in N_{\xi_t} \times N_{\xi_p} \text{ and } H(\eta) = \omega, \text{ then}$$
$$\text{for all } A \in \Gamma_{t,p}, H(A_{x_1,\ldots,x_{k+m}}(\eta)) = t\};$$

$$\Omega = \bigcup_{H \in \mathscr{X}, \xi_e RH} \Omega_H; \text{ and } \mathscr{F} = \mathscr{P}(\Omega).$$

Next we define $N(\cdot): \mathscr{F} \to \mathscr{P}(N_{\xi_t} \times N_{\xi_p})$ by

$$N(B) = \{\eta \in N_{\xi_t} \times N_{\xi_p} : \eta \text{ is the name of some } \omega \in B\}, \qquad B \in \mathscr{F};$$

and $\tilde{Q}(\cdot): \mathscr{F} \to [0, 1]$ by

$$\tilde{Q}(B) = P^{\mathscr{L}}(\{H \in \mathscr{X} : \xi_e RH \text{ and, for some } \eta \in N(B),$$
$$H(A_{x_1,\ldots,x_{k+m}}(\eta)) = \text{t for all } A \in \Gamma_{t,p}\} | \varphi(K, \xi_e))$$

for each and every $B \in \mathscr{F}$. Then $\tilde{Q}(\cdot)$ is well defined and σ-additive on $\mathscr{F}$. Finally, we let $\tilde{P}(\cdot): \mathscr{F} \to [0, 1]$ be defined by

$$\tilde{P}(B) = \tilde{Q}(B)/\tilde{Q}(\Omega), \qquad B \in \mathscr{F}.$$

Then $\tilde{P}(\cdot)$ is a well-defined, σ-additive probability measure on $\mathscr{F}$.

So much for Ω, $\mathscr{F}$, and $\tilde{P}(\cdot)$. Next we let S be a set and F a one-to-one vector-valued mapping $F(\cdot): S \to \Omega$. S may, but need not, come with a structure. In the intended interpretation of S, S is a sample space, e.g., a set of consumers or a set of planetary orbits. If all observations are to be taken at one and the same place and time, S need not have a structure. However, if the observations are to be obtained over time and at different locations, S must be endowed with a structure.

As to $F(\cdot)$: This function assigns to each $s \in S$ a vector of attributes. If we let $F(\cdot) = (F_t(\cdot), F_p(\cdot))$, where $F_t(\cdot)$ contains the first k components of $F(\cdot)$ and F_p contains the last m components of $F(\cdot)$, then $F_t(s)$ and $F_p(s)$, respectively, satisfy the interpretation of Γ_t and Γ_p in all $H \in \mathscr{X}$ that are in the relation R to ξ_e. Moreover, there is an $H \in \mathscr{X}$ that is in relation R to ξ_e and is such that $F(s)$ satisfies the interpretation of $\Gamma_{t,p}$ in H; i.e., there is an $\eta \in N_{\xi_t} \times N_{\xi_p}$ and an $H \in \mathscr{X}$ such that $H(\eta) = F(s)$ and such that, for all $A \in \Gamma_{t,p}$, $H(A_{x_1,\ldots,x_{k+m}}(\eta)) = \text{t}$. It is possible that there is only one such H;

i.e., there need not exist an $H' \in \mathscr{X}$ such that $H' \neq H$, HRH' and $F(s) \in \Omega_{H'}$.

The mapping F and the triple $(\Omega, \mathscr{F}, \tilde{P}(\cdot))$ determine an experiment $(S, \mathscr{F}_S)$ and a σ-additive probability measure $Q(\cdot)$ on $(S, \mathscr{F}_S)$. To wit: $\mathscr{F}_S$ is the smallest σ-field of subsets of S that contains all sets of the form

$$A_S = \{s \in S : F(s) \in A\}, \qquad A \in \mathscr{F}.$$

Moreover, $Q(\cdot): \mathscr{F}_S \to [0, 1]$ is well defined by

$$Q(A_S) = \tilde{P}(A), \qquad A \in \mathscr{F}.$$

In the intended interpretation of $(S, \mathscr{F}_S, Q(\cdot))$, $Q(A_S)$ is the probability of observing an $s \in A_S$. Furthermore, to sample in S in accordance with a meaningful probability measure means to sample in accordance with $Q(\cdot)$.

If our choice of the constants θ_{ij}, ξ, and the structures in $\mathscr{X}$ that are in the relation R to ξ_e is bad, $(\Omega, \mathscr{F}, \tilde{P}(\cdot))$ and $(S, \mathscr{F}_S, Q(\cdot))$ need not be interesting. Keep, therefore, in mind that the θ_{ij}, ξ, and the H's are chosen at the discretion of "the experimenter." These entities ought to be chosen such that $\{s\} \in \mathscr{F}_S$ for all $s \in S$.

Step 3: In this step we assume that the θ_{ij}'s, ξ, and the H's have been chosen so that $(\Omega, \mathscr{F}, \tilde{P}(\cdot))$ and $(S, \mathscr{F}_S, Q(\cdot))$ are interesting from the viewpoint of testing the validity of $T(\Gamma_t)$. The problem we now face is twofold: (1) We must decide on a sampling scheme and formalize it mathematically; e.g., we must determine whether to sample at random in S or to use time series of observations on the elements of S. (2) We must introduce assumptions concerning the characteristics of $\tilde{P}(\cdot)$ that will make it possible to perform a statistical test of Γ_t; e.g., we may specify the signs of means and covariances of certain kinds of individuals in the universe of ξ. The necessity for such assumptions often arises because of errors of observations, the existence of unobservable factors, and/or simultaneous relations. I shall give examples of the problems caused by errors of observations and unobservable factors in chapters 27 and 28. Here I shall give an example of the simultaneity problem which is due to Haavelmo (1947, pp. 105–122), who was the first to formulate the economic simultaneous-equations model as a statistical hypothesis (1944, chapter III).

E 25.7 Suppose that Wright's Law gives a true description of the relationship between an economy's aggregate consumption c and aggregate personal disposable income y. Specifically, suppose that there are constants α and β and a sequence of random variables u_t, $t = 1, 2, \ldots,$ such that in each period t

(i) $c_t = \alpha + \beta y_t + u_t$

and such that $0 < \alpha$, $0 < \beta < 1$, $Eu_t = 0$, $Eu_t^2 < \infty$ and $Eu_t u_{t+s} = 0$ for $s \neq 0$ and $t + s \geqslant 1$. Suppose also that c, y, and the economy's aggregate investment expenditures z satisfy the accounting identity,

(ii) $y = c + z$.

Finally, suppose that the z_t, $t = 1, 2, \ldots$, are randomly independent of the u_t.

We wonder whether we can use (i) above to estimate α and β by applying the method of least squares to data on c and y. The answer is "no" because of the (simultaneous) relation between c and y described in (ii). To obtain reasonable estimates of α and β, we must first regress c on z to obtain least-squares estimates of $(\alpha/(1-\beta))$ and $(\beta/(1-\beta))$, say $\hat{a}$ and $\hat{b}$, and then solve

(iii) $\hat{a} = [\alpha/(1-\beta)]$ and $\hat{b} = [\beta/(1-\beta)]$

for α and β.

The probability spaces $(\Omega, \mathscr{F}, \tilde{P}(\cdot))$ and $(S, \mathscr{F}_s, Q(\cdot))$, together with the required assumptions concerning sampling schemes and the properties of $\tilde{P}(\cdot)$, provide us with a formal apparatus by which we can use $L_{t,p}$ and $T(\Gamma_t, \Gamma_p, \Gamma_{t,p})$ to test a scientific theory, $T(\Gamma_t)$. This formal apparatus is intended for situations in which a theory can be tested only by indirect means. In terms of $L_{t,p}$ the idea of an indirect test is to find a wff A in L_p which is a theorem of $T(\Gamma_t, \Gamma_p, \Gamma_{t,p})$ but not of $T(\Gamma_p)$ and to test the validity of Γ_t by testing the validity of A. The import of such a test can be illustrated as follows: Let $\models B$ mean that our data satisfy B and let B and C be the families of wffs used in the proof of A. Assume that the formulas in B and C are closed and that $C \subset \Gamma_t$. Suppose also a further fact:

We know that $\models B$ and we wonder whether $\models C$.

By assumption, $B, C \vdash A$. Hence, by the Deduction Theorem,

$\vdash [[B \wedge C] \supset A]$.

But, if that is so, then PLA 3 and Modus Ponens imply that

$\vdash [\sim A \supset [\sim B \vee \sim C]]$

and hence that

$\models [\sim A \supset [\sim B \vee \sim C]$.

Since $\models B$, we conclude that $\models [A \vee \sim C]$; i.e., if not A, then not C, and if A, the possibility of C cannot be rejected.

In many situations we cannot be sure that $\models B$. Note, therefore, that the validity of the preceding test depends on the validity of $\models B$. Because, if $\models \sim B$, A cannot be used to provide an indirect test of C since then $\models [\sim A \supset [\sim B \vee \sim C]]$ no matter whether $\models A$ or $\models \sim A$.[3]

With this much said about indirect tests we conclude our discussion of $L_{t,p}$, SEL, and the way these two languages can be used to formulate tests of scientific hypotheses. In the next three chapters I shall demonstrate how useful an informal version of the formal apparatus we have created can be in testing economic theories.

25.8 Appendix: Proof of The Completeness Theorem for Many-Sorted Languages

The main purpose of this appendix is to prove the Completeness Theorem for many-sorted languages. To do that we must first construct a predicate-calculus alias of L.

25.8.1 Predicate-Calculus Aliases of Many-Sorted Languages

A predicate-calculus alias of L is a first-order language $\hat{L}$ with the property that every wff A of L has a translation $\hat{A}$ in $\hat{L}$ such that A is a theorem of L if and only if $\hat{A}$ is a theorem of $\hat{L}$.

To construct $\hat{L}$ we must first construct two auxiliary multisorted languages $\tilde{L}$ and L_0. We begin with $\tilde{L}$: Let c_{i_j} be the jth constant of the ith kind in L and let S^{i_j} be a unary predicate symbol such that

$$LC(i,j)\colon [S_c^{i_j}(x_{i_j}) \equiv [x_{i_j} = c_{i_j}]], \qquad i = 1, \ldots, k;\ j = 1, 2, \ldots.$$

Also, for each n and every $i \in I_n$, let $S_f^{i_0, i_1, \ldots, i_n}$ be an $(n+1)$-ary predicate symbol such that

$$Lf(i_0, \ldots, i_n)\colon [S_f^{i_0, i_1, \ldots, i_n}(x_{i_0}, x_{i_1}, \ldots, x_{i_n}) \equiv [x_{i_0} = f^{i_0, i_1, \ldots, i_n}(x_{i_1}, \ldots, x_{i_n})]].$$

Finally, assume that the $S_c^{i_j}$ and the $S_f^{i_0, i_1, \ldots, i_n}$ are different from one another and from the P^j and $R^{j_1, \ldots, j_n}$ in L. Then $\tilde{L}$ is the multisorted language we obtain by adding first the $S_c^{i_j}$ and the $S_f^{i_0, i_1, \ldots, i_n}$ to the nonlogical vocabulary of L and then the $LC(i,j)$ and the $Lf(i_0, i_1, \ldots, i_n)$ as axioms to the axioms of L.

Next we construct L_0. The multisorted language L_0 is a language with k kinds of individuals, the same logical vocabulary as L, no constants and function symbols, and a list of predicate symbols that consists of the predicate symbols of L and all the $S_c^{i_j}$ and the $S_f^{i_0, i_1, \ldots, i_n}$ described above. The terms of L_0 are the variables of its logical vocabulary; and the wffs of L_0 are defined inductively by MPFR 1; MPFR 2; MPFR 3, with R replaced by R_0 and with R_0 varying through the $S_c^{i_j}$ and the $S_f^{i_0, i_1, \ldots, i_n}$ as well as the $R^{j_1, \ldots, j_n}$ of L; and MPFR 4–MPFR 6. Finally, the axioms of L_0 are given by the axiom schemata of L and the following lists of axioms concerning the $S_c^{i_j}$ and the $S_f^{i_0,i_1,\ldots,i_n}$:

L_0 1 For each constant symbol c_{i_j} of L,

$$(\exists x_{i_j}) S_c^{i_j}(x_{i_j}), \qquad i = 1, \ldots, k, j = 1, 2, \ldots.$$

L_0 2 For each constant symbol c_{i_j} of L,

$$(\forall x_{i_j})(\forall y_{i_j})[[S_c^{i_j}(x_{i_j}) \wedge S_c^{i_j}(y_{i_j})] \supset [x_{i_j} = y_{i_j}]].$$

L_0 3 For each n and every $i \in I_n$,

$$(\forall x_{i_1}) \cdots (\forall x_{i_n})(\exists x_{i_0}) S_f^{i_0,i_1,\ldots,i_n}(x_{i_0}, x_{i_1}, \ldots, x_{i_n}).$$

L_0 4 For each n and every $i \in I_n$,

$$(\forall x_{i_1}) \cdots (\forall x_{i_n})(\forall x_{i_0})(\forall y_{i_0})[[S_f^{i_0,i_1,\ldots,i_n}(x_{i_0}, x_{i_1}, \ldots, x_{i_n}) \wedge S_f^{i_0,i_1,\ldots,i_n}(y_{i_0}, x_{i_1}, \ldots, x_{i_n})] \supset [x_{i_0} = y_{i_j}]].$$

If we start from L_0, we can introduce the symbols c_{i_j} and $f^{i_0,i_1,\ldots,i_n}$ in L_0 by postulating $LC(i, j)$ and $Lf(i_0, i_1, \ldots, i_n)$. Let $\tilde{L}_0$ be the resulting extension of L_0 and observe that $\tilde{L}_0$ and $\tilde{L}$ have the same nonlogical vocabulary. Moreover, the axiom schemata L_0 1 — L_0 4 of L_0 are theorem schemata of $\tilde{L}$. From this it follows that a wff A is a theorem in $\tilde{L}_0$ if and only if it is a theorem in $\tilde{L}$. We will use this fact and the following metatheorem to establish a useful relationship between the wffs of L_0 and the wffs of L.

TM 25.13 Let $\tilde{L}$ and $\tilde{L}_0$ be as described above; and let A and B, respectively, be wffs of L and L_0. Then A is a theorem in $\tilde{L}$ if and only if A is a theorem in L. Also B is a theorem in $\tilde{L}_0$ if and only if B is a theorem in L_0.

The proof of this theorem is, with only obvious modifications, identical to the proof of TM 7.1 and TM 7.2. So I omit the proof here and refer the reader to Shoenfield 1967 (pp. 67–61) for details.

For our purposes, the relationship between L_0 and L can be characterized as follows: First we take TM 25.14:

TM 25.14 Let A be a wff in L_0. The *alias in* L of A is the wff A^0 that we obtain from A by replacing each occurrence of an $S_c^{i_j}(x)$ by $[x = c_{i_j}]$ and each occurrence of an $S_f^{i_0,i_1,\ldots,i_n}(x_{i_0}, x_{i_1}, \ldots, x_{i_n})$ by $[x_{i_0} = f^{i_0,i_1,\ldots,i_n}(x_{i_1}, \ldots, x_{i_n})]$. If A is a theorem of L_0, A^0 is a theorem of L and conversely.

The validity of this theorem is an easy consequence of TM 25.13 and the equivalence of $\tilde{L}_0$ and $\tilde{L}$. To wit: By TM 25.13 and TM 25.6, A^0 is a theorem of $\tilde{L}_0$ if and only if A is a theorem of L_0. By the equivalence of $\tilde{L}_0$ and $\tilde{L}$, A^0 is a theorem of $\tilde{L}_0$ if and only if it is a theorem of $\tilde{L}$. Finally, by TM 25.13, A^0 is a theorem of $\tilde{L}$ if and only if it is a theorem of L.

Next we consider a theorem concerning wffs in L and their representatives in L_0:

TM 25.15 Let B be a wff in L. *A representative of B in L_0* is a wff A whose alias in L, A^0, contains the same constants and function and nonlogical predicate symbols as B and is such that $[A^0 \equiv B]$ is a theorem of L. Every wff B of L has a representative wff A in L_0, and B is a theorem of L if and only if A is a theorem of L_0.

We shall prove, by induction on the length of terms, that the theorem is valid when B has the form $[x_i = b]$, where b is a term of the ith kind. With only obvious modifications, the same arguments suffice to show that the theorem is valid for any atomic formula B. The remainder of the proof can be obtained by induction on the length of B. I leave those details to the reader.

So suppose B is $[x_{i_0} = b]$, where b is a term of the i_0th kind. If b is a variable, there is nothing to prove; and if b is a constant, the validity of TM 25.15 for the given B follows from TM 25.14. If b is not a constant and not a variable, there is an n-ary function symbol $f^{i_0,i_1,\ldots,i_n}$ and terms $t_{i_1}, \ldots, t_{i_n}$ such that b is $f^{i_0,i_1,\ldots,i_n}(t_{i_1},\ldots,t_{i_n})$ and B is $[x_{i_0} = f^{i_0,i_1,\ldots,i_n}(t_{i_1},\ldots,t_{i_n})]$. Let B^* be the wff

$$(\exists x_{i_1})\cdots(\exists x_{i_n})[[x_{i_1} = t_{i_1}] \wedge [[x_{i_2} = t_{i_2}]\cdots \wedge [[x_{i_n} = t_{i_n}] \wedge [x_{i_0} = f^{i_0,i_1,\ldots,i_n}(x_{i_1},\ldots,x_{i_n})]]\cdots]].$$

We can use TM 25.3, MPLA 1, MPLA 2, and MPLA 5 to show that $[B \equiv B^*]$ is a theorem of L. Also, by the induction hypothesis, there are wffs A_j, $j = 1, \ldots, n$, of L_0 such that the alias of A_j in L, A_j^0, has the same constants and function symbols as $[x_{i_j} = t_{i_j}]$ and is such that $[A_j^0 \equiv [x_{i_j} = t_{i_j}]]$ is a theorem of L. Next, let A^0 be B^* with the $[x_{i_j} = t_{i_j}]$ replaced by A_j^0 and let A be the formula

$$(\exists x_{i_1})\cdots(\exists x_{i_n})[A_1 \wedge [A_2 \wedge [\cdots[A_n \wedge S_f^{i_0,i_1,\ldots,i_n}(x_{i_0}, x_{i_1},\ldots,x_{i_n})]\cdots]]].$$

Then A is a wff in L_0, A^0 is the alias of A, and A^0 has the same constants and function symbols as B. Also, by TM 25.6, $[A^0 \equiv B^*]$ is a theorem of L. Hence, by TM 25.5, $[B \equiv A^0]$ is a theorem of L. Since A^0 is the alias of A, it follows from this and TM 25.14 that B is a theorem of L if and only if A is a theorem of L_0. Thus we have shown that the theorem is true when B is $[x_{i_0} = b]$ for some $i_0 \in \{1,\ldots,k\}$.

We can use L_0 to construct $\hat{L}$. To wit: Let S_i, $i = 1, \ldots, k$, be a unary predicate symbol such that $S_i(x)$ if and only if x is an individual of the ith kind. then $\hat{L}$ is the first-order language whose nonlogical vocabulary consists of the predicate symbols of L_0 and the S_i described above, The terms if $\hat{L}$ are the variables of $\hat{L}$; and the wffs of $\hat{L}$ are as described in PFR 1–PFR 4 of section 5.1.2. Also, the axioms of $\hat{L}$ are given by PLA 1–PLA 7, the appropriate translations of L_0 1–L_0 4 in $\hat{L}$ and the following axioms

L̂A 1 For each $i = 1, \ldots, k$, $(\exists x)S_i(x)$.

L̂A 2 For each pair (i, j) such that $i \neq j$ and $i, j = 1, \ldots, k$,
$(\exists x)(\forall y)[[S_i(x) \wedge S_j(y)] \supset \sim[x = y]]$.

If A is a wff of L_0, a translation of A in $\hat{L}$, $\tilde{A}$, is a wff in which each subformula of A of the form $(\forall x_i)[-x_i-]$, $i \in \{1, \ldots, k\}$, is replaced by a wff of $\hat{L}$ of the form $(\forall x)\ [S_i(x) \supset [-x-]]$ in such a way that distinct variables of A are replaced by distinct variables in $\hat{A}$. The syntactic relationship between A and $\hat{A}$ is described in the following theorem (see Wang 1952, p. 107):

TM 25.16 Let A be a wff of L_0 and let $\hat{A}$ be a translation of A in $\hat{L}$. Then A is a theorem of L_0 if and only if $\hat{A}$ is a theorem of $\hat{L}$.

The proof of TM 25.16 is involved, so I omit it here and refer the reader to Wang 1952 (pp. 106–111) for details.

Let B be a wff of L and let A be its representative in L_0. We can think of a translation of A in $\hat{L}$ as a translation of B as well. If we do, TM 25.15 and TM 25.16 establish the fact that a wff B in L has a translation A in $\hat{L}$ such that A is a theorem of $\hat{L}$ if and only if B is a theorem of L.

25.8.2 The Completeness Theorem

In this section we shall sketch a proof of our completeness theorem, TM 25.8. For the purposes of the proof we let B be a wff of L. Also we let A be a representative of B in L_0. Finally, we let $\hat{A}$ be a translation of A in $\hat{L}$.

Let $\mathscr{D}$ be a structure for L. We can use $\mathscr{D}$ to construct a structure $\mathscr{D}_0$ for L_0. A structure for L_0 is a $(2k + 1)$-tuple

$$\mathscr{D}_0 = (U_1, \ldots, U_k, N_{U_1}, \ldots, N_{U_k}, G^{\mathscr{D}_0}),$$

where the U_i and the N_{U_i} are as in our description of a structure of L and where $G^{\mathscr{D}_0}$ contains the interpretations of the predicate symbols of L_0. To construct $\mathscr{D}_0$ from $\mathscr{D}$, we let the U_i, N_{U_i}, and the predicates of L be as described in $\mathscr{D}$. Also, for each pair i, j, we interpret $S_c^{i_j}$ as $\{\mathscr{D}(c_{i_j})\}$ and, for each n and every $i \in I_n$, we interpret $S_f^{i_0, i_1, \ldots, i_n}$ as the graph of

$(f^{i_0, i_1, \ldots, i_n})^{\mathscr{D}}$. Finally, we interpret $=$ in $L_0(\mathscr{D}_0)$ in the same way we interpreted $=$ in $L(\mathscr{D})$.

Above we started with a structure $\mathscr{D}$ for L and constructed $\mathscr{D}_0$. It is clear that, if $\mathscr{D}$ is a model of L, then $\mathscr{D}_0$ is a model of L_0 (i.e., a structure for L_0 in which all the axioms of L_0 are valid). It is also clear that we could have reversed the process; i.e., we could have started with a model of L_0 and constructed the corresponding model of L. From this it follows that B is valid in L if and only if A is valid in every model of L_0.

Let $\mathscr{D}$ and $\mathscr{D}_0$ be as above. Also let $U = \bigcup_{i=1}^{k} U_i$; let $N_U = \bigcup_{i=1}^{k} N_{U_i}$; let $\hat{S}_i(x)$ if and only if $x \in U_i$, $i = 1, \ldots, k$; and let $G^{\hat{\mathscr{D}}} = G^{\mathscr{D}_0} \cup \{\hat{S}_i, \ldots, \hat{S}_k\}$. Then

$$\hat{\mathscr{D}} = (U, N_U, G^{\hat{\mathscr{D}}})$$

is a structure for $\hat{L}$. Also $\hat{\mathscr{D}}$ is a model of $\hat{L}$ (i.e., a structure for $\hat{L}$ in which all the axioms of $\hat{L}$ are valid) if $\mathscr{D}_0$ is a model of L_0.

We can also start out with a structure $\hat{\mathscr{D}}$ that is a model of $\hat{L}$ and construct a model of L_0. Then we let $U_i = \{x \in U : \hat{S}_i(x)\}$, $i = 1, \ldots, k$, and let N_{U_i} consist of the names of the elements of U_i. We pick the names in N_{U_i}, $i = 1, \ldots, k$, so that $N_{U_i} \cap N_{U_j} = \varnothing$ if $i \neq j$. Since the U_i must be disjoint, N_U equals $\bigcup_{i=1}^{k} N_{U_i}$. Finally, we interpret the predicates of L_0 in the same way they are interpreted in $\hat{\mathscr{D}}$. The structure that we obtain in this way—i.e.,

$$\hat{\mathscr{D}}_0 = (U_1, \ldots, U_n, N_{U_1}, \ldots, N_{U_k}, G^{\hat{\mathscr{D}}_0}),$$

with $G^{\hat{\mathscr{D}}_0} = G^{\hat{\mathscr{D}}} - \{\hat{S}_1, \ldots, \hat{S}_n\}$—determines a model of L_0.

From the preceding two paragraphs we deduce that if A is a wff of L_0, then A is valid in every model of L_0 if and only if its translation $\hat{A}$ is valid in every model of $\hat{L}$. But, according to TM 6.11, $\hat{A}$ is valid in every model of $\hat{L}$ if and only if it is a theorem. Hence, by TM 25.16, A is valid in every model of L_0 if and only if it is a theorem. From this, TM 25.15, and the easily established fact that B is valid if and only if A is valid in every model of L_0 it follows that B is valid if and only if B is a theorem, as was to be shown.

VII

Econometrics I: Empirical Analysis of Economic Theories

26 Empirical Analysis of Economic Theories

In this chapter we see how the axiomatic method can be used to confront an economic theory with data. To do so, we build an axiomatic superstructure that contains the axioms of the theory and also delineates characteristic features of our data. *This superstructure represents an informal version of the formal apparatus for testing theories that we created in chapter 25. It is designed so that, if a model of its axioms exists, the model will describe one set of circumstances under which a particular interpretation of the theory can be applied.*

26.1 Four Kinds of Theorems

When constructing the desired axiomatic superstructure, a good way to begin is by sorting the theorems of the theory into groups. Usually there are three kinds.

1. *First there are theorems that can be used to test the empirical validity of the theory.*

One example of such a theorem in the standard theory of consumer choice is Samuelson's Fundamental Theorem, T 10.16. Another is T 10.9, which asserts that the consumer's demand function satisfies Houthakker's Strong Axiom of Revealed Preference. A third example is Savage's Expected Utility Theorem T 19.3, which concerns the theory of choice under uncertainty. A final example is a theorem from Modigliani and Brumberg's theory of the consumption function. We paraphrase that theorem in E 26.1.

E 26.1 Modigliani and Brumberg's theory of the consumption function (see Modigliani and Brumberg 1955, pp. 388–436) is an interpretation of T(H 1, ..., H 6) with the additional axiom

H 7 $V(\cdot)$ is homothetic.

In Modigliani and Brumberg's interpretation, $n = M - \alpha + 1$ and $x = (C_t, \ldots, C_{t+M-\alpha})$, where C_{t+i}, $i = 0, \ldots, M - \alpha$, denotes the consumer's expenditures on goods and services in year $t + i$, M denotes his expected life span in years, and α denotes his age in year t. Furthermore, $p = (1, 1/(1 + r), \ldots, [1/(1 + r)]^{M-\alpha})$, where r denotes the going interest rate, and

$$\hat{A} = A_{t-1} + y_t + \sum_{i=1}^{M-\alpha} [1/(1 + r)]^i y_{t+i},$$

where A_{t-1} and y_{t+i}, $i = 0, \ldots, M - \alpha$, denote, respectively, the consumer's net worth at the end of year $t - 1$ and his labor income during year $t + i$.

According to T 11.9, there is a continuous function, $g(\cdot)\colon R^n_{++} \to R^n_+$, such that the consumer's demand function, $f(\cdot)$, satisfies

$$f(p, \hat{A}) = g(p)\hat{A} \text{ for } (p, \hat{A}) \in R^n_{++} \times R_+.$$

Therefore, if we let $H(r) = g_1(1, 1/(1 + r), \ldots, [1/(1 + r)]^{M-\alpha})$, the consumer's demand for C_t can be written as

$$C_t = H(r)[A_{t-1} + y_t + (M - \alpha)y_t^e], \qquad r > 0, \tag{26.1}$$

where $(M - \alpha)y_t^e = \sum_{i=1}^{M-\alpha} [1/(1 + r)]^i y_{t+i}$.

We conclude: if H 1–H 7 hold and x, p, n, and $\hat{A}$ are interpreted as above, the consumer's demand for current consumption satisfies equation 26.1.

Besides theorems that provide bases for testing the empirical validity of an interpreted theory, there is another group of theorems:

2. *There are theorems that can be used to obtain factual information concerning properties of the theoretical constructs of the theory.*

One example of such a theorem is T 13.12 in the standard theory of consumer choice; this theorem establishes necessary and sufficient conditions on a consumer's demand function that his utility function be homothetic. A second example of such a theorem is T 12.7; it establishes on a consumer's demand for risky assets necessary and sufficient conditions that his absolute risk-aversion function be a decreasing function of net worth.

Strictly speaking, theorems such as T 13.12 and T 12.7 mentioned above cannot be used to establish conclusively that a given theoretical construct (e.g., the consumer's utility function) has a specific structural property. They can only be used in conjunction with data to show that certain hypotheses concerning the structural properties of the theoretical constructs in question are empirically untenable. For instance, the data we use to test Arrow's theory suggest that Arrow's conjecture that a consumer's proportional risk-aversion function increases with his net worth is false.

There is a third group of theorems that provide neither testable hypotheses nor indirect information about the properties of theoretical constructs of the theory.

3. *There are theorems that guide the economist in his search for good ways to confront his theory with data.*

For instance, if we use regression analysis to estimate a consumer's demand function, the values of the parameters we estimate must satisfy several linear equalities and nonlinear inequalities. Some of these are easily derived from the equality, $pf(p, A) = A$. Others can be deduced from T 10.16.

The econometrician, besides heeding linear and nonlinear restrictions on the values of the parameters he estimates, must also worry about problems of aggregation. These occur in many disguises. For instance, while economic theories of choice usually concern choice of well-defined commodities, such as sugar and salt, and specific securities, such as shares in IBM or Ford Motor, the econometrician's data often refer to expenditures on groups of commodities and groups of securities. Some theorems are sensitive to aggregation. Others are not. The Hicks-Leontief Aggregation Theorem in the standard theory of consumer choice, T 10.17, shows that the main theorems of that theory are true of composite commodities, if the prices of the components of the composite commodities vary proportionately within the respective groups. However, Arrow's and Pratt's theorems concerning the monotonic properties of the absolute and proportional risk-aversion functions and the consumer's demand for safe and risky assets are untrue if the risky asset is interpreted as an aggregate of many risky securities. Therefore, one of the main problems we face in testing Arrow's theory, is to delineate the class of utility functions that would render his consumer's demand for risky assets insensitive to such aggregation problems. Theorems T 12.14–T 12.18 provide the required characterization of utility functions.

In the cases cited, the existence of the relevant aggregates is obvious. In other situations the existence of the aggregates that are needed for the empirical analysis may be hard to establish. Cases in point are meaningful index numbers in consumer theory and capital aggregates in production theory and in macroeconomic theory. Below I give an example of a theorem that establishes necessary and sufficient conditions on a firm's single-vintage production functions for the existence of a capital aggregate. Prescriptions for constructing capital aggregates—when they exist—are given in Stigum 1967 (pp. 349–367).

E 26.2 Consider a firm that utilizes n vintages of a single capital good, k_i, $i = 1, \ldots, n$, and assume that the production opportunities available to this firm can be represented by n *single-vintage production functions* of capital and labor,

$$f_i(\cdot)\colon R_+^2 \to R_+, \qquad i = 1, \ldots, n$$

that are nondecreasing, continuous, and satisfy

(i) $f_i(0, L_i) = f_i(k_i, 0) = 0$ for $(k_i, L_i) \in R_+^2$, and

(ii) $f_i(k_i, \cdot)$ is a concave function for each fixed $k_i \in R_+$.

Then the firm's *multivintage production function*, $H(\cdot): R_+^{n+1} \to R_+$, is given by

$$H(k, L) = \max_{\sum_{i=1} L_i \leqslant L, L_i \geqslant 0} \sum_{i=1}^{n} f_i(k_i, L_i),$$

where $k = (k_1, \ldots, k_n)$. Moreover, $j(\cdot): R_+^n \to R_+$ is a *capital aggregate of* $H(\cdot)$ if and only if there exists a function, $H^*(\cdot): R_+^2 \to R_+$, such that $H^*(j(k), L) = H(k, L)$ for all $(k, L) \in R_+^{n+1}$.

We can show: Let $j_i(\cdot)$, $i = 1, \ldots, n$, be nondecreasing, continuous functions from R_+ onto R_+. Then there exists a capital aggregate $j(\cdot)$ such that

$$j(k) = \sum_{i=1}^{n} j_i(k_i), \qquad k \in R_+^n$$

if and only if there exists a nondecreasing, continuous function, $F(\cdot): R_+^2 \to R_+$, that is homogeneous of degree 1 and satisfies $f_i(k_i, L_i) = F(j_i(k_i), L_i)$, $(k_i, L_i) \in R_+^2$, $i = 1, \ldots, n$. For a proof see Stigum 1967 (p. 356).

The three groups of theorems described above, constitute the main body of an economic theory. There is a fourth group:

4. *There are theorems that are relevant to the import of factors for which the theory does not account.*

These are usually obtained by adding simplifying assumptions to the original set of axioms. For instance, when the standard theory of consumer choice is interpreted as in chapter 11, we can determine the effect of age on current consumption if the consumer's utility function has a simple additive structure (see T 11.8). Similarly, we can determine the import of education if we make assumptions about how education affects the consumer's income stream. For later reference, I give an example of the simplifying assumptions concerning consumer behavior that Modigliani and Brumberg proposed in Modigliani and Brumberg 1955 (pp. 394–397). Other examples can be obtained with the help of T 11.7 and T 11.9.

E 26.3 Modigliani and Brumberg suggested several simplifying assumptions for the analysis of their consumer's behavior. Two of them were

$$r = 0 \text{ and } \frac{g_i(p)}{g_j(p)} = (1 + r)^{i-j} \qquad i, j = 0, \ldots, M - \alpha.$$

If they hold, equation 26.1 becomes

$$C_t = (M - \alpha + 1)^{-1}[A_{t-1} + y_t + (M - \alpha)y_t^e].$$

With respect to confronting theory with data, the fourth group of theorems is open-ended. The economist may prove some such theorems to determine what kind of information he can extract from real-life observations. He may prove other such theorems after he has analyzed his data; in that case his objective is to find assumptions that can be used to rationalize certain characteristics of the data. Whatever an economist's motives for establishing the theorems in the fourth group are, such theorems play an important role in the dynamics of theory formation.

26.2 The Structure of an Empirical Analysis

We have sorted our theorems into groups. Next we interpret them and put them in four boxes T_1, T_2, T_3 and T_4, according to the order in which we discussed them. In that way we complete the left side of the schematic process illustrated in figure 26.1. The top half of this figure repeats the relevant part of the schema presented in figure 2.1: three boxes, one with the undefined terms, one with the axioms, and one with the theorems. On the right side of the schema, we interpret the undefined objects and axioms of the original theory and distribute them on three boxes with universal names. We then add a box of axioms concerning the interpreted objects that contains the simplifying assumptions of the theorems in T_4 to complete the right side of the schema.

In looking at figure 26.1, one observation is especially important: What is a theoretical construct in the context of one empirical analysis need not be a theoretical construct in another. For example, when we confront T(H 1, ..., H 6) with data, $V(\cdot)$ will always designate a theoretical construct. On the other hand, if we were to add to H 1, ..., H 6 an axiom A that insists that $V(x)=\prod_{i=1}^{n} x_i^{\alpha_i}$, then in an empirical analysis of T(H 1, ..., T 6, A), $V(\cdot)$ would denote a theoretical construct only if the α_i were not estimable. The α_i may be estimable in one situation and not in another.

It is also important to observe that whatever the interpreted versions of the undefined objects may be, it is about them that the theorems in T_1, ..., T_4 talk, and it is they that we put in the boxes for "observable objects" and "theoretical constructs." With that in mind we continue the construction of our axiomatic superstructure.

First we use information stored in a "design" box to single out the objects that are to play the role of undefined terms in the theory-data confrontation. Some of these terms will denote objects in the "observable objects" and "theoretical constructs" boxes. Others will denote objects for which the "design" box insists that we have records. Next we use ideas

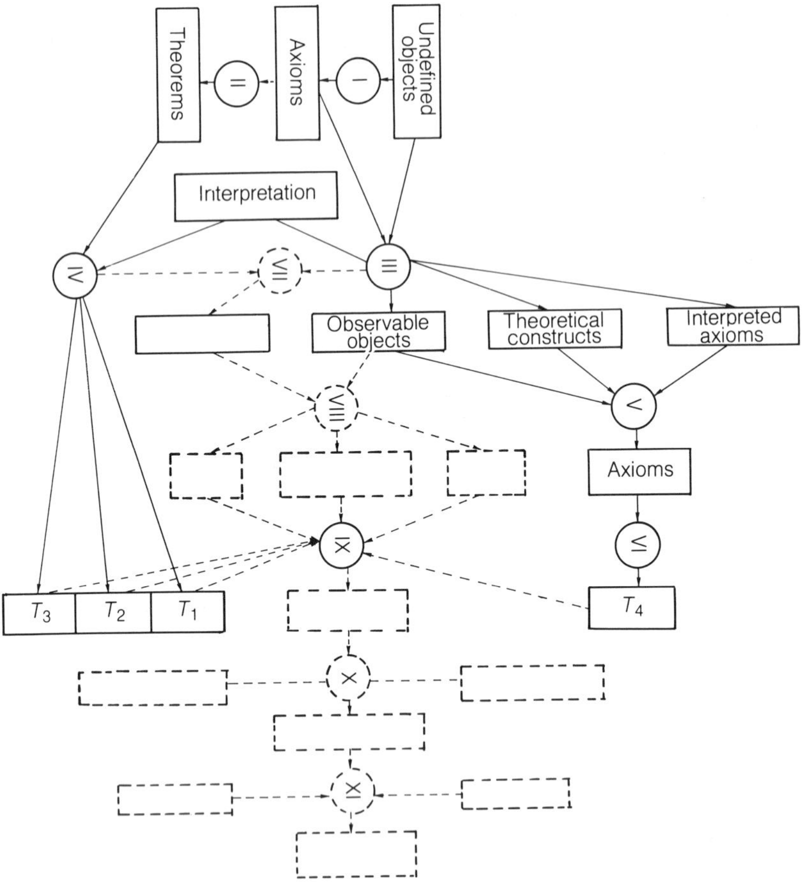
Theorems
II
Axioms
I
Undefined objects
Interpretation
IV
VII
III
Observable objects
Theoretical constructs
Interpreted axioms
VIII
V
Axioms
IX
VI
T_3
T_2
T_1
T_4
X
XI

Figure 26.1

contained in the T_i boxes and information from the "design" box to write the axioms of the empirical analysis. Finally, we place the axioms into an "axioms" box and proceed to use them and the necessary universal theorems to derive useful theorems for the theory-data confrontation. We call such theorems *sample theorems* and store them in a box with this name.

The "sample theorems" box puts the finishing touch on our axiomatic superstructure. To use it in empirical analysis, we must first interpret the undefined terms and collect data. When that is done, we use the data and the sample theorems to test the validity of the proposed model of the original theory. (See figure 26.2.)

We have described briefly an axiomatic superstructure that can be used as a basis for testing an economic theory. Our superstructure is pictured in figures 26.1 and 26.2. We shall next describe in more detail the contents of the "axioms," "sample theorems," and "tests" boxes in figure 26.2.

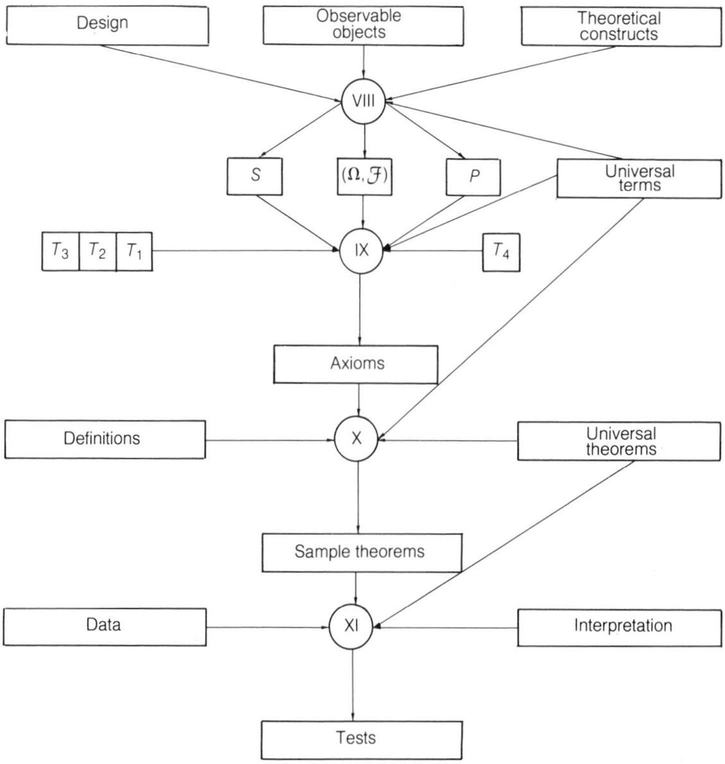

Figure 26.2

26.2.1 The Undefined Terms: S, $(\Omega, \mathscr{F})$, and $P(\cdot)$

In the schema depicted in figure 26.2, the undefined objects are the *sample population* S, the *sample space* $(\Omega, \mathscr{F})$, the *sampling distribution* $P(\cdot)$, and two vectors, ω_T and ω_P. In the intended interpretation, $\Omega = \Omega_T \times \Omega_P$, $\omega_T \in \Omega_T$, and $\omega_P \in \Omega_P$. Also, interpreted versions of the undefined terms of the original theory are components of ω_T; components of ω_P denote the objects of the empirical investigation. Hence the subscripts T and P may be read, respectively, as theory and population.

There are components in ω_T for each of the objects in the "observable objects" and "theoretical constructs" boxes and for other objects as well. How many components there are depends on the kind of empirical analysis we envisage. For instance, if we were to use budget data to obtain information concerning characteristics of a consumer's demand function, ω_T would have one component for each of the components of the vector, (p, x, A, V), where the respective letters refer to prices, commodities, income, and the utility function. The vector might also have one component for each of the factors age, profession, education, race, and region, and several components of error terms. If instead of cross-section data, we were to use time-series data to study consumer behavior, ω_T would have components for each of the components of the vector, $(A(M-1), p(M), y(M), \ldots, p(K), y(K))$, where $[M, K]$ denotes the time interval over which we have observations and $A(i-1)$, $p(i)$, and $y(i)$ denote, respectively, net worth at the beginning of period i and prices and income in period i. Also, ω_T would have components for error terms and whatever factors we think might be relevant for our analysis.

How many components ω_P must have will depend on the characteristics of the empirical analysis undertaken. Certainly, ω_P will have components which the econometrician associates with specific components of ω_T. For instance, in a budget study of consumer behavior, ω_P will have one component for each component of p and components for such aggregates as expenditures on cheese, shoes, and skis. In addition, ω_P will have components that represent instrumental variables and other extralogical observable variables that play a role in the empirical analysis. That is so even though these variables are not mentioned in the interpretation of the theory. Finally, ω_P may have components that denote unobservable factors such as risk and entrepreneurship, factors that need not have any representative components in ω_T.

E 26.4 The preceding comments concerning S, $(\Omega, \mathscr{F})$, $P(\cdot)$, and (ω_T, ω_P) are reflected in the first six axioms of the axiomatic superstructure that we shall use to test Modigliani and Brumberg's theory of the consumption function, which we described in E 26.1:

M 1 Let $\#S$ denote the number of elements in S. Then $S \in \{1, 2, \dots\}$.

M 2 $\Omega \subset R^{16}$ and $\mathscr{F}$ is a σ field of subsets of Ω.

M 3 $P(\cdot)$ is a probability measure on $(\Omega, \mathscr{F})$.

M 4 $\omega_T = (r, c_t, y_t, y_t^e, A_{t-1}, M, \alpha, u, v, \eta, \delta)$,

$\omega_P = (\tilde{r}, \tilde{c}_t, \tilde{y}_t, \tilde{A}_{t-1}, \tilde{\alpha})$, and $(w_T, w_P) \in \Omega$.

M 5 There is a one-to-one mapping,

$F(\cdot): S \to \Omega$.

In the interpretation of these axioms that we intend, the components of ω_T represent the interpreted versions of r, C_t, y_t, y_t^e, A_{t-1}, M, and α in Modigliani and Brumberg's theory and four error terms: u, v, η, and δ. Also, the components of ω_P represent the observed counterparts of r, c_t, y_t, and A_{t-1} and an age group.

Note that in the preceding example the observed values of w_P will depend both on the sample design and on the population from which the sample is drawn. We shall test Modigliani and Brumberg's theory using data collected by the Federal Reserve Board.[1] These data pertain to economic choices made by a group of U.S. consumers during 1962 and 1963. For each consumer in the sample, the data provide information on 1962 end-of-year net worth, which we take to be the denotation of $\tilde{A}_{t-1}$; on 1963 disposable income, which will be the denotation of $\tilde{y}_t$; on the change in his net worth during 1963; and on the age of the head of the household in 1963, which we take as the age of the consumer. In our test we let the denotation of $\tilde{c}_t$ equal $\tilde{y}_t$ minus the change in the consumer's net worth during 1963. The values of $\tilde{c}_t$ that we observe are different from the values we would have observed in a budget study of the same consumers.

26.2.2 The Axioms concerning Ω

For our testing the empirical relevance of an economic theory, there are two sets of axioms in the "axioms" box of figure 26.2. First we have two sorts of axioms concerning Ω. One kind specifies the denotation of the components of $\omega = (\omega_T, \omega_P)$. These axioms may assert that some of the components of ω can take on one value only, that others can take on values in a subset of R or in certain abstract spaces. For instance, in a study based on budget data of consumer-demand functions, the econometrician may assume that prices do not vary over his sample of consumers. If he does, he will postulate that the price components of ω_T equal some arbitrary constant vector. Similarly, if the econometrician denotes a consumer by a household and the age of the consumer by the age of the head of the household, and if the latter is recorded in years, he will postulate that the age component of ω_T can take on only a certain number of integral values.

The second kind of axioms concerning Ω specifies the functional relationships that hold between the components of ω. For instance, some axioms may define aggregation operators which transform components of ω_T representing, say, ages, different kinds of corporate shares, and different kinds of shoes into components of ω_P which, when interpreted, will denote age groups, investments in stocks, and expenditures on shoes. Still other axioms may postulate the existence of "errors-in-variable" operators and "partial-adjustment" operators. In the simplest cases an operator of the former kind uses an error-term component, v, of ω_T to transform a component, a, of ω_T into a component, b, of ω_P according to the equation, $b = a + v$. An operator of the latter kind generally uses a subvector, $z = (z_0, \ldots, z_k)$, of ω_P, an error-term component, η, of ω_T, and a $(k + 1)$-tuple of constants, $(\alpha_0, \ldots, \alpha_k)$, to transform a component, d, of ω_T into a component, e, of ω_P according to the equation,

$$e = \alpha_0(d - z_0) + \sum_{i=1}^{k} \alpha_1 z_i + \eta.$$

Finally, there are axioms that postulate functional relationships between the components of ω_T; these can be derived from the $T_1 - T_4$ boxes. Examples of such axioms are given in E 26.5 below.

E 26.5 In E 26.4 we recorded the first five axioms of the superstructure we shall use to test Modigliani and Brumberg's theory. Here we present seven more. Together with M 2 and M 4, these provide a complete characterization of the components of (ω_T, ω_P). In reading these axioms, note that the ω_T components of $F(s)$ must satisfy equations 26.2–26.6 for all $s \in S$ with $F(s) \in \Omega(\alpha)$. Note also that equation 26.3 is the sample analogue of equation 26.1; and finally note that, if we were to use equation 26.6 to define v, the values assumed by v would, for a given pair $(v, f(\alpha))$, depend on y_t^e but not on A_{t-1} and y_t. The importance of this observation will become apparent later.

M 6 $\alpha \in \{15, \ldots, 100\}$.

M 7 There is a one-to-one mapping

$G(\cdot)\colon \{15, \ldots, 100\} \to \{76, \ldots, 200\}$

such that, for all (ω_T, ω_P),

$$M = G(\alpha). \qquad (26.2)$$

M 8 Let $\Omega(\hat{\alpha}) = \{(\omega_T, \omega_P) \in \Omega\colon \alpha = \hat{\alpha}\}, \qquad \hat{\alpha} \in \{15, \ldots, 100\}$.

There exists a function

$H(\cdot): R_{++} \times \{15, \ldots, 100\} \to R_{++}$

such that, for all $(\omega_T, \omega_P) \in \Omega(\alpha)$,

$$c_t = H(r, \alpha)\{A_{t-1} + y_t + (M - \alpha)y_t^e\}. \tag{26.3}$$

M 9 Let

$$f(\alpha) = \begin{cases} 25 & \text{if } \alpha < 35 \\ 5(i+6)+2 & \text{if } 5(i+6) \leqslant \alpha < 5(i+7), \qquad i = 1, \ldots, 6 \\ 70 & \text{if } 65 \leqslant \alpha. \end{cases}$$

Then for all $\alpha \in \{15, \ldots, 100\}$,

$$H(r, f(\alpha)) = H(r, \alpha), \qquad r \in R_{++} \tag{26.4}$$

$$G(f(\alpha)) = G(\alpha). \tag{26.5}$$

M 10 For all $(\omega_T, \omega_P) \in \Omega$,

$$c_t = H(r, f(\alpha))\{A_{t-1} + y_t + (M - f(\alpha))y_t^e\} + v. \tag{26.6}$$

M 11 $r = \bar{r}$.

M 12 For all $(\omega_T, \omega_P) \in \Omega$,

$$(\tilde{r}, \tilde{c}_t, \tilde{y}_t, \tilde{A}_{t-1}, \tilde{\alpha}) = (r, c_t, y_t, A_{t-1}, f(\alpha)).$$

In the interpretation of the axioms that we intend, M 6 postulates that consumers in the sample population are between 15 and 100 of age. M 7 insists that consumers of the same age have the same expected life span (in years), M, and that M belongs to the interval [76, 200]. M 8 (together with M 7) postulates that consumers of the same age have the same consumption function. Finally, M 9, M 10, and M 11 describe how the consumption function varies over consumers within a given age group, e.g., over consumers who are less than 35 years of age or over consumers who are between 50 and 55 years of age.

With respect to the last example, recall that we intend to interpret the components of ω_T as denoting interpreted versions of the undefined terms of Modigliani and Brumberg's theory and the components of ω_P as denoting their observed counterparts. Therefore M 12 does not assert that the given components of ω_T and ω_T are identical. Instead, M 12 postulates that, whatever interpretation we give to the undefined terms of Modigliani and Brumberg's theory, we shall be able to obtain an accurate record of their values in the sample population.

26.2.3 The Axioms concerning $P(\cdot)$ and $(\Omega, \mathscr{F})$

The second set of axioms concern $P(\cdot)$ and $(\Omega, \mathscr{F})$. In most theory-data confrontations in economics, $P(\cdot)$ is an N-tuple, $\{P_i(\cdot)\}$, where N denotes the number of observations on (ω_T, ω_P) which the econometrician envisions and $P_i(\cdot)$ denotes the sampling distribution of the ith observation,

$i = 1, \ldots, N$. Therefore, one of the axioms concerning $P(\cdot)$ may postulate that the $P_i(\cdot)$ are probability measures on $(\Omega, \mathscr{F})$ that satisfy the condition, $P(A_1 \times \cdots \times A_N) = \prod_{i=1}^{N} P_i(A_i)$. In different words, the axiom may insist that the sample is a random sample. The data we use to test Modigliani and Brumberg's theory were obtained by a stratified random sampling scheme, the details of which are described in E 26.6.

E 26.6 The Federal Reserve survey was carried out according to a stratified random sampling scheme in which consumers were stratified by income. Some of the characteristics of this sampling scheme are reflected in the next three axioms of the superstructure we build for Modigliani and Brumberg's theory.

M 13 Let a_i be one of the numbers \$3000, \$5000, \$7500, \$10,000, \$15,000, \$25,000, \$50,000, and \$100,000, with $a_1 < a_2 < \cdots < a_8$. Moreover, let I_i be defined by

$$I_1 = \{(\omega_T, \omega_P) \in \Omega : y_t < a_1\},$$

$$I_i = \{(\omega_T, \omega_P) \in \Omega : a_{i-1} \leqslant y_t < a_i\}, \qquad i = 2, \ldots, 8$$

$$I_9 = \{(\omega_T, \omega_P) \in \Omega : y_t \geqslant a_8\}.$$

Then $I_i \in \mathscr{F}$ and $P(I_i) > 0$, $i = 1, \ldots, 9$.

M 14 There are N observations with n_i observations from I_i, $i = 1, \ldots, 9$. The probability distribution of the sample is given by

$$\prod_{i=1}^{9} (P(\cdot \mid I_i))^{n_i},$$

where $P(\cdot \mid I_i)$ denotes the conditional probability measure on Ω, given I_i.

M 15 Let $\Omega_{\tilde{\alpha}} = \{(\omega_T, \omega_P) \in \Omega : \tilde{\alpha} = f(\alpha)\}$, $\tilde{\alpha} = 25, 37, \ldots, 70$. Then $\Omega_{\tilde{\alpha}} \in \mathscr{F}$ and $P(I_i \cap \Omega_{\tilde{\alpha}}) > 0$ for all $(i, \tilde{\alpha})$, $i = 1, \ldots, 9$ and $\tilde{\alpha} = 25, 37, \ldots, 70$.

In the interpretation of the axioms that we intend, M 13 (together with M 5) delineates a partition of S according to income:

$$S_i = F^{-1}(I_i), \qquad i = 1, \ldots, 9.$$

Moreover, M 14 insists that we have sampled within income groups according to a random sampling scheme. Finally, M 15 postulates that if we partition the sample population into age groups according to the value of $f(\cdot)$ (see M 9) such that

$$S(\tilde{\alpha}) = F^{-1}(\Omega_{\tilde{\alpha}}), \qquad \tilde{\alpha} = 25, 37, \ldots, 70$$

then the probability of sampling a consumer in $S_i \cap S(\tilde{\alpha})$ is positive for all $i = 1, \ldots, 9$ and $\tilde{\alpha} = 25, 37, \ldots, 70$; e.g., the probability of sampling a consumer whose disposable income is between \$15,000 and \$25,000 and whose age is between 45 and 50 years is positive.

Besides axioms describing characteristics of the sampling distribution, an econometrician uses axioms that specify the joint distribution of error terms and certain other components of ω_T. He may use still others that characterize the stochastic relationship of a given set of instrumental variables to some of the unobservable components of ω_T. And if he employs factor analysis as one method to test his theory, he will also need axioms that specify the joint distribution of the components of ω_T that represent the factors of the analysis. Finally, the econometrician may use axioms that impose restrictions on the variances and the covariances of components of ω_T. In econometric text books, such restrictions are usually dealt with under the heading "heteroscedasticity," "collinearity," and "problems of identification."

E 26.7 We complete in this example the axioms of the superstructure we use to test Modigliani and Brumberg's theory.

M 16 Relative to $P(\cdot|I_i \cap \Omega_{\tilde{\alpha}})$, $i = 1, \ldots, 9$, $\tilde{\alpha} = 25, 37, \ldots, 70$, the variance of A_{t-1} is positive, and the variances of y_t and y_t^e are both positive and independent of i. All three variances are finite.

M 17 Relative to $P(\cdot|I_i \cap \Omega_{\tilde{\alpha}})$, $i = 1, \ldots, 9$, $\tilde{\alpha} = 25, 37, \ldots, 70$, the variable v in M 10 has mean zero and finite variance; the covariances of v and A_{t-1} and v and y_t are zero; and the variance of v is independent of i.

M 18 For each pair, $(i, \tilde{\alpha})$, $i = 1, \ldots, 9$, $\tilde{\alpha} = 25, 37, \ldots, 70$, there exist constants, $\gamma_{i\tilde{\alpha}}$ and $\beta_{\tilde{\alpha}}$, and a random variable u such that, in $I_i \cap \Omega_{\tilde{\alpha}}$,

$$y_t^e = \gamma_{i\tilde{\alpha}} + \beta_{\tilde{\alpha}} y_t + u. \tag{26.7}$$

Also, relative to $P(\cdot|I_i \cap \Omega_{\tilde{\alpha}})$, the covariances of the pairs (y_t, u) and (A_{t-1}, u) are zero; the variance of u and the covariance of u and v are finite and independent of i; and the mean of u is zero.

M 19 Relative to $P(\cdot|I_i \cap \Omega_{\tilde{\alpha}})$, $i = 1, \ldots, 9$, $\tilde{\alpha} = 25, 37, \ldots, 70$, the covariance matrix of A_{t-1} and y_t is nonsingular.

With respect to the postulates in E 26.7, note that the properties of u imply that $\gamma_{i\tilde{\alpha}}$ and $\beta_{\tilde{\alpha}}$ in equation 26.7 are the regression coefficients of y_t^e and y_t relative to $P(\cdot|I_i \cap \Omega_{\tilde{\alpha}})$. The existence of such regression coefficients is an immediate consequence of M 16; the proof of this is a standard theorem in statistics. Strictly speaking, we assume in M 18 only that $\beta_{\tilde{\alpha}}$ is independent of i, and that relative to $P(\cdot|I_i \cap \Omega_{\tilde{\alpha}})$ u is stochastically orthogonal to A_{t-1} and the covariance of u and v is independent of i. We also note that M 16 and M 18 imply that the covariance of y_t and y_t^e relative to $P(\cdot|I_i \cap \Omega_{\tilde{\alpha}})$ is independent of i.

To conclude our discussion of the axioms concerning $P(\cdot)$ and $(\Omega, \mathscr{F})$, we note that the sample distribution $P(\cdot)$ induces a probability distribution on S in accordance with

$$Q(F^{-1}(B)) = P(B), \qquad B \in \mathscr{F}. \tag{26.8}$$

If we let $\mathscr{F}_S$ be the σ field of subsets of S that consists of all subsets of S that are inverse images under $F(\cdot)$ of sets that belong to $\mathscr{F}$, then $Q(\cdot)$ is a probability measure on $(S, \mathscr{F}_S)$. In the intended interpretation of M 1–M 19, $Q(F^{-1}(I_i))$ measures the probability that the surveyors assign to observing a consumer with disposable income in $[a_{i-1}, a_i)$; $Q(B|F^{-1}(I_i))$ measures the probability of observing a consumer in B in a sample of consumers with disposable income in $[a_{i-1}, a_i)$. Note that, in our particular interpretation of the axioms, the probabilities $Q(F^{-1}(I_i))$, $i = 1, \ldots, 9$, do not equal the proportion of U.S. consumers that in 1963 had disposable incomes in the respective sets $[a_{i-1}, a_i)$, $i = 1, \ldots, 9$. The Federal Reserve Board surveyors designed their sampling scheme so that families in the upper income brackets would be overrepresented in the sample. Specifically, they attempted to obtain a sample with each n_i in M 15 as close to 400 as possible.[2]

26.2.4 Sample Theorems

There are roughly four kinds of sample theorems. First there are the axioms. Then there are theorems that assert that certain functional relationships exist between the components of ω_P. For later use, I give an example of the latter kind in E 26.8.

E 26.8 In this example, we assume that M 1–M 19 are valid. If that is so, we can establish the following theorem:

T 26.1 There exist constants, $\varphi_{i\tilde{\alpha}}$, $\psi_{1\tilde{\alpha}}$, and $\psi_{2\tilde{\alpha}}$, and random variables, $\delta_{\tilde{\alpha}}$, $i = 1, \ldots, 9$, $\tilde{\alpha} = 25, 37, \ldots, 70$, such that

$$\varphi_{i\tilde{\alpha}} = H(\overline{r}, \tilde{\alpha})(M - \alpha)\gamma_{i\tilde{\alpha}}, \qquad i = 1, \ldots, 9,\ \tilde{\alpha} = 25, 37, \ldots, 70 \tag{26.9}$$

$$\psi_{1\tilde{\alpha}} = H(\overline{r}, \tilde{\alpha}), \qquad \tilde{\alpha} = 25, 37, \ldots, 70 \tag{26.10}$$

$$\psi_{2\tilde{\alpha}} = H(\overline{r}, \tilde{\alpha})[1 + (M - \tilde{\alpha})\beta_{\tilde{\alpha}}], \qquad \tilde{\alpha} = 25, 37, \ldots, 70 \tag{26.11}$$

and

$$\delta_{\tilde{\alpha}} = v + (M - \tilde{\alpha})H(\overline{r}, \tilde{\alpha})u, \qquad \tilde{\alpha} = 25, 37, \ldots, 70 \tag{26.12}$$

and such that, for all pairs $(i, \tilde{\alpha})$,

$$\tilde{c}_t = \varphi_{i\tilde{\alpha}} + \psi_{1\tilde{\alpha}}\tilde{A}_{t-1} + \psi_{2\tilde{\alpha}}\tilde{y}_t + \delta_{\tilde{\alpha}} \tag{26.13}$$

is the regression of $\tilde{c}_t$ on $\tilde{A}_{t-1}$ and $\tilde{y}_t$ relative to $P(\cdot|I_i \cap \Omega_{\tilde{\alpha}})$; i.e., $\delta_{\tilde{\alpha}}$ has mean zero, finite variance, and zero covariance with $\tilde{A}_{t-1}$ and $\tilde{y}_t$. The variance of $\delta_{\tilde{\alpha}}$ relative to $P(\cdot|I_i \cap \Omega_{\tilde{\alpha}})$ is independent of i.

An econometrician uses a third group of sample theorems, and whatever universal theorems are needed, to decide what the relevant test statistics are and to determine the qualitative properties of these statistics. Such theorems may, for example, determine whether a given test statistic is biased, and if not, whether it is best linear unbiased. Other theorems may specify whether an estimator is asymptotically unbiased, consistent, and asymptotically efficient. Examples of such theorems are readily found in the literature. For later reference, I give an example here.

E 26.9 In E 26.8 the error terms, u and v, the constant, M, and the function, $H(\cdot)$, are unobservable. Hence it is impossible to determine whether a given interpretation of $\tilde{c}_t$, $\tilde{A}_{t-1}$, and $\tilde{y}_t$ satisfies equation 26.13 with $\delta_{\tilde{\alpha}}$, $\psi_{1\tilde{\alpha}}$, $\psi_{2\tilde{\alpha}}$, and the $\varphi_{i\tilde{\alpha}}$ as specified in equations 26.9–26.12. However, we can make probabilistic inferences about this by using the observed values of $\tilde{c}_t$, $\tilde{A}_{t-1}$, and $\tilde{y}_t$ to estimate the coefficients in

$$\tilde{c}_{ts} = a + \sum_{i=1}^{8} b_i \xi_{is} + d\tilde{A}_{t-1,s} + e\tilde{y}_{ts} + \varepsilon_{ts}, \qquad s \in F^{-1}(\Omega_{\tilde{\alpha}}) \tag{26.14}$$

for $\tilde{\alpha} = 25, 37, \ldots, 70$, where

$$\xi_{is} = \begin{cases} 1 & \text{if } s \in F^{-1}(I_i) \\ 0 & \text{otherwise.} \end{cases}$$

According to T 26.2 below, the least-quares estimates of a, d, e, and the b_i are consistent estimates of $\varphi_{9\tilde{\alpha}}$, $\psi_{1\tilde{\alpha}}$, $\psi_{2\tilde{\alpha}}$, and $\varphi_{i\tilde{\alpha}} - \varphi_{9\tilde{\alpha}}$, $i = 1, \ldots, 8$, respectively. Hence, for a sufficiently large number of observations, the signs of the estimated values of a, d, e, and the b_i ought to equal the signs of their theoretical counterparts.

T 26.2 Let n be the number of observed consumers in $F^{-1}(\Omega_{\tilde{\alpha}})$, and let $n(I_i \cap \Omega_{\tilde{\alpha}})$be the corresponding number in $F^{-1}(I_i \cap \Omega_{\tilde{\alpha}})$, $i = 1, \ldots, 9$. Also, let $\hat{a}^n$, $\hat{d}^n$, $\hat{e}^n$, and $\hat{b}_i^n$ be the least-squares estimates of a, d, e, and b_i, $i = 1, \ldots, 8$; and suppose that as the number N of observations goes to ∞,

$$\lim n(I_i \cap \Omega_{\tilde{\alpha}})/n = P(I_i|\Omega_{\tilde{\alpha}}), \qquad i = 1, \ldots, 9. \tag{26.15}$$

Finally, suppose that the given interpretation of $\tilde{c}_t$, $\tilde{A}_{t-1}$, and $\tilde{y}_t$ satisfies equation 26.13. Then in terms of $P(\cdot|\Omega_{\tilde{\alpha}})$,

$$\lim \hat{a}^n = \varphi_{9\tilde{\alpha}} \quad \text{a.e.},$$

$$\lim(\hat{a}^n + \hat{b}_i^n) = \varphi_{i\tilde{\alpha}} \quad \text{a.e.}, \qquad i = 1, \ldots, 8$$

$$\lim \hat{d}^n = \psi_{1\tilde{\alpha}} \quad \text{a.e.},$$

and

$$\lim \hat{e}^n = \psi_{2\tilde{\alpha}} \quad \text{a.e.}$$

Depending on the econometrician's attitude toward his data, the fourth group of sample theorems concern either the distribution of the test statistics that he proposed in his third group of theorems or the posterior distributions of the parameters which he associates with his test statistics. If the econometrician is a frequentist, he will be concerned with the distribution of test statistics. If he is a Bayesian, he will compute posterior distributions. The probabilistic evaluation of the model of the theory depends on the theorems the econometrician uses in his tests. This fact was illustrated in section 18.3.2 when we discussed the difference between the frequentist and the Bayesian approach to estimating the parameters of a normal distribution.

26.2.5 Testing an Economic Theory

To test an economic theory means to check whether a given interpretation of the theory has empirical relevance. It does if the interpretation which we intend for the undefined terms of the associated axiomatic superstructure is a model of the axioms of the superstructure.

The natural way to see if a given interpretation of an axiom system is valid is to check the axioms one by one to determine whether each is a true statement about an interpreted object. Often this is easy for some axioms because they are true by definition: axioms M 2–M 5 in E 26.4 are such axioms. Other axioms ought to be true by design, but need not be. Examples are M 1, M 6, and M 11–M 15. We intend them to be true by design; however, it is difficult to design a stratified random sampling scheme, and harder still to carry it out in the manner described in M 14. The researchers at the Federal Reserve Board failed in this respect; they intended each n_i in M 14 to equal 400, but obtained sample sizes ranging from 325 for $i = 3$ to 453 for $i = 5$. Thus in their sampling scheme, the n_i were random variables, not constants.

Of the remaining axioms, some make assertions as to the stochastic properties of the data; examples are M 16–M 19 in E 26.7. The validity of such axioms ought to be tested directly if possible. Other axioms concern both the interpretation of the original theory and characteristics of the sample population; cases in point are M 7 and M 8 in E 26.5. If Modigliani and Brumberg's theory is true, and if all consumers of the same age, α, order commodity bundles the same way, then M 5 and M 7 imply that M 8 is true for all consumers $s \in F^{-1}(\Omega(\alpha))$. Most axioms of the last kind contain hypotheses about theoretical constructs and cannot be tested directly; instead they must be tested indirectly by checking whether the interpreted objects satisfy sample theorems derived from the axiom system as a whole. Indirect tests were discussed briefly in section 25.6. An example of such a test is given below:

E 26.10 In this example, we assume that the axioms in T(M 1, ..., M 19) that are "true by design" are "true in fact." Thus we disregard the failure of the researchers at the Federal Reserve Board to obtain exactly 400 observations in each income group. We also ignore the possibility that our data do not satisfy

M 12. We do this because Modigliani and Brumberg ignored such a possibility and because we want to test their theory in accordance with their own prescriptions. Finally, we assume that M 16–M 19 are valid. Our purpose is to describe an indirect test of {M 5, . . . , M 10}. In terms of the characterization of such tests in section 25.6, B is {M 1, . . . , M 4, M 11, . . . , M 19}, C is {M 5, . . . , M 10}, and A is T 26.1.

We used the Federal Reserve Board data with our interpretation of $\tilde{c}_t$, $\tilde{A}_{t-1}$, and $\tilde{y}_t$ to estimate a, d, e, and the b_i in equation 26.14. The estimates, with their respective t values in parentheses underneath, are presented in table 26.1. In reading it, note that D.F. stands for residual degrees of freedom.

According to T 26.1 and equation 26.10, $\psi_{1\tilde{\alpha}} > 0$. From this and from T 26.2, it follows that our interpretation of M 1–M 19 cannot be valid unless our estimates of d for the various age groups are positive and differ significantly from zero. In table 26.1 we see that, with one exception, the d's are positive and differ significantly from zero at the 0.01 level of significance. The estimate of d for the $\geqslant 65$ age group is negative but does not differ significantly from zero. Since our sample is large, these results represent favorable evidence for the validity of our interpretation of M 1, . . . , M 19; i.e., they do not allow us to reject {M 5, . . . , M 10}.

If we had no idea of how equation 26.13 was derived, we might have insisted (on the basis of introspective arguments alone) that $\psi_{2\tilde{\alpha}}$ should be positive. Note, therefore, that T 26.2 does not assert this for the simple reason that $\psi_{2\tilde{\alpha}}$ is not a *behavioral parameter*; it is a product of $\psi_{1\tilde{\alpha}}$ with the factor $(1 + (M - \tilde{\alpha})\beta_{\tilde{\alpha}})$. While $\psi_{1\tilde{\alpha}}$ must be positive on theoretical grounds, the sign of $(1 + (M - \tilde{\alpha})\beta_{\tilde{\alpha}})$ depends on both the sign and the size of $\beta_{\tilde{\alpha}}$ and $\beta_{\tilde{\alpha}}$ is not a behavioral parameter. It is a statistical parameter, the value of which depends on the stochastic properties of y_t^e and y_t in the sample population. Thus we cannot determine the sign or value of $\beta_{\tilde{\alpha}}$ by searching our innermost feelings or by appealing to analogy.

As the preceding observations would lead us to expect, the signs of the estimates of e in table 26.1 are not uniformly positive. The estimate of e is positive and significantly different from zero at the 0.01 level of significance for the <35 and the $\geqslant 65$ age groups. It is negative and significantly different from zero at the 0.01 level of significance for the 35–39, 50–54, 55–59, and 60–64 age groups. Finally, it is, for all practical purposes, zero for the 40–44 and 45–49 age groups. The corresponding values of $\beta_{\tilde{\alpha}}$ are given in table 26.2 below for different values of M, where M is as specified in equations 26.2 and 26.5.

The axioms concerning the theory and the characteristics of the sample population are not the only axioms that involve theoretical constructs. Some axioms specifying the stochastic properties of the data may also involve such unobservable constructs. If they do, we can test them only indirectly. E 26.11 gives an example of such a test.

E 26.11 In E 26.10 axioms M 5–M 10 passed the indirect test proposed there. However, the negative values of $\beta_{\tilde{\alpha}}$ in table 26.2 are disconcerting. Therefore in this example we construct an indirect test of M 18.

Table 26.1
Least-squares estimates of the coefficients in $c_{ts} = a + \sum_{i=1}^{8} b_i \xi_{is} + d\tilde{A}_{t-1,s} + e\tilde{y}_{ts} + \varepsilon_{ts}$.

Age groups	$\hat{a}$	$\hat{b}_1$	$\hat{b}_2$	$\hat{b}_3$	$\hat{b}_4$	$\hat{b}_5$	$\hat{b}_6$	$\hat{b}_7$	$\hat{b}_8$	$\hat{d}$	$\hat{e}$	R^2	D.F.
	Coefficients												
<35	1138	779	902	1138	1068	1229	2101	−15509	11390	0.0610	0.6399		
	(1.206)	(−0.454)	(−0.461)	0	(−0.132)	(0.102)	(0.517)	(−4.446)	(1.303)	(9.839)	(3.830)	0.78976	329
35–39	370762	9256	17040	25026	32778	43896	64051	101112	−26241	0.1171	−3.6937		
	(8.746)	(−8.626)	(−8.658)	(−8.656)	(−8.613)	(−8.530)	(−8.407)	(−7.850)	(−15.330)	(31.923)	(−9.090)	0.92745	182
40–44	817	1255	2318	3748	5411	6742	13944	6514	39027	0.0269	0.1944		
	(0.022)	(0.119)	(0.413)	(0.831)	(0.133)	(0.177)	(0.415)	(0.206)	(1.741)	(8.113)	(0.516)	0.6068	211
45–49	19504	918	327	1084	1234	2391	2167	−995	11891	0.0474	0.5453		
	(9.521)	(−0.503)	(−0.530)	(−0.523)	(−0.533)	(−0.517)	(−0.564)	(−0.789)	(−0.400)	(9.481)	(1.205)	0.6594	214
50–54	42095	3461	4703	7749	10339	13333	15657	24069	59807	0.0586	−0.6056		
	(2.250)	(−2.019)	(−1.993)	(−1.867)	(−1.747)	(−1.638)	(−1.518)	(−1.084)	(1.225)	(14.672)	(−3.481)	0.6764	225
55–59	121162	1590	6390	9321	12980	17644	25521	48711	68889	0.0214	−0.9007		
	(4.835)	(−4.717)	(−4.667)	(−4.656)	(−4.598)	(−4.588)	(−4.488)	(−3.946)	(−3.304)	(5.558)	(−3.082)	0.4614	228
60–64	121424	3421	6088	9248	13236	16744	30868	49738	9321	0.0191	−0.9461		
	(6.058)	(−5.835)	(−5.726)	(−5.624)	(−5.407)	(−5.588)	(−5.016)	(−4.370)	(−4.656)	(12.381)	(−4.196)	0.6828	184
≥65	−67496	−1738	−4302	−5468	−8762	−15665	−19381	−35553	−74403	−0.0022	2.3151		
	(−3.191)	(3.140)	(3.068)	(3.034)	(2.889)	(2.631)	(2.594)	(2.066)	(−0.581)	(−0.809)	(8.172)	0.5623	348

Note: The t values in the b_i column are t values of $\hat{b}_i - \hat{a}$, $i = 1, \ldots, 8$.

Table 26.2
Estimated values of $\beta_{\tilde{\alpha}} = [(\psi_{2\tilde{\alpha}} - \psi_{1\tilde{\alpha}})/(M - \tilde{\alpha})\psi_{1\tilde{\alpha}}]$.

	Age groups							
$M = G(\tilde{\alpha})$	<35	35–39	40–44	45–49	50–54	55–59	60–64	$\geqslant 65$
75	0.2109	−0.8564	0.1887	0.3752	−0.4928	−2.3938	−3.8872	−210.4636
80	0.1898	−0.7568	0.1639	0.3183	−0.4048	−1.8736	−2.8074	−105.3318
85	0.1725	−0.6780	0.1448	0.2764	−0.3439	−1.5389	−2.1971	−70.2212
90	0.1582	−0.6140	0.1297	0.2443	−0.2983	−1.3057	−1.8048	−52.6659

Table 26.3
F ratio results of covariance analysis.

	Age							
	<35	35–39	40–44	45–49	50–54	55–59	60–64	⩾65
F	1.27	5.17	2.74	5.92	0.57	1.10	0.84	0.65

If all the axioms of T(M 1, ..., M 19) except M 18 are valid, then M 18 is true only if $\psi_{2\tilde{\alpha}}$ in equation 26.13 is independent of i. To test whether it is, we first obtain the least-squares estimates of the coefficients in

$$\tilde{c}_{ts} = a + \sum_{i=1}^{8} b_i \xi_{is} + d\tilde{A}_{t-1} + \sum_{i=1}^{9} e_i \tilde{y}_{is} + \zeta_s, \qquad s \in F^{-1}(\Omega_{\tilde{\alpha}}), \quad \tilde{\alpha} = 25, 37, \ldots, 70, \tag{26.16}$$

where

$$\tilde{y}_{is} = \begin{cases} y_{ts} & \text{if } s \in F^{-1}(I_i) \\ 0 & \text{otherwise.} \end{cases}$$

Then we construct the standard covariance table and consult the F distribution to determine whether going from equation 26.14 to equation 26.16 significantly decreases the variance of the error component. Table 26.3 presents the results of this analysis. The critical value of F for a 0.01-level significance test lies in the interval (2.5, 2.6) for every class. Hence the results show a significant decrease in the variance of the error component at the 0.01 level of significance in the 35–39, 40–44, and 45–49 age groups.

Whether this evidence provides a sufficient basis for rejecting M 18 for the given age groups is debatable. In the regressions pertaining to these age groups the estimates of e_i for $i = 1, \ldots, 7$ equal zero for all practical purposes. Also, the number of consumers in $F^{-1}(I_8 \cap \Omega_{\tilde{\alpha}})$ and $F^{-1}(I_9 \cap \Omega_{\tilde{\alpha}})$ is small for these age groups.

26.3 New Axioms and New Tests

Once he has tested a theory, an econometrician faces the arduous task of deciding what parts of the theory to keep, what parts to reject, and what new parts to add.

26.3.1 New Axioms versus New Tests

A researcher's tests may be inconclusive, as they were in our tests of Modigliani and Brumberg's theory. In that case there is no need to reject the theory. Instead the researcher must devise new and better tests.

Alternatively, the researcher's tests may confirm the theory and add useful information concerning the properties of the theoretical constructs of the theory. In that case the researcher has a choice. Either he can leave the theory as it is and try to devise different and perhaps more stringent tests. Or he can keep the old axioms and add new ones that put additional restrictions on the characteristics of the undefined objects.

Finally, the researcher's tests may show that the theory as it stands does not fit reality. What the researcher does then will depend both on the nature of his evidence and on his temperament. He may be so attached to his axioms that he decides to keep them and to change only his interpretation of the undefined objects. Examples of such behavior abound in the struggle by theorists to keep the quantity theory of money alive. Alternatively, the researcher may believe that his original axioms are correct, but that he must add new undefined objects and new axioms that postulate some of their characteristics and some of their relationships to the old undefined objects. A good example of such a revision is Arrow and Debreu's suggested modification of the standard certainty model of consumer behavior (i.e., H 1–H 6, section 10.2.1) to allow for the fact that consumers make decisions under uncertainty (see Debreu 1959, pp. 30–40 and pp. 70–80). If tests of a model are sufficiently devastating, the researcher may be led to make drastic changes in his theory. One example of such a sequence of events (i.e., unfavorable tests and revolution in theory) is Keynes's writing of his General Theory in response to the great depression.

Whatever the outcome of the researcher's testing and its implications with respect to his theory, testing the theory represents only one step in an unending search for truth. Once he has tested his theory and, guided by the test, written a new axiom system with his intended interpretation of it, the researcher must think of ways to test his new theory.

26.3.2 An Example

What it means in terms of axiomatic superstructures to devise new tests of a theory may be nonobvious. So in the remainder of this section, we discuss a new test of Modigliani and Brumberg's theory which the authors themselves proposed.

Many reasons exist for looking for new tests of Modigliani and Brumberg's theory. First, the test we performed in E 26.11 left us feeling ambivalent about the validity of M 18. Second, the low values in the R^2 column of table 26.1 suggest that important explanatory variables have been omitted from equation 26.13. These observations do not imply that the theory is false, but rather that the axiomatic superstructure we used in testing the theory was inadequate. Third, Modigliani and Brumberg's fundamental conjecture (see E 26.5) that $\psi_{1\tilde{\alpha}}$ is an increasing function of $\tilde{\alpha}$ is not supported by our statistical results.

New tests of Modigliani and Brumberg's theory may be devised in many different ways:

1. We can derive additional sample theorems from M 1–M 19 and check whether the undefined terms, as we interpret them, satisfy the assertions of these theorems.

2. We can sample anew from the same population and repeat the tests performed in E 26.10 with new data. In this case the observed values of $\tilde{c}_t$, $\tilde{A}_{t-1}$, and $\tilde{y}_t$ will differ from the original values, but our interpretation of the undefined objects of M 1–M 19 will not.

3. We can retain the axioms but change our interpretation of the undefined terms. One way to do so is to use the same data but change the denotation of the ω_P components (e.g., change the assignment of numbers to blank response boxes, change from book values to market values in measuring a firm's net worth, and add imputed income from own home to estimates of disposable income for 1963) to the extent this is permitted by the prescribed measurement of the interpreted objects of Modigliani and Brumberg's theory. Another way to change the interpretation of the undefined terms is to obtain a similar sample from a different population (e.g., the 1962–1963 population of Norwegian consumers or the 1976–1977 population of U.S. consumers). A third way to do the same thing is to obtain entirely different data from the same population or from a different population (e.g., we could obtain budget data that contain direct estimates of $\tilde{c}_t$ as well as of $\tilde{A}_{t-1}$ and $\tilde{y}_t$).

4. We can change the axioms with or without changing the specification of (ω_T, ω_P).

From our point of view, alternative 4 presents the most interesting way of devising new tests, since by adding one component to ω_P, three components to ω_T, and a few axioms to M 1–M 19, we can construct a test that is essentially one that Modigliani and Brumberg proposed themselves.

The three new components of ω_T are y_{t-1}, y_{t-1}^e, and ε_y. In the interpretation we intend of the new axiom system, y_{t-1} denotes the consumer's disposable income in period $t-1$; y_{t-1}^e denotes the average level of income the consumer in period $t - 1$ expects to receive during the rest of his life; and ε_y denotes the consumer's elasticity of income expectations in period t.

The new component of ω_P is $\tilde{y}_{t-1}$. It is intended to denote the observed value of y_{t-1}.

Having noted these remarks about the new undefined terms, we are now ready to write down the axioms of the tests. To begin, we must rephrase M 4 and M 12 to account for the changes we have made in ω_T and ω_P; assuming that has been done, we shall refer to the new axioms as M 4* and M 12*. Axioms M 1–M 3, M 5–M 11, and M 13–M 17 we leave as they are. To incorporate Modigliani and Brumberg's ideas, we must rephrase M 18 and M 19 and add three postulates concerning the new components of ω_T:

M 18* For all $(\omega_T, \omega_P) \in I_i \cap \Omega_{\tilde{\alpha}}$, $i = 1, \ldots, 9$, $\tilde{\alpha} = 25, 37, \ldots, 70$, there exist constants, $\gamma_{i\tilde{\alpha}}$ and $\beta_{\tilde{\alpha}}$ such that

$$y_{t-1}^e = \gamma_{i\tilde{\alpha}} + \beta_{\tilde{\alpha}} y_{t-1} + u.$$

Relative to $P(\cdot | I_i \cap \Omega_{\tilde{\alpha}})$, u has mean zero and finite variance; the variance of u is independent of i; the covariances of u with y_{t-1}, y_t, and A_{t-1} are zero; and the covariance of u and v is independent of i.

M 19* Relative to $P(\cdot | I_i \cap \Omega_{\tilde{\alpha}})$, $i = 1, \ldots, 9$, $\tilde{\alpha} = 25, 37, \ldots, 70$, the covariance matrix of A_{t-1}, y_t and y_{t-1} is nonsingular.

M 20 For all $(\omega_T, \omega_P) \in \Omega$,

$$y_t^e = (1 - \varepsilon_y) y_{t-1}^e + \varepsilon_y y_t.$$

M 21 There exists a one-to-one mapping,

$$K(\cdot): \{15, \ldots, 100\} \to R$$

such that, for all $(\omega_T, \omega_P) \in \Omega$,

$$\varepsilon_y = K(\alpha), \text{ and } K(f(\alpha)) = K(\alpha), \qquad \alpha \in \{15, \ldots, 100\}.$$

M 22 Relative to $P(\cdot | I_i \cap \Omega_{\tilde{\alpha}})$, the variances of y_{t-1} and y_{t-1}^e are positive, finite, and independent of i; and the covariance of v and y_{t-1} is zero.

The new axiom system consists of the axioms M 1–M 3, M 4*, M 5–M 11, M 12*, M 13–M 17, M 18*, M 19*, and M 20–M 22.

To see how the new axiom system differs from M 1–M 19, we observe that in the interpretation of the new system that we intend, M 18* describes how in period $t - 1$ consumer income expectations vary over the sample population. M 20 characteristizes the way each consumer in period t adjusts his income expectations in accordance with the new information provided by y_t. And M 21 insists that the elasticity of income expectations does not vary within age groups. Together these three axioms imply that, for all $(w_T, w_P) \in I_i \cap \Omega_{\tilde{\alpha}}$, $i = 1, \ldots, 9$ and $\tilde{\alpha} = 25, 37, \ldots, 70$,

$$y_t^e = (1 - \varepsilon_y^{\tilde{\alpha}})\gamma_{i\tilde{\alpha}} + (1 - \varepsilon_y^{\tilde{\alpha}})\beta_{\tilde{\alpha}} y_{t-1} + \varepsilon_y^{\tilde{\alpha}} y_t + \tilde{u}, \tag{26.17}$$

where $\tilde{u} = (1 - \varepsilon_y^{\tilde{\alpha}})u$. Comparing equations 26.7 and 26.17 we obtain a formal account of the way the new system differs from M 1–M 19 and note that the differences have to do with the statistical specifications of the sample population and not with the theory we are about to test.

Our new test of Modigliani and Brumberg's theory is based on a simple theorem stated below.

T 26.3 There exist constants, $\varphi_{i\tilde{\alpha}}$, $\psi_{1\tilde{\alpha}}$, $\psi_{2\tilde{\alpha}}$, and $\psi_{3\tilde{\alpha}}$, and random variables, $\delta_{\tilde{\alpha}}$, $i = 1, \ldots, 9$, $\tilde{\alpha} = 25, 37, \ldots, 70$, such that, with $\varepsilon_y^{\tilde{\alpha}} = K(\tilde{\alpha})$,

$$\varphi_{i\tilde{\alpha}} = H(\bar{r}, \tilde{\alpha})(M - \tilde{\alpha})(1 - \varepsilon_y^{\tilde{\alpha}})\gamma_{i\tilde{\alpha}}, \qquad i = 1, \ldots, 9,\ \tilde{\alpha} = 25, 37, \ldots, 70 \tag{26.18}$$

$$\psi_{1\tilde{\alpha}} = H(\bar{r}, \tilde{\alpha}), \qquad \tilde{\alpha} = 25, 37, \ldots, 70 \tag{26.19}$$

$$\psi_{2\tilde{\alpha}} = H(\bar{r}, \tilde{\alpha})(1 + (M - \tilde{\alpha})\varepsilon_y^{\tilde{\alpha}}), \qquad \tilde{\alpha} = 25, 37, \ldots, 70 \tag{26.20}$$

$$\psi_{3\tilde{\alpha}} = H(\bar{r}, \tilde{\alpha})(M - \tilde{\alpha})(1 - \varepsilon_y^{\tilde{\alpha}})\beta_{\tilde{\alpha}}, \qquad \tilde{\alpha} = 25, 37, \ldots, 70 \tag{26.21}$$

and

$$\delta_{\tilde{\alpha}} = v + (M - \tilde{\alpha})(1 - \varepsilon_y^{\tilde{\alpha}})H(\bar{r}, \tilde{\alpha})u, \qquad \tilde{\alpha} = 25, 37, \ldots, 70$$

and such that, for all pairs $(i, \tilde{\alpha})$,

$$\tilde{c}_t = \varphi_{i\tilde{\alpha}} + \psi_{1\tilde{\alpha}}\tilde{A}_{t-1} + \psi_{2\tilde{\alpha}}\tilde{y}_t + \psi_{3\tilde{\alpha}}\tilde{y}_{t-1} + \delta_{\tilde{\alpha}}, \qquad i = 1, \ldots, 9;\ \tilde{\alpha} = 25, 37, \ldots, 70. \tag{26.22}$$

Moreover, relative to $P(\cdot | I_i \cap \Omega_{\tilde{\alpha}})$, $\delta_{\tilde{\alpha}}$ has mean zero, positive and finite variance that is independent of i, and covariance with $\tilde{A}_{t-1}$, $\tilde{y}_t$ and $\tilde{y}_{t-1}$ equal to zero.

We can use theorem T 26.3 to test the validity of any given interpretation of the new axiom system in the same way we used T 26.1 to test our interpretation of M 1–M 19. We assume that our observations satisfy equation 26.22 and estimate the values of the coefficients in the equation

$$\tilde{c}_{ts} = a + \sum_{i=1}^{8} b_i \xi_{is} + d\tilde{A}_{t-1,s} + e\tilde{y}_{ts} + g\tilde{y}_{t-1,s} + \varepsilon_{ts}, \quad s \in F^{-1}(\tilde{\alpha}) \tag{26.23}$$

for $\tilde{\alpha} = 25, 37, \ldots, 70$. The estimates of d, e, g, a, and the b_i, $i = 1, \ldots, 8$, in equation 26.23 are estimates of the $\psi_{1\tilde{\alpha}}$, $\psi_{2\tilde{\alpha}}$, $\psi_{3\tilde{\alpha}}$, $\varphi_{9\tilde{\alpha}}$, and $\varphi_{i\tilde{\alpha}} - \varphi_{9\tilde{\alpha}}$ in equation 26.22 for $i = 9$ and $i = 1, \ldots, 8$, respectively. Moreover, in accordance with equations 26.18–26.21, we can use them to estimate indirectly $\gamma_{i\tilde{\alpha}}$, $i = 1, \ldots, 9$, $\beta_{\tilde{\alpha}}$, and $\varepsilon_y^{\tilde{\alpha}}$. If our interpretation of the new axioms is valid, an analogue of T 26.2 will show that, for a large enough number of observations, the estimates ought to have the same sign as their theoretical counterparts. The latter are as follows:

$$\psi_{1\tilde{\alpha}} > 0; \tag{26.24}$$

$$\varphi_{i\tilde{\alpha}} > 0, \text{ iff } \varepsilon_y^{\tilde{\alpha}} < 1 \text{ and } \gamma_{i\tilde{\alpha}} > 0, \text{ or } \varepsilon_y^{\tilde{\alpha}} > 1 \tag{26.25}$$

and

$$\gamma_{i\tilde{\alpha}} < 0, \qquad i = 1, \ldots, 9;$$

$$\psi_{2\tilde{\alpha}} > 0, \text{ if } 0 \leqslant \varepsilon_y^{\tilde{\alpha}}; \tag{26.26}$$

and

$$\psi_{3\tilde{\alpha}} > 0, \text{ iff } \varepsilon_y^{\tilde{\alpha}} < 1 \text{ and } \beta_{\tilde{\alpha}} > 0 \text{ or } \varepsilon_y^{\tilde{\alpha}} > 1 \text{ and } \beta_{\tilde{\alpha}} < 0. \tag{26.27}$$

In our particular interpretation of the new axiom system, the interpretation of $\tilde{c}_t$, $\tilde{y}_t$, and $\tilde{A}_{t-1}$ is as in section 26.2.1 and the interpretation of $\tilde{y}_{t-1}$ is the one given to a consumer's 1962 disposable income by the Federal Reserve Board researchers. Our estimates of a, d, e, g, and the b_i are presented in table 26.4. The corresponding indirect estimates of $\gamma_{i\tilde{\alpha}}$, $i = 1, \ldots, 9$, $\beta_{\tilde{\alpha}}$, and $\varepsilon_y^{\tilde{\alpha}}$ are given in table 26.5.

In table 26.4 all estimates of d except one are positive and differ significantly from zero as they ought to according to equation 26.24. The one exception is the estimate of d for the $\geqslant 65$ age group; it is negative but does not differ significantly from zero at the 0.01 level of significance. With regard to the other estimates and the corresponding values of $\varepsilon_y^{\tilde{\alpha}}$, $\gamma_{i\tilde{\alpha}}$, and $\beta_{\tilde{\alpha}}$ in table 26.5, our findings for $\tilde{\alpha} = 25, 37, \ldots, 62$, do support Modigliani and Brumberg's theory. In the $\geqslant 65$ age group we find estimates of e, $\varepsilon_y^{\tilde{\alpha}}$, and g that do not satisfy the relations of equations 26.26 and 26.27.

26.4 Superstructures, Data-Generating Mechanisms, the Encompassing Principle, and Meaningful Sampling Schemes

In this chapter we have described one way in which the axiomatic method can be used to confront an economic theory with data; and we have illustrated the usefulness of our ideas in two tests of Modigliani and Brumberg's theory of the consumption function. We shall conclude the chapter with a few remarks concerning T_4 theorems (i.e., the theorems in the T_4 box of figure 26.1), the problem of comparing data-generating mechanisms, and meaningful sampling schemes.

First T_4-*theorems*: The T_4 theorems are supposed to be relevant to the import of factors for which the theory does not account. In Modigliani and

Table 26.4
Least-squares estimates of the coefficients in $\tilde{c}_{ts} = a + \sum_{i=1}^{8} b_i \xi_{is} + d\tilde{A}_{t-1,s} + e\tilde{y}_{ts} + gy_{t-1,s} + \varepsilon_{ts}$.

	Coefficients													
Age groups	$\hat{a}$	$\hat{b}_1$	$\hat{b}_2$	$\hat{b}_3$	$\hat{b}_4$	$\hat{b}_5$	$\hat{b}_6$	$\hat{b}_7$	$\hat{b}_8$	$\hat{d}$	$\hat{e}$	$\hat{g}$	R^2	D.F.
<35	1440	975	1088	—	1377	1654	2224	−14031	12555	0.0631	0.7462	−0.1725		
	(1.515)	(−0.588)	(−0.688)		(−0.120)	(0.242)	(0.423)	(−4.103)	(1.380)	(10.089)	(4.286)	(−2.055)	0.7924	328
35–39	328609	3976	13072	22629	27968	38022	62466	89387	−19434	0.1037	−6.4768	3.447		
	(7.943)	(−7.903)	(−7.857)	(−7.767)	(−7.786)	(−7.710)	(−7.343)	(−7.103)	(−12.699)	(21.876)	(−8.416)	(4.191)	0.9339	181
40–44	−19389	419	894	1671	2727	2677	9004	−1921	23925	0.0255	0.2004	0.3805		
	−(0.511)	(0.530)	(0.556)	(0.587)	(0.632)	(0.652)	(0.885)	(0.626)	(1.973)	(7.594)	(0.5375)	(2.253)	0.6161	210
45–49	21784	1703	1172	1956	2047	3551	3984	927	12169	0.0531	1.0740	−0.7070		
	(0.589)	(−0.550)	(−0.577)	(−0.571)	(−0.583)	(−0.558)	(−0.587)	(−0.813)	(−0.511)	(9.792)	(2.180)	(−2.549)	0.6695	213
50–54	51652	4066	5387	8784	11272	15080	17965	27345	65425	0.0631	−0.2751	−0.5158		
	(2.647)	(−2.401)	(−2.379)	(−2.252)	(−2.142)	(−2.019)	(−1.882)	(−1.431)	(0.943)	(13.097)	(−1.039)	(−1.652)	0.6802	224
55–59	94635	424	4911	6805	9692	13400	18942	38065	51311	0.0188	−1.026	0.574		
	(3.483)	(−3.459)	(−3.386)	(−3.403)	(−3.366)	(−3.357)	(−3.337)	(−2.924)	(−3.071)	(4.765)	(−3.491)	(2.393)	0.4746	227
60–64	149226	4744	7755	12133	18136	20478	36471	61482	88715	0.0217	−0.2418	−1.1558		
	(7.274)	(−7.025)	(−6.913)	(−6.791)	(−6.523)	(−6.771)	(−6.180)	(−5.386)	(−3.778)	(13.384)	(−0.863)	(−3.973)	0.7080	183
⩾65	−81976	−2108	−5051	−6782	−9948	−17456	−20686	−42326	−82742	−0.0026	1.940	0.5465		
	(−3.752)	(3.696)	(3.622)	(3.576)	(3.441)	(3.184)	(3.147)	(2.528)	(−0.640)	(−0.972)	(6.032)	(2.409)	0.5695	347

Note: The t values in the $\hat{b}_i$ column are the t values of $\hat{b}_i - \hat{a}_i$, $i = 1, \ldots, 8$.

Table 26.5
Indirect least-squares estimates of $\varepsilon_y^{\tilde{a}}$, $\beta_{\tilde{a}}$, and $\gamma_{i\tilde{a}}$, $i = 1, \ldots, 9$.

	Age groups							
Coefficients	<35	35–39	40–44	45–49	50–54	55–59	60–64	⩾65
$\varepsilon_y^{\tilde{a}}$	0.2406	−0.6699	0.2078	0.6866	−0.2330	−3.0875	−0.9341	−149.4308
$\beta_{\tilde{a}}$	−0.0800	0.3276	0.5708	−1.5175	−0.2882	0.4150	−2.1184	−0.2795
$\gamma_{1\tilde{a}}$	832	82235	−21880	15252	36793	266123	506814	5389999
$\gamma_{2\tilde{a}}$	871	84484	−21332	14907	37665	278685	516725	5578654
$\gamma_{3\tilde{a}}$	496	86847	−20436	15416	39908	283987	531135	5689616
$\gamma_{4\tilde{a}}$	970	88167	−19218	15475	41551	292069	550895	5892564
$\gamma_{5\tilde{a}}$	1066	90653	−19275	16452	44066	265419	558604	6373846
$\gamma_{6\tilde{a}}$	1262	96697	−11978	16733	45971	317965	611247	6580898
$\gamma_{7\tilde{a}}$	−4338	103354	−24579	14748	52165	371501	693575	7968077
$\gamma_{8\tilde{a}}$	4718	76447	5232	22048	77310	408584	783216	10558846
$\gamma_{9\tilde{a}}$	496.11	81252	−22363	14146	34108	264936	491198	5254872

Brumberg's theory there are three such factors: age, income expectations, and the elasticity of income expectations. The T_4 theorems concerning α, y_t^e, y_{t-1}^e, and ε_y, which Modigliani and Brumberg derived, and their fate in our two tests are, therefore, of considerable interest in the context of this chapter.

In E 26.3 we introduced two of Modigliani and Brumberg's simplifying assumptions:

(i) $r = 0$ and $\dfrac{g_i(p)}{g_j(p)} = (1 + r)^{i-j}, \qquad i, j = 0, 1, \ldots, M - \alpha.$

From them we conclude the following:

T₄ 1 $H(r, \alpha) = (M - \alpha + 1)^{-1}$.

T₄ 2 $(M - \alpha)y_t^e = \sum_{i=1}^{M-\alpha} y_{t+i}$.

T₄ 3 $(M + 1 - \alpha)y_{t-1}^e = \sum_{i=1}^{M+1-\alpha} y_{t-1+i}$.

If we add to condition i the simplifying assumption

(ii) $y_t^e = (1 - \varepsilon_y)y_{t-1}^e + \varepsilon_y y_t$,

which Modigliani and Brumberg postulated in Modigliani and Brumberg 1955 (equation II.12, p. 413) and which we insisted on in M 20, then we have another T_4 theorem:

T₄ 4 $\varepsilon_y = \dfrac{-1}{M - \alpha}$.

From the point of view of the test we performed with T(M 1, ..., M 19), the specifics of T_4 1 are of no consequence. What matters, and ought to be tested, is the idea that $H(r, \cdot)$ increases with age. Similarly, the specifics of T_4 4 are not important to the test we performed with T(M 1, ..., M 22). However, we may ask and test whether ε_y is negative and decreases with age. Judging from the *d* columns of tables 26.1 and 26.4, our tests reject the suggestion that $H(r, \cdot)$ increases with age. Moreover, the estimates of ε_y in table 26.5 certainly do not support the hypothesis that ε_y is negative and decreases with age.

Next *data-generating mechanisms and the encompassing principle*: One way to view the superstructure we construct to test an economic theory is as an axiomatic characterization of the chance mechanism by which our data are generated. For example, in M 1–M 19, only M 8 postulates a theorem of the theory which we are about to test. The other axioms delineate relevant characteristics of the sample population. Seen as a whole, M 1–M 19 provide an axiomatic characterization of the *data-generating mechanism* underlying the FRB data we use to test Modigliani and Brumberg's theory.

There are situations in which it is important to dispose of a method by which different characterizations of a data-generating mechanism can be compared. For example, M 1–M 19 and M 1–M 22 provide two axiomatic characterizations of the same data-generating mechanism. How are we to choose between them if we are to carry out a new test of Modigliani and Brumberg's theory with "similarly" generated data from the 1976 U.S. population? At the moment there exists no general method for comparing data-generating mechanisms of the kind we have in mind, and devising such a method is beyond the scope of this chapter. However, I shall comment briefly on one relevant aspect that is of importance to us: the relation between viewing a test of hypothesis from within and from without an axiomatic superstructure.

One of the most interesting ideas for comparing data-generating mechanisms is compressed in the *Encompassing Principle* as developed by Graham Mizon, David F. Hendry, J. F. Richard, and others (Mizon 1984, pp. 135–172; Hendry and Richard 1989). Here the principle may be expressed roughly as follows: Let $\mathscr{M}_1$ and $\mathscr{M}_2$ be superstructures and let δ be a parameter. Moreover, let $\tilde{\delta}$ be an estimate of δ in $\mathscr{M}_2$ and let

$$\delta_1 = p\lim\tilde{\delta}$$

with respect to the probability distribution of $\tilde{\delta}$ determined in $\mathscr{M}_1$. Finally, let $\tilde{\delta}_1$ be an estimate of δ_1 in $\mathscr{M}_1$ and suppose that both $\tilde{\delta}$ and $\tilde{\delta}_1$ are consistent within their respective superstructures. Then $\mathscr{M}_1$ encompasses $\mathscr{M}_2$ with respect to δ if $(\tilde{\delta} - \tilde{\delta}_1)$ does not differ significantly from zero in terms of the probability distribution of $(\tilde{\delta} - \tilde{\delta}_1)$ determined within $\mathscr{M}_1$.

Here is an example to fix our ideas. The example paraphrases an observation that we found in Hendry and Richard 1989.

E 26.12 Let y be a random variable that in $\mathscr{M}_1$ is normally distributed with mean μ and variance 1 and that in $\mathscr{M}_2$ is normally distributed with mean 0 and variance σ^2. Suppose that the values of both μ and σ^2 are unspecified in their respective structures, and let δ denote the true variance of y. Finally, suppose that we have n observations on y, $y_1, \ldots, y_n$, and that these observations are independently distributed with the same probability distribution as y. Then in $\mathscr{M}_2$ the maximum likelihood estimator of δ is

$$\tilde{\delta} = n^{-1} \sum_{i=1}^{n} y_i^2 .$$

According to the distribution of $\tilde{\delta}$ in $\mathcal{M}_1$,

$$\delta_1 = 1 + \mu^2$$

and the maximum likelihood estimate of δ_1 in $\mathcal{M}_1$ is given by

$$\tilde{\delta}_1 = 1 + \bar{y}^2,$$

where $\bar{y} = n^{-1} \sum_{i=1}^{n} y_i$. Consequently, $\mathcal{M}_1$ encompasses $\mathcal{M}_2$ with respect δ if and only if the value of

$$(\tilde{\delta} - \tilde{\delta}_1) = n^{-1} \sum_{i=1}^{n} (y_i - \bar{y})^2 - 1$$

is not significantly different from zero in terms of the probability distribution of $(\tilde{\delta} - \tilde{\delta}_1)$ in $\mathcal{M}_1$.

With this example in mind we can now illustrate the relevance of the Encompassing Principle for our purposes. Let $\mathcal{M}_1$ be M 1–M 19, let $\mathcal{M}_2$ be M 1–M 22, and let δ denote a vector of parameters from the distribution of y_t^e in the sample population. Moreover, let $\tilde{\delta}$ be the estimate of δ in $\mathcal{M}_2$ and suppose that $\tilde{\delta}$ is a function of both y_t and y_{t-1}. Then δ_1 does not exist and we cannot determine whether $\mathcal{M}_1$ encompasses $\mathcal{M}_2$ with respect to δ. This is so because the random variable y_{t-1} is unmentionable within $\mathcal{M}_1$. To compare $\mathcal{M}_1$ and $\mathcal{M}_2$ with respect to δ we must step *outside* $\mathcal{M}_1$—for example, by adding y_{t-1} and $\tilde{y}_{t-1}$ to the list of variables of $\mathcal{M}_1$ and by adding several postulates to $\mathcal{M}_1$ concerning the probability distribution of y_{t-1} and $\tilde{y}_{t-1}$, one of which might insist that equation 26.7 delineates the orthogonal projection of y_t^e on the linear space spanned by y_t *and* y_{t-1}.

The preceding remark is not as strange as it sounds. Within M 1–M 19, equation 26.7 depicts the orthogonal projection of y_t^e on the linear space of random variables spanned by y_t. Within M 1–M 22 equation 26.17 depicts the orthogonal projection of y_t^e on the linear space of random variables spanned by y_t and y_{t-1}. We cannot compare the relations in equations 26.7 and 26.17 within $\mathcal{M}_1$. We cannot even compare them within $\mathcal{M}_2$. To compare the relations in equations 26.7 and 26.17 within $\mathcal{M}_2$ we must add to equation 26.7 the hypothesis that the relation there is in fact the orthogonal projection on the linear space of random variables spanned by y_t and y_{t-1} (see Mizon 1984, pp. 135–172, for a discussion of analogous problems).

The need to step outside a superstructure when performing tests of hypotheses arises in many contexts. I described one situation in which such a need might arise in our discussion of the Encompassing Principle. Other examples are given in the next two chapters. Thus in chapter 27 we step *outside* the superstructure to obtain consistent estimates of statistics that live *within* the structure. In chapter 28 we step *outside* the superstructure in order to use statistics that live *within* the structure to determine the relative degrees of risk aversion in various groups of consumers. As we shall see, moving in and out of a given superstructure can be as exciting to an econometrician as moving in and out of a given nonstandard hyperspace is to a mathematician.

Finally, *meaningful sampling schemes*: We presented the idea of meaningful sampling schemes in section 25.3 and pointed out its relevance for statistical inference. In the context of M 1–M 19, a sampling scheme $Q(\cdot): \mathscr{F}_S \to [0, 1]$ that satisfies equation 26.8 and M 13–M 15 is meaningful if and only if it is designed to satisfy the conditions

$$\lim_{N\to\infty} n(I_i)/N = P(I_i), \quad i = 1, \dots, 9 \tag{26.28}$$

where $n(\cdot): \mathscr{F} \to R_+$ and $n(A)$ records the number of observed consumers who belong to $F^{-1}(A)$.

A sampling scheme that satisfies M 13–M 15 and is designed to satisfy equation 26.28 will ensure that the conditions of equation 26.15 are satisfied a.e. in the sample space. To see why, pick an arbitrary $\tilde{\alpha} \in \{25, 37, \dots, 70\}$ and observe that, by M 13 and the definition of conditional probabilities,

$$P(\Omega_{\tilde{\alpha}}) = \sum_{i=1}^{9} P(\Omega_{\tilde{\alpha}}|I_i)P(I_i), \tag{26.29}$$

and that, by M 14, equation 26.28, and T 16.6,

$$\lim_{N\to\infty} n(\Omega_{\tilde{\alpha}} \cap I_i)/n(I_i) = P(\Omega_{\tilde{\alpha}}|I_i) \quad \text{a.e.,} \quad i = 1, \dots, 9. \tag{26.30}$$

Next deduce from equations 26.28–26.30 that

$$\lim_{N\to\infty} n(\Omega_{\tilde{\alpha}})/N = P(\Omega_{\tilde{\alpha}}) \quad \text{a.e.} \tag{26.31}$$

Then use equations 26.31, 26.30, and 26.28 and the obvious relation

$$(n(\Omega_{\tilde{\alpha}} \cap I_i)/n(\Omega_{\tilde{\alpha}}))(n(\Omega_{\tilde{\alpha}})/N) = (n(\Omega_{\tilde{\alpha}} \cap I_i)/n(I_i))(n(I_i)/N)$$

to establish

$$\lim_{N\to\infty} n(\Omega_{\tilde{\alpha}} \cap I_i)/n(\Omega_{\tilde{\alpha}}) = P(I_i|\Omega_{\tilde{\alpha}}) \quad \text{a.e.} \quad i = 1, \dots, 9,$$

which is equation 26.15 with n replaced by $n(\Omega_{\tilde{\alpha}})$.

It is easy to demonstrate that a sampling scheme that satisfies M 13–M 15 and is designed to satisfy the conditions of equation 26.15 need not satisfy equation 26.28. In the statement of T 26.2 we have appealed to equation 26.15 rather than equation 26.28 because of the way the conditions in equation 26.15 enter the proof of T 26.2.

27 The Permanent-Income Hypothesis

There are two versions of the permanent-income hypothesis, a certain-world model and an uncertainty model. Friedman presents both in chapter II of *A Theory of the Consumption Function* (1957, pp. 7–18). The certainty model is clearly delineated, the uncertainty model less so. We shall test the empirical relevance of both of Friedman's hypotheses.

The data we use to test Friedman's permanent-income hypothesis are the same as those we used to test Modigliani and Brumberg's theory, but the statistical analysis differs for two reasons. First, we want to allow for *errors in the variables*, i.e., for the possibility that the values assumed by the interpreted undefined objects of the empirical analysis need not equal the true values of their theoretical counterparts. We did not allow for this possibility in testing the life-cycle hypothesis because we wanted to follow as closely as possible Modigliani and Brumberg's own suggestions for testing their theory. Second, we want to include in our analysis unobservable as well as observable factors and to study their impact on consumer behavior. In analyzing Modigliani and Brumberg's theory, we did not do this because the unobservable variables that appeared there were either assumed to be constant over the sample (e.g., the going interest rate) or were substituted out on the basis of statistical arguments (e.g., expected future income).

27.1 Formulation of the Hypothesis

Friedman's theory of consumer choice is a model of the standard axioms of consumer choice with the additional postulate that the utility function is homothetic, i.e., a model of H 1–H 6 and the H 7 of E 26.1. Specifically, Friedman's commodity bundle is

$x = (C_0, \ldots, C_{n-1}),$

where C_i denotes the consumer's total expenditures on goods and services in year i, $i = 0, 1, \ldots, n - 1$. His price vector is

$$p = (1, 1/(1 + r), \ldots, [1/(1 + r)]^{n-1}),$$

where r denotes the going interest rate. Friedman's consumer is an ordinary household that has a utility function, $V(\cdot): R_+^n \to R$, which satisfies H 6 and H 7, and that has the economic resources,

$$\hat{A} = A_{-1} + \sum_{i=0}^{n-1} [1/(1 + r)]^i z_i, \tag{27.1}$$

where A_{-1} denotes the consumer's initial net worth in year 0, and where z_i denotes his labor income in year $i = 0, 1, \ldots, n - 1$. Finally, for each pair (p, A), the associated consumption bundle represents the consumer's optimal expenditure strategy for the years 0 to $n - 1$.

In Friedman's model the demand function,

$$f(\cdot): R_{++}^n \times R_+ \to R_+^n,$$

records for each pair, $(p, A) \in R_{++}^n \times R_n$, the consumer's optimal expenditure strategy. Friedman's model, like that of Modigliani and Brumberg, contains a function, $g(\cdot): R_{++}^n \to R_+^n$, that is continuous and homogeneous of degree -1 and that satisfies

$$f(p, A) = g(p)A, \qquad (p, A) \in R_{++}^n \times R_+.$$

Thus, if we let

$$h(r) = g_1(1, 1/(1 + r), \ldots, [1/(1 + r)]^{n-1}), \qquad r \geqslant 0$$

and write

$$c = h(r)\hat{A}, \qquad r \geqslant 0 \tag{27.2}$$

then c denotes the consumer's optimal expenditure on consumer goods in year 0 when the going interest rate equals r.

The function $h(\cdot)(\cdot): R_+^2 \to R$ in equation 27.2 ought to be called the consumption function, but in Friedman's model is not because it is a function of the wrong variables. To derive the consumption function from equation 27.2, Friedman proceeds as follows. He observes that the "designation of current receipts as 'income' in statistical studies is an expedient enforced by the limitation of data. On a theoretical level, income is generally defined as the amount a consumer unit could consume (or believes that it could) while maintaining its wealth intact" (Friedman 1957,

p. 10). Consequently, the consumer's true current period ($\equiv$ year 0) income should be defined, not as z_0, but as

$$y_p = (r/(1 + r))\hat{A}. \tag{27.3}$$

Income so defined Friedman named *permanent income* and used it to define *the* consumption function as follows:

$$c = k(r)y_p, \qquad (r, y_p) \in R_{++} \times R_+$$

where

$$k(r) = ((1 + r)/r) \cdot h(r), \qquad r > 0.$$

In a given period a consumer's *measured income* is ordinarily taken to equal his salary plus any rent, interest, and/or dividends he earns. Friedman calls the difference between measured income and permanent income *transitory income*. Thus, if y denotes measured income and y_t transitory income, then

$$y = y_p + y_t. \tag{27.4}$$

In Friedman's model

$$y = (r/(1 + r))A_{-1} + z_0$$

in year 0, and

$$\begin{aligned} y_t &= (r/(1 + r))A_{-1} + z_0 - y_p \\ &= \left(\frac{1}{1 + r}\right)\left[z_0 - r\sum_{i=1}^{n-1}\left(\frac{1}{1 + r}\right)^i z_i\right], \end{aligned}$$

which, for large n, is negative (positive) if the value of z_0 is small (large) relative to the values of the z_i in year $i = 1, 2, \ldots, n - 1$.

Friedman also hypothesized that a consumer's expenditures on goods and services during a given period c can be decomposed into a permanent component c_p and a transitory component c_t; i.e.,

$$c = c_p + c_t, \tag{27.5}$$

where c_p satisfies the relation

$$c_p = k(r)y_p, \qquad r > 0,\ y_p \geqslant 0 \tag{27.6}$$

and transitory consumption is essentially unrelated to income. In Friedman's certainty model, c_t may differ from zero "because of additions to or subtractions from the stock of consumer goods" (Friedman 1957, p. 11). In the uncertainty model, c_t may differ from zero for additional reasons such as sickness, favorable opportunities to buy, changes in the weather, and errors of measurement (see Friedman 1957, pp. 22–23).

The relations 27.4–27.6 constitute the certainty version of Friedman's Permanent-Income Hypothesis. A few comments on it are in order. First, once we state an ideal procedure for measuring the components of $\hat{A}$, equation 27.3 unambiguously determines a procedure for measuring y_p. Thus in the certainty case y_p is both an observable and a measurable variable. The permanent component of consumption, however, only partially shares these properties. Under certainty the value of c_p equals the value of actual consumption minus the value of changes in the stock of consumer goods. To the extent that consumption is observable and measurable, c_p is observable and measurable. But from the point of view of budget data on consumer expenditures, c_p remains an unobservable theoretical construct so long as $V(\cdot)$ is taken to be such a construct.

Second, when we test the empirical relevance of the certainty case, we are testing its relevance for and using data from an uncertain world. Thus from our data we cannot hope to extract the consumer's permanent consumption and his supposedly "observable and measurable" permanent income. We can only look at the data and make statements such as, whatever the value of y_p is, "it reflects the effect of those factors that the (consumer) regards as determining [his] capital value or wealth" (Friedman 1957, p. 21). However, according to Friedman, the inability to extract permanent components need not be damaging. "It seems neither necessary nor desirable to decide in advance the precise meaning to be attached to 'permanent.' The distinction between permanent and transitory is intended to interpret actual behavior." We should "treat consumer units as if they regarded their income and their consumption as the sum of two such components, and as if the relation between the permanent components is the one suggested by our theoretical analysis. The precise line to be drawn between permanent and transitory components is best left to be determined by the data themselves, to be whatever seems to correspond to consumer behavior" (Friedman 1957, p. 23).

Friedman admits that "introduction of uncertainty blurs the sharp lines" (Friedman 1957, p. 15) of the certainty model. He insists, however, that the "effect of uncertainty establishes no presumption against the shape assigned to the consumption function, and thus casts no shadow on the 'simplicity' that recommends it" (Friedman 1957, p. 15). To account for uncertainty all we need do is to introduce new arguments into the function $k(\cdot)$ in equation 27.6.

To determine what arguments to add to $k(\cdot)$, Friedman observes that "uncertainty adds a new reason for holding wealth to the two motives present under certainty ... straightening out the consumption stream and earning interest" (Friedman 1957, p. 16)—namely, providing a reserve for emergencies. The need for such a reserve depends on the consumer's financial resources and can, according to Friedman, be represented as a function of the ratio of the consumer's nonhuman wealth to his permanent income. The larger this ratio, all else being constant, the less urgent the need for a reserve against unforeseen contingencies.

Besides unforeseen contingencies, the consumer faces uncertainty with respect to future receipts and prices and the resulting uncertainty with respect to his future standard of living and to his ability to repay debts. However, "on the present level of analyses," Friedman says, "there seems no way to judge whether these factors would tend to make consumption a larger or a smaller fraction of [permanent income]" (Friedman 1957, p. 15). Consequently, there is no need to add arguments to $k(\cdot)$ to account for these factors. Friedman considers only those uncertainties mentioned above and proposes at the end of his discussion of the uncertainty model that equation 27.6 be replaced by

$$c_p = \tilde{k}(r, w)y_p, \qquad r > 0$$

where w denotes the ratio of nonhuman wealth to permanent income. Since the consumer's nonhuman wealth is his initial net worth, as we have used the term,

$$w = A_{-1}/y_p,$$

and

$$c_p = \tilde{k}(r, A_{-1}/y_p)y_p, \qquad r > 0. \tag{27.7}$$

Thus equations 27.4, 27.5, and 27.7 constitute the uncertainty version of Friedman's permanent-income hypothesis.

27.2 The Axioms of a Test of the Certainty Model: F 1, . . . , F 17

In this section we present a set of axioms for a test of the certainty version of Friedman's permanent-income hypothesis, i.e., of equations 27.4–27.6.

The undefined terms of the axioms are the sample population S, the sample space $(\Omega, \mathscr{F})$, the sampling distribution $P(\cdot)$, and two vectors ω_T and ω_P.

F 1 Let $\#S$ denote the number of elements in S. Then $\#S \in \{1, 2, \ldots\}$.

F 2 $\Omega \subset R^{17}$ and $\mathscr{F}$ is a σ field of subsets of Ω.

F 3 $P(\cdot)$ is a probability measure on $(\Omega, \mathscr{F})$.

F 4 $\omega_T = (r, y, y_p, y_t, c, c_p, c_t, \hat{A}, A_{-1}, \alpha, u, v, \delta)$,

$\omega_P = (\tilde{y}, \tilde{c}, \tilde{A}_{-1}, \tilde{\alpha})$,

and

$(\omega_T, \omega_P) \in \Omega$.

F 5 There is a one-to-one mapping

$F(\cdot): S \to \Omega$.

As in chapter 26, we shall denote $F(s)$ by $(\omega_{Ts}, \omega_{Ps})$. Moreover, if x is a component of (ω_T, ω_P), we let x_s denote the corresponding component of $(\omega_{Ts}, \omega_{Ps})$.

In the interpretation of the axioms we intend, the variables r, y, y_p, y_t, c, c_p, and c_t denote the interpreted versions of the corresponding variables in equations 27.4–27.6. Also $\hat{A}$, A_{-1}, and α are to be, respectively, the consumer's total wealth (as specified in equation 27.1), his initial net worth in the current period, and his age. Finally, u, v, and δ are error terms whose denotations are specified in the axioms. It may be unimportant to say in advance how y_t, y_p, c_p, and c_t are to be measured (see Friedman's comments above). However, the interpretation of r, y, c, A_{-1}, and α should provide a detailed prescription for measuring them under ideal circumstances.

In the intended interpretation of ω_P, $\tilde{y}$, $\tilde{c}$, and $\tilde{A}_{-1}$ are the observed counterparts of y, c, and A_{-1}. Moreover, $\tilde{\alpha}$ denotes an age group which will be specified in the axioms. In our particular interpretation of the axioms, $\tilde{y}$ and $\tilde{A}_{-1}$ denote, respectively, the consumer's 1963 disposable income and initial net worth as recorded in the Federal Reserve survey. We also let $\tilde{c}$ denote the difference between the consumer's 1963 disposable income and the change in his net worth during 1963.[1]

The components of (ω_T, ω_P) must satisfy the following postulates:

F 6 $\alpha \in \{15, 16, \ldots, 100\}$.

F 7 Let $\Omega(\hat{\alpha})$: $\{(\omega_T, \omega_P) \in \Omega: \alpha = \hat{\alpha}\}$, $\quad \hat{\alpha} \in \{15, 16, \ldots, 100\}$.

There exists a function

$k(\cdot): R_{++} \times \{15, 16, \ldots, 100\} \to R_{++}$

such that, for all $(\omega_T, \omega_P) \in \Omega(\alpha)$,

$$c_p = k(r, \alpha)y_p. \tag{27.8}$$

F 8 Let $f(\cdot)$ be defined by

$$f(\alpha) = \begin{cases} 25 & \text{if } \alpha < 35, \\ 5(i+6)+5 & \text{if } (i+6)5 \leqslant \alpha < (i+8)5,\ i = 1, 3, 5 \\ 70 & \text{if } 65 \leqslant \alpha. \end{cases}$$

For all $\alpha \in \{15, 16, \ldots, 100\}$,

$$k(r, f(\alpha)) = k(r, \alpha), \qquad r > 0. \tag{27.9}$$

Moreover, for all $(\omega_T, \omega_P) \in \Omega$,

$$\tilde{\alpha} = f(\alpha), \qquad \alpha \in \{15, 16, \ldots, 100\}. \tag{27.10}$$

F 9 There are constants $q(\tilde{\alpha})$, $\tilde{\alpha} = 25, 40, \ldots, 70$, such that

$$A_{-1} = q(\tilde{\alpha}) + \hat{A} + u. \tag{27.11}$$

Moreover,

$$\hat{A} = ((1 + r)/r)y_p. \tag{27.12}$$

F 10 $r = \overline{r}$ and $\overline{r} > 0$.

F 11 For all $(\omega_T, \omega_P) \in \Omega$,

$$y = y_p + y_t, \tag{27.13}$$

$$c = c_p + c_t, \tag{27.14}$$

and

$$(\tilde{y}, \tilde{c}, \tilde{A}_{-1}) = (y, c, A_{-1}). \tag{27.15}$$

With respect to F 6–F 11, note that in the intended interpretation of the axioms, equations 27.13, 27.14, and 27.8 represent the sample analogues of equations 27.4–27.6, and equation 27.12 is the sample analogue of equation 27.3. According to equations 27.9 and 27.1, the consumption function and the constant in equation 27.11 do not vary within age groups. Note also that equation 27.11 postulates a relationship between A_{-1} and $\hat{A}$ that is satisfied in the sample population. The validity of this postulate is of no consequence for Friedman's hypothesis. However, it establishes the intriguing possibility of using A_{-1} as an instrumental variable in a factor-analytic test of the permanent-income hypothesis. In doing that, it also illustrates how "outside" information can be introduced into our axiomatic superstructure and used in the testing of a theory.

Since we use the same data to test Friedman's theory that we used to test Modigliani and Brumberg's ideas, some of the postulates concerning the sampling distribution will be identical with those asserted in M 1–M 19. For ease of reference, we repeat them here.

F 12 Let a_i be one of the numbers \$3000, \$5000, \$7500, \$10,000, \$15,000, \$25,000, \$50,000, and \$100,000, with $a_1 < a_2 < \cdots < a_8$. Moreover, let I_i be defined by

$$I_1 = \{(\omega_T, \omega_P) \in \Omega : y < a_1\},$$

$$I_i = \{(\omega_T, \omega_P) \in \Omega : a_{i-1} \leqslant y < a_i\}, \qquad i = 2, \ldots, 8$$

$$I_9 = \{(\omega_T, \omega_P) \in \Omega : y \geqslant a_8\}.$$

Then $I_i \in \mathscr{F}$ and $P(I_i) > 0$, $i = 1, \ldots, 9$.

F 13 There are N observations with n_i observations from I_i, $i = 1, \ldots, 9$. The probability distribution of the sample is given by

$$\prod_{i=1}^{9} (P(\cdot|I_i))^{n_i},$$

where $P(\cdot|I_i)$ denotes the conditional probability measure on Ω, given I_i.

F 14 Let $\Omega_{\tilde{\alpha}} = \{(\omega_T, \omega_P) \in \Omega : \tilde{\alpha} = f(\alpha)\}$, $\tilde{\alpha} = 25, 40, \ldots, 70$. Then $\Omega_{\tilde{\alpha}} \in \mathscr{F}$ and $P(I_i \cap \Omega_{\tilde{\alpha}}) > 0$ for all $(i, \tilde{\alpha})$, $i = 1, \ldots, 9$ and $\tilde{\alpha} = 25, 40, \ldots, 70$.

The interpretation we intend of these axioms is identical with the one proposed for M 13–M 15.

The sample distribution of (ω_T, ω_P) relative to $P(\cdot)$ has definite characteristics, which we record in F 15–F 17:

F 15 Relative to $P(\cdot|\Omega_{\tilde{\alpha}})$, the variances of y_p, y_t, c_p, and c_t are positive and finite. Moreover, the covariances of the pairs (y_p, y_t), (y_p, c_t), and (c_t, y_t) are zero, $\tilde{\alpha} = 25, 40, \ldots, 70$.

F 16 Relative to $P(\cdot|\Omega_{\tilde{\alpha}})$, the variance of u is positive and finite, and the covariances of the pairs, $(u, \hat{A})$, (u, y_t), and (u, c_t), are zero, $\tilde{\alpha} = 25, 40, \ldots, 70$.

F 17 Relative to $P(\cdot|\Omega_{\tilde{\alpha}})$, the means of y_t, c_t, and u are zero, and the means of y, c, and A_{-1} are positive, $\tilde{\alpha} = 25, 40, \ldots, 70$.

Axiom F 15 and the assertion concerning y_t and c_t in F 17 formalize for the present axiom system the assumptions that Friedman introduced in Friedman 1957 (assumption 3.3 on p. 26 and assumption 3.4 on p. 30). Also the fact that $E((y_p - E_{\tilde{\alpha}} y_p)u|\Omega_{\tilde{\alpha}}) = 0$, $E(c_t u|\Omega_{\tilde{\alpha}}) = 0$, and $((1 + r)/r) > 0$ implies that the variable A_{-1} satisfies the conditions we usually impose on an instrumental variable.

The axioms F 1–F 17 constitute the axiom system of our test of the certainty version of Friedman's permanent-income hypothesis. We describe in the next section how we shall use them.

27.3 Theorems of T(F 1, . . . , F 17)

There are many interesting theorems in T(F 1, . . . , F 17). In stating the first two we make use of the following notation: First, $E_{\tilde{\alpha}}(\cdot)$ denotes the expected value of $(\cdot)$ with respect to $P(\cdot|\Omega_{\tilde{\alpha}})$, $\sigma^2_{(\cdot)}(\tilde{\alpha}) = E_{\tilde{\alpha}}((\cdot) - E_{\tilde{\alpha}}(\cdot))^2$, and

$$P_y(\tilde{\alpha}) = \sigma^2_{\tilde{y}_p}(\tilde{\alpha})/\sigma^2_{\tilde{y}}(\tilde{\alpha}). \tag{27.16}$$

Second, the regression relation of $\tilde{c}$ on $\tilde{y}$ relative to $P(\cdot|\Omega_{\tilde{\alpha}})$ is written as

$$\tilde{c} = a(\tilde{\alpha}) + \beta(\tilde{\alpha})\tilde{y} + \eta_{\tilde{\alpha}}. \tag{27.17}$$

T 27.1 Let

$$k_{\tilde{\alpha}} = k(\bar{r}, \tilde{\alpha}). \tag{27.18}$$

For all $\tilde{\alpha} = 25, 40, \ldots, 70,$

$$k_{\tilde{\alpha}} = E_{\tilde{\alpha}}\tilde{c}/E_{\tilde{\alpha}}\tilde{y} \tag{27.19}$$

T 27.2 For all $\tilde{\alpha} = 25, 40, \ldots, 70,$

$$\beta(\tilde{\alpha}) = k_{\tilde{\alpha}}P_y(\tilde{\alpha}). \tag{27.20}$$

Moreover, if $E_{\tilde{\alpha}}\tilde{c} \leqslant E_{\tilde{\alpha}}\tilde{y}$, then

$$0 < a(\tilde{\alpha}) \quad \text{and} \quad 0 \leqslant \beta(\tilde{\alpha}) < 1 \tag{27.21}$$

if and only if $\sigma^2_{\tilde{y}_t}(\tilde{\alpha}) > 0$.

Note that equation 27.19 follows from equations 27.8, 27.9, 27.10, 27.18, and 27.13–27.15 and from F 17. Moreover, equation 27.20 follows from equations 27.8, 27.9, 27.10, 27.16, 27.18, and 27.13–27.15 and from F 15 and the relation

$$\beta(\tilde{\alpha}) = E_{\tilde{\alpha}}(\tilde{c} - E_{\tilde{\alpha}}c)(\tilde{y} - E_{\tilde{\alpha}}y)/\sigma^2_{\tilde{y}}(\tilde{\alpha}).$$

Finally, equation 27.21 follows from equations 27.19 and 27.20 and the relation

$$\begin{aligned} a(\tilde{\alpha}) &= E_{\tilde{\alpha}}\tilde{c} - \beta(\tilde{\alpha})E_{\tilde{\alpha}}\tilde{y} \\ &= E_{\tilde{\alpha}}\tilde{y}\cdot(k_{\tilde{\alpha}} - \beta(\tilde{\alpha})) \\ &= E_{\tilde{\alpha}}\tilde{y}\cdot(1 - P_y(\tilde{\alpha}))\cdot k_{\tilde{\alpha}}. \end{aligned}$$

Friedman took for granted that $E_{\tilde{\alpha}}\tilde{c} \leqslant E_{\tilde{\alpha}}\tilde{y}$ and $\sigma^2_{\tilde{y}_t}(\tilde{\alpha}) > 0$, and deduced the inequalities in equation 27.21. The savings relation that results from equations 27.17 and 27.21 satisfies all the conditions of Wright's Law (see section 25.23). Note, therefore, that the savings relation that results from equation 27.17 is a statistical relation, not a behavioral relation.

In a world in which consumers can both borrow and invest, there is no theoretical reason why $E_{\tilde{\alpha}}\tilde{c}$ ought to be smaller than or equal to $E_{\tilde{\alpha}}y$. When $E_{\tilde{\alpha}}y < E_{\tilde{\alpha}}c$ and $\sigma^2_{y_t}(\tilde{\alpha}) > 0$, $0 < a(\tilde{\alpha})$ and $0 \leqslant \beta(\tilde{\alpha})$ as before, but $\beta(\tilde{\alpha})$ need not be less than 1.

The next theorem shows that there exist consistent estimates, $\hat{k}^n(\tilde{\alpha}) = \bar{c}^n(\tilde{\alpha})/\bar{y}^n(\tilde{\alpha})$, $\hat{\beta}^n(\tilde{\alpha})$, and $\hat{P}^n_r(\tilde{\alpha}) = \hat{\beta}^n(\tilde{\alpha})\cdot\bar{y}^n(\tilde{\alpha})/\bar{c}^n(\tilde{\alpha})$ of $k_{\tilde{\alpha}}$, $\beta(\tilde{\alpha})$, and $P_y(\tilde{\alpha})$, respectively. In reading the theorem, note that equation 27.24 is a consequence of equations 27.19 and 27.23, F 13–F 15, F 17, T 16.6, and the relation

$$E_{\tilde{\alpha}}z = \sum_{i=1}^{9} E(z|I_i \cap \Omega_{\tilde{\alpha}})P(I_i|\Omega_{\tilde{\alpha}}), \tag{27.22}$$

which is valid for all random variables z on $(\Omega, \mathscr{F})$ with $E_{\tilde{\alpha}}z < \infty$. In addition, equation 27.25 is obtained from equations 27.22 and 27.23, and from F 13–F 15 by applying the Strong Law of Large Numbers, T 16.6, to the components of $\hat{\beta}^n(\tilde{\alpha})$. I leave the details of the proof to the reader.

T 27.3 Let n and $n(I_i \cap \Omega_{\tilde{\alpha}})$, respectively, denote the number of observations that we have on consumers in $F^{-1}(\Omega_{\tilde{\alpha}})$ and $F^{-1}(I_i \cap \Omega_{\tilde{\alpha}})$, $i = 1, \ldots, 9$. Also, let $\bar{y}^n(\tilde{\alpha})$ and $\bar{c}^n(\tilde{\alpha})$ denote the sample means of $\tilde{y}$ and $\tilde{c}$ in $F^{-1}(\Omega_{\tilde{\alpha}})$, and let $\hat{\beta}^n(\tilde{\alpha})$ denote the least-squares estimate of $\beta(\tilde{\alpha})$. Finally, assume that as the number N of observations goes to ∞,

$$\lim n(I_i \cap \Omega_{\tilde{\alpha}})/n = P(I_i|\Omega_{\tilde{\alpha}}), \quad i = 1, \ldots, n. \tag{27.23}$$

For any valid interpretation of F 1–F 17,

$$\lim \bar{c}^n(\tilde{\alpha})/\bar{y}^n(\tilde{\alpha}) = k_{\tilde{\alpha}} \quad \text{a.e.} \tag{27.24}$$

and

$$\lim \hat{\beta}^n(\tilde{\alpha}) = \beta(\tilde{\alpha}) \quad \text{a.e.} \tag{27.25}$$

with respect to $P(\cdot|\Omega_{\tilde{\alpha}})$.

Some of the ingredients we need to construct a factor-analytic test of Friedman's theory are described in T 27.1–T 27.3. We provide additional ingredients in theorems T 27.4–T 27.6. Of these, T 27.5 is a universal theorem in mathematical statistics (see Cramér 1946, p. 351, and use T 16.6); T 27.6 is a universal theorem of factor analysis (see Lawley and Maxwell 1971, pp. 86–93, and Anderson and Rubin 1956, pp. 111–150); and T 27.4 follows from axioms F 6–F 17 and the following definitions:

$$x = (\tilde{c} - E_{\tilde{\alpha}}\tilde{c}, \tilde{y} - E_{\tilde{\alpha}}\tilde{y}, \tilde{A}_{-1} - E_{\tilde{\alpha}}\tilde{A}_{-1})',$$

$$f = y_p - E_{\tilde{\alpha}}y_p,$$

$\eta = (c_t, y_t, u)'$,

$\Sigma = (\Sigma_{ij}) = E_{\tilde{\alpha}} xx'$,

$\psi = E_{\tilde{\alpha}} \eta\eta'$,

and

$\Lambda = (k_{\tilde{\alpha}}, 1, (1 + \overline{r})/\overline{r}))'$.

T 27.4 Let x, f, η, $\sum$, ψ, and Λ be as defined above. With respect to $P(\cdot|\Omega_{\tilde{\alpha}})$, x has mean zero and covariance matrix Σ. Also x and Σ satisfy the relations

$$x = \Lambda f + \eta \tag{27.26}$$

and

$$\Sigma = \sigma^2_{y_p}(\tilde{\alpha})\Lambda\Lambda' + \psi, \tag{27.27}$$

where ψ is diagonal.

Since ψ is diagonal, equations 27.26 and 27.27 form a restricted factor-analysis model (see Lawley and Maxwell 1971, pp. 86–104) with three scores, x_1, x_2, and x_3, and one factor f.[2] The structure of this model is exactly identified, and the values of its parameters can be estimated even though f and η are unobservable. The necessary steps are outlined in T 27.5 and T 27.6 below.

T 27.5 Let x and Σ be as in T 27.4, and suppose that in $\Omega_{\tilde{\alpha}}$ we have n observations on x, $x_1, \ldots, x_n$. In addition, let $\overline{x}(n) = n^{-1} \sum_{i=1}^{n} x_i$, and let

$$S(n) = (n - 1)^{-1} \sum_{i=1}^{n} [x_i - \overline{x}(n)][x_i - \overline{x}(n)]'. \tag{27.28}$$

Finally, let $n(I_i \cap \Omega_{\tilde{\alpha}})$ denote the number of observations that we have on consumers in $F^{-1}(I_i \cap \Omega_{\tilde{\alpha}})$, $i = 1, \ldots, 9$, and suppose that as the number N of our observations goes to ∞,

$$\lim n(I_i \cap \Omega_{\tilde{\alpha}})/n = P(I_i|\Omega_{\tilde{\alpha}}), \qquad i = 1, \ldots, n. \tag{27.29}$$

For any valid interpretation of F 1–F 17,

$$E_{\tilde{\alpha}} S(n) = \Sigma \tag{27.30}$$

and

$$\lim S(n) = \Sigma \quad \text{a.e. } (P(\cdot|\Omega_{\tilde{\alpha}}) \text{ measure}). \tag{27.31}$$

According to T 27.4, the Σ of T 27.5 satisfies equation 27.27. Factor-analytic estimates of the parameters in the latter equation can be obtained as suggested in T 27.6. In reading theorem T 27.6, note that $\Lambda\Lambda' = \Lambda a^2 \Lambda'$ for $a = \pm 1$. We impose the condition $\Lambda_2 = 1$ for theoretical reasons.

Doing so, we avoid the inherent indeterminacy of the signs of the components of Λ.

Note also that when the x_i in T 27.5 are independent, normally distributed vectors, then $(n-1)S(n)$ has a Wishart distribution, with $(n-1)$ degrees of freedom and a log likelihood function,

$$\log L(S(n)|\Sigma) = g(x_1, \ldots, x_n) - \left(\frac{n-1}{2}\right)[\log|\Sigma| + \operatorname{tr}(S(n)\Sigma^{-1})],$$

where $g(\cdot)$ is a function of the observations and $|(\cdot)|$ and $\operatorname{tr}((\cdot))$ denote, respectively, the determinant and trace of $(\cdot)$. In T 27.6 we do not insist that x is normally distributed. We use the log likelihood function of the Wishart distribution only to generate estimates of the parameters in equation 27.27. Such estimates we shall refer to as *factor-analytic estimates.*

T 27.6 Let x, Σ, Λ, ψ, $\sigma_{y_p}^2(\tilde{\alpha})$, and $S(n)$ be as in T 27.4 and T 27.5. Well-defined estimates of Λ, ψ, and $\sigma_{y_p}^2(\tilde{\alpha})$ can be obtained by minimizing

$$\log|\Sigma| + \operatorname{tr}(S(n)\Sigma^{-1}) - \log|S(n)| - 3$$

subject to the conditions

$$\Sigma = \Lambda\sigma_{y_p}^2(\tilde{\alpha})\Lambda' + \varphi, \tag{27.32}$$

$$\Lambda = (\Lambda_1, 1, \Lambda_3)', \tag{27.33}$$

$$\psi = \begin{pmatrix} \psi_1 & 0 & 0 \\ 0 & \psi_2 & 0 \\ 0 & 0 & \psi_3 \end{pmatrix}, \quad \psi_i \geqslant 0, \quad i = 1, 2, 3. \tag{27.34}$$

Whenever the equation

$$S(n) = \Lambda\sigma_{y_p}^2(\tilde{\alpha})\Lambda' + \psi \tag{27.35}$$

has a solution that satisfies equations 27.33 and 27.34, the factor-analytic estimates of Λ, $\sigma_{y_p}^2(\tilde{\alpha})$, and ψ will satisfy equation 27.35. From this, equation 27.31, the fact that Σ_{21}, Σ_{31}, and Σ_{32} must be positive, and the relations

$$(k_2, 1, ((1+\overline{r})/\overline{r})) = (\Sigma_{31}/\Sigma_{32}, 1, \Sigma_{31}/\Sigma_{21}), \tag{27.36}$$

$$\sigma_{y_p}^2(\tilde{\alpha}) = \Sigma_{32}\Sigma_{21}/\Sigma_{32}, \tag{27.37}$$

and

$$\psi = \psi - \sigma_{y_p}^2(\tilde{\alpha})\Lambda\Lambda' \tag{27.38}$$

follows the validity of the next theorem.

T 27.7 Let x, Σ, Λ, ψ, $\sigma_{y_p}^2(\tilde{\alpha})$, and $S(n)$ be as in T 27.4 and T 27.5. Moreover, let $\hat{\Lambda}^n$, $\hat{\sigma}_{y_p}^n(\hat{\alpha})$, and $\hat{\psi}^n$ be the factor-analytic estimates of Λ, σ_{y_p}, and ψ. Finally, let $n(I_i \cap \Omega_{\tilde{\alpha}})$ be as in T 27.5 and suppose that, as the number N of our observations goes to ∞, $n(I_i \cap \Omega_{\tilde{a}})/n$ satisfies equation 27.29. Then, with respect to $P(\cdot|\Omega_{\tilde{a}})$,

$\lim \hat{\Lambda}^n = \Lambda$ a.e.,

$\lim \hat{\sigma}^n_{y_p} = \sigma_{y_p}$ a.e.,

and

$\lim \hat{\psi}^n = \psi$ a.e.

E 27.1 In our statistical analysis of the whole sample,

$$S(n) = \begin{pmatrix} 18.17954 & 4.37500 & 235.82715 \\ 4.37500 & 3.61420 & 111.12758 \\ 235.82715 & 111.12758 & 8115.44629 \end{pmatrix};$$

and the factor-analytic estimates of Λ, $\sigma^2_{y_p}$ and ψ,

$\hat{\Lambda} = (2.12214, 1, 53.90317)'$,

$\sigma^2_{y_p} = 2.06160$,

and

$(\hat{\psi}_1, \hat{\psi}_2, \hat{\psi}_3) = (8.89515, 1.55259, 2125.36516)$

satisfy equations 27.33–27.35.[3]

27.4 Confronting T(F 1, . . . , F 17) with Data

In this section we use our data to test the certainty version of Friedman's permanent-income hypothesis. Originally Friedman proposed the hypothesis as a way to reconcile the conflicting evidence that budget and time-series data give concerning the shape of the consumption function, $c = C(y)$. We begin by presenting Friedman's resolution of this controversy. Then we use T 27.1–T 27.4 to develop a factor-analytic test of Friedman's theory. Finally, we show how a population's mean rate of time preference and mean human-wealth/nonhuman-wealth ratio can be estimated. Estimates of these parameters for the U.S. population are listed in table 27.1 in section 27.4.2.

27.4.1 Budget Data versus Time-Series Data

Budget studies provide information concerning consumer income and expenditures on goods and services over a given period (e.g., the year 1875). Most such studies report that average disposable income exceeds average consumer expenditures. From this and from theorems T 27.1–T 27.3 we see how Friedmann's permanent-income hypothesis can be used to explain why regressions of c on y based on budget data confirm the consumption version of Wright's Law, which we may reformulate as

$$s = y - C(y); \quad C(0) > 0; \quad \text{and} \quad 0 \leqslant C'(y) < 1.$$

Time-series data on aggregate national consumption and disposable income provide information on a nation's total consumer expenditures and aggregate disposable income during each of a sequence of equally long time periods (e.g., each and every year from 1897 to 1949, as in figure 27.1 below). Such data do not agree with Wright's Law; they show that the ratio of savings to disposable income is stable over time even when income rises steadily.

E 27.2 Figure 27.1 relates personal saving to personal disposable income in the United States for the years 1897–1949, a period during which per capita disposable income rose from \$367 to \$826 (1928 dollars). The annual savings-income

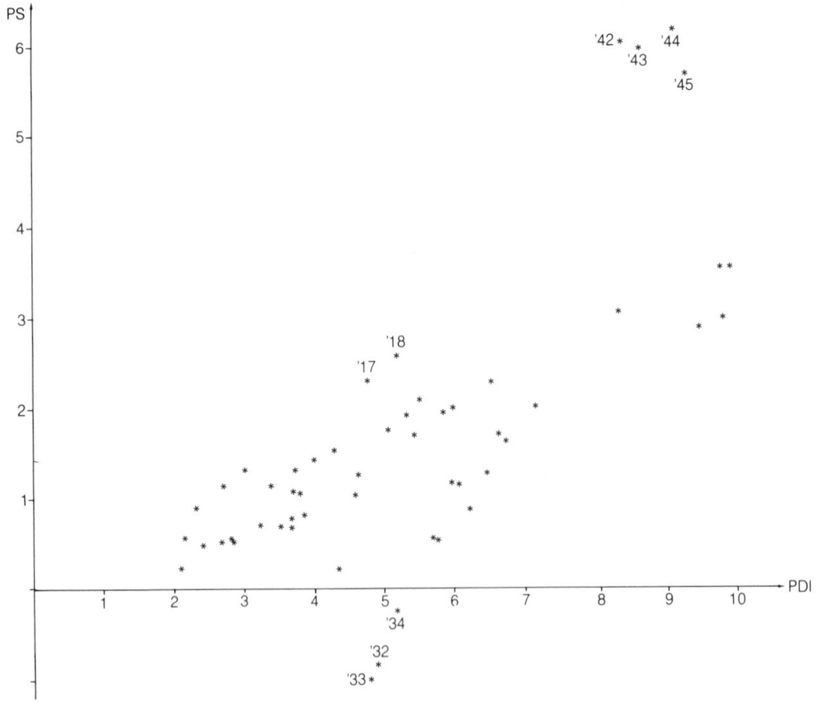

Figure 27.1
Scatter diagram of savings and income in the United States, 1897–1949. PDI units are \$12,500; PS units are \$5000.

ratio plotted in the figure shows no marked trend, as witnessed by the regression relation derived from these data minus the 1932–1934 and 1942–1945 years:

$$\text{Savings} = \hat{a} + \hat{\beta}y + u = -1460.9 + 0.137y + u,$$

where $\hat{a} < 0$ but not significantly different from zero. The t value of $\hat{a}$ is -1.5291, and $t_{0.01} = 2.660$ with 50 degrees of freedom for a two-tailed test.

Friedman's permanent-income hypothesis can be used to rationalize the observed time-series relationship between aggregate savings and income. Let Y, Y_p, Y_t, C, and C_t be, respectively, the national aggregates of y, y_p, y_t, c, and c_t; and suppose that the values of $k(\cdot)$ and y_p in the population are independently distributed relative to the probability measure on S that assigns probability $(\# S)^{-1}$ to each individual in S. Then there exists a constant k^* such that

$$Y - C = (1 - k^*)Y_p + (Y_t - C_t)$$

and

$$(Y - C)/Y = (1 - k^*)(Y_p/Y) + [(Y_t - C_t)/Y].$$

The constant k^* may vary from year to year for various reasons (e.g., fluctuations in the interest rate and changes in the structure of the population) but it need not. Friedman gives good reasons to believe that k^* remained relatively stable in the United States throughout the period 1897–1949.

Over a period of years in which k^* is nearly constant, the observed $(Y - C)/Y$ ratio will be largely determined by the values of Y_t and C_t. In wartime years, with inflation and scarcity, we would expect Y_t and C_t to be positive and negative, respectively. The corresponding values of $(Y - C)/Y$ would tend to be relatively high, as they are in figure 27.1 (see the observations for the years 1942–1945 and 1917, 1918). In years of depression, we would expect Y_t to be negative and the observed values of $(Y - C)/Y$ to be low, as they are in figure 27.1 (see the observations for the years 1931–1935). Finally, in prosperous years we would expect the values of Y_t and C_t to be small and the observed values of $(Y - C)/Y$ to be close to a constant $(=(1 - k^*))$, as they are in figure 27.1, with $k^* = 0.863$.

27.4.2 A Factor-Analytic Test

The preceding arguments show how Friedman's permanent-income hypothesis can be used to rationalize the conflicting descriptions of the behavior of the personal savings/disposable income ratio that budget data and time-series data yield. However, these arguments do not provide a serious test of Friedman's theory. We shall use T 27.1–T 27.7 to construct such a test.

To set up the test we begin by dividing the sample population in groups according to age. For each group we use the Liserel factor-analysis program (see Jöreskog and Sörbom 1978, pp. 1–56) to compute the factor-analytic estimates of the various parameters in equations 27.26 and 27.27; that is, $\hat{k}_{\tilde{\alpha}}$, $\widehat{((1+\overline{r})/\overline{r})}(\tilde{\alpha})$, $\hat{\sigma}^2_{c_t}(\tilde{\alpha})$, $\hat{\sigma}^2_{y_p}(\tilde{\alpha})$, $\hat{\sigma}^2_{y_t}(\tilde{\alpha})$, and $\hat{\sigma}^2_u(\tilde{\alpha})$. With one exception, these estimates satisfy equations 27.33–27.35. In the exceptional case, equation 27.35 does not have a solution which satisfies equation 27.34. How well our estimates of Σ, $\hat{\Sigma}$, in this case approximate $S(n)$ we can measure by the value of

$$\lambda(\hat{\Sigma}) = -2[\log L(S(n)|\hat{\Sigma}) - \log L(S(n)|S(n))]. \quad (27.39)$$

A high value of $\lambda(\hat{\Sigma})$ indicates that the approximation is poor and a low value that it is good. When (1) x, f, and η are jointly normally distributed, (2) equations 27.26 and 27.27 are valid, and (3) $\psi_{11} = \hat{\sigma}^2_{c_t}(\tilde{\alpha})$, $\psi_{22} = \hat{\sigma}^2_{y_t}(\tilde{\alpha})$, and $\psi_{33} = \hat{\sigma}^2_u(\tilde{\alpha})$, $\lambda(\cdot)$ is distributed approximately as a χ^2 variable with 3 degrees of freedom. Hence we shall look for a critical value of $\lambda(\hat{\Sigma})$ in the χ^2 table.

Next we compute

$$\hat{P}_y(\tilde{\alpha}) = \frac{\hat{\sigma}^2_{y_p}(\tilde{\alpha})}{\hat{\sigma}^2_{y_p}(\tilde{\alpha}) + \hat{\sigma}^2_{y_t}(\tilde{\alpha})}$$

and

$$b(\tilde{\alpha}) = \hat{k}_{\tilde{\alpha}} \cdot \hat{P}_y(\tilde{\alpha})$$

for the different values of $\tilde{\alpha}$. Here $\hat{P}_y(\tilde{\alpha})$ is the factor-analytic estimate of $P_y(\tilde{\alpha})$ in equation 27.16 and $b(\tilde{\alpha})$ denotes the factor-analytic estimate of the regression parameter, $\beta(\tilde{\alpha})$, in equation 27.17. We record the values of $\hat{P}_y(\tilde{\alpha})$ and $b(\tilde{\alpha})$, together with the values of $\hat{k}_{\tilde{\alpha}}$, $\hat{\beta}^n(\tilde{\alpha})$, and $\overline{c}^n(\tilde{\alpha})/\overline{y}^n(\tilde{\alpha})$ in table 27.1 below.

Our test of Friedman's hypothesis consists in comparing first $b(\tilde{\alpha})$ with $\hat{\beta}^n(\tilde{\alpha})$—the least-squares estimate of $\beta(\tilde{\alpha})$—and then $\hat{k}_{\tilde{\alpha}}$ with $\overline{c}(\tilde{\alpha})/\overline{y}(\tilde{\alpha})$. If Friedman's theory is correct, the values of $(b(\tilde{\alpha}) - \hat{\beta}(\tilde{\alpha}))$ and $(\hat{k}_{\tilde{\alpha}} - (\overline{c}(\tilde{\alpha})/\overline{y}(\tilde{\alpha})))$ must, for large n, be close to zero.

The interesting aspect of the comparisons suggested above is that they complement each other. In comparing $b(\tilde{\alpha})$ with $\hat{\beta}(\tilde{\alpha})$, we test a set of conditions A, and in comparing $\hat{k}(\tilde{\alpha})$ with $\bar{c}(\tilde{\alpha})/\bar{y}(\tilde{\alpha})$, we test both A and a condition B. If A passes the first test, and A and B fail the second test, it is likely that B rather than one of the conditions of A is the cause of failure. We shall next show what the conditions of A are and what B is.

To describe A we first observe that the components of (ω_T, ω_P) have finite means and variances relative to $P(\cdot|\Omega_{\tilde{\alpha}})$. This implies that there exist pairs of constants, (a_1, b_1), (a_2, b_2), and (a_3, b_3), and random variables, ξ_1, ξ_2, and ξ_3, such that, for all $s \in F^{-1}(\Omega_{\tilde{\alpha}})$,

$$\begin{pmatrix} \tilde{c}_s \\ \tilde{y}_s \\ \tilde{A}_{-1,s} \end{pmatrix} = \begin{pmatrix} a_1 \\ a_2 \\ a_3 \end{pmatrix} + \begin{pmatrix} b_1 \\ b_2 \\ b_3 \end{pmatrix} y_{ps} + \begin{pmatrix} \xi_{1s} \\ \xi_{2s} \\ \xi_{3s} \end{pmatrix}, \tag{27.40}$$

and such that the means of the ξ_i's and the covariances of (y_p, ξ_i), $i = 1, 2, 3$, are zero relative to $P(\cdot|\Omega_{\tilde{\alpha}})$. Consequently,

$$\left(\begin{pmatrix} \tilde{c}_s \\ \tilde{y}_s \\ \tilde{A}_{-1,s} \end{pmatrix} - \begin{pmatrix} E_{\tilde{\alpha}}\tilde{c} \\ E_{\tilde{\alpha}}\tilde{y} \\ E_{\tilde{\alpha}}\tilde{A}_{-1} \end{pmatrix}\right) = \begin{pmatrix} b_1 \\ b_2 \\ b_3 \end{pmatrix} \cdot (y_{ps} - E_{\tilde{\alpha}} y_p) + \begin{pmatrix} \xi_{1s} \\ \xi_{2s} \\ \xi_{3s} \end{pmatrix}, \quad s \in F^{-1}(\Omega_{\tilde{\alpha}}). \tag{27.41}$$

We shall choose as A the wff which asserts F 1–F 6, F 9–F 17, and "the ξ_i are uncorrelated."

To demonstrate that A is valid only if $\hat{\beta}(\tilde{\alpha})$ and $b(\tilde{\alpha})$ are nearly alike, we first observe that the second equation of 27.41 implies that

$$E_{\tilde{\alpha}}(\tilde{y} - E_{\tilde{\alpha}}\tilde{y})(y_p - E_{\tilde{\alpha}} y_p) = b_2 \sigma^2_{y_p}(\tilde{\alpha}). \tag{27.42}$$

From equations 27.42, 27.13, and 27.15 and from F 15 it follows that

$$b_2 = 1. \tag{27.43}$$

Consequently, if A is valid, then (1) equation 27.41 constitutes a factor-analysis model that satisfies equation 27.27 with $\Lambda = (b_1, 1, b_3)'$ and $\psi = E_{\tilde{\alpha}}\xi \cdot \xi'$, where $\xi = (\xi_1, \xi_2, \xi_3)'$; (2) $\hat{k}_{\tilde{\alpha}}$ is an estimate of b_1; and (3) $b(\tilde{\alpha})$ is an estimate of $b_1(\sigma^2_{y_p}(\tilde{\alpha})/\sigma^2_y(\tilde{\alpha}))$.

Next we note that if $E_{\tilde{\alpha}}\xi_1\xi_2 = 0$, then the first two equations of 27.41 and equation 27.43 imply that

$$E_{\tilde{\alpha}}(\tilde{c} - E_{\tilde{\alpha}}\tilde{c})(\tilde{y} - E_{\tilde{\alpha}}\tilde{y}) = b_1 \sigma^2_{y_p}(\tilde{\alpha}).$$

Hence

$$\beta(\tilde{\alpha}) = b_1(\sigma^2_{y_p}(\tilde{\alpha})/\sigma^2_y(\tilde{\alpha})). \tag{27.44}$$

From equation 27.44, the results of the preceding paragraph, and equations 27.31, 27.36–27.38, and 27.25, it follows that A is valid only if, for large n, $\hat{\beta}(\tilde{\alpha})$ is approximately equal to $b(\tilde{\alpha})$.

We shall choose as B the wff that asserts F 7 and F 8. To show that the second step in our test of the permanent-income hypothesis is a test of A *and* B we proceed as follows: First we note that the second equation in 27.40 implies that

$$E_{\tilde{\alpha}}\tilde{y} = a_2 + E_{\tilde{\alpha}}y_p.$$

From this equation, equations 27.13 and 27.15, and F 17 it follows that

$$a_2 = 0 \qquad \text{and} \qquad \xi_2 = y_t. \tag{27.45}$$

Next we deduce from equations 27.40, 27.43, and 27.45 that

$$E_{\tilde{\alpha}}\tilde{c} = a_1 + b_1 E_{\tilde{\alpha}}\tilde{y}.$$

Consequently, if $E_{\tilde{\alpha}}y > 0$, as asserted in F 17,

$$b_1 = (E_{\tilde{\alpha}}\tilde{c}/E_{\tilde{\alpha}}\tilde{y}) - (a_1/E_{\tilde{\alpha}}\tilde{y}). \tag{27.46}$$

From equations 27.46, 27.24, and 27.36 it follows that if A is valid, then for large n. $\hat{k}_{\tilde{\alpha}}$ is close to $\overline{c}(\tilde{\alpha})/\overline{y}(\tilde{\alpha})$ if and only if $a_1 = 0$. But $a_1 = 0$ if F 7 and F 8 are true. Thus—as was to be shown—when we record the values of $(\hat{k}_{\tilde{\alpha}} - (\overline{c}(\tilde{\alpha})/\overline{y}(\tilde{\alpha}))$, we are checking the validity of A *and* F 7 and F 8.

The two-stage test of Friedman's hypothesis, which we described above, can be formulated as a statistical test in several ways. The simplest way is the following: For a given $\tilde{\alpha}$, let $\hat{\Lambda}$, $\hat{\sigma}_{y_p}$, and $\hat{\psi}$ be the factor-analytic estimates of Λ, σ_{y_p}, and ψ, and let $\hat{b}$ be the corresponding estimate of $b(\tilde{\alpha})$. Then in the first step of the test the null hypothesis is

$$\mathrm{H}_{10} \quad A, \Lambda = \hat{\Lambda}, \sigma_{y_p} = \hat{\sigma}_{y_p} \text{ and } \psi = \hat{\psi},$$

and the alternative hypothesis is

$$\mathrm{H}_{11} \quad \beta \neq \hat{b}.$$

If Friedman's hypothesis passes the first step of the test, then in the second step the null hypothesis is

$$\mathrm{H}_{20} \quad A, B, \Lambda = \hat{\Lambda}, \sigma_{y_p} = \hat{\sigma}_{y_p} \text{ and } \psi = \hat{\psi},$$

and the alternative hypothesis is

$$\mathrm{H}_{21} \quad a_1 \neq 0.$$

From the values of $(b(\tilde{\alpha}) - \hat{\beta}(\tilde{\alpha}))$ we see that F 1–F 6, F 9–F 17, and the subsidiary condition on the ξ_i passed the first test with flying colors. However, F 1–F 6, F 9–F 17, the subsidiary conditions on the ξ_i, and F 7 and F 8 performed miserably on the second test. To see how badly Friedman's hypothesis fared on the second test we recorded the values of a_1 for the various groups. These values with the corresponding standard errors in parentheses below are displayed in table 27.1. They show that, for all groups, a_1 is significantly different from zero at the 0.05 level of confidence. From this we conclude that our data do not satisfy the certainty version of Friedman's permanent-income hypothesis.

In reading our test, note that we have used our estimate of a_1, $\hat{a}_1$, as a test statistic rather than $(\hat{k}_{\tilde{\alpha}} - \bar{c}(\tilde{\alpha})/\bar{y}(\tilde{\alpha}))$. The implications of this can be seen as follows: We can without loss in generality assume the following for the U.S. population of 1962–1963:

(i) For any one of the relevant groups, the probability of obtaining a sample in which $\bar{y}(\tilde{\alpha}) < 1$ is zero.

If that is true and if H_{20} is valid, then in terms of the sampling distribution of $\hat{k}_{\tilde{\alpha}}$, $\bar{c}(\tilde{\alpha})$, $\bar{y}(\tilde{\alpha})$, and $a_1(\tilde{\alpha})$, we have a further condition:

(ii) For any $\varepsilon > 0$, the probability that $|\hat{k}_{\tilde{\alpha}} - \bar{c}(\tilde{\alpha})/\bar{y}(\tilde{\alpha})| \geqslant \varepsilon$ is not larger than the probability of $|\tilde{a}_1| \geqslant \varepsilon$.

Consequently, if condition i is true, then at any level of significance the probability of rejecting H_{20} with H_{21} as specified is not smaller than the probability of rejecting H_{20} if the alternative hypothesis were to insist that $k_{\tilde{\alpha}} \neq E_{\tilde{\alpha}}c/E_{\tilde{\alpha}}y$.

27.4.3 The Rate of Time Preference and the Human-Nonhuman Wealth Ratio

The factor-analytic estimates of the parameters in equations 27.26 and 27.27 enable us both to propose tests of the permanent-income hypothesis and to estimate other interesting parameters in Friedman's model. Specifically, from the estimates of the third component of Λ, Λ_3, and from

$$\Lambda_3 = \frac{1 + \bar{r}}{\bar{r}},$$

we can find the implicit values of $\bar{r}$ for various groups in the sample population. These estimates of $\bar{r}$ can be interpreted as the mean rate of time preference of the groups studied. Similarly, from

Table 27.1
Test of the certainty version of the permanent-income hypothesis.

	Estimates										
Age groups	$10^{-8}\sigma^2_{y_p}$	$10^{-8}\sigma^2_{y_t}$	b	$\hat{\beta}$	$\hat{k}_{\tilde{a}}$	$\bar{c}/\bar{y}$	$\hat{a}_1$	$P_f = \sigma^2_{y_p}/(\sigma^2_{y_p} + \sigma^2_{y_t})$	$P_r = \hat{\beta}\cdot(\bar{y}/\bar{c})$	χ^2	D.F.
<35	0.0955	0.0782	0.9342	0.9342	1.6994	0.8609	−5402	0.5497	1.0852	0	362
	(0.012)	(0.006)		(0.050)	(0.104)		(267)				
35–44	0.4640	1.2566	1.9178	1.6015	7.1114	1.1793	−69091	0.2697	1.3580	8.4069	408
	(0.082)			(0.209)	(0.631)		(4297)				
45–54	2.2128	1.8128	1.1349	1.1351	2.0647	1.1135	−14046	0.5497	1.0194	0	426
	(0.260)	(0.149)		(0.075)	(0.123)		(1748)				
55–64	3.1757	2.5346	1.0433	1.0433	1.8760	1.0418	−14307	0.5561	1.0014	0	403
	(0.389)	(0.231)		(0.069)	(0.124)		(1926)				
⩾65	5.5672	0.4727	1.3516	1.3516	1.4664	1.1301	−4883	0.9217	1.1959	0	313
	(0.540)	(0.246)		(0.076)	(0.100)		(1877)				
All	2.0616	1.5526	1.2105	1.2105	2.1221	1.0855	−13464	0.5704	1.1152	0	1912
	(0.119)	(0.074)		(0.043)	(0.074)		(912)				

Note: The numbers in parentheses are estimates of standard errors. The χ^2 column records the values of $\lambda(\cdot)$ in equation 27.39.

$$E_{\tilde{\alpha}}A_{-1} = q(\tilde{\alpha}) + E_{\tilde{\alpha}}\hat{A}$$
$$= q(\tilde{\alpha}) + ((1+\bar{r})/\bar{r})E_{\tilde{\alpha}}y, \tag{27.47}$$

we can obtain the implicit value of $q(\tilde{\alpha})$ by substituting the sample means of $\tilde{A}_{-1}$ and $\tilde{y}$ for $E_{\tilde{\alpha}}A_{-1}$ and $E_{\tilde{\alpha}}y$ in equation 27.47. The value of $q(\tilde{\alpha})$ is of particular interest since

$$-q(\tilde{\alpha})/E_{\tilde{\alpha}}A_{-1} = [E_{\tilde{\alpha}}(\hat{A} - A_{-1})/E_{\tilde{\alpha}}A_{-1}] \tag{27.48}$$

and since the right-hand side of equation 27.48 equals

$$\frac{E_{\tilde{\alpha}}\ (\text{human wealth})}{E_{\tilde{\alpha}}\ (\text{nonhuman wealth})}$$

in our intended interpretation of the axiom system.

It follows from the discussion of our sequential test of Friedman's theory that the indirect estimates of $\bar{r}$ and $q(\tilde{\alpha})$ are meaningful regardless of whether F 7 and F 8 are true. In particular, they would be meaningful in F 1–F 17 if equations 27.8 and 27.9, respectively, were changed to

$$c_p = a_1(\tilde{\alpha}) + b_1(r, \tilde{\alpha})y_p, \text{ with } a_1(\tilde{\alpha}) \neq 0, \tag{27.8}^*$$

and

$$a_1(f(\tilde{\alpha})) = a_1(\alpha) \quad \text{and} \quad b_1(r, f(\alpha)) = b_1(r, \alpha), \quad r > 0. \tag{27.9}^*$$

Since the first test suggests that our data satisfy F 1–F 17 with these changes, we can use our data to obtain meaningful estimates of $\bar{r}$ and $q(\tilde{\alpha})$ in the way suggested above.

Table 27.2 presents the estimates of $\bar{r}$, $q(\tilde{\alpha})$, and $|q(\tilde{\alpha})/E_{\tilde{\alpha}}A_{-1}|$ that we obtain for various groups in the U.S. population. It is interesting to search for patterns in the observed values of $\bar{r}$ and $|q(\tilde{\alpha})/E_{\tilde{\alpha}}A_{-1}|$. The latter ought to decrease with age, and it does. As to the former, we may take low (high) values of $\bar{r}$ to indicate that the consumer places a high premium on current (future) consumption. If this is correct, $\bar{r}$ ought to decrease up to a point where the consumer's income stops rising and where the demands of family living level out; it should increase thereafter. This pattern occurs in table 27.2.

27.4.4 Concluding Remarks

We have tested the certainty version of the permanent-income hypothesis for various groups and rejected it. We have also estimated the rate of time preference and the human/nonhuman wealth ratio for the same groups.

Table 27.2
Estimates of the rate of time preference and the human wealth-nonhuman wealth ratio.

	Estimates						
Age groups	$10^{-4}\bar{A}_{-1}$	$10^{-4}q(\bar{\alpha})$	$\hat{\Lambda}_3$	$10^{-4}\bar{y}$	r	$E_{\hat{\alpha}}(\hat{A} - A_{-1})/E_{\hat{\alpha}}A_{-1}$	D.F.
<35	0.8970	−7.0076 (0.2264)	12.2689 (0.7738)	0.6443	0.0887	7.8126	362
35–44	10.7684	−81.4855 (4.4029)	79.2077 (6.4702)	1.1647	0.0128	7.5671	408
45–54	13.9745	−34.4984 (2.2643)	32.8252 (1.9000)	1.4767	0.0314	2.4687	426
55–64	32.3511	−94.3699 (6.9248)	73.8885 (4.8157)	1.7150	0.0137	2.9171	403
⩾65	31.3004	−22.7029 (4.0263)	37.1841 (2.3107)	1.4523	0.0276	0.7253	313
All	17.5240	−52.4838 (1.8635)	53.9032 (1.8162)	1.2988	0.0189	2.9950	1912

Note: The numbers in parentheses are estimates of standard errors.

Whether our results are meaningful for the group whose $\hat{\Sigma}$ differs from $S(n)$ is uncertain. For this group we estimated ψ with an SPSS program (see Nie et al. 1975, pp. 398–410) and, under the presupposition that the estimated value of ψ is the population value, we estimated Λ and $\sigma_{y_p}^2$ with a Liserel program. The standard errors of Λ' and $\sigma_{y_p}^2$ are small, but the value of $\lambda(\hat{\Sigma})$ for the given group is much too high for comfort. In fact, if we had used $\lambda(\hat{\Sigma})$ as a test statistic in the first step of our test, then for the age group 35–44 years, we would have rejected A and ended up without a test of Friedman's hypothesis.

27.5 A Test of the Uncertainty Version of Friedman's Theory

The certainty version of the permanent-income hypothesis failed to pass our tests. In this section we propose and apply to our data a factor-analytic test of the uncertainty version of Friedman's hypothesis. Since this test involves several new variables, the system of axioms of the last section must be changed.

27.5.1 New Axioms

The undefined terms of our new axiom system are the sample population S, the sample space $(\Omega, \mathscr{F})$, the sampling distribution $P(\cdot)$, and two vectors

ω_T and ω_P. These terms satisfy axioms, F 1, F 3, F 5, F 6, F 10, F 12–F 15, and F 2, with R^{17} replaced by R^{21} as specified in section 27.2. The new axioms that the components of (ω_T, ω_P) must satisfy are

SF 4 $\omega_T = (r, y, y_p, y_t, c, c_p, c_t, A_{-1}, J, K, \alpha, u, v, \eta_1, \eta_2)$,

$\omega_P = (\tilde{y}, \tilde{c}, \tilde{A}_{-1}, \tilde{J}, \tilde{K}, \tilde{\alpha})$, and

$(\omega_T, \omega_P) \in \Omega$.

SF 7 Let $\Omega(\hat{\alpha}) = \{(\omega_T, \omega_P) \in \Omega : \alpha = \hat{\alpha}\}$, $\hat{\alpha} \in \{15, \ldots, 100\}$.

There exists a function,

$k(\cdot): R_{++} \times R \times \{15, 16, \ldots, 100\} \rightarrow R_{++}$

such that, for all $(\omega_T, \omega_P) \in \Omega(\alpha)$,

$$c_p = k(r, A_{-1}/y_p, \alpha) \cdot y_p \tag{27.49}$$

SF 8 Let $f(\cdot)$ be as in F 8. For all $\alpha \in \{15, 16, \ldots, 100\}$,

$$k(r, A_{-1}/y_p, f(\alpha)) = k(r, A_{-1}/y_p, \alpha), \qquad (r, A_{-1}/y_p) \in R_{++} \times R. \tag{27.50}$$

Moreover, for all $(\omega_T, \omega_P) \in \Omega$,

$\tilde{\alpha} = f(\alpha), \qquad \alpha \in \{15, 16, \ldots, 100\}$.

Finally, there are constants $a(\tilde{\alpha})$ and $b(\tilde{\alpha})$, $\tilde{\alpha} = 25, 40, \ldots, 70$, such that, for all $(\omega_T, \omega_P) \in \Omega$ with $f(\alpha) = \tilde{\alpha}$,

$$k(r, A_{-1}/y_p, \tilde{\alpha}) = a(\tilde{\alpha}) + b(\tilde{\alpha})(A_{-1}/y_p). \tag{27.51}$$

SF 9 There exist triples of constants $(g_1(\tilde{\alpha}), a_1(\tilde{\alpha}), b_1(\tilde{\alpha}))$ and $(g_2(\tilde{\alpha}), a_2(\tilde{\alpha}), b_2(\tilde{\alpha}))$ such that, for all $(\omega_T, \omega_P) \in \Omega$ with $f(\alpha) = \tilde{\alpha}$, $\tilde{\alpha} = 25, 40, \ldots, 70$,

$$J = g_1(\tilde{\alpha}) + a_1(\tilde{\alpha})y_p + b_1(\tilde{\alpha})A_{-1} + \eta_1, \tag{27.52}$$

and

$$K = g_2(\tilde{\alpha}) + a_2(\tilde{\alpha})y_p + b_2(\tilde{\alpha})A_{-1} + \eta_2. \tag{27.53}$$

SF 11 For all $(\omega_T, \omega_P) \in \Omega$,

$$y = y_p + y_t, \tag{27.54}$$

$$c = c_p + c_t, \tag{27.55}$$

$$(\tilde{y}, \tilde{c}, \tilde{J}, \tilde{K}) = (y, c, J, K), \tag{27.56}$$

$$\tilde{A}_{-1} = A_{-1} + u. \tag{27.57}$$

In the interpretation we intend for the axioms, J and K denote the consumer's investment in risky and liquid assets respectively, and $\tilde{J}$ and $\tilde{K}$ are their observed counterparts. Moreover, u, v, η_1, and η_2 are error terms, and the "familiar" variables have the same denotation as in the preceding test. In our interpretation we have identified $\tilde{K}$ with the Federal Reserve

Board's definition of liquid assets, and we have identified $\tilde{J}$ with the consumer's investments in such varied items as real estate, bonds, shares, etc. Roughly speaking, $\tilde{J}$ corresponds to the Federal Reserve Board's definition of investment assets minus debts secured by them (see Projector and Weiss 1966, pp. 45–47).

When reading SF 4, SF 7–SF 9 and SF 11, note that in their intended interpretation, equations 27.49, 27.54, and 27.55 represent the sample analogue of the uncertainty version of Friedman's permanent-income hypothesis, equations 27.7, 27.4, and 27.5. According to equations 27.49, 27.50 and 27.51, the consumption function does not vary within age groups and can be written as a linear function of the ratio of nonhuman wealth, A_{-1}, to permanent income y_p. The coefficients in equation 27.51, $a(\cdot)$ and $b(\cdot)$, depend on both $\overline{r}$ and $\tilde{\alpha}$. However, since $\overline{r}$ is to be kept constant throughout our analysis, we have for notational simplicity omitted the $\overline{r}$ arguments of $a(\cdot)$ and $b(\cdot)$. Note also that it follows from SF 17 below that the relations we postulate in equations 27.52 and 27.53 are the least-squares relation between J and (y_p, A_{-1}) and between K and (y_p, A_{-1}). Finally, note that equation 27.56 insists that we have accurate observations on y, c, J, and K, while equation 27.57 suggests that our observations on A_{-1} are marred by errors.

We intend to use J and K as instrumental variables in estimating Friedman's consumption function. It is, therefore, important to us that, in a statistical sense, we can distinguish J and K from one another and from c, y, and A_{-1}. So we postulate SF 16.

SF 16 For all $\tilde{\alpha}$, the 2×2 matrices that can be formed by rows of the matrix

$$\Lambda = \begin{pmatrix} a(\tilde{\alpha}) & b(\tilde{\alpha}) \\ a_1(\tilde{\alpha}) & b_1(\tilde{\alpha}) \\ a_2(\tilde{\alpha}) & b_2(\tilde{\alpha}) \\ 1 & 0 \\ 0 & 1 \end{pmatrix}$$

are nonsingular.

In addition to the preceding postulates, we must also specify how the components of (ω_T, ω_P) are distributed relative to $P(\cdot)$. We do this in the next axioms.

SF 17 Relative to $P(\cdot|\Omega_{\tilde{\alpha}})$, the variances of y_p, A_{-1}, y_t, c_t, u, η_1, and η_2 are positive and finite; the covariances matrix of y_p and A_{-1} is nonsingular; and the covariances of the pairs (u, A_{-1}), (u, y_p), (η_i, A_{-1}), (η_i, y_p), (η_i, u), (η_i, y_t), (η_i, c_t), $i = 1, 2$, (u, y_t), (u, c_t), (y_t, A_{-1}), (y_t, y_p), and (y_t, c_t) are zero, $\tilde{\alpha} = 25, 40, \ldots, 70$.

SF 18 Relative to $P(\cdot|\Omega_{\tilde{\alpha}})$, the means of y_t, c_t, η_i, $i = 1, 2$, and u are zero, and the means of y, c, J, K, and A_{-1} are positive, $\tilde{\alpha} = 25, 40, \ldots, 70$.

In reading these axioms note that SF 16 and SF 17 ensure that J and K satisfy the conditions we usually impose on instrumental variables; that is, $E_{\tilde{\alpha}}c_t\eta_i = 0$, $i = 1, 2$, $E_{\tilde{\alpha}}\eta_1\eta_2 = 0$, and the matrix $\begin{pmatrix} a_1(\tilde{\alpha}) & b_1(\tilde{\alpha}) \\ a_2(\tilde{\alpha}) & b_2(\tilde{\alpha}) \end{pmatrix}$ is nonsingular.[4]

27.5.2 New Theorems

The axioms F 1–F 3, SF 4, F 5, F 6, SF 7–SF 9, F 10, SF 11, F 12–F 15, and SF 16–SF 18 constitute the axiom system of the test we shall perform in this section. For the purpose of the test we must record six theorems. In the statement of the first,

$$x \equiv (\tilde{c} - E_{\tilde{\alpha}}\tilde{c}, \tilde{J} - E_{\tilde{\alpha}}\tilde{J}, \tilde{K} - E_{\tilde{\alpha}}\tilde{K}, \tilde{y} - E_{\tilde{\alpha}}\tilde{y}, \tilde{A}_{-1} - E_{\tilde{\alpha}}\tilde{A}_{-1})';$$

$$\varepsilon \equiv (c_t, \eta_1, \eta_2, y_t, u)' \quad \text{and} \quad f = (y_p - E_{\tilde{\alpha}}y_p, A_{-1} - E_{\tilde{\alpha}}A_{-1})';$$

$$\Sigma = E_{\tilde{\alpha}}xx' \quad \text{and} \quad \psi = E_{\tilde{\alpha}}\varepsilon\varepsilon'.$$

T 27.8 Let x, f, ε, Λ, Σ, and ψ be as defined above. The vector x has mean zero and covariance matrix Σ. Moreover, x and Σ satisfy the relations

$$x = \Lambda f + \varepsilon \tag{27.58}$$

and

$$\Sigma = \Lambda M \Lambda' + \psi, \tag{27.59}$$

where $M = E_{\tilde{\alpha}}ff'$ and ψ is diagonal.

In this theorem equation 27.58 is deduced from equations 27.49–27.57 and SF 18; and equation 27.59 is an easy consequence of equation 27.58 and SF 17.

Since ψ is diagonal, equations 27.58 and 27.59 describe the structure of a restricted factor-analysis model. This model is overidentified from the point of view of factor analysis. However, as we see, with the given restrictions on Λ, the factor-analytic estimates of the parameters of the model are well defined.

When we compare T 27.8 and T 27.4, we see that if, for the x in T 27.8 and T 27.9, we define $S(n)$ as in equation 27.28, then $S(n)$ has all the properties ascribed to it in T 27.5; that is, $ES(n) = \Sigma$ and $\lim S(n) = \Sigma$ a.e., as insisted in equations 27.30 and 27.31, respectively. Thus T 27.5 is valid verbatim for the present case. Theorem T 27.6, however, is not. We state the correct version below.

T 27.9 Let x, Σ, Λ, ψ, M, and $S(n)$ be as in T 27.8 and equation 27.28. Well-defined estimates of Λ, ψ, and M, can be found by minimizing

$$\log|\Sigma| + \mathrm{tr}(S\Sigma^{-1}) - \log|S| - 5$$

subject to the following conditions:

$$\Sigma = \Lambda M \Lambda' + \psi; \tag{27.60}$$

$$\Lambda = \begin{pmatrix} \Lambda_1 & \\ 1 & 0 \\ 0 & 1 \end{pmatrix}, \tag{27.61}$$

where Λ_1 is a 3×2 matrix; and

$$\psi \text{ is diagonal and } \psi \geqslant 0. \tag{27.62}$$

In reading the theorem note that, for the true Σ, T 27.8 insists that there is a solution to equation 27.60 that satisfies equations 27.61 and 27.62, SF 17 postulates that $\psi_{ii} > 0$, $i = 1, \ldots, 5$, and the conditions of SF 16 ensure that the solution to equation 27.60 is unique. The uniqueness of the solution to equation 27.60 can be established as follows: Let B be a nonsingular 2×2 matrix that satisfies $B'B = M$ and let $\varphi = \Lambda B'$. Then $\Sigma = \varphi\varphi' + \psi$. According to a universal theorem in Anderson and Rubin 1956 (theorem 5.7, p. 129), a necessary and sufficient condition that $\varphi\varphi'$ and ψ be indentified is that, if any row of φ is deleted, the remaining rows of φ can be arranged to form two disjoint matrices of rank 2. Since the determinant of the product of two 2×2 matrices equals the product of the determinants of the respective matrices, SF 16 implies that $\Lambda B'$ satisfies the condition of Anderson and Rubin. Consequently, if SF 16 holds, $\varphi\varphi'$ and ψ are identified. But if that is so, then M and Λ are uniquely determined, since by T 27.8

$$M = \begin{pmatrix} \Sigma_{44} - \psi_4 & \Sigma_{45} \\ \Sigma_{54} & \Sigma_{55} - \psi_5 \end{pmatrix} \quad \text{and} \quad \Lambda_1 = \begin{pmatrix} \Sigma_{14} & \Sigma_{15} \\ \Sigma_{24} & \Sigma_{25} \\ \Sigma_{34} & \Sigma_{35} \end{pmatrix} M^{-1}.$$

From the preceding observations, T 27.5, and equation 27.60, we can deduce that if n is sufficiently large and if $\hat{\Lambda}$, $\hat{M}$, and $\hat{\psi}$ are the factor-analytic estimates of T 27.9,[5] then

$$S(n) = \hat{\Lambda}\hat{M}\hat{\Lambda}' + \hat{\psi} \tag{27.63}$$

and $\hat{\Lambda}$, $\hat{M}$, and $\hat{\psi}$ are the only matrices that satisfy equations 27.61–27.63. Moreover, as n tends to infinity, the solutions to equations 27.61–27.63 converge, a.e., in $P(\cdot|\Omega_{\tilde{\alpha}})$ measure to the solutions to equations 27.60, 27.61, and 27.62, with $\psi_{ii} > 0$, $i = 1, \ldots, 5$.

To see why the last assertion is true, let Σ_{ij} be the ijth component of Σ and observe first that the nonsingularity of M, SF 16, and equation 27.59 imply that the matrices

$$\begin{pmatrix} \Sigma_{41} & \Sigma_{42} \\ \Sigma_{51} & \Sigma_{52} \end{pmatrix}, \quad \begin{pmatrix} \Sigma_{41} & \Sigma_{43} \\ \Sigma_{51} & \Sigma_{53} \end{pmatrix}, \quad \text{and} \quad \begin{pmatrix} \Sigma_{42} & \Sigma_{43} \\ \Sigma_{52} & \Sigma_{53} \end{pmatrix}$$

are nonsingular. Then show that, for a given value of $\tilde{\alpha}$,

$$\begin{pmatrix} a \\ b \end{pmatrix} = \begin{pmatrix} \Sigma_{42} & \Sigma_{52} \\ \Sigma_{43} & \Sigma_{53} \end{pmatrix}^{-1} \begin{pmatrix} \Sigma_{21} \\ \Sigma_{31} \end{pmatrix}, \tag{27.64}$$

$$\begin{pmatrix} a_1 \\ b_1 \end{pmatrix} = \begin{pmatrix} \Sigma_{41} & \Sigma_{51} \\ \Sigma_{43} & \Sigma_{53} \end{pmatrix}^{-1} \begin{pmatrix} \Sigma_{21} \\ \Sigma_{32} \end{pmatrix}, \tag{27.65}$$

$$\begin{pmatrix} a_2 \\ b_2 \end{pmatrix} = \begin{pmatrix} \Sigma_{41} & \Sigma_{51} \\ \Sigma_{42} & \Sigma_{52} \end{pmatrix}^{-1} \begin{pmatrix} \Sigma_{31} \\ \Sigma_{32} \end{pmatrix}, \tag{27.66}$$

and

$$M^{-1} = \left(\begin{pmatrix} \Sigma_{42} & \Sigma_{52} \\ \Sigma_{43} & \Sigma_{53} \end{pmatrix}^{-1} \begin{pmatrix} \Sigma_{21} \\ \Sigma_{31} \end{pmatrix} \begin{pmatrix} \Sigma_{41} & \Sigma_{51} \\ \Sigma_{42} & \Sigma_{52} \end{pmatrix}^{-1} \begin{pmatrix} \Sigma_{31} \\ \Sigma_{32} \end{pmatrix} \right) \begin{pmatrix} \Sigma_{41} & \Sigma_{43} \\ \Sigma_{51} & \Sigma_{53} \end{pmatrix}^{-1}. \tag{27.67}$$

From these relations, equation 27.31, and the equations

$$\psi = \Sigma - \Lambda M \Lambda' \tag{27.68}$$

follows the validity of our assertion. We record this fact in the next theorem.

T 27.10 Let x, Σ, Λ, M, and ψ be as in T 27.8; let n be the number of observations that we have on consumers in $F^{-1}(\Omega_{\tilde{\alpha}})$; and let $S(n)$ be as defined in equation 27.28. Moreover, for each n, let $\hat{\Lambda}^n$, $\hat{M}^n$, and $\hat{\psi}^n$ be the factor-analytic estimates of Λ, M, and ψ. Finally, let $n(I_i \cap \Omega_{\tilde{\alpha}})$ denote the number of observations that we have on consumers in $F^{-1}(I_i \cap \Omega_{\tilde{\alpha}})$, $i = 1, \ldots, 9$, and suppose that as the number N of observations goes to infinity, $\lim n(I_i \cap \Omega_{\tilde{\alpha}})/n = P(I_i|\Omega_{\tilde{\alpha}})$. Then, relative to $P(\cdot|\Omega_{\tilde{\alpha}})$,

$\lim \hat{\Lambda}^n = \Lambda$ a.e.,

$\lim \hat{M}^n = M$ a.e.,

and

$\lim \hat{\psi}^n = \psi$ a.e.

Equations 27.58 and 27.59 are for the present test the analogues of equations 27.26 and 27.27 and play the same role as the latter did in our test of T(F 1,…,F 17). The analogue of equation 27.40 is provided by T 27.11. We state the theorem without proof since the arguments we used to establish the properties of the ξ in equation 27.40 can be applied almost verbatim to prove T 27.11.

T 27.11 Suppose that the components of (ω_T, ω_P) have finite means and variances relative to $P(\cdot|\Omega_{\tilde{\alpha}})$. Then there exist a 5×1 matrix $d(\tilde{\alpha})$, a 3×2 matrix $A_1(\tilde{\alpha})$, and a 2×2 matrix $A_2(\tilde{\alpha})$, and a random vector $\xi = (\xi_1, \ldots, \xi_5)'$ such that, for all $s \in F^{-1}((\Omega_{\tilde{\alpha}})$,

$$\begin{pmatrix} \tilde{c}_s \\ \tilde{J}_s \\ \tilde{K}_s \\ \tilde{y}_s \\ \tilde{A}_{-1,s} \end{pmatrix} = d(\tilde{\alpha}) + \begin{pmatrix} A_1(\tilde{\alpha}) \\ A_2(\tilde{\alpha}) \end{pmatrix} \begin{pmatrix} y_{ps} \\ A_{-1,s} \end{pmatrix} + \xi_s, \tag{27.69}$$

and such that, relative to $P(\cdot|\Omega_{\tilde{\alpha}})$, the components of ξ have zero means, finite variances, and zero correlations with y_p and A_{-1}.

From T 27.11 and equation 27.69 we obtain the following analogue of equation 27.41:

$$x_s = \begin{pmatrix} A_1(\tilde{\alpha}) \\ A_2(\tilde{\alpha}) \end{pmatrix} f_s + \xi_s, \qquad s \in F^{-1}(\Omega_{\tilde{\alpha}}). \tag{27.70}$$

In comparing equations 27.70 and 27.58, note that equation 27.70 is a consequence of the conditions specified in T 27.11, not of the axioms in our present axiom system. Thus $A_2(\tilde{\alpha})$ need not be the 2×2 identity matrix, and ξ need not have a diagonal covariance matrix. However, it is easy to show the following:

T 27.12 If F 1–F 3, SF 4, F 5, F 6, SF 9, F 10, SF 11, F 12–F 15, and SF 16–SF 18 are valid, then

$$A_2(\tilde{\alpha}) = \begin{pmatrix} 1 & 0 \\ 0 & 1 \end{pmatrix}$$

$$(d_4(\tilde{\alpha}), d_5(\tilde{\alpha})) = 0, \qquad \text{and} \qquad (\xi_4, \xi_5) = (y_t, u).$$

For the present test the last three equations are the analogues of equations 27.43 and 27.45.

The vector (y_p, A_{-1}) is nonobservable. To construct our test, we must establish an analogue of T 27.11 in which the observable vector $(\tilde{y}, \tilde{A}_{-1})$ takes the place of (y_p, A_{-1}).

T 27.13 Suppose that the components of (ω_T, ω_P) have finite means and variances relative to $P(\cdot|\Omega_{\tilde{\alpha}})$. Then there exist a 3×1 matrix $e(\tilde{\alpha})$, a 3×2 matrix

$B(\tilde{\alpha})$, and a three-dimensional vector of random variables δ such that, for all $s \in F^{-1}(\Omega_{\tilde{\alpha}})$,

$$\begin{pmatrix} \tilde{c}_s \\ \tilde{J}_s \\ \tilde{K}_s \end{pmatrix} = e(\tilde{\alpha}) + B(\tilde{\alpha}) \begin{pmatrix} \tilde{y}_s \\ \tilde{A}_{-1,s} \end{pmatrix} + \delta_s, \tag{27.71}$$

and such that, relative to $P(\cdot|\Omega_{\tilde{\alpha}})$, the components of δ have zero means, finite variances, and zero correlations with $\tilde{y}$ and $\tilde{A}_{-1}$.

The relationship between $B(\tilde{\alpha})$ and $A_1(\tilde{\alpha})$ is of fundamental importance to our test. As we show in T 27.14, this relationship is analogous to the relationship between $b(\tilde{\alpha})$ and $k_{\tilde{\alpha}}$.

T 27.14 Suppose that the components of (ω_T, ω_P) have finite means and variances relative to $P(\cdot|\Omega_{\tilde{\alpha}})$. Also, let $A_i(\tilde{\alpha})$, $i = 1, 2$, and ξ be as in equation 27.69 and let $B(\tilde{\alpha})$ be as in equation 27.71. Finally, let ξ_1 and ξ_2 be, respectively, the first three and the last two components of ξ and suppose that

$$E_{\tilde{\alpha}}\xi_1\xi_2' = 0$$

and

$$A_2(\tilde{\alpha}) = \begin{pmatrix} 1 & 0 \\ 0 & 1 \end{pmatrix}.$$

Then, with $\varphi = E_{\tilde{\alpha}}\xi_2\xi_2'$,

$$B(\tilde{\alpha}) = A_1(\tilde{\alpha})M(M + \varphi)^{-1}. \tag{27.72}$$

27.5.3 The Test

Like our test of the certainty version of Friedman's permanent-income hypothesis, our test of the uncertainty version proceeds in two steps. First we compute the least-squares estimate of $B(\tilde{\alpha})$ in $F^{-1}(\Omega_{\tilde{\alpha}})$, $\hat{B}_r(\tilde{\alpha})$, and the factor-analytic estimates of M, Λ, and ψ,

$$\hat{M},\ \hat{\Lambda} = \begin{pmatrix} & \hat{\Lambda}_1 & \\ 1 & & 0 \\ 0 & & 1 \end{pmatrix} \quad \text{and} \quad \hat{\psi} = \begin{pmatrix} \hat{\psi}_1 & 0 \\ 0 & \hat{\psi}_2 \end{pmatrix}.$$

Here $\hat{\Lambda}_1$, $\hat{\psi}_1$, and $\hat{\psi}_2$ are, respectively, 3×2, 3×3, and 2×2 matrices, and both $\hat{\psi}_1$ and $\hat{\psi}_2$ are diagonal. If the conditions of T 27.12 are satisfied and the components of ξ are independently distributed, then $A_2(\tilde{\alpha})$ is the identity matrix, $\hat{\Lambda}_1$ is an estimate of $A_1(\tilde{\alpha})$, the φ in equation 27.72 equals ψ_2, and

$$\hat{B}_f(\tilde{\alpha}) = \hat{\Lambda}_1(\tilde{\alpha})\hat{M}(\tilde{\alpha})[\hat{M}(\tilde{\alpha}) + \hat{\psi}_2(\tilde{\alpha})]^{-1}$$

is a factor-analytic estimate of $B(\tilde{\alpha})$. By comparing $\hat{B}_r(\tilde{\alpha})$ and $B_f(\tilde{\alpha})$, we check whether the conditions of T 27.12 are satisfied and whether ξ satisfies the distributional requirement we stated. That test does not involve SF 7 and SF 8.

Suppose that our data satisfy the conditions specified in the first test. Then we can see if they satisfy SF 7 and SF 8 as well. This we do by checking whether $\hat{d}_1(\tilde{\alpha}) = 0$—i.e., by seeing whether the first component of

$$\hat{d}(\tilde{\alpha}) = \begin{pmatrix} \bar{c}(n) \\ \bar{J}(n) \\ \bar{K}(n) \end{pmatrix}(\tilde{\alpha}) - \hat{\Lambda}_1(\tilde{\alpha})\begin{pmatrix} \bar{y}(n) \\ \bar{A}_{-1}(n) \end{pmatrix}(\tilde{\alpha})$$

for the various age groups differs significantly from zero.

With our Federal Reserve Board data we performed all the calculations suggested above. Table 27.3 presents the results of our analysis. There

$$\hat{B}_f(\tilde{\alpha}) = \begin{pmatrix} \hat{a}_f & \hat{b}_f \\ \hat{a}_{1f} & \hat{b}_{1f} \\ \hat{a}_{2f} & \hat{b}_{2f} \end{pmatrix}, \qquad \hat{B}_r(\tilde{\alpha}) = \begin{pmatrix} \hat{a}_r & \hat{b}_r \\ \hat{a}_{1r} & \hat{b}_{1r} \\ \hat{a}_{2r} & \hat{b}_{2r} \end{pmatrix}, \qquad \hat{d}(\tilde{\alpha}) = \hat{d}.$$

Evidently, the pairs $(\hat{a}_f, \hat{b}_f)$ are not identical with the pairs $(\hat{a}_r, \hat{b}_r)$. However, for all groups in the table, the standard errors of $(\hat{a}_r, \hat{b}_r)$ imply that the hypothesis $(B_{11}, B_{12})(\tilde{\alpha}) = (\hat{a}_f, \hat{b}_f)$ cannot be rejected at the 0.05 level of significance. Hence the uncertainty version of the permanent-income hypothesis passes the first test. On the second test the uncertainty version of Friedman's hypothesis fares no better than the certainty version. To wit: the values of $\hat{d}$ for the various groups are significantly different from zero at the 0.05 level of significance.

27.5.4 Concluding Remarks

The test we proposed above is valid only if our data satisfy the axioms we postulated. In that respect several comments are in order.

First, in SF 8 I insisted that $k(r, \cdot, \alpha)$ be a linear function of A_{-1}/y_p. Hence, strictly speaking, we have rejected a linear version of Friedman's hypothesis.

Second, we include in our analysis two variables J and K that we claim are linearly related to the two unobservable factors, y_p and A_{-1}. We can check whether our data satisfy SF 9 and the parts of SF 11 and SF 16–SF 18 that concern J and K by comparing the values of the components of

$$\begin{pmatrix} \hat{a}_{1f} & \hat{b}_{1f} \\ \hat{a}_{2f} & \hat{b}_{2f} \end{pmatrix} \quad \text{and} \quad \begin{pmatrix} \hat{a}_{1r} & \hat{b}_{1r} \\ \hat{a}_{2r} & \hat{b}_{2r} \end{pmatrix}.$$

That we do in table 27.4. The figures in the last eight columns show that the two matrices differ numerically. However, the standard erros of the $\hat{a}_{ir}$ and $\hat{b}_{ir}$, $i = 1, 2$, suggest that the matrices are not statistically different at the 0.05 level of significance. Hence we cannot reject the hypothesis that our data satisfy the given postulates.

Third, the standard errors of the components of $\hat{\Lambda}$ are conditional upon the observed values of ψ. The values of the components of ψ were obtained by the factor-analysis program of SPSS; and the standard errors were computed by the Liserel factor-analysis program. We used both programs because Liserel does not heed the condition $\psi \geqslant 0$ and SPSS does not produce test statistics.[6]

Unfortunately, the Liserel estimates of standard errors need not be consistent unless x, f, and ε are normally distributed. Therefore, since it is relevant for the import of the test to ascertain how precise our factor-analytic estimates are, we shall in the next section present estimates of their standard errors that are consistent if our axioms are valid.

27.6 Appendix: Standard Errors of Factor-Analytic Estimates

In this appendix we present bootstrap estimates of the standard errors of the factor-analytic estimates displayed in tables 27.1 and 27.3. The significance of these bootstrap estimates can be deduced from three theorems, T 27.15–T 27.17, which we state below. Theorem T 27.15 is a special case of a universal theorem of statistics (see Muirhead 1982, pp. 18); theorem T 27.17 is an application of a theorem of Rudolf Beran and Muni S. Srivastava (see Beran and Srivastova 1985, pp. 96–97); and theorem T 27.16 is an analogue of a theorem of Petter Laake's (see Laake 1987, theorem 2, p. 82). The arguments I use to prove these theorems are as much Petter Laake's as they are my own.

27.6.1 The Asymptotic Distribution of the Sample Covariance Matrix

We do not know the probability distribution $F(\cdot)$ of x in T 27.4 and T 27.8. Hence we cannot describe the probability distribution of the sample covariance matrix of our observations on x. However, we can determine the asymptotic distribution of this matrix. To see how: For a given age group $\tilde{\alpha}$, let x and Σ be as in T 27.4 or T 27.8, as the case may be; let x_{ij} denote the jth observation on x in $I_i \cap \Omega_{\tilde{\alpha}}$; and let n and $n(I_i \cap \Omega_{\tilde{\alpha}})$, respec-

Table 27.3
A test of the uncertainty version of the permanent-income hypothesis.

	Parameters											
Age groups	$\hat{L}_{11}$	$\hat{L}_{12}$	$10^{-8}\hat{M}_{11}$	$10^{-8}\hat{M}_{12}$	$10^{-8}\hat{M}_{22}$	$\psi_1 \cdot 10^{-8}$	a_f	a_r	b_f	b_r	d	D.F.
< 35	0.4791 (0.053)	0.0691 (0.005)	0.1682 (0.013)	1.1731 (0.118)	20.6077 (1.571)	0.0930	0.4721	0.4761 (0.049)	0.0678	0.0679 (0.004)	1841 (164)	362
35–44	−0.4331 (0.159)	0.0935 (0.004)	1.6913 (0.121)	36.7774 (3.957)	2910.8199 (204.531)	12.3190	−0.4166	−0.4297 (0.150)	0.0930	0.0950 (0.004)	8717 (1744)	408
45–54	0.2190 (0.093)	0.0510 (0.004)	3.9074 (0.276)	72.6643 (6.096)	2563.9827 (179.167)	6.2169	0.2400	0.1975 (0.084)	0.0495	0.0520 (0.003)	6082.28 (1222)	426
55–64	0.4512 (0.079)	0.0144 (0.002)	5.6934 (0.403)	234.6587 (21.460)	22741.5243 (1606.593)	8.1985	0.4505	0.4321 (0.078)	0.0144	0.0149 (0.001)	5462 (1429)	403
≥65	4.7271 (0.467)	−0.0554 (0.009)	4.1387 (0.459)	205.6347 (19.222)	12063.6984 (968.939)	0.1535	1.1853	1.1890 (0.118)	0.0050	0.0047 (0.003)	−34896 (3696)	313
All	10.1515 (0.989)	−0.1116 (0.014)	1.6643 (0.098)	112.1591 (4.681)	8086.7540 (262.538)	0.09666	0.5407	0.5475 (0.052)	0.0216	0.0216 (0.001)	−98184 (3245)	1912

Note: The numbers in parentheses are estimates of standard errors.

Table 27.4
A test of the validity of using J and K as instrumental variables.

	Estimates												
Age groups	$\hat{L}_{21}$	$\hat{L}_{22}$	$\hat{L}_{31}$	$\hat{L}_{32}$	$\hat{a}_{1f}$	$\hat{a}_{1r}$	$\hat{b}_{1f}$	$\hat{b}_{1r}$	$\hat{a}_{2f}$	$\hat{a}_{2r}$	$\hat{b}_{2f}$	$\hat{b}_{2r}$	D.F.
<35	0.3133	0.0136	1.1858	0.9639	0.3007	0.2900	0.0140	0.0166	1.3722	1.3906	0.9307	0.9298	362
	(0.045)	(0.004)	(0.174)	(0.016)		(0.042)		(0.004)		(0.162)		(0.015)	
35–44	0.4703	0.0046	1.5606	0.8990	0.4597	0.4584	0.0047	0.0048	1.5864	1.5744	0.8966	0.8969	408
	(0.043)	(0.001)	(0.162)	(0.004)		(0.042)		(0.001)		(0.158)		(0.004)	
45–54	0.4459	0.0146	0.9616	1.0060	0.4294	0.3917	0.0148	0.0170	1.5739	1.5879	0.9705	0.9710	426
	(0.089)	(0.003)	(0.396)	(0.015)		(0.082)		(0.003)		(0.364)		(0.014)	
55–64	0.8421	0.0011	0.9060	1.0147	0.8380	0.8313	0.0011	0.0013	1.0153	1.0214	1.0120	1.0120	403
	(0.068)	(0.001)	(0.241)	(0.004)		(0.068)		(0.001)		(0.241)		(0.004)	
⩾65	1.7442	−0.0154	1.5657	0.9749	0.4387	1.5042	0.0069	−0.0129	0.6474	−0.4956	0.9874	1.0068	313
	(0.3657)	(0.0068)	(0.648)	(0.012)		(0.145)		(0.003)		(0.324)		(0.007)	
All	1.0659	−0.0018	−8.5965	1.1298	0.0587	0.8374	0.0122	0.0018	−0.2594	0.7016	1.0106	0.9974	1912
	(0.215)	(0.003)	(1.010)	(0.014)		(0.038)		(0.02)		(0.128)		(0.003)	

Note: The numbers in parentheses are estimates of standard errors.

tively, denote the number of observations on x in $\Omega_{\tilde{\alpha}}$ and the number of observations on x in $I_i \cap \Omega_{\tilde{\alpha}}$. Then the sample covariance matrix $S(n)$ is given by

$$S(n) = (n-1)^{-1} \sum_{i=1}^{9} \sum_{j=1}^{n(I_i \cap \Omega_{\tilde{\alpha}})} [x_{ij} - \overline{x}(n)][x_{ij} - \overline{x}(n)]', \tag{27.73}$$

where

$$\overline{x}(n) = n^{-1} \sum_{i=1}^{9} \sum_{j=1}^{n(I_i \cap \Omega_{\tilde{\alpha}})} x_{ij}. \tag{27.74}$$

Next let $\mu = E(x|\Omega_{\tilde{\alpha}})$ and $\Sigma_i = E((x-\mu)(x-\mu)'|(I_i \cap \Omega_{\tilde{\alpha}}))$, $i = 1, \ldots, 9$. Then

$$E(S(n)|\Omega_{\tilde{\alpha}}) = \Sigma, \tag{27.75}$$

$$\Sigma = \sum_{i=1}^{9} P(I_i|\Omega_{\tilde{\alpha}})\Sigma_i, \tag{27.76}$$

and

$$S(n) = \frac{n}{n-1}\left[n^{-1} \sum_{i=1}^{9} \sum_{j=1}^{n(I_i \cap \Omega_{\tilde{\alpha}})} (x_{ij}-\mu)(x_{ij}-\mu)' - (\overline{x}(n)-\mu)(\overline{x}(n)-\mu)'\right]. \tag{27.77}$$

Consequently,

$$\frac{n-1}{n} S(n) - \Sigma = \sum_{i=1}^{9} \frac{n(I_i \cap \Omega_{\tilde{\alpha}})}{n} \left(n(I_i \cap \Omega_{\tilde{\alpha}})^{-1} \sum_{j=1}^{n(I_i \cap \Omega_{\tilde{\alpha}})} (x_{ij}-\mu)(x_{ij}-\mu)' - \Sigma_i \right)$$
$$+ \sum_{i=1}^{9} \left(\frac{n(I_i \cap \Omega_{\tilde{\alpha}})}{n} - P(I_i|\Omega_{\tilde{\alpha}}) \right) \Sigma_i - [\overline{x}(n)-\mu][\overline{x}(n)-\mu]'. \tag{27.78}$$

Finally, for any $p \times p$ symmetric matrix $A = (a_{ij})$, let uvec A denote the $p(p+1)/2$ dimensional column vector $\{a_{ij}, 1 \leqslant i \leqslant j, 1 \leqslant j \leqslant p\}$ formed from the elements in the upper triangular half of A (including the diagonal elements), let cov$(\cdot)$ denote the covariance matrix of $(\cdot)$, and relative to $P(\cdot|I_i \cap \Omega_{\tilde{\alpha}})$, $i = 1, \ldots, 9$, and $P(\cdot|\Omega_{\tilde{\alpha}})$ let

$$\Xi_i = \text{cov}(\text{uvec}(x-\mu)(x-\mu)'), \qquad i = 1, \ldots, 9, \tag{27.79}$$

and

$$\Xi = \text{cov}(\text{uvec}(x-\mu)(x-\mu)'), \tag{27.80}$$

respectively. Then

$$\Xi = \sum_{i=1}^{9} P(I_i|\Omega_{\tilde{\alpha}})\Xi_i. \tag{27.81}$$

Since $p\lim \sqrt{n}(\overline{x}(n) - \mu)(\overline{x}(n) - \mu)' = 0$, equations 27.73–27.81 and standard arguments suffice to establish the asymptotic distribution of $S(n)$. Hence we have T 27.15.

T 27.15 Let x and Σ be as in T 27.4 or T 27.8, as the case may be, and let n and $n(I_i \cap \Omega_{\tilde{\alpha}})$, respectively, denote the number of observations on x in $\Omega_{\tilde{\alpha}}$ and the number of observations on x in $I_i \cap \Omega_{\tilde{\alpha}}$. Moreover, let $S(n)$ and $\overline{x}(n)$ be as described in equations 27.73 and 27.74 and let Ξ_i and Ξ be as defined in equations 27.79 and 27.80. Finally, suppose that the probability distribution of x, $F(\cdot)$, has finite fourth moments and that as the number N of observations increases to infinity,

$$\lim \sqrt{n}\left(\frac{n(I_i \cap \Omega_{\tilde{\alpha}})}{n} - P(I_i|\Omega_{\tilde{\alpha}})\right) = 0, \qquad i = 1, \ldots, 9. \tag{27.82}$$

Then the random matrix $\sqrt{n}[S(n) - \Sigma]$ converges in distribution to a normally distributed symmetric random matrix with mean zero and covariance matrix Ξ.

27.6.2 The Asymptotic Distribution of Factor-Analytic Estimates

From the preceding theorem, equations 27.30 and 27.31, the relations in 27.36–27.38 and 27.64–27.68, and theorems T 27.7 and T 27.10, it follows that if our axioms are valid and if n goes to infinity in accordance with equation 27.82, then our factor-analytic estimates are asymptotically normally distributed. We shall show why first for the certainty case and then for the uncertainty case.

The certainty case: Let n be large and suppose that equation 27.35 has a solution for the given n. Moreover, let

$$\theta = (\psi_{11}, k_{\tilde{\alpha}}, \psi_{22}, \sigma^2_{y_p}(\tilde{\alpha}), ((1 + \overline{r})/\overline{r})), \psi_{33})'; \tag{27.83}$$

let $\hat{\theta}^n$ denote the factor-analytic estimate of θ; and let θ_i and $\hat{\theta}_i^n$, respectively, denote the ith component of θ and $\hat{\theta}^n$, $i = 1, \ldots, 6$. Finally, let $\hat{A}(n)$ be given by

$$\hat{A}(n) = \begin{pmatrix} 1 & \hat{\theta}_4^n(\hat{\theta}_2^n + \theta_2) & 0 & \theta^2 & 0 & 0 \\ 0 & \theta_4 & 0 & \hat{\theta}_2^n & 0 & 0 \\ 0 & 0 & 1 & 1 & 0 & 0 \\ 0 & \theta_4\theta_5 & 0 & \theta_2\theta_5 & \hat{\theta}_2^n\hat{\theta}_4^n & 0 \\ 0 & 0 & 0 & \hat{\theta}_5^n & \theta_4 & 0 \\ 0 & 0 & 0 & \theta_5^2 & \hat{\theta}_4^n(\hat{\theta}_5^n + \theta_5) & 1 \end{pmatrix}$$

and let

$$\Delta(\theta) = (\partial \,\mathrm{uvec}\, \Sigma/\partial\theta_1, \ldots, \partial \,\mathrm{uvec}\, \Sigma/\partial\theta_6). \tag{27.84}$$

Then, for a given $\tilde{\alpha}$, it is easy to show that

$$\hat{A}(n)(\hat{\theta}^n - \theta) = \mathrm{uvec}(S(n) - \Sigma), \tag{27.85}$$

$$\lim \hat{A}(n) = \Delta(\theta) \quad \text{a.e.} \quad (P(\cdot|\Omega_{\tilde{\alpha}}) \text{ measure}), \tag{27.86}$$

and

$$\det(\Delta(\theta)) = -\theta_2\theta_5\theta_4^2. \tag{27.87}$$

From equations 27.83–27.87 and T 27.15 it follows that, if the conditions of T 27.15 are satisfied, then the random vector $\sqrt{n}(\hat{\theta}^n - \theta)$ converges in distribution to a normally distributed vector with mean zero and covariance matrix

$$\Delta(\theta)^{-1}\Xi\,\Delta(\theta)^{-1}.$$

The uncertainty case: Let n be large and suppose that equation 27.63 has a solution. Moreover, let

$$\theta = (\psi_{11}, a, \psi_{22}, M_{11}, b, \psi_{33}, M_{12}, a_1, b_1, \psi_{44}, M_{22}, a_2, b_2, \psi_{55})'; \tag{27.88}$$

let $\hat{\theta}^n$ denote the factor-analytic estimate of θ; and let $\hat{A}(n)$ be the 15×14 matrix defined by

$$\hat{A}(n)(\hat{\theta}^n - \theta) = \mathrm{uvec}((\hat{\Lambda}\hat{M}\hat{\Lambda}' + \hat{\psi}) - (\Lambda M \Lambda' + \psi)).$$

Moreover, let Ξ be as defined in equation 27.80 and let

$$\Delta(\theta) = (\partial \,\mathrm{uvec}\, \Sigma/\partial\theta_1, \ldots, \partial \,\mathrm{uvec}\, \Sigma/\theta_{14}), \tag{27.89}$$

where θ_i denotes the ith component of θ, $i = 1, \ldots, 14$. Then

$$\hat{A}(n)(\hat{\theta}^n - \theta) = \mathrm{uvec}(S(n) - \Sigma) \tag{27.90}$$

and it is easy to verify that our axioms imply that

$$\lim \hat{A}(n) = \Delta(\theta) \quad \text{a.e.,} \quad (P(\cdot|\Omega_{\tilde{\alpha}}) \text{ measure}) \tag{27.91}$$

and that the 15×14 matrix $\Delta(\theta)$ is of full rank. From this it follows that, for large enough n, $\hat{A}(n)$ is of full rank and

$$(\hat{\theta}^n - \theta) = [\hat{A}(n)'\Xi^{-1}\hat{A}(n)]^{-1}A(n)'\Xi^{-1}\mathrm{uvec}(S(n) - \Sigma). \tag{27.92}$$

Consequently, if n goes to infinity in accordance with equation 27.82 and if the other conditions of T 27.15 are satisfied, then equations 27.90–27.92 and T 27.15 imply that $\sqrt{n}(\hat{\theta} - \theta)$ converges in distribution to a normally distributed vector with covariance matrix

$[\Delta(\theta)'\Xi^{-1}\Delta(\theta)]^{-1}$.

For ease of reference we summarize the preceding results in the following theorem:

T 27.16 Let x and Σ be as in T 27.4 or T 27.8, as the case may be; and let n and $n(I_i \cap \Omega_{\tilde{\alpha}})$, respectively, denote the number of observations on x in $\Omega_{\tilde{\alpha}}$ and $I_i \cap \Omega_{\tilde{\alpha}}$, $i = 1, \ldots, 9$. Moreover, let $S(n)$ and Ξ, respectively, be as defined in equations 27.73 and 27.80; and let θ and $\Delta(\theta)$, respectively, be as described in equations 27.83 and 27.84 or 27.88 and 27.89, as the case may be. Finally, suppose that the probability distribution of x, $F(\cdot)$, has finite fourth moments, and that as the number N of observations increases to infinity

$$\lim \sqrt{n}\left(\frac{n(I_i \cap \Omega_{\tilde{\alpha}})}{n} - P(I_i|\Omega_{\tilde{\alpha}})\right) = 0.$$

Then the random vector $\sqrt{n}(\hat{\theta}^n - \theta)$ converges in distribution to a normally distributed vector with covariance matrix

$[\Delta(\theta)'\Xi^{-1}\Delta(\theta)]^{-1}$.

27.6.3 Bootstrap Estimates of Factor-Analytic Parameters

In this section we discuss certain bootstrap estimates of our factor-analytic parameters. Let x_i, $i = 1, \ldots, n$ denote our observations on x in $\Omega_{\tilde{\alpha}}$; let $\hat{P}_n(\cdot): \mathscr{P}(\{x_1, \ldots, x_n\}) \to [0, 1]$ be the sample probability measure which assigns probability n^{-1} to $\{x_i\}$, $i = 1, \ldots, n$; and let $\hat{F}_n$ denote the corresponding probability distribution. Then $\bar{x}(n)$ and $S(n)$ are, respectively, the mean vector and the covariance matrix of $\hat{F}_n$, and at all continuity points a of $F(\cdot)$, the probability distribution of x,

$$\lim \hat{F}_n(a) = F(a). \tag{27.93}$$

Next let x_i^*, $i = 1, \ldots, m$, be a random sample from $\{x_1, \ldots, x_n\}$ and let

$$\bar{x}_i^*(m) = m^{-1}\sum_{i=1}^{m} x_i^*$$

and

$$S_i^*(m) = (m-1)^{-1}\sum_{i=1}^{m} [x_i^* - \bar{x}_n^*(m)][x_i^* - \bar{x}_n^*(m)]'. \tag{27.94}$$

Then in terms of $\hat{P}_n(\cdot)$

$$E\bar{x}_n^*(m) = \bar{x}(n) \quad \text{and} \quad \lim_{m\to\infty} \bar{x}_n^*(m) = \bar{x}(n) \quad \text{a.e.} \tag{27.95}$$

and

$$ES_n^*(m) = S(n) \quad \text{and} \quad \lim_{m\to\infty} S_n^*(m) = S(n) \quad \text{a.e.} \tag{27.96}$$

Finally, let θ be a vector whose components are the free parameters on the right-hand side of equation 27.27 (or 27.59, as the case may be); let $\hat{\theta}_n$ denote our factor-analytic estimate of θ; and let $\theta_n^*(m)$ denote the factor-analytic estimate of θ that we obtain when we replace $S(n)$ in T 27.6 (or T 27.9) by $S_n^*(m)$. If $\hat{\theta}_n$ satisfies equation 27.35 (or 27.63 and SF 16), then in terms of $\hat{P}_n(\cdot)$

$$\lim_{m\to\infty} \theta_n^*(m) = \hat{\theta}_n \quad \text{a.e.} \tag{27.97}$$

Consequently, if our axioms are valid, then equation 27.31, T 27.7, T 27.10, and equation 27.96 imply that equation 27.97 is valid for large enough n. However, if n is not that large and $\hat{\theta}^n$ does not satisfy equation 27.35 (or 27.63 and SF 16), we may not assert equation 27.97.

The matrix $S_n^*(m)$ and the vectors $\bar{x}_i^*(m)$ and $\theta_n^*(m)$ are bootstrap estimates of Σ, μ, and θ, respectively. We can use independently generated replicas of them to estimate the parameters of the asymptotic distribution of $\hat{\theta}_n$. To show how, we begin by recording a useful theorem, the validity of which can be intuited from T 27.15 and equations 27.93–27.97.

T 27.17 Let x and Σ be as in T 27.4 or T 27.8, as the case may be; let Ξ be as defined in equation 27.80; and let n and $n(I_i \cap \Omega_{\tilde{a}})$, respectively, denote the number of observations in $\Omega_{\tilde{a}}$ and $I_i \cap \Omega_{\tilde{a}}$. Moreover, let x_i, $i = 1, \ldots, n$, be our sample of observations on x in $\Omega_{\tilde{a}}$; let $S(n)$ be as defined in equation 27.28; and let $\hat{P}_n(\cdot)$: $\mathscr{P}(\{x_1, \ldots, x_n\}) \to [0, 1]$ be the sample probability measure which assigns probability n^{-1} to $\{x_i\}$, $i = 1, \ldots, n$. Finally, let x_i^*, $i = 1, \ldots, m$, be a random sample from $\{x_1, \ldots, x_n\}$ and the $\bar{x}_n^*(m)$ and $S_n^*(m)$ be as defined in equation 27.94. Then, if the probability distribution of x, $F(\cdot)$ has finite fourth moments and if n increases in accordance with equation 27.82, for large n and m the distribution of $\sqrt{n}(S_n^*(m) - S(n))$ relative to $\hat{P}_n(\cdot)$ approximates the distribution of a normally distributed symmetric random matrix with mean zero and covariance matrix Ξ. Moreover, the distribution of $\sqrt{m}\,(\theta_n^*(m) - \hat{\theta}^n)$ relative to $\hat{P}_n(\cdot)$ approximates the distribution of a normally distributed vector with mean zero and covariance matrix

$[\Delta(\theta)'\Xi^{-1}\Delta(\theta)]^{-1}$.

Unless the x in T 27.4 (or T 27.8, as the case may be) is normally distributed, the Liserel estimate of the covariance matrix of $\sqrt{n}(\hat{\theta}^n - \theta)$ need not, as n tends to infinity, converge in probability to $(\Delta(\theta)'\Xi^{-1}\Delta(\theta))^{-1}$. From this fact and T 27.16, it follows that we cannot assert that, for large n, the Liserel estimate is with high probability approximately equal to the covariance matrix of $\sqrt{n}(\hat{\theta}^n - \theta)$. Consequently, the Liserel estimate of $\text{cov}(\sqrt{n}(\hat{\theta}^n - \theta))$ is not a good estimate.

To obtain a good estimate of $\text{cov}(\sqrt{n}(\hat{\theta}^n - \theta))$, we appeal to T 27.16 and T 27.17 and proceed as follows: First we pick an n so large that equation 27.35 (or 27.63, as the case may be) has a solution and compute $\hat{\theta}^n$. Then we pick an m so large that $\sqrt{m}(\theta_n^*(m) - \hat{\theta}^n)$ is approximately normally distributed with covariance matrix $(\Delta(\theta)'\Xi^{-1}\Delta(\theta))^{-1}$. Finally, we perform $\hat{N}$ independent m sequences of drawings from our sample observations $\{x_1, \ldots, x_n\}$. For each m sequence we estimate θ, denote it by $\theta_n^*(m, j)$, $j = 1, \ldots, \hat{N}$, and compute

$$\bar{\theta}_n^*(m) = \hat{N}^{-1} \sum_{j=1}^{\hat{N}} \theta_n^*(m, j) \tag{27.98}$$

and

$$\hat{\text{cov}}(\theta_n^*(m) - \hat{\theta}^n) = (\hat{N} - 1)^{-1} \sum_{j=1}^{\hat{N}} [\theta_n^*(m, j) - \bar{\theta}_n^*(m)][\theta_n^*(m, j) - \bar{\theta}_n^*(m)]'. \tag{27.99}$$

As m and n and then $\hat{N}$ go to infinity, $\hat{\text{cov}}(\theta_n^*(m) - \hat{\theta}^n)$ converges in probability to $(\Delta(\theta)'\Xi^{-1}\Delta(\theta))^{-1}$. Hence, for large m, n, and $\hat{N}$, $\hat{\text{cov}}(\theta_n^*(m) - \hat{\theta}^n)$ is a good estimate or $\text{cov}(\sqrt{n}(\hat{\theta}^n - \theta))$ since the probability that any one of the elements of $\hat{\text{cov}}(\theta_n^*(m) - \hat{\theta}^n)$ differs by more than a given $\varepsilon > 0$ from the corresponding element of $\text{cov}(\sqrt{n}(\hat{\theta}^n - \theta))$ can be made arbitrarily small by choosing m, n, and $\hat{N}$ large enough.

The estimates described in equations 27.98 and 27.99 are *bootstrap estimates* of θ and $(\Delta(\theta)'\Xi^{-1}\Delta(\theta))^{-1}$, respectively. Petter Laake generated

Table 27.5
Factor-analytic estimates and their bootstrap standard errors: The certainty case.

	Estimates			
Age groups	$\hat{\Lambda}$	$\hat{\sigma}^2_{y_p} \cdot 10^{-8}$	$\hat{\sigma}^2_{y_r} \cdot 10^{-8}$	$\hat{a}_1$
<35	1.6994	0.0955	0.0782	−5402
	(0.568)	(0.046)	(0.044)	(260)
35–44	7.1114	0.4640	1.2566	−69091
	(4.286)	(0.242)	(0.452)	(4070)
45–54	2.0647	2.2128	1.8128	−14046
	(1.066)	(1.598)	(0.457)	(1800)
55–64	1.8760	3.1757	2.5346	−14307
	(0.835)	(1.573)	(1.364)	(1890)
⩾65	1.4664	5.5672	0.4727	−4883
	(0.282)	(1.408)	(0.402)	(1950)
All	2.1221	2.0616	1.5526	−13464
	(0.505)	(0.498)	(0.354)	(800)

Table 27.6
Factor-analytic estimates and their bootstrap standard errors: The uncertainty case.

	Estimates						
Age groups	$\hat{L}_{11}$	$\hat{L}_{12}$	$10^{-8}\hat{M}_{11}$	$10^{-8}\hat{M}_{12}$	$10^{-8}\hat{M}_{22}$	$\hat{\psi}_1 \cdot 10^{-8}$	d
<35	0.4791	0.0691	0.1682	1.1731	20.6077	0.0930	1841
	(0.141)	(0.039)	(0.042)	(0.702)	(13.384)		(170)
35–44	−0.4331	0.0935	1.6913	36.7774	2910.819	12.319	8717
	(0.551)	(0.039)	(0.495)	(12.406)	(1494.88)		(1560)
45–54	0.2190	0.0510	3.9074	72.6643	2563.9827	6.2169	1837
	(0.264)	(0.017)	(1.679)	(42.529)	(1125.23)		(1210)
55–64	0.4512	0.0144	5.6934	234.6587	22741.5243	8.1985	5462
	(0.244)	(0.009)	(1.035)	(84.096)	(12229.972)		(1350)
>65	4.7271	−0.0554	4.1387	205.6347	12063.6984	0.1535	−34896
	(2.964)	(0.101)	(0.950)	(78.941)	(7463.015)		(3400)
All	10.1515	−0.1116	1.6643	112.1591	8086.754	0.0966	−98184
	(13.396)	(0.221)	(0.355)	(27.146)	3425.625		(3180)

bootstrap estimates of the parameters of the permanent-income hypothesis and their covariance matrix both for the certainty case and the uncertainty case. For each age group he chose $m = n$ and generated $N = 100$ independent mm sequences of drawings from our sample population. In tables 27.5 and 27.6 we record in parentheses squares of the diagonal components of Laake's $\hat{\text{cov}}(\cdot)$ matrix for the certainty and the uncertainty case, respectively. In comparing Laake's estimate of $\text{cov}(\sqrt{n}(\hat{\theta}^n - \theta))$ with the corresponding Liserel estimate, recall that bootstrap estimates for a given age group are consistent estimates of the model parameters only if equation 27.35 (or 27.63) is satisfied. Equation 27.35 is not satisfied in the 45–54 age group and equation 27.63 is not satisfied in any age group. Consequently, Petter Laake's bootstrap estimate of $\text{cov}(\sqrt{n}(\hat{\theta}^n - \theta))$ cannot be interpreted as an estimate of the covariance matrix of the model parameters for the 35–44 age group in the certainty case and not for any age group in the uncertainty case. However, except for the 35–44 age group, the standard errors recorded in table 27.5 are good estimates of the standard errors of the respective model parameters. These estimates are larger than the corresponding Liserel estimates without throwing doubts on our rejection of Friedman's hypothesis.

28 An Empirical Analysis of Consumer Choice among Risky and Nonrisky Assets

Theorems T 12.7–T 12.9 are the sort econometricians dream of but rarely find. They give conditions on consumer *behavior* that are necessary and sufficient to ensure that a consumer's *utility function* has specific and interesting characteristics. Moreover, these conditions should be easy to test.

In this chapter we shall use data from the Federal Reserve Board and the multidimensional analogues of T 12.1–T 12.9 to demonstrate the empirical relevance of Arrow's theory of choice among risky and nonrisky asserts. In the process we establish monotonic properties of a consumer's absolute and proportional risk-aversion functions, and we test Arrow's hypothesis that a consumer's absolute (proportional) risk aversion decreases (increases) with his net worth (see Arrow 1965, pp. 43–44). We also determine whether consumers who differ in age, education, race, tenure, or profession are likely to differ in their absolute and proportional aversion to risk.

28.1 The Axioms of the Empirical Analysis

The undefined terms of the axioms of our empirical analysis of Arrow's theory are the sample population S, the sample space $(\Omega, \mathscr{F})$, the sampling distribution $P(\cdot)$, and the sample design (ω_T, ω_P, F). To begin, we postulate the following:

SA 1 Let $\#S$ denote the number of elements in S. Then $\#S \in \{1, 2, \ldots\}$.

SA 2 $\Omega \subset R^d$ and $\mathscr{F}$ is a σ field of subsets of Ω, where $d = 2(n + v) + p + 9$.

SA 3 $P(\cdot)$ is a probability measure on $(\Omega, \mathscr{F})$.

SA 4 $\omega_T = (a_1, \ldots, a_n, \mu, m_1, \ldots, m_n, A, y, b_1, \ldots, b_v, \delta, \varepsilon, \eta_1, \ldots, \eta_p)$;

$\omega_P = (\tilde{\mu}, \tilde{m}, \tilde{A}, \tilde{y}, \tilde{b}_1, \ldots, \tilde{b}_v)$, and $(\omega_T, \omega_P) \in \Omega$.

SA 5 F is a one-to-one mapping $F(\cdot)\colon S \to \Omega$.

For clarity, we shall denote $F(s)$ by $(\omega_{Ts}, \omega_{Ps})$. Also if x is a component of (ω_T, ω_P), we let x_s denote the corresponding component of $(\omega_{Ts}, \omega_{Ps})$.

In our intended interpretation of ω_T, ε, δ, and the η_ν, $\nu = 1, \ldots, p$, denote error terms; μ, A and the pairs (a_i, m_i), $i = 1, \ldots, n$, denote the interpreted versions of the same variables in Arrow's extended axiom system (i.e., A 1–A 4, A 5*, A 6* and A 7, section 12.4); y denotes the consumer's income; and the b_j, $j = 1, \ldots, v$, denote measures that are used to describe characteristics of the consumer (e.g., age, education, and profession). Note that n, the number of risky assets, equaled 2 in chapter 12. Here we allow n to be any integer larger than 1. Note also that while the error terms are unobservable, the other variables are, in principle, observable and ought to be measurable under ideal circumstances.

28.1.1 Axioms concerning the Components of ω_T

The components of ω_T must satisfy many conditions:

SA 6 Let $b = (b_1, \ldots, b_v)$ and $\tilde{b} = (\tilde{b}_1, \ldots, \tilde{b}_v)$, and let B, $\tilde{B}$, and Y denote, respectively, the range of b, $\tilde{b}$, and y in Ω. There is a denumerable subset of R, denoted W, such that

$$Y \times B \times \tilde{B} \subset W \times W^v \times W^v.$$

SA 7 Let $a \equiv (a_1, \ldots, a_n)$, $m = (m_1, \ldots, m_n)$, and $am = \sum_{i=1}^{n} a_i m_i$. There exist a set $D \subset R_{++}^{n+1}$ and continuous functions

$$h(\cdot): D \times W^v \to R_{++}$$

and

$$g(\cdot): D \times W^v \to R_{++}$$

such that, for all $(\omega_T, \omega_P) \in \Omega$,

$$am = h(a, A, b), \tag{28.1}$$

$$g(a, A, b) = h(a, A, b)/A, \tag{28.2}$$

and

$$g(a, A^*, b) > g(a, A, b) \text{ whenever } A < A^*. \tag{28.3}$$

SA 8 For all $(\omega_T, \omega_P) \in \Omega$,

$$(\mu, m) \in R_{++}^{n+1}, \tag{28.4}$$

and

$$\mu + a \cdot m = A. \tag{28.5}$$

A few comments on these axioms are called for. In our intended interpretation of the axioms, $h(\cdot)$ represents a consumer's demand for risky assets.

Therefore it is a function of the individual consumer's characteristics as well as of his net worth and the prices of his assets. Note also that, if the consumer behaves in accordance with Arrow's axioms, if his utility function possesses the separation property, and if his risk-aversion functions are monotonic, the inequality in equation 28.3 can happen only if both risk-aversion functions are strictly decreasing functions of their respective arguments.

Arrow's and Pratt's theorems concerning risk aversion and consumer choice among risky and nonrisky assets apply to choice in price–net worth situations in which the consumer invests in both safe and risky assets. Note, therefore, that in the intended interpretation of the axioms, SA 7 and SA 8 insist that D and W be chosen such that, for all $(a, A, b) \in D \times W^{v}$,

$$0 < h(a, A, b) < A \qquad \text{and} \qquad m_{\mathfrak{i}} > 0, \qquad \mathfrak{i} = 1, \ldots, \mathfrak{n}.$$

When the consumer's utility function satisfies the separation property, then $0 < h(a, A, b) < A$ only if $m_{\mathfrak{i}} > 0$ for all $\mathfrak{i} = 1, \ldots, \mathfrak{n}$.

28.1.2 Axioms concerning the Components of ω_P

In our intended interpretation of the axioms, the components of ω_P denote observed counterparts of components of ω_T. Thus $\tilde{\mu}$, $\tilde{A}$, and the $\tilde{b}_{\mathfrak{j}}$, $\mathfrak{j} = 1, \ldots, v$ denote observed values of μ, A, and the $b_{\mathfrak{j}}$. Similarly, $\tilde{m}$ denotes the observed value of am. These variables must also satisfy several conditions, which we specify in SA 9:

SA 9 For all $(\omega_T, \omega_P) \in \Omega$, $\tilde{y} = y$, $\tilde{b} = b$, and

$$(\tilde{\mu}, \tilde{m}) \in R_{+}^{2} - \{0\}, \tag{28.6}$$

$$\tilde{m} = h(a, \tilde{A}, b) + \varepsilon, \tag{28.7}$$

$$\tilde{A} = A + \delta, \tag{28.8}$$

and

$$\tilde{\mu} + \tilde{m} = \tilde{A}. \tag{28.9}$$

When interpreted, this axiom postulates that we have accurate observations on y and b, but not on μ, am, and A. We delineate in equations 28.7 and 28.8 the way in which observations on am and A are likely to be marred by errors. And in equations 28.6 and 28.9 we insist that our observations on $\tilde{\mu}$, $\tilde{m}$, and $\tilde{A}$ are consistent in the sense that they satisfy the consumer's budget constraint. From this is follows that, while ε and δ may be unrelated, the errors of observation on μ, am, and A cannot be unrelated.

28.1.3 Axioms concerning the Images of F

In the intended interpretation of the axioms, $F(\cdot)$ identifies the consumers in the sample population, with vectors in the sample space. The range of values of $F(\cdot)$ depends on the sampling scheme that the researchers in the "design" box of figure 26.2 have designed. In our case some of the properties of this sampling scheme are described in the following two axioms:

SA 10 For all $(\omega_T, \omega_P) \in \{\text{range of } F(\cdot)\}$

$a = \bar{a}$ for some $\bar{a} \in R^n_{++}$.

SA 11 There are p relevant partitions of $Y \times B$, $\mathscr{G}_v$, $v = 1, \ldots, p$. For each such partition there is a function $f_v(\cdot)\colon \mathscr{G}_v \to \tilde{B}$ such that, for all $(\omega_T, \omega_P) \in \{\text{range of } F(\cdot)\}$,

$$h(a, A, f_v(G)) = h(a, A, b) + \eta_v(b), \qquad G \in \mathscr{G}_v,\ (y, b) \in G, \tag{28.10}$$

where $\eta_v(\cdot)\colon B \to R_+$ and $\sup \eta_v(b) < \infty$, $v = 1, \ldots, p$.

The partitions of $Y \times B$ and $F(\cdot)$ induce partitions of S. Axiom SA 11 postulates the way consumer-demand functions for risky assets vary over consumers within groups and between groups that are components of a given partition of S. Since $a = \bar{a}$ in the range of $F(\cdot)$, the important thing to note is that $\eta_v(\cdot)$ is independent of A.

28.1.4 An Example

It is not at all obvious that there are ways of generating classes of demand functions which satisfy equations 28.1–28.5 and 28.10. In E 28.1 below we see how it can be done in a simple case. We also see that the axioms SA 1–SA 11 have a model. Hence they are consistent.

E 28.1 Suppose that the utility functions of the consumers in a given sample population belong to the following family:

$$U_b(A) = \log(b + A), \qquad -1 < b \leqslant -\tfrac{1}{2}, \qquad A \geqslant 1.$$

Suppose also that these consumers share the same subjective probability distribution of r:

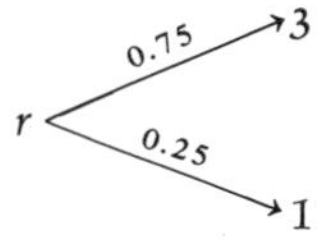

Finally, suppose that a consumer with characteristic b chooses pairs (μ, m) that will maximize

$$0.75 \log(b + A + m(3 - a)) + 0.25 \log(b + A + m(1 - a))$$

subject to $0 \leqslant m \leqslant A/a$ and $\mu = A - am$. For $A \geqslant 1$ and $2 \leqslant a < 2.5$, the optimal values of m are given by

$$m = \left(\frac{10 - 4a}{4(3 - a)(a - 1)}\right)(b + A).$$

We shall use the sample population that we described above to construct a model of SA 1–SA 11. To do so we consider one axiom at a time, and we begin with SA 1, SA 4, SA 6, and SA 7: Let S denote the given sample population; assume that S is finite; and let n, v, and p in SA 4 equal 1. Also let the Y, B, and $\tilde{B}$ in SA 6 satisfy $Y = \{0\}$, $B \subset (-1, -\frac{1}{2}]$, and $\tilde{B} \subset (-1, \frac{1}{2}]$, and assume that B consists of a finite number of points. Finally, let the functions $h(\cdot)$ and $g(\cdot)$ in SA 7 be defined for each and every $b \in B$ by

$$h(a, A, b) = [(10 - 4a)a/4(3 - a)(a - 1)](b + A) \tag{28.11}$$

if $1 < a < 2.5$ and $A \geqslant 1$, and

$$g(a, A, b) = h(a, A, b)/A$$

if $1 < a < 2.5$ and $A \geqslant 1$.

Then $h(\cdot)$ and $g(\cdot)$ are strictly increasing functions of A.

Next we consider SA 10 and SA 11. Since $p = 1$, there is only one partition of $Y \times B$, $\{G_1, \ldots, G_q\}$. So let the $f(\cdot)$ in SA 11 be defined by

$$f(G_i) = -\tfrac{1}{2}, \qquad i = 1, \ldots, q$$

and use equations 28.10 and 28.11 to deduce that, for each

$b \in B$ and $a \in (1, 2.5)$,

$$\eta(b) = -[(10 - 4a)a/4(3 - a)(a - 1)](\tfrac{1}{2} + b).$$

Also let $\bar{a} = 2$. For this value of a, $\eta(b)$ reduces to $-(\frac{1}{2} + b)$. Evidently, $\eta(\cdot)$: $B \to R_+$ as required.

To conclude our model of SA 1–SA 11 we must discuss SA 8 and SA 9. We can adopt the conditions of these axioms verbatim. We only note that equations 28.11, 28.4, and 28.5 put restrictions on the allowed values of (a, A, b); e.g., only those values of a, A, and b that satisfy $h(a, A, b) < A$ are allowed. Similarly, for $a = 2$, equations 28.6, 28.7, and 28.9 imply that $b + \varepsilon \leqslant 0$. From the point of view of this example, SA 2 and SA 3 are purely descriptive. Hence the arguments above suffice to establish the existence of a model of SA 1–SA 11.

28.1.5 Axioms concerning $P(\cdot)$ and $\mathscr{F}$

The probability measure $P(\cdot)$ and the family $\mathscr{F}$ of subsets of Ω must satisfy the following conditions:

SA 12 Let $\{G_1, \ldots, G_q\}$ be one of the partitions $\mathscr{G}$ of $Y \times B$, and let $\Omega_G = \{(\omega_T, \omega_P) \in \Omega : (y, b) \in G\}$ Then

$$\Omega_{G_i} \in \mathscr{F} \quad \text{and} \quad P(G_i) > 0, \qquad i = 1, \ldots, q.$$

SA 13 Let $\{G_1, \ldots, G_q\}$ be as in SA 12 and let $P(\cdot|\Omega_G)$ denote the conditional probability measure on $(\Omega, \mathscr{F})$ given that we are in Ω_G. Moreover, let $E_G f$ denote the expected value of f with respect to $P(\cdot|\Omega_G)$. Then

$$E_{G_i}\varepsilon = E_{G_i}\delta = 0, \qquad i = 1, \ldots, q.$$

SA 14 Let $\{G_1, \ldots, G_q\}$ be as in SA 12. The variables A, ε, δ, and η are independently distributed relative to $P(\cdot|\Omega_{G_i})$, $i = 1, \ldots, q$.

SA 15 Let $\{G_1, \ldots, G_q\}$ be as in SA 12. The variables am, A, μ/A, ε, δ, and η have finite positive variances with respect to $P(\cdot|\Omega_{G_i})$, $i = 1, \ldots, q$.

In reading these axioms, note that if $\mathscr{G}_v$ *is* the partition $\{G_1, \ldots, G_q\}$ in SA 12, then the η in SA 14 and SA 15 *is* the $\eta_v(\cdot)$ of equation 28.10. Note also that the inequalities which the first eleven axioms impose on ε and δ are not such that S 1–S 13 are inconsistent. For example, if $a = 2$, then the ε and δ of E 28.1 satisfy the inequalities

$$\varepsilon \leqslant -b, \qquad -(b + A) \leqslant \delta + \varepsilon, \qquad \text{and} \qquad -A \leqslant \delta,$$

none of which contradicts SF 13 since $A \geqslant 1$ and $b \in (-1, -\frac{1}{2}]$. Finally, note that the intended interpretation of $P(\cdot)$ is like the interpretation we gave to $P(\cdot)$ in M 1–M 19. Specifically, let $Q(F^{-1}(D)) = P(D)$, $D \in \mathscr{F}$; and let $\mathscr{F}_S$ denote the σ field of subsets of S that consists of all subsets of S that are inverse images under $F(\cdot)$ of sets which belong to $\mathscr{F}$. Then $Q(\cdot)$ is a probability measure on $(S, \mathscr{F}_S)$. As in chapters 26 and 27 we interpret $Q(F^{-1}(D))$ as the probability which the samplers assign to the chance of abserving a consumer with a (ω_T, ω_P) vector in D (e.g., a consumer with at least twelve years of education or a consumer with a yearly income of more than \$100,000).

The data we intend to use to test Arrow's theory were obtained in accordance with a stratified random sampling scheme in which consumers were stratified by their 1960 income. Some of the characteristics of this sampling scheme are described in the next three axioms.

SA 16 Let a_r be one of the numbers \$3000, \$5000, \$7500, \$10,000, \$15,000, \$25,000, \$50,000, and \$100,000, with $a_1 < a_2 \cdots < a_8$. Moreover, let I_r be defined by

$$I_1 = \{(\omega_T, \omega_P) \in \Omega : y < a_1\},$$

$$I_r = \{(\omega_T, \omega_P) \in \Omega : a_{r-1} \leqslant y < a_r\}, \qquad r = 2, \ldots, 8$$

$$I_9 = \{(\omega_T, \omega_P) \in \Omega : a_8 \leqslant y\}.$$

There is a $v \in \{1, \ldots, p\}$ such that $\mathscr{G}_v = \{G_1, \ldots, G_9\}$ and such that $\Omega_{G_r} = I_r$, $r = 1, \ldots, 9$. Also, for all partitions $\mathscr{G}_v$, $v = 1, \ldots, p$, and for any $G \in \mathscr{G}_v$, $P(I_r \cap \Omega_G) > 0$, $r = 1, \ldots, 9$.

SA 17 There are N observations with n_r observations from I_r, $r = 1, \ldots, 9$. The probability distribution of the sample is given by

$$\prod_{r=1}^{9} (P(\cdot|I_r))^{n_r}.$$

Axioms SA 1–SA 17 are all the axioms we need to carry out the tests we have in mind. Of these axioms, only SA 7 and SA 8 pertain to Arrow's theory *per se*. The others concern properties of $P(\cdot)$ and the way consumers in the sample population differ among themselves. Note, therefore, that the implications of our empirical analysis for Arrow's theory and for his hypothesis concerning the monotonic properties of a consumer's risk-aversion functions stand and fall with the validity of axioms SA 9–SA 17.

28.2 Arrow's Risk-Aversion Functions and the Data

In this section we describe a test of Arrow's hypothesis that a consumer's absolute risk-aversion function is strictly decreasing and that his proportional risk-aversion function is strictly increasing. The test is based on several theorems concerning characteristics of the sample population that are easy consequences of the axioms and of well-known theorems in mathematical statistics.

28.2.1 The Data and the Axioms

To test Arrow's hypothesis we shall use data that were collected by the Federal Reserve Board in two reinterview surveys of consumer finances (see Projector and Weiss 1966 and Projector 1968). In these a consumer was taken to be a "consumer unit" as defined by the Bureau of the Budget, i.e. either a family living together and having a common budget or a single individual living alone. For each such consumer the surveyors recorded the value of his assets and liabilities at the end of 1962 and 1963, the level of his income in 1962 and 1963, and the values of many of his most important characteristics, such as age and education. The assets comprised major financial assets plus others such as equity in farm and nonfarm sole proprietorships and company savings plans. The debts consisted of debt secured by a home and /or investment assets, including life insurance, installment debt, and unsecured loans to doctors, hospitals, and banks.

This extraordinary supply of information on consumer finances leaves us with a serious problem of interpretation which we resolve as follows: We identify Arrow's consumer with the two surveys' consumers and we adopt our intended interpretation of y, μ, A, and the pairs (a_i, m_i), $i = 1, \ldots, n$.

Moreover, we let $\tilde{y}$ and $\tilde{\mu}$ denote, respectively, the consumer's income in 1963 and the value of his liquid assets (as specified in Projector 1968, pp. 45–46) at the end of 1963; we identify $\tilde{m}$ with the end-of-1963 value of those of the consumer's investment assets that were covered by the two surveys (see Projector 1968, pp. 45–47 and our interpretation of $\tilde{J}$ in section 27.5.1) minus the value of debt secured by these assets, and minus, liquid assets; and we define $\tilde{A}$ to equal $\tilde{\mu} + \tilde{m}$. Finally, we interpret b, $\tilde{b}$, B, and $\tilde{B}$ in such a way that the inverse images under $F(\cdot)$ of the sets of the various $\mathscr{G}$ partition the sample population into renters and homeowners, self-employed and employed by others, whites and nonwhites, consumers whose head of the household has $\leqslant 8$, 9–12, or > 12 years of education, and consumers whose head of the household was < 35, 35–44, 45–54, 55–64, or $\geqslant 65$ years old in 1962.

Our interpretation satisfies axioms SA 1–SA 5, SA 10, SA 12, and SA 15–SA 17 since they are true by design. It satisfies SA 6, SA 8, and (except for equation 28.7) SA 9 as if by definition, because in delineating the denotation of the components of (ω_T, ω_P) we made sure that these axioms were satisfied. Whether our interpretation satisfies axioms SA 7, SA 11, and SA 13–SA 14 is harder to say. Since these axioms involve so many unobservables, we can test their validity only in indirect ways.

28.2.2 Sample Theorems

To obtain an indirect test of SA 7, SA 11, SA 13, and SA 14 we next record two sample theorems.

The first theorem concerns the monotonic properties of $h(\bar{a}, \cdot, b)$. We have postulated that this function is an increasing function of A. The theorem asserts that, if this is so, any interpretation of the axioms which satisfies SA 8–SA 17 must agree that the covariance of $\tilde{m}$ and $\tilde{A}$ is positive.

T 28.1 Let $\{G_1, \ldots, G_q\}$ be one of the partitions $\mathscr{G}_v$ of $Y \times B$, and let

$$\tilde{m} = \alpha_{G_i} + \beta_{G_i}\tilde{A} + u \qquad (28.12)$$

denote the regression relation of $\tilde{m}$ on $\tilde{A}$ relative to $P(\cdot|\Omega_{G_i})$. Then

$$\beta_{G_i} > 0, \qquad i = 1, \ldots, q. \qquad (28.13)$$

In reading the theorem, note the existence of a pair $(\alpha_{G_i}, \beta_{G_i})$ and a variable u which satisfy equation 28.12 and the additional conditions

$$E_{G_i}u = E_{G_i}(\tilde{A} - E_{G_i}\tilde{A})u = 0$$

follows from the fact that both $\tilde{m}$ and $\tilde{A}$ have finite mean and variance. The inequality in equation 28.13 is a consequence of the monotonicity of $h(\overline{a}, \cdot, b)$ and SA 12–SA 14. To wit: Fix v and i and observe that

$$E_{G_i}(\tilde{m} - E_{G_i}\tilde{m})(\tilde{A} - E_{G_i}\tilde{A})$$
$$= E_{G_i}(h(\overline{a}, \tilde{A}, b) - E_{G_i}\tilde{m})(\tilde{A} - E_{G_i}\tilde{A}) + E_{G_i}(\varepsilon((A - E_{G_i}A) + (\delta - E_{G_i}\delta))$$
$$= E_{G_i}(h(\overline{a}, \tilde{A}, f_v(G_i)) - h(\overline{a}, E_{G_i}\tilde{A}, f_v(G_i)))(\tilde{A} - E_{G_i}\tilde{A}) - E_{G_i}\eta_v(\tilde{A} - E_{G_i}\tilde{A})$$
$$= E_{G_i}(h(\overline{a}, \tilde{A}, f_v(G_i)) - h(\overline{a}, E_{G_i}\tilde{A}, f_v(G_i)))(\tilde{A} - E_{G_i}\tilde{A}) > 0.$$

Our next theorem concerns the monotonic properties of $g(\cdot)$. Axiom SA 7 insists that $g(\overline{a}, \cdot, b)$ is an increasing function of A. If that is correct, then (according to the theorem) any interpretation of the axioms which satisfies SA 8–SA 17 must agree that the covariance of $(\tilde{\mu}/\tilde{A})$ and $\tilde{A}$ is negative.

T 28.2 Let $\{G_1, \ldots, G_q\}$ be any one of the partitions $\mathscr{G}_v$ of $Y \times B$ and let

$$(\tilde{\mu}/\tilde{A}) = \gamma_{G_i} + \varphi_{G_i}\tilde{A} + \xi \tag{28.14}$$

denote the regression relation of $(\tilde{\mu}/\tilde{A})$ on $\tilde{A}$ relative to $P(\cdot|\Omega_{G_i})$. Then

$$\varphi_{G_i} < 0, \qquad i = 1, \ldots, q. \tag{28.15}$$

Again the existence of a pair $(\gamma_{G_i}, \varphi_{G_i})$ and a variable ξ which satisfy equation 28.14 and the additional relations

$$E_{G_i}\xi = E_{G_i}(\tilde{A} - E_{G_i}\tilde{A})\xi = 0$$

follows from the fact that both $(\tilde{\mu}/\tilde{A})$ and $\tilde{A}$ have finite mean and variance. The inequality in equation 28.15 is a consequence of the monotonicity of $g(\overline{a}, \cdot, b)$ and of SA 11–SA 13. To wit: Fix v and i and observe first that

$$E_{G_i}((\tilde{m}/\tilde{A}) - E_{G_i}(\tilde{m}/\tilde{A}))(\tilde{A} - E_{G_i}\tilde{A})$$
$$= E_{G_i}([h(\overline{a}, \tilde{A}, b)/A] - E_{G_i}(\tilde{m}/\tilde{A}))(\tilde{A} - E_{G_i}\tilde{A}) + E_{G_i}(\varepsilon/\tilde{A})(\tilde{A} - E_{G_i}\tilde{A})$$
$$= E_{G_i}(g(\overline{a}, \tilde{A}, f_v(G_i)) - g(\overline{a}, E_{G_i}\tilde{A}, f_v(G_i)))(\tilde{A} - E_{G_i}\tilde{A})$$
$$- E_{G_i}(\eta_v/\tilde{A})(\tilde{A} - E_{G_i}\tilde{A})$$
$$= E_{G_i}(g(\overline{a}, \tilde{A}, f_v(G_i)) - g(\overline{a}, E_{G_i}\tilde{A}, f_v(G_i)))(\tilde{A} - E_{G_i}\tilde{A})$$
$$- E_{G_i}\eta_v(1 - (E_{G_i}\tilde{A} \cdot E_{G_i}\tilde{A}^{-1})).$$

Next observe that, by Schwartz's Inequality,

$$E_{G_i}\tilde{A} \cdot E_{G_i}\tilde{A}^{-1} = E_{G_i}(\tilde{A}^{1/2})^2 E_{G_i}(\tilde{A}^{-1/2})^2 \geqslant (E_{G_i}\tilde{A}^{1/2}\tilde{A}^{-1/2})^2 = 1.$$

Hence $E_{G_i}((\tilde{m}/\tilde{A}) - E_{G_i}(\tilde{m}/\tilde{A}))(\tilde{A} - E_{G_i}\tilde{A}) > 0$. But if that is so, then

$$E_{G_i}((\tilde{\mu}/\tilde{A}) - E_{G_i}(\tilde{\mu}/\tilde{A}))(\tilde{A} - E_{G_i}\tilde{A})$$
$$= E_{G_i}(1 - (\tilde{m}/\tilde{A}) - 1 + E_{G_i}(\tilde{m}/\tilde{A}))(\tilde{A} - E_{G_i}\tilde{A})$$
$$= -E_{G_i}((\tilde{m}/\tilde{A}) - E_{G_i}(\tilde{m}/\tilde{A}))(\tilde{A} - E_{G_i}\tilde{A}) < 0,$$

as was to be shown.

28.2.3 An Indirect Test of SA 7 and SA 11–SA 17

Theorems T 28.1 and T 28.2 suggest one way to test whether our interpretation of the undefined terms of SA 1–SA 17 satisfies SA 7 and SA 11–SA 17: Use least squares to estimate the parameters in equations 28.12 and 28.14, and check whether the estimates satisfy equations 28.13 and 28.15. For large enough samples, the signs of the estimated values of β and φ must equal the signs of the true of β and φ, as witnessed by the following theorem.

T 28.3 Let $\{G_1, \ldots, G_q\}$ be one of the partitions $\mathscr{G}$ of $Y \times B$; and let G_i be a group belonging to this partition. Suppose that we have $n = n(\Omega_{G_i})$ observations from $F^{-1}(\Omega_{G_i})$ and $n(\Omega_{G_i} \cap I_r)$ observations from $F^{-1}(\Omega_{G_i} \cap I_r)$ and let $\hat{\beta}^n_{G_i}$ and $\hat{\varphi}^n_{G_i}$ denote the ordinary least squares estimates of β_{G_i} and φ_{G_i}. Finally, suppose that as the number N of our observations goes to ∞,

$$\lim n(\Omega_{G_i} \cap I_r)/n = P(I_r|\Omega_{G_i}), \qquad r = 1, \ldots, 9.$$

Then with respect to $P(\cdot|\Omega_{G_i})$,

$$\lim \hat{\beta}^n_{G_i} = \beta_{G_i} \quad \text{a.e.;}$$

and

$$\lim \hat{\varphi}^n_{G_i} = \varphi_{G_i} \quad \text{a.e.}$$

We carried out the suggested calculations for the various partitions of the sample population. Our results are presented in table 28.1. A close look at the table reveals that—with one exception—the estimated values of β and φ are significantly different from zero at the 0.05 level of significance and satisfy equations 28.13 and 28.15. Thus, if we ignore the one exception, our calculations allow us to assume that our interpretation is a model of SA 1–SA 17.

28.2.4 A Test of Arrow's Hypotheses

For the purpose of testing Arrow's hypotheses concerning the monotonic properties of the absolute and proportional risk-aversion functions, theorems T 28.1 and T 28.2 may be rephrased as follows: Suppose that SA 1–SA 17 are valid assertions concerning a given sample population. Suppose

Table 28.1
Estimates of the regression coefficients in $m = \alpha + \beta\tilde{A} + \xi$ and $(\mu/A) = \gamma + \varphi\tilde{A} + \xi$.[1]

Groups	Coefficients α	β	R^2	γ	φ	R^2	D.F.
Age, years	5.375	0.977		0.313	−3.039 E-04		
<35	(0.000)	(0.000)	0.992	(0.000)	(0.012)	0.023	271
35–44	6.168	0.986		0.166	−5.262 E-05		
	(0.009)	(0.000)	0.996	(0.000)	(0.019)	0.016	338
45–54	4.312	0.985		0.159	−3.392 E-05		
	(0.1403)	(0.000)	0.997	(0.000)	(0.005)	0.021	360
55–64	0.822	0.991		1.174	−1.514 E-05		
	(0.844)	(0.000)	0.998	(0.000)	(0.040)	0.145	287
⩾65	15.401	0.975		0.246	−7.416 E-05		
	(0.222)	(0.000)	0.986	(0.000)	(0.005)	0.075	104
Self-employed	−11.453	0.986		0.104	−2.532 E-05		
	(0.000)	(0.000)	0.999	(0.000)	(0.000)	0.041	358
Employed by	−4.416	0.993		0.231	−2.496 E-05		
others	(0.000)	(0.000)	0.9999	(0.000)	(0.009)	0.007	1006
Homeowners	−7.692	0.991		0.092	−1.048 E-05		
	(0.000)	(0.000)	0.9997	(0.002)	(0.001)	0.012	1009
Renters	36.515	0.976		0.499	−1.194 E-04		
	(0.000)	(0.000)	0.989	(0.000)	(0.000)	0.046	355
Education, years	1.378	0.987		0.241	−1.117 E-04		
⩽8	(0.2837)	(0.000)	0.995	(0.000)	(0.100)	0.011	239
9–12	3.686	0.973		0.231	−1.304 E-04		
	(0.001)	(0.000)	0.993	(0.000)	(0.002)	0.018	541
>12	5.417	0.989		0.159	−2.211 E-05		
	(0.142)	(0.000)	0.997	(0.000)	(0.001)	0.021	583
Race, white	8.269	0.989		0.192	−3.124 E-05		
	(0.000)	(0.000)	0.997	(0.000)	0.000	0.014	1279
Race, nonwhite	2.629	0.825		0.403	−0.007		
	(0.000)	(0.000)	0.909	(0.000)	(0.001)	0.152	70
All	8.542	0.987		0.198	−3.217 E-05		
	(0.000)	(0.000)	0.997	(0.000)	(0.000)	0.015	1365

Note: The numbers in parentheses record the level of significance at which the estimates differ from zero. Moreover, $aE - 05 = a \cdot 10^{-5}$.

also that the consumers in the population behave in accordance with Arrow's extended axiom system, and that their utility functions possess the strict separation property. Then their absolute risk-aversion functions are decreasing only if $\beta_{G_i} > 0$, and their proportional risk-aversion functions are strictly decreasing only if $\varphi_{G_i} < 0$.

To test Arrow's hypotheses, we must be able to replace the "only if" in the last assertion with "if and only if."

T 28.4 Suppose that SA 1–SA 6, SA 8–SA 17, and SA 7 without equation 28.3 are valid assertions about a given sample population. Suppose also that, for all $b \in B$, $h(\bar{a}, \cdot, b)$ and $g(\bar{a}, \cdot, b)$ are either strictly increasing, constant, or strictly decreasing functions of A. Then, for any partition $\mathcal{G}_v$, $v = 1, \ldots, p$, and any $G \in \mathcal{G}_j$,

(i) $\beta_G > (= (\text{or} <))\, 0$ if and only if $h(\bar{a}, \cdot, f_v(G))$ is a strictly increasing (constant (or strictly decreasing)) function of A.

(ii) $\varphi_G < (= (\text{or} >))\, 0$ if and only if $g(\bar{a}, \cdot, f_v(G))$ is a strictly increasing (constant (or strictly decreasing)) function of A.

To prove the theorem we observe first that T 28.4 (i) is an immediate consequence of

$$E_{G_i}(\tilde{m} - E_{G_i}\tilde{m})(\tilde{A} - E_{G_i}\tilde{A})$$
$$= E_{G_i}(h(\bar{a}, \tilde{A}, f_v(G_i)) - h(\bar{a}, E_{G_i}\tilde{A}, f_v(G_i)))(\tilde{A} - E_{G_i}\tilde{A}),$$

which is valid for all $v = 1, \ldots, p$ and $G_i \in \mathcal{G}_v$. To prove T 28.4 (ii), we fix v and i and let

$$H(\bar{a}, \tilde{A}) = h(\bar{a}, \tilde{A}, f_v(G_i)) - E_{G_i}\eta_v,$$

and

$$G(\bar{a}, \tilde{A}) = H(\bar{a}, \tilde{A})/\tilde{A}.$$

Then $G(\bar{a}, \cdot)$ is strictly increasing (constant (or strictly decreasing)) according as $g(\bar{a}, \cdot, f_v(G_i))$ is strictly increasing (constant (or strictly decreasing)). Also,

$$E_{G_i}((\tilde{m}/\tilde{A}) - E_{G_i}(\tilde{m}/\tilde{A}))(\tilde{A} - E_{G_i}\tilde{A})$$
$$= E_{G_i}(G(\bar{a}, \tilde{A}) - G(\bar{a}, E_{G_i}\tilde{A}))(\tilde{A} - E_{G_i}\tilde{A})$$
$$- E_{G_i}(\eta_v - E_{G_i}\eta_v)(1 - E_{G_i}\tilde{A} \cdot E_{G_i}\tilde{A}^{-1})$$
$$= E_{G_i}(G(\bar{a}, \tilde{A}) - G(\bar{a}, E_{G_i}\tilde{A}))(\tilde{A} - E_{G_i}\tilde{A}).$$

Consequently, $E_{G_i}((\tilde{\mu}/\tilde{A}) - E_{G_i}(\tilde{\mu}/\tilde{A}))(\tilde{A} - E_{G_i}\tilde{A}) < (= (\text{or} >))\, 0$ according as $g(\bar{a}, \cdot, f_v(G_i))$ is strictly increasing (constant (or strictly decreasing)), as was to be shown.

It is clear that if our interpretation of the undefined terms of SA 1–SA 17 is a model of these axioms, it is also a model of SA 1–SA 6, SA 8–SA 17, and SA 7 with the changes described in T 28.4. Therefore T 28.4 and our indirect test of SA 7, SA 11, SA 13, and SA 14 suggest that Arrow's hypth-eses are not both true of our sample populaton. Specifically, if consumers in this population behave in accordance with Arrow's axioms and have utility functions that possess the separation property, their absolute risk-aversion functions are strictly decreasing functions of A—as Arrow hypothesized. Their proportional risk-aversion functions are also strictly decreasing functions of A—*not* increasing, as Arrow suggested.

28.3 Comparative Risk Aversion

In this section we proceed on the assumption that our interpretation of SA 1–SA 17 is valid. We also assume throughout that the following three assertions are true:

(i) Consumers in the sample population behave in accordance with Arrow's extended axiom system, with the number of risky assets equal to n.
(ii) They have utility functions that possess the separation property.
(iii) Both within and across groups, differences in the subjective probability distributions of future values of the a_i, $i = 1, \ldots, n$, are insignificant in the context of the present empirical analysis.

From assertions i–iii and from theorems T 12.5 and T 12.6, it follows that, if two consumers in the same group have the same value of A, one of them will invest (proportionately) more in risky assets than the other if and only if his (proportional) absolute risk aversion at the given value of A is less than that of the other consumer. The same is true of two consumers who belong to different groups. Consequently, if assumptions i–iii are true, and if our interpretation of SA 1–SA 17 is valid, we should be able to use our data to ascertain differences in degrees of risk aversion of consumers in the population. In this section we shall, therefore, attempt to determine to what extent the risk aversion of consumers varies with age, profession, education, race, and tenure.

28.3.1 One-Way Analysis of Variance: Theory

Before we begin our analysis, several preliminary remarks are called for. In T 28.4 we established a unique relationship between the signs of β_G and φ_G and the monotonicity of $h(\overline{a}, \cdot, b)$ and $g(\overline{a}, \cdot, b)$ for $b \in G$. Note, therefore, in T(SA 1, ..., SA 17) *the parameters we have estimated,* α_G, β_G, γ_G, *and* φ_G, *are statistical parameters, not behavioral parameters!* Thus on the basis of our postulates, i.e., SA 1–SA 17, we cannot interpret β_G as the marginal propensity to invest in risky assets of a representative individual in G. Similarly, if G_1 and G_2 belong to one of the partitions $\mathscr{G}$, $\beta_{G_1} > \beta_{G_2}$ does not imply that group G_1's marginal propensity to invest in risky assets is larger than that of group G_2. More importantly, we cannot infer from $\beta_{G_1} > \beta_{G_2}$ that consumers in $F^{-1}(\Omega_{G_1})$ are, on the average, less risk-averse than consumers in $F^{-1}(\Omega_{G_2})$; nor can we infer from $\varphi_{G_1} < \varphi_{G_2}$ that the proportional risk aversion of consumers in $F^{-1}(\Omega_{G_1})$ is less than that of consumers in $F^{-1}(\Omega_{G_2})$.

When we add assertions i–iii to SA 1–SA 17, the status of the α_G, β_G, γ_G, and φ_G of equations 28.12 and 28.14 changes dramatically, as can be intuited from T 28.5.

T 28.5 Suppose that SA 1–SA 17 and assertions i–iii above are valid. Suppose also that the function $h(\cdot, b)\colon D \to R_{++}$ in SA 7 is the demand function for *am* of a consumer with characteristic b. Finally, suppose that the number of partitions of $Y \times B$ in SA 11 is at least two. Then two of these partitions, say $\{H_1, \ldots, H_q\}$ and $\{K_1, \ldots, K_k\}$, satisfy the relations

$$H_i \cap K_j \neq \emptyset, \qquad i = 1, \ldots, q \quad \text{and} \quad j = 1, \ldots, k. \tag{28.16}$$

Moreover, if $\{G_1, \ldots, G_q\}$ is one of the partitions of $Y \times B$ in SA 11, there exist constants α, α_i, $i = 1, \ldots, q-1$, and β and a random variable τ that is orthogonal to $\tilde{A}$, has mean zero and finite variance and satisfies

$$\tilde{m}_s = \alpha + \sum_{i=1}^{q-1} \alpha_i G_{is} + \beta \tilde{A}_s + \tau_s, \qquad s \in S \tag{28.17}$$

where

$$G_{is} = \begin{cases} 1 & \text{if } (y_s, b_s) \in G_i \\ 0 & \text{otherwise.} \end{cases}$$

The proof is as follows: The existence of two partitions of $Y \times B$ that satisfy equation 28.16 is an immediate consequence of SA 16 and the supposition that there are at least two partitions of $Y \times B$. Hence the only claim in need of proof is equation 28.17. For that purpose consider a consumer with characteristic b and utility function $U^b(\cdot)\colon R_{++} \to R$. It follows from equation 28.3 and T 12.14–T 12.16 that there exist constants $D(b)$, $e(b)$, $c(b)$, and $\gamma(b)$ such that

$$\frac{dU^b(A)}{dA} = D(b)(e(b) + c(b)A)^{\gamma(b)}.$$

Consequently, if $(\bar{a}, A) \in D$, if $\bar{a}m = h(\bar{a}, A, b)$ and m denotes the consumer's choice of risky assets, then $0 < \bar{a}m < A$ and m is a solution to the equations

$$D(b)E(r_i - \bar{a}_i)(e(b) + c(b)A + c(b)m(r - \bar{a}))^{\gamma(b)} = 0, \qquad i = 1, \ldots, n.$$

But if that is so and if $u \in R^n_+$ is a solution to

$$E(r_i - \bar{a}_i)(1 + u(r - \bar{a}))^{\gamma(b)} = 0, \qquad i = 1, \ldots, n$$

then $u = m/((e(b)/c(b)) + A)$ and u depends on $\gamma(b)$ but not on A, $e(b)$, and $c(b)$. Let $\varphi(b) = (e(b)/c(b))\bar{a}u$ and $\psi(\gamma(b)) = \bar{a}u$. Then, for the given value of a, $\bar{a}$,

$$h(\bar{a}, A, b) = \varphi(b) + \psi(\gamma(b))A, \tag{28.18}$$

which, for an appropriately chosen D in SA 7, holds for all $A \in R_{++}$ such that $(\bar{a}, A) \in D$.[2] Next observe that SA 11 implies that $\psi(\gamma(b))$ is constant on each of the G. Note also that this and relations in equation 28.16 imply that ψ does not vary with b. Hence from equations 28.18 and 28.7 and SA 11 follows the validity of equation 28.17. The fact that τ and $\tilde{A}$ are orthogonal is a consequence of equations 28.7, 28.8, 28.10, and 28.18 and of SA 13 and SA 14.

It follows easily from the arguments we used in the proof of T 28.5 that if we add assertions i–iii to SA 1–SA 17, we can interpret β_G as the marginal propensity to invest in risky assets of a representative individual in G. From the same arguments it also follows that we cannot use the estimated value of β_G to infer how absolute risk aversion varies across groups. To wit: if SA 1–SA 17 and assertions i–iii are valid, the absolute risk-aversion function of a consumer with characteristics b, $R(\cdot, b)$, satisfies the relation

$$R(A, b) = \frac{c(b)\gamma(b)}{e(b) + c(b)A},$$

where A varies over the domain of definition of $R(\cdot, b)$. This risk-aversion function depends on A, $c(b)$, and $e(b)$ as well as on the value of $\gamma(b)$.

To measure the relative degree of risk aversion in different groups, we must search for parameters other than those that appeared in our regression analysis. Our search is based on the following idea:

Consider two disjoint groups of consumers in the sample population, G_1 and G_2, and suppose that there is a way to eliminate the effect of A from the observed values of $(\tilde{\mu}, \tilde{m})$ and let $(\tilde{\mu}^*, \tilde{m}^*)$ denote the value of $(\tilde{\mu}, \tilde{m})$ after this effect has been adjusted for. Then our commentary on assumptions i–iii above implies that, if the (proportional) absolute risk-aversion functions in G_1 are generally higher than the (proportional) absolute risk-aversion functions in G_2, we would expect the mean value of $(\tilde{\mu}^*/\tilde{m}^*)\tilde{m}^*$ to be (larger) smaller in G_1 than in G_2.

This idea suggests that we begin our search by figuring out a way to eliminate the effect of A from the observed values of $(\tilde{\mu}, \tilde{m})$. Thereafter we can look for a statistical method to determine whether the group means of $\tilde{m}^*$ and $(\tilde{\mu}^*/\tilde{m}^*)$ differ from one another.

Since we cannot observe A, it is difficult to adjust our observations on $(\tilde{\mu}, \tilde{m})$ for the influence of A. Instead we shall use equation 28.17 and

$$\tilde{\mu}_s = -\alpha - \sum_{i=1}^{q-1} \alpha_i G_{is} + (1-\beta)\tilde{A}_s - \tau_s$$

to adjust $(\tilde{\mu}_s, \tilde{m}_s)$ for the influence of $\tilde{A}$. To see how, let $\{G_1, \ldots, G_q\}$ be one of the partitions $\mathscr{G}_v$, $v = 1, \ldots, p$; and suppose that the conditions of T 28.5 hold. In addition, let

$$\tilde{\xi}_s = \tilde{m}_s - \beta(\tilde{A}_s - \tilde{A}^0), \qquad s \in S$$

and

$$\tilde{\psi}_s = \frac{\tilde{\mu}_s - (1-\beta)(\tilde{A}_s - \tilde{A}^0)}{\tilde{\xi}_s}, \qquad s \in S$$

where $\tilde{A}^0$ is some appropriately chosen value of $\tilde{A}$, e.g., the unweighted or weighted mean of the group means of $\tilde{A}$. Then

$$\tilde{\xi}_s + (\tilde{\xi}_s \cdot \tilde{\psi}_s) = A^0, \qquad s \in S \tag{28.19}$$

and

$$\begin{aligned}\tilde{\xi}_s &= \varphi(b_s) + \beta\tilde{A}^0 + \varepsilon_s \\ &= h(\overline{a}, \tilde{A}^0, b_s) + \varepsilon_s, \qquad s \in S.\end{aligned} \tag{28.20}$$

From equations 28.19 and 28.20 it follows that, except for errors of observation, $\tilde{\xi}_s$ represents consumer s's demand for risky assets at $A = \tilde{A}^0$. It also follows that, except for errors of observations, $\xi_s \cdot \psi_s$ represents consumer s's demand for safe assets at $A = \tilde{A}^0$.

Next, let $\varphi_i = \varphi(f_v(G_i))$, $i = 1, \ldots, q$, and observe that α and the α_i in equation 28.17 satisfy the relations,

$$\alpha = \varphi_q - E(\eta_v(b)|G_q)$$

and

$$\alpha + \alpha_i = \varphi_i - E(\eta_v(b)|G_i), \qquad i = 1, \ldots, q-1$$

where $f_v(\cdot)$ and $\eta_v(\cdot)$ are as described in equation 28.11. Consequently,

$$\tilde{\xi}_s = \varphi_i + \beta\tilde{A}^0 - \eta_v(b_s) + \varepsilon_s, \qquad s \in F^{-1}(\Omega_{G_i}), i = 1, \ldots, q$$

and

$$E(\tilde{\xi}|G_i) = E(h(\overline{a}, \tilde{A}^0, b)|G_i) + E(\varepsilon|G_i)$$

$$= \begin{cases} \alpha + \beta\tilde{A}^0 \text{ if } i = q \\ \alpha + \alpha_i + \beta\tilde{A}^0 \text{ otherwise} \end{cases} \tag{28.21}$$

since, by SA 13, $E(\varepsilon|G_i) = 0$, $i = 1, \ldots, q$. From equation 28.21 and T 12.18, it follows that we can determine the relative degree of absolute risk aversion in different groups of consumers by comparing the respective values of α and $\alpha + \alpha_i$, $i = 1, \ldots, q - 1$. Specifically, the consumers in G_i have on the average a higher degree of absolute risk aversion than the consumers in G_j if and only if $\alpha_i < \alpha_j$.

Since, except for errors of observation, $\tilde{\xi}_s$ and $\tilde{\xi}_s\tilde{\psi}_s$ represent, respectively, consumer s's demand for risky and nonrisky assets at $\tilde{A}^0$, we can appeal to the analogue of T 12.8 in Arrow's extended axiom system and use $\tilde{\psi}_s$ as a means to measure the relative degree of proportional risk aversion in different groups. This we do in the following way. Suppose that

$$E(\tilde{\xi}^{-1}|G_i) < \infty, \qquad i = 1, \ldots, q.$$

Then there exist constants ψ_i, $i = 1, \ldots, q$, and a random variable ζ on $(S, \mathscr{F}_S)$ such that

$$\tilde{\psi}_s = \psi_i + \zeta_s, s \in F^{-1}(\Omega_{G_i}), \qquad i = 1, \ldots, q$$

and

$$E(\zeta|G_i) = 0, \qquad i = 1, \ldots, q.$$

These relations and equations 28.19 and 28.20 justify our insisting that, on the average, consumers in G_i have a higher degree of proportional risk aversion than consumers in G_j if and only if $\psi_j < \psi_i$.

We do not know the value of β. Hence we have no way of obtaining accurate observations on $\tilde{\xi}$ and $\tilde{\psi}$. However, we can regress $\tilde{m}$ on $\tilde{A}$ in accordance with equation 28.17, compute the least-squares estimate of β, and use the estimate of β to form reasonable estimates of $\tilde{\xi}$ and $\tilde{\psi}$. This is evidenced in T 28.6, which is stated without proof.

T 28.6 Suppose that the conditions of T 28.5 are satisfied, and let $\{G_1, \ldots, G_q\}$ be any one of the partitions $\mathscr{G}$ of $Y \times B$. Suppose also that we have $N(G_i)$ observations from $F^{-1}(\Omega_{G_i})$, $i = 1, \ldots, q$. Finally, suppose that as the number N of our observations goes to ∞,

$\lim N(G_i)/N = P(G_i), \qquad i = 1, \ldots, q.$

Then if $\hat{\alpha}_N$, $\hat{\alpha}_{iN}$ and $\hat{\beta}_N$, respectively, denote the least-squares estimates of α, α_i and β,

$$\lim_{\infty \to \infty} \hat{\alpha}_N = \alpha \quad \text{a.e.,}$$

$$\lim_{N \to \infty} \hat{\alpha}_{iN} = \alpha_i \quad \text{a.e.,} \qquad i = 1, \ldots, q-1$$

and

$$\lim_{N \to \infty} \hat{\beta}_N = \beta \quad \text{a.e.}$$

Moreover, with ξ and ψ defined by

$$\xi_s = \tilde{m}_s - \hat{\beta}_N(\tilde{A}_s - \tilde{A}^0), \qquad s \in S$$

and

$$\psi_s = (\tilde{\mu}_s - (1 - \hat{\beta}_N)(\tilde{A}_s - \tilde{A}^0))/\xi_s, \qquad s \in S$$

it is the case that

$$\tilde{\xi}_s - \xi_s = (\hat{\beta}_N - \beta)(\tilde{A}_s - \tilde{A}^0), \qquad s \in S$$

$$\tilde{\psi}_s - \psi_s = \tilde{A}^0(\xi_s - \tilde{\xi}_s)/\xi_s \cdot \tilde{\xi}_s, \qquad s \in S$$

and

$$E(\tilde{\xi}_s - \xi_s | G_i) = 0, \qquad i = 1, \ldots, q.$$

We shall use observations on the values of ξ and ψ to determine the relative degrees of risk aversion in groups that belong to some given partition of S. Let $\{G_1, \ldots, G_q\}$ be one of the partitions $\mathcal{G}_v$, $v = 1, \ldots, p$; let N_i denote the number of observations in $F^{-1}(\Omega_{G_i})$, $i = 1, \ldots, q$; and let $N = \sum_{i=1}^{q} N_i$. Moreover, denote the lth observation on ξ and ψ in $F^{-1}(\Omega_{G_i})$ by ξ_{il} and ψ_{il}, respectively, and let

$$\bar{\xi}_i = N_i^{-1} \sum_{l=1}^{N_i} \xi_{il} \qquad \text{and} \qquad \bar{\psi}_i = N_i^{-1} \sum_{l=1}^{N_i} \psi_{il}, \qquad i = 1, \ldots, q.$$

Finally, let

$$\bar{\xi} = N^{-1} \sum_{i=1}^{q} \sum_{l=1}^{N_i} \xi_{il} \qquad \text{and} \qquad \bar{\psi} = N^{-1} \sum_{i=1}^{q} \sum_{l=1}^{N_i} \psi_{il}.$$

Then

$$\bar{\xi} = \hat{\alpha} + \sum_{i=1}^{q-1} (N_i/N)\hat{\alpha}_i + \hat{\beta}\tilde{A}^0,$$

$$\sum_{i=1}^{q} \sum_{l=1}^{N_i} (\xi_{il} - \bar{\xi})^2 = \sum_{i=1}^{q} \sum_{l=1}^{N_i} (\xi_{il} - \bar{\xi}_i)^2 + \sum_{i=1}^{q} N_i(\bar{\xi}_i - \bar{\xi})^2, \tag{28.23}$$

and

$$\sum_{i=1}^{q}\sum_{\hat{l}=1}^{N_i}(\psi_{i\hat{l}}-\bar{\psi})^2=\sum_{i=1}^{q}\sum_{l=1}^{N_i}(\psi_{il}-\bar{\psi}_i)^2+\sum_{i=1}^{q}N_i(\bar{\psi}_i-\bar{\psi})^2. \qquad (28.24)$$

The first right-hand term in equations 28.23 and 28.24, respectively, measures the *within-groups variation* in ξ and ψ. The second right-hand term in equations 28.23 and 28.24 measures, respectively, the *between-groups variation* in ξ and ψ. We can check whether the group means of $\xi(\psi)$ are all equal by comparing the relative size of the between-group and within-groups variation in $\xi(\psi)$.

The test we have in mind for ξ can be formally described as follows: First we suppose that there exist constants μ and a_i and independently distributed random variables ε_{il}, $l = 1, \ldots, N_i$, and $i = 1, \ldots, q$, such that

$$\xi_{i\hat{l}} = \mu + a_i + \varepsilon_{i\hat{l}}, \qquad l = 1, \ldots, N_i \quad \text{and} \quad i = 1, \ldots, q \qquad (28.25)$$

$$\sum_{i=1}^{q}(N_i/N)a_i = 0, \qquad (28.26)$$

and

$$E(\varepsilon_{i\hat{l}}) = 0 \quad \text{and} \quad E(\varepsilon_{i\hat{l}}^2) = \sigma^2, \quad l = 1, \ldots, N_i, \quad \text{and} \quad i = 1, \ldots, q. \qquad (28.27)$$

Then we observe that

$$\sum_{i=1}^{q}\sum_{\hat{l}=1}^{N_i}(\xi_{il}-\mu-a_i)^2$$
$$=\sum_{i=1}^{q}\sum_{\hat{l}=1}^{n_i}(\xi_{il}-\bar{\xi}_i)^2+N(\bar{\xi}-\mu)^2+\sum_{i=1}^{q}N_i((\bar{\xi}_i-\bar{\xi})-a_i)^2 \qquad (28.28)$$

and deduce that the least-squares estimates of μ and the a_i are given by

$$\hat{\mu} = \bar{\xi} \qquad \text{and} \qquad \hat{a}_i = (\bar{\xi}_i - \bar{\xi}), \qquad i = 1, \ldots, q. \qquad (28.29)$$

Finally, we let $\mathscr{S}_\Omega$ and $\mathscr{S}_{\Omega_a}$ denote, respectively, the minimum value of the left-hand side of equation 28.28, with no assumptions on the values of μ and the a_i and under the presumption that all the a_i equal zero. Then

$$\mathscr{S}_\Omega = \sum_{i=1}^{q}\sum_{\hat{l}=1}^{N_i}(\xi_{il}-\bar{\xi}_i)^2$$

and

$$\mathscr{S}_{\Omega_a} - \mathscr{S}_\Omega = \sum_{i=1}^{q}N_i(\bar{\xi}_i-\bar{\xi})^2.$$

Under the null hypothesis that equations 28.25–28.27 are valid and all the a_i equal zero, the statistic

$$F_\xi = (N - q)(\mathscr{S}_{\Omega_a} - \mathscr{S}_\Omega)/(q - 1)\mathscr{S}_\Omega$$

is for large N approximately F-distributed with $(q - 1)$ and $(N - q)$ degrees of freedom. The null hypothesis is to be rejected for large values of the test statistic.

Similar arguments apply to our observations on ψ. In particular, under the null hypothesis that (1) the variance of ψ does not vary across groups and (2) the group means of ψ are all equal, the statistic

$$F_\psi = \frac{N-q}{q-1}\left(\sum_{i=1}^{q} N_i(\bar{\psi}_i - \bar{\psi})^2 \Big/ \sum_{i=1}^{q}\sum_{l=1}^{N_i} (\psi_{il} - \bar{\psi}_i)^2\right)$$

has, for large N, approximately the F distribution with $(q - 1)$ and $(N - q)$ degrees of freedom. Again the null hypothesis is to be rejected for large values of the test statistic.

The preceding tests provide us with a method by which we can determine the relative degrees of absolute and proportional risk aversion in groups that belong to some partition of S. To make sure that they do, we need only observe that the $\hat{\alpha}_N$ and $\hat{\alpha}_{iN}$ of T 28.6 and the $\hat{\mu}$ and $\hat{a}_i$ of equation 28.29 satisfy the relations

$$(\hat{\alpha}_N + \hat{\beta}_N\tilde{A}^0) + \hat{\alpha}_{iN} = \hat{\mu} + \hat{a}_i, \qquad i = 1, \ldots, q - 1$$

and

$$(\hat{\alpha}_N + \hat{\beta}_N\tilde{A}^0) = \hat{\mu} + \hat{a}_q.$$

Hence, when we test whether all the $\hat{a}_i$ are significantly different from zero, we are at the same time testing whether all the $\hat{\alpha}_{iN}$ are equal to zero.

28.3.2 One-Way Analysis of Variance of the Data

We used our data and our interpretation of SA 1–SA 17 to estimate $\bar{\xi}_i$, $\bar{\psi}_i$, F_ξ, and F_ψ for the partitions of S described in the preceding section. Tables 28.2 and 28.3 present our results for partitions of S according to age and profession, respectively.. Similar results for partitions of S based on tenure, education, and race are recorded in tables 28.4–28.6.

We cannot be sure that the variances of the respective ξ (and ψ) do not vary across groups. We also cannot be certain that N is large enough for the F_ξ (and the F_ψ) to be distributed approximately like an F-distributed

Table 28.2
S partition: Age, with $A^\circ = 232.22324562$.

Component	Number of cells, *N*	Cell mean	Sum of squares	D.F.	Mean squares
ANOVA analysis of ξ					
Age group					
<35	272	228.57			
35–44	339	226.08			
45–54	361	223.36			
55–64	288	219.88			
$\geqslant 65$	105	211.79			
Total	1365				
Grand mean		223.45			
Between groups			27466.0425	4	6866.5106
Within groups			399339.3003	1360	293.6318
Total			426805.3428	1364	
F					23.385

ANOVA analysis of ψ

Age group					
< 35	272	0.02			
35–44	339	0.03			
45–54	361	0.05			
55–64	288	0.07			
⩾65	105	0.12			
Total	1365				
Grand mean		0.05			
Between groups			1.0653	4	0.2663
Within groups			15.6660	1360	0.0115
Total			16.7313	1364	
F					23.119

Table 28.3
S partition: Employment, with $A^\circ = 264.96776199$.

Component	Numbers of cells, N	Cell mean	Sum of squares	D.F.	Mean squares
ANOVA analysis of ξ					
Employment group					
Self-employed	359	249.01			
Employed by others	1007	258.14			
Total	1366				
Grand mean		255.74			
Between groups			22059.2618	1	22059.2618
Within groups			416785.5410	1364	305.5612
Total			438844.8028	1365	
F					72.193
ANOVA analysis of ψ					
Employment group					
Self-employed	359	0.08			
Employed by others	1007	0.03			
Total	1366				
Grand mean		0.04			
Between groups			0.6253	1	0.6253
Within groups			11.2460	1364	0.0082
Total			11.8613	1365	
F					75.840

Table 28.4
S partition: Tenure, with $A^{\circ} = 266.98374939$.

Components	Number of cells, N	Cell mean	Sum of squares	D.F.	Mean squares
ANOVA analysis of ξ					
Tenure group					
Homeowners	1010	256.91			
Renters	356	260.03			
Total	1366				
Grand mean		257.72			
Between groups			2558.4119	1	2558.4119
Within groups			440285.6660	1364	322.7901
Total			442844.0779	1365	
F					7.926
ANOVA analysis of ψ					
Tenure group					
Homeowners	1010	0.04			
Renters	356	0.03			
Total	1366				
Grand mean		0.04			
Between groups			0.0688	1	0.0688
Within groups			11.3029	1364	0.0083
Total			11.3717	1365	
F					8.306

Table 28.5
S partition: Education, with $A^\circ = 255.44019890$.

Component	Number of cells, N	Cell mean	Sum of squares	D.F.	Mean squares
ANOVA analysis of ξ					
Education group					
$\leqslant 8$ years	240	248.98			
9–12 years	542	248.47			
12 years	584	243.23			
Total	1366				
Grand mean		246.32			
Between groups			9787.9091	2	4893.9545
Within groups			429924.9215	1363	315.4255
Total			439712.8306	1365	
F					15.515
ANOVA analysis of ψ					
Education group					
$\leqslant 8$ years	240	0.02			
9–12 years	542	0.03			
> 12 years	584	0.06			
Total	1366				
Grand mean		0.04			
Between groups			0.3349	2	0.1674
Within groups			12.8078	1363	0.0094
Total			13.1427	1365	
F					17.819

Table 28.6
S partition: Race, with $A^\circ = 184.07860947$.

Component	Number of cells, N	Cell mean	Sum of squares	D.F.	Mean squares
ANOVA analysis of ξ					
Racial group					
White	1280	176.61			
Nonwhite	70	180.75			
Total	1350				
Grand mean		176.83			
Between groups			1153.2109	1	1153.2109
Within groups			310778.8727	1349	230.3772
Total			311932.0836	1350	
F					5.006
ANOVA analysis of ψ					
Racial group					
White	1280	0.05			
Nonwhite	70	0.02			
Total	1350				
Grand mean		0.05			
Between groups			0.0739	1	0.0739
Within groups			17.3186	1349	0.0128
Total			17.3925	1350	
F					5.756

variable. Still we may infer from the tables that in all partitions the between-groups variation is a significant source of variation in the dependent variable. The tables and the columns of cell means underneath them, therefore, suggest the following inductive generalizations:

IG 1 Absolute risk aversion increases with age and education. Moreover, the absolute risk aversion of the self-employed, homeowners, and white consumers tends to be higher than that of consumers who are, respectively, employed by others, renters, and nonwhite.

IG 2 Proportional risk aversion tends to increase with age and education. Moreover, proportional risk aversion tends to be higher among the self-employed, homeowners, and white consumers than among those who are, respectively, employed by others, renters, and nonwhite.

These inductive generalizations are interesting. So a few remarks concerning their validity are in order.

Psychologists believe that people become more conservative as they grow older. Hence our finding that absolute risk aversion increases with age seems reasonable. Our observation in IG 2 that consumers' proportional risk aversion increases with age is reasonable for the same reason. However, the strength of the statistical result is surprising. Since the income and expenditure streams of younger people are less predictable than the income and expenditure streams of older people, everything else being equal, the demand for liquid funds should decrease with age. If it does, our statistics indicate that this decrease in demand has been swamped by the import of changes in the proportional risk aversion of consumers in the sample.

It is difficult to understand why self-employed individuals (SEIs) should have a higher absolute risk aversion than those who are employed by others (EOIs). To explain why, Richard Manning has ventured the following hypothesis: In the business world only a few are very successful and many fail. Chances are that the predominant portion of those who survive, survive because they act conservatively. If that is true, a random sample of SEIs is likely to contain a large proportion of individuals whose investment behavior is characteristic of people with a relatively high absolute risk aversion.

Richard Manning's hypothesis is plausible. However, equally reasonable scenarious suggest that our findings concerning the relative absolute risk aversion of SEIs and EOIs are due to a statistical artifact: SEIs function in a riskier environment than EOIs do; e.g., the SEIs face more variable income streams and possess more highly levered portfolios than EOIs do. If that is true, our fundamental assumption concerning the similarity of subjective probability distributions is false, and our observations that SEIs have a higher absolute risk aversion than EOIs do cannot be maintained.

A second statistical artifact might be the reason why homeowners seem to have a higher absolute risk aversion than renters. Even though cars and homes are not financial assets, a consumer's choice of financial assets might depend on the cars and houses he owns. For example, the extent to which a consumer has mortgaged his house and used loans to finance his car purchase will be an important determining factor of his optimal mix of safe and risky assets.[3] The same mix will also vary with the degree of uncertainty he faces with respect to future repairs and renovations of his house.

Finally, it seems unreasonable that absolute risk aversion increases with years of education. So we hypothesize that our findings concerning education and absolute risk aversion are due to a statistical artifact: Income expectations increase with education. If that is true, we should have added an estimate of human capital when we calculated the value of $\tilde{A}_s$ for the consumers in our sample.

The upshot of the preceding remarks is that we cannot accept IG 1 and IG 2 without further tests. Two such tests are described in sections 28.3.4 and 28.3.5.

28.3.3 Two-Way Analysis of Variance: Theory

In this section we shall prepare the ground for a five-way analysis of variance of our data by discussing the ideas behind a two-way analysis of variance of ξ. The same ideas carry over to Ψ as well.

Consider two partitions of $Y \times B$, $\{G_1^*, \dots, G_q^*\}$ and $\{D_1^*, \dots, D_k^*\}$, and write $\tilde{m}_s$ as

$$\tilde{m}_s = \alpha + \sum_{i=1}^{q-1} \sum_{j=1}^{k} \alpha_{ij} G_{ijs} + \sum_{j=1}^{k-1} \alpha_{qj} G_{qjs} + \beta \tilde{A}_s + \gamma_s, \qquad s \in S \tag{28.30}$$

where, for $i = 1, \dots, q-1$, $j = 1, \dots, k$, and for $i = q$ and $j = 1, \dots, k-1$,

$$G_{ijs} = \begin{cases} 1 & \text{if } s \in F^{-1}(\Omega_{G_i^*} \cap \Omega_{D_j^*}) \\ 0 & \text{otherwise.} \end{cases}$$

Then obtain the least-squares estimates of the parameters in equation 28.30—$\hat{\alpha}$; $\hat{\alpha}_{ij}$, $i = 1, \dots, q-1$, $j = 1, \dots, k$; $\hat{\alpha}_{qj}$, $j = 1, \dots, k-1$; and $\hat{\beta}$—and use the estimated value of $\hat{\beta}$ to construct ξ in accordance with 28.22.

Next let

$$G_i = F^{-1}(\Omega_{G_i^*}), \quad i = 1, \ldots, q; \qquad \text{and} \qquad D_j = F^{-1}(\Omega_{D_j^*}), \quad j = 1, \ldots, k.$$

Then $G_1, \ldots, G_q$ and $D_1, \ldots, D_k$ are partitions of S. Suppose that we have N_{ij} observations in $G_i \cap D_j$, $i = 1, \ldots, q$, $j = 1, \ldots, k$, and let

$$N_{i*} = \sum_{j=1}^{k} N_{ij}, \qquad N_{*j} = \sum_{i=1}^{q} N_{ij}, \qquad \text{and} \qquad N = \sum_{i=1}^{q} N_{i*}.$$

Suppose also that

$$N_{ij} = (N_{i*} \cdot N_{*j})/N, \qquad i = 1, \ldots, q, \quad j = 1, \ldots, k \tag{28.31}$$

and let $\xi_l(i,j)$ denote the lth observation of ξ in $G_i \cap D_j$, $i = 1, \ldots, q$, $j = 1, \ldots, k$ Finally, let

$$\bar{\xi}_{ij} = N_{ij}^{-1} \cdot \sum_{l=1}^{N_{ij}} \xi_l(i,j),$$

$$\bar{\xi}_{i*} = N_{i*}^{-1} \sum_{j=1}^{k} \sum_{l=1}^{N_{ij}} \xi_l(i,j),$$

$$\bar{\xi}_{*j} = N_{*j}^{-1} \sum_{i=1}^{q} \sum_{l=1}^{N_{ij}} \xi_l(i,j),$$

and

$$\bar{\xi}_{**} = N^{-1} \sum_{i=1}^{q} \sum_{j=1}^{k} \sum_{l=1}^{N_{ij}} \xi_l(i,j).$$

Then it can be shown that

$$\begin{aligned}
&\sum_{i=1}^{q} \sum_{j=1}^{k} \sum_{l=1}^{N_{ij}} [\xi_l(i,j) - \bar{\xi}_{**}]^2 \\
&\quad = \sum_{i=1}^{q} \sum_{j=1}^{k} \sum_{l=1}^{N_{ij}} [\xi_l(i,j) - \bar{\xi}_{ij}]^2 \\
&\qquad + \sum_{i=1}^{q} N_{i*}(\bar{\xi}_{i*} - \bar{\xi}_{**})^2 \\
&\qquad + \sum_{j=1}^{k} N_{*j}(\bar{\xi}_{*j} - \bar{\xi}_{**})^2 \\
&\qquad + \sum_{i=1}^{q} \sum_{j=1}^{k} N_{ij}\{\bar{\xi}_{ij} - [(\bar{\xi}_{i*} - \xi_{**}) + (\bar{\xi}_{*j} - \bar{\xi}_{**}) + \bar{\xi}_{**}]\}^2.
\end{aligned} \tag{28.32}$$

In the last equation, the first term on the right-hand side records that part of the variation in $\xi_l(i,j)$'s that is due to variation in $\xi_l(i,j)$ within groups.

The next two terms represent, respectively, that part of the variation in $\xi_l(i,j)$ that is due to variation in the group means of the two partitions. Finally, whenever

$$(\bar{\xi}_{i*} - \bar{\xi}_{**}) + (\bar{\xi}_{*j} - \bar{\xi}_{**}) \neq \bar{\xi}_{ij} - \xi_{**}$$

for some pair i, j, the last term on the right-hand side differs from zero and measures that part of the variation in $\xi_l(i,j)$ that is due to interaction between the two factors which determine the partitions of S we are considering.

In standard statistical terminology, the first term on the right-hand side of equation 28.32 is referred to as the *residual* or *within-class effect*; the next two terms are called the *main effect*, or the *between-class variation*; and the last term is called the *two-way interaction effect*. When we consider more than two partitions of S, there will be one residual term as above, more main effects, several two-way interaction effects, one or more *three-way interaction effects*, etc.

The significance of the various effects is measured by an F statistic. For instance, the significance of the between-class variation over the G_i is measured by

$$F_i = \frac{N - qk}{q - 1}\left(\frac{\sum_{i=1}^{q} N_{i*}(\bar{\xi}_{i*} - \bar{\xi}_{**})^2}{\sum_{i=1}^{q}\sum_{j=1}^{k}\sum_{l=1}^{N_{ij}} [\xi_l(i,j) - \bar{\xi}_{ij}]^2}\right),$$

and the significance of the two-way interaction effect is measured by

$$F_{ij} \equiv \frac{N - qk}{(q - 1)(k - 1)}\left(\frac{\sum_{i=1}^{q}\sum_{j=1}^{k} N_{ij}\{\bar{\xi}_{ij} - [(\bar{\xi}_i - \bar{\xi}_{**}) + (\bar{\xi}_{*j} - \bar{\xi}_{**}) + \bar{\xi}_{**}]\}}{\sum_{i=1}^{q}\sum_{j=1}^{k}\sum_{l=1}^{N_{ij}} (\xi_l(i,j) - \bar{\xi}_{ij})^2}\right).$$

Under the hypothesis that the respective effects are nonexistent, these statistics are approximately F-distributed with $(q - 1, N - qk)$ and $((q - 1)(k - 1), (N - qk))$ degrees of freedom.

Since the preceding tests are not easy to understand, we shall be a bit more specific. As we did in the one-way analysis-of-variance case, we begin by supposing that there are constants, μ, a_i, b_j, and γ_{ij} and independently distributed random variables $\varepsilon_l(i,j)$ such that, for $l = 1, \ldots, N_{ij}$,

$$\xi_l(i,j) = \mu + a_i + b_j + \gamma_{ij} + \varepsilon_l(i,j), \quad i = 1, \ldots, q, \quad j = 1, \ldots, k \tag{28.33}$$

$$\sum_{i=1}^{q} N_{i*}a_i = \sum_{j=1}^{k} N_{*j}b_j = 0, \tag{28.34}$$

$$\sum_{i=1}^{q} N_{i*}\gamma_{ij} = 0, \quad j = 1, \ldots, k, \qquad \text{and} \qquad \sum_{j=1}^{k} N_{*j}\gamma_{ij} = 0, \quad i = 1, \ldots, k \tag{28.35}$$

and

$$E\varepsilon_l(i,j) = 0 \quad \text{and} \quad E\varepsilon_l(i,j)^2 = \sigma^2, \quad i = 1, \ldots, q, \quad j = 1, \ldots, k. \tag{28.36}$$

Then we observe that

$$\begin{aligned}
&\sum_{i=1}^{q}\sum_{j=1}^{k}\sum_{l=1}^{N_{ij}} (\xi_l(i,j) - \mu - a_i - b_j - \gamma_{ij})^2 \\
&\quad = \sum_{i=1}^{q}\sum_{j=1}^{k}\sum_{l=1}^{N_{ij}} (\xi_l(i,j) - \overline{\xi}_{ij})^2 + N(\overline{\xi}_{**} - \mu)^2 \\
&\qquad + \sum_{i=1}^{q} N_{i*}((\overline{\xi}_{i*} - \overline{\xi}_{**}) - a_i)^2 + \sum_{j=1}^{k} N_{*j}((\overline{\xi}_{*j} - \overline{\xi}_{**}) - b_j)2 \\
&\qquad + \sum_{i=1}^{q}\sum_{j=1}^{k} N_{ij}((\overline{\xi}_{ij} - \overline{\xi}_{i*} - \overline{\xi}_{*j} + \xi_{**}) - \gamma_{ij})^2
\end{aligned} \tag{28.37}$$

and deduce that the least-squares estimates of the constants in equations 28.33–28.35 are given by

$$\hat{\mu} = \xi_{**}; \qquad \hat{a}_i = (\overline{\xi}_{i*} - \overline{\xi}_{**}), \qquad i = 1, \ldots, q$$

$$\hat{b}_j = (\overline{\xi}_{*j} - \xi_{**}), \qquad j = 1, \ldots, k$$

and

$$\hat{\gamma}_{ij} = (\overline{\xi}_{ij} - \overline{\xi}_{i*} - \xi_{*j} + \xi_{**}), \qquad i = 1, \ldots, q, \qquad j = 1, \ldots, k. \tag{28.38}$$

Next we let $\mathscr{S}_\Omega$, $\mathscr{S}_{\Omega_a}$, and $\mathscr{S}_{\Omega_\gamma}$, respectively, denote the minimum value of the left-hand side in equation 28.37 under no additional restrictions on the constants in equations 28.33–28.35, when the a_i are taken to be zero and when the γ_{ij} are presumed to be zero. Then it is easy to see that

$$\mathscr{S}_\Omega = \sum_{i=1}^{q}\sum_{j=1}^{k}\sum_{l=1}^{N_{ij}} (\xi_l(i,j) - \overline{\xi}_{ij})^2,$$

$$\mathscr{S}_{\Omega_a} - \mathscr{S}_\Omega = \sum_{i=1}^{q} N_{i*}(\overline{\xi}_{i*} - \xi_{**})^2,$$

and

$$\mathscr{S}_{\Omega_\gamma} - \mathscr{S}_\Omega = \sum_{i=1}^{q}\sum_{j=1}^{k} N_{ij}(\overline{\xi}_{ij} - \overline{\xi}_{i*} - \overline{\xi}_{*j} + \xi_{**})^2.$$

Under the null hypothesis that equations 28.33–28.36 are valid and all

a_i equal zero, $(N - qk)(\mathscr{S}_{\Omega_a} - \mathscr{S}_{\Omega})/(q - 1)\mathscr{S}_{\Omega}$ equals F_i and has for large N approximately the F distribution with $(q - 1)$ and $(N - qk)$ degrees of freedom. The null hypothesis is to be rejected for large values of the statistics. Similarly, under the null hypothesis that equations 28.33–28.36 are valid and all the γ_{ij} are zero, the statistic $(N - qk)(\mathscr{S}_{\Omega_\gamma} - \mathscr{S}_{\Omega})/(q - 1)(k - 1)\mathscr{S}_{\Omega}$ equals F_{ij} and is for large N approximately F-distributed with $(q - 1)(k - 1)$ and $(N - qk)$ degrees of freedom. Again the null hypothesis is to be rejected for large values of the statistic.

The preceding tests provide us with a way to measure the relative risk aversion of consumers who belong to different groups in a given partition of S. To see that they do, we need only delineate the relationship between the least-squares estimates of the coefficients in equation 28.30 and the values of $\hat{\mu}$, $\hat{a}_i$, $\hat{b}_j$, and $\hat{\gamma}_{ij}$ in equation 28.38. We do that in equations 28.39–28.44:

$$\hat{a}_i + \hat{\mu} = \sum_{j=1}^{k} (N_{*j}/N)\hat{\alpha}_{ij} + (\hat{\alpha} + \hat{\beta}\tilde{A}^0), \qquad i = 1, \ldots, q - 1 \tag{28.39}$$

$$\hat{a}_q + \hat{\mu} = \sum_{j=1}^{k-1} (N_{*j}/N)\hat{\alpha}_{qj} + (\hat{\alpha} + \hat{\beta}\tilde{A}^0), \tag{28.40}$$

$$\hat{b}_j + \hat{\mu} = \sum_{i=1}^{q} (N_{i*}/N)\hat{\alpha}_{ij} + (\hat{\alpha} + \hat{\beta}\tilde{A}^0), \qquad j = 1, \ldots k - 1 \tag{28.41}$$

$$\hat{b}_k + \hat{\mu} = \sum_{i=1}^{q-1} (N_{i*}/N)\alpha_{ik} + (\hat{\alpha} + \hat{\beta}\tilde{A}^0), \tag{28.42}$$

and

$$\hat{\gamma}_{ij} = (\hat{\alpha} + \hat{\beta}\tilde{A}^0) + \hat{\alpha}_{ij} - \hat{a}_i - \hat{b}_j - \hat{\mu}, \quad i = 1, \ldots, q, j = 1, \ldots, k \quad (i, j \neq (q, k) \tag{28.43}$$

$$\hat{\gamma}_{qk} = (\hat{\alpha} + \hat{\beta}\tilde{A}^0) - \hat{a}_q - \hat{b}_q - \hat{\mu}. \tag{28.44}$$

These equations explicate the import of the two-way analysis-of-variance tests described above.

28.3.4 Multiple-Classification Analysis of the Data

In our statistical analysis we consider five factors—age, education, tenure, profession, and race. For us the analogue of equation 28.31 is not satisfied. Hence the details of the decomposition of the variance of $\xi_l(i, j)$ and (with the obvious notation) $\psi_l(i, j)$ differ from the natural extension of equation 28.32 for five factors. The ideas of it, however, carry over to our case.

Therefore I will be content to present our results next and refer the reader to a text on the analysis of variance for further details concerning both the theory and the computational aspects of the analysis (see, for instance, Scheffé 1959, pp. 90–145).

Our results are presented in tables 28.7 and 28.8. Table 28.7 supports the conclusions of IG 1 with respect to age, profession, and education; i.e., absolute risk aversion increases with age and education, and individuals who are self-employed have a higher absolute risk aversion than those who are employed by others. However, differences in the characteristics of tenure and race provide little if any information as to the relative degree of consumer's absolute risk aversion.

Table 28.8 confirms the conclusion of IG 2 that proportional risk aversion tends to increase with age and education. The table also upholds the conclusion of IG 2 with respect to profession; i.e., the proportional risk aversion tends to be higher among the self-employed consumers than among those who are employed by others. Finally, table 28.8 suggests that the conclusion of IG 2 that homeowners and white consumers have a higher proportional risk aversion than renters and nonwhite consumers cannot be maintained.

28.3.5 Education and Income

Our data do not allow us to test whether the expected income streams of SEIs in 1963 were more variable than the expected income streams of EOIs. However, we can test whether our result concerning education and absolute and proportional risk aversion is a statistical artifact. This we do by introducing four new covariates in our statistical analysis. They are defined as follows:

$I_s^1 = 1$ or 0 according as $s \in F^{-1}(I_2 \cup I_3)$ or not;

$I_s^2 = 1$ or 0 according as $s \in F^{-1}(I_4 \cup I_5)$ or not;

$I_s^3 = 1$ or 0 according as $s \in F^{-1}(I_6 \cup I_7)$ or not;

$I_s^4 = 1$ or 0 according as $s \in F^{-1}(I_8 \cup I_9)$ or not.

When we include these covariates in our analysis, we first use all our data to regress ξ and ψ on I_s^i, $i = 1, \ldots, 4$. Then we perform an analysis of variance of the resulting error terms. Thus we adjust our observations on $\tilde{m}$ and $\tilde{\mu}/\tilde{A}$ for the effect of both income and net worth and perform the analysis of variance with respect to age, profession, tenure, education, and race of the adjusted observations.

Table 28.7
Five-way analysis of variance of ξ with age, employment, tenure, education, and race.

Source of variation	Sum of squares	D.F.	Mean square	F	Significance of F
Main effects	48160.963	9	5351.218	18.587	0.000
Age	20888.989	4	5222.247	18.139	0.000
Employment	8641.104	1	8641.104	30.014	0.000
Tenure	39.917	1	39.917	0.139	0.710
Education	7469.153	2	3734.576	12.972	0.000
Race	530.241	1	530.241	1.842	0.175
2-way interactions	12886.385	29	444.358	1.543	0.033
Explained	61047.348	38	1606.509	5.580	0.000
Residual	382040.399	1327	287.898		
Total	443087.747	1365	324.606		

Group Means

Age	N	$\bar{\xi}$	Employment	N	$\bar{\xi}$	Education	N	$\bar{\xi}$
<35 years	272	245.84	Self-employed	359	234.22	$\leqslant 8$ years	240	243.35
35–44 years	339	243.45	Employed by others	1007	243.12	9–12 years	542	242.85
45–54 years	362	240.49				>12 years	584	237.81
55–64 years	288	237.39	Tenure	N	$\bar{\xi}$			
$\geqslant 65$ years	105	229.35	Homeowners	1010	239.97	Race	N	$\bar{\xi}$
			Renters	356	243.08	White	1295	240.70
						Nonwhite	71	245.73

Table 28.8
Five-way analysis of variance of ψ with age, employment, tenure, education, and race.

Source of variation	Sum of squares	D.F.	Mean square	F	Significance of F
Main effects	1.597	9	0.177	20.086	0.000
Age	0.662	4	0.165	18.727	0.000
Employment	0.292	1	0.292	33.004	0.000
Tenure	0.001	1	0.001	0.160	0.689
Education	0.277	2	0.138	15.658	0.000
Race	0.015	1	0.015	1.722	0.190
2-way interactions	0.472	29	0.016	1.841	0.004
Explained	2.068	38	0.054	6.162	0.000
Residual	11.722	1327	0.009		
Total	13.791	1365	0.010		

Group Means

Age	N	$\bar{\psi}$	Employment	N	$\bar{\psi}$	Education	N	$\bar{\psi}$
<35 years	272	0.01	Self-employed	359	0.08	$\leqslant 8$ years	240	0.02
35–44 years	339	0.03	Employed by others	1007	0.03	9–12 years	542	0.03
45–54 years	362	0.04				>12 years	584	0.06
55–64 years	288	0.06	Tenure	N	$\bar{\psi}$			
$\geqslant 65$ years	105	0.10	Homeowners	1010	0.04	Race	N	$\bar{\psi}$
			Renters	356	0.03	white	1295	0.04
						nonwhite	71	0.01

Our results are presented in tables 28.9 and 28.10. Table 28.9 differs from table 28.7 in two ways: The explanatory power of education has come to naught and the two-way interactions have become statistically insignificant. Otherwise tables 28.9 and 28.7 tell the same story. We conclude that the education effect in table 28.7 was an (expected) income effect.

Table 28.10 confirms the finding of table 28.8 that profession and age are important factors in determining consumer demand for liquid funds. It also shows that the explanatory power of education is insignificant. Hence, whatever effect we might have attributed to education on the basis of table 28.8 was in fact an (expected) income effect.

Here it is worth remarking that we have also performed a one-way covariance analysis with covariates $I_1, \ldots, I_4$ as defined above and the S partitions age, employment, tenure, education, and race. According to the printouts, for ξ and ψ alike, we have the following:

1. The variations due to I_1 and I_2 are not significant, while the variations due to I_3 and I_4 are both highly significant; and
2. the main effects due to age and to employment are both highly significant, while the main effects due to tenure, to education, and to race are all not significant.

These results suggest that the inductive generalizations concerning tenure and race recorded in IG 1 and IG 2 might be based on the same statistical artifact as our ideas about education. This is not unreasonable since chances are good that income expectations are, on the average, higher among homeowners (white consumers) than among renters (nonwhite consumers).

28.4 Concluding Remarks

This concludes our empirical analysis of consumer choice among risky and nonrisky assets. In looking back at the results, we should make several mental notes.

First, Arrow consumers and the separation property: The assumption that our sample consumers are Arrow consumers whose utility functions possess the separation property must be viewed as a shorthand specification of the contents of the top three boxes in figure 26.1. Thus the theory whose empirical relevance we are testing in this chapter is T(A 1, ..., A 4, A 5″, A 6″, A 7, A 8) (section 12.1.1), where A 8 insists that the utility functions in A 6 and A 7 possess the separation property and where A 5″ and A 6″ are A 5* and A 6* (section 12.4) with n risky assets instead of two. The

Table 28.9
Analysis of variance of ξ by age, employment, tenure, education, and race with income variates.

Source of variation	Sum of squares	D.F.	Mean square	F	Significance of F
Covariates	52926.263	4	13231.566	48.236	0.000
I^1	3.352	1	3.352	0.012	0.912
I^2	219.874	1	219.874	0.802	0.371
I^3	12485.672	1	12485.672	45.517	0.000
I^4	11855.422	1	11855.422	43.219	0.000
Main effects	16600.024	9	1844.447	6.724	0.000
Age	13311.409	4	3327.852	12.132	0.000
Employment	1885.285	1	1885.285	6.873	0.009
Tenure	158.663	1	158.663	0.578	0.447
Education	322.258	2	161.129	0.587	0.556
Race	168.492	1	168.492	0.614	0.433
2-way interactions	10652.466	29	367.326	1.339	0.108
Age + Employment	2436.889	4	609.222	2.221	0.065
Age + Tenure	77.088	4	19.272	0.070	0.991
Age + Education	5426.819	8	678.352	2.473	0.012
Age + Race	274.662	4	68.666	0.250	0.910
Employment + Tenure	22.707	1	22.707	0.083	0.774
Employment + Education	1962.862	2	981.431	3.578	0.028
Employment + Race	45.718	1	45.718	0.167	0.683
Tenure + Education	428.678	2	214.339	0.781	0.458
Tenure + Race	8.581	1	8.581	0.031	0.860
Education + Race	58.073	2	29.037	0.106	0.900
Explained	80178.753	42	1909.018	6.959	0.000
Residual	362908.994	1323	274.308		
Total	443087.747	1365	324.606		

Table 28.10
Analysis of variance of ψ by age, employment, tenure, education, and race with income variates.

Source of variation	Sum of squares	D.F.	Mean square	F	Significance of F
Covariates	2.025	4	0.506	61.307	0.000
I^1	0.000	1	0.000	0.013	0.910
I^2	0.005	1	0.005	0.630	0.428
I^3	0.366	1	0.366	44.320	0.000
I^4	0.649	1	0.649	78.627	0.000
Main effects	0.476	9	0.053	6.402	0.000
Age	0.380	4	0.095	11.514	0.000
Employment	0.056	1	0.056	6.831	0.009
Tenure	0.006	1	0.006	0.676	0.411
Education	0.010	2	0.005	0.614	0.541
Race	0.004	1	0.004	0.479	0.489
2-way interactions	0.364	29	0.013	1.521	0.038
Age + Employment	0.072	4	0.018	2.182	0.069
Age + Tenure	0.010	4	0.002	0.299	0.879
Age + Education	0.208	8	0.026	3.148	0.002
Age + Race	0.007	4	0.002	0.201	0.938
Employment + Tenure	0.000	1	0.000	0.000	0.987
Employment + Education	0.058	2	0.029	3.538	0.029
Employment + Race	0.003	1	0.003	0.382	0.536
Tenure + Education	0.016	2	0.008	0.941	0.391
Tenure + Race	0.001	1	0.001	0.067	0.795
Education + Race	0.002	2	0.001	0.117	0.890
Explained	2.865	42	0.068	8.261	0.000
Residual	10.925	1323	0.008		
Total	13.791	1365	0.010		

pivotal role which A 8 plays in our investigations must not be overlooked. Without A 8 we could not have tested Arrow's hypotheses concerning the monotonicity properties of an average consumer's absolute and proportional risk-aversion functions. Similarly, without A 8 we could not have carried out our comparative study of absolute and proportional risk aversion in various subgroups of the sample population.[4]

Then subjective probability distributions: The assumption that the sample consumers' subjective probability distributions of future values of the a_i, $i = 1, \ldots, n$, differ insignificantly plays no role in our tests of Arrow's hypotheses in section 28.2.4 but is of primary importance to our study of the way absolute and proportional risk aversion vary across disjoint subgroups of the sample population. This assumption can be viewed as a restriction on the range values of one of the components of b that we could have spelled out in SA 10, e.g., by insisting that the relevant component assume one and only one value.

In conclusion, we also ought to point out that the results we obtained in T 28.4 have independent interest. They demonstrate that the monotonicity properties of a function of just one variable can be determined by applying least squares to a finite sample of independent observations from the graph of the function. Analogous results for functions of more than one variable cannot be obtained without putting restrictions on the data-generating mechanism!

VIII

Economic Theory II: Determinism, Uncertainty, and the Utility Hypothesis

29 Time-Series Tests of the Utility Hypothesis

Much of economic theory is based on three questionable assumptions:

1. The world is deterministic.
2. Decision makers act as if they know the value of all relevant parameters.
3. Consumers and firms, respectively, act as if they were maximizing utility and profit.

In part VIII we shall first discuss the possibility of using time-series data on consumer behavior to test the utility hypothesis. Then we shall determine how sensitive some of the fundamental theorems of economics are to a relaxation of assumptions 1 and 2 above.

We tried in chapters 10 and 13 to establish an equivalence between the utility hypothesis and certain assumptions concerning the characteristics of a consumer's demand function. In chapter 29 we pose two related questions: When does a finite time series of price-quantity pairs belong (1) to the graph of a demand function and (2) to the graph of an excess demand function? The answer to (1) provides us with a nonparametric test of the utility hypothesis. The answer to (2) shows that most time-series data on the consumption expenditures of groups of consumers cannot be used to test the utility hypothesis.

Chapters 30 and 31 are devoted to determining the sensitivity of several economic doctrines to a relaxation of the first two assumptions above. We begin in chapter 30 by introducing uncertainty into the environment of economic decision makers. Our results demonstrate among other things that theorems T 10.9, T 10.16, and T 14.4 are not valid in such an environment. Hence the second assumption above is crucical for the general validity of both the fundamental theorem of consumer choice and the hallmark of welfare economics, which insists that competitive equilibria allocate resources Pareto-optimally.

In chapter 31 we relax the first assumption and study economic growth in a nondeterministic world. The results we obtain demonstrate that a deterministic theory of growth of an economy has a bearing on phenomena in the real world only if the probability distributions of the variables of the economy satisfy rather stringent conditions.

Philosophers argue about the deterministic nature of the world and economists derive theorems, make predictions, and suggest economic policies using arguments which explicitly or implicitly postulate the validity of the three assumptions posed above. The essays of chapters 29–31 will not convince philosophers that the world is nondeterministic nor persuade economists to scrap their certainty theories. The significance of these essays is based on three facts: Chapter 29 presents operational tests of the utility hypothesis. Chapter 30 contains discussions of real-life phenomena which our uncertainty theory can deal with and the standard certainty theories cannot. And chapter 31 establishes the existence of a parameter that can be used to determine whether a given economy, when large enough, will grow deterministically.

Chapters 29–31 belong to speculative economics because in them we use the axiomatic method to *speculate* about the autonomy of well-established doctrines of economic theory. By doing that we exhibit uses of the axiomatic method in economics and econometrics that we have not discussed before.

29.1 A Nonparametric Test of the Utility Hypothesis

In this section I present a nonparametric test of the utility hypothesis which is due to Sidney Afriat. The arguments I use to establish the validity of the test are borrowed from two of Hal Varian's papers (Varian 1982, pp. 945–973, and Varian 1983, pp. 99–110).

We begin with a few preliminary remarks and several useful definitions. Suppose that we have observed m pairs,

$$(x^i, p^i) \in R_+^n \times R_{++}^n, \qquad i = 1, \ldots, m \tag{29.1}$$

where x^i and p^i, respectively, denote the commodity bundle which a given consumer acquired in period i and the price he paid for x^i. Moreover, let $u(\cdot)\colon R_+^n \to R$ be a function which, for all $x \in R_+^n$, satisfies

$$u(x^i) \geqslant u(x) \quad \text{if} \quad p^i x^i \geqslant p^i x, \qquad 1, \ldots, m. \tag{29.2}$$

Then $u(\cdot)$ *rationalizes* our observations on p and x.

A function $u(\cdot)$ that rationalizes our data need not satisfy the conditions of H 6 in chapter 10. We shall show that if one function rationalizes our data, we can find a continuous, monotone, concave function with differentiable level sets at the boundary of $(R_+^n - \{0\})$ which also rationalizes the data. Whether we can find a function $u(\cdot)$ that satisfies both equation 29.2 and H 6 depends on the given data. Consequently, we shall be able to deduce from equation 29.1 that the observed pairs belong to the graph of some demand *correspondence* but not that they belong to the graph of a demand *function*.

There exists a function $u(\cdot)$ which rationalizes our observations only if the latter satisfy a certain consistency condition. To express this condition succinctly, we let x^iQx mean that there exists a sequence i_j, $j = 1, \ldots, k$, such that $p^ix^i \geqslant p^ix^{i_1}$, $p^{i_1}x^{i_1} \geqslant p^{i_1}x^{i_2}$, $\ldots$, $p^{i_k}x^{i_k} \geqslant p^{i_k}x$. The consistency condition, which Hal Varian calls GARP, insists that, for any pair, $1 \leqslant i$, $j \leqslant m$,

$$x^iQx^j \text{ implies that } p^jx^j \leqslant p^jx^i. \tag{29.3}$$

GARP is short for Generalized Axiom of Revealed Preference. The appropriateness of the name can be established by looking back at D 1 in chapter 13. There the x^i were consumption bundles, and x^iQx^j, $x^i \neq x^j$, and the Strong Axiom of Revealed Preference implied that $p^jx^j < p^jx^i$. The weaker requirement of GARP allows the possibility that the x^i and x^j of equation 29.3 satisfy $x^i \neq x^j$ and both $p^ix^i = p^ix^j$ and $p^jx^j = p^jx^i$.

Varian shows in Varian 1982 (p. 968) that the following universal theorem concerning GARP is valid:

UT 22 If the pairs (x^i, p^i), $i = 1, \ldots, m$, in equation 29.1 satisfy GARP, then there exist pairs of numbers, $(U^i, \lambda^i) \in R \times R_{++}$, $i = 1, \ldots, m$, such that

$$U^i \leqslant U^j + \lambda^j p^j(x^i - x^j), \qquad 1 \leqslant i, j \leqslant m. \tag{29.4}$$

Interestingly enough, Varian proves UT 22 by describing a finite computer program which, for any sequence of pairs (x^i, p^i) that satisfy GARP, will generate pairs (U^i, λ^i) that satisfy equation 29.4.

With a little bit of thought it is easy to imagine that the U^i and U^j in equation 29.4 represent utility levels and that the components of $\lambda^j p^j$ are marginal utilities. To see why, let $u(\cdot)$: $R_+^n \to R$ be a differentiable concave function and let $\partial u/\partial x = (\partial u/\partial x_1, \ldots, \partial u/\partial x_n)$. Then, for all $x \in R_+^n$ and $i = 1, \ldots, m$,

$$u(x) \leqslant u(x^i) + \left(\frac{\partial u(x^i)}{\partial x}\right)(x - x^i).$$

Moreover, if the x^i belong to R^n_{++} and maximize $u(\cdot)$ subject to the condition $p^i x \leqslant p^i x^i$, then there exist $\mu^i \in R_{++}$ such that

$$\frac{\partial u(x^i)}{\partial x} = \mu^i p^i, \qquad i = 1, \ldots, m.$$

When this is the case, we may let $U^i = u(x^i)$ and $\lambda^i = \mu^i$, $i = 1, \ldots, m$.

The preceding introductory remarks serve as motivation for the following fundamental theorem of Afriat. In the statement of the theorem, $u(\cdot)$ is taken to be *nonsatiated* if it is locally nonsatiated at every $x \in R^n_+$. Moreover, $u(\cdot)$ is *locally nonsatiated* at $x \in R^n_+$ if and only if in every neighborhood of x there is a y such that $u(y) > u(x)$.

T 29.1 Let our data consist of pairs $(x^i, p^i) \in R^n_+ \times R^n_{++}$. Then the following conditions are equivalent:

(i) There exists a nonsatiated utility function $u(\cdot)$: $R^n_+ \to R$ which rationalizes the data.

(ii) The data satisfy GARP.

(iii) There exist pairs of numbers, $(U^i, \lambda^i) \in R \times R_{++}$, such that, for all pairs $1 \leqslant i, j \leqslant m$,

$$U^i \leqslant U^j + \lambda^j p^j (x^i - x^j). \tag{29.5}$$

(iv) There exists a nonsatiated, continuous, concave monotonic function $u(\cdot)$: $R^n_+ \to R$ which rationalizes the data.

It is obvious that condition iv implies condition i. Moreover, UT 22 insists that condition iii follows from condition ii. Therefore, to prove the theorem we need only show that condition i implies ii and that condition iv follows from iii.

We begin by showing that condition i implies ii: Suppose that $u(\cdot)$ rationalizes the data and that $x^i Q x^j$. Then $u(x^i) \geqslant u(x^j)$. Suppose also that $p^j x^j > p^j x^i$. Then, by local nonsatiation, there is a $y \in R^n_+$ such that $p^j x^j > p^j y > p^j x^i$ and $u(x^i) < u(y) \leqslant u(x^j)$, which contradicts $u(x^i) \geqslant u(x^j)$. Hence $x^i Q x^j$ and $p^j x^j > p^j x^i$ cannot happen if condition i is valid.

To show that condition iv follows from iii, we define $u(\cdot)$: $R^n_+ \to R$ by

$$u(x) = \min_{1 \leqslant i \leqslant m} \{U^i + \lambda^i p^i (x - x^i)\}, \qquad x \in R^n_+. \tag{29.6}$$

Then $u(\cdot)$ is continuous. To show that $u(\cdot)$ is nonsatiated and monotonic, we pick $x, y \in R^n_+$ such that $x \leqslant y$ and $x \neq y$ and assume that

$$u(x) = U^i + \lambda^i p^i (x - x^i) \tag{29.7}$$

and

$$u(y) = U^j + \lambda^j p^j (y - x^j). \tag{29.8}$$

Since $p^j \in R^n_{++}$, it follows from equations 29.6–29.8 that

$$u(x) \leqslant U^j + \lambda^j p^j (x - x^j) < U^j + \lambda^j p^j (y - x^j) = u(y).$$

To show that $u(\cdot)$ is concave we pick $x, y \in R^n_+$ and $\alpha \in (0, 1)$ and let i, j, and k be such that equations 29.7, 29.8, and

$$u(\alpha x + (1 - \alpha)y) = U^k + \lambda^k p^k ((\alpha x + (1 - \alpha)y) - x^k) \tag{29.9}$$

are satisfied. Then equations 29.6–29.8 and 29.9 imply that

$$\begin{aligned} u(\alpha x + (1 - \alpha)y) &= \alpha(U^k + \lambda^k p^k (x - x^k)) + (1 - \alpha)(U^k + \lambda^k p^k (y - x^k)) \\ &\geqslant \alpha u(x) + (1 - \alpha)u(y), \end{aligned}$$

as was to be shown.

To conclude the proof that condition iv follows from iii, we must show that the $u(\cdot)$ we defined in equation 29.6 rationalizes our data. This we do as follows: The inequalities in equations 29.5 and 29.6 imply that

$$u(x^i) = U^i, \qquad i = 1, \ldots, m. \tag{29.10}$$

From equations 29.10 and 29.6 and the inequalities

$$u(x) \leqslant u(x^i) + \lambda^i p^i (x - x^i), \qquad i = 1, \ldots, m$$

it follows that $p^i x^i \geqslant p^i x$ implies $u(x^i) \geqslant u(x)$, $i = 1, \ldots, m$, as was to be shown.

Theorem T 29.1 has many interesting implications. I shall detail three of them: The utility hypothesis insists that the consumer (1) ranks commodity bundles in accordance with the values of a nonsatiated (utility) function, $u(\cdot)\colon R^n_+ \to R$, and (2) acquires a commodity bundle which maximizes the value of $u(\cdot)$ subject to his budget constraint. Afriat's theorem describes a way in which we can use finite time series of observations on the behavior of single consumers to test the empirical relevance of the utility hypothesis: Check whether the data satisfy GARP. In addition, the theorem shows that if we accept the utility hypothesis, we can without loss in generality assume that $u(\cdot)$ is continuous, concave, and monotonic. Finally, the theorem demonstrates that cross-section data on the behavior of different consumers who face the same price vector cannot be used to test the utility hypothesis! The reason is that such data necessarily satisfy GARP.

As our last remark suggests, T 29.1 has interesting implications for the empirical analyses of chapters 27 and 28. For example, T 29.1 implies that, in the context of chapter 28, the assumption that a consumer ranks (μ, m) pairs in accordance with the values of a continuous, concave, monotonic function, $V(\cdot)$: $R_+^2 \to R$, and acquires the (μ, m) pair which maximizes $V(\cdot)$ subject to his budget constraint, $\mu + am = A$ and $(\mu, m) \geqslant 0$, is innocuous and cannot be tested. The only issues at stake are (1) whether $V(\cdot)$ can be written as an integral of a function $u(\cdot)$: $R_+ \to R$ that satisfies the conditions of axiom A 7 and (2) whether the absolute and proportional risk-aversion functions determined by $u(\cdot)$ are monotonic.

29.2 Testing for Homotheticity of the Utility Function

In order to ascertain the implications of T 29.1 for our test of the permanent-income hypothesis, we must state and prove another theorem.

T 29.2 Suppose that we have observed the pair $(x^i, p^i) \in R_+^n \times R_{++}^n$, $i = 1, \ldots, m$, and let

$$q^i = (p^i/p^ix^i), \qquad i = 1, \ldots, m.$$

Then the following conditions are equivalent:

(i) The data can be rationalized by a nonsatiated homothetic function $u(\cdot)$: $R_+^n \to R$.

(ii) For all distinct choices of $i, j, \ldots, k$, we have

$$(q^ix^j)(q^jx^l)\cdots(q^kx^i) \geqslant 1.$$

(iii) There exist numbers $U^i > 0$, $i = 1, \ldots, m$, such that

$$U^i \leqslant U^jq^jx^i, \qquad 1 \leqslant i, j \leqslant m. \tag{29.11}$$

(iv) The data can be rationalized by a nonsatiated, continuous, concave, monotonic homothetic function $u(\cdot)$: $R_+^n \to R$.

This theorem is the joint product of S. Afriat, W. E. Diewert, and H. Varian. The proof I sketch below is due to Varian (see Varian 1983, pp. 102–104).

We begin by showing that condition i implies ii: Suppose that $u(\cdot)$: $R_+^n \to R$ is a nonsatiated homothetic function that rationalizes the data and let $i, j, l, \ldots, t, k$ be a sequence of distinct members of $\{1, \ldots, m\}$. Moreover, let

$$s^j = q^ix^j,$$

$$s^l = (q^ix^j)(q^jx^l) = s^j(q^jx^l)$$

$$\vdots$$

$$s^k = (q^ix^j)(q^jx^l)\cdots(q^tx^k) = s^t(q^tx^k)$$

and note that, since $1 = q^i x^i = q^i(x^j/s^j)$, $u(x^i) \geqslant u(x^j/s^j)$. Finally, note that the homotheticity of $u(\cdot)$ implies that, for any $a > 0$ and $j = 1, \ldots, m$,

$$u(x^j) \geqslant u(x) \text{ for all } x \in R_+^n \text{ such that } q^j x^j \geqslant q^j x \text{ implies that}$$

$$u(x^j/a) \geqslant u(y) \text{ for all } y \in R_+^n \text{ such that } (aq^j)(x^j/a) \geqslant (aq^j)y.$$

Consequently, since $1 = (s^j q^j)(x^j/s^j) = (s^j q^j)(x^l/s^l)$, we have $u(x^j/s^j) \geqslant u(x^l/s^l)$. Continuing in this way, we deduce at last that

$$u(x^i) \geqslant u(x^k/s^k) \qquad \text{and} \qquad u(s^k x^i) \geqslant u(x^k). \tag{29.12}$$

From equation 29.12 and the fact that $u(\cdot)$ is nonsatiated follows

$$1 = q^k x^k \leqslant q^k(s^k x^i) = s^k(q^k x^i)$$

and the validity of condition ii in T 29.2.

To show that condition ii implies iii we let

$$U^i = \min_{\{j,l,\ldots,k,i\}} \{(q^j x^l)(q^l x^t) \cdots (q^k x^i)\}, \qquad i = 1, \ldots, m$$

where the minimum is over all sequences of integers in $\{1, \ldots, m\}$, starting somewhere and terminating in i. By condition ii we need only consider sequences without cycles. Hence the U^i are well defined. Moreover, they satisfy the inequalities in equation 29.11, since if

$$U^i = (q^j x^l)(q^l x^t) \cdots (q^k x^i)$$

and

$$U^j = (q^r x^s)(q^s x^0) \cdots (q^e x^j),$$

then the defining equation for U^i, $i = 1, \ldots, m$, implies that

$$U^i = (q^j x^l)(q^l x^t) \cdots (q^k x^i) \leqslant (q^r x^s)(q^s x^0) \cdots (q^e x^j)(q^j x^i) = U^j q^j x^i.$$

In order to show that condition iii implies iv we let

$$u(x) = \min_{1 \leqslant i \leqslant m} U^i q^i x, \qquad x \in R_+^n.$$

Then it is a routine matter to verify that $u(\cdot)$ satisfies all the requirements of condition iv.

Since condition iv obviously implies i, our proof of T 29.2 is complete.

With T 29.2 assured, we can ascertain the implication of T 29.1 for our tests of the permanent-income hypothesis. Theorem T 29.1 demonstrates that cross-section data on the expenditures of consumers who face the same price vector cannot be used to test the utility hypothesis. However, if we accept the utility hypothesis, T 29.2 shows that we cannot use such data to determine whether the utility function is homothetic either. The reason is that such data always satisfy condition (ii).[1] It is, therefore, interesting to recall that in chapter 27 we carried out factor-analytic tests of the homotheticity of Friedman's utility function with different kinds of data—data consisting of triples (c^i, y^i, A^i) and quintuples $(c^i, J^i, K^i, y^i, A^i)$ that were marred by errors of observation.

29.3 Testing for Homothetic Separability of the Utility Function

In theorems T 11.10 and T 11.11 we characterized the behavior of a consumer whose utility function is homothetically separable. Next we shall propose a nonparametric test to determine whether a consumer's utility function is homothetically separable.

T 29.3 Suppose that $n = \xi k$ and that our data consists of m ξ-tuples $((x_1^i, p_1^i), \ldots, (x_\xi^i, p_\xi^i))$, $i = 1, \ldots, m$, where $(x_j^i, p_j^i) \in R_+^k \times R_{++}^k$, $j = 1, \ldots, \xi$. Moreover, let

$$C_j^i = p_j^i x_j^i \qquad \text{and} \qquad q_j^i = p_j^i / C_j^i, \qquad j = 1, \ldots, \xi, \quad i = 1, \ldots, m.$$

Then the following assertions are equivalent:

(i) There exist nonsatiated, continous, concave monotonic functions, $V(\cdot)\colon R_+^\xi \to R$, $u_j(\cdot)\colon R_+^k \to R_+$, $j = 1, \ldots, \xi$, such that the $u_j(\cdot)$ are linearly homogeneous and $V(u_1(\cdot), \ldots, u_\xi(\cdot))$ rationalizes the data.

(ii) There exist m ξ-tuples, $((U_1^i, P_1^i), \ldots, (U_\xi^i, P_\xi^i))$, $i = 1, \ldots, m$, which satisfy the following conditions:

a. $(U_j^i, P_j^i) \in R_{++}^2$, $\quad j = 1, \ldots, \xi, \quad i = 1, \ldots, m.$

b. $U_j^i \leqslant U_j^r q_j^r x_j^i, \quad 1 \leqslant i, r \leqslant m, \quad j = 1, \ldots, \xi.$

c. $P_j^i = C_j^i / U_j^i, \quad j = 1, \ldots, \xi, \quad i = 1, \ldots, m.$

d. The ξ-tuples $((U_1^i, P_1^i), \ldots, (U_\xi^i, P_\xi^i))$, $\quad i = 1, \ldots, m$, satisfy GARP.

For brevity I shall only sketch a proof of the theorem. Suppose first that condition i is true. Then it must be case that, for each j, $j = 1, \ldots, \xi$, $u_j(\cdot)$ rationalizes the m pairs (x_j^i, p_j^i), $i = 1, \ldots, m$. Consequently, since the $u_j(\cdot)$ are linearly homogeneous, we can appeal to T 29.2 and deduce the existence of numbers U_j^i, $j = 1, \ldots, \xi$ and $i = 1, \ldots, m$, which satisfy condition iib. In fact, we can show that the U_j^i can be chosen so that they satisfy both condition iib and

$$U_j^i = u_j(x_j^i), \qquad i = 1, \ldots, m, \quad j = 1, \ldots, \xi. \tag{29.13}$$

To establish equation 29.13 we fix i and j and use the properties of $u_j(\cdot)$ and a standard theorem in concave programming (Karlin 1959, p. 201) to deduce that there exists a $\lambda \in R_{++}$ such that

$$u_j(x) + \lambda(p_j^i x_j^i - p_j^i x) \leqslant u_j(x_j^i), \qquad x \in R_+^k. \tag{29.14}$$

From equation 29.14 and the homogeneity of $u_j(\cdot)$, it follows that

$$\alpha(u_j(x) - \lambda p_j^i x) \leqslant u(x_j^i) - \lambda p_j^i x_j^i, \qquad x \in R_+^n \text{ and } \alpha \in R_+.$$

Consequently,

$$u_j(x_j^i) = \lambda p_j^i x_j^i, \tag{29.15}$$

and

$$u_j(x) \leqslant \lambda p_j^i x, \qquad x \in R_+^n. \tag{29.16}$$

From equations 29.15 and 29.16 it follows that we can choose the U_j^i so that they satisfy equation 29.13.

Suppose that we have chosen the U_j^i in accordance with equation 29.13 and defined the P_j^i by condition ii-c. Then the pairs (U_j^i, P_j^i), $i = 1, \ldots, m$, and $j = 1, \ldots, \xi$, satisfy condition ii-a. Moreover, $V(\cdot)$ rationalizes the vectors $((U_1^i, P_1^i), \ldots, (U_\xi^i, P_\xi^i))$, $i = 1, \ldots, m$. To establish this fact we let

$$U^i = (U_1^i, \ldots, U_\xi^i) \qquad \text{and} \qquad P^i = (P_1^i, \ldots, P_\xi^i), \quad i = 1, \ldots, m$$

and we intend to show that, for each $i = 1, \ldots, m$,

$$P^i U^i \geqslant P^i U,\ U \in R_+^\xi, \text{ implies } V(U^i) \geqslant V(U). \tag{29.17}$$

To begin, we fix i and let

$$A = \sum_{j=1}^{\xi} C_j^i.$$

Then we use the optimality of x_j^i, $j = 1, \ldots, \xi$, and the homogeneity of the $u_j(\cdot)$ to show that

$$V(u_1(x_1^i/C_1^i)C_1^i, \ldots, u_\xi(x_\xi^i/C_\xi^i)C_\xi^i)$$
$$= \max_{A_j \geqslant 0,\, j=1,\ldots,\xi,\, \sum_{j=1}^{\xi} A_j = A} V(u_1(x_1^i/C_1^i)A_1, \ldots, u_\xi(x_\xi^i/C_\xi^i)A_\xi). \tag{29.18}$$

Finally, we choose $U^0 \in R_+^\xi$ such that $P^i U^0 = P^i U^i$ and

$$V(U^0) = \max_{U \in R_+^\xi,\, P^i U = P^i U^i} V(U). \tag{29.19}$$

Then $\sum_{j=1}^{\xi} (P_j^i U_j^0) = A$ and equation 29.18 imply that

$$V(U^0) = V(u_1(x_1^i/C_1^i)P_1^i U_1^0, \ldots, u_\xi(x_\xi^i/C_\xi^i)P_\xi^i U_\xi^0)$$
$$\leqslant V(u_1(x_1^i/C_1^i)C_1^i, \ldots, u_\xi(x_\xi^i/C_\xi^i)C_\xi^i) = V(U^i); \tag{29.20}$$

and equations 29.19 and 29.20 imply that

$$V(U^i) = V(U^0). \tag{29.21}$$

From equations 29.19 and 29.21 follows the validity of equation 29.17 for the given i. Since i was chosen arbitrarily, we conclude from the preceding arguments that $V(\cdot)$ rationalizes the ξ-tuples, $((U_1^i, P_1^i), \ldots, (U_\xi^i, P_\xi^i))$, $i = 1, \ldots, m$, as was to be shown.

To conclude the proof that condition i implies condition ii, we use the preceding result and theorem T 29.1 to show that the ξ-tuples, $((U_1^i, P_1^i), \ldots, (U_\xi^i, P_\xi^i))$, $i = 1, \ldots, m$, satisfy GARP.

In order to establish the converse we first define

$$u_j(x) = \min_{1 \leqslant i \leqslant m} U_j^i q_j^i x, \qquad j = 1, \ldots, \xi, \ x \in R_+^k$$

and observe that the $u_j(\cdot)$ are continuous, nonsatiated, concave, and monotonic linearly homogeneous functions which rationalize the respective data subsets, (x_j^i, p_j^i), $i = 1, \ldots, m$, for each $j = 1, \ldots, \xi$. Evidently,

$$u_j(x_j^i) = U_j^i, \qquad j = 1, \ldots, \xi, \text{ and } \quad i = 1, \ldots, m.$$

Next we let $U^i = (U_1^i, \ldots, U_\xi^i)$ and $P^i = (P_1^i, \ldots, P_\xi^i)$, $i = 1, \ldots, m$, and use T 29.1 and condition iid to find pairs, $(V^i, \lambda^i) \in R_{++}^2$, $i = 1, \ldots, m$, that satisfy

$$V^i \leqslant V^r + \lambda^r P^r(U^i - U^r), \qquad 1 \leqslant i, r \leqslant m.$$

Finally, we define $V(\cdot)\colon R_+^\xi \to R$ by

$$V(U) = \min_{1 \leqslant i \leqslant m} \{V^i + \lambda^i P^i(U - U^i)\}.$$

Then it is easy to see that

$$V(U^i) = V^i, \qquad i = 1, \ldots, m$$

and that $V(\cdot)$ is a nonsatiated, continuous, concave, monotonic function. It is also evident that, for each $i = 1, \ldots, m$,

$P^i U^i \geqslant P^i U$ implies that $V(U^i) \geqslant V(U)$.

This fact and the properties of the $u_j(\cdot)$ suffice to give a simple proof that

$V(u_1(\cdot), \ldots, u_\xi(\cdot))$ rationalizes our data. Those arguments I leave to the reader.

The preceding theorem is an analogue of a theorem of Varian's (see Varian 1983, theorem 5, p. 107). Varian also proposes a test for additively separable utility functions (see Varian 1983, p. 107–108).

29.4 Excess Demand Functions and the Utility Hypothesis

Above we discussed the use of time-series observations on *single* consumers to test the utility hypothesis. In the process I presented several nonparametric tests of the empirical relevance of the standard interpretation of H 1–H 6.

Next we shall discuss the use of time-series observations on the income and expenditures of *groups* of consumers to test the empirical relevance of the standard interpretation of a slightly modified version of H 1–H 6. In this version a commodity bundle is a pair $(x, y) \in R_+^{n-1} \times [0, T]$, and a price is a pair $(p, w) \in R_{++}^{n-1} \times R_{++}$. Also, the $\hat{A}$ in H 3 is replaced by a vector, $(\omega, T) \in R_+^{n-1} \times R_{++}$, and $p\omega + wT$ is substituted for the A in H 4 so that $\Gamma(p, A)$ becomes

$$\Gamma(p, w, p\omega + wT) = \{(x, y) \in R_+^{n-1} \times [0, T] : px + wy \leqslant p\omega + wT\}.$$

In the intended interpretation of the axioms, the components of x denote so many units of ordinary commodities and y denotes hours of leisure time. Also, ω is taken to be the consumer's initial holdings of commodities and T measures the total amount of leisure time available to the consumer.

If we adopt the version of H 1–H 6 described above, the consumer's behavior can be characterized by the relation

$$(z, -L) = h(p, w), \qquad p \in R_{++}^{n-1} \text{ and } w \in R_{++}$$

where L denotes so many hours of labor, $h(\cdot): R_{++}^n \to R^{n-1} \times R$ is defined by

$$h(p, w) = f(p, w, p\omega + wT) - (\omega, T), \qquad p \in R_{++}^{n-1} \text{and } w \in R_{++}$$

and $f(\cdot): R_{++}^n \times R_+ \to R_+^n$ is the demand function. As we shall see, the significance of this representation of consumer behavior stems from the fact that $h(\cdot)$ satisfies the following conditions:

(C) $h(\cdot)$ is continuous;
(H) $h(\cdot)$ is homogeneous of degree zero;

(W) $h(\cdot)$ satisfies Walras's Law; i.e., $(p, w)h(p, w) = 0$; and
(B) $h(\cdot)$ is bounded from below.

Any function which satisfies (H) and (W) is called an *excess demand function.*

Suppose now that we have obtained a time series, (z^i, L^i, p^i, w^i), $i = 1, \ldots, m$, of observations on consumer behavior. If our data represent the choices which a single consumer made during the time from $i = 1$ to $i = m$, we can apply T 29.1 and construct a test of the utility hypothesis. If our data pertain to the choices which a group of consumers made during the same time period, the analysis of sections 29.1–29.3 does not apply. We shall next discuss some of the alternatives open to us.

29.4.1 Testing the Utility Hypothesis with Group Data That Satisfy GARP

Let G denote a group of consumers and assume that

$$\#G \geqslant n.$$

Moreover, let z^i and L^i, respectively, denote the total *purchases* of the components of z, *which we assume to be positive*, and the aggregate supply of hours of labor in period i by consumers in G. Finally, let p^i and w^i, respectively, denote the price of z and the wage rate which the same consumers faced in period i. We assume that our data consist of the quadruples, (z^i, L^i, p^i, w^i), $i = 1, \ldots, m$, and we want to determine how we can use these data to test the utility hypothesis.

It seems reasonable that if we have obtained information on the number of hours which the consumers in G supplied in period i, we should be able to determine the value of T for each consumer and hence the value of T for the group as a whole. It is also reasonable to assume that the total amount of leisure time available to the consumers in G does not change from one period to the next. So from now on we assume that we have determined the value of T for the group as a whole and define $y^i \in R_+$, $i = 1, \ldots, m$ by

$$y^i = T - L^i, \qquad i = 1, \ldots, m.$$

Then, for each period i, y^i measures the total amount of leisure time of which the consumers in G actually disposed.

Suppose now that the sequence of data (z^i, y^i, p^i, w^i), $i = 1, \ldots, m$, satisfy GARP. Then we can find a nonsatiated, monotonic, continuous, concave function, $u(\cdot)\colon R^n_+ \to R$, which rationalizes our data.

The existence of $u(\cdot)$ shows that it is possible that the z and y aggregates for the given group are chosen as if the group as a whole maximized utility subject to the group's budget constraint. That is interesting, but it does not help us determine whether each consumer in the group is a utility maximizer. And it is the latter problem about which the utility hypothesis is concerned.

To test the utility hypothesis we proceed as follows. We let $N = \#G$ and $\lambda = 1/N$ and observe that if our data satisfy GARP, the sequence $(\lambda z^i, \lambda y^i, p^i, w^i)$, $i = 1, \ldots, m$, must satisfy GARP as well. Consequently, there exists a nonsatiated, monotonic, continuous, concave function, $\tilde{u}(\cdot)$: $R_+^n \to R$, which rationalizes $(\lambda z^i, \lambda y^i, p^i, w^i)$, $i = 1, \ldots, m$, and is such that if each consumer in G chose his consumption bundle by maximizing $\tilde{u}(\cdot)$ subject to the constraint,

$$pz + wy \leqslant w(\lambda T), \qquad z \in R_+^{n-1} \quad \text{and} \quad y \in [0, \lambda T]$$

then for each $i = 1, \ldots, m$, the quadruple (z^i, y^i, p^i, w^i) would belong to the graph of the aggregate demand correspondence of the consumers in G.[2]

The relationship between the $\tilde{u}(\cdot)$ of the members of G and the $u(\cdot)$ of G is not uniquely determined. A possible choice of $\tilde{u}(\cdot)$ can be intuited from the following arguments: Consider a group of (H 1–H 6) consumers, $(R_+^n, V_l(\cdot), \hat{A}_l)$, $l = 1, \ldots, N$. Moreover, let $f^l(\cdot)$: $R_{++}^n \times R_+ \to R_+^n$ denote the demand function of consumer l, $l = 1, \ldots, N$, and assume that the aggregate income of the group, A, is always divided so that the income of each consumer equals A/N. Finally, assume that the utility functions of the consumers are identical. Then the aggregate demand function of the group, $F(\cdot)$: $R_{++}^n \times R_+ \to R_+^n$, which is defined by

$$F(p, A) = \sum_{l=1}^{N} f^l(p, A/N),$$

is the demand function of a consumer, $(R_+^n, \tilde{V}(\cdot), \sum_{i=1}^{N} \hat{A}_i)$, whose utility function satisfies the relation,

$$\tilde{V}(x) = V_1(x/N), \qquad x \in R_+^n.$$

Now the $u(\cdot)$ of G need not satisfy H 6. Still we may chose $\tilde{u}(\cdot)$ such that

$$\tilde{u}(x/N) = u(x), \qquad x \in R_+^n$$

and demonstrate that (z^i, y^i, p^i, w^i) belong to the graph of the aggregate demand correspondence of the consumers in G. Those details I leave to the reader.

From the preceding arguments it follows that a sufficient condition that our group data be consistent with the utility hypothesis is that they satisfy GARP.

29.4 Testing for the Homotheticity of Individual Utility Functions with Group Data That Satisfy GARP

Next let $x^i = (z^i, y^i), \qquad i = 1, \ldots, m$

$$q^i = (p^i, w^i) \Big/ \left(\sum_{j=1}^{n-1} p_j^i z_j^i + w^i y^i \right), \qquad i = 1, \ldots, m.$$

Moreover, suppose that the pairs (x^i, q^i), $i = 1, \ldots, m$, satisfy condition ii of T 29.2. Then we can find a nonsatiated, continuous, concave, homothetic, and monotonic function, $u(\cdot)\colon R_+^n \to R$, which rationalizes our data. From this and from arguments like those used above, we deduce that our data are consistent with the hypothesis that the consumers in G determine their consumption bundles by maximizing one and the same homothetic utility function $\tilde{u}(\cdot)\colon R_+^n \to R_+$, subject to their respective budget contraints.

When the $u(\cdot)$ of G is homothetic, the $\tilde{u}(\cdot)$ of the members of G can be taken to equal $u(\cdot)$. This fact can be intuited from the next theorem:

T 29.4 Consider a set of H 1–H 6 consumers, $(R_+^n, V_l(\cdot), \hat{A}_l)$, $l = 1, \ldots, k$, and assume that the $V_l(\cdot)$ satisfy the conditions of H 6. Moreover, let $f^l(\cdot)\colon R_{++}^n \times R_+ \to R_+^n$ denote the demand function of the lth consumer, $l = 1, \ldots, k$, and let $F(\cdot)\colon R_{++}^n \times R_+^k \to R_+^n$ be defined by

$$F(p, A_1, \ldots, A_k) = \sum_{l=1}^{k} f^l(p, A_l).$$

Then there exists a function $H(\cdot)\colon R_{++}^n \times R_+ \to R_+^n$ such that, for all $(p, A_1, \ldots, A_k) \in R_{++}^n \times R_+^n$,

$$H\left(p, \sum_{l=1}^{k} A_l\right) = F(p, A_1, \ldots, A_k) \tag{29.22}$$

if and only if the $V_l(\cdot)$ (1) are homothetic and (2) induce the same ordering of R_+^n.

This theorem is due to G. Antonelli (see Antonelli 1971, pp. 344–345) and the proof is as follows: If the $V_i(\cdot)$ are homothetic and induce the same ordering of R_+^n, then T 11.9 implies that there exists a continuous function $g(\cdot)\colon R_{++}^n \to R_+^n$ such that

$$f^l(p, A) = g(p) \cdot A, \qquad (p, A) \in R_{++}^n \times R_+, \; l = 1, \ldots, k \tag{29.23}$$

from which it follows that $F(\cdot)$ satisfies equation 29.22 with

$$H\left(p, \sum_{l=1}^{k} A_l\right) = g(p) \sum_{l=1}^{k} A_l. \tag{29.24}$$

Conversely, suppose that there is a function $H(\cdot)$: $R^n_{++} \times R \to R^n_+$ which satisfies equation 29.22 for all $(p, A_1, \ldots, A_k) \in R^n_{++} \times R^k_+$. Then

$$H(p, A) = f^l(p, A), \qquad (p, A) \in R^n_{++} \times R_+, \qquad l = 1, \ldots, k. \tag{29.25}$$

Moreover, for all $(A_1, A_2) \in R^2_+$ and $p \in R^n_{++}$,

$$H(p, A_1 + A_2) = H(p, A_1) + H(p, A_2),$$

from which it follows by standard arguments that there is a continuous function $g(\cdot)$: $R^n_{++} \to R^n_+$ which satisfies equation 29.23. But if this is true, then equations 29.23 29.25 and T 13.12 imply that the $V_l(\cdot)$ are homothetic and induce the same ordering of R^n_+.

29.4.3 A Characterization of Excess Demand Functions

To test the utility hypothesis with group data that cannot be rationalized by a utility function, we must generate new ideas. The most interesting of those ideas is described in the next theorem, which is due to D. McFadden, A. Mas-Colell, R. Mantel, and M. K. Richter:

T 29.5 A function $h(\cdot)$: $R^n_{++} \to R^n$ satisfies conditions (*H*), (*W*), and (B) if and only if there exist n preference-maximizing consumers whose excess demand functions satisfy (B) and sum to $h(\cdot)$.

It is obvious that if the excess demand functions of n preference-maximizing consumers satisfy (B) and sum to $h(\cdot)$, then $h(\cdot)$ will satisfy (H), (W), and (B). Hence we need only prove the converse.

The proof of the necessity part of T 28.5 which McFadden et al. gave in McFadden, Mas-Colell, Mantel, and Richter 1974 (pp. 364–366) is informative. Hence I shall repeat it here: We begin by envisioning a sphere with center $-q \in \{x \in R^n : x < 0\}$ and radius $2\|q\|$ and by observing that the intersection of this sphere with R^n_{++}, i.e.,

$$Q = \{p \in R^n_{++} : \|p + q\| = 2\|q\|\},$$

has the following interesting properties:

(i) for each $p \in R^n_{++}$, there is a unique $\lambda \in R_{++}$ such that $\lambda p \in Q$;
(ii) for each $p \in R^n_{++}$, there is a unique pair $(r, \lambda) \in Q \times R_{++}$ such that that $p = \lambda r$;
(iii) $q \in Q$;

(iv) if $p, r \in Q$ and $p \neq r$, then $(r+q)(p+q) < 4\|q\|^2$; and
(v) if $p \in Q$, $p \cdot q \leqslant q \cdot q$ and $p \cdot (p+q) \geqslant 2q \cdot q$.

Since these properties are easily established, I leave their verification to the reader.

Next we pick a $q \in R^n_{++}$ such that, for all $p \in R^n_{++}$, $h(p) + q > 0$, and define $\beta_l(\cdot)$: R_{++}, $l = 1, \ldots, n$, by

$$h(p) + p + q = \sum_{l=1}^{n} \beta_l(p) e^l, \tag{29.26}$$

where e^l is the lth unit vector, $l = 1, \ldots, n$. Since $ph(p) = 0$,

$$p \cdot (p+q) = \sum_{l=1}^{n} \beta_l(p) p e^l.$$

Consequently, for all $p \in Q$,

$$\begin{aligned} h(p) &= \sum_{l=1}^{n} \beta_l(p) e^l - (p+q) \\ &= \sum_{l=1}^{n} \beta_l(p) e^l - (p+q)\left(\sum_{l=1}^{n} \beta_l(p) p' e^l / p \cdot (p+q)\right) \\ &= \sum_{l=1}^{n} \beta_l(p)[I - ((p+q)p'/p \cdot (p+q))] e^l \\ &= \sum_{l=1}^{n} h^l(p), \end{aligned}$$

where I is the $n \times n$ identity matrix and

$$h^l(p) = \beta_l(p)\{I - [(p+q)p'/p \cdot (p+q)]\} e^l, \qquad p \in Q, \qquad l = 1, \ldots, n. \tag{29.27}$$

For each $l = 1, \ldots, n$, the function $h^l(\cdot)$: $Q \to R^n$ has three interesting properties:

(i) $ph^l(p) = 0$;
(ii) $h^l(\cdot)$ is bounded below; and
(iii) $h^l(\cdot)$ satisfies the Strong Axiom of Revealed Preference.

The validity of conditions i and ii is obvious. Hence it suffices to prove condition iii. Let r, p be two vectors in Q. In order that $h^l(r)$ be directly revealed preferred to $h^l(p)$, we must have $h^l(r) \neq h^l(p)$ and

$$0 \geqslant rh^l(p) = \beta_l(p)\{re^l - [r(p+q)/p(p+q)]pe^l\}. \tag{29.28}$$

Since $pe^l > 0$ and (see property iv of Q)

$$r(p+q) - p(p+q) = (r+q)(p+q) - (p+q)(p+q) < 0,$$

the inequality in equation 29.28 implies that

$$re^l < pe^l. \tag{29.29}$$

Hence $h^l(r)$ is directly revealed preferred to $h^l(p)$ only if equation 29.29 holds.

If $h^l(r)$ is indirectly revealed preferred to $h^l(p)$, it is obvious that r and p must satisfy equation 29.29 again. And from equation 29.29 we deduce that

$$0 = ph^l(p) < ph^l(r),$$

as was to be known.

In order to conclude the proof we must show that the $h^l(p)$ can be extended to R^n_{++} in such a way that they satisfy (H), (W), (B), and the Strong Axiom of Revealed Preference. For each $p \in R^n_{++}$ we find the $\lambda \in R_{++}$ with $\lambda p \in Q$ and let

$$h^l(p) = h^l(\lambda p). \tag{29.30}$$

Then properties (i) and (ii) of Q imply that $h^l(\cdot)\colon R^n_{++} \to R^n$ is well defined. Moreover, if $p \in R^n_{++}$ and $\lambda p \in Q$, then $\lambda > 0$ and

$$0 = \lambda p h^l(\lambda p) = \lambda p h^l(p)$$

imply that $h^l(\cdot)$ satisfies (W). For the same p and any $\mu \in R_{++}$,

$$h^l(\mu p) = h^l\left(\frac{\lambda}{\mu}(\mu p)\right) = h^l(\lambda p) = h^l(p).$$

Hence $h^l(\cdot)$ satisfies (H) as well. To show that $h^l(\cdot)$ satisfies the Strong Axiom of Revealed Preference, let p and $r \in R^n_{++}$ and λ and $\mu \in R_{++}$ be such that $\lambda p \in Q$ and $\mu r \in Q$. Moreover, suppose that

$$0 = ph^l(p) \geqslant ph^l(r).$$

Then $\lambda p h^l(p) = \lambda p h^l(\lambda p) \geqslant \lambda p h^l(r) = \lambda p h^l(\mu r)$ implies that

$$0 = \mu r h^l(\mu r) < \mu r h^l(\lambda p)$$

and hence that $rh^l(r) < rh^l(p)$. This shows that $h^l(\cdot)$ satisfies the Weak Axiom of Revealed Preference. The same argument with only obvious modifications suffices to ascertain that $h^l(\cdot)$ satisfies the Strong Axiom as well.

To show that $h^l(\cdot)$ satisfies (B) we use equations 29.27, 29.26 and condition (v) in our description of Q and deduce that, for all $p \in Q$,

$$h^l(p) \geqslant -(p+q)[p_l h_l(p) + p_l^2 + p_l q_l]/p(p+q)$$

$$\geqslant -(p+q)(pq + p_l^2 + p_l q_l)/p(p+q)$$

$$\geqslant -3(p+q) \geqslant -6\|q\|e, \qquad l = 1, \ldots, n$$

where $e \in R^n_{++}$ is a vector all of whose components equal 1. These inequalities and equation 29.30 demonstrate that the $h^l(\cdot)$ are bounded from below.

It remains to show that each $h^l(\cdot)$ is the excess demand function of a preference-maximizing consumer. To that end, we define $x^l(\cdot)\colon R^n_{++} \to R^n_+$ by

$$x^l(p) = h^l(p) + 6\|q\|e, \qquad p \in R^n_{++}.$$

Then $x^l(\cdot)$ is a function that satisfies the Strong Axiom of Revealed Preference, and $px^l(p) = 6\|q\|pe$ for all $p \in R^n_{++}$. From this and a theorem of M. K. Richter's (Richter 1966, theorem 1, p. 639), it follows that there exists a total, reflexive, and transitive ordering of R^n_+, $\lesssim$, that rationalizes $x^l(\cdot)$ in the sense that, for all $p \in R^n_{++}$ and all $x \in R^n_+$ such that $px \leqslant 6\|q\|pe$, $x \lesssim x^l(p)$. This concludes the proof since $\lesssim$ and the initial quantities $6\|q\|e$ obviously rationalize $h^l(\cdot)$ as well as $x^l(\cdot)$.

Several remarks are in order in reading T 29.5 and its proof. First, neither the preference order, $\lesssim$, nor the initial quantities, $6\|q\|e$, that rationalize $h^l(\cdot)$ are uniquely determined. For the applications of T 29.5 that we have in mind only two things matter: (1) $\lesssim$ exists and (2) $h^l(\cdot)$ satisfies the Strong Axiom of Revealed Preference.

Second, we established the existence of a preference order, $\lesssim$, not of a utility function. Moreover, we established the existence of n preference-maximizing consumers whose excess demand functions add up to $h(\cdot)$. The significance of n and the possibility of finding a group of utility-maximizing consumers whose excess demand functions add up to $h(\cdot)$ are explored in the following remarkable theorem of G. Debreu's.

T 29.6 Suppose that $h(\cdot)\colon R^n_{++} \to R^n$ satisfies (C), (H), and (W) and let $S_\varepsilon = \{p \in R^n_{++} : (p/\|p\|) > \varepsilon\}$. Then we have:

(i) For every $\varepsilon > 0$, there exist n consumers with unspecified initial quantities of commodities and monotonic, continuous, strictly quasi-concave utility functions whose excess demand functions on S_ε add to $h(\cdot)$.

(ii) There are a function $h(\cdot)$: $R^n_{++} \rightarrow R^n_+$ which satisfies (C), (H), and (W) and an $\varepsilon > 0$ such that $h(\cdot)$ cannot be expressed as a sum of fewer than n individual excess demand functions on S_ε.

Since the proof of this theorem is involved, I omit it here and refer the reader to Debreu 1974 (pp. 15–21) for Debreu's own proof. The interested reader should also consult Geanakoplos 1984 (pp. 1–9). For twice-differentiable functions $h(\cdot)$ that satisfy (H) and (W), Geanakoplos finds explicit uncomplicated utility functions that give rise to Debreu's individual excess demands on S_ε.

29.4.5 Constructing a "Test" of the Utility Hypothesis When the Group Data Do Not Satisfy GARP.

Theorem T 29.5 provides almost all the arguments we need for demonstrating that even data that do not satisfy GARP cannot be used to reject the utility hypothesis. To see why, consider first the following system of equations:

$$\begin{pmatrix} p_1 z_1 \\ \vdots \\ -wL \end{pmatrix} = \begin{pmatrix} \alpha_1 \\ \vdots \\ \alpha_n \end{pmatrix} w + \begin{pmatrix} \beta_{11} & \cdots & \beta_{1(n-1)} \\ \vdots & & \vdots \\ \beta_{n1} & & \beta_{n(n-1)} \end{pmatrix} p + \begin{pmatrix} \eta_1 \\ \vdots \\ \eta_n \end{pmatrix}, \tag{29.31}$$

where $(\eta_1, \ldots, \eta_n)$ is a vector of error terms. We can use our data, $(z^i, -L^i, p^i, w^i)$, $i = 1, \ldots, m$, to obtain constrained least-squares estimates of the parameters in equation 29.31—$\hat{\alpha}_j$, $j = 1, \ldots, n$; $\hat{\beta}_{jk}$, $1 \leqslant j, k \leqslant n$; and $\hat{\eta}^i_j$, $j = 1, \ldots, n$, $i = 1, \ldots, m$, which satisfy the relations

$$\begin{pmatrix} p^i_1 z^i_1 \\ \vdots \\ -w^i L^i \end{pmatrix} = \begin{pmatrix} \hat{\alpha}_1 \\ \vdots \\ \hat{\alpha}_n \end{pmatrix} w^i + \begin{pmatrix} \hat{\beta}_{11} & \cdots & \hat{\beta}_{1(n-1)} \\ \vdots & & \vdots \\ \hat{\beta}_{n1} & \cdots & \hat{\beta}_{n(n-1)} \end{pmatrix} p^i + \begin{pmatrix} \hat{\eta}^i_1 \\ \vdots \\ \hat{\eta}_n \end{pmatrix}, \quad i = 1, \ldots, m \tag{29.32}$$

and

$$\sum_{j=1}^{n} \hat{\alpha}_j = \sum_{j=1}^{n} \hat{\beta}_{jk} = \sum_{j=1}^{n} \hat{\eta}^i_j = 0, \quad k = 1, \ldots, n-1, i = 1, \ldots, m. \tag{29.33}$$

From equations 29.32 and 29.33 it follows that if we assume that $(p^i, w^i)/\|(p^i, w^i)\| \neq (p^j, w^j)/\|(p^j, w^j)\|$ if $i \neq j$, $1 \leqslant i, j \leqslant m$, and if for all $(p, w) \in R^n_{++} \times R_{++}$, we let

$$\tilde{\eta}_j^i = \begin{cases} \hat{\eta}_j^i/p_j^i, & j = 1, \ldots, n-1, \qquad i = 1, \ldots, m \\ \hat{\eta}_n^i/w^i, & j = n,\ i = 1, \ldots, m \end{cases}$$

$$f_j(p,w) = \begin{cases} \hat{\alpha}_j(w/p_j) + \sum_{k=1}^{n-1} \hat{\beta}_{jk}(p_k/p_j) + \sum_{i=1}^{m} \delta(((p,w)/\|(p,w)\|) \\ \quad - ((p^i,w^i)/\|(p^i,w^i)\|))\tilde{\eta}_j^i \qquad j = 1, \ldots, n-1 \\ \text{and (for } j = n) \\ \hat{\alpha}_n + \sum_{k=1}^{n-1} \hat{\beta}_{nk}(p_k/w) + \sum_{i=1}^{m} \delta(((p,w)/\|(p,w)\|) \\ \quad - ((p^i,w^i)/\|(p^i,w^i)\|))\tilde{\eta}_n^i, \end{cases}$$

where $\delta(\cdot): R^n \to \{0, 1\}$ and $\delta(s) = 1$ or 0 according as $s = 0$ or not, and

$$f(p,w) = (f_1(p,w), \ldots, f_n(p,w))',$$

then $f(\cdot): R_{++}^n \times R_{++} \to R^n$ is well defined and satisfies (H) and (W). Moreover, $f(\cdot)$ satisfies (B) on any compact subset of R_{++}^n.

Next, let A be a cone in R_{++}^n with vertex at the origin and assume that A is closed and contains in its interior p^i, $i = 1, \ldots, m$. Moreover, define $g(\cdot): R_{++}^{n-1} \times R_{++} \to R^n$ by

$$g(p,w) = \begin{cases} f(p,w) & \text{if } (p,w) \in A \\ 0 & \text{otherwise.} \end{cases}$$

Then $g(\cdot)$ satisfies (H), (W), and (B) and, by T 29.5, there exist functions $h^l(\cdot): R_{++}^{n-1} \times R_{++} \to R^n$, $l = 1, \ldots, n$, which are the excess demand functions of n preference-maximizing consumers and satisfy

$$\sum_{l=1}^{n} h^l(p,w) = g(p,w), \qquad (p,w) \in R_{++}^{n-1} \times R_{++}.$$

In particular,

$$\sum_{l=1}^{n} h^l(p^i,w^i) = \begin{pmatrix} z^i \\ -L^i \end{pmatrix}, \qquad i = 1, \ldots, m.$$

Finally, for each $l = 1, \ldots, n$, add a vector $q^l \in R_{++}^n$ to $h^l(\cdot)$ and obtain a function $f^l(\cdot): R_{++}^n \to R_+^n$ which satisfies (H),

$$(p,w)f^l(p,w) = (p,w)q^l, \qquad (p,w) \in R_{++}^{n-1} \times R_{++}$$

and the Strong Axiom of Revealed Preference. From the last two conditions it follows that, for each $l = 1, \ldots, n$, the pairs

$$(f^l(p^i, w^i), (p^i, w^i)), \qquad i = 1, \ldots, m \tag{29.34}$$

must satisfy GARP. But if this so, we can find n nonsatiated, continuous, concave, monotonic functions, $u_l(\cdot)$: $R^n_+ \to R$, $1 = 1, \ldots, n$, such that, for each l, $u_{l_l}(\cdot)$ rationalizes the data in equation 29.34 and $u_l(x - q^l)$, $x \in R^n_+$, rationalizes $(h^l(p^i, w^i), (p^i, w^i))$, $i = 1, \ldots, m$, in the set $\{y \in R^n : y \geqslant -q^l\}$.

If $\#G = n$, the preceding arguments demonstrate that our data are consistent with the utility hypothesis. If $\#G > n$, we can obtain the same result in several ways. For example, we can pick an $l \in \{1, \ldots, n\}$ and apply arguments we used in section 29.4.1 to the data in equation 29.34 and produce any number of consumers with nonsatiated, monotonic, continuous, concave utility functions whose aggregate demand and excess demand at (p^i, w^i), respectively, equal $f^l(p^i, w^i)$ and $h^l(p^i, w^i)$, $i = 1, \ldots, m$. In that way we succeed in showing that our data are consistent with the utility hypothesis.

29.4.6 Summing Up

The result we obtained in the last section and the results we obtained in sections 29.4.1 and 29.4.2 demonstrate that *any* finite sequence of data $(z^i, -L^i, p^i, w^i)$, $i = 1, \ldots, m$, on the purchases of commodities and supply of labor of a group of consumers which satisfy the conditions $(p^i, w^i)/\|(p^i, w^i)\| \neq (p^j, w^j)/\|(p^j, w^j)\|$, $1 \leqslant i, j \leqslant m$, $i \neq j$, is consistent with the utility hypothesis. It goes without saying that such data cannot be used to test the utility hypothesis.

In obtaining the preceding result we left unspecified the initial commodity bundles and the values of the various T facing the individual consumers in G. The importance of this omission is brought out in an example, E 29.1, which we discuss in our concluding remarks.

29.5 Nonparametric versus Parametric Tests of the Utility Hypothesis and a Counterexample

In sections 29.1–29.3 we presented nonparametric tests of the utility hypothesis as it applies to the behavior of individual consumers. According to J. R. Hicks, such tests cannot be taken seriously because to "assume that the representative consumer acts like an ideal consumer is a hypothesis worth testing; to assume that an actual person, the Mr. Brown or Mr. Jones who lives round the corner, does in fact act in such a way does not deserve a moment's consideration" (Hicks 1956, p. 55). Hicks's authority notwithstanding, we believe in such tests. They are analogues of the "laboratory" tests of the expected utility hypothesis which we discussed in chapter 19. They are also true in spirit to the tests we described in chapters 26–28 in which we postulated the existence of a representative consumer and used him to specify how the Browns and the Joneses of the sample population differed from one another.

The representative consumer appears in many disguises. One in which he seems to frequent most time-series tests of the utility hypothesis is described by John Muellbauer in Muellbauer 1976 (p. 979) as follows: "A representative consumer exists if the market behaviour of an aggregate of different consumers is as if it were the market behavior of a number of identical hypothetical consumers each with the same level of income." But if that is so, then the tests of the utility hypothesis which we presented in sections 29.4.1, 29.4.2, and 29.4.5 were nonparametric tests of the existence of such a representative consumer.

Parametric tests of the utility hypothesis are tests in which the researcher—explicitly or implicitly—postulates the form of the utility function of the representative consumer and demands to know whether such a consumer exists. In these tests, therefore, the utility hypothesis per se is not at stake, only the particular form of the utility function. Examples of utility functions that have been postulated are (1) the linear logarithmic function,

$$V(x) = F\left(\sum_{i=1}^{n} \log x_i, t\right),$$

which according to Dale Jorgenson and Lawrence Lau (Jorgenson and Lau 1977, p. 392) can be used to rationalize the Rotterdam system of demand functions of A. P. Barten and H. Theil (see Theil 1965, pp. 67–87); and (2) the transcendental logarithmic function of Lauritz Christensen, D. Jorgenson, and L. Lau (see Christensen, Jorgenson, and Lau 1975, p. 370),

$$V(x) = \exp\left(\alpha_0 + \sum_{j=1}^{n} \alpha_i \log x_i + \sum_{i,j=1}^{n} \beta_{ij} \log x_i \log x_j\right).$$

Time-series tests have usually concluded that the required representative consumer does not exist (see, for example, Christensen, Jorgenson, and Lau 1975, p. 381, and Brown and Deaton 1972, pp. 1188–1216).

We have claimed that our results demonstrate that most time-series data on the consumption expenditures of groups of consumers cannot be used to test the utility hypothesis. Note, therefore, that "most" instead of "all" account for two provisos: (1) the data, (z^i, L^i, p^i, w^i), $i = 1, \ldots, m$, must be observations on the aggregate excess demand for x and L of the consumers in the group G; i.e., they must satisfy the conditions

$$p^i z^i - w^i L^i = 0, \qquad i = 1, \dots, m$$

and (2) the pairs (p^i, w^i), $i = 1, \dots, m$, must satisfy the conditions

$$(p^i, w^i)/\|(p^i, w^i)\| \neq (p^j, w^j)/\|(p^j, w^j)\|, \qquad 1 \leqslant i, j \leqslant m,\ i \neq j. \tag{29.35}$$

Both provisos need further comments. First, the second proviso: The conditions in equation (29.35) make sure that the data cannot be used to test for the homogeneity restriction (H) on community excess demand functions. Only data that fail to satisfy (all) the conditions in equation 29.35 could force us to reject the homogeneity restriction (H) and with it the utility hypothesis.[3]

Then the first proviso: The arguments we used in section 29.4.4 took into account one important characteristic of our data: The observations on z record the *purchases* of commodities which the consumers in G as a group carried out in the m observation periods. Pairs of purchased quantities and prices need not belong to the graph of an aggregate demand function unless the commodities in question are nonstorable. These days most commodities can be stored and many consumers keep stocks of various commodities all the time. Consequently, it is reasonable to interpret the z^i as measures of the aggregate excess demand at p^i of the consumers in G.

To strees both the import and the relevance of the last remark, I conclude this section and the chapter by observing that the analogue of T 29.5 for aggregate demand functions is not valid. To wit: Example E 29.1, which is due to D. McFadden, demonstrates that there are functions $f(\cdot)\colon R^n_{++} \to R^n_+$ which satisfy (H) and $pf(p) = p\omega$ for some $\omega \in R^n_+$ and all $p \in R^n_{++}$ but cannot be decomposed into a sum of individual demand functions (McFadden, Mas-Colell, Mantel, and Richter 1974, p. 369).

E 29.1 Suppose that $n = 3$ and let $\omega \in R^n_+$ and $f(\cdot)\colon R^3_{++} \to R^3_+$, respectively, denote a commodity bundle and a function which satisfies (H) and $pf(p) = p\omega$, $p \in R^3_{++}$. Moreover, assume that

$$\omega = (0, 0, 1)$$

and that the values of $f(\cdot)$ at $p^1 = (1, 2, 1)$ and $p^2 = (2, 1, 1)$ satisfy the inequalities

$$f_1(p^1) \leqslant 1/8, \qquad f_3(p^1) \leqslant 1/8, \tag{29.36}$$

and

$$f_2(p^2) \leqslant 1/8, \qquad f_3(p^2) \leqslant 1/8. \tag{29.37}$$

Then $(f(p^1), p^1)$ and $(f(p^2), p^2)$ do not satisfy GARP. We shall show that $f(\cdot)$ cannot be written as the sum of demand functions.

Suppose that there exist m consumers, $i = 1, \ldots, m$, with initial endowments $\omega^i = (0, 0, \alpha_i)$ and consumption bundles x^{i1} and x^{i2}, respectively, at $(p^1, p^1\omega^i)$ and $(p^2, p^2\omega^i)$. Suppose also that $\sum_{i=1}^{m} \alpha_i = 1$ and that

$$f(p^1) = \sum_{i=1}^{m} x^{i1} \qquad \text{and} \qquad f(p^2) = \sum_{i=1}^{m} x^{i2}.$$

Then, if individual i's demand function satisfies the Strong Axiom of Revealed Preference, his consumption bundles of p^1 and p^2 must satisfy one of the following three conditions:

(i) $p^1x^{1i} < p^1x^{2i}$,

(ii) $p^2x^{2i} < p^2x^{1i}$,

(iii) $x^{1i} = x^{2i}$.

Consequently, if we let A, B, and C, respectively, contain all the consumers whose consumption bundles satisfy conditions i, ii, and iii, and if A and B are not empty, then

$$p^1f(p^2) - p^1f(p^1) > \sum_{i \in B} (p^1x^{2i} - p^1x^{1i}) \geqslant -\sum_{i \in B} (\alpha_i/2) \tag{29.38}$$

and

$$p^2f(p^1) - p^2f(p^2) > \sum_{i \in A} (p^2x^{1i} - p^2x^{2i}) \geqslant -\sum_{i \in A} (\alpha_i/2). \tag{29.39}$$

From the inequalities in equations 29.36 and 29.37 and $p^if(p^i) = 1$, $i = 1, 2$, we can deduce

$$p^1f(p^2) \leqslant 3/4 \qquad \text{and} \qquad p^2f(p^1) \leqslant 3/4. \tag{29.40}$$

But then equations 29.38 and 29.39 imply that

$$3/4 > 1 - \sum_{i \in B} (\alpha_i/2) \qquad \text{and} \qquad 3/4 > 1 - \sum_{i \in A} (\alpha_i/2)$$

and hence that $\sum_{i \in B} \alpha_i > 1/2$ and $\sum_{i \in A} \alpha_i > 1/2$, which cannot happen since, by assumption, $\sum_{i=1}^{m} \alpha_i = 1$.

The fact that neither A nor B can be empty follows from equation 29.40, $p^1f(p^1) = p^2f(p^2) = 1$, and our insisting that individual demand functions must satisfy the Strong Axiom of Revealed Preference.

McFadden's counterexample demonstrates that it may be impossible to write a *given* $f(\cdot)$ as a sum of demand functions of consumers whose initial quantities add to a *specified* aggregate stock of commodites. Note, therefore, that in section 29.4.5 we took for granted that data on initial stocks of commodities did not exist. This allowed us to vary initial stocks at will in our proof of the impossibility of testing the utility hypothesis with group data.

30 Temporary Equilibria under Uncertainty

K. Arrow (Arrow 1964, pp. 91–96), G. Debreu (Debreu 1959, pp. 98–102), and R. Radner (Radner 1968, pp. 31–50) have proposed interesting theories of resource allocation under uncertainty. In this chapter we discuss Arrow's, Debreu's, and Radner's theories and demonstrate that they are based on inadequate ideas of the behavior of consumers and firms in a nondeterministic environment. I also present my own theories of consumer and entrepreneurial choice under uncertainty, and describe a production economy in which consumers and firms who behave in accordance with my axioms can function successfully.[1]

My purpose of writing this essay in speculative economics is to formulate a theoretical basis for exploring the problems of resource allocation under uncertainty that from a nomological point of view is better than the ones proposed by Arrow, Debreu, and Radner. Several of the essay's features are particularly noteworthy: (1) The theories of consumer and entrepreneurial choice presented are extensions of the theories of Arrow, Debreu, and Radner. (2) My theories pertain to agents who function in a nondeterministic environment that has many characteristics in common with the economic environment in which we live; e.g., there are markets only for currently available goods and securities, and firms produce, invest, and make decisions as to how best to finance their production-investment plans. (3) I demonstrate that fundamental theorems concerning resource allocation in a deterministic environment have no natural analogues for resource allocation in the nondeterministic environment considered here; e.g., it is possible that the economy's agents are better off (i.e., obtain a higher expected utility) in one temporary equilibrium than in another.

30.1 The Arrow-Debreu Consumer[2]

For the purpose of discussing Arrow's and Debreu's consumer we must first say what the terms "state of nature" and "event" mean.

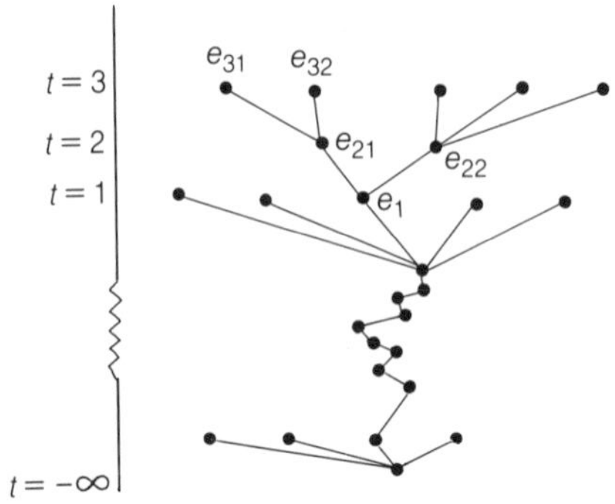

Figure 30.1

30.1.1 Nature

A *state of nature* is a description of the environment which leaves no relevant detail undescribed. It describes the environment as it was in the past, as it is in the present, and as it will be in the future. From this definition it follows that there can exist only one true state of nature. No individual living in the present, however, can know with certainty what this state is. Such an individual, even if he possessed complete knowledge of the evolution of the environment from the beginning of time through the present, could always think of an infinite number of ways in which the environment might evolve in the future; and he would have no way of knowing which was the true state of nature.

Strictly speaking, an *event* is any subset of the set of all possible states of nature. For the purpose of discussing Arrow's and Debreu's consumer, however, it suffices to think of an event as a description of the environment as it was from the beginning of time up to and including some period t. To see this, consider figure 30.1: Here e_1 represents the event that occurs in the current period; e_{21} and e_{22} represent two events that might occur in period $t = 2$; and e_{32} and e_{31}, two events that might occur in period $t = 3$, if e_{21} occurred in period $t = 2$.

30.1.2 The Consumer

Using the notion of a state of nature and an event as defined above, Arrow and Debreu construct an exceedingly simple theory of consumer choice under uncertainty. First they introduce uncertainty into their theory by characterizing all commodities and services not only in terms of their physical properties but also in terms of events. More specifically, they create a universe of commodities and services which consists of all available commodities and services multiplied by the number of events (assumed to be finite) that might occur. Next they assume that a consumer's decisions about the commodities he will consume and the services he will offer during the current and each future period within his planning horizon take the form of irrevocable purchases and sales consummated during the *current* period. Moreover, they specify that during each future period the consumer will receive—among all the commodities he has purchased—and that he will supply—among all the services he has sold—only those that correspond to the event that actually occurs during that period. Finally, they postulate that the consumer's decisions about the commodities he will consume and the services he will offer are such that they maximize his utility subject to the budget constraint he faces.

Except for the fact that Arrow's and Debreu's consumer does not know which of the many contracts he made during the current period will actually be fulfilled during future periods, the uncertainty theory of Arrow and Debreu is formally identical with the certainty theory of consumer choice which we discussed in chapter 10. Moreover, it is completely free of any explicit notion of subjective probability.

30.1.3 Markets and Expenditure Plans

As our description suggests, Arrow and Debreu are concerned about an uncertain world in which consumers trade not only in current commodities and services but also in contingent claims on future commodities and services. In the real world, however, markets for contingent claims on future goods rarely exist; for this reason the Arrow-Debreu theory will represent realistically the behavior of consumers only if the purchases and sales that an Arrow-Debreu consumer actually makes relative to each possible contingency are identical with the purchases and sales that he would plan to make under each such contingency if he were restricted to trading in current goods and in currently available securities.

For the Arrow-Debreu consumer such an identity can—superficially at least—be established. To show how, consider a consumer with a two-period planning horizon; suppose that this consumer has observed the event e_1 in the current period, and that he knows that only two events, e_{21} and e_{22}, could occur in the next period. Let q_1 denote a vector of commodities available to the consumer in the current period; let q_{21} denote a vector of commodities which would be available to him in period 2 if the event e_{21} were to obtain; and let q_{22} be defined similarly relative to the event e_{22}. In addition, let W^i, $i = 1, 2$, denote a security, each unit of which would pay a dollar in period 2 if e_{2i} were to obtain and nothing if some other event were to obtain. Finally, let p_1 denote the current price of q_1; let p_{2i}, $i = 1, 2$, denote the price of q_{2i} in the current period; and let $(1/1 + r_i)$, $i = 1, 2$, denote the current price of W^i.

Then—according to the Arrow-Debreu model—if the consumer were permitted to trade in contingent claims on future goods, he would behave during the current period as if he were attempting to choose a budget vector that would maximize a continuous, strictly increasing, strictly quasi-concave function $V(q_1, q_{21}, q_{22})$ subject to the following constraints:

$$p_1 q_1 + p_{21} q_{21} + p_{22} q_{22} \leqslant Y_1 + Y_{21} + Y_{22}, \qquad (q_1, q_{21}, q_{22}) \geqslant 0$$

where Y_1 represents the consumer's current income and Y_{2i} represents his claim on income in period 2 contingent on the event e_{2i}.

On the other hand, however, if the consumer were restricted to trading in current goods and in currently available securities, and if his price-income expectations were point expectations, he would behave during the current period as if he were attempting to maximize $V(q_1, q_{21}, q_{22})$ subject to the following contraints:

$$p_1 q_1 + \left(\frac{1}{1 + r_1}\right) W^1 + \left(\frac{1}{1 + r_2}\right) W^2 \leqslant Y_1,$$

$$p_{21}^e q_{21} \leqslant Y_{21}^e + W^1,$$

$$p_{22}^e q_{22} \leqslant Y_{22}^e + W^2,$$

and

$$(q_1, q_{21}, q_{22}) \geqslant 0, \quad W^1 \geqslant -Y_{21}^e, \quad W^2 \geqslant -Y_{22}^e,$$

where p_{2i}^e and Y_{2i}^e, respectively, denote the price and income which the consumer expects to observe in period 2 if e_{2i} obtains, $i = 1, 2$.

While the two models I have just sketched differ in form, both give identical pictures of how the consumer would behave or would plan to behave under different contingencies. Specifically, if

$$p_{2i}^e = (1 + r_i) p_{2i} \qquad \text{and} \qquad Y_{2i}^e = (1 + r_i) Y_{2i}, \qquad i = 1, 2$$

then $(q_1^0, q_{21}^0, q_{22}^0, W^{10}, W^{20})$ represents an optimal choice in the second model only if $(q_1^0, q_{21}^0, q_{22}^0)$ is an optimal choice in the first. Similarly, if $(q_1^*, q_{21}^*, q_{22}^*)$ represents an optimal allocation in the first model, then if we let $W^{1^*} = p^e_{21}q^*_{21} - Y^e_{21}$ and $W^{2^*} = p^e_{22}q^*_{22} - Y^e_{22}$, the vector $(q^*_1, q^*_{21}, q^*_{22}, W^{1^*}, W^{2^*})$ is an optimal choice in the second. Thus, if we view the two models as planning models, they are equivalent.

30.1.4 Concluding Remarks

Despite the fact that the Arrow-Debreu model represents consumer behavior well in the kind of world they consider, and despite the equivalence we have just established, a fundamentally different model is still needed. This is so because the "equivalent" model sketched out above does not adequately characterize consumer choice in a world where markets for contingent claims on future goods do not exist.

The main reason for the inadequacy of the Arrow-Debreu model of consumer choice is the following: Since the Arrow-Debreu model concerns a world in which both current and future prices are determined in the present, it need not incorporate any assumptions about how a consumer forms his expectations about future prices. In contrast, a model which purports to describe the way consumers behave when future prices are determined in future periods should provide some notion of how the consumer's expectations about future prices are determined. The "equivalent" model, however, does not do this, and so must be judged inadequate.

30.2 The Radner Consumer

A Radner consumer is an Arrow-Debreu consumer in disguise who roams around in a world slightly more complicated than the one he is used to. We shall discuss his behavior here because his disguise is so interesting.

30.2.1 Notational Matters

Radner's consumer is a consumer with a T-period planning horizon. To describe his behavior I must introduce several new terms. First, an act and a price system: Let S denote the set of states of nature and assume that $\# S < \infty$. Then an *act* is a T-tuple, $\alpha = (\alpha_1(\cdot), \ldots, \alpha_T(\cdot))$, where $\alpha_i(\cdot)\colon S \to R^n_+$, $i = 1, \ldots, T$. Moreover, a *price system* is a T-tuple, $p = (p_1(\cdot), \ldots, p_T(\cdot))$, where $p_i(\cdot)\colon S \to R^n$, $i = 1, \ldots, n$.

Next an information structure: Let a *partition* of S be a family of subsets of S, $\{A_1, \ldots, A_m\}$, such that $A_i \cap A_j = \varnothing$ if $i \neq j$ and $\bigcup_{i=1}^m A_i = S$. Then an *information structure* is a T-tuple of partitions of S, $\mathscr{S} = (\mathscr{S}_1, \ldots, \mathscr{S}_T)$.

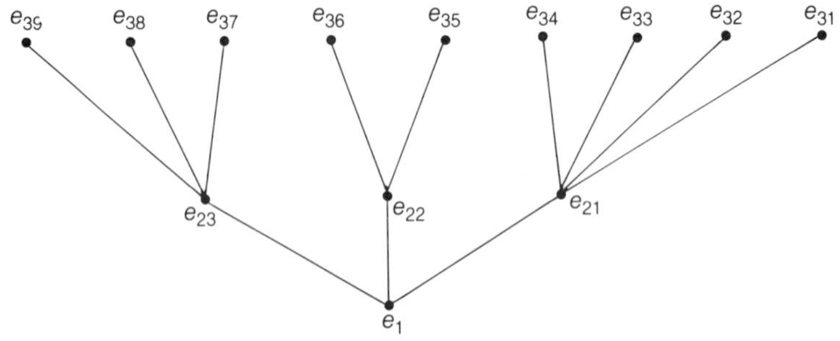

Figure 30.2

An information structure $\mathscr{S} = (\mathscr{S}_1, \ldots, \mathscr{S}_T)$ is *expanding* if and only if, for all $1 \leqslant i < j \leqslant T$, (1) $\mathscr{S}_i \neq \mathscr{S}_j$ and (2) $A \in \mathscr{S}_i$ and $B \in \mathscr{S}_j$ imply that either $B \subset A$ or $A \cap B = \varnothing$. An example of an expanding information structure is pictured in figure 30.2. There $T = 3$, $S = e_1$, and $\mathscr{S} = (\mathscr{S}_1, \mathscr{S}_2, \mathscr{S}_3)$, where $\mathscr{S}_1 = e_1$, $\mathscr{S}_2 = \{e_{21}, e_{22}, e_{23}\}$, and $\mathscr{S}_3 = \{e_{31}, \ldots, e_{39}\}$. An example of a nonexpanding information structure is $\mathscr{T} = (\mathscr{T}_1, \mathscr{T}_2, \mathscr{T}_3)$, where $\mathscr{T}_1 = e_1$, $\mathscr{T}_2 = \{e_{21}, e_{22} \cup e_{23}\}$, and $\mathscr{T}_3 = \{e_{31} \cup e_{32}, \bigcup_{i=3}^{5} e_{3i}, e_{36} \cup e_{37}, e_{38} \cup e_{39}\}$.

Finally, an act, $\alpha = (\alpha_1(\cdot), \ldots, \alpha_T(\cdot))$, is *compatible with an information structure*, $\mathscr{S} = (\mathscr{S}_1, \ldots, \mathscr{S}_T)$ if and only if, for all $1 \leqslant i \leqslant T$ and $A \in \mathscr{S}_i$, s, $s' \in A$ implies that $\alpha_i(s) = \alpha_i(s')$. We denote by $\mathscr{A}(\mathscr{S})$ the collection of all acts that are compatible with $\mathscr{S}$.

30.2.2 The Consumer

With these concepts in mind we can characterize a *Radner consumer* as a quadruple, $(\mathscr{S}, X, V(\cdot), w)$, where $\mathscr{S} = (\mathscr{S}_1, \ldots, \mathscr{S}_T)$ is an expanding information structure, $X \subset \mathscr{A}(\mathscr{S})$, $V(\cdot): X \to R$, and $w \in \mathscr{A}(\mathscr{S})$. When faced with a price system, $p = (p_1(\cdot), \ldots, p_T(\cdot))$, Radner's consumer will choose an act in X which maximizes the value of $V(\cdot)$ subject to his budget constraint,

$$\Gamma(p, w) = \left\{x \in X : \sum_{s \in S} \sum_{i=1}^{T} p_i(s) x_i(s) \leqslant \sum_{s \in S} \sum_{i=1}^{T} p_i(s) w_i(s)\right\}. \tag{30.1}$$

Radner's theory of consumer choice under uncertainty has several interesting features:

1. The consumer never forgets any information that he has received. This is so because $\mathscr{S}$ is expanding.

2. The price system, which the consumer faces, carries no information about the environment and need not be compatible with $\mathscr{S}$.

3. In searching for an optimal act, the consumer only considers acts that are compatible with his information structure. This is so because $X \subset \mathscr{A}(\mathscr{S})$.

4. The consumer's decisions about the commodities he will consume during the current and each future period within his planning horizon take the form of irrevocable purchases and/or sales consummated during the current period. These purchases and sales can vary with the state of nature but no more than is allowed by $\mathscr{S}$; i.e., if the consumer in period t will not be able to distinguish s from s', the contingent claims on t-period commodities, which he purchases in the current period, will also not distinguish between s and s'.

We criticized Arrow and Debreu's theory for involving too many markets. Judging from feature 2, the looks of $\Gamma(\cdot)$ in equation 30.1, and the first half of feature 4, Radner's theory suffers from the same defect. It is, therefore, interesting to note (see the second half of feature 4 and E 30.1 below) that the information structures which the consumers face determine how many markets an economy needs in order to achieve an optimal allocation of resources. In Arrow and Debreu's economy, consumers face the same expanding information structure. In Radner's economy, different consumers may face different information structures, and if they do, the required number of markets is reduced. This is so because "the net trade between any group of agents and the group of all other agents in the economy can at most depend upon information that is common to both groups of agents (Radner 1968, p. 50).

In the next example we illustrate the import of Radner's remark concerning the net trades of consumers facing different information structures. We also raise a fundamental question concerning the meaning of Radner's price system.

E 30.1 Let $S = \{s_1, s_2, s_3\}$ and suppose that $T = n = 1$. Moreover, let $A = (\mathscr{S}^A, X^A, V^A(\cdot), w^A)$ and $B = (\mathscr{S}^B, X^B, V^B(\cdot), w^B)$ be two consumers and assume that

$$\mathscr{S}^A = \{s_1, \{s_2, s_3\}\} \qquad \text{and} \qquad \mathscr{S}^B = \{\{s_1, s_2\}, s_3\};$$

$$X^A = R_+^3 \cap \{x \in R^3: x_2 = x_3\} \text{ and } X^B = R_+^3 \cap \{x \in R^3: x_1 = x_2\};$$

$$V^A(\cdot): X^A \to R_+ \qquad \text{and} \qquad V^B(\cdot): X^B \to R_+;$$

and

$$w^A = (1, 2, 2) \qquad \text{and} \qquad w^B = (3, 3, 1).$$

Finally, assume that, for all $x \in X^A$,

$V^A(x) = x_1^{1/2} x_2^{1/4} x_3^{1/4}$,

and for all $x \in X^B$,

$V^B(x) = x_1^{1/6} x_2^{1/6} x_3^{2/3}$.

Then consider an exchange economy populated by just A and B. A competitive equilibrium in this economy is a triple, $(\hat{p}, \hat{x}^A, \hat{x}^B)$, which satisfies the conditions

(i) $\hat{p} \in R^3$;

(ii) $\hat{x}^A \in X^A$ and $\hat{x}^B \in X^B$;

(iii) $\hat{p} \cdot \hat{x}^A \leqslant \hat{p} w^A$ and $\hat{p}\hat{x}^B \leqslant \hat{p} w^B$;

(iv) $V^A(\hat{x}^A) = \max_{x \in X^A, \hat{p}x \leqslant \hat{p}w^A} V^A(x)$ and $V^B(\hat{x}^B) = \max_{x \in X^B, \hat{p}x \leqslant \hat{p}w^B} V^B(x)$;

and

(v) $\hat{x}^A + \hat{x}^B = w^A + w^B$.

It is easy to demonstrate that if $\hat{p} = (2/3, -11/21, 6/7)$, then $(\hat{p}, w^A, w^B)$, is a competitive equilibrium in which net trades equal zero in each state of nature. In this equilibrium, consumer A "observes" the pair of prices $(\hat{p}_1 = 2/3, \hat{p}_2 + \hat{p}_3 = 1/3)$ and consumer B "observes" the prices $(\hat{p}_1 + \hat{p}_2 = 1/7, \hat{p}_3 = 6/7)$.

The negative value of $\hat{p}_2$ is disconcerting. Note, therefore, that (w^A, w^B) is a Pareto-optimal allocation of the given economy's resources; i.e., the pair $(x^A = w^A, x^B = w^B)$ satisfies two conditions:

(i) $x^A \in X^A$, $x^B \in X^B$, and $x^A + x^B = w^A + w^B$; and

(ii) there exists no pair (z^A, z^B) such that $z^A \in X^A$, $z^B \in X^B$, $z^A + z^B = w^A + w^B$ and

$V^A(z^A) \geqslant V^A(x^A)$ and $V^B(z^B) \geqslant V^B(x^B)$

with strict inequality for either A or B.

In fact, any positive initial distribution of resources which is compatible with $\mathscr{S}^A$ and $\mathscr{S}^B$ represents a Pareto-optimal allocation of the resulting economy's resources. This is a reflection of the fact that in equilibrium net trades between A and B can "at most depend upon information that is common" to A and B.

We do not know what it means in E 30.1 that $-11/21$ is an equilibrium price of x_2 when the utility functions of A and B are strictly increasing in x_2. We also do not understand what it means that in equilibrium A faces the price pair $(\hat{p}_1 = 2/3, \hat{p}_2 + \hat{p}_3 = 1/3)$ and B faces the price pair $(\hat{p}_1 + \hat{p}_2 = 1/6, \hat{p}_3 = 6/7)$. It looks like there is something fundamentally wrong with the role of prices in Radner's theory.

30.2.3 Markets and Expenditure Plans

Although we cannot understand Radner's price system, we can construct a different theory which both makes sense and becomes equivalent to

Radner's theory when we reinterpret his as a theory of consumer choice of optimal expenditure plans. In the "equivalent" theory the terms "act," "price system," "information structure," and "$\mathscr{A}(\mathscr{S})$" mean the same as in Radner's theory. In addition, an *expenditure sequence* is a T-tuple,

$$(x, W) = ((x_1, W_1)(\cdot), \ldots, (x_{T-1}, W_{T-1})(\cdot), x_T(\cdot)),$$

where $x_i(\cdot): S \to R_+^n$, $i = 1, \ldots, T$, and $W_i(\cdot): S \to R$, $i = 1, \ldots, T-1$; an *expected price system* is a T-tuple,

$$(p^e, \beta^e) = ((p_1, \beta_1), (p_2^e, \beta_2^e)(\cdot), \ldots, (p_{T-1}^e, \beta_{T-1}^e)(\cdot), p_T^e(\cdot)),$$

where $(p_1, \beta_1) > 0$, $p_i^e(\cdot): S \to R_{++}^n$, $i = 2, \ldots, T$, and $\beta_i^e(\cdot): S \to R_{++}$, $i = 2, \ldots, T-1$; and a *consumer* is a quintuple,

$$(\mathscr{S}, X, V(\cdot), w, (p^e, \beta^e)), \tag{30.2}$$

where $\mathscr{S} = (\mathscr{S}_1, \ldots, \mathscr{S}_T)$ is an expanding information structure; $X \subset \mathscr{A}(\mathscr{S})$; $V(\cdot): X \to R$; $w \in \mathscr{A}(\mathscr{S})$; and (p^e, β^e) is an expected price system which is compatible with $\mathscr{S}$. We assume that $V(\cdot)$ is continuous, strictly increasing, and strictly quasi-concave and insist that the consumer is to choose an expenditure sequence (x, W) which maximizes the value of $V(\cdot)$ subject to the following conditions:

(i) (x, W) is compatible with $\mathscr{S}$.
(ii) $x \in X$.
(iii) for all $s \in S$, (x, W) satisfies the inequalities

$$p_1 x_1(s) + \beta_1 W_1(s) \leqslant p_1 w_1(s),$$

$$p_i^e(s) x_i(s) + \beta_i^e(s) W_i(s) \leqslant p_i^e(s) w_i(s) + W_{i-1}(s), \qquad i = 2, \ldots, T-1,$$

and

$$p_T^e x_T(s) \leqslant p_T^e w_T(s) + W_{T-1}(s).$$

In the intended interpretation of this theory, $x_i(s)$ is a commodity vector; $W_i(s)$ is a contingent claim on the $(i+1)$-period unit of account; p_1 and β_1 denote the prices of x_1 and W_1 which the consumer faces in the first period; and $p_i^e(s)$ and $\beta_i^e(s)$ denote the prices of $x_i(s)$ and $W_i(s)$ which the consumer expects to face in period i. Moreover, if (x^0, W^0) maximizes $V(\cdot)$ subject to conditions i–iii and if the consumer observes the event $A \in \mathscr{S}_1$, we suppose that he will purchase the components of $(x_1^0, W_1^0)(s)$ and plan to purchase $(x_i^0, W_i^0)(s)$ if $s \in B$, $B \in \mathscr{S}_i$, $B \subset A$ and B were to happen in period i. In this respect, note that $(x_1^0, W_1^0)(s)$ does not vary with $s \in A$ and $(x_i^0, W_i^0)(s)$ does not vary with $s \in B$.

To establish the equivalence of the preceding theory and Radner's theory, we first let

$$(\mathscr{S}, X, V(\cdot), w)$$

be the Radner alias of the consumer in equation 30.2. Next we use (p^e, β^e) to define a price system $\hat{p} = (\hat{p}_1(\cdot), \ldots, \hat{p}_T(\cdot))$ by the relations

$$\hat{p}_1(s) = p_1 \qquad \text{and} \qquad \hat{p}_i(s) = \beta_1\left(\prod_{j=2}^{i-1} \beta_j^e(s)\right)p_i^e(s), \qquad i = 2, \ldots, T.$$

Then $\hat{p}$ is compatible with $\mathscr{S}$ and satisfies the conditions

$$\hat{p}_i(\cdot)\colon S \to R_{++}^n.$$

Finally, we let $p = (p_1(\cdot), \ldots, p_T(\cdot))$ be a price system which satisfies the condition

$$\text{for all } A \in \mathscr{S}_i \quad \text{and} \quad \tilde{s} \in A,\ (\# A)^{-1} \sum_{s \in A} p_i(s) = \hat{p}_i(\tilde{s}), \quad i = 1, \ldots, T. \tag{30.3}$$

Then the equivalence of the two theories can be summarized as follows:

If (x^0, W^0) maximizes $V(\cdot)$ subject to conditions i–iii, then x^0 maximizes the value of $V(\cdot)$ subject to the following conditions:

1. $x \in X$.

2. $\sum_{s \in S} \sum_{i=1}^{T} p_i(s)x_i(s) \leqslant \sum_{s \in S} \sum_{i=1}^{T} p_i(s)w_i(s)$.

Conversely, if $x^* \in X$ maximizes the value of $V(\cdot)$ subject to conditions 1 and 2 above, then there is a $W^* = (W_1^*(\cdot), \ldots, W_{T-1}^*(\cdot))$ such (x^*, W^*) is an expenditure sequence which maximizes the value of $V(\cdot)$ subject to the first set of conditions, i–iii.

The preceding equivalence is similar to the equivalence we exhibited in our discussion of Arrow and Debreu's theory. It is also similar to the equivalence described in T 14.11. For brevity's sake I leave the proof to the reader.

30.2.4 Concluding Remarks

As we judge the import of this equivalence, several facts are significant. The consumer's price expectations in equation (30.2) are positive point expectations with respect to the state of nature and compatible with the consumer's information structure. The price system in equation (30.3) need not be positive and need not be compatible with $\mathscr{S}$. The equivalence demonstrates that these characteristics of p need not concern us when we interpret Radner's theory as a theory of consumer choice of optimal expenditure *plans*. However, it is another matter when p surfaces as a general equilibrium price of a well-defined exchange economy in which the consumers' utility functions are increasing, strictly quasi-concave, continuous functions (as in E 29.1). Then the equivalence does not dispel our qualms about the properties of p.

30.3 Consumer Choice under Uncertainty

In this section I shall present a theory of consumer choice under uncertainty that is similar to Radner's theory in some respects and differs in others. Specifically, as in Radner's theory, our consumer never forgets information that he receives and he searches for an optimal act among the acts that are compatible with his information structure. Unlike the consumer in Radner's theory, our consumer receives information from the prices he faces and in each period he trades only in currently available commodities and securities and not in contingent claims on future commodities. I demonstrate in the discussion of the axioms that my theory is a natural extension of Radner's to a world in which consumers trade only in currently available commodities and securities and entertain price expectations that are multivalued with respect to the states of nature.

30.3.1 Definitional Axioms

My axioms for consumer choice concern many undefined terms: *the world*, a *commodity bundle*, a *security bundle*, a *share bundle*, a *price system*, *dividends*, a *consumer*, an *expenditure sequence*, and a *consumption-investment strategy*. These terms are described in the first eight axioms of my axiom system.

CBS 1 The world is an experiment, $(\Omega, \mathscr{F})$, where $\mathscr{F}$ is a σ field.

CBS 2 A commodity bundle is a vector, $x \in \bigcup_{i=1}^{M} (R_+^n \times R_-)^i$, where $R_- = \{r \in R : r \leqslant 0\}$. When $x \in (R_+^n \times R_-)^i$, we often write x as an i-tuple of pairs,

$((q, L)(1), \ldots, (q, L)(i))$,

where $q \in R_+^n$ is a commodity vector, $L \in R_-$ denotes units of labor, and $(q, L)(j)$ is a commodity-service vector for period j, $j = 1, \ldots, i$.

CBS 3 A security bundle is a vector, $\mu \in R^k$.

CBS 4 A share bundle is a vector, $m \in R_+^l$.

CBS 5 Let $T = \{1, 2, \ldots\}$. Then a price system is a vector-valued function,

$(p_q, w, \alpha, p_m)(\cdot) : T \times \Omega \to R^n_{++} \times R_{++} \times R^k_{++} \times R^l_{++}.$

Moreover, dividends is a vector-valued function

$d(\cdot) : T \times \Omega \to R^l_{+}.$

Finally, for all $t \in T$, $\mathscr{F}((p_q, w, \alpha, p_m, d)(t)) \subset \mathscr{F}$.

CSB 6 A consumer is a 6-tuple,

$$(X, V, A, Q, \xi, (N_L, N_\mu)), \tag{30.4}$$

where

(i) $X = \bigcup_{i=1}^{M} ((R^n_+ \times R_-)^i \times R)$;

(ii) $V(\cdot) : X \to R$;

(iii) $A(\cdot) : \Omega \to R_{++}$ and $\mathscr{F}(A) \subset \mathscr{F}$;

(iv) $Q(\cdot) : \mathscr{F} \to [0, 1]$ is a σ-additive probability measure;

(v) $\xi(\cdot) : \Omega \to \{1, \ldots, M\}$ and $\mathscr{F}(\xi) \subset \mathscr{F}$;

(vi) $(N_L, N_\mu)(\cdot) : T \times \Omega \to R_{++} \times R^k_{++}$ and, for all $t \in T$, $\mathscr{F}((N_L, N_\mu)(t)) \subset \mathscr{F}$.

CBS 7 An expenditure sequence is a vector-valued function,

$(q, L, \mu, m)(\cdot) : \{1, \ldots, M\} \times \Omega \to R^n_+ \times R_- \times R^k \times R^l_+,$

which, for all $t \in \{1, \ldots, M\}$, satisfies the following conditions:

(i) $\mathscr{F}((q, L, \mu, m)(t)) \subset \mathscr{F}(A, (p_q, w, \alpha, p_m, d, N_L, N_\mu)(s), 1 \leqslant s \leqslant t, I_{\geqslant t}(\xi))$, where $I_{\geqslant t}(\xi)$ is a random variable which assumes the values 1 or 0 according as $\xi \geqslant t$ or $\xi < t$.

(ii) On the set $\{\omega \in \Omega : \xi(\omega) \leqslant t\}$,

$$(q, L, \mu, m)(s, \omega) = 0, \qquad s = t + 1, \ldots, M.$$

(iii) On the set $\{\omega \in \Omega : \xi(\omega) = t\}$,

a. $$p_q(1, \omega)q(1, \omega) + w(1, \omega)L(1, \omega) + \alpha(1, \omega)\mu(1, \omega) + p_m(1, \omega)m(1, \omega) \leqslant A(\omega);$$

b. for $1 < s \leqslant t$,

$$p_q(s, \omega)q(s, \omega) + w(s, \omega)L(s, \omega) + \alpha(s, \omega)\mu(s, \omega) + p_m(s, \omega)m(s, \omega)$$
$$\leqslant \mu_1(s - 1, \omega) + \sum_{j=1}^{k-1} \alpha_j(s, \omega)\mu_{j+1}(s - 1, \omega)$$
$$+ (p_m + d)(s, \omega)m(s - 1, \omega);$$

c. for $1 \leqslant s \leqslant t$,

$$-N_L(s, \omega) \leqslant L(s, \omega) \quad \text{and} \quad -M_\mu(s, \omega) \leqslant \mu(s, \omega).$$

CSB 8 For all $i = 1, \ldots, M$, let $U_i(\cdot)$: $(R_+^n \times R_-)^i \times R \to R$ be defined by

$$U_i(x, y) = V(x, y), \qquad x \in (R_+^n \times R_-)^i,\ y \in R. \tag{30.5}$$

Then a consumption-investment strategy is an expenditure sequence, $(q, L, \mu, m)(\cdot)$, such that if $(q^*, L^*, \mu^*, m^*)(\cdot)$ is any other expenditure sequence, then

$$\begin{aligned}
&\sum_{\xi=1}^{M} E\Big\{U_\xi\Big[(q, L)(1, \omega), \ldots, (q, L)(\xi, \omega), \mu_1(\xi, \omega) + \sum_{j=1}^{k-1} \alpha_j(\xi + 1, \omega)\mu_{j+1}(\xi, \omega) \\
&\quad + (p_m + d)(\xi + 1, \omega)m(\xi, \omega)\Big] \Big| A, (p_q, w, \alpha, p_m, d, N_L, N_\mu)(1), \xi(\omega) = \xi\Big\} \\
&\qquad \times Q\Big(\{\omega \in \Omega : \xi(\omega) = \xi\} \Big| A, (p_q, w, \alpha, p_m, d, N_L, N_\mu)(1)\Big) \\
&\geqslant \sum_{\xi=1}^{M} E\Big\{U_\xi\Big[(q^*, L^*)(1, \omega), \ldots, (q^*, L^*)(\xi, \omega), \mu_1^*(\xi, \omega) + \sum_{j=1}^{k-1} \alpha_j(\xi + 1, \omega)\mu_{j+1}^*(\xi, \omega) \\
&\quad + (p_m + d)(\xi + 1, \omega)m^*(\xi, \omega)\Big] \Big| A, (p_1, w, \alpha, p_m, d, N_L, N_\mu)(1), \xi(\omega) = \xi\Big\} \\
&\qquad \times Q\Big(\{\omega \in \Omega : \xi(\omega) = \xi\} \Big| A, (p_q, w, \alpha, p_m, d, N_L, N_\mu)(1)\Big).
\end{aligned}$$

30.3.2 The Intended Interpretation

The preceding axioms call for several comments. First, the state of nature: A *state of nature* is a description of the environment as it was in the past, as it is in the present, and as it will be in the future. In the preceding axioms, the environment is represented by the triple $(A, \xi, \{(N_L, N_\mu)(t, \omega); t \in T\})$. Hence in the intended interpretation of the axioms, a state of nature is a description of (1) the consumer's initial claim on first-period units of account, $A(\omega)$, (2) the period in which the consumer will die, $\xi(\omega)$, and (3) the values of the institutional constraints, $(N_L, N_\mu)(t, \omega)$, which the consumer will face in the labor and loan markets in period t, $t = 1, 2, \ldots$.

Next, the world: A *state of the world* is an $\omega \in \Omega$. In the intended interpretation of the axioms, a state of the world is a complete description (i.e., one that leaves no relevant details undescribed) of the world as it was in the past, as it is in the present, and as it will be in the future. We assume that a description of the world describes the state of nature and the values of prices and dividends in all relevant periods. However, the state of the world does not describe the actions of individual consumers in the economy.

Then *price expectations*: To say that a consumer has expectations concerning what the price of a particular commodity might be in each period under every set of circumstances that might occur is, in the context of the preceding axioms, equivalent to saying that, for each t, there exists a function $p(t, \omega) : \Omega \to R_{++}$ such that $p(t, \omega)$ represents the price which the consumer believes this commodity would assume in period t if the true state of the world were ω. Since we intend that the description of the world associated with ω specify the value of the price assumed by the given commodity in each and every period, the value of $p(t, \cdot)$ at ω must necessarily coincide with the value of this price specified in the description of the world.

As suggested by the preceding remarks, in the intended interpretation of the axioms the consumer's price expectations are point expectations with respect to the state of the world and multivalued with respect to the state of nature. These price expectations do not appear in our description of "a consumer," equation 30.4, as they did in equation 30.2. The place of (p^e, β^e) has been taken by $Q(\cdot)$, which in the intended interpretation of the axioms represents the consumer's subjective probability measure on $(\Omega, \mathscr{F})$.

Finally, *expenditure sequences*: These sequences describe possible sequences of acquisitions of commodities and securities that both satisfy the consumer's budget constraint and are compatible with the consumer's information structure. Except for differences in information structures, an expenditure sequence in CBS 1–CBS 8 is like an expenditure sequence in the modified version of Radner's theory which we discussed above.

Here is an example to help our intuition about the meaning of the axioms:

E 30.2 Let $M = 3$, $X = \bigcup_{i=1}^{3} (R_+^i \times R)$, $k = 1$, $l = 0$, $\Omega = \{\omega_1, \ldots, \omega_8\}$, and $\mathscr{F} = \mathscr{P}(\Omega)$. Then suppose that $A(\omega) = 50$ for all $\omega \in \Omega$, and that the ranges of $\xi(\cdot)$ and $(p_q, \alpha, N_\mu)(t, \cdot)$, $t = 1, 2, 3$, are as specified in table 30.1. Moreover, suppose that the $U_i(\cdot)$ in equation 30.5 are given by

Table 30.1

ω	$(p, \alpha, N_\mu)(1, \cdot)$	$(p, \alpha, N_\mu)(2, \cdot)$	$(p, \alpha, N_\mu)(3, \cdot)$	$\xi(\cdot)$
ω_1	(1, 0.9, 10)	(1.1, 0.8, 12.5)	(1.2, 0.85, 15)	1
ω_2	(1, 0.9, 10)	(1.1, 0.8, 12.5)	(1, 0.9, 15)	1
ω_3	(1, 0.9, 10)	(1.1, 0.8, 12.5)	(1, 0.95, 15)	1
ω_4	(1, 0.9, 10)	(1.1, 0.9, 11.5)	(1.2, 0.9, 16)	2
ω_5	(1, 0.9, 10)	(1.1, 0.9, 11.5)	(1.2, 0.75, 16)	2
ω_6	(1, 0.9, 10)	(1.1, 0.9, 11.5)	(1.2, 0.75, 16)	3
ω_7	(1, 0.9, 10)	(0.905, 1, 12)	(0.85, 1.1, 14)	3
ω_8	(1, 0.9, 10)	(0.905, 1, 12)	(1, 0.95, 14)	3

$$U_1(x, y) = (1 + x)^{1/8}(2.855 + y)^{3/8}, \qquad x \in R_+, y \geqslant -2.855;$$

$$U_2(x, y) = (1 + x_1)^{1/8}(1 + x_2)^{1/8}(1.95 + y)^{1/4}, \qquad x \in R_+^2, y \geqslant -1.95;$$

and

$$U_3(x, y) = (1 + x_1)^{1/8}(1 + x_2)^{1/8}(1 + x_3)^{1/8}(1 + y)^{1/8}, \qquad x \in R_+^3, y \geqslant -1.$$

Finally, suppose that $Q(\cdot)$ is a probability measure on $(\Omega, \mathscr{F})$ that assigns the values given in table 30.2 to the various states of the world.

In this example there are four states of nature, $s_1 = \{\omega_1, \omega_2, \omega_3\}$, $s_2 = \{\omega_4, \omega_5\}$, $s_3 = \{\omega_6\}$, and $s_4 = \{\omega_7, \omega_8\}$. Moreover, the consumer faces the information structure exhibited in figure 30.3, where e_{ij} is an event that might occur in period i, $i = 1, 2, 3$. Finally, the main characteristics of expenditure sequences are displayed in the equations below, where we record the consumer's consumption-investment strategy.

$$(q, \mu)(1, \omega) = (12.392375, 41.78625) \quad \text{for all } \omega \in \Omega.$$

$$(q, \mu)(2, \omega) = \begin{cases} (15.442449, 27.810833) & \text{if } \omega \in e_{21}; \\ (12.527652, 31.117593) & \text{if } \omega \in e_{22}; \text{ and} \\ (0, 0) & \text{if } \omega \in e_{23}. \end{cases}$$

$$(q, \mu)(3, \omega) = \begin{cases} (13.880417, 14.663596) & \text{if } \omega \in e_{31}; \\ (16.506372, 12.527651) & \text{if } \omega \in e_{32}; \\ (12.778164, 21.045062) & \text{if } \omega \in e_{33}; \text{ and} \\ (0, 0) & \text{if } \omega \in e_{23} \cup e_{34}. \end{cases}$$

Table 30.2

$\{\omega\}$	$\{\omega_1\}$	$\{\omega_2\}$	$\{\omega_3\}$	$\{\omega_4\}$	$\{\omega_5\}$	$\{\omega_6\}$	$\{\omega_7\}$	$\{\omega_8\}$
$Q(\{\omega\})$	1/18	1/18	1/18	1/9	1/9	4/9	1/12	1/12

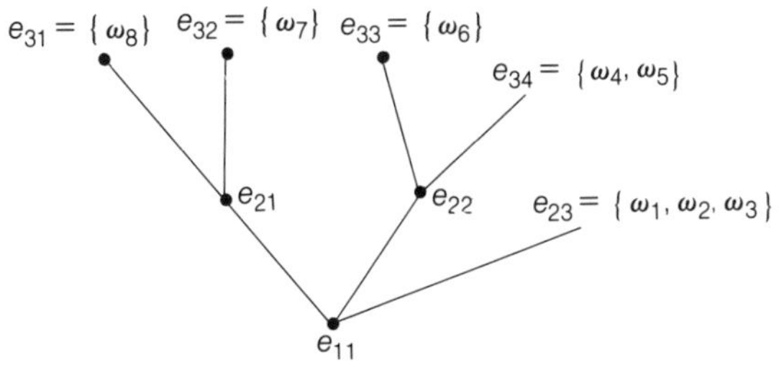

Figure 30.3

30.3.3 Axioms concerning the Properties of $V(\cdot)$ and $Q(\cdot)$

Faced with a vector $(A, (p_q, w, \alpha, p_m, d, N_L, N_\mu)(1))$ and knowing that $\xi \geqslant 1$, the consumer determines his consumption-investment strategy and goes to the market to acquire the corresponding vector $(q, L, \mu, m)(1)$. In order to be sure that the consumer has a consumption-investment strategy, we must introduce more axioms. First, $V(\cdot)$:

CBS 9 $V(\cdot)$ is strictly increasing and bounded above on X. Moreover, for each $i = 1, \ldots, M$, $V(\cdot)$ is continuous and strictly concave on $(R_+^n \times R_-)^i \times R$.

Next, $Q(\cdot)$: In stating the axioms for $Q(\cdot)$, we let

$$\gamma(t, \omega) = ((p_q, w, \alpha, p_m, d, N_L, N_\mu)(1, \omega), \ldots, (p_q, w, \alpha, p_m, d, N_L, N_\mu)(t, \omega)),$$
$$t = 1, 2, \ldots. \tag{30.6}$$

Moreover, for a random variable x and a random vector y, $Q\{x \in A | y \in B\}$ $(Q(x \in A|y))$ and $E\{x|y \in B\}$ $(E(x|y))$ denote, respectively, the conditional probability that x in A and the conditional expectation of x (with respect to $Q(\cdot)$) given that $y \in B$ (with respect to $\mathscr{F}(y)$).

CBS 10 For each $t = 1, \ldots, M$,

(i) $Q\{\{\omega \in \Omega : \xi(\omega) = t\} | A, \gamma(1)\} > 0$; and

(ii) $$Q\left\{\left\{\omega \in \Omega : N_{\mu_1}(t, \omega) + \sum_{i=1}^{k-1} \alpha_i(t+1, \omega) N_{\mu_{i+1}}(t, \omega) \leqslant w(t+1, \omega) N_L(t+1, \omega) + \alpha(t+1, \omega) N_\mu(t+1, \omega)\right\} \middle| A, \gamma(t), \xi \geqslant t\right\} = 1.$$

CBS 11 Let $R_a^k = \{r \in R^k : r \geqslant a\}$ and, for $t = 1, \ldots, M$, let $h_t(\cdot)$ be a bounded, continuous, real-valued function on the set

$$\{(s, A, \gamma(t), x, \mu, m) \in \{1, \ldots, M\} \times \{\text{range of } (A, \gamma(t))\} \times (R_+^n \times R_-)^t \times R^k \times R_+^l : \mu \geqslant -N_\mu(t)\},$$

and let

$$g_t(\cdot): \{\text{range of } (A, \gamma(t+1))\} \times (R_+^n \times R_-)^t \times R \to R$$

be a bounded, continuous function. Then, for each t,

(i) the ranges of $A(\cdot)$ and $\gamma(t, \cdot)$ are independent of the value of $\xi(\cdot)$;

(ii) there exists a version of

$$E\{h_t(\xi, A, \gamma(t), (q, L)(1), \ldots, (q, L)(t), \mu, m) | A, \gamma(t), \xi \geqslant t\}$$

which is a continuous function of $(A, \gamma(t), (q, L)(1), \ldots, (q, L)(t), \mu, m)$; and

(iii) there exists a version of

$$E\left\{g_t\left[A, \gamma(t+1), (q, L)(1), \ldots, (q, L)(t), \mu_1 + \sum_{j=1}^{k-1} \alpha_j(t+1)\mu_{j+1} + (p_m + d)(t+1)m\right] \Bigg| A, \gamma(t), \xi\right\},$$

which, for each value of $\xi \in \{t, \ldots, M\}$, is a continuous function of $(A, \gamma(t), (q, L)(1), \ldots, (q, L)(t), \mu, m)$.

CBS 12 The probability distribution induced by $(1, (\alpha_1, \ldots, \alpha_{k-1}), (p_m + d))(t+1, \cdot))$ and $Q\{\cdot | A, \gamma(t), \xi = t\}$ is nondegenerate, $t = 1, \ldots, M$.

In the intended interpretation of the axioms, axioms CBS 9 and CBS 11 and CBS 12 can be viewed as the uncertainty version of the sixth axioms in T(H 1, ..., H 6). Thus CBS 9 specifies that the consumer's utility function in T(CBS 1, ..., CBS 12) has properties analogous to the properties of the utility function in T(H 1, ..., H 6) and CBS 11 and CBS 12 insist that consumer's expectations vary continuously with the information he possesses. As to CBS 10, it declares that the consumer is convinced that he might die during any one of the periods $t = 1, \ldots, M$ and that he believes his creditors will never force him into bankruptcy.

When $V(\cdot)$ and $Q(\cdot)$ satisfy the axioms CBS 9–CBS 12, we can demonstrate that there exists a consumption-investment strategy for each value of $(A, (p_q, w, \alpha, p_m, d, N_L, N_\mu)(1))$. That is, we have T 30.1:

T 30.1 If CBS 1–CBS 12 are valid, then for each value of A and $(p_q, w, \alpha, p_m, d, N_L, N_\mu)(1)$, there is a consumption-investment strategy.

A review of E 30.2 suffices to ascertain that our axioms are consistent. Hence the assertion of T 30.1 is not vacuous. We sketch a proof of the theorem in the appendix (section 30.7.1).

30.3.4 The Fundamental Theorem of Consumer Choice under Uncertainty

We have demonstrated that the axioms CBS 1–CBS 12 are consistent and that there exists a consumption-investment strategy for all values of the vector $(A, \gamma(1))$. However, this does not mean that our axioms necessarily can be used as a basis for an empirical analysis of consumer behavior. To show that they can, I shall next establish what may justly be called the *fundamental theorem* of my theory of consumer choice under uncertainty:

T 30.2 Let $\gamma(\cdot)$ be as defined in equation 30.6 and suppose that CBS 1–CBS 12 are valid. Then there exists a continuous, real-valued function, $\tilde{V}(\cdot)$, on the set

$\{(A, \gamma(1), q, L, \mu, m) \in \{\text{range of } (A, \gamma(1))\} \times R_+^n \times R_- \times R^k \times R_+^l : \mu \geqslant -N_\mu\}$,

which for each value of $(A, \gamma(1))$ satisfies the conditions:

(i) $\tilde{V}(A, \gamma(1), \cdot)$ is a strictly increasing, strictly concave function on $R_+^n \times R_- \times R_{-N_\mu(1)}^k \times R_+^l$; and

(ii) the consumer can determine the $(q, L, \mu, m)(1)$ component of his consumption-investment strategy by setting it equal to the (q, L, μ, m) vector which maximizes the value of $\tilde{V}(A, \gamma(1), \cdot)$ subject to the conditions

$p_q(1)q + w(1)L + \alpha(1)\mu + p_m(1)m \leqslant A;$

and

$(q, L, \mu, m) \in R_+^n \times (R_{-N_L(1)} \cap R_-) \times R_{-N_\mu(1)}^k \times R_+^l.$

This theorem is an analogue of T 14.11. Since proving it is an involved process, I relegate the proof to the appendix (section 30.71).

To determine the main empirical implications of T 30.2, I record a simple analogue of T 10.5:

T 30.3 If CBS 1–CBS 12 are valid, there exists a continuous function,

$(q, L, \mu, m)(\cdot)$: $\{\text{range of } (A, \gamma(1))\} \to R_+^n \times R_- \times R^k \times R_+^l$,

which, for each value of $(A, \gamma(1))$, satisfies the conditions:

(i) $(q, L, \mu, m)(\lambda(A, (p_q, w, \alpha, p_m)(1)), (N_L, N_\mu)(1)) = (q, L, \mu, m)(A, \gamma(1)), \lambda > 0;$

(ii) $(p_q, w, \alpha, p_m)(1)(q, L, \mu, m)(A, \gamma(1)) = A$; and

(iii) $\tilde{V}(A, \gamma(1), (q, L, \mu, m)(A, \gamma(1))) = \max_{x \in \Gamma(A, \gamma(1))} \tilde{V}(A, \gamma(1), x),$

where

$$\Gamma(A, \gamma(1)) = \{x \in R_+^n \times (R_{-N_L(1)} \cap R_-) \times R_{-N_\mu(1)}^k \times R_+^l : (p_q, w, \alpha, p_m)(1)x \leqslant A\}.$$

With some obvious modifications, the proof of T 30.3 is almost like the proof of T 10.5. The only thing we need to add is the observation that the conditional distribution of $(p_q, w, \alpha, p_m, d, N_L, N_\mu)(t, \cdot)$, $t \geqslant 2$, on $\mathscr{F}(A, (p_q, w, \alpha, p_m, d, N_L, N_\mu)(1), I_{\geqslant 1}(\xi))$ is invariant under changes in the current-period unit of account. Hence $\tilde{V}(\cdot)$ is invariant under changes in the current-period unit of account.

The two preceding theorems demonstrate that $(q, L, \mu, m)(\cdot)$ is the consumer's demand function for q, L, μ, and m in the first period. This function has several interesting properties:

1. In the intended interpretation of the axioms, $(q, L, \mu, m)(\cdot)$ is a function of parameters whose values are observable. Hence the demand function

of our consumer can be used as a basis for an econometric analysis of consumer choice under uncertainty.

2. $(q, L, \mu, m)(\cdot)$ satisfies neither the Strong nor the Weak Axiom of Revealed Preference. Therefore, in the intended interpretation of the axioms, the consistency of our consumer's market behavior cannot be tested by the Strong (or Weak) Axiom of Revealed Preference.

The reason property 2 is true is simple: The first-period prices (i.e., current price) of q, L, μ, and m are components of $\gamma(1)$. As current prices change, $\gamma(1)$ changes, and as $\gamma(1)$ changes, the consumer's ordering of first-period budget vectors also changes.

3. $(q, L, \mu, m)(\cdot)$ does not satisfy Samuelson's fundamental theorem of consumer choice, T 10.16. Hence, in the intended interpretation of the axioms, it is not sufficient to consult our consumer's Engel curves to determine whether he will respond to a fall in the price of a commodity by buying more of that commodity.

To demonstrate the validity of property 3 it suffices to observe that our consumer's response to a change in the price of a commodity or security can be analyzed as a sum of three different effects. First, there is the *substitution effect*. It determines how the consumer would react to a price change if (1) his expectations (i.e., if the $(A, \gamma(1))$ argument of $\tilde{V}(\cdot)$) were not allowed to change and if (2) his initial net worth were adjusted so that he could maintain the same level of expected utility after the price change as before. Then there is the *income effect* which determines the reaction of the consumer when we undo the net-worth compensation but keep expectations constant. Finally, there is the *expectation effect*, which determines the consumer's response when we at last remove the lid on his expectations. Since $\tilde{V}(A, \gamma(1), \cdot)$ is increasing and strictly concave, the substitution effect is always negative. The signs of the other two effects, however, are indeterminate. Only if *both* signs are positive can we be sure that our consumer would respond to a fall in the price of a commodity by buying more of that commodity.

30.3.5 Concluding Remarks

It follows easily from our discussion in sections 30.3.1–30.3.3 that our theory of consumer choice under uncertainty is an extension of Radner's theory to a world in which consumers trade only in currently available commodities and securities and entertain price expectations that are multivalued with respect to the states of nature. It is also clear from our discussion in section (30.3.4) that T(CBS 1–CBS 12) is an extension of T(A 1–A 7). In that respect, one last remark is in order.

An Arrow consumer's ordering of (μ, m) pairs differs in two ways from our consumer's ordering of (q, L, μ, m) vectors. First, the utility function $V(\cdot)$ of an Arrow consumer is a function of (μ, m) and not of the current-period prices of μ and m, $(1, a)$. Second, $V(\cdot)$ can be written as an integral; that is, $V(\mu, m) = EU(\mu + mr)$. In contrast, $\tilde{V}(\cdot)$ is a function of $(A, \gamma(1))$ as well as (q, L, μ, m). Moreover, it is, in general, impossible to write $\tilde{V}(A, \gamma(1), q, L, \cdot)$ as an integral of a function of the consumer's second-period net worth. The latter fact, which can be substantiated by a careful perusal of the proof of T 30.2, prevents us from giving a meaningful definition of an absolute and a proportional risk-aversion function in the present axiom system and hence from establishing analogues of T 12.6–T 12.9.

30.4 The Arrow-Debreu Producer

In the next section I shall develop a theory of entrepreneurial choice under uncertainty. My theory is an extension of the Arrow-Debreu theory of the perfectly competitive firm which Debreu presents in chapters 3 and 7 of his *Theory of Value* (Debreu 1959, pp. 37–49 and pp. 98–102). Arrow and Debreu's theory has several shortcomings, which I detail below.

The standard theory of choice under certainty views the firm as a closed convex subset of R^n which exhibits all feasible ways of combining inputs to produce various outputs. The firm is owned by consumers who insist that the manager of the firm—the producer—choose the input-output combination which maximizes the firm's profits. All profits are distributed to the owners.

In an Arrow-Debreu uncertainty economy, a firm is a closed convex subset of R^N, where $N = n \cdot \{\text{number of possible events}\}$. Like the certainty firm, Arrow and Debreu's firm is owned by consumers who insist that the manager of the firm choose the inputs and outputs that maximize the firm's profits and distribute all profits to them. Moreover, all decisions about current and future inputs and outputs take the form of irrevocable purchases and sales consummated during the current period. Unlike the certainty firm, the Arrow-Debreu uncertainty firm deals both in currently available inputs and outputs and in contingent claims on future inputs and outputs. The contingent claims specify that during each future period the firm will receive—among all the inputs it has purchased—and that it will supply—among all the goods it has sold—only those that correspond to the event that actually occurs during the period.

While a superficial equivalence can be established between the Arrow-Debreu consumer theory—seen as a theory of choice of expenditure plans—and a theory of consumer choice in a world in which the consumer can trade only in current goods and currently available securities, no similar equivalence can be established for the Arrow-Debreu uncertainty theory of the firm. This lack of equivalence is to be explained by the fact that if an Arrow-Debreu producer were to incur a funds deficit during the current period, he would in general have no meaningful basis for choosing what securities he should issue in order to cover this deficit. Similarly, if he were to incur a funds surplus, he would have no meaningful basis for choosing what securities he should buy in order to absorb this surplus. To enable the Arrow-Debreu producer to make such choices, we would have to provide him (through the introduction of a new function) with risk preferences and expectations as to the likelihood of different future events.

To show why the preceding observations are valid, we consider a manager of a privately owned firm with a two-period planning horizon. Suppose that the producer has observed the event e_1 in the current period and that he knows that only two events, e_{21} and e_{22}, could occur in the next period. Suppose also that his firm in each period produces one output y, using one fixed factor of production K and one variable factor L, according to an instantaneous point-input–point-output production function $g(\cdot)$: $R_+^2 \to R_+$. Finally, suppose that (1) K does not depreciate; (2) the firm cannot store its output from one period to the next; and (3) during period 1 the firm can buy units of K, denoted I, but it cannot sell old units of K.

If we denote the current prices of y, L, and I by p_1, w_1, and p_I and the (current) second-period prices of Y and L by p_{2i} and w_{2i}, $i = 1, 2$, then in an Arrow-Debreu uncertainty economy the manager of the firm will choose a production plan,

$$(\tilde{I}, \tilde{L}_1, \tilde{y}_1, \tilde{L}_{12}, \tilde{y}_{12}, \tilde{L}_{22}, \tilde{y}_{22}), \tag{30.7}$$

which maximizes the value of

$$\{p_1 y_1 - w_1 L_1 - p_I I\} + \{p_{21} y_{21} - w_{21} L_{21}\} + \{p_{22} y_{22} - w_{22} L_{22}\} \tag{30.8}$$

subject to the constraints

$$0 \leqslant y_1 \leqslant g(K, L_1), \qquad L_1 \geqslant 0 \tag{30.9}$$

$$0 \leqslant y_{21} \leqslant g(K + I, L_{21}), \qquad L_{21} \geqslant 0 \tag{30.10}$$

and

$$0 \leqslant y_{22} \leqslant g(K + I, L_{22}), \qquad L_{22} \geqslant 0. \tag{30.11}$$

Of this plan the producer will in the first period purchase $(\tilde{I}, \tilde{L}_1)$ and contingent claims on $(\tilde{L}_{21}, \tilde{L}_{22})$, and he will sell $\tilde{y}_1$ and contingent claims on $\tilde{y}_{21}$ and $\tilde{y}_{22}$. In period 2—if e_{2i} occurs—he will receive $\tilde{L}_{2i}$, carry out the production plan $(\tilde{L}_{2i}, \tilde{y}_{2i})$, and deliver $\tilde{y}_{2i}$ as promised.

Consider next a situation in which the same firm functions in an economy where consumers and producers trade only in current goods and currently available securities. Suppose that the manager of the firm entertains single-valued price expectations with respect to the two events e_{21} and e_{22} that might occur in period 2. Suppose also that these expectations are independent of the first-period prices of y, L, I, and W^i, $i = 1, 2$, where W^i denotes a security, each unit of which will pay one unit of the unit of account in period 2 if e_{2i} occurs and nothing otherwise. If we denote the price of W^i by $(1/1 + r_i)$ and the expected prices of y and L by (p_{2i}^e, w_{2i}^e), $i = 1, 2$, and if we let δ denote the dividends paid to the owners of the firm, the producer would attempt to choose an expenditure strategy,

$$(\hat{I}, \hat{L}_1, \hat{y}_1, \hat{W}^1, \hat{W}^2, \hat{L}_{21}, \hat{y}_{21}, \hat{L}_{22}, \hat{y}_{22}, \hat{\delta}_1, \hat{\delta}_{21}, \hat{\delta}_{22}), \tag{30.12}$$

which maximizes the value of

$$\delta_1 + \left(\frac{1}{1 + r_1}\right)\delta_{21} + \left(\frac{1}{1 + r_2}\right)\delta_{22} \tag{30.13}$$

subject to the conditions,

$$p_I I + \delta_1 + \left(\frac{1}{1 + r_1}\right)W^1 + \left(\frac{1}{1 + r_2}\right)W^2 \leqslant p_1 y_1 - w_1 L_1,$$

$$(\delta_1, I) \in R_+^2; \tag{30.14}$$

$$0 \leqslant y_1 \leqslant g(K, L_1), \qquad L_1 \geqslant 0 \tag{30.15}$$

$$0 \leqslant \delta_{21} \leqslant W^1 + p_{21}^e y_{21} - w_{21}^e L_{21}, \tag{30.16}$$

$$0 \leqslant y_{21} \leqslant g(K + I, L_{21}), \qquad L_{21} \geqslant 0 \tag{30.17}$$

$$0 \leqslant \delta_{22} \leqslant W^2 + p_{22}^e y_{22} - w_{22}^e L_{22}, \tag{30.18}$$

and

$$0 \leqslant y_{22} \leqslant g(K + I, L_{22}), \qquad L_{22} \geqslant 0. \tag{30.19}$$

In this case, the manager of the firm would pay $\hat{\delta}_1$ dividends, buy $(\hat{I}, \hat{W}^1, \hat{W}^2)$, and carry out the production plan $(\hat{y}_1, \hat{L}_1)$ in period 1. And he would plan to pay $\hat{\delta}_{2i}$ dividends and carry out the production plan $(\hat{y}_{2i}, \hat{L}_{2i})$ if e_{2i} occurs and the period-2 prices of y and L actually equal (p^e_{2i}, w^e_{2i}), $i = 1, 2$.

If we view the Arrow-Debreu theory of the firm as a theory of how the manager of the firm chooses an optimal production plan, and if $p_{2i} = (1/1 + r_i)p^e_{2i}$, $i = 1, 2$, the two models of the firm described above are equivalent in the following sense: (1) the subvector $(\hat{I}, \hat{L}_1, \hat{y}_1, \hat{L}_{21}, \hat{y}_{21}, \hat{L}_{22}, \hat{y}_{22})$ in equation 30.12 is a solution to the maximum problem of equations 30.8–30.11; and (2) there exists a vector $(\tilde{W}^1, \tilde{W}^2, \tilde{\delta}_1, \tilde{\delta}_{21}, \tilde{\delta}_{22})$ such that if we expand the vector in equation 30.7 to $(\tilde{I}, \tilde{L}_1, \tilde{y}_1, \tilde{W}^1, \tilde{W}^1, \tilde{L}_{21}, \tilde{y}_{21}, \tilde{L}_{22}, \tilde{y}_{22}, \tilde{\delta}_1, \tilde{\delta}_{21}, \tilde{\delta}_{22})$, then the resulting vector solves the maximum problem of equations 30.13–30.19. I claim that the import of this equivalence is slight for the following reason: When we substitute the vector $(\tilde{I}, \tilde{L}_1, \tilde{y}_1, \tilde{y}_{21}, \tilde{L}_{21}, \tilde{y}_{22}, \tilde{L}_{22})$ into equations 30.14–30.19, its components will satisfy the inequalities in equations 30.15, 30.17, and 30.19. That leaves us with three inequalities, equations 30.14, 30.16, and 30.18, to determine the values of $\tilde{\delta}_1$, $\tilde{\delta}_{21}$, $\tilde{\delta}_{22}$, $\tilde{W}^1$, and $\tilde{W}^2$. The two degrees of freedom involved in the choice of dividends and securities imply that the manager in the second model of the firm has no meaningful basis for choosing an optimal expenditure strategy.

If the producer's price expectations had been multivalued with respect to the events e_{21} and e_{22}, he would have had to choose among uncertain multivalued income streams. An Arrow-Debreu producer would not know how to do that unless we modified his objective somewhat, e.g., by endowing him with a utility function and a subjective probability distribution and by insisting that he maximize expected utility subject to both financial and production constraints. Sample utility functions for risk-neutral and risk-averse producers, respectively, are

$$\delta_1 + \left(\frac{1}{1 + r(\omega)}\right)\delta_2 \qquad \text{and} \qquad f(\delta_1) + \left(\frac{1}{1 + r(\omega)}\right)f(\delta_2),$$

where ω is a pair (e, p), with e and p denoting an event and a price vector, and $f(\cdot)\colon R_+ \to R_+$ is an increasing, strictly concave function. However, there are many other possibilities, one of which I adopt in my own theory of the perfectly competitive firm.

30.5 Entrepreneurial Choice under Uncertainty

To develop a theory of *entrepreneurial choice under uncertainty* we must make assumptions about the kinds of things that an entrepreneur can do and about the objectives that motivate him. We shall assume in this section that the entrepreneur can engage in the following activities: (1) he can produce a finite number of different outputs by combining a finite number of different variable and fixed inputs according to a production function of the instantaneous point-input–point-output variety; (2) he can invest in a finite number of different fixed assets; (3) he can raise funds by issuing stock or selling a finite number of different debt obligations; (4) he can invest in a finite number of debt securities issued by consumers and other firms.

So far as the entrepreneur's motivation is concerned, the natural assumption to make would be that the entrepreneur—choosing among the alternative plans his firm might pursue over time—picks the one that will best *serve the interests of his stockholders.*

In the Arrow-Debreu uncertainty economy, this assumption leads to a clear-cut rule. There the present value of a firm's profit stream is, by the assumptions of Arrow and Debreu, earned and paid out to consumers (i.e., stockholders) during the current period. The larger the present value of a firm's profit stream, the larger the current income of its stockholders will be. And, all other things being equal, the larger the current income of stockholders, the greater their well-being. Thus in the Arrow-Debreu world, the entrepreneur who wants to serve the best interests of his stockholders will always choose the plan that maximizes the present value of the profit stream earned by the firm over time.

Unfortunately, in a world such as ours, in which an entrepreneur cannot trade in contingent claims on future goods, the entrepreneur's objective of serving his stockholders' best interests cannot be translated into this simple rule. The reason is that our entrepreneur associates with each plan of action he might undertake a whole subjective probability distribution of possible earnings streams, and so he is unable to assign a unique present-value-of-future-profits figure to any such plan. One might think, of course, that the entrepreneur could get around this difficulty by picking the plan whose anticipated earnings would be capitalized by the market at the highest value, i.e., by picking the plan that would maximize the market value of the firm's outstanding shares. But this approach, too, presents difficulties. The entrepreneur might not be able to guess accurately how the market would respond to different plans. Also, even if he could, he might not agree with the market's view of the "best" plan. For example, he might believe, given his knowledge and expectations (which differ from those of investors in the market), that a plan which would maximize the market value of the firm's stock today would depress it in the future.

Because the future is uncertain and because our entrepreneur's appreciation of the future may differ from that of the market, we must—to make precise our assumption that the entrepreneur seeks to serve his stockholders' best interests—take the entrepreneur's own judgment, expectations, and risk preferences into account. This we do by assuming that the entrepreneur possesses a subjective probability measure $Q(\cdot)$—defined on subsets of the set of all states of the world—and a utility function $V(\cdot)$, whose arguments are (1) the dividends which the firm pays out in all periods within the entrepreneur's planning horizon and (2) the market value of the firm at the end of the entrepreneur's planning horizon.

30.5.1 Definitional Axioms

Having made the preceding comments about the entrepreneur's activities and motivation, I proceed to state the definitional axioms of my theory of entrepreneurial choice. These axioms concern the following undefined terms: the *world*, a *production plan*, a *security bundle*, the *stock*, a *firm*, *dividends*, a *price system*, an *expenditure sequence*, and a *production-investment strategy*.

FBS 1 The world is an experiment, $(\Omega, \mathcal{F})$, where $\mathcal{F}$ is a σ field.

FBS 2 A production plan is a triple, $(y, x, L) \in R_+^v \times R_+^l \times R_+$.

FBS 3 A security bundle is a vector, $\mu \in R^k$.

FBS 4 The stock is a number, $M \in [1, \infty)$, and dividends is a vector $d \in R_+^N$.

FBS 5 Let $T = \{1, 2, \ldots\}$. Then a price system is a vector-valued function,
$(p_y, p_x, w, p_I, \alpha, p_M)(\cdot)\colon T \times \Omega \to R_{++}^v \times R_{++}^l \times R_{++} \times R_{++}^h \times R_{++}^k \times R_{++}$.
Moreover, for all $t \in T$, $\mathcal{F}((p_y, p_x, w, p_I, \alpha, p_M)(t)) \subset \mathcal{F}$.

FBS 6 A firm is a 9-tuple,

$$(g, Y, V, A, \hat{K}, \hat{M}, Q, N_\mu, N_M), \tag{30.20}$$

where

(i) $g(\cdot)\colon R_+^h \times R_+^l \times R_+ \to R_+^v$;

(ii) $Y = \{(y, K, x, L) \in R_+^v \times R_+^h \times R_+^l \times R_+ : y \leqslant g(K, x, L)\}$;

(iii) $V(\cdot)\colon R_+^N \times R \to R$;

(iv) $A(\cdot)\colon \Omega \to R_{++}$ and $\mathcal{F}(A) \subset \mathcal{F}$;

(v) $\hat{K} \in R_{++}^h$ and $\hat{M} \in (1, \infty)$;

(vi) $Q(\cdot)\colon \mathcal{F} \to [0, 1]$ is a δ-additive probability measure;

(vii) $(N_\mu, N_M)(\cdot)\colon T \times \Omega \to R_{++}^k \times \{r \in R : r > \hat{M}\}$ and, for all $t \in T$, $\mathcal{F}((N_\mu, N_M)(t)) \subset \mathcal{F}$.

FBS 7 An expenditure sequence is a vector-valued function,

$(y, x, L, d, I, \mu, M)(\cdot): \{1, \ldots, N\} \times \Omega \to R_+^{v+l+1+1} \times R_+^h \times R^k \times R_1$,

which for all $t \in \{1, \ldots, N\}$ satisfies the conditions,

(i) $\mathscr{F}((y, x, L, d, I, \mu, M)(t)) \subset \mathscr{F}(A, (p_y, p_x, w, p_I, \alpha, p_M, N_\mu, N_M)(s), 1 \leqslant s \leqslant t)$;

(ii) $y(t, \omega) \leqslant g(K(t, \omega), x(t, \omega), L(t, \omega))$,

where

$K(1, \omega) \equiv \hat{K}$;

and

$K(t, \omega) = K(t-1, \omega) + I(t-1, \omega), \qquad t = 2, \ldots, N$;

(iii) $$p_I(t, \omega)I(t, \omega) + d(t, \omega) + \alpha(t, \omega)\mu(t, \omega) + p_M(t, \omega)(M(t-1, \omega) - M(t, \omega))$$

$$\leqslant A(\omega)\delta(t-1) + \mu_1(t-1, \omega) + \sum_{i=1}^{k-1} \alpha_i(t, \omega)\mu_{i+1}(t-1, \omega)$$

$$+ p_y(t, \omega)y(t, \omega) - p_x(t, \omega)x(t, \omega) - w(t, \omega)L(t, \omega),$$

where $\delta(t-1) = 0$ or 1 according as $t \neq 1$ or $t = 1$, $M(0, \omega) = \hat{M}$, and $\mu(0, \omega) = 0$;

(iv) $-N_\mu(t, \omega) \leqslant \mu(t, \omega)$ and $1 \leqslant M(t, \omega) \leqslant N_M(t, \omega)$.

FBS 8 A production-investment strategy is an expenditure sequence, $(y, x, L, d, I, \mu, M)(\cdot)$, with the property that if $(\tilde{y}, \tilde{x}, \tilde{L}, \tilde{d}, \tilde{I}, \tilde{\mu}, \tilde{M})(\cdot)$ is any other expenditure sequence, then

$$E\{V[d(1, \omega), \ldots, d(N, \omega), p_M(N+1, \omega)M(N, \omega)] | A, (p_y, p_x, w, p_I, \alpha_M, p_M, N_\mu, N_M)(1)\}$$
$$\geqslant E\{V[\tilde{d}(1, \omega), \ldots, \tilde{d}(N, \omega), p_M(N+1, \omega)\tilde{M}(N, \omega)] | A, (p_y, p_x, w, p_I, \alpha_M, p_M, N_\mu, N_M)(1)\}$$

30.5.2 The Intended Interpretation

In the intended interpretation of the axioms, a state of the world is as described in section 30.3.2; and a state of nature is a complete description of the entrepreneur's initial claim on first-period purchasing power, $A(\cdot)$, and the institutional constraints, $(N_\mu, N_M)(t, \cdot)$, that he will face in the loan and stock markets in each and every period $t \in T$. Moreover, $V(\cdot)$ is the entrepreneur's utility function, $Q(\cdot)$ is his subjective probability measure on $(\Omega, \mathscr{F})$, and $g(\cdot)$ is his *production function*. The arguments of $g(\cdot)$ denote fixed factors K, intermediate goods x, and labor L; and Y contains all feasible input-output combinations. Finally, an expenditure sequence is a possible sequence of sales of outputs y, issues of shares M, purchases of factors of production (I, x, L) and securities μ, and distribution of dividends d in each period within the firm's planning horizon that satisfies the firm's production and financial constraints and is compatible with the entrepreneur's information structure.

Our firm's *production set* Y is much simpler than the production sets we met in Arrow and Debreu's theory of the firm. We could have generalized Y by dating inputs and outputs and allowing production processes that require more than one period to complete themselves. However, if we had done so, we would have succeeded in complicating our notation without gaining more insight into the problems of entrepreneurial choice under uncertainty and thus performed a useless exercise in generalities.

In respect of Y, note also that we have "prohibited" the firm from carrying inventories of intermediate goods and final outputs and insisted that capital equipment which is bought and installed in one period cannot be used before the next. Moreover, the components of $\underset{\sim}{K}$ do not depreciate and cannot be resold by the firm.

The entrepreneur's information structure is expanding. It differs from the consumer's information structure only to the extent that the components of $(A, p_y, p_x, w, p_I, \alpha, p_M, N_\mu, N_M)$ differ from the components of $(A, \xi, p_q, w, \alpha, p_m, d, N_L, N_\mu)$. This difference is of no concern to us here. However, our discussion of Radner's theory suggests that we pay attention to it when we begin our search for first-period temporary equilibria.

Finally—and most importantly (!)—in the intended interpretation of the axioms, the components of d denote so many units of the respective periods' units of account. These units of account are specified in advance (i.e., before the beginning of period 1) and are independent of the state of the world. When we later (e.g., in T 30.6) hypothesize about the effect of changes in the current-period unit of account, we are not envisioning changes in our interpretation of the components of d. The components of d will always denote so many units of the originally specified units of account. Hypothetical changes in the current-period unit of account, therefore, have no effect on $V(\cdot)$, but they will affect the firm's budget equation in the obvious way.

30.5.3 Axioms concerning the Properties of $g(\cdot)$, $V(\cdot)$, and $Q(\cdot)$

Faced with a vector $(A, (p_y, p_x, w, p_I, \alpha, p_M, N_\mu, N_M)(1))$, the entrepreneur determines his production-investment strategy and proceeds to carry out that part of it which pertains to period 1. In order to be sure that the entrepreneur has a production-investment strategy, I must introduce more axioms. These axioms concern the properties of $g(\cdot)$, $V(\cdot)$, and $Q(\cdot)$. First, $g(\cdot)$ and $V(\cdot)$:

FBS 9 $g(\cdot)$ is a bounded, strictly concave, continuous function which is strictly increasing on $R^h_{++} \times R^l_+ \times R_{++}$ and satisfies the condition $g(K, x, 0) = 0$.

FBS 10 $V(\cdot)$ is a strictly increasing, strictly concave, bounded continuous function.

Next, $Q(\cdot)$: In stating the axioms for $Q(\cdot)$ we let

$$\psi(t, \omega) = ((p_y, p_x, w, p_I, \alpha, p_M, N_\mu, N_M)(1, \omega), \ldots,$$
$$(p_y, p_x, w, p_I, \alpha, p_M, N_\mu, N_M)(t, \omega)) \quad (30.21)$$

for all $t \in T$. Moreover, for a random variable x and a random vector y, we let $Q\{x \in A | y \in B\}$ $(Q(x \in A|y))$ and $E\{x|y \in B\}$ $(E(x|y))$ be as described in section 30.3.3:

FBS 11 For each $t = 1, \ldots, N$,

(i) $Q\{\{\omega \in \Omega : N_{\mu_1}(t, \omega) + \sum_{i=1}^{k-1} \alpha_i(t+1, \omega) N_{\mu_{i+1}}(t, \omega) \leqslant \alpha(t+1, \omega) N_\mu(t+1, \omega)$ and $N_M(t, \omega) \leqslant N_M(t+1, \omega)\} | A, \psi(t)\} = 1$; and

(ii) the probability distribution induced by

$Q\{\cdot | A, \psi(t)\}$ and $(1, (\alpha_1, \ldots, \alpha_{k-1}, p_M)(t+1, \cdot))$

is nondegenerate.

FBS 12 Let

$h_t(\cdot)$: $\{\text{range of } (A, \psi(t+1))\} \times R^l_+ \times R^h_{++} \times R \to R, \qquad t = 1, \ldots, N$

and

$f(\cdot)$: $R^N_+ \times R_+ \to R$

be bounded, continuous functions. Then

(i) for each $t = 1, \ldots, N-1$, there exists a version of

$$E\left\{h_t(A, \psi(t+1), d(1), \ldots, d(t), K, \mu_1 + \sum_{j=1}^{k-1} \alpha_j(t+1, \omega)\mu_{j+1} - p_M(t+1, \omega)M) \middle| A, \psi(t)\right\}$$

which is a continuous function of $(A, \psi(t), d(1), \ldots, d(t), K, \mu, M)$; and

(ii) there exists a version of

$E\{f(d(1), \ldots, d(N), p_M(N+1, \omega)M) | A, \psi(N)\}$

which is a continuous function of $(A, \psi(N), d(1), \ldots, d(N), M)$.

These postulates are the firm analogues of CBS 9–CBS 12. They are, therefore, self-explanatory and imply that the entrepreneur has a production-investment strategy. That is, we have our next theorem:

T 30.4 If FBS 1–FBS 12 are valid, then for each value of $(A, \psi(1), \hat{K}, \hat{M})$, there exists a production-investment strategy.

The arguments needed to prove this theorem are similar to those used to establish T 30.1. Hence I omit the proof for brevity's sake.

30.5.4 The Fundamental Theorem of Entrepreneurial Choice under Uncertainty

In the preceding section we developed a multistage model of a firm which operates under uncertainty. This model seems discouragingly intricate and without much empirical content. Fortunately, however, we can use the methods of dynamic programming to reduce the given multistage model to a much simpler one-stage model. The latter provides a basis for an empirical analysis of entrepreneurial choice under uncertainty. That is, we have T 30.5:

T 30.5 Let $\psi(\cdot)$ be as defined in equation 30.21 and assume that $N \geqslant 2$ and that the axioms FBS 1–FBS 12 are valid. Then there exists a continuous, real-valued function $\tilde{V}(\cdot)$ on the set

$$\{(A, \psi(1), d, K, \mu, M) \in \{\text{range of } (A, \psi(1))\} \times R_+ \times R^h_{++} \times R^k \times R_1 : \\ \mu \geqslant -N_\mu(1), M \leqslant N_M(1)\}$$

which, for each value of $(A, \psi(1), d, K, \mu, M)$, satisfies the conditions:

(i) $\hat{V}(A, \psi(1), \cdot)$ is a strictly concave function;

(ii) $\hat{V}(A, \psi(1), \cdot, M)$ is strictly increasing;

(iii) $\hat{V}(A, \psi(1), d, K, \mu, \cdot)$ is strictly decreasing; and

(iv) the entrepreneur can determine the $(y, x, L, d, I, \mu, M)(1)$ component of his production-investment strategy by setting it equal to the (y, x, L, d, I, μ, M) vector, which maximizes the value of $\hat{V}(A, \psi(1), d, \hat{K} + I, \mu, M)$ subject to the conditions,

$$p_I(1)I + d + p_M(1)(\hat{M} - M) + \alpha(1)\mu \leqslant A + p_y(1)y - p_x(1)x - w(1)L;$$

$$\mu \geqslant -N_\mu(1) \quad \text{and} \quad 1 \leqslant M \leqslant N_M(1);$$

and

$$0 \leqslant y \leqslant g(\hat{K}, x, L), \quad (I, d, x, L) \geqslant 0.$$

This theorem plays the same role for the firm as T 30.2 plays for the consumer. Hence T 30.5 is the *fundamental theorem* of my theory of entrepreneurial choice under uncertainty. The proof of the theorem, which I sketch in the appendix (section 30.7.2) is similar to the proof of T 30.2.

For later purposes and to describe some of the empirical implications of T 30.5, I record the following analogue of T 30.3.

T 30.6 If FBS 1–FBS 12 are valid, there exists a continuous function,

$$(y, x, L, d, I, \mu, M)(\cdot)\colon \{(A, \psi(1), \hat{K}, \hat{M}) \in \{\text{range of } (A, \psi(1))\} \times R^h_{++} \times R_1 : \hat{M} < N_M(1)\} \to R^{v+l+1+1+h}_{+} \times R^k \times R_1,$$

which, for each value of $(A, \psi(1), \hat{K}, \hat{M})$, satisfies the following conditions:

(i) $(y, x, L, d, I, \mu, M)(\cdot)$ is invariant under changes in the current-period unit of account.[3]

(ii) $$p_I(1)I(\cdot) + d(\cdot) + p_M(1)(\hat{M} - M(\cdot)) + \alpha(1)\mu(\cdot) = A + p_y(1)y(\cdot) - p_x(1)x(\cdot) - w(1)L(\cdot).$$

(iii) $$\hat{V}(A, \psi(1), d(\cdot), \hat{K} + I(\cdot), \mu(\cdot), M(\cdot)) = \max_{(y,x,L,d,I,\mu,M) \in \hat{\Gamma}(A,\psi(1),\hat{K},\hat{M})} \hat{V}(A, \psi(1), d, \hat{K} + I, \mu, M),$$

where

$$\hat{\Gamma}(A, \psi(1), \hat{K}, \hat{M}) = \{(y, x, L, d, I, \mu, M) \in R^{v+l+1+1+h}_{+} \times R^k \times R_1 : p_I(1)I + d + p_M(1)(\hat{M} - M) + \alpha(1)\mu \leqslant A + p_y(1)y - p_x(1)x - w(1)L, \quad \mu \geqslant -N_\mu(1), \quad M \leqslant N_M(1), \quad \text{and} \quad y \leqslant g(\hat{K}, x, L)\}.$$

The proof of this theorem is, with only obvious modifications, similar to the proof of T 30.3. Hence I omit it for brevity's sake.

It follows from T 30.4 and T 30.5 that the components of $(y, x, L, d, I, \mu, M)(\cdot)$ represent the current-period supply-demand functions of the firm. These functions have several interesting properties:

1. In the intended interpretation of FBS 1–FBS 12, the arguments of the vector-valued function $(y, x, L, I, d, \mu, M)(\cdot)$ are observable. Hence this function can be used as a basis for an empirical analysis of entrepreneurial choice under uncertainty.

2. For each value of $(A, \psi(1), \hat{K}, \hat{M})$, the vector $(y, x, L)(A, \psi(1), \hat{K}, \hat{M})$ represents the solution to the maximum problem:

$$\max p_y(1)y - p_x(1)x - w(1)L$$

subject to the conditions

$$(y, x, L) \in R^{v+l+1}_{+} \quad \text{and} \quad y \leqslant g(\hat{K}, x, L).$$

Hence the entrepreneur always chooses his $(y, x, L)(1)$ vector such that he maximizes profit in the current period. This fact is an obvious consequence of the monotonicity properties of $\hat{V}(A, \psi(1), \cdot)$.

3. Let $P = (p_y, p_x, w)(1)$; let

$$Y = (y, x, L)(A, \psi(1), \hat{K}, \hat{M}) \cdot \begin{pmatrix} I_v & 0 & 0 \\ 0 & -I_l & 0 \\ 0 & 0 & -1 \end{pmatrix};$$

and let $\Delta P = (0, \ldots, 0, \Delta P_i, 0, \ldots, 0) \in R^{v+l+1}$. Moreover, let

$$\Delta Y = (y, x, L)(A, P + \Delta P, (p_I, \alpha, p_M, N_\mu, N_M)(1), \hat{K}, \hat{M}) \begin{pmatrix} I_v & 0 & 0 \\ 0 & -I_l & 0 \\ 0 & 0 & -1 \end{pmatrix} - y.$$

Then the result obtained in property 2 and the arguments used by Debreu to establish 2′ in Debreu 1959 (p. 47) suffice to establish the inequality

$$\Delta P \cdot \Delta Y \leqslant 0.$$

Consequently, if the current-period price of an output (input) increases, the firm will increase the production of the output (decrease the use of the input).

4. Consider the firm at $(y, x, L, d, I, \mu, M)(A, \psi(1), \hat{K}, \hat{M})$, and let λ_1 denote the marginal utility to the entrepreneur of paying out an extra dollar of dividends in period 1. Moreover, let λ_2 denote the cost of this dollar, which we take to be the expected value of the marginal utility to the entrepreneur of the income foregone if this dollar is not invested in the firm. Finally, let r_1 be defined by $(1/1 + r_1) = \alpha_1(1)$. Then we can show that $((\lambda_1 - \lambda_2)/\lambda_2) \geqslant r_1$. Hence—in the jargon of economists—the entrepreneur will chose his production-investment strategy such that in the first period the firm's marginal efficiency of capital (i.e., $((\lambda_1 - \lambda_2)/\lambda_2)$ equals or exceeds the interest on one-period loans, r_1.

For a formal proof of the last assertion and for a derivation of other characteristics of the entrepreneur's production-investment strategy, I refer the reader to Stigum 1990, where I subject Norwegian firms to an empirical analysis based on the ideas outlined in FBS 1–FBS 12.

30.6 Temporary Equilibria under Uncertainty

I have presented a theory of consumer choice under uncertainty and a theory of entrepreneurial choice under uncertainty. To establish the nomological adequacy of these theories, I must describe a *production economy* in which CBS 1–CBS 12 consumers and FBS 1–FBS 12 entrepreneurs can function successfully. In this section I formulate such an economy.

30.6.1 Notational Matters

I begin by specifying (1) the number of consumers and firms in the economy, (2) the number and kinds of goods produced, and (3) the number and kinds of securities traded in the economy. First, goods:

1. I assume that the firms in the economy produce $(n + h)$ final outputs, n of which are consumer goods and h of which are investment goods, and l intermediate goods. In producing these outputs, they use as inputs fixed factors (i.e., initial stocks of investment goods), intermediate goods, and labor. I shall denote a *commodity bundle* by a pair,

$$(x, L) \in R_+^{n+h+l} \times R_-,$$

and a *production vector* by a pair

$$(y, L) \in R_+^{n+h} \times R^l \times R_-.$$

Moreover, I insist that the first n components of x and y denote *consumer goods*, the next h *investment goods*, and the following l *intermediate goods*, while L denotes *labor*.

Next, securities:

2. I assume (1) that consumers and entrepreneurs in the economy can issue k different debt securities, (2) that consumers can invest in S different stock, and (3) that each firm can obtain equity funds by issuing one kind of stock. I denote the *debt securities* by

$$\mu \in R^k$$

and the *shares* by

$$m \in R_+^S.$$

Moreover, I insist that the ith component of μ matures in i periods and that the jth component of m represents the shares issued by the jth firm.

Then, prices and dividends:

3. I denote the *price of* (x, L) (*and* (y, L)) by the pair

$$(p, w) \in R_+^{n+h+l} \times R_+,$$

and the *price of* (μ, m) by the pair

$$(\alpha, p_m) \in R_+^k \times R_+^S.$$

Moreover, I denote the *dividends* on m by

$d \in R_+^S$

and the *institutional constraints on labor supply and the issue of securities* by

$(N_L, N_\mu, N_m) \in R_{++} \times R_{++}^k \times R_{++}^S.$

These prices, dividends, and institutional constraints are the components of the vector

$$\varphi = (p, w, \alpha, p_m, d, N_L, N_\mu, N_m). \tag{30.22}$$

Finally, the consumers and firms: In describing them, I assume for simplicity that the integers n, k, S, h, l of this section satisfy the conditions,

$n =$ the n of CBS 2;

$k =$ the k of CBS 3 and FBS 3;

$S =$ the l of CBS 4;

$h =$ the h of FBS 5 and FBS 6 (v);

and

$l > \max l_j$, where $l_j =$ the l of FBS 2 corresponding to the jth firm.

4. In the present economy, a consumer is a quintuple,

$\mathscr{C} = (\chi, \tilde{U}, \bar{m}, N_L, N_\mu),$

where

(i) $\bar{m} \in (R_+^S - \{0\})$ and $(N_L, N_\mu) \in R_{++} \times R_{++}^k$;

(ii) $\chi = ((R_+^{n+h+l} \times R_{-N_L}) \cap (R_+^n \times R_-^{h+l} \times R_-)) \times R_{-N_\mu}^k \times R_+^S$; and

(iii) $\tilde{U}(\cdot): (R_+^{n+h+l+1+k+S} - \{0\}) \times R_+^S \times R_{++}^{1+k+S} \times \chi \to R.$

I assume that there are T consumers in the economy and denote them by the quintuples $\mathscr{C}^i = (\chi^i, \tilde{U}^i, \bar{m}^i, N_L^i, N_\mu^i)$, $i = 1, \ldots, T$. Different consumers face different institutional constraints in the labor and securities' markets, and they possess different pairs $(\tilde{U}, \bar{m})$.

5. In the present economy, a firm is an 8-tuple,

$\mathscr{Y} = (Y, \hat{U}, Z, \bar{x}, \hat{K}, \overline{M}, N_\mu, N_M)$

where

(i) $\overline{M} \in (1, \infty)$, $(N_\mu, N_M) \in R^k_{++} \times R_1$, $\hat{K} \in R^h_+$, and

$\overline{x} \in (R^{n+h+l+1}_+ \cap (R^{n+h}_- \times R^l_{++} \times R_-))$;

(ii) $Z = R_+ \times R^h_+ \times R^k_{-N_\mu} \times [1, N_M]$;

(iii) $\hat{U}(\cdot)$: $(R^{n+h+l+1+k+S}_+ - \{0\}) \times R^{1+k+S}_{++} \times Z \to R$; and

(iv) $Y \subset R^{n+h+l} \times R_-$.

I assume that there are S firms in the economy and denote them by the 8-tuples, $\mathscr{Y}^j = (Y^j, \hat{U}^j, Z^j, \overline{x}^j, \hat{K}^j, \overline{M}^j, N^j_\mu, N^j_M)$, $j = 1, \ldots, S$. Different firms face different production sets and different institutional constraints in the securities and stock markets. Moreover, different firms may possess different utility functions and they issue different stock.

30.6.2 Axioms for a Production Economy

So much for symbols and agents. Next I shall present axioms that will enable us to establish the existence of a temporary equilibrium in our production economy. I begin with the consumers.

MCBS 1 For each $i = 1, \ldots, T$, let $A^i(\cdot)$: $\Omega \to R_+$ be the $A(\cdot)$ of CBS 6 (iii). Then the observed value of $A^i(\cdot)$ equals the market value of consumer i's initial share holdings, $\overline{m}^i$, plus the dividends i earns on them; that is,

$A^i = (p_m + d)\overline{m}^i$.

MCBS 2 For each $i = 1, \ldots, T$, $\tilde{U}^i(\cdot)$ is a continuous function which satisfies the following conditions:

(i) Let φ be as in equation 30.22. Then for each $(x, L, \mu, m) \in \chi^i$ and $(\lambda, N_L, N_\mu, N_m) \in R^{2+k+S}_{++}$,

$$\tilde{U}^i(\lambda p, \lambda w, \lambda \alpha, \lambda p_m, \lambda d, N_L, N_\mu, N_m, x, L, \mu, m) = \tilde{U}^i(\varphi, x, L, \mu, m). \tag{30.23}$$

(ii) For each $\varphi \in (R^{n+h+l+1+k+S}_+ - \{0\}) \times R^S_+ \times R^{1+k+S}_{++}$, $\tilde{U}^i(\varphi, \cdot)$ is a strictly increasing, strictly concave function.

(iii) Let $\gamma = (p_1, \ldots, p_n, w, \alpha, p_m, d, N_L, N_\mu)$ and let $\gamma(1, \cdot)$ be as in equation 30.6. Then for each $((p_m + d)\overline{m}^i, \gamma)$ in the range of $(A^i(\cdot), \gamma(1, \cdot))$ and for each $(x, L, \mu, m) \in \chi^i$,

$$\tilde{U}^i(\varphi, x, L, \mu, m) = \tilde{V}^i((p_m + d)\overline{m}^i, \gamma, x_1, \ldots, x_n, L, \mu, m), \tag{30.24}$$

where $\tilde{V}^i(\cdot)$ is the $\tilde{V}(\cdot)$ of T 30.2 corresponding to the ith consumer.

MCBS 3 For each $i = 1, \ldots, T$,

$(N^i_L, N^i_\mu) \in R_{++} \times R^k_{++}$.

Note that equation 30.24 insists that $\tilde{U}^i(\cdot)$ is an extension of $\tilde{V}^i(\cdot)$ to the domain of $\tilde{U}^i(\cdot)$. We shall discuss the existence of such an extension later. Moreover, recall that the expectations of a CBS 1–CBS 12 consumer are invariant under changes in the current-period unit of account. Hence, for all $(p_q, w, \alpha, p_m, d, N_L, N_\mu)$ in the range of $\gamma(1, \cdot)$ and $\lambda \in R_{++}$,

$$\tilde{V}^i(\lambda A, \lambda p_q, \lambda w, \lambda\alpha, \lambda p_m, \lambda d, N_L, N_\mu, \cdot) = \tilde{V}^i(A, p_q, w, \alpha, p_m, d, N_L, N_\mu, \cdot).$$

From this it follows that equations 30.23 and 30.24 are consistent.

Next, the axioms for the firms:

MFBS 1 For each $j = 1, \ldots, S$, let $A^j(\cdot): \Omega \to R_+$ be the $A(\cdot)$ of FBS 6 (iv) corresponding to the jth firm. Then the observed value of $A^j(\cdot)$ equals the market value of the jth firm's initial stock of intermediate goods; i.e.,

$$A^j = p_x \bar{x}^j.$$

Moreover, every intermediate good is used to produce some final output.

MFBS 2 For each $j = 1, \ldots, S$, let $g^j(\cdot)$ and $\hat{K}^j$ be, respectively, the $g(\cdot)$ and $\hat{K}$ of FBS 6 (i) and (v) corresponding to the jth firm. Moreover, for each production vector (y, L), let y_{n+h+j_k}, $k = 1, \ldots, l_j$, be the components that represent the intermediate goods employed by the jth firm; and let y_{j^i}, $i = 1, \ldots, v_j$, be the components that represent the jth firm's outputs. Then, for all $j = 1, \ldots, S$,

(i) $j^i \neq n + h + j_k$, $k = 1, \ldots, l_j$, $i = 1, \ldots, v_j$; that is, an intermediate good cannot be both an input and an output in the same firm.

(ii) $(y, L) \in Y^j$ if and only if the following conditions are satisfied:

a. $(y_{n+h+j_1}, \ldots, y_{n+h+j_{l_j}}, L) \in R_{-}^{l_j+1}$;

b. $(y_{j1}, \ldots, y_{jv_j}) \in R_+$ and $y_s = 0$ if $s \neq j^i$,

$i = 1, \ldots, v_j$, and $s \neq n + h + j_k$, $k = 1, \ldots, l_j$; and

c. $y_{ji} \leqslant g_i^j(\hat{K}^j, -y_{n+h+j_1}, \ldots, -y_{n+h+j_{l_j}}, -L)$, $i = 1, \ldots, v_j$.

(iii) In its domain of definition, $g^j(\cdot)$ satisfies the conditions we imposed on $g(\cdot)$ in FBS 9.

MFBS 3 For each $j = 1, \ldots, S$, $\hat{U}^j(\cdot)$ is a continuous function which satisfies the following conditions:

(i) Let $\beta = (p, w, \alpha, p_m, N_L, N_\mu, N_m)$. Then for each $(d, I, \mu, M) \in Z^j$ and

$(\lambda, N_L, N_\mu, N_m) \in R_{++}^{2+k+S}$,

$$\hat{U}^j(\lambda p, \lambda w, \lambda\alpha, \lambda p_m, N_L, N_\mu, N_m, d, I, \mu, M) = \hat{U}^j(\beta, d, I, \mu, M). \quad (30.25)$$

(ii) For each $\beta \in (R_+^{n+h+l+1+k+S} - \{0\}) \times R_{++}^{1+k+S}$, $\hat{U}^j(\beta, \cdot)$ is a strictly concave function which is strictly increasing in (d, I, μ) and strictly decreasing in M.

(iii) Let $\psi^j(1, \cdot)$ be the current-period component of the $\psi(\cdot)$ of equation 30.21 corresponding to the jth firm, and for each β, let $\beta_\psi j$ be the corresponding vector in the range space of $\psi^j(1, \cdot)$. Then for each β such that $(p\bar{x}^j, \beta_\psi j)$ is in the range of $(A^j(\cdot), \psi^j(1, \cdot))$, and for each $(d, I, \mu, M) \in R_+^{1+h} \times R_{-N_\mu}^k \times R_1$,

$$\hat{U}^j(\beta, d, I, \mu, M) = \hat{V}(p\bar{x}^j, \psi(1)^j, d\bar{M}^j, \hat{K} + I, \mu, M), \tag{30.26}$$

where $\hat{V}^j(\cdot)$ is the $\hat{V}^j(\cdot)$ of T 30.5 corresponding to the jth firm.

MFBS 4 For each $j = 1, \ldots, S$,

$(N^j_\mu, N^j_M) \in R^k_{++} \times (\bar{M}^j, \infty)$.

Axioms MFBS 1–MFBS 4 embed the firm of FBS 1–FBS 12 and T 30.5 in a larger commodity space. In reading the axioms, note that MFBS 2 and FBS 9 imply that Y^j is closed, convex, bunded above, and satisfies

$$Y^j \cap R^{n+h+l+1}_+ = \{0\}.$$

In fact, MFBS 2 and FBS 9 imply that the aggregate production set, $Y = \sum_{j=1}^{s} Y^j$ is closed, convex, bounded above, and satisfies

$$Y \cap R^{n+h+l+1}_+ = \{0\}$$

and

$$Y \cap (-Y) = \{0\}.$$

Hence in this economy, production cannot be arranged in such a way that some output appear to be produced without inputs and some production processes are reversible.

Note also that MFBS 3 insists that there exists an extension of $\hat{V}^j(\cdot)$ to the domain of $\hat{U}^j(\cdot)$ which possesses the same continuity and monotonicity properties as $\hat{V}^j(\cdot)$. Since the expectations of the entrepreneur in FBS 1–FBS 12 are invariant under changes in the current-period unit of account, the assertions made in equations 30.25 and 30.26 are consistent.

So much for the economy's consumers and firms. To conclude our list of axioms we must add an axiom concerning (1) the distribution of outstanding shares and (2) the institutional constraints on the issue of shares:

MMBS 1 For each $j = 1, \ldots, S$,

$$\sum_{i=1}^{T} \bar{m}^i_j = \bar{M}^j \qquad \text{and} \qquad N^j_M = N_{m_j}.$$

Hence each firm's outstanding shares are owned by the consumers in the economy.

30.6.3 The Existence of Temporary Equilibria

In the economy described above, a temporary equilibrium is a set of prices and dividends and an allocation of current commodities, labor, and securities which conforms to the following conditions:

1. Each consumer receives the vector of commodities and securities and supplies the amount of labor which at the given set of prices and dividends would maximize the consumer's expected utility subject to his budget constraint.

2. Each firm is allocated a vector of dividends, capital goods, securities, and inputs and outputs which at the given set of prices would maximize the firm's profits and the entrepreneur's expected utility subject to the firm's financial and production constraints.

3. All dividends, commodities, securities, and labor which would be supplied at the given set of prices are allocated to the respective consumers and firms in the economy.

Finding such an equilibrium is more involved than finding a temporary equilibrium in the exchange economy of chapter 14. There are several reasons for this. First of all, the present economy is a production economy in which the supply of goods is not fixed, as in chapter 14, but is to be determined by the market mechanism. Second, allocating resources in the present economy involves allocating some goods, dividends, for which there are no markets.

We demonstrate in the appendix (section 30.7.3) that there exists a temporary equilibrium in the economy described in sections 30.6.1 and 30.6.2. Specifically, we establish the validity of T 30.7.

T 30.7 The economy described in MCBS 1–MCBS 3, MFBS 1–MFBS 4, and MMBS 1 possesses a temporary equilibrium.

In order that the import of this theorem be understood, several remarks are called for. They concern problems of bankruptcy, the range of prices on the various experiments $(\Omega, \mathscr{F})$ which the agents in the economy face, and the extensions of individual utility functions postulated in MCBS 2 and MFBS 3. We begin with bankruptcy.

One characteristic feature of an uncertainty economy in which the agents can borrow and lend loanable funds is the possibility that, in any one period, one or more agents might go bankrupt; i.e., the possibility exists that in some period there might not exist a temporary equilibrium at which all agents are solvent. Note, therefore, that postulates MCBS 1, MFBS 1 and MFBS 4 make sure that bankruptcy will not be a problem in the present economy. The first two insist that the agents in the economy enter the current period without debt, and the third maintains that each firm's upper limit on stock issues exceeds the firm's initial supply of stock.

I decided not to wrestle with the bankruptcy problem both for reasons of simplicity and because I have dealt with the problem at length elsewhere (see, for instance, Stigum 1972, pp. 431–459, and section 14.4.4 of this text).

Next, $(\Omega, \mathscr{F})$ and the price system: In reading T 30.7 and the axioms postulated for our production economy, it is interesting to note that the experiments $(\Omega, \mathscr{F})$ and the subjective probability measures $Q(\cdot)$ that figure in CBS 1, CBS 6 and FBS 1, FBS 6 play no essential role in T 30.7. The same is true of the vector-valued functions that represented the price system and dividends in CBS 5 and the price system in FBS 5. This is in keeping with the way we think about theories of individual choice and the use of temporary equilibrium theory to determine their nomological adequacy, but is cause for concern anyway. Here is why: The triple $(\Omega, \mathscr{F}, Q(\cdot))$ and the price-dividend functions in CBS 1–CBS 12 as well as the triple $(\Omega, \mathscr{F}, Q(\cdot))$ and price functions in FBS 1–FBS 12 serve as descriptive references for generating the conditional probability distributions which the respective agents face when they search for their optimal expenditure sequences. In addition, $Q(\cdot)$ and the range of values of the price-dividend functions in CBS 5 and $Q(\cdot)$ and the range of values of the price functions in FBS 5 determine the set of values of prices and dividends upon which the individual agents' conditional expectations are well defined. A temporary equilibrium in T 30.7 with a set of prices and dividends at which some agent's conditional probability distribution of next-period prices and dividends are not well defined is of little use in establishing the nomological adequacy of our individual theories of choice.

Temporary equilibrium prices and dividends, respectively, must in the present economy be positive and nonnegative. This is as it ought to be, since the conditional distributions of CBS 1–CBS 12 consumers are defined on sets of positive prices and nonnegative dividends, and the conditional distributions of FBS 1–FBS 12 firms are defined on sets of positive prices. However, to use T 30.7 to establish the nomological adequacy of our theories of individual behavior, these sets of positive prices and nonnegative dividends must be so large that they include at least one multiple of each and every possible vector of temporary equilibrium prices and dividends. More specifically, for each possible vector of temporary equilibrium prices and dividends in the economy of T 30.7, there must exist a unit of account by which we can measure prices and dividends and verify that they belong to the domain of definition of the conditional expectations of the various agents in the economy.

Finally, the extensions of $\tilde{V}(\cdot)$ and $\tilde{V}(\cdot)$ whose existence is postulated in MCBS 2 and MFBS 3: Suppose that the ranges of values of the price systems and dividends in CBS 5 and FBS 5 are so large that the domain of definition of the conditional expectations of the various agents in the economy actually include appropriate constant multiples of each and every possible vector of temporary equilibrium prices and dividends in the economy of T 30.7. These ranges might still not be large enough for a systematic search for temporary equilibria. If they are not, we must look for ways to compensate for this deficiency. We do that in MCBS 2 and MFBS 3 by postulating the existence of extensions of the $\tilde{V}(\cdot)$ of T(CBS 1–CBS 12) and the $\tilde{V}(\cdot)$ of T(FBS 1–FBS 12) whose domains of definition are large enough for us to search successfully for temporary equilibria in the economy of T 30.7. Whether such extensions exist depends on $Q(\cdot)$ and the price system and dividends in CBS 5 and on $Q(\cdot)$ and the price system in FBS 5. To show how, I shall give two examples in which the required extension of the $\tilde{V}(\cdot)$ of T(CBS 1, ..., CBS 12) exists. Similar examples for the required existence of an extension of $\hat{V}(\cdot)$ are equally easy to construct.

E 30.3 Consider a CBS 1–CBS 12 consumer and suppose that, relative to $Q(\cdot)$, the vector-valued family of random variables,

$$\Xi = \{(p_q, w, \alpha, p_m, d, N_L, N_\mu)(t);\ t = 1, 2, \ldots\} \tag{30.27}$$

is a stationary Markov process.[4] Moreover, for each $t \in T$, let $\mathscr{R}_t$ denote the {range of $(p_q, w, \alpha, p_m, d, N_L, N_\mu)(t)$}; assume that $\mathscr{R}_t$ is a Borel set and let $\mathscr{B}(\mathscr{R}_t)$ be the σ field of Borel subsets of $\mathscr{R}_t$. Finally, let

$$\tilde{Q}(\cdot, \cdot)\colon \mathscr{R}_t \times \mathscr{B}(\mathscr{R}_{t+1}) \to [0, 1] \tag{30.28}$$

be defined by

$$\tilde{Q}(z, B) = Q\{\omega \in \Omega : (p_q, w, \alpha, p_m, d, N_L, N_\mu)(t + 1, \omega) \in B \mid (p_q, w, \alpha, p_m, d, N_L, N_\mu)(t) = z\} \tag{30.29}$$

for $z \in \mathscr{R}_t$ and $B \in \mathscr{B}(\mathscr{R}_{t+1})$, and assume that, for all $t \in T$,

$$Q\{\omega \in \Omega : (p_q, w, \alpha, p_m, d, N_L, N_\mu)(t + 1, \omega) \in B \mid A, (p_q, w, \alpha, p_m, d, N_L, N_\mu)(t) = z\} = \tilde{Q}(z, B). \tag{30.30}$$

Then the required extension of $\tilde{V}(\cdot)$ in MCBS 3 exists if $\tilde{Q}((p_q, w, \alpha, p_m, d, N_L, N_\mu)(t), \cdot)$ does not vary with $(p_q, w, \alpha, p_m, d)(t)$.

It is not easy to envision situations in which a consumer's expectations of future prices are independent of the level of current prices. Hence E 30.3 is interesting mainly because it demonstrates that it is not difficult to construct models of the economy of T 30.7. In the next example, we shall consider a case in which the consumer's expectations vary in more intriguing ways with current prices. The ideas underlying the example I learned from J. M. Grandmont and K. A. Brekke (see Grandmont 1974, pp. 216–219, and Brekke 1983).

In writing E 30.4 below, I make use of several new concepts, the meanings of which I must explain carefully. Let $\mathscr{B}(\mathscr{R}_{t+1})$ and $\mathscr{R}_t$ be as in E 30.3; let $\mathscr{M}(\mathscr{R}_{t+1})$ be the set of all σ-additive probability measures on $\mathscr{B}(\mathscr{R}_{t+1})$; and suppose that $\mathscr{M}(\mathscr{R}_{t+1})$ is endowed with the *weak topology*. In the weak topology, a sequence of probability measures $\mu_n(\cdot) \in \mathscr{M}(\mathscr{R}_{t+1})$, $n = 1, 2, \ldots$, converges to a probability measure $\mu(\cdot) \in \mathscr{M}(\mathscr{R}_{t+1})$ if and only if, for all bounded continuous functions $f(\cdot): \mathscr{R}_{t+1} \to R$,

$$\lim_{n\to\infty} \int_{\mathscr{R}_{t+1}} f(z)\, d\mu_n(z) = \int_{\mathscr{R}_{t+1}} f(z)\, d\mu(z).$$

Next, let $\tilde{q}(\cdot): \mathscr{R}_t \to \mathscr{M}(\mathscr{R}_{t+1})$ be defined by

$$\tilde{q}(z) = \tilde{Q}(z, \cdot), \qquad z \in \mathscr{R}_t. \tag{30.31}$$

We shall say that $\tilde{q}(\cdot)$ is continuous if and only if for all convergent sequences $z_n \in \mathscr{R}_t$, $n = 1, 2, \ldots$, the conditions

$$z \in \mathscr{R}_t \qquad \text{and} \qquad z = \lim z_n$$

imply that in the weak topology

$$\tilde{q}(z) = \lim_{n\to\infty} \tilde{q}(z_n).$$

Finally, for each $\mu(\cdot) \in \mathscr{M}(\mathscr{R}_{t+1})$, let

$$\operatorname{supp} \mu = \bigcap \{B \in \mathscr{B}(\mathscr{R}_{t+1}): B \text{ is closed and } \mu(B^c) = 0\}.^5 \tag{30.32}$$

Then our second example of sufficient conditions for the existence of an appropriate extension of the $\tilde{V}(\cdot)$ of T(CBS 1–CBS 12) can be phrased as follows:

E 30.4 Consider again a CBS 1–CBS 12 consumer, let Ξ and $\tilde{Q}(\cdot, \cdot)$ be as defined in equations 30.27–30.29, and assume that Ξ is a stationary Markov process and that $\tilde{Q}(\cdot, \cdot)$ satisfies equation 30.30. Moreover, let $\mathscr{M}(\mathscr{R}_{t+1})$ be the topological space of all σ-additive probability measures on $\mathscr{B}(\mathscr{R}_{t+1})$ endowed with the weak topology; let $\tilde{q}(\cdot)$ be as defined in equation 30.31; and for all $\mu \in \mathscr{M}(\mathscr{R}_{t+1})$, let supp μ be as defined in equation 30.32. Finally, make the following assumptions:

(i) $\tilde{q}(\cdot)$ is continuous.

(ii) There is a compact set $G \subset \mathscr{R}_{t+1}$ such that, for all $z \in \mathscr{R}_t$,

$$\operatorname{supp} \tilde{q}(z) \subset G.$$

(iii) For all $\varepsilon > 0$, there is a $\delta > 0$ such that, for all closed subsets B of G and for all $z, \mu \in \mathscr{R}_t$, $\|z - u\| < \delta$ implies that $|\tilde{Q}(z, B) - \tilde{Q}(u, B)| < \varepsilon$.[6]

(iv) For each pair $(\bar{N}_L, \bar{N}_\mu) \in R_{++}^{1+k}$, there is an $a \in R_{++}$ such that, for all $t \in T$,

$$\mathscr{R}_t \cap \{(p_q, w, \alpha, p_m, d, N_L, N_\mu) \in R_+^{n+2(1+k+m)} : (N_L, N_\mu) = (\bar{N}_L, \bar{N}_\mu)\}$$

$$= \left(\left\{u \in R_+^{n+1+k+m} : \sum_{i=1}^{n+1+k+m} u_i = a\right\} \cap R_{++}^{n+1+k+m}\right) \times R_+^m \times \{(\bar{N}_L, \bar{N}_\mu)\}.$$

Then condition ii and Parthasarathy's theorem (Parthasarathy 1967, theorem 6.7, p. 47) ensure that the closure of the family $\{\tilde{q}(z); z \in \mathscr{R}_t\}$ is a compact subset of $\mathscr{M}(\mathscr{R}_{t+1})$. From this, from the boundedness of $V(\cdot)$, from the fact that $G \subset R_{++}^{n+2(1+k+m)}$, and from conditions iii and iv above follows the existence of the required extension of $\tilde{V}(\cdot)$ in MCBS 2 for each value of (N_L, N_μ). That is all that is required for the purposes of T 30.7.

30.6.4 Concluding Remarks

The price system and dividends of CBS 5 and the pair $(Q(\cdot), V(\cdot))$ of CBS 6 are undefined terms of CBS 1–CBS 12. Similarly, the price system of FBS 5 and the pair $(Q(\cdot), V(\cdot))$ of FBS 6 are undefined terms of FBS 1–FBS 12. Therefore, the remarks made above about various characteristics of the agents in the economy of T 30.7 concerned both the relevance of T 30.7 and the possibility of finding nomologically adequate models of CBS 1–CBS 12 and FBS 1–FBS 12. For the purpose of our concluding remarks, we shall now assume that we are dealing with an uncertainty economy for which T 30.7 is relevant. Specifically, we assume that a vector of prices and dividends and an allocation of resources in the uncertainty economy is a temporary equilibrium for that economy if and only if it is a temporary equilibrium in the economy of T 30.7. Our intent is to check whether such equilibria have the same properties as competitive equilibria in a deterministic environment. We begin with stability.

The problem of the stability of a temporary equilibrium in an economy populated by CBS 1–CBS 12 consumers and FBS 1–FBS 12 entrepreneurs must be resolved by determining the stability of temporary equilibria in E, the economy of T 30.7. In that respect, the following observations are relevant:

1. The temporary equilibria in E cannot be more stable than competitive equilibria in a deterministic environment. Example E 14.5, therefore, demonstrates that we cannot be sure that the set of temporary equilibria in E is stable.

2. Since the consumers in E have no initial quantities of consumer goods, the excess demand function of E is not continuous on all of $R_+^{n+h+l+1+k+S}$ –

$\{0\}$. Consequently, neither T 14.8 nor T 14.9 have analogues that are valid for E.

Our inability to establish the stability of temporary equilibria in our uncertainty economy is as much a concern to us as was our failure in chapter 14 to establish the stability of competitive equilibria in a deterministic environment. However, here as in chapter 14 we are left with the feeling that our inability might be a reflection of deficiencies in the dynamic model we use to model the price-adjustment process. Therefore we shall not pursue the matter any further.

Next, the characteristic feature of resource allocation in an economy populated by CBS 1–CBS 12 consumers and FBS 1–FBS 12 firms: For such an economy an allocation of its current-period resources is admissible if no feasible reallocation of them would increase one agent's expected utility without simultaneously decreasing somebody else's. We demonstrated in T 14.17 that a temporary equilibrium in a deterministic environment achieves an admissible allocation of resources. This is not true of the economy we now consider. The reason is that in the present economy the expected utility which each agent associates with his sales and purchases of goods and securities depends in part on current prices. Therefore, it is possible that one set of equilibrium prices might provide a higher level of satisfaction for all agents in the economy than some other set. In other words, if the economy could attain more than one temporary equilibrium, it is possible that one and not the other might be admissible.

In reading the preceding observation, we should make several mental notes. First, in the definition of an admissible allocation of resources, the expected utilities of entrepreneurs count as much as the expected utilities of consumers. This is controversial since the standard notion of a Pareto-optimal allocation of resources—under uncertainty as well as certainty—is explicated in terms of production possibility sets and consumer preferences only. We have no qualms with the standard optimality criteria as such. They are the natural criteria to apply to the economies about which the standard certainty and uncertainty theories are concerned. However, I believe that they cannot be applied to the kind of uncertainty economy I have in mind. My reasons for that are essentially the reasons I gave for introducing an entrepreneurial utility function in section 30.5 and need not be repeated here.

Second, even though a temporary equilibrium need not be admissible, it still allocates resources efficiently in the usual sense. To wit: Fix prices and dividends as prescribed by some given temporary equilibrium. The corresponding equilibrium allocation of goods and securities is obviously efficient in the sense that there exists no feasible redistribution of goods and securities that will provide some (consumers and entrepreneurs) with higher utility without causing a loss of utility to others.

Third, if one temporary equilibrium is admissible and another is not, the reason need not be that the conditional expectations of consumers and entrepreneurs in one equilibrium is "better" than in the other by, for example, corresponding more closely to the true distribution of future prices. Thus there is no trace of the idea of a rational expectations equilibrium undelying my notion of an admissible allocation of resources. Inasmuch as the expectations of the agents in our uncertainty economy are multivalued with respect to the states of nature, there cannot be such a thing as a rational expectations equilibrium in our economy. Pertinent references in this respect are Radner 1979 (pp. 655–677), Jordan 1985 (pp. 257–276), Kihlstrom and Mirman 1975 (pp. 357–376), and Stigum 1974 (pp. 98–105).

30.7 Appendix: Proofs of Theorems

In this appendix we shall sketch proofs of theorems T 30.1, T 30.2, T 30.5, and T 30.7. We begin with T 30.1 and T 30.2, which we treat as if they were different parts of one and the same theorem.

30.7.1 Proof of T 30.1 and T 30.2

Our proof of T 30.1 and T 30.2 is obtained in several steps, the first seven of which concern the existence of $\tilde{V}(\cdot)$. Throughout the proof, we let $x(t) = (q, L)(t)$. Also, with z short for $(p, w, \alpha, p_m, d, N_L, N_\mu)$, we let

$$\Gamma(z, r) = \{(q, L, \mu, m) \in R_+^n \times R_- \times R^k \times R_+^l : (L, \mu) \geqslant -(N_L, N_\mu) \text{ and } (p_q, w, \alpha, p_m)(q, L, \mu, m) \leqslant r\}.$$

Finally, we shall write $z(t)$, $\alpha(t)$, $p_m(t)$, $d(t)$, $\gamma(t)$, and A for the values assumed, respectively, by $(p_q, w, \alpha, p_m, d, N_L, N_\mu)(t, \cdot)$, $\alpha(t, \cdot)$, $p_m(t, \cdot)$, $d(t, \cdot)$, $\gamma(t, \cdot)$, and $A(\cdot)$, $t = 1, \ldots, M + 1$; and we shall argue as if $M > 2$.

Step 1: It is clear that $\Gamma(\cdot)$ is convex. It is equally clear that $\Gamma(\cdot)$ is compact if $(p_q, w, \alpha, p_m) > 0$. Finally, it follows from UT 7 and only obvious additional arguments that $\Gamma(\cdot)$ is continuous on the set

$$\{(z, r) \in R_+^{n+1+k+l+l+1+k} \times R : (p_q, w, \alpha, p_m) > 0, (N_L, N_\mu) > 0 \text{ and } r \geqslant -wN_L - \alpha N_\mu\}.$$

Step 2: For each $\xi = 1, \ldots, M$, let

$$f_0(\xi, A, \gamma(\xi), x(1), \ldots, x(\xi), \mu, m)$$

$$= E\left\{U_\xi\left(x(1), \ldots, x(\xi), \mu_1 + \sum_{i=1}^{k-1} \alpha_i(\xi + 1)\mu_{i+1} + (p_m + d)(\xi + 1)m\right)\middle| A, \gamma(\xi), \xi\right\}.$$

It follows from CBS 9 and CBS 11 (i) and (iii) that, for each value of ξ, $f_0(\xi, \cdot)$ is a well-defined, bounded, continuous function on the set

$$\{\text{range of } (A, \gamma(\xi))\} \times (R_+^n \times R_-)^\xi \times R^k \times R_+^l,$$[7]

and that, for each $(A, \gamma(\xi)) \in \{\text{range of } (A, \gamma(\xi))\}$, $f_0(\xi, A, \gamma(\xi), \cdot)$ is a strictly increasing, concave function on the set

$$(R_+^n \times R_-)^\xi \times R^k \times R_+^l.$$

Moreover, if the conditional distribution of $(1, \alpha_1(\xi + 1, \cdot), \ldots, \alpha_{k-1}(\xi + 1, \cdot), (p_m + d)(\xi + 1, \cdot))$, given $(\xi, A, \gamma(\xi))$, is nondegenerate, then $f_0(\xi, A, \gamma(\cdot), \cdot)$ is a strictly concave function on $(R_+^n \times R_-)^\xi \times R^k \times R_+^l$. Hence, by CBS 12, $f_0(t, A, \gamma(t), \cdot)$ is a strictly concave function on $(R_+^n \times R_-)^t \times R^k \times R_+^l$, $t = 1, \ldots, M$.

Step 3: Let

$$f_1^*(M, A, \gamma(M), x(1), \ldots, x(M-1), r)$$

$$= \max_{(x(M), \mu, m) \in \Gamma(z(M), r)} f_0(M, A, \gamma(M), x(1), \ldots, x(M), \mu, m).$$

Then it follows from step 1 and C. Berge's theorems VI. 3.1 and VI 3.2 (Berge 1959, pp. 121–122) that $f_1^*(M, \cdot)$ is a well-defined, bounded, continuous function on the set

$$\{(A, \gamma(M), u, r) \in \{\text{range of } (A, \gamma(M))\} \times (R_+^n \times R_-)^{M-1} \times R: r \geqslant -w(M)N_L(M) - \alpha(M)N_\mu(M)\}.$$

Moreover, for each $(A, \gamma(M)) \in \{\text{range of } (A, \gamma(M))\}$, $f_1^*(M, A, \gamma(M), \cdot)$ is strictly increasing and strictly concave on the set

$$(R_+^n \times R_-)^{M-1} \times \{r \in R : r \geqslant -w(M)N_L(M) - \alpha(M)N_\mu(M)\}.$$

Step 4: In this step we shall define two functions, $f_1^{**}(\xi, \cdot)$, $\xi = M-1, M$, and $f_1(M-1, \cdot)$ and derive their properties. Let

$$f_1^{**}(\xi, A, \gamma(M-1), x(1), \ldots, x(M-1), \mu, m)$$
$$= \begin{cases} f_0(\xi, A, \gamma(M-1), x(1), \ldots, x(M-1), \mu, m) & \text{if } \xi = M-1 \\ E\left\{f_1^*\left(M, A, \gamma(M), x(1), \ldots, x(M-1), \mu_1 + \sum_{i=1}^{k-1} \alpha_i(M)\mu_{i+1}\right.\right. & \\ \qquad \left.\left. + (p_m + d)(M)m\right) \middle| A, \gamma(M-1), \xi\right\} & \text{if } \xi = M. \end{cases}$$

Moreover, let

$$f_1(M-1, A, \gamma(M-1), x(1), \ldots, x(M-1), \mu, m)$$
$$= E\{ f_1^{**}(\xi, A, \gamma(M-1), x(1), \ldots, x(M-1), \mu, m) | A, \gamma(M-1),$$
$$\xi \geqslant M-1\}.$$

Then the properties of $f_0(M-1, \cdot)$ and $f_1^*(M, \cdot)$, together with CBS 10 (ii), CBS 11 (iii), and CBS 12 imply that, for $\xi = M-1$ and M, $f_1^{**}(\xi, \cdot)$ is a well-defined, bounded, continuous function on the set

$$\{(A, \gamma(M-1), u, \mu, m) \in \{\text{range of } (A, \gamma(M-1))\} \times (R_+^n \times R_-)^{M-1}$$
$$\times R^k \times R_+^l : \mu \geqslant -N_\mu(M-1)\}.$$

Moreover, for each $(A, \gamma(M-1)) \in \{\text{range of } (A, \gamma(M-1))\}$, $f_1^{**}(\xi, A, \gamma(M-1), \cdot)$ is a strictly increasing, strictly concave function on the set

$$(R_+^n \times R_-)^{M-1} \times R^k_{-N_\mu(M-1)} \times R_+^l.$$

From the properties of $f_1^{**}(\cdot)$ and CBS 11 (ii), it follows that $f_1(M-1, \cdot)$ is a well-defined, bounded, continuous function on the set

$$\{(A, \gamma(M-1), u, \mu, m) \in \{\text{range of } (A, \gamma(M-1))\} \times (R_+^n \times R_-)^{M-1}$$
$$\times R^k \times R_+^l : \mu \geqslant -N_\mu(M-1)\},$$

and that, for each $(A, \gamma(M-1)) \in \{\text{range of } (A, \gamma(M-1))\}$, $f_1(M-1, A, \gamma(M-1), \cdot)$ is a strictly increasing, strictly concave function on the set

$$(R_+ \times R_-)^{M-1} \times R^k_{-N_\mu(M-1)} \times R_+^l.$$

Step 5: Note that, conditional upon the observed value of $(A, \gamma(M-1))$, $f_1(M-1, A, \gamma(M-1), x(1), \ldots, x(M-1), \mu, m)$ represents the maximum expected utility which the consumer can obtain over the remainder of his life if he chooses the vector $(x(M-1), \mu, m)$ in period $M-1$ after having chosen $x(1), \ldots, x(M-2)$ in the preceding periods.

Step 6: Since $f_1(M-1, \cdot)$ has the same properties as $f_0(M-1, \cdot)$, it is evident that, by working backward on the tree structure of events facing the consumer, we can use the same arguments used above to construct real-valued functions $f_s(M-s, \cdot)$ on the respective sets

$$\{(A, \gamma(M-s), u, \mu, m) \in \{\text{range of } (A, \gamma(M-s))\} \times (R^n_+ \times R_-)^{M-s}$$

$$\times R^k \times R^l_+ : \mu \geqslant -N_\mu(M-s)\},$$

$s = 2, \ldots, M-1$, with the following properties:

(i) $f_s(M-s, \cdot)$ is bounded and continuous;

(ii) for each pair $(A, \gamma(M-s)) \in \{\text{range of } (A, \gamma(M-s))\}$, $f_s(M-s, A, \gamma(M-s), \cdot)$ is strictly increasing and strictly concave on the set

$$(R^n_+ \times R_-)^{M-s} \times R_{-N_\mu(M-s)} \times R^l_+;$$

(iii) for each vector $(A, \gamma(M-s), x(1), \ldots, x(M-s), \mu, m)$ in the domain of $f_s(M-s, \cdot)$, $f_s(M-s, A, \gamma(M-s), x(1), \ldots, x(M-s), \mu, m)$ measures the maximum expected utility which the consumer, conditional upon the event $(\{\xi \geqslant M-s\} \cap \{(A, \gamma(M-s))(\omega) = (A, \gamma(M-s))\})$, could obtain over the remainder of his life if he chose $(x(M-s), \mu, m)$ in period $M-s$ after having chosen $x(1), \ldots, x(M-s-1)$ in the preceding periods.

Step 7: From step 1–step 6 it follows that if we let

$$\tilde{V}(A, \gamma(1), x(1), \mu, m) = f_{M-1}(1, A, \gamma(1), x(1), \mu, m),$$

then $\tilde{V}(\cdot)$ has all the properties required of $\tilde{V}(\cdot)$ in T 30.2 (i).

To demonstrate that $\tilde{V}(\cdot)$ satisfies the condition described in T 30.2 (ii), we assume that the consumer has a consumption-investment strategy, which we denote by

$$\text{CIS} = \{(\hat{q}, \hat{L}, \hat{\mu}, \hat{m})(t, \omega), t = 1, \ldots, M\},$$

and proceed as follows:

Step 8: Let $(q, L, \mu, m)(M, \cdot)$ be the real vector-valued function on the set

$$\{(A, \gamma(M), x(1), \ldots, x(M-1), r) \in \{\text{range of } (A, \gamma(M))\} \times (R^n_+ \times R_-)^{M-1}$$

$$\times R : r \geqslant -\alpha(M)N_\mu(M) - w(M)N_L(M)\},$$

which at each value of its arguments solves the associated maximum problem in step 3. It is an easy consequence of the properties of $\Gamma(\cdot)$ and $f_0(M, \cdot)$ and C. Berge's Théoreme du Maximum (Berge 1959, p. 122) that

$(q, L, \mu, m)(M, \cdot)$ is a continuous function of its arguments. Consequently, when we substitute $(\hat{q}, \hat{L})(t, \cdot)$ for $x(t)$, $t = 1, \ldots, M-1$, and $\hat{\mu}_1(M-1, \cdot) + \sum_{i=1}^{k-1} \alpha_i(M)\hat{\mu}_{i+1}(M-1, \cdot) + (p_m + d)(M)\hat{m}(M-1, \cdot)$ for r in $(q, L, \mu, m)(M, \cdot)$, we obtain a function,

$$(\tilde{q}, \tilde{L}, \tilde{\mu}, \tilde{m})(M, \cdot) : \Omega \to R_+^n \times R_- \times R^k \times R_+^l,$$

which satisfies the condition $\mathscr{F}((\tilde{q}, \tilde{L}, \tilde{\mu}, \tilde{m})(M)) \subset \mathscr{F}(A, \gamma(M), I_{\xi \geqslant M})$. But if this is so, it is a routine matter to verify that

$$(\tilde{q}, \tilde{L}, \tilde{\mu}, \tilde{m})(M, \omega) = (\hat{q}, \hat{L}, \hat{\mu}, \hat{m})(M, \omega) \quad \text{a.e.}$$

Step 9: Let

$$f_2^*(M-1, A, \gamma(M-1), x(1), \ldots, x(M-2), r)$$
$$= \max_{(x(M-1), \mu, m) \in \Gamma(z(M-1), r)} f_1(M-1, A, \gamma(M-1), x(1), \ldots, x(M-1), \mu, m).$$

Then it follows from the properties of $\Gamma(\cdot)$ and $f_1(M-1, \cdot)$ and from C. Berge's theorems VI. 3.1, VI. 3.2, and Théoreme du Maximum that the following assertions are true:

(i) $f_2^*(M-1, \cdot)$ is well defined and continuous on the set

$$\hat{\Gamma} = \{(A, \gamma(M-1), x(1), \ldots, x(M-2), r) \in \{\text{range of } (A, \gamma(M-1))\}$$
$$\times (R_+^n \times R_-)^{M-2} \times R : r \geqslant -\alpha(M-1)N_\mu(M-1)$$
$$- w(M-1)N_L(M-1)\}.$$

Moreover, for each value of $(A, \gamma(M-1)$, $f_2^*(M-1, A, \gamma(M-1), \cdot)$ is a strictly increasing, strictly concave function.

(ii) The vector-valued function on $\hat{\Gamma}$, $(q, L, \mu, m)(M-1, \cdot)$, which at each value of its arguments solves the associated maximum problem in the definition of $f_2^*(M-1, \cdot)$, is well defined and continuous.

Step 10: From steps 8 and 9 we deduce that if we substitute $(\hat{q}, \hat{L})(t, \cdot)$ for $x(t)$, $t = 1, \ldots, M-2$, and $\hat{\mu}_1(M-2, \cdot) + \sum_{i=1}^{k-1} \alpha_i(M-1)\hat{\mu}_{i+1}(M-2, \cdot) + (p_m + d)(M-1)\hat{m}(M-2, \cdot)$ for r in $(q, L, \mu, m)(M-1, A, \gamma(M-1), \cdot)$ we obtain a function,

$$(\tilde{q}, \tilde{L}, \tilde{\mu}, \tilde{m})(M-1, \cdot) : \Omega \to R_+^n \times R_- \times R^k \times R_+^l,$$

which satisfies the condition $\mathscr{F}((\tilde{q}, \tilde{L}, \tilde{\mu}, \tilde{m})(M-1)) \subset \mathscr{F}(A, \gamma(M-1), I_{\xi \geqslant M-1})$. Moreover, if we substitute $(\hat{q}, \hat{L})(t, \cdot)$ for $x(t)$, $t = 1, \ldots, M-2$, $(\tilde{q}, \tilde{L})(M-1, \cdot)$ for $x(M-1)$, and $\tilde{\mu}_1(M-1, \cdot) + \sum_{i=1}^{k-1} \alpha_i(M)\tilde{\mu}_{i+1}(M-$

$1, \cdot) + (p_m + d)(M)\tilde{m}(M-1, \cdot)$ for r in $(q, L, \mu, m)(M, A, \gamma(M), \cdot)$, we obtain a function,

$$(\tilde{\tilde{q}}, \tilde{\tilde{L}}, \tilde{\tilde{\mu}}, \tilde{\tilde{m}})(M, \cdot): \Omega \to R_+^n \times R_- \times R^k \times R_+^l,$$

which satisfies the condition $\mathscr{F}((\tilde{\tilde{q}}, \tilde{\tilde{L}}, \tilde{\tilde{\mu}}, \tilde{\tilde{m}})(M)) \subset \mathscr{F}(A, \gamma(M), I_{\xi \geqslant M})$. But if this is so, then it is a routine matter to verify that

$$(\tilde{\tilde{q}}, \tilde{\tilde{L}}, \tilde{\tilde{\mu}}, \tilde{\tilde{m}})(M, \omega) = (\hat{q}, \hat{L}, \hat{\mu}, \hat{m})(M, \omega) \quad \text{a.e.}$$

and

$$(\tilde{q}, \tilde{L}, \tilde{\mu}, \tilde{m})(M-1, \omega) = (\hat{q}, \hat{L}, \hat{\mu}, \hat{m})(M-1, \omega) \quad \text{a.e.}$$

Step 11: Proceeding as above, we can establish the existence of a sequence of vector-valued functions $(q, L, \mu, m)(M-s, \cdot)$, $s = 2, \ldots, M-1$, that are, respectively, well defined and continuous on the set

$$\{(A, \gamma(M-s), x(1), \ldots, x(M-s-1), r) \in \{\text{range of } (A, \gamma(M-s))\}$$
$$\times (R_+^n \times R_-)^{M-s-1} \times R: r \geqslant -\alpha(M-s)N_\mu(M-s)$$
$$- w(M-s)N_L(M-s)\}$$

and maximize the value of $f_{M-s}(M-s, A, \gamma(M-s), x(1), \ldots, x(M-s-1), \cdot)$ subject to the conditions of $\Gamma(z(M-s), r)$. Moreover, by substituting $(\hat{q}, \hat{L})(t, \cdot)$ for $x(t)$, $t = 1, \ldots, M-s-1$, and $\hat{\mu}_1(M-s-1) + \sum_{i=1}^{k-1} \alpha_i(M-s)\hat{\mu}_{i+1}(M-s-1, \cdot) + (p_m + d)(M-s)\hat{m}(M-s-1, \cdot)$ for r in $(q, L, \mu, m)(M-s, A, \gamma(M-s), \cdot)$, $s = 2, \ldots, M-1$ (with $\hat{\mu}(0, \cdot) = \hat{m}(0, \cdot) = 0$ and A substituted for r when $s = M-1$), we obtain a sequence of functions,

$$(\tilde{q}, \tilde{L}, \tilde{\mu}, \tilde{m})(M-s, \cdot): \Omega \to R_+^n \times R_- \times R^k \times R_+^l, \quad s = 2, \ldots, M-1,$$

that satisfy the conditions

(i) $\mathscr{F}((\tilde{q}, \tilde{L}, \tilde{\mu}, \tilde{m})(M-s)) \subset \mathscr{F}(A, \gamma(M-s), I_{\xi \geqslant M-s})$ and

(ii) $(\tilde{q}, \tilde{L}, \tilde{\mu}, \tilde{m})(M-s, \omega) = (\hat{q}, \hat{L}, \hat{\mu}, \hat{m})(M-s, \omega)$ a.e.

These results and the definition of $\tilde{V}(\cdot)$ establish the validity of T 30.2 (ii).

Step 12: The validity of T 30.2 (ii) would be vacuous if T 30.1 were false. In this step we establish the validity of T 30.1. We begin by observing that

$$\mathscr{F}((q, L, \mu, m)(1)) \subset \mathscr{F}(A, \gamma(1), I_{\xi \geqslant 1})$$

and by letting

$$(\mathring{q}, \mathring{L}, \mathring{\mu}, \mathring{m})(1, \omega) = (q, L, \mu, m)(1, A(\omega), \gamma(1, \omega)), \qquad \omega \in \Omega.$$

Next we substitute $(\mathring{q}, \mathring{L})(1)$ for $x(1)$ and $\mathring{\mu}_1(1, \cdot) + \sum_{i=1}^{k-1} \alpha_i(2)\mathring{\mu}_{i+1}(1, \cdot) + (p_m + d)(2)\mathring{m}(1, \cdot)$ for r in $(q, L, \mu, m)(2, A, \gamma(2), \cdot)$ to obtain a function,

$$(\mathring{q}, \mathring{L}, \mathring{\mu}, \mathring{m})(2, \cdot) : \Omega \to R_+^n \times R_- \times R^k \times R_+^l,$$

which satisfies the condition $\mathscr{F}((\mathring{q}, \mathring{L}, \mathring{\mu}, \mathring{m})(2)) \subset \mathscr{F}(A, \gamma(2), I_{\xi \geqslant 2})$. Continuing in the obvious way, we obtain a family of random variables,

$$\text{OCIS} = \{(\mathring{q}, \mathring{L}, \mathring{\mu}, \mathring{m})(s, \omega); s = 1, \ldots, M\},$$

with the following properties:

(i) If $(\mathring{q}, \mathring{L})(t, \cdot)$ is substituted for $x(t)$, $t = 1, \ldots, s$, and $\mathring{\mu}_1(s, \cdot) + \sum_{i=1}^{k-1} \alpha_i(s+1)\mathring{\mu}_{i+1}(s, \cdot) + (p_m + d)(s+1)\mathring{m}(s, \cdot)$ is substituted for r in $(q, L, \mu, m)(s+1, A, \gamma(s+1), \cdot)$, we obtain $(\mathring{q}, \mathring{L}, \mathring{\mu}, \mathring{m})(s+1, \cdot)$, $s = 1, \ldots, M-1$; and

(ii) $\mathscr{F}((\mathring{q}, \mathring{L}, \mathring{\mu}, \mathring{m})(s)) \subset \mathscr{F}(A, \gamma(s), I_{\xi \geqslant s}), \qquad s = 1, \ldots, M.$

It is evident that OCIS constitutes an expenditure sequence, and that the arguments we outlined in steps 9–11, with only obvious modifications, suffice to show that OCIS is a consumption-investment strategy.

30.7.2 Proof of T 30.5

The proof of T 30.5 is similar to the proof of T 30.2. Throughout the proof we let z be short for $(p_y, p_x, w, p_I, \alpha, p_M, N_\mu, N_M)$ and we let

$$\tilde{\Gamma}(z, K, r) = \{(y, x, L, d, I, \mu, M) \in R_+^v \times R_+^l \times R_+ \times R_+ \times R_+^h \times R_{-N_\mu}^k \times [1, N_M] : p_I I + d + \alpha\mu - p_M M \leqslant r + p_y y - p_x x - wL, y \leqslant g(K, x, L)\}.$$

Moreover, we let $z(t)$, $\alpha(t)$, $p_M(t)$, $\psi(t)$, and A denote values assumed, respectively, by $(p_y, p_x, w, p_I, \alpha, p_M, N_\mu, N_M)(t, \cdot)$, $\alpha(t, \cdot)$, $p_M(t, \cdot)$, $\psi(t, \cdot)$, and $A(\cdot)$, $t = 1, \ldots, N+1$. The proof is obtained in several steps as follows:

Step 1: Since $g(\cdot)$ is continuous and does not vary with z, we can use UT 7 and only obvious additional arguments to demonstrate that $\tilde{\Gamma}(\cdot)$ is convex, compact, and continuous on the set

$$\{(z, K, r) \in R_{++}^{v+l+1+h+k+1+k+1} \times R_{++}^h \times R : r \geqslant -p_M N_M - \alpha N_\mu\}.$$

Step 2: In this step we shall define three functions, $f_0(\cdot)$, $f_1^*(\cdot)$, and $f_1(\cdot)$, and derive their properties. First $f_0(\cdot)$:

$$f_0(A, \psi(N), d(1), \ldots, d(N), M)$$
$$= E\{V(d(1), \ldots, d(N), p_M(N+1)M) | A, \psi(N)\}.$$

From FBS 10 and FBS 12 (ii) it follows that

(i) $f_0(\cdot)$: {range of $(A, \psi(N))$} $\times R_+^N \times R_+ \to R$ is well defined, bounded, and continuous; and

(ii) for each value of $(A, \psi(N)), f_0(A, \psi(N), \cdot)$ is a strictly increasing, strictly concave function.

Next $f_1^*(\cdot)$:

$$f_1^*(A, \psi(N), d(1), \ldots, d(N-1), K, r)$$
$$= \max_{(y,x,L,d,I,\mu,M) \in \Gamma(z(N),K,r)} f_0(A, \psi(N), d(1), \ldots, d(N-1), d, M).$$

Then it follows from the properties of $\tilde{\Gamma}(\cdot)$ and from C. Berge's theorems VI. 3.1 and VI. 3.2 that

(iii) $f_1^*(\cdot)$ is a well-defined, bounded, continuous real-valued function on the set,

$$\{(A, \psi(N), u, K, r) \in \{\text{range of } (A, \psi(N))\} \times R_+^{N-1} \times R_{++}^h$$
$$\times R : r \geqslant -\alpha(N)N_\mu(N) - p_M(N)N_M(N)\};$$

(iv) for each value of $(A, \psi(N), f_1^*(A, \psi(N), \cdot)$ is a strictly increasing, strictly concave function.

Finally $f_1(\cdot)$:

$$f_1(A, \psi(N-1), d(1), \ldots, d(N-1), K, \mu, M)$$
$$= E\left\{f_1^*\left(A, \psi(N), d(1), \ldots, d(N-1), K, \mu_1 + \sum_{i=1}^{k-1} \alpha_i(N)\mu_{i+1}\right.\right.$$
$$\left.\left. - p_M(N)M\right) \middle| A, \psi(N-1)\right\}.$$

It follows from the properties of $f_1^*(\cdot)$ and from FBS 11 and FBS 12 (i) that

(v) $f_1(\cdot)$ is a well-defined, bounded, continuous real-valued function on the set

$$\{(A, \psi(N-1), u, K, \mu, M) \in \{\text{range of } (A, \psi(N-1))\} \times R_+^{N-1} \times R_{++}^h$$
$$\times R^k \times R_1 : \mu \geqslant -N_\mu(N-1), M \leqslant N_M(N-1)\};$$

(vi) for each value of $(A, \psi(N-1)), f_1(A, \psi(N-1), \cdot)$ is a strictly concave function;

(vii) for each value of $(A, \psi(N-1), M), f_1(A, \psi(N-1), \cdot, M)$ is a strictly increasing function; and

(viii) for each value of $(A, \psi(N-1), d(1), \ldots, d(N-1), K, \mu), f_1(A, \psi(N-1), d(1), \ldots, d(N-1), K, \mu, \cdot)$ is a strictly decreasing function.

If $N = 2$, we can proceed directly to step 4. Otherwise we must continue as described in step 3.

Step 3: In this step we work backward on the tree structure of events facing the entrepreneur. We begin with $f_1(\cdot)$ and use arguments like those we used above to construct real-valued functions $f_s(\cdot)$, $s = 2, \ldots, N-1$, that satisfy the conditions:

(i) $f_s(\cdot)$ is a well-defined, bounded, continuous function on the set

$$\{(A, \psi(N-s), u, K, \mu, M) \in \{\text{range of } (A, \psi(N-s))\} \times R_+^{N-s} \times R_{++}^h \times R^k \times R_1 : \mu \geqslant N_\mu(N-s), M \leqslant N_M(N-s)\};$$

(ii) for each value of $(A, \psi(N-s)), f_s(A, \psi(N-s), \cdot)$ is strictly concave function;

(iii) for each value of $(A, \psi(N-s), M), f_s(A, \psi(N-s), \cdot, M)$ is a strictly increasing function;

(iv) for each value of $(A, \psi(N-s), d(1), \ldots, d(N-s), K, \mu), f_1(A, \psi(N-s), d(1), \ldots, d(N-s), K, \mu, \cdot)$ is a strictly decreasing function; and

(v) for each vector $(A, \psi(N-s), d(1), \ldots, d(N-s), K+I, \mu, M)$ in the domain of $f_s(\cdot), f_s(A, \psi(N-s), d(1), \ldots, d(N-s), K+I, \mu, M)$ measures the maximum expected utility which the entrepreneur, conditional upon the event $\{\omega \in \Omega : (A, \psi(N-s))(\omega) = (A, \psi(N-s))\}$, could obtain over the remainder of his planning horizon if he chose $(d(N-s), I, \mu, M)$ in period $N-s$ after having paid out $(d(1), \ldots, d(N-s-1)$ in dividends and accumulated a stock of capital equal to K in the preceding periods.

Step 4: From steps 1–3, it follows that if we let

$$\tilde{V}(A, \psi(1), d(1), \hat{K}+I, \mu, M) = f_{N-1}(A, \psi(1), d(1), \hat{K}+I, \mu, M),$$

then $\hat{V}(\cdot)$ has all the properties required of it in T 30.5 (i)–(iii). The proof of T 30.5 (iv) is, with only obvious modifications, like the proof of T 30.2 (ii). Those details I leave to the reader.

30.7.3 Proof of T 30.7

In this subsection we shall establish the existence of a temporary equilibrium in a production economy which satisfies the conditions of MCBS 1–MCBS 3, MFBS 1–MFBS 4 and MMBS 1. The arguments we need to obtain this result are essentially the arguments I used to establish Proposition III in Stigum 1969 (pp. 551–553).

In the economy of T 30.7 a temporary equilibrium is a vector,

$$(\hat{p}, \hat{w}, \hat{\alpha}, \hat{p}_m, (\tilde{x}, \tilde{L}, \tilde{\mu}, \tilde{m})^1, \ldots, (\tilde{x}, \tilde{L}, \tilde{\mu}, \tilde{m})^T, (\hat{y}, \hat{L}, \hat{d}, \hat{I}, \hat{\mu}, \hat{M})^1, \ldots, (\hat{y}, \hat{L}, \hat{d}, \hat{I}, \hat{\mu}, \hat{M})^S),$$

which satisfies the following conditions:

(i) $(\hat{p}, \hat{w}, \hat{\alpha}, \hat{p}_m) \in R_{++}^{n+h+l+1+k+S} \cap P$, where

$$P = \left\{ u \in R_{+}^{n+h+l+1+k+S} : \sum_{i=1}^{n+h+l+1+k+S} u_i = 1 \right\};$$

(ii) for each $i = 1, \ldots, T$,

$$(\tilde{x}, \tilde{L}, \tilde{\mu}, \tilde{m})^i \in \chi^i;$$

$$(\tilde{x}, \tilde{L}, \tilde{\mu}, \tilde{m})^i \in \Gamma^i(\hat{p}, \hat{w}, \hat{\alpha}, \hat{p}_m, \hat{d}, \overline{m}^i, N_L^i, N_\mu^i), \quad \text{where}$$

$$\hat{d} = (\hat{d}^1, \ldots, \hat{d}^S), \quad \text{and}$$

$$\Gamma^i(p, w, \alpha, p_m, d, \overline{m}^i, N_L^i, N_\mu^i) = \{(x, L, \mu, m) \in \chi^i : px + wL + \alpha\mu + p_m m \leqslant (p_m + d)\overline{m}^i\};$$

$$\tilde{U}^i(\hat{p}, \hat{w}, \hat{\alpha}, \hat{p}_m, \hat{d}, N_L^i, N_\mu^i, N_m^i, (\tilde{x}, \tilde{L}, \tilde{\mu}, \tilde{m})^i) = \max_{(x, L, \mu, m) \in \Gamma^i(\hat{p}, \hat{w}, \hat{\alpha}, \hat{p}_m, \hat{d}, \overline{m}^i, N_L^i, N_\mu^i)} \tilde{U}^i(\hat{p}, \hat{w}, \hat{\alpha}, \hat{p}_m, \hat{d}, N_L^i, N_\mu^i, N_m^i, x, L, \mu, m);$$

(iii) for each $j = 1, \ldots, S$,

$$(\hat{y}, \hat{L})^j \in Y^j;$$

$$\hat{p}\hat{y}^j + \hat{w}\hat{L}^j = \max_{(y, L) \in Y^j} \hat{p}y + \hat{w}L;$$

$$(\hat{d}, \hat{I}, \hat{\mu}, \hat{M})^j \in Z^j,$$

$$\hat{U}^j(\hat{p}, \hat{w}, \hat{\alpha}, \hat{p}_m, N_L^j, N_\mu^j, N_m^j, (\hat{d}, \hat{I}, \hat{\mu}, \hat{M})^j) = \max_{(d, I, \mu, M) \in \Gamma^j(\hat{p}, \hat{w}, \hat{\alpha}, \hat{p}_m, N_\mu^j, N_M^j, \overline{M}^j, \overline{x}^j)} \hat{U}^j(\hat{p}, \hat{w}, \hat{\alpha}, \hat{p}_m, N_L^j, N_\mu^j, N_m^j, d, I, \mu, M),$$

where

$$\Gamma^j(p, w, \alpha, p_m, N_\mu^j, N_M^j, \overline{M}^j, \overline{x}^j)$$
$$= \{(d, I, \mu, M) \in Z^j : (p_{n+1}, \ldots, p_{n+h})I + d\overline{M}^j + p_m(\overline{M}^j - M)$$
$$+ \alpha\mu \leqslant p\overline{x}^j + p\hat{y}^j + w\hat{L}^j\};$$

(iv) let 0_{hn} and 0_{hl} be, respectively, $h \times n$ and $h \times l$ matrices whose components equal zero; let I_h denote the $h \times h$ identity matrix; and let

$D = (0_{hn}, I_h, 0_{hl})$. Then

$$\sum_{i=1}^{T} \tilde{x}^i + \sum_{j=1}^{S} (\hat{I}^j D - \hat{y}^j - \overline{x}^j) = 0;$$

$$\sum_{i=1}^{T} \tilde{L}^i - \sum_{j=1}^{S} \hat{L}^j = 0;$$

$$\sum_{i=1}^{T} \tilde{\mu}^i + \sum_{j=1}^{S} \hat{\mu}^j = 0; \quad \text{and}$$

$$\sum_{i=1}^{T} \tilde{m}_j^i - \hat{M}^j = 0, \quad j = 1, \ldots, S.$$

Let E denote the economy we described in sections 30.6.1 and 30.6.2. To establish T 30.7 we must construct two auxiliary economies, $E(C)$ and $E(C, \delta)$. We begin with $E(C)$.

To construct $E(C)$ and for later reference, we first observe that our assumptions concerning the firms' production sets, i.e., MFBS 2 and FBS 9, imply that

$$\left(\sum_{j=1}^{S} Y^j\right) \subset \{r \in R : r \leqslant C\}^{n+h+l+1} \qquad \text{for some } C \in R_{++}. \tag{30.33}$$

From this it follows that we can find a $C \in R_{++}$ which is so large that it satisfies equation 30.33 and the following conditions:

$$\text{If } (y, L) \in Y^j, \text{ then } S \cdot |y_i| < C, \qquad i = 1, \ldots, n + h + l; \tag{30.34}$$

and

$$(n + h + l) + \sum_{i=1}^{T} (N_L^i + \|N_\mu^i\| + \|N_m\|) + \sum_{j=1}^{S} (\|\overline{x}^j\| + \|N_\mu^j\| + N_M^j)$$
$$+ (S + T) < (C/(S + T)). \tag{30.35}$$

Let C be a constant which satisfies equations 30.33–30.35. Then $E(C)$ is an economy which is populated by the consumers and firms in E but in which (1) consumers are required to choose their budget vectors (x, L, μ, m) from

$$\chi^i \cap \{r \in R : |r| \leqslant C\}^{n+h+l+1+k+S}, \qquad i = 1, \ldots, T;$$

and (2) firms are required to choose their budget vectors (y, L, d, I, μ, M) from

$$\{r \in R : |r| \leqslant C\}^{n+h+l+1} \times (Z^j \cap (R_+ \times \{r \in R : |r| \leqslant C\}^{h+k+1})),$$

$$j = 1, \ldots, S.$$

So much for $E(C)$. To construct $E(C, \delta)$ we pick a $\delta \in R_{++}$ such that

$$\delta < N_L^i, \quad i = 1, \ldots, T; \quad \text{and} \quad (T + S)\delta < N_M^j - \overline{M}^j, \quad j = 1, \ldots, S.$$

Then we give each consumer i, $i = 1, \ldots, T$, in $E(C)$ an additional endowment,

$$\delta_c^i = ((\delta, \ldots, \delta), -\delta, (0, \ldots, 0), (\delta, \ldots, \delta)) \in R_+^{n+h+l} \times R_- \times R_+^k \times R_+^S.$$

We also give each firm j, $j = 1, \ldots, S$, in $E(C)$ an additional endowment,

$$\delta_f^j = ((\delta, \ldots, \delta), (T/S)\delta, (0, \ldots, 0), (\delta, \ldots, \delta), -(T + S - 1)\delta,$$
$$(\delta, \ldots, \delta)), \in R_+^{n+h+l} \times R_+ \times R_+^k \times R_+^{j-1} \times R_- \times R_+^{S-j}.$$

The economy which results from these changes in the initial endowments of the consumers and firms in $E(C)$ is $E(C, \delta)$.

It is easy to demonstrate that in $E(C, \delta)$ each consumer's choice of budget vector is a continuous function of prices, dividends, initial endowments, and institutional constraints. Similarly, each firm's choice of dividends is a continuous function of prices, initial endowments, and institutional constraints. If we substitute the firm's equilibrium dividends for the consumer's dividend parameters, each consumer's choice of budget vector becomes a continuous function of prices, initial endowments, and institutional constraints. Since the arguments needed to establish these facts are easy to come by, I leave the proof of the preceding assertions to the reader.

If we hold initial endowments and institutional constraints fixed and if we substitute the firms' equilibrium dividend rates for the consumer's dividend parameters, we can represent the $E(C, \delta)$ economy's excess demand for commodities, labor, and securities by a multi-valued function,

$$z(\cdot): P \to \mathscr{P}(R^{n+h+l+1+k+S}).$$

$z(\cdot)$ is upper semi-continuous on P and a continuous function on $(P \cap$

$R_{++}^{n+h+l+1+k+S}$). Moreover, for each $u \in P$, $z(u)$ is convex and $uz = 0$ for all $z \in z(u)$. Finally, if $u \in P$ and $u_j = 0$ for some j, there is a $z \in z(u)$ such that $z_j > 0$. But if that is so, and if every intermediate good is used in the production of some final output, we can apply Debreu's Theorem 5.7.1 (1959, pp. 83–84) and standard arguments to demonstrate that there exists a strictly positive $\hat{u} \in P$, which we denote by $(p, w, \alpha, p_m)(\delta)$, such that $z((p, w, \alpha, p_m)(\delta)) = 0$. For later reference the associated equilibrium allocation is described in

$$((p, w, \alpha, p_m)(\delta), (x, L, \mu, m)^1(\delta), \ldots, (x, L, \mu, m)^T(\delta),$$
$$(y, L, I, \mu, M)^1(\delta), \ldots, (y, L, I, \mu, M)^S(\delta)).$$

We now pick a sequence of numbers δ_n that converge to zero. Using this sequence, we can show that the monotonic properties of the $\tilde{U}^i(\cdot)$, the $\hat{U}^j(\cdot)$, and the firm's production functions imply that there exists a subsequence of the δ_n, δ_{n_k} such that

(i) $(p, w, \alpha, p_m)(\delta_{n_k})$ converges to a positive price vector, $(\hat{p}, \hat{w}, \hat{\alpha}, \hat{p}_m) \in P$;

(ii) $(x, L, \mu, m)^i(\delta_{n_k})$ converges to a vector,

$$(\tilde{x}, \tilde{L}, \tilde{\mu}, \tilde{m})^i \in \chi^i \cap \{r \in R : |r| \leqslant C\}^{n+h+l+1+k+S}, \qquad i = 1, \ldots, T;$$

(iii) $(y, L, I, \mu, M)^j(\delta_{n_k})$ converges to a vector,

$$(\hat{y}, \hat{L}, \hat{I}, \hat{\mu}, \hat{M})^j \in (Y^j \times R_+^h \times R_{-N_\mu^j} \times [1, N_M^j]) \cap \{r \in R : |r|$$
$$\leqslant C\}^{n+h+1+h+k+1}, \qquad j = 1, \ldots, S; \qquad \text{and}$$

(iv) with $\hat{d} = (\hat{d}^1, \ldots, \hat{d}^S)$ denoting equilibrium dividends in $E(C)$ at $(\hat{p}, \hat{w}, \hat{\alpha}, \hat{p}_m)$,

$$((\hat{p}, \hat{w}, \hat{\alpha}, \hat{p}_m), (\tilde{x}, \tilde{L}, \tilde{\mu}, \tilde{m})^1, \ldots, (\tilde{x}, \tilde{L}, \tilde{\mu}, \tilde{m})^T, (\hat{y}, \hat{L}, \hat{d}, \hat{I}, \hat{\mu}, \hat{M})^1, \ldots,$$
$$(\hat{y}, \hat{L}, \hat{d}, \hat{I}, \hat{\mu}, \hat{M})^S)$$

is a temporary equilibrium in $E(C)$. The arguments needed to establish these facts are also easy to come by, and I leave it to the reader to provide them.

To conclude the proof of T 30.7, we need only observe that we have chosen C so large that a temporary equilibrium in $E(C)$ is also a temporary equilibrium in E.

31 Balanced Growth under Uncertainty[1]

In two path-breaking articles on economic growth, Samuelson and Solow suggested that one approach economists might take in studying the behavior over time of an economy would be to study the solutions to nonlinear difference equations of the form

$$x(t+1) = H(x(t)), \qquad t = 0, 1, \ldots, \tag{31.1}$$

where $x(t) = (x_1, \ldots, x_n)(t)$, $H(x(t)) = (H_1(x(t)), \ldots, H_n(x(t)))$, and each $H_i(\cdot)$ is a linearly homogeneous, nondecreasing function of its arguments. Depending on the economic system under study, the x_i's might denote various things. In most cases, however, the components of $x(t)$ would denote the economy's aggregate stock at time t of labor and various capital goods, and equations 31.1 would thus describe the behavior of these stocks over time (see Solow and Samuelson 1953, pp. 412–424, and Solow 1956, pp. 65–94).

The system of equations 31.1 is said to be *decomposable* if $H(\cdot)$ is decomposable; it is said to be *indecomposable* if $H(\cdot)$ is indecomposable. The definitions of indecomposable and decomposable functions are as follows:

D 31.1 Let $M = \{1, 2, \ldots, n\}$ and, for $x, y \in R_+^n$, let $N(x, y) = \{i \in M : x_i > y_i\}$. The vector-valued function $H(\cdot)$: $R_+^n \to R_+^n$ is called *indecomposable* if, for any x, $y \in R_+^n$ such that $x \geqslant y$, $x \neq y$, and $N(x, y)$ is a proper subset of M, $H_i(x) \neq H_i(y)$ for some $i \notin N(x, y)$. Moreover, $H(\cdot)$ is called *decomposable* if and only if it is not indecomposable.

Two simple economies which illustrate this definition can be obtained as follows: Let $x_1(t)$ denote an economy's stock of labor at time t; $x_2(t)$ the same economy's aggregate capital stock at time t; and $F(\cdot)$: $R_+^2 \to R_+$ the economy's aggregate production function, which we assume to be linearly homogeneous and increasing. If in the economy, labor is "produced" by labor alone and capital is produced by combining both labor and capital, then the behavior of the economy can be described by the following two equations:

$$x_1(t+1) = \lambda x_1(t),$$

and

$$x_2(t+1) = x_2(t) + sF(x_1(t), x_2(t)),$$

in which λ denotes the rate of growth of the labor force, s the average propensity of consumers to save. Applying the above definition to these equations, we see that the economy whose behavior they represent is clearly a decomposable economy.

Now let us make a slight switch in our assumptions. Let us think of labor as being produced both by labor and consumption. Then the behavior of the economy would be described by the following system of equations:

$$x_1(t+1) = G(x_1(t), (1-s)F(x_1(t), x_2(t))),$$

and

$$x_2(t+1) = x_2(t) + sF(x_1(t), x_2(t)),$$

in which $G(\cdot)$ is taken to be a linearly homogeneous, increasing function of its arguments. Our definition tells us that the above equations represent the behavior of an indecomposable economy.

Of the preceding models, the first turns out to be the difference-equation analogue of the system of differential equations proposed by Solow in Solow 1956, while the second is just a particular realization of the general systems studied by Solow and Samuelson in Solow and Samuelson 1953.

In studying the behavior of solutions to equations 31.1, Samuelson and Solow found that, under "reasonable" conditions on $H(\cdot)$, there exists a positive number λ, a positive vector V, and a real-valued function $\gamma(\cdot)$ such that, for each nonnegative, nonzero initial vector $x(0)$,

$$\lim_{t\to\infty} (x(t)/\lambda^t) = \gamma(x(0))V.$$

This they interpreted to imply that if an economy behaves in accordance with equations 31.1, then regardless of where it starts out, it will, for large t, approach closely a *balanced growth* pattern. Also this balanced growth configuration will be independent of the economy's initial starting point.

In their papers, Samuelson and Solow did not specify whether or not their equation systems would apply to an economy which operates under uncertainty. It seems quite unlikely, however, that the relationship implied by the system 31.1 would hold exactly for an "uncertainty" economy. The best one could ever hope for would be that it would hold "on the average" in the sense that the conditionally expected value of $x(t + 1)$, given $x(0), \ldots, x(t)$, would equal some linearly homogeneous function $H(\cdot)$ of $x(t)$.

To see why, let us take a closer look at Solow's model. First the labor equation: In any economy which operates under uncertainty, the size of the labor force in any given period t would depend not just on the size of the labor force in period $t - 1$ but also on the composition of the population in $t - 1$. Moreover, this composition would have been determined by many random events that occurred in the past such as wars, droughts, and severe depressions. Also, even if the composition of the population and the size of the labor force in period $t - 1$ were known, the size of the labor force in period t would still depend on such imponderables as the extent to which students decided to stay in school one more year, the number of highway accidents, the occurrence of an earthquake, and the successful termination of a war in period $t - 1$. Therefore in an uncertainty economy, Solow's labor equation—seen as a description of the actual growth of the economy's labor force—could at best hold in the sense of "on the average" suggested above.

Next the savings-investment equation: It is true that, in an economy without government and international trade, investment in period t ex post, $(x_2(t + 1) - x_2(t))$, must equal savings in period t. It is not true, however, that actual investment need equal the average propensity to save times national income. One reason is that, while the savings function $S = sY$ (where Y denotes national income) might be a good "long-run" assumption in the sense that over time consumers tend on the average to allocate a constant proportion of their disposable income to savings, it is maybe a poor approximation of consumer behavior in any one short-run period. Second, even if $S = sY$ represented a true short- as well as long-run relationship, there is no reason why in an uncertainty economy investors need choose to invest exactly that amount in each period. Thus—seen as a description of the allocation of savings and investment in an uncertainty economy—Solow's equation is suspect on the one hand because it might not represent the true equilibrium relationship between savings and investment and on the other hand because an economy operating under uncertainty need not ever be in equilibrium. Conclusion: for an uncertainty economy, the best one could ever hope for is that Solow's investment-savings equation might hold "on the average" in the sense suggested above.

If equation 31.1 holds only on the average, then it becomes important to determine whether or not the assumption that this relationship is exact is "crucial", i.e., whether or not Samuelson and Solow's results are sensitive to this feature of their models. In this chapter we test this sensitivity of Samuelson and Solow's result. Specifically, we ask the following question: Suppose that the behavior over time of an economy can be represented by a family of vector-valued random variables $\{x(t), t = 0, 1, \ldots\}$. Moreover, suppose that there exists a linearly homogeneous, nondecreasing vector-valued function $H(\cdot)$ such that, for each $t = 0, 1, \ldots,$

$$E\{x(t+1)|x(0), \ldots, x(t)\} = H(x(t)) \quad \text{with probability 1},$$

where $E\{x(t+1)|x(0), \ldots, x(t)\}$ denotes the expected value of $x(t+1)$ conditional upon the observed values of $x(0), \ldots, x(t)$. Then does there exist a random variable g, a positive vector V, and a positive constant λ such that

$$\lim_{t\to\infty} (x(t)/\lambda^t) = gV \quad \text{with probability 1},$$

and such that

$$E\{g|x(0) = x\} > 0 \qquad \text{for all } x \geqslant 0, \quad x \neq 0?$$

If the answer to this equation is "yes," then Samuelson and Solow's assumption that equation 31.1 holds exactly is in fact not crucial.

To answer this question, we have to point up one other aspect of Samuelson and Solow's theories which might not be apparent in the general formulation (31.1) but which comes out clearly in Solow's model. This aspect concerns the relationship between flows and stocks. In any period in which the two equations in Solow's model are satisfied, the demand for stocks of labor and capital is equal to the supply of labor and capital. Thus there is "stock equilibrium." Moreover, the supply and demand for output (flows) are equal. Thus there is also a "flow equilibrium." However, the relationship between stocks and flows need not be one of equilibrium. In fact, stocks and flows cannot be in equilibrium vis-à-vis each other unless the economy travels along the *balanced growth path.*

Solow has shown for his economy that if flows and stocks are not in equilibrium vis-à-vis each other, then there exists an inexorable force which in each period moves stocks and flows closer to an equilibrium configuration. Such a "gravitational" force also operates in the economy studied in this paper (see T 31.2 and T 31.4). However, since in our economy there need be neither a stock nor a flow equilibrium in any given period, we must—to establish the existence of a balanced growth path—introduce an assumption on the variance of the distribution of the $x(t)$'s that ensures that the economy will, with large probability, move within the "sphere of influence" of this force. Such an assumption is stated in equation 31.31 for the case $\lambda > 1$.

31.1 Balanced Growth under Certainty

In this section we shall discuss salient characteristics of solutions to equation 31.1. We begin with the case when $H(\cdot)$ is indecomposable.

31.1.1 The Indecomposable Case

The study of solutions to equations 31.1 is essentially a study of the properties of nonnegative, linearly homogeneous, vector-valued functions and their iterates.

Nonnegative, linearly homogeneous, vector-valued functions have much in common with nonnegative square matrices. For example, let A be an $n \times n$ symmetric, nonnegative matrix and assume that there is an integer $t \geqslant 1$ such that the components of A^t are positive. Then A has a strictly positive eigenvalue ρ which is simple and exceeds all other eigenvalues in absolute value. Moreover, there exist $u, v \in R^n_{++}$ such that

$$Av = \rho v; \qquad uA = \rho u; \tag{31.2}$$

and

$$u \cdot v = 1. \tag{31.3}$$

Solow and Samuelson showed in Solow and Samuelson 1953 (pp. 415–416) that nonegative, linearly homogeneous, vector-valued functions have analogous properties. To wit, they gave us T 31.1:

T 31.1 Let $H(\cdot)$: $R^n_+ \to R^n_+$ be a continuous, nondecreasing function which is homogeneous of degree 1 and indecomposable. Then there exist a $\lambda \in R_{++}$ and a $V \in R^n_{++}$ such that

$$H(V) = \lambda V. \tag{31.4}$$

The λ is unique and V is determined up to a multiplicative positive constant.

If $H(\cdot)$ in addition is differentiable at V and the components of

$$H'(V) = (H_{ij}(V)) = \left(\frac{\partial H_i(V)}{\partial x_j}\right)$$

are positive, then there is a $U \in R^n_{++}$ such that

$$UH'(V) = \lambda U;$$

and

$UV = 1.$

The iterates of linearly homogeneous, vector-valued functions also have much in common with the iterates of nonnegative square matrices. For example, let A, v, ρ, and u be as in equations 31.2 and 31.3. Then there exist constants k and α such that $0 < \alpha < 1$ and, for all $t = 1, 2, \ldots$ and all $1 \leqslant i, j \leqslant n$,

$$|(A^t/\rho^t)_{i,j} - v_i u_j| < k\alpha^t. \tag{31.5}$$

The iterates of a linearly homogeneous, vector-valued function $H(\cdot)$, which we denote by $H^t(\cdot)$, have analogous properties. Consider T 31.2:

T 31.2 Let $H(\cdot)$: $R^n_+ \to R^n_+$ be a continuous, nondecreasing function which is homogeneous of degree 1, and indecomposable. Moreover, let λ and V be as in equation 31.4 and assume that $H(\cdot)$ has a derivative at V, $H'(V)$, whose components are positive. Finally, assume that

$$H(x) > 0 \quad \text{whenever} \quad x \in (R^n_+ - \{0\}).$$

Then there exist a continuous, nondecreasing function $\gamma(\cdot)$: $R^n_+ \to R_+$ and constants K, K^*, and α such that $0 < \alpha < 1$ and, for all $t = 1, 2, \ldots,$ and $x \in R^n_+$,[2]

$$\|(H^t(x)/\lambda^t) - \gamma(x)V\| \leqslant K\alpha^t\|x\|;^2 \tag{31.6}$$

and

$$\|(H^t(x)/\|H^t(x)\|) - (V/\|V\|)\| \leqslant K^*\alpha^t. \tag{31.7}$$

We shall assume the validity of T 31.1 and sketch a proof of equation 31.6. Proofs of T 31.1 and equation 31.7, respectively, can be found in Solow and Samuelson 1953 and Stigum 1972 (pp. 55–56).

In order to establish equation 31.6 we must first establish the existence of a function $\gamma(\cdot)$: $R^n_+ \to R_+$ which satisfies

$$\lim_{t\to\infty} \frac{H^t(x)}{\lambda^t} = \gamma(x)V, \qquad x \in R^n_+. \tag{31.8}$$

To do that we let

$$\alpha(t,x) = \min_{1\leqslant i\leqslant n} \frac{(H^t(x))_i}{\lambda^t V_i}, \qquad t = 0, 1, \ldots, \quad x \in R^n_+, \text{ and}$$

$$\beta(t,x) = \min_{1\leqslant i\leqslant n} \frac{(H^t(x))_i}{\lambda^t V_i}, \qquad t = 0, 1, \ldots, \quad x \in R^n_+.$$

Then, for each $t = 0, 1, \ldots, \alpha(t,\cdot)$ and $\beta(t,\cdot)$ are nondecreasing, continuous functions which, for all $x \in R^n_+$, satisfy

$$\alpha(0,x) \leqslant \cdots \leqslant \alpha(t,x) \leqslant \cdots \leqslant \beta(t,x) \leqslant \cdots \leqslant \beta(0,x).$$

We shall show that

$$\lim_{t\to\infty} \alpha(t,x) = \lim_{t\to\infty} \beta(t,x). \tag{31.9}$$

In order to establish equation 31.9, we first note that

$$\frac{H^t(x)}{\lambda^t} = \alpha(t,x)V + (\beta(t,x) - \alpha(t,x))y(t,x), \tag{31.10}$$

for some vector $y(t,x)$ with $0 \leqslant y_i(t,x) \leqslant V_i$, $i = 1, \ldots, n$, and $y_k(t,x) \geqslant V_k$ for some k, $k = 1, \ldots, n$. Then we observe that, for any nonnegative y,

$$H(V+y) = H(V) + H'(V)y + o(y) \quad \text{(see note 3)} \tag{31.11}$$

and that, for some sufficiently small $\varepsilon > 0$ and all y such that $0 \leqslant y \leqslant \varepsilon V$,

$$H(V+y) \geqslant H(V) + (1/2)H'(V)y. \tag{31.12}$$

These observations can be used to establish equation 31.9 in the following way: Deduce from equation 31.10 that

$$\begin{aligned}\frac{H^{t+1}(x)}{\lambda^{t+1}} &= \frac{H(H^t(x)/\lambda^t)}{\lambda}\\ &= \left(\frac{1}{\lambda}\right)H(\alpha(t,x)V + (\beta(t,x) - \alpha(t,x))y(t,x))\\ &\geqslant \left(\frac{1}{\lambda}\right)\alpha(t,x)H\left(V + \left(\frac{\beta(t,x) - \alpha(t,x)}{\alpha(t,x)}\right)\varepsilon' y(t,x)\right),\end{aligned} \tag{31.13}$$

where ε' is chosen so that, for all $x \geqslant 0$, $x \neq 0$,

$$0 < \varepsilon'\left(\frac{\beta(1,x) - \alpha(1,x)}{\alpha(1,x)}\right) \leqslant \varepsilon, \text{ and } \varepsilon' < 1. \tag{31.14}$$

Next, deduce from equations 31.11–31.14 that

$$\begin{aligned}\frac{H^{t+1}(x)}{\lambda^{t+1}} &\geqslant \left(\frac{1}{\lambda}\right)\alpha(t,x)\left(H(V) + (1/2)H'(V)\left(\frac{\beta(t,x) - \alpha(t,x)}{\alpha(t,x)}\right)\varepsilon' y(t,x)\right)\\ &= \alpha(t,x)V + \left(\frac{\varepsilon'}{2\lambda}\right)(\beta(t,x) - \alpha(t,x))H'(V)y(t,x)\\ &\geqslant \alpha(t,x)V + \left(\frac{\varepsilon'\delta}{2\lambda}\right)(\beta(t,x) - \alpha(t,x))V,\end{aligned} \tag{31.15}$$

where $\delta > 0$ is chosen so small that with $e_i = (0, \ldots, 0, e_{ii} = 1, 0, \ldots, 0)$,

$$H'(V)e_i V_i \geqslant \delta V, \qquad i = 1, \ldots, n.$$

Finally, deduce from equation 31.15 that

$$\alpha(t+1, x) \geqslant \alpha(t, x) + \left(\frac{\varepsilon'\delta}{2\lambda}\right)(\beta(t, x) - \alpha(t, x)).$$

Hence, since $\beta(t + 1, x) \leqslant \beta(t, x)$, we get

$$\beta(t + 1, x) - \alpha(t + 1, x) \leqslant (\beta(t, x) - \alpha(t, x))\left(\frac{1 - \varepsilon'\delta}{2\lambda}\right),$$

which by iteration gives

$$\beta(t + 1, x) - \alpha(t + 1, x) \leqslant (\beta(1, x) - \alpha(1, x))\left(1 - \frac{\varepsilon'\delta}{2\lambda}\right)^t. \tag{31.16}$$

From equation 31.16 and the fact that $n\delta \leqslant \lambda$ follows the validity of equation 31.9.

Next we let

$$\gamma(x) = \lim_{t\to\infty} \alpha(t, x), \qquad x \in R^n_+,$$

and observe that $\gamma(\cdot)\colon R^n_+ \to R_+$ is well defined and nondecreasing and satisfies equation 31.8. Moreover, since $\gamma(\cdot)$ is the limit of both a decreasing and an increasing sequence of continuous functions, $\gamma(\cdot)$ is a continuous function as well.

To conclude the proof of equation 31.6, we now let $\tilde{x} = x/\|x\|$, $x \in (R^n_+ - \{0\})$, and observe that

$$\begin{aligned}\left\|\left(\frac{H^t(x)}{\lambda^t}\right) - \gamma(x)V\right\| &= \sum_{i=1}^n V_i \left|\frac{H_i^t(x)}{\lambda^t V_i} - \gamma(x)\right| \\ &\leqslant \left(\sum_{i=1}^n V_i\right)(\beta(t, x) - \alpha(t, x)) \\ &= \left(\sum_{i=1}^n V_i\right)(\beta(t, \tilde{x}) - \alpha(t, \tilde{x}))\,\|x\|. \end{aligned} \tag{31.17}$$

From equations 31.17 and 31.16 and from the fact that $(\beta(1, x) - \alpha(1, x))$ is bounded on the set $\{x \in R^n_+ : \|x\| = 1\}$ follows the validity of equation 31.6.

Equations 31.6–31.8 tell us all we need to know here about balanced growth under certainty in an indecomposable economy. From them we deduce that (1) $\lim_{t\to\infty} x(t)/\lambda^t = \gamma(x(0))V$, (2) $\lim_{t\to\infty}(x(t)/\|x(t)\|) = (V/\|V\|)$, and hence that the direction of growth of a large economy is nearly independent of its starting point. Moreover, both equation 31.6 and equation 31.7 explicate the idea that there is a gravitational force which drives an economy toward its balanced growth path.

E 31.1 Let A, v, ρ, and u be as in equations 31.6 and 31.7, and let the function $H(\cdot): R^n_+ \to R^n_+$ be defined by

$$H(x) = Ax. \tag{31.18}$$

Then equation 31.5 and the definition,

$$\gamma(x) = ux, \qquad x \in R^n_+, \tag{31.19}$$

can be used to show that

$$\lim_{t\to\infty} \frac{H^t(x)}{\rho^t} = \gamma(x)v, \qquad x \in R^n_+. \tag{31.20}$$

The relations in 31.18–31.20 explicate the correspondence of equation 31.6 to 31.5.

31.1.2 The Decomposable Case

The decomposable case is much more involved than the indecomposable case. To deal with it, I must introduce additional notation. Let $1 \leqslant n_1 < n$ and, for $x \in R^n_+$, let $x = (x^1, x^2)$, where $x^1 \in R^{n_1}_+$ and $x^2 \in R^{n-n_1}_+$. Moreover, let $H(\cdot) = (H^1(\cdot), H^2(\cdot))$, where $H^1(\cdot) = (H_1(\cdot), \ldots, H_{n_1}(\cdot))$ and $H^2(\cdot) = (H_{n_1+1}(\cdot), \ldots, H_n(\cdot))$. Throughout this section we assume that

$$H^1(\cdot): R^{n_1}_+ \to R^{n_1}_+; \tag{31.21}$$

and

$$H^2(\cdot): R^n_+ \to R^{n-n_1}_+. \tag{31.22}$$

It follows from T 31.1 that if $H^1(\cdot)$ and $H^2(0^1. \cdot)$ are continuous, nondecreasing functions which are homogeneous of degree 1 and indecomposable, then there exist vectors, $V^1 \in R^{n_1}_{++}$ and $\overline{V}^2 \in R^{n-n_1}_{++}$, and numbers, λ_1 and λ_2 in R_{++}, such that

$$H^1(V^1) = \lambda_1 V^1, \tag{31.23}$$

and

$$H^2(0^1, \overline{V}^2) = \lambda_2 \overline{V}^2. \tag{31.24}$$

Moreover, λ_1 and λ_2 are uniquely determined and V^1 and $\overline{V}^2$ are determined up to positive multiplicative constants. Finally,

$$H(0^1, \bar{V}^2) = \lambda_2(0^1, \bar{V}^2).$$

Hence $(0^1, \bar{V}^2)$ and λ_2, respectively, are an eigenvector and an eigenvalue of $H(\cdot)$.

Whether there exists a pair $(\lambda, W) \in R_{++} \times R^n_{++}$ which satisfies

$$H(W) = \lambda W, \tag{31.25}$$

depends on the values of λ_1 and λ_2. If $\lambda_2 > \lambda_1$, such a pair does not exist. This is so because then

$$H^1(W^1) = \lambda W^1$$

and that cannot happen unless $\lambda = \lambda_1$. If $\lambda_1 = \lambda_2$ and $H^2(x^1, \bar{V}^2)$ does not vary with x^1, then $(\lambda_2, (V^1, \bar{V}^2))$ satisfies equation 31.25. However, if $\lambda_1 = \lambda_2$ and $H^2(x^1, \bar{V}^2)$ varies with x^1, the pair $(\lambda, W) \in R^{n+1}_{++}$ does not exist. Finally, if $\lambda_1 > \lambda_2$, it follows from a theorem of Frank Fisher's that we can find a $V^2 \in R^{n-n_1}_{++}$ such that $(\lambda_1, (V^1, V^2))$ satisfies equation 31.25. Specifically, we have T 31.3:

T 31.3 Let $H(\cdot) = (H^1(\cdot), H^2(\cdot))$ and assume that $H^1(\cdot)$ satisfies equation 31.21 and that $H^2(\cdot)$ satisfies equation 31.22. Moreover, suppose that $H^1(\cdot)$ and $H^2(\cdot)$ are continuous, nondecreasing functions which are homogeneous of degree 1 and suppose that both $H^1(\cdot)$ and $H^2(0^1, \cdot)$ are indecomposable. Finally, let (λ_1, V^1) and $(\lambda_2, \bar{V}^2)$, be as in equations 31.23 and 31.24, respectively, and assume that

$$\lambda_1 > \lambda_2 \tag{31.26}$$

and that, for any $x, y \in R^n_+$ with $x \geqslant y$, $N(x, y) \neq \emptyset$ and $\{n_1 + 1, \ldots, n\}$ not contained in $N(x, y)$, there is an $i \in \{n_1 + 1, \ldots, n\}$ such that $i \notin N(x, y)$ and

$$H_i^2(x) > H_i^2(y).$$

Then there exists a unique vector $V^2 \in R^{n-n_1}_{++}$ such that

$$H^2(V^1, V^2) = \lambda_1 V^2. \tag{31.27}$$

The proof of this theorem is involved. Therefore, since the meaning of the theorem is clear, I omit the proof and refer the reader to Fisher 1963 (pp. 79–81) for the details of Fisher's own proof.

In order to study growth in decomposable economies, we must establish analogues of T 31.2 for the iterates of $(H^1(\cdot), H^2(\cdot))$. We shall do that for the case $\lambda_1 > \lambda_2$ and present two examples from the case $\lambda_1 = \lambda_2$. For details concerning the case $\lambda_1 < \lambda_2$, the interested reader is referred to Kesten and Stigum 1974 (pp. 356–361) for details.

T 31.4 Suppose that $H(\cdot) = (H^1(\cdot), H^2(\cdot))$ satisfies the conditions of T 31.3 and that

$x^1 \in (R_+^{n_1} - \{0\})$ implies $H(x^1, x^2) > 0.$

Suppose also that the matrix

$\{H_{ij}(V^1, V^2)\} = \{\partial H_i(V^1, V^2/\partial x_j\}$

exists with

$H_{ij}(V^1, V^2) > 0, \qquad 1 \leqslant i, j \leqslant n_1 \quad \text{and} \quad n_1 \leqslant i \leqslant n, 1 \leqslant j \leqslant n.$

Then for each $\varepsilon > 0$ and $\varepsilon < (\|V^1\|/\|(V^1, V^2)\|)$, there exist finite positive constants K_1 and α and a continuous, nondecreasing, linearly homogeneous function $\gamma(\cdot)$: $R_+^{n_1} \to R_+$ such that $0 < \alpha < 1$ and such that, for all $t \geqslant 1$ and all $x \in (R_+^n - \{0\})$ for which $\varepsilon \leqslant (\|x^1\|/\|x\|)$,

$$\|(H^t(x)/\lambda_1^t) - \gamma(x^1)(V^1, V^2)\| \leqslant K_1\alpha^t\|x\|. \tag{31.28}$$

Moreover, there exists a constant K_2 which depends on ε but not t and x such that, for $(\|x^1\|/\|x\|) > \varepsilon$,

$$\|(H^t(x)/\|H^t(x)\|) - ((V^1, V^2)/\|(V^1, V^2)\|)\| \leqslant K_2(\varepsilon)\alpha^t. \tag{31.29}$$

Since the meaning of the theorem is clear and since the ideas of the proof are similar to the ideas of the proof of T 31.2, I refer the reader to Kesten and Stigum 1974 (pp. 352–356) for a detailed proof and omit the proof here.

For the purposes of this chapter equations 31.28 and 31.29 tell us all we need to know about balanced growth under certainty in a decomposable economy which satisfies equations 31.21–31.24 and 31.26. From them we deduce that

$$\lim_{t\to\infty} (x(t)/\lambda_1^t) = \gamma(x^1)(V^1, V^2),$$

and

$$\lim_{t\to\infty} (x(t)/\|x(t)\|) = ((V^1, V^2)/\|(V^1, V^2)\|).$$

Hence the direction of growth of a large economy which satisfies equations 31.21–31.24 and 31.26 is nearly independent of its starting point. In addition, there is a gravitational force which drives the economy toward its balanced growth path.

The behavior of a decomposable economy for which the λ_1 in equation 31.23 differs from the λ_2 in equation 31.24 is like the behavior of an indecomposable economy. The behavior of a decomposable economy for which $\lambda_1 = \lambda_2$ is very different from that of an indecomposable economy. The next two examples will establish that fact.

E 31.2 Suppose that $\lambda > 0$ and that $n = 2$. Moreover, suppose that $0 < \alpha < 1$ and that

$x_1(t+1) = \lambda x_1(t), \qquad t = 0, 1, \ldots;$

and

$x_2(t+1) = p x_1(t)^{\alpha} x_2(t)^{1-\alpha} + \lambda x_2(t), \qquad t = 0, 1, \ldots.$

Then $x_1(t) = x_1(0)\lambda^t$, and if $x_2(0) \neq 0$, then

$\lim_{t\to\infty} (x_2(t)/t^{(1/\alpha)}\lambda^t) = (p x_1(0)^{\alpha}(\alpha/\lambda))^{(1/\alpha)}.$

E 31.3 Suppose that $\lambda > 0$ and that $n = 2$. Moreover, let p_k and α_k, $k = 1, 2, \ldots$, be constants such that $p_k > 0$, $0 < \alpha_k < 1$, $k = 1, 2, \ldots$, $\sum_{k=1}^{\infty} p_k < \infty$, and $\lim_{k\to\infty} \alpha_k = 0$. Finally, let

$x_1(t+1) = \lambda x_1(t), \qquad t = 0, 1, \ldots;$

and

$$x_2(t+1) = \sum_{k=1}^{\infty} p_k x_1(t)^{\alpha_k} x_2(t)^{(1-\alpha_k)} + \lambda x_2(t), \qquad t = 1, 2, \ldots.$$

Then

$x_1(t) = x_1(0)\lambda^t,$

and $x_2(t)/\lambda^t$ grows faster any power of t.

These examples are borrowed from Kesten and Stigum 1974 (pp. 361–362).

31.2 Balanced Growth under Uncertainty in an Indecomposable Economy

In this section we study growth under uncertainty in an indecomposable economy and establish sufficient conditions for balanced growth. We assume that the behavior of the economy can be represented by a vector-valued random process $\{x(t, \omega);\ t = 0, 1, \ldots\}$ which satisfies the condition

$$E\{x(t+1)|x(0), \ldots, x(t)\} = H(x(t)) \quad \text{a.e.}, \qquad t = 0, 1, \ldots, \tag{31.30}$$

where $H(\cdot)\colon R_+^n \to R_+^n$ is a continuous, nondecreasing, linearly homogeneous, indecomposable function. Our intent is to show that if

(i) $H(\cdot)$ satisfies the conditions of T 31.2 and a weak Lipschitz condition,
(ii) λ and V satisfy equation 31.4 and $\lambda > 1$,
(iii) the probability of growth is positive, and
(iv) there exist finite positive constants K and δ such that $0 < \delta < 1$ and such that, for all $t = 0, 1, \ldots$, and $i = 1, \ldots, n$,

$$E\{|x_i(t+1) - H_i(x(t))|^2 | x(0), \ldots, x(t)\} \leqslant K\|x(t)\|^{2(1-\delta)}, \tag{31.31}$$

we can establish the existence of a random variable $g(\cdot)$ such that

$$\lim_{t \to \infty} x(t, \omega)/\lambda^t = g(\omega) V \quad \text{a.e.},$$

and

$$E\{g|x(0)\} > 0.$$

It might not be obvious that there are stochastic processes which satisfy the conditions we listed above. So here is an example to demonstrate that such processes exist.

E 31.4 Let Z denote the set of all n-dimensional vectors whose components are nonegative integers, and let $(\Omega, \mathscr{F}, P(\cdot))$ be a probability space. Moreover, let $\{x(t, \omega); t = 0, 1, \ldots\}$ be a vector-valued random process and assume that, for all $t = 0, 1, \ldots,$

$$x(t, \cdot): \Omega \to Z.$$

In addition, assume that the probability distributions induced by $P(\cdot)$ and the $x(t, \cdot)$ satisfy the probability law of a multitype Galton-Watson process and let

$$a_{ij} = E\{x_i(1)|x(0) = e_j\}, \qquad 1 \leqslant i, j \leqslant n,$$

where $e_j = (0, \ldots, e_{jj} = 1, \ldots, 0)$. Then the $x(t, \cdot)$ satisfy equation 31.30 with

$$H(x) = Ax,$$

and $A = (a_{ij})$. This H-function satisfies the required Lipschitz condition but it need not satisfy the other conditions we listed above; e.g., A may be decomposable and λ may be less than 1. However, there are Galton-Watson processes which satisfy conditions i, ii, and iii above; and any square-integrable Galton-Watson process will satisfy condition iv with $\delta = 1/2$ (see Kesten and Stigum 1967, pp. 309–338, and Kesten and Stigum 1966, pp. 1211–1223).

31.2.1 Balanced Growth When $n = 1$

In order that the reader get a good understanding of the generality of our sufficient condition, we begin our study of balanced growth under uncertainty by presenting several simple examples concerning the case $n = 1$.

Let $T = \{0, 1, \ldots\}$ and let $\{L(t, \omega); t \in T\}$ be a sequence of nonnegative random variables on a probability space $(\Omega, \mathscr{F}, P(\cdot))$. Here $L(t)$ might be taken to denote the size of the economy's labor force in period t. Assume that

$$L(0) = 1,$$

and that, for all $t \geqslant 0$,

$$E\{L(t+1)|L(0), \ldots, L(t)\} = \lambda L(t) \quad \text{a.e.},$$

where $1 < \lambda < \infty$. Then

$$E\{L(t+1)/\lambda^{t+1})|L(0),\ldots,L(t)\} = (L(t)/\lambda^t)$$

and

$$E\{(L(t)/\lambda^t)|L(0)\} = 1.$$

Hence the sequence $\{(L(t)/\lambda^t);\ t \in T\}$ is a nonnegative martingale with uniformly bounded means. From this and from Doob's Theorem 4.1 (see Doob 1953, p. 319), it follows that there exists a random variable φ such that

$$\lim_{t\to\infty} (L(t)/\lambda^t) = \varphi \quad \text{a.e.} \tag{31.32}$$

and

$$E\{\varphi|L(0)\} \leqslant 1.$$

Whether or not $E\{\varphi|L(0)\} > 0$ depends on the distribution of the $L(t)$'s. We consider three different cases.

1. Suppose that the probability distributions induced by the $L(t)$'s and $P(\cdot)$ satisfy the probability law of a Galton-Watson process. Then it can be shown that the distribution of φ has a jump at the origin equal to $q \in [0, 1]$ and allows a continuous density function on the set of positive real numbers (see Stigum 1966, p. 697). Moreover,

$$q < 1 \text{ iff } E\{L(1)\log L(1)|L(0)\} < \infty$$

(see Kesten and Stigum 1966, pp. 1211–1212). Thus in this case, $E\{\varphi|L(0)\}$ might be positive even if $E\{(L(1) - \lambda L(0))^2|L(0)\} = \infty$.

2. Suppose that there exists a sequence of independently and identically distributed, nondegenerate random variables $\{\theta(t,\omega);\ t = 1, 2, \ldots\}$ that are distributed independently of the $L(t)$'s and have mean λ. Moreover, suppose that

$$L(t+1) = \theta(t+1)L(t), \qquad t \geqslant 0, \tag{31.33}$$

and that

$$E|\log\theta(t)| < \infty.$$

It is easy to see that if the $L(t)$'s satisfy equation 31.33, they do not satisfy equation 31.31. It is also easy to see that, by the Law of Large Numbers (see T 16.6),

$$\lim_{t\to\infty} (1/t)\log L(t) = \lim_{t\to\infty} (1/t)\sum_{i=1}^{t} \log\theta(i) = \mu \quad \text{a.e.,} \tag{31.34}$$

where $\mu = E\log\theta(t) < \log E\theta(t) = \log\lambda$. Finally, if we let $f(t,\omega) = \log L(t,\omega) - \mu t$, then the equality

$$L(t, \omega)/\lambda^t = \exp(\mu - \log \lambda + (f(t, \omega)/t))t \tag{31.35}$$

and equation 31.34 can be seen to imply that in this case $\varphi = 0$ a.e..

In interpreting the preceding result, note that equations 31.34 and 31.35 imply that w. pr. 1 lim $\lim_{t\to\infty} L(t, \omega)/\alpha^t = 0$ or ∞ according as $\log \alpha > \mu$ or $\log \alpha < \mu$. If $\log \alpha = \mu$, $L(t)/\alpha^t$ does not converge to a random variable. The most we can say is that, if $E|\log \theta(t)|^2 < \infty$ and $\log \alpha = \mu$, then the Central Limit Theorem (see T 16.8) and equation 31.35 imply that, for any $K > 1$ and $0 < \tilde{K} < 1$,

$$\lim_{t\to\infty} P(\{\omega \in \Omega : L(t, \omega)/\alpha^t \geqslant K\}) = \tfrac{1}{2} \qquad \text{and}$$

$$\lim_{t\to\infty} P(\{\omega \in \Omega : L(t, \omega)/\alpha^t \leqslant \tilde{K}\}) = \tfrac{1}{2}.$$

If $E|\log \theta(t)|^2 = \infty$ and $\log \alpha = \mu$, the "limiting distribution" of $(L(t)/\alpha^t)$ either does not exist or is concentrated on 0 and $+\infty$. From these observations it follows that, for the case under study, there is no "right" normalizing constant α which ensures that $(L(t)/\alpha^t)$ converges to a random variable whose distribution is concentrated on $[0, \infty)$ with some positive mass on $(0, \infty)$.

3. Suppose that the $L(t)$ satisfy the conditions

$$E\{(L(t+1) - \lambda L(t))^2 | L(0), \ldots, L(t)\} \leqslant K_0 L(t)^{2(1-\delta)}, \qquad t = 0, 1, \ldots,$$

for some finite constants K_0 and δ with $\delta \in (0, 1)$.[4] Then the following proposition is valid:

$\mathscr{P}$. For each $\eta \in (0, 1)$ there exists a finite constant K_η such that, on the set where $L(t) \geqslant K_\eta$, $P\{\varphi > 0 | L(0), \ldots, L(t)\} \geqslant 1 - \eta$. Moreover, for each K_η, there exists an integer t_η such that $P\{L(t_\eta) \geqslant K_\eta | L(0)\} > 0$.

To establish the first half of $\mathscr{P}$, we proceed as follows. First we let $\eta \in (0, 1)$ be fixed and choose K_η so large that

$$K_\eta^{-(\delta/2)} \leqslant \frac{\lambda - 1}{2}$$

and

$$\prod_{a=0}^{\infty} \left[1 - K_0 K_\eta^{-\delta} \left(\frac{\lambda + 1}{2}\right)^{-a\delta}\right] \geqslant 1 - \eta.$$

Then we assume that $L(t_0) \geqslant K_\eta$ for some $t_0 \geqslant 1$ and that the following statement, which we refer to as equation 31.36(a), is valid for some positive integer a:

1. $|L(t+1) - \lambda L(t)| \leqslant L(t)^{1-(\delta/2)}, \qquad t_0 \leqslant t < t_0 + a,$

and (31.36(*a*))

2. $L(t) \geqslant \left(\frac{\lambda + 1}{2}\right)^{t-t_0} K_\eta, \qquad t_0 \leqslant t < t_0 + a.$

If equation 31.36(*a*) is true,

$$L(t_0 + a) \geqslant \lambda L(t_0 + a - 1) - L(t_0 + a - 1)^{1-(\delta/2)}$$
$$\geqslant \left(\frac{\lambda + 1}{2}\right) L(t_0 + a - 1) \geqslant \left(\frac{\lambda + 1}{2}\right)^{\alpha} K_\eta. \tag{31.37}$$

Moreover,

$$P\{|L(t_0 + a + 1) - \lambda L(t_0 + a)| \leqslant L(t_0 + a)^{1-(\delta/2)} | L(0), \ldots, L(t_0 + a)\}$$
$$\geqslant 1 - K_0 L(t_0 + a)^{-\delta}$$
$$\geqslant 1 - K_0 K_\eta^{-\delta} \left(\frac{\lambda + 1}{2}\right)^{-a\delta}. \tag{31.38}$$

From equations 31.37 and 31.38 it follows that on the set where equation 31.36(*a*) holds,

$$P\{31.36(a + 1) \text{ holds } | L(0), \ldots, L(t_0 + a)\} \geqslant 1 - K_0 K_\eta^{-\delta} \left(\frac{\lambda + 1}{2}\right)^{-a\delta}$$

Hence, once we observe that on the set where $L(t_0) \geqslant K_\eta$,

$$P\{31.36(1) \text{ holds } | L(0), \ldots, L(t_0)\} \geqslant 1 - K_0 K_\eta^{-\delta},$$

then it follows by simple iteration from equations 31.37 and 31.38 that

$$P\{31.36(a) \text{ holds for all } a \geqslant 1 | L(0), \ldots, L(t_0), L(t_0) \geqslant K_\eta\}$$
$$\geqslant \prod_{a=0}^{\infty} \left(1 - K_0 K_\eta^{-\delta} \left(\frac{\lambda + 1}{2}\right)^{-a\delta}\right) \geqslant 1 - \eta. \tag{31.39}$$

Next we let ω^* be a sample point at which equation 31.36(*a*) holds for all $a \geqslant 1$ and observe that for each $r \geqslant t_0$

$$L(r + 1, \omega^*) = \lambda L(r, \omega^*) + \theta_{1r} L(r, \omega^*)^{1-(\delta/2)}$$
$$= \lambda L(r, \omega^*)[1 + \theta_{2r} K_4 [(\lambda + 1)/2]^{-((r-t_0)\delta/2)}],$$

where $|\theta_{ir}| \leqslant 1$, $i = 1, 2$, and $K_4 = (\lambda K_\eta^{(\delta/2)})^{-1}$. By simple iteration we can show that, for all $r \geqslant 1$ and all $a \geqslant 0$,

$$\frac{(L(t_0 + r + a, \omega^*)/\lambda^{t_0+r+a})}{(L(t_0 + a, \omega^*)/\lambda^{t_0+a})} = \prod_{s=a}^{a+r-1} \left(1 + K_4 \theta_{2s} \left(\frac{\lambda + 1}{2}\right)^{-(s\delta/2)}\right). \tag{31.40}$$

By choosing a large enough, we can make the right-hand side of equation 31.40 converge to a positive number as r goes to infinity. This shows that

$$\lim_{t \to \infty} \frac{L(t, \omega^*)}{\lambda^t} > 0$$

for all ω^* for which equation 31.36(a) holds for all $a \geqslant 1$. But if that is true, then equations 31.32 and 31.39 imply the validity of the first half of $\mathscr{P}$.

The validity of the second half of $\mathscr{P}$ is obvious: For all t,

$$E\{L(t)|L(0)\} = \lambda^t.$$

Therefore $P\{L(t) \geqslant \lambda^t|L(0)\} > 0$. So we can choose $t_\eta > \log K_\eta - \log \lambda$.

31.2.2 Balanced Growth When $n \geqslant 2$

So much for balanced growth of a univariate economy. Next we discuss balanced growth in an indecomposable multivariate economy. We begin by establishing a theorem concerning the *possibility* of growth in such economy.

T 31.5 Suppose that $n \geqslant 2$ and let $\{x(t, \omega);\, t \in T\}$ be an n-vector-valued random process on a probability space $(\Omega, \mathscr{F}, P(\cdot))$. Assume that there exists a continuous, nondecreasing, linearly homogeneous function, $H(\cdot)$: $R_+^n \to R_+^n$, such that, for all $t \in T$,

$$E\{x(t+1)|x(0), \ldots, x(t)\} = H(x(t)) \quad \text{a.e.}$$

In addition, assume that $H(\cdot)$ satisfies the conditions of T 31.2 and that the λ of equation 31.4 satisfies $\lambda > 1$. Finally, assume that, for all $t \in T$,

$$P\{x(t+1) \geqslant H(x(t))|x(0), \ldots, x(t)\} > 0. \tag{31.41}$$

Then for each $0 < k < \infty$ and $x \in (R_+^n - \{0\})$, there exists a finite t (depending on k and x) such that

$$P\{\|x(t)\| \geqslant k|x(0) = x\} > 0.$$

The proof goes as follows: Let λ, V, and $\gamma(\cdot)$ be as in equation 31.6 and observe that

$$\gamma(H(x))V = \lim_{t \to \infty} H^t\left(\frac{H(x)}{\lambda^t}\right) = \lambda \lim_{t \to \infty} \frac{H^{t+1}(x)}{\lambda^{t+1}} = \lambda\gamma(x)V.$$

Consequently, for all $x \in R_+^n$,

$$\gamma(H(x)) = \lambda\gamma(x). \tag{31.42}$$

Next let

$$\varphi(x) = P\{x(1) \geqslant H(x)|x(0) = x\}, \qquad x \in R_+^n,$$

and let $\varphi_0 = \varphi(x(0))$. From equations 31.42 and 31.41 it follows that

$$P\{\gamma(x(1)) \geqslant \lambda\gamma(x(0))|x(0)\} \geqslant \varphi_0 > 0.$$

In addition, let

$$\varphi_1(x(1)) = P\{x(2) \geqslant H(x(1))|x(0), x(1)\},$$

and let $\varphi_1 = E\{\varphi_1(x(1))|x(1) \geqslant H(x(0)), x(0)\}$. Then, by equation 31.41, $\varphi_1(x(1)) > 0$ for all $x(1) \in ((R_+^n - \{0\}) \cap (\text{range of } x(1,\cdot))$ and

$$\begin{aligned} P\{x(2) \geqslant H^2(x(0))|x(0)\} &\geqslant P\{x(2) \geqslant H^2(x(0)), x(1) \geqslant H(x(0))|x(0)\} \\ &\geqslant \varphi_0 P\{x(2) \geqslant H(x(1))|x(1) \geqslant H(x(0)), x(0)\} \\ &= \varphi_0 E\{P\{x(2) \geqslant H(x(1))|x(1), x(0)\}|x(1) \geqslant H(x(0)), x(0)\} \\ &= \varphi_0 E\{\varphi_1(x(1))|x(1) \geqslant H(x(0)), x(0)\} = \varphi_0\varphi_1 > 0. \end{aligned} \tag{31.43}$$

From equation 31.43 we find that

$$P\{\gamma(x(2)) \geqslant \lambda^2\gamma(x(0))|x(0)\} \geqslant \varphi_0\varphi_1 > 0.$$

By continuing the process begun above, we can find positive numbers $\varphi_2, \ldots, \varphi_t$ such that, for all $t \geqslant 2$,

$$P\{\gamma(x(t)) \geqslant \lambda^t\gamma(x(0))|x(0)\} \geqslant \prod_{i=0}^{t} \varphi_i.$$

To conclude the proof of the theorem, we need only observe that if $\gamma(x(t)) \geqslant \lambda^t\gamma(x(0))$, then

$$\|x(t)\| \geqslant \lambda^t \frac{\gamma(x(0)}{\gamma(x(t)/\|x(t)\|)} \geqslant K_{14}\lambda^t,$$

where $K_{14} = \gamma(x(0))/\max_{\|x\|=1}\gamma(x)$. Because then, for t so large that $K_{14}\lambda^t > k$, we find that

$$P\{\|x(t)\| \geqslant k|x(0)\} \geqslant P\{\gamma(x(t)) \geqslant \lambda^t\gamma(x(0))|x(0)\} \geqslant \prod_{i=0}^{t} \varphi_i > 0.$$

The assertion made in T 31.5 is an analogue of the last half of proposition $\mathscr{P}$. Next I shall introduce a weak Lipschitz condition on $H(\cdot)$ and establish a theorem that corresponds to the first half of proposition $\mathscr{P}$.

T 31.6 Suppose that $n \geqslant 2$ and let $\{x(t, \omega); t \in T\}$ be an n-vector-valued random process on a probability space $(\Omega, \mathscr{F}, P(\cdot))$. Assume that there exists a continuous, nondecreasing, linearly homogeneous function, $H(\cdot)$: $R_+^n \to R_+^n$, such that, for all $t \in T$,

$$E\{x(t+1)|x(0), \ldots, x(t)\} = H(x(t)) \quad \text{a.e.}$$

In addition, assume that $H(\cdot)$ satisfies the conditions of T 31.2 and that the λ of equation 31.4 satisfies $\lambda > 1$. Finally, assume that (1) the $x(t, \cdot)$ satisfy the variance condition described in condition iv in section 31.2 and (2) for each $\varepsilon > 0$, there is a constant $K(\varepsilon)$ such that, for all $x, y \in R_+^n$ with $\|x\| = \|y\| = 1$ and $x \geqslant \varepsilon, y \geqslant \varepsilon$,

$$\|H(x) - H(y)\| \leqslant K(\varepsilon)\|x - y\|. \tag{31.44}$$

Then, with

$$K_5 = \left(\min_{\substack{1 \leqslant i \leqslant n \\ \|z\|=1}} \frac{H_i(z)}{n}\right)\left(\max_{\substack{1 \leqslant i \leqslant n \\ \|z\|=1}} H_i(z)\right)^{-1}$$

for each $0 < \varepsilon < K_5$ and $\eta \in (0, 1)$, there exists a positive integer $K(\eta, \varepsilon)$ such that on the set where $\varepsilon \leqslant (x(t)/\|x(t)\|)$ and $\|x(t)\| \geqslant K(\eta, \varepsilon)$,

$$P\left\{\lim_{s\to\infty} (x(s, \omega)/\lambda^s) = g(\omega)V \text{ for some finite } g(\omega) > 0|x(0), \ldots, x(t)\right\} \geqslant 1 - \eta.$$

With some obvious modifications, this theorem can be established by using arguments similar to those used by H. Kesten in proving theorem 6.1 in Kesten 1970 (pp. 91–98). Since these arguments are involved and since the ideas of the proof generalize upon the ideas of the proof I gave of the first half of $\mathscr{P}$, I omit the proof of T 31.6 for brevity's sake.

With T 31.5 and T 31.6 well in hand, we can establish the promised theorem on balanced growth in an indecomposable economy.

T 31.7 Suppose that $n \geqslant 2$ and let $\{x(t, \omega); t \in T\}$ be an n-vector-valued random process on a probability space $(\Omega, \mathscr{F}, P(\cdot))$. Assume that the $x(t, \cdot)$ satisfy the conditions of T 31.6. Then

$$P\left\{\|x(t, \omega)\| \text{ will remain bounded or } \lim_{t\to\infty} \frac{x(t, \omega)}{\lambda^t} = g(\omega)V \text{ for some finite } g(\omega) > 0|x(0)\right\} = 1. \tag{31.45}$$

If the $x(t, \cdot)$ also satisfy equation 31.41, then for all $x(0) \in (R_+^n - \{0\})$,

$$P\left\{\lim_{t\to\infty} (x(t, \omega)/\lambda^t) = g(\omega)V \text{ for some finite } g(\omega) > 0|x(0)\right\} > 0. \tag{31.46}$$

The proof goes as follows: It is clear that on the Ω set where lim $\sup_{t\to\infty} \|x(t, \omega\| < \infty$, the random variable $g(\cdot)$ defined by

$$g(\omega)V = \lim_{t\to\infty} \frac{x(t,\omega)}{\lambda^t}$$

is well defined and equal to zero. Therefore, to establish the validity of equation 31.45 we need only show that $g(\cdot)$ is well defined, finite, and positive, a.e. on the Ω set where $\lim\sup_{t\to\infty} \|x(t,\omega)\| = \infty$. This we will do by showing that for each $\eta > 0$ and $x \geqslant 0$, $x \neq 0$, $x(0) = x$,

$$P\left\{\omega \in \Omega : \lim_{t\to\infty} \sup \|x(t,\omega)\| = \infty \text{ and there exists no finite, positive } g(\omega) \text{ such that } \lim_{t\to\infty} \frac{x(t,\omega)}{\lambda^t} = g(\omega)V | x(0)\right\} \leqslant 2\eta. \quad (31.47)$$

To establish equation 31.47 we begin by fixing $x(0) = x$, $x \geqslant 0$, $x \neq 0$, $\eta > 0$, and $0 < \varepsilon < K_5$. Next, we let "$x(t)$ n. r. l. b." mean that there exists no finite positive g such that $\lim_{t\to\infty} (x(t)/\lambda^t) = gV$. Finally, we let

$$A_k = \{x : \|x\| \geqslant k, (x_i/\|x\|) < \varepsilon \text{ for some } i\},$$

and

$$B_k = \{x : \|x\| \geqslant k, (x/\|x\|) \geqslant \varepsilon\},$$

and note that

$$\left\{\omega \in \Omega : \lim_{t\to\infty} \sup \|x(t,\omega)\| = \infty\right\}$$
$$\subset \{\omega \in \Omega : x(t,\omega) \text{ in each } B_k,\ k = 1, \ldots, \text{i.o.}\}$$
$$\cup \{\omega \in \Omega : x(t,\omega) \text{ in each } A_k,\ k = 1, 2, \ldots, \text{i.o.}\}, \quad (31.48)$$

where "i.o." means infinitely often.

It is easy to show that, for each pair (k, m) with k large and greater than m, we can find a positive constant $\delta_{k,m}$ such that for $t = 0, 1, \ldots,$

$$P\{x(t+s) \in B_m \text{ for some } s \geqslant 1 | x(0), \ldots, x(t), x(t) \in A_k\} \geqslant \delta_{k,m}.$$

Hence (see Breiman 1968, chapter 5, problem 9, p. 97) if we "throw out" a null Ω set, then

$$\{\omega \in \Omega : x(t,\omega) \in A_k \text{i.o.}\} \subset \{\omega \in \Omega : x(t,\omega) \in B_m \text{i.o.}\}. \quad (31.49)$$

From equation 31.49 it follows that, if we "throw out" a null Ω set, then for each fixed m,

$$\{\omega \in \Omega : x(t,\omega) \text{ in each } A_k,\ k = 1, 2, \ldots, \text{i.o.}\} \subset \{\omega \in \Omega : x(t,\omega) \in B_m \text{i.o.}\}.$$

The preceding result can be used to establish equation 31.47 in the following way: First, for the pair (η, ε) let $k_\eta = K(\eta, \varepsilon)$ be chosen as in T 31.6. Then it follows from T 31.6 that

$$P\{x(t) \in \text{each } B_k \text{ i.o. but } x(t) \text{ n. r. l. b.} | x(0)\}$$

$$\leqslant P\{x(t) \in B_{k_\eta} \text{ for some } t \text{ but } x(t) \text{ n. r. l. b.} | x(0)\}$$

$$\leqslant \sum_{s=1}^{\infty} P\{x(t) \in B_{k_\eta} \text{ for the first time at } t = s | x(0)\}$$

$$\times P\{x(t) \text{n. r. l. b.} | x(0), \ldots, x(s), x(s) \in B_{k_\eta}\} \leqslant \eta, \quad (31.50)$$

and

$$P\{x(t) \in \text{each } A_k \text{ i. o. but } x(t) \text{ n. r. l. b.} | x(0)\}$$

$$\leqslant P\{x(t) \in \text{each } A_k \text{ i. o. but } x(t) \text{ not in } B_{k_\eta} \text{ i. o.} | x(0)\}$$

$$+ P\{x(t) \in B_{k_\eta} \text{ i. o. and } x(t) \text{ n. r. l. b.} | x(0)\}$$

$$\leqslant 0 + P\{x(t) \in B_{k_\eta} \text{ for some } t \text{ but } x(t) \text{ n. r. l. b.} | x(0)\} \leqslant \eta. \quad (31.51)$$

The validity of equation 31.47 is an immediate consequence of equations 31.50, 31.51, and 31.48, and the proof of the validity of equation 31.45 under the conditions stated is complete.

The validity of equation 31.46 can be established by observing that, under the conditions stated in T 31.7, theorems T 31.5 and T 31.6 imply that, for all $x \geqslant 0$, $x \neq 0$, and $x(0) = x$,

$$P\left\{\omega \in \Omega : \limsup_{t \to \infty} \|x(t, \omega)\| = \infty | x(0)\right\} > 0.$$

Theorem T 31.7 can be interpreted to say: If an uncertainty economy satisfies the conditions of T 31.7, then with positive probability the economy will, for large enough t, come arbitrarily close to balanced growth. Moreover—and this is definitely the most interesting aspect—both the eventual rate of growth and the eventual balanced growth configuration of the uncertainty economy will be identical with those that the certainty theory of Samuelson and Solow would have predicted.

The conditions we imposed on the $x(t, \cdot)$ in T 31.7 are in one sense the best possible sufficient conditions for balanced growth under uncertainty. Specifically, there are processes which satisfy equations 31.30, 31.41, and 31.44 and for which equation 31.46 is false. Here is one case in point:

E 31.5 Let $\{\theta(t, \omega);\ t = 1, 2, \ldots\}$ be an n-variate, purely random process on a probability space $(\Omega, \mathscr{F}, P(\cdot))$ and assume that the $\theta(t, \cdot)$ are nonnegative and have a finite positive mean and a finite diagonal covariance matrix with positive diagonal entries. Moreover, let $w(0) \in R^n_{++}$ be a fixed vector; let $w_i(t + 1, \omega) = G_i(\theta_i(t + 1, \omega), w(t))$, $t = 0, 1, \ldots$, $i = 1, \ldots, n$, where $w(t) = (w_1(t), \ldots, w_n(t))$, and assume that $G_i(\cdot)\colon R^{n+1}_+ \to R_+$ is continuous, that $G_i(\cdot, w(t))$ is bounded, and that $G_i(\theta_i(t + 1), \cdot)$ is increasing, linearly homogeneous, and strictly quasi-concave, $i = 1, \ldots, n$. Finally, assume that the $\theta(t, \cdot)$ are distributed independently of the $w(t)$, and let

$$H_i(w(t)) = E\{G_i(\theta_i(t + 1), w(t))|w(t)\},\ i = 1, \ldots, n,$$

and $H(w(t)) = (H_1(w(t)), \ldots, H_n(w(t)))$. Then it is easy to verify that $H(\cdot)$ is increasing, continuous, linearly homogeneous, and strictly quasi-concave and satisfies equation 31.44. It is also clear that the probability distributions of the $w(t)$ satisfy equation 31.41 and that, for all $t = 0, 1, \ldots$,

$$E\{w(t + 1)|w(0), \ldots, w(t)\} = H(w(t)) \quad \text{a.e..}$$

Finally, if the pair $(\lambda, V) \in R_{++} \times R^n_{++}$ is such that $H(V) = \lambda V$, then the preceding observations and theorem 1 in Stigum 1972a (p. 47) imply that there exists a random variable g such that

$$\lim_{t\to\infty} \frac{w(t)}{\lambda^t} = gV \quad \text{a.e.,}$$

and

$$E\{g|w(0)\} < \infty.$$

The random process, $\{w(t, \omega);\ t \in T\}$ does not satisfy equation 31.46 and it can be shown that $g = 0$ a.e.

There are also vector-valued random processes which satisfy equations 31.30, 31.41, and 31.44 and approach a balanced growth pattern even though they do not satisfy equation 31.46. Here is one case in point:

E 31.6 Let $\{x(t, \omega);\ t \in T\}$ be as in E 31.4 and suppose that there exists an integer $t \geqslant 1$ such that $A^t > 0$. Moreover, let $u, v \in R^n_{++}$ and $\rho \in R_{++}$ be such that

$$Av = \rho v; \qquad uA = \rho u; \qquad u \cdot v = 1; \qquad \rho > 1.$$

Then there exists a random variable g such that

$$\lim_{t\to\infty} \frac{x(t, \omega)}{\rho^t} = gu \quad \text{a.e.}$$

The probability distribution of g can be described as follows: Let $e_i = (0, \ldots, e_{ii} = 1, \ldots, 0)$, $i = 1, \ldots, n$. Then

$$E\{g|x(0) = e_i\} = v_i, \qquad i = 1, \ldots, n, \tag{31.52}$$

or

$g = 0$ a.e.

Moreover, equation 31.52 holds if and only if

$$E\{x_j(1)\log x_j(1)|x(0) = e_i\} < \infty, \qquad 1 \leqslant i, j \leqslant n. \tag{31.53}$$

Finally, if $x(0) = e_j$, if equation 31.53 holds, and if there is an i_0 such that, for at least two values of $a \in R_+$,

$$P\left\{\sum_{i=1}^{n} x_i(1)v_i = a|x(0) = e_{i_0}\right\} \neq 1, \tag{31.54}$$

then g has a jump at the origin and a continuous density function on R_{++}. If equation 31.54 does not hold for any i_0, then the distribution of g is concentratedon one point.

For a proof of the assertions of E 31.6, the interested reader is referred to Kesten and Stigum 1966 (pp. 1211–1223).

31.3 Balanced Growth under Uncertainty in a Decomposable Economy

In this section we shall study growth under uncertainty in a decomposable economy and establish sufficient conditions for balanced growth. We assume that the behavior of the economy can be represented by a vector-valued random process $\{x(t, \omega); t \in T\}$ which satisfies the condition

$$E\{x(t + 1)|x(0), \ldots, x(t)\} = H(x(t)) \quad \text{a.e.}, \qquad t = 0, 1, \ldots, \tag{31.55}$$

where $H(\cdot)$: $R_+^n \to R_+^n$ is a continuous, nondecreasing, linearly homogeneous, decomposable function. We also assume that there is an integer $n_1 \in [1, n)$ and two nondecreasing, continuous, linearly homogeneous functions, $H^1(\cdot)$: $R_+^{n_1} \to R_+^{n_1}$ and $H^2(\cdot) R_+^n \to R_+^{n-n_1}$, such that $H(\cdot) = (H^1(\cdot), H^2(\cdot))$ and such that both $H^1(\cdot)$ and $H^2(0^1, \cdot)$ are indecomposable. Finally, we assume that if $(\lambda_1, V^1) \in R_{++} \times R_{++}^{n_1}$ and $(\lambda_2, \overline{V}^2) \in R_{++} \times R_{++}^{n-n_1}$ are such that

$$H^1(V^1) = \lambda_1 V^1 \qquad \text{and} \qquad H^2(0^1, \overline{V}^2) = \lambda_2 \overline{V}^2,$$

then $\lambda_1 > \lambda_2$. An example of such an economy is given here.

E 31.7 Let $n = 2$ and let $\{x(t, \omega); t \in T\}$ be a two-variate random process whose components $x_1(t)$ and $x_2(t)$, respectively, represent an economy's labor force and aggregate capital stock in period t, $t = 0, 1, \ldots$. Assume first that there exists a constant $\rho > 1$ such that

$$x_1(t + 1, \omega) = \rho x_1(t, \omega) \quad \text{a.e.}, \tag{31.56}$$

for all $t \in T$. Next let $\{A_t; t \in T\}$ be a purely random process of nonnegative, nondegenerate, square-integrable random variables and assume that the aggregate production function can be represented by a continuous function, $G(\cdot)$: $R_+^2 \times R_+ \to R_+$, with the property that, for all $A \in R_+$, $G(\cdot, A)$ is nondecreasing and linearly homogeneous. Finally, assume that there is a constant $s \in (0, 1)$ such that, for all $t \in T$ and a.e. in Ω,

$$x_2(t+1, \omega) = x_2(t, \omega) + sG(x(t, \omega), A_t). \tag{31.57}$$

Then, if $H^1(x_1) = \rho x_1$, $F(y) = P\{A_t < y\}$, $y \in R_+$, and

$$H^2(x) = x_2 + s\int_{R_+} G(x, y)\, dF(y), \qquad x \in R_+^2,$$

we find that, with $H(\cdot) = (H^1(\cdot), H^2(\cdot))$ and for all $t \in T$,

$$E\{x(t+1)|x(0), \ldots, x(t)\} = H(x(t)) \quad \text{a.e.} \tag{31.58}$$

The economy whose behavior is represented by equations 30.56–31.58 is a simplified version of an economy which L. J. Mirman studied in Mirman 1973.

For the decomposable economies I have in mind, we can establish the following analogue of T 31.7:

T 31.8 Let $\{x(t, \omega); t \in T\}$ be an n-vector-valued random process on a probability space $(\Omega, \mathscr{F}, P(\cdot))$ and assume that the $x(t, \cdot)$ satisfy equation 31.55 and that the $H(\cdot)$ in equation 31.55 satisfies the conditions of T 31.4. Moreover, suppose that, for all $x^1 \in (R_+^{n_1} - \{0\})$,

$$H^1(x^1) > 0 \qquad \text{and} \qquad H^2(x^1, x^2) > 0. \tag{31.59}$$

Finally, let V^1, V^2, and λ_1 be as in equation 31.27 and assume that there exists a neighborhood U of $((V^1, V^2)/\|(V^1, V^2)\|)$ in $\{x \in R_+^n : \|x\| = 1\}$ and constants K and δ such that $0 < \delta < 1$ and such that (1) for $1 \leqslant i \leqslant n_1$ and all $t \in T$,

$$E\{|x_i^1(t+1) - H_i^1(x^1(t))|^2 | x(0), \ldots, x(t)\} \leqslant K\|x^1(t)\|^{2(1-\delta)}, \tag{31.60}$$

(2) for $n_1 + 1 \leqslant i \leqslant n$ and all $t \in T$,

$$E\{|x_i(t+1) - H_i^2(x(t))|^2 | x(0), \ldots, x(t)\} \leqslant K\|x(t)\|^{2(1-\delta)} \tag{31.61}$$

and (3) for all $x, y \in U$,

$$\|H(x) - H(y)\| \leqslant K\|x - y\|. \tag{31.62}$$

Then there exists a random variable g such that

$$\lim_{t\to\infty} (x(t, \omega)/\lambda_1^t) = g((V^1, V^2)/\|(V^1, V^2)\|) \tag{31.63}$$

with probability 1. Moreover,

$$E\{g|x(0)\} > 0 \qquad \text{and} \qquad P\{g > 0|x(0)\} > 0 \tag{31.64}$$

whenever $x^1(0) \neq 0$, $\|x(0)\| \geqslant M(\|x^1(0)\|/\|x(0)\|)$ for a suitable finite function $M(\cdot)$: $(0, 1] \to (0, \infty)$. If

$$P\{\|x^1(s)\|/\|x(s)\|) \geqslant \varepsilon, \|x(s)\| \geqslant M(\varepsilon) \text{ for some } s|x(0)\} > 0 \tag{31.65}$$

for some $\varepsilon > 0$ and all $x(0)$ with $x^1(0) \neq 0$, then equation 31.64 holds for all $x^1(0) \neq 0$. On the other hand,

$$x^1(t) = 0 \text{ for all } t \text{ and } g = 0 \quad \text{a.e. on } \{x^1(0) = 0\}.$$

Finally,

$$E\{g|x(0)\} < \infty$$

if the functions $H_i(\cdot)$, $1 \leqslant i \leqslant n_i$ are concave.

It follows from T 31.7 that if $x^1(0) \neq 0$ and there is an $\varepsilon > 0$ for which equation 31.65 is satisfied, then equations 31.59, 31.60 and 31.62 and the conditions of T 31.4 imply that there exists a random variable g_1 such that

$$\lim_{t\to\infty} (x^1(t,\omega)/\lambda_1^t) = g_1 V^1 \quad \text{a.e.,}$$

and such that $E\{g_1|x^1(0)\} > 0$ and $P\{g_1 > 0|x^1(0)\} > 0$. It also follows from T 31.7 that the conditions of T 31.4 and equations 31.59, 31.61, and 31.62 imply that on the set $\{x^1(0) = 0\}$

$$\lim_{t\to\infty} (x^2(t,\omega)/\lambda_1^t) = 0 \quad \text{a.e.} \tag{31.66}$$

In order to establish the theorem, we must show first that on the set where $\limsup x^1(t) < \infty$, equation 31.66 must hold and then that on the set where $\limsup x^1(t) = \infty$,

$$\lim_{t\to\infty} (x^2(t,\omega)/\lambda_1^t) = g_1 V^2 \quad \text{a.e..}$$

The arguments needed for that purpose are involved (see Kesten and Stigum 1974, pp. 373–380), so I omit them and conclude this section with a few pertinent comments concerning the generality of our sufficient conditions for the validity of equations 31.63 and 31.64.

From one point of view, our sufficient conditions for equations 31.63 and 31.64 are the best obtainable sufficient conditions. Specifically, there exist processes that satisfy all but one of these conditions whose asymptotic behavior cannot be described by equations 31.63 and 31.64. Here is an example.

E 31.8 Consider the economy in E 31.7 and make assumptions on $G(\cdot)$ that will ensure that $H(\cdot)$ satisfies the conditions of T 31.4, equation 31.59, and equation 31.62. Assume also that the distribution of A_t is absolutely continuous with respect to Lebesgues measure and concentrated on a compact interval, and that the corresponding density function is continuous and positive on this interval. Then the $x_1(t,\cdot)$ satisfy equation 31.60. However, the $x_2(t,\cdot)$ do not satisfy equation 31.61, and it follows trivially from theorem 3.3 in Mirman 1973

(p. 111) that $(x(t)/\rho^t)$ converges in distribution to a random vector whose distribution is not concentrated along a single ray from the origin in R_+^2.

On the other hand, there exist processes that satisfy some but not all the conditions of T 31.8 whose asymptotic behavior can be described as in equation 31.63 and 31.64. Here is an example:

E 31.9 Let $\{x(t, \omega); t \in T\}$ be a two-variate decomposable Galton-Watson process with first-moment matrix

$$A = \begin{pmatrix} \lambda_1 & 0 \\ m & \lambda_2 \end{pmatrix}$$

and let $H(x) = Ax$, $x \in R_+^2$. Moreover, suppose that $\lambda_1 > 1$, $\lambda_2 > 0$, $\lambda_1 > \lambda_2$, and $m > 0$. Then $H(\cdot)$ satisfies the conditions of T 31.4, equation 31.60, and equation 31.62; and equations 31.63 and 31.64 hold (see Kesten and Stigum 1967, pp. 335–336, for a proof) if and only if

$$E\{x_1(1) \log x_1(1) | x_1(0) = 1\} < \infty.$$

It is not intuitively obvious that any economy ever would satisfy conditions 31.60 and 31.61. Next we describe a simple economy that does. This hypothetical economy can be thought of as a free translation of Edward Bellamy's USA year 2000 (Bellamy 1967). It was first discussed in Kesten and Stigum 1974, pp. 348–350).

E 31.10 Consider an economy in which there are two primary inputs, labor x_1 and capital x_2. These factors can be combined to produce output ($\equiv$ net national product) according to a continuous, strictly quasi-concave, linearly homogeneous function $F(\cdot)$ that is increasing on $\{x_1 > 0, x_2 \geqslant 0\}$. We assume (1) that capital and output are both publicly owned, (2) that workers share equally in national output, each one's share being equal to a fraction of labor's average product, and (3) that the general surplus (i.e. net national product—wage allotments) is used in toto by government to augment the nation's capital stock.

Assume in addition that the share of national output credited on the public books to each worker is so ample that a worker is "more likely not to spend it all." If a worker does not fully expend his credit, the balance is turned into general surplus. Under extraordinary circumstances a worker might be allowed to spend more than his allotment but never more than labor's average product. The excess above the usual allotment would be taken out of the general surplus.

More precisely we are assuming (4) that the fraction of labor's average product consumed in each period by the ith worker can be represented by a random variable c_i with range (0, 1], and (5) that, if $x_1(t)$ and $x_2(t)$ denote the labor and capital in period t, then for all t:

$$x_2(t+1) = x_2(t) + \sum_{i=1}^{x_1(t)} (1 - c_i)[F(x_1(t), x_2(t))/x_1(t)].$$

We will also assume (6) that the distribution of c_i is independent of i and constant over time and that, for each pair (i, j), c_i and c_j are distributed independently of each other and of labor and capital. Finally, we assume (7) that the growth of the labor force can be represented by a Galton-Watson process with mean $\lambda > 1$ and finite variance σ^2.

The preceding assumptions allow us to describe the development over time of our utopian economy in terms of a random process, $\{(x_1(t, \omega), x_2(t, \omega)); t \in T\}$, with the following properties:

$$E\{x_1(t+1)|x(0), \ldots, x(t)\} = \lambda x_1(t) \quad \text{a.e.,} \tag{31.67}$$

and

$$E\{x_2(t+1)|x(0), \ldots, x(t)\} = x_2(t) + sF(x(t)) \quad \text{a.e.,} \tag{31.68}$$

where $s = E(1 - c_1)$. Moreover,

$$E\{[x_1(t+1) - \lambda x_1(t)]^2|x(0), \ldots, x(t)\} = \sigma^2 x_1(t), \quad \text{a.e.,} \tag{31.69}$$

and

$$E\{(x_2(t+1) - x_2(t) - sF(x(t)))^2|x(0), \ldots, x(t)\} \leqslant K\|x(t)\| \quad \text{a.e.} \tag{31.70}$$

for a suitable finite constant K.

In concluding the chapter it is interesting to observe that equations 31.63 and 31.64 may obtain even if equation 31.55 is not valid. In order that a vector-valued random process satisfy equations 31.63 and 31.64, it is sufficient that there exist functions $H(\cdot)$, $H^1(\cdot)$, and $H^2(\cdot)$ that satisfy equations 31.59–31.62 and the conditions of T 31.4. To bring this point home, we consider the following variation on the theme of E 31.10, which also comes from Kesten and Stigum 1974.

E 31.11 Consider the economy of E 31.10 and modify the assumption concerning the probability distribution of the c_i as follows: Let $y_1, y_2, \ldots$ be identically and independently distributed, nonnegative random variables and assume that

$$0 < E\{y_i\} = \mu < 1,$$

and

$$E\{(y_i - \mu)^2\} = \sigma_y^2 < \infty.$$

Assume also that the y_i's are distributed independently of $x(t)$, $t \in T$, where $x(t)$ is as defined in E 31.10. Finally, assume that in each period t the distribution of the c_i's conditional upon the observed value of $x_1(t)$, satisfies the following condition:

$$P\{(c_1, \ldots, c_{x_1(t)}) \in A\} = P\left\{(y_1, \ldots, y_{x_1(t)}) \in A \,\middle|\, \sum_{i=1}^{x_{t,1}} y_i \leqslant x_1(t)\right\},$$

for all Borel subsets A of $(R_+)^{x_1(t)}$.

When we make the above modification, but leave the economy otherwise unchanged, the relations 31.67 and 31.69 are still valid. Moreover, with $s =$

$(1 - \mu)$, it is fairly easy to show that equation 31.70 is still valid. However, equation 31.68 is generally false unless the range of the y_i belongs to $(0, 1]$. Thus $\{(x_1(t, \cdot), x_2(t, w)), t \in T\}$ need not satisfy equation 31.55. However, the arguments used to establish T 31.8 can be used to demonstrate that the $x(t, \cdot)$ satisfy equations 31.63 and 31.64.

IX

Econometrics II: Prediction, Distributed Lags, and Stochastic Difference Equations

32 Distributed Lags and Wide-Sense Stationary Processes

In part IX we shall use the axiomatic method to discuss four topics of fundamental importance to the analysis of economic time series: prediction, optimal distributed lags, modeling trends, cycles and seasonals, and estimating parameters of a stochastic difference equation. This task involves us in delineating three classes of random processes—wide-sense stationary processes, ARIMA processes, and dynamic stochastic processes—and in establishing many interesting limit theorems for nonstationary processes.

Chapter 32 is devoted to prediction and distributed lags. We begin by deriving the spectral representation of wide-sense stationary processes. Then I present the theory of best linear prediction in a wide-sense stationary environment, prove Herman Wold's Decomposition Theorem, and establish A. Kolmogorov's spectral characterization of the best linear predictor. Finally, we apply the ideas of linear prediction to a stochastic control problem and obtain a solution that provides us with an economic-theoretic way of rationalizing various distributed-lag models in econometrics.

Chapter 33 concerns the problem of how best to model trends, cycles, and seasonals in economic time series. We begin by describing various ways in which trends, cycles, and seasonals have been modeled in econometrics and demonstrate that they can be rationalized by assuming that an economic time series is a partial realization of an ARIMA process or a dynamic stochastic process. Then we derive the salient characteristics of such processes and show that it is unlikely that an economic time series is generated by an ARIMA process but possible that it is generated by a dynamic stochastic process.

Chapter 34 deals with least squares and the estimation of parameters of a stochastic difference equation. We study the limiting behavior of such estimates and show that some of them converge exponentially fast, others with probability 1, and still others in probability to well-defined limiting values that need not equal the true values of the parameters in question. We also derive the limiting distribution of these estimates and demonstrate that it can, but need not, be normal and that it is often degenerate. These results exhibit the importance of asymptotic theory in econometrics and suggest many interesting questions; e.g., how good is an inconsistent best linear unbiased estimate, and what is the power of a finite-sample test of the sizes (or signs) of a set of parameters when the test is based on estimates whose limiting distribution is degenerate?

The essays in part IX illustrate uses of the axiomatic method that we have not dealt with before, e.g., developing stochastic optimal control theory for a wide-sense stationary environment and demonstrating how asymptotic theory can help us determine the reasonableness of standard hypotheses concerning the mechanisms by which economic time series are generated. The results we obtain are partly universal theorems of mathematical statistics and partly T_4 theorems, i.e., theorems that belong in a T_4 box of an axiomatic superstructure. All of them provide relevant information to econometricians engaged in constructing axiomatic superstructures for testing economic theories with time-series data. In that way, the chapters of part IX complete the discussion of axiomatic superstructures that we began in chapter 26.

32.1 A Characterization of Wide-Sense Stationary Processes

In this section we shall obtain an integral representation of wide-sense stationary processes. We begin with a definition and several useful examples.

32.1.1 Examples

Let $\bar{a}$ denote the complex conjugate of the complex number a, and let $X = \{x(t,\omega); t \in T\}$ be a complex or real-valued random process on a probability space $(\Omega, \mathscr{F}, P(\cdot))$. Then X is a *wide-sense stationary process* relative to $P(\cdot)$ if and only if the functions,

$$m(t) = Ex(t), \qquad t \in T,$$

and

$$r(t, t+s) = Ex(t)\overline{x(t+s)} - m(t)\overline{m(t+s)}, \qquad (t, t+s) \in T \times T,$$

are finite and independent of t. In that case we write m for $m(t)$, $r(s)$ for $r(t, t+s)$, and refer to $r(\cdot)$ as the *covariance function* of X.

A strictly stationary random process with finite means and variances is wide-sense stationary. However, not all wide-sense stationary processes are strictly stationary. We see that in E 32.1:

E 32.1 Let $a(\cdot)$ and $b(\cdot)$ be real random variables on a probability space $(\Omega, \mathscr{F}, P(\cdot))$, and assume that, relative to $P(\cdot)$, $a(\cdot)$ and $b(\cdot)$ are identically and independently distributed with mean zero and variance σ^2. Moreover, let $\theta \in (0, \pi)$ be such that $t\theta$ is not an integer multiple of either π or $(\pi/2)$ for any $t \geqslant 1$. Finally, let $X = \{x(t, \omega); t = 0, 1, \dots\}$ be defined by

$$x(t, \omega) = a(\omega) \cos t\theta + b(\omega) \sin t\theta, \qquad t = 0, 1, \dots. \tag{32.1}$$

Then X is a wide-sense stationary process since, for all $t, s = 0, 1, \dots,$

$$Ex(t) = 0;$$

and

$$Ex(t)x(t + s) = \sigma^2 \cos s\theta.$$

However, X is obviously not strictly stationary.

The wide-sense stationary process in E 32.1 has several disguises. For example, if we define $\alpha(\cdot)\colon \Omega \to R_+$ and $\beta(\cdot)\colon \Omega \to (-\pi, \pi)$ by the relations,

$$a(\omega) = \alpha(\omega) \cos \beta(\omega) \qquad \text{and} \qquad b(\omega) = -\alpha(\omega) \sin \beta(\omega), \qquad \omega \in \Omega,$$

then we can write the $x(t, \omega)$ of equation 32.1 as

$$x(t, \omega) = \alpha(\omega) \cos(t\theta + \beta(\omega)), \qquad t = 0, 1, \dots, \qquad \omega \in \Omega.$$

Hence X can be thought of as having been generated by an experiment that determines the amplitude $\alpha(\omega)$ and the phase $(-\beta(\omega)/\theta)$ of the cosine curve which describes the behavior of $x(\cdot, \omega)$ as t varies over nonnegative integers.

We obtain a second disguise if we let $U(\cdot)\colon [0, \pi] \times \Omega \to R$ and $V(\cdot)\colon [0, \pi] \times \Omega \to R$ be defined by

$$U(\lambda, \omega) = \begin{cases} 0 & \text{if } \lambda \in [0, \theta] \\ \pi a(\omega) & \text{if } \lambda \in (\theta, \pi] \end{cases} \quad \text{and} \quad V(\lambda, \omega) = \begin{cases} 0 & \text{if } \lambda \in [0, \theta] \\ \pi b(\omega) & \text{if } \lambda \in (\theta, \pi] \end{cases}.$$

Then $U(\cdot, \omega)$ and $V(\cdot, \omega)$ are nondecreasing and continuous from the left for all $\omega \in \Omega$ and satisfy $E\,dU(\lambda) = E\,dV(\lambda) = 0$, $\lambda \in [0, \pi]$ and

$$E\{dU(\lambda)\, dU(\mu)\} = E\{dV(\lambda)\, dV(\mu)\} = 0, \qquad 0 \leqslant \lambda, \mu \leqslant \pi,\ \lambda \neq \mu; \tag{32.2}$$

$$E\{dU(\lambda)\}^2 = E\{dV(\lambda)\}^2 = dG(\lambda), \qquad \lambda \in [0, \pi); \tag{32.3}$$

$$E\{dU(\lambda)\}^2 = dG(\lambda), \qquad \lambda \in [0, \pi], \tag{32.4}$$

and

$$E\{dU(\lambda)\,dV(\mu)\} = 0, \qquad 0 \leqslant \lambda, \mu \leqslant \pi, \tag{32.5}$$

where $G(\lambda)$ equals 0 or $\sigma^2\pi^2$ according as $\lambda \leqslant \theta$ or $\lambda > \theta$. Moreover, for each $t = 0, 1, \ldots$, and $\omega \in \Omega$, $x(t, \omega)$ can be written as

$$x(t, \omega) = \pi^{-1} \int_0^{\pi} \cos t\lambda\, dU(\lambda, \omega) + \sin t\lambda\, dV(\lambda, \omega). \tag{32.6}$$

The interesting aspect of equation 32.6 is that all real-valued wide-sense stationary processes can be decomposed into similar forms of "weighted averages" of $\cos(\cdot)$ and $\sin(\cdot)$ functions with weights that satisfy equations 32.2–32.5 for some nondecreasing function $G(\cdot)$: $[0, \pi] \to R$. Moreover, all complex-valued wide-sense stationary processes can be decomposed into analogous forms, the characteristics of which can be intuited from the complex version of equation 32.6.

To obtain the complex version of equation 32.6 we first let C denote the set of complex numbers and define $A(\cdot)$: $\Omega \to C$ and $B(\cdot)$: $\Omega \to C$ by

$$A(\omega) = (a(\omega) - ib(\omega))/2 \quad \text{and} \quad B(\omega) = \overline{A(\omega)}, \qquad \omega \in \Omega.$$

Then the $x(t, \cdot)$ of E 32.1 can be written as

$$x(t, \omega) = A(\omega)e^{it\theta} + B(\omega)e^{-it\theta}, \qquad t = 0, 1, \ldots, \qquad \omega \in \Omega,$$

which is the complex form of equation 32.1. Next we let

$$Z(\lambda, \omega) = \begin{cases} 0 & \text{for } \lambda \in [-\pi, -\theta]; \\ 2\pi B(\omega) & \text{for } \lambda \in (-\theta, \theta]; \text{ and} \\ 2\pi(A(\omega) + B(\omega)) & \text{for } \lambda \in (\theta, \pi]; \end{cases}$$

and

$$F(\lambda) = \begin{cases} 0 & \text{if } \lambda \in [-\pi, -\theta]; \\ \pi\sigma^2 & \text{if } \lambda \in (-\theta, \theta]; \quad \text{and} \\ 2\pi\sigma^2 & \text{if } \lambda \in (\theta, \pi]. \end{cases} \tag{32.7}$$

Then, for all $\omega \in \Omega$, $Z(\cdot, \omega)$ is nondecreasing and continuous from the left and satisfies $E\,dZ(\lambda) = 0$, $\lambda \in [-\pi, \pi]$, and

$$E\{dZ(\lambda)\,\overline{dZ(\mu)}\} = 0, \qquad -\pi \leqslant \lambda, \mu \leqslant \pi, \ \lambda \neq \mu, \tag{32.8}$$

and

$$E|dZ(\lambda)|^2 = 2\pi\, dF(\lambda), \qquad \lambda \in [-\pi, \pi]. \tag{32.9}$$

Moreover, the $x(t, \cdot)$ of E 31.1 can be written as

$$x(t,\omega) = (2\pi)^{-1} \int_{-\pi}^{\pi} e^{it\lambda}\, dZ(\lambda,\omega), \qquad \omega \in \Omega, \tag{32.10}$$

which is the complex analogue of equation 32.6.

It is easy to understand the meaning of equations 32.6 and 32.10 when $x(t)$ is as described in E 32.1, but it is hard to intuit their meaning in the general case. The following theorem will later help our intuition and provide means to establish the general validity of equations 32.6 and 32.10.

UT 23 Let $(\Omega, \mathscr{F}, P(\cdot))$ be a probability space and let $\mathscr{L}_2$ denote the set of all random variables $x(\cdot): \Omega \to C$ that satisfy

$$E|x|^2 = \int_{\Omega} |x(\omega)|^2\, dP(\omega) < \infty.$$

Moreover, let $x_n(\cdot) \in \mathscr{L}_2$, $n = 1, 2, \ldots$, be such that

$$\lim_{n,m\to\infty} E|x_n - x_m|^2 = 0.$$

Then there exists an $x(\cdot) \in \mathscr{L}_2$ such that

$$\lim_{n\to\infty} E|x_n - x|^2 = 0.$$

The required $x(\cdot)$ is uniquely determined up to a set of P-measure zero.

In reading this theorem, note that UT 23 is an analogue of UT 16 for square-integrable, complex-valued functions. For a proof of the theorem, I refer the reader to Loève 1960 (p. 161).

32.1.2 Orthogonal Set Functions and Stochastic Integrals[1]

To establish the general validity of equation 32.10, we must first explicate the meaning of a stochastic integral over $[-\pi, \pi]$. To this end, let $(\Omega, \mathscr{F}, P(\cdot))$ be a probability space, let $\mathscr{B}$ denote the σ field of Borel subsets of $[-\pi, \pi]$, and let $\mu(\cdot): \mathscr{B} \to R_+$ be a bounded σ-additive measure on $([-\pi, \pi], \mathscr{B})$. Moreover, let $z(\cdot): \mathscr{B} \times \Omega \to C$ be a random process which, for all A, B, $\in \mathscr{B}$, satisfies the conditions:

$$z((A \cup B), \omega) = z(A,\omega) + z(B,\omega) \quad \text{a.e.} \quad \text{if } (A \cap B) = \varnothing;$$

$$Ez(A) = 0;$$

and

$$Ez(A)\overline{z(B)} = \mu((A \cap B)).$$

Then $z(\cdot)$ is an *orthogonal set function*. We shall determine the meaning of

$$\int_{-\pi}^{\pi} f(\lambda)\, dz(\lambda, \omega) \tag{32.11}$$

when $f(\cdot)\colon [-\pi, \pi] \to C$ satisfies the condition,

$$\int_{-\pi}^{\pi} |f(\lambda)|^2\, d\mu(\lambda) < \infty. \tag{32.12}$$

To begin, we consider indicator functions and simple functions. For each $A \in \mathscr{B}$, let $I_A(\cdot)\colon [-\pi, \pi] \to \{0, 1\}$ denote the indicator function of A. Then $I_A(\cdot)$ satisfies equation 32.12, and we let

$$\int_{-\pi}^{\pi} I_A(\lambda)\, dz(\lambda, \omega) = z(A, \omega), \qquad \omega \in \Omega.$$

Next, let $A_i \in \mathscr{B}$, $i = 1, \dots, m$, be such that $(A_i \cap A_j = \emptyset$ for $i \neq j$; let a_i, $i = 1, \dots, m$, be complex constants; and let $f(\lambda) = \sum_{i=1}^{m} a_i I_{A_i}(\lambda)$, $\lambda \in [-\pi, \pi]$. Then $f(\cdot)$ is a simple function which satisfies equation 32.12, and we let

$$\int_{-\pi}^{\pi} f(\lambda)\, dz(\lambda, \omega) = \int_{-\pi}^{\pi} \sum_{i=1}^{m} a_i I_{A_i}(\lambda)\, dz(\lambda, \omega) = \sum_{i=1}^{m} a_i z(A_i, \omega), \qquad \omega \in \Omega.$$

To define the integral in equation 32.11 generally, we observe that if $f(\cdot)\colon [-\pi, \pi] \to C$ satisfies equation 32.12, then there exists a sequence of simple functions, $f_n(\cdot)\colon [-\pi, \pi] \to C$, $n = 1, 2, \dots$, such that

$$\lim_{n \to \infty} \int_{-\pi}^{\pi} |f(\lambda) - f_n(\lambda)|^2\, d\mu(\lambda) = 0. \tag{32.13}$$

But if this is so and if we let

$$J_n(\omega) = \int_{-\pi}^{\pi} f_n(\lambda)\, dz(\lambda, \omega), \quad \omega \in \Omega,\ n = 1, 2, \dots,$$

then it is easy to see that

$$E|J_n|^2 = \int_{-\pi}^{\pi} |f_n(\lambda)|^2\, d\mu(\lambda), \qquad n = 1, 2, \dots, \tag{32.14}$$

and

$$\lim_{n, m \to \infty} E|J_n - J_m|^2 = \lim_{n, m \to \infty} \int_{-\pi}^{\pi} |f_n(\lambda) - f_m(\lambda)|^2\, d\mu(\lambda) = 0. \tag{32.15}$$

From equations 32.13–32.15 and UT 23, it follows that there exists a random variable $J(\cdot): \Omega \to C$ such that

$$\lim_{n\to\infty} E|J - J_n|^2 = 0$$

and

$$E|J|^2 = \lim_{n\to\infty} E|J_n|^2 = \int_{-\pi}^{\pi} |f(\lambda)|^2\, d\mu(\lambda).$$

We observe that $J(\cdot)$ is uniquely determined up to a set of P-measure zero and let

$$\int_{-\pi}^{\pi} f(\lambda)\, dz(\lambda, \omega) = J(\omega), \qquad \omega \in \Omega. \tag{32.16}$$

The integral in equation 32.16 is well defined up to a set of P-measure zero. To see why, let $f_n'(\cdot): [-\pi, \pi] \to C$, $n = 1, 2, \ldots$, be another sequence of simple functions that satisfy

$$\lim_{n\to\infty} \int_{-\pi}^{\pi} |f(\lambda) - f_n'(\lambda)|^2\, d\mu(\lambda) = 0,$$

and define the random variables $J_n'(\cdot): \Omega \to C$, $n = 1, 2, \ldots$, by

$$J_n'(\omega) = \int_{-\pi}^{\pi} f_n'(\lambda)\, dz(\lambda, \omega).$$

Then it is a routine matter to verify that

$$\lim_{n\to\infty} E|J - J_n'|^2 = 0$$

and hence that our assertion is true.

Our stochastic integral has standard properties. To wit: If $f(\cdot): [-\pi, \pi] \to C$ and $g(\cdot): [-\pi, \pi] \to C$ satisfy equation 32.12, then for all α, β, ε C,

$$\int_{-\pi}^{\pi} (\alpha f(\lambda) + \beta g(\lambda))\, dz(\lambda, \omega)$$

$$= \alpha \int_{-\pi}^{\pi} f(\lambda)\, dz(\lambda, \omega) + \beta \int_{-\pi}^{\pi} g(\lambda)\, dz(\lambda, \omega) \quad \text{a.e.}$$

Moreover, for the same $f(\cdot)$ and $g(\cdot)$,

$$E\left(\int_{-\pi}^{\pi} f(\lambda)\,dz(\lambda)\overline{\int_{-\pi}^{\pi} g(\lambda)\,dz(\lambda)}\right) = \int_{-\pi}^{\pi} f(\lambda)\overline{g(\lambda)}\,d\mu(\lambda).$$

Finally, if $f_n(\cdot): [-\pi, \pi] \to C$, $n = 1, 2, \ldots$, and $f(\cdot): [-\pi, \pi] \to C$ satisfy equation 32.12, then

$$\lim E\left(\left|\int_{-\pi}^{\pi} f_n(\lambda)\,dz(\lambda, \omega) - \int_{-\pi}^{\pi} f(\lambda)\,dz(\lambda, \omega)\right|^2\right) = 0$$

if and only if

$$\lim \int_{-\pi}^{\pi} |f_n(\lambda) - f(\lambda)|^2\,d\mu(\lambda) = 0.$$

Since these relations are easy to establish, I leave their verification to the reader.

32.1.3 The Spectral Distribution Function

Let $X = \{x(t, \omega); t \in T\}$ be the wide-sense stationary process of E 32.1 and let $r(s) = Ex(t)\overline{x(t+s)}$, $s = 0, 1, \ldots$. Then it follows easily from equation 32.8–32.10 that

$$r(s) = (2\pi)^{-1}\int_{-\pi}^{\pi} e^{-is\lambda}\,dF(\lambda), \qquad s = 0, 1, \ldots. \tag{32.17}$$

In this subsection we shall establish the general validity of equation 32.17 for all complex-valued wide-sense stationary processes. We begin with an auxiliary theorem concerning an important property of the covariance function.

T 32.1 Let $X = \{x(t, \omega); t \in T\}$ be a real- or complex-valued wide-sense stationary process and assume that $Ex(t) = 0$, $t \in T$. Moreover, let

$$r(s) = Ex(t)\overline{x(t+s)}, \qquad (t, t+s) \in T \times T \tag{32.18}$$

and assume that $T = \{\ldots, -1, 0, 1, \ldots\}$. Then

$$r(-s) = \overline{r(s)}, \qquad s \in T; \tag{32.19}$$

and for all $n = 1, 2, \ldots$, and complex numbers, α_i, $i = 1, 2, \ldots, n$,

$$\sum_{i,j=1}^{n} \alpha_i\overline{\alpha_j}r(j-i) \geqslant 0. \tag{32.20}$$

Since $Ex(t)\overline{x(t-s)} = \overline{Ex(t-s)\overline{x(t)}}$, the validity of equation 32.19 is obvious; and the validity of equation 32.20 follows from

$$\sum_{i,j=1}^{n} \alpha_i \overline{\alpha_j} r(j-i) = \sum_{i,j=1}^{n} \alpha_i \overline{\alpha_j}\, Ex(t+i)\overline{x(t+j)}$$

$$= E\left|\sum_{i=1}^{n} \alpha_i x(t+i)\right|^2 \geqslant 0.$$

The fact that the $r(\cdot)$ of equation 32.18 can be expressed in the form of an integral like the right-hand side of equation 32.17 is a consequence of the following theorem.

T 32.2 Let $X = \{x(t,\omega); t \in T\}$ be a real- or complex-valued wide-sense stationary process and assume that $Ex(t) = 0$, $t \in T$. Moreover, let

$$r(s) = Ex(t)\overline{x(t+s)}, \qquad (t, t+s) \in T \times T$$

and assume that $T = \{\ldots, -1, 0, 1, \ldots\}$. Then there exists a nondecreasing function $F(\cdot)\colon [-\pi, \pi] \to R$ that is continuous from the left and satisfies

$$F(-\pi) = 0, \qquad F(\pi) = 2\pi \cdot r(0), \tag{32.21}$$

and

$$r(s) = (2\pi)^{-1} \int_{-\pi}^{\pi} e^{-is\lambda}\, dF(\lambda), \qquad s \in T. \tag{32.22}$$

$F(\cdot)$ is uniquely determined by equations 32.21 and 32.22.

To prove this theorem we let, for each $N = 1, 2, \ldots,$

$$F_N(\lambda) = r(0)(\lambda + \pi) + \sum_{\substack{s=-N \\ s \neq 0}}^{N} r(s)\left(\frac{e^{is\lambda} - e^{-is\pi}}{is}\right)\left(1 - \frac{|s|}{N}\right), \qquad \lambda \in [-\pi, \pi].$$

Then $F_N(-\pi) = 0$, $F_N(\pi) = 2\pi r(0)$, and, for $-\pi \leqslant \lambda_1 < \lambda_2 \leqslant \pi$,

$$F_N(\lambda_2) - F_N(\lambda_1) = r(0)(\lambda_2 - \lambda_1) + \sum_{\substack{s=-N \\ s \neq 0}}^{N} r(s)\left(\frac{e^{is\lambda_2} - e^{is\lambda_1}}{is}\right)\left(1 - \frac{|s|}{N}\right)$$

$$= \int_{\lambda_1}^{\lambda_2} \sum_{s=-N}^{N} r(s) e^{is\lambda}\left(1 - \frac{|s|}{N}\right) d\lambda$$

$$= \int_{\lambda_1}^{\lambda_2} N^{-1} \sum_{k,j=1}^{N+1} r(j-k) e^{i(j-k)\lambda}\, d\lambda \geqslant 0.$$

Hence $F_N(\cdot)\colon [-\pi, \pi] \to R$ is nondecreasing and satisfies equation 32.21. From this and a universal theorem, (see Loève 1960, p. 179), it follows that there exists a nondecreasing function $F(\cdot)\colon [-\pi, \pi] \to R$ that satisfies the conditions in 32.21 and a subsequence $F_{N_m}(\cdot)$ of the $F_N(\cdot)$ that converges to $F(\cdot)$ at the set of continuity points of $F(\cdot)$ and satisfies

$$\lim_{m\to\infty} \int_{-\pi}^{\pi} e^{-is\lambda}\, dF_{N_m}(\lambda) = \int_{-\pi}^{\pi} e^{-is\lambda}\, dF(\lambda), \qquad s \in T. \tag{32.23}$$

Since, for any given s and m,

$$(2\pi)^{-1} \int_{-\pi}^{\pi} e^{-is\lambda}\, dF_{N_m}(\lambda) = \begin{cases} r(s)\left(1 - \dfrac{|s|}{N_m}\right) & \text{if } |s| \leqslant N_m, \quad \text{and} \\ 0 & \text{if } |s| > N_m, \end{cases} \tag{32.24}$$

it follows from equations 32.23 and 32.24 that $F(\cdot)$ satisfies equation 32.22 as well. Finally, by adjusting the values of $F(\cdot)$ at its discontinuity points in $(-\pi, \pi)$ such that $F(\cdot)$ is continuous from the left, we obtain an $F(\cdot)$ which satisfies all the conditions of the theorem.

The function $F(\cdot)$, whose existence we have established, is called the *spectral distribution function* of X. Examples of such functions are the $F(\cdot)$ of equation 32.7 and the $F(\cdot)$ in E 32.2 below.

E 32.2 Let $X = \{x(t, \omega); t \in T\}$ be a wide-sense stationary process and assume that $Ex(t) = 0$, $t \in T$, and that

$$Ex(t)\overline{x(t+s)} = \begin{cases} \sigma^2 & \text{if } s = 0, \quad \text{and} \\ 0 & \text{otherwise.} \end{cases}$$

Then X is an *orthogonal* random process and

$$F(\lambda) = \sigma^2(\lambda + \pi), \qquad \lambda \in [-\pi, \pi].$$

When X is real-valued, then $r(s) = r(-s)$ for all $s \in T$ and $dF(\cdot)$ is symmetric around 0. Consequently, when X is real-valued, the integral representation of $r(\cdot)$ can be written as

$$r(s) = \pi^{-1} \int_{0}^{\pi} \cos s\lambda\, dF(\lambda), \qquad s \in T.$$

32.1.4 The Spectral Representation of a Wide-Sense Stationary Process

We shall use the results of the last two sections to establish an integral representation of complex-valued wide-sense stationary processes. We begin by describing a σ-additive measure $\mu_F(\cdot): \mathscr{B} \to R_+$ that we can substitute for $F(\cdot)$ in equation 32.22.

Let X, $r(\cdot)$, and $F(\cdot)$ be as described in T 32.2 and let $\mathscr{B}^0$ be the smallest field of subsets of $[-\pi, \pi]$ that contains all sets of the form $[a, b)$, $-\pi \leqslant a < b \leqslant \pi$, and finite disjoint unions of such sets. Moreover, let $\tilde{\mu}_F(\cdot)$: $\mathscr{B}^0 \to R_+$ be an additive measure that satisfies

$$\tilde{\mu}_F([a, b)) = F(b) - F(a), \qquad -\pi \leqslant a < b \leqslant \pi,$$

and

$$\tilde{\mu}_F([-\pi, \pi]) = F(\pi) - F(-\pi).$$

It can be shown that there is only one such measure and that $\tilde{\mu}(\cdot)$ is σ-additive on $\mathscr{B}^0$. Moreover, $\mathscr{B}$ is the smallest σ field that contains $\mathscr{B}^0$. Consequently, by UT 15, there exists one and only one σ-additive measure $\mu_F(\cdot)\colon \mathscr{B} \to R_+$ such that, for all $A \in \mathscr{B}^0$,

$$\mu_F(A) = \tilde{\mu}_F(A).$$

It is a fact (Loève 1960, pp. 166–167) that we can substitute $\mu_F(\cdot)$ in equation 32.22 and write

$$r(s) = (2\pi)^{-1} \int_{-\pi}^{\pi} e^{-is\lambda}\, d\mu_F(\lambda), \qquad s \in T.$$

Next we shall use $\mu_F(\cdot)$ and the $x(t, \cdot)$ in X to construct an orthogonal set function on $([-\pi, \pi], \mathscr{B})$. To this end, let $L_2([-\pi, \pi])$ denote the set of all Borel-measurable functions $f(\cdot)\colon [-\pi, \pi] \to C$ that satisfy the condition,

$$\int_{-\pi}^{\pi} |f(\lambda)|^2\, d\mu_F(\lambda) < \infty,$$

and observe that $L_2([-\pi, \pi])$ is spanned by the family of functions, $\{e^{is\lambda}; s \in T\}$ i.e., observe that any function in $L_2([-\pi, \pi])$ can be approximated arbitrarily closely by functions that are linear combinations of a finite number of the $e^{is(\cdot)}$. Moreover, let A be an arbitrary set in $\mathscr{B}$ and note that, since obviously $I_A(\cdot) \in L_2([-\pi, \pi])$, there is a sequence of functions,

$$f_n(\lambda) = \sum_{j=1}^{n} a_j^{(n)} e^{is_{n_j}\lambda},\ \lambda \in [-\pi, \pi]; \qquad s_{n_j} \in T;\ n = 1, 2, \ldots,$$

such that

$$\lim \int_{-\pi}^{\pi} |I_A(\lambda) - f_n(\lambda)|^2\, d\mu_F(\lambda) = 0. \tag{32.25}$$

Finally, let $z_n(\cdot)\colon \Omega \to C$, $n = 1, 2, \ldots$, be defined by

$$z_n(\omega) = 2\pi \sum_{j=1}^{n} a_j^{(n)} x(s_{n_j}, \omega), \qquad \omega \in \Omega,$$

and ascertain that

$$E|z_n|^2 = 2\pi \int_{-\pi}^{\pi} |f_n(\lambda)|^2 \, d\mu_F(\lambda), \qquad n = 1, 2, \ldots, \text{and} \tag{32.26}$$

$$\lim_{n,m\to\infty} E|z_n - z_m|^2 = \lim_{n,m\to\infty} 2\pi \int_{-\pi}^{\pi} |f_n(\lambda) - f_m(\lambda)|^2 \, d\mu_F(\lambda) = 0. \tag{32.27}$$

From equations 32.25–32.27 and UT 23, it follows that there exists a random variable, $z(A, \cdot): \Omega \to C$, such that

$$\lim_{n\to\infty} E|z(A) - z_n|^2 = \lim_{n\to\infty} 2\pi \int_{-\pi}^{\pi} |I_A(\lambda) - f_n(\lambda)|^2 \, d\mu_F(\lambda) = 0,$$

and

$$E|z(A)|^2 = 2\pi \int_{-\pi}^{\pi} |I_A(\lambda)|^2 \, d\mu_F(\lambda).$$

We can establish the existence of $z(A, \cdot)$ for all $A \in \mathcal{B}$ and demonstrate that $z(A, \cdot)$ is well defined up to a set of P-measure zero. Suppose that we have done that. Then it is easy to verify that, for all $A, B \in \mathcal{B}$,

$$Ez(A) = 0;$$

$$E\{z(A)\overline{z(B)}\} = \mu_F((A \cap B));$$

and that if $(A \cap B) = \varnothing$, then

$$E|z((A \cup B)) - z(A) - z(B)|^2 = 2\pi \int_{-\pi}^{\pi} |I_{(A\cup B)}(\lambda) - I_A(\lambda) - I_B(\lambda)|^2 \, d\mu_F(\lambda)$$
$$= 0.$$

Hence, $z(\cdot): \mathcal{B} \times \Omega \to C$ is an orthogonal set function.

The orthogonal set function constructed above satisfies the integral equations,

$$x(t, \omega) = (2\pi)^{-1} \int_{-\pi}^{\pi} e^{it\lambda} \, dz(\lambda, \omega) \quad \text{a.e.}, \quad t \in T.$$

To establish this fact, we first verify that, for each $A \in \mathcal{B}$,

$$Ex(t)\overline{z(A)} = \int_{-\pi}^{\pi} e^{it\lambda} I_A(\lambda) \, d\mu_F(\lambda). \tag{32.28}$$

Next we let

$$y(t, \omega) = (2\pi)^{-1} \int_{-\pi}^{\pi} e^{it\lambda} \, dz(\lambda, \omega)$$

and observe that there exists a sequence of simple functions,

$$g_n(\lambda) = \sum_{j=1}^{n} b_j^{(n)} I_{B_j^{(n)}}(\lambda), \qquad \lambda \in [-\pi, \pi], \qquad n = 1, 2, \ldots,$$

such that

$$\lim_{n\to\infty} \int_{-\pi}^{\pi} |e^{it\lambda} - g_n(\lambda)|^2 \, d\mu_F(\lambda) = 0. \tag{32.29}$$

Finally, we define a sequence of random variables, $J_n(\cdot)\colon \Omega \to C$, by

$$J_n(\omega) = (2\pi)^{-1} \int_{-\pi}^{\pi} g_n(\lambda)\, dz(\lambda, \omega), \qquad n = 1, 2, \ldots,$$

and use equations 32.28 and 32.29 to demonstrate that

$$\lim_{n\to\infty} E|y(t) - J_n|^2 = 0,$$

and

$$\begin{aligned} Ex(t)\overline{y(t)} &= \lim_{n\to\infty} Ex(t)\overline{J_n} \\ &= \lim_{n\to\infty} (2\pi)^{-1} \int_{-\pi}^{\pi} e^{it\lambda}\overline{g_n(\lambda)}\, d\mu_F(\lambda) = r(0). \end{aligned} \tag{32.30}$$

From equation 32.30 and the fact that $E|y(t)|^2 = r(0)$ follows

$$E|x(t) - y(t)|^2 = 0,$$

as was to be shown. Since $t \in T$ was chosen arbitrarily, we can assert the following theorem:

T 32.3 Let $X = \{x(t, \omega); t \in T\}$ be a complex-valued wide-sense stationary process and assume that $Ex(t) = 0$, $t \in T$, and that $T = \{\ldots, -1, 0, 1, \ldots\}$. Then there exists an orthogonal set function, $z(\cdot)\colon \mathscr{B} \times \Omega \to C$ such that, for all $t \in T$,

$$x(t, \omega) = (2\pi)^{-1} \int_{-\pi}^{\pi} e^{it\lambda}\, dz(\lambda, \omega) \quad \text{a.e.},$$

and such that, for all $\lambda \in [-\pi, \pi]$,

$$E|dz(\lambda)|^2 = 2\pi\, dF(\lambda),$$

where $F(\cdot)\colon [-\pi, \pi] \to R$ is the spectral distribution function of X.

Often the spectral representation of one process can be written in terms of the stochastic set function of another process whose spectral distribution function has a particularly simple structure. A case in point is described in the next example.

E 32.3 Let $X = \{x(t, \omega); t \in T\}$ and $\eta = \{\eta(t, \omega); t \in T\}$ be wide-sense stationary processes and assume that $Ex(t) = 0$, $t \in T$, $T = \{\ldots, -1, 0, 1, \ldots\}$ and η is an orthogonal random process. Moreover, let $z_j = 1, \ldots, m$, be complex numbers; let

$$z^m A(z) = \sum_{k=0}^{m} a_k z^{m-k} = \sum_{j=1}^{m} (z - z_j), \qquad z \in C, \tag{32.31}$$

and assume that $|z_j| \neq 1$, $j = 1, \ldots, m$. Finally, let $z_\eta(\cdot)\colon \mathscr{B} \times \Omega \to C$ be the orthogonal set function of η, and suppose that, for all $t \in T$,

$$\sum_{i=1}^{m} a_k x(t - k, \omega) = \eta(t, \omega).$$

Then X is an *autoregressive process*. Moreover, it is easy to verify that

$$x(t, \omega) = (2\pi)^{-1} \int_{-\pi}^{\pi} e^{it\lambda} A(e^{i\lambda})^{-1}\, dz_\eta(\lambda, \omega) \quad \text{a.e.,} \qquad t \in T, \tag{32.32}$$

and that the covariance function of X, $r(\cdot)\colon T \to C$, satisfies

$$r(s) = (\mathrm{E}|\eta(t)|^2/2\pi) \int_{-\pi}^{\pi} e^{-is\lambda} |A(e^{i\lambda})|^{-2}\, d\mu(\lambda), \qquad s \in T,$$

where $\mu(\cdot)\colon \mathscr{B} \to [0, 2\pi]$ is the Lebesgue measure on $([-\pi, \pi], \mathscr{B})$.

In closing this section, we note that when $X = \{x(t, \omega); t \in T\}$ is real-valued, then there exist two orthogonal set functions, $U(\cdot)\colon \mathscr{B} \times \Omega \to R$ and $V(\cdot)\colon \mathscr{B} \times \Omega \to R$, that satisfy equations 32.2–32.5 with $G(\cdot)$ replaced by $F(\cdot)$ in equation 32.3.

32.2 Linear Least-Squares Prediction

In this section we consider a real- or complex-valued wide-sense stationary process, $X = \{x(t, \omega); t \in T\}$, on some probability space $(\Omega, \mathscr{F}, P(\cdot))$, with covariance function, $r(\cdot)\colon T \to C$ and spectral distribution function, $F(\cdot)\colon [-\pi, \pi] \to R$. We assume (1) that $T = \{\ldots, -1, 0, 1, \ldots\}$, (2) that $Ex(t) = 0$, $t \in T$, and (3) that X and $r(\cdot)$ can be represented by

$$x(t, \omega) = (2\pi)^{-1} \int_{-\pi}^{\pi} e^{it\lambda}\, dz(\lambda, \omega) \quad \text{a.e.,} \qquad t \in T,$$

and

$$r(s) = (2\pi)^{-1} \int_{-\pi}^{\pi} e^{-is\lambda}\, d\mu_F(\lambda), \qquad s \in T,$$

where $z(\cdot)\colon \mathscr{B} \times \Omega \to C$ is the orthogonal set function determined by the $x(t, \cdot)$, and $\mu_F(\cdot)\colon \mathscr{B} \to R_+$ is the countably additive measure on

$([-\pi, \pi], \mathscr{B})$ determined by $F(\cdot)$. Our intent is to characterize the random variable $\phi_{t,v}(\cdot)\colon \Omega \to C$ which minimizes $E|x(t+v) - \phi|^2$ over all random variables ϕ that are either linear combinations of the $x(s, \cdot)$ for $s \leqslant t$ or limits of such linear combinations.

32.2.1 The Best Linear Least-Squares Predictor

For each $t \in T$ and $v \in (T \cap R_{++})$, $\phi_{t,v}$ is the *best linear least-squares predictor of* $x(t+v, \cdot)$ *based on the knowledge of* $x(s, \cdot)$ *for* $s \leqslant t$ *that we possess*. To establish the existence of $\phi_{t,v}$, I must first introduce several new terms. Let

$$_t\mathscr{M}^0 = \mathscr{M}(x(s); s \leqslant t), \qquad t \in T,$$

denote the linear manifold generated by the $x(s, \cdot)$ for $s \leqslant t$. Then $y \in {}_t\mathscr{M}^0$ if and only if there exist integers m, s_j, $j = 1, \ldots, m$, and complex constants, a_j, $j = 1, \ldots, m$, such that $s_j \leqslant t$, $j = 1, \ldots, m$, and

$$y(\omega) = \sum_{j=1}^{m} a_j x(s_j, \omega), \qquad \omega \in \Omega.$$

Next, for each $t \in T$, let $_t\mathscr{M}$ denote the closure of $_t\mathscr{M}^0$ in the following sense: $y \in {}_t\mathscr{M}$ if and only if there exists a sequence of random variables, $y_n(\cdot)\colon \Omega \to C$, $n = 1, 2, \ldots$, such that

$$y_n \in {}_t\mathscr{M}^0, \quad n = 1, 2, \ldots, \qquad \text{and} \qquad \lim_{n \to \infty} E|y - y_n|^2 = 0.$$

Finally, let

$$_\infty\mathscr{M}^0 = \mathscr{M}(x(s); s < \infty)$$

denote the linear manifold generated by X; let $_\infty\mathscr{M}$ denote the closure of $_\infty\mathscr{M}^0$ in the same sense as $_t\mathscr{M}$ is the closure of $_t\mathscr{M}^0$; and let

$$_{-\infty}\mathscr{M} = \bigcap_{t=-\infty}^{\infty} {}_t\mathscr{M}.$$

Then the following theorem is true:

T 32.4 Let $X = \{x(t, \omega); t \in T\}$ be a real- or complex-valued wide-sense stationary process on some probability space $(\Omega, \mathscr{F}, P(\cdot))$, and assume that $T = \{\ldots, -1, 0, 1, \ldots\}$ and that $Ex(t) = 0$, $t \in T$. Moreover, let the $_t\mathscr{M}$ be as described above. Then for each pair $(t, v) \in T \times (T \cap R_{++})$, there exists a random variable, $\phi_{t,v}(\cdot) \in {}_t\mathscr{M}$, such that, for all $\phi \in {}_t\mathscr{M}$,

$$E|x(t+v) - \phi_{t,v}|^2 \leqslant E|x(t+v) - \phi|^2. \tag{32.33}$$

$\phi_{t,v}$ is uniquely determined up to a set of P-measure zero. In addition,

$$E(x(t+v) - \phi_{t,v})\bar{\phi} = 0 \tag{32.34}$$

for all $\phi \in {}_t\mathcal{M}$.

Since ${}_t\mathcal{M}$ is a closed linear manifold, T 32.4 is a standard theorem in functional analysis. Hence I shall only sketch the ideas of the proof. We begin with the existence of $\phi_{t,v}$. Fix t and v and let

$$\sigma_v^2 = \min_{\phi \in {}_t\mathcal{M}} E|x(t+v) - \phi|^2.$$

Then observe that there exists a sequence of random variables, $\phi_n \in {}_t\mathcal{M}$, $n = 1, 2, \ldots$, such that

$$\lim_{n\to\infty} E|x(t+v) - \phi_n|^2 = \sigma_v^2.$$

Since $(\phi_n + \phi_m)/2 \in {}_t\mathcal{M}$, and since $|\phi_n - \phi_m|^2 = |(\phi_n - x(t+v)) - (\phi_m - x(t+v))|^2$ and $|x(t+v) - (\phi_n + \phi_m)/2|^2 = \frac{1}{4}|(\phi_n - x(t+v)) + (\phi_m - x(t+v))|^2$, this sequence must, for all $n, m = 1, 2, \ldots$, satisfy

$$E|x(t+v) - (\phi_n + \phi_m)/2|^2 \geqslant \sigma_v^2,$$

and

$$E|\phi_n - \phi_m|^2 = 2E|x(t+v) - \phi_n|^2 + 2E|x(t+v) - \phi_m|^2 - 4E|x(t+v) - (\phi_n + \phi_m)/2|^2.$$

Consequently,

$$\lim_{n,m\to\infty} E|\phi_n - \phi_m|^2 = 0. \tag{32.35}$$

The existence of $\phi_{t,v}$ now follows from equation 32.35 and UT 23. The uniqueness is established by standard arguments.

To show that $\phi_{t,v}$ satisfies equation 32.34, observe that, for all $\alpha \in C$ and $y \in {}_t\mathcal{M}$, $\phi_{t,v} + \alpha y \in {}_t\mathcal{M}$ and

$$\begin{aligned} 0 &\leqslant E|x(t+v) - \phi_{t,v} - \alpha y|^2 - E|x(t+v) - \phi_{t,v}|^2 \\ &= -\bar{\alpha}E(x(t+v) - \phi_{t,v})\bar{y} - \alpha E y(\overline{x(t+v) - \phi_{t,v}}) + |\alpha|^2 E|y|^2. \end{aligned}$$

Consequently, if we let $\alpha = \beta E(x(t+v) - \phi_{t,v})\bar{y}$, $\beta \in R$, then

$$0 \leqslant 2\beta|E(x(t+v) - \phi_{t,v})\bar{y}|^2 + \beta^2|E(x(t,v) - \phi_{t,v})\bar{y}|^2 \cdot E|y|^2,$$

which cannot be the case for small positive values of β unless $E(x(t+v) - \phi_{t,v})\bar{y} = 0$.

We learn from T 32.4 that $\phi_{t,v}$ exists and that $(x(t+v,\cdot)-\phi_{t,v}(\cdot))$ is orthogonal to ${}_t\mathscr{M}$. Next we shall determine how $\phi_{t,v}$ and the prediction error,

$$\sigma_{t,v}^2 = E|x(t+v)-\phi_{t,v}|^2, \qquad t \in T, \tag{32.36}$$

vary with t.

T 32.5 Let $X = \{x(t,\omega); t \in T\}$ be a real- or complex-valued wide-sense stationary process on a probability space $(\Omega, \mathscr{F}, P(\cdot))$ and assume that $T = \{\dots, -1, 0, 1, \dots\}$ and that $Ex(t) = 0$, $t \in T$. Moreover, let $\phi_{t,v}(\cdot)$ and $\sigma_{t,v}^2$ be as described in equations 32.33, 32.34, and 32.36. Then, for all $(t,s) \in T \times T$,

$$\sigma_{t,v}^2 = \sigma_{s,v}^2.$$

It suffices to prove the theorem for some t and for $s = t+1$. So fix $t \in T$ and observe that since $\phi_{t,v} \in {}_t\mathscr{M}$ and $\phi_{(t+1),v} \in {}_{(t+1)}\mathscr{M}$, there exist sequences of random variables, $\phi_{n,t} \in {}_t\mathscr{M}^0$ and $\phi_{n,(t+1)} \in {}_{(t+1)}\mathscr{M}^0$, $n = 1, 2, \dots$, such that

$$\lim_{n\to\infty} E|\phi_{n,t}-\phi_{t,v}|^2 = \lim_{n\to\infty} E|\phi_{n,(t+1)}-\phi_{(t+1),v}|^2 = 0;$$

$$\lim_{n\to\infty} E|\phi_{n,t}|^2 = E|\phi_{t,v}|^2 \qquad \text{and} \qquad \lim_{n\to\infty} E|\phi_{n,(t+1)}|^2 = E|\phi_{(t+1),v}|^2.$$

For each n, there exist integers m, s_j, $j = 1, \dots, m$; p, s_k, $k = 1, \dots, p$; and complex numbers, a_j, $j = 1, \dots, m$ and b_k, $k = 1, \dots, p$, such that

$$\phi_{n,t} = \sum_{j=1}^{m} a_j x(s_j) \qquad \text{and} \qquad \phi_{n,(t+1)} = \sum_{k=1}^{p} b_k x(s_k),$$

where $s_j \leqslant t$, $j = 1, \dots, m$, and $s_k \leqslant t+1$, $k = 1, \dots, p$. If we let

$$\phi_{n,t}^+ = \sum_{j=1}^{m} a_j x(s_j+1) \qquad \text{and} \qquad \phi_{n,t+1}^- = \sum_{k=1}^{p} b_k x(s_k-1),$$

$n = 1, 2, \dots$, then for all n and for all $s \in T$,

$$E|\phi_{n,t}^+|^2 = E|\phi_{n,t}|^2 \qquad \text{and} \qquad E|\phi_{n,(t+1)}^-|^2 = E|\phi_{n,(t+1)}|^2$$

$$E\phi_{n,t}^+\overline{x(s+1)} = E\phi_{n,t}\overline{x(s)} \qquad \text{and} \qquad E\phi_{n,(t+1)}^-\overline{x(s-1)} = E\phi_{n,(t+1)}\overline{x(s)}.$$

Moreover, there exist random variables, $\phi_{t,v}^+ \in {}_{(t+1)}\mathscr{M}$ and $\phi_{(t+1),v}^- \in {}_t\mathscr{M}$, such that

$$\lim_{n\to\infty} E|\phi_{n,t}^+-\phi_{t,v}^+|^2 = \lim_{n\to\infty} E|\phi_{n,(t+1)}^- - \phi_{(t+1),v}^-|^2 = 0; \tag{32.37}$$

$$E|\phi_{t,v}^+|^2 = E|\phi_{t,v}|^2 \qquad \text{and} \qquad E|\phi_{(t+1),v}^-|^2 = E|\phi_{(t+1)v}|^2. \tag{32.38}$$

But if this is so, then it is easy to verify the relations,

$$\begin{aligned}\sigma_{t,v}^2 &= E|x(t+v) - \phi_{t,v}|^2 = E|x(t+1+v) - \phi_{t,v}^+|^2 \\ &\geqslant \sigma_{(t+1),v}^2 = E|x(t+1+v) - \phi_{(t+1),v}|^2 \\ &= E|x(t+v) - \phi_{(t+1),v}^-|^2 \geqslant \sigma_{t,v}^2,\end{aligned}$$

which establish the theorem.

With some obvious additions, the proof of T 32.5 suffices to establish the following useful result:

T 32.6 Let $X = \{x(t,\omega); t \in T\}$ and $\phi_{t,v}$ be as described in T 32.5. Moreover, let $\phi_{t,v}^+$ and $\phi_{(t+1),v}^-$ be as in equations 32.37 and 32.38. Then

$$\phi_{t,v}^+(\omega) = \phi_{(t+1),v}(\omega) \quad \text{a.e.,} \qquad \text{and} \qquad \phi_{(t+1),v}^-(\omega) = \phi_{t,v}(\omega) \quad \text{a.e.}$$

Moreover, for all $s = 0, 1, \ldots$, $Ex(t)\overline{\phi_{(t+s),v}}$ is independent of t.

32.2.2 Examples

The preceding theorems leave many questions unanswered; e.g., what is in ${}_{-\infty}\mathcal{M}$ and how *good* is the *best* linear least-squares predictor of $x(t+v)$? We shall answer these questions and others in due course, but first some examples to help our intuition.

E 32.4 Let $X = \{x(t,\omega); t \in T\}$ be an orthogonal random process and assume that $T = \{\ldots, -1, 0, 1, \ldots\}$ and that $E|x(t)|^2 = 1$. Then $Ex(t) = 0$ (by assumption) and it is easy to verify that

$${}_{-\infty}\mathcal{M} = \{0\}$$

and that, for all $(t,v) \in T \times (T \cap R_{++})$,

$$\phi_{t,v}(\omega) = 0 \quad \text{a.e.}$$

In reading this example, recall from T 32.4 that $\phi_{t,v}(\cdot)$ minimizes a quadratic function over all random variables that belong to ${}_t\mathcal{M}$. The ranges of the members of ${}_t\mathcal{M}$ need not be subsets of the range of $x(t+v,\cdot)$. Hence it is possible that the range of $\phi_{t,v}(\cdot)$ has no points in common with the range of $x(t+v,\cdot)$. If in E 32.4, 0 does not belong to the range of $x(t+v,\cdot)$, the value of the *best* linear least-squares predictor in E 32.4 is questionable.[2]

E 32.5 Let $X = \{x(t,\omega); t \in T\}$ be a complex-valued wide-sense stationary process and assume that $T = \{\ldots, -1, 0, 1, \ldots\}$ and that $Ex(t) = 0$, $t \in T$. Moreover, let $\xi = \{\xi(t,\omega); t \in T\}$ be an orthogonal wide-sense stationary process and assume that there exists a complex constant β such that $0 < |\beta| < 1$ and such that

$$x(t,\omega) = \xi(t,\omega) - \beta\xi(t-1,\omega), \qquad \omega \in \Omega,\ t \in T.$$

Then, for all $\omega \in \Omega$,

$$\xi(t, \omega) = x(t, \omega) + \sum_{s=1}^{\infty} \beta^s x(t - s, \omega), \qquad t \in T,$$

and it is easy to verify that

$$\phi_{t,1}(\omega) = -\sum_{s=0}^{\infty} \beta^{s+1} x(t - s, \omega) \quad \text{a.e.}, \qquad t \in T;$$

and

$$\phi_{t,v}(\omega) = 0 \quad \text{a.e.}, \qquad v > 1 \text{ and } t \in T.$$

Moreover, ${}_{-\infty}\mathscr{M} = \{0\}$.

If we define the $\phi_{t,v}(\cdot)$ of E 32.4 to equal 0 for all $\omega \in \Omega$, then $\phi_{t,v}(\omega)$ is well defined everywhere. Similarly, if we define that $\phi_{t,1}(\cdot)$ of E 32.5 to equal $-\sum_{s=1}^{\infty} \beta^s x(t - s + 1, \omega)$ for all $\omega \in \Omega$, then $\phi_{t,1}(\omega)$ is well defined for almost all $\omega \in \Omega$. Note, therefore, that in T 32.4 $\phi_{t,v}(\cdot)$ is characterized as a random variable that is defined up to a set of P-measure zero. A random variable which is defined a.e. need not be well defined anywhere and exists only as an equivalence class of well-defined functions. Consequently, $\phi_{t,v}(\omega)$ need not have a meaning at any particular $\omega \in \Omega$.

The last remark sounds strange. To see that it is true, consider the following theorem:

T 32.7 Let $\xi = \{\xi(t, \omega); t \in T\}$ be an orthogonal wide-sense stationary process on some probability space $(\Omega, \mathscr{F}, P(\cdot))$ and assume that $T = \{\ldots, -1, 0, 1, \ldots\}$. Moreover, let c_j, $j = 0, 1, \ldots$, be complex constants such that $c_0 = 1$. Then for each $t \in T$, there exists a random variable, $x(t, \cdot): \Omega \to C$, that satisfies the relation

$$\lim_{n \to \infty} E|x(t) - \sum_{j=0}^{n} c_j \xi(t - j)|^2 = 0 \tag{32.39}$$

if and only if

$$\sum_{j=0}^{\infty} |c_j|^2 < \infty. \tag{32.40}$$

If the c_j satisfy equation 32.40 and the $x(t, \cdot)$ satisfy equation 32.39, then $X = \{x(t, \omega); t \in T\}$ constitutes a wide-sense stationary process with $Ex(t) = 0$, $t \in T$, and covariance function

$$r(s) = \sum_{j=\max(0, -s)}^{\infty} c_j \bar{c}_{s+j}, \qquad s \in T. \tag{32.41}$$

In that case we shall write

$$x(t, \omega) = \sum_{j=0}^{\infty} c_j \xi(t - j, \omega), \qquad t \in T. \tag{32.42}$$

To establish the first half of the theorem observe that, for each $t \in T$,

$$E\left|\sum_{j=0}^{n} c_j\xi_{t-j} - \sum_{j=0}^{m} c_j\xi_{t-j}\right|^2 = E|\xi(t)|^2 \sum_{j=\min(m,n)+1}^{\max(m,n)} |c_j|^2. \tag{32.43}$$

From equation 32.43 and UT 23, it follows that $x(t, \cdot)$ exists and is determined up to a set of P-measure zero if and only if the c_j satisfy equation 32.40.

To establish the second half, we must show that $Ex(t) = 0$, $t \in T$, and verify equation 32.41. Since that is easy, I leave the second half of the proof to the reader.

For our purpose the important thing to notice is that even though $x(t, \cdot)$ is determined up to a set of P-measure zero, the right-hand side of equation 32.42 need not be well defined at any particular $\omega \in \Omega$. It probably is not if $c_j = (j+1)^{-1}$, $j = 0, 1, \ldots$, and it is if $c_j = \beta^j$, $j = 0, 1, \ldots$, and $|\beta| < 1$ as in E 32.4. A sufficient condition that the right-hand side of equation 32.42 is well defined for almost all $\omega \in \Omega$ is that

$$\sum_{j=0}^{\infty} |c_j|^2(\log(j+1))^2 < \infty.$$

For a proof of this fact, I refer the reader to Doob 1953 (pp. 157–158).

E 32.6 Let $X = \{x(t, \omega); t \in T\}$ be a complex-valued wide-sense stationary process and assume that $T = \{\ldots, -1, 0, 1, \ldots\}$ and $Ex(t) = 0$. Next, let $V = \{v(t, \omega); t \in T\}$ be another wide-sense stationary process and suppose that there exist numbers $\theta_j \in (-\pi, \pi)$, $j = 1, \ldots, m$, and complex-valued random variables A_j, $j = 1, \ldots,$ that satisfy the relations

(i) $EA_j = 0$, $E|A_j|^2 < \infty$ and $EA_j\bar{A}_k = 0$,

$k \neq j$, $j = 1, \ldots, m$;

(ii) $v(t, \omega) = \sum_{j=1}^{m} A_j(\omega)e^{it\theta_j}$, $t \in T$.

Finally, let $\xi = \{\xi(t, \omega); t \in T\}$ be an orthogonal random process and assume that

(iii) $E\xi(t)\bar{A}_j = 0$, $j = 1, \ldots, m$, $t \in T$;

and

(iv) $x(t, \omega) = \xi(t, \omega) + v(t, \omega)$, $t \in T$.

Then it can be shown (see the proof of T 32.8 below) that $v(t, \cdot) \in {}_{-\infty}\mathcal{M}$ for all $t \in T$ and that $w \in {}_{-\infty}\mathcal{M}$ if and only if w belongs to the closure of the linear manifold generated by the $v(t, \cdot)$. Moreover,

$$\phi_{t,v}(\omega) = v(t+v, \omega) \quad \text{a.e.}$$

To see why, observe first that, by condition iii and equation 32.34,

$$\begin{aligned} E|v(t+v)|^2 &= Ex(t+v)\overline{v(t+v)} = E\phi_{t,v}\overline{v(t+v)} \\ &= E\phi_{t,v}\overline{x(t+v)} = E|\phi_{t,v}|^2. \end{aligned}$$

From these equalities it follows that

$$E|x(t+v) - v(t+v)|^2 = E|x(t+v) - \phi_{t,v}|^2,$$

which establishes our assertion.

In reading E 32.6, note that X is written as the sum of two mutually orthogonal wide-sense stationary processer, ξ and V. The first has an absolutely continuous spectral distribution function,

$$F_\xi(\lambda) = \sigma_\xi^2 \int_{-\pi}^{\lambda} d\mu(\lambda),\ \lambda \in [-\pi, \pi],$$

where $\sigma_\xi^2 = E|\xi(t)|^2$ and $\mu(\cdot): \mathscr{B} \to [0, 2\pi]$ is the Lebesgue measure on $([-\pi, \pi], \mathscr{B})$. The second has a discrete spectral distribution,

$$F_v(\lambda) = 2\pi \sum_{\theta_j < \lambda} \sigma_j^2, \qquad \lambda \in [-\pi, \pi],$$

where $\sigma_j^2 = E|A_j|^2$, $j = 1, \ldots, m$. Moreover, all of the components of V and none of the components of ξ belong to ${}_{-\infty}\mathscr{M}$. This example can be generalized, and we see how in the next section.

32.2.3 Wold's Decomposition Theorem

If $F(\cdot): [-\pi, \pi] \to R$ is the spectral distribution function of a wide-sense stationary process, $X = \{x(t, \omega); t \in T\}$, then (by Lebesgue's Decomposition Theorem)[3] $F(\cdot)$ can be decomposed into a sum of three functions,

$$F(\lambda) = F_{ac}(\lambda) + F_d(\lambda) + F_{cs}(\lambda), \qquad \lambda \in [-\pi, \pi],$$

whose components satisfy the conditions:

(i) $F_{ac}(\lambda) = \int_{-\pi}^{\lambda} F'(\lambda)\, d\mu(\lambda), \qquad \lambda \in [-\pi, \pi];$

(ii) $F_d(\lambda) = \sum_{\lambda_j < \lambda} \Delta F(\lambda_j), \qquad \lambda \in [-\pi, \pi],$

where $\Delta F(\lambda_j) = F(\lambda_j +) - F(\lambda_j)$ and $\{\lambda_1, \lambda_2, \ldots\}$ is the set of discontinuity points of $F(\cdot)$; and

(iii) $F_{cs}(\cdot)$ is the continuous, monotone, nondecreasing singular component of $F(\cdot)$.

The decomposition of $F(\cdot)$ implies a corresponding decomposition of X into a sum of three mutually orthogonal wide-sense stationary processes, $X_{ac} = \{x_{ac}(t, \omega); t \in T\}$, $X_d = \{x_d(t, \omega); t \in T\}$ and $X_{cs} = \{x_{cs}(t, \omega); t \in T\}$, such that

$$x(t, \omega) = x_{ac}(t, \omega) + x_d(t, \omega) + x_{cs}(t, \omega) \quad \text{a.e.,} \quad t \in T,$$

and such that $F_{ac}(\cdot)$, $F_d(\cdot)$, and $F_{cs}(\cdot)$ are, respectively, the spectral distribution functions of X_{ac}, X_d, and X_{cs}. In T 32.8 we demonstrate (1) that all of the components of X_d and X_{cs} belong to $_{-\infty}\mathcal{M}$, and (2) that if $\sigma_{t,1}^2 > 0$, then none of the components of X_{ac} belong to $_{-\infty}\mathcal{M}$. This remarkable theorem is due to H. Wold (Wold 1938, p. 89).

T 32.8 Let $X = \{x(t, \omega); t \in T\}$ be a real- or complex-valued wide-sense stationary process on a probability space $(\Omega, \mathcal{F}, P(\cdot))$ and assume that $T = \{\ldots, -1, 0, 1, \ldots\}$ and that $Ex(t) = 0$, $t \in T$. Moreover, let the $_t\mathcal{M}$ be as defined above and assume that

$$\sigma_1^2 = E|x(t+1) - \phi_{t,1}|^2 > 0.$$

Then there exist three wide-sense stationary processes, $\xi = \{\xi(t, \omega); t \in T\}$, $U = \{u(t, \omega); t \in T\}$ and $V = \{v(t, \omega); t \in T\}$, and a sequence of complex numbers, γ_n, $n = 0, 1, \ldots$, such that

(i) $\gamma_0 = \sigma_1$ and $\sum_{j=0}^{\infty} |\gamma_j|^2 < \infty$;

(ii) $\gamma_j = Ex(t)\overline{\xi(t-j)}$, $\quad j = 0, 1, \ldots, \quad t \in T$;

(iii) $E\xi(t)\overline{\xi(s)} = 0$ or 1 according as $t \neq s$ or $t = s$, $\quad t, s \in T$;

(iv) $E\xi(t)\overline{v(s)} = 0$, $\quad t, s \in T$;

(v) $u(t, \omega) = \sum_{j=0}^{\infty} \gamma_j \xi(t-j, \omega)$, $\quad t \in T$;

(vi) $x(t, \omega) = u(t, \omega) + v(t, \omega)$ a.e., $\quad t \in T$;

(vii) $v(t, \cdot) \in {}_{-\infty}\mathcal{M}$ for all $t \in T$; and

(viii) $\xi(t, \cdot) \in {}_t\mathcal{M}$, $\quad t \in T$.

Moreover, there is only one sequence of constants, γ_j, $j = 0, 1, \ldots$, and only one family of random variables, ξ, that satisfy conditions i–viii.

To prove this theorem we let $\xi(t, \cdot): \Omega \to C$, $t \in T$, be defined by

$$\sigma_1 \xi(t, \omega) = (x(t, \omega) - \phi_{(t-1),1}(\omega)).$$

Then $\xi = \{\xi(t, \omega); t \in T\}$ satisfies condition iii and $E|\xi(t)|^2 = 1$ for all $t \in T$. Hence the $\xi(t, \cdot)$ form an orthonormal set. From this it follows that, for each $t \in T$, we can write $x(t, \cdot)$ as a Fourier series in the $\xi(s, \cdot)$, $s \in T$, plus a remainder; i.e.,

$$x(t, \omega) = \sum_{j=-\infty}^{\infty} \gamma_{tj} \xi(t-j, \omega) + v(t, \omega), \qquad t \in T, \tag{32.44}$$

where

$$\gamma_{tj} = Ex(t)\overline{\xi(t-j)}, \qquad j \in T \qquad \text{and} \qquad \sum_{j=-\infty}^{\infty} |\gamma_{tj}|^2 < \infty. \tag{32.45}$$

It follows from T 32.4 that $\xi(s, \cdot)$ is orthogonal to ${}_t\mathcal{M}$ for all $t < s$. Hence $\gamma_{tj} = 0$ for $j = -1, -2, \ldots$. Moreover, we deduce from T 32.5 and T 32.6 that $Ex(t)\overline{\xi(t-j)}$ is independent of t for all $j = 0, 1, \ldots$. Hence $\gamma_{tj} = \gamma_j$ for $j = 0, 1, \ldots$, and equations 32.44 and 32.45 become

$$x(t, \omega) = \sum_{j=0}^{\infty} \gamma_j \xi(t-j, \omega) + v(t, \omega), \qquad t \in T; \tag{32.46}$$

$$\gamma_j = Ex(t)\overline{\xi(t-j)}, \quad j \in T \cap R_+, \qquad \text{and} \qquad \sum_{j=0}^{\infty} |\gamma_j|^2 < \infty.$$

Moreover, $\gamma_0 = \sigma_1$. Consequently, the $\xi(t, \cdot)$ and the γ_j satisfy conditions i–iii; and if we define $u(t, \cdot)$, $t \in T$, by condition v, then conditions v and vi are satisfied as well.

It is easy to verify that the $u(t, \cdot)$ as defined constitute a wide-sense stationary process. It is also easy to demonstrate that if we define $v(\cdot)$: $T \times \Omega \to C$ by equation 32.44, then the $v(t, \cdot)$ constitute a wide-sense stationary process that satisfies condition iv. These details I leave to the reader.

Next we show that $w \in {}_{-\infty}\mathcal{M}$ if and only if w is orthogonal to every $\xi(t, \cdot)$, $t \in T$. To do that, we recall that, for all $t \in T$, $\xi(t, \cdot)$ is orthogonal to ${}_{(t-1)}\mathcal{M}$. Consequently, if $w \in {}_{-\infty}\mathcal{M}$, w is orthogonal to each and every $\xi(t, \cdot)$. Conversely, suppose that w is orthogonal to every $\xi(t, \cdot)$ and that $w \in {}_t\mathcal{M}$ for some t. Then w is in the linear manifold generated by $\xi(t, \cdot)$ and the $x(s, \cdot)$ for $s \leqslant t - 1$. Since w is orthogonal to $\xi(t, \cdot)$, w must belong to ${}_{(t-1)}\mathcal{M}$. Continuing this argument, we find that $w \in {}_s\mathcal{M}$ for all $s \leqslant t$ and hence for all $s \in T$; that is, $w \in {}_{-\infty}\mathcal{M}$, as was to be shown.

From the preceding paragraph and condition iv it follows that $v(t, \cdot) \in {}_{-\infty}\mathcal{M}$ for all $t \in T$. Since it is obvious that $\xi(t, \cdot) \in {}_t\mathcal{M}$, $t \in T$, we conclude the proof of T 32.8 by establishing the uniqueness of ξ and the γ_j. To do that we observe that if ξ, V and the γ_j satisfy conditions i–viii, then necessarily

(i) $\phi_{(t-1),1}(\omega) = \sum_{j=1}^{\infty} \gamma_j \xi(t-j, \omega) + v(t, \omega)$ a.e., $\quad t \in T$; and

(ii) $\gamma_0 \xi(t, \omega) = x(t, \omega) - \phi_{(t-1),1}(\omega)$, $\quad t \in T$.

From condition ii above, T 32.4, and $|\gamma_0|^2 = \sigma_1^2 > 0$ follows the uniqueness of γ_0 and the $\xi(t, \cdot)$, $t \in T$. But if this is so, the uniqueness of γ_j, $j = 1, 2, \ldots$, is an immediate consequence of condition ii in T 32.8.

Wold's remarkable theorem calls for an example. In reading the example, note that if one of the z_j in equation 32.48 has absolute value greater than 1, then $\eta(t+1,\cdot)$ is not orthogonal to ${}_t\mathcal{M}$. Hence we cannot use the a_k to construct a best linear least-squares predictor of $x(t+1,\cdot)$ based on ${}_t\mathcal{M}$. Note also that equations 32.47–31.49 show how the ξ of T 32.7 can be constructed when X satisfies the conditions of E 32.3.

E 32.7 Let $X = \{x(t,\omega); t \in T\}$ and $\eta = \{\eta(t,\omega); t \in T\}$ be the two wide-sense stationary processes of E 32.3, and let $A(\cdot)\colon C \to C$ be as defined in equation 32.31. By expanding $A(e^{i\lambda})^{-1}$ in a power series and using equation 32.32, we find that there exist complex constants c_l, $l \in T$, and β such that, for some $K \in R_{++}$,

$$|\beta| < 1, \quad |c_l| < K\cdot|\beta|^{|l|}, \quad l \in T, \quad \text{and}$$

$$x(t,\omega) = \sum_{j=0}^{\infty} c_l \eta(t-l,\omega) \quad \text{a.e.,} \qquad t \in T.$$

If $|z_j| < 1$, $j = 1, \ldots, m$, then $c_l = 0$ for all $l < 0$. Otherwise, $c_l \neq 0$ for all but a finite number of negative l.

Suppose now that $|z_j| > 1$ for at least one j, and for each $j = 1, \ldots, m$, let

$$w_j = \begin{cases} z_j & \text{if } |z_j| < 1, \quad \text{and} \\ z_j^{-1} & \text{if } |z| > 1. \end{cases} \tag{32.47}$$

In addition, let $B(\cdot)\colon C \to C$ be defined by

$$z^m B(z) = \sum_{k=0}^{m} b_k z^{m-k} = \prod_{j=1}^{m} (z - w_j), \tag{32.48}$$

and define $\xi = \{\xi(t,\omega); t \in T\}$ by

$$\xi(t,\omega) = \sum_{k=0}^{m} b_k x(t-k,\omega), \qquad \omega \in \Omega,\ t \in T. \tag{32.49}$$

Then it is easy to verify that ξ is an orthogonal wide-sense stationary process and that there exist complex constants γ_l, $l = 0, 1, \ldots$, and α such that $|\alpha| < 1$, $|\gamma_l| < K|\alpha|^l$, $l = 0, 1, \ldots$, for some K and

$$x(t,\omega) = \sum_{l=0}^{\infty} \gamma_l \xi(t-l,\omega) \quad \text{a.e.,} \qquad t \in T.$$

Moreover,

$$\phi_{t,1}(\omega) = -\sum_{k=1}^{m} b_k x(t+1-k,\omega) \quad \text{a.e.,} \qquad t \in T.$$

Next we record an important corollary of T 32.8, the proof of which I leave to the reader:

T 32.9 Let $X = \{x(t,\omega); t \in T\}$, $\xi = \{\xi(t,\omega); t \in T\}$, and $V = \{v(t,\omega); t \in T\}$ be as described in T 32.8; and let $\phi_{t,v}(\cdot)$ denote the linear least-squares predictor of

$x(t+v, \cdot)$ based on our knowledge of $x(s, \cdot)$ for $s \leqslant t$. Then, for all $t \in T$,

$$\phi_{t,v}(\omega) = \sum_{j=v}^{\infty} \gamma_j \xi(t+v-j, \omega) + v(t+v, \omega) \quad \text{a.e.};$$

and

$$\sigma_v^2 = \sum_{j=0}^{v-1} |\gamma_j|^2.$$

32.2.4 Kolmogorov's Theorem

The preceding theorem presents one characterization of $\phi_{t-v,v}(\cdot)$. Since we cannot observe the $\xi(t, \cdot)$, this characterization is not good enough for the purpose I have in mind. To obtain a better characterization, I must introduce new terms. Let

$$\mathscr{M}_t^0 = \mathscr{M}(e^{is\lambda}, \lambda \in [-\pi, \pi], s \leqslant t)$$

denote the linear manifold generated by the $e^{is(\cdot)}$ for $s \leqslant t$. Then $f(\cdot)$: $[-\pi, \pi] \to C$ belongs to $\mathscr{M}_t^0$ if and only if there exist integers m, s_j, $j = 1, \ldots, m$, and complex constants, a_j, $j = 1, \ldots, m$, such that $s_j \leqslant t$, $j = 1, \ldots, m$, and

$$f(\lambda) = \sum_{j=1}^{m} a_j e^{is_j\lambda}, \qquad \lambda \in [-\pi, \pi].$$

Next let $\mathscr{M}_t$ denote the closure of $\mathscr{M}_t^0$ in the following sense: $g(\cdot)$: $[-\pi, \pi] \to C$ belongs to $\mathscr{M}_t$ if and only if there exists a sequence of functions, $g_n(\cdot)$: $[-\pi, \pi] \to C$, $n = 1, 2, \ldots$, such that

$$g_n(\cdot) \in \mathscr{M}_t^0, \; n = 1, 2, \ldots, \quad \text{and} \quad \lim_{n\to\infty} \int_{-\pi}^{\pi} |g_n(\lambda) - g(\lambda)|^2 \, d\mu_F(\lambda) = 0.$$

Finally, let

$$\mathscr{M}_\infty^0 = \mathscr{M}(e^{is\lambda}, \lambda \in [-\pi, \pi], s \in T)$$

be the linear manifold generated by the $e^{is(\cdot)}$ for $s \in T$; let $\mathscr{M}_\infty$ denote the closure of $\mathscr{M}_\infty^0$ in the same way $\mathscr{M}_t$ is the closure of $\mathscr{M}_t^0$; and let

$$\mathscr{M}_{-\infty} = \bigcap_{t=-\infty}^{\infty} \mathscr{M}_t.$$

Then the following theorem is true for $v = 1, 2, \ldots$.

T 32.10 Let $X = \{x(t, \omega); t \in T\}$ and $\xi = \{\xi(t, \omega); t \in T\}$ be as described in T 32.8, and let

$$X(t,\omega) = (2\pi)^{-1} \int_{-\pi}^{\pi} e^{it\lambda}\, dz(\lambda,\omega), \qquad t \in T,$$

be the integral representation of X. Then there exists a set $S_v \subset [-\pi, \pi]$ of Lebesgue-measure zero and a function $\varnothing_v(\cdot) \in \mathscr{M}_0$ such that

$$\varnothing_v(\lambda) = \begin{cases} e^{iv\lambda} & \text{if } \lambda \in S_v, \text{ and} \\ e^{iv\lambda} \sum_{j=v}^{\infty} \gamma_j e^{-ij\lambda} \Big/ \sum_{j=0}^{\infty} \gamma_j e^{-ij\lambda} & \text{if } \lambda \in S_v^c \end{cases}$$

and such that, for all $t \in T$,

$$\phi_{t,v}(\omega) = (2\pi)^{-1} \int_{-\pi}^{\pi} e^{it\lambda} \varnothing_v(\lambda)\, dz(\lambda,\omega) \quad \text{a.e.}$$

To prove this theorem, we observe first that there is a one-to-one mapping of ${}_{\infty}\mathscr{M}$ onto $\mathscr{M}_{\infty}$ that is linear, maps $x(t,\cdot)$ into $e^{it(\cdot)}$, $t \in T$, and preserves distance between the elements in the following sense: let $y, z \in {}_{\infty}\mathscr{M}$ be mapped into $f_y, f_z \in \mathscr{M}_{\infty}$. Then

$$E|y - z|^2 = (2\pi)^{-1} \int_{-\pi}^{\pi} |f_y(\lambda) - f_z(\lambda)|^2\, d\mu_F(\lambda).$$

In particular, for each $v = 1, 2, \ldots,$ there is a function $\varnothing_v(\cdot) \in \mathscr{M}_0$ that corresponds to $\phi_{0,v}(\cdot) \in {}_0\mathscr{M}$ and satisfies

$$E|x(v) - \phi_{0,v}|^2 = (2\pi)^{-1} \int_{-\pi}^{\pi} |e^{iv\lambda} - \varnothing_v(\lambda)|^2\, d\mu_F(\lambda). \tag{32.50}$$

It follows easily from equation 32.50 and the nature of the given correspondence that since

$$E|x(v) - \phi_{0,v}|^2 \leqslant E|x(v) - \phi|^2$$

for all $\phi \in {}_0\mathscr{M}$, it must be the case that

$$(2\pi)^{-1} \int_{-\pi}^{\pi} |e^{iv\lambda} - \varnothing_v(\lambda)|^2\, d\mu_F(\lambda) \leqslant (2\pi)^{-1} \int_{-\pi}^{\pi} |e^{iv\lambda} - f(\lambda)|^2\, d\mu_F(\lambda)$$

for all $f(\cdot) \in \mathscr{M}_0$. But, if this is the case, it is clear that if $\varnothing_v(\cdot)$ corresponds to $\phi_{0,v}(\cdot)$, then $e^{it(\cdot)}\varnothing_v(\cdot)$ must correspond to $\phi_{t,v}(\cdot)$ for all $t \in T$. We shall use this observation below.

Next let

$$\xi(t,\omega) = (2\pi)^{-1} \int_{-\pi}^{\pi} e^{it\lambda}\, dz_{\xi}(\lambda,\omega), \qquad t \in T,$$

be the integral representation of ξ and recall from E 32.1 that

$$E|dz_\xi(\lambda)|^2 = d\mu(\lambda), \qquad \lambda \in [-\pi, \pi],$$

where $\mu(\cdot)\colon \mathscr{B} \to [0, 2\pi]$ is the Lebesgue measure. Moreover, let $V = \{v(t, \omega); t \in T\}$ be as described in T 32.8; and let

$$v(t, \omega) = (2\pi)^{-1} \int_{-\pi}^{\pi} e^{it\lambda}\, dz_v(\lambda, \omega), \qquad t \in T,$$

be the integral representation of V. Since $v(t, \cdot)$ is orthogonal to $\xi(s, \cdot)$ for all $s \in T$,

$$\int_{-\pi}^{\pi} e^{is\lambda} E\, dz_v(\lambda)\, \overline{dz_\xi(\lambda)} = 0, \qquad s \in T,$$

from which it follows that $E\, dz_v(\lambda)\, \overline{dz_\xi(\lambda)} = 0$ for all $\lambda \in [-\pi, \pi]$.

It follows from T 32.8 and T 32.9 that

$$x(t, \omega) = (2\pi)^{-1} \int_{-\pi}^{\pi} e^{it\lambda} \left\{ \sum_{j=0}^{\infty} \gamma_j e^{-ij\lambda}\, dz_\xi(\lambda, \omega) + dz_v(\lambda, \omega) \right\}, \qquad t \in T.$$

Moreover, if in the correspondence between ${}_\infty\mathscr{M}$ and $\mathscr{M}_\infty$, $\xi(t, \cdot)$ corresponds to $\varnothing(\cdot) \in \mathscr{M}_t$, then

$$\xi(t, \omega) = (2\pi)^{-1} \int_{-\pi}^{\pi} \varnothing(\lambda) \left\{ \sum_{j=0}^{\infty} \gamma_j e^{-ij\lambda}\, dz_\xi(\lambda, \omega) + dz_v(\lambda, \omega) \right\}$$

$$= (2\pi)^{-1} \int_{-\pi}^{\pi} e^{it\lambda}\, dz_\xi(\lambda, \omega).$$

Hence, for almost all $\lambda \in [-\pi, \pi]$ (Lebesgue measure),

$$\varnothing(\lambda) \sum_{j=0}^{\infty} \gamma_j e^{-ij\lambda} = e^{it\lambda};$$

and for almost all $\mu_{F_v}(\cdot)$ measure, $\varnothing(\lambda) = 0$, where $F_v(\cdot)$ is the spectral distribution function of V. These two conditions are incompatible unless there is a set $S_v \subset [-\pi, \pi]$ of Lebesgue-measure zero such that

$$\int_{S_v} d\mu_{F_v}(\lambda) = 2\pi \cdot Ev(t)\overline{v(t)}.$$

From this and T 32.9 we conclude that

$$\varnothing_v(\lambda) = \begin{cases} e^{iv\lambda} \sum_{j=v}^{\infty} \gamma_j e^{-ij\lambda} \Big/ \sum_{j=0}^{\infty} \gamma_j e^{-ij\lambda} & \text{if } \lambda \in S_v^c \\ e^{iv\lambda} & \text{if } \lambda \in S_v \end{cases}$$

We have obtained a spectral representation of the best linear least-squares predictor when

$$E|x(t+1) - \phi_{t,1}|^2 > 0, \qquad t \in T. \tag{32.51}$$

In the next and last theorem of this section we state necessary and sufficient conditions for the inequality in equation 32.51. This remarkable theorem is due to A. Kolmogorov. A proof of the theorem is given in Doob 1953 (pp. 577–578).

T 32.11 Let $X = \{x(t, \omega); t \in T\}$ be a wide-sense stationary process with spectral distribution function, $F(\cdot): [-\pi, \pi] \to R$, and assume that $T = \{\ldots, -1, 0, 1, \ldots\}$ and that $Ex(t) = 0$. Then X satisfies the conditions in equation 32.51 if and only if $F'(\lambda) > 0$ a.e. in $[-\pi, \pi]$ (Lebesgue measure) and

$$\int_{-\pi}^{\pi} \log F'(\lambda)\, d\mu(\lambda) > -\infty. \tag{32.52}$$

The power of T 32.11 and the import of T 32.10 are exemplified in the following example, which concludes our discussion of prediction with wide-sense stationary processes.

E 32.8 Let $X = \{x(t, \omega); t \in T\}$ and $\xi = \{\xi(t, \omega); t \in T\}$ be wide-sense stationary process and assume that $T = \{\ldots, -1, 0, 1, \ldots\}$, $Ex(t) = 0$, $t \in T$, and ξ is an orthogonal random process. In addition, suppose that

$$x(t, \omega) = \xi(t, \omega) - \xi(t-1, \omega), \qquad \omega \in \Omega,\ t \in T.$$

Then the spectral distribution function of X, $F(\cdot): [-\pi, \pi] \to R$, is given by

$$F(\lambda) = E|\xi(t)|^2 \int_{-\pi}^{\lambda} |1 - e^{-i\lambda}|^2\, d\mu(\lambda),$$

where $\mu(\cdot): \mathscr{B} \to [0, 2\pi]$ is Lebesgue measure. Since

$$\int_{-\pi}^{\pi} \log|1 - e^{-i\lambda}|^2\, d\mu(\lambda) = 0,$$

X satisfies equation 32.52 and

$$\phi_{t,1}(\omega) = (2\pi)^{-1} \int_{-\pi}^{\pi} e^{it\lambda} \left(\frac{-1}{1 - e^{-i\lambda}} \right) dz_x(\lambda, \omega) \quad \text{a.e.}, \qquad t \in T, \tag{32.53}$$

where $z_x(\cdot): \mathscr{B} \times \Omega \to C$ is the orthogonal set function of X.

It is clear from equation 32.53 that $\phi_{t,1}(\cdot)$ cannot be written as a linear combination of $x(s, \cdot)$ for $s \leqslant t$. However, if we let

$$\phi_n(\omega) = -\sum_{j=0}^{n-1} \left(\frac{n-j}{n+1} \right) x(t-j, \omega), \qquad \omega \in \Omega,\ n = 1, 2, \ldots, \tag{32.54}$$

then $\phi_n(\cdot) \in {}_t\mathscr{M}^0$ for all $n = 1, 2, \ldots$, and it is easy to verify that

$$\lim_{n \to \infty} E|\phi_{t,1} - \phi_n|^2 = 0.$$

In reading this example, it is interesting to observe that the ϕ_n of equation 32.54 is the best linear least-squares predictor of $x(t + 1, \cdot)$ from $x(s, \cdot)$, $s = t, t - 1, \ldots, t - (n - 1)$ (see Whittle 1963, pp. 43–44, for a discussion of this fact).

32.3 Distributed Lags and Optimal Stochastic Control

In this section we shall use the basic ideas of linear least-squares prediction to solve a problem in stochastic control theory. The solution provides an economic-theoretic way of rationalizing various distributed-lag models in econometrics. Both the formulation of the problem and its solution are due to Keith McLaren (McLaren 1979, pp. 183–191).

32.3.1 Distributed Lags

For our purpose the general distributed-lag model in econometrics can be formulated as follows: Let $Y = \{y(t, \omega); t \in T\}$, $X = \{x(t, \omega); t \in T\}$ and $\eta = \{\eta(t, \omega); t \in T\}$ be real-valued wide-sense stationary processes on some probability space, $(\Omega, \mathscr{F}, P(\cdot))$, and assume that $T = \{\ldots, -1, 0, 1, \ldots\}$ and that

(i) $E\eta(t) = 0, \qquad t \in T;$ and

(ii) $Ex(t)\eta(s) = 0, \qquad (t, s) \in T \times T.$

Moreover, let $c_j \in R$, $j = 0, 1, \ldots,$ be *square-summable constants*; that is, $\sum_{j=0}^{\infty} |c_j|^2 < \infty$, and assume that

(iii) $y(t, \omega) = \sum_{j=0}^{\infty} c_j x(t - j, \omega) + \eta(t, \omega), \qquad t \in T.$

Then Y, X and η constitute a *general distributed-lag model.*

32.3.2 Examples

Distributed-lag models arise in many different econometric contexts. Two cases in point are described below.

E 32.9 Consider an econometrician who wants to test the permanent-income hypothesis. He has data on various consumers' expenditures on consumer goods in periods t and $t - 1$, which we denote by C_t and C_{t-1}, and he has data on the same consumers' income in period t, y_t. To carry out his test, he hypothesizes that there exists a constant $\lambda \in (0, 1)$ such that he can write each consumer's permanent income as a weighted average of current and past income,

$$y_p(v) = (1 - \lambda) \sum_{s=0}^{\infty} \lambda^s y_{v-s}, \quad v = t - 1, t, \tag{32.55}$$

where y_{v-s} denotes income in period $v - s$. Then he uses equations 32.55, 27.5, and 27.6 to establish the following distributed-lag relations for C_t and C_{t-1}:

$$C_v = k(r)(1 - \lambda) \sum_{s=0}^{\infty} \lambda^s y_{v-s} + \eta_v, \qquad v = t - 1, t, \tag{32.56}$$

where η_v denotes transitory consumption in period v. Finally, he shows that the C_v in equation 32.56 satisfy the difference equation,

$$C_t - \lambda C_{t-1} = k(r)(1 - \lambda)y_t + (\eta_t - \lambda\eta_{t-1}),$$

which he will use to formulate his test of Friedman's hypothesis.

We are not convinced that the y_p we defined in equation 27.3 necessarily satisfies equation 32.55. It is, therefore, interesting that equation 32.55 is the discrete version of Friedman's own definition of permanent income (Friedman 1957, p. 143, equations 5.11 and 5.13). Moreover, with $(1 - \lambda)$ equal to the consumer's elasticity of income expectations, ε_y, as defined in equation 26.17, $y_p(v)$ is simply Modigliani and Brumberg's mean expected income, y_v^e, in disguise. Hence the hypothesis expressed in equations 32.55 and 32.56 belongs to the main stream of economic thought.

E 32.10 Consider an econometrician who sets out to study the dynamics of supply of a given agricultural commodity. For each period $t = 0, 1, \ldots, N$, he has data on the actual supply of the commodity, y_t, and its price, p_t. He postulates that the desired level of production in any period t, y_t^d, is a constant multiple of the price which the farmers expect to face in that period, p_t^e; i.e., there exists a constant $\alpha \in R_{++}$ such that

$$y_t^d = \alpha p_t^e. \tag{32.57}$$

In addition, he assumes that there is a constant $\gamma \in (0, 1)$ such that the way farmers in period $(t - 1)$ determine the value of p_t^e can be represented by the equation,

$$p_t^e - p_{t-1}^e = \gamma(p_{t-1} - p_{t-1}^e). \tag{32.58}$$

Finally, he hypothesizes that because of the exigencies of the weather and the fact that farmers tend to hedge their bets, the actual level of production in period t will differ from y_t^d. The way it differs is described in

$$y_t - y_{t-1} = \phi(y_t^d - y_{t-1}) + u_t, \tag{32.59}$$

where ϕ is a constant in (0, 1) and u_t is a random variable with mean zero and finite variance that is distributed independently of the p_s and the y_s for $s < t$. If these hypotheses are true for all $t = \ldots, -1, 0, 1, \ldots$, and if the u_t and the p_t constitute wide-sense stationary processes, then it follows that the behavior over time of the production of the given agricultural commodity can be represented by a distributed-lag model. In fact, for all $t = \ldots, -1, 0, 1, \ldots$,

$$y_t = \frac{\alpha\phi\gamma}{(1-(1-\phi)S^{-1})(1-(1-\gamma)S^{-1})} p_{t-1} + \frac{1}{(1-(1-\phi)S^{-1})} u_t,$$

where S^{-1} shifts p_s and u_s to p_{s-1} and u_{s-1}, respectively. Our econometrician records the equation for y_t and transforms it into a difference equation,

$$y_t - (2-\phi-\gamma)y_{t-1} + (1-\gamma)(1-\phi)y_{t-2} = \alpha\phi\gamma p_{t-1} + (u_t - (1-\gamma)u_{t-1}),$$

to which he decides to apply his data and estimate the values of ϕ, λ, and α.

This example also belongs to the main stream of economic thought. To wit: The relation between actual and expected prices which we delineate in equation 32.71 is called the *adaptive expectations hypothesis*. It is usually attributed to P. Cagan (Cagan 1956, p. 37) and has appeared in various disguises throughout the development of the rational expectations hypothesis. In Cagan's study of the monetary dynamics of hyperinflation, p and p^e are interpreted, respectively, as the actual and expected rate of change in prices; and in M. Nerlove's study of adaptive expectations and the cobweb phenomena, p, and p^e are taken to be, respectively, the actual price and the expected normal price of a given agricultural commodity (Nerlove 1956, p. 231).

One way the adaptive expectations hypothesis has been rationalized is like this (see Nerlove and Wage 1964, pp. 207–224): Let $T = \{1, 2, \ldots\}$; and let $P = \{p_t;\, t = 0, 1, \ldots\}$ and $\eta = \{\eta_t;\, t \in T\}$ be random processes on some probability space $(\Omega, \mathscr{F}, P(\cdot))$. Moreover, suppose that η is purely random with mean zero and finite variance and that P has finite mean and variances and satisfies the conditions

$$p_t = \gamma \sum_{s=0}^{t-1} (1-\gamma)^s p_{t-1-s} + \eta_t, \qquad t \in T; \tag{32.60}$$

$$E\eta_t p_{t-1-s} = 0, \qquad s = 0, 1, \ldots, \qquad t-1,\ t \in T; \tag{32.61}$$

and

$p_0 \in R_{++}$ is a constant,

where $\gamma \in (0, 1)$. Finally, suppose that $p^e = \{p_t^e;\, t \in T\}$ is a random process which satisfies the adaptive expectations hypothesis; that is, $p_0^e = p_0$ and

$$p_t^e - p_{t-1}^e = \gamma(p_{t-1} - p_{t-1}^e), \qquad t \in T.$$

Then for each $t \in T$, p_t^e is the best linear least-squares predictor of p_t.

We have difficulties with this rationalization of equation 32.58 for the following reasons: Besides satisfying equations 32.60 and 32.61, P and η also satisfy the relations

$$p_1 = p_0 + \eta_1,$$

and

$$p_t = p_{t-1} + \eta_t - (1 - \gamma)\eta_{t-1}, \qquad t = 2, 3, \ldots.$$

Hence P is an ARIMA process. Such processes are not wide-sense stationary. We shall discuss their characteristics in chapter 33 and give reasons why they should not be used to represent the behavior over time of economic variables.

The hypothesis delineated in equations 32.57 and 32.59 is called the *partial adjustment hypothesis* and appears in many disguises in the econometric literature. For example, in H. Chenery's study of the investment behavior of firms (Chenery 1952, pp. 11–13), p^e becomes expected output (or sales), y^d is desired capital stock, and y denotes actual capital stock. In J. K. Lintner's study of corporáte financing behavior (Lintner 1956, pp. 97–113), p^e becomes (current) profits after taxes, y^d is desired dividends, and y denotes actual dividend payments. Finally, in M. Nerlove's study of the supply of agricultural commodities (Nerlove 1958, pp. 53 and 62), p^e, y^d, and y are interpred, respectively, as the expected normal price, the long-run equilibrium output, and the actual output of an agricultural commodity.

In E 32.10 our econometrician justified the u_t in equation 32.59 by the weather and $\phi(y_t^d - y_{t-1})$ by the farmer's tendency to hedge his bet. There is another way of justifying the latter. Suppose that farmers incur two kinds of cost: (1) foregone profits, which we measure by $a(y_t - y_t^d)^2$, and (2) cost of change, which we measure by $b(y_t - y_{t-1})^2$. To minimize their costs, farmers must choose y_t so that

$$y_t = \left(\frac{a}{a + b}\right)y_t^d + \left(\frac{b}{a + b}\right)y_{t-1}.$$

If they do, y_t, y_t^d, and y_{t-1} will satisfy

$$y_t - y_{t-1} = \phi(y_t^d - y_{t-1})$$

with $\phi = (a/a + b)$. For a discussion of this justification of equation 32.59 and related matters, see Griliches 1967, pp. 42–45.

32.3.3 A Stochastic Control Problem

It is clear that the two econometricians we described above will have difficulties obtaining good estimates of their respective parameters. However, this is of no concern to us here. What bothers us is the ad hoc nature of the hypotheses which form the basis of these econometricians' empirical work. It is doubtful that the distributed-lag models we derived from them depict anything but statistical relationships between the variables involved.

In this section we shall solve a stochastic control problem, which we formulate in T 32.12. The solution to this problem will enable us to determine situations in which we can represent the behavior over time of an economic agent by a distributed-lag model of a given kind.

To state the theorem succinctly, I must introduce a new symbol and explicate a useful concept. First the concept: We shall say that a wide-sense stationary process X is *nondeterministic* if it satisfies the inequality in equation 32.51. Moreover, X is *purely nondeterministic* if it satisfies equation 32.51 and if the deterministic component (i.e., V in T 32.8) of the Wold decomposition of X is nonexistent.

Next the new symbol: Let $X = \{x(t, \omega); t \in T\}$ be a wide-sense stationary process with mean zero and $T = \{\ldots, -1, 0, 1, \ldots\}$ and let ${}_t\mathscr{M}^0$ and ${}_t\mathscr{M}$, $t \in T$, be as defined in section 32.2. Moreover, let WSSP be short for wide-sense stationary process. Then

$$\Xi = \{Z = \{z(t, \omega); t \in (T \cap R_+)\}: Z \text{ is a WSSP and}$$
$$z(t, \cdot) \in {}_t\mathscr{M} \text{ for all } t \in (T \cap R_+)\}.$$

With Ξ and the idea of a purely nondeterministic process in mind, we can formulate our stochastic control theorem, T 32.12. In studying the theorem and its proof, it is interesting to observe that T 32.12 is a discrete-time, stochastic control analogue of a continuous-time, optimal investment strategy theorem which R. Eisner and R. Strotz formulated and proved in Eisner and Strotz 1963. It is also interesting to note that the problem we solve in T 32.12 generalizes upon the minimum-cost problem used to justify equation 32.59 above.

T 32.12 Let $X = \{x(t, \omega); t \in T\}$ and $Y^d = \{y^d(t, \omega); t \in T\}$ be real-valued wide-sense stationary processes on some probability space $(\Omega, \mathscr{F}, P(\cdot))$, and assume that $Ex(t) = 0$, $t \in T$, $T = \{\ldots, -1, 0, 1, \ldots\}$, and that there exists a constant $a \in R_{++}$ such that

$y^d(t, \omega) = ax(t, \omega), \qquad \omega \in \Omega,\ t \in T.$

Moreover, let $Y = \{y(t, \omega); t \in (T \cap R_+)\}$ be a WSSP in Ξ, let $r \in R_{++}$ and $c \in R_{++}$ be given constants, and suppose that, for all $Z \in \Xi$,

$$E\left\{\sum_{t=0}^{\infty} (1 + r)^{-t}[(y(t) - y^d(t))^2 + c(y(t) - y(t - 1))^2]\right\}$$

$$\leqslant E\left\{\sum_{t=1}^{\infty} (1 + r)^{-t}[(z(t) - y^d(t))^2 + c(z(t) - z(t - 1))^2]\right\}.$$

Finally, let $\xi = \{\xi(t, \omega); t \in T\}$ be the orthogonal random process in the Wold decomposition of X; let $\gamma_j = Ex(t)\xi(t - j)$, $j = 0, 1, \ldots$; and assume that X is purely nondeterministic, $\gamma_0 = 1$, $\sum_{j=0}^{\infty} |\gamma_j| < \infty$ and $\sum_{j=0}^{\infty} \gamma_j z^j \neq 0$ for all $z \in C$ such that $|z| \leqslant 1$. Then there exist constants, $e_j \in R$, $j = 0, 1, \ldots$, that satisfy the conditions,

(i) $\sum_{j=0}^{\infty} |e_j| < \infty$;

(ii) $y(t, \omega) = \sum_{j=0}^{\infty} e_j x(t - j, \omega)$ a.e., $t \in T$; and

(iii) $e(z) = \dfrac{a}{p(z)\gamma(z)}\left[\dfrac{\gamma(z)}{p(z^{-1})}\right]_+$

where $e(z) = \sum_{j=0}^{\infty} e_j z^j$, $\gamma(z) = \sum_{j=0}^{\infty} \gamma_j z^j$, $p(z) = K(1 - pz)$,

$K = (c/p)^{1/2}$, $p = (2c)^{-1}[1 + 2c - (1 + 4c)^{1/2}]$, z varies over all $z \in C$ such that $|z| \leqslant 1$ and $[\cdot]_+$ is the operation which extracts only the nonnegative powers of the Laurent expansion of the bracketed expression.

For the sake of brevity, I shall only outline the ideas of the proof of this theorem. We begin by observing that, for each $Z \in \Xi$, there exist constants b_j, $j = 0, 1, \ldots$, such that $\sum_{j=0}^{\infty} |b_j|^2 < \infty$ and

$$z(t, \omega) = \sum_{j=0}^{\infty} b_j \xi(t - j, \omega), \qquad t \in (T \cap R_+). \tag{32.62}$$

Hence there exist constants $\hat{b}_j$, $j = 0, 1, \ldots$, such that $\sum_{j=0}^{\infty} |\hat{b}_j|^2 < \infty$ and

$$y(t, \omega) = \sum_{j=0}^{\infty} \hat{b}_j \xi(t - j, \omega), \qquad t \in (T \cap R_+). \tag{32.63}$$

Next we shall find a way of expressing the $\hat{b}_j$ in terms of the γ_j. To do that, we first use the wide-sense stationarity of the members of Ξ and the monotone convergence theorem (section 15.6) to show that, for each $Z \in \Xi$,

$$E\left\{\sum_{t=1}^{\infty} (1 + r)^{-t}[[z(t) - y^d(t)]^2 + c(z(t) - z(t - 1))^2]\right\}$$

$$= E\left\{\sum_{t=1}^{\infty} (1 + r)^{-t}[(z(t) - ax(t))^2 + c(t) - z(t - 1))^2]\right\}$$

$$= (1/r)E\{z(t) - ax(t))^2 + c(z(t) - z(t - 1))^2\}. \qquad (32.64)$$

Then we substitute equation 32.62 into equation 32.64 and deduce that

$$E\left\{\left(\sum_{j=0}^{\infty} (b_j - a\gamma_j)\xi(t - j)\right)^2 + c\left(b_0\xi(t) + \sum_{j=1}^{\infty} (b_j - b_{j-1})\xi(t - j)\right)^2\right\}$$

$$= E|\xi(t)|^2\left[\sum_{j=0}^{\infty} (b_j - a\gamma_j)^2 + c\left(b_0^2 + \sum_{j=1}^{\infty} (b_j - b_{j-1})^2\right)\right]. \qquad (32.65)$$

But if this is so, then for all sequences b_j, $j = 0, 1, \ldots$, such that $\sum_{j=0}^{\infty} |b_j|^2 < \infty$, we must have

$$\left[\sum_{j=0}^{\infty} (\hat{b}_j - a\gamma_j)^2 + c\left(\hat{b}_0^2 + \sum_{j=1}^{\infty} (\hat{b}_j - \hat{b}_{j-1})^2\right)\right]$$

$$\leqslant \left[\sum_{j=0}^{\infty} (b_j - a\gamma_j)^2 + c\left(b_0^2 + \sum_{j=1}^{\infty} (b_j - b_{j-1})^2\right)\right].$$

Hence we can find the $\hat{b}_j$ of equation 32.63 by minimizing the right-hand side of equation 32.65 with respect to b_j, $j = 0, 1, \ldots$.

Necessary conditions that the $\hat{b}_j$, $j = 0, 1, \ldots$, constitute a minimum of the right-hand side of equation 32.65 in the closed linear manifold of square-summable sequences b_j, $j = 0, 1, \ldots$, are that they satisfy the following system of equations:

$$\hat{b}_1 - \left(\frac{1 + 2c}{c}\right)\hat{b}_0 = -\left(\frac{a}{c}\right)\gamma_0; \qquad (32.66)$$

and

$$\hat{b}_{j+1} - \left(\frac{1 + 2c}{c}\right)\hat{b}_j + \hat{b}_{j-1} = -\left(\frac{a}{c}\right)\gamma_j, \qquad j = 1, 2, \ldots, \qquad (32.67)$$

which we obtain by differentiating the right-hand side of equation 32.65 with respect to b_j and insisting that the derivative equal zero. From equations 32.66 and 32.67, it follows that the $\hat{b}_j$ must satisfy a second-order difference equation whose particular solution is a function of the γ_j and the two roots of the associated characteristic polynomial, z_1 and z_2, where

$$z_1 = \frac{(1 + 2c) - (1 + 4c)^{1/2}}{2c};$$

and

$$z_2 = \frac{(1 + 2c) + (1 + 4c)^{1/2}}{2c}.$$

To obtain the particular solution, we let

$$b(z) = \sum_{j=0}^{\infty} \tilde{b}_j z^j, \qquad z \in C, |z| \leqslant 1,$$

multiply each equation in 32.66 and 32.67 by z^j, sum over all j, and deduce that

$$z^{-1}(z - z_1)(z - z_2)b(z) - \tilde{b}_0 z^{-1} = -\left(\frac{a}{c}\right)\gamma(z)$$

and hence (since $z_1 z_2 = 1$) that, for all $z \in C$ such that $|z| \leqslant 1$,

$$(1 - z_1 z^{-1})(1 - z_1 z)b(z) = -(\tilde{b}_0 z_1)z^{-1} + a\left(\frac{z_1}{c}\right)\gamma(z). \tag{32.68}$$

By equating coefficients in equation 32.68 and letting $p = z_1$ and $K = (c/p)^{1/2}$, we find that, for all $z \in C$ such that $|z| \leqslant 1$,

$$b(z) = (K^2(1 - pz))^{-1}\left[\frac{a\gamma(z)}{1 - pz^{-1}}\right]_+, \tag{32.69}$$

which determines the values of the $\tilde{b}_j$ as functions of the γ_j.

The $\tilde{b}_j$, $j = 0, 1, \ldots,$ constitute the particular solution to equations 32.66 and 32.67. We shall next demonstrate that $\hat{b}_j = \tilde{b}_j$ for all j. Suppose that this is not the case, and let $h_j = \hat{b}_j - \tilde{b}_j$, $j = 0, 1, \ldots.$ Then the h_j must satisfy the equations

$$h_1 - \left(\frac{1 + 2c}{c}\right)h_0 = 0,$$

and

$$h_{j+1} - \left(\frac{1 + 2c}{c}\right)h_j + h_{j-1} = 0, \qquad j = 1, 2, \ldots.$$

Consequently, there are constants A and B such that

$$h_j = Az_1^j + Bz_2^j, \qquad j = 0, 1, \ldots.$$

Since $\sum_{j=0}^{\infty} |\gamma_j| < \infty$ implies $\sum_{j=0}^{\infty} |\hat{b}_j| < \infty$ and since $|x_2| > 1$, the square summability of the $\hat{b}_j$ implies that $B = 0$. But if this is the case, then the fact that

$$Az_1 - \left(\frac{1 + 2c}{c}\right) A = 0$$

cannot happen unless $A = 0$ implies that $h_j = 0$ for all $j = 0, 1, \ldots$.

We insisted that the conditions in equations 32.66 and 32.67 were necessary for the $\hat{b}_j$ to constitute a minimum of the right-hand side of equation 32.65. Next we show that they are sufficient as well.[4] To that end we let l^2 denote the set of all vectors $b = (b_0, b_1, \ldots)$ such that $\sum_{j=0}^{\infty} |b_j|^2 < \infty$, and define $f(\cdot)$: $l^2 \to R$ by

$$f(b) = \sum_{j=0}^{\infty} (b_j - a\gamma_j)^2 + c\left(b_0^2 + \sum_{j=1}^{\infty} (b_j - b_{j-1})^2\right), \qquad b \in l^2.$$

Moreover, we let $\gamma = (\gamma_0, \gamma_1, \ldots)$ and define the infinite-dimensional symmetrix A by

$$A = \begin{pmatrix} (1 + 2c) & -c & 0 & 0 & \ldots & . & . \\ -c & (1 + 2c) & -c & 0 & \ldots & . & . \\ 0 & -c & (1 + 2c) & -c & \ldots & . & . \\ \vdots & \vdots & \vdots & \vdots & \vdots & \vdots & \vdots \end{pmatrix}$$

Finally, we let $\|\cdot\|$ denote the norm in l^2 (that is, $\|b\|^2 = \sum_{j=0}^{\infty} b_j^2$) and observe that

$$f(b) = bAb' - 2a\gamma b' + a^2 \|\gamma\|^2; \quad \hat{b}A = a\gamma;$$

and hence that

$$f(b) - f(\hat{b}) = (b - \hat{b})A(b - \hat{b})'.$$

But if this is the case and if $\lambda = \sqrt{cz_2}$ and $\mu = \sqrt{cz_1}$, then it is easy to verify that

$$f(b) - f(\hat{b}) = \lambda^2(b_0 - \hat{b}_0)^2 + \sum_{j=1}^{\infty} (\lambda(b_j - \hat{b}_j) - \mu(b_{j-1} - \hat{b}_{j-1}))^2$$

$$= cz_2\{(b_0 - \hat{b}_0)^2 + \sum_{j=1}^{\infty} ((b_j - \hat{b}_j) - z_1(b_{j-1} - \hat{b}_{j-1}))^2\}.$$

Hence $f(b) \geqslant f(\hat{b})$ for all $b \in l^2$ and $f(b) = f(\hat{b})$ if and only if $b = \hat{b}$, as was to be shown.

We conclude the proof by observing that the $e(\cdot)$ in condition ii of T 32.12 must satisfy the equation

$$e(z) = \frac{b(z)}{\gamma(z)}, \qquad z \in C, |z| \leqslant 1. \tag{32.70}$$

If $c(\cdot)$ satisfies equation 32.70, the properties of $b(\cdot)$ and $\gamma(\cdot)$ imply that $c(\cdot)$ satisfies conditions i and iii of the theorem as well.

To help the reader's intuition concerning the import of equations 32.69 and 32.70, I shall conclude this subsection with two simple examples and a remark.

E 32.11 Let $X = \{x(t,\omega); t \in T\}$ and $\xi = \{\xi(t,\omega); t \in T\}$ be as described in T 32.12 and assume that

$$x(t,\omega) = \xi(t,\omega), \qquad t \in T.$$

Then it follows from equations 32.69 and 32.70 that

$$e(z) = b(z) = \left(\frac{a}{K^2}\right) \sum_{j=0}^{\infty} p^j z^j, \qquad z \in C, |z| \leqslant 1,$$

and hence that

$$y(t,\omega) = \left(\frac{a}{K^2}\right) \sum_{j=0}^{\infty} p^j x(t-j,\omega) \quad \text{a.e.,} \qquad t \in (T \cap R_+).$$

For the applications of T 32.12 that we have in mind, e.g., corporate investments and agricultural production, it is disconcerting that $Ex(t) = 0$. Hence a clarifying remark is called for. To that end, let $\{X(t,\omega); t \in T\}$ be a random process which satisfies the relations

$$X(t,\omega) = \mu_x(t) + x(t,\omega), \qquad \omega \in \Omega \text{ and } t \in T,$$

where $\mu_x(\cdot)\colon T \to R$ is square-summable and $\{x(t,\omega); t \in T\}$ is a purely nondeterministic wide-sense stationary process with $Ex(t) = 0$. Moreover, let Ξ be as defined above and let

$$\tilde{\Xi} = \{V(\cdot)\colon (T \cap R_+) \times \Omega \to R\colon V(t,\omega) = f(t) + z(t,\omega),\ t \in (T \cap R_+) \text{ and }$$
$$\omega \in \Omega, \text{ for some square-summable } f(\cdot)\colon (T \cap R_+) \to R \text{ and } Z \in \Xi\}.$$

Finally, let $\{Y(t,\omega); t \in (T \cap R_+)\}$ be a random process which satisfies the conditions:

(i) $Y(t,\omega) = \mu_y(t) + y(t,\omega), \qquad \omega \in \Omega$ and $t \in (T \cap R_+)$;

(ii) $\mu_y(\cdot)\colon (T \cap R_+) \to R$ is the solution of the deterministic minimization problem in equation 32.71, where s. q. is shorthand for square-summable:

$$\min_{\text{s.q.} f(\cdot):T\to R} \sum_{t=1}^{\infty} (1+r)^{-t}[(f(t) - a\mu_x(t))^2 + c(f(t) - f(t-1))^2]; \tag{32.71}$$

and

(iii) $\{y(t,\omega); t \in (T \cap R_+)\}$ is the wide-sense stationary solution of the stochastic control problem:

$$\min_{Z \in \Xi} E\left\{\sum_{t=1}^{\infty} (1+r)^{-t}[(z(t) - ax(t))^2 + c(z(t) - z(t-1))^2]\right\}. \tag{32.72}$$

Then $\{Y(t,\omega); t \in (T \cap R_+)\}$ constitutes the solution of the following stochastic control problem:

$$\min_{V(\cdot) \in \tilde{\Xi}} E\left\{\sum_{t=1}^{\infty} (1+r)^{-t}[(V(t) - aX(t))^2 + c(V(t) - V(t-1))^2\right\} \tag{32.73}$$

Hence we can think of T 32.12 as providing a characterization of the random component of the solution of the stochastic control problem described in equation 32.73.

When $\mu_x(t) = A$ for all $t \in (T \cap R_+)$, $\mu_y(t) = aA$ and we can obtain a solution of equation 32.73 by adding a constant, aA, to the solution of equation 32.72. Here is an example to illustrate this fact.

E 32.12 Let $X = \{x(t,\omega); t \in T\}$ and $\xi = \{\xi(t,\omega); t \in T\}$ be as described in T 32.12 and suppose that there is a constant $\beta \in (0, 1)$ such that

$$x(t,\omega) - \beta x(t-1,\omega) = \xi(t,\omega); \qquad t \in T.$$

Moreover, let $\{X(t,\omega); t \in T\}$ be a random process which satisfies the relations,

$$X(t,\omega) = A + x(t,\omega), \qquad \omega \in \Omega \text{ and } t \in T.$$

Then

$$\gamma(z) = \sum_{j=0}^{\infty} \beta^j z^j, \qquad z \in C, |z| \leqslant 1;$$

$$b(z) = (K^2(1-pz))^{-1} \frac{a}{(1-\beta p)(1-\beta z)},$$

and (32.74)

$$e(z) = \left(\frac{a}{K^2}\right)((1-pz)(1-\beta p))^{-1}, \qquad z \in C, |z| \leqslant 1.$$

Consequently,

$$y(t,\omega) = \frac{a}{K^2(1-\beta p)} \sum_{j=0}^{\infty} p^j x(t-j,\omega), \quad \text{a.e.}, \qquad t \in (T \cap R_+) \tag{32.95}$$

is the wide-sense stationary solution of equation 32.72, and

$$Y(t, \omega) = aA + y(t, \omega), \qquad \omega \in \Omega \text{ and } t \in (T \cap R_+),$$

constitutes the solution of equation 32.73.

32.3.4 Rational Distributed Lags and Control

Dale Jorgenson has suggested (see Jorgenson 1966, pp. 135–149) that most distributed-lag models can be approximated arbitrarily close by a so-called rational distributed-lag model. Consequently, there is little loss in generality if we assume that most econometric distributed-lag models are rational.

A distributed-lag model,

$$y(t, \omega) = \sum_{j=0}^{\infty} c_j x(t - j, \omega) + \eta(t, \omega), \qquad t \in T,$$

is *rational* if and only if there exist polynomials, $A(\cdot)$: $C \to C$ and $B(\cdot)$: $C \to C$, such that

(i) $A(z) = \sum_{k=0}^{n} a_k z^k$ and $A(\hat{z}) = 0$ only if $|\hat{z}| > 1$;

(ii) $B(z) = \sum_{l=0}^{m} b_l z^l$; and

(iii) $C(z) = \sum_{j=0}^{\infty} c_j z^j = \dfrac{B(z)}{A(z)}, \qquad z \in C, |z| \leqslant 1.$

Jorgenson's claim is that even when $C(\cdot)$ is not rational, for every $\varepsilon > 0$, we can find two polynomials, $A(\cdot)$ and $B(\cdot)$, such that if

$$\sum_{j=0}^{\infty} d_j z^j = \frac{B(z)}{A(z)},$$

then, for all $j = 0, 1, \ldots, |c_j - d_j| < \varepsilon$.

Dale Jorgenson's interesting idea has two drawbacks: (1) There is no a priori argument that in any particular case will determine the values of n and m. (2) Estimating the parameters of a distributed-lag model is simplified by assuming that the model is rational only if n and m can be chosen to be small. From this it follows that it is important to find theoretical arguments that will help us determine appropriate values of m and n. We shall do that for economic agents whose behavior satisfies the conditions of T 32.12. Our main result is stated in T 32.13. Both the idea of the theorem and the proof I give are due to Keith McLaren (see McLaren 1979, pp. 188–189). However, my statement of the theorem differs from McLaren's original formulation in that I allow for the possibility that $k > 1$ in condition iv. This modification is due to H. Lütkepohl.

T 32.13 Let $X = \{x(t, \omega); t \in T\}$ and $\xi = \{\xi(t, \omega); t \in T\}$ be as described in T 32.12; let $\gamma_j = Ex(t)\xi(t-j)$, $j = 0, 1, \ldots$, and assume that $\gamma_0 = 1$ and that there exist polynomials, $A(\cdot)\colon C \to C$ and $B(\cdot)\colon C \to C$, which have no common factors, satisfy conditions i and ii above,

$$\gamma(z) = \sum_{j=0}^{\infty} \gamma_j z^j = \frac{B(z)}{A(z)}, \qquad z \in C, |z| \leqslant 1,$$

and are such that $\gamma(z) \neq 0$ for all $z \in C$ with $|z| \leqslant 1$. Moreover, let $Y = \{y(t, \omega); t \in T\}$ and $e(\cdot)\colon C \to C$ be as described in T 32.12. Then there exist polynomials, $D(\cdot)\colon C \to C$ and $H(\cdot)\colon C \to C$, such that

(i) $D(z) = \sum_{k=0}^{r} d_k z^k$ and $D(\hat{z}) = 0$ only if $|\hat{z}| > 1$;

(ii) $H(z) = \sum_{l=0}^{s} h_l z^l$;

(iii) $e(z) = \dfrac{H(z)}{D(z)}, \qquad z \in C, |z| \leqslant 1;$

(iv) $(r, s) = \begin{cases} (m+1, n-k) & \text{for some } 1 \leqslant k \leqslant n \text{ if } n > m, \text{ and} \\ (m+1, m) & \text{if } n \leqslant m; \end{cases}$

(v) $H(\cdot)$ is related to both $A(\cdot)$ and $B(\cdot)$, and $D(z) = K^2 p(z) B(z)$, where K^2 and $p(\cdot)\colon C \to C$ are as described in T 32.12.

We shall prove this theorem under the additional assumption that the roots of $A(\cdot)$ are distinct. The proof for the case of repeated roots can be obtained in the same way by using a result of P. Whittle (see Whittle 1963, theorem 1, p. 93).

Suppose that

$$A(z) = \prod_{j=1}^{n} (1 - z_j z), \quad |z_j| < 1, \quad j = 1, \ldots, n,$$

and assume that the z_j are distinct. Suppose also that $A(\cdot)$ and $B(\cdot)$ have no common factors. Then there exist a polynomials $G_0(\cdot)\colon C \to C$ and constants e_j, $j = 1, \ldots, n$, such that

$$\frac{B(z)}{A(z)} = G_0(z) + \sum_{j=1}^{n} e_j (1 - z_j z)^{-1}, \qquad z \in C, |z| \leqslant 1,$$

and such that if $n > m$, $G_0(\cdot) = 0$, and if $m \geqslant n$, $G_0(\cdot)$ is of degree $m - n$. But if this is so, then the arguments needed to establish equation 32.74 and the linearity of $[\cdot]_+$ imply that

$$\left[\frac{\gamma(z)}{1-pz^{-1}}\right]_+ = G(z) + \sum_{j=1}^{n} e_j((1-z_jp)(1-z_jz))^{-1}, \qquad z \in C, |z| \leqslant 1, \tag{32.75}$$

where $G(\cdot)\colon C \to C$ is identically 0 if $n > m$ and a polynomial of degree $m - n$ if $m \geqslant n$. From equation 32.75 it follows that there is a $1 \leqslant k \leqslant n$ and a polynomial $F(\cdot)\colon C \to C$ of degree $n - k$ such that

$$\left[\frac{\gamma(z)}{1-pz^{-1}}\right]_+ = \frac{G(z)A(z) + F(z)}{A(z)}, \qquad z \in C, |z| \leqslant 1.$$

Consequently, by condition iii of T 32.12,

$$e(z) = a\left(\frac{G(z)A(z) + F(z)}{K^2p(z)B(z)}\right), \qquad z \in C, |z| \leqslant 1;$$

and we can conclude the proof by letting $D(z) = K^2p(z)B(z)$, which is a polynomial of degree $(m + 1)$, land by letting $H(z) = a(G(z)A(z) + F(z))$, which is a polynomial of degree $n - k$, if $n > m$, and of degree m, if $m \geqslant n$.

Theorem T 32.13 establishes a remarkably simple relationship between the spectral representation of X and the structure of the distributed lag that relates the solution of equation 32.72 to X. This relationship is exemplified in E 32.11, where $(n, m) = (0, 0)$ and $(r, s) = (1, 0)$, and in E 32.12, where $(n, m) = (1, 0)$ and $(r, s) = (1, 0)$. Another example is provided by E 32.13, where $(n, m) = (0, 1)$ and $(r, s) = (2, 1)$.

E 32.13 Let $X = \{x(t, \omega); t \in T\}$ and $\xi = \{(t, \omega); t \in T\}$ be as described in T 32.12 and suppose that there is a constant $\beta \in (0, 1)$ such that

$$x(t, \omega) = \xi(t, \omega) - \beta\xi(t - 1, \omega), \qquad \omega \in \Omega, t \in T.$$

Then for all $z \in C$ such that $|z| \leqslant 1$,

$$\gamma(z) = 1 - \beta z;$$

$$b(z) = \frac{a((1 - p\beta) - \beta z)}{K^2(1 - pz)};$$

and

$$e(z) = \frac{H(z)}{D(z)},$$

where

$$H(z) = a((1 - p\beta) - \beta z) \quad \text{and} \quad D(z) = K^2(1 - pz)(1 - \beta z).$$

In commenting on McLaren's results, H. Lütkepohl gives an example where the k in T 32.13 (iv) is bigger than 1 (Lütkepohl 1984, pp. 504–506).

He also observes that $H(\cdot)$ and $D(\cdot)$ may have common factors even if $A(\cdot)$ and $B(\cdot)$ do not. A $k > 1$ and common factors of $H(\cdot)$ and $D(\cdot)$ simplify the structure of $c(\cdot)$ but are hard to determine on a priori grounds alone. Hence assuming $k = 1$ and disregarding common factors of $H(\cdot)$ and $D(\cdot)$ are probably the only options available to an econometrician.

33 Trends, Cycles, and Seasonals in Economic Time Series and Stochastic Difference Equations

In this chapter we begin by discussing various ways of modeling trends, cycles, and seasonals in economic time series. All of them can be rationalized by assuming that an economic time series is a partial realization of a family X of random variables which satisfy a stochastic difference equation. If the initial conditions of the difference equation are fixed, X is an ARIMA process. If the initial conditions are random, X is a dynamic stochastic process.

Two sections of the chapter are given to determining the adequacy of different schemes for modeling trends, cycles, and seasonals; we study the salient characteristics first of ARIMA processes and then of dynamic stochastic processes. Our conclusion is that an economic time series may be generated by a dynamic stochastic process, but it is unlikely that it can be generated by an ARIMA process.

33.1 Modeling Trends, Cycles, and Seasonals in Economic Time Series

In this section we consider the behavior over time of a single economic variable x. We assume that a time series of observations on x can be decomposed and written as a sum of four components,

$$x_t = p_t + c_t + s_t + \eta_t, \tag{33.1}$$

where p, c, s, and η, respectively, denote the trend, cycle, seasonal, and random component of the behavior of x. Our objective is to discuss various ways of modeling the behavior over time of p, c, and s.

33.1.1 Trends

The terms "trend," "cycles," and "seasonals" have a more or less definite meaning in economics. Following E. Malinvaud (see Malinvaud 1966,

p. 440), we say that the *trend* is "a slow variation in some specific direction which is maintained over a long period of years." The *cycle* is "a movement, quasi-periodic in appearance, alternately increasing and decreasing." The *seasonal movement* is "composed of regular weekly, monthly, or yearly variations."

Mathematically the trend is often represented as a polynomial in t whose coefficients are either constant or vary exponentially with t; for example,

$$p_t = \alpha + \gamma t, \qquad t \in T; \tag{33.2}$$

or (more generally),

$$p_t = \sum_{i=1}^{m} \sum_{j=0}^{n_i-1} \alpha_{ij}(t^j z_i^t), \qquad t \in T. \tag{33.3}$$

Then there exist an integer n and constants a_k, $k = 0, 1, \ldots, n$, such that $n = \sum_{i=1}^{m} n_i$, $a_0 = 1$, and

$$\sum_{k=0}^{n} a_k p_{t-k} = 0, \qquad t \in T.$$

In the case of equation 33.2, the a_k are obtained by equating coefficients in

$$\sum_{k=0}^{2} a_k z^{-k} = z^{-2}(z-1)^2;$$

and in the case of equation 33.3 we determine the a_k from

$$\sum_{k=0}^{n} a_k z^{-k} = z^{-n} \prod_{i=1}^{m} (z - z_i)^{n_i}.$$

Some econometricians believe that the preceding view of the trend is much too simplistic. For example, instead of equation 33.2, they may postulate the following system of equations:[1]

$$p_0 = \alpha \qquad \text{and} \qquad \beta_1 = \beta; \tag{33.4}$$

$$p_t = p_{t-1} + \beta_t, \qquad t = 1, 2, \ldots; \tag{33.5}$$

and

$$\beta_t = \beta_{t-1} + \xi_t, \qquad t = 2, 3, \ldots, \tag{33.6}$$

where the ξ_t constitute a purely random process with mean zero and finite variance σ_ξ^2. Then the β_t determine how the slope of the trend changes from one period to the next, and the trend is characterized by equation 33.4, $p_1 = p_0 + \beta_1$ and

$$(1 - S^{-1})^2 p_t = \xi_t, \qquad t = 2, 3, \ldots, \tag{33.7}$$

where S is a shift operator that shifts p_t to p_{t+1}.

The econometricians, who believe that the equations in 33.4–33.6 represent a preferable alternative to equation 33.2, would also replace equation 33.3 with a system of equations that is similar to equations 33.4–33.6 but contains more variables and more equations. For our purpose here it is not important to know exactly what the preferable alternative to equation 33.3 looks like. What matters to us is that in most cases the alternative to equation 33.3 will determine (1) a constant d; (2) two polynomials in negative powers of z, $M(z)$, and $N(z)$, whose roots lie, respectively, outside the unit circle and on or inside the unit circle; and (3) a sequence of identically and independently distributed random variables ξ_t such that, for some positive integer q and constants $\overline{p}_t$, $t = 0, 1, \ldots, q$, the p_t satisfy the equations,

$$p_t = \overline{p}_t, \qquad t = 0, 1, \ldots, q, \tag{33.8}$$

and

$$M(S)(1 - S^{-1})^d p_t = N(S)\xi_t, \qquad t = q + 1, q + 2, \ldots. \tag{33.9}$$

In comparing equation 33.7 with equation 33.2 and equation 33.9 with equation 33.3, note that the solution to equation 33.7 satisfies equation 33.4, $p_1 = \alpha + \beta$, and

$$p_t = \alpha + \beta t + u_t, \qquad t = 2, 3, \ldots, \tag{33.10}$$

where the u_t are random variables which constitute a solution to the equations,

$$(1 - S^{-1})^2 u_t = \xi_t, \qquad t = 2, 3, \ldots, \qquad u_0 = 0, \text{ and } u_1 = 0.$$

Similarly, the p_t in equations 33.8 and 33.9 will satisfy a relation of the form,

$$p_t = \sum_{i=1}^{m} \sum_{j=0}^{n_i - 1} \alpha_{ij}(t^j z_i^t) + v_t, \qquad t = q + 1, q + 2, \ldots, \tag{33.11}$$

where the v_t are random variables which constitute a solution to the equations,

$$M(S)(1 - S^{-1})^d v_t = N(S)\xi_t, \qquad t = q + 1, q + 2, \ldots, \qquad \text{and}$$

$$v_t = 0, \; t = 0, \ldots, q.$$

In section 33.2 below we shall see that the behavior of p_t in equation

32.10 and p_t in equation 33.11 is for large t completely determined by the behavior of the u_t and the v_t, respectively.

33.1.2 Cycles and Seasonals

The cycle and the seasonal components of an economic time series are often represented mathematically as finite trigonometric series whose coefficients are constants if the corresponding components are not trending and polynomials in t whenever the associated components are trending. The period of each component of the cycle series is greater than one year and the period of each of the components of the seasonal series is less than or equal to one year.

Suppose first that the cycle and seasonal component of x are nontrending. Then the preceding description of cycles and seasonals can be expressed as follows: There exist complex constants b_j, $j = 1, \ldots, m$, and real numbers $\lambda_j \in [-\pi, \pi)$ such that

$$c_t + s_t = \sum_{j=1}^{m} b_j e^{it\lambda_j}, \qquad t \in T. \tag{33.12}$$

Which part of the right-hand sum in equation 33.12 represents the nontrending seasonal component of x and which part represents the nontrending cyclical component of x depends on the length of the period in which time is measured. Suppose that time is measured in months and that $-\pi \leqslant \lambda_1 < \lambda_2 < \cdots < \lambda_m < \pi$. Moreover, let A and B be a partition of $\{1, \ldots, m\}$; that is,

$$A \cap B = \varnothing \qquad \text{and} \qquad A \cup B = \{1, \ldots, m\}, \tag{33.13}$$

and suppose that, for all $j = 1, \ldots, m$, $\lambda_j \in A$ if and only if

$$(2\pi/|\lambda_j|) \leqslant 12, \qquad \text{and} \qquad (1 - S^{-12})e^{it\lambda_j} = 0. \tag{33.14}$$

Then the seasonal component of x can be represented by

$$s_t = \sum_{j \in A} b_j e^{it\lambda_j}, \qquad t \in T, \tag{33.15}$$

and the cyclical component by

$$c_t = \sum_{j \in B} b_j e^{it\lambda_j}, \qquad t \in T. \tag{33.16}$$

The assignment of frequencies to s_t and c_t is not always as clear-cut as it seems to be in equations 33.13–33.16. To see why, observe first that equations 33.13–33.15 imply that

$$(1 - S^{-12})s_t = 0, \qquad t \in T, \tag{33.17}$$

a condition on which most econometricians would insist. Next observe that there may exist a constant $c > 12$ which is not divisible by 12 and satisfies both

$$(1 - S^{-c})c_t = 0, \qquad t \in T,$$

and

$$(1 - S^{-c})e^{it\lambda_j} = 0, \qquad t \in T,$$

for some $j \in A$. If such a constant exists, assigning λ_j to s_t rather than c_t in order to satisfy equation 33.14 seems arbitrary.

It is also important to observe that in many instances some work is required to show that a given representation of the seasonal component of a time series is a special case of equation 33.15. Here is one case in point:

E 33.1 Frequently the seasonal component of a time series is represented by the following equations:

$$s_t = \sum_{k=1}^{12} d_k s_{k,t}, \qquad t \in T, \tag{33.18}$$

where t is measured in months, $s_{k,t}$ equals 1 for $t - k$ divisible by 12 and 0 otherwise, and

$$\sum_{k=1}^{12} d_k = 0. \tag{33.19}$$

After a little reflection, we see that the s_t in equation 33.18 satisfies equation 33.17. Consequently, there exist constants b_j, $j = -6, \ldots, -1, 1, \ldots, 5$, such that

$$s_t = \sum_{\substack{j=-6 \\ j \neq 0}}^{5} b_j e^{it(2\pi j/12)}, \qquad t \in T,$$

and we can conclude that the representation of a seasonal determined by equations 33.18 and 33.19 is a special case of equation 33.15.

Equations 33.12 describe the behavior over time of a nontrending cycle and seasonal component of an economic time series. If the cycle and seasonal components of x are trending, the equations in 33.12 must be changed to

$$c_t + s_t = \sum_{j=1}^{m} \sum_{l=0}^{n_j - 1} b_{jl}(t^l e^{it\lambda_j}), \qquad t \in T. \tag{33.20}$$

Which part of the right-hand sum of equation 33.28 belongs to s_t and which part to c_t is determined in the same way we decomposed equation

33.12 into equations 33.15 and 33.16. We need not repeat those details here.

If the behavior over time of c_t and s_t can be represented by the equations in 32.20, then there exist an integer n and constants a_k, $k = 0, 1, \ldots, n$, such that $a_0 = 1$, $n = \sum_{j=1}^{m} n_j$ and

$$\sum_{k=0}^{n} a_k(c_{t-k} + s_{t-k}) = 0, \qquad t \in T.$$

The a_k are obtained by equating coefficients in

$$\sum_{k=0}^{n} a_k z^{-k} = z^{-n} \prod_{j=1}^{m} (z - e^{i\lambda_j})^{n_j}.$$

Again there are many econometricians who believe that the behavior over time of the cycle and seasonal components of x cannot be described by a deterministic model such as equation 33.20. They agree that the cyclical and seasonal characteristics of economic time series are caused by ever-recurring phenomena, e.g., the yearly round of climatic seasons and religious festivals. However, these recurring phenomena change over time, and this change injects an irregular pattern in the behavior of c_t and s_t that we must account for. To do that when time is measured in months, the econometrician might propose the following model for the cycle;

$$\begin{aligned}
&c_t = c_{t-18} + \gamma_t, \qquad t = 18, 19, \ldots \\
&\gamma_t = \gamma_{t-1} + \xi_t, \qquad t = 1, 2, \ldots \\
&\gamma_0 = 0, \\
&c_t = \bar{c}_t, \qquad t = 0, 1, \ldots, 17,
\end{aligned} \tag{33.21}$$

where the ξ_t constitute a purely random process with mean zero and finite variance σ_ξ^2. For the seasonal, the econometrician might propose

$$\begin{aligned}
&s_t = s_{t-1} + \phi_t, \qquad t = 1, 2, \ldots \\
&\sum_{k=0}^{11} \phi_{t-k} = \eta_t, \qquad t = 12, 13, \ldots \\
&\eta_t = \eta_{t-1} + \varepsilon_t, \qquad t = 12, 13, \ldots \\
&s_0 = \bar{s} \\
&\phi_i = 0, \qquad i = 0, 1, \ldots, 11 \\
&\eta_i = 0, \qquad i = 0, 1, \ldots, 11,
\end{aligned} \tag{33.22}$$

where the ε_t constitute a purely random process with mean zero and finite variance $\sigma^2_{\varepsilon_t}$. By solving equations 33.21 and 33.22, we find that

$$(1 - S^{-1})(1 - S^{-18})c_t = \xi_t, \qquad t = 19, 20, \ldots;$$

and

$$(1 - S^{-1})(1 - S^{-12})s_t = \varepsilon_t, \qquad t = 13, 14, \ldots.$$

Consequently, there exist constants b_j, $j = 0, 1, \ldots, 18$, and d_k, $k = 0, 1, \ldots, 12$, and numbers $\lambda_j \in [-\pi, \pi)$, $j = 1, \ldots, 18$, and $\mu_k \in [-\pi, \pi)$, $k = 1, \ldots, 12$, such that

$$c_t = b_0 + \sum_{j=1}^{18} b_j e^{it\lambda_j} + u_t, \qquad t = 0, 1, \ldots;$$

and

$$s_t = d_0 + \sum_{k=1}^{12} d_k e^{it\mu_k} + v_t, \qquad t = 0, 1, \ldots,$$

where the u_t and the v_t, respectively, are solutions to the system of equations,

$$(1 - S^{-1})(1 - S^{-18})u_t = \xi_t, \quad t = 19, 20, \ldots; u_t = 0, \quad t = 0, 1, \ldots, 18;$$

and

$$(1 - S^{-1})(1 - S^{-12})v_t = \varepsilon_t, \quad t = 13, 14, \ldots; v_t = 0, \quad t = 0, 1, \ldots, 12.$$

The models we described in equations 33.22 and 33.21 are two of many possible substitutes for equations 33.15 and 33.16. Most of these substitutes have the following characteristics in common: There exist (1) integers q_c and q_s; (2) triples of integers, (d_c, c, e_c) and (d_s, s, e_s); (3) pairs of polynomials in negative powers of z, $(M_c(z), N_c(z))$ and $(M_s(z), N_s(z))$; and (4) purely random prosesses, $\{\xi_t; t = q_c + 1, q_c + 2, \ldots\}$ and $\{\varepsilon_t; t = q_s + 1, q_s + 2, \ldots\}$ such that

$$(1 - S^{-1})^{d_c}(1 - S^{-c})^{e_c} M_c(S)c_t = N_c(S)\xi_t, \quad t = q_c + 1, q_c + 2, \ldots; \quad (33.23)$$

and

$$(1 - S^{-1})^{d_s}(1 - S^{-s})^{e_s} M_s(S)s_t = N_s(S)\varepsilon_t, \quad t = q_s + 1, q_s + 2, \ldots. \quad (33.24)$$

Here both c and s depend on the length of the periods in which time is measured; for example, s may be 4 or 12, according as the time is measured in quarters or months. Moreover, the roots of $M_c(z)$ and $M_s(z)$ are usually taken to lie inside the unit circle. Finally, when the appropriate initial conditions are added to equations 33.23 and 33.24, the c_t and s_t constitute two GARIMA processes, where G stands for generalized and ARIMA is short for autoregressive integrated moving average.[2]

33.1.3 Concluding Remarks

In the preceding sections we have described various ways of modeling trends, cycles, and seasonals in economic time series. It remains to observe that if we substitute the right-hand side of equations 33.3 and 33.12, respectively, for p_t and $(c_t + s_t)$ in equation 33.1 and assume that the η_t in equation 33.1 constitute a wide-sense stationary process, we obtain a dynamic stochastic representation of the behavior of x. On the other hand, if we (1) substitute the right-hand side of equation 33.11 for p_t in equation 33.1; (2) substitute solutions to equations 33.39 and 33.40, respectively, for c_t and s_t in equation 33.1; and (3) assume that the η_t in equation 33.1 constitute a wide-sense stationary process, then we obtain a GARIMA-process representation of the behavior over time of x. In the next two sections we shall study the salient characteristics of ARIMA processes and dynamic stochastic processes to determine the appropriateness of using them, or generalizations of them, to model trends, cycles, and seasonals in economic time series.

33.2 ARIMA Processes

In this section we study the asymptotic behavior of so-called autoregressive integrated moving average processes. These processes constitute a large class of stochastic difference equations, which includes among many other well-known processes the simple one-dimensional random walk. They were dubbed by G. E. P. Box and G. M. Jenkins who found them to provide useful models for studying and controlling the behavior of certain economic variables and various chemical processes (Box and Jenkins 1970, pp. 85–125).

An autoregressive integrated moving average process (hereafter an ARIMA process) is defined as follows:

Let $X = \{x(t, \omega): t = -n + 1, -n + 2, \dots\}$ be a family of real-valued random variables on some probability space $(\Omega, \mathscr{F}, P(\cdot))$. Then X is an ARIMA process if and only if it satisfies the following conditions:

(i) There exist constants $\bar{x}_t$, $-n + 1 \leqslant t \leqslant 0$, such that

$$x(t, \omega) = \bar{x}_t \quad \text{a.e.,} \qquad t = -n + 1, \dots, 0.$$

(ii) There exists on $(\Omega, \mathscr{F}, P(\cdot))$ a real-valued, purely random process $\eta = \{\eta(t, \omega): t = \ldots, -1, 0, 1, \ldots\}$ with mean zero and finite positive variance σ_η^2, and two sequences of constants $\{a_k: k = 0, \ldots, n\}$, $\{\alpha_s: s = \ldots, -1, 0, 1, \ldots\}$ such that $a_0 = \alpha_0 = 1$, $a_n \neq 0$, and

$$\sum_{s=-\infty}^{\infty} \alpha_s^2 < \infty, \tag{33.25}$$

$$\sum_{k=0}^{n} a_k x(t-k, \omega) = \sum_{s=-\infty}^{\infty} \alpha_s \eta(t+s, \omega), \qquad t = 1, 2, \ldots. \tag{33.26}$$

(iii) There exist a positive integer l_0, nonnegative integers l_j, and complex constants z_j, $j = 1, \ldots, l$, such that

$$\sum_{k=0}^{n} a_k z^{n-k} = (z-1)^{l_0} \prod_{j=1}^{l} (z - z_j)^{l_j}, \tag{33.27}$$

$$|z_j| < 1, \qquad j = 1, \ldots, l. \tag{33.28}$$

In interpreting this definition, note that, when $n = 1$ and $\alpha_s = 0$ for $s \neq 0$, then x is a simple one-dimensional random walk. Note also that Box and Jenkins always assume that $n = l_0$, that $\alpha_s = 0$ for $s > 0$, and that $|\alpha_s| \leqslant K\beta^{|s|}$ for some $\beta \in (0, 1)$ and some suitably large constant K.

33.2.1 The Short and Long Run Behavior of ARIMA Processes

The short run behavior of an ARIMA process is delineated in T 33.1.

T 33.1 Suppose that $\{x(t, \omega); t = -n+1, -n+2, \ldots\}$ is an ARIMA process and let $\{\eta(t, \omega); t = 1, 2, \ldots\}$ be the associated η process. Also let

$$y(t, \omega) = \sum_{s=-\infty}^{\infty} \alpha_s \eta(t+s, \omega), \qquad t = 1, 2, \ldots. \tag{33.29}$$

Then there exist a function $\varphi(\cdot)$ and a sequence of real constants γ_s such that

$$\gamma_0 = 1, \tag{33.30}$$

$$\sum_{k=0}^{v} a_k \gamma_{v-k} = 0, \qquad v = 1, \ldots, n-1, \tag{33.31}$$

$$\sum_{k=0}^{n} a_k \gamma_{v-k} = 0, \qquad v = n, n+1, \ldots, \tag{33.32}$$

$$\varphi(t) = \bar{x}_{t'}, \qquad t = -n+1, \ldots, 0, \tag{33.33}$$

$$\sum_{k=0}^{n} a_k \varphi(t-k) = 0, \qquad t = 1, 2, \ldots, \tag{33.34}$$

$$x(t, \omega) = \varphi(t) + \sum_{s=0}^{t-1} \gamma_s y(t - s, \omega), \qquad t = 1, 2, \ldots. \tag{33.35}$$

The existence of a function $\varphi(\cdot)$ and a set of constants γ_s that satisfy equations 33.33 and 33.35 is easy to verify. So we will not prove it here. To establish equations 33.30–33.32 and 33.34 we use equations 33.26, 33.29, and 33.35 to note that, for all $t = 1, 2, \ldots$ and $n' = \min\{n, t-1\}$,

$$\begin{aligned}
y(t, \omega) &= \sum_{k=0}^{n} a_k x(t - k, \omega) \\
&= \sum_{k=0}^{n} a_k \varphi(t - k) + \sum_{k=0}^{n'} a_k \sum_{s=0}^{t-k-1} \gamma_s y(t - k - s, \omega) \\
&= \sum_{k=0}^{n} a_k \varphi(t - k) + \sum_{k=0}^{n'} a_k \sum_{v=k}^{t-1} \gamma_{v-k} y(t - v, \omega) \\
&= \sum_{k=0}^{n} a_k \varphi(t - k) + \sum_{v=0}^{n'-1} \left(\sum_{k=0}^{v} a_k \gamma_{v-k} \right) y(t - v, \omega) \\
&\quad + \sum_{v=n'}^{t-1} \left(\sum_{k=0}^{n'} a_k \gamma_{v-k} \right) y(t - v, \omega).
\end{aligned} \tag{33.36}$$

Since equation 33.36 is an identity in ω, it implies the validity of equations 33.30–33.32 and 33.34.

Theorem T 33.1, can be used to study the long-run behavior of ARIMA processes. To see how, let $x(t, \cdot)$ and $y(t, \cdot)$ be as in T 33.1 and note first that equations 33.33, 33.34, and 33.27 imply that there exist constants A_{jk}, $j = 1, \ldots, l$; $k = 0, \ldots, l_j - 1$, and B_k, $k = 0, \ldots, l_0 - 1$, such that

$$\varphi(t) = \sum_{j=1}^{l} \sum_{k=0}^{l_j - 1} A_{jk}(t^k z_j^t) + \sum_{k=0}^{l_0 - 1} B_k t^k, \qquad t = -n + 1, \ldots. \tag{33.37}$$

Since by 33.28, $|z_j| < 1$ for all j, equation 32.37 implies that the "trend line" $\varphi(\cdot)$ satisfies the asymptotic relation

$$\varphi(t) t^{-(l_0 - 1)} \sim B_{l_0 - 1}, \tag{33.38}$$

the sign $\sim$ indicating that the ratio of the two sides in equation 33.38 tends to unity as $t \to \infty$.

Next , note that equations 33.30–33.32, 33.26, and 33.27 imply that there exist constants C_{jk}, $j = 1, \ldots, l$; $k = 0, \ldots, l_j - 1$, and d_k, $k = 0, \ldots, l_0 - 1$, such that

$$D_{l_0-1} \neq 0, \tag{33.39}$$

and

$$\gamma_s = \sum_{j=1}^{l} \sum_{k=0}^{l_j-1} C_{jk}(s^k z_j^s) + \sum_{k=0}^{l_0-1} D_k s^k, \qquad s = 0, 1, \ldots. \tag{33.40}$$

Thus γ_s, for large enough s, satisfies the approximate relation

$$\gamma_s s^{-(l_0-1)} \sim D_{l_0-1}. \tag{33.41}$$

Finally, note that if we assume that

$$0 < \left| \sum_{s=-\infty}^{\infty} \alpha_s \right| \tag{33.42}$$

and that the function

$$f_y(\lambda) = \left| \sum_{s=-\infty}^{\infty} \alpha_s e^{-is\lambda} \right|^2 \sigma_\eta^2, \qquad \lambda \in [-\pi, \pi), \tag{33.43}$$

is piecewise continuous on $(-\pi, \pi)$ and continuous in a neighborhood of $\lambda = 0$, then, by lemma 1 in Stigum 1974, for all nonnegative integers q,

$$\lim_{T\to\infty} P\left(\left\{\omega \in \Omega : \sum_{t=1}^{T} t^q y(t, \omega) \left\{\frac{T^{2q+1} f_y(0)}{2q+1}\right\}^{-1/2} < z\right\}\right)$$
$$= (2\pi)^{-1/2} \int_{-\infty}^{z} \exp\left[\frac{1}{2}u^2\right] du. \tag{33.44}$$

Consequently, if we denote $D_{l_0-1} \sum_{s=0}^{t-1} s^{l_0-1} y(t-s)$ by $\tilde{S}_t$ and observe that

$$\tilde{S}_t(\omega) = D_{l_0-1} \sum_{k=0}^{l_0-1} \binom{l_0 - 1}{k} t^{l_0-1-k} \sum_{v=1}^{t} (-v)^k y(v, \omega), \tag{33.45}$$

we find that there exists a normally distributed random variable ρ with mean zero and variance

$$\tilde{\sigma}^2 = f_y(0) D_{l_0-1}^2 \sum_{k=0}^{l_0-1} \sum_{m=0}^{l_0-1} \binom{l_0 - 1}{k} \binom{l_0 - 1}{m} (-1)^{k+m} (k + m + 1)^{-1}$$
$$= \frac{f_y(0) D_{l_0-1}^2}{2l_0 - 1} \tag{33.46}$$

such that, for large enough t and for all $a \in (-\infty, \infty)$,

$$P(\{\omega \in \Omega : \tilde{S}_t(\omega)t^{-(l_0-1/2)} < a\}) \sim F_\rho(a)$$

$$= (2\pi\tilde{\sigma}^2)^{-1/2} \int_{-\infty}^{a} \exp[-(1/2\tilde{\sigma}^2)u^2]\,du. \qquad (33.47)$$

Evidently, if equation 33.42 is satisfied, then equations 33.38, 33.39, 33.41, and 33.44–33.47 imply that, for large t, the behavior of $x(t)$ is completely dominated by the behavior of $\tilde{S}_t$. From this fact and from equation 33.47 we infer the validity of T 33.2 below. A formal proof of it is given in Stigum 1975 (p. 327).

T 33.2 Suppose that $\{x(t, \omega); t = -n + 1, -n + 2, \ldots\}$ is an ARIMA process and let $\{\eta(t, \omega); t \in T$ be the associated η process. Also, let $\{y(t, \omega); t \in T\}$, $f_y(\cdot)$ and $\tilde{\sigma}^2$, respectively, be as described in equations 33.29, 33.43, and 33.46. Finally, assume that $f_y(\cdot)$ is piecewise continuous on $[-\pi, \pi)$ and continuous in a neighborhood of $\lambda = 0$. Then, for all $z \in R$,

$$\lim_{t\to\infty} P(x(t)\tilde{\sigma}^{-1}t^{-(l_0-1/2)} < z) = \lim_{t\to\infty} P((x(t) - \varphi(t))\tilde{\sigma}^{-1}t^{-(l_0-1/2)} < z)$$

$$= (2\pi)^{-1/2} \int_{-\infty}^{z} \exp\left[\frac{1}{2}u^2\right] du. \qquad (33.48)$$

This theorem characterizes the asymptotic distribution of $x(t)$. We can also characterize the asymptotic behavior of x by giving upper bounds on the growth of $|x(t)|$ and by estimating the fraction of time $x(t)$ spends above the trend line $\varphi(\cdot)$. This is done in theorems T 33.3 and T 33.4.

33.2.2 An Invariance Principle and the Associated Wiener Measures

Before I state T 33.3, I must introduce certain notational conventions and state an invariance principle. Let $C([0, 1])$ denote the set of continuous functions on $[0, 1]$ to R, and let distances between functions in $C([0, 1])$ be measured by the sup norm; i.e., for each x, $y \in C([0, 1])$, let the distance between x and y be given by $\|x - y\| = \sup_{t\in[0,1]}|x(t) - y(t)|$. Also let $\mathscr{C}$ denote the class of Borel sets in $C([0, 1])$; i.e., let $\mathscr{C}$ be the smallest σ field that contains all the subsets of $C([0, 1])$ that are open in the topology determined by $\|\cdot\|$. Finally, for each $\tau \in [0, 1]$, let $\pi^\tau(\cdot)$: $C([0, 1]) \to R$ be defined by $\pi^\tau(x) = x(\tau)$, $x \in C([0, 1])$. Then the $\pi^\tau(\cdot)$ are continuous functions on $C([0, 1])$ and, by T 22.21, $\mathscr{C}$ is the smallest σ field of subsets of $C([0, 1])$ with respect to which the $\pi^\tau(\cdot)$ are measurable.

For the invariance principle I have in mind, the experiment $(C([0,1]), \mathscr{C})$ is not large enough. The experiment I require can be described as follows: Let $D([0, 1])$ be the set of functions on $[0, 1]$ to R that are right-continuous and have left-hand limits; and let Δ denote the set of strictly increasing, continuous functions from [0, 1] onto [0, 1]. Also let $d(\cdot)$ denote the function that measures distances of functions in $D([0, 1])$ and define $d(\cdot)$ by

$$d(x, y) = \inf_{\lambda \in \Delta} \left(\sup_{t \in [0,1]} |x(t) - y(\lambda(t))| + |t - \lambda(t)| \right).$$

The topology for $D([0, 1])$ determined by $d(\cdot)$ is called the *Skorohod topology* and is described in detail in Parthasarathy 1967, pp. 231–248. Finally, let $\mathscr{D}$ denote the class of Borel sets in $D([0, 1])$; i.e., let $\mathscr{D}$ be the smallest σ field of subsets of $D([0, 1])$ that contains all the sets that are open in the Skorohod topology. Then $\mathscr{D}$ is the smallest σ field of subsets of $D([0, 1])$ with respect to which the extensions to $D([0, 1])$ of the $\pi^{\tau}(\cdot)$ are measurable; and $(D([0, 1]), \mathscr{D})$ is the experiment for which we search.

In section 22.5.3 we established the existence of the Wiener measure on $(C([0, 1]), \mathscr{C})$. This result can be extended as follows.

UT 24 For each $q = 0, 1, \ldots$, there exists a probability measure $\hat{W}_q(\cdot)$ on $(D([0, 1]), \mathscr{D})$ with the following properties:

(i) For each $\tau \in (0, 1]$ and $\alpha \in (-\infty, \infty)$,

$$\hat{W}_q(\{x \in D([0, 1]) : x(\tau) < \alpha\}) = (2\pi\tau^{2q+1})^{-1/2} \int_{-\infty}^{\alpha} \exp[(-1/2)u^2\tau^{-(2q+1)}]\, du,$$

and for $\tau = 0$,

$$\hat{W}_q(\{x \in D([0, 1]) : x(0) = 0\}) = 1.$$

(ii) For each finite m-tuple $(\tau_1, \ldots, \tau_m)$ such that $0 \leqslant \tau_1 < \cdots < \tau_m \leqslant 1$, the vector $(x(\tau_1), \ldots, x(\tau_m))$ is normally distributed with mean zero and covariance matrix

$$\Gamma(\tau_1, \ldots, \tau_m) = \{\mu_{\tau_i, \tau_j}\}_{1 \leqslant i, j \leqslant m},$$

where, for $k = \min\{i, j\}$ and $p = \max\{i, j\}$,

$$\mu_{\tau_i, \tau_j} = (2q + 1)\tau_k^{q+1} \sum_{u=0}^{q} \binom{q}{u} (\tau_p - \tau_k)^u \tau_k^{q-u} (2q + 1 - u)^{-1}.$$

(iii) The stochastic process $\{x(\tau): \tau \in [0, 1]\}$ is continuous a.e. under $\hat{W}_q(\cdot)$.

I state this theorem here for ease of reference and without proof. A detailed proof is given in Stigum 1975 (pp. 327–330).

The invariance principle I seek to establish concerns all processes consisting of independently and identically distributed random variables with finite fourth moments. I state the principle in the form of a universal theorem:

UT 25 Let $(\Omega, \mathscr{F}, P(\cdot))$ be a probability space; let $\{\eta(t,\omega); -\infty < t < \infty\}$ be a purely random process on $(\Omega, \mathscr{F}, P(\cdot))$ with mean zero and finite variance σ_η^2; let $A_0 = 0$; and let

$$A_i = \sum_{j=1}^{i} (i-j)^q \eta(j), \qquad i = 1, 2, \ldots.$$

Moreover, for each $\tau \in [0,1]$ and $n = 1, 2, \ldots$, let $[n\tau]$ denote the largest integer k such that $k \leqslant n\tau$; and let

$$\hat{X}_n(\tau) = (2q+1)^{1/2}\sigma_\eta^{-1} n^{-(q+1/2)} A_{[n\tau]}, \; \tau \in [0,1],$$

Finally, let $\hat{P}_n(\cdot)$ denote the distribution of $\hat{X}_n(\cdot)$ on $(D([0,1]), \mathscr{D})$, and assume that $E\eta(t)^4 < \infty$. Then the $\hat{P}_n(\cdot)$ converge weakly to $\hat{W}_q(\cdot)$.

For $q = 0$ this invariance principle (without the fourth moment assumption on the $\eta(t)$) is due to Donsker (1967). A proof of UT 25 as stated is given in Stigum 1975 (p. 330).

Donsker called his theorem an invariance principle because the limiting distribution of the $\hat{P}_n(\cdot)$ is independent of the $\eta(t)$'s probability distribution. Often Donsker's theorem is referred to as *the* invariance principle. The reason is that if $h(\cdot)$: $C([0,1]) \to R$ is a continuous function, e.g., if $h(x) = \sup_{t \in [0,1]} x(t)$, the limiting probability distribution of $h(\hat{X}_n(\cdot))$ as $n \to \infty$ is the distribution of $h(\cdot)$ on $(D([0,1], \mathscr{D})$ determined by $\hat{W}_q(\cdot)$; and the latter distribution is independent of the $\eta(t)$'s probability distribution. This is interesting because it allows us to make simplifying assumptions on the distribution of the $\hat{X}_n$ when we compute the limiting distribution of $h(\hat{X}_n)$. And if such simplifying assumptions are of no help, the possibility still exists that we can find the limiting distribution directly by computing the distribution of $h(\cdot)$ on $(D([0,1], \mathscr{D})$ under $\hat{W}_q(\cdot)$.

33.2.3 The Invariance Principle and the Long Run of ARIMA Processes

For the purpose of studying the long-run behavior of ARIMA processes we must establish an analogue of UT 25 in which the η process is replaced by a wide-sense stationary process. The required theorem is UT 26.

UT 26 Suppose that $\{y(t,\omega), t = 1, 2, \ldots\}$ satisfies equations 33.29, 33.25, and 33.42. Suppose also that the $\eta(t)$ in equation 33.29 constitute a purely random process with mean zero, finite variance σ_η^2, and finite fourth moments and that the function $f_y(\cdot)$ defined in equations 33.43 is piecewise continuous on $[-\pi, \pi]$ and continuous in a neighborhood of $\lambda = 0$. Finally, let

$$\psi(s) = \begin{cases} 1 & \text{if } s > 0 \\ 0 & \text{otherwise} \end{cases} \tag{33.49}$$

let

$$S_T = \sum_{s=1}^{T} (T-s)^q y(s), \qquad T = 1, 2, \ldots,$$

where q is a nonnegative integer, and let

$$h(x) = \int_{\{\tau\in[0,1]:x(\tau)>0\}} d\tau, \qquad x \in D([0,1]). \tag{33.50}$$

Then

$$\lim_{T\to\infty} P\left(\left\{\omega\in\Omega : T^{-1}\sum_{t=1}^{T}\Psi(S_t) < \beta\right\}\right) = \hat{W}_q(\{x\in D([0,1]) : h(x) < \beta\}), \tag{33.51}$$

where $\beta \in [0, 1]$ ranges over the set of continuity points of the distribution of $h(\cdot)$ under $\hat{W}_q(\cdot)$ and where $\hat{W}_q(\cdot)$ is as described in UT 25.

A proof of UT 26 is given in Stigum 1975 (pp. 330–336). In reading UT 26, it is interesting to observe that equation 33.51 represents a generalization of the Arc Sine Law of T 16.3. To see why, observe that if

$$x(t) = x(t-1) + \eta(t), \qquad t = 1, 2, \ldots,$$

and the $\eta(t)$ constitute a purely random process with mean zero and finite variance. Then, for $t = 1, 2, \ldots,$

$$x(t) = x(0) + \sum_{s=1}^{t}\eta(s) = x(0) + \sum_{s=1}^{t}(t-s)^0\eta(s),$$

which suggests that the limiting distribution in equation 33.51 reduces to the Arc Sine Law when $q = 0$. That this is in fact the case is asserted in the last half of the next theorem, and is a consequence of T 16.3 and UT 25.

T 33.3 Suppose that $\{x(t,\omega); t = -n+1, -n+2, \ldots\}$ is an ARIMA process that satisfies the conditions of T 33.2. Suppose also that the associated $\eta(t,\omega)$ have finite fourth moments. Finally, let $\Psi(\cdot): R \to \{0, 1\}$ be as defined in equation 33.49 and let

$$N_T = \sum_{t=1}^{T}\Psi(x(t) - \varphi(t)), \qquad T = 1, 2, \ldots.$$

Then

$$\lim_{T\to\infty} P(\{\omega\in\Omega : N_T/T < \beta\}) = \hat{W}_{l_0-1}(\{x\in D([0,1]) : h(x) < \beta\}), \tag{33.52}$$

where $h(x)$ is as defined in equation 33.50 and β ranges over the set of continuity points of the distribution of $h(\cdot)$ under $\hat{W}_{l_0-1}$. When $l_0 = 1$,

$$\hat{W}_q(\{x\in D([0,1]) : h(x) < \beta\}) = (2/\pi)\arcsin\beta^{1/2}, \ \beta\in[0,1]. \tag{33.53}$$

The proof of this theorem is involved. So I shall only sketch a few of the details here: We first appeal to equation 33.38 and deduce that

$$\lim_{t\to\infty} \varphi(t)t^{-(l_0-1/2)} = 0. \tag{33.54}$$

Next we use Stigum 1972 (lemma 6) and some algebra to show that, for all $j = 1, \ldots, l$ and $k = 0, \ldots, l_j - 1$,

$$\lim_{t\to\infty} t^{-(l_0-1/2)} \sum_{s=0}^{t-1} s^k z_j^s y(t-s) = 0 \quad \text{a.e.} \tag{33.55}$$

Finally, we let $R_y(t-s) = Ey(t)y(s)$ and observe that, for $k = 0, 1, \ldots, l_0 - 1$,

$$E\{t^{-(l_0-1/2)} \sum_{s=0}^{t-1} s^k y(t-s)\}^2 = t^{-(2l_0-1)} \sum_{s,r=0}^{t-1} s^k r^k R_y(r-s); \tag{33.56}$$

$$\lim_{t\to\infty} t^{-(2k+1)} \sum_{s,r=0}^{t-1} s^k r^k R_y(r-s) = (2k+1)^{-1} f_y(0); \tag{33.57}$$

and

$$2l_0 - 1 - 2k - 1 = 2(l_0 - k) - 2. \tag{33.58}$$

From equations 33.54–33.58 and the Borel-Cantelli lemma (i.e., T 16.1), it follows that if $l_0 > 1$, then for $k = 0, \ldots, l_0 - 2$,

$$\lim_{t\to\infty} t^{-(l_0-1/2)} \sum_{s=0}^{t-1} s^k y(t-s) = 0 \quad \text{a.e.} \tag{33.59}$$

But if equations 33.54, 33.55, and 33.59 are true, then the validity of T 33.3 becomes an immediate consequence of equations 33.39, 33.40 and 33.46 and UT 26.

Theorem T 33.3 is, from an econometric point of view, a very interesting theorem. From our discussion of T 16.3 it follows that when $l_0 = 1$, equations 33.52 and 33.53 imply that the chances are 1 in 10 that $x(t)$ will be larger than $\varphi(t)$ for more than 97.6 percent of the time. The chances are 1 in 5 that $x(t)$ will be larger than $\varphi(t)$ for at least 90.5 percent of the time. Similar estimates hold for the likelihood that $x(t)$ will be less than $\varphi(t)$. The fact that $x(t)$ with such a large probability will either be greater than $\varphi(t)$ most of the time or smaller than $\varphi(t)$ most of the time, and the fact that $\varphi(t)$ for large t is dominated by $\tilde{S}_t$ (see equation 33.45) makes it nearly impossible, when $l_0 = 1$, to use observations on $x(t)$ to estimate $\varphi(t)$.

We have not been able to derive the distribution of $h(\cdot)$ under $\hat{W}_{l_0-1}$ for $l_0 > 1$. However, the results of the simulation experiment on an ARIMA process with $l_0 = 2$ presented in E 33.2 below suggest that the chances of estimating $\varphi(t)$ from time-series observation on $x(\cdot)$ are, if anything, poorer when $l_0 > 1$ than when $l_0 = 1$. To see why, compare the result of Feller's simultation experiment on the standard random walk (Feller 1957, figure 5, p. 84) with the result of my simulation experiment (see figures 33.1 and 33.2). One striking difference is that Feller's process seems to change sign much more frequently than my process. In fact, the number of changes of sign of an ordinary random walk grows (very roughly speaking) as some constant multiple of $\sqrt{t}$, while the number of changes of sign of my process for $l_0 > 1$ grows as some constant multiple of $\log t$.

E 33.2 Let $\{x(t); t = -2, -1, \ldots\}$ be an ARIMA process which satisfies the equations,

$$x(t) - 2.5x(t-1) + 2x(t-2) - 0.5x(t-3) = \eta(t),$$

$$x(-2) = 1, \quad x(-1) = 0.7, \quad x(0) = 0.5.$$

In this case $n = 3$ and

$$\sum_{k=0}^{3} a_k z^{3-k} = (z-1)^2(z-0.5).$$

Moreover,

$$\varphi(t) = 0.4 - 0.1t + 0.1(0.5)^t, \quad t = -2, -1, \ldots,$$

$$\gamma_s = 0.2 + 1.9s + 0.8(0.5)^s, \quad s = 0, 1, \ldots,$$

$$\tilde{\sigma}^2 = \tfrac{1}{3}(1.9)^2\sigma_\eta^2.$$

Consequently, by equation 33.47, for all $z \in (-\infty, \infty)$,

$$\lim_{t\to\infty} P\left(x(t)\left[\frac{1}{3}(1.9)^2\sigma_\eta^2 t^3\right]^{-1/2} < z\right) = (2\pi)^{-1/2}\int_{-\infty}^{z} \exp\left[-\frac{1}{2}u^2\right] du. \tag{33.60}$$

Moreover, by equation 33.52, for all $\beta \in (0, 1]$ which are continuity points of the distribution of $h(\cdot)$ under $\hat{W}_1$,

$$\lim_{T\to\infty} P\left(T^{-1}\sum_{t=1}^{T} \psi(x(t) - 0.4 + 0.1t - 0.1(0.5)^t) < \beta\right)$$
$$= \hat{W}_1(x \in D([0, 1]) : h(x) < \beta). \tag{33.61}$$

To bring home the implications of equations 33.60 and 33.61 for time-series analysis of X, I have simulated the behavior of $x(t)$, for $t = 1, 2, \ldots, 10{,}000$. The results of the simulations are presented in the two graphs of figures 33.1 and 33.2 which picture one (!) realization of X under the assumption that η is a (pseudo-) Bernoulli process with

$$P\left\{\eta(t) = 1\right\} = P\left\{\eta(t) = -1\right\} = \frac{1}{2}.$$

Dr. Jaffar Al-Abdulla wrote the required computer program for me. He used the generating method described in the reference manual for the 1108 computer at

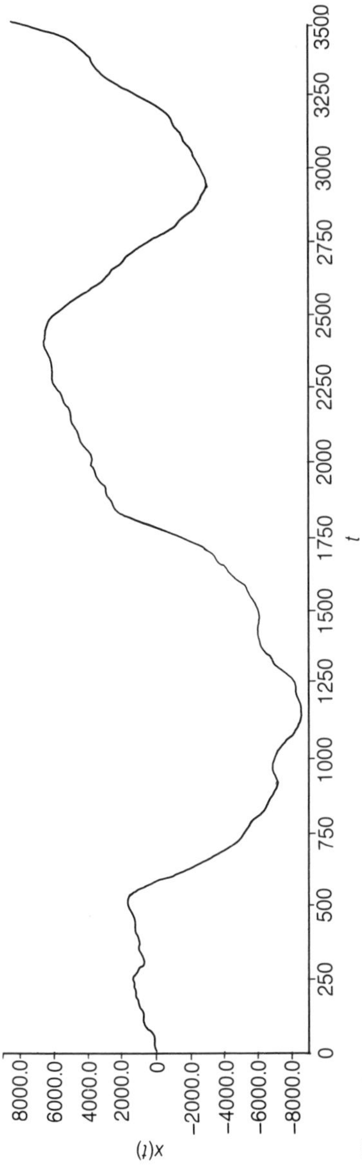

Figure 33.1
Sample path of $x(t)$ for $0 \leqslant t \leqslant 3500$.

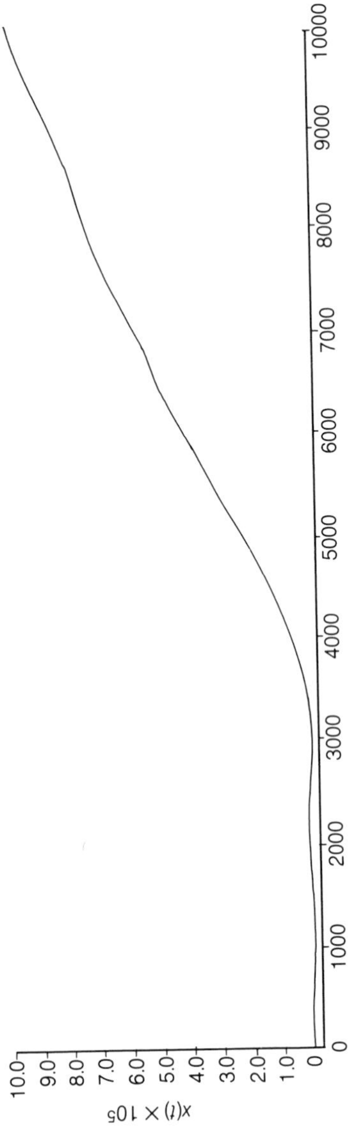

Figure 33.2
Sample path of $x(t)$ for $0 \leqslant t \leqslant 10{,}000$.

the University of Wisconsin Computing Center. In studying the figures, note that the maximum value of $x(\cdot)$ in figure 33.2 is 985236.0. In contrast, $\varphi(10000\} = -999.6$.

So much for T 33.3. The next and last theorem of this section establishes bounds on the growth pattern of an ARIMA process. The theorem insists that, whatever the positive value of ε, with probability 1

$$\varphi(t) - [2\tilde{\sigma}^2 t^{2l_0-1} \log\log t]^{1/2}(1+\varepsilon) \leqslant x(t)$$

$$\leqslant \varphi(t) + [2\tilde{\sigma}^2 t^{2l_0-1} \log\log t]^{1/2}(1+\varepsilon)$$

for all but a finite number of values of t, and for infinitely many t, either

$$x(t) \leqslant \varphi(t) - [2\tilde{\sigma}^2 t^{2l_0-1} \log\log t]^{1/2}(1-\varepsilon),$$

or

$$x(t) \geqslant \varphi(t) + [2\tilde{\sigma}^2 t^{2l_0-1} \log\log t)^{1/2}(1-\varepsilon).$$

Since the proof of the theorem is involved and has been published elsewhere (see Stigum, 1975, pp. 337–343), I omit it here.

T 33.4 Suppose that $\{x(t,\omega); t = -1+1, -n+2, \ldots\}$ is an ARIMA process which satisfies the conditions of T 33.2 and let $\tilde{\sigma}^2$ be as defined in equation 33.46. Then

$$\limsup_{t\to\infty} \{|(x(t,\omega) - \varphi(t))/(2\tilde{\sigma}^2 t^{2l_0-1} \log\log t)^{1/2}|\} = 1 \quad \text{a.e.}$$

I believe that the characteristics of an ARIMA process which are described in T 33.1–T 33.4 are such that it would be unreasonable to postulate that an economic time series is generated by an ARIMA process. Since a GARIMA process is simply a process $\{x(t); t = -m+1, -m+2, \ldots\}$ for which there exist an ARIMA process $\{y(t); t = -n+1, -n+2, \ldots\}$ and nonnegative integers, s, d_s, c, and d_c, such that

$$x(t) = (1 - S^{-s})^{d_s}(1 - S^{-c})^{d_c} y(t),$$

a GARIMA process cannot generate an economic time series either.

33.3 Dynamic Stochastic Processes

In this section we shall characterize the behavior of a dynamic stochastic process. We begin with a few remarks concerning second-order processes. Unless otherwise stated, the time parameter varies over $T = (\ldots, -1, 0, 1, \ldots)$.

A second-order stochastic process is a family of real- or complex-valued random variables, $X = \{x(t, \omega); t \in T\}$, on some probability space $(\Omega, \mathcal{F}, P(\cdot))$ with the property that

$$E|x(t, \omega)|^2 = \int_\Omega |x(t, \omega)|^2 \, dP(\omega) < \infty$$

for all $t \in T$. If, in addition, $Ex(t, \omega) = 0$, $t \in T$, and the numbers $Ex(t + s, \omega)\overline{x(t, \omega)}$, $s \in T$ are independent of t, then X is called a wide-sense stationary process. Finally, if X is wide-sense stationary and the $x(t, \cdot)$ are independently and identically distributed, then X is a purely random process. The theory of second-order processes was first developed by M. Loève (see Loève 1960, chapter X).

When $X = \{x(t, \omega); t \in T\}$ is a second-order process, X generates a Hilbert space in the following way: let L_x be the linear manifold of all random variables of the form $\sum_{j=1}^n b_j x(t_j, \omega)$, where $t_j \in T$ and the b_j's are complex constants.[3] Moreover, define the inner product on L_x by

$$\langle z, v \rangle = \int_\Omega z(\omega)\overline{v(\omega)} \, dP(\omega).$$

Finally, let

$$\|z\|^2 = \langle z, z \rangle.$$

Then $\|\cdot\|$ defines a norm on L_x. The completion of L in this norm[4] is a Hilbert space.[5] We will denote it by $L\{x(t, \omega)\colon t \in T\}$.

Associated with a given second-order process X there is a linear operator S on L with the property that, for all $t \in T$,

$$x(t + 1, \omega) = Sx(t, \omega) \text{ a.e. with respect to } P.$$

S is called a *shift operator*.[6] Moreover, S is said to be uniquely defined if it is uniquely defined modulo an ω set of P-measure zero. Finally, S is said to be null-preserving if $z(\omega) = v(\omega)$ a.e. implies that $Sz(\omega) = Sv(\omega)$ a.e. The shift operators dealt with in this chapter are always assumed to be null-preserving.

33.3.1 A Definition and Illustrative Examples

Let $X = \{x(t, \omega); t \in T\}$ be a second-order process and let $X_2 = L\{x(t, \omega); t \in T\}$. We say that X is a *dynamic stochastic process* if

(i) the $x(t, \omega)$'s can be represented by the relation

$$x(t, \omega) = y(t, \omega) + f_x(t, \omega), \qquad t \in T, \tag{33.62}$$

where $Y = \{y(t, \omega); t \in T\}$ is a wide-sense stationary process, and where $F = \{f_x(t, \omega); t \in T\}$ is a nonstationary stochastic process of the form

$$f_x(t, \omega) = \sum_{j=1}^{\alpha} \sum_{k=0}^{n_j - 1} A_{jk}(\omega)(z_j^t t^k), \qquad t \in T; \tag{33.63}$$

and

(ii) $X_2 = L\{y(t, \omega); t \in T\} \oplus L\{f_x(t, \omega); t \in T\}$, where $\oplus$ is used instead of $+$ to indicate that the two spaces are linearly independent whenever $y(t, \omega)$ and/or $f_x(t, \omega)$ do not vanish a.e. for all $t \in T$.

Note that in this definition it is not necessary to assume that $T = (\ldots, -1, 0, 1, \ldots)$. So in examples E 33.3 and E 33.4 below we let t range over the set $\{0, 1, \ldots\}$.

Note also that the z_j in equation 33.63 are complex constants, and that the $x(t, \omega)$ need not be real. Since we would not gain anything by restricting our remarks to real-valued processes, we will here argue as if X were complex. The results obtained will be valid for real processes too.

To derive the properties of dynamic stochastic processes we begin by discussing two simple examples.

E 33.3 Let $X = \{x(t, \omega); t = 0, 1, \ldots\}$ be a second-order stochastic process. Moreover, suppose that there exists a constant a such that

$$x(t, \omega) - ax(t-1, \omega) = 0, \qquad t = 1, 2, \ldots. \tag{33.64}$$

By simple iteration we find that $x(t, \omega)$ has the following functional form:

$$x(t, \omega) = x(0, \omega)a^t, \qquad t \geqslant 0. \tag{33.65}$$

Hence X is a dynamic stochastic process.

The conceptual experiment underlying the X process of E 33.3 can be thought of as determining the value of $x(0)$. Thereafter the values of the other $x(t)$'s are determined by equation 33.65.

A general characterization of dynamic stochastic processes which satisfy an equation of the form of equation 33.64 is obtained in the following theorem:

T 33.5 Let $\{x(t, \omega); t \in T\}$ be a second-order stochastic process. Then there exist constants $a_1, \ldots, a_n$ such that (with $a_0 \equiv 1$)

$$\sum_{k=0}^{n} a_k x(t-k, \omega) = 0, \qquad t \in T, \tag{33.66}$$

if and only if there are constants z_j, $j = 1, \ldots, \alpha$, and random variables $A_{jk}(\omega)$, $j = 1, \ldots, \alpha$, $k = 0, 1, \ldots, n_j - 1$, with finite second moments such that

$$x(t, \omega) = \sum_{j=1}^{\alpha} \sum_{k=0}^{n_j - 1} A_{jk}(\omega)(z_j^t t^k), \qquad t \in T. \tag{33.67}$$

Except for the appearance of ω in equations 33.66 and 33.67, this theorem can be recognized as a standard theorem in the theory of linear difference equations. The z_j's are the roots of the characteristic polynomial $\sum_{k=0}^{n} a_k z^{n-k}$, n_j is the multiplicity of z_j, and the $A_{jk}(\cdot)$'s can be written as linear combinations of n different $x(t, \cdot)$'s—the so-called initial values.

Next consider the following example:

E 33.4 Suppose that $X = \{x(t, \omega); t = 0, 1, \ldots\}$ is a second-order process. Suppose also that X satisfies the equation

$$x(t, \omega) - ax(t - 1, \omega) = \eta(t, \omega), \qquad t = 1, 2, \ldots, \tag{33.68}$$

where $a > 1$ and $\eta = \{\eta(t, \omega); t = 1, 2, \ldots\}$ is a purely random process. By simple iteration we find that

$$x(t, \omega) = \sum_{s=0}^{t-1} a^s \eta(t - s, \omega) + x(0, \omega)a^t, \qquad t \geqslant 1. \tag{33.69}$$

Since $\{\sum_{s=0}^{t-1} a^s \eta(t - s, \omega); t = 1, 2, \ldots\}$ is not a wide-sense stationary process, the equations in 33.69 seem to preclude the possibility that X is a dynamic stochastic process. However, if we let

$$y(t, \omega) = -\sum_{s=1}^{\infty} a^{-s} \eta(t + s, \omega), \qquad t = 0, 1, \ldots, \tag{33.70}$$

and

$$f_x(t, \omega) = x(t, \omega) - y(t, \omega), \qquad t = 0, 1, \ldots,$$

we find that $Y = \{y(t, \omega); t \in T\}$ is a wide-sense stationary process which satisfies equation 33.68, and that

$$f_x(t, \omega) - af_x(t - 1, \omega) = 0, \qquad t = 0, 1, \ldots.$$

Thus the $x(t, \omega)$ can be represented by

$$x(t, \omega) = y(t, \omega) + f_x(0, \omega)a^t, \qquad t = 0, 1, \ldots.$$

Consequently, if $f_x(t, \omega) \notin L\{y(t, \omega); t \in T\}$, then X is, in fact, a dynamic stochastic process on account of equations 33.62 and 33.63.

It we let $y(t, \omega)$ be as defined in equation 33.70, and let

$$u(t, \omega) = y(t, \omega) + \eta(s, \omega)a^t, \qquad t \geqslant 0,$$

for some $s \in \{1, 2, \ldots\}$, then $U = \{u(t, \omega); t \in T\}$ is a second-order process which satisfies equation 33.68 and yet is not a dynamic stochastic process. The reason is that $\eta(s, \omega)a^t \in L\{y(t, \omega); t \in T\}$ for all $t \geqslant 0$.

33.3.2 Fundamental Theorems

The preceding examples serve to motivate my main theorem, T 33.6.[7]

T 33.6 Let $X = \{x(t, \omega); t \in T\}$ be a second-order process and suppose that

(i) the shift operator S associated with X is uniquely defined on L_x, has a unique extension to X_2 that is continuous, and has a continuous inverse S^{-1};

(ii) the complex polynomial $M(z) = \sum_{j=0}^{n} b_j z^{-j}$ has no roots of modulus equal to 1, and X satisfies

$$M(S)x(t, \omega) = \eta(t, \omega), \qquad t \in T, \tag{33.71}$$

where $\eta = \{\eta(t, \omega); t \in T\}$ is a wide-sense stationary process. Then X is a dynamic stochastic process.

Conversely, if X is a dynamic stochastic process and if the z_j in equation 33.63 satisfy $|z_j| \neq 1$, then the shift operator S associated with X satisfies assumption (i), and there is a minimal polynomial $M(z)$ with all roots different from 1 such that $\{M(S)x(t, \omega); t \in T\}$ is a wide-sense stationary process.

The proof of this theorem follows. First a few preliminary observations: Let $L_2 = L\{\eta(t, \omega); t \in T\}$. We observe that the assumptions of the theorem imply that $L_2 \subset X_2$ and that L_2 reduces S in the sense that S maps L_2 into itself. Next, let S_1 be the restriction of S to L_2. We use equation 33.71 to show that S_1 is uniquely defined by the relation $S_1\eta(t, \omega) = \eta(t + 1, \omega)$, $t \in T$. Finally, we observe that S_1 is a unitary operator with $\|S_1\| = \|S_1^{-1}\| = 1$ and deduce that, for all a such that $|a| \neq 1$, $(a - S_1)^{-1}$ is a well-defined bounded operator taking L_2 into L_2. But if that is so, we can expand $M^{-1}(z)$ in partial fractions and use assumption (ii) to ascertain that $M^{-1}(S_1)$ is a well-defined bounded operator taking L_2 into itself.

From the preceding observations it follows that equation 33.71 has a uniquely defined solution in L_2,

$$y(t, \omega) = M^{-1}(S_1)\eta(t, \omega), \qquad t \in T.$$

Obviously, $L\{y(t, \omega); t \in T\} \subset L_2$, and the inverse relation follows from $\eta(t, \omega) = \sum_{j=0}^{n} b_j y(t - j, \omega)$. Hence $L\{y(t, \omega); t \in T\} = L_2$.

Next, let $f_x(t, \omega)$ be defined by the equations,

$$f_x(t, \omega) = x(t, \omega) - y(t, \omega), \qquad t \in T.$$

If $f_x(t, \omega) = 0$ a.e. for all $t \in T$, we say that $x(t, \omega)$ is a centered dynamic stochastic process. Suppose not. Then $f_x(t, \omega)$ satisfies the relation,

$$M(S)f_x(t, \omega) = 0, \qquad \text{all } t \in T.$$

Hence, by the general theory of difference equations, we deduce that

$$f_x(t,\omega) = \sum_{j=1}^{\alpha} \sum_{k=0}^{n_j-1} A_{jk}(z_j^t t^k),$$

where $\{z_j\}_{j=1}^{\alpha}$ are distinct roots of the equation $\sum_{j=0}^{n} b_j z^{n-j} = 0$, and n_j is the multiplicity of z_j; and we deduce that the system of equations,

$$\left\{ f_x(t,\omega) = \sum_{j=1}^{\alpha} \sum_{k=0}^{n_j-1} A_{jk}(z_j^t t^k) \right\}_{t=1}^{n},$$

can be solved uniquely for each A_{jk} in terms of the $f_x(t,\omega)$'s.

From this it follows that the coefficients A_{jk} are indeed random variables in X_2, and that

$$x(t,\omega) = y(t,\omega) + \sum_{j=1}^{\alpha} \sum_{k=0}^{n_j-1} A_{jk}(\omega)(z_j^t t^k), \qquad t \in T.$$

The process, $f_x(t,\omega)$, is clearly deterministic since for all $t \in T$,

$$f_x(t,\omega) = -\sum_{j=1}^{n} (b_j/b_0) f_x(t-j,\omega).$$

It remains to be shown that $X_2 = L_2 \oplus F_2$.

Suppose L_2 and F_2 are two linearly independent spaces and let $Y_2 = L_2 \oplus F_2$. Since L_2 is closed and F_2 is finite-dimensional, we know that Y_2 is closed. Clearly $X \subset Y_2$. This gives the relation $X_2 \subset Y_2$. Since $F_2 \subset X_2$ and $L_2 \subset X_2$, $Y_2 \subset X_2$. Hence $X_2 = L_2 \oplus F_2$ if L_2 and F_2 are linearly independent.

That L_2 and F_2 are indeed linearly independent follows from the following considerations. Let $E = F_2 \cap L_2$. E is finite-dimensional and clearly reduces S. Let $\{S_1^t u(\omega); t \in T\}$ be a wide-sense stationary process in E. Then $u(t)$ has the representation,

$$u(t,\omega) = \sum_{j=1}^{p} e^{it\lambda_j} d_j(\omega),$$

where the $d_j(\omega)$'s are mutually orthogonal and the λ_j's are real. On the other side, $u(t) \in F_2$ and hence satisfies the equation,

$$M(S)u(t,\omega) = 0, \qquad \text{for all } t \in T,$$

which is impossible since $M(z)$ has no root of modulus equal to 1.

For an econometrician it is important to know whether the representation of a dynamic stochastic process as a sum of a nonstationary process and wide-sense stationary process is uniquely determined. The next two theorems address themselves to this problem.

T 33.7 If $\{x(t, \omega); t \in T\}$ is a dynamic stochastic process, then there exists a linear difference operator, $M(S)$, of lowest order such that $M(S)x(t, \omega) \in L_2$ for all $t \in T$. $M(S)$ is uniquely determined up to a multiplicative constant.

The proof is as follows: Let S be the shift operator defined by $Sx(t, \omega) = x(t + 1, \omega)$, $t \in T$. S is clearly uniquely defined on X and can be extended to all of X_2. We note that it is easily deduced from the definition of dynamic stochastic processes that L_2 reduces S. Furthermore, from the general representation, $f_x(t, \omega) = \sum_{j=1}^{\alpha} \sum_{k=0}^{n_j-1} A_{jk}(\omega)(z_j^t t^k)$, we see immediately that there exists at least one finite difference operator with constant coefficients taking $x(t, \omega)$ into L_2. Hence there must be at least one of lowest order. Suppose there are two, $M(S)$ and $N(S)$. It is clear that $a \cdot N(S)$, where a is an arbitrary constant, is a third operator with the same properties, and that $\{M(S) - aN(S)\}x(t, \omega) \in L_2$. If $M(z) = \sum_{j=0}^{n} b_j z^{-j}$ and $N(z) = \sum_{j=0}^{n} v_j z^{-j}$, we can choose a such that $b_0 = a \cdot v_0$. It is now evident that $\{M(S) - a \cdot N(S)\}$ is an operator of lower order than both $M(S)$ and $N(S)$ unless $M(S) = a \cdot N(S)$.

In T 33.7 we do not rule out the possibility that one or more of the roots of $M(z)$ lie on the unit circle. Roots of modulus 1 in equation 33.63 make it impossible to insist on the uniqueness of the representation of X in equation 33.62. To see why, suppose that $z_j = e^{i\lambda_j}$ and consider the process

$$z(t, \omega) = y(t, \omega) + A_{j_0}(\omega)e^{it\lambda_j}, \qquad t \in T.$$

If $A_{j_0}(\cdot)$ is orthogonal to $y(t, \cdot)$ for all $t \in T$, then $\{z(t, \omega); t \in T\}$ is a wide-sense stationary process.

The preceding observation is the reason why in T 33.8 we assume that the moduli of the z_j in equation 33.63 differ from 1.

T 33.8 Let $X = \{x(t, \omega); t \in T\}$ be a dynamic stochastic process whose representation is as described in equations 33.62 and 33.63. If the moduli of the z_j in equation 33.63 differ from 1, then the representation of X is uniquely determined.

The only thing left to prove is the uniqueness of $y(t, \omega)$. Suppose that we have two operators, $M(S)$ and $N(S)$, neither of which has zeros of modulus equal to 1, such that $x(t, \omega)$ satisfies the two relations,

$$M(S)x(t, \omega) = \eta(t, \omega),$$

and

$$N(S)x(t, \omega) = \xi(t, \omega).$$

We have to prove that $L\{\eta(t, \omega); t \in T\} = L\{\xi(t, \omega); t \in T\}$.

Clearly, $N(S)\eta(t,\omega) = M(S)\xi(t,\omega)$, and if S_1^M and S_1^N are the restrictions of S to the two spaces respectively, then $\xi(t,\omega) = M^{-1}(S_1^M)N(S_1^M)\eta(t,\omega)$, which gives

$$L\{\xi(t,\omega); t \in T\} \subset L\{\eta(t,\omega); t \in T\},$$

and

$$\eta(t,\omega) = N^{-1}(S_1^N)M(S_1^N)\xi(t,\omega),$$

which gives the converse relation.

This, together with the proof of T 33.7, establishes the validity of T 33.8.

ARIMA processes as well as dynamic stochastic processes are solutions to stochastic difference equations. Even so, an ARIMA process differs from a dynamic stochastic process in many ways. For us the most important difference is displayed in figures 33.1 and 33.2 and figures 33.3 and 33.4: The random component of an ARIMA process swamps the deterministic component, while the deterministic component of a dynamic stochastic process will swamp the stochastic component if one of the z_j in equation 32.63 has modulus greater than 1.

T 33.9 Let $\{x(t); t = 0, 1, \ldots\}$ be a random process which satisfies the equations

$$x(t) = y(t) + (1.02)^t, \qquad t = 0, 1, \ldots, 700, \tag{33.72}$$

where

$$y(t) = -\sum_{s=1}^{400} (1.02)^{-s}\eta(t+s), \qquad t = 0, 1, \ldots, 700, \tag{33.73}$$

and $\{\eta(t); t = 1, \ldots, 1100\}$ constitutes a purely random process with mean 0 and variance 1. Then, for all $t = 1, \ldots, 700$,

$$x(t) - (1.02)x(t-1) = y(t) - (1.02)y(t-1),$$

and

$$y(t) - (1.02)y(t-1) = \eta(t) - (1.02)^{-400}\eta(t+400).$$

With the help of Anders Ekeland I simulated the behavior of the $\eta(t)$ under the additional assumption that $\eta(t) \in \{-1, 1\}$ and that $\Pr\{\eta(t) = -1\} = \Pr\{\eta(t) = 1\} = 1/2$, and used equations 33.72 and 33.73 to obtain 700 observations on $x(t)$ and $y(t)$. My observations on $y(t)$ and $x(t)$ are displayed in figures 33.3 and 33.4, respectively.

33.4 Concluding Remarks on Multivariate Dynamic Stochastic Processes

There are two features of our discussion of trends, cycles, and seasonals that may detract from the generality and hence the import of our observa-

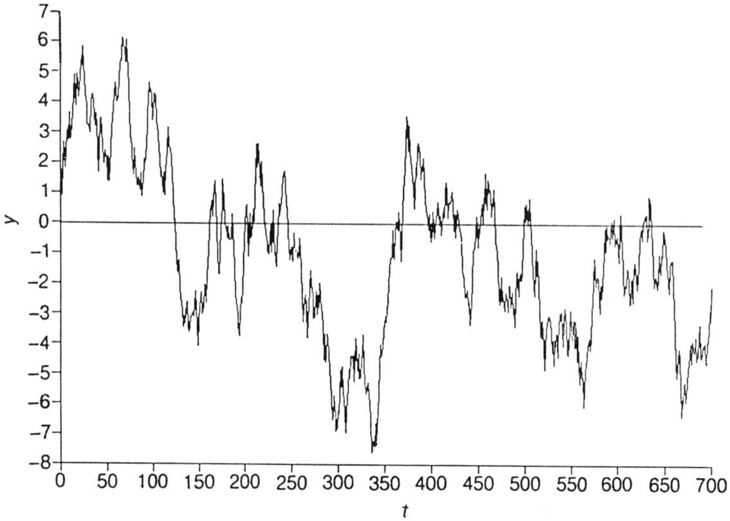

Figure 33.3
Sample path of $y(t)$.

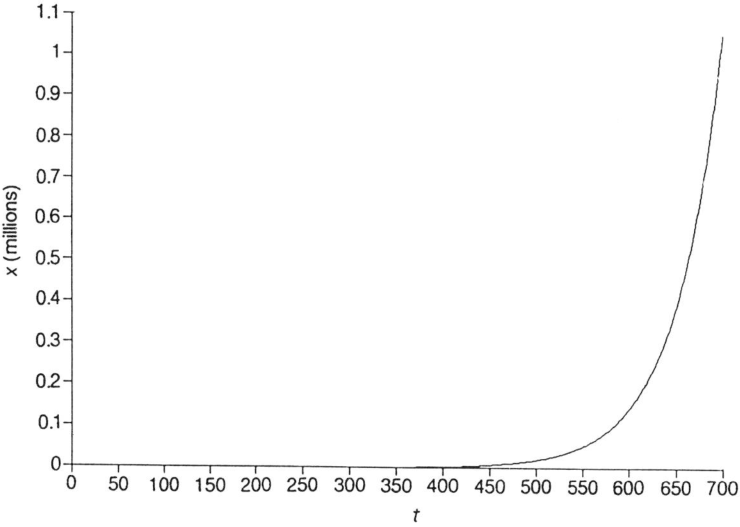

Figure 33.4
Sample path of $x(t)$

tions on ARIMA processes and dynamic stochastic processes:

1. Equation (33.1) ignores the possible systematic influence on x of other economic variables.

2. The representation for trends, cycles, and seasonals by a dynamic stochastic process was derived from a single-equation dynamic model of the behavior of x. In contrast, the ARIMA and GARIMA models of the trend, cycle, and seasonal components of x were solutions to reduced-form models of a set of dynamic structural equations.

But appearances can deceive. In order to show how deceptive the preceding two observations are, I shall conclude the chapter with a discussion of multivariate dynamic stochastic processes.

Let $U = \{u(t); t \in T\}$ be a p-variate column-vector-valued second-order stochastic process, that is, a process whose components are all second-order processes. Also let $\mathscr{U}$ be the linear manifold generated by U, that is, the linear manifold of all random vectors of the form, $\sum_{j=1}^{n} B_j u(t_j)$, where the B_j's are $p \times p$ matrices with complex entries. The ordinary inner product is not very important in the theory of multivariate processes. Instead we introduce the Gramian matrix,

$$(u(t), u(s)) = \{(u_i(t), u_j(s))\} = \{Eu_i(t)\overline{u_j(s)}\},$$

and define the norm on $\mathscr{U}$ by

$$\|u(t)\| = [\tau(u(t), u(t))]^{1/2},$$

where $\tau(u(t), u(t))$ denotes the trace of the Gramian matrix, $(u(t), u(t))$.When $\mathscr{U}$ is completed in this norm, we denote its completion by $\mathscr{L}\{u(t); t \in T\}$.

Next let $Y = \{y(t); t \in T\}$ be a p-variate column-vector-valued second-order process with mean 0 and covariance matrix,

$$\Gamma(t, s) = (y(t), y(s)), \qquad (t, s) \in T \times T.$$

Then Y is a p-variate column-vector-valued wide-sense stationary process if and only if $\Gamma(t, s)$ depends on $t - s$ only. Evidently, if Y is wide-sense stationary, then for each i, $i = 1, \ldots, p$, $\{y_i(t); t \in T\}$ is a wide-sense stationary process. In addition, for each pair i, j such that $1 \leqslant i, j \leqslant p$, and for all pairs $(t, s) \in T \times T$, the covariance $Ey_i(t)\overline{y_j(s)}$ is a function of $t - s$ only.[8]

Finally, let $X = \{x(t, \omega); t \in T\}$ be a p-variate column-vector-valued second-order stochastic process on some probability space $(\Omega, \mathscr{F}, P(\cdot))$, let $\mathscr{X}_2 = \mathscr{L}\{x(t, \omega); t \in T\}$, and observe that $\mathscr{X}_2$ is well defined. We say that X is a *p-variate discrete dynamic stochastic process* if,

(i) $x(t, \omega)$ can be represented by the relation

$$x(t, \omega) = y(t, \omega) + f_x(t, \omega),$$

where $y(t, \omega)$ is a p-variate column-vector-valued wide-sense stationary stochastic process, and $f_x(t, \omega)$ is a p-variate column-vector-valued deterministic nonstationary stochastic process of the form,

$$f_x(t, \omega) = \sum_{j=1}^{\alpha} \sum_{k=0}^{n_j-1} A_{jk}(\omega)(z_j^t t^k), \tag{33.74}$$

the $A_{jk}(\omega)$'s being p-dimensional column vectors,

(ii) $\mathscr{X}_2 = \mathscr{L}_2 \oplus \mathscr{F}_2$, where $\mathscr{L}_2 = \mathscr{L}\{y(t, \omega); t \in T\}$ and $\mathscr{F}_2 = \mathscr{L}\{f_x(t, \omega); t \in T\}$.

We note that if the "matrix polynomial" $M(z)$ is defined by $M(z) = \sum_{j=0}^{n} B_j z^{-j}$, where the B_j's are $p \times p$ matrices with complex entries, then $M(z) = \{M_{ij}(z)\}$, where the $M_{ij}(z)$'s are ordinary polynomials in z. The determinant of $M(z)$ is denoted by $\det M(z) = W(z)$. $W(z) = \sum_{j=0}^{m} w_j z^{-j}$, where the w_j's are complex constants. Whenever $W(z) \neq 0$,

$$M^{-1}(z) = \frac{V(z)}{W(z)} = \left\{\frac{V_{ij}(z)}{W(z)}\right\},$$

is well defined.

If S_1 is a unitary operator on $\mathscr{L}_2$, and $W(z)$ has no roots of modulus $= 1$, then $M(S_1)$ has an inverse:

$$M^{-1}(S_1) = \frac{V(S_1)}{W(S_1)} = \{W^{-1}(S_1)V_{ij}(S_1)\} = \{V_{ij}(S_1)W^{-1}(S_1)\}.$$

T 33.10 Suppose that

(i) $\{x(t, \omega); t \in T\}$ is a p-variate column-vector-valued second-order stochastic process such that $\mathscr{X}_2 = \mathscr{L}\{x(t, \omega); t \in T\}$ is well defined;

(ii) the shift operator S on the linear manifold of random vectors generated by X is uniquely defined by the relation $Sx(t, \omega) = x(t + 1, \omega)$, can be extended to all of $\mathscr{X}_2$, and has a continuous inverse S^{-1};

(iii) the matrix polynomial $M(z) = \sum_{j=0}^{n} B_j z^{-j}$, where the B_j's are $p \times p$ matrices with complex entries, is such that $\det M(z) = W(z) = \sum_{j=0}^{m} w_j z^{-j}$ has no roots of modulus $= 1$, and $x(t, \omega)$ satisfies the relation,

$$M(S)x(t, \omega) = \eta(t, \omega), \qquad \text{all } t \in T,$$

where $\{\eta(t, \omega); t \in T\}$ is a p-variate column-vector-valued wide-sense stationary stochastic process,

Then $x(t, \omega)$ is a p-variate discrete dynamic stochastic process.

To prove the theorem, we first let $\mathscr{L}_2 = \mathscr{L}\{\eta(t, \omega); t \in T\}$ and observe that $\mathscr{L}_2 \subset X_2$ and that $\mathscr{L}_2$ reduces S. It is then straightforward to show that if S_1 is the restriction of S to $\mathscr{L}_2$, then S_1 is uniquely defined by $S_1\eta(t,\omega) = \eta(t+1,\omega)$, $t \in T$, and is a unitary operator. Using the proof of T 33.6, it is, therefore, clear that the equation $M(S)x(t,\omega) = \eta(t,\omega)$, has a uniquely defined solution in $\mathscr{L}_2$,

$$y(t,\omega) = M^{-1}(S_1)\eta(t,\omega) = \{W^{-1}(S_1)V_{ij}(S_1)\}\eta(t,\omega),$$

and that $\mathscr{L}\{y(t,\omega); t \in T\} = \mathscr{L}_2$.

Let $f_x(t,\omega)$ be defined by the relation, $x(t,\omega) - y(t,\omega) = f_x(t,\omega)$. If $f_x(t,\omega) = 0$ a.e., we say that $x(t,\omega)$ is a centered dynamic process. We note that some of the components may be centered, but this is of no importance as far as the rest of the proof goes.

It is clear that $f_x(t,\omega)$ satisfies the difference relation,

$$M(S)f_x(t,\omega) = 0;$$

but then in particular it satisfies the difference equation,

$$W(S)f_x(t,\omega) = 0.$$

Hence again, as in the univariate case, we can write

$$f_x(t,\omega) = \sum_{j=1}^{\alpha}\sum_{k=0}^{n_j-1} A_{jk}(z_j^t t^k),$$

where the A_{jk}'s are now p-dimensional column vectors. Finally, the system of equations,

$$\left\{f_x(t,\omega) = \sum_{j=1}^{\alpha}\sum_{k=0}^{n_j-1} A_{jk}(z_j^t, t^k)\right\}_{t=1}^{n},$$

can be solved uniquely for the A_{jk}'s in terms of the $f_x(t,\omega)$'s which proves that the A_{jk}'s are indeed random vectors in $\mathscr{X}_2$. Hence

$$x(t,\omega) = y(t,\omega) + \sum_{j=1}^{\alpha}\sum_{k=0}^{n_j-1} A_{jk}(\omega)(z_j^t t^k), \qquad t \in T.$$

It is clear from the representation of $f_x(t,\omega)$ that the last half of the proof of theorem T 33.6 carries over to the multivariate case with only obvious modifications. We have therefore proved that $x(t,\omega)$ is a p-variate dynamic stochastic process.

The order of the matrix operator $M(S)$ is defined by the order of its determinant operator $W(S)$. Since the finite dimensionality of $\mathscr{F}_2$ implies that for some sequence of complex matrices $\{B_j\}$ and some sequence $\{t_j\}$,

$$f_x(t, \omega) = \sum_{j=1}^{n} B_j f_x(t_j, \omega), \qquad \text{all } t \in T,$$

the existence of a finite ordered matrix-valued operator taking $x(t, \omega)$ into $\mathscr{L}_2$ is immediate. In addition, as far as the corresponding determinant operator is concerned, T 33.7 carries over directly to the multivariate case:

T 33.11 Let $\{x(t, \omega); t \in T\}$ be a p-variate dynamic stochastic process. There exists a minimal polynomial $W(z)$ in negative powers of z with leading coefficient 1 such that if

$$\xi_i(t, \omega) = W(S)x_i(t, \omega), \qquad t \in T, \qquad i = 1, \ldots, p;$$

and $\xi(t, \omega) = (\xi_1(t, \omega), \ldots, \xi_p(t, \omega))'$, then

$$\xi(t, \omega) \in \mathscr{L}_2, \qquad t \in T.$$

But if T 33.11 is true, then we can use an obvious analogue of our reasoning in the proof of T 33.8 to establish the following theorem:

T 33.12 Let $X = \{x(t, \omega); t \in T\}$ be a p-variate dynamic stochastic process and suppose that the z_j in equation 33.74 have moduli different from 1. Then X has one and only one centering function.

Theorems T 33.10–T 33.12 demonstrate that if the x in equation 33.1 is one of the components of a p-variate dynamic stohastic process, then (1) the relation depicted in equation 33.1 does not ignore the possible systematic influence on x of other economic variables; and (2) the trend, cycle, and seasonal components of x can be viewed as solutions to reduced-form models of a set of dynamic structural equations. However, these theorems do not tell us how best to decompose a given time series into a sum of trend, cycle, seasonal, and random components. In the next chapter we shall treat several aspects of that problem when the time series constitutes a partial realization of a dynamic stochastic process. For an authoritative and interesting account of possible solutions to the problem when the time series is generated by an ARIMA process or a GARIMA process, I refer the reader to Svend Hylleberg's recent book, *Seasonality in Regression* (see, in particular, pp. 160–220).

34 Least Squares and Stochastic Difference Equations

In this chapter we study the asymptotic properties of least-squares estimates of parameters of the solution to a stochastic difference equation,

$$\sum_{k=0}^{n} a_k x(t-k) = \eta(t), \tag{34.1}$$

with fixed or random initial conditions.

We begin by assuming that the solution to equation 34.1 is a dynamic stochastic process and by focusing on the parameters of the centering function $f_x(\cdot)$ and the deterministic component of $y(\cdot)$. It is known that (generalized) least-squares estimates of these parameters are best linear unbiased (see Jorgenson 1964, pp. 681–724). We see here that some of the least-squares estimates converge either exponentially fast or in probability to the true parameter values. Others converge in probability to false values of their respective parameters. Since inconsistent best linear unbiased estimates cannot be good estimates, these results illustrate the importance of asymptotic theory in econometrics.

Next we focus on the coefficients in $M(z) = \sum_{k=0}^{n} a_k z^{-k}$. When the initial conditions of equation 34.1 are fixed and the $\eta(t)$ are independently and identically distributed with mean zero and finite variance, it is known (see Muench 1974, pp. 1–41) that the least-squares estimates of $a = (a_1, \ldots, a_n)$ converge in probability to a. We show that the convergence to a will happen with probability 1 if $M(z)$ has no roots of modulus equal to 1. When (1) the initial conditions of equation 34.1 are random, (2) the moduli of the roots of $M(z)$ differ from 1, and (3) the $\eta(t)$ constitute a purely random process, then the least-squares estimates of a converge either exponentially fast or with probability 1 to well-defined parameter values. Sometimes these limiting values are equal to the values of the respective a_k. Other times they are not.

Finally, we study the asymptotic distribution of the least-squares estimates of a, $\hat{a}(N)$, $N = n + 1, \ldots$, when the $\eta(t)$ constitute a purely random process and the moduli of the roots of $M(z)$ differ from 1. It is known (see Anderson 1959, pp. 676–687)) that if the initial conditions are fixed and if the roots of $M(z)$ have moduli less than 1, then as $N \to \infty$, $\sqrt{N}(\hat{a}(N) - a)$ converges in distribution to an n-dimensional normally distributed vector. We see that if the moduli of the roots of $M(z)$ lie on both sides of the unit circle, then $\sqrt{N}(\hat{a}(N) - a)$ converges in distribution to a degenerate, normally distributed vector. When (1) the initial conditions of equation 34.1 are random, (2) $c = \lim \hat{a}(N)$, and (3) the moduli of the roots of $M(z)$ are not all greater than 1, then $\sqrt{N}(\hat{a}(N) - c)$ converges to a normally distributed vector. The limiting distribution is degenerate if and only if the roots of $M(z)$ lie on both sides of the unit circle.

To save space, I shall state theorems without proofs and use examples and simulation studies to illustrate the import of the results. Detailed proofs of all the theorems can be found in Stigum 1972c (pp. 19–39), Stigum 1976 (pp. 60–74), Stigum 1974c (pp. 364–381), and Stigum 1976a (pp. 355–369).

34.1 The Elimination of Trend, Cycle, and Seasonal Factors in Time Series

Recall that in economics a *trend* is a slow variation in some specific direction which is maintained over a long period of years. A *cycle* is a seemingly quasi-periodic movement, alternately increasing and decreasing. And a *seasonal* is a movement composed of more or less regular weekly, monthly, or yearly variations. When the behavior of an economic variable can be represented as a dynamic stochastic process, then the components of the cycle and seasonal series with constant coefficients are reflected in the discrete part of the spectral distribution of $y(\cdot)$. The trending cyclical and seasonal components and the trend itself are completely represented by $f_x(\cdot)$.

34.1 Basic Assumptions

In this section we shall study the asymptotic properties of linear procedures for eliminating seasonal, cyclical, and trend components of time series generated by a dynamic stochastic process. The assumptions we make about the underlying process are as follows: Let $\{x(t, \omega); t \in T\}$ be a dynamic stochastic process on a probability space $(\Omega, \mathscr{F}, P(\cdot))$. Moreover, let the $x(t, \cdot)$ be represented by

$$x(t, \omega) = f_x(t, \omega) + y(t, \omega), \qquad t \in T, \tag{34.2}$$

where $\{ y(t, \omega); t \in T\}$ is a wide-sense stationary process and

$$f_x(t, \omega) = \sum_{p=1}^{h} \sum_{q=0}^{n_p - 1} A_{pq}(\omega)(t^q z_p^t), \qquad t \in T. \tag{34.3}$$

We always hold to certain assumptions:

(i) The $x(t, \cdot)$ are complex-valued.

(ii) There exists a wide-sense stationary process, $\{u(t, \omega); t \in T\}$, with absolutely continuous spectral distribution function, $G(\cdot)$, and a wide-sense stationary process, $\{z(t, \omega), t \in T\}$, of the form

$$z(t, \omega) = \sum_{j=1}^{m} B_j(\omega) e^{it\lambda_j}, \qquad t \in T, \lambda_j \in (-\pi, \pi), \qquad j = 1, \ldots, m, \tag{34.4}$$

such that

$$y(t, \omega) = u(t, \omega) + z(t, \omega), \qquad t \in T, \tag{34.5}$$

(iii) If $p \in \{1, \ldots, h\}$ and $z_p = e^{i\theta_p}$, then $\theta_p \neq \lambda_j$, $j = 1, \ldots, m$.

(iv) The $u(t, \omega)$ are distributed independently of the $z(t, \cdot)$ and the $f_x(t, \cdot)$.

For some purposes we shall also insist that the $u(t, \cdot)$ satisfy the following condition:

(v) There is a finite positive pair (K, δ) such that, for all $q = 1, \ldots, \max_{1 \leqslant p \leqslant h_1} (n_p - 1)$,

$$E|S^{-(q+1)} \sum_{t=1}^{S} t^q u(t, \omega)|^2 \leqslant KS^{-\delta}, \qquad S \geqslant 1. \tag{34.6}$$

Subsidiary conditions on the $u(t, \cdot)$ that will ensure the validity of equation 34.6 are easy to obtain. Here is one example:

E 34.1 Suppose that there is an orthogonal process $\eta = \{\eta(t, \omega); t \in T\}$ and constants ϕ_s, $s \in T$, such that

$$u(t, \omega) = \sum_{s=-\infty}^{\infty} \phi_s \eta(t + s, \omega), \qquad t \in T, \tag{34.7}$$

and

$$\sum_{s=-\infty}^{\infty} |\phi_s| < \infty. \tag{34.8}$$

Then

$$\sum_{s=-\infty}^{\infty} |R_u(s)| < \infty, \tag{34.9}$$

where $R_u(s) = Eu(t)\overline{u(t-s)}$, $s \in T$, and lemma 4 in Stigum 1972c implies that the $u(t,\cdot)$ satisfy equation 34.6 with $\delta = 1$.

In reading this example, it is interesting to note that if the $x(t,\cdot)$ constitute a solution to equation 34.1 with independently and identically distributed $\eta(t)$, then the $u(t,\cdot)$ will satisfy equations 34.7–34.9 if $\sum_{k=0}^{n} a_k z^{-k}$ has no roots of modulus equal to 1 and if the $\eta(t)$ have mean zero and finite variance.

34.1.2 Linear SCT-Adjustment Procedures

Suppose now that $\{x(t,\omega); t \in T\}$ is a dynamic stochastic process, and that we have observed the value of $x(t,\omega)$ for $t = 1, 2, \ldots, S$. Moreover, denote these observations by the vector $x_S(\omega) = (x_1, \ldots, x_S)$. Finally, let "SCT-adjusted" mean adjusted for seasonal, cyclical, and trend factors.

A linear procedure for eliminating the seasonal, cyclical, and trend components of a time series such as $x_S(\omega)$ is a square matrix $\mathscr{A}$ which transforms $x_S(\omega)$ into a SCT-adjusted set of observations x^s according to

$$x^s = \mathscr{A} x_S(\omega). \tag{34.10}$$

Here is an example to fix our ideas:

E 34.2 Let $\{x(t,\omega); t \in T\}$ be a dynamic stochastic process, where $T = \{0, 1, \ldots\}$, and assume that

$$x(0,\omega) = \alpha \quad \text{and} \quad x(t,\omega) = y(t,\omega) + \alpha a^t \quad \text{for } t \geqslant 1. \tag{34.11}$$

Suppose that we have $(S+1)$ observations on the $x(t,\cdot)$ and let $x = (x(0,\omega), x(1,\omega), \ldots, x(S,\omega))'$ and

$$\mathscr{A} = \begin{pmatrix} 1 & 0 & & \cdots & 0 \\ -a & 1 & 0 & \cdots & 0 \\ \cdot & \cdot & \cdot & \cdots & \cdot \\ -a^S & 0 & 0 & \cdots & 1 \end{pmatrix}.$$

Then $x^s = \mathscr{A} a$ is an SCT-adjusted set of observations on $x(\cdot)$. In fact,

$$x^s = (\alpha, y(1,\omega), \ldots, y(S,\omega))'$$

for the relevant value of ω.

In equation 34.11 we observe the value of α and use this observation to formulate an exact SCT-adjustment procedure for $x_S(\cdot)$. When we cannot observe the value of α we must obtain an estimate of α and use the estimate to design an approximate SCT-adjustment procedure for $x_S(\cdot)$. One way to do that is described in E 34.3.

E 34.3 Let $\{x(t,\omega); t \in T\}$ be a dynamic stochastic process which satisfies the equations,

$$x(t,\omega) = y(t,\omega) + A(\omega)a^t, \qquad t \in T, a > 1.$$

Moreover, for all $S \geqslant 1$, let $a_S = (a, a^2, \ldots, a^S)'$ and let

$$\begin{aligned}\mathscr{L}(S,\omega) &= \sum_{t=1}^{S} x(t,\omega)a^t / \sum_{t=1}^{S} a^{2t} \qquad (34.12)\\ &= A(\omega) + \left(\frac{1-a^{-2}}{1-a^{-2S}}\right)a^{-2S}\sum_{t=1}^{S} a^t y(t,\omega)\\ &= A(\omega) + \left(\frac{1-a^{-2}}{1-a^{-2S}}\right)a^{-S}\sum_{v=0}^{S-1} a^{-v}y(S-v,\omega).\end{aligned}$$

Since $a > 1$, it follows from lemma 4 in Stigum 1976 (pp. 48–75) that

$$\lim_{S\to\infty} S^{-1}\sum_{v=0}^{S-1} a^{-v}y(S-v,\omega) = 0 \quad \text{a.e. } (P \text{ measure}). \qquad (34.13)$$

Consequently, by equations 34.12 and 34.13, there exists a bounded random variable $k(\omega)$ and a $\lambda \in (0,1)$ such that $a^{-1} < \lambda$ and such that

$$|\mathscr{L}(S,\omega) - A(\omega)| \leqslant k(\omega)\lambda^S, \qquad S \geqslant 1, \quad \text{a.e. } (P \text{ measure}).$$

But if that is so, we obtain an approximately SCT-adjusted time series of observations on $x(t,\cdot)$ by letting

$$x^s = x_S(\omega) - a_S\mathscr{L}(S,\omega). \qquad (34.14)$$

As S tends to ∞, x^s tends componentwise to $y_S(\omega)$ a.e. (P measure), where $y_S(\omega) = (y(1,\omega),\ldots,y(S,\omega))'$.

In reading E 34.3, note that equation 34.14 represents a prototype of the kind of adjustment procedures we envision in this section. The two significant features of the procedure are (1) $\mathscr{L}(S,\omega)$ is the least-squares estimate of $A(\omega)$ and (2) a is a known constant. In the more general context of equations 34.2–34.5, $\mathscr{L}(S,\omega)$ becomes the least-squares estimate of the $A_{pq}(\omega)$ in equation 34.3 and the $B_j(\omega)$ in equation 34.4 and a becomes a known vector of parameters whose components are the $(t^q z_p)$ in equation 34.3 and the e^{λ_j} in equation 34.4. We shall study the asymptotic properties of the least-squares estimates of the $A_{pq}(\omega)$ in equation 34.3 and the $B_j(\omega)$ in equation 34.4 next; I begin by introducing symbols for the vectors and matrices that appear in the pertinent regressions.

34.1.3 Notational Matters

To study linear SCT-adjustment procedures for time series generated by a dynamic stochastic process, it will be convenient to write our basic model (that is, equations 34.2–34.5) in a different way. For this purpose, let

$$C_j(S) = (e^{i\lambda_j}, \ldots, e^{iS\lambda_j})', \qquad j = 1, \ldots, m,$$

$$D_{pq}(S) = (z_p, 2^q z_p^2, \ldots, S^q z_p^S)', \quad S \geqslant 1, p = 1, \ldots, h; q = 0, 1, \ldots, n_p - 1,$$

and let h_1 and h_2 be such that

$$|z_p| = 1, \qquad p = 1, \ldots, h_1; \tag{34.15}$$

$$|z_p| < 1, \qquad p = h_1 + 1, \ldots, h_2; \tag{34.16}$$

and

$$|z_p| > 1, \qquad p = h_2 + 1, \ldots, h. \tag{34.17}$$

Moreover, let

$$C(S) = \{C_1(S), \ldots, C_m(S), D_{10}(S), \ldots, D_{1(n_1-1)}(S), \ldots, D_{h_1 0}(S), \ldots,$$
$$D_{h_1(n_{h_1}-1)}(S)\}, \qquad S \geqslant 1;$$

$$D(S) = \{D_{(h_1+1)0}(S), \ldots, D_{(h_1+1)(n_{h_1+1}-1)}(S), \ldots, D_{h_2 0}(S), \ldots,$$
$$D_{h_2(n_{h_2}-1)}(S)\}, \qquad S \geqslant 1;$$

and

$$G(S) = \{D_{(h_2+1)0}(S), \ldots, D_{(h_2+1)(n_{h_2+1}-1)}(S), \ldots, D_{h0}(S), \ldots,$$
$$D_{h(n_h-1)}(S)\}, \qquad S \geqslant 1.$$

Finally, let

$$\alpha(\omega) = (B_1(\omega), \ldots, B_m(\omega), A_{10}(\omega), \ldots, A_{1(n_1-1)}(\omega), \ldots,$$
$$A_{h_1 0}(\omega), \ldots, A_{h_1(n_{h_1}-1)}(\omega))';$$

$$\beta(\omega) = (A_{(h_1+1)0}(\omega), \ldots, A_{(h_1+1)(n_{h_1+1}-1)}(\omega), \ldots, A_{h_2 0}(\omega), \ldots, A_{h_2(n_{h_2}-1)}(\omega))';$$

$$\gamma(\omega) = (A_{(h_2+1)0}(\omega), \ldots, A_{(h_2+1)(n_{h_2+1}-1)}(\omega), \ldots, A_{h0}(\omega), \ldots, A_{h(n_h-1)}(\omega))';$$

$$x_S(\omega) = (x(1, \omega), \ldots, x(S, \omega))', \qquad S \geqslant 1;$$

$$z_S(\omega) = (z(1, \omega), \ldots, z(S, \omega))', \qquad S \geqslant 1;$$

and

$$u_S(\omega) = (u(1, \omega), \ldots, u(S, \omega))', \qquad S \geqslant 1.$$

Then we can rewrite equations 34.2–34.5 for $1 \leqslant t \leqslant S$ as

$$x_S(\omega) = C(S)\alpha(\omega) + D(S)\beta(\omega) + G(S)\gamma(\omega) + u_S(\omega), \qquad S \geqslant 1. \qquad (34.18)$$

In this expression,

$$C(S)\alpha(\omega) = z_S(\omega) + f_{xS}^1(\omega),$$

where $f_{xS}^1(\omega) = (f_x^1(1,\omega), \ldots, f_x^1(S,\omega))'$, $f_x^1(t,\omega) = \sum_{p=1}^{h_1} \sum_{q=0}^{n_p-1} A_{pq}(\omega)(t^q z_p^t)$, $t = 1, \ldots, S$, and, by equation 34.15, $|z_p| = 1$, $p = 1, \ldots, h_1$;

$$D(S)\beta(\omega) = f_{xS}^2(\omega),$$

where $f_{xS}^2(\omega) = (f_x^2(1,\omega), \ldots, f_x^2(S,\omega))'$, $f_x^2(t,\omega) = \sum_{p=h_1+1}^{h_2} \sum_{q=0}^{n_p-1} A_{pq}(\omega)$ $(t^q z_p^t)$, $t = 1, \ldots, S$, and, by equation 34.16, $|z_p| < 1$, $p = h_1 + 1, \ldots, h_2$;

$$G(S)\gamma(\omega) = f_{xS}^3(\omega),$$

where $f_{xS}^3(\omega) = (f_x^3(1,\omega), \ldots, f_x^3(S,\omega))'$, $f_x^3(t,\omega) = \sum_{p=h_2+1}^{h} \sum_{q=0}^{n_p-1} A_{pq}(t^q z_p^t)$, $t = 1, \ldots, S$, and, by equation 34.17, $|z_p| > 1$, $p = h_2 + 1, \ldots, h$. Since $|z_p| = 1$ for $p = 1, \ldots, h_1$, $C(S)\alpha(\omega)$ represents the trending and constant cyclical and seasonal components of $x_S(\omega)$. The trend, i.e., the nonseasonal and noncyclical trending components of $x_S(\cdot)$, is given by $G(S)\gamma(\omega)$.

34.1.4 Least-Squares Estimates of the Deterministic Components of a Time Series

So much for new symbols. Now we shall determine the asymptotic properties of the least-squares estimates of $\alpha(\cdot)$, $\beta(\cdot)$, and $\gamma(\cdot)$ in equation 34.18. To that end, let $H(S) = \{C(S), G(S), D(S)\}$ land $H^*(S)$ denote the complex conjugate of $H(S)$. Then the least-squares estimate of $(\alpha(\omega), \gamma(\omega), \beta(\omega))$ is given by

$$(\hat{\alpha}(S,\omega), \hat{\gamma}(S,\omega), \hat{\beta}(S,\omega)) = \{H^*(S)H(S)\}^{-1} H^*(S) x_S(\omega), \qquad S > n + m, \qquad (34.19)$$

where m is the m of equation 34.4, $n = \sum_{p=1}^{h} n_p$, and n_p is the n_p of equation 34.3. The asymptotic properties of the estimate are described in the following thorem:

T 34.1 Let $\{x(t,\omega); t \in T\}$ be a dynamic stochastic process and assume that assumptions i–iv listed in section 34.1.1 hold. Moreover, let $\hat{\alpha}(S.\cdot)$, $\hat{\beta}(S,\omega)$, and $\hat{\gamma}(S,\omega)$ be as defined in equation 34.19. Then $\hat{\beta}(S,\cdot)$ is inconsistent; in fact, there is a random variable $\varphi(\omega) \neq \beta(\omega)$ such that in P measure

$$p\lim \hat{\beta}(S,\omega) = \varphi(\omega). \qquad (34.20)$$

Moreover,

$$p\lim \hat{\alpha}(S,\omega) = \alpha(\omega) \quad (P \text{ measure}); \qquad (34.21)$$

and

$$\|\hat{\gamma}(S,\omega) - \gamma(\omega)\| \leqslant K_1(\omega)\lambda^S, \qquad S > n + m \quad \text{a.e. } (P \text{ measure}) \tag{34.22}$$

for some bounded random variable $K_1(\omega)$ and constant $\lambda \in (0, 1)$. Finally, if the $u(t, \cdot)$ satisfy equation 34.6, then

$$\lim_{S\to\infty} \hat{\alpha}(S,\omega) = \alpha(\omega) \quad \text{a.e. } (P \text{ measure}). \tag{34.23}$$

In interpreting T 34.1, it is important to note that $\hat{\beta}(S,\cdot)$ is not just inconsistent. It converges in probability to a random variable which is different from $\beta(\cdot)$. Moreover, while $\hat{\alpha}(S,\cdot)$ converges in probability to $\alpha(\cdot)$, $\hat{\gamma}(S,\cdot)$ converges exponentially fast to $\gamma(\cdot)$. The first of these two results implies that, even when $(\hat{\alpha}(S,\cdot), \hat{\beta}(S,\cdot), \hat{\gamma}(S,\cdot))$ is the best linear, unbiased estimate of $(\alpha(\cdot), \beta(\cdot), \gamma(\cdot))$, $\hat{\beta}(\cdot)$ is not a reasonable estimate of $\beta(\cdot)$. The two results together also show that the standard large-sample theory of least-squares estimates cannot be applied to $(\hat{\alpha}(S,\cdot), \hat{\beta}(S,\cdot), \hat{\gamma}(S,\cdot))$. In fact (see theorem T 34..2 below), the standard large-sample theory of least-squares estimates can be applied to $\hat{\alpha}(S,\cdot)$ only.

Theorem T 34.1 needs an illustration, so here is a simple example for that purpose.

34.4 Let $\{x(t,\omega); t \in T\}$ be a dynamic stochastic process which satisfies the relations,

$$x(t,\omega) = u(t,\omega) + \tilde{\beta}(\omega)a^t + \gamma(\omega)b^t, \qquad t \in T, \tag{34.24}$$

and

$$b > 1 \geqslant a > 0, \tag{34.25}$$

where $\tilde{\beta}(\omega) = \alpha(\omega)$ if $a = 1$ and $\tilde{\beta}(\omega) = \beta(\omega)$ if $a < 1$. There are two cases to consider:

Case 1: $a < 1$. If $a < 1$, it is easy to show that

$$\hat{\beta}(S,\omega)$$

$$= \tilde{\beta}(\omega) + \left\{\left[\sum_{t=1}^{S} u(t,\omega)a^t \sum_{t=1}^{S} b^{2t} - \sum_{t=1}^{S} u(t,\omega)b^t \sum_{t=1}^{S} (ab)^t\right] \Big/ \left[\sum_{t=1}^{S} a^{2t} \sum_{t=1}^{S} b^{2t} - \left(\sum_{t=1}^{S} (ab)^t\right)^2\right]\right\}$$

$$= \tilde{\beta}(\omega) + \frac{[(1-b^{-2S})/(1-b^{-2})] \sum_{t=1}^{S} a^t u(t,\omega) - [(b^{-S}-a^S)/(1-(ab)^{-1})] \sum_{v=0}^{S-1} b^{-v}u(S-v,\omega)}{\{a^2[(1-a^{2S})/(1-a^2)][(1-b^{-2S})/(1-b^{-2})] - [(b^{-S}-a^S)/(1-(ab)^{-1})]^2\}} \tag{34.26}$$

and that

$$\hat{\gamma}(S,\omega) = \gamma(\omega) + \frac{[(b^{-S}-a^S)/(1-(ab)^{-1})]b^{-S} \sum_{t=1}^{S} a^t u(t,\omega) + a^2[(1-a^{2S})/(1-a^2)]b^{-S} \sum_{v=0}^{S} b^{-v}u(S-v,\omega)}{a^2[(1-a^{2S})/(1-a^2)][(1-b^{-2S})/(1-b^{-2})] - [(b^{-S}-a^S)/(1-(ab)^{-1})]^2}. \tag{34.27}$$

It follows easily from equations 34.25–34.27, and from an analogue of equation 34.13 that a.e. (P measure)

$$\lim_{S\to\infty} \hat{\beta}(S,\omega) = \tilde{\beta}(\omega) + \frac{[1/(1-b^{-2})]\sum_{t=1}^{\infty} a^t u(t,\omega)}{[a^2/(1-a^2)][1/(1-b^{-2})]} \neq \tilde{\beta}(\omega),$$

and that there exists a bounded random variable $k_1(\omega)$ and a constant $\lambda \in (0,1)$, $b^{-1} < \lambda$ such that

$|\hat{\gamma}(S,\omega) - \gamma(\omega)| \leqslant k_1(\omega)\lambda^S, \qquad S > 2, \quad$ a.e. (P measure).

Consequently, for this case, $\hat{\gamma}(S,\cdot)$ satisfies equation 34.22 and there is a random variable $\varphi(\cdot) \neq \tilde{\beta}(\cdot)$ such that $\hat{\beta}(\cdot)$ satisfies equation 34.20 as predicted by T 34.1.

Case 2: $a = 1$. If $a = 1$,

$$\hat{\beta}(S,\omega) = \tilde{\beta}(\omega) + \frac{[(1-b^{-2S})/(1-b^{-2})]S^{-1}\sum_{t=1}^{S} u(t,\omega) - [(1-b^{-S})/(1-b^{-1})]S^{-1}\sum_{v=0}^{S} b^{-v}u(S-v,\omega)}{[(1-b^{-2S})/(1-b^{-2})] - S^{-1}[(1-b^{-S})/(1-b^{-1})]^2}, \tag{34.28}$$

and

$$\hat{\gamma}(S,\omega) = \gamma(\omega) + \frac{-[(1-b^{-S})/(1-b^{-1})]S^{-1}b^{-S}\sum_{t=1}^{S} u(t,\omega) + b^{-S}\sum_{v=0}^{S-1} b^{-v}u(S-v,\omega)}{[(1-b^{-2S})/(1-b^{-2})] - S^{-1}[(1-b^{-S})/(1-b^{-1})]^2}. \tag{34.29}$$

From equations 34.28 and 34.29, from Doob's theorem X.6.2 (see Doob 1953, p. 492), and from an analogue of equation 34.13, it follows that

$p\lim \hat{\beta}(S,\omega) = \tilde{\beta}(\omega) \quad$ (P measure),

and that there exist a bounded random variable $k_2(\omega)$ and a constant $\lambda \in (0,1)$ such that

$|\hat{\gamma}(S,\omega) - \gamma(\omega)| \leqslant k_2(\omega)\lambda^S, \quad S \geqslant 2, \quad$ a.e. (P measure).

Moreover, if the $u(t,\cdot)$ satisfy equation 34.6,

$\lim_{S\to\infty} \hat{\beta}(S,\omega) = \tilde{\beta}(\omega) \quad$ a.e. (P measure).

Thus for this case, $\hat{\beta}(S,\cdot)$, satisfies equation 34.21 or equation 34.23 as the case may be, and $\hat{\gamma}(S,\cdot)$ satisfies equation 34.22 just as predicted by T 34.1.

Both the inconsistency of $\hat{\beta}(S,\cdot)$ and the different behavior of $\hat{\alpha}(S,\cdot)$ and $\hat{\gamma}(S,\cdot)$ in equations 34.21 and 34.22 are surprising. Since these characteristics have an important bearing on the large-sample theory of least squares, to help the reader's intuition I shall next present an interesting simulation study of the large-sample behavior of $\hat{\alpha}(S,\omega)$, $\hat{\gamma}(S,\omega)$, and $\hat{\beta}(S,\omega)$.

E 34.5 Let $\{y(t,\omega); t \in T\}$ be a wide-sense stationary solution to the equations,

$$y(t,\omega) - (1.52)y(t-1,\omega) + 0.56y(t-2,\omega) = \eta(t,\omega); \qquad t \in T,$$

where $\{\eta(t,\omega); t \in T\}$ is a purely random process of normally distributed variables with mean 0 and variance 1. Moreover, let $\{x(t,\omega); t \in T\}$ be a dynamic stochastic process which satisfies the equation,

$$x(t,\omega) = 4\cos(t\pi/3) + 2(0.5)^t + (1.02)^t + y(t,\omega), \qquad t \in T.$$

With the help of Dr. Jaffar Al-Abdulla I simulated the behavior of the $x(t,\cdot)$ for $t = 0, 1, \ldots, 700$, and estimated the coefficients $\alpha = 4$, $\beta = 2$, and $\gamma = 1$ by the method of least squares. Figures 34.1–34.3 below show plots of the values of the estimates obtained from the first N observation on the $x(t,\cdot)$, $N = 10, 20, \ldots, 700$. Here $A(\cdot)$ is the estimate of α, while $B(\cdot)$ and $C(\cdot)$ are, respectively, the estimates of β and γ. The exponential convergence of $C(\cdot)$ to γ and the inconsistent behavior of $B(\cdot)$ are dramatically displayed in figures 34.2 and 34.3.

The hopeless asymptotic behavior of $\hat{\beta}(S,\cdot)$ suggests that we ought to ignore $D(S)\beta(\omega)$ when we estimate $\alpha(\cdot)$ and $\gamma(\cdot)$; i.e., it suggests that we let $\tilde{H}(S) = \{C(S), G(S)\}$ and estimate $(\alpha(\cdot), \gamma(\cdot))$ by

$$(\tilde{\alpha}(S,\omega), \tilde{\gamma}(S,\omega)) = \{\tilde{H}(S)\tilde{H}^*(S)\}\tilde{H}^* x_S(\omega), \qquad S > n. \tag{34.30}$$

The asymptotic behavior of this estimate is described in T 34.2.

T 34.2 Suppose that $\{x(t,\omega); t \in T\}$ is a dynamic stochastic process which satisfies i–iv, the basic assumptions given in section 34.1.1, and let $\tilde{\alpha}(S,\omega)$ and $\tilde{\gamma}(S,\omega)$ be as described in equation 34.30. Suppose also that $\eta = \{\eta(t,\omega); t \in T\}$ is a purely random process with mean zero and positive, finite variance σ_η^2, that $\{\alpha_s : s \in T\}$ are real constants, and that η and the α_s satisfy the conditions

$$u(t,\omega) = \sum_{s=-\infty}^{\infty} \alpha_s \eta(t-s,\omega), \quad t \in T, \qquad \text{and} \qquad \sum_{s=-\infty}^{\infty} |\alpha_s| < \infty.$$

Finally, suppose that the spectral density $g(\cdot)$ of the $u(t,\cdot)$ is positive and continuous on $[-\pi,\pi]$ and let $\Phi(S)$, A, C, and $\tilde{\Gamma}$ be as defined in equations 34.34–34.38 below. Then

$$\lim_{S\to\infty} \tilde{\alpha}(S,\omega) = \alpha(\omega), \quad \text{a.e. } (P \text{ measure}) \tag{34.31}$$

and, for some bounded random variable $K_2(\omega)$ and constant $\lambda \in (0,1)$,

$$\|\tilde{\gamma}(S,\omega) - \gamma(\omega)\| \leqslant K_2(\omega)\lambda^S, \qquad S > n, \quad \text{a.e. } (P \text{ measure}). \tag{34.32}$$

Moreover, there exist an $(m + \sum_{p=1}^{h_1} n_p)$-dimensional, normally distributed vector $\mathscr{G}$ with mean zero and covariance matrix $\Gamma = C^{-1}\tilde{\Gamma}\, C'^{-1}$ and an $(\sum_{p=h_2+1}^{h} n_p)$-dimensional random vector ξ with mean zero and finite second moments such that

$$\begin{pmatrix} \Phi(S) & 0 \\ 0 & A^{*S} \end{pmatrix} ((\tilde{\alpha}(S,\omega), \tilde{\gamma}(S,\omega)) - (\alpha(\omega), \gamma(\omega)))' \tag{34.33}$$

converges in distribution to $(\mathscr{G}', \xi')'$ as $S \to \infty$.

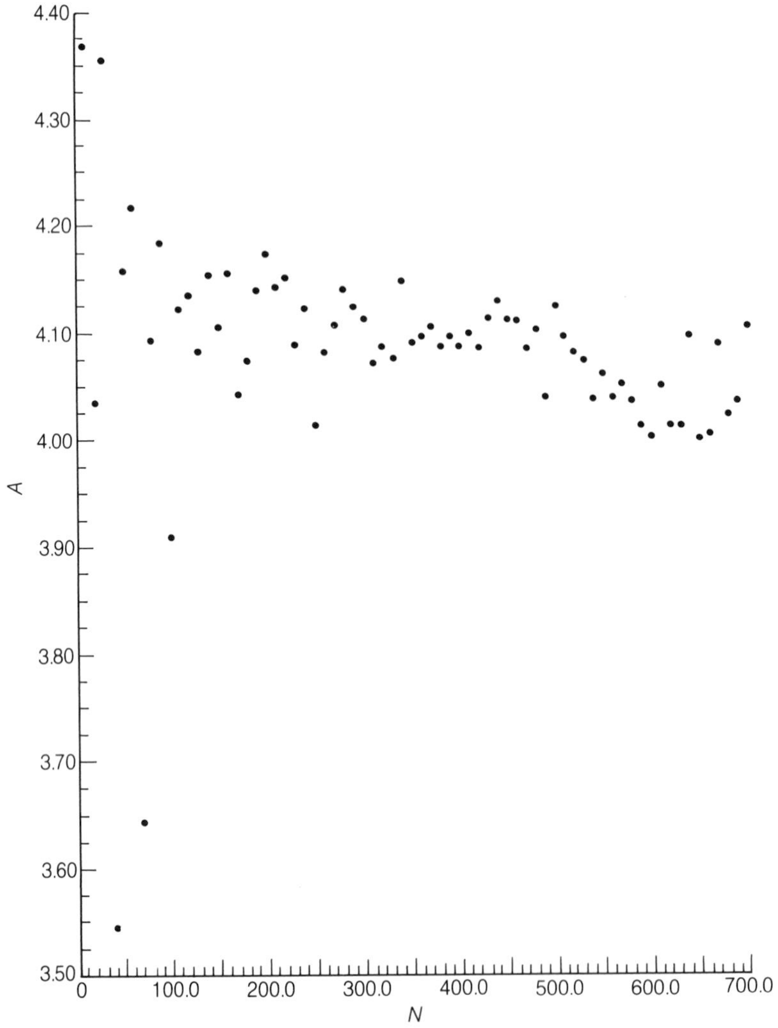

Figure 34.1
Least-squares estimates of A in $x(t) = A\cos(t\pi/3) + B(0.5)^t + C(1.02)^t + y(t)$, $t \in T$.

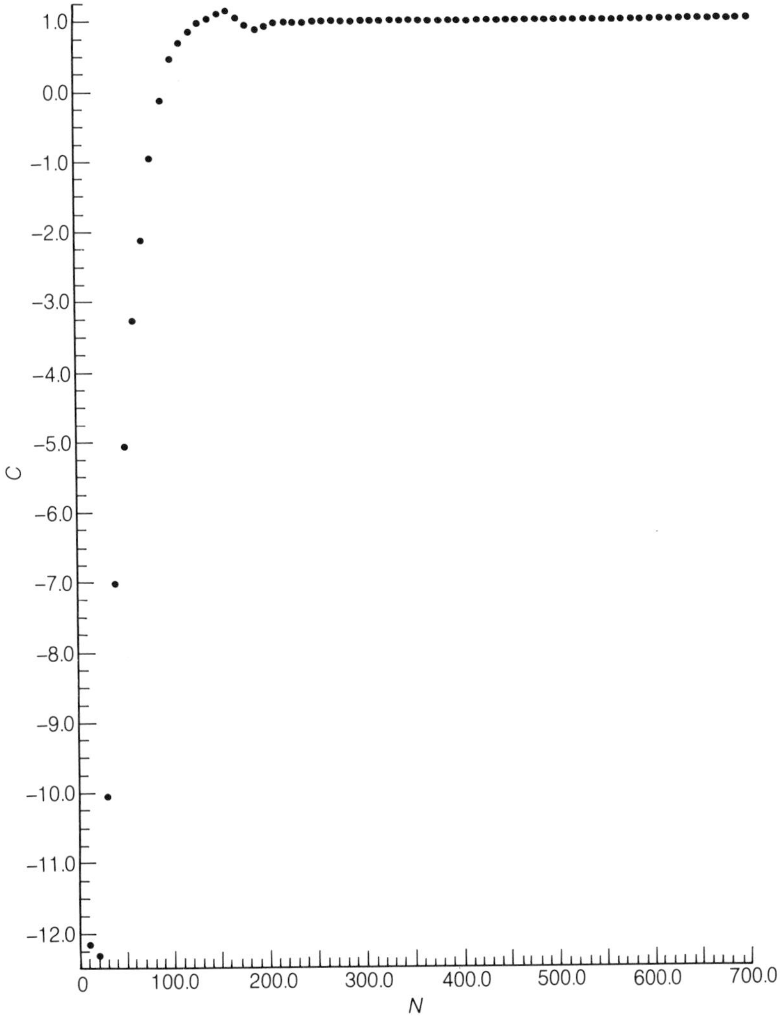

Figure 34.2
Least-squares estimates of C in $x(t) = A\cos(t\pi/3) + B(0.5)^t + C(1.02)^t + y(t)$, $t \in T$.

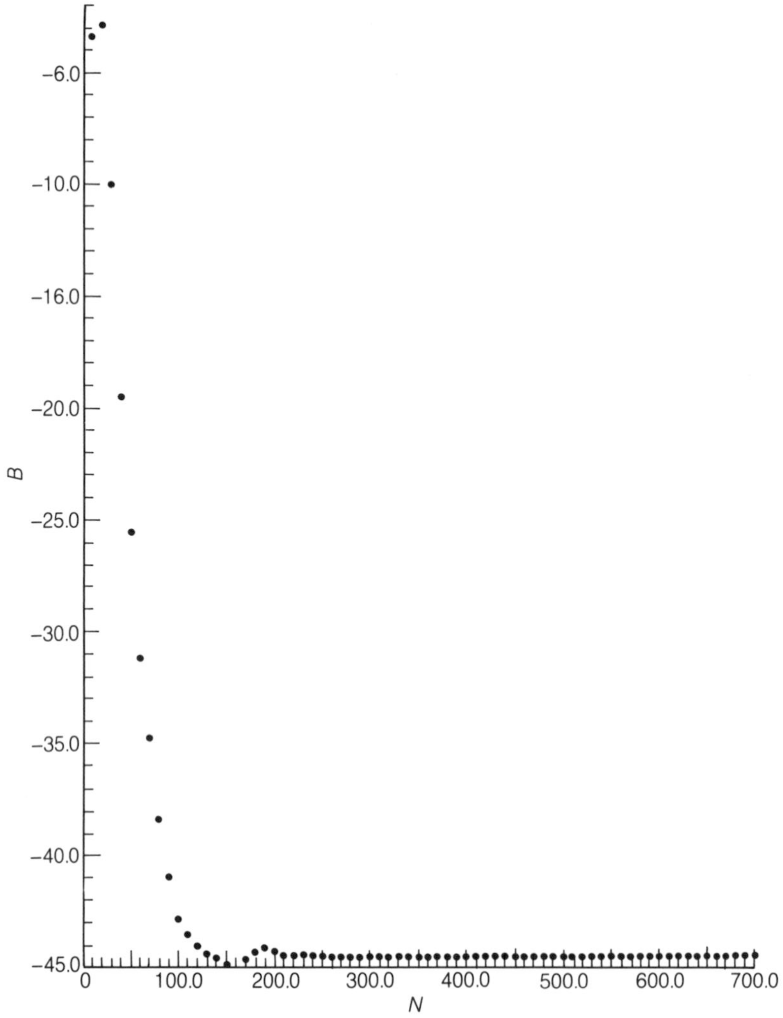

Figure 34.3
Least-squares estimates of B in $x(t) = A\cos(t\pi/3) + B(0.5)^t + C(1.02)^t + y(t)$, $t \in T$.

In the statement of this theorem, the matrices $\Phi(S)$, A, C, and Γ are defined as follows:

$$\Phi(S) = \begin{pmatrix} \phi_1^c(S) & 0 & \cdots & 0 & 0 & \cdots & 0 \\ 0 & \phi_2^c(S) & & & & & \cdot \\ \cdot & \cdot & & \phi_m^c(S) & \cdot & \cdots & \cdot \\ \vdots & \vdots & & \vdots & \phi_{1,0}^D(S) & \cdots & \vdots \\ 0 & 0 & & 0 & 0 & & \phi_{h_1,n_{h_1}-1}^D(S) \end{pmatrix}, \quad S \geqslant 1 \tag{34.34}$$

where $\phi_j^c(S) = \sqrt{S}$, $j = 1, \ldots, m$, $S \geqslant 1$, and $\phi_{p,q}^D(S) = \sqrt{\sum_{t=1}^S t^{2q}}$, $p = 1, \ldots, h_1$; $q = 0, 1, \ldots, n_p - 1$; $S \geqslant 1$;

$$A = \begin{pmatrix} A_{h_2+1} & 0 & \cdots & 0 \\ 0 & A_{h_2+2} & \cdots & 0 \\ \cdot & \cdot & \cdots & \cdot \\ 0 & 0 & \cdots & A_h \end{pmatrix} \tag{34.35}$$

where $A_p = \{\alpha_{ks}(p)\}_{1 \leqslant k,s \leqslant n_p}$, $p = h_2 + 1, \ldots, h$,

and

$$\alpha_{ks}(p) = \begin{cases} \binom{k-1}{s-1} \bar{z}_p & \text{for } k = 1, \ldots, n_p;\ s = 1, \ldots, k, \\ 0 & \text{for } k = 1, \ldots, n_p;\ s = k+1, \ldots, n_p, \end{cases}$$

$p = h_2 + 1, \ldots, h$;

$$C = \begin{pmatrix} I_m & 0 \\ 0 & \{[\sqrt{(2q+1)(2l+1)}/q + l + 1]\delta(p - s)\}_{1 \leqslant p,s \leqslant h_1; 0 \leqslant q \leqslant n_p - 1; 0 \leqslant l \leqslant n_s - 1} \end{pmatrix}, \tag{34.36}$$

where $\delta(x) = 1$ or 0 according as $x = 0$ or $x \neq 0$, and I_m is the $m \times m$ identity matrix; and

$$\tilde{\Gamma} = \begin{pmatrix} \tilde{\Gamma}_{11} & \tilde{\Gamma}_{12} \\ \tilde{\Gamma}_{21} & \tilde{\Gamma}_{22} \end{pmatrix}, \tag{34.37}$$

where (with $g(\cdot)$ being the spectral density of the $u(t, \cdot)$)

$$\tilde{\Gamma}_{11} = \{g(-\lambda_j)\delta(\lambda_j + \lambda_k)\}_{1\leqslant j,k\leqslant m};$$

$$\tilde{\Gamma}_{12} = \{g(-\theta_p)\delta(\theta_p + \lambda_j)/(q+1)\}_{1\leqslant j\leqslant m; 1\leqslant p\leqslant h_1; 0\leqslant q\leqslant n_p - 1} = \tilde{\Gamma}'_{12} \qquad (34.38)$$

$$\tilde{\Gamma}_{22} = \{g(-\theta_p)\delta(\theta_p + \theta_v)/(l+q+1)\}_{1\leqslant p,v\leqslant h_1, 0\leqslant q\leqslant n_p-1; 0\leqslant l\leqslant n_v - 1}.$$

We note in passing that the nonsingularity of $\tilde{\Gamma}$ was established by Grenander and Rosenblatt in Grenander and Rosenblatt 1957 (pp. 245–247). We also note that equation 34.33 explicates why standard large-sample theory cannot be applied to all of $(\tilde{\alpha}(S,\cdot), \tilde{\gamma}(S,\cdot))$ but only to $\tilde{\alpha}(S,\cdot)$.

34.1.5 Removal of Seasonal, Cyclical, and Trend Factors in Time Series

Our intention in this first section of the chapter was to study the asymptotic properties of three linear SCT-adjustment procedures for time series generated by a dynamic stochastic process. Above we determined the asymptotic properties of least-squares estimates of the relevant parameters of such a process. Now we shall use our results to study characteristics of the three adjustment procedures.

Recall first the definition of a linear SCT-adjustment procedure in section 34.1.2 and take a second look at equations 34.10 and 34.14. Then suppose that we have observed $x_S(\omega)$ and that we want to eliminate all trace of the seasonal and cyclical components of $x_S(\cdot)$. For that purpose we use the following "rough" least-squares estimate of $\alpha(\cdot)$:

$$\mathscr{L}_1(S,\omega) = \{C^*(S)C(S)\}^{-1}C^*(S)x_S(\omega), \qquad S > m. \qquad (34.39)$$

On the ω set where $\gamma(\omega) = 0$, $\mathscr{L}_1(S,\cdot)$ is a consistent estimator of $\alpha(\cdot)$ and the associated linear SCT-adjustment procedure, defined by

$$\mathscr{A}_1(S)x_S(\omega) = x_S(\omega) - C(S)\mathscr{L}_1(S,\omega), \qquad (34.40)$$

has desirable properties. That is seen in T 34.3:

T 34.3 Let $\{x(t,\omega); t \in T\}$ be a dynamic stochastic process which satisfies the basic assumptions i–iv, and let $\mathscr{L}_1(\cdot)$ and $\mathscr{A}_1(\cdot)$ be as defined in equations 34.39 and 34.40. Moreover, let $S_\gamma = \{\omega \in \Omega : \gamma(\omega) = 0\}$ and assume that $P(S_\gamma) > 0$. Then

$$\lim_{S\to\infty} E\{\|\alpha(\omega) - \mathscr{L}_1(S,\omega)\|^2 | S_\gamma\} = 0, \qquad (34.41)$$

and

$$p\lim_{S\to\infty} \mathscr{A}_1(S)x_S(\omega) = \lim_{S\to\infty} \{u_S(\omega) + D(S)\beta(\omega)\} \quad (P_{S_\gamma} \text{ measure}), \qquad (34.42)$$

where the limit in equation 34.42 is componentwise.

In the statement of this theorem, $E\{\|\cdot\|^2|S_\gamma\}$ denotes the conditional expectation of $\|\cdot\|^2$ given S_γ. Moreover, $P_{S_\gamma}(\cdot)$ denotes the conditional probability measure of events given S_γ.

Since the $u(t,\cdot)$ are distributed independently of $\alpha(\cdot)$, $\beta(\cdot)$, and $\gamma(\cdot)$, the assertion in equation 34.41 is a simple consequence of a theorem of Grenander and Rosenblatt (Grenander and Rosenblatt 1957, pp. 245–248) whenever, for some fixed vector α, $S_\gamma = \{\omega: \alpha(\omega) = \alpha,\ \beta(\omega) = 0,\ \gamma(\omega) = 0\}$, and the spectral density $g(\cdot)$ is positive and piecewise continuous. Note, therefore, that we do not assume that $\alpha(\omega) \equiv \alpha$ (a fixed vector) and $\beta(\omega) \equiv 0$ on S_γ. We also make no restriction on the spectral distribution function of the $u(t,\cdot)$ other than that it must be absolutely continuous.

Grenander and Rosenblatt also showed for their case that $\mathscr{L}_1(S,\omega)$ is an asymptotically efficient estimator of $\alpha(\omega)$. It can be shown that $\mathscr{L}_1(S,\omega)$ is an asymptotically efficient estimator of $\alpha(\cdot)$ even if $\beta(\omega) \neq 0$, provided the spectral density $g(\cdot)$ is positive and continuous.

Suppose next that we have observed $x_S(\omega)$ and want to remove all trace of the trend components of $x_S(\cdot)$. To that end we use the following "rough" least-squares estimate of $\gamma(\cdot)$:

$$\mathscr{L}_2(S,\omega) = \{G^*(S)G(S)\}G^*(S)x_S(\omega), \qquad S > n. \tag{34.43}$$

On almost all of Ω, $\mathscr{L}_2(S,\omega)$ converges exponentially fast to $\gamma(\cdot)$, and the associated SCT-adjustment procedure, defined by

$$\mathscr{A}_2(S)x_S(\omega) = x_S(\omega) - G(S)\mathscr{L}_2(S,\omega), \qquad S > n, \tag{39.44}$$

has desirable properties, as evidenced in the following theorem:

T 34.4 Let $\{x(t,\omega);\ t \in T\}$ be a dynamic stochastic process which satisfies assumptions i–iv and let $\mathscr{L}_2(\cdot)$ and $\mathscr{A}_2(\cdot)$ be as defined in equations 34.43 and 34.44. Then there exist a bounded random variable $K(\omega)$ and a constant $\lambda \in (0, 1)$ such that

$$\|\mathscr{L}_2(S,\omega) - \gamma(\omega)\| \leqslant K(\omega)\lambda^S, \quad S > n, \quad \text{a.e. } (P \text{ measure}).$$

Consequently,

$$\lim_{S\to\infty} \mathscr{A}_2(S)x_S(\omega) = \lim_{S\to\infty} \{u_S(\omega) + C(S)\alpha(\omega) + D(S)\beta(\omega)\}, \quad \text{a.e. } (P \text{ measure}), \tag{34.45}$$

where the limit in equation 34.45 is componentwise.

Suppose at last that we want to erase in one swoop all trace of seasonal, cyclical, and trend factors from our observations on the $x(t,\cdot)$. Then we define $\mathscr{L}_3(S,\omega)$ by

$$\mathscr{L}_3(S,\omega) = (\tilde{\alpha}(S,\omega), \tilde{\gamma}(S,\omega)), \qquad S > n + m, \tag{34.46}$$

where $\tilde{\alpha}(\cdot)$ and $\tilde{\gamma}(\cdot)$ are as described in equation 34.30; and we let the corresponding SCT-adjustment procedure, $\mathscr{A}_3$, be defined by

$$\mathscr{A}_3(S)x_S(\omega) = x_S(\omega) - \tilde{H}(S)\mathscr{L}_3(S, \omega), \qquad S > n + m. \tag{34.47}$$

Then $\mathscr{L}_3(S, \cdot)$ converges in proabability to $(\alpha(\cdot), \gamma(\cdot))$, and the SCT-adjustment procedure has equally agreeable properties. That is, we have T 34.5:

T 34.5 Let $\{x(t, \omega); t \in T\}$ be a dynamic stochastic process that satisfies assumptions i–iv. In addition, let $\mathscr{L}_3(\cdot)$ and $\mathscr{A}_3(\cdot)$ be as defined in equations 34.46 and 34.47. Then

$$p\lim \mathscr{L}_3(S, \omega) = (\alpha(\omega), \gamma(\omega));$$

and

$$p\lim \mathscr{A}_3(S)x_S(\omega) = \lim \{u_S(\omega) + D(S)\beta(\omega)\}, \tag{34.48}$$

where the limit in equation 34.48 is componentwise.

34.2 Estimating the Coefficients in a Stochastic Difference Equation: Consistency

In this section I present various theorems concerning the asymptotic properties of least-squares estimates of the a_k in equation 34.1. My purpose is to contrast the properties of these estimates when the initial conditions are fixed with their properties when the initial conditions are random. The fact that the properties vary with our assumptions about the initial conditions can be intuited from the discussion of stochastic difference equations in section 33.3.

34.2.1 Equations with Fixed Initial Conditions

We begin by assuming that the initial conditions of equation 34.1 are fixed. If this is the case, then we can assert the following:

T 34.6 Let $\{x(t); t = -n + 1, -n + 2, \dots\}$ be a family of real-valued random variables which satisfy the conditions:

(i) $x(t) = \overline{x}_t$, w. pr. 1 (i.e., with probability 1), $t = -n + 1, \dots, 0$;

(ii) $0 < Ex(t)^2 < \infty$, $t = 1, 2, \dots$; and

(iii) $\sum_{k=0}^{n} a_k x(t - k) = \eta(t)$, $t = 1, 2, \dots$,

where $\overline{x}_t$ and a_k are real constants with $a_0 = 1$, and where $\{\eta(t); t = 1, 2, \dots\}$ is a family of nondegenerate, independently and identically distributed real random variables with mean zero. Next, let $a = (a_1, \dots, a_n)$ and let $\hat{a}(N) = (\hat{a}_1(N), \dots,$

$\hat{a}_n(N))$, $N > n$, be a sequence of random vectors which, for each N and "almost all" realizations of the $x(t)$, satisfy

$$\sum_{t=1}^{N}\left(x(t) - \sum_{k=1}^{n} \hat{a}_k(N)x(t-k)\right)^2$$

$$= \min_{\alpha_1,\ldots,\alpha_n} \sum_{t=1}^{N}\left(x(t) - \sum_{k=1}^{N} \alpha_k x(t-k)\right)^2. \tag{34.49}$$

Then $\hat{a}(N)$ converges in probability to $-a$; that is,

$$p\lim \hat{a}(N) = -a. \tag{34.50}$$

This theorem was orginally established by Mann and Wald (Mann and Wald 1943) under the additional assumption that $E\eta(1)^4 < \infty$ and that the moduli of the roots of the polynomial $M(z) = \sum_{k=0}^{n} a_k z^{-k}$ are all less than 1. T. W. Anderson established the theorem for the case when the roots of $M(z)$ are all distinct and have moduli greater than 1 (Anderson 1959), and M. M. Rao proved the theorem for the case when $M(z)$ has two roots, one with modulus less than 1 and one with modulus greater than 1 (Rao 1961). Finally, H. Rubin proved the theorem for $n = 1$ (Rubin 1950), and T. J. Muench proved it for an arbitrary n (Muench 1974).

The important thing to notice about T 34.6 is that the least-squares estimate of $-a$ is consistent and that the consistency of $\hat{a}(N)$ is independent of the values of the moduli of the roots of $M(z)$. By making assumptions about the moduli of the roots of $M(z)$, we can obtain a stronger result.

T 34.7 Let $\{x(t); t = -n+1, -n+2, \ldots\}$ be a family of real-valued random variables that satisfies conditions i–iii of T 34.6. Moreover, let $M(z) = \sum_{k=0}^{n} a_k z^{-k}$ and assume that the moduli of the roots of $M(z)$ differ from 1. Finally, let a and $\hat{a}(N)$ be as defined in T 34.6. Then

$$\lim \hat{a}(N) = -a \quad \text{w. pr. 1.} \tag{34.51}$$

Moreover, if the moduli of the roots of $M(z)$ are all greater than 1, then there exist positive constants K and λ such that $\lambda \in (0, 1)$ and

$$\|\hat{a}(N) + a\| \leqslant K\lambda^N \quad \text{w. pr. 1,} \qquad N = n+1, n+2, \ldots. \tag{34.52}$$

In interpreting the conditions of T 34.6, Mann and Wald, Anderson, Rao, Rubin, and Muench took the distribution of the $\eta(t)$ to be independent of the values assumed by $x(t)$ at $t = -n+1, \ldots, 0$. This means that the $x(t)$ should be thought of as representing an experiment which starts at time $t = 1$ with fixed (i.e., nonrandom) initial conditions $x_{-n+1}, \ldots, x_0$. Such experiments occur frequently in physics and chemistry. However, they are uncommon in sciences such as astronomy, meteorology, and economics. In the latter, researchers are more likely to observe "ongoing" processes than experiments with a fixed initial date.

34.2.2 Equations with Random Initial Conditions: Special Cases

Next we shall investigate the asymptotic properties of $\hat{a}(N)$ when the $x(t)$ represent an ongoing process rather than an experiment with a fixed initial date. This means that we want to ascertain the limit of $\hat{a}(N)$ if the $x(t)$ satisfy conditions ii and iii of T 34.6 for all $t \in \{\ldots, -1, 0, 1, \ldots\}$ but not condition i. To do that we must introduce some notation: Let the a_k be as in equation (34.1) and let z_p and n_p, $p = 1, \ldots, h$, be such that

$$\sum_{k=0}^{n} a_k z^{n-k} = \prod_{p=1}^{h} (z - z_p)^{n_p} = z^n M(z). \tag{34.53}$$

Moreover, let $w_p = z_p$ if $|z| \leqslant 1$ and let $w_p = z_p^{-1}$ if $|z_p| > 1$. Then define b_k, $k = 0, \ldots, n$, by

$$\sum_{k=0}^{n} b_k z^{n-k} = \prod_{p=1}^{h} (z - w_p)^{n_p}. \tag{34.54}$$

Finally, let $(\Omega, \mathscr{F}, P(\cdot))$ be a probability space, and let $\{x(t, \omega);\ t \in T\}$ be a dynamic stochastic process on $(\Omega, \mathscr{F}, P(\cdot))$ with the representation

$$x(t, \omega) = y(t, \omega) + f_x(t, \omega), \qquad t \in T, \tag{34.55}$$

where $\{y(t, \omega);\ t \in T\}$ is a wide-sense stationary process and $\{f_x(t, \omega);\ t \in T\}$ is a nonstationary stochastic process which satisfies

$$f_x(t, \omega)) = \sum_{p=1}^{h} \sum_{j=0}^{n_p - 1} A_{pj}(\omega)(t^j z_p^t), \qquad t \in T, \tag{34.56}$$

and assume that

(i) the $x(t, \cdot)$ are real-valued; and
(ii) $|z_p| \neq 1$, $p = 1, \ldots, h$.

Then observe that

$$\sum_{k=0}^{n} a_k f_x(t - k, \omega) = 0, \qquad t \in T,$$

and recall that if condition ii above holds, then the representation of the $x(t, \cdot)$ in equation 34.55 is uniquely determined.

To provide the right setting for our main result, we begin by considering two special cases. First the *autoregressive case*:

T 34.8 Let $\{x(t, \omega);\ t \in T\}$ be a dynamic stochastic process which satisfies equations 34.55 and 34.56 and conditions i and ii above. Moreover, let

$a = (a_1, \ldots, a_n)'$ and $b = (b_1, \ldots, b_n)'$, respectively, be as in equations 34.53 and 34.54 and let

$$\hat{a}(N, \omega) = (B_N'(\omega) B_N(\omega))^{-1} B_N'(\omega) x_N(\omega), \tag{34.57}$$

where $x_N(\omega) = (x(1, \omega), \ldots, x(N, \omega))'$; $B_N'(\omega) = \{\tilde{x}(0, \omega), \ldots, \tilde{x}(N-1, \omega)\}$; and

$\tilde{x}(t, \omega) = (x(t, \omega), \ldots, x(t - n + 1, \omega))'$ $t = 0, 1, \ldots, N-1$.

Finally, let

$$\eta(t, \omega) = \sum_{k=0}^{n} a_k x(t-k, \omega), \qquad t \in T,$$

and

$$\mathscr{A} = \{\omega \in \Omega : f_x(t, \omega) = 0, t \in T\};$$

and assume that $\{\eta(t, \omega); t \in T\}$ is a purely random process whose variables are distributed independently of the $f_x(t, \omega)$ in equation 34.56 and that $P(\mathscr{A}) > 0$. Then

$$\lim_{N \to \infty} \hat{a}(N, \omega) = -b \quad \text{a.e. } (P_{\mathscr{A}} \text{ measure}), \tag{34.58}$$

where $P_{\mathscr{A}}(\cdot)$ denotes the conditional probability measure on $(\Omega, \mathscr{F})$ given $\mathscr{A}$.

In interpreting the theorem, note that, when $\mathscr{A} = \Omega$, $\{x(t, \omega); t \in T\}$ is an autoregressive process. When $\mathscr{A} \neq \Omega$ and the conditions of the theorem are satisfied, then relative to $P_{\mathscr{A}}(\cdot)$, the $x(t, \cdot)$ behave as an autoregressive process. Note also that in estimating the parameters of an autoregressive process, statisticians usually assume that the process is stable, i.e., that $a = b$. Theorem T 34.8 shows that this assumption cannot be tested in any meaningful way if the parameter estimates are least-squares estimates. Finally, note that E. J. Hannan has established equation 34.58 for the case $a = b$ and $\mathscr{A} = \Omega$ (see Hannan 1970, theorem VI. 1, p. 329). The relation 34.58 for $a \neq b$ was established in Stigum 1976 (pp. 49–75).

Here is an example to fix our ideas:

E 34.6 Let $\{x(t, \omega); t \in T\}$ be a wide-sense stationary solution to the equations,

$$x(t, \omega) + ax(t-1, \omega) = \eta(t, \omega), \qquad t \in T,$$

where $a > 1$ and $\eta = \{\eta(t, \omega); t \in T\}$ is a purely random process with mean zero and finite variance σ_η^2. Also let $\hat{a}(N, \cdot)$ be as described in equation 34.57. Then

$$\begin{aligned} \hat{a}(N, \omega) &= \sum_{t=1}^{N} x(t, \omega) x(t-1, \omega) \Big/ \sum_{t=1}^{N} x(t-1, \omega)^2 \\ &= -a + \left(\sum_{t=1}^{N} x(t-1, \omega) \eta(t, \omega) \Big/ \sum_{t=1}^{N} x(t-1, \omega)^2 \right). \end{aligned}$$

Moreover (by lemma 3 in Stigum 1976, p. 61),

$$\lim_{N\to\infty}\left(\frac{1}{N}\right)\sum_{t=1}^{N} x(t-1,\omega)\eta(t,\omega) = +a^{-1}\sigma_\eta^2 \quad \text{a.e.,}$$

and

$$\lim_{N\to\infty}\left(\frac{1}{N}\right)\sum_{t=1}^{N} x(t-1,\omega)^2 = \frac{\sigma_\eta^2}{a^2-1} \quad \text{a.e.}$$

Consequently,

$$\lim_{N\to\infty} \hat{a}(N,\omega) = -a + \frac{a^2-1}{a} = -a^{-1} \quad \text{a.e.}$$

Next the *purely explosive case*:

T 34.9 Let $\{x(t,\omega);\, t \in T\}$ be a real-valued dynamic stochastic process which satisfies equations 34.55 and 34.56 and let $a = (a_1, \dots, a_n)$ and $\hat{a}(N,\omega)$, respectively, be as in equations 34.53 and 34.57. Moreover, suppose that

$$|z_p| > 1, \qquad p = 1, \dots, h;$$

and

$$|A_{pj}(\omega)| > 0 \quad \text{a.e.,} \qquad p = 1, \dots, \alpha, \qquad j = 0, \dots, n_p - 1.$$

Then there exist a constant λ and a bounded random variable $K(\cdot)$ such that $0 < \lambda < 1$, and

$$\|\hat{a}(N,\omega) + a\| \leqslant K(\omega)\lambda^N \qquad \text{a.e. for } N > n. \tag{34.59}$$

In interpreting this theorem, note first that in form 34.59 is identical to 34.52. Then observe that if we let

$$\eta(t,\omega) = \sum_{k=0}^{n} a_k x(t-k,\omega), \qquad t \in T,$$

and let $\eta = \{\eta(t,\omega);\, t \in T\}$, then η is a wide-sense stationary process. However, in contradistinction to the $\eta(t)$ of T 34.7 the $\eta(t,\cdot)$ we defined above need not constitute a purely random process. In fact, η need not even have an absolutely continuous spectral distribution function. This might seem surprising. So here is an example to show why it is not strange at all.

E 34.7 Let $\{x(t,\omega);\, t \in T\}$ be a dynamic stochastic process with the representation

$$x(t,\omega) = -\sum_{s=1}^{\infty} a^{-s}\eta(t+s,\omega) + A(\omega)a^t, \qquad t \in T$$

where $a > 1$, where $\{\eta(t,\omega);\, t \in T\}$ is an arbitrary real-valued wide-sense stationary process, and where $A(\omega)^2 > 0$ a.e. Also let $\hat{a}(N,\cdot)$ be as described in equation 34.57. Then

$$x(t,\omega) - ax(t-1,\omega) = \eta(t,\omega), \qquad t \in T,$$

and

$$\hat{a}(N,\omega) = a + \left(\sum_{t=1}^{N} x(t-1,\omega)\eta(t,\omega) \Big/ \sum_{t=1}^{N} x(t-1,\omega)^2 \right).$$

Moreover (by lemma 4 in Stigum 1976, p. 62), Tchebichev's Inequality, Borel's 0–1 Criterion, and some algebra),

$$\lim_{N\to\infty} (N^{1/2}a^N)^{-1} \sum_{t=1}^{N} x(t-1,\omega)\eta(t,\omega) = 0 \quad \text{a.e.,}$$

and

$$\lim_{N\to\infty} a^{-2N} \sum_{t=1}^{N} x(t-1,\omega)^2 = \frac{A(\omega)^2}{a^2-1} > 0 \quad \text{a.e.}$$

From this it follows easily that there are a bounded random variable $K(\cdot)$ and a constant $\lambda \in (0,1)$ such that

$$|\hat{a}(N,\omega) - a| \leqslant K(\omega)\lambda^N \quad \text{a.e. for } N \geqslant 1.$$

The differences in the behavior of $\hat{a}(N,\cdot)$ in E 34.6 and E 34.7 are interesting. In the next example we record the results of a simulation experiment which show how dramatic these differences can be.

E 34.8 Let $\{\eta(t,\omega); t \in T\}$ be a purely random process of normally distributed variables with mean 0 and variance 1. Moreover, let

$$y(t,\omega) = -\sum_{s=1}^{400} (1.02)^{-s}\eta(t+s,\omega), \qquad t = 0, 1, \ldots; \tag{34.60}$$

$$w(t,\omega) = \sum_{s=0}^{400} (1.02)^{-s}\eta(t-s,\omega), \qquad t = 0, 1, \ldots; \tag{34.61}$$

$$x(t,\omega) = y(t,\omega) + (1.02)^t, \qquad t = 0, 1, \ldots; \tag{34.62}$$

and observe that, for $t = 1, 2, \ldots, 700$,

$$y(t,\omega) - (1.02)y(t-1,\omega) = \eta(t,\omega) - (1.02)^{-400}\eta(t+400);$$

$$w(t,\omega) - (1.02)^{-1}w(t-1,\omega) = \eta(t,\omega) - (1.02)^{-400}\eta(t-400);$$

$$x(t,\omega) - (1.02)x(t-1,\omega) = y(t,\omega) - (1.02)y(t-1,\omega).$$

By a pseudo-random sampling scheme, which Anders Ekeland programmed for me, I obtained one observation on each of the $\eta(t,\cdot)$ from $t = -400$ to $t = 1100$. Those observations and equations 34.60–34.62 provided me with one observation on each of the triples $(y(t,\cdot), w(t,\cdot), x(t,\cdot))$ from $t = 0$ to $t = 700$ which I used to compute

$$\hat{a}_z(N) = \sum_{t=1}^{N} z(t)z(t-1) \Big/ \sum_{t=1}^{N} z(t-1)^2, \qquad N = 1, 2, \ldots, 700,$$

for $z = y, w$, and x. According to T 34.8, $\hat{a}_y(N)$ and $\hat{a}_w(N)$ converge with prob-

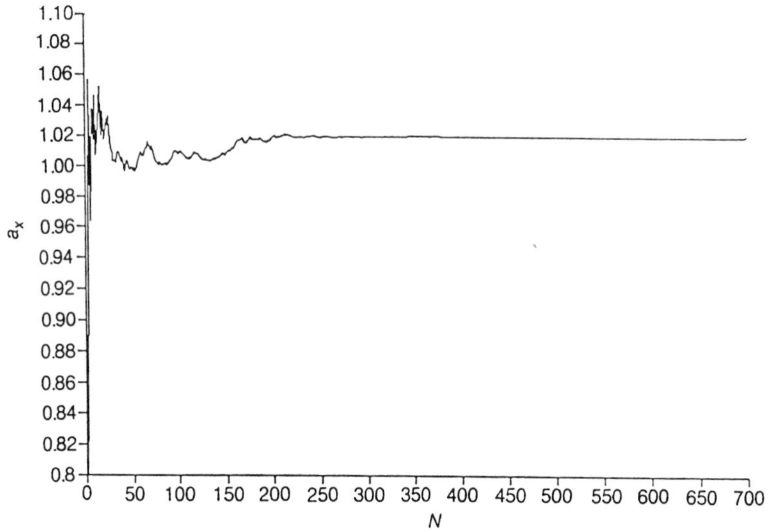

Figure 34.4
Least-squares estimates of a_x in $x(t) - a_x x(t-1) = \eta(t)$, $t \in T$.

ability 1 to $(1.02)^{-1}$, and according to T 34.9, $\hat{a}_x(N)$ converges exponentially fast to (1.02). These predictions are borne out in figures 34.4–34.6.

34.2.3 Equations with Random Initial Conditions: The Fundamental Theorem

For my main result, I need more notation. Let $\{x(t, \omega); t \in T\}$ be a real-valued dynamic stochastic process which satisfies equations 34.55, 34.56, and

$$P(\{\omega: A_{p(n_p-1)}(\omega) \neq 0\}) > 0, \qquad p = 1, \ldots, h. \tag{34.63}$$

Moreover, for a given ω, let $Q(z, \omega)$ be the polynomial of least order with leading coefficient 1 such that

$$Q(S, \omega) f_x(t, \omega) = 0, \qquad t \in T, \tag{34.64}$$

and let m, m_p, $p = 1, \ldots, h$; q_k, $k = 0, \ldots, m$ be such that

$$\sum_{k=0}^{m} q_k z^{-k} = Q(z, \omega) = z^{-m} \prod_{p=1}^{h} (z - z_p)^{m_p}. \tag{34.65}$$

Finally, let the z_p be numbered so that

$$|z_p| < 1, \quad p = 1, \ldots, h_1, \qquad \text{and} \qquad |z_p| > 1, \quad h_1 + 1, \ldots, h,$$

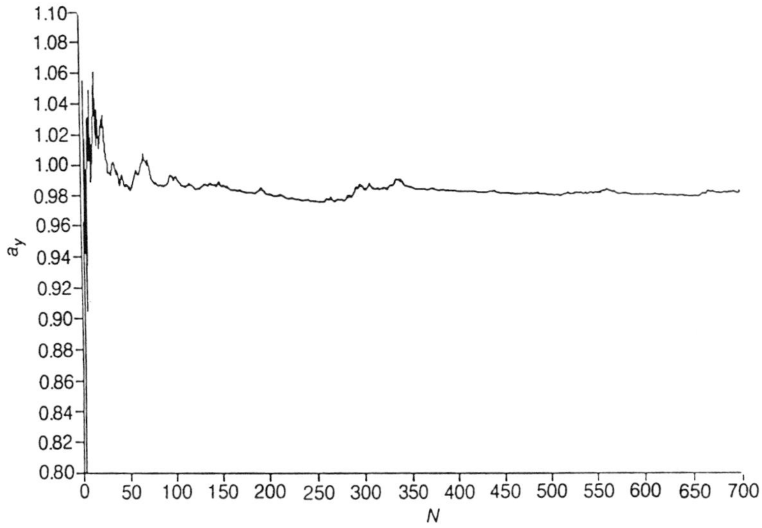

Figure 34.5
Least-squares estimates of a_y in $y(t) - a_y y(t-1) = \eta(t)$, $t \in T$.

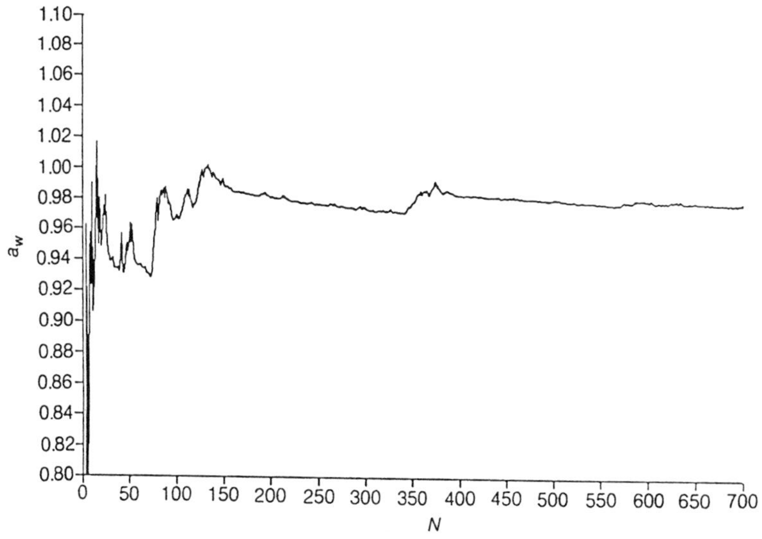

Figure 34.6
Least-squares estimates of a_w in $w(t) - a_w w(t-1) = \eta(t)$, $t \in T$.

and let $m^* = \sum_{p=h_1+1}^{h} m_p$, $w_p = z_p^{-1}$, $p = h_1 + 1, \ldots, h$,

$$\psi(z) = \sum_{k=0}^{m^*} \psi_k z^{-k} = z^{-m^*} \prod_{p=h_1+1}^{h} (z - z_p)^{m_p}, \text{ and}$$

$$\sum_{k=0}^{n} c_k z^{-k} = z^{-n+m^*}\psi(z)\left(\prod_{p=1}^{h_1} (z - z_p)^{n_p}\right)\left(\prod_{p=h_1+1}^{h} (z - w_p)^{n_p - m_p}\right). \tag{34.66}$$

With the preceding notation, I can state my main result as in T 34.10. In reading it, note that equation 34.63 implies that $M(z)$ is the minimal polynomial with leading coefficient 1 such that $M(S) f_x(t, \omega) = 0$ a.e. Thus, if $m \neq n$ and

$$z(t, \omega) = \sum_{k=0}^{m} q_k x(t - k, \omega), \qquad t \in T,$$

then $\{z(t, \omega); t \in T\}$ is not a wide-sense stationary process. Similarly, if $M(z) \neq \sum_{k=0}^{n} c_k z^{-k}$, and if

$$v(t, \omega) = \sum_{k=0}^{n} c_k x(t - k, \omega), \qquad t \in T,$$

then $\{v(t, \omega); t \in T\}$ is not a wide-sense stationary process.

T 34.10 Let $\{x(t, \omega); t \in T\}$ be a real-valued dynamic stochastic process which satisfies equations 34.55, 34.56, and 34.63; define $\{\eta(t, \omega); t \in T\}$ by

$$\eta(t, \omega) = \sum_{k=0}^{n} a_k x(t - k, \omega), \qquad t \in T; \tag{34.67}$$

let q_k, $k = 0, 1, \ldots, m$, be as defined in equations 34.64 and 34.65; and let $c' = (c_1, \ldots, c_n)$, where the c_k are as in equation 34.66. Moreover, let

$$\mathscr{S} = \{\omega \in \Omega : \textstyle\sum_{k=0}^{m} q_k f_x(t - k, \omega) = 0,\ t \in T, \text{ and there is no polynomial } N(z) \text{ of lower order than } m \text{ such that } N(S) f_x(t, \omega) = 0;\ t \in T\}.$$

Finally, let $\hat{a}(N, \cdot)$ be as described in equation 34.57 and assume that

(i) the $\eta(t, \cdot)$ constitute a purely random process and are distributed independently of the $f_x(t, \cdot)$; and

(ii) $P(\mathscr{S}) > 0$.

Then

$$\lim_{N \to \infty} \hat{a}(N, \omega) = -c \quad \text{a.e. } (P_{\mathscr{S}} \text{ measure}), \tag{34.68}$$

where $P_{\mathscr{S}}(\cdot)$ denotes the conditional probability measure on $(\Omega, \mathscr{F})$ given $\mathscr{S}$.

In interpreting this theorem, note that when $h_1 = h$, $c = a$. For this case, E. J. Hannan established equation 34.68 in Hannan 1970 (chapter VI, theorem VI.1, p. 329). Note also that when $\mathscr{S} = \Omega$ and $M(z) = \sum_{k=0}^{n} q_k z^{-k}$, then again $c = a$. Finally, note that T 34.10 suggests that Ω can be partitioned into a finite number of sets on which $\hat{a}(N, \cdot)$ converges a.e. to different vectors. For instance, on the set $\{\omega: A_{jk}(\omega) = 0, j = h_1 + 1, \ldots, h, k = 0, 1, \ldots, n_j - 1\}$, $\hat{a}(N, \cdot)$ converges to $-b$, where b is as defined in theorem T 34.8. On the set $\{\omega: A_{jk}(\omega) \neq 0, j = h_1 + 1, \ldots, h, k = 0, 1, \ldots, n_j - 1\}$, $\hat{a}(N, \cdot)$ converges to $-a$. All intermediate cases are described by the definition of $\mathscr{S}$ and c. Thus even when $\hat{a}(N, \cdot)$ is inconsistent in the sense that $p\lim_{N\to\infty} \hat{a}(N, \omega) \neq -a$, $\hat{a}(N, \cdot)$ always converges on each of the sets of the partition to something definite.

E 34.9 Let $\{x(t, \omega); t \in T\}$ be a dynamic stochastic process with the representation

$$x(t, \omega) = y(t, \omega) + A(\omega)z^t + B(\omega)w^t, \qquad t \in T,$$

where $z > w > 1$. Moreover, let

$$a' = (a_1, a_2) = (-(z + w), zw),$$

and

$$\eta(t, \omega) = x(t, \omega) + a_1 x(t - 1, \omega) + a_2(t - 2, \omega), \qquad t \in T.$$

Finally, let

$$\mathscr{S}_1 = \{\omega \in \Omega : A(\omega) \neq 0, B(\omega) \neq 0\},$$

$$\mathscr{S}_2 = \{\omega \in \Omega : A(\omega) \neq 0, B(\omega) = 0\},$$

$$\mathscr{S}_3 = \{\omega \in \Omega : A(\omega) = 0, B(\omega) \neq 0\},$$

$$\mathscr{S}_4 = \{\omega \in \Omega : A(\omega) = 0, B(\omega) = 0\},$$

and

$$b' = (b_1, b_2) = [-(1/z + 1/w), 1/zw].$$

Assume now that $\{\eta(t, \omega); t \in T\}$ is a purely random process which is indenpendently distributed of $A(\cdot)$ and $B(\cdot)$. Assume also that $P(\mathscr{S}_i) > 0$, $i = 1, \ldots, 4$, and let $\hat{a}(N, \cdot)$ be as described in equation 34.57. Then

$$\lim_{N\to\infty} \hat{a}(N, \omega) = \begin{cases} -a & \text{a.e. on } \mathscr{S}_1, \\ -[-(z + (1/w)), z/w] & \text{a.e. on } \mathscr{S}_2, \\ -[-((1/z) + w), w/z] & \text{a.e. on } \mathscr{S}_3, \text{ and} \\ -b & \text{a.e. on } \mathscr{S}_4. \end{cases}$$

34.2.4 Concluding Remarks

From all appearance it looks like the processes considered in theorems T 34.7 and T 34.10 differ from one another only in that the initial conditions in one are fixed (i.e., nonrandom) while the initial conditions in that the other are random. This and the fact that the limit in equations 34.51 is completely independent of the values assumed by $x(t)$ for $t = -n + 1, \ldots, 0$, make it hard to intuit the reason the conclusions drawn in the two theorems are so different. The following simple arguments will show why.

Let $\{x(t); t = -n + 1, -n + 2, \ldots\}$ be as specified in theorem T 34.7, and let $X \equiv \{x(t, \omega); t \in T\}$ be as specified in theorem T 34.10. Then observe that condition iii of theorem T 34.6 and equation 34.67 imply that there exist constants γ_s, $s = 0, 1, \ldots$, and real-valued functions $\varphi(\cdot)$ on $\{-n + 1, -n + 2, \ldots\}$ and $\tilde{\varphi}(\cdot)$ on $\{-n + 1, -n + 2, \ldots\} \times \Omega$ such that

(i) a. $x(t) = \varphi(t) + \sum_{s=0}^{t-1} \gamma_s \eta(t - s)$, $t = 1, 2, \ldots;$

b. $\varphi(t) = \bar{x}_t$, $t = -n + 1, \ldots, 0$; and

c. $\sum_{k=0}^{n} a_k \varphi(t - k) = 0$, $t = 1, 2, \ldots.$

(ii) a. $x(t, \omega) = \tilde{\varphi}(t, \omega) + \sum_{s=0}^{t-1} \gamma_s \eta(t - s, \omega)$, $t = 1, 2, \ldots;$

b. $\tilde{\varphi}(t, \omega) = x(t, \omega)$, $t = -n + 1, \ldots, 0$; and

c. $\sum_{k=0}^{n} a_k \tilde{\varphi}(t - k, \omega) = 0 \qquad$ for all $\omega \in \Omega$ and $t = 1, 2, \ldots.$

Assertions i and ii here make precise what it means to say that the two processes in theorems T 34.7 and T 34.10 differ in that one has fixed initial conditions while the other has random initial conditions.

Next observe that there is a wide-sense stationary solution to equation 34.67. This solution is unique in the sense that any other solution can differ from it only on an Ω set of P-measure 0. Thus we may pick the Y process in equation 34.55 as the wide-sense stationary solution of equation 34.67. If we do, we can also find constants $\tilde{\gamma}_s$, $s \in T$ such that

$$y(t, \omega) = \sum_{s=-\infty}^{\infty} \tilde{\gamma}_s \eta(t - s, \omega) \quad \text{a.e.,} \qquad \text{for all } t \in T,$$

and assert that

$$x(t, \omega) = f_x(t, \omega) + \sum_{s=-\infty}^{\infty} \tilde{\gamma}_s \eta(t - s, \omega) \quad \text{a.e.,} \qquad \text{for all } t \in T.$$

If the z_p in equation 34.56 satisfy $|z_p| < 1$, $p = 1, \ldots, h$, $\tilde{\gamma}_s = 0$ for $s < 0$. If the z_p satisfy $|z_p| > 1$, $p = 1, \ldots, h$, $\tilde{\gamma}_s = 0$ for $s \geqslant 0$. Otherwise $\tilde{\gamma}_s \neq 0$ for $s \geqslant 0$ and for $s \leqslant -k$ where k is a positive integer which depends on the multiplicity of the z_p with $|z_p| > 1$.

Finally, observe that the last equation and conditions ii above imply that

$$\tilde{\varphi}(t, \omega) = f_x(t, \omega) + \sum_{s=-\infty}^{\infty} \tilde{\gamma}_s \eta(t - s, \omega) \qquad \text{for } t = -n + 1, \ldots, 0,$$

and that there exist random variables $\tilde{A}_{pk}(\cdot)$, $p = 1, \ldots, h$, $k = 0, \ldots, n_p - 1$, such that

$$\tilde{\varphi}(t, \omega) = \sum_{p=1}^{h} \sum_{k=0}^{n_p} \tilde{A}_{pk}(\omega)(t^k z_p^t), \qquad \text{for all } \omega \in \Omega \text{ and}$$

$$t = -n + 1, -n + 2, \ldots.$$

From the last two equations and from (iib) we can draw the following conclusions:

1. If $|z_p| < 1$ for all $p = 1, \ldots, j$, the $\tilde{A}_{pk}(\cdot)$ are linear functions of the $f_x(t, \cdot)$, $t = -n + 1, \ldots, 0$, and of the $\eta(t, \cdot)$ for $t \leqslant 0$.

2. If $|z_p| > 1$ for all $p = 1, \ldots, h$, the $\tilde{A}_{pk}(\cdot)$ are linear functions of the $f_x(t, \cdot)$, $t = -n + 1, \ldots, 0$, and the $\eta(t, \cdot)$ for $t + n > k$, where k is a positive integer which depends on the multiplicity of the various z_p.

3. If some of the z_p have moduli smaller than 1 and some greater than 1, the $\tilde{A}_{pk}(\cdot)$ are linear functions of the $f_x(t, \cdot)$, $t = -n + 1, \ldots, 0$, and of the $\eta(t, \cdot)$ for $t \leqslant 0$ and for $t + n > k$, where k is a positive integer which depends on the multiplicity of the z_p with $|z_p| > 1$.

The preceding observations allow us to point out one other way in which the processes in theorem T 34.7 and T 34.10 differ. In theorem T 34.7 the $\eta(t)$, $t = 1, 2, \ldots$, are implicitly assumed to be independently distributed of $\varphi(t)$, $t = -n + 1, -n + 2, \ldots, 0$, and hence of $\varphi(t)$ for $t \geqslant 1$ as well. In theorem T 34.10, the $\eta(t, \cdot)$ are assumed to be independently distributed of the $f_x(t, \cdot)$. This means that, if $|z_p| < 1$ for all p, the $\eta(t, \cdot)$ for $t \geqslant 1$ are independently distributed of the $\tilde{\varphi}(t, \cdot)$ for $t = -n + 1, -n + 2, \ldots$. In all other cases the distribution of the $\eta(t, \cdot)$ for $t \geqslant 1$ is not independent of the values assumed by $\tilde{\varphi}(t, \cdot)$ for $t = -n + 1, \ldots, 0$. Evidently, in these cases the process considered in theorem T 34.10 differs in a second fundamental way from the process considered in theorem

T 34.7. It is, therefore, revealing to observe that the conclusions of the two theorems differ only when at least one of the z_p has modulus greater than 1.

In interpreting the conclusions of theorem T 34.10, note also that the set $\mathscr{S}$ is defined in terms of values assumed by the $A_{pq}(\cdot)$'s (and not the $\tilde{A}_{pq}(\cdot)$'s!).

34.3 Estimating the Coefficients in a Stochastic Difference Equation: Limiting Distributions

In this section I present theorems concerning the asymptotic distribution of least-squares estimates of the a_k in equation 34.1. My primary aim is to contrast the properties of the limiting distributions when the initial conditions are fixed with their properties when the initial conditions are random.

34.3.1 Equations with Fixed Initial Conditions

We begin by assuming that the initial conditions are fixed. For this case we can assert the following theorem:

T 34.11 Let $\{x(t); t = -n+1, -n+2, \ldots\}$ be a family of real-valued random variables which satisfy conditions i–iii of T 34.6. Moreover, let $\hat{a}(N)$ and $M(z)$, respectively, be as in equations 34.49 and 34.53. Then the following assertions are true:

(i) If the moduli of the roots of $M(z)$ are all less than 1, the matrix

$$\Gamma_1 = \lim_{N\to\infty} \left(N^{-1} \sum_{t=1}^{N} Ex(t-i)x(t-j) \right)_{1\leqslant i,j\leqslant n} \tag{34.69}$$

is well defined (i.e., the limit exists) and positive-definite. Moreover, the random vectors $\sqrt{N}(\hat{a}(N) + a)$ converge in distribution to an $n \times 1$ normally distributed vector $\mathscr{G}$ with mean zero and covariance matrix $\sigma_\eta^2 \Gamma_1^{-1}$, where $\sigma_\eta^2 = E\eta(t)^2$.

(ii) If the moduli of the roots of $M(z)$ are all greater than 1, if 0_k denotes the zero vector in R^k, if

$$\tilde{x}(t) = (x(t), \ldots, x(t-n+1))', \qquad t = 0, 1, \ldots;$$

$$\tilde{\eta}(t) = (\eta(t), 0_{n-1})', \qquad t = 1, \ldots;$$

and

$$A = \begin{pmatrix} -a_1 & -a_2 & \cdots & -a_n \\ 1 & 0 & \cdots & 0 \\ 0 & 1 & \cdots & 0 \\ \cdot & \cdot & \cdots & \cdot \\ 0 & 0 & 1 & 0 \end{pmatrix}; \tag{34.70}$$

and if

$$U = \sum_{t=1}^{\infty} A^{-t}\left(\tilde{x}(0) + \sum_{v=1}^{\infty} A^{-v}\hat{\eta}(v)\right)\left(\tilde{x}(0) + \sum_{k=1}^{\infty} A^{-k}\hat{\eta}(k)\right)' A'^{-t},$$

and

$$w = p \lim_{T\to\infty} \sum_{t=1}^{T} A^{-t}\left(\tilde{x}(0) + \sum_{m=1}^{\infty} A^{-m}\hat{\eta}(m)\right)\eta(T-t+1),$$

then U is nonsingular and positive-definite w. pr. 1 and

$$p \lim_{N\to\infty} A^N(\hat{a}(N) + a)' = U^{-1}w.$$

The first half of this theorem was proved by Mann and Wald under the additional assumption that all the moments of $\eta(1)$ exist and are finite. Anderson established the first half as stated and the second half under the additional assumption that U is nonsingular w. pr. 1. Finally, Muench showed that U must be nonsingular w. pr. 1 if the distribution of $\eta(t)$ is nondegenerate.[1]

In the next theorem, we determine the asymptotic distribution of $\sqrt{N}(\hat{a}(N) + a)$ when the roots of $M(z)$ lie on both sides of the unit circle. For that purpose, we let $M(z)$ be as in equation 34.53 and assume that

$$|z_p| < 1, \qquad p = 1, \ldots, h_1; \tag{34.71}$$

and

$$|z_p| > 1, \qquad p = h_1 + 1, \ldots, h. \tag{34.72}$$

We also make use of several new symbols:

$$\psi(z) = \sum_{k=0}^{m} \psi_k z^{-k} = z^{-m} \prod_{p=h_1+1}^{h} (z - z_p)^{n_p}, \tag{34.73}$$

$$D(z) = \sum_{k=0}^{n-m} d_k z^{-k} = \frac{M(z)}{\psi(z)}, \tag{34.74}$$

and the $n \times n$ matrix

$$\tilde{R} = \begin{bmatrix} 1 & 0 & 0 & \cdots & 0 & 1 & 0 & 0 & \cdots & 0 \\ d_1 & 1 & 0 & \cdots & 0 & \psi_1 & 1 & 0 & \cdots & 0 \\ \cdot & d_1 & 1 & \cdots & 0 & \cdot & \psi_1 & 1 & \cdots & \cdot \\ \cdot & \cdot & \cdot & \cdots & \cdot & \cdot & \cdot & \cdot & \cdots & \cdot \\ \cdot & \cdot & \cdot & \cdots & 1 & \psi_m & \cdot & \cdot & \cdots & \cdot \\ \cdot & \cdot & \cdot & \cdots & d_1 & 0 & \psi_m & \cdot & \cdots & \cdot \\ \cdot & \cdot & \cdot & \cdots & \cdot & \cdot & \cdot & \psi_m & \cdots & \cdot \\ d_{n-m} & \cdot & \cdot & \cdots & \cdot & \cdot & \cdot & \cdot & \cdots & 1 \\ 0 & d_{n-m} & \cdot & \cdots & \cdot & \cdot & \cdot & \cdot & \cdots & \psi_1 \\ \cdot & \cdot & d_{n-m} & \cdots & \cdot & \cdot & \cdot & \cdot & \cdots & \cdot \\ \cdot & \cdot & \cdot & \cdots & \cdot & \cdot & \cdot & \cdot & \cdots & \cdot \\ \cdot & & & & & & & & & \\ 0 & 0 & 0 & \cdots & d_{n-m} & 0 & 0 & 0 & \cdots & \psi_m \end{bmatrix} \tag{34.75}$$

With the additional notation, our result can be stated as follows:

T 34.12 Let $\{x(t);\, t = -n+1, -n+2, \ldots\}$ be a family of real-valued random variables which satisfy conditions i–iii of T 34.6. Moreover, let $\hat{a}(N)$ and $M(z)$ be as defined in equations 34.49 and 34.53, and assume that $M(z)$ satisfies equations 34.71 and 34.72. Finally, let $\psi(z)$, $D(z)$, and $\tilde{R}$ be as defined in equations 34.73–34.75 and let

$$u(t) = \sum_{k=0}^{m} \psi_k x(t-k), \qquad t = -(n-m)+1, \ldots,$$

and

$$\Gamma_2 \equiv \lim_{N\to\infty} \left(N^{-1} \sum_{t=1}^{N} Eu(t-i)u(t-j) \right)_{1 \leqslant i,j \leqslant n-m} \tag{34.76}$$

Then Γ_2 is well defined and positive-definite. Also the random vectors $\sqrt{N}(\hat{a}(N)+a)$ converge in distribution to

$$\tilde{x} = (0_m, \mathscr{G})\tilde{R}',$$

where $\mathscr{G} = (\mathscr{G}_1, \ldots, \mathscr{G}_{n-m})$ is an $(n-m)$-dimensional, normally distributed random vector with mean zero and covariance matrix $\sigma_\eta^2 \Gamma_2^{-1}$.

As illustration of the preceding theorem consider the following example:

E 34.10 Let $\{x(t);\, t = -n+1, -n+2, \ldots\}$, a, and $\hat{a}(N)$ be as in T 34.12 and assume that

$$M(z) = z^{-3}(z - z_1)(z - z_2)(z - z_3),$$

where $0 < z_1 < 1 < z_2 < z_3$. Also let $\psi(\cdot)$, $D(\cdot)$, and $\tilde{R}$ be as defined in equations 34.73–34.75, and let the $u(t)$ be as described in T 34.12. Then in the present case $m = 2$,

$$\psi(z) = 1 - (z_2 + z_3)z^{-1} + z_2 z_3 z^{-2}, \tag{34.77}$$

$$D(z) = 1 - z_1 z^{-1}, \tag{34.78}$$

and

$$\tilde{R} = \begin{pmatrix} 1 & 0 & 1 \\ -z_1 & 1 & -(z_2 + z_3) \\ 0 & -z_1 & z_2 z_3 \end{pmatrix}. \tag{34.79}$$

Moreover,

$$u(t) = x(t) - (z_2 + z_3)x(t - 1) + z_2 z_3 x(t - 2), \qquad t = 0, 1, \ldots,$$

and

$$\Gamma_2 = \lim_{N\to\infty} N^{-1} \sum_{t=1}^{N} Eu(t - 1)^2 = \frac{\sigma_\eta^2}{1 - z_1^2}. \tag{34.80}$$

Finally, by theorem T 34.12, there is a normally distributed random variable with mean zero and variance $\sigma_\eta^2 \Gamma_2^{-1}$ such that the random vectors $\sqrt{N}(\hat{a}(N) + a)$ converge in distribution to $\tilde{x} = (0, 0, \mathscr{G})\tilde{R}' = \mathscr{G}\cdot(1, -(z_2 + z_3), z_2 z_3)$.

34.3.2 Equations with Random Initial Conditions

Next we shall consider the limiting distribution of the least-squares estimate of $-a$ when the $x(t)$ in equation 34.1 represent an ongoing process rather than an experiment with a fixed initial date. We begin with the purely explosive case:

T 34.13 Let $\{x(t, \omega); t \in T\}$ be a real-valued dynamic stochastic process which satisfies equations 34.55 and 34.56 and let $a = (a_1, \ldots, a_n)$ and $\hat{a}(N, \cdot)$, respectively, be as in equations 34.53 and 34.57. Moreover, suppose that

$$|z_j| > 1, \qquad j = 1, \ldots, h;$$

and

$$|A_{ji}(\omega)| \neq 0 \quad \text{a.e.,} \qquad j = 1, \ldots, h, \qquad i = n_j - 1;$$

and let

$$\eta(t, \omega) = \sum_{k=0}^{n} a_k x(t - k, \omega), \qquad t \in T.$$

Finally, let $\tilde{f}_x(t, \omega) = (f_x(t, \omega), \ldots, f_x(t - n + 1, \omega))'$; $t \in T$; let $F_{-\infty}(\omega) = \{\tilde{f}_x(0, \omega), \tilde{f}_x(-1, \omega), \ldots\}$; let A be as in equation 34.70, and assume that the $\eta(t, \cdot)$ constitute a purely random process whose variables are distributed independently of the $f_x(t,\cdot)$ with mean zero and positive finite variance. Then $F_{-\infty}(\omega)$ is of full rank a.e., and for all $z \in R^n$,

$$\lim_{N\to\infty} P(\{\omega \in \Omega : A^N(\hat{a}(N,\omega) + a)' \leqslant z\})$$

$$= P\left(\left\{\omega \in \Omega : [F_{-\infty}(\omega)'F_{-\infty}(\omega)]^{-1}\left[-\sum_{s=1}^{\infty} A^{-s}\tilde{f}_x(0,\omega)\eta(s,\omega)\right] \leqslant z\right\}\right).$$

This theorem is a complete analogue of the second half of T 34.11. To see why, let $\tilde{x}(t,\omega) = (x(t,\omega),\ldots,x(t-n+1,\omega))'$ and $\hat{\eta}(t,\omega) = (\eta(t,\omega),0,\ldots,0)'$ and observe that

$$\tilde{x}(t,\omega) = A\tilde{x}(t-1,\omega) + \hat{\eta}(t,\omega), \qquad t \in T,$$

and

$$\tilde{f}_x(t,\omega) = A\tilde{f}_x(t-1,\omega), \qquad t \in T.$$

Consequently, if we let $\tilde{y}(t,\omega) = (y(t,\omega),\ldots,y(t-n+1,\omega))'$, $t \in T$, then

$$\tilde{y}(t,\omega) + A^t\tilde{f}_x(0,\omega) = A^t\tilde{x}(0,\omega) + \sum_{s=0}^{t-1} A^s\hat{\eta}(t-s,\omega).$$

From this it follows by obvious arguments that with probability 1

$$\tilde{f}_x(0,\omega) = \tilde{x}(0,\omega) + \sum_{v=1}^{\infty} A^{-v}\hat{\eta}(v,\omega),$$

and

$$\tilde{f}_x(-t,\omega) = A^{-t}\{\tilde{x}(0,\omega) + \sum_{v=1}^{\infty} A^{-v}\hat{\eta}(v,\omega)\}, \qquad t = 1, 2, \ldots,$$

which suffices to establish the validity of our assertion.

In order to state our main theorem, we need still more notation: Let

$$0 \leqslant m_p \leqslant n_p, \qquad p = 1,\ldots,h;$$

and

$$\tilde{Q}(z) = \sum_{k=0}^{r} q_k z^{-r} = z^{-r}\prod_{p=1}^{h}(z-z_p)^{m_p}. \tag{34.81}$$

Moreover, redefine (!) $\psi(\cdot)$ in terms of $\tilde{Q}(\cdot)$ as

$$\psi(z) = \sum_{k=0}^{m^*} \psi_k z^{-k} = z^{-m^*}\prod_{p=h_1+1}^{h}(z-z_p)^{m_p}, \tag{34.82}$$

and let $D(z) = M(z)/\psi(z)$ as in equation 34.74 with $\psi(z)$ as in equation 34.82. Finally, let

$$C(z) = \sum_{k=0}^{n} c_k z^{-k} = z^{-n+m^*}\psi(z) \prod_{p=1}^{h_1} (z - z_p)^{n_p} \prod_{p=h_1+1}^{h} (z - z_p^{-1})^{n_p - m_p}. \quad (34.83)$$

When $h_1 = h$, $\psi(z)$ is taken to equal 1 and $C(z)$ to equal $M(z)$. When $m^* = 0$ and $h_1 \neq h$, $c_k = b_k$, $k = 1, \ldots, n$, where the b_k are as defined in equation 34.54.

T 34.14 Let $\{x(t, \omega); t \in T\}$ be a real-valued dynamic stochastic process which satisfies equations 34.55 and 34.56; let $M(z)$ and the z_p be as in equation 34.53, 34.71, and 34.72; and let $a = (a_1, \ldots, a_n)$ and $\hat{a}(N, \cdot)$, respectively, be as in equations 34.53 and 34.57. Moreover, let

$$\eta(t, \omega) = \sum_{k=0}^{n} a_k x(t - k, \omega), \qquad t \in T,$$

and assume the $\eta(t, \cdot)$ constitute a purely random process whose variables are distributed independently of the $f_x(t, \cdot)$ with mean zero and positive variance. Finally, let $\tilde{Q}(\cdot)$, $\psi(\cdot)$, $D(\cdot)$, and $C(\cdot)$ be as specified above in equations 34.81–34.83; let

$$\xi(t, \omega) = \sum_{k=0}^{n} b_k y(t - k, \omega), \qquad t \in T;$$

$$\zeta(t, \omega) = \sum_{k=0}^{n} c_k y(t - k, \omega), \qquad t \in T;$$

and

$$y_2(t, \omega) = \sum_{k=0}^{m^*} \psi_k y(t - k, \omega), \qquad t \in T;$$

let

$\mathscr{S} = \{\omega \in \Omega : \sum_{k=0}^{r} q_k f_x(t - k, \omega) = 0, t \in T$, and there is no polynomial $N(z) = \sum_{k=0}^{s} \tilde{q}_k z^{-k}$ such that $s < r$, $\sum_{k=0}^{s} \tilde{q}_k f_x(t - k, \omega) = 0$, $t \in T$, and $\tilde{q}_s \neq 0\}$;

and assume that $P(\mathscr{S}) > 0$. Then the following assertions are true.

(i) If $m^* = 0$, for all $z \in R^n$,

$$\lim_{N\to\infty} P(\{\omega \in \Omega : \sqrt{N}(\hat{a}(N, \omega) + b) \leqslant z\}|\mathscr{S})$$

$$= (2\pi\sigma_\xi^2)^{-n/2}|\Gamma_3|^{1/2} \int_{\{u \in R^n : u \leqslant z\}} \exp -(1/2\sigma_\xi^2)(u'\Gamma_3 u)\, du,$$

where $\sigma_\xi^2 = E\xi(t, \omega)^2$; $|\Gamma_3|$ is the determinant of Γ_3;

$$\Gamma_3 = \{E\{y(t - i, \omega)y(t - j, \omega)|\mathscr{S}\}\}_{1 \leqslant i, j \leqslant n}; \quad (34.84)$$

and $E\{\cdot|\mathscr{S}\}$ denotes the expected valued of $(\cdot)$ with respect to $P\{\cdot|\mathscr{S}\}$.
(ii) If $0 < m^* < n$, if $\sigma_\zeta^2 = E\zeta(t, \omega)^2$, and if

$$\Gamma_4 = \{E\{y_2(t-i,\omega)y_2(t-j,\omega)|\mathscr{S}\}\}_{1\leqslant i,j\leqslant n-m^*}, \tag{34.85}$$

then there exists a normally distributed vector $\mathscr{G} = (\mathscr{G}_1, \ldots, \mathscr{G}_{n-m^*})$ with mean zero and covariance matrix $\sigma_\zeta^2\Gamma_4^{-1}$ such that the vector $\sqrt{N}(\hat{a}(N,\omega) + c)$ converge in distribution to

$$\tilde{x} = (0_{m^*}, \mathscr{G})\tilde{R}',$$

where $\tilde{R}$ is as defined in equation 34.75 with $\psi(\cdot)$ and $D(\cdot)$ as specified in equations 34.82 and 34.74, and where $c = (c_1, \ldots, c_n)$ with the c_k as defined in equation 34.83.

The first half of T 34.14 is related to the first half of T 34.11 in the following way. Suppose that $|z_p| < 1$ for all $p = 1, \ldots, h$. Then $\psi(z) \equiv 1$, $m^* = 0$, $b_k = a_k$, $k = 1, \ldots, n$, and $\xi(t,\omega) = \eta(t,\omega)$ for all $t \in T$. Moreover, it is easy to show that, if the variance of the $\eta(t.\cdot)$ is the same as the variance of the $\eta(t)$ of T 34.11, then Γ_3 as defined in equation 34.84 equals Γ_1 as defined in equation 34.69.

Consequently, if $|z_p| < 1$, $p = 1, \ldots, h$, *and if the variance of the* $\eta(t,\cdot)$ *and the* $\eta(t)$ *are identical, the limiting distribution of the vector* $\sqrt{N}(\hat{a}(N,\omega) + a)$ *is the same as the limiting distribution of the random vector* $\sqrt{N}(\hat{a}(N) + a)$ *of T 34.11 (i).*

The second half of T 34.14 is related to the conclusions of T 34.12 in the following way. Suppose that $\tilde{Q}(z) = M(z)$, and that $M(z)$ satisfies equations 34.71 and 34.72. Then $0 < m^* < n$, and

$$\mathscr{S} = \{\omega \in \Omega : A_{pq}(\omega) \neq 0,\ p = 1, \ldots, h,\ q = n_p - 1\}.$$

Moreover $m^* = m$, $c_k = a_k$, $k = 1, \ldots, n$, $\zeta(t,\omega) = \eta(t,\omega)$ for all $t \in T$, and the $\psi(\cdot)$, $D(\cdot)$, and $\tilde{R}$ of T 34.14 are identical with the $\psi(\cdot)$, $D(\cdot)$, and $\tilde{R}$ of T 34.12. Finally, it is easy to show that, if the variance of $\eta(t,\cdot)$ is the same as the variance of the $\eta(t)$ of T 34.12, then Γ_4 as defined in equation 34.85 equals Γ_2 as defined in equation 34.76.

Consequently, *if* $\tilde{Q}(z) = M(z)$, *if* $M(z)$ *satisfies equations 34.71 and 34.72, and if the variance of* $\eta(\cdot)$ *is identical with the variance of* $\eta(t)$, *then the limiting distribution of the vectors* $\sqrt{N}(\hat{a}(N,\omega) + a)$ *is the same as the limiting distribution of the random vectors* $\sqrt{N}(\hat{a}(N) + a)$ *of T 34.12.*

E 34.11 Let $\{x(t,\omega); t \in T\}$, $\{\eta(t,\omega); t \in T\}$, a, and $\hat{a}(N,\cdot)$ be as in T 34.14 and suppose that

$$M(z) = z^{-3}(z - z_1)(z - z_2)(z - z_3),$$

where $0 < z_1 < 1 < z_2 < z_3$. Also let $\tilde{Q}(\cdot)$, $\psi(\cdot)$, and $C(\cdot)$ and $D(\cdot)$ and $\tilde{R}$, respectively, be as specified in equations 34.81–34.83 and 34.74 and 34.75 and let $\zeta(t,\cdot)$, $y_2(t,\cdot)$, and Γ_4 be as described in T 34.14. Then

$x(t, \omega) = y(t, \omega) + A_{10}(\omega)z_1^t + A_{20}(\omega)z_2^t + A_{30}(\omega)z_3^t,$

and there are two interesting special cases to consider.

Case 1: Suppose that $\tilde{Q}(z) = M(z)$. Then $m^* = 2$, $c = a$,

$\mathscr{S} = \{\omega \in \Omega : A_{i0}(\omega) \neq 0, i = 1, 2, 3\},$

and $\psi(\cdot)$, $D(\cdot)$, and $\tilde{R}$ are as described in equations 34.77–34.79. Moreover,

$\zeta(t, \omega) = \eta(t, \omega), \qquad t \in T;$

$y_2(t, \omega) = y(t, \omega) - (z_2 + z_3)y(t - 1, \omega) + z_2 z_3 y(t - 2, \omega), \qquad t \in T;$

and

$y_2(t, \omega) - z_1 y_2(t - 1, \omega) = \eta(t, \omega), \qquad t \in T.$

From this it follows that

$$y_2(t, \omega) = \sum_{s=0}^{\infty} z_1^s \eta(t - s, \omega), \qquad t \in T,$$

and hence that

$$\Gamma_4 = \frac{\sigma_\eta^2}{1 - z_1^2},$$

which equals Γ_2 as defined in equation 34.80 if the variance of the $\eta(t, \cdot)$ equals the variance of the $\eta(t)$ of E 34.10. Finally, from T 34.14 it follows that the limiting distribution of the vectors $\sqrt{N}(\hat{a}(N, \omega) + a)$ equals the distribution of the vector $(0, 0, \mathscr{G})\tilde{R}'$, where $\mathscr{G}$ is normally distributed with mean zero and variance $\sigma_\eta^2 \Gamma_4^{-1}$. This limiting distribution is the same as the limiting distribution of the $\sqrt{N}(\hat{a}(N) + a)$ of E 34.10 if the variance of $\eta(t)$ equals the variance of $\eta(t, \cdot)$.

Case 2: Suppose that

$\tilde{Q}(z) = z^{-2}(z - z_1)(z - z_2).$

Then $m^* = 1$,

$\mathscr{S} = \{\omega \in \Omega : A_{i0}(\omega) \neq 0, i = 1, 2; A_{30}(\omega) = 0\},$

$\psi(z) = 1 - z_2 z^{-1},$

$D(z) = 1 - (z_1 + z_3)z^{-1} + z_1 z_3 z^{-2},$

$C(z) = 1 - (z_1 + z_2 + z_3^{-1})z^{-1} + (z_2 z_3^{-1} + z_1(z_2 + z_3^{-1}))z^{-2} - z_1 z_2 z_3^{-1} z^{-3},$

and

$$\tilde{R} = \begin{pmatrix} 1 & 1 & 0 \\ -(z_1 + z_3) & -z_2 & 1 \\ z_1 z_3 & 0 & -z_2 \end{pmatrix}.$$

Moreover,

$y_2(t, \omega) = y(t, \omega) - z_2 y(t - 1, \omega), \qquad t \in T,$

and

$$\zeta(t,\omega) = y(t,\omega) - (z_1 + z_2 + z_3^{-1})y(t-1,\omega) + (z_2 z_3^{-1} + z_1(z_2 + z_3^{-1}))y(t-2,\omega) - z_1 z_2 z_3^{-1} y(t-3,\omega).$$

Finally, if we let

$$\xi(t,\omega) = y_2(t,\omega) - (z_1 + z_3^{-1})y_2(t-1,\omega) + z_1 z_3^{-1} y_2(t-2,\omega),$$

and

$$A^* = \begin{pmatrix} (z_1 + z_3^{-1}) & -z_1 z_3^{-1} \\ 1 & 0 \end{pmatrix},$$

then it is easy to see that

$$\Gamma_4 = \sum_{s=0}^{\infty} A^{*s} \begin{pmatrix} \sigma_\xi^2 & 0 \\ 0 & 0 \end{pmatrix} A^{*\prime s}.$$

T 34.14 now implies that there exists a normally distributed random vector $\mathscr{G} = (\mathscr{G}_1, \mathscr{G}_2)$ with mean zero and covariance matrix $\sigma_\xi^2 \Gamma_4^{-1}$ such that $\sqrt{N}(\hat{a}(N,\omega) + c)$ converges in distribution to

$$\tilde{x} = (0, \mathscr{G})\tilde{R}' = (\mathscr{G}_1, \mathscr{G}_2 - z_2\mathscr{G}_1, -z_2\mathscr{G}_2).$$

Evidently, if $\tilde{x} = (\tilde{x}_1, \tilde{x}_2, \tilde{x}_3)$, then

$$\tilde{x}_3 = -z_2^2\tilde{x}_1 - z_2\tilde{x}_2 \text{ w. pr. } 1.$$

34.3.3 A Simulation Experiment

The conclusions of T 34.14 in the generality in which they are stated were first established in Stigum 1974 (pp. 360–361). Note, however, that the first half of T 34.14 under the additional assumption that $|z_p| < 1$, $p = 1, \ldots, h$, is an immediate consequence of a theorem which is proved by Hannan and by Anderson (see Hannan 1970, theorem VI.1, p. 329, and Anderson 1958, theorem 5.5.7, p. 200). When $E\eta(t,\omega)^4 < \infty$ and $|z_p| < 1$, $p = 1, \ldots, h$, the first half of theorem T 34.14 is an immediate consequence of a theorem of Grenander and Rosenblatt (see Grenander and Rosenblatt 1957, pp. 111–114).

The condition $m^* < n$ is crucial for the validity of theorem T 34.14, as can be seen by rereading the statement of T 34.13.

Since the preceding results have an important bearing on the possibility of using finite samples to test hypotheses concerning the roots of $M(z)$, we conclude this section by recording the results of a simple simulation experiment.

E 34.12 Let $\{\eta(t); t = -41, \ldots, -1, 0, 1, \ldots, 60\}$ be independent, normally distributed random variables with mean 0 and variance 1. Moreover, let

$$u(t) = -\sum_{s=0}^{40} (0.5)^s \eta(t-s), \qquad t = -1, 0, 1, \ldots, 20;$$

$$v(t) = -\sum_{s=1}^{40} (1.5)^{-s} \eta(t+s), \qquad t = -1, 0, 1, \ldots, 20;$$

$$y(t) = 0.5u(t) + 1.5v(t), \qquad t = -1, 0, 1, \ldots, 20; \tag{34.86}$$

$$x(t) = y(t) + 2(0.5)^t + (1.5)^t, \qquad t = -1, 0, 1, \ldots, 20, \tag{34.87}$$

and observe that both $y(\cdot)$ and $x(\cdot)$ approximately satisfy the equation

$$z(t) + a_1 z(t-1) + a_2 z(t-2) = \eta(t) \tag{34.100}$$

with $a_1 = -2$ and $a_2 = 0.75$. Finally, let $\hat{a}_x(N)$ and $\hat{a}_y(N)$, respectively, denote the least-squares estimate of (a_1, a_2) based on observations on $x(\cdot)$ and $y(\cdot)$. According to T 34.14, $\lim_N \hat{a}_x(N) = (2, -0.75)$ and $\lim_N \hat{a}_y(N) = (7/6, -1/3)$; for large N the distribution of $\hat{a}_x(N)$ is concentrated on the line $a_2 = -1.5a_1 + 2.25$.

By a pseudo-random sampling scheme, which Dr. Jaffar Al-Abdulla programmed for me, I obtained fifty independently distributed sets of observations on the $\eta(t)$ from $t = -41$ to $t = 60$. Those observations and equations 34.86 and 34.87 were used to generate fifty independently distributed sets of observations on the pairs $(y(t), x(t))$ from $t = -1$ to $t = 20$. Finally, I used each set of observations on $(y(t), x(t))$ to compute fifty values of $(\hat{a}_y(20), \hat{a}_x(20))$. The $\hat{a}_y(20)$ values are displayed in figure 34.7 and the $\hat{a}_x(20)$ values are displayed in figure 34.8.

34.4 Concluding Remarks

In the last two sections we have only paid lip service to the case when $M(z)$ has roots of modules equal to 1. We have also ignored the possibility that the difference equation in 34.1 might contain a constant term; and we have steered clear of all the estimation problems that arise when the $\eta(t)$ do not constitute a purely random process. Hence a few remarks concerning these omissions are called for.

First, roots of modulus equal to 1: We know from Lai and Wei 1983 (theorem 1, pp. 2–3) that if we add to the assumptions of T 34.6 the condition "$E|\eta(t)|^{2+\delta} < \infty$ for some $\delta > 0$," the convergence in equation 34.50 will happen with probability 1. We also know from Chan and Wei 1988 that if we add the same condition to the assumptions of T 34.11, we can determine the limiting distribution of the $\hat{a}(N)$ when the roots of $M(z)$ are all less than or equal to 1 in absolute value. However, in this case both the sequence of normalizing constants and the limiting distributions are too involved to describe in a few words.

Next, constant terms: Judging from the results described in Fuller, Hasza, and Goebel 1981, adding a constant term to T 34.6 (iii) would not affect the limiting behavior of the least-squares estimate of a in any essential way.

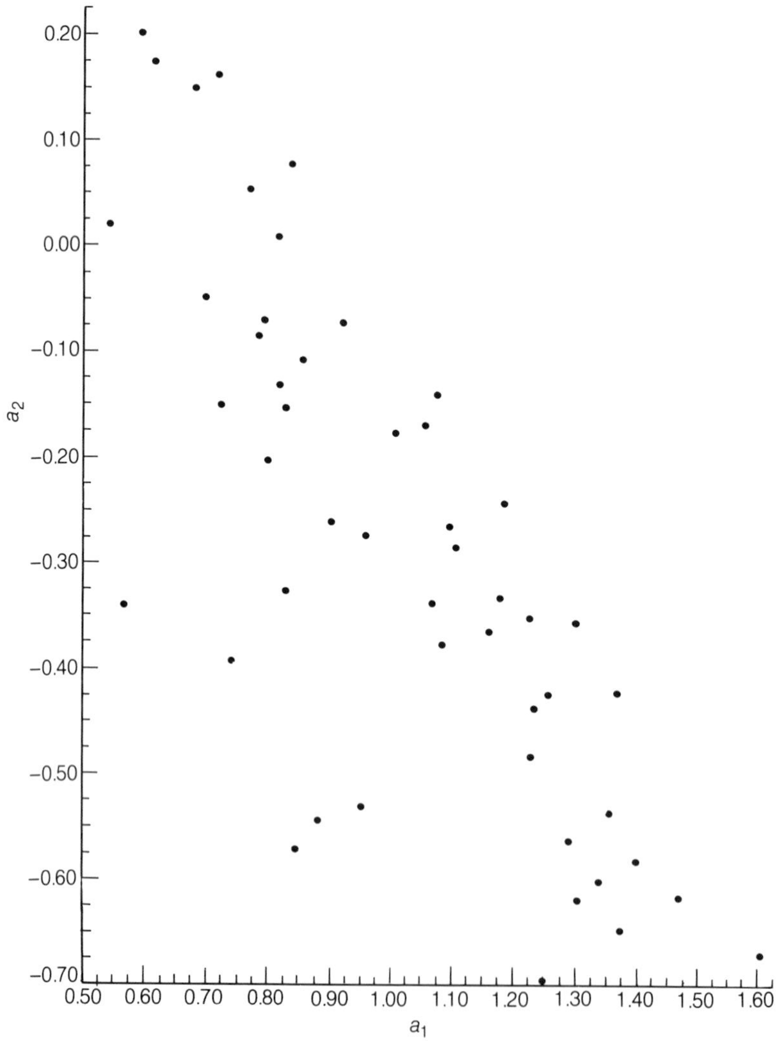

Figure 34.7
$\hat{a}_y(20)$ values.

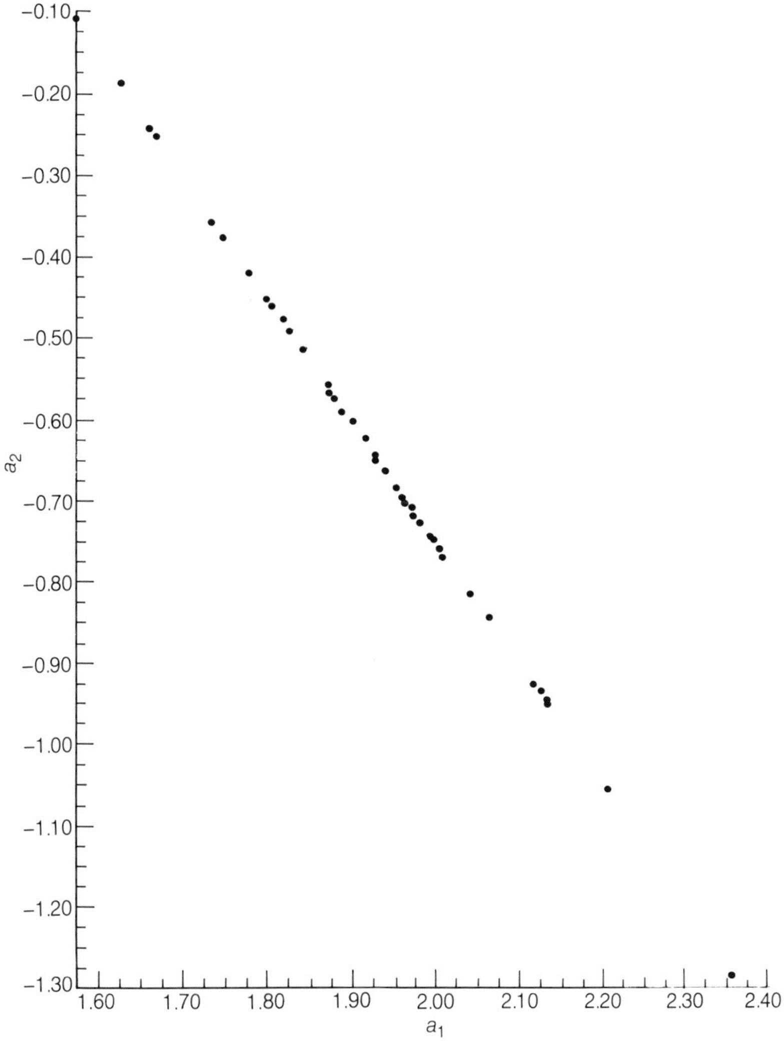

Figure 34.8
$\hat{a}_x(20)$ values.

The estimator is always consistent and has a limiting distribution that is normal or hard to describe according as the moduli of the roots of $M(z)$ are all less than 1 or some are greater than or equal to 1. For a discussion of these and related matters, I refer the reader to W. A. Fuller's interesting survey article (Fuller 1985).

Finally, serially correlated $\eta(t)$'s: I know of no published general results concerning the asymptotic properties of the $\hat{a}(N)$ in equation 34.50 when the $\eta(t)$ in T 34.6 (iii) are serially correlated. However, judging from T 34.7, T 34.11, and Edmond Malinvaud's interesting discussion in Malinvaud 1966 (pp. 458–466), it must be the case that $\hat{a}(N)$ converges in probability to a well-defined vector c. When the roots of $M(z)$ are all less than 1 in absolute value, c differs from $-a$ and $\sqrt{N}(\hat{a}(N) - c)$ has a normal limiting distribution. When the moduli of the roots of $M(z)$ are all greater than 1, $c = -a$ and, with A and U as described in T 34.11 (ii), $A^N(\hat{a}(N) - c)$ has a well-defined limiting distribution whenever U is a.e. invertible.

The preceding omissions notwithstanding, we have in this chapter achieved what we set out to do: Demonstrate the importance of asymptotic theory in time-series analysis. In addition, we have concluded the book with a most important observation: Seemingly innocuous assumptions, such as the fixed initial conditions in T 34.6, can be as misleading in econometrics as is the assumption of a measure space of agents in mathematical economics. So watch out, young econometricians! The specter of useless asymptotic results is very much like the specter of topological artifacts that haunts mathematical economists. Intuitive knowledge gained from empirically irrelevant Gedanken experiments has no scientific cash value!

Notes

Chapter 1

1. Here "the life-cycle hypothesis" is a synonym for "the Modigliani-Brumberg theory of the consumption function" (Modigliani and Brumberg 1955).

Chapter 2

1. Some of these terms might not be that "universal." Cases in point are collection, imply, and assertion. For the purposes of the present example, a *collection* may be taken to be something that has been gathered into a (possibly empty) mass or pile; an *assertion* is a positive statement as exemplified in UT 1, A 1–A 5, and T 1–T 4; and *imply* is short for "materially imply," which is a synonym of "either not … or … ." I shall explicate the meaning of material implication in chapter 4.

Chapter 3

1. I shall explicate the meaning of a relation in chapter 9. Here it suffices to say that a *relation* is a structured predicate. Relations may be binary as in "grass is (one of those things that are) green," ternary as in "Belgium lies between France and Germany," and *n*-ary as in the graph of an $(n - 1)$-ary function. They may also be hard to describe, as is the relation predicated in "either the spruce tree in my garden is green or the spruce tree in my garden is not green."

2. J. Hintikka (1979, pp. 150–151) has elaborated on this idea.

Chapter 5

1. Usually a structure $\mathscr{D}$ for L comes without $N_{\mathscr{D}}$, i.e., without the names of the individuals in $|\mathscr{D}|$. I have added $N_{\mathscr{D}}$ for ease of reference.

2. The propositional and first-order predicate calculus of the Dutch intuitionists will be discussed in some detail in section 23.4.1.

Chapter 7

1. Let A be a wff in L. Then A^c denotes the closure of A. The closure of A is defined on p. 97.

Chapter 8

1. The reference here is to Gödel 1931 and Rosser 1936.

2. A wff is *open* if it contains no quantifier.

3. An *existensial* wff is a wff with only existential quantifiers all of which appear at the beginning of the formula. Here the class of existential wffs in P′ is taken to include the open wffs in P′.

Chapter 9

1. I have borrowed this example from Halmos's *Naive Set Theory* (1974, p. 3).

2. The proof is due to Barwise (1975, pp. 12–13).

Chapter 10

1. Debreu's proof of the lower semicontinuity of his consumer's budget correspondence can be reworded so that it also constitutes a proof of UT 7 (Debreu 1959, pp. 64–65).

2. This lemma is due to K. J. Arrow and A. C. Enthoven (theorems 1 and 2, 1961, pp. 783 and 789).

3. Let $f(\cdot): R^n_+ \to R$ be a continuous, strictly increasing, and strictly quasi-concave function. A *level set* of $f(\cdot)$ is a set of the form $\{x \in R^n_+ : f(x) \geqslant f(y)\}$, where $y \in R^n_+$. We shall say the level sets of $f(\cdot)$ are *differentiable* in $(R^n_+ - R^n_{++}) - \{0\}$ if and only if, for all $y \in (R^n_+ - R^n_{++}) - \{0\}$, there exists a vector $a \in R^n_{++}$ (depending on y) such that

$\{x \in R^n_+ : f(x) \geqslant f(y)\} \subset \{x \in R^n_+ : ax \geqslant ay\}$.

4. L. McKenzie (1956, pp. 185, 186) established the existence of $A(\cdot, p^0, A^0)$, which he denoted by $M_x(\cdot)$, and observed that $A(\cdot, p^0, A^0)$ is well defined and concave.

5. See Leontief (1936, pp. 53–59) and Hicks (1946, pp. 312–313). An analytic proof of a version of the theorem is given in Wold (1953, pp. 109, 110). The ideas of Wold's proof differ from the ideas of my proof.

Chapter 11

1. Here "almost everywhere" means "everywhere except possibly in a set of (n + 2)-dimensional Lebesgue measure zero."

2. Let $f(\cdot)$: $R_+^n \to R$ be a continuous function. Then $f(\cdot)$ is homogeneous of degree m if and only if, for all $\lambda \in R_+^n$, $f(\lambda x) = \lambda^m f(x)$. Moreover, $f(\cdot)$ is linearly homogeneous if $f(\cdot)$ is homogeneous of degree 1.

3. This theorem is due to Blackorby, Primont, and Russell (see corollary 5.6.2, 1983, p. 205). The arguments I use to prove it, however, are my own.

Chapter 12

1. Theorem T 12.2 is my version of a theorem of Arrow's (see Arrow 1965, pp. 38–39).

2. The data underlying figures 12.1 and 12.2 were computed by Ron Gilbert of Loyola University in 1972.

3. The data underlying figures 3 through 9 were computed by Professor Lois B. Rall of the University of Wisconsin while I was a research associate at the Mathematics Research Center in Madison during the summer of 1972.

4. The ideas underlying my proof of T 12.5 are due to J. Pratt (1964, p. 136).

5. The basic ideas underlying this part of my proof of T 12.17 are due to O. D. Hart (1975, pp. 615–621).

Chapter 13

1. A different example was constructed by L. Hurwicz and M. K. Richter. In their example the "exceptional" commodity bundle lies at the boundary of X. (See example 3 in Hurewicz and Richter 1971, pp. 64–66.)

2. We have discussed those aspects of revealed preference theory which are particularly important in the context of my methodological essay. For a broader discussion of revealed preference the interested reader is referred to Fuchs-Seliger 1976.

Chapter 14

1. An interesting discussion of envious consumers and fair allocations can be found in Varian (1974, pp. 63–70). Theorems T 14.2 and T 14.3 are analogues of Varian's theorems 2.1 and 2.3.

2. Let $x_n \in R$, $n = 1, 2, \ldots$. We say that the x_n constitute a Cauchy sequence if and only if $\lim_{m,n\to\infty} |x_n - x_m| = 0$.

3. The scenario I have in mind is similar to the scenario which Hicks (1946, chapters IX and X) describes. The results I present are for choice-under-certainty analogues of the results I obtained for an uncertainty economy in Stigum (1974, pp. 301–331).

Chapter 15

1. Shafer calls the rule by which belief functions are combined in T 15.5 "Dempster's Rule of Combination." He refers to my definition of conditional belief by the name "Dempster's Rule of Conditioning." See A. P. Dempster's discussion of these concepts (Dempster 1967, pp. 325–339).

2. For a proof of this assertion, see Loève (1960, pp. 96–98).

3. Equation 15.47 follows because

$$\Delta_{b-a}F_{x_1,\ldots,x_n}(a) = P(\{\omega \in \Omega : a_i \leqslant x_i(\omega) < b_i, i = 1, \ldots, n\})$$

Chapter 16

1. This discussion of the ruin problem borrows freely from Feller 1957 (pp. 311–318).

Chapter 17

1. I use the term "prior" as short for "prior measure" or "prior distribution" as the case may be.

2. I have learned of this system of axioms from Koopman and Kimball (1959, pp. 188 and 199).

3. Lindley's scenario was much more involved than the one I describe in E 17.5. My version is similar to the one Shafer (1982, pp. 325–334) analyzed by means of belief functions.

Chapter 18

1. Strictly speaking, this assertion does not follow from T 18.7. However, it can be established in the obvious way by generalizing upon Olshen's proof of T 18.7.

2. The version of the Radon–Nikodym theorem that I apply here is formulated in theorem B of Loève 1960 (p. 132).

Chapter 19

1. Strictly speaking, the observation that $U(\cdot)$ is bounded is due to Fishburn and Savage. Savage did not know this when he first published his expected-utility

theorem (see Fishburn 1967, pp. 1054–1060). In this respect I note that a complete proof of Savage's subjective probability and expected-utility representations (including the fact that Savage's utility function must be bounded) is given in chapter 14 of Fishburn's book *Utility Theory for Decision Making* (1970, pp. 191–210).

2. This theorem is a strong version of theorem 2 in Stigum (1972b, p. 257). The strengthening of my original result was made possible by Debreu and Koopmans' discoveries (see Debreu and Koopmans 1982, pp. 9, 10–11, and 30).

3. The idea of such risk preferences I owe to Kjell Arne Brekke.

4. The integral in equation 19.31 is called the *Choquét integral*. Both Chateauneuf and Gilboa obtain a similar integral representation of their decision maker's risk preferences.

Chapter 21

1. I learned of this proof from Albeverio et al. (1986, p. 46).

2. The results I record in T 21.20–T 21.22 are due to Brown and Robinson (1974, p. 47).

3. This comment I owe to Tom Lindstrøm.

Chapter 22

1. The name truthfully suggests that Peter Loeb was the originator of this line of inquiry into nonstandard probability theory. Both T 21.3 and T 21.4 are due to Loeb (see, for instance, Loeb 1975, p. 115).

2. See in this respect proposition 3.4.2 and corollary 3.4.3 in Albeverio et al. 1986 (pp. 87–88).

3. The basic ideas of T 22.6 I have borrowed from Albeverio et al. 1986.

4. A proof of the continuity of $V(t,\cdot)$ can be obtained from A. Robinson's proof of theorem 4.5.10 (Robinson 1966, p. 116).

5. This comment I owe to Tom Lindstrøm.

6. This observation is substantiated by T 21.28, T 21.30, and the equivalences between nonstandard and measure-theoretic economies obtained in Rashid 1979.

7. Let $X = \{x(t,\omega); t = 0, 1, \ldots\}$ be a family of real-valued integrable random variables. Then X is a *martingale* if and only if, for all $t = 0, 1, \ldots$, $E\{x(t+1)|x(0), \ldots, x(t)\} = x(t)$ a.e. Hence a hypermartingale is the nonstandard version of a standard martingale.

Chapter 23

1. R. Nozick calls this puzzle "the puzzle of the ship of Theseus" and discusses its implications in Nozick 1981 (pp. 33–34).

2. Russell's ideas concerning knowledge by acquaintance and knowledge by description are presented in Russell 1976 (pp. 25–32).

3. Strictly speaking, a variable hypothetical is a for-all sentence that cannot be written as a finite conjunction (see Ramsey 1954a, pp. 237–241). For simplicity I use "variable hypothetical" to designate a "for-all sentence."

4. We discussed Senior and his four fundamental postulates of political economy in chapter 1.

Chapter 24

1. This formulation of PLV is due to C. Broad (1928, pp. 25–26).

2. The idea of this example I learned from Peirce 1955 (p. 207).

Chapter 25

1. I learned of this example from Russell 1948.

2. I learned of this example from Broad 1928.

3. In reading my explication of indirect tests it is important to keep in mind that the assertion "$\models A$" insists that our data *satisfy* A. It does not claim that our data *confirm* $(\forall x)A$ in the way *confirm* is used in Hempel 1965 (pp. 3–51). Thus, if A is $[R(x) \supset B(x)]$ and if A asserts that either x is not a raven or x is black, and if a, a black pen, is the data we have, $\models A$ even though A does not confirm $(\forall x)A$ in Hempel's terminology.

Chapter 26

1. The reference here is to Projector and Weiss 1966 and Projector 1968.

2. See in this respect Projector and Weiss 1966, pp. 60–70.

Chapter 27

1. The reference here is to Projector and Weiss 1966 and Projector 1968.

2. I call the model a restricted factor-analytic model instead of a restricted factor-analysis model because we do not assume that η is a normally distributed vector.

3. For the computation of S matrices in this chapter I rescaled the relevant FRB data by the factor 10^{-4}.

4. An illuminating discussion of the need for an axiom like SF 16 in factor analysis is given in Anderson and Rubin 1956 (pp. 100–110).

5. As in the case of T 27.6, I shall refer to the estimates of T 27.9 as factor-analytic estimates. Whenever the ε of equation 27.58 is a normally distributed vector, the estimates of T 27.9 are also factor-analysis estimates.

6. It is relevant here that some of the most important breakthroughs in analyzing covariance structures during the last two decades have come at the hands of Karl G. Jöreskog (see, for example, Jöreskog 1970, pp. 239–251, and Jöreskog 1981, pp. 65–92, the latter of which contains a discussion of Liserel).

Chapter 28

1. For the statistical analysis in this chapter I rescaled the relevant FRB data by the factor 10^{-3}.

2. It is relevant here that Cass and Stiglitz observed that in their theory the separation property of the utility function of a decision maker implies that his demand for Arrow-Debreu securities is a linear function of initial wealth (Cass and Stiglitz 1970, p. 145).

3. This remark I owe to R. D. Terrell.

4. The last remark I owe to Harald Goldstein.

Chapter 29

1. This was pointed out to me by Jørgen Aasnes.

2. Since we do not have data on the initial commodity bundles of the consumers in G, we are free to assume that they were nonexistent.

3. I owe this remark to Jørgen Aasnes.

Chapter 30

1. These theories were first presented in Stigum 1969a (pp. 533–561) and Stigum 1969 (pp. 426–442).

2. Formally, Arrow's and Debreu's theories of choice under uncertainty are not alike. However, the basic ideas are essentially the same. That is why the theory of resource allocation developed in Debreu 1959 (pp. 98–102) has become known as the Arrow-Debreu theory, and why in this chapter we refer to Arrow's and Debreu's consumer as the Arrow-Debreu consumer and to Debreu's producer as the Arrow-Debreu producer.

3. Recall that such changes affect the "price" of *d* but not *d* itself.

4. Let $X = \{x(t, \omega); t = 0, 1, \ldots\}$ be a random process on some probability space $(\Omega, \mathscr{F}, P(\cdot))$. Then X is a *Markov process* if and only if, for any sequence of integers, $t_i, i = 1, \ldots, n$, such that $t_1 < t_2 < \cdots < t_n$, the conditional probability of $\mathscr{F}(x(t_n))$ sets with respect to $\mathscr{F}(x(t_1), \ldots, x(t_{n-1}))$ varies only with the values assumed by $x(t_{n-1})$.

5. Supp μ is called the support of $\mu(\cdot)$. If $F(\cdot): R_+ \to [0, 1]$ is a probability distribution, if $\mathscr{B}$ is the Borel field of subsets of R_+, and if $\mu_F(\cdot): \mathscr{B} \to [0, 1]$ is the probability measure on $(R_+, \mathscr{B})$ induced by $F(\cdot)$, then we say that $F(\cdot)$ has compact support if and only if $\mu_F(\cdot)$ has compact support.

6. Conditions ii and iii imply the validity of condition i. A proof of this can be found in Billingsley 1968 (pp. 11–14). I have included condition i to make the reading of E 30.4 easier.

7. Here and in the remainder of the chapter, it is understood that we always pick a version of the relevant conditional expectations that satisfy the conditions we specify.

Chapter 31

1. The contents of this chapter have been taken from Stigum 1972a and Kesten and Stigum 1974.

2. Throughout this chapter the norm of a vector $x \in R^n$, $\|x\|$, is defined to equal $\sum_{i=1}^n |x_i|$.

3. In expansions, $o(\cdot)$ means "terms of smaller order than."

4. Note that if the $L(t)$'s constituted a Galton-Watson process and if $E(L(1) - \lambda L(0))^2 < \infty$, then they would satisfy these conditions with $\delta = 1/2$. Hence these conditions are meaningful.

Chapter 32

1. The ideas which we discuss in section 31.1.2–31.1.4 are well known. I learned of them first in Grenander and Rosenblatt 1957 (pp. 25–29 and 33–36).

2. I first learned of the questionable properties of the best linear least-squares predictor in Furstenberg 1960 (pp. 1–7).

3. Lebesgue's Decomposition Theorem is stated and proved in Loève 1960 (pp. 130–132). The application of this theorem to distribution functions is described in Loève 1960 (pp. 176–178).

4. The arguments we use in proving sufficiency are due to Arne Strøm.

Chapter 33

1. With the exception that A. C. Harvey adds an error term to equation 33.5 and uses different symbols, equations 33.5 and 33.6 are identical to equations 3.2a and 3.2b in Harvey 1985a.

2. For a discussion of the properties of such models and the problems involved in estimating their parameters, I refer the reader to Engle 1978 (pp. 281–295) and Hylleberg 1986 (pp. 175–350).

3. Let L be a complex linear manifold and let x, y, and z denote elements in L. An *inner product* of elements of L is a complex-valued function $\langle \cdot, \cdot \rangle$ on $(L \times L)$ that satisfies the following conditions:

(i) $\langle x + y, z \rangle = \langle x, z \rangle + \langle y, z \rangle$;

(ii) $\langle x, y \rangle = \overline{\langle y, x \rangle}$;
(iii) $\langle \alpha x, y \rangle = \alpha \langle x, y \rangle$ for all complex constants α; and
(iv) $\langle x, x \rangle \geqslant 0$ and $\langle x, x \rangle \neq 0$ if $x \neq 0$.

A complex linear manifold with an associated inner product is called an *inner-product space*.

4. Let L be an inner-product space; let x, y denote elements of L; and let $\langle x, y \rangle$ denote the inner product of x and y. The inner product determines a function $\|\cdot\|: L \to R_+$ by $\|x\| = \sqrt{\langle x, x \rangle}$, $x \in L$. It is easy to verify that $\|\cdot\|$ satisfies conditions (i)–(iv) of UT 1 (see chapter 10) with a ranging over complex constants. Hence we are justified in referring to $\|x\|$ as the norm of x. We shall say that $\hat{L}$ is the completion in norm of L if, for all sequences x_n *of elements of* L, the condition $\lim_{n,m \to \infty} \|x_n - m_m\| = 0$ implies that there is an $x \in \hat{L}$ such that $\lim_{n \to \infty} \|x_n - x\| = 0$, and if all the elements of $\hat{L}$ are limit points of sequences of elements of L. If $\hat{L}$ is the completion of L, $\hat{L}$ is said to be a *complete inner-product space*.

5. A Hilbert space is an infinite-dimensional, complete inner-product space. Two Hilbert spaces, L_1 and L_2, are linearly independent if and only $L_1 \cap L_2 = \{0\}$.

6. Recall that section 18.5 described how such a shift operator can be generated by a so-called "translation of events."

7. Theorem T 33.6 and the theorems that follow, i.e., T 33.7–T 33.11, were first etablished in Stigum 1963 (pp. 274–283).

8. For an authoritative account of multivariate wide-sense stationary processes and the associated prediction theory the reader should consult Wiener and Masani 1957 (pp. 111–150) and 1958 (pp. 93–137).

Chapter 34

1. The references here are to Mann and Wald 1943, Anderson 1959, and Muench 1974.

Bibliography

Afriat, Sidney N. 1965. "The Equivalence in Two Dimensions of the Strong and Weak Axioms of Revealed Preference." *Metroeconomica* 17.

Afriat, Sidney N. 1976. *The Combinatorial Theory of Demand*. London: Input-Output.

Albeverio, Sergio, Jens E. Fenstad, Raphael Høegh-Krohn, and Tom Lindstrøm. 1986. *Nonstandard Methods in Stochastic Analysis and Mathematical Physics*. New York: Academic.

Allais, Maurice. 1979. "The So-Called Allais Paradox and Rational Decisions under Uncertainty." In *Expected Utility Hypotheses and the Allais Paradox*, ed. M. Allais and O. Hagen. Boston: Reidel.

Allais, Maurice. 1983. "Frequency, Probability and Chance." In *Foundations of Utility and Risk Theory with Applications*, ed. B. P. Stigum and F. Wenstøp. Boston: Reidel.

Allais, Maurice. 1988. "The General Theory of Random Choices in Relation to the Invariant Cardinal Utility Function and the Specific Probability Function. The (U, O) Model, a General Overview. "In *Risk, Decision and Rationality*, ed. B. R. Munier. Dordrecht: Reidel.

Allen, R. G. D., and A. Bowley. 1935. *Family Expenditure*. London: Staples.

Anderson, Robert M. 1976. "A Non-Standard Representation for Brownian Motion and Itô Integration." *Israel Journal of Mathematics* 25.

Anderson, Robert M. 1977. Star-Finite Probability Theory. Ph.D. thesis, Yale University.

Anderson, Robert M. 1986. "Notions of Core Convergence." In *Contributions to Mathematical Economics in Honor of Gerard Debreu*, ed. W. Hildebrand and A. Mas-Colell. Amsterdam: North-Holland.

Anderson, T. W. 1971. *The Statistical Analysis of Time Series*. New York: Wiley.

Anderson, T. W. 1959. "On Asymptotic Distributions of Estimates of Parameters of Stochastic Difference Equations." *Annals of Mathematical Statistics*, 30.

Anderson, T. W., and H. Rubin. 1956. "Statistical Inference in Factor Analysis." In *Proceedings of the Third Berkeley Symposium on Mathematical Statistics and Probability* 5. ed. J. Neyman.

Antonelli, Giovanni B. 1971. "On the Mathematical Theory of Political Economy." In *Preferences, Utility, and Demand*, ed. J. S. Chipman, L. Hurwicz, M. K. Richter, and H. F. Sonnenschein. New York: Harcourt Brace Jovanovich.

Aristotle. 1964. *Prior and Posterior Analytics*, ed. trans. John Warrington. London: Dent.

Aristotle. 1978. *Metaphysics*, ed. trans. John Warrington. London: Dent.

Aristotle. 1980. *Physics*, trans. Hippocrates G. Apostle. Grinnel, Iowa: Peripatetic.

Arrow, Kenneth J. 1964. "The Role of Securities in the Optimal Allocation of Risk Bearing." *Review of Economic Studies* 31.

Arrow, Kenneth J. 1965. *Aspects fo the Theory of Risk-Bearing*, Helsinki: Academic Book Store.

Arrow, Kenneth J., H. D. Block, and Leonid Hurwicz. 1959. "On the Stability of the Competetive Equilibrium, II." *Econometrica* 27.

Arrow, Kenneth J., and Alain C. Enthoven. 1961. "Quasi-Concave Programming." *Econometrica* 29.

Arrow, Kenneth J., and Leonid Hurwicz. 1958. "On the Stability of the Competetive Equilibrium, I." *Econometrica* 26.

Arrow, Kenneth J., and Leonid Hurwicz. 1960. "Some Remarks on the Equilibria of Economic Systems." *Econometrica* 28.

Aumann, Robert J. 1964. "Markets with a Continuum of Traders." *Econometrica* 32.

Aumann, Robert J. 1966. "Existence of Competitive Equilibria in Markets with a Continuum of Traders." *Econometrica* 34.

Ayer, A. J. 1968. *The Origins of Pragmatism*, San Fransisco: Freeman, Cooper.

Barwise, Jon. 1975. *Admissible Sets and Structures*. New York: Springer-Verlag.

Barwise, Jon, and John Perry. 1983. *Situations and Attitudes*, Cambridge: MIT Press.

Beatty, John. 1980. "Optimal-Design Models and the Strategy of Model Building in Evolutinary Biology." *Philosophy of Science* 47.

Bell, J. L., and M. Machover. 1977. *A Course in Mathematical Logic*. Amsterdam: North-Holland.

Bellamy, E. 1967. *In Looking Backward 2000-1778*, ed. John L. Thomas, Cambridge: Harvard University Press.

Beran, Rudolf, and Muni S. Srivastava. 1985. "Bootstrap Tests and Confidence Regions for Functions of a Covariance Matrix." *Annals of Statistics* 13.

Berge, Claude. 1959. *Espaces Topologiques*. Paris: Dunod.

Billingsley, Patrick. 1968. *Convergence of Probability Measures*, New York: Wiley.

Bllingsley, Patrick. 1979. *Probability and Measures*. New York: Wiley.

Blackorby, Charles, Daniel Primot, and R. Robert Russell. 1978. *Duality, Separability and Functional Structure: Theory and Economic Applications*. New York: North-Holland.

Boole, George. 1847. *The Mathematical Analysis of Logic*. Cambridge: MacMillan, Barclay and MacMillan.

Boolos, George, and Richard Jeffrey. 1974. *Computability and Logic*. Cambridge University Press.

Borel, Emile. 1964. "Apropos of a Treatise on Probability." In *Studies in Subjective Probability*, ed. H. E. Kyburg, Jr., and H. E. Smokler, trans. H. E. Smokler. New York: Wiley.

Box, George E. P., and G. M. Jenkins. 1970. *Time Series Analysis, Forecasting and Control*. San Fransisco: Holden-Day.

Box, George, and George C. Tiao. 1973. *Bayesian Inference in Statistical Analysis*. Reading: Addison-Wesley.

Breiman, L. 1968. *Probability*. Reading: Addison-Wesley.

Brekke, Kjell A. 1983. "Temporary Equilibria in a Monetary Economy with Infinite Horizon and the Possibility of Bankruptcy." Institute of Mathematics, University of Oslo.

Brier, G. W. 1950. "Verification of Forecasts Expressed in Terms of Probability." *Monthly Weather Review* 78.

Broad, C. D. 1928. "The Principles of Problematic Induction." *Proceeding of the Aristotelian Society* 28.

Brown, Alan, and Angus Deaton. 1972. "Surveys in Applied Economics: Models of Consumer Behaviour." *Economic Journal* 82.

Brown, Donald J. 1976. "Existence of a Competetive Equilibrium in a Nonstandard Exchange Economy." *Econometrica* 44.

Brown, Donald J., and M. Ali Kahn. 1980. "An Extension of the Brown-Robinson Equivalence Theorem." *Applied Mathematics and Computation* 6.

Brown, Donald J., and Abraham Robinson. 1975. "Nonstandard Exchange Economies." *Econometrica* 43.

Burali-Forti, M. 1897. "Una questione sui numeri transfinit." *Rendiconti del Circolo Matematico di Palermo* 11.

Cagan, Philip. 1956. "The Monetary Dynamics of Hyperinflation." In *Studies in the Quantity Theory of Money*, ed. M. Friedman. University of Chicago Press.

Cantor, Georg. 1895 and 1897: "Beiträge zur Begründung der transfiniten Mengenlehre, Parts I and II." *Mathematische Annalen* 46 and 47.

Carnap, Rudolf. 1936. "Testability and Meaning." *Philosophy ad Science* 3.

Carnap, Rudolf. 1956. *Meaning and Necessity*, 2d ed. University of Chicago Press.

Cass, David, and Joseph E Stiglitz. 1970. "The Structure of Investor Preferences and Asset Returns, and Separability in Portfolio Allocation: A Contribution to the Pure Theory of Mutual Funds." *Journal of Economic Theory* 2.

Chan, N. H., and C. Z. Wei. 1988. "Limiting Distributions of Least Squares Estimates of Unstable Autoregressive Processes." *Annals of Statistics* 15.

Chateauneuf, Alain. 1986. Uncertainty Aversion and Risk Aversion in Models with Nonadditive Probabilities. Mimeographed paper, Université de Paris.

Chenery, Hollis B. 1952. "Overcapacity and the Acceleration Principle." *Econometrica* 20.

Chisholm, Roderick M. 1977. *Theory of Knowledge*, 2d ed. Englewood Cliffs: Prentice-Hall.

Chisholm, Roderick M. 1982. *The Foundations of Knowing*. University of Minnesota Press.

Choquet, Gustave. 1953. "Theory of Capacities." *Annals de l'Institut du Fourier* 5.

Christensen, Laurits R., Dale W. Jorgenson, and Lawrence J. Lau. 1975. "Transcendental Logarithmic Utility Functions." *American Economic Review* 65.

Church, Alonzo. 1940. "On the Concept of a Random Sequence." *Bulletin of the American Mathematical Society* 46.

Church, Alonzo. 1956. *Introduction to Mathematical Logic*. Princeton University Press.

Cobb, C. W., and P. H. Douglas. 1928. "A Theory of Production." *American Economic Review*, supplement.

Cohen, I. Bernard. 1981. "Newton's Discovery of Gravity." *Scientific American* 244.

Cramér, Harald. 1936. "Über eine Eigenschaft der normalen Verteilungsfunktion." *Mathematische Zeitschrift* 41.

Cramér, Harald. 1946. *Mathematical Methods of Statistics*. Princeton University Press.

Debreu, Gerard. 1959. *Theory of Value*, New York: Wiley.

Debreu, Gerard. 1959a. "Topological Methods in Cardinal Utility Theory." In *Mathematical Methods in the Social Sciences*, ed. K. J. Arrow, S. Karlin, and P. Suppes. Stanford University Press.

Debreu, Gerard. 1974. "Excess Demand Functions." *Journal of Mathematical Economics* 1.

Debreu, Gerard, and Tjalling C. Koopmans. 1982. "Additively Decomposed Quasiconvex Functions." *Mathematical Programming* 24.

Debreu, Gerard, and Herbert Scarf. 1963. "A Limit Theorem on the Core of an Economy." *International Economic Review* 4.

Dempster, A. P. 1967. "Upper and Lower Probabilities Induced by a Multivalued Mapping." *Annals of Mathematical Statistics* 38.

Diaconis, Persi, and David Freedman. 1986. "On the Consistency of Bayes Estimates." *Annals of Statistics* 14.

Diewert, W. E. 1973. "Afriat and Revealed Preference Theory." *Review of Economic Studies* 40.

Donsker, Monroe D. 1951. "An Invariance Principle for Certain Probability Limit Theorems." *Memoirs of the American Mathematical Society* 6.

Doob, J. L. 1936. "Note on Probability." *Annals of Mathematics* 37.

Doob. J. L. 1949. "Application of the Theory of Martingales." In *Colloques Internationaux du Centre National de la Recherche Scientifique, Lyon 1948,* XIII Paris: Centre National de la Recherche Scientifique.

Doob, J. L. 1953. *Stochastic Processes.* New York: Wiley.

Drake, Frank R. 1974. *Set Theory.* London: North-Holland.

Dwyer, Gerald P., Jr., and Cotton M. Lindsay. 1984. "Robert Giffen and the Irish Potato." *American Economic Review* 74.

Edgeworth, F. Y. 1884. "The Philosophy of Chance." *Mind* 4.

Edwards, Ward. 1955. "The Prediction of Decisions among Bets." *Journal of Experimental Psychology* 50.

Eisner, Robert, and Robert Strotz. 1963. "Determinants of Business Investment." In *Impacts of Monetary Policy.* Englewood Cliffs: Prentice-Hall.

Ellsberg, Daniel. 1961. "Risk, Ambiguity and the Savage Axioms." *Quarterly Jounral of Economics* LXXV.

Engel, Ernst. 1857. *Die Produktions- und Consumtionsverhältnisse des.* Königreichs Sachsen. "*Zeitschrift des Statistischen Büreaus des Königlich Sächsischen Ministeriums des Innern,* Dresden.

Engle, Robert F. 1978. "Estimating Structural Models of Seasonality." In *Seasonal Analysis of Econometric Time Series,* ed. A. Zellner. Washington, D.C: Bureau of the Census.

Erdøs, P., and M. Kac. 1947. "On the Number of Positive Sums of Independent Random Variables." *Bulletin of the American Mathematical Society* 53.

Feller, William. 1957. *An Introduction to Probability Theory and Its Applications,* Vol. 1, 2d ed. New York: Wiley.

Feller, William. 1966. *An Introduction to Probability Theory and Its Applications,* Vol. 2, New York: Wiley.

Fellner, William. 1961. "Distortion of Subjective Probabilities as a Reaction to Uncertainty." *Quarterly Journal of Economics* 75.

Fenstad, Jens E. 1967. "Representations of Probabilities Defined on First Order Languages." In *Sets, Models and Recursion Theory,* ed. J. N. Crossle. Amsterdam: North-Holland.

Fenstad, Jens E. 1968. "The Structure of Logical Probabilities." *Synthese* 18.

Feynman, Richard P., Robert B. Leighton, and Matthew Sands. 1963. *The Feynman Lectures on Physics,* Vol. 1. Reading: Addison-Wesley.

Finetti, Bruno de. 1964. "La prévision: ses Lois Logiques, ses Sources Subjectives." In *Studies in Subjective Probability,* ed. H. E. Kyburg, Jr., and H. E. Smokler. New York: Wiley.

Fishburn, Peter C. 1967. "Bounded Expected Utility." *Annals of Mathematical Statistics* 38.

Fishburn, Peter C. 1970. *Utility Theory for Decision Making.* New York: Wiley.

Fishburn, P. C., and A. M. Odlyzko. 1989. Unique Subjective Probability on Finite Sets. *Journal of the Ramanujan Mathematical Society* 2.

Fisher, Frank M. 1963. "Decomposability, Near Decomposability, and Balanced Price Change under Constant Returns to Scale." *Econometrica* 31.

Fisher, Irving. 1961. *The Theory of Interest,* New York: Kelley.

Freedman, David A. 1963. "On the Asymptotic Behaviour of Bayes Estimates in the Discrete Case." *Annals of Mathematical Statistics* 34.

Freedman, David A. 1965. "On the Asymptotic Behaviour of Bayes Estimates in the Discrete Case II." *Annals of Mathematical Statistics* 35.

Frege, Gottlob. 1879. *Begriffsschrift eine der arithmetischen nachgebildete Formelsprache des reinen Denkens.* Halle a/S: Nebert.

Frege, Gottlob. 1884. *Die Grundlagen der Arithmetik.* Breslau: Verlag Wilhelm Koebner.

Frege, Gottlob. 1893. *Grundgesetze der Arithmetik begriffsschriftlich abgeleitet,* Band I. Jena: Verlag Hermann Pohle.

Friedman, Milton. 1953. "The Methodology of Positive Economics." In *Essays in Positive Economics*, Univeristy of Chicago Press.

Friedman, Milton. 1957. *A Theory of the Consumption Function*. Princeton University Press.

Frisch, Ragnar. 1955. "Trygve Haavelmo's Contributions to Economics and Econometrics during the Period 1938–47." In *University of Oslo, Annual Report July '47–June '48*. Oslo: Akademisk Forlag.

Fuchs-Seliger, Susanne. 1976. *Zur Theorie der Revealed Preference*. Meisenheim am Glan: Verlag Anton Hein.

Fuller, Wayne A. 1985. "Nonstationary Autoregressive Time Series." In *Handbook of Statistics*, Vol. 5, ed. E. J. Hannan, P. R. Krishnaiah, and M. M. Rao. New York: Elsevier Science.

Fuller, Wayne A., David P. Hasza, and J. Jeffery Goebel. 1981. "Estimation of the Parameters of Stochastic Difference Equations." *Annals of Statistics* 9.

Furstenberg, Harry. 1960. *Stationary Processes and Prediction Theory*. Princeton Universtiy Press.

Galambos, Janos. 1978. *The Asymptotic Theory of Extreme Order Statistics*. New York: Wiley.

Gale, David. 1960. "A Note on Revealed Preference." *Economica* 27.

Geanakoplos, John. 1984. "Utility Functions for Debreu's Excess Demands." *Journal of Mathematical Economics* 13.

Gentzen, Gerhard. 1969. *The Collected Papers of Gerhard Gentzen*, ed. M. E. Szabo. Amsterdam: North-Holland.

Gettier, Edmund L. 1963. "Is Justified True Belief Knowledge?" *Analysis* 23.

Gilboa, Itzhak. 1987. "Expected Utility with Purely Subjective Non-additive Probabilities." *Journal of Mathematical Economics* 16.

Gödel, Kurt. 1931. Über formal unentscheidbare Sätze der Principia Mathematica und verwandter Systeme I. *Monatschrift der Mathematischen Physik* 38.

Grandmont, Jean-Michel 1974. "On the Short Run Equilibrium in a Monetary Economy." In *Allocation under Uncertainty: Equilibrium and Optimality*, ed. Jacques H. Drèze. New York: Halstead.

Grassmann, Hermann. 1862: *Die Ausdehnungslehre*, Berlin: Verlag von Th. Chr. Fr. Enslin.

Graves, Lawrence M. 1956. *The Theory of Functions of Real Variables* 2d ed. New York: McGraw-Hill.

Grenander, Ulf, and Murray Rosenblatt. 1957. *Statistical Analysis of Stationary Time Series*. New York: Wiley.

Griliches, Zvi. 1967. "Distributed Lags: A Survey." *Econometrica* 35.

Haavelmo, Trygve. 1944. *The Probability Approach in Econometrics. Econometrica* 12 (supplement).

Haavelmo, Trygve. 1947. "Methods of Measuring the Marginal Propensity to Consume." *Journal of the American Statistical Association* 42.

Haberler, Gottfried von. 1937. *Prosperity and Depression.* Geneva: League of Nations.

Hacking, Ian. 1975. *The Emergence of Probability.* Cambridge University Press.

Halmos, Paul R. 1974. *Naive Set Theory.* New York: Springer-Verlag.

Hannan, E. J. 1970. *Multiple Time Series.* New York: Wiley.

Hart, Oliver D. 1975. "Some Negative Results on the Existence of Comparative Statics Results in Portfolio Theory." *The Review of Economic Studies* 42.

Harvey, A. C. 1985. "Applications of the Kalman Filter in Econometrics." Invited paper, Fifth World Congress of the Econometric Society.

Harvey, A. C. 1985a. "Trends and Cycles in Macroeconomic Time Series." *Journal of Business and Economic Statistics* 3.

Hempel, Carl G. 1952: *Fundamentals of Concept Formation in Empirical Science.* University of Chicago Press.

Hempel, Carl G. 1965. "Studies in the Logic of Confirmation." In *Aspects of Scientific Explanation and Other Essays in the Philosophy of Science.* New York: Free Press.

Hendry, D. F., and J. F. Richard. 1989. "Recent Developments in the Theory of Encompassing." In *Contributions to Operations Research and Econometrics. The xxth Anniversary of CORE,* ed. B. Cornet and H. Tulkens. Cambridge: MIT Press.

Heyting, A. 1956. *Intuitionism, an Introduction.* Amsterdam: North-Holland.

Hicks, J. R. 1946. *Value and Capital,* 2d ed. Oxford University Press.

Hicks, J. R. 1956. *A Revision of Demand Theory.* Oxford University Press.

Hildebrand, George H., and Ta-Chung Liu. 1965. *Manufacturing Production Functions in the United States, 1957.* Ithaca: New York State School of Industrial and Labor Relations. Cornell University.

Hintikka, Jaakko. 1962. *Knowledge and Belief.* Cornell University Press.

Hintikka, Jaakko. 1969. *Models for Modalities.* Boston: Reidel.

Hintikka, Jaakko. 1974. *Knowledge and the Known.* Boston: Reidel.

Hintikka, Jaakko. 1979. "Semantics for Propositional Attitudes." In *Reference and Modality,* ed. L. Linsky. Oxford University Press.

Hirsch, Morris W., and Stephen Smale. 1974. *Differential Equations, Dynamical Systems, and Linear Algebra*. New York: Academic.

Houthakker, Henrik S. 1950. "Revealed Preference and the Utility Function." *Economica* 17.

Huber, Peter J., and Volker Strassen. 1973. "Minimax Tests and the Neyman Pearson Lemma for Capacities." *Annals of Statistics* 1.

Hurwicz, Leonid, and Marcel K. Richter. 1971. "Revealed Preference without Demand Continuity Assumption." In *Preferences, Utiltity and Demand*, ed. J. S. Chipman, L. Hurwicz, M. K. Richter, and H. F. Sonnenschein. New York: Harcourt Brace Jovanovich.

Huxley, Aldous. 1954. *The Doors of Perception*. London: Chatto and Windus LTD.

Hylleberg, Svend. 1986. *Seasonality in Regression*. New York: Academic.

Johansen, Leif. 1960. *A Multi-Sectoral Study of Economic Growth*. Amsterdam: North-Holland.

Johansen, Leif. 1972. *Production Functions*, Amsterdam: North-Holland.

Jones, Andrew J. I. 1983. *Communication and Meaning*. Boston: Reidel.

Jordan, James S. 1985. "Learning Rational Expectations: The Finite State Case." *Journal of Economic Theory* 36.

Jorgenson, Dale W. 1964. "Minimum Variance, Linear, Unbiased Seasonal Adjustment of Economic Time Series." *Journal of the American Statistical Association* 59.

Jorgenson, Dale W. 1966. "Rational Distributed Lag Functions." *Econometrica* 32.

Jorgenson, Dale W., and Lawrence J. Lau. 1977. "Statistical Tests of the Theory of Consumer Behaviour." In *Quantitative Wirtschaftsforschung*, ed. H. Albach, E. Helmstädter, and R. Henn. Tübingen: Mohr.

Jöreskog, Karl G. 1970. "A General Method for Analysis of Covariance Structures." *Biometrica* 57.

Jöreskog, Karl G. 1981. "Analysis of Covariance Structures." *Scandinavian Journal of Statistics* 8.

Jöreskog, Karl G., and Dag Sörbom. 1978. *LISEREL IV, Analysis of Linear Structural Relationships by the Method of Maximum Likelihood*. Department of Statistics, University of Uppsala.

Kahneman, Daniel, and Amos Tversky. 1972. "Subjective Probability: A Judgement of Representativeness." *Cognitive Psychology* 3.

Karlin, Samuel. 1959. *Mathematical Methods and Theory in Games, Programming and Economics, Vol. 1*. Reading: Addison-Wesley.

Keisler, H. Jerome. 1976. *Foundations of Infinitesimal Calculus*. Boston: Prindle, Weber and Schmidt.

Keisler, H. Jerome. 1984. "An Infinitesimal Approach to Stochastic Analysis." *Memoirs of the American Mathematical Society* 297.

Kelley, John L. 1955. *General Topology*. New York: American Book, Van Nostrand Reinhold.

Kendall, David G. 1967. "On Finite and Infinite Sequences of Exchangeable Events." *Studia Scientiarum Mathematicarum Hungarica* 2.

Kesten, Harry. 1970 "Quadratic Transformations: A Model for Population Growth I and II." *Advances in Applied Probability* 2.

Kesten, Harry, and Bernt P. Stigum. 1966. "A Limit Theorem for Multidimensional Galton-Watson Processes." *Annals of Mathematical Statistics* 37.

Kesten, Harry, and Bernt P. Stigum, 1967. "Limit Theorems for Decomposable Multidimensional Galton-Watson Processes." *Journal of Mathematical Analysis and Applications* 17.

Kesten, Harry, and Bernt P. Stigum. 1974. "Balanced Growth under Uncertainty in Decomposable Economies." In *Essays on Economic Behavior under Uncertainty*, ed. M. S. Balch, D. L. McFadden, and S. Y. Wu. New York: North-Holland/American Elsevier.

Keynes, John M. 1921. *A Treatise on Probability*, London: MacMillan.

Keynes, John M. 1936. *The General Theory of Employment, Interest and Money*. New York: Harcourt, Brace.

Keynes, John N. 1897. *The Scope and Method of Political Economy*, 2d ed., London: MacMillan.

Kihlstrom, Richard E., and Leonard J. Mirman. 1975. "Information and Market Equilibrium." *The Bell Journal of Economics* 6.

Kingman, J. F. C. 1978. "Uses of Exchangeability." *Annals of Probability* 6.

Klein, L, and A. S. Goldberger. 1955. *An Econometric Model of the United States 1929-1952*. Amsterdam: North-Holland.

Kolmogorov, A. 1933. *Grundbegriffe der Wahrscheinlichkeitsrechnung*. Berlin: Chelsea.

Koopman, Bernard O., and George E. Kimball. 1959. "Information Theory." In *Notes on Operations Research 1959*. Cambridge: Technology Press.

Kraft, Charles H., John W. Pratt, and A. Seidenberg. 1959. "Intuitive Probability on Finite Sets." *Annals of Mathematical Statistics* 30.

Kripke, Saul A. 1971. "Semantical Considerations on Modal Logic." In *Reference and Modality*, ed. L. Linsky. Oxford University Press.

Kuznets, Simon. 1934. *Gross Capital Formation, 1919-1933*. National Bureau of Economic Research, Bulletin 52.

Kuznets, Simon. 1937. *National Income, 1919-1935*. National Bureau of Economic Research, Bulletin 66.

Laake, Petter. 1987. *Studies of Performance in Models with Non-Linear Covariance Structure: A Non-Robust and a Robust Approach*. University of Oslo.

Lai, T. L., and C. Z. Wei. 1983. "Asymptotic Properties of General Autoregressive Models and Strong Consistency of Least Squares Estimates of Their Parameters." *Journal of Multivariate Analysis* 13.

Lambalgen, Michiel van. 1987. "von Mises' Definition of Random Sequences Reconsidered." *Journal of Symbolic Logic* 52.

Laplace, Pierre S. 1951. *A Philosophical Essay on Probabilities*, New York: Dover.

Lawley, D. N., and A. E. Maxwell. 1971. *Factor Analysis as a Statistical Method*, New York: American Elsevier.

Leong, Y. S. 1935. "Indices of the Physical Volume of Production of Producers' Goods, Consumers' Goods, Durable Goods and Transient Goods." *Journal of the American Statistical Association* 30.

Leontief, Wassily W. 1936. "Composite Commodities and the Problem of Index Numbers." *Econometrica* 4.

Leontief, Wassily. 1941. *The Structure of the American Economy, 1919-1929*. Oxford University Press.

Lewis, David. 1973. *Counterfactuals*. Oxford: Basil Blackwell.

Lin, Winston. 1976. *Econometric Factor Analysis*, Ph.D. thesis, Department of Economics, Northwestern University.

Lindley, Dennis V. 1957. "A Statistical Paradox." *Biometrica* 44.

Lindley, Dennis V. 1977. "A Problem in Forensic Science." *Biometrica* 64.

Lintner, John K. 1956. "Distribution of Incomes of Corporations among Dividends, Retained Earnings and Taxes." Papers and *Proceedings of the Sixty-eigth Annual Meeting of the American Economic Association* 46.

Liviatan, Nissan. 1968. "Tests of the Permanent-Income Hypothesis Based on a Reinterview Savings Survey." In *Readings in Economic Statistics and Econometrics*, ed. A. Zellner. Boston: Little, Brown.

Lobatschefskij, Nikolaj I. 1829. "Über die Anfangsgründe der Geometrie." *Kasaner Bote*, Theil 25; translated by F. Engel and published in Vol. 1 of *Urkunden zur Geschichte der Nichteuklidischen Geometrie*. Leipzig 1898: Druck und Verlag von B. G. Teubner.

Loeb, Peter A. 1975. "Conversion from Nonstandard to Standard Measure Spaces and Applications in Probability Theory." *Transactions of the American Mathematical Society* 211.

Loève, Michel. 1960. *Probability Theory,* 2d ed. Princeton: Van Nostrand

Łos, Jerzy. 1963. "Remarks on Foundations of Probability." *Proceedings 1962 of the International Congress of Mathematicians.*

Lütkepohl, Helmut. 1984. "The Optimality of Rational Distributed Lags: A Comment." *International Economic Review* 25.

McCord, Mark, and Richard de Neufville. 1983. "Empirical Demonstration That Expected Utility Decision Analysis Is not Operational." In *Foundations of Utility and Risk Theory with Applications,* ed. B. P. Stigum and F. Wenstøp. Boston: Reidel.

McFadden, Daniel, Andreu Mas-Colell, Rolf Mantel, and Marcel K. Richter. 1974. "A Characterization of Community Excess Demand Functions." *Journal of Economic Theory* 9.

McKenzie, Lionel, 1956–1957. "Demand Theory without a Utility Index." *Review of Economic Studies* 24.

McLaren, Keith. R. 1979. "The Optimality of Rational Distributed Lags." *International Economic Review* 20.

Malinvaud, Edmond. 1970. *Statistical Methods of Econometrics.* 2nd revised ed. New York: North-Holland.

Malthus, T. R. 1973. *An Essay on the Principle of Population.* London: Dent.

Mann, H. B., and Abraham Wald. 1943. "On the Statistical Treatment of Linear Stochastic Difference Equations." *Econometrica* 11.

Marschak, Jacob, and William H. Andrews. 1944. "Random Simultaneous Equations and the Theory of Production." *Econometrica* 12.

Mas-Colell, Andreu. 1977. "The Recoverability of Consumers' Preferences from Market Demand Behavior." *Econometrica* 45.

Mill, John S. 1973. *A System of Logic Ratiocinative and Inductive.* Toronto: University of Toronto Press and Routledge and Kegan Paul.

Mirman, Leonard J. 1973. "The Steady State Behavior of a Class of One Sector Growth Models with Uncertain Technology." *Journal of Economic Theory* 6.

Mises, Richard von. 1951. *Probability, Statistics and Truth,* 2d ed. London: Allen and Unwin.

Mizon, Graham E. 1984. "The Encompassing Approach in Econometrics." In *Econometrics and Quantitative Economics,* ed. D. F. Hendry and K. F. Wallis. London: Basil Blackwell.

Modigliani, Franco, and Richard Brumberg. 1955. "Utility Analysis and the Consumption Function: An Interpretation of Cross-Section Data." In *Post-Keynesian Economics*, ed. K. K. Kurihara. London: Allen and Unwin.

Montague, Richard. 1974. *Formal Philosophy, Selected Papers*, ed. R. H. Thomason. Yale University Press.

Mosteller, Frederick C., and Philip Nogee. 1951. "An Experimental Measurement of Utility." The *Journal of Political Economy* 59.

Muellbauer, John. 1976. "Community Preferences and the Representative Consumer." *Econometrica* 44.

Muench, Thomas J. 1974. Consistency of Least Squares Estimates of Coefficients of a Stochastic Difference Equation. Unpublished manuscript, Department of Economics, University of Minnesota.

Muirhead, R. J. 1982. *Aspects of Multivariate Statistical Theory*. New York: Wiley.

Nagel, Ernest. 1939. "The Formation of Modern Conceptions of Formal Logic in the Development of Geometry." *Osiris* 7.

Nagel, Ernest. 1961. *The Structure of Science*. New York: Harcourt, Brace & World.

Nerlove, Marc. 1956. "Adaptive Expectations and Cobweb Phenomena." *Quarterly Journal of Economics* 70.

Nerlove, Marc. 1958. *The Dynamics of Supply: Estimation of Farmer's Response to Price*. The Johns Hopkins University Press.

Nerlove, Marc, and S. Wage. 1964. "On the Optimality of Adaptive Forecasting." *Management Science* 10.

Newton, Isaac. 1968. *The Mathematical Principles of Natural Philosophy*, Vol. 1, trans. Andrew Motte. London: Dawsons.

Nie, Norman H., C. Hadlai Hull, Jean G. Jenkins, Karin Steinbrenner, and Dale H. Bent. 1975. *Statistical Package for the Social Sciences*, 2d ed. (SPSS). New York: McGraw-Hill.

Nozick, Robert. 1981. *Philosophical Explanations*. Belknap Press of Harvard University Press.

Olshen, Richard. 1974. "A Note on Exchangeable Sequences." *Zeitschrift Zur Wahrscheinlichkeitstheorie und verwandte Gebiete* 28.

Parthasarathy, K. R. 1967. *Probability Measures on Metric Spaces*. New York: Academic Press.

Pasch, M. 1882. *Vorlesungen über Neuere Geometrie*. Leipzig: Verlag von B. G. Teubner.

Peano, Giuseppe. 1889. *Arithmetices Principia Nova Methodo Exposita*. Turin: Bocca.

Peirce, Charles S. 1955. *Philosophical Writings of Peirce,* ed. Justus Buckler. New York: Dover.

Peterson, Cameron R., Wesley M. DuCharme, and Ward Edwards. 1968. "Sampling Distributions and Probability Revisions." *Journal of Experimental Psychology* 76.

Plato 1974. *The Republic,* translated by Desmond Lee, 2nd revised ed. London: Penguin Books.

Pletcher, Galen K. 1973. "Mysticism, Contradiction and Ineffability." *American Philosophical Quarterly* 10.

Prais, S. J., and H. S. Houthakker. 1955. *The Analysis of Family Budgets.* Cambridge University Press.

Pratt, John W. 1964. "Risk Aversion in the Small and in the Large." *Econometrica* 32.

Projector, Dorothy S. 1968. *Survey of Changes in Family Finances.* Washington, D.C.: Board of Governors of the Federal Reserve System.

Projector, Dorothy S., and Gertrude S. Weiss. 1966. *Survey of Financial Characteristics of Consumers.* Washington, D.C.; Board of Governors of the Federal Reserve System.

Przelecki, Marian. 1969. *The Logic of Empirical Theories.* London: Routledge and Kegan Paul.

Quine, W. V. O. 1979. "Reference and Modality." In *Reference and Modality,* ed. L. Linsky. Oxford University Press.

Radhakrishnan, Sarvepalli, and Charles Moore. 1957. *Sourcebook in Indian Philosophy.* Princeton University Press.

Radner, Roy. 1968. "Competitive Equilibrium under Uncertainty." *Econometrica* 36.

Radner, Roy. 1979. "Rational Expectations Equilibrium: Generic Existence and the Information Revealed by Prices." *Econometrica* 47.

Raiffa, Howard. 1961. "Risk, Ambiguity and the Savage Axioms: Comment." *Quarterly Journal of Economics* 75.

Raiffa, Howard. 1969. "Assessments of Probabilites." Unpublished manuscript, Harvard University.

Ramsey, Frank P. 1954. "Truth and Probability." In *The Foundations of Mathematics and Other Logical Essays,* ed. R. B. Braithwaite. London: Routledge and Kegan Paul.

Ramsey, Frank P. 1954a. *The Foundations of Mathematics and Other Logical Essays.* London: Routledge and Kegan Paul.

Rao, M. M. 1961. "Consistency and Limit Distributions of Estimators of Parameters in Explosive Stochastic Difference Equations." *Annals of Mathematical Statistics* 32.

Rashid, Salim. 1979. "The Relationship between Measure-Theoretic and Non-Standard Exchange Economies." *Journal of Mathematical Economics* 6.

Rényi, Alfred. 1970. *Foundations of Probability*. San Francisco: Holden-Day.

Rényi, A., and P. Révész. 1963. "A Study of Sequences of Equivalent Events as Special Stable Sequences." *Publicationes Mathematicae* 10.

Richter, Marcel K. 1966. "Revealed Preference Theory." *Econometrica* 34.

Riemann, Bernhard. 1854. *Über die Hypothesen welche der Geometrie zu Grunde liegen*. Berlin: Verlag von Julius Springer.

Robinson, Abraham. 1966. *Non-Standard Analysis*, Amsterdam: North-Holland.

Rosser, J. B. 1936. "Estensions of some Theorems of Gödel and Church. *Journal of Symbolic Logic* 1.

Rubin, Herman. 1950. "Consistency of Maximum Likelihood Estimates in the Explosive Case." *In Statistical Inference in Dynamic Economic Models Models*, ed. T. C. Koopmans. New York: Wiley.

Rudin, Walter. 1964. *Principles of Mathematical Analysis*, 2d ed. New York: McGraw-Hill.

Russell, Bertrand. 1903. *Principles of Mathematics*. New York: Norton.

Russell, Bertrand. 1976. *The Problems of Philosophy*. Oxford University Press.

Russell, Bertrand. 1948. *Human Knowledge*. New York: Simon and Shuster.

Russell, Bertrand, and Alfred N. Whitehead. 1910–1913. *Principia Mathematica*. Cambridge University Press.

Samuelson, Paul A. 1947. *Foundations of Economic Analysis*. Harvard University Press.

Samuelson, Paul A. 1953. "Consumption Theorems in Terms of Overcompensation Rather Than Indifference Comparisons." *Economica* 20.

Sanders, Frederick. 1963. "On Subjective Probability Forecasting." *Journal of Applied Meteorology* 2.

Sanders, Frederick. 1967. "The Verification of Probability Forecasts." *Journal of Applied Meteorology* 6.

Sandvik, Bjørn. 1988. "The Choice Consequences of Completely Separable Utility." The Norwegian School of Business, Bergen.

Savage, Leonard J. 1954. *The Foundations of Statistics*. New York: Wiley.

Scarf, H. 1960. "Some Examples of Global Instability of the Competitive Equilibrium." *International Economic Review* 1.

Scheffé, Henry. 1959. *The Analysis of Variance*. New York: Wiley.

Schnorr, Claus P. 1971. *Zufälligkeit und Wahrscheinlichkeit*. Lecture notes in mathematics. Heidelberg: Springer-Verlag.

Schröder, Ernst. 1890. *Vorlesungen über die Algebra der Logik*. Leipzig: Druck und Verlag von B. G. Teubner.

Schultz, H. 1938. *The Theory and Measurement of Demand*. University of Chicago Press.

Schumpeter, Joseph A. 1954. *History of Economic Analysis*. Oxford University Press.

Senior, N. William. 1850. *Political Economy*, London: Griffin.

Shafer, Glenn. 1976. *A Mathematical Theory of Evidence*. Princeton University Press.

Shafer, Glenn. 1982. "Lindley's Paradox." *Journal of the American Statistical Association* 77.

Shannon, C. E. 1948. "A Mathematical Theory of Communication." *Bell System Technology Journal* 27.

Shoenfield, Joseph R. 1967. *Mathematical Logic*, Reading: Addison-Wesley.

Skolem, Thoralf 1920. "Logisch-kombinatorische Untersuchungen über die Erfüllbarkeit und Beweisbarkeit mathematischen Sätze nebst einem Theoreme über dichte Mengen." In *Selected Works in Logic by Th. Skolem*, ed. J. E. Fenstad. Oslo 1970: Universitetsforlaget.

Skolem, Thoralf. 1922. "Einige Bemerkungen zur axiomatischen Begründung der Mengenlehre." Proceedings of the 5th Scandinavian Mathematics Congress in Helsinki. Helsingfors: Akademiska Bokhandelen.

Skolem, Thoralf. 1933. "Über die Unmöglichkeit einer Characterisierung der Zahlenreihe mittels eines endlichen Axiomensystems." *Norsk Matematisk Forenings Skrifter* 2.

Skolem, Thoralf. 1934. "Über die Nicht-characterisierbarkeit der Zahlenreihe mittels endlich oder abzählbar unendlich vieler Aussagen mit Ausschliesslich Zahlenvariabeln. *Fundamenta Mathematicae* 23.

Solow, Robert M. 1956. "A contribution to the Theory of Economic Growth." *Quarterly Journal of Economics* 70.

Solow, Robert M., and Paul A. Samuelson. 1953. "Balanced Growth under Constant Returns to Scale." *Econometrica* 21.

Sonnenschein, Hugo. 1972. "Market Excess Demand Functions." *Econometrica* 40.

Stace, W. T. 1961. *Mysticism and Philosophy*. London: MacMillan and Co. LTD.

Staël von Holstein, Carl-Axel S. 1970. *Assessment and Evaluation of Subjective Probability Distributions.* Stockholm: Economic Research Institute.

Stigler, George J. 1965. "The Early History of Empirical Studies of Consumer Behavior." *Journal of Political Economy* 42.

Stigler, George J. 1965a. *Essays in the History of Economics.* University of Chicago Press.

Stigum, Bernt P. 1963. "Dynamic Stochastic Processes." *Annals of Mathematical Statistics* 34.

Stigum, Bernt P. 1966. "A Theorem on the Galton-Watson Process." *Annals of Mathematical Statistics* 37.

Stigum, Bernt P. 1967. "On Certain Problems of Aggregation." *International Economic Review* 8.

Stigum, Bernt P. 1969. "Entrepreneurial Choice over Time under Conditions of Uncertainty." *International Economic Review* 10.

Stigum, Bernt P. 1969a, "Competitive Equilibria under Uncertainty." The *Quarterly Journal of Economics* 83.

Stigum, Bernt P. 1972. "Resource Allocation under Uncertainty." *International Economic Review* 13.

Stigum, Bernt P. 1972a. "Balanced Growth under Uncertainty." *Journal of Economic Theory* 5.

Stigum, Bernt P. 1972b. "Finite State Space and Expected Utility Maximization." *Econometrica* 40.

Stigum, Bernt P. 1972c. "Asymptotic Properties of Dynamic Stochastic Parameter Estimates II." *Technical Summary Report No. 1269.* Mathematics Research Center, University of Wisconsin.

Stigum, Bernt P. 1973. "Revealed Preference—A Proof of Houthakker's Theorem." *Econometrica* 41.

Stigum, Bernt P. 1974. Comments on R. Radner's paper, "Market Equilibrium under Uncertainty: Concepts and problems." In *Frontiers of Quantitative Economics,* Vol. 2, ed. M. D. Intriligator and D. A. Kendrick. Amsterdam: North-Holland.

Stigum, Bernt P. 1974a. "An Arc Sine Law and a Law of the Iterated Logarithm for Non-Stationary Process." *Technical Summary Report No. 1380.* Mathematics Research Center, University of Wisconsin.

Stigum, Bernt P. 1974b. "Competitive Resource Allocation over Time under Uncertainty." In *Essays on Economic Behavior under Uncertainty,* ed. M. Balch, D. McFadden, and S. Wu. New York: North-Holland.

Stigum, Bernt P. 1974c. "Asymptotic Properties of Dynamic Stochastic Parameter Estimates III." *Journal of Multivariate Analysis* 4.

Stigum, Bernt P. 1975. "Asymptotic Properties of Autoregressive Integrated Moving Average Processes." *Stochastic Processes and Their Applications* 3.

Stigum, Bernt P. 1976. "Asymptotic Properties of Dynamic Stochastic Parameter Estimates I." *Annals of the Institute of Statistical Mathematics* 28.

Stigum, Bernt P. 1976a. "Least Squares and Stochastic Difference Equations." *Journal of Econometrics* 4.

Stigum, Bernt P. 1990. "Enterpreneurial Choice in Norway." Unpublished memo, Department of Economics, University of Oslo.

Strotz, Robert H. 1957. "The Empirical Implications of a Utility Tree." *Econometrica* 25.

Suppe, Frederick 1974. "The Search for Philosophic Understanding of Scientific Theories." In *The Structure of Scientific Theories*, ed. F. Suppe. Urbana: University of Illinois Press.

Suppes, Patrick 1967. "What is a Scientific Theory." In *Philosophy of Science Today*, ed. S. Morgenbesser. New York: Basic Books.

Suppes, Patrick 1968. "The Desirability of Formalization in Science. " *Journal of Philosophy* 65.

Tarski, Alfred. 1964. "The Semantic Conception of Truth and the Foundations of Semantics." In *Readings in Philosophical Analysis*, ed. H. Feigel and W. Sellars. New York: Appleton-Century-Crofts.

Theil, Henri. 1961. *Economic Forecasts and Policy*, 2d ed. Amsterdam: North-Holland.

Theil, Henri. 1965. "The Information Approach to Demand Analysis." *Econometrica* 33.

Tinbergen, Jan. 1939. *Business Cycles in the United States of America, 1919–1932*. Geneva: League of Nations.

Toulmin, Stephen. 1959. *The Philosophy of Science*. New York: Harper and Row.

Uzawa, Hirofumi. 1960. "Preference and Rational Choice in the Theory of Consumption." In *Mathematical Methods in the Social Sciences*, ed. K. J. Arrow, S. Karlin, and P. Suppes. Stanford University Press.

Varian, Hal R. 1974. "Equity, Envy and Efficiency." *Journal of Economic Theory* 9.

Varian, Hal R. 1982. "The Nonparametric Approach to Demand Analysis." *Econometrica* 50.

Varian, Hal R. 1983. "Non-parametric Tests of Consumer Bahavior." *Review of Economic Studeis* 50.

Ville, J. 1939. *Étude Critique de la Notion de Collectif.* Paris: Gauthier-Villars.

Wang, Hao. 1952. "Logic of Many-Sorted Theories." *Journal of Symbolic Logic* 17.

Weber, Max. 1949. *The Methodology of the Social Sciences,* trans. E. Shils and H. Finch. New York: Free Press.

Weyl, Herman. 1963. *Philosophy of Mathematics and Natural Science,* rev. ed. trans. Olaf Helmer. Princeton University Press.

Whittle, P. 1963. *Prediction and Regulation.* Princeton: Van Nostrand.

Wiener, N. and P. Masani 1957 and 1958. "The Prediction Theory of Multivariate Stochastic Processes, I and II." *Acta Mathematica* 98 and 99.

Wilder, Raymond L. 1965. *Introduction to the Foundations of Mathematics,* 2d ed. New York: Wiley.

Wold, Herman. 1938. *A Study in the Analysis of Stationary Time Series.* Uppsala: Almquist and Wiksell.

Wold, Herman. 1943. "A Synthesis of Pure Demand Analysis, Part I." *Skandinavisk Aktuarietidsskrift* 26.

Wold, Herman. 1943. "A Synthesis of Pure Demand Analysis, Part I." *Skandinavisk Aktuarietidsskrift* 26.

Wolfowitz, Jacob. 1962. "Bayesian Inference and Axioms of Consistent Decision." *Econometrica* 30.

Wright, Caroll. 1875. *Sixth Annual Report of the Bureau of Labor Statistics.* Boston.

Zellner, Arnold. 1971. *An Introduction to Bayesian Inference in Econometrics* New York: Wiley.

Index